LANDLORD AND TENANT LAW IN CONTEXT

This new work, a successor to the author's earlier book (co-written with Geoff Gilbert) *Landlord and Tenant Law: The Nature of Tenancies* (1995), though now the work of a single author and completely updated and rewritten, shares the same aim of setting leases in their wider context by weaving together matters of law and policy. The book provides a clear understanding of the main principles of landlord and tenant law in each sector.

The style of this book is distinctive. First of all, it explains the law of landlord and tenant law by showing how the statutory and common law rules have been shaped by wider commercial, social, economic and policy considerations, by the growth in human rights law and by changing concepts of community and justice. The other innovative feature of the book is that the law is explained by reference to the different stages of the relationship: entering a lease, regulating leases, managing leasehold property, and so on. The stages of the relationship provide the structure for the book. Most landlord and tenant books set out the 'common law' rules in the opening chapters and then deal with the legislative regime for each individual sector later in the book. By instead setting the law in the different stages of the relationship, this book is able to show where the shared issues faced by landlord and tenant receive a common legal response, and where the different context of the leasehold relationship has led to a variety of legal rules.

Landlord and tenant law is now very different from the common law of 100 years ago. In describing the modern law (or laws), the unique style of this book enables the reader to see how the commonalities and the contrasts between the law in the different sectors can be explained by reference to the way that leases are differently used and regulated.

Landlord and Tenant
Law in Context

SUSAN BRIGHT

·HART·
PUBLISHING
OXFORD AND PORTLAND, OREGON
2007

Published in North America (US and Canada) by
Hart Publishing
c/o International Specialized Book Services
920 NE 58th Avenue, Suite 300
Portland, OR 97213-3786
USA
Tel: +1 503 287 3093 or toll-free: (1) 800 944 6190
Fax: +1 503 280 8832
E-mail: orders@isbs.com
Website: www.isbs.com

Hart Publishing, 16C Worcester Place, OX1 2JW
Telephone: +44 (0)1865 517530 Fax: +44 (0)1865 510710
E-mail: mail@hartpub.co.uk
Website: http://www.hartpub.co.uk

British Library Cataloguing in Publication Data
Data Available
ISBN: 978-1-84113-722-3

Typeset by Forewords, Oxford
Printed and bound in Great Britain by
TJ International Ltd, Padstow, Cornwall

PREFACE

This book is written as a 'law in context' book so that the reader will not simply learn the rules of landlord and tenant law but will understand how leases are typically used in practice and what the role of the law is within the landlord and tenant relationship. The book is based around the different stages of the relationship – from entering into a tenancy, through the various management issues that arise during the relationship, to the point where the tenancy is brought to an end. As well as describing the law applicable to each of these stages, the book draws on policy, empirical research and statistical surveys to show what goals the law is seeking to achieve and to assess its effectiveness in regulating issues that arise between the landlord and tenant.

The focus is on the law relating to residential and business tenancies, although some reference is also made to agricultural tenancy law.

I owe an enormous debt of thanks to Geoff Gilbert. Many years ago we together wrote the forerunner to this book. It was Geoff who was inspired to theme the book around the stages of the relationship, an approach which I have retained in this book. Although this book has been almost completely re-written, odd passages survive from the earlier book and I am grateful to Geoff for allowing me to take forward this new project, building on our earlier work.

In addition to re-structuring the chapters (from 12 to the current 25), updating and rewriting, there is much that is completely new in this book. Quite apart from the numerous law reports, there have been enormous changes to the shape of landlord and tenant law over the last fifteen years or so. The enactment of the human rights legislation means that there have been many cases exploring the impact of this area of law on the leasehold relationship. In the social housing sector landlords have become more involved with managing communities, and anti-social behaviour has come to be seen as a problem which landlords are expected to control. The transfer of local authority stock to the housing association sector has continued, and the adoption of the decent homes standard has done much to improve the condition of rented housing. There are changes underway relating to how social housing is allocated and how rents are set. Tenant empowerment has become a new buzz phrase, with increasing recognition of the importance of allowing tenants a voice through consultation and participation in management. In the private residential sector, compulsory licensing has been introduced for houses in multiple occupation, and deposit taking is now regulated. Ombudsmen have an important role in dealing with complaints against residential landlords. The 'tolerated trespasser' has been born and has multiplied rapidly. Enfranchisement laws, including the right to buy, have been amended. In the commercial sector, original tenant liability has gone, statutory protection for tenants is optional, and voluntary codes of practice have been promoted for the negotiation of leases and for managing service charges (arguably to stave off legislative intervention). Extensive research has been carried out by a team at the University of Reading investigating the operation of the commercial leases market. Disability discrimination laws now affect the way that tenanted property is managed. The Law Commission has been engaged in projects impacting on most aspects of residential renting, as well as on the state and condition of tenanted property, and on the termination of tenancies.

This is not a 'text and materials' book, but in some parts selected materials are quoted, either where it is important to know the precise wording used (for example in a statutory provision) or where it is more useful to quote the original than to paraphrase points made by others.

As Geoff recently pointed out to me, law books have in-built obsolescence: within two days of handing the manuscript in there had already been important new policy developments. Where possible, I have included changes in the text. For the most part, the law and policy is stated as at the end of July 2007. Since then, the much anticipated Court of Appeal decision in *Cadogan v Sportelli* [2007] EWCA Civ 1042 has confirmed the approach taken by the Lands Tribunal in relation to setting the deferment rate in leasehold enfranchisement claims (chapter 25). The Department for Communities and Local Government has issued a consultation paper on tolerated trespassers that looks at options for remedying the situation both in the future and for existing tolerated trespassers. A new priority has been given to housing under Gordon Brown's leadership of the Labour party. The pace of building new social homes is to grow and the new Homes and Communities Agency (mentioned, but without a name, in chapter 5) is to oversee the delivery of 45,000 new social homes per year by 2010–11. A new social housing watchdog, recommended by the Cave Review, and called the Office for Tenants and Social Landlords is to be created.

In addition to Geoff, there are many others to whom I owe thanks. The law and policy in this area is fast changing and in the rush of busy academic (and family) life it is difficult to keep on top of developments, yet alone have time to absorb and reflect on them. I have been tremendously privileged to benefit from a British Academy Research Readership during the period 2005–2007, which has enabled me to immerse myself in landlord and tenant law and policy. My thanks go not only to the British Academy, but also to my employers, the University of Oxford and New College, for allowing me to take up this opportunity. My colleagues at New College – Dori Kimel, Rowena Meager and Paul Yowell – have nobly let me enjoy my research leave without troubling me in relation to college business. The Oxford Law Faculty enabled me to employ a research assistant, Rhonda Powell, who had the unenviable job of reading through the entire book in an area of law she was unfamiliar with in order to comment on style and formatting. You were a star, Rhonda; thanks. The team at Hart Publishing, and in particular Richard himself and Mel Hamill, have been great.

Various people have read through particular parts and chapters for me: Professor David Clarke of Bristol University, Tim Horsley of Housing Quality Network and Ben McFarlane of Trinity College, Oxford. Others have fielded mad-cap questions or problems: Camilla Lamont of Landmark Chambers, David Keene (who has helped me understand farming vocabulary), David Martin of Bower & Bailey solicitors and Pamela Stanworth at Oxford University Computing Services who has rescued me from the random behaviour of Word documents in moments of crisis. The staff at the Bodleian Law Library have been unfailingly helpful, especially Angela Carritt, Margaret Watson and Sandy Meredith who have helped me to navigate around various databases. Many have given permission for me to refer to their work; and additionally organisations have consented to me using illustrations from their web-sites or precedents (Graham White of Slaughter and May, John Stephenson of Bircham Dyson Bell LLP and Peter Haler of LEASE).

Writing this book has been a joy. Landlord and tenant law is an interesting subject as it not only involves so many areas of law, but it really matters to a substantial part of the population and a majority of businesses. But it must be said that the joy wore off as the project moved from research and writing to finishing, checking for compliance with style conventions and the like. It is especially for the help, patience, encouragement and child care during this time, when family life was put on hold, that I must thank the various members of my family, particularly Chris and my parents, for their emotional and practical support. I have promised a special mention to my youngest child, Jacob, who kept me laughing and smiling throughout.

Susan Bright
November 2007

CONTENTS

Table of Abbreviations   vii
List of Tables, Figures and Charts   xi
Table of Cases   xxiii
Table of Statutes   xlv
Table of Statutory Instruments   lxxiii

PART ONE: INTRODUCING THE RELATIONSHIP   **1**

1   Introduction to Landlord and Tenant Law   3

   1.1   Understanding Leases in Context   3

   1.2   The Language of Leases   4

   1.3   The Variety of Letting Arrangements   5

   1.4   Key Issues and Trends in the Different Sectors   7

   1.5   Explaining the Structure of the Book   20

   1.6   Some more Terminology on Leases   22

2   Keys to Understanding Leases   25

   2.1   Introduction   25

   2.2   Leases in a Map of the Law   26

   2.3   The Hybrid Nature of Leases: Part Property, Part Contract   27

   2.4   The Private Law Relationship and the Common Law   29

   2.5   Landlord and Tenant Law as Regulatory Law   41

   2.6   The Public Law Dimension   41

   2.7   Leases and Land   46

   2.8   Leases as Split-ownership   48

   2.9   Intervention in the Landlord and Tenant Relationship   51

   2.10   Interpretation of Leases and Leasehold Notices   59

PART TWO: ENTERING THE RELATIONSHIP   **65**

3   Identifying Leasehold Relationships   67

   3.1   The Essential Elements of a Lease   67

   3.2   Different Categories of Occupation   77

3.3   Categorising a Relationship   95

4   Entering the Tenancy: Allocation, Formalities and Content   103

4.1   Allocation and Choice   103

4.2   Formalities on Entering into the Landlord and Tenant Relationship   105

4.3   The Effect of Non-observance of the Formality Requirements   110

4.4   Vitiating Factors and Leases   112

4.5   Construction and Rectification   113

4.6   Providing Information to Tenants   117

4.7   The Structure of Leases   120

4.8   Fairness and Contract Terms   124

4.9   The Structure of Commercial Leases   130

4.10   The Structure of Residential Leases   138

4.11   Variation of Lease Terms   139

PART THREE: REGULATING THE RELATIONSHIP   141

The Structure of Part Three   141

The Importance of Policy in the Wider Context   141

What is Policy?   143

Avoiding Statutory Protection   144

5   Renting Homes: The Policy Background   149

5.1   Introduction   149

5.2   Tenure Division   150

5.3   Social Renting and Private Renting   151

5.4   The Period to 1980   155

5.5   From 1980 Onwards   160

5.6   Current Housing Issues   168

5.7   Current Issues and Directions in the Different Tenures   177

5.8   Summary: Rented Housing in 2007   181

6   Renting Homes: Legislative Controls   183

6.1   Introduction   183

6.2   Legislative History of Housing Law   184

6.3   Allocation of Housing   190

6.4   The Housing Act 1988: The Private Rented Sector   203

6.5   The Housing Act 1985: Local Authorities and the Secure Tenancy   210

	6.6	The Housing Association Sector	218
	6.7	Statutory Control of Rented Homes	219
	6.8	Future Directions	222
7		Long Residential Leases	225
	7.1	The Reasons for Using Long Leases	225
	7.2	Problems with Long Leasehold	226
	7.3	The Case for Reform	227
	7.4	Reform at Last	229
	7.5	An Overview of Legislative Controls of Residential Long Leases	232
	7.6	The Future?	232
8		Business Tenancies	235
	8.1	Policy and Legislative History in the Commercial Property Sector	235
	8.2	The Operation of the Landlord and Tenant Act 1954, Part II	244
	8.3	Tenancies to which Part II of the 1954 Act applies	244
	8.4	Future Directions	252
9		Agricultural Tenancies	257
	9.1	Policy and Legislative History in the Agricultural Sector	257
	9.2	Farm Business Tenancies	263
	9.3	The Impact of the ATA 1995	267
	9.4	Future Directions	269
10		Human Rights in Landlord and Tenant Law	271
	10.1	Introduction: Human Rights	271
	10.2	Human Rights in Domestic Law	271
	10.3	The Meaning of Public Authority	273
	10.4	Interpreting Convention Rights	277
	10.5	The Convention Rights	279
	10.6	Interpretation of Legislation	291
	10.7	International Rights to Housing	293
PART FOUR: MANAGING THE RELATIONSHIP			**297**
11		Managing the Leasehold Relationship	299
	11.1	What is Management?	299
	11.2	Management and Disability Legislation	303
	11.3	Leasehold Estate Management	305

11.4	Management and Long Residential Leasehold	310
11.5	Managing Anti-social Behaviour	314
11.6	Landlords and Third Parties	326
11.7	Ensuring Effective Management	333
11.8	Disputes	341

12 Repair and Maintenance — 347

12.1	Introduction: Standards and Repair	347
12.2	The State of Tenanted Housing	348
12.3	Ensuring Good Standards in Rented Property	353
12.4	The Duty to Repair	364
12.5	Regulatory Controls	383
12.6	Beyond Landlord and Tenant Law	391
12.7	Enforcing Repairing Obligations	394
12.8	Landlord's Remedies for Breach of Tenant's Repairing Covenant	394
12.9	Tenant's Remedies for Breach of Landlord's Repairing Covenant	400
12.10	Improvements and Alterations	406

13 Using, Insuring and Servicing Tenanted Property — 415

13.1	Introduction	415
13.2	User	415
13.3	Insurance	426
13.4	Service Charges	432

14 Rent — 443

14.1	Introduction	443
14.2	Setting the Rent	443
14.3	Fixing Initial Rent Levels	444

15 Residential Rents — 449

15.1	Setting Rents in the Social Sector	449
15.2	Rent Control	453
15.3	Ensuring Affordability through Welfare Payments	465
15.4	The Tolerated Trespasser and Payment for Occupation	470

16 Varying the Rent and Ensuring Payment — 471

| 16.1 | Introduction | 471 |
| 16.2 | Variation of the Rent during a Tenancy | 471 |

16.3	Overpaying the Rent	499
16.4	Ensuring Payment	499
16.5	Remedies for Non-payment	505
16.6	Cesser of Rent	513

PART FIVE: CHANGING THE PARTIES TO THE RELATIONSHIP   **515**

17 Alienation, Transfer and Succession   517

17.1	General Introduction	517
17.2	Change of Tenant	517
17.3	Obtaining Consent	519
17.4	Covenants against Alienation	522
17.5	Alienation Covenants in Particular Sectors	530
17.6	Disposition in Breach of an Alienation Clause	542
17.7	Formalities and Alienation	544
17.8	The Position of Sub-tenants	545
17.9	Statutory Succession on Death	546
17.10	Change of Landlord	551
17.11	Transfer of Local Authority Housing to New Social Landlords	552

18 Enforcing Leasehold Covenants   559

18.1	Introduction	559
18.2	The Problem of Continuing Liability	560
18.3	New and Old Leases	562
18.4	Anti-avoidance	563
18.5	Liability of the Original Tenant under Old (Pre-1996) Leases	563
18.6	Liability of the Original Tenant under New (Post-1995) Leases	568
18.7	The Position of the Assignee Tenant under Old (Pre-1996) Leases	570
18.8	The Position of the Assignee Tenant under New (Post-1995) Leases	574
18.9	The Position of the Original Landlord in Old (Pre-1996) Leases	575
18.10	The Position of the Original Landlord in New (Post-1995) Leases	576
18.11	The Position of the New Reversioner in Old (Pre-1996) Leases	578
18.12	The Position of the New Reversioner in New (Post-1995) Leases	580
18.13	The New Reversioner and Pre-assignment Breaches	581
18.14	The Position of Guarantors	583
18.15	The Impact of the 1995 Act	585

18.16   Enforcement of Covenants by and against Management Companies under New (Post-1995) Leases   586

18.17   The Position of the Superior Landlord   586

18.18   Enforcing Covenants between Tenants?   587

18.19   The Effect of Disclaimer upon Liability   589

PART SIX: CONTINUING THE RELATIONSHIP   **591**

The Right to Stay   591

Why is Security Important?   591

Trends in Security   593

19   Security and Residential Tenancies   595

   19.1   Introduction   595

   19.2   Scheme of Protection   596

   19.3   Grounds for Possession   613

20   Security and Long Residential Leases   641

   20.1   Continuing Rights of Occupation for Long Leaseholders   641

   20.2   Qualifying for Protection   642

   20.3   Continuing or Ending the Tenancy   643

21   Security and Business Leases   645

   21.1   Introduction   645

   21.2   Obtaining Information   645

   21.3   The End of the Contractual Term   646

   21.4   Agreeing a New Tenancy   650

   21.5   Applying for an Interim Rent   651

   21.6   Applying to Court   652

   21.7   Opposing a New Tenancy   652

   21.8   Compensation for Non-renewal   658

   21.9   The Terms of the New Tenancy   660

PART SEVEN: ENDING THE RELATIONSHIP   **667**

22   Ending a Lease   669

   22.1   Introduction   669

   22.2   Periodic Tenancies   669

   22.3   Fixed Term Leases   674

   22.4   Statutory Requirements for Residential Tenants   674

22.5   Disability and Possession   678

22.6   Other Landlord Remedies if the Tenant Refuses to Leave   679

23 Unlawful Eviction and Harassment   681

23.1   Introduction   681

23.2   The Type of Behaviour that Goes On   682

23.3   The Size of the Problem   683

23.4   The Victims of Unlawful Eviction and Harassment   684

23.5   The Background to Regulation   684

23.6   The Offences of Unlawful Eviction and Harassment   686

23.7   The Response of the Agencies   689

23.8   Civil Remedies for Illegal Eviction and Harassment   691

23.9   Other Remedies   698

23.10   Reform?   698

24 Ending a Lease Early   701

24.1   Introduction   701

24.2   Ending a Lease for Tenant Breach: Forfeiture   702

24.3   The Law Commission's Termination Scheme for Tenant Default   719

24.4   Tenant Termination for Landlord Default?   723

24.5   Ending a Lease for Breach: Repudiation   723

24.6   Tenant Insolvency   725

24.7   Mortgagee Possession and Residential Leases   728

24.8   Surrender   729

24.9   Abandonment   732

24.10   Break Clauses   732

24.11   Merger   735

24.12   Frustration   736

24.13   The Effect of Termination on Sub-tenants   737

25 Enfranchisement and the Right to Buy   743

25.1   Introduction   743

25.2   Social Tenants and Enfranchisement   745

25.3   The Right to Buy   749

25.4   The Right to Acquire   758

25.5   The Preserved Right to Buy   758

25.6   Enfranchisement of Long Leasehold Houses – the Leasehold Reform Act 1967 759

25.7   Enfranchisement of Flats   768

25.8   Limited Rights under the Landlord and Tenant Act 1987   769

25.9   Enfranchisement of Flats under the Leasehold Reform, Housing and Urban
       Development Act 1993   774

25.10 The Future of Renting and Long Leaseholds   784

Bibliography   787

Index   803

TABLE OF ABBREVIATIONS

ADR	Alternative Dispute Resolution
Adv Q	Advocates Quarterly
AGA	Authorised Guarantee Agreement
AHA	Agricultural Holdings Act
ALMO	Arms Length Management Organisation
ALR	American Law Reports
ARLA	The Association of Residential Letting Agents
ASBO	Anti-Social Behaviour Order
BVHH	Best Value in Housing and Homelessness Framework
BPF	British Property Federation
BRC	British Retail Consortium
CAAV	Central Association of Agricultural Valuers
CAB	Citizens Advice Bureau
CBL	Choice Based Lettings
CML	Council of Mortgage Lenders
Conv	The Conveyancer and Property Lawyer
CRAR	Commercial Rent Arrears Recovery
DCA	Department for Constitutional Affairs
DCH	Defend Council Housing
DCLG	Department for Communities and Local Government
DEFRA	Department for Environment, Food and Rural Affairs
DETR	Department of the Environment, Transport and the Regions
DHS	Decent Homes Standard
DoE	Department of Environment
DoH	Department of Health
DSS	Department of Social Security
DWP	Department for Work and Pensions
ECHR	European Convention for the Protection of Human Rights and Fundamental Freedoms
ECtHR	European Court of Human Rights
EDMO	Empty Dwelling Management Order
EG	Estates Gazette
EGCS	Estates Gazette Case Summaries

EGLR	Estates Gazette Law Reports
EHRLR	European Human Rights Law Review
FBT	Farm Business Tenancy
HAG	Housing Association Grant
HAT	Housing Action Trusts
HHSRS	Housing Health and Safety Rating System
HLR	Housing Law Reports
HMO	Houses in Multiple Occupation
HRA	Housing Revenue Account
ICESCR	UN Committee on Economic, Social and Cultural Rights
IHOS	Independent Housing Ombudsman Scheme
IPD	Investment Property Databank
IPF	Investment Property Forum
ISMI	Income Support Mortgage Interest
JSWFL	Journal of Social Welfare and Family Law
JSWL	Journal of Social Welfare Law
KLE	Key Lines of Enquiry
L & TR	Landlord and Tenant Reports
LCHO	Low-cost Home Ownership
LGO	Local Government Ombudsman
LHA	Local Housing Allowance
LRR	Local Reference Rent
LSVT	Large Scale Voluntary Transfer
LVT	Leasehold Valuation Tribunal
MITR	Mortgage Interest Tax Relief
MMC	Monopolies and Mergers Commission
NACAB	National Association of Citizens Advice Bureaux
NRDF	National Rent Deposit Forum
NSP	Notice Seeking Possession
ODPM	Office of the Deputy Prime Minister
OFT	Office of Fair Trading
P & CR	Property and Compensation Reports
PFI	Private Finance Initiative
PLR	Planning Law Reports
PRTB	Preserved Right to Buy
RAC	Rent Assessment Committee
REIT	Real Estate Investment Trust
RICS	Royal Institution of Chartered Surveyors

ROOF	Shelter's housing magazine
RPI	Retail Price Index
RSL	Registered Social Landlord
RTA	Right to Acquire
RTB	Right to Buy
RTE	Right to Enfranchise
RTM	Right to Manage
SAA	Suitable Alternative Accommodation
SHG	Social Housing Grant
SIPP	Self Invested Personal Pension
SRR	Single Room Rent
TMO	Tenant Management Organisation
TRIG	Tenancy Reform Industry Group
TPC	Tenant Participation Compact
UORR	Upward Only Rent Review
VAO	Valuation Office Agency

LIST OF TABLES, FIGURES AND CHARTS

Figure 3.1   Key Questions in Categorising Single Occupancy

Figure 3.2   Multiple Occupation: Licences, Tenancies or Joint Tenancy?

Table 4.1   Formalities and Registration Requirements for all Leases

Figure P3   Which Statutory Code?

Figure 5.1   Trends in Housing Tenure

Figure 5.2   Rental by Stock Tenure

Table 5.1   Housing Stock by Tenure

Table 5.2   Help with Housing Costs in all Tenures in Great Britain

Table 5.3   Housing Decency by Tenure

Figure 6.1   Private Rental Sector by Tenancy Type

Table 6.1   Homelessness Duties

Table 6.2   Main Statutory Controls for Residential Tenancies

Table 7.1   Outline of Statutory Controls for Long Residential Leases

Table 12.1   Non-decent Homes by Tenure

Table 12.2   Vulnerable Households and Non-decent Homes

Table 13.1   Controls on Insurance Charges

Table 13.2   Controls on Service Charges

Table 14.1   Annualised Total Rates of Return in Great Britain, 2000

Table 14.2   Range of Commercial Rents mid 2006

Table 15.1   Mean Weekly Rent in £, Net of Services

Figure 16.1   Rent Review in Assured Periodic Tenancy

Figure 16.2   Statutory Increase Mechanism for Periodic Tenancy, Housing Act 1988 sections 13 and 14

Figure 16.3   Rent Review for Fixed Term and Statutory Assured Tenancy

Table 16.1   Average Rents (£ per Hectare) 2001-06

Figure 18.1   The Facts in *London Diocesan Fund v Phithwa*

Table 19.1   (Public Sector) Secure Tenancies: Grounds for Possession

Table 19.2   (Private sector) Assured Tenancies: Grounds for Possession

Table 19.3   Actions Entered in Court and Evictions by Local Authorities and Housing Associations in 2002/03: Breakdown by Reason for Action

Table 19.4   After the Tenancy: Trespasser or Tolerated Trespasser?

Table 21.1   Tenant Options as End of Lease Approaches

Chart 24.1   Forfeiture other than for Non-payment of Rent

Chart 24.2   Forfeiture for Non-payment of Rent
Chart 24.3   Summary Termination Procedure under the Law Commission Scheme
Chart 24.4   Termination Claims under the Law Commission Scheme
Figure 25.1   Right to Buy Sales of Local Authority Dwellings to Owner Occupation:
               England
Table 25.1   Setting the Price of Enfranchisement
Table 25.2   Enfranchisement of Long Leasehold Houses
Table 25.3   How the Original Valuation Basis Works
Table 25.4   How the Market Valuation Basis Works
Table 25.5   The Cost of Collective Enfranchisement

TABLE OF CASES

A Plesser & Co Ltd v Davis [1983] 2 EGLR 70 (QB) 500
Abbeyfield (Harpenden) Society Ltd v Woods [1968] 1 WLR 374 (CA) 81
Abbott v Bayley (1999) 32 HLR 72 (CA) 694
Abdul Amarjee v Barrowfen Properties Ltd [1993] 2 EGLR 133 (Cty Ct) 484
Abidogun v Frolan Health Care Ltd [2001] EWCA Civ 1821 . . . . 702, 716, 717, 725
Acme Housing Association and Royal Borough of Kensington and Chelsea v Chevska,
   Legal Action 17 (June 1987) 742
Active Estates v Parness [2002] EWHC 893 (Ch) 727
Addiscombe Garden Estates Ltd v Crabbe [1958] 1 QB 513 (CA) 250
Adler v Blackman [1953] 1 QB 146 (CA) 92
Afzal Mohammed Madarbakus (1992) 13 Cr App R (S) 542 (CA) 688
AG Securities v Vaughan [1990] 1 AC 417 (HL) 61, 70, 71, 97, 98, 100, 101, 146, 464
Air India v Balabel [1993] 2 EGLR 66 (CA) 521
Akici v LR Butlin Ltd [2005] EWCA Civ 1296; [2006] 1 WLR 201 . . . . 62, 522, 705, 706, 707, 721
Ala Anufrijeva v Southwark [2003] EWCA Civ 1406 . . . . 332, 333
Alker v Collingwood Housing Association [2007] EWCA Civ 343 382
Allied Dunbar Assurance plc v Homebase Ltd [2002] EWCA Civ 666 . . . . 519, 525, 532, 543
Allied London Investments Ltd v Hambro Life Assurance Ltd (1985) 50 P & CR 207 (CA) 563
Allnatt London Properties Ltd v Newton [1984] 1 All ER 423 (CA) 533
Amoah v London Borough of Barking and Dagenham (2001) 82 P & CR D12 (Ch) 213
Amsprop Trading Ltd v Harris Distribution Ltd [1997] 1 WLR 1025 (Ch) 586
Anderson v Oppenheimer (1880) 5 QBD 602 122
Antoniades v Villiers [1990] 1 AC 417 (HL) 70, 71, 97, 98, 100, 101, 146, 464
Arbib v Earl Cadogan [2005] 3 EGLR 139 (Lands Trib) 763
Armit Holdings Co Ltd v Shahbakhti (Feraidoun) [2005] EWCA Civ 339 629
Artemiou v Procopiou [1966] 1 QB 878 (CA) 657
Artesian Residential Development Ltd v Beck [2000] 1 QB 541 (CA) 607
Artizans, Labourers and General Dwellings Co v Whitaker [1919] 2 KB 301 (KB) 205
Ashburn Anstalt v Arnold [1989] Ch 1 (CA) 443
Ashworth Frazer Ltd v Gloucester City Council [1997] 1 EGLR 104 (CA) 473
Ashworth Frazer Ltd v Gloucester City Council [2001] UKHL 59; [2001] 1 WLR 2180 . . . . . 419, 420,
                                                                                                          527, 528
Aslan v Murphy (Nos 1 and 2), Wynne v Duke (1990) 1 WLR 766 (CA) 776 . . . . 71, 79, 100, 145
Aspley Hall Estate Ltd v Nottingham Rent Officers [1992] 2 EGLR 187 (Rent Assessment Com) . . 461
Associated British Ports v CH Bailey plc [1990] 2 AC 703 (HL) 396, 708, 709
Associated Provincial Picture Houses Ltd v Wednesbury Corporation [1948] 1 KB 223 (CA) 496
Aston Cantlow and Wilmcote with Billesley Parochial Church Council v Wallbank [2003]
   UKHL 37; [2004] 1 AC 546 . . . . 273, 274, 276, 277
Attorney-General v Blake [2001] 1 AC 268 (HL) 78
Aubergine Enterprises Ltd v Lakewood International Ltd [2002] EWCA Civ 177; [2002] 1 WLR 2149
   520

Auwoth v Johnson (1832) 5 C & P 239; 172 ER 955 257
Bacchiocchi v Academic Agency Ltd [1998] 1 WLR 1313 (CA). 247, 659
Backhouse v Lambeth LBC (1972) 116 Sol Jo 802 (QB). 496
Bagettes Ltd v GP Estates Co Ltd [1956] Ch 290 249
Bain & Co v Church Commissioners (1988) 21 HLR 29 (Ch) 603
Bairstow Eves (Securities) Ltd v Ripley [1992] 2 EGLR 47 (CA). 733
Baker v Merckel [1960] 1 QB 657 (CA). 731
Balfour v Balfour [1919] 2 KB 571 (CA). 69
Balfour v Kensington Gardens Mansions Ltd (1932) 49 TLR 29 (KB) 529
Bandar Property Holdings Ltd v J S Darwen (Successors) Ltd [1968] 2 All ER 305 (QB) 428
Banjo v Brent LBC [2005] EWCA Civ 292; [2005] 1 WLR 2520. . . . . 188, 205, 212
Bank of England v Cutler [1908] 2 KB 208 (CA) 94
Bank of Ireland Home Mortgages v South Lodge Developments [1996] 1 EGLR 91 (Ch) 715, 718
Bankway Properties Ltd v Pensfold-Dunsford [2001] EWCA Civ 528; [2001] 1 WLR 169. 147, 491, 492
Barclays Bank plc v Bee [2001] EWCA Civ 1126; [2002] 1 WLR 332. . . . . 62, 649
Bardrick v Haycock (1976) 31 P & CR 420 (CA). 209
Barnes v City of London Real Property Co [1918] 2 Ch 18 (Ch) 374, 436
Barnett v O'Sullivan [1995] 1 EGLR 93 (CA) 209
Barrett v Lounova (1982) Ltd [1990] 1 QB 348 (CA) 370, 374
Barrett v Morgan [2000] 2 AC 264 (HL) 729, 730, 738, 739, 740
Barrow v Isaacs & Son [1891] 1 QB 417 (CA). 542
Basildon DC v Wahlen [2006] EWCA Civ 326. 750
Basingstoke & Deane BC v Host Group Ltd [1988] 1 WLR 348 (CA). 60, 61, 485, 486
Basingstoke & Deane BC v Paice (1995) 27 HLR 433 (CA) 210
Bass Ltd v Morton Ltd [1988] 1 Ch 493 (CA) 706, 707
Bater v Bater [1999] 4 All ER 944 (CA) 749, 756
Bates v Donaldson [1896] 2 QB 241 (CA) 526, 527, 529
Baxter v Camden LBC (No 2) [2001] 1 AC 1 (HL) . . 35, 45, 122, 278, 329, 354, 359, 363, 365, 392, 393
Bayley v Bradley (1848) 5 CB 396. 78
Baynton v Morgan (1888) 22 QBD 74 563
Beacon Carpets Ltd v Kirby (1984) 48 P & CR 445 (CA). 431
Begum (FC) v Tower Hamlets LBC [2003] UKHL 5; [2003] 2 AC 430 . . . . 280, 281
Bell v General Accident Fire and Life Assurance Corporation Ltd [1998] 1 EGLR 69 (CA). 245
Bell London and Provincial Properties Ltd v Reuben [1946] 2 All ER 547 (CA). 599
Bellcourt Estates Ltd v Adesina [2005] EWCA Civ 208 730
Belvedere Court Management Ltd v Frogmore Developments Ltd [1997] QB 858 (CA) 311, 772,
                                                                                        773, 774
Berrycroft Management Company Ltd and Girling v Sinclair Gardens Investments
    (Kensington) Ltd (1998) 75 P & CR 210 (CA) 428
Betty's Cafes Ltd v Phillips Furnishing Stores Ltd [1959] AC 20 (HL). 653, 656
Bhojwani v Kingsley Investment Trust Ltd [1992] 39 EG 138 (Ch). 715
Bhopal v Walia (1999) 32 HLR 302 (CA) 145
BHP Petroleum GB Ltd v Chesterfield Properties Ltd [2001] EWCA Civ 1797; [2002] Ch 194. . . . 109,
                                                                                        576, 577, 580
Bickel v Duke of Westminster [1977] QB 517 (CA) 420, 526, 527, 528
Bickenhall Engineering Co Ltd v Grandmet Restaurants Ltd [1995] 1 EGLR 110 (CA). 48
Billson v Residential Apartments Ltd [1992] 1 AC 494 (CA, HL). 36, 708, 710, 711, 712, 713
Bird v Hildage [1948] 1 KB 91 (CA). 614
Birmingham City Council v Doherty [2006] EWCA Civ 1739 . . . . 612, 613

Birmingham City Council v McCann [2003] EWCA Civ 1783 670
Birmingham City Council v Oakley [2001] 1 AC 617 (HL) 385
Birmingham DC v Kelly (1985) 17 HLR 572 (DC) 385
Birmingham, Dudley and District Banking Co v Ross (1888) 38 Ch D 295 123
Blawdziewicz v Diodon Establishment [1988] 2 EGLR 52 (Ch) 402
Blockbuster Entertainment Ltd v Barnsdale Properties Ltd [2003] EWHC 2912 (Ch). 521
Blythewood Plant Hire Ltd v Spiers [1992] 2 EGLR 103 (Cty Ct) 483
Boldack v East Lindsey DC (1999) 31 HLR 41 (CA) 381
Bon Apettito Ltd v Poon; Speedhold Ltd v Bon Apettito Ltd, Cuscani (Newcastle Cty Ct)
     18 January 2005 83
Booker v Palmer [1942] 2 All ER 674 (CA) 68
Boots the Chemists Ltd v Pinkland Ltd [1992] 28 EG 118 (Cty Ct) 483
Boswell v Crucible Steel of America [1925] 1 KB 119 (CA) 378
Boustany v Piggott [1993] EGCS 85 (PC) 30, 112
Boyer v Warbey [1953] 1 QB 234 (CA) 511, 573
Boyle, Greer, Jackson and Laird's Application for Judicial Review, Re [2005] NIQB 22; [2006]
     NI 16 . . . . 54, 272, 285, 290
Bracey v Read [1963] 1 Ch 88 (Ch) 246
Bracknell Development Corporation v Greenlees Lennerds Ltd [1981] 2 EGLR 105 (Ch) 499
Braddon Towers v International Stores Ltd [1987] 1 EGLR 209 (Ch) 424, 425
Bradford MCC v McMahon [1994] 1 WLR 52 (CA) 756
Bradney v Birmingham City Council [2003] EWCA Civ 1783 . . . . 670, 671, 672
Brann v Westminster Anglo-Continental Investment Co Ltd [1976] 2 EGLR 72 (CA) 528
Bratchett v Beaney [1992] 3 All ER 910 (CA) 693
Braythwayte v Hitchcock (1842) 10 M & W 494 87
Breams Property Investment Co Ltd v Strougler [1948] 2 KB 1 (CA) 92, 93
Brent LBC v Knightley (1997) 29 HLR 857 (CA). 606
Bretherton v Paton (1986) 18 HLR 257 (CA) 82
Brew Bros v Snax [1970] 1 QB 612 (CA). 366
Brick Farm Management Ltd v Richmond Housing Partnership Ltd (No 2) [2006] EWHC
     1004 (Ch). 780
Bristol City Council v Hassan, Bristol City Council v Glastonbury [2006] EWCA Civ 656;
     [2006] 1 WLR 2582 . . . . 605, 607
Bristol City Council v Lovell [1998] 1 WLR 446 (HL) 750, 756
Bristol and West Building Society v Marks and Spencer plc [1991] 2 EGLR 57 (Ch). 305
Britannia Building Society v Earl [1990] 2 All ER 469 (CA). 636
British Anzani (Felixstowe) Ltd v International Marine Management (UK) Ltd [1980] QB 137 (QB)
     403
British Gas Corporation v Universities Superannuation Scheme Ltd [1986] 1 WLR 398 (Ch). . 60, 485,
     486, 488
British Movietonews Ltd v London and District Cinemas [1952] AC 166 (HL) 498
British Telecommunications plc v Sun Life Assurance Society plc [1996] Ch 69 (CA). 372
Broadgate Square plc v Lehman Brothers Ltd [1995] 1 EGLR 97 (CA) 485, 490
Broadway Investments Hackney Ltd v Grant [2006] EWCA Civ 1709. 251
Bromley Park Garden Estates Ltd v Moss [1982] 1 WLR 1019 (CA) 521, 527
Brown v Liverpool Corporation [1969] 3 All ER 1345 (CA) 378
Brown v Wilson (1949) 208 LT Jo 144 (CA) 738
Brown & Root Technology Ltd v Sun Alliance & London Assurance Co Ltd [2001] Ch 733 (CA)
     . . . . 544, 545

Browne v Flower [1911] 1 Ch 219 (Ch) 122
Bruton v London and Quadrant Housing Trust [1998] QB 834 (CA); [2000] 1 AC 406 (HL)... 29, 68, 71, 72, 77, 84, 95, 377, 378, 739, 741
Buchmann v May [1978] 2 All ER 993 (CA).. 208
Buckley v Buckley (1787) 1 TR 647 .... 728, 729
Burford Midland Properties Ltd v Marley Extrusions Ltd [1995] 2 EGLR 15 (Ch) 565
Burman v Mount Cook Land Ltd [2001] EWCA Civ 1712; [2002] Ch 256..................... 63
Burrows v Brent LBC [1996] 1 WLR 1448 (HL) 70, 85, 86, 405, 406, 606, 607
Buswell v Goodwin [1971] 1 WLR 92 (CA) 363
Cadogan v Morris (1998) 77 P & CR 336 (CA)...................................... 782
Caerns Motor Services Ltd v Texaco Ltd [1994] 1 WLR 1249 (Ch)............. 422, 546, 579, 580
Caerphilly Concrete Products Ltd v Owen [1972] 1 WLR 372 (CA) 94
Camden LBC v Goldenberg (1996) 28 HLR 727 (CA)................................. 547
Camden LBC v McBride [1999] CLY 3737 (Cty Ct) 393
Camden LBC v Shortlife Community Housing Ltd (1993) 25 HLR 330 (Ch) 77, 82, 212
Camden Nominees v Forcey [1940] Ch 352 (Ch) 403
Campden Hill Towers Ltd v Gardner [1977] QB 823 (CA)......................... 379, 432
Canary Riverside PTE Ltd v Schilling [2006] Lands Tribunal LRX/65/2005 434
Canary Wharf Investments (Three) v Telegraph Group Ltd [2003] EWHC 1575 (Ch) ... 485, 487, 488
Canlin and Gray v Berkshire Holdings, September 1990, Legal Action 10 694
Canterbury City Council v Lowe (2001) 33 HLR 53 (CA)............................. 323
Capital and Counties Bank Ltd v Rhodes [1903] 1 Ch 631 (CA) 735
Cardiothoracic Institute v Shrewdcrest Ltd [1986] 1 WLR 368 (Ch) 88, 90, 91
Carega Properties SA v Sharratt [1979] 1 WLR 928 (HL) 550
Carroll v Manek and Bank of India (2000) 79 P & CR 173 (Ch) 83
Cassell & Co Ltd v Broome [1972] AC 1027 (HL)................................. 693
Cavalier v Pope [1906] AC 428 (HL) 380
Centaploy v Matlodge [1974] Ch 1 (Ch)....................................... 92, 93
Central Estates (Belgravia) Ltd v Woolgar (No 2) [1972] 1 WLR 1048 (CA) 704, 714, 715
Central Estates Ltd v Secretary of State for the Environment [1997] 1 EGLR 239 (CA)........ 489
Chalmers, Guthrie and Co v Guthrie (1923) LTJ 382............................... 98
Chamberlain v Farr [1942] 2 All ER 567 (CA) 87
Chappel v Panchall, December 1991, Legal Action 19............................... 694
Chartered Trust plc v Davies [1997] 2 EGLR 83 (CA) 33, 121, 123, 254, 306, 307, 308, 328, 330, 402, 724
Chelsea Yacht & Boat Co Ltd v Pope [2000] 1 WLR 1941 (CA) 761
Cheryl Investments v Saldanha [1978] 1 WLR 1329 (CA) 208, 251
Cheshire Lines Committee v Lewis & Co (1880) 50 LJQB 121 .... 92, 93
Chester v Buckingham Travel Ltd [1981] 1 WLR 96 (Ch) 110
Cheverell Estates Ltd v Harris [1998] 1 EGLR 27 (QB)........................... 500, 584
Chinwe Gil v Baygreen Properties Limited [2002] EWCA Civ 1340 601
Christopher Moran Holdings Ltd v Bairstow [2000] 2 AC 172 (HL) 727
Church Commissioners for England v Meya [2006] EWCA Civ 821 .... 596, 637
CIN Properties Ltd v Gill [1993] 2 EGLR 97 (QB) 521
CIN Properties Ltd v Rawlins [1995] 2 EGLR 130 (CA)........................... 308, 309
Circle 33 Housing Trust Ltd v Ellis [2005] EWCA Civ 1233.......................... 609
City and Metropolitan Properties Ltd v Greycroft Ltd [1987] 1 WLR 1085 (Ch) 582
City of London Corporation v Bown (1990) 22 HLR 32 (CA) 535, 544
City of London Corporation v Fell [1994] 1 AC 458 (HL); [1993] QB 589 ...... 37, 38, 560, 565, 566,

570, 571, 647

City of Westminster v Peart (1992) 24 HLR 389 (CA) 537, 545

City Permanent Building Society v Miller [1952] Ch 840 (CA) 112

Clark v Novacold Ltd [1999] 2 All ER 977 (CA) 621

Clear Channel UK Ltd v Manchester CC [2005] EWCA Civ 1304 81

Clegg v Hands (1890) 44 Ch D 503 (CA) 580

Co-operative Insurance Society Ltd v Argyll Stores (Holdings) Ltd [1996] Ch 286 (CA); [1998]
    AC 1 (HL). 399, 424, 425, 475

Co-Operative Wholesale Society Ltd v National Westminster Bank plc [1995] 1 EGLR 97 (CA) . . 485,
    490

Coatsworth v Johnson (1886) 55 LJQB 220. 112

Cobb v Lane [1952] 1 All ER 1199 (CA). 68

Cobstone Investments Ltd v Maxim [1985] QB 140 (CA) 618

Cocks v Thanet DC [1983] 2 AC 286 (HL) 43, 44

Cody v Philips, (unreported) discussed in *Private Renter* Issue 4 March 2006. 405

Cole v Kelly [1920] 2 KB 106 (CA). 580

Collins v Barrow (1831) 1 M & Rob 112; 174 ER 38 35

Commercial Union Life Assurance Co Ltd v Moustafa [1999] 2 EGLR 44 (QB) 566

Commission for New Towns v R Levy & Co Ltd [1990] 2 EGLR 121 (Ch) 489

Commissioners of Revenue and Customs v Abbey National plc [2006] EWCA Civ 886 16

Connaught Restaurants Ltd v Indoor Leisure Ltd [1994] 1 WLR 501 (CA) 405

Conquest v Ebbetts [1896] AC 490 (HL). 397

Continental Property Ventures Inc v White [2006] 1 EGLR 85 (Lands Tribunal) 438

Contour Homes Ltd v Rowen, [2007] EWCA Civ 842 . . . . 491 Cook v Mott (1961) 178 EG
    637 (CA) 656

Coppen v Bruce-Smith (1988) 77 P & CR 239 (CA) 656

Coronation Street Industrial Properties Ltd v Ingall Industries plc [1989] 1 WLR 304 (HL) 584

Costain Property Developments Ltd v Finlay & Co Ltd (1988) 57 P & CR 345 (QB) 424

Cottage Holiday Associates Ltd v Customs and Excise Commissioners [1983] QB 735 73

Council of Civil Service Unions and Others v Minister for Civil Service [1985] AC 374 (HL) . . 43, 332

Cox v Bishop (1857) 8 De GM & G 815 574

Crago v Julian [1992] 1 WLR 372 (CA) 544

Cramas Properties v Connaught Fur [1965] 1 WLR 892 (HL). 658

Crawley BC v B (2000) 32 HLR 636 (CA). 195

Crawley BC v Sawyer (1987) 20 HLR 98 (CA) 210, 213

Crawley BC v Ure [1996] QB 13 (CA) 670

Credit Suisse v Beegas Nominees Ltd [1994] 4 All ER 803 (Ch). 61, 366, 368

Creery v Summersell and Flowerdew & Co Ltd [1949] Ch 751 (Ch) 542, 718

Crehan v Inntrepreneur Pub Company [2003] EWHC 1510 (Ch); [2006] UKHL 38; [2007]
    1 AC 333 . . . . 422, 423

Cremin v Barjack Properties Ltd [1985] 1 EGLR 30 (CA) 714

Crestfort Ltd v Tesco Stores Ltd [2005] EWHC 805 (Ch) 525, 529, 532, 542, 543

Cricket Ltd v Shaftesbury plc [1999] 3 All ER 283 (Ch). 250

Cricklewood Property and Investment Trust Ltd v Leighton's Investment Trust Ltd [1945]
    AC 221 (HL). 31, 736

Croydon LBC v Moody (1998) 31 HLR 738 (CA) 599

Cruse v Mount [1933] Ch 278 (Ch). 359, 361

Cumming v Danson [1942] 2 All ER 653 (CA). 599

Cunliffe v Goodman [1950] 2 KB 237 (CA) 656

Curl v Angelo [1948] 2 All ER 189 (CA)..205
Curtis v London Rent Assessment Committee [1999] QB 92 (CA)....................461, 462
Cuthbertson v Irving (1859) 4 H & N 742 95
DAF Motoring Centre (Gosport) Ltd v Hatfield and Wheeler Ltd [1982] 2 EGLR 59 (CA)........656
Daley, James, Wiseman, Reynolds v Mahmood and Rahman, unreported, 12 August 2005
     (Central London Cty Ct)..693
Davenport v R (1877) 3 App Cas 115 704
Davies v Price [1958] 1 WLR 434 (CA)...593
Dawncar Investments Ltd v Plews (1993) 25 HLR 639 (CA) 629
De Markozoff v Craig (1949) 93 Sol Jo 693 (CA) 629
De Mattos v Gibson (1858) 4 De G & J 276 38
Dean and Chapter of the Cathedral and Metropolitan Church of Christ Canterbury v
     Whitbread plc [1995] 1 EGLR 82 (Ch)....................................78, 89
Deanplan Ltd v Mahmoud [1993] Ch 151 565
Debenhams Retail Plc v Sun Alliance & London Assurance Co Ltd [2005] EWCA Civ 868 . . . 474, 475
Delgable Ltd v Perinpanathan [2005] EWCA Civ 1724 369
Dellneed v Chin (1987) 53 P & CR 172 (Ch) 83
Demetriou v Robert Andrews (Estate Agencies) Ltd (1990) 62 P & CR 536 (CA)..............374
Denetower Ltd v Toop [1991] 1 WLR 945 (CA)...............................771, 773
Dennett v Atherton (1872) LR 7 QB 316...122
Design Progression Ltd v Thurloe Properties Ltd [2004] EWHC 324 (Ch); [2005] 1 WLR 1 . . 520, 522
Desnousse v LB of Newham [2006] EWCA Civ 547; [2006] QB 831.............675, 676, 677, 678
Din (Taj) v Wandsworth BC [1983] 1 AC 657 (HL)..........................676, 677
Dinefwr BC v Jones (1987) 19 HLR 445 (CA).....................................379
Dobson v Jones (1844) 5 Man & G 112 83
Doe d Aslin v Summersett (1830) 1 B & Ad 135 40
Doe d Cheny v Batten (1775) 1 Cowp 243 680
Doe d Lord v Crago (1848) 6 CB 90 ....88, 89
Dollar v Winston [1950] Ch 236..528
Dong Bang Minerva (UK) Ltd v Davina Ltd [1996] 2 EGLR 31 (CA)...................521
Donnelly's Application for Judicial Review, Re [2003] NICA 55; [2004] NI 189 ....283, 332, 619
Douglas Shelf Seven Ltd v Co-Operative Wholesale Society Ltd & Kwik Save Group Plc [2007]
     CSOH 53 425
Drane v Evangelou [1978] 1 WLR 455 (CA) 691, 693
Dresden Estates Ltd v Collinson (1988) 55 P & CR 47 (CA)......................80, 476
Dudley MBC v Bailey (1990) 22 HLR 424 (CA) 598
Duke of Westminster v Birrane [1995] QB 262 (CA).............................761
Duke of Westminster v Guild [1985] QB 688 (CA)........................374, 375, 436
Dukeminster (Ebbgate House One) Ltd v Somerfield Property Co Ltd (1997) 75 P & CR 154
     (CA)...481
Duncliffe v Caerfelin Properties Ltd [1989] 2 EGLR 38 (Ch)....................582
Dunn v Bradford MDC [2002] EWCA Civ 1137 393
Dyer v Dorset County Council [1988] QB 346 (CA)..............................752
Earl Cadogan and Cadogan Estates Ltd v 26 Cadogan Square Ltd [2007] EWCA Civ 499 781
Earl Cadogan and Cadogan Estates Ltd v Sportelli [2006] RVR 382 (Lands Trib).......763, 767, 779
Earle v Charalambous [2006] EWCA Civ 1090................................372, 400
East v Pantiles Plant Hire Ltd [1982] 2 EGLR 111 (CA).........................114
Eastern Telegraph Co v Dent [1899] 1 QB 835 (CA).............................542
Eaton v Lyon (1798) 3 Ves Jun 691 712

Edlington Properties v Fenner & Co Ltd [2006] EWCA Civ 403; [2006] 1 WLR 1583 . . . . 582, 583
Edmonton Corporation v W M Knowles & Son Ltd (1961) 60 LGR 124 (QB). 375, 395, 436
Edward H Lewis & Son v Morelli [1948] 2 All ER 1021 (CA) 94
Edwards v Etherington (1825) Ry & M 268; 171 ER 1016 35
Eker v Becker (1946) 174 LT 410 73
Electricity Supply Nominees Ltd v IAF Group Ltd [1993] 1 WLR 1059 (QB) 125, 405
Elite Investments v TI Silencers [1986] 2 EGLR 43 (Ch) 366
Elitestone v Morris [1997] 1 WLR 687 (HL) 413
Eller v Grovecrest Investments Ltd [1995] QB 272 (CA). 404, 511
Elsden v Pick [1980] 1 WLR 898 (CA) 674
Elvidge v Coventry City Council (1993) 26 HLR 281 (CA). 210, 215
Equity & Law Life Assurance Society Plc v Bodfield Ltd (1987) 54 P & CR 290 (CA) 486
Escalus Properties Ltd v Robinson [1996] QB 231 (CA) 718
Esselte AB v Pearl Assurance plc [1997] 1 WLR 891 (CA) 648, 659
Essex Plan Ltd v Broadminster (1988) 56 P & CR 353 (Ch). 82
Esso Petroleum Co Ltd v Harper's Garage (Stourport) Ltd [1968] AC 269 (HL). 422
Estates Gazette Ltd v Benjamin Restaurants Ltd [1994] 1 WLR 1528 (CA). 572
Expert Clothing Service & Sales Ltd v Hillgate House [1986] Ch 340 (CA) 705, 706, 707
Fairweather v Ghafoor [2001] CLY 4164 (Cty Ct) 697
Family Housing Association v Jones [1990] 1 WLR 779 (CA) 72
Featherstone v Staples [1986] 1 WLR 861 (CA). 263
Fernandez v McDonald [2003] EWCA Civ 1219; [2004] 1 WLR 1027 637
Finch v Underwood (1876) 2 Ch D 310 (CA) 733
Finchbourne v Rodrigues [1976] 3 All ER 581 (CA) 436
First Penthouse Ltd v Channel Hotels and Properties (UK) Ltd [2003] EWHC 2713 (Ch) 562
First Property Growth Partnership Ltd v Royal and Sun Alliance Property Services Ltd [2002]
    EWCA Civ 1687; [2003] 1 All ER 533 489
Fitzpatrick v Sterling Housing Association Ltd [2001] 1 AC 27 (HL) 292, 550
Fitzroy House Epworth Street (No 1) Ltd v The Financial Times Ltd [2006] EWCA Civ 329;
    [2006] 1 WLR 2207. 733
Flexman v Corbett [1930] 1 Ch 672 (Ch) 110
Footwear Corp Ltd v Amplight Properties Ltd [1999] 1 WLR 551 (Ch). 521
Forbouys plc v Newport BC [1994] 1 EGLR 138 (Cty Ct) 483
Francis v Brown (1998) 30 HLR 143 (CA). 694, 697
Francis Jackson Developments Ltd v Stemp [1943] 2 All ER 601 (CA) 87, 205
Francke v Hackmi [1984] CLY 1906 208
Friends' Provident Life Office, Re [1999] 1 All ER (Comm) 28 (Ch). 29, 735
Friends' Provident Life Office v British Railways Board [1996] 1 All ER 336 (CA). 564, 565, 567,
                                                                                    568, 731
Fuller v Judy Properties Ltd (1991) 64 P & CR 176 (CA). 715
FW Woolworth and Co Ltd v Lambert [1938] Ch 883 (CA). 407, 408
FW Woolworth plc v Charlwood Alliance Properties Ltd [1987] 1 EGLR 53 (Ch) 305
G Orlik (Meat Products) Ltd v Hastings and Thanet BS (1974) 29 P & CR 126 (CA) 663
Garston v Scottish Widows Fund & Life Assurance Society [1998] 1 WLR 1583 (CA). 62, 651
Gaudy v Jubber (1865) 9 B & S 15 89
Gay v Sheeran [2000] 1 WLR 673 (CA) 539
Geddes v Texaco Ltd [1994] 1 WLR 1249 (Ch) 422, 579
Gentle v Faulkner [1900] 2 QB 267 (CA) 544
Ghaidan v Godin-Mendoza [2004] UKHL 30; [2004] 2 AC 557 . . . . 272, 278, 285, 292, 293, 547

Gilbert-Ash (Northern) Ltd v Modern Engineering (Bristol) [1974] AC 689 (HL) 405
Gilje v Charlgrove Securities Ltd [2001] EWCA Civ 1777 61
Gisborne v Burton [1989] QB 390 (CA) 263
Gladstone v Bower [1960] 1 QB 170 (QB); [1960] 2 QB 384 (CA). 259, 262, 268
Glasgow Corporation v Johnstone [1965] AC 609 (HL) 83
Go West Ltd v Spigarolo [2003] EWCA Civ 17; [2003] QB 1140 521
Gold v Brighton Corporation [1956] 3 All ER 442 (CA) 663
Goldmile Properties Ltd v Lechouritis [2003] EWCA Civ 49 . . . . 122, 371
Gouldsworth v Knights (1843) 11 M & W 337 95
Governors of the Peabody Donation v Grant (1982) 6 HLR 43 (CA) 213
Granby Village (Manchester) Management Co Ltd v Unchained Growth III plc [2000]
    1 WLR 739 (CA). 126
Gray v Taylor [1998] 1 WLR 1093 (CA) 84
Graysim Ltd v P & O Property Holdings Ltd [1996] AC 329 (HL) 244, 246, 248, 249
Great Peace Shipping Ltd v Tsavliris Salvage (International) Ltd [2002] EWCA Civ 1407 30
Greater London Council v Connolly [1970] 2 QB 100 (CA) 477
Green v Eales (1841) 2 QB 225 378
Greene v Church Commissioners [1974] 1 Ch 467 (CA) 519
Greenwich LBC v McGrady (1982) 46 P & CR 223 (CA). 40
Greenwich LBC v Regan (1996) 28 HLR 469 (CA) 87, 406, 606
Gregson v Cyril Lord [1963] 1 WLR 41 (CA) 656
Griffiths v St Helens MBC [2006] EWCA Civ 160; [2006] 1 WLR 2233 . . . . 188, 196, 197
Groveside Properties Ltd v Westminster Medical School (1983) 47 P & CR 507 (CA). 250
Habermann v Koehler [2000] EGCS 125 (CA) 110
Hackney LBC v Side by Side (Kids) Ltd [2003] EWHC 1813 (QB); 1 WLR 363 603
Hafton Properties Ltd v Camp [1994] 1 EGLR 67 (QB). 374
Hagee (London) Ltd v A B Erikson and Larson [1976] QB 209 (CA) 87, 240, 245
Hale v Hale [1975] 1 WLR 931 (CA) 540
Hall v King (1987) 19 HLR 440 (CA) 539
Hamilton v Martell Securities Ltd [1984] Ch 266 (Ch) 395, 396, 709
Hammersmith and Fulham LBC v Clarke (2001) 33 HLR 881 (CA) 213
Hammersmith and Fulham LBC v Creska Ltd (1999) 78 P & CR D 46 (Ch) 394
Hammersmith and Fulham LBC v Monk [1992] 1 AC 478 (HL) 39, 40, 76, 670, 672, 734, 749
Hampshire v Wickens (1878) 7 Ch D 555 . . . . 109, 110
Hand v Hall (1877) 2 Ex D 355 106
Hankey v Clavering [1942] 2 KB 326 (CA) 61
Hannon v 169 Queen's Gate Ltd [2000] 1 EGLR 40 (Ch). 374
Hanson v Newman [1934] Ch 298 (CA). 397
Haringey LBC v Hickey [2006] EWCA Civ 373 217
Haringey LBC v Stewart (1991) 23 HLR 557 (CA) 404
Harlow DC v Hall [2006] EWCA Civ 156; [2006] 1 WLR 2116 605
Harmer v Jumbil (Nigeria) Tin Areas [1921] 1 Ch 200 (CA) 123
Harrison v Hammersmith and Fulham LBC [1981] 1 WLR 650 (CA). 188, 189
Harrow LBC v Johnstone [1997] 1 WLR 459 (HL) 670
Harrow LBC v Qazi [2003] UKHL 43; [2004] 1 AC 983 . . . . 281, 282, 610, 611, 670, 671, 672
Harrow LBC v Tonge (1992) 25 HLR 99 (CA). 548
670 Hart v Emelkirk Ltd [1983] 1 WLR 1289 (Ch) 402
Hart v Windsor (1843) 12 M & W 68; (1844) 152 ER 1114 . . . . 35, 184, 358
Hastie v City of Edinburgh 1981 SLT 61 378

Havenridge Ltd v Boston Dyers Ltd [1994] 2 EGLR 73 (CA) 428
Haviland v Long [1952] 2 QB 80 (CA) 397
Heath v Drown [1973] AC 498 (HL) 655
Helena Housing Ltd v Pinder [2005] EWCA Civ 1010 . . . . 70, 86, 87, 470, 606
Hemingway Realty Ltd v Clothworkers Co [2005] EWHC 299 (Ch) 61
Hemingway Securities Ltd v Dunraven Ltd (1996) 71 P & CR 30 (Ch). 543
Herbert v Byrne [1964] 1 WLR 519 (CA) 643
Herbert Duncan Ltd v Cluttons [1993] 2 WLR 710 (CA) 566, 647
Herne v Bembow (1913) 128 ER 531 376
Heslop v Burns [1974] 1 WLR 1241 (CA) 68, 81, 88
Hill v Barclay (1810) 16 Ves 402 . . . . 398, 399
Hill v East and West India Dock Co (1884) 9 App Cas 448 590
Hilton v James Smith & Sons (Norwood) Ltd [1979] 2 EGLR 44 (CA) 124, 328, 330
Hilton v Plustitle [1988] 3 All ER 1053 (CA). 206
Hindcastle v Barbara Attenborough Associates Ltd [1997] AC 70 (HL) 561, 589, 590, 726, 727
Hodgkinson v Crowe (1875) 10 Ch App 622. 109
Hoffman v Fineberg [1949] Ch 245 (Ch) 706
Holbeck Hall Hotel Ltd v Scarborough Borough Council [2000] QB 836 (CA) 736
Holding & Barnes plc v Hill House Hammond Ltd [2001] EWCA Civ 1334 . . . . . . 114, 227, 369, 370
Holme v Brunskill (1878) 3 QBD 495. . . . . 583, 584, 731
Hopcutt v Carver (1969) 209 EG 1069 (CA) 653
Hopwood v Cannock Chase DC [1975] 1 WLR 373 (CA) 378
Horford Investments Ltd v Lambert [1976] Ch 39 (CA) 205
Houlder Brothers & Co Ltd v Gibbs [1925] Ch 575 (CA). 526, 529
Hounslow LBC v McBride (1999) 31 HLR 143 (CA) 599, 601
Hounslow LBC v Pilling [1993] 1 WLR 1242 (CA) 670, 674, 682, 695, 697, 734
Howard de Walden Estates Ltd v Les Aggio [2007] EWCA Civ 499 781
Howard de Waldon Estates Ltd v Pasta Place Ltd [1995] 1 EGLR 79 (Ch) 583
Howard v Fanshawe [1895] 2 Ch 581 716
Hua Chiao Commercial Bank Ltd v Chiaphua Industries Ltd [1987] AC 99 (PC) 571, 579
Hughes v LB of Greenwich (1994) 26 HLR 99 (HL) 215
Hughes v Liverpool CC (1988) *The Times* 30 March (CA). 379
Hunter v Canary Wharf Ltd [1997] AC 655 (HL) 49
Hurstfell v Leicester Square Property Co [1988] 2 EGLR 105 (CA) 653
Hussain v Lancaster City Council [2000] QB 1 (CA) 327, 328, 329, 332
Hussein v Mehlman [1992] 2 EGLR 87 (Cty Ct) 32, 33, 378, 402, 724
Hussey v Camden LBC (1994) 27 HLR 5 (CA) 213
Huwyler v Ruddy (1995) 28 HLR 550 (CA) 79
Hyde Housing Assocation Ltd v Harrison (1990) 23 HLR 57 (CA). 215, 216
Hyman v Rose [1912] AC 623 (HL) 713
I & H Caplan Ltd v Caplan (No 2) [1963] 1 WLR 1247 (Ch). 247
Industrial Properties (Barton Hill) Ltd v Associated Electrical Industries Ltd [1977] QB
    580 (CA). 94, 110
Ingram v Inland Revenue Commissioners [1997] 4 All ER 395 (CA) 28, 736
International Drilling Fluids Ltd v Louisville Investments (Uxbridge) Ltd [1986] Ch 513 . . . . 407, 419,
    420, 421, 520, 526, 528
Inverugie Investments v Hackett [1995] 1 WLR 713 (PC) 78
Investors Compensation Scheme Ltd v West Bromwich Building Society [1988] 1 WLR 896 (HL). . 60,
    61, 113, 370

Iqbal v Thakrar [2004] EWCA Civ 592 . . . . 407, 408
Isaac v Hotel de Paris Ltd [1960] 1 WLR 239 (PC) 89, 91
Islington LBC v Honeygan-Green [2007] EWHC 1270 (QB). 750, 751, 756
Islington LBC v Uckac [2006] EWCA Civ 340; [2006] 1 WLR 1303 . . . . 624, 625
Issa v Hackney BC [1997] 1 WLR 956 (CA). 385, 391
Ivorygrove Ltd v Global Grange Ltd [2003] EWHC 1409 (Ch); [2003] 1 WLR 2090. 657
Janes (Gowns) Ltd v Harlow Development Corporation [1980] 1 EGLR 52 (Ch) 483, 661
Janet Reger International Ltd v Tiree Ltd [2006] EWHC 1743 (Ch) 114, 365
Jaquin v Holland [1960] 1 WLR 258 (CA). 397, 398
Javad v Mohammed Aqil [1999] 1 WLR 1007 (CA) 82, 87, 88, 90, 91, 245
Jenkins R Lewis Ltd v Kerman [1971] 1 Ch 477 (CA). 39, 731
Jervis v Harris [1996] Ch 195 (CA) 396, 397, 507
Jeune v Queen's Cross Ltd [1974] Ch 97 (Ch) 399, 401
Johnson v Moreton [1980] AC 37 (HL) 145, 146, 258, 259, 262, 263, 268
Johnston & Sons Ltd v Holland [1988] 1 EGLR 264 (CA) 416
Jones v Jones (1997) 29 HLR 561 (CA). 539
Jones v Miah (1992) 24 HLR 578 (CA) 692, 696
Joyner v Weeks [1891] 2 QB 31 (CA) 397
JT Developments v Quinn (1991) 62 P & CR 33 (CA). 110
Junction Estates Ltd v Cope (1974) 27 P & CR 482 (QB) 500, 647
K v K [1992] 1 WLR 530 (CA). 540
Kataria v Safeland plc [1998] 1 EGLR 39 (CA) 711
Kay v LB of Lambeth [2006] UKHL 10; [2006] 2 AC 465 . . . . . . 272, 277, 282, 283, 284, 610, 611, 612,
                                                                                    613, 671, 729, 738, 741
Kay Green v Twinsectra Ltd [1996] 1 WLR 1587 (CA) 771
Kaye v Massbetter [1991] 39 EG 129 (CA) 206
Keepers and Governors of John Lyon Grammar School v Secchi [1999] 3 EGLR 49 (CA). 63
Kened Ltd v Connie Investments Ltd (1995) 70 P & CR 370 (CA) 519
Kenny v Preen [1963] 1 QB 499 (CA). 122
Khar v Delbounty Ltd (1998) 75 P & CR 232 (CA). 722
Killick v Roberts [1991] 1 WLR 1146 (CA). 30, 112, 625
King, Re decd [1963] Ch 459 (CA) 431, 581
King v Jackson (1997) 30 HLR 541 (CA). 692, 696
King v South Northamptonshire DC (1992) 64 P & CR 35 (CA). 373
Kingston v Prince [1999] 1 FLT 539 (CA). 548
Kleinwort Benson Ltd v Lincoln City Council [1999] 2 AC 349 (HL) 499, 648
Knight ex p Voisey, In Re (1882) 21 Ch D 442. 106
Knowsley Housing Trust v McMullen [2006] EWCA Civ 539. . . . . 323, 324, 604, 609
KPMG LLP v Network Rail Infrastructure Ltd [2007] EWCA Civ 363 . . . . 114, 115, 116
Kumar v Dunning [1989] QB 193 (CA) 584
Kushner v Law Society [1952] 1 KB 264 (DC). 106
Kuwait Airways Corporation v Iraqi Airways Company [2004] EWHC 2603 (Comm) 78
Lace v Chantler [1944] KB 368 (CA) 37, 72, 73, 75
Laconia, The [1977] AC 850 (HL) 36
Ladbroke Group plc v Bristol CC [1998] 1 EGLR 126 (CA). 114
Lambert v Keymood Ltd [1997] 2 EGLR 70 (QB) 429
Lambeth LBC v O'Kane [2005] EWCA Civ 1010 . . . . 70, 86, 87, 470, 606
Lambeth LBC v Rogers (2000) 32 HLR 361 (CA). 406, 606
Land Reclamation Co v Basildon District Council [1979] 1 WLR 767 (CA) 247, 248

Landlords Association for Northern Ireland's Application for Leave to Apply for Judicial Review, Re
    [2005] NIQB 22; [2006] NI 16. . . . . 54, 272, 285, 290, 390, 391
Langford Property Co Ltd v Tureman [1949] 1 KB 29 (CA) 206
Langford v Selmes (1857) 3 K & J 220 519
Latimer v Carney [2006] EWCA Civ 1417. 397
Lavender v Betts [1942] 2 All ER 72 (KB) 122
Lawrence v Carter (1956) 167 EG 222 (Cty Ct). 654
Lay v Ackerman [2004] EWCA Civ 184 62
Leadenhall Residential 2 Ltd v Stirling [2001] EWCA Civ 1011; [2002] 1 WLR 499. . . . . 84, 86
Lee v K Carter Ltd [1949] 1 KB 85 (CA). 528
Lee v Leeds CC [2002] EWCA Civ 6; [2002] 1 WLR 1488 . . . . 45, 272, 278, 283, 368, 374, 381, 392
Lee-Parker v Izzet [1971] 1 WLR 1688 (Ch) 403
Leeds CC v Price [2006] UKHL 10; [2006] 2 AC 465. . . . . . 272, 277, 282, 283, 284, 610, 613, 671, 729,
                                                                                                      738, 741
Levy v Vesely [2007] EWCA Civ 367. 69
Ley v Peter (1858) 3 H&N 101 . . . . 68, 87
Linden v Department of Health and Social Security [1986] 1 WLR 164 (Ch). 250
Linden Gardens Trust Ltd v Lenesta Sludge Disposals Ltd [1994] 1 AC 85 (HL). 25
Lippiatt v South Gloucestershire Council [2000] QB 51 (CA) 329
Lipton v Whitworth (1994) 26 HLR 293 (CA) 634
Lister v Lane and Nesham [1893] 2 QB 212 (CA) 367
Littman v Aspen Oil (Broking) Ltd [2005] EWCA Civ 1579 . . . . 30, 115, 116
Liverpool CC v Irwin [1977] AC 239 (HL). 122, 373, 374
Liverpool CC v Slavin, 29 April 2005, *Legal Action* (July 2005). 622
Liverpool CC v Walton Group plc [2002] 1 EGLR 149 (Ch) 110
Llanelly Rly & Dock Co v London & N W Rly Co (1875) LR 7 HL 550 75
Lloyd v Dugdale [2002] 2 P & CR 13 (CA). 110
Lobb (Alec) (Garages) Ltd v Total Oil GB Ltd [1985] 1 WLR 173 (CA) 422
Lock v Pearce [1893] 2 Ch 271 (CA). 705
Lohan v Hilton [1994] EGCS 83 (CA) 634
London & Argyll Developments v Mount Cook Land Ltd [2003] EWHC 1404 (Ch) 420
London & County (A & D) Ltd v Wilfred Sportsman Ltd [1971] Ch 764 (CA) 581
London & Quadrant Housing Trust v Ansell [2007] EWCA Civ 326. . . . . 606, 607
London Baggage Company v Railtrack plc (2000) 80 P & CR D38 (Ch). 88, 90
London Diocesan Fund v Phithwa [2005] UKHL 70; [2005] 1 WLR 3956 . . . . . 561, 562, 563, 577, 578
Long v Tower Hamlets LBC [1998] Ch 197 (Ch). 107
Long Acre Securities Ltd v Karet [2004] EWHC 442 (Ch); [2005] Ch 61 771
Lord Strathcona SS Co v Dominion Coal Co [1926] AC 108 (PC). 38
Lotteryking Ltd v AMEC Properties Ltd [1995] 2 EGLR 13 (Ch). 579
Lowe v Lendrum (1950) 159 EG 423 (CA) 624
Lower Street Properties Ltd v Jones (1996) 28 HLR 877 (CA) 637
Luganda v Service Hotels Ltd [1969] 2 Ch 209 (CA) 71
Lurcott v Wakely and Wheeler [1911] 1 KB 905 (CA) 366, 371
McAuley v Bristol City Council [1992] QB 134 (CA). 378, 380
McCall v Abelesz [1976] QB 585 (CA) 691
McCann v Birmingham City Council [2004] EWHC 2156 (Admin). 671, 672
McCarrick v Liverpool Corporation [1947] AC 219 (HL) 362
McCarthy v Bence [1990] 1 EGLR 1 (CA) 80
McCormack v Namjou [1990] CLY 1725 (Cty Ct). 698

McDonald v Fernandez [2003] EWCA Civ 1219; [2004] 1 WLR 1027 63
McIntyre v Hardcastle [1948] 2 KB 82 (CA) 629
McMillan v Singh (1985) 17 HLR 120 (CA). 692, 693
McNerny v Lambeth LBC [1989] 1 EGLR 81 (CA) 363
Majorstake Ltd v Monty Curtis [2006] EWCA Civ 1171; [2006] 3 WLR 1114. 783
Malekshad v Howard De Walden Estates Ltd [2002] UKHL 49. . . . . 760, 761
Mallett & Sons (Antiques) Ltd v Grosvenor West End Properties [2006] EWCA Civ 594; [2006] 1 WLR
    2848 760
Malzy v Eicholz [1916] 2 KB 308 (CA) 308, 329
Mancetter Development Ltd v Garmanson Ltd [1986] QB 1212 (CA). 375, 413
Manchester Bonded Warehouse Co v Carr 5 CPD 507 359
Manchester Brewery v Coombs [1901] 2 Ch 608 (Ch). 573
Manchester City Council v Cochrane [1999] 1 WLR 809 (CA) 214
Manchester City Council v Higgins [2005] EWCA Civ 1423; [2006] 1 All ER 841 . . . 284, 323, 324, 618
Manchester City Council v Romano and Samari [2004] EWCA Civ 834; [2005] 1 WLR 2775 284,
                                                                                       621, 622, 678
Mannai Investments Co Ltd v Eagle Star Life Assurance Co Ltd [1997] AC 749 (HL) . . . 59, 61, 62, 63,
                                                                      113, 370, 649, 679, 705, 734
Marchant v Charters [1977] 1 WLR 1181 (CA) 70, 71, 81
Marcroft Wagons Ltd v Smith [1951] 2 KB 496 (CA) 69
Marjorie Burnett Ltd v Barclay [1981] 1 EGLR 41 (Ch). 94
Mark Rowlands Ltd v Berni Inns Ltd [1986] QB 211 (CA) 429
Marks v Warren [1979] 1 All ER 29 (Ch) 522
Marsden v Edward Heyes Ltd [1927] 2 KB 1 (CA) 370
Marshall v Bradford Metropolitan DC [2001] EWCA Civ 595 606
Marston v Leeds City Council [2002] EWCA Civ 1137 393
Martin v Smith (1874) LR 9 Ex 50 . . . . 91, 111
Mason v Skilling [1974] 1 WLR 1437 (HL). 462
Mayho v Buckhurst (1617) Cro Jac 438. 571
Mayor and Burgesses of LB of Lewisham v Malcolm [2007] EWCA Civ 763 678
Meadows v Clerical Medical & General Life Assurance Society [1981] Ch 70 (Ch) 703
Mellor v Watkins (1874) LR 9 QB 400. . . . . 739, 741
Melville v Bruton (1996) 29 HLR 319 (CA) 692, 696
Merton LBC v Cook, December 2006 (Croydon Cty Ct) 605
Methuen-Campbell v Walters [1979] 2 WLR 113 (CA) 761
Metropolitan Properties Company (Regis) Ltd v Bartholomew and Dillon (1996) 72 P & CR
    380 (CA) 565
Metropolitan Property Holdings Ltd v Finegold [1975] 1 WLR 349 (CA) 461
Midland Railway Co's Agreement, In Re; Charles Clay & Sons Ltd v British Railways Board
    [1971] Ch 725 (CA). 76, 92, 93
Mikeover Ltd v Brady [1989] 3 All ER 618 (CA) 98, 101
Milmo v Carreras [1946] KB 306 (CA). 28, 72, 519, 544
Ministry of Defence v Asham (1993) 66 P & CR 195 (CA) 78
Minja Properties Ltd v Cussins Property Ltd [1998] 2 EGLR 52 (Ch) 365
Moat v Martin [1950] 1 KB 175 (CA) 522, 529
Moat Housing Group South Ltd v Harris [2005] EWCA Civ 287; [2006] QB 606. . . 284, 320, 321, 324,
    619, 620
Mohamed v Manek (1995) 27 HLR 439 (CA). 677
Mohammadi v Anston Investments Limited [2003] EWCA Civ 981. 717

Moorcock, The (1889) 14 PD 64 . . . . 361, 373
Morgan v Liverpool Corporation [1927] 2 KB 131 (CA) 363
Morris v Liverpool City Council (1988) 20 HLR 498 (CA) 379
Morrow v Nadeem [1986] 1 WLR 1381 (CA) 649
Mount Eden Land Ltd v Folia Ltd, Prohibition London Ltd [2003] EWHC 1815 (Ch) 521
Mount Eden Land Ltd v Straudley Investments Ltd (1997) 74 P & CR 306 (CA) 527
Mountain v Hastings (1993) 25 HLR 427 (CA) 598
Mowan v Wandsworth (2001) 33 HLR 56 (CA) 42, 330, 345
Mumford Hotels Ltd v Wheler [1964] 1 Ch 117 (Ch) 430
Murray v Aslam (1994) 27 HLR 284 (CA) 692
Muscat v Smith [2003] EWCA Civ 962; [2003] 1 WLR 2853 . . . . 31, 404, 582, 583
National Car Parks Ltd v Trinity Development Company (Banbury) Ltd [2001] EWCA Civ 1686 80, 81
National Carriers Ltd v Panalpina (Northern) Ltd [1981] AC 675 (HL) 32, 736, 737
National Provincial Bank Ltd v Ainsworth [1965] AC 1175 (HL) 1248 756
National Trust the Places of Historic Interest or Natural Beauty v Knipe [1998] 1 WLR 230 (CA) . 675
National Westminster Bank plc v Arthur Young McClelland Moores & Co [1985] 1 EGLR 61
    (Ch) 488
NCB v Neath BC [1976] 2 All ER 478 (HL) 386
NCR Ltd v Riverland No 1 Ltd [2004] EWHC 921 (Ch) 532
NCR Ltd v Riverland Portfolio No 1 Ltd [2005] EWCA Civ 312 521
Neale v Del Soto [1945] KB 144 (CA) 205
New England Properties plc v Portsmouth New Shops Ltd [1993] 1 EGLR 84 (Ch) 366
Newham LBv Hawkins [2005] EWCA Civ 451 86
Newham LB v Khatun, Zeb and Iqbal [2004] EWCA Civ 55; [2005] QB 37 . . . . 30, 126, 127, 193
Newham LB v Kibata [2003] EWCA Civ 1785 . . . . 670, 672
Newlon Housing Trust v Al-Sulaimen [1999] 1 AC 313 (HL) 540, 671
Newtons of Wembly Ltd v Williams [1965] 1 QB 560 54
9 Cornwall Crescent London Ltd v Kensington and Chelsea LBC [2005] EWCA Civ 324;
    [2006] 1 WLR 1186 782
99 Bishopsgate v Prudential Assurance (1985) 273 EG 984 (CA) 490
No 1 Albemarle Street, Re [1959] Ch 531 (Ch) 539 . . . . 662, 663
Nordenfelt v Maxim Nordenfelt Guns and Ammunition Co [1894] AC 535 (HL) 422
Norfolk v Trinity College, Cambridge (1976) 32 P & CR 147 (Lands Trib) 766
Norfolk Capital Group Ltd v Kitway [1977] QB 506 (CA) 528
Norris (t/a J Davis & Son) v Checksfield [1991] 1 WLR 1241 (CA) 83, 674
North British Housing Association Ltd v Matthews [2004] EWCA Civ 1736; [2005] 1 WLR 3133 . . 615
Northampton BC v Lovatt [1998] 2 FCR 177 (CA) 618
Northcote Laundry Ltd v Frederick Donelly Ltd [1968] 1 WLR 562 (CA) 107
Northway Flats Management Co (Camden) Ltd v Wimpey Pension Trustees [1992] 2 EGLR 42
    (CA) 433
Norwich City Council v Famuyiwa [2004] EWCA Civ 1770 601
Norwich City Council v Secretary of State for the Environment [1982] QB 808 (CA) 758
Norwich Union Insurance Society v British Railways Board [1987] 2 EGLR 137 (Ch) 61
Norwich Union Life Insurance Ltd v Low Profile Fashions Ltd (1991) 64 P & CR 187 (CA) 563
Norwich Union Life Insurance Society v British Railways Board [1987] 2 EGLR 137 (Ch) . 356, 368, 369
Norwich Union Life Insurance Society v Shopmoor Ltd [1999] 1 WLR 531 (Ch) 519, 521
Norwich Union Life Insurance Society v Sketchley plc [1988] 2 EGLR 126 (Ch) 489
Norwich Union Life Insurance Society v Trustee Savings Bank Central Board [1986] 1 EGLR
    136 (Ch) 482, 487

Norwich Union Linked Life Assurance Co Ltd v Mercantile Credit Co Ltd [2003] EWHC
    3064 (Ch)... 521
Notting Hill Housing Trust v Roomus [2006] EWCA Civ 407; [2006] 1 WLR 1375 637
Nunes v Davies Laing & Dick Ltd [1986] 1 EGLR 127 (Ch)............................. 489
Nunn v Dalrymple (1989) 21 HLR 569 (CA) 69
Nurdin & Peacock plc v DB Ramsden & Co Ltd [1999] 1 WLR 1249 (Ch).................. 499
Nwokorie v Mason (1993) 26 HLR 60 (CA) 681, 692, 696, 697
Nynehead Developments Ltd v RH Fibreboard Containers Ltd [1999] 1 EGLR 7 (Ch) 402, 724
Oakfern Properties Ltd v Ruddy [2007] EWCA Civ 1389; [2006] 1 All ER 337 .... 437, 442
Oceanic Village v Shirayama Shokusan Co Ltd [2001] L & TR 35 (Ch).................. 124, 417
O'Connor v Old Etonian Housing Association Ltd [2002] EWCA Civ 150; [2002] Ch 295 378
Official Custodian of Charities v Goldridge (1973) 26 P & CR 191 (CA) 765
Old Grovebury Manor Farm Ltd v W Seymour Plant Sales and Hire Ltd (No 2) [1979] 1 WLR
    1397 (CA) 542
O'Leary v LB of Islington (1983) 9 HLR 83 (CA) 327
Oliver Ashworth (Holdings) Ltd v Ballard (Kent) Ltd [2000] Ch 12 (CA)............... 679, 680
Olympia & York Canary Wharf Ltd v Oil Property Investments Ltd [1994] 2 EGLR 48 (CA) 528
O'May v City of London Real Property Co Ltd [1983] 2 AC 726 (HL)............. 441, 663, 664
Onyx (UK) Ltd v Beard [1996] EGCS 55 (Ch) 77
O'Reilly v Mackman [1983] 2 AC 237 (HL) 43, 344, 345
Orlando Investments Ltd v Grosvenor Estate Belgravia [1989] 2 EGLR 74 (CA)............... 529
Owen v Gadd [1956] 2 QB 99 (CA) 122
P & A Swift Investments v Combined English Stores Group plc [1989] 1 AC 632 (HL) .. 571, 572, 584
P & S Amusements Ltd v Valley House Leisure Ltd [2006] EWHC 1510 (Ch) 423
Panayi & Pyrkos v Roberts (1993) 25 HLR 421 (CA)................................ 636
Parc Battersea Ltd v Hutchinson [1999] L & TR 554 (Ch)............................ 544
Parker v Camden LBC [1985] 2 All ER 141 (CA) 402
Parker v Taswell (1858) 2 De G & J 559 .... 110, 111, 112
Parkins v Westminster City Council [1998] 1 EGLR 22 (CA) 70
Parsons v Trustees of Henry Smith's Charity [1973] 1 WLR 845 (CA)................... 761
Patel v Newham LB (1978) 13 HLR 77 (CA)...................................... 379
Patel v Pirabakaran [2006] EWCA Civ 685; [2006] 1 WLR 3112................ 208, 675, 676, 710
Peabody Donation Fund Governors v Higgins [1983] 1 WLR 1091 (CA).................. 542
Peer Freeholds Ltd v Clean Wash International Ltd [2005] EWHC 179 (Ch) 62
Pelosi v Newcastle Arms Brewery (Nottingham) Ltd (1982) 43 P & CR 18 (CA) 412
Pemberton v Southwark LBC [2000] 1 WLR 1672 (CA)............................ 85, 406
Pembery v Lamdin [1940] 2 All ER 434 367
Pennell v Payne [1995] QB 192 (CA) 738, 740, 741
Petra Investments Ltd v Jeffrey Rogers plc [2000] 3 EGLR 120 (Ch) 124, 307, 402, 416, 417
Petrofina (UK) Ltd v Magnaload Ltd [1984] 1 QB 127 (QB) 429
Pimms Ltd v Tallow Chandlers Company [1964] 2 QB 547 .... 420, 527
Plinth Property Investments Ltd v Mott, Hay and Anderson (1979) 38 P & CR 361 (CA) 418, 482
Plymouth Corporation v Harvey [1971] 1 WLR 549 (Ch)............................. 706
Pointon York Group plc v Poulton [2006] EWCA Civ 1001...................... 246, 247, 248
Pole Properties Ltd v Feinberg (1982) 43 P & CR 121 (CA) 433, 498
Poplar Housing and Regeneration Community Association Ltd v Donoghue [2001] EWCA
    Civ 595; [2002] QB 48 (CA) 274, 275, 276, 610, 611
Port v Griffith [1938] 1 All ER 295 (Ch) 416, 417
Porter v Commissioner of Police of the Metropolis [1999] All ER (D) 1129 (CA).......... 309, 310

Post Office v Aquarius Properties Ltd [1987] 1 All ER 1055 (CA). 359, 365, 367, 371
Powely v Walker (1793) 5 Term Rep 373; 101 ER 208 257
Princes House Ltd v Distinctive Clubs Ltd [2006] All ER (D) 117 (Sep) (Ch). 433
Proforce Recruit Ltd v The Rugby Group Ltd [2006] EWCA Civ 69. 114
Proudfoot v Hart (1890) 25 (QBD) 371, 378, 397
Prudential Assurance Co Ltd v London Residuary Body [1992] 2 AC 386 (HL) . . 28, 37, 72, 73, 74, 75,
    76, 91, 92, 93, 674
Prudential Assurance Co Ltd v PRG Powerhouse Ltd [2007] EWHC 1002 (Ch). 728
Prudential Nominees Ltd v Greenham Trading Ltd [1995] 1 EGLR 97 (CA) 485, 490
Pumperninks of Piccadilly Ltd v Land Securities plc [2002] EWCA Civ 621; [2002] Ch 332 . . 655, 656,
    657
Purchase v Lichfield Brewery [1915] 1 KB 184 (KB) 573
PW & Co v Milton Gate Investments Ltd [2004] EWHC 1994 (Ch); [2004] Ch 142. 272, 293, 731, 738,
    739, 740
Queen's Club Garden Estates v Bignell [1924] 1 KB 117 (DC). 89
Queensway Housing Association v Chairman of the Chilterns, Thames and Eastern Rent
    Assessment Committee (1999) 31 HLR 945 (QB). 461
Quick v Taff Ely BC [1986] QB 809 (CA). 362, 365, 367, 369, 371, 380, 392
R v Bristol City Council ex p Everett [1999] 2 All ER 193 (CA) 385
R v Burke [1991] 1 AC 135 (HL) 688
R v Cardiff City Council ex p Cross (1982) 6 HLR 1 (CA). 384
R v Housing Benefit Review Board for East Devon DC ex p Gibson and Gibson (1993) 25
    HLR 487 (CA) 467
R v Housing Benefit Review Board of the London Borough of Brent ex p Connery [1990] 2
    All ER 353 (QB) 467
R v Local Commissioner for Local Government for North and North-east England ex p
    Liverpool City Council [2001] 1 All ER 462 (CA) 343
R v London Borough of Croydon ex p Jarvis (1993) 26 HLR 194 (QB) 677
R v Newham LBC ex p Khan [2000] All ER (D) 580 (QB). 677
R v Newham LBC ex p Ojuri (No 3) (1999) 31 HLR 631 (QB) 675
R v Newham LBC ex p Ugbo (1993) 26 HLR 263 (QB) 676
R v Panel on Take-overs and Mergers ex p Datafin plc [1987] QB 815 (CA). 275
R v Parnell (1881) 14 Cox CC 508 403
R v Rent Officer for LB of Camden ex p Plant [1981] EGLR 73 (QB). 208
R v Rent Officer of Nottingham Registration Area ex p Allen [1985] 2 EGLR 153 (QB); (1985) 17 HLR
    481 (QB). 206, 761
R v Secretary of State for the Environment ex p Royal Borough of Kensington and
    Chelsea (1987) 19 HLR 161 (QB) 698
R v Secretary of State for the Environment ex p Walters (1998) 30 HLR 328 (CA) 554, 555
R v Welwyn Hatfield DC ex p Slough Estates plc [1991] EGCS 38 (QB). 42
R v Worthing BC ex p Bruce (1993) 26 HLR 223 (CA) 213
R v Yuthiwattana (1984) 80 Cr App R 55 (CA). 687, 688, 689
R (on the application of Beale) v Camden LB [2004] EWHC 6 (Admin) 335
R (on the application of Bempoa) v Southwark LB [2002] EWHC 153 (Admin) 692
R (on the application of Clays Lane Housing Cooperative Ltd) v Housing Corporation [2004]
    EWCA Civ 1658 180
R (on the application of Gangera) v Hounslow LBC [2003] EWHC 794 (Admin) 549
R (on the application of Kilby) v Basildon DC [2007] EWCA Civ 479 139
R (on the application of Rowe) v Vale of White Horse DC [2003] EWHC 388 (Admin). 432

R (on the application of Vella) v Lambeth LBC [2005] EWHC 2473 (Admin) 385, 386, 392
R (Badu) v Lambeth LBC [2005] EWCA Civ 1184; [2006] 1 WLR 505. 293
R (Limbuela) v Secretary of State for the Home Department [2005] UKHL 66; [2006] 1 AC 396
    . . . . 279, 280, 296
R (McCann) v Manchester Crown Court [2001] 1 WLR 358 (QB) 321
R (McLellan) v Bracknell Forest B C [2001] EWCA Civ 1510; [2002] QB 1129 . . . . . 214, 281, 610, 611
R (Morris) v Westminster City Council [2005] EWCA Civ 1184; [2006] 1 WLR 505 293
Rainbow Estates Ltd v Tokenhold Ltd [1999] Ch 64 (Ch). 398, 399
Ramdath v Daley (1993) 25 HLR 273 (CA) 692, 693
Ramnarace v Lutchman [2001] UKPC 25; [2001] 1 WLR 1651 . . . . 68, 87
Ratcliffe v Sandwell MBC [2001] EWCA Civ 6; [2002] 1 WLR 1488 . . 272, 278, 283, 368, 374, 381, 392
Ravenseft Properties Ltd v Davstone (Holdings) Ltd [1980] QB 12 (QB) 367, 368
Ravenseft Properties Ltd v Hall [2001] EWCA Civ 2034. . . . . 62, 63
Rawlin's Case (1587) Jenk 254 95
Receiver for the Metropolitan Police District v Palacegate Properties Ltd [2000] 13 EGLR
    187 (CA) 251
Redfern v Reeves [1978] 2 EGLR 52 (CA). 655
Regalgrand Ltd v Dickerson (1997) 29 HLR 620 (CA). 683, 688, 697
Regis Property Co Ltd v Dudley [1958] 1 QB 346 (CA). 370
Regus (UK) Ltd v Epcot Solutions Ltd [2007] EWHC 938 (Comm) 80, 126
Reichman v Beveridge [2006] EWCA Civ 1659 . . . . 33, 39, 254, 402, 506, 507, 508, 509, 724
Reid v Dawson [1955] 1 QB 214 (CA) 259
Reigate and Banstead BC v Benfield [2001] EWCA Civ 1510; [2002] QB 1129 281
Reohorn v Barry Corporation [1956] 2 All ER 742 (CA). 656
Rich v Basterfield (1847) 4 CB 783 329
Richard Clarke & Co v Widnall [1976] 1 WLR 845 (CA) 706, 712
Richmond Court (Swansea) Ltd v Williams [2006] EWCA Civ 1719 . . . . 303, 304, 410
Rimmer v Liverpool City Council [1985] QB 1 (CA) 380
Ritz Hotel (London) Ltd v Ritz Casino Ltd [1989] 2 EGLR 135 (CA). 487
Riverside Housing Association Ltd v White [2007] UKHL 20. . . . . 472, 475
Rogers v Rice [1892] 2 Ch 170 (CA). 718
Romulus Trading Co Ltd v Comet Properties Ltd [1996] 2 EGLR 70 (QB). 416
Rookes v Barnard [1964] AC 1129 (HL) 692
Ropemaker Properties Ltd v Noonhaven Ltd [1989] 2 EGLR 50 (Ch) 714, 715
Rugby School (Governors) v Tannahill [1935] 1 KB 87 (CA). 707
Rye v Rye [1962] AC 496 (HL). 28, 735, 736
St Brice v LB of Southwark [2001] EWCA Civ 1138; [2002] 1 WLR 1527. 608
St Catherine's College v Dorling [1980] 1 WLR 66 (CA) 205
St Martins Property Investments Ltd v CIB Properties Ltd [1999] 1 L & T R 1 (CA) 487
Salisbury v Marshall (1829) 4 Ca & P 65, NP 35
Sampson v Wilson [1996] Ch 39 (CA) 694
Samrose Properties Ltd v Gibbard [1958] 1 WLR 235 (CA). 207
Sanctuary Housing Association v Campbell [1999] 3 All ER 460 (CA). 540
Sargeant v Macepark (Whittlebury) Ltd [2004] EWHC 1333 (Ch); [2004] 4 All ER 662 . . . . . 420, 421
Savile Settled Estates, In Re [1931] 2 Ch 210 731
Savoy Hotel Ltd, Re [1981] Ch 351 54
Savva v Houssein [1996] 2 EGLR 65 (CA) 66. . . . . 706, 707
Saxby v McKinley (1996) 29 HLR 569 (CA) 691
Say v Smith (1530) 1 Plowden 269 72

Scala House & District Property Co Ltd v Forbes [1974] QB 575 (CA)................707, 708
Scandinavian Trading Tanker Co AB v Flota Petrolera Ecuatoriana (The Scaptrade) [1983]
    QB 529 (CA); [1983] 2 AC 694 (HL)......................................36
Scaptrade, The *see* Scandinavian Trading Tanker Co AB v Flota Petrolera Ecuatoriana
Schon v L B of Camden (1986) 18 HLR 341 (QB)...............................688, 689
Scottish & Newcastle plc v Raguz [2006] EWHC 821 (Ch)............................586
Scottish & Newcastle plc v Raguz [2007] EWCA Civ 150.....................564, 566, 567
Scottish Amicable Life Assurance Society v Middleton Potts [1995] 1 EGLR 97 (CA).......485, 490
Scottish Mutual v Jardine Public Relations......................................366
Scribes West Ltd v Relsa Anstalt (No 3) [2004] EWCA Civ 1744; [2005] 1 WLR 1847 (CA)......580
Secretary of State for Communities and Local Government v Swords [2007] EWCA Civ 795.....555
Secretary of State for Defence v Guardian Newspapers Limited [1985] AC 339 (HL)............54
Secretary of State for the Environment v Associated Newspapers Holdings Ltd (1996) 72
    P & CR 395 (CA)...485
Sevenoaks, Maidstone and Tunbridge Railway Co v London, Chatham and Dover Railway Co
    (1879) 11 Ch D 625...74
Shanly v Ward (1913) 29 TLR 714 (CA)..527, 528
Sharp v McArthur (1987) 19 HLR 364 (CA)...89
Shaw v Groom [1970] 2 QB 504 (CA)...117
Sheffield City Council v Smart [2002] EWCA Civ 4; [2002] HLR 639................610, 612
Sheldrake v DPP, Attorney General's Reference No 4 of 2004 [2004] UKHL 43; [2005] 1 AC 264..293
Shell-Mex & BP Ltd v Manchester Garages [1971] 1 WLR 612 (CA).................81, 245
Shelley v London County Council [1948] 1 KB 274 (CA); [1949] AC 56 (HL).........188, 191, 301
Sherrin v Brand [1956] 1 QB 403 (CA)...608
Shiloh Spinners Ltd v Harding [1973] AC 691 (HL)...............................713, 714
Shirayama Shokusan Co Ltd v Danovo Ltd [2005] EWHC 2589 (Ch)..................708, 714
Shrimpton v Rabbits (1924) 131 LT 478 (KB).....................................599
Siddiqui v Rashid [1980] 3 All ER 184 (CA).......................................629
Sidnell v Wilson [1966] 2 QB 67..395
Sight & Sound Education Ltd v Books etc Ltd [1999] 3 EGLR 45 (Ch)...............658, 659
Simons v Associated Furnishers Ltd [1931] 1 Ch 379 (Ch).............................733
Skeet v Powell-Sneddon [1988] 2 EGLR 112 (CA)...................................657
Sleafer v Lambeth B C [1960] 1 QB 43 (CA)..........................374, 375, 436
Slough BC v Robbins [1996] 12 CL 353 (Cty Ct)...................................598
Slough Estates plc v Welwyn Hatfield DC [1996] 2 PLR 50 (QB).........................42
Smallwood v Sheppards [1895] 2 QB 627..73
Smith v Bradford Metropolitan Council (1982) 44 P & CR 171 (CA)...................381
Smith v Marrable (1843) 11 M & W 5; 152 ER 693.....................35, 121, 358, 359
Smith v Scott [1973] Ch 314 (Ch)...327, 329
Snook v London & West Riding Investments Ltd [1967] 2 QB 786 (CA)..................145
Solle v Butcher [1950] 1 KB 671 (CA)..30
Somma v Hazelhurst [1978] 1 WLR 1014 (CA).......................................99
Sopwith v Stuchbury (1985) 17 HLR 50 (CA)....................................89, 91
Southern Depot Co Ltd v British Railways Board [1990] 2 EGLR 39 (Ch)................714
Southwark LBC v Edem [1999] CLY 3713..406
Southwark LBC v Tanner [2001] 1 AC 1 (HL)..35, 45, 122, 123, 278, 329, 354, 359, 363, 365, 392, 393
Spath Holme Ltd v Chairman of the Greater Manchester and Lancashire Rent Assessment
    Committee (1995) 28 HLR 107 (CA).................................461, 462
Speedwell Estates Ltd v Dalziel [2001] EWCA Civ 1277...........................62, 63

Spenborough UDC's Agreement, Re [1968] Ch 139 (Ch) 76
Spencer's Case (1583) 5 Co Rep 16a.................................. 37, 560, 571, 573, 574
Spook Erection Ltd v British Railways Board [1988] 1 EGLR 76 (CA) 656
Sportoffer Ltd v Erewash BC [1999] 3 EGLR 136 (Ch) 418, 419, 420, 421, 529
Stacey v Hill [1901] 1 KB 660 (CA) 589
Staffordshire Area Health Authority v South Staffordshire Waterworks Co [1978] 1 WLR 1387
    (CA)... 498
Star Rider Ltd v Inntrepreneur Pub Co [1998] 1 EGLR 53 (Ch) 125, 405
Starmark Enterprises Ltd v CPL Distribution Ltd [2001] EWCA Civ 1252; [2002] Ch 306 489
Starsin, The [2003] UKHL 12; [2004] 1 AC 715................................. 113, 114
Sterling Land Office Developments Ltd v Lloyds Bank plc [1984] 2 EGLR 135 (Ch)........... 480
Stratford v Syrett [1958] 1 QB 107 (CA)... 205
Street v Mountford [1985] 1 AC 809 (HL) 68, 69, 70, 71, 75, 81, 82, 83, 89, 90, 91, 96, 97, 99, 101,
                                                    145, 186, 208, 211, 258, 519
Stuart v Joy [1904] 1 KB 362 (CA) 582
Stuchbery v General Accident Fire and Life Assurance Corp Ltd [1949] 2 KB 256 (CA) 236
Sun Life Assurance plc v Thales Tracs Ltd [2001] EWCA Civ 704; [2002] 1 WLR 1562.......... 658
Sutton v Temple (1843) 12 M & W 52; 152 ER 1108 .... 35, 358
Sutton (Hastoe) Housing Association v Williams (1988) 20 HLR 321 (CA) 437
Swainland Builders Ltd v Freehold Properties Ltd [2002] 2 EGLR 71 (CA) 115
Swanson v Forton [1949] Ch 143 (CA)... 528
Swinburne v Milburn (1884) 9 App Cas 844....................................... 94
Swindon BC v Aston [2002] EWCA Civ 1850 .... 86, 606
Swiss Bank Corpn v Lloyds Bank Ltd [1979] Ch 548 (Ch)............................. 38
Swords v Secretary of State for Communities and Local Government and others [2007]
    EWHC 771 (Admin)... 555
Tagro v Cafane [1991] 1 WLR 378 (CA) 693, 694, 696, 697
Tandon v Trustees of Spurgeon's Homes [1982] AC 755 (HL)........................... 761
Teasdale v Walker [1958] 1 WLR 1076 (CA) 247
Tegerdine v Brooks [1977] 36 P & CR 261 (CA) 266................................. 649
Tennant Radiant Heat Ltd v Warrington Development Corporation [1988] 1 EGLR 41 (CA)..... 374
Terrell v Murray (1901) 45 Sol Jo 579 (DC) 370
Thomas Bates & Sons Ltd v Wyndham's (Lingerie) Ltd [1981] 1 WLR 505 (CA) 115
Thompson v Elmbridge BC [1987] 1 WLR 1425 (CA) 605
Torminster Properties Ltd v Green [1983] 1 WLR 676 (CA) 501
Torridge DC v Jones (1985) 18 HLR 107 (CA) 598
Total Oil Great Britain Ltd v Thompson Garages (Biggin Hill) Ltd [1972] 1 QB 318 (CA) 31, 723
Tower Hamlets LBC v Abdi (1993) 25 HLR 80 (CA)................................. 216
Tower Hamlets LBC v Miah [1992] QB 622 (CA) 216
Trafford MBC v Total Fitness (UK) Ltd [2002] EWCA Civ 151 62
Transworld Land Co Ltd v J Sainsbury plc [1990] 2 EGLR 255 (Ch).................... 306, 425
Tulk v Moxhay (1848) 2 Ph 774.. 546, 573
Turner v Wandsworth LBC (1995) 69 P & CR 433 (CA) 656
Ujima Housing Association v Anash (1998) 30 HLR 831 (CA) 207
Unchained Growth III plc v Granbyvillage (Manchester) Management Co Ltd [2000] 1 WLR
    739 (CA) 405
United Scientific Holdings Ltd v Burnley B C [1978] AC 904 (HL) 30, 443, 479, 488
Uratemp Ventures Ltd v Collins [2001] UKHL 43; [2002] 1 AC 301 .... 205, 206, 211
Van Haarlam v Kasner Charitable Trust (1992) 64 P & CR 214 (Ch) 707, 715

Verrall v Great Yarmouth BC [1981] QB 202 (CA) 78
Viscount Tredegar v Harwood [1929] AC 72; [1928] All ER Rep 11 420
Vural Ltd v Security Archives Ltd (1989) 60 P & CR 258 (Ch) 430
W G Clark (Properties) Ltd v Dupre Properties Ltd [1992] Ch 297 (Ch) 124, 711, 716, 717
Wallace v Manchester City Council [1998] 3 EGLR 38 (CA) 400
Wallis Fashion Group Ltd v CGU Life Assurance Ltd [2000] 2 EGLR 49 (Ch) 665, 666
Walls v Atcheson (1826) 11 Moore CP and Exch Rep 379 507
Walsh v Lonsdale (1882) 21 Ch D 9 . . . . 111, 112, 474
Waltham Forest Community Based Housing Association v Fanning [2001] L & TR 41 (QB) 207
Waltham Forest LBC v Thomas [1992] 2 AC 198 (HL) 547
Wandsworth LBC v Michalak [2002] EWCA Civ 271; [2003] 1 WLR 617 . . . . 548, 549, 612
Wandsworth LBC v Osei-Bonsu [1999] 1 WLR 1011 (CA) 682, 688, 695, 696, 697
Wandsworth LBC v Winder [1985] 1 AC 461 (HL) 44, 345
Wansbeck DC v Marley (1988) 20 HLR 247 (CA) 631
Ward v Warnke (1990) 22 HLR 496 (CA) 69
Warder v Cooper [1970] 1 Ch 495 691
Warmington v Miller [1973] QB 877 (CA) 112
Warner v Sampson [1959] 1 QB 297 (CA) 716
Warren v Keen [1954] 1 QB 15 (CA) 376
Wedd v Porter [1916] 2 KB 91 (CA) 376
Welsh v Greenwich LBC (2001) 33 HLR 40 (CA) 369
West Ham Central Charity Board v East London Waterworks Co [1900] 1 Ch 624 (Ch) 375
West Horndon Industrial Park Ltd v Pheonix Timber Group plc [1995] 1 EGLR 137 (Ch) 583
West Layton Ltd v Ford [1979] QB 593 527
Westminster City Council v Basson (1990) 62 P & CR 57 (CA) 77
Westminster City Council v Clarke [1992] 2 AC 288 (HL) 79, 80, 211, 212
Westminster City Council v HSBC Bank Plc [2003] EWHC 393 (TCC) 62
Wettern Electric Ltd v Welsh Development Agency [1983] QB 796 (QB) 358, 361
Wheeler v Mercer [1957] AC 416 (HL) 78, 87, 88, 245
White v Knowsley Housing Trust [2007] EWCA Civ 404 . . . . 85, 86, 188, 405, 607, 608
White and Carter (Councils) Ltd v McGregor [1962] AC 413 (HL) 507, 509
White and White v Riverside Housing Association Ltd [2007] UKHL 20 . . . . 60, 495
Whitely v Stumbles [1930] AC 554 (HL) 246
Whiteman Smith Motor Co v Chaplin [1934] 2 KB 35 (CA) 237
Whiteminster Estates Ltd v Hodges Menswear Ltd (1974) 232 EG 715 (Ch) 421
Williams v Kiley (t/a CK Supermarkets Ltd) [2002] EWCA Civ 1645 . . . . 588, 589
Willingale v Globalgrange Ltd [2000] 2 EGLR 55 (CA) 780, 781
Willis v Association of the Universities of the British Commonwealth [1965] 1 QB 140 (CA) 657
Winch v Mid Bedfordshire DC [2002] All ER (D) 380 (QB) 329
Winter Garden Theatre (London) Ltd v Millennium Productions Ltd [1948] AC 173 (HL) 76, 78
Wolfe v Hogan [1949] 2 KB 194 (CA) 704
Wolverhampton Corporation v Emmons [1901] 1 QB 515 (CA) 399
Woodspring DC v Taylor (1982) 4 HLR 95 (CA) 614
Woolworth (FW) plc v Charlwood Alliance Properties Ltd [1987] 1 EGLR 53 (Ch) 528
Wright v Howell (1947) 204 LTJ 299 (CA) 205
Wycombe Area Health Authority v Barnett (1982) 5 HLR 84 (CA) 378, 379
Yankwood Ltd v L Bof Havering, 6 May 1998 (Ch) 308
YL v Birmingham City Council [2007] UKHL 27 . . . . 276, 277
York v Casey (1999) 31 HLR 209 (CA) 636

Zafiris v Liu [2005] EWCA Civ 1698. 657

Australia

J and S Chan Pty Ltd v McKenzie and McKenzie [1994] ANZ Conv Rep 610 (ACTSC) 507
Legione v Hateley (1983) 46 ALR 1 (HC). 36
Progressive Mailing House Pty Ltd v Tabali Pty Ltd (1985) 157 CLR 17; 57 ALR 609 (HC
    Australia) 40, 41, 508, 711, 725, 737
Radiach v Smith (1959) 101 CLR 209 (HCA) 70, 71
Shevill v Builders Licensing Board (1982) 149 CLR 620 (HC of Australia). 723
Smith v Leurs (1945) 70 CLR 256 (HC Aust) 331
Tall-Bennett & Co Pty Ltd v Sadot Holdings Pty Ltd (1988) NSW Conv Rep 57, 881 510
Vickers v Stichtenoth Investments Pty Ltd (1989) 52 SASR 90 (SASC). 509
Western Australia v Ward [2002] HCA 28. 71
Wood Factory Pty Ltd v Kiritos Pty Ltd 508

Canada

Globe Convestra v Vucetic (1990) 15 RPR (2d) 220 (Onto CJ). 506, 510
Grouse Mechanical Co v Griffith (1990) 14 RPR (2d) 233 (BCSC) 508
Highway Properties Ltd v Kelly, Douglas & Co Ltd [1971] SCR 562; (1971) 17 DLR (3d)
    710 (SC Canada) 506, 508, 725
607190 Ontario Inc v First Consolidate Holdings Corp (1992) 26 RPR (2d) 298 (ODC) 509
Transco Mills Ltd v Percan Enterprises Ltd (1993) 100 DLR (4th) 359 (BCCA) 509
Vinland Holdings Ltd v Wisniowski (1990) 9 RPR (2d) 194 (SCNS) 509

European Union

Anderson v United Kingdom (App No 44958/98) (1998) 25 EHRR CD 172. 308
Antoniades v United Kingdom (App No 15434/89) 15 February 1990 (ECtHR) 101, 464
Appleby v United Kingdom (App No 44306/98) (2003) 37 EHRR 38 (ECtHR) 272, 308, 309
Blecic v Croatia (2004) 41 EHRR 185 284
Broniowski v Poland [(App No 31443/96) (2006) 43 EHRR 1 457
Buckley v United Kingdom (App No 20348/92) (1996) 23 EHRR 101 281
Chapman v United Kingdom (App No 27238/95) (2001) EHRR 399 (ECtHR). 283
Connors v United Kingdom (App No 66746/01) (2004) 40 EHRR 189 (ECtHR) . . . 281, 282, 284, 324,
                                                                                                         620
Di Palma v United Kingdom (App No 11949/86) (1988) 10 EHRR 149 . . . . 272, 288
DP v United Kingdom see Di Palma v United Kingdom
Guerra v Italy (App No 14967/89) (1998) 26 EHRR 357 (ECtHR) 282, 333
Hatton v United Kingdom (App No 36022/97) (2003) 37 EHRR 28 . . . . 45, 278, 331
Hutten-Czapska v Poland (App No 35014/97) (2007) 45 EHRR 4 (ECtHR) 49, 456, 457, 460
Iatridis v Greece (App No 31107/96) (2000) 30 EHRR 97. . . . . 286, 287
James v United Kingdom (App No 8793/79) (1986) 8 EHRR 123 (ECtHR) . . . 272, 286, 287, 288, 289,
                                                                                                         766

Larkos v Cyprus (App No 29515/95) (1999) 30 EHRR 597 (ECtHR) 285
Lopez Ostra v Spain (App No 16798/90) (1995) 20 EHRR 277 (ECtHR). 282, 333
Marzari v Italy (36448/97) (1999) 28 EHRR 175 282
Mellacher and Others v Austria (App Nos 10522/83, 11011/84 and 11070/84) (1990) 12
    EHRR 391 (ECtHR). 287, 457
Moreno Gomez v Spain (App No 4143/02) (2005) 41 EHRR 40 (ECtHR). 283, 331
Neimietz v Germany (App No 13710/88) (1992) 16 EHRR 235 281
Oneryildiz v Turkey (App No 48939/99) (2005) 41 EHRR 20 288
O'Rourke v United Kingdom (App No 39022/97), 26 June 2001 (ECtHR) 280
P v United Kingdom (Application No 14751/89) 12 December 1990 612
Papamichalopoulos v Greece (App No 14556/89) (1993) 16 EHRR 40 279
Spath Holme Ltd v United Kingdom (App No 78031/01) 14 May 2002 (ECtHR) 289
Sporrong and Lonnroth v Sweden (App Nos 7151/75 and 7152/75) (1983) 5 EHRR 35 (ECtHR) . . 286
Stretch v United Kingdom (App No 44277/98) (2004) 38 EHRR 12 . . . . 290, 291
Surugiu v Romania (App No 48995/99) 20 April 2004 (ECtHR). 283, 331
Tsfayo v UK (App No 60860/00), 14 November 1996 (ECtHR) 281
Ure v United Kingdom (App No 28027/95), unreported, 27 November 1996 . . . . 612, 672
X and Y v The Netherlands (App No 8978/80) (1986) 8 EHRR 235 282

Ireland

Blake v Attorney General [1982] IR 117 (ISC). 289, 290, 458

South Africa

Government of the Republic of South Africa v Grootboom [2001] 1 SA 46 (CC) 296

United States of America

Armstrong v United States 364 US 40; 80 S Ct 1563 (1960) 49 458
Block v Hirsch 256 US 135, 41 S Ct 458 (1921). 458
Davidow v Inwood North Professional Group 747 SW 2d 373 (1988) (SC Texas) 34, 360
Delamater v Foreman 239 NW 148 (1931) (SC Minn) 33, 359
Edwards v Habib 397 F 2d 687 (1968) (CA DC) 34
Helmsley v Ft Lee 78 NJ 200; 394 A 2d 65 (1978) (NJ SC); 440 US 978; 99 S Ct 182 (1979)
    (US SC) 460
Hutton Park Gardens v Town Council 68 NJ 543; 350 A2d 1 (1975) (New Jersey SC) 458
Javins v First National Realty Corporation 428 F 2d 1071 (DC Cir 1970) 33, 34, 359, 360
Kelo v City of New London 545 US 469, 125 S Ct 2655 (2005) 288
Lingle v Chevron USA Inc 544 US 528; 125 S Ct 2074 (2005). 458, 459
Old Town Development Company v Langford 349 N E 2d 744 (1976) (Court of Appeals Indiana). . 32
Parrino v Lindsay 29 NY 2d 30; 323 NYS 2d 689 (1971) (NYCA) 35 460
Penn Central Transport Co v New York City 438 US 104; 98 S Ct 2646 (1978). 459
Pennell v City of San Jose 485 US 1; 108 S Ct 849 (1988) (US SC) 289
Pines v Perssion 14 Wis 2d 590 (1961) (SC Wis) 33, 359

Pittsburgh Allied Fabricators Inc v Haber 440 Pa 545; 271 A 2d 217 (1970) (SC Pa)............ 476
Pugh v Holmes 486 Pa 272; 405 A 2d 897 (1979) (SC Pennsylvania) 907 725
Rich v Don-Ron Trousers Corp 74 Misc 2d 259; 343 NYS 2d 684 (1973) (NYC Civ Ct) 476
Steele v Latimer 214 Kan 329; 521 P 2d 304 (1974) (SC Kansas) 725
Stoddard v Illinois Improvement & Ballast Co 113 NE 913; 275 Ill 199 (1916) (SC Ill).......... 475
Teller v McCoy 162 WVa 367; 253 SE 2d 114 (1978) (SC of Appeals West Virginia) 725
Whetzel v Jess Fisher Management Co 282 F 2d 943 (1960) (CA DC) 34
Witmer v Exxon Corp 495 Pa 540; 434 A 2d 1222 (1981) (SC Pa) 477
Yee v City of Escondido, California 503 US 519; 112 S Ct 1522 (1992) (S Ct)................. 459

TABLE OF STATUTES

Addison's Act *see* Housing and Town Planning Act 1919
Agricultural Holdings Act 1948 258
Agricultural Holdings Act 1984 551
Agricultural Holdings Act 1986. . . . 142, 145, 146, 257, 258, 259, 260, 263, 264, 266, 268, 270, 357, 382,
395, 411, 412, 496, 497, 593, 740
    s 1 258
    s 1(2) 259
    s 2 259
    s 3 259
    s 3(a) 259
    s 5 142
    ss 7–8 382
    s 12 496
    s 26(2) 259
    s 27(2) 259
    s 27(3) 259, 260
    s 27(3)(a) 260, 593
    s 27(3)(e) 260
    s 96 . . . . 259, 382
    Sch 2 496
        para 1(3)(a) 463
    Sch 3
        Part I 259
        Part II 259
            para 9 593
Agricultural Holdings (England) Act 1875 . . . . 258, 411
Agricultural Tenancies Act 1995 . . . . 19, 142, 257, 261, 262, 263, 264, 266, 267, 268, 269, 270, 342, 395,
411, 412, 496, 593, 677
    s 1(a) 264
    s 1(2)–(4) 264
    s 1(8) 264
    s 1(8) 257, 263
    s 4 265
    ss 5–6 . . . . 265, 497
    s 9(a)–(b) 497
    s 9(c) 265
    s 9(c)(ii) 265, 497
    s 10 . . . . 265, 497
    s 13(2) 497
    s 13(3) 497
    s 13(4) 265, 498
    s 13(4)(a)–(b) 265, 498

Agricultural Tenancies Act 1995 (continued)
　　s 15 411
　　s 15(a)–(b) 266
　　ss 16–17 . . . . 265, 411
　　s 18 412
　　s 18(1)(a)–(c) 267
　　s 19(5) 266, 411
　　s 20 412
　　s 20(1)–(3) 266
　　s 20(4) 412
　　s 21 412
　　s 21(1) 267
　　s 26 266
　　ss 28–29 . . . . 267, 344
　　s 30 344
　　s 38(1) 264
Agriculture Act 1947 258
Anti-social Behaviour Act 2003 . . . . 190, 214, 218, 317, 318, 323, 595, 618
　　s 12 317
　　ss 25A–25B 319
　　s 26A 319
Arbitration Act 1950 343
Arbitration Act 1979 343
Arbitration Act 1996 . . . . 341, 478
Artisans' and Labourers' Dwellings Improvement Act 1875 155
Caravan Sites Act 1968 206
Charities Act 1993 . . . . 623, 633
Children Act 1989 535
　　Sch 1
　　　　para 1(2)(d)–(e) 540
　　　　para 4(1) 540
Civil Partnerships Act 2004 . . . . 285, 547
　　Part 54 45
Common Law Procedure Act 1852
　　s 210 . . . . 715, 716
　　s 212 716
Commonhold and Leasehold Reform Act 2002 . . . . 13, 230, 231, 312, 314, 437, 717, 774, 775, 780
　　Part II 233
　　s 71 313
　　s 72 . . . . 312, 313
　　s 72(1)–(5) 312
　　ss 73–74 313
　　s 75 313
　　s 75(2) 313
　　s 76 . . . . 313, 428, 717
　　s 76(2) 313
　　s 77 . . . . 313, 428, 717
　　ss 78–95 313
　　s 96 313

s 96(b) 313
s 96(5)–(6) 313
ss 97–113 313
s 158 . . . . 435, 439
s 164 . . . . 230, 233, 427, 428, 430, 432
s 166 505
s 167 . . . . 233, 435, 440, 717
s 168 . . . . 233, 717
ss 169–171 233
Sch 6
    para 1 313
    paras 3–4 313
Sch 11 . . . . 435, 439
Competition Act 1998 . . . . 422, 423
Contracts (Rights of Third Parties) Act 1999 . . . . 546, 587, 588
s 1(1)(a)–(b) 587, 588
s 1(2) 587
Conveyancing Act 1881, s 14(2) 713
Counter-Inflation Act 1973, s 11 465
County Courts Act 1984
s 138 716
s 139(2) 716
Crime and Disorder Act 1998
s 1 320
s 1(1A) 321
s 1(6) 321
s 1(9) 322
s 1(10) 321
s 6 302
Criminal Law Act 1977
s 2 703
s 6 710
s 6(1) 680
Cross Act *see* Artisans' and Labourers' Dwellings Improvement Act 1875
Defective Premises Act 1972 . . . . 380, 406
s 4 . . . . 380, 381
s 4(1) 380
s 4(2)–(4) 381
s 4(5)–(6) 380
Disability Discrimination Act 1995 . . . . 104, 303, 409, 481, 620
s 1 303
s 18A 410
s 21 410
s 22 104
s 22(3) 678
s 22(3)(c) 318, 621
s 22(4) 520
s 23 104
s 24 . . . . 104, 621, 678

Disability Discrimination Act 1995 (continued)
 s 24(2)–(3) 319
 s 24B(3)–(4) 304
 s 24C 303
 s 24D 303, 410
 s 24E 303, 409
 s 24F 304
 s 24H 304
 s 24H(3)–(4) 304
 s 24K 304
 s 49A 104, 304
 s 49B 305
 s 49G 410
 s 49G(2)–(5) 410
 s 49H 410
Disability Discrimination Act 2005 410
Distress for Rent Act 1737 679
 s 18 . . . . 679, 680
Enterprise Act 2002 127
Environmental Protection Act 1990 . . . . 383, 385
 s 79 385
 s 80 . . . . 385, 388
 s 82 385
Equality Act 2006 104
 s 47 104
 s 48(1) 104
Factories Act 1961 357
Family Law Act 1996 . . . . 539, 540
 s 30 . . . . 538, 539
 s 30(3)–(4) 538
 s 30(7) 538
 s 33 539
 s 35 . . . . 538, 539
 s 36 539
 s 53 . . . . 538, 672
 Sch 7 . . . . 538, 539, 672
  para 1 539
  paras 4–5 539
  para 10 539
 Sch 8
  para 7(2) 539
  para 11 539
Finance Act 1988 . . . . 168, 173
Fires Prevention (Metropolis) Act 1774 430
 s 83 430
Health and Safety at Work Act 1974 357
Homelessness Act 2002 . . . . 193, 198, 216
 ss 1–3 193
 s 14 192

Housing Act 1935 159
Housing Act 1936 159
Housing Act 1957
  s 111. 477
  s 111(1) 496
  s 113. 477
Housing Act 1961 186
  s 32(1) 381
Housing Act 1966. . . . . 195, 553
  s 122. 467
  s 188. 677
  s 190(2)(a) 677
  s 192(3) 195
Housing Act 1974. . . . . 159, 451
  ss 121–122 118
Housing Act 1980 . . . . 7, 23, 26, 55, 154, 186, 335, 542, 595, 747, 757
  s 52 769
  s 79 502
  s 89. . . . . 603, 607
  s 105. 339
  s 106A 335
  Sch 3A 335
Housing Act 1985 . . . . . . 142, 189, 192, 210, 215, 221, 321, 323, 364, 383, 413, 547, 548, 611, 613, 618,
                                                   623, 626, 719, 749, 756, 757, 775

  Part V 220, 631
  Part VII 193
  s 5(1) 637
  s 5(4)–(5) 633
  s 21 402
  s 24 . . . . 450, 472, 477
  s 24(3) 451
  s 27 339
  s 79 . . . . 210, 211, 214, 554, 742
  s 79(1) 210
  s 79(3). 211, 215
  s 80 . . . . 210, 214, 554
  s 80(1). 212, 545
  s 80(2) 545
  s 81 . . . . 189, 211, 214
  s 82 . . . . 220, 596, 625
  s 82(2) 605, 607, 608
  s 82(3) 597
  s 82A 214
  s 83. . . . . 597, 631
  s 83(3)(b) 598
  s 83(4)(b) 598
  s 84 . . . . 189, 220
  s 84(1) 596
  s 84(2). 218, 599

Housing Act 1985 (continued)
s 85 606
s 85(1) 603
s 85(2) 84, 86, 603, 606, 607
s 85(3) 603
s 85(3)(a) 470
s 85(4) 603
s 85A 324, 325, 617, 618
s 85A(1)–(2) 617
s 86 597
s 86(2)(a)–(b) 596
s 87 . . . . 213, 220, 538, 545, 547
s 87(a) 548, 630
s 87(b) 548, 630, 631
s 88(1) 549
s 89 631
s 89(2) 547
s 89(3) 549
s 90(3) 549
s 91(1) 535
s 91(1)(b) 540
s 91(2) 535
s 91(3) 672
s 91(3)(a)–(b) 535
s 91(3)(c) 535, 538, 545
s 92 535
s 92(3)–(6) 535
s 93 220
s 93(1)(a) 537
s 93(1)(b) 536
s 93(2) 207, 214, 536, 543, 545, 678
s 94 220
s 94(2) 536
s 94(5) 525, 536
s 94(6)(a)–(b) 537
s 95 . . . . 220, 537
s 96 401
s 97 . . . . 409, 410
s 98 410
s 98(1)–(2) 409
s 99 409
s 100 413
s 101(2) 412
s 102 597
s 102(1)(a)–(b) 139
s 103 597
s 103(2) 139
s 104 119
s 104(2) 118, 119

s 105. 220
s 106A 554
s 112(1)–(2) 211
s 113 . . . . 548, 551
s 118(1)–(2) 751
s 119. 749
s 121 . . . . 749, 750
s 122. 756
s 123. 751
s 124. 756
s 125 . . . . 438, 757
ss 125A–125B 214
s 126. 753
s 127. 753
s 127(1)(b) 753
s 128. 756
s 129. 754
s 131. 754
s 138 . . . . 750, 753, 756
s 138(2) 756
s 138(3) 757
ss 140–141 758
ss 143D–143G. 215
s 153A 757
s 155. 754
s 155A 755
s 155C 755
s 156A. 755, 757
s 157. 755
ss 159–160 754
s 163A 755
s 164 . . . . 160, 757
ss 165–166. . . . . 160, 758
ss 167–170 758
s 171. 749
ss 171A–171B 554, 758
s 171C 554, 750, 758
ss 171D–171H 554, 758
s 183(2) 751
s 207. 384
s 268. 384
s 332 . . . . 117, 119
s 346. 386
ss 348B–348F 386
s 450A–450C 757
s 604 . . . . 348, 383
s 610. 409
Sch 1 214
    paras 1A–1B. 214, 595

Housing Act 1985 (continued)
   Sch 2 . . . . 189, 220, 633
      Part I 201, 543, 600
      Part II 600, 631
      Part III 600
      Part IV 599, 628
      Part V 632
      Part X 630
      para 3 630
      Ground 1 . . . . 543, 600, 613, 617
      Ground 2 . . . . 322, 600
      Ground 2A 600, 623
      Grounds 3–4 . . . . 600, 624
      Ground 5 . . . . 600, 625
      Ground 6 . . . . 600, 625, 626, 632, 633
         paras (a)–(b) 632
      Ground 7 . . . . 600, 626, 627
      Ground 8 . . . . 600, 629
      Ground 9 . . . . 600, 630
      Grounds 10–10A 600, 631, 632
      Ground 11 600
      Ground 12 . . . . 600, 626, 627
      Ground 13 . . . . 600, 633, 634
      Ground 14 600
      Ground 15 . . . . 600, 633, 634
      Ground 16 . . . . 548, 600, 630
   Sch 3 535
   Sch 3A 554
      para 3 554
      paras 5–6 555
   Sch 4 749
   Sch 5 . . . . 752, 753
      para 5(1)(a) 752
      para 7 752
      paras 9–11 752
   Sch 5A 753
   Sch 6 757
      Part III 751, 757
      para 12(3) 751
      para 16A 438
   Sch 6A 757
   Sch 9A 749
Housing Act 1986, Sch 3, Part I 260
Housing Act 1988 . . . . 8, 9, 22, 23, 55, 57, 63, 142, 147, 154, 163, 165, 167, 168, 173, 185, 187, 188, 189,
      203, 205, 206, 207, 210, 211, 214, 218, 451, 462, 464, 466, 491, 493, 494, 502, 547, 552, 555, 595,
         608, 618, 623, 624, 625, 626, 629, 637, 643, 677, 685, 688, 691, 699, 769
   s 1 545
   s 2 206
   s 3 . . . . 97, 206, 211

s 4 545
s 5. . . . . 220, 494, 596, 625
s 5(1) 210
s 5(2) 210, 493, 597
s 5(3) 596
s 5(3)(d). 596
s 5(3)(e) 493, 596
s 6 596
s 6A 637
s 7 . . . . 220, 596, 599
s 7(3)–(4) 210
s 7(5A) 599
s 7(6) 597, 599, 632
s 7(7) 607
s 8. . . . . 597, 614
s 8(1)(b) 613, 614
s 8(3)(c) 598
s 9(2) 84, 86, 604, 607
s 9(3) 470, 604, 608
s 9(4) 604
s 9A 324, 617, 618
s 9A(1)–(2). 617
s 11. . . . . 628, 632
s 13 . . . . 220, 464, 492, 493, 498
s 13(1) 494
s 13(1)(a) 493, 494
s 13(1)(b) 491, 493
s 13(3) 492
s 14. . . . . 478, 492
s 14(1) 493
s 15 220
s 15(1)–(2) 537
s 15(3)(a)–(b). 537
s 17. . . . . 220, 500, 547, 634
s 17(1) 547
s 17(2) 547
s 17(2)(b) 547
s 17(3)–(4) 547
s 18 . . . . 500, 741
s 18(1)–(2) 741
s 19 . . . . 500, 512
s 19A. 187, 204
s 20. . . . . 62, 636
s 20A 317
s 20B 219, 317, 637
s 21 . . . . 220, 389, 504, 596, 638
s 21(1) 636
s 21(3) 607
s 21(4). 611, 636

Housing Act 1985 (continued)
  s 21(5) 636
  s 22 . . . . 220, 464
  s 22(2)–(3) 464
  s 27 . . . . 691, 694, 695
  s 27(1)–(3) 694
  s 27(5)–(6) 697
  s 27(7) 698
  s 27(7)(a) 696
  s 27(8) 695
  s 28 . . . . 691, 694, 695, 696, 697
  s 28(1)–(3) 695
  s 28(6) 695
  s 45 545
  s 45(1) 205
  Sch 1 . . . . 204, 207
    Part III 208
    para 1 207
    paras 2–3 . . . . 207, 215
    paras 3A–3C 207
    para 4 . . . . 208, 216
    para 4A 216
    para 5 216
    para 6 . . . . 208, 216
    para 6(a)–(b) 217
    para 7 . . . . 208, 217
    para 8 . . . . 208, 217, 635
    para 9 . . . . 208, 217
    para 10 . . . . 209, 545
    para 11 . . . . 210, 217
    para 12 . . . . 210, 643
    para 13 207
  Sch 2 . . . . 210, 220, 597
    Part I 210, 600, 602, 643
    Part II 210, 600, 643
    Part III 628
    Ground 1 . . . . 493, 599, 600, 628, 634
    Ground 2 . . . . 493, 597, 599, 600, 621, 628, 635
    Grounds 3–4 . . . . 493, 599, 600, 628, 635
    Ground 5 . . . . 493, 599, 600, 627, 628
    Ground 6 . . . . 599, 600, 632, 643
    Ground 7 . . . . 547, 599, 600, 634
    Ground 8 . . . . 187, 218, 555, 597, 598, 599, 600, 613, 614, 615, 639
    Ground 9 . . . . 597, 628, 630
    Ground 10 . . . . 597, 599, 600, 602, 613, 628, 630
    Ground 11 . . . . 597, 599, 600, 602, 614, 628, 630
    Ground 12 . . . . 543, 599, 600, 617
    Ground 13 . . . . 599, 600, 624
    Ground 14 . . . . 322, 599, 600, 617

    Ground 14A 599, 600, 623
    Ground 15. . . . . 599, 600, 624
    Ground 16 . . . . 597, 599, 600, 627
    Ground 17. . . . . 599, 600, 625
  Sch 2A. 204, 636
  Sch 4, Parts I–II 633
Housing Act 1995
  s 82A 317
  s 143A 317
Housing Act 1996 . . . . 23, 190, 192, 193, 311, 317, 614, 615, 636, 678, 744, 758, 773
  Part I 623
  Part VI. 193, 195, 196, 200, 536
  Part VII 193, 195, 216
  s 16 758
  s 17. . . . . 750, 758
  s 27A 172
  s 36 164
  s 81. . . . . 435, 440, 717, 718
  s 115. 215
  s 124 . . . . 214, 317
  s 125 . . . . 214, 317
  s 125(5)(a) 543
  s 125(6) 543
  s 125B 317
  s 126. 214
  s 127. 214
  s 127(2) 611
  s 128. 214
  s 128A 316
  ss 129–133 214
  s 134. 535
  s 134(2)(a)–(b). 535
  ss 143A–143B 214
  s 153A 215, 319, 320
  s 153A(4) 320
  s 153B. 215, 320
  s 153C 320
  ss 153D–153E. 319
  s 153E(2)(a) 320
  s 153E(7)–(8) 319
  s 160. . . . . 201, 317
  s 160A. 201, 317
  s 160A(7) 201
  s 167(1) 198
  s 167(1A) 199
  s 167(2)–(2A) 198
  s 167(2C) 198
  s 167(2E). 199, 200
  s 167(4A) 199

Housing Act 1996 (continued)
  s 167(8) 198
  s 169 . . . . 198, 536
  s 170 198
  s 171 625
  s 175 195
  s 177 195
  s 179 194
  s 182(2) 193
  ss 183–184 194
  s 185(1) 194
  s 185(4) 293
  s 188 194
  s 189 195
  s 190 194
  s 190(2)(a) 194
  s 191 . . . . 194, 195
  s 192 194
  s 192(3) 194
  s 193 194
  s 193(2) 200
  s 193(5)–(7) 196
  s 193(7D) 196
  s 193(7F) 196
  s 196 673
  ss 198–201 195
  s 206(1) 195
Housing Act 2004 . . . . . 26, 58, 172, 214, 224, 317, 326, 334, 348, 352, 362, 364, 384, 390, 391, 749, 750,
                                                        752, 753, 754, 755
  Part 2 . . . . 386, 387
  Part 3 387
  Part 4 389
  ss 3–4 384
  s 56 387
  s 56(2) 387
  s 57(2)–(4) 388
  s 58(1) 388
  s 64 388
  s 64(3) 388
  s 65 388
  s 66 . . . . 388, 389
  s 67 389
  ss 72–76 389
  s 77 . . . . 387, 389
  s 78 389
  s 79 389
  s 79(3) 388
  s 80 . . . . 388, 389
  s 80(3)–(4) 388

s 80(6)–(7) 388
s 81 389
s 81(2)–(4) 388
s 82 389
s 82(1) 388
ss 83–84 389
s 88(3) 388
ss 89–90 389
ss 101–131 389
s 212. 502
s 212(8)–(9) 503
s 213. 502
s 213(5)–(6) 503
s 214 . . . . 502, 504
s 214(4) 504
s 215. 502
s 254 . . . . 377, 387, 390
ss 255–256 387
s 257 . . . . 387, 390
s 258 . . . . 386, 387
s 259. 387
Sch 1 384
Sch 10 502
    paras 3–7. 503
    para 10 504
Housing Act 2006 177
Housing Associations Act 1985 . . . . 623, 633
Housing Finance Act 1972 . . . . 55, 159, 450, 451, 465, 496
Housing (Homeless Persons) Act 1977 . . . . 157, 162, 191
Housing Repairs and Rents Act 1954, s 33. 188
Housing and Town Planning Act 1919 156
Housing of the Working Classes Act 1885. 362
    s 12 184
Human Rights Act 1998 . . . . 45, 271, 273, 274, 276, 278, 292, 296, 332, 333, 392, 612, 729
    s 3 . . . . 272, 273, 291, 292, 293, 547, 621, 678
    s 3(1) 291, 293
    s 3(2) 291
    s 4. . . . . 291, 293
    s 4(1)–(6) 292
    s 6 . . . . 273, 274, 275, 277, 392
    s 6(1) 273, 276
    s 6(3) 273, 274, 276
    s 6(3)(b). 273, 275, 276
    s 6(5) 273, 275
    s 6(6) 273
    s 7(5)(a)–(b) 45
    s 19 272
Immigration and Asylum Act 1999
    Part VI 216

Immigration and Asylum Act 1999 (continued)
   s 4 216
Increase of Rent and Mortgage Interest (Restrictions) Act 1938 185
Increase of Rent and Mortgage Interest (War Restrictions) Act 1915 . . . . 156, 185, 460
Insolvency Act 1986
   s 6(1)(a) 728
   s 178 589
   s 178(2) 726
   s 178(4) 589, 726
   s 178(6) 728
   ss 179–180 589
   s 181 . . . . 589, 590
   s 181(2) 726
   s 182 589
   s 315 589
   s 315(2) 726
   s 315(3)(b) 726
   s 315(4) 726
   ss 316–319 589
   s 320 . . . . 589, 590
   s 320(2) 726
   s 321 589
Judicature Act 1873 573
Land Compensation Act 1973
   s 29 632
   s 32(7B) 632
Land Registration Act 1925 112
   s 24 570
   s 24(1)(b) 563
Land Registration Act 2002 . . . . 108, 112
   s 4 . . . . 108, 544
   s 4(1)(a)–(b) 552
   s 6 552
   s 7 . . . . 108, 552
   s 27 . . . . 108, 544, 552
   s 27(1) 105
   s 27(2)(d) 105
   s 27(2)(e) 702
   s 27(5) 552
   ss 32–33 105
   s 134(2) 563
   Sch 3
      para 1 . . . . 112, 729
      para 2 729
   Sch 12, para 20 564
Landlord and Tenant Act 1730 680
   s 1 679
Landlord and Tenant Act 1927 . . . . 236, 519, 524, 530, 532
   Part I 235, 660

s 1 .... 235, 412
s 1(b) 412
s 2(1)(c) 412
s 3 412
s 17 246
s 17(1) 412
s 18 398
s 18(1) 397, 398
s 18(2) 706
s 19 .... 19, 236, 525, 530, 537, 562, 570
s 19(1) 125, 524, 526, 530, 537, 542
s 19(1)(a) 418, 524
s 19(1)(b) 524
s 19(1A) 526, 530, 531, 570
s 19(1B) 526, 531
s 19(1C) 526
s 19(1D) 524, 526
s 19(1E) 526
s 19(2) 407, 408, 409, 418
s 19(3) 418, 419
s 19(4) 419, 524
Landlord and Tenant Act 1954 ...... 62, 230, 239, 240, 241, 244, 250, 252, 253, 264, 475, 483, 532, 545,
                                             641, 642, 645, 646, 656, 658, 660, 663, 664, 734
Part I 229, 233, 641, 642, 643, 759, 766
Part II 19, 56, 62, 142, 208, 235, 238, 239, 244, 246, 249, 251, 270, 546, 645, 646, 677, 761, 775
s 20(1)(f) 239
s 22(3) 643
s 23 .... 246, 251, 546, 647
s 23(1) 244, 545
s 23(1A) 249
s 23(2) 244
s 23(3) 244, 662
s 23(4) 244
s 24 .... 251, 564, 565, 646, 648, 652
s 24(1) 649, 650
s 24(1)(a) 650
s 24(2) 647
s 24(2A) 650
s 24A 651
s 24A(3) 652
ss 24B–24C 651
s 25 .... 62, 244, 251, 646, 648, 649, 650, 651, 652, 659
s 25(1)–(2) 648
s 25(3) 649
s 25(3)(b) 649
s 25(4) 649
s 25(6)–(7) 649
s 25(8) 650
s 26 .... 244, 251, 646, 648, 650, 651, 652, 659

Landlord and Tenant Act 1954 (continued)

s 26(1) 650
s 26(2) 651
s 26(3) 650, 651
s 26(5) 651
s 26(6) 651, 652
s 27 . . . . 251, 646, 647
s 27(1A) 646, 647, 648
s 27(2) 647, 648
s 28 . . . . 251, 651, 660
s 29(1) 649
s 29(5) 650
s 29A 649
s 29A(2)(a)–(b) 652
s 29A(3) 652
s 29B 649, 652
s 30 . . . . 244, 734
s 30(1) 734
s 30(1)(a) 652, 653, 654
s 30(1)(b)–(c) 652, 653
s 30(1)(d)–(e) 652, 654
s 30(1)(f) 631, 652, 655, 656, 657
s 30(1)(g) 652, 657
s 30(1A)–(1B) 657
s 30(2) 658
s 30(2A) 657
s 31(1) 653
s 31A 655
s 31A(1)(b) 655
s 31A(2) 655
s 32 666
s 32(1) 244, 662
s 32(2)–(3) 662
s 33 . . . . 660, 666
s 34 . . . . 478, 652, 661, 666
s 34(1)–(4) 661
s 35 . . . . 441, 660, 663, 664, 665, 666
s 35(1) 660
s 35(2) 660, 665
s 37 . . . . 244, 658, 659
s 37(3) 659
s 37(7) 659
s 37A 658
s 38 653
s 38(1) 533
s 38(2) 659
s 38(4) 240, 251, 546
s 38(A) 251, 546, 730
s 40 646

s 41 249
s 41A 250
s 42 250
s 42(2)–(3) 657
s 43 250
s 43(1)(aa) 250
s 43(1)(b) 250
s 43(2)–(3) 250
s 44 646
s 57 653
s 69 546
s 69(2) 652
Landlord and Tenant Act 1985 . . . . 230, 233, 377, 379, 438
s 1 118
s 1(1)–(2) 118
s 2 118
s 3 . . . . 552, 580
s 3(3) 552
s 3A 552, 580
s 4 . . . . 117, 119
s 4(3) 117
s 5(1) 117
s 7 117
s 8 . . . . 362, 363
s 8(1) 362
s 8(5) 362
s 10 362
s 11 . . . . 71, 125, 138, 208, 219, 220, 356, 362, 365, 377, 378, 379, 380, 381, 389, 402, 724
s 11(1) 377
s 11(1)(c) 378
s 11(1A)–(1B) 379
s 11(2)(a) 379
s 11(2)(b)–(c) 378
s 11(3) 379
s 11(3)(A) 379
s 11(4)–(5) 378
s 11(6) 377
s 12 378
s 12(2) 378
s 13 377
s 14(3) 380
s 14(4) 208, 220, 380
s 14(5) 380
s 17 401
s 17(1)–(2) 437
s 18(1)–(2) 437
s 19 . . . . 435, 437
s 19(1)-(2) 435, 437
s 20 . . . . 435, 438

Landlord and Tenant Act 1985 (continued)
  s 20(1) 439
  s 20ZA 439
  s 21 . . . . 435, 439
  s 21A 439
  s 21B 437
  s 22 . . . . 435, 439
  s 25 439
  s 26 . . . . 435, 437
  s 27A 437
  s 30B 435
  s 32(2) 380
  s 58 435
  s 604(1) 362
  Sch 427
      paras 2–3 430
      paras 8–9 430
Landlord and Tenant Act 1987 . . . . 13, 57, 230, 311, 312, 437, 743, 769, 773, 776, 783
  Part I 233, 769, 772
  Part II 233, 772
  Part III 233, 311, 769, 773
  Part IV 139, 311
  s 1 . . . . 769, 770
  s 1(2)–(3) 770
  s 1(4) 770, 771
  s 3 769
  s 4 769
  s 4(1) 769
  s 4(2) 770
  s 4A 770
  s 5 771
  s 5A(5) 771
  s 5B 771
  s 6 771
  s 7 772
  s 8(3) 771
  s 10A 772
  s 11(3) 772
  ss 12A–12C 772
  s 13 772
  s 18A 771
  ss 19–20 230
  s 21 311
  s 25 311
  s 25(4) 772
  s 26 772
  s 27(4) 773
  s 29 . . . . 311, 772
  s 31(2) 773

s 35 311
s 42 . . . . 435, 438
ss 42A–42B 438
s 46 118
s 47 . . . . 118, 437
s 47(2)–(3) 118
s 48 118
s 48(3) 118
s 58(1) 770
s 58(2) 771
s 59(3) 772
Landlord and Tenant Act 1988 . . . . 520, 521, 537
s 1 . . . . 19, 531
s 1(3) 521
s 1(3)(b) 521
s 1(5) 529
s 1(6) 521
s 1(6)(c) 527
s 2 19
s 2(1) 521
ss 3–4 . . . . 19, 521
s 5(3) 520
Landlord and Tenant (Covenants) Act 1995 . . . 37, 38, 254, 500, 518, 524, 526, 531, 534, 545, 560, 562,
                              563, 566, 568, 584, 585, 586, 646, 660, 661, 665, 666, 727, 731
s 2(a) 575
s 2(1)(a) 580
s 3(1) 574
s 3(2) 574, 575
s 3(5) 546, 586
s 3(6)(a) 575, 580
s 5 586
s 5(2) 568
s 5(3) 575
s 6 . . . . 576, 578
s 6(3) 581
s 7 . . . . 576, 578
s 8 . . . . 576, 577, 578
s 11(1) 569
s 11(3) 577
s 12 586
s 13(1) 575
s 13(3) 575
s 14 570
s 15 581
s 15(1) 581
s 16 . . . . 531, 569
s 16(2)-(4) 569
s 16(5) 569
s 16(5)(c) 569

Landlord and Tenant (Covenants) Act 1995 (continued)
    s 17 . . . . 566, 567, 570, 572, 575, 584, 585
    s 17(2) 567
    s 18. . . . . 565, 567, 570, 572, 575, 584
    s 18(3) 567
    s 19. . . . . 567, 570, 572, 575, 584, 590
    s 19(1) 568
    s 19(2) 568
    s 19(2)(a) 568
    s 19(8) 572
    s 20 . . . . 567, 570, 572, 575, 584
    s 22 526
    s 23 583
    s 23(1) 581
    s 23(2)–(3) 582
    s 24(2). 569, 585
    s 25. . . . . 142, 146, 531, 563, 585, 586
    s 25(1) 563
    s 28 . . . . 545, 574, 577, 580, 586
    s 28(2) 575
    s 30 564
    s 30(4) 546
Landlord and Tenant (Licensed Premises) Act 1990. 250
Landlord and Tenant (Termination of Tenancies) Bill (draft) 720
Law of Distress Amendment Act 1888 184
Law of Distress Amendment Act 1895 184
Law of Property Act 1922
    s 145 . . . . 37, 73, 93
    Sch 15 93
Law of Property Act 1925 5
    s 1 . . . . 4, 68
    s 1(1)(a) 4, 27
    s 1(1)(b) 4, 27, 67
    s 1(2) 574
    s 1(2)(e). 702
    s 1(6) 77, 548
    s 40 109
    s 52. . . . . 106, 107, 552, 730
    s 52(1) 544
    s 52(2)(c) 730
    s 52(2)(g) 544
    s 53(1)(a) 544
    s 54(1) 111
    s 54(2) 106, 107, 109, 544
    s 56(1) 587
    s 77 570
    s 77(1)(c) 563
    s 78 546
    s 84 421

s 84(12) 589
s 101. 635
s 136. 583
s 139(1) 740
s 141. . . . . 37, 272, 578, 579, 580, 584
s 141(2)–(3) 581
s 142 . . . . 37, 272, 578, 579, 580, 581, 582
s 144 . . . . 19, 519
s 145 . . . . 728, 729
s 146 . . . . 62, 396, 703, 705, 706, 708, 709, 717, 719
s 146(1) 705
s 146(2) 710, 713, 718
s 146(4). 718, 737
s 146(5)(e) 718
s 146(7) 706
s 146(8)–(9) 705
s 146(11). 432, 705
s 146(12) 705
s 147. 709
s 147(1) 709
s 147(2)(ii)–(iii) 709
s 149(3) 73
s 149(6) 37, 73
s 150. 740
s 185. 735
s 196. 706
s 205 76
s 205(1)(xix). 5, 107
s 205(1)(xxvii) 37, 68, 73
Law of Property Act 1969, s 7. 655
Law of Property (Miscellaneous Provisions) Act 1989 545
s 2 . . . . 109, 544, 730
s 2(1)–(3). 109
Leasehold Property (Repairs) Act 1938 . . . . 395, 396, 398, 400, 704, 708, 709, 721
s 1 396
s 1(5) 396, 708
s 3 395
s 7(1) 395
Leasehold Reform Act 1967. . . . . 12, 62, 142, 228, 229, 230, 233, 272, 528, 743, 745, 759, 760, 761, 762,
764, 766, 775, 778, 780, 783
s 1 764
s 1(1) 764
s 1(1)(a) 764
s 1(1)(b). 761
s 1(1B) 759, 761
s 1(1ZB) 759
s 1(1ZC). 761
s 1(3)–(3A) 762
ss 1A–1AA 764

Leasehold Reform Act 1967 (continued)
    s 1B 764
    s 2 760
    s 2(1) 760
    s 2(2)–(3) 761
    s 2(5) 761
    s 4(1) 764
    s 9 229
    s 9(1) 764
    s 9(1A) 764, 766
    s 9(1D)–(1E) 766
    s 14 766
    s 15 766
    s 15(2)(a) 766
    s 15(2)(b) 767
    s 16 767
    s 17 768
    s 17(1) 768
    s 18 768
    s 19 . . . . 229, 768
    s 23 768
    ss 32–32A 762
    s 33 762
Leasehold Reform, Housing and Urban Development Act 1993 . . . . 13, 62, 63, 142, 231, 553, 743, 745,
                  759, 762, 766, 773, 774, 776, 777, 778, 779, 780, 781, 783, 784, 785
    Part I 233, 774, 781
    s 1(3)(b) 777
    s 1(5) 777
    s 1(7) 777
    s 1(8) 780
    s 2 777
    s 3(1)(a) 775
    s 3(1)(b)–(c) 776
    s 4(1) 776
    s 4(4) 776
    ss 4A–4C 780
    s 5(2)(a) 775
    s 5(2)(b) 776
    s 5(5) 775
    ss 7–8 775
    s 10 776
    s 11 780
    s 12A 780
    s 13 780
    s 13(2)(b)(ii) 777, 780
    s 13(3)(g) 780
    s 15 780
    s 21 780
    s 21(1) 780

s 21(4) 777
s 23 781
s 31 776
s 33 778
s 36 778
s 39 . . . . 781, 783
s 39(4) 781
ss 40–41 782
s 45 783
s 45(2)(c) 783
s 47 783
s 54 781
s 56 782
s 59 782
s 61 783
s 69 781
s 72(1) 781
s 73 781
s 76 435
s 87 . . . . 333, 438
s 87(7) 333
s 94 777
s 95 776
s 96 777
s 101. 775
Sch 6
    para 3 778
    para 4(2)–(2A) 778
    para 5 780
Sch 9, Parts II–III 778
Sch 13 782
    para 4(2)–(2A) 782
Sch 14 783
Local Government Act 1999, s 3 342
Local Government Act 2000. 175
    s 4 302
Local Government and Housing Act 1989 . . . . 142, 643
    s 186. 641
    s 186(4) 643
    Sch 10. . . . . 233, 599, 633, 641, 644, 677, 766, 767
        para 1 643
        para 1(2A). 642
        para 1(7) 643
        para 2 642
        para 2(4) 642
        para 3 643
        para 4 643
        para 4(5)–(6) 643
        para 5 643

Local Government and Housing Act 1989 (continued)
      para 5(1)(b).. 643
      para 5(4).. 643
      paras 8–10.. 643
      para 16... 642
      para 22... 643
Matrimonial Causes Act 1973
  s 24... 539, 671
  s 25... 539
  s 37... 671
Matrimonial Homes Act 1983 540
Metropolitan Police Courts Act 1839 184
Mobile Homes Act 1983... 206
National Assistance Act 1948 549
National Health Service and Community Care Act 1990, s 60(7) 627
National Immigration and Asylum Act 2002............................ 280
  s 55... 280
Offices, Shops and Railway Premises Act 1963......................... 357
Official Secrets Acts 715
Police and Justice Act 2006... 319
Protection from Eviction Act 1964 .... 185, 685
Protection from Eviction Act 1977 .... 41, 680, 685, 698
  s 1... 674, 686, 689, 691, 710
  s 1(1)... 687
  s 1(2)... 685, 686, 687, 688
  s 1(3)... 685, 687, 688
  s 1(3A)–(3C)... 687, 688
  s 2.................................. 220, 675, 702, 709, 717
  s 3.................................. 209, 219, 220, 675, 676, 677
  s 3(1)... 676
  s 3(2)–(2B)... 676
  s 3(7A)–(7C)... 675
  s 3(8)... 675
  s 3A.. 209, 675, 677
  s 3A(2)–(3).. 675
  s 3A(6)... 675
  s 3A(7)(a)–(b)... 675
  s 5.. 219, 220, 674, 675
  s 5(1)–(1A)... 674
  s 5(1B)... 209
  s 6... 689
  s 8(1)... 677
Protection from Harassment Act 1997 698
  ss 1–3.. 698
  s 7(2).. 698
Race Relations Act 1976 .... 104, 191
  s 1... 104
  s 3... 104
  s 21(1)... 104

s 24 519
s 71(1) 104
Rent Act 1957 185
Rent Act 1965 185
   Part III 685
Rent Act 1977 . . . . 55, 67, 186, 188, 206, 207, 208, 285, 292, 462, 464, 490, 501, 548, 550, 624, 677, 689
   s 12 209
   s 20 209
   s 70 461
   s 70(1) 462
   s 70(2) 461
   ss 119–120 464
   s 123. 464
   s 126. 464
   s 128(1)(c) 502
   s 147. 512
   Sch 1 633
      para 2 550
      para 6 550
Rent (Agriculture) Act 1976 539
   s 4 633
Rent and Mortgage Interest Restrictions (Amendment) Act 1933 185
Rentcharges Act 1977. 73
Rented Homes Bill (Draft) 540, 545, 638
Sex Discrimination Act 1975 104
   ss 1–2 104
   s 30 104
   s 31 . . . . 104, 520
   s 32 104
   s 76A 104
Small Tenements Recovery Act 1838 184
Social Security Contributions and Benefits Act 1992
   s 130A 468
   s 130B 318
Sunday Trading Act 1994, s 3 306
Supply of Goods and Services Act 1982, s 13. 393
Supreme Court Act 1981 402
   s 37(1) 402
   s 38(1) 716
Torts (Inerference with Goods) Act 1977 691
Tribunals, Courts and Enforcement Act 2007 432
   s 71 . . . . 511, 513
   s 72 511
   ss 75–78 513
   s 80 513
   Sch 12 511
Unfair Contract Terms Act 1977 . . . . 80, 125, 126, 405
   ss 2–4 125
Validation of Wartime Leases Act 1944 75

Welfare Reform Act 2007
  s 30 468
  s 31 318

Australia

Anti-social Behaviour (Miscellaneous Amendments) Act 2006 325
Retail Tenancies Act 1986 (Victoria) 475

European Union

EC Treaty
  art 81 . . . . 422, 423
  art 82 422
Social Charter (1961), art 31 296
Directive 93/13/EC. 126

South Africa

Constitution of the Republic of South Africa Act 108 1996, s 26(1)–(3). 296

United States of America

Constitution (1776), Amendment V (1791) 458
Texas Property Code, s 91.006 509

International

Convention on the Elimination of All Forms of Discrimination against Women (1979), art 14(2) . 295
Convention relating to the Status of Refugees (1951), art 21 296
Convention on the Rights of the Child (1989)
  art 27(1)–(2) 295
  art 27(3). 296
European Convention on Human Rights . . 45, 54, 271, 272, 273, 277, 279, 285, 291, 292, 293, 331, 332,
  390, 678, 2778
  art 1 272
  art 2 . . . . 332, 334
  art 3. . . . . 277, 279, 280
  art 6. . . . . 278, 280, 281
  art 6(1). 280
  art 8 . . . 45, 46, 48, 54, 278, 279, 281, 282, 283, 284, 285, 286, 287, 292, 293, 324, 330, 331, 332, 392,
                               548, 549, 610, 611, 612, 619, 620, 671, 672
  art 8(1) 281, 283

art 8(2) 281, 283, 284, 610, 611, 612, 613

art 10 . . . . 279, 309

art 11 . . . . 279, 308, 309

art 14 . . . . 45, 272, 278, 285, 292, 293, 548, 549

Protocol 1, art 1 . . . . 45, 54, 101, 180, 278, 286, 287, 288, 289, 290, 291, 309, 455, 456, 457, 464, 672

Protocol 4, art 2 309

International Convention on the Elimination of All Forms of Racial Discrimination (1965), art 5 . 295

International Covenant on Economic, Social and Cultural Rights (1966) 293, 294

art 11(1) 293, 294

UN Universal Declaration of Human Rights (1948) 271

art 12 271

art 25 271

TABLE OF STATUTORY INSTRUMENTS

Assured Tenancies and Agricultural Occupancies (Forms) Regulations 1977 (SI 1977/194). 598
Civil Procedure Rules 1998 (SI 1998/3132) 343
Competition Act 1998 (Land Agreements Exclusion and Revocation) Order 2004 (SI 2004/1260) . 423
Disability Discrimination (Premises) Regulations 2006 (SI 2006/887) 304
Disability Discrimination (Public Authorities) (Statutory Duties) Regulations 2005 (SI 2005/2966) 305
Electrical Equipment (Safety) Regulations 1994 (SI 1994/3260). 358
Electricity at Work Regulations 1989 (SI 1989/635). 357
Furniture and Furnishings (Fire) (Safety) Regulations 1988 (SI 1988/1324) 358
Gas Safety (Installation and Use) Regulations 1998 (SI 1998/2451) 358
Homelessness (Suitability of Accommodation) (England) Order 2003 (SI 2003/3326) 196
Houses in Multiple Occupation (Certain Converted Blocks of Flats) (Modifications to the
    Housing Act 2004 and Transitional Provisions for section 257 HMOs) (England) Regulations
    2007 (SI 2007/1904) 390
Housing (Empty Dwelling Management Orders) (Prescribed Exceptions and Requirements)
    (England) Order 2006 (SI 2006/367) 389
Housing, Health and Safety Rating System (England) Regulations 2005 (SI 2005/3208) 384
Housing (Interim Management Orders) (Prescribed Circumstances) (England) Order 2006
    (SI 2006/369). 340, 389
Housing (Management Orders and Empty Dwelling Management Orders) (Supplemental
    Provisions) (England) Regulations 2006 (SI 2006/368). 389
Housing (Northern Ireland) Order 1992 (SI 1992/1725) 290
    art 75G(1) 290
Housing (Prescribed Forms) Regulations 1990 (SI 1990/447) 117
Housing (Right to Buy) (Limits on Discount) (Amendment) Order 1998 (SI 1998/2997). 754
Housing (Right to Buy) (Limits on Discount) (Amendment) Order 2003 (SI 2003/498). 754
Housing (Right to Manage) Regulations 1994 (SI 1994/627) 342
Land Registration Rules 2003
    r 58A 108
    r 77 702
Landlord and Tenant Act 1954, Part 2 (Notices) Regulations 2004 (SI 2004/1005). 648, 650
Landlord and Tenant (Covenants) Act 1995 (Notices) Regulations 1995 (SI 1995/2964) 566
Leasehold Reform (Collective Enfranchisement and Lease Renewal) Regulations 1993
    (SI 1993/2407), Sch 2 782
Licensing of Houses in Multiple Occupation (Prescribed Descriptions) (England) Order 2006
    (SI 2006/371). 327, 386
Licensing and Management of Houses in Multiple Occupation and Other Houses
    (Miscellaneous Provisions) (England) Regulations 2006 (SI 2006/373) 386, 388
Licensing and Management of Houses in Multiple Occupations (Additional Provisions)
    (England) Regulations 2007 (SI 2007/1903). 389
Management of Houses in Multiple Occupation (England) Regulations 2006 (SI 2006/372). . 377, 387, 389

Notice to Quit etc (Prescribed Information) Regulations 1988 (SI 1988/2201) 674
Plugs and Sockets (Safety) Regulations 1994 (SI 1994/1768) 358
Race Relations Act (Amendment) Regulations 2003 (SI 2003/1626) 104
Regulatory Reform (Business Tenancies) (England and Wales) Order 2003 (SI 2003/3096) . . . 241, 251,
    252, 649, 651, 652, 658, 661
    Schs 1–2 251
    Schs 3–4 730
Regulatory Reform (Fire Safety) Order 2005 (SI 2005/1541) 357
Rent Acts (Maximum Fair Rent) Order 1999 (SI 1999/06) 289, 462, 463
Rent Book (Forms of Notice) Regulations 1982 (SI 1982/1474) 117
Rights of Re-entry and Forfeiture (Prescribed Sum and Period) (England) Regulations 2004
    (SI 2004/3086) 440, 717
Secure Tenancies (Designated Courses) (Amendment) Regulations 1993 SI 1993/931 217
Secure Tenancies (Designated Courses) Regulations 1980 SI 1980/1407 217
Secure Tenancies (Notices) Regulations 1987 (SI 1987/755) 598
Secure Tenants of Local Authorities (Compensation for Improvements) Regulations 1994
    (SI 1994/613) 413
Secure Tenants of Local Housing Authorities (Rights to Repair) Regulations 1994 (SI 1994/133) . . 401
Selective Licensing of Houses (Specified Exemptions) (England) Order 2006 (SI 2006/370) 388
Service Charges (Consultation Requirements) (England) Regulations 2003 (SI 2003/1987) 439
Service Charges (Summary of Rights and Obligations, and Transitional Provision) (England)
    Regulations 2007 (SI 2007/1257) 437
Supply of Beer (Loan Licensed Premises and Wholesale Prices) Revocation Order 2003
    (SI 2003/52) 423
Supply of Beer (Loan Ties, Licensed Premises and Wholesale Prices) Order 1989 (SI 1989/2558) . . 423
Supply of Beer (Tied Estate) Order 1989 (SI 1989/2390) 423
Supply of Beer (Tied Estate) Revocation Order 2002 (SI 2002/3204) 423
Unfair Terms in Consumer Contracts Regulations 1994 (SI 1994/3159) 30, 126, 127, 393
Unfair Terms in Consumer Contracts Regulations 1999 (SI 1999/2083) 30, 125, 126, 127, 128,
                                         130, 138, 147, 223, 254, 405, 434, 435, 477, 494, 618
    reg 4 126
    reg 4(2) 128
    reg 5 128
    reg 5(1)–(4) 129
    reg 6(2) 128
    reg 7 61
    reg 7(1)–(2) 129
    reg 8 129
    Sch 2 129

PART ONE

INTRODUCING THE RELATIONSHIP

1

INTRODUCTION TO LANDLORD AND TENANT LAW

1.1   Understanding leases in context
1.2   The language of leases
1.3   The variety of letting arrangements
1.4   Key issues and trends in the different sectors
1.5   Explaining the structure of the book
1.6   Some more terminology on leases

1.1 Understanding Leases in Context

This book takes a fresh look at the principles of landlord and tenant law and is built on the belief that in order to have a full understanding of how leases are regulated it is necessary to go beyond matters that are within the traditional domain of landlord and tenant law. This means that it is important to refer to other areas of law that touch upon the landlord and tenant relationship, even if they are traditionally seen as belonging to different branches of the law. So, for example, it is impossible to understand the way that a modern social landlord relates to its tenants without having an awareness of the laws relating to housing conditions, disability laws and human rights, and those designed to promote greater social cohesion and reduce anti-social behaviour.

In addition, it is necessary to go beyond the law to understand how these laws have come about and to understand the way that landlords and tenants relate to one another. This book discusses the wider social, policy, commercial and economic environments, as well as the law, in order to provide a richer picture. Two examples follow to illustrate why this is important; the first relates to renting commercial property, and the second to renting housing.

1.1.1 Context and Business Tenancies

The relationship between the landlord and tenant of commercial property is largely shaped by the contractual terms of the lease negotiated between them. The agreement between the landlord and tenant will be influenced by all sorts of considerations: market practice, fiscal matters, the state of the economy and professional advice received, as well as the legislative framework in which leases operate. By looking at the wider context in which leases are negotiated it is possible to understand why business tenancies tend to be drafted in a particular way and how this impacts on the legal relationship between the landlord and tenant. So, for example, when business tenancies provide for rent to be adjusted during the life of the lease it is almost universal for the rent to be capable only of going up: even in a falling market the rent cannot go down. The upward only nature of rent review has been much criticised in recent years but its continued prevalence in business tenancies reflects the role of institutional investors in the commercial property market and the strength of the landlord lobby. Understanding the wider context of leasing is also important to legal analysis, as many leasehold disputes revolve around matters of contractual interpretation and courts in recent years have emphasised the need to interpret contractual documents in the light of the wider commercial context.

1.1.2 Context and Renting Homes

Modern residential tenancy law equally cannot be understood without an appreciation of wider policy considerations. The dramatic decline in the amount of housing privately rented throughout the last century is accounted for in part by the legal regime – rent control limiting the amount of rent that a landlord could charge and security of tenure laws giving a tenant the right to stay beyond the end of the contractual tenancy – but is also part of the larger story of the growth in subsidised local authority housing and the promotion of owner occupation. Nor is housing management any longer (if it ever was) simply a matter of receiving rents and maintaining the physical fabric of a property but, in tune with the government's 'respect' agenda, it is increasingly concerned with managing the wider environment, engaging with the community of tenants and controlling anti-social behaviour.

This is a book, then, about landlord and tenant law in context. In answer to the question sometimes asked, 'what is context?', it is law 'linked to the interests or needs of its time.'[1]

1.2 The Language of Leases

The relationship of landlord and tenant arises when one person, the tenant, has the right to exclusive possession of the land of another, the landlord, for a period of time. Usually, but not always, this will be in return for some kind of monetary payment, the rent.

A lease is one of the two estates capable of existing at law in accordance with section 1 of the Law of Property Act 1925.[2] The distinction between the leasehold estate and other (lesser) interests in land that also give a right to occupation is discussed in chapter 3.

The person with the right to occupy is variously referred to as the tenant, the lessee or (usually only for longer leases) the leaseholder. In this book the word 'leaseholder' is reserved for the residential occupier who has a lease of more than 21 years, although this leaseholder is also sometimes referred to as 'tenant' as this is the language used in some of the relevant statutory provisions.

---

[1] D Nelken, 'Getting the Law out of Context' (1996) 19 *Socio-Legal Newsletter* 12, 12.
[2] Referred to in s 1(1)(b) as 'a term of years absolute'. The other legal estate is the freehold, 'the fee simple absolute in possession': Law of Property Act 1925 s 1(1)(a).

The tenant's interest can be described as a tenancy or a lease or, more formally, as a 'term of years' or 'leasehold estate'. The words 'tenancy' and 'lease' mean the same thing, but the expression tenancy is more often used in the case of short term lettings. Many leases are recorded in a written contract: this document is also sometimes referred to as the lease or the tenancy, but from the context it will be clear whether it is the leasehold interest itself or the contractual agreement that is being referred to.

The person granting the interest is known as the landlord, the lessor or the reversioner. After the landlord has granted the lease he still retains what is known as the 'reversion', which is 'an estate in possession for the purposes of the Law of Property Act 1925': although he is not entitled to physically occupy the land, possession 'is defined[3] so as to include not only physical possession of the land but also the receipt of rents and profits or the right to receive them, if any'.[4]

The tenant may be able to transfer (or assign) his interest to another; if he does so, the transferee will become the tenant and is known as the assignee. Alternatively, the tenant may be able to create a new, shorter, interest out of his own lease by granting a further lease. This is referred to as a sub-lease or an under-lease, and the grantee as the sub-tenant/lessee or under-tenant/lessee. In this situation, the tenant remains as a tenant under the 'head-lease' and the sub-tenant is in a direct relationship only with the tenant and not with the 'head-landlord'.

At the end of this chapter there is a list explaining some more of the terms used throughout the book.

1.3 The Variety of Letting Arrangements

There is a wide variety within the landlord and tenant relationship. A lease of a house is likely to be very different from a lease of a department store. A tenant who rents a house in order to let out individual rooms to others has a quite different perspective than a tenant renting the house to provide a home for his family. Some tenancies may be intended to last for only a short period, such as a let of holiday accommodation, and some may be for extremely long periods, such as a 999 year lease. Some may be granted in return for a substantial capital payment (known as a premium) and only a nominal rent, others for no premium but for a market rent. Some landlords are motivated primarily by financial considerations, others by social concerns.

It is important to have an overview of how leases are used in practice as different types of lease raise very different legal issues. The student renting a room for the year would, for example, rightly expect the landlord to be responsible for solving the problem of a leaking roof. In contrast, the commercial tenant with a 125 year lease of an entire building would usually be responsible for the maintenance and repair of the property itself. For the landlord, also, the length of the lease will affect its expectations; with a short lease the freehold (or reversion) has a high capital value and so the landlord may take an active role in managing the property in order to preserve this capital value, but with very long term

---

[3] By the Law of Property Act 1925 s 205 (1)(xix).
[4] C Harpum, *Megarry & Wade, The Law of Real Property* 6th edn (London, Sweet & Maxwell, 2000) 297 and 113.

leases the capital value of the reversion will be minimal, and so the landlord may show less interest in managing the property.

At the risk of over-generalisation, there are three broad categories of lease that can be identified based on the length of the lease.[5] The expectations of landlords and tenants in terms of what the relationship provides will differ according to which category the lease comes within. First, there are tenancies for short term occupation which usually involve the payment of a market rent and will be either periodic (weekly, monthly or annual) or for a fixed term of up to five years (commercial) or seven years (residential). The tenant pays for occupation and exclusive possession for the term, while the landlord's reversion retains all, or nearly all, of the capital value of the property. Second, medium term leases are generally used to provide occupation for the tenant for up to, say, 25 years for commercial leases and 21 years for residential leases. Again, these leases will usually be at a market rent, with provision for the rent to be reviewed at regular intervals. A premium (a capital sum) may be paid for the grant of the lease, but this would be unusual. The reversion again continues to have a substantial value. In the last category, long leases, there is greater divergence between the commercial and residential models. The longer commercial lease, typically for a term of 125 years, may involve the payment of a 'ground rent', that is, a market rent that reflects the value of the land only (the site value). In this arrangement, the lessee will often construct the buildings on the site, and the cost of doing so will be written off over the life of the lease, with the expectation that the building's useful life will draw to an end as the lease does. Notwithstanding the length of the lease, the reversion will carry a significant capital value because of the substantial and reviewable ground rent. In contrast, the long residential lease is typically granted for terms of 99, 125 or 999 years and a substantial premium will be paid to purchase this interest, similar to the amount that would be paid to buy a freehold interest. Here it is the lease that will have a significant capital value, rather than the reversion. Indeed, the leaseholder will usually perceive of himself as the 'owner' of the property, as a purchaser rather than a renter or tenant. The lease is primarily being used in this context because it enables covenants, such as obligations to repair and financial commitments to contribute towards the cost of shared facilities, to be enforced against successive owners (English common law does not permit positive covenants to be attached to freehold land).[6]

The rights and responsibilities of the landlord and tenant will be most affected by the type of letting, whether it is short term rented housing, a home purchased on a long lease, commercial property or agricultural land. Within these main divisions, there will be further differentiation according to the status of the landlord. Understanding the characteristics of these relationships is an important step in understanding the law of landlord and tenant. The following section, therefore, provides some background material on the main rental

---

[5] This adopts the breakdown used by David Clarke: D Clarke, 'Long Residential Leases: Future Directions' in S Bright (ed), *Landlord and Tenant Law. Past, Present and Future* (Oxford, Hart, 2006). Peter Sparkes regards the distinction between long and short leases as 'fundamental' to an understanding of modern landlord and tenant law, drawing the line at 21 years as the divide between long and short, but this requires commercial letting to be set outside this divide as an 'intermediate group': P Sparkes, *A New Landlord and Tenant* (Oxford, Hart, 2001) Preface.

[6] It is now possible to sell flats on a commonhold (freehold) basis but the use of commonholds is yet to take off (see ch 7).

sectors: short term residential renting, long term residential leases, business tenancies and agricultural leases.

1.4 Key Issues and Trends in the Different Sectors

1.4.1 The Public Sector and Social Rented Housing

1.4.1.1 Local Authority Housing

Before 1989, the public sector comprised residential properties let by local authorities and similar public institutions, such as New Towns, along with residential accommodation let by housing associations. The public sector was synonymous with social housing, where the landlord was not trying to make a profit out of renting accommodation. Although it is widely assumed that social housing has always been low-rent housing for low-income households, providing long term security, the picture is actually much more complex (see chapter 5). Indeed, since the early days of council housing the role of local authorities in housing has been subject to debate: are they general landlords or are they landlords for the poor and needy only? Until the mid-1950s local authorities were building good quality homes and charging rents beyond the reach of the very poor; notwithstanding the common perception, council housing was in fact providing homes for the skilled, better-off working class house-holds. Central government has had to push local authorities into more of a welfare-oriented role, and since 1977 there have been statutory duties in relation to housing the homeless.

Local authority lettings were negligible before the end of World War I, but by 1979 they comprised 32 per cent of all households in England and Wales and local authorities were the biggest residential landlords by a significant margin. Since then, the shape and nature of local authority housing has undergone considerable change. The Right to Buy (RTB) was introduced in the Housing Act 1980, giving council tenants the right to become owner-occupiers or long leaseholders of their home at a discounted price. This was (and remains) very popular. Many council tenants exercised the right and became 'owner-occupiers' in the early part of the 1980s, leading to the loss of much local authority housing stock. Stock lost through the RTB has not been replaced. Inevitably it tended to be the better-off stock that was bought by the better-off tenants. Council housing is now mainly occupied by those unable to afford to own their own homes. The long term legacy of the RTB is that the council house stock is run down and occupied by the most economically disadvantaged and vulnerable.

1.4.1.2 Housing Associations

Housing associations are described as 'independent, non-profit-distributing organisations governed by voluntary boards to provide mainly rented housing at below market rents'.[7] Historically they were mainly philanthropic organisations providing low cost housing for the poor and disadvantaged. Until the 1980s they played only a small part in the overall provision of housing, mainly providing housing for particular groups who could not afford market

---

[7] D Mullins and A Murie, *Housing Policy in the UK* (Basingstoke, Palgrave Macmillan, 2006) 178.

rents, such as the elderly or disabled. The enactment of the Housing Act 1988, described as a defining moment in the history of the housing association movement, moved housing associations firmly into the private sector and enabled them to borrow private sector finance. Since then the sector has undergone considerable expansion. In addition to its traditional role of providing housing for special needs it is now an important provider of general needs social housing.

Although part of the private sector, most housing associations are registered with the Housing Corporation (and known as registered social landlords, RSLs). This regulates the basis upon which they rent property, so that in practice housing association tenants remain more like 'council tenants' than market rent private sector tenants.

The rapid growth in the share of the rental market that it is owned by RSLs is in part accounted for by the transfer of much local authority housing stock to housing associations through the large scale voluntary transfer (LSVT) programme, designed to enable local authorities to concentrate on strategic housing functions rather than the provision of housing itself.[8] Most of these transfer associations have large stock holdings, which explains why only 27 per cent of housing associations hold the vast majority (97 per cent) of housing association stock.[9]

Since 1979 the role of local authorities in the provision of housing has diminished, and the role of housing associations has grown. Local authorities now let fewer dwellings than private sector landlords (around 2.2 million local authority lettings in England in 2005, compared to 2.5 million private sector lettings)[10] and the housing association sector, which played a very small role in the provision of housing until the 1980s, continues to expand (providing over 1.8 million dwellings in England in 2005).[11]

1.4.1.3 Social Housing

Both local authority and RSL tenants tend to have short term (weekly or monthly) periodic tenancies, but in practice tenancies can offer life-long security. The role of social housing has changed considerably over the last few decades. It has become the home for many of the marginalised within society. Social tenants are much more likely to have low incomes and to be unemployed than are private tenants and owner-occupiers; they have high rates of disability; are more likely than others to be vulnerable – lone parents or single, to be over 60 years of age, and to belong to a black or ethnic minority household.[12] This presents new challenges, particularly in relation to management.

A major report into the role of social housing, the Hills Review, was published in 2007.[13] This affirms many of the positive benefits of social housing: providing a higher quality of

---

[8] In 2004/05 around two-thirds of units new to the housing association sector were acquired through LSVT: J Spenceley and C Whitehead, 'Housing Associations in 2005' (Cambridge, Dataspring, April 2006) 7.

[9] These are associations that each own more than 250 units: C Kiddle, 'RSR Briefing Paper 1: The Population of Registered Social Landlords 1989–2005' Dataspring Briefing Paper (Cambridge Centre for Housing and Planning Research, July 2006) available at http://www.dataspring.org.uk. Just under one half of RSLs own fewer than 50 dwellings.

[10] S Wilcox, *UK Housing Review 2006/07* (Coventry, Chartered Institute of Housing and London, Council of Mortgage Lenders, 2006) Table 17a.

[11] S Wilcox, *UK Housing Review 2006/07* (Coventry, Chartered Institute of Housing and London, Council of Mortgage Lenders, 2006) Table 17a.

[12] J Hills, 'Ends and means: The future roles of social housing in England' (CASE Report 34, February 2007) 54.

[13] J Hills, 'Ends and means: The future roles of social housing in England' (CASE Report 34, February 2007).

housing than tenants on low incomes could afford in the private sector, providing stability and security for households, and, through the activities of social landlords, taking a lead role in the renewal and regeneration of deprived areas. It also notes the need for further debate in relation to how existing stock is managed and how it accommodates the 'voice power' of tenants, how to promote a better income mix amongst social tenants, how housing can better support livelihoods, and how social housing can be used to offer greater choices (not simply life-long renting).

Housing policy is moving away from the image of council and housing association tenants as inactive recipients of welfare-based housing towards a model in which tenants are seen as consumers, having greater choice, but also carrying greater responsibility. Choice-based letting policies are being introduced and tenants are increasingly given the opportunity to participate in management, but at the same time a greater degree of social control is being achieved through the legislative regime; long term secure housing is available, but only to those who prove themselves to be good and responsible tenants. These themes are explored throughout the book.

1.4.2 The Private Rental Sector

The private rented sector provides around 12 per cent of housing in England.[14] This represents a dramatic change from the position a hundred years ago: in 1914 about 90 per cent of housing was privately rented. A variety of reasons explain the decline (see chapter 5). Part of the explanation lies in the impact of legislative controls, first introduced in 1915, which meant that throughout much of the twentieth century some measure of rent control and security of tenure applied through different Rent Acts. These regulatory measures are often portrayed as causing the decline of the sector as landlords were unable to make a satisfactory return on their investment. The true story is much more complex. Although the Rent Acts were undoubtedly a contributory factor, other policies (in particular the promotion of owner-occupation and the birth of council housing) also play an important part in explaining the decline in the size of the sector. Since the late 1980s, the sector has undergone a very slow (and small) expansion. Again, there are several factors contributing to this pattern. Landlord and tenant legislation plays an important part. The Housing Act of 1988, often – slightly misleadingly – said to 'deregulate' the private rented sector,[15] went a long way to removing rent control and, in effect, made the grant of long term security of tenure optional for landlords. There was also a property market crash at the beginning of the 1990s which made many cautious about entering owner-occupation and left many owners renting out homes that they were unable to sell.

The private rented market is extremely diverse. It is dominated by younger households,[16] and more than two-thirds of tenants are in employment.[17] While the majority of tenants in

---

[14] This is the figure for 2006, according to the DCLG, Survey of English Housing, Live Tables, S101, 'Trends in Tenure'.

[15] Regulation in the private sector now takes a different form: licensing has been introduced for certain properties, and tenancy deposit schemes are compulsory.

[16] P Kemp, *Private Renting in Transition* (Coventry, Chartered Institute of Housing, 2004) 115–16.

[17] S Wilcox, *UK Housing Review 2006/07* (Coventry, Chartered Institute of Housing and London, Council of Mortgage Lenders, 2006) Table 31c.

social housing are in the lower half of the income distribution (indeed, concentrated in the bottom three deciles), households in the private rented sector are drawn from across the income distribution, including those in the highest group.[18] On the other hand, over one-fifth of private tenants are in receipt of housing benefit. The sector tends to house either the economically weak who are unable to afford owner-occupation yet do not fall into priority categories for social housing (or, increasingly, have been excluded from social housing or wish to avoid the 'stigma' of social housing), or those who wish to remain mobile, for example, students and people who frequently move jobs or who are settling into a new area. Much private sector housing is in worse condition than social housing, and will house those unable to access social housing. It is also the case, however, that some very good quality housing can be found in the private rented sector. For some it is the tenure of choice. In practice, it is better to think of it as comprising many sub-sectors: providing for the student market, the overspill social housing market and the executive market.[19]

The diversity of the market poses challenges for regulation. In order for regulation of the private rented sector to be effective it is necessary to take account of the profile of private landlords. According to the English House Condition Survey 2003, a third of the sector is owned by companies and other organisations.[20] Although not defined in the survey, this presumably covers the traditional (or stewardship) landlords,[21] employer landlords,[22] property companies,[23] and institutions.[24] There is increasing recognition of the need for a vibrant private sector to help meet the housing needs of the nation and for many years there have been attempts to encourage more institutional investment.

The majority of private landlords, however, are private individuals (67 per cent).[25] Of these most own only a few properties: almost half let only a single dwelling.[26] This pattern

---

[18] S Wilcox, *UK Housing Review 2006/07* (Coventry, Chartered Institute of Housing and London, Council of Mortgage Lenders, 2006) Table 38.

[19] There are other ways of classifying the roles of private rental sector housing. Rhodes, for example, refers to five main roles: a traditional role housing people who have rented privately for many years (which is small and declining); flexible, easy access housing for young and mobile people; accommodation linked to employment; a 'residual role' housing people who are unable to access owner occupation or social renting; and an 'escape route' from social housing: D Rhodes, 'The Modern Private Rented Sector' (York, Joseph Rowntree Foundation, 2006) 12–13.

[20] ODPM, 'English House Condition Survey 2003: Private Landlords Survey' (April 2006) Appendix 1, Table 1. The survey is relatively small scale but provides a sufficient picture of the make up of the private rented sector for our purposes.

[21] Who 'tend to operate with a sense of stewardship and long-term commitment to maintain the estate': P Kemp, *Private Renting in Transition* (Coventry, Chartered Institute of Housing, 2004) 103.

[22] Historically, industrialists provided housing for their workforce on the grounds that it would improve production if employees lived in good housing. An example is Port Sunlight on Merseyside which was built by Lever Brothers to provide homes for the workers at the soap factory and their families. The aim of employers today is more likely to be to ensure that workers who are needed outside working hours, such as park keepers or school caretakers, are available or simply to provide housing as a perk of the job. 10% of private sector housing is for employees, and amongst dwellings owned by organisations more than 40% are viewed as employee housing: ODPM, 'English House Condition Survey 2003: Private Landlords Survey' (April 2006) 27.

[23] Only a small number of property companies invest in property but they tend to hold several thousand properties in their portfolios. Some private individuals may also create small companies to hold their properties.

[24] Financial institutions invest only a very small part of their portfolio in private housing – 1% according to Kemp: P Kemp, *Private Renting in Transition* (Coventry, Chartered Institute of Housing, 2004) 108.

[25] ODPM, 'English House Condition Survey 2003: Private Landlords Survey' (April 2006) 13.

[26] ODPM, 'English House Condition Survey 2003: Private Landlords Survey' (April 2006) Table 3.

has been fuelled by the easier availability of finance through 'buy-to-let' mortgages,[27] a financial product which was launched by a group of mortgage lenders in conjunction with the Association of Residential Letting Agents in the late 1990s and which has brought more private individuals into the letting market.[28]

The fact that so much of the private rental market is owned by private individuals with few properties can make it harder to ensure high standards of service delivery for tenants. Most landlords are 'hobby' or 'amateur' landlords; for these the bulk of their income comes from other activities and owning a property for rental is very much a 'sideline' activity providing a supplementary income and a pension for the future.[29] Many of those with only one or two properties:

> … operate in ignorance of the law of landlord and tenant, and some are not aware of even basic market information such as prevailing rent levels.[30]

The amateurism of private landlords poses challenges in ensuring that that there is compliance with the increasing levels of regulation: licensing schemes, tenancy deposit schemes, safety testing of gas installations and so on. Part of the problem is that landlords may not have the knowledge and skills to comply with the various regulatory requirements set. There is also a body of landlords who choose not to comply. The size of this group is unknown. Landlordism suffered from very negative images during the 1960s, particularly following the exposure of 'Britain's most notorious landlord', Peter Rachman, during the political crisis of the Profumo affair.[31] In recent years, the image of landlordism has become much more respectable. New landlords tend to bring more modern properties in better condition into the sector.[32] 'Buy to let' has helped in this respect; the growing competition it has brought appears to have led to higher levels of tenant satisfaction.[33] Nonetheless, there appears to remain a tail of landlords who are not renting responsibly and recent government publications have adopted a discourse which contrasts the majority of 'good well-intentioned' landlords with a minority of bad and disreputable landlords (see further chapter 11).

Private lettings tend to be either short term periodic lettings (weekly or monthly) – although these may continue for many years – or lettings for fixed terms. In practice, these tend to be relatively short term arrangements: a recent survey found that more than three quarters of tenants (77 per cent) remain in the same property for between 10 and 18 months.[34] Long term occupation is unusual. According to Kemp:

[27] Prior to its launch it was much harder for individuals to borrow money at good rates specifically to buy property for renting out.

[28] Before buy-to-let was introduced, less than half of privately rented dwellings were owned by individuals: M Ball, 'Buy to Let. The Revolution – 10 Years On' (ARLA, September 2006) i.

[29] Fewer than a quarter of landlords earn 50% or more of their income from rent; 72% of private landlords see the property as an investment or pension: ODPM, 'English House Condition Survey 2003: Private Landlords Survey' (April 2006) 13, 27.

[30] P Kemp, *Private Renting in Transition* (Coventry, Chartered Institute of Housing, 2004) 105.

[31] Profumo was forced to resign as Secretary of State and as an MP following a political 'sex scandal'. One of the call girls involved had also been Rachman's mistress. It was this scandal that brought to light Rachman's unsavoury behaviour as landlord.

[32] ODPM, 'English House Condition Survey 2003: Private Landlords Survey' (April 2006) 17.

[33] M Ball, 'Buy to Let. The Revolution – 10 Years On' (ARLA, September 2006) 12.

[34] Based on a survey of members of ARLA (The Association of Residential Letting Agents): O Carey Jones, 'ARLA Members Survey, Source and Tenure of Property in the Residential Rental Market, First Quarter 2005' (Leeds, ARLA, March 2005). It is difficult to know how representative this is.

… three-fifths of tenants have lived at their current address for less than three years, compared with only one in six owner occupiers and a quarter of social housing tenants.[35]

The ease of mobility to and from the private rental sector is, for many, an attraction. In contrast, the difficulty in moving within the social sector is seen as inhibiting employment opportunities for those in social housing.[36] On the other hand, there will be some private tenants who are forced to move against their wishes; the consequence of 'liberalising' the private rented market by removing security of tenure has made it difficult for some house-holds to put down roots in a community.

1.4.3 Long Leases of Residential Property

Many residential properties are sold on a 'long leasehold' basis. The purchasers may think of themselves as 'owners' but they are nonetheless tenants in a leasehold relationship.

The way in which long leases are used for the sale of residential property has changed considerably during the last century. Long leases were often used for housing developments, originally under the building lease system,[37] and more recently by landlords with a long term perspective on investment. There has, however, always been a level of dissatisfaction with the long leasehold system and, as is seen in chapter 7, campaigners sought for long leaseholders to have enfranchisement rights, that is the right to buy the freehold to the property, as long ago as the end of the nineteenth century. The ground of complaint has varied but in the latter half of the twentieth century crystallised around two major problems. The first problem is that a lease is a 'wasting asset'. The sum paid to purchase a 99 year lease will not be much different (if at all) from a 999 year lease: in both cases the lease-holder will perceive of himself as 'owner', not tenant, but the value and marketability of the 99 year lease will diminish as the lease gets shorter, contrary to the expectations of the owner-occupier.[38] The problem was first addressed in 1954 when long leaseholders were given a right to remain at the end of the lease on payment of a market rent. This did not, however, go to the root of the problem and further, and more extensive, reform followed in 1967 when the Leasehold Reform Act gave long leaseholders of houses (but not flats) the right to buy the freehold. Since then few houses have been sold on a leasehold basis, and enfranchisement rights have been extended to owners of flats on a collective basis.

The second problem with long leases has emerged with their increasing use for flat sales. In the past, flats were mainly used for rental but since the 1950s it has been increasingly common for flats and maisonettes to be purpose-built for sale on long leases and for existing buildings to be converted into flats. Blocks built for rental in earlier times have been 'broken-up' for long leasehold sales and many of these buildings now contain flats of mixed tenure, some rental and some long leasehold. In 1985 the Nugee Committee traced several reasons for this development: the restriction on rents imposed by the Rent Acts made renting less attractive to landlords, there was rapid escalation in the capital values of flats

---

[35] P Kemp, *Private Renting in Transition* (Coventry, Chartered Institute of Housing, 2004) 119.

[36] J Hills, 'Ends and means: The future roles of social housing in England' (CASE Report 34, February 2007).

[37] Where the tenant is granted a long lease of vacant land for a ground rent and erects the building at its own expense.

[38] A 999 year lease is so long that value will not be affected for hundreds of years.

with vacant possession, owner-occupation was of growing popularity, and financial institutions were more willing to lend on the security of long leasehold flats.[39]

With flats there is an interdependency that simply does not exist with houses. There are shared entrance areas and other communal spaces, lifts, access ways and so on that must be maintained, and the maintenance needs paying for. Leases need to be carefully drafted to ensure that good management structures are in place. The management function can be performed either by (or on behalf of) the landlord or by a management company run by the leaseholders. In practice, many modern developments are sold on 99 or 125 year leases with management being transferred on completion to a company controlled by the leaseholders, but there are also developments in which control of management is retained by the developer landlord. With long leaseholds, management problems are commonplace, and often serious, particularly where control of the management has been retained by the landlord. Landlords may neglect repair and maintenance, charge exorbitant costs to the leaseholders, or the lease may be badly drafted and make inadequate provision for recovering the costs of good management. In addition, where 99 year leases have been used for the sale of flats they suffer from the wasting asset problem. Although 999 year leases give much greater security to leaseholders, they are by no means the normal method for selling flats.

As will be seen, long leaseholders of flats have been given a variety of (consumer)[40] rights to seek to overcome both the 'wasting asset' problem and the management troubles commonly experienced. The first measures were contained in the Landlord and Tenant Act 1987, focusing on addressing problems with management and service charges. Since then there have been two further major legislative provisions: the Leasehold Reform, Housing and Urban Development Act 1993, giving rights for flat leaseholders to extend their leases or to collectively purchase the freehold; and the Commonhold and Leasehold Reform Act 2002, giving a 'no fault' right to manage.

The result is that the law applicable to residential leaseholds is hugely complex. It had been hoped that the implementation of the commonhold proposals (enabling flats to be sold on a freehold basis within a scheme designed specifically to provide for good management) would mean that over time leasehold would be phased out. Commonhold suffers from a number of technical defects, however, which means that it is hardly being used in practice. This means that new developments continue to be sold as leaseholds, with all the attendant difficulties.

1.4.4 Commercial Property

1.4.4.1 The Diversity of Commercial Property: Size and Categories

The leasehold commercial property market is hugely diverse. On the one hand, it includes

---

[39] Nugee Committee, 'Report of the Committee of Enquiry on the Management of Privately Owned Blocks of Flats' (London, 1985).

[40] The consumer protection thrust of much of the legislation is remarked upon by Davey and Clarke: M Davey, 'Long Residential Leases: Past and Present' in S Bright (ed), *Landlord and Tenant Law. Past, Present and Future* (Oxford, Hart, 2006) and D Clarke, 'Long Residential Leases: Future Directions' in S Bright (ed), *Landlord and Tenant Law. Past, Present and Future* (Oxford, Hart, 2006).

small corner shops and workshop units. At the other end of the scale it includes properties of very substantial value. Two examples follow.

The freehold of CityPoint, a 36 storey skyscraper with the largest amount of rentable commercial office floorspace in the City of London, was sold for £520 million at the beginning of 2006. The building houses several commercial tenants, the largest amount of space being taken by the law firm Simmons & Simmons (which has sub-let some of its space). Average rents per square foot are around £49 per annum,[41] with most leases expiring after 2020.

Bluewater Shopping Centre covers 1.6 million square feet, with more than 300 shop units (including large 'flagship' or 'anchor' stores let to John Lewis, Marks & Spencer and House of Fraser). The company that built Bluewater, Lendlease, is an international property and financial services company based in Australia which is involved internationally in the long-term management of 44 shopping centres and has relationships with over 4,000 retail tenants.[42]

The commercial property market is traditionally divided into three main sectors (sometimes known as 'core commercial'): office, retail and industrial.[43] A fourth, much smaller, category of 'leisure centres' has also emerged more recently. These sectors can be further subdivided. For example, retail will include large out-of-town retail warehouses and parks, shopping centres and the traditional high street shop. A report compiled by the Investment Property Forum (IPF) states that:

> … the overall result sets the capital value of the commercial property stock at £611 billion [this includes owner occupied and leased], of which £489 billion (80%) is in the core commercial categories of retail (one third of the total), office (one quarter of the total) and industrial (one fifth of the total). That core commercial stock is in turn made up of 1.5 million separate tenancies, a floor space of 659 million square meters, commanding a total rental value of £42 billion, valued at an average reversionary yield of 8.5%.[44]

The remaining 20 per cent (£122 billion) covers a wide range including hotels, pubs, leisure, utilities and public service buildings.[45]

Finding reliable figures on the size of the leasehold commercial property market is, however, extremely difficult. It is often said that a majority of commercial property is rented; information from the Valuation Office Agency (VOA) supports this, suggesting that close to 60 per cent of non-domestic property is rented.[46] Other studies suggest, however,

---

[41] The UK Trade and Investment website describes rents in the UK office market thus: 'The basic rent on a conventional office lease usually ranges from £130 to £500 per square metre per annum (approximately £13 to £50 per square foot per annum) depending on location and facilities.'

[42] M Evamy, *Bluewater: Vision to Reality* (London, Lendlease, 1999).

[43] For a more detailed breakdown of the principal characteristics of these sectors see A Baum, *Commercial Real Estate Investment* (Oxford, Chandos Publishing, 2000) 4–8.

[44] Investment Property Forum, 'The Size and Structure of the UK Property Market' (Research Findings, July 2005) 28.

[45] Investment Property Forum, 'The Size and Structure of the UK Property Market' (Research Findings, July 2005) 28.

[46] The VAO holds comprehensive information collected for rating purposes. There were 1,750,197 non domestic properties in the Rating List as at 18th April 2006; investigation of the tenure details on 31st May 2006 showed 812,672 were rented, 618,654 were owner occupied or subject to a ground rent. There was no tenure information on 318,871 properties. Information supplied to the author in reply to an e-mail request.

that a smaller proportion of commercial property is leased. A report produced for the Royal Institution of Chartered Surveyors (RICS), *Property in Business*, states that 64 per cent of commercial and industrial property in the United Kingdom is owner occupied (therefore, only 36 per cent leased).[47] Similarly, the IPF report, while noting a very large degree of uncertainty over the figures, estimates 43 per cent of the total stock by value is in the 'investment market' (around £265 billion at the end of 2003), comprising just over 60 per cent of the retail and office sectors, but a little less than 25 per cent in the industrial sector.[48]

The definitions used in the IPF report are interesting for our purposes. The investment market includes only stock that can be rated as 'investment grade' ('a fuzzy concept embracing transferability of use between tenants, lot size, and building quality'), that is, 'that part of the total invested stock in the hands of those large, professionally managed investors which can be identified from industry sources'. Excluded from this definition are those leasehold properties at:

> ... the lower end of the range, [where] many small landlords hold stock which in terms of lot size, building quality, and quality of covenant will fall below the conventional thresholds applied by institutions, listed property companies and other large investors.[49]

A more common way of distinguishing 'investment grade' property from other properties is to talk of prime, secondary and tertiary markets. Prime property is the top quality property, favoured by investors: property with a high specification and in a good location which commands the highest rentals and attracts the strongest tenants. This is not to say that property in the secondary and tertiary markets (in less good condition, with fewer facilities and a poorer location) does not also attract outside investment, but it is the prime property market that has drawn in the big institutional investors and, as will be seen below, this has had a marked impact on the pattern of commercial leases. At the lower end of the market, landlords are more likely to be small property companies and private individuals.

The IPF report notes that with commercial property a 'very large element of the owner occupied stock is below the quality considered investible' and that while there remain some opportunities for further investor involvement in stock these opportunities are relatively limited apart from in particular sub-sectors such as public service buildings (notably schools and hospitals).[50]

1.4.4.2 Why Rent rather than Purchase Outright?

Renting, rather than buying, can be advantageous for businesses. It provides greater flexibility than outright purchase, both in terms of the amount of property occupied and of the

---

[47] R Bootle and S Kalyan, *Property in Business – a Waste of Space?* (London, RICS, 2002) 42. Retail property does not appear to be included in this. According to this report the value of the investment market was £180 billion in the United Kingdom.

[48] Investment Property Forum, 'The Size and Structure of the UK Property Market' (Research Findings, July 2005) 51.

[49] Investment Property Forum, 'The Size and Structure of the UK Property Market' (Research Findings, July 2005) 13.

[50] Investment Property Forum, 'The Size and Structure of the UK Property Market' (Research Findings, July 2005) 63–65.

opportunities for financing land acquisition and business expansion. A company that foresees expansion may lease more space than currently needed, and sub-let part until it is needed. Also, 'sale and leaseback' arrangements are quite common; with owner-occupiers selling the freehold to an investor, and renting it back. This latter kind of sale and leaseback arrangement is, in fact, not an unusual way of releasing capital that can then be invested in the main business.[51] Renting can also be a way of separating the property management function of a business from its main activities. In recent years a number of substantial hotel chains have, for example, sold their property portfolios while retaining management of the hotels, enabling the hotel operators to concentrate on their area of expertise.[52] There are other commercial reasons for renting. Many businesses do not have the kind of capital needed for outright purchase of premises, and renting means that capital can be used for investment in business development instead of being tied up in property. In addition, whereas the rent payable will be deductible from profits in computing income and corporation tax charges, the purchase cost of land with a building would not normally be tax deductible (although some capital allowance may be available). Further, the report, *Property in Business*, found that leasehold property is occupied more efficiently than owner-occupied property.[53]

1.4.4.3 Investing in Commercial Property

Investment has not always been the primary factor underlying landlordism. In his study of the history of the British commercial property sector,[54] Scott notes that before the nineteenth century most property took the form of 'estate management' by aristocratic and other traditional landlords – a strategy that was influenced by social and political considerations as well as monetary ones. Scott refers to a study of landlordism by Massey and Catalono[55] who identify three forms of large scale commercial landownership in Britain: former landed property, industrial landownership and financial landownership. For the group comprising former landed property, property is not simply an investment but reflects a social role. This explains, for example, the reluctance to sell agricultural land that Scott found in papers of the Church Commissioners: the proposed sale made sense on the basis of monetary considerations but the lands were retained by them for other reasons ('the ancient link between the Church and the land; flooding the market; "letting down" British agriculture and the landlord-tenant system...').[56]

---

[51] In 2000 the Abbey National sold most of its property portfolio (freehold and leasehold) on a sale and leaseback basis for £457 million. It leased back those properties it occupied itself. In fact, because of the restrictions on alienation in some of the leases, the particular form of this arrangement was highly unusual. For a summary of the perceived commercial benefits, see *Commissioners of Revenue and Customs v Abbey National plc* [2006] EWCA Civ 886 [12]. For more information on the Abbey National transactions (and other property 'outsourcing' deals), see C Edwards and P Krendel, *Institutional Leases in the 21st Century* (London, EG Books, 2007) ch 11.

[52] Many are intended as only 'management back' deals but because of the degree of devolution of powers to the hotels they are at risk of being construed as 'lease backs': see S Bright, 'Managing or Leasing' [2005] 69 *Conv* 352.

[53] R Bootle and S Kalyan, *Property in Business – a Waste of Space?* (London, RICS, 2002) 35.

[54] P Scott, *The Property Masters* (London, E & FN Spon, 1996).

[55] D Massey and A Catalono, *Capital and Land: Landownership by Capital in Great Britain* (London, Edward Arnold, 1978).

[56] Internal papers of 1962, referred to in P Scott, *The Property Masters* (London, E & FN Spon, 1996) 140.

Since the late 1970s, however, the commercial property market has changed considerably. The traditional owners – the landed estates, such as the Church, the Crown and Oxbridge colleges – have become much less significant.[57] Murdoch notes how commercial property came to be seen as an attractive investment for financial institutions:

There have been ... major shifts in ownership patterns culminating in large elements of the higher value properties moving to major investing institutions and property companies. The insurance companies and pension funds did not seriously enter the property market until the 1960s. In 1964, they owned just £851 million of property; by 1970, their property holdings had risen to £2 billion; and, by 1982, these had climbed to £17.5 billion. They have continued to have a significant presence ever since.[58]

The institutional investors – pension funds and insurance companies – were most interested in 'prime property' and during the 1980s they had a considerable impact on the letting market:

... the institutional investor dominated the higher levels of the industry, controlling the larger transaction business and (in collaboration with chartered surveying businesses) driving best practice and forming industry lobbies.[59]

The investment criteria of the institutional investors demanded long term secure income, and this led to the development of a standard form of lease being offered to occupational tenants which required a long term commitment (25 years), regular rent review (but only capable of going up), and that all uncertain costs (repair and maintenance) should be borne by the tenant. This style of lease, known as the 'institutional lease', became the norm in the prime property market but also influenced the structure of leases used in the secondary and tertiary markets. It is discussed more fully in the next section and in chapter 4. Certainty of income is also important; hence the 'strong' tenant covenants provided by Government departments and blue-chip companies are very attractive to landlords.

The institutions still have a strong presence, owning 29 per cent of commercial property by value,[60] but the pattern of ownership has changed again in the last couple of decades. There has been a big growth in overseas investment in UK commercial property, and in investment through pooled funds.[61] Real estate investment traditionally took the form of direct investment in property as an asset, but it has over recent years become a significant sector in the capital markets through vehicles for indirect property investment, such as property unit trusts and securitisation. The problem with direct investment in property is that it is illiquid, has given relatively poor returns compared to other forms of investment,

---

[57] A Baum, *Commercial Real Estate Investment* (Oxford, Chandos Publishing, 2000) 17.

[58] S Murdoch, 'Commercial Leases: Future Directions' in S Bright (ed), *Landlord and Tenant Law. Past, Present and Future* (Oxford, Hart, 2006) 84.

[59] A Baum, *Commercial Real Estate Investment* (Oxford, Chandos Publishing, 2000) 17.

[60] Investment Property Forum, 'The Size and Structure of the UK Property Market' (Research Findings, July 2005) 52.

[61] Investment Property Forum, 'The Size and Structure of the UK Property Market' (Research Findings, July 2005) 52; C Lizieri and N Kutsch, *Who Owns the City 2006* (University of Reading Business School, March 2006) 1. The latter report focuses on ownership in the City of London – this is a special market and will not necessarily reflect wider trends. There is, for example, a disproportionately high number of overseas investors in City properties compared to the rest of the UK: see the IPF report 52.

and investing through corporate structures is not always tax efficient. In recent years a number of vehicles have been developed with:

> ... the primary objective of reducing tax, of achieving liquidity or of aligning the interests of the investors and the managers. They may exist to permit co-mingling of investors, or may be special-purpose vehicles for the use of one investor acting alone.[62]

The most significant development is the recent introduction of REITs, Real Estate Investment Trusts. A REIT is an organisation established to own and manage property investments in a tax efficient way. Shares in REITs can be traded on the stock market.[63] It is expected that REITs will be a popular medium for investing in commercial property.

1.4.4.4 The Commercial Lease

The dominance of institutional investors and the lending criteria applied by banks lending to property companies have played an important part in shaping lease structures, particularly in the prime market. It was the desire to avoid risk that led to the development of the 'institutional lease', a 'near perfect investment vehicle'.[64] The landlord's position was further strengthened by 'original tenant liability', by which the first tenant (who the landlord would select for its covenant strength) would remain liable to perform the leasehold covenants throughout the lease, even after assigning its interest to another tenant. The investor was therefore, in effect, guaranteed a rent net of all expenses for the 25 year length of the lease. Although focused on the prime market this lease structure, dominant during the 1980s, also 'trickled down into leases of lower grade premises'.[65]

Since the late 1980s the market has undergone considerable change. As already noted, there has been a shift in the spread of investors, with a decline in new investment by the pension funds and insurance companies. Second, the recession of the early 1990s and oversupply of new commercial property space effected a change in the bargaining relationship between investor landlords and prospective tenants. Third, regulatory and fiscal changes have impacted on lease structures. Original tenant liability was 'abolished' for leases entered into after 1995 (see chapter 18). As a result there is greater diversity in lease structures. Leases have become much shorter across the commercial property market; average lease lengths are now below fifteen years in all three sectors, with the retail sector retaining the longest leases.[66] Break clauses (giving the tenant the opportunity to end the lease early, but at a prescribed time and on certain conditions being met) were almost unheard of in the early 1980s but are now common, especially in the secondary and tertiary markets.

The content of any particular lease will, therefore, be the product of a complex mix of factors, including the relative negotiating strength of the parties. In a weak market,

---

[62] A Baum, *Commercial Real Estate Investment* (Oxford, Chandos Publishing, 2000) 9.

[63] Introduced in 2007, REITs can invest in commercial or residential property, but certainly for now, most REITs are concerned with commercial property. For an outline of other property investment vehicles, see A Baum, *Commercial Real Estate Investment* (Oxford, Chandos Publishing, 2000) 8–21.

[64] S Murdoch, 'Commercial Leases: Future Directions' in S Bright (ed), *Landlord and Tenant Law. Past, Present and Future* (Oxford, Hart, 2006) 85. See further ch 4.

[65] S Murdoch, 'Commercial Leases: Future Directions' in S Bright (ed), *Landlord and Tenant Law. Past, Present and Future* (Oxford, Hart, 2006) 86.

[66] N Crosby, C Hughes and S Murdoch, 'Monitoring the 2002 Code of Practice for Commercial Leases' (ODPM, March 2005) 79.

landlords have had to use inducements to attract tenants, such as rent-free periods (with no rent being payable for an initial period) and financial contributions towards the tenant's costs in fitting out the property for occupation. Although there is legislation to address the vulnerability of commercial tenants both on the expiry of the lease[67] and when seeking to dispose of a lease[68] the overall policy towards business tenancies is largely to leave things to market forces, but with increasing emphasis being placed on compliance with voluntary Codes of Practice. There has been none of the 'consumer protection' style legislation found, or being promoted, in the residential market. Recent studies of the commercial property market reveal, however, that small business tenants do not enjoy leases that best protect their commercial interests and the question must be asked whether it is now time to offer greater protection to this sub-group.[69]

1.4.5 Agricultural Leases

Historically, most agricultural land was farmed by tenants but, as with the private residential sector, the twentieth century witnessed a move away from renting to owner-occupation. In 1979 it was thought that only 35 per cent to 40 per cent of agricultural land was tenanted, as against 88 per cent in 1914.[70] Again, as with the private rental sector, there has been debate as to the role of legislative intervention in this decline. From the mid-twentieth century the position of agricultural tenants was strengthened by statute as a matter of deliberate public policy; maintaining an efficient and competitive national agricultural industry was seen as important to the national economy and well-being. As part of this overall policy, tenants were given a degree of security of tenure, succession rights, and, in order to encourage investment in the production process, the right to compensation for improvements.

The Northfield Committee, reporting in 1979, predicted that the downward trend in tenanted land would continue but considered it important to the agricultural community to maintain a variety of tenure types, and therefore recommended that the government should try to ensure that by 2020 the overall percentage of tenanted land should not have fallen below 20 per cent to 25 per cent. By 1994, only 24 per cent of agricultural holdings were tenanted and the transfer of land from the rented sector into owner occupation was continuing.[71]

The nature of farming is also changing. With membership of the European Union, and the increasing availability of cheap agricultural imports, the pressures on domestic farmers have changed. Environmentally-friendly farming practices are encouraged, and farmers increasingly need to be able to diversify beyond traditional agricultural concerns in order to survive. These various pressures led to the Agricultural Tenancies Act of 1995 moving away from the interventionist style of earlier legislation, to support a model based on free market negotiation of tenancy terms with very little regulation over the content. This new regime

---

[67] Landlord and Tenant Act 1954 Part II.

[68] Landlord and Tenant Act 1927 s 19; Law of Property Act 1925 s144; Landlord and Tenant Act 1988 ss 1–4. See ch 17.

[69] See ch 8, and S Bright, 'Protecting the Small Business Tenant' [2006] 70 *Conv* 137.

[70] Northfield Committee, 'Report of the Committee of Inquiry into the Acquisition and Occupancy of Agricultural Land' (Cmnd 7599, 1979).

[71] See J Kerr, *Farm Business Tenancies: New Farms and Land 1995–97* (London, RICS, 1994) paras 2.1 and 5.2.

makes it easier for tenant farmers to undertake non-farming activities, such as using barns for commercial storage or opening a farm shop, without being in breach of the tenancy, and income from non-agricultural activities is increasingly important in enabling tenants to meet rent payments.[72]

1.5 Explaining the Structure of the Book

Landlord and tenant law is now very different from the common law of 100 years ago. Then it made sense to see it as one subject based around the common law principles of landlord and tenant law, supplemented by a few statutory provisions. Few would think of landlord and tenant law in this way now. As already seen in this chapter, the law and practice of leasing property has developed very differently in each of the main property sectors in response to different commercial, social and economic pressures. For this reason, the pattern adopted by most modern landlord and tenant books is to set out the 'common law' rules (many of which are in fact statutory) in the opening chapters and then deal separately with the legislative regime for each sector later in the book.

This book takes a different approach. The law is explained by reference to the different stages of the relationship: entering a lease, regulating leases, managing leasehold property, and so on. The stages of the relationship provide the structure for the book; and each stage is introduced by a section that explains themes and legal issues common to the different sectors. In some parts of the book the different sectors are discussed in separate chapters as the laws are very different; in other parts chapters are divided by reference to topic. For those readers interested in a particular sector, the place to start will be (in addition to the relevant part of this chapter), the relevant chapter in Part Three of the book. This explains the key legislative controls operating in that sector and will direct the reader to other parts of the book that relate to that particular sector.

By exploring what the law is and how it has come about by reference to the different stages of the landlord and tenant relationship, this book is able to show where the shared issues faced by landlord and tenant receive a common legal response, and where the different context of the leasehold relationship has led to a variety in the legal rules.

This book is mainly about residential and commercial landlord and tenant law. There are chapters on tenanted agricultural land but, as seen in chapter 9, the practice of farming and agricultural land use is now heavily influenced by European agricultural and environmental policy, and a comprehensive explanation of the law in this area is beyond the scope of this book. Agricultural tenancies will be referred to mainly as a point of contrast – to illustrate where a different approach has been adopted towards the relevant issue.

The next chapter of this book encourages the reader to think about the nature of leases: where they belong in a map of the law, to what extent tenants (and landlords) enjoy rights conventionally associated with property ownership, and how effective legislative measures

---

[72] IPD UK Let Land Index 2006, Market Commentary. The leasing records collected by the Investment Property Databank (IPD) provide a comprehensive and detailed source of information on property occupied by 'major tenants'.

are in furthering policy goals. The later chapters are then structured around the different stages of the landlord and tenant relationship.

Part Two: Entering the Relationship
Chapter 3 discusses which occupancy relationships give rise to the relationship of landlord and tenant by explaining the essential elements of a lease and how the courts determine if a right to occupy constitutes a leasehold estate or some other, non-proprietary, relationship. Chapter 4 looks at the formalities requirements for entering into a legal lease, as well as factors that influence the negotiation and structure of leases.

Part Three: Regulating the Relationship
Part Three looks at how landlord and tenant relationships are regulated. Chapters 5 to 9 are divided up by the main property sectors: for each of rental homes, long leasehold residential, business tenancies and agricultural tenancies there is a separate chapter setting out the policy initiatives that have led to the major legislative controls introduced in each sector. These chapters also give an outline of the main statutory protection. Chapter 10 discusses how human rights law impacts on landlord and tenant law, something that is followed through in later chapters as appropriate.

Part Four: Managing the Relationship
During the tenancy relationship, management issues are at the fore. This means not only maintaining the fabric of the property and collecting rents but, particularly if the landlord rents out more than one property in a particular area, looking after any communal parts and controlling the behaviour of other tenants. These wider aspects of management are discussed in chapter 11. Chapter 12 then covers the law relating to the repair and maintenance of property, and chapter 13 looks at other servicing issues, such as the recovery of service charges, insurance and regulating what the property can be used for. The remaining three chapters of this part discuss matters relating to rent: chapter 14 covers introductory material on rent; chapter 15 looks at residential rents, particularly rent setting and affordability issues; and chapter 16 looks at how rents can be varied and how landlords can improve the prospects of payment.

Part Five: Changing the Parties to the Relationship
Chapter 17 looks at how leases control the freedom of landlords and tenants to transfer their interest, or create further interests. Chapter 18 looks at the consequential impact this has on the enforceability of the contractual promises contained in the lease.

Part Six: Continuing the Relationship
Part Six discusses what is often referred to as 'security of tenure', essentially rights that are given to tenants to remain in the property even after the contractual term has expired. As the rules are quite different between the sectors, there is a chapter on each of residential tenancies (short term tenancies, chapter 19), long residential leases (chapter 20), and business tenancies (chapter 21).

Part Seven: Ending the Relationship
Chapter 22 describes how leases can be brought to an end in the normal course of events. The following chapter shows how the landlord's behaviour is constrained in the residential

sector to prevent him from circumventing these rules and unlawfully evicting the tenant. Chapter 24 describes how the lease can be ended early, including the law on forfeiture for breach of a tenant covenant. The final chapter discusses the various rights that residential tenants and leaseholders have been given to 'upgrade' their leasehold interests – either into longer leases or freeholds.

1.6 Some more Terminology on Leases

AGA: authorised guarantee agreement. A guarantee that is provided by a tenant who is assigning the lease by which he guarantees performance of the leasehold covenants by his immediate successor.

Alienation: the act of transferring, or disposing of an interest in a property. An alienation covenant contains restrictions on the tenant's ability to dispose of the leasehold interest and often controls acts less than outright disposition, such as sub-letting.

Assignment: transferring the interest in the property for the whole of the period for which it is held.

Assured tenancy: a tenancy regulated by the Housing Act 1988 which the landlord can end only on certain specified grounds for possession.

Assured shorthold tenancy: a tenancy regulated by the Housing Act 1988 which, after the contractual term, the landlord is able to end on two months' notice (subject to a six months' minimum term).

Break clause: a clause giving either party (but most commonly the tenant) an option to end the lease early.

Commonhold: a system of freehold ownership introduced in 2004 and which is designed for buildings in multiple occupation.

Demise: the technical term used for lease.

Enfranchisement: the process of a leaseholder (or leaseholders collectively) buying the freehold.

Forfeiture: the contractual right to bring a lease to an end early following a breach of covenant by the tenant.

FRI: full repair and insuring lease. Under this the uncertain costs of repair and insurance are placed on the tenant, either through an obligation to repair and insure or to pay the costs through a service charge.

Ground rent: a rent payable that, broadly, reflects the site value but not the value of the site with a building on it.

Institutional lease: the form of lease of commercial property favoured by investors during the 1980s. The aim was to provide a long term secure income stream. Typically it would be a 25 year lease with upward only rent review on an FRI basis.

Large Scale Voluntary Transfer: the transfer of local authority housing stock to a registered social landlord or housing association.

Market rent: a rent that reflects the full value of the site and building.

Mesne landlord: an intermediate landlord, for example where a tenant has sub-let the property and becomes the mesne landlord of the sub-tenant.

Peppercorn rent: a nominal rent.

Privity of contract/original liability/continuing liability: different terminology to refer to the fact that the original parties to the lease remain liable on the leasehold covenants throughout the term of the lease, even if there is a new landlord/tenant. This has changed for leases entered into since 1996.

Rack rent: the best market rent obtainable.

Registered social landlord: a housing organisation (usually a housing association) registered with the Housing Corporation under the Housing Act 1996 and which provides social housing.

Rent Acts: the collective name used to describe the various Acts regulating private sector residential tenancies prior to the Housing Act 1988.

Reversion: the landlord's interest in the property remaining after the lease has been granted.

Right to acquire: a statutory right to purchase the freehold (or a long leasehold) at a discount given to certain tenants of registered social landlords.

Right to buy: a statutory right to purchase the freehold (or a long leasehold) at a discount given to certain tenants of local authorities.

Secure tenancy: a tenancy between a local authority landlord and a tenant coming within the Housing Act 1980.

Security of tenure: a right given to the tenant to remain after the expiry of the lease.

Shelter: the housing and homelessness charity.

Sub-letting: when the tenant creates a new lease for a shorter term out of his own leasehold interest.

Upward only rent review: a provision in a lease for rents to be adjusted to market levels at intervals during the lease but which states that the rent can not be adjusted in a downward direction.

2
KEYS TO UNDERSTANDING LEASES

2.1   Introduction
2.2   Leases in a map of the law
2.3   The hybrid nature of leases: part property, part contract
2.4   The private law relationship and the common law
2.5   Landlord and tenant law as regulatory law
2.6   The public law dimension
2.7   Leases and land
2.8   Leases as split-ownership
2.9   Intervention in the landlord and tenant relationship
2.10   Interpretation of leases and leasehold notices

2.1 Introduction

Although this is a book primarily about landlord and tenant law, it is helpful to spend some time thinking about the nature of leases more broadly. This chapter therefore looks at some key issues in relation to leases: where they fit in a map of the law, how they relate to wider understandings of property and ownership, and the kinds of justification that are given for intervention in the landlord and tenant relationship. The final section of this chapter has more of a legal focus and considers how courts approach issues of interpretation in relation to leasehold contracts and notices.

As a legal concept, the lease has a particular meaning. The origins of the lease lie in the law of contract, but it was recognised as creating an estate in land hundreds of years ago. Doctrinally, it has a hybrid nature, as Lord Browne-Wilkinson observed in *Linden Gardens Trust Ltd v Lenesta Sludge Disposals Ltd*: 'A lease is a hybrid, part contract, part property.'[1] In England it tends to be seen as belonging in the land law camp because of its proprietary characteristics, but many of the day to day issues arising in relation to leases are really matters of contract law and, as will be seen, other branches of law may also be important when it comes to understanding broader legal questions affecting landlords and tenants. The first part of this chapter will consider where leases fit in a map of the law.

---

[1] [1994] 1 AC 85 (HL) 108.

2.2 Leases in a Map of the Law

Until just over a century ago most of the law on leases was based around the common law principles of landlord and tenant law, with little statutory regulation. Landlord and tenant law is now very different from the common law subject of the nineteenth century. It has become a much more complex body of law with discrete and specialised branches governed by detailed statutory codes. This process of transformation of leasehold law is set to continue, as human rights legislation, social housing measures, judicial developments, extensive Law Commission activity and changing economic and trade policies all impact on the regulation and uses of leases. For the most part, this book concentrates on those legislative provisions that directly relate to landlord and tenant law, but the growing complexity of modern law and society means that there are many other areas of law that touch upon the landlord and tenant relationship and which have considerable impact upon the rights and responsibilities of both parties. Examples can be found in the disability discrimination legislation, regulations designed to protect consumers from unfair contracts, regulation of housing standards, and ever growing attempts to control anti-social behaviour. With local authority landlords there is also a public law dimension to the relationship; so, for example, a tenant may be able to seek judicial review of a decision made by his landlord.

Although historically rooted in the private law relationship between landlord and tenant the subject has, therefore, now grown beyond this. The contract of tenancy containing the covenants, both express and implied (by common law and statute), remains at the core: it is this agreement that sets out those rights and obligations that are legally enforceable between the parties. There are, however, myriad other laws that impact upon the relationship between the landlord and tenant, even if not all give rise to rights that are directly legally enforceable between them. Some of these laws, external to the contract, generate legally enforceable claims, such as the well known right to buy[2] or the right to statutory damages for unlawful eviction.[3] Others impose legal obligations but do not create a right in the other party. So, for example, under the licensing regime introduced for houses in multiple occupation by the Housing Act 2004 the landlord may be required to improve the physical and safety standards at the property, but this does not give a tenant the right to claim against the landlord for failure to provide the prescribed level of amenities.[4] Others still may be aspirational, such as the setting of performance targets for social landlords in the delivery of housing management services.

Blandy uses three Rs to describe the alternative or overlapping policy approaches used in the context of controlling private rented sector housing conditions:

> … *regulation* by an outside agency; persuading private landlords and tenants to take *responsibility* by themselves; and/or giving tenants enforceable individual *rights* to use against defaulting landlords.[5]

---

[2] That is the statutory right to buy the freehold (or a long lease) at a discount, given to council tenants by the Housing Act 1980: see ch 25.

[3] See ch 23.

[4] See ch 11.

[5] S Blandy, 'Housing standards in the private rented sector and the three Rs: regulation, responsibility and rights' in D Cowan and A Marsh (eds), *Two Steps Forward* (Bristol, The Policy Press, 2001) 73. At p 78 she also refers to work by Stewart who has 'identified three "spheres" of housing law: contractual, statutory and regulatory. Contract

As the illustrations given suggest, it is the law in relation to rented housing that has been most supplemented by these regulatory laws and aspirational targets. But in all sectors there are areas of law, practice and policy that touch upon the workings of the landlord and tenant relationship which fall outside the private law relationship. In discussing the law of landlord and tenant law this book, therefore, similarly encompasses these wider 'regulatory laws' in addition to the more traditional landlord and tenant diet that concentrates on the private law relationship.

2.3 The Hybrid Nature of Leases: Part Property, Part Contract

2.3.1 History and Classification

Although it is now one of the two legal estates in land permitted by the 1925 legislation,[6] the lease has historic roots in the law of contract. Prior to the thirteenth century, leases for a term of years were generally given by landowners as security for borrowing, in order to circumvent the church's prohibition on usury. The rights given to the lessee were then solely contractual. Over time, the lease was increasingly used to grant rights over agricultural land for farming purposes and with this change of function it became necessary to provide remedies to protect the tenant's possession of land. Remedies *in personam* (damages) were no longer adequate; what the tenant needed now was a right *in rem*, that is, a right to recover the land itself. During the fifteenth century, the action of ejectment became available to tenants so that, if dispossessed, they could recover the land itself and not just claim damages.[7] For the lawyer this distinction between property and non-property, *in rem* and *in personam* rights, is an important one. Peter Birks summarises why it matters:

> The practical difference bears on this question. Against whom can the right be demanded? 'Demandability' is intelligible but not really English. But another word for 'to demand' is 'to exact', which gives us 'exigible' and 'exigibility'. A right *in rem* is a right the exigibility of which is defined by the location of a thing. The exigibility of a right *in personam* is defined by the location of the person …
>
> Most of the landowner's legitimate desires can be achieved only if the law allows them to be given effect *in rem* – that is, as proprietary rights …
>
> If I grant you a lease of my land for twenty-one years and then sell and convey my fee simple, the purchaser from me will take subject to your lease. The reason is that your slice of time is a proprietary interest, an interest *in rem*, exigible against the land itself and hence against my successors in title.[8]

As seen, it took some time for leases to be recognised as giving real rights. By then,

---

or statute can provide the basis for rights, whereas regulation can only lead to consumer rights which depend on external enforcement.'

[6] Law of Property Act 1925 s 1(1)(b). The other legal estate is the fee simple absolute in possession: s 1(1)(a).

[7] See the very useful discussion in P Birks, 'Before We Begin: Five Keys to Land Law' in S Bright and J Dewar (eds), *Land Law. Themes and Perspectives* (Oxford, OUP, 1998) 470–75. For the historical development of English law, see C Harpum, *Megarry & Wade, The Law of Real Property* 6th edn (London, Stevens & Sons, 2000) Appendix.

[8] P Birks, 'Before We Begin: Five Keys to Land Law' in S Bright and J Dewar (eds), *Land Law. Themes and Perspectives* (Oxford, OUP, 1998) 473–75.

however, the classification of leases as personalty had already set. Hence, leases have an unusual (and unhelpful) classification in law, simply as a result of history. Most personalty cannot be specifically recovered, but leases can be. Further, in law the word 'chattels' tends to be used for personalty; leases are known as 'chattels real', reflecting their historic status as personalty but also their connection with land.[9]

2.3.2 Leases as Contracts

As seen, leases began as purely contractual arrangements; and their contractual nature persists in the modern law notwithstanding that the contract also creates an interest in land. In the words of Lord Templeman in *Prudential Co Ltd v London Residuary Body*, a 'demise for years is a contract for the exclusive possession and profit of land for some determinate period'.[10] In *Rye v Rye* Lord Denning said: 'every tenancy is based upon an agreement between two persons and contains covenants expressed or implied by the one person with the other'.[11]

It is nowadays widely stated that all tenancies are contractual.[12] It is, however, possible for a lease to be created by grant, as Millet LJ stated in *Ingram v Inland Revenue Commissioners*:

> There is no doubt that a lease is property. It is a legal estate in land. It may be created by grant or attornment as well as by contract and need not contain any covenants at all. The mortgage term and the portions term are examples of leases which contain no covenants and which consist of nothing more than the vesting of a term of years …
>
> It normally arises by agreement, but it can be created by statute, and the obligations to which it gives rise are enforceable by privity of estate alone.[13]

It is hard to imagine a lease that does not contain any promises, implied if not express, on the part of the tenant.

2.3.3 Leases as Estates

Once it had become accepted that leases were proprietary, it was generally assumed that all leases were proprietary in the sense that they create an estate in land. This assumption has often been referred to judicially. In *Milmo v Carreras*, Lord Greene MR stated:

> I myself find it impossible to conceive of a relationship of landlord and tenant that has not got that essential element of tenure in it, and that implies that the tenant holds of his landlord, and he can only do that if the landlord has a reversion. You cannot have a purely contractual tenure.[14]

---

[9] C Harpum, *Megarry & Wade, The Law of Real Property* 6th edn (London, Stevens & Sons, 2000) 6.
[10] [1992] 2 AC 386 (HL) 390.
[11] [1962] 1 AC 496 (HL) 514.
[12] See, for example, C Harpum, *Megarry & Wade, The Law of Real Property* 6th edn (London, Stevens & Sons, 2000) 752.
[13] [1997] 4 All ER 395 (CA) 421–22. It is probably the case that not all deeds are contractual: see discussion in R Stevens, 'The Contracts (Rights of Third Parties) Act 1999' (2004) 120 *LQR* 292, 313.
[14] [1946] KB 306 (CA) 310.

More recently, Neuberger J stated in *Re Friends Provident Life Office*, that 'a lease involves not only a contract, but also an estate in land'.[15]

The universality of this must now be questioned. In *Bruton v London and Quadrant Housing Trust* the House of Lords held that there was a tenancy even though the grantor itself held only a licence (which is a contractual obligation), and therefore appeared incapable of granting a lease under the principle of *nemo dat quod non habet* ('no one can give a better title than he has').[16] Lords Hoffmann and Hobhouse both clearly state, however, with little discussion of the point, that, though usual, an estate in land is not an essential element of a lease. A lease, in the words of Lord Hoffmann:

> … describes a relationship between two parties who are designated landlord and tenant. It is not concerned with the question of whether the agreement creates an estate or other propri-etary interest which may be binding upon third parties.[17]

Chapter 3 discusses the question of when a right to use the land of another constitutes a lease rather than a (mere) (contractual) licence. The question matters, in addition to the fact of exigibility referred to by Birks, for a number of reasons: as in *Bruton* itself, statutory provisions often bite only on leases and not on licences; leasehold covenants are enforceable by and against successor landlords and tenants; and the range of remedies available for breach differ according to whether the agreement remains purely contractual or also creates a proprietary estate in land.

In practice, the vast majority of leases do involve the creation of an estate and this has important consequences for the discussion about whether leases should be viewed as predominantly contractual or proprietary, an issue explored in the next few sections.

2.4 The Private Law Relationship and the Common Law

2.4.1 Introduction

Leases are special kinds of contracts. They are contracts that (generally)[18] create estates in land. This has made for a complex legal history. The fact that an estate is created has generated an element of mystery around the legal rules applicable to leases. There are many rules that apply to leases that do not apply to contracts more generally, reflecting the fact that the leasehold contract creates a proprietary interest in land. Because it is a system which has its own set of rules there has also been a tendency to see the law applicable to leasehold contracts as somehow set apart from the general principles of contract law. Until relatively recently there was, for example, considerable doubt as to whether a lease could be ended by frustration or repudiation, doubts which have now (largely) been cast aside.[19] The reality is that a leasehold contract is both contract and property. The ordinary rules of contract law apply, but they are supplemented by particular property-based rules.

---

[15] [1999] 1 All ER (Comm) 28 (Ch) 36.
[16] [2000] 1 AC 406 (HL).
[17] [2000] 1 AC 406 (HL) 415.
[18] But not always: *Bruton v London and Quadrant Housing Trust* [2000] 1 AC 406 (HL).
[19] See further ch 24.

2.4.2 The Changing Nature of Leases and Contract Law

2.4.2.1 The Application of Contract Law to Leases

Leases have always been a part of contract law. This means that the ordinary rules of contract law apply to leases: offer and acceptance, rectification,[20] the doctrine of mistake,[21] rescission for misrepresentation[22] and unconscionability.[23] The Unfair Terms in Consumer Contracts Regulations 1999 apply to leases in the same way as to other contracts.[24] In *United Scientific Holdings Ltd v Burnley Borough Council*, the House of Lords decided that, in accordance with general contractual principles, there was a presumption that time was not of the essence in relation to rent review clauses.[25] Lord Diplock states:

> I see no relevant difference between the obligation undertaken by a tenant under a rent review clause in a lease and any other obligation in a synallagamatic contract that is expressed to arise upon the occurrence of a described event, where a postponement of that event beyond the time stipulated in the contract is not so prolonged as to deprive the obligor of substantially the whole benefit that it was intended he should obtain by accepting the obligation.[26]

This does not mean that the application of contract rules to leases has always been straightforward. As the nature and purpose of leases has developed, from being commonly the grant of rural land alone to become complex commercial bargains involving the use of serviced premises, so the application of contract rules to leases has varied. This story of the evolution of leases best explains the previous uncertainty as to whether contractual rules on termination apply to leases.

2.4.2.2 Leases as Contracts for Possession Only

Historically, leases usually involved no more than the 'grant of land for a time'. There were no promises from the landlord beyond granting possession and, in return, the tenant promised to pay the rent. The contract was, on the landlord's side, a simple one of grant of an estate, and no more. Covenants were implied[27] – the duty not to derogate from grant and the covenant of quiet enjoyment – but the aim of these was simply to protect the tenant's possession and enjoyment of the estate. The simple nature of this relationship is described in the following quotation from Quinn and Phillips:

> The landlord's primary obligation was to turn over possession of the land to the tenant and to agree to leave him in peaceful possession. The tenant, in turn, was expected to pay the 'rent'. In

---

[20] *Littman v Aspen Oil (Broking) Ltd* [2005] EWCA Civ 1579.
[21] The famous case of *Solle v Butcher* [1950] 1 KB 671 (CA) involved a tenancy, although the particular development in that case of the doctrine of mistake in equity must now be read subject to *Great Peace Shipping Ltd v Tsavliris Salvage (International) Ltd* [2002] EWCA Civ 1407.
[22] *Killick v Roberts* [1991] 1 WLR 1146 (CA).
[23] *Boustany v Piggott* [1993] EGCS 85 (PC).
[24] SI 1999/2083; *Newham LB v Khatun, Zeb and Iqbal* [2004] EWCA Civ 55, [2005] QB 37. There were, however, many doubts expressed as to whether the earlier Regulations, the Unfair Terms in Consumer Contracts Regulations 1994 SI 1994/3159, applied to land contracts, although it was argued by some that since their inception the Regulations have applied to leases: S Bright and C Bright, 'Unfair Terms in Land Contracts: Copy-out or Cop Out?' (1995) 111 *LQR* 655.
[25] [1978] AC 904 (HL).
[26] [1978] AC 904 (HL) 930.
[27] See ch 4.

technical terms, the tenant 'covenanted' to pay the rent while the landlord 'covenanted' to keep him in quiet possession.

Significantly, the landlord was not being paid to do anything. He was turning over the land to the tenant with the rent serving as continuous compensation for the transfer. The landlord was *not* expected to assist in the operation of the land. Quite the reverse, he was expected to stay as far away as possible. In other words, for the term of the lease, the lands were subject to the tenant's, not the landlord's care and concern. Should the landlord interfere, he risked violating real property law ...

The point that emerges and which bears emphasis is that the basic remedies peculiar to landlord-tenant law are possession oriented. The tenant who failed to pay rent was evicted from possession [provided the landlord had reserved the power to terminate in this event]. In turn, the landlord violated the law when he deprived the tenant of possession.[28]

Seen in this light, the contract was executed at the time of grant: the tenant received what was bargained for, and the law would protect the tenant's possession of the land to ensure that the grant was not denied. Beyond this the law did little to recognise that the tenant might lose other aspects of the bargain. This view persisted for a considerable time. In the 1975 edition of Megarry and Wade the fact that a lease is an executed contract was used to explain why leases could not be ended by frustration:

In general, the doctrine [of frustration] does not apply to executed leases: for a lease creates an estate which vests in a lessee ... In other words, the lessor's principal obligation is executed when he grants the lease and puts the tenant into possession. The doctrine of frustration can apply to obligations which are executory and which can therefore be rendered impossible of performance by later events. [29]

Similarly, Lord Denning MR said, in *Total Oil Great Britain Ltd v Thompson Garages (Biggin Hill) Ltd*:

A lease is a demise. It conveys an interest in land. It does not come to an end like an ordinary contract on repudiation and acceptance.[30]

2.4.2.3 Leases as Contracts for Possession 'Plus'

This view has become much harder to sustain as leases have come to contain many other promises beyond the grant itself. The modern lease of a retail unit in a shopping centre is far more than the grant of an estate; it is a much bigger package which includes not only possession, but promises to clean, to erect signs, to provide security and utilities and so on. In the residential sector, there is an important statutory covenant implied into leases for fewer then seven years that requires the landlord to repair the exterior and structure of the property.[31] It is now recognised that leases involve more than simply the grant of the land for a time. In *Muscat v Smith*, Sedley LJ stated:

---

[28] TM Quinn and E Phillips, 'The Law of Landlord-Tenant: A Critical Evaluation of the Past with Guidelines for the Future' (1969) 38 *Fordham L Rev* 225, 227–230, footnotes omitted.

[29] R Megarry and HWR Wade, *The Law of Real Property* 4th edn (London, Stevens & Sons, 1975) 673. For judicial support for this view see Lord Goddard in *Cricklewood Property and Investment Trust Ltd v Leighton's Investment Trust Ltd* [1945] AC 221 (HL) 245.

[30] [1972] 1 QB 318 (CA) 324.

[31] See ch 12.

... rent today is correctly regarded as consideration not merely for granting possession but for *undertaking obligations which go with the reversion.* (emphasis added)[32]

In America during the late 1960s and early 1970s there was, similarly, increasing judicial recognition of the fact that leases involve far more than the grant of possession. The following quotation from *Old Town Development Company v Langford* refers to a 'transformation' of the essence of leases:

Since 16th century feudal England a lease has been considered a conveyance of an interest in land, carrying with it the doctrine of *caveat emptor* ...

[The landlord] made a conveyance which ordinarily involved no covenants or warranties, express or implied (except a right to convey and quiet enjoyment), leaving the tenant to the tender mercy of *caveat emptor.* However, the tenant in that agrarian feudal society was likely to be an artisan capable of shifting for himself in inspecting the land and relatively simple improvements. The improvements were incidental; it was the land that was sought ...

During and following the Industrial revolution, the population migration from rural to urban areas accentuated the importance of the structural improvements on the premises, and a corresponding decrease in the significance of the land itself. Leases often developed into complex transactions. The typical lease began to look more like a contract than a conveyance of real estate, often containing numerous express covenants ...

Reevaluation of the lessor-lessee relationship was inevitable for various reasons. Probably the single most important reason was recognition that the lease had been gradually transformed from essentially a conveyance to a contract, ie, that its essential nature is contractual.[33]

This change in leases from being (only) contracts of 'estate' to become contracts of 'estate plus' has had a considerable impact on the application of the common law principles of contract. It does not mean that leases have suddenly become 'contractual' as against 'proprietary' (although this is close to what is suggested in some of the American jurisprudence), but as the content of the contract has expanded to incorporate servicing obligations, so this has affected the application of contractual principles. It can be seen at work in a number of different areas, particularly, as seen in the following paragraphs, in relation to ending leases early.

Reservations about whether leases can be ended by frustration were laid to rest by the House of Lords in *National Carriers Ltd v Panalpina (Northern) Ltd*, Lord Simon acknowledging that a lease involves more than the grant of an estate:

A fully executed contract cannot be frustrated; and a sale of land is characteristically such a contract. But a lease is partly executory: rights and obligations remain outstanding on both sides throughout its currency. Even a partly executed contract is susceptible of frustration in so far as it remains executory: there are many such cases in the books.[34]

More recently, in *Hussein v Mehlman*, Sedley QC (sitting as an assistant recorder) accepted that the landlord's failure to repair amounted to a repudiatory breach because the obligation to repair was seen an essential part of the contract:

---

[32] [2003] EWCA Civ 962 [30]; [2003] 1 WLR 2853.
[33] *Old Town Development Company v Langford* 349 N E 2d 744 (1976) (Court of Appeals Indiana) 753–756, footnotes omitted.
[34] [1981] AC 675 (HL) 705.

... the defects in the ceilings were such as to render the house as a whole unfit to be lived in and ... the defendant's conduct, in the classic language, evinced an intention not to be bound by the implied covenant to repair. The breach, in my judgment, vitiated the *central purpose* of the contract of letting. (emphasis added)[35]

By recognising that the landlord is not only granting an estate, but is making various promises and generating expectations about management, the transformation has also influenced the construction of the implied covenant of the duty not to derogate from grant (a duty placed on the landlord not to do something that effectively takes away what he has granted to the tenant; see chapter 4). Previously, the doctrine had only ever been used to impose a duty on the landlord not to interfere, but in *Chartered Trust Plc v Davies*, the Court of Appeal held that the landlord had derogated from its grant by failing to control the nuisance created by a pawnbroker's business, in effect imposing an obligation to act on the landlord even though this had not been expressly bargained for.[36]

2.4.2.4 The 'Transformation' of Landlord and Tenant Law in the US

The approach of the English judiciary has, however, been relatively cautious and they have been reluctant to use the common law as a force for change and enhanced tenant protection. In contrast, the process that is sometimes described as the 'contractualisation of leases' has been embraced in other common law jurisdictions, particularly in the US where courts have been willing to invoke contractual principles to develop a model of housing law based upon more general consumer protection measures. In the landmark case of *Javins v First National Realty* a landlord was seeking possession from tenants who had not paid their rent.[37] The tenants claimed that there were approximately 1,500 violations of Housing Regulations at the premises (housing codes laying down minimum standards), and that they were withholding the rent as a protest against the defective state of the apartments. There had been a few earlier cases eroding the caveat lessee rule and imposing a warranty of habitability on the landlord,[38] but these had received relatively little publicity. It was the *Javins* decision that had the greatest impact upon future legal development. The case was important for changing several common law rules. First, Judge Skelly Wright (for the District of Columbia Court of Appeals) held that a warranty of habitability was implied into the lease of urban dwellings covered by the Housing Regulations. Second, breach of this warranty gave rise to 'the usual remedies for breach of contract'. This meant that a tenant's obligation to pay rent may be suspended if the landlord has broken a repairing obligation.

In addition to the actual decision in *Javins*, the case is interesting for the reasoning followed. Judge Skelly Wright traced the change from conveyance to contract but additionally observed that the urban tenant was not simply buying land but also:

---

[35] *Hussein v Mehlman* [1992] 2 EGLR 87 (Cty Ct) 91. There may, however, remain some doubts as to whether repudiation does apply to leases: see *Reichman v Beveridge* [2006] EWCA Civ 1659; see ch 24.
[36] (1998) 76 P & CR 396 (CA).
[37] 428 F 2d 1071 (1970) 1079.
[38] *Delamater v Foreman* 239 NW 148 (1931) (SC Minn) 149; *Pines v Perssion* 14 Wis 2d 590 (1961) (SC Wis).

... 'shelter' ... a well known package of goods and services – a package which includes not merely walls and ceilings, but also adequate heat, light and ventilation, serviceable plumbing facilities, secure windows and doors, proper sanitation, and proper maintenance.[39]

Although courts had widened a seller's responsibility for quality in relation to other goods and services through implied warranties of fitness and merchantability, there had been a reluctance to apply this approach to leases because the lease was seen as a proprietary interest. The time had come for this to change:

> In our judgment the common law itself must recognise the landlord's obligation to keep his premises in a habitable condition. This conclusion is compelled by three separate considerations. First, we believe that the old rule was based on certain factual assumptions which are no longer true; on its own terms, it can no longer be justified. Second, we believe that the consumer protection cases discussed above require that the old rule be abandoned in order to bring residential landlord-tenant law into harmony with the principles on which those cases rest. Third, we think that the nature of today's urban housing market also dictates abandonment of the old rule ...
>
> Today's urban tenants, the vast majority of whom live in multiple dwelling houses, are interested, not in the land, but solely in a 'house suitable for occupation'.[40]

Several factors are important in the line of reasoning: the analogy with consumer law, recognition of the contractual nature of leases, inequality within the bargaining relationship and the fact that through the housing codes the legislature had made a policy judgment about housing standards. The warranty of habitability in *Javins* is not an isolated development. Over forty jurisdictions in the US now give private law rights and remedies to tenants whose homes do not meet minimum standards of habitability. Based on this approach, there have also been significant judicial developments in other areas. Tort immunity for landlords has disappeared.[41] Leasehold covenants are seen as dependent and not independent, meaning that the tenant will not be under an obligation to pay rent if the landlord is in substantial breach. And the doctrine of retaliatory eviction has been developed, making it unlawful for the landlord to evict a tenant for making a complaint about the property.[42] Further, although most States have declined to apply the approach in *Javins* to commercial leases, a few States have done so. So, for example, the Supreme Court of Texas, in *Davidow v Inwood North Professional Group*, held that there was an implied warranty of suitability for purpose in a commercial lease, and that this warranty and the tenant's obligation to pay rent were mutually dependent.[43] Spears J said that in view of the 'the many similarities between residential and commercial tenants and the modern trend towards consumer protection' there was no reason not to imply a similar warranty in commercial leases. Collectively, the changes in US landlord and tenant law have been described as transforming the nature of the law.[44]

---

[39] 428 F 2d 1071 (1970) 1074, footnotes omitted.

[40] See 428 F 2d 1071 (1970) 1075–1079, footnotes omitted.

[41] See, for example, *Whetzel v Jess Fisher Management Co* 282 F 2d 943 (1960) (CA DC) (tenant tort action based on landlord's violation of housing code).

[42] *Edwards v Habib* 397 F 2d 687 (1968) (CA DC).

[43] 747 SW 2d 373 (1988) (SC Texas).

[44] M Glendon, 'The Transformation of American Landlord-Tenant Law' (1982) 23 *Boston Common L Rev* 503. For further reading on the American position, see the following, although there appears to be relatively little recent

2.4.2.5 *The Conservative Response of English Judges*

In creating private law rights out of the statutory codes, US courts have taken a much more pro-active part in legal development than English courts have done.

Things could have developed very differently here. An important case in the story is *Hart v Windsor*, decided in 1843. The tenant argued that he did not have to pay rent because the property, being infested with bugs, was not fit to live in. This argument was in line with a number of cases decided earlier that impliedly accepted that a landlord was under a degree of responsibility to ensure that property let for residential occupation was habitable. In each of *Edwards v Etherington*,[45] *Salisbury v Marshall*,[46] *Collins v Barrow*,[47] and *Smith v Marrable*,[48] it was held that the tenant was not liable in an action for use and occupation after he quit premises that were unfit for occupation. But in 1843, with *Hart v Windsor* and an agricultural tenancy case, *Sutton v Temple*,[49] the tide turned. In *Sutton v Temple* the farmland that was let poisoned the tenant's cattle. The court held the tenant still liable to pay the rent notwithstanding the condition of the land, and impliedly overruled the earlier cases. In *Hart v Windsor* Baron Parke withdrew from the notion that there might be an implied warranty in housing cases. *Smith v Marrable* was now explained as a case which turned on the fact that the letting was for land *and* furniture.[50] Since this case, English judges have been unwilling to develop the common law to address the problems of housing conditions, as shown by the following remark of Lord Hoffmann in *Southwark LBC v Tanner; Baxter v Camden LBC (No 2)*:

> … in a field such as housing law, which is very much a matter for the allocation of resources in accordance with democratically determined priorities, the development of the common law should not get out of step with legislative policy.[51]

2.4.3 **Property Based Rules**

2.4.3.1 *Forfeiture and Relief against Forfeiture*[52]

The most notable remedial difference between leasehold and other contracts is in relation to termination for breach. In contract law, termination provisions in a contract are strictly applied: if there is express provision for termination on a particular event happening and that event occurs then the non-defaulting party is entitled to end the contract even though he has

---

debate on this: JF Hicks, 'The Contractual Nature of Real Property Leases' (1972) 24 *Baylor L Rev* 443; C Donahue Jr, 'Change in the American Law of Landlord and Tenant' (1974) 37 *MLR* 242; L Berger, 'The New Residential Tenancy Law – Are Landlords Public Utilities?' (1981) 60 *Nebraska L Rev* 707; EH Rabin, 'The Revolution in Residential Landlord-Tenant Law: Causes and Consequences' (1984) 69 *Cornell L Rev* 517 (and the following symposium responses).

[45] (1825) Ry & M 268, 171 ER 1016.
[46] (1829) 4 Ca & P 65, NP.
[47] (1831) 1 M & Rob 112, 174 ER 38.
[48] (1843) 11 M &W 5, 152 ER 693.
[49] (1843) 12 M & W 52, 152 ER 1108.
[50] Even though in *Smith v Marrable* itself it was the fact that the letting was for 'occupation' that mattered in the reasoning, not the inclusion of furniture in the agreement.
[51] [2001] 1 AC 1 (HL) 9–10; see also Lord Millett, 26.
[52] See ch 24.

suffered little, if any, prejudice and the breach is only minor. In landlord and tenant law a different approach is followed. Although leases are usually drafted in such a way that the landlord has a right of 're-entry' (to forfeit) in the event of breach of any covenants on the tenant's part, both equity and statute have intervened so as to provide the tenant with possible relief against forfeiture which would allow him to keep his tenancy.

The emergence of the right to relief against forfeiture stemmed from the general jurisdiction of equity to prevent unconscionable insistence on strict legal rights,[53] on the basis that it will often be unjust for a landlord to secure the windfall benefit of recovering the property for what is a relatively minor breach which causes little harm. In the words of Lord Templeman in *Billson v Residential Apartments Ltd*:

> In 1881 Parliament interfered to supplement equity and to enable any tenant to be relieved from forfeiture. The need for such intervention was and is manifest because otherwise a tenant who had paid a large premium for a 999-year lease at a low rent could lose his asset by a breach of covenant which was remediable or which caused the landlord no damage. The forfeiture of any lease, however short, may unjustly enrich the landlord at the expense of the tenant. In creating a power to relieve against forfeiture for breach of covenant Parliament protected the landlord by conferring on the court a wide discretion to grant relief on terms or to refuse relief altogether.[54]

Although the same points could equally be said to apply to many contractual breaches, the availability of relief has been confined to contracts involving possessory or proprietary rights. Using the analogy of leases[55] it has, for example, been argued that equitable relief against forfeiture should be available following breach of charterparty as the charterer pays for hire of the ship in much the same way as the tenant pays for the hire of land. The House of Lords rejected this argument in *The Scaptrade*.[56] It is not entirely clear why equitable relief is confined to contracts involving possessory or proprietary rights. In practice it was probably not the proprietary nature of leases *per se* that led to the intervention of equity but the desire to prevent an injustice, due to a landlord taking advantage of a trivial or easily remedied breach. In the case of commercial contracts, the courts have generally been more concerned to uphold freedom of contract and encourage certainty.[57]

The Law Commission has recommended the abolition of the current law of forfeiture and its replacement with a statutory scheme for the termination of tenancies following tenant default.[58] If enacted, it will give further statutory force to the differential treatment of leases.

---

[53] RP Meagher, WMC Gummow and JRF Lehane, *Equity Doctrines and Remedies* 3rd edn (Sydney, Butterworths, 1992) ch 18, esp [1805]-[1815].

[54] [1992] 1 AC 494 (HL) 535.

[55] Drawing on the suggestion from Lord Simon in *The Laconia* [1977] AC 850 (HL).

[56] *The Scaptrade (Scandinavian Trading Tanker Co AB v Flota Petrolera Ecuatoriana* [1983] 2 AC 694 (HL) 702. Another reason given was that relief would be tantamount to an order of specific performance, a remedy not available where the contract includes the provision of services: 702. This is not a convincing ground on which to distinguish charterparties as leases also include services and specific performance is not the usual remedy.

[57] Robert Goff LJ in the Court of Appeal spoke of the need for a shipowner to be able to act swiftly and irrevocably following breach to take advantage of a favourable market: [1983] QB 529 (CA) 540–541, cited with approval in the House of Lords. Property can not be swiftly traded and so certainty is less essential. See also the Australian case of *Legione v Hateley* (1983) 46 ALR 1 (HC) 31.

[58] Law Commission, 'Termination of Tenancies for Tenant Default' (Law Com No 303, 2006).

2.4.3.2 Distress[59]

Another remedy peculiar to leases is distress which is available for non-payment of rent, under which the landlord can enter the premises and remove the tenant's goods. The justification for this is that, unlike other creditors, a landlord cannot quickly cease to supply the goods as a response to non-payment and so needs a swift method of recovering its loss. Although distress is shortly to be abolished, it will be replaced in the case of commercial leases by a new remedy, Commercial Rent Arrears Recovery.

2.4.3.3 Certainty of Term[60]

The duration of a lease must be certain in the sense that it can be predicted what the maximum duration of the lease is.[61] This is a rule peculiar to leases and the need for this degree of certainty is said to follow from the proprietary nature of leases, although it is not a very convincing argument. The rule is consistent with the policy of the 1925 property legislation which requires a lease to have a predictable end-date. Hence the reference in the definition of a 'term of years absolute' to a term 'either certain or liable to determination by notice, etc';[62] the statutory conversion of leases for life or until marriage into leases for ninety years,[63] and the conversion of perpetually renewable leases into leases for two thousand years.[64]

2.4.3.4 Covenant Enforceability[65]

Covenants are enforceable between the current landlord and tenant even if there is no relationship of contract between the parties. The tenant is able to assign the lease, the landlord is able to assign the reversion, and the new assignee/owner will both be liable under covenants in the lease and able to enforce covenants against the other party so long as they are not personal covenants. Until recently, this was achieved through a combination of common law and statute,[66] but it is now the consequence of statute.

Without covenants being enforceable against successors, there could be no market in leases. As Lord Templeman said in *City of London Corp v Fell*:

> The system of leasehold tenure requires that the obligations in the lease shall be enforceable throughout the term, whether those obligations are affirmative or negative. The owner of a reversion must be able to enforce the positive covenants to pay rent and keep in repair against an assignee who in turn must be able to enforce any positive covenants entered into by the original landlord …
>
> … Nourse LJ neatly summarised the position when he said in an impeccable judgment ([1993] QB 589, 604):

---

[59] See ch 16.

[60] See ch 3.

[61] *Lace v Chantler* [1944] KB 368 (CA); *Prudential Assurance Co Ltd v London Residuary Body* [1992] 2 AC 386 (HL).

[62] Law of Property Act 1925 s 205(xxvii).

[63] Law of Property Act 1925 s 149(6).

[64] Law of Property Act 1922 s 145.

[65] See ch 18.

[66] For leases entered into before 1 January 1996 liability rules flowed from the common law and statute: *Spencer's Case* (1583) 5 Co Rep 16a; Law of Property Act 1925 ss 141 and 142. For leases entered into on or after 1 January 1996 liability is governed by the Landlord and Tenant (Covenants) Act 1995.

'The contractual obligations which touch and concern the land having become imprinted on the estate, the tenancy is capable of existence as a species of property independently of the contract.'[67]

It is the fact that it is crucially important for parties to a lease to have a remedy against the current owner/occupier that explains the early development of these enforceability rules.[68] Of course, there are some non-leasehold contractual situations in which it would also be useful for contractual promises to be enforceable against successive owners, but this is only exceptionally allowed, and then not by contract law but by holding the successor bound by constructive trust or liable in tort.[69]

2.4.3.5 Release from Covenant Liability[70]

Until the Landlord and Tenant (Covenants) Act 1995 the original parties to the lease would usually remain liable on the leasehold covenants throughout the term. Of course, this is no different from the usual contractual position, but the impact was very different. Leases are often long term relationships which regularly change hands; something much less common in the wider contractual world. The burden of the rule (often misleadingly called 'privity of contract' but better described as 'original liability') would fall heavily on the original tenant who could find himself having to pay even though he had ceased to benefit from the contract and had no control over the current use of the property. The harshness of this became apparent during the early 1990s as tenant insolvency rates were high and landlords frequently turned to original tenants to pay substantial rent arrears. Even before the economic climate brought things to a head, the Law Commission had, in 1986, set out arguments against continuing liability:

> 3.1 Some people see the continuing liability of the privity of contract principle as intrinsically unfair. They regard the contractual obligations undertaken in a lease as only properly regulating the terms on which the owner for the time being of a property permits the tenant for the time being to occupy and use it, or as the case may be, to sublet and profit from it. They see no reason why responsibility should last longer than ownership of the particular interest in the property. Furthermore, as the facts seem to indicate that the continuing responsibility in practice falls more on tenants than on landlords, those of this view see the principle as operating in an unfair way, being biased against tenants ...[71]

The principle enshrined in the 1995 Act is that tenants are automatically released from liability on assignment (although they can be made to guarantee their immediate successor).[72]

---

[67] [1994] 1 AC 458 (HL) 465.

[68] See S Gardner, 'The Proprietary Effect of Contractual Obligations under Tulk v Moxhay and De Mattos v Gibson' (1982) 98 *LQR* 279, 320; and HWR Wade, 'The Future of Certiorari' (1958) 17 *CLJ* 169, 170.

[69] *De Mattos v Gibson* (1858) 4 De G & J 276; *Lord Strathcona SS Co v Dominion Coal Co* [1926] AC 108 (PC); *Swiss Bank Corpn v Lloyds Bank Ltd* [1979] Ch 548 (Ch).

[70] See ch 18.

[71] Law Commission, 'Landlord and Tenant: Privity of Contract and Estate' (Law Com No 174, 1988) paras 3.5–3.23.

[72] Landlords are not automatically released but can apply to be released. In practice, landlord liability is seldom in issue.

2.4.3.6 No Recovery of Lost Rent after Acceptance of Tenant Abandonment[73]

If a tenant moves out of leasehold property and ceases to pay the rent, the landlord is able to treat the lease as at an end. In some respects it is similar to the idea that there has been a repudiatory breach by the tenant, but it is treated as a rule of property. Further, it has been held in England that if the landlord does bring the lease to an end, he is unable to sue the tenant for losses that he suffers after that point in time, perhaps because there is a void for a while, or because he has to relet the premises at a lower rent. This is quite different from the position in contract law generally where the innocent party is able to claim damages for post-repudiation losses. Further, the landlord is under no duty to accept the tenant's abandonment as a repudiatory act and can simply continue to sue for rent as it falls due. It has sometimes been argued that the landlord should come under a duty to mitigate in this situation, which will usually require him to re-let the property. In *Reichman v Beveridge*, however, the Court of Appeal held that this duty to mitigate was not part of English landlord and tenant law.[74]

2.4.3.7 Surrender[75]

If the landlord and tenant agree to vary the lease by adding further land to it or by extending the term this will amount in law to an implied surrender and re-grant, irrespective of whether the parties intended for the arrangement to be a new lease or whether the changes are significant. In contract law, whether a variation has the effect of creating a new contract will depend upon how fundamental the changes are. The explanation given for the leasehold rule by Russell LJ in *Jenkins R Lewis Ltd v Kerman* is that variations that alter the 'pre-existing item of property' will lead to the creation of a new tenancy.[76]

2.4.4 Leases as Property and Contract

The fact that leases are now seen as to do with more than simply the grant of an estate, does not mean that leases are now primarily situated within the law of contract. The hybrid nature of leases means that both property-based rules and contractual rules apply to leases.

The correct approach is that followed by Lord Bridge in *Hammersmith and Fulham LBC v Monk*.[77] Mr Monk and Mrs Powell had a weekly tenancy of a flat which they held as joint tenants. After their relationship broke down, Mrs Powell served a notice to quit on the landlord without Mr Monk's knowledge or concurrence. The question before the court was whether one joint tenant acting alone could determine the joint tenancy. Lord Browne-Wilkinson presented the issue as one involving a tension between a property-based approach and a contractual approach: the property approach finding revulsion in the idea that Mrs Powell could end Mr Monk's right to live in his home by her unilateral action, and the contract-based approach disliking the idea that she could be held to a contract by the will of the other party. In fact, there was not really a tension between property and contract,

---

[73] See ch 16.
[74] [2006] EWCA Civ 1659.
[75] See ch 24.
[76] [1971] 1 Ch 477 (CA).
[77] [1992] 1 AC 478 (HL).

at least not in a legally meaningful sense. The only sense in which it was a 'property approach' was that the decision would impact on the use of the 'home'. This is not to say that it is not an important factor, but it had no particular legal significance (although it might have a stronger weight now in the light of human rights legislation, see below and chapter 10).

Lord Bridge approached the issue first by asking how it would be answered in contract law, before asking whether there:

> ... is any principle of the English law of real property and peculiar to the contractual relationship of landlord and tenant which refutes that expectation.[78]

Looked at from a contractual perspective, the notice to quit would be effective. For renewal of the contract (the periodic tenancy), the consent of both parties is required and the fact that one party had served a notice to quit showed that there was not joint consent for renewal. Although it might have been expected that in property law joint action would be required, the law had not developed this way. Lords Bridge and Browne-Wilkinson referred to authority for the view that joint *landlords* of a periodic tenancy had to *all* agree individually to *renew*[79] and that joint *tenants* of a periodic tenancy had to *all* agree individually to *renew*.[80] There was no property rule, however, that joint action was necessary to serve a notice to quit, and so the answer remained that provided by contract law and Mrs Powell's notice was effective to end the tenancy.

As many of the property-based rules are to do with remedies and enforceability, they tend to be more in issue with longer term leases. For short tenancies property related issues will arise less frequently. Indeed, the Law Commission has proposed reform of the law relating to rented homes which proposes a consumer approach to the law, under which everyone renting a home would have access to a definitive written agreement clearly setting out their rights and obligations.[81] Within this scheme what would matter is that there is a contract for renting a home; the question as to whether it is a proprietary interest is irrelevant to the scheme.

Deane J, in the Australian case of *Progressive Mailing House Pty Ltd v Tabili Pty Ltd*, commented on the way that the nature of the lease affects how the contractual principles apply (in the context of how the principles of frustration apply to leases):

> ... it should be accepted that, as a general matter and subject to one qualification, the ordinary principles of contract law are applicable to contractual leases. The qualification is that the further one moves away from the case where the rights of the parties are, as a matter of substance, essentially defined by executory covenant or contractual promise to the case where the tenant's rights are, as a matter of substance, more properly to be viewed by reference to their character as an estate (albeit a chattel one) in land with a root of title in the executed demise, the more difficult it will be to establish that the lease has been avoided or terminated pursuant to the operation of the ordinary principles of frustration or fundamental breach. Indeed, one may reach the case where it would be quite artificial to regard the tenant's rights as anything

---

[78] [1992] 1 AC 478 (HL) 483.
[79] *Doe d Aslin v Summersett* (1830) 1 B & Ad 135.
[80] *Greenwich LBC v McGrady* (1982) 46 P & CR 223 (CA).
[81] Law Commission, 'Renting Homes: The Final Report. Volume 1: Report' (Law Com No 297, 2006).

other than an estate or interest in land (eg, a 99 year lease of unimproved land on payment of a premium and with no rent, or only a nominal rent, reserved).[82]

2.5 Landlord and Tenant Law as Regulatory Law

In her chapter on the three Rs, Blandy refers to regulatory law as a new type of law.[83] It is difficult to be precise in defining what regulatory law is, but broadly it is concerned with state control directed to social and individual action to address problems of social risk or market failure. Regulatory law tends not to be concerned with control through actionable private law rights, but with control through agencies. There are many examples of this kind of regulation in the housing sector such as the recent licensing of houses in multiple occupation which is enforced by local authorities.

Blandy suggests that as 'rights' have reduced, so regulation has stepped in:

> Tuebner's 'emergence of new structures of law' … can be seen throughout the private rented sector. This is because the withdrawal of legal provisions from some aspects of the private rented sector has led to the need for other forms of regulation. For example, in 1988 new tenants lost the rights and security which went with Rent Act tenancies, but landlords who harassed or unlawfully evicted their tenants were to be regulated by local authorities enforcing the strengthened 1977 Protection from Eviction Act. The fitness standard changed in 1989, and grants to landlords became discretionary, but local authorities continued to regulate physical conditions and management in the sector. Rents were deregulated in 1988, but Housing Benefit reforms set up 'backdoor rent regulation' by rent officers and local authorities.[84]

What the most appropriate methods of intervention are is a matter for debate. As is discussed later in this chapter, there are often gaps between policy objectives and the reality of experience. Nonetheless, regulatory law and 'rights' based law can supplement one another. Whether regulatory law alone is sufficient must, however, be doubted. In the absence of energetic enforcement, tenants can be left feeling stranded and without a voice. Blandy describes regulation of private landlords as 'second hand' rights for tenants:

> … this type of right – neither contractual nor statutory, but dependent on complaints to the regulatory body – can be described as a *regulatory right*. For tenants, this is not a satisfactory way of ensuring that standards in the private rented sector are maintained and improved. It falls far short of the 'consumerist' model of regulation …[85]

2.6 The Public Law Dimension

More than a third of rented homes are rented from a local authority. Local authorities also

---

[82] (1985) 57 ALR 609 (HC Australia) 635–636. See also Mason J at 621, Brennan J at 626 *et seq.*

[83] S Blandy, 'Housing standards in the private rented sector and the three Rs: regulation, responsibility and rights' in D Cowan and A Marsh (eds), *Two Steps Forward* (Bristol, The Policy Press, 2001).

[84] S Blandy, 'Housing standards in the private rented sector and the three Rs: regulation, responsibility and rights' in D Cowan and A Marsh (eds), *Two Steps Forward* (Bristol, The Policy Press, 2001) 87.

[85] S Blandy, 'Housing standards in the private rented sector and the three Rs: regulation, responsibility and rights' in D Cowan and A Marsh (eds), *Two Steps Forward* (Bristol, The Policy Press, 2001) 88.

rent out a significant number of commercial properties. This brings the landlord and tenant relationship into the public law realm, and the interaction of public and private law remedies is not always straightforward. There are two main ways in which this public law dimension may impact on the landlord and tenant relationship: enabling the tenant to question the decision of public landlords, and using public law as a means to force landlords to take action.

2.6.1 Questioning the Decisions of Public Authorities

2.6.1.1 Public Law: An Additional Ground of Challenge?

Judicial review provides a route for challenging the 'legality' of a decision made by a public authority. If a local authority has decided to evict all tenants with red hair this would seem to fall within the scope of a judicial review challenge. It is here that the distinction between private and public landlords becomes visible. If a private landlord decides to evict a tenant, the question falls to be resolved only as a matter of private law (has the tenancy ended, has a court order been obtained, and so on.) Eviction can be challenged this way, too, by a council tenant, but public law may provide an additional remedy if the decision is illegal, irrational or offends the principles of natural justice.

  Mowan v Wandsworth provides an illustration of how the issue could arise.[86] Mrs Mowan had exercised her right to buy and become a long residential leaseholder with the local authority as her landlord. She lived beneath Miss Abrahart who was renting from the council and who was mentally disturbed. Mrs Mowan's flat was regularly flooded with sewage from the flat above, she suffered persistent noise, and a death threat was made against her. Her claim against the council in negligence and nuisance for having failed to stop the problem failed (see chapter 11), but Sir Christopher Staughton and Peter Gibson LJ hinted that Mrs Mowan might have got further had she sought a remedy in public law, perhaps by judicially reviewing the legality of the Council's decision not to take possession proceedings against Miss Abrahart.

  Public law may also impinge on commercial lettings. In *R v Welwyn Hatfield DC, ex p Slough Estates plc*, a commercial tenant, Slough Estates plc, had been assured by its landlord, the local authority, that it would enforce a 'tenant mix agreement' in relation to another (potentially competing) development site.[87] This agreement permitted the council, for a five year period, to restrict the classes of tenant allowed at the other site so as to minimise competition between the two developments. Although the council had represented to Slough Estates that it intended to enforce the agreement, it secretly relaxed the tenant mix agreement by a side-letter. Slough Estates plc brought a successful judicial review action to quash this relaxation. Kennedy J held that the decision of the council to relax the tenant mix agreement by issuing the side letter amounted to an abuse of power. The case then proceeded by writ in a claim for damages for misrepresentation, which resulted in liability of some £48 million.[88]

---

[86] *Mowan v Wandsworth* [2000] EWCA Civ 357.
[87] [1991] EGCS 38 (QB).
[88] *Slough Estates plc v Welwyn Hatfield DC* [1996] 2 PLR 50 (QB) 92.

In practice, however, a tenant seeking to challenge a local authority decision on public law grounds is unlikely to succeed. Courts are unwilling to second guess decisions taken by the local authority. Provided that the local authority has taken a decision in a manner compatible with the three basic tenets of judicial review – adopting Lord Diplock's classic exposition, legality, rationality and natural justice[89] – a court will not interfere. It is only in extreme cases, such as the 'red hair' example given above, that a local authority tenant is likely to get very far with a public law challenge. The discretionary nature of public law remedies and the constitutional tightrope that the judges are navigating in their roles as guardians of administrative law, mean that in reality it will be difficult – but not impossible – for a tenant successfully to challenge a decision by a local authority.

2.6.1.2 Public Law: Constraining Private Law Challenges?

The availability of a remedy through public law may, however, also limit a tenant's ability to pursue a private action. In *O'Reilly v Mackman* (a prisoner case) the House of Lords set out the principle that a person who seeks a remedy for infringement of public law rights must, as a general rule, proceed by way of judicial review rather than pursuing a common law action.[90] This is to support the public policy underlying the protections given by judicial review, in the words of Lord Diplock:

> … viz., the need, in the interests of good administration and of third parties who may be indirectly affected by the decision, for speedy certainty as to whether it has the effect of a decision that is valid in public law.[91]

The fact that a judicial review claim must be brought within three months of the decision being challenged brings finality to decision-making within a short time.

The assumption underlying this approach is that it is possible to distinguish between public rights and private rights, but this boundary is not clearly defined. Beatson suggests that the distinction may turn on whether the issue involves challenging a power which has been committed to the jurisdiction of the authority in question (a public law issue) or an individuated Hohfeldian claim right (a private law issue).[92] This suggestion follows from what is known as the 'collateral challenge exception' stemming from the remarks of Lord Diplock in *O'Reilly v Mackman* that there may be exceptions to the general rule:

> … particularly where the invalidity of the decision arises as a collateral issue in a claim for infringement of a right of the plaintiff arising under private law …[93]

In the very next reported decision, *Cocks v Thanet DC*, the House of Lords developed this further.[94] The particular case concerned the homelessness legislation. Lord Bridge divided a local authority's functions into two: decision-making and executive. Decision-making

---

[89] *Council of Civil Service Unions and Others v Minister for Civil Service* [1985] AC 374 (HL) 410–411.

[90] [1983] 2 AC 237 (HL) 285.

[91] [1983] 2 AC 237 (HL) 284.

[92] J Beatson, '"Public" and "Private" in English Administrative Law' (1987) 103 *LQR* 34. Hohfeld famously develops a more refined language of rights than is commonly used, that builds on the idea that all legal claim rights involve correlative legal duties on others: see WN Hohfeld, 'Some Fundamental Legal Conceptions as Applied in Judicial Reasoning' (1913) 23 *Yale LJ* 16.

[93] [1983] 2 AC 237 (HL) 285.

[94] [1983] 2 AC 286 (HL) 292–3.

referred to the local authority's obligation to investigate a genuine claim for homelessness to see if a duty to rehouse had arisen. Since statute conferred exclusive jurisdiction on the local authority to reach the decision, its decision was of a public law nature and could only be challenged by judicial review.[95]

> On the other hand, the housing authority are charged with executive functions. Once a decision has been reached by the housing authority which gives rise to the temporary, the limited or the full housing duty, rights and obligations are immediately created in the field of private law. Each of the duties referred to, once established, is capable of being enforced by injunction and breach of it will give rise to a liability in damages. But it is inherent in the scheme of the [homelessness legislation] that an appropriate public law decision of the housing authority is a condition precedent to the establishment of the private law duty.[96]

The effect is that a local authority tenant is not confined to pursuing public law remedies if a private law duty is in issue, which usually will be the case in disputes between landlord and tenant.

Further, as *Wandsworth LBC v Winder* illustrates, a local authority tenant can challenge local authority decisions on public law grounds as a defence to private law proceedings.[97] The local authority had issued notices of rent increases which the tenant considered excessive and so he had continued to pay the old rent. Wandsworth London Borough Council sued for possession and for the arrears. Winder's defence was that he was not liable for arrears since the rent increases were *ultra vires* and counterclaimed for a declaration to that effect. At first instance the counterclaim and defence were struck out as an abuse of process since a challenge to the council's policies should be initiated by judicial review. The judgment, however, was reversed by the Court of Appeal and the House of Lords. Lord Fraser held that a local authority could be challenged on its policies in a private, as opposed to public, action, at least by way of defence where there is 'a pre-existing private law right':[98]

> It would in my opinion be a very strange use of language to describe the respondent's behaviour in relation to this litigation as an abuse or misuse by him of the process of the court. He did not select the procedure to be adopted. He is merely seeking to defend proceedings brought against him by the appellants. In so doing he is seeking only to exercise the ordinary right of any individual to defend an action against him on the ground that he is not liable for the whole sum claimed by the plaintiff. Moreover, he puts forward his defence as a matter of right, whereas in an application for judicial review, success would require an exercise of the court's discretion in his favour. … I find it impossible to accept that the right to challenge the decision of a local authority in the course of defending an action for non-payment can have been swept away by Order 53, which was directed to introducing a procedural reform.[99]

The only constraint is that the private law rights must dominate the proceedings when seeking to enforce performance of a public law duty in an action commenced by writ.

---

[95] A large number of judicial review challenges are brought in relation to homelessness decisions, but this is beyond the scope of this book.
[96] [1983] 2 AC 286 (HL) 292–3.
[97] [1985] 1 AC 461 (HL).
[98] [1985] 1 AC 461 (HL) 508.
[99] [1985] 1 AC 461 (HL) 509. The decision in *Winder* is criticised by Woolf: H Woolf, 'Public Law – Private Law: why the divide?' [1986] *PL* 220.

2.6.1.3 Human Rights Law

The advent of human rights law provides further scope to challenge local authority decision making. If, for example, the local authority brings eviction proceedings, the tenant may claim that this violates his right to respect for home under Article 8 of the European Convention on Human Rights and Fundamental Freedoms (ECHR). As Arden and Partington state, human rights law has the potential to make a big impact on housing law:

> Housing lawyers have been amongst the most eager to test the extent to which the provisions of the European Convention on Human Rights and Fundamental Freedoms are able to protect housing rights. Cases have sought to raise issues in relation to access, security, rents, conditions and management; in other words, to test the extent to which the Human Rights Act 1998 can be superimposed on domestic housing law.
>
> The two key articles which housing lawyers have sought to employ are the rights to a fair hearing in article 6 and to respect for private and family life and the home in article 8. Other potentially relevant articles include the article 14 right not to be discriminated against (where another Convention article is in play), and article 1 of Protocol 1 which protects the right to peaceful enjoyment of possessions.[100]

There are procedural advantages to proceeding through the Human Rights Act 1998 rather than through Part 54 judicial review; for instance, the time limit for proceedings is one year rather than three months,[101] and the victim can apply directly to the court without the need for a cumbersome leave procedure.[102] There has been a large number of housing cases in which Article 8 of the ECHR, in particular, has been argued as a defence against local authority action, but in practice human rights law has had little impact on substantive outcomes. In human rights cases there is always a need to undertake a balancing exercise:

> ... regard must be had to the fair balance that has to be struck between the competing interests of the individual and of the community as a whole ... [The] State enjoys a certain margin of appreciation in determining the steps to be taken to ensure compliance with the Convention.[103]

Ordinarily, the courts will uphold the decisions taken by local authorities, particularly in the area of housing policy which is seen as very much a matter for the allocation of resources in accordance with democratically determined priorities.[104]

2.6.2 Compelling Local Authorities to Take Action[105]

A further question is whether public law can be used to compel local authorities to act.

---

[100] A Arden and M Partington, 'Housing Law: Past and Present' in S Bright (ed), *Landlord and Tenant Law. Past, Present and Future* (Oxford, Hart, 2006) 208.

[101] It is not clear from when the one year time limit before which proceedings must be brought under the Human Rights Act 1998 s 7(5)(a) would run in cases of failure to act. Presumably it would run from the time when a complaint was first made, though the court could use its discretion under s 7(5)(b) to extend this if unfairness would result.

[102] This is especially important for those victims whose complaints to the local authority have been ignored.

[103] *Hatton v UK* (App No 36022/97) (2002) 34 EHRR 1 [96]. See also *Lee v Leeds CC* [2002] EWCA Civ 6, [2002] 1 WLR 1488 [48].

[104] *Southwark LBC v Tanner, Baxter v Camden LBC (No 2)* [2001] 1 AC 1 (HL) 9–10 (Lord Hoffmann). See also D Rook, 'Property Law and the Human Rights Act 1998: a Review of the First Year' [2002] *Conv* 316.

[105] See also ch 11.

Recent years have seen, for example, a growth in complaints about anti-social behaviour and local authorities (and housing associations) have large armouries of weapons to use in the fight against bad behaviour. It may be that the victim wants to force the local authority to take action, and the question is whether public law remedies might help. The tenant is very unlikely to be able to use traditional public law remedies in this way, but there is now the possibility that a tenant might try to use the human rights legislation to compel a local authority to act.

As will be seen in later chapters, Article 8 of the ECHR, which refers to the right to respect for the home, can be used not only when the claim is that a local authority has infringed a tenant's rights but also to impose a positive obligation to act on a local authority. This means that the tenant does not need to be seeking to impugn a particular decision but could use human rights law to require the local authority to do something. In practice, however, judges have been reluctant to intervene with housing matters, leaving the exercise of judgement as to the appropriate use of scarce housing resources to those more closely involved with decision-making.

2.7 Leases and Land

Quite apart from the doctrinal classification of leases as proprietary estates, leases also involve property in a much more everyday sense as they involve the use of land. Later chapters of this book focus on the law relating to the landlord and tenant relationship and it is useful to think about ways in which the fact that leases relate to the use of land may have contributed to the shape of the law.

As the tenant has the right to the present use of the land during the term of the lease and the landlord has the right to the income, it could be said that for the tenant the physicality of the land is important whereas for the landlord the lease represents an investment asset. There is some truth in this, but this approach underestimates how important landholding can be to both parties.

2.7.1 Landlords: Land and Wealth

For most landlords the lease is important because of its worth as an investment. Maintaining the value of this investment, both in terms of income stream and the capital value of the reversion, will be important to the landlord. This means that the landlord will seek a reliable tenant who will be able to pay the rent and also look after the property. The law on alienation supports the notion that the landlord is entitled to preserve the value of his reversionary interest by allowing the landlord to refuse consent to an assignment of the lease if the assignee would be an unsatisfactory tenant.[106] On the other hand, in one instance the law restricts the landlord's rights to control what the tenant does during the lease if this has no impact on the reversionary value: if a long lease has three or more years left to run, the landlord's ability to obtain a remedy for breach of a tenant repairing covenant is restricted.

---

[106] See ch 18.

One of the grounds on which action is possible is where immediate repair is necessary to prevent a substantial diminution in the value of the reversion.[107]

Even for landlords, the reversionary interest will often have a value beyond the mere investment value that it represents, reflecting the fact that the rights exist in relation to land. A substantial minority of private sector residential landlords have a 'personal connection' with the property, as a former or future-intended home, or as an inheritance.[108] The law recognises this by providing grounds for recovery of possession based on the landlord's former or intended use of the property as a home.[109] Even for 'investment landlords' property is often not simply 'an' investment, as good as any other so long as the financial return is right, but there is a value to owning 'bricks and mortar'. The work by Scott, referred to in chapter 1, found that for many traditional commercial landlords (who still have substantial property holdings), property is not simply an investment but has a social role. The final chapter of this book discusses various statutory rights that tenants have to acquire freeholds (known as enfranchisement): these laws are resisted not only if the compensation package is seen as inadequate but more fundamentally on the grounds that landlords should not be compulsorily dispossessed of their property rights.[110] Famously, the Duke of Westminster, who owns large parts of Mayfair and Belgravia in Central London through his property company, Grosvenor, staunchly opposed enfranchisement reform as the land has formed part of his family's estates for centuries. For social landlords, there is a further dimension. For them the housing stock enables them to fulfil a political function and perform a welfare role, although in the course of doing so they will also need to balance the books.

It is not the case, therefore, that the law adequately protects the landlord's interests by preserving only the investment value (or equivalent). It is not an investment that can always be substituted by a pot of money. For many landlords it is important that, as he wishes, he is able to sell the property or to keep it, to let it, or to bring a tenancy to an end.

2.7.2 Tenants: Land and Wealth

For the tenant, the lease may also represent wealth. In the case of a long residential leasehold, the lease is likely to have been purchased for a substantial premium and it may well be the only significant financial asset that the leaseholder owns. By contrast, in most cases where the tenant is paying a market rent there is no financial value in the tenancy. Whether or not the lease does represent wealth for the tenant it will, however, nearly always carry a worth beyond any financial value that might attach to the lease.

Security is obviously important in this context; whether it is a home or a business, moving is expensive, disturbing and time consuming. For the business tenant, having to move premises will carry significant financial cost but may also, particularly in a location-sensitive business such as retailing, lead to a loss of goodwill that could spell

---

[107] See ch 12, especially the discussion relating to the Leasehold Property (Repairs) Act 1938.
[108] ODPM, 'Private Landlords Survey: English House Condition Survey 2001' (Housing Research Summary Number 205, 2003).
[109] See ch 19.
[110] See ch 25.

financial disaster. For the farmer, security is important to encourage long term efficiency in farming methods. As will be seen, the policy towards 'security' in leases has fluctuated, but at various times the law has given tenants, in all sectors, the right to remain in the rented property after the lease expires.

For the residential tenant the property will be both shelter and home, both important concepts. Shelter focuses on the physical aspects: the fact that it provides a weatherproof and safe environment providing the necessary level of amenities. Both policy and the law will feed into this concept. To ensure that this shelter is accessible there may need to be rules about allocation of housing, and the property will need to be rented out at affordable rates (or else welfare payments available for low income groups). The quality of the shelter will be affected by construction standards, but also by the standards of repair and improvement, something that the law has much to say about. Home is a much broader concept than shelter. There have been numerous studies in other disciplines showing the importance of 'home': in addition to meeting the basic need for shelter, to have a secure home enables the building of links within the community, it provides a sense of place, belonging and identity, and supports psychological well-being. One way in which home may now find a voice in law is through human rights law, as Article 8 of the ECHR gives a right to respect for home.

Several studies suggest that the 'home experience' is much stronger for home owners than renters. This is because home owners generally have a greater degree of control, status and security than renters.[111] It is clear that the legislative scheme in place for rented homes will have a significant impact on the home experience as the social and cultural benefits of 'home' will be enhanced by a legal regime that supports security and promotes control/choice. Renters of social housing generally have much greater security than private renters, giving greater opportunities to develop community links. Social renters have more opportunity to participate in management decisions. But, negatively, social renters are also likely to suffer from a poorer status image as social housing is increasingly used to house those unable to access other tenures and is increasingly associated with social deprivation and exclusion.

Security, shelter and home are therefore all important. One question to think about is whether landlord and tenant law gives sufficient support to renters to ensure not only that they have shelter, but also that they have security and, in the case of residential properties, the opportunity to create a home.

2.8 Leases as Split-ownership

Ownership is often described as consisting of a 'bundle of rights' in relation to a thing.[112] Although in a strict sense, land law has no concept of ownership as the law is one of

---

[111] In her book exploring the concept of home, Fox notes that the extent to which home meanings are 'tenure-specific' is controversial: L Fox, *Conceptualising Home* (Oxford, Hart, 2007). These points are brought out at 228–41, particularly in the discussion of the work done by Marcuse.

[112] L Underkuffler-Freund explores 'bundle of rights' theories in 'Takings and the Nature of Property' (1996) 9 *Canadian J L & Juris* 161, esp 169–171. For criticism, see J Penner, 'The "Bundle of Rights" Picture of Property' (1996) 43 *UCLA L Rev* 711.

possession,[113] it is helpful at a more abstract level to think about the kind of rights that landlords and tenants have in relation to land and how they are split between them. Clarke sees leases as primarily concerned with the dividing up of the 'ownership interest':

> ... it is submitted that a, perhaps the, principal purpose of a lease (and a vital feature), is to achieve a division of interests, or a split in ownership, in the property as a whole.[114]

During the life of the lease many of the rights most strongly associated with property are held by the tenant: the right to exclude non-owners, the right to license others to use the property (in terms of allowing access, and also alienating the tenant's interest), and the right to use the land. In this sense, there is no doubt that the tenant has 'property' rights in relation to the land. Indeed, what for many is seen as one of the most fundamental rights of property,[115] the right to exclude non-owners, is doctrinally central; as will be seen in chapter 3 it is *the* tool used to distinguish the lease from the (merely contractual) licence to occupy.

The landlord also, however, enjoys many rights in relation to the land even while he holds only the reversionary interest. He does, for example, have the right to receive the rent, and the right to profit has been accepted by the Grand Chamber of the ECtHR as an important aspect of property ownership.[116] He also enjoys rights of alienation as he is free to dispose of his reversionary interest. Interestingly, what he does not enjoy during the life of the lease is the right to exclude, for he has granted this right to the tenant. Yet even though this right is often seen as a fundamental aspect of property, there is no doubting that the landlord does have property in the reversionary interest.

Clarke rightly describes leases as involving a split in 'ownership'. The variety of rights that together make up ownership are split between the landlord and the tenant during the life of the lease. But it must also be recognised that leases involve the splitting of the rights in a way that creates two separate objects of ownership; the leasehold estate that is enjoyed by the tenant, and the reversionary interest that is enjoyed by the landlord. One of the jobs of policy in the field of landlord and tenant law is to ensure that the way that ownership is split provides an appropriate balance between the landlord and tenant, giving due recognition to the interest that each also separately owns. So, for example, there has been much concern that landlords of long residential leases retain too much control and power in relation to management, given that the leaseholder has a long term interest in the property that carries a significant capital value. The unacceptability of this division of interest has led to several

---

[113] W Swadling, 'Property: General Principles' in P Birks (ed), *English Private Law* (Oxford, OUP, 2000) vol 1, 218. This view reflects the fact that 'property' is protected by protecting the right to possession. In *Hunter v Canary Wharf Ltd* [1997] AC 655 (HL) 703, Lord Hoffmann approved the following summary: 'As it is said in *Cheshire and Burn's Modern Law of Real Property*, 15th ed. (1994), p. 26: "All titles to land are ultimately based upon possession in the sense that the title of the man seised prevails against all who can show no better right to seisin. Seisin is a root of title, and it may be said without undue exaggeration that so far as land is concerned there is in England no law of ownership, but only a law of possession."'

[114] D Clarke, 'Long Residential Leases: Future Directions' in S Bright (ed), *Landlord and Tenant Law. Past, Present and Future* (Oxford, Hart, 2006) 172.

[115] For some it is *the* defining right: I W Merrill, 'Property and the Right to Exclude' (1998) 77 *Nebraska L Rev* 730.

[116] In *Hutten-Czapaska v Poland* (App No 35014/97) (2006) 20 BHRC 493 [239] the Grand Chamber directed the Polish government to amend its rental legislation (that contained an extreme form of rent control preventing landlords from even recovering their costs) to ensure that a fair balance was achieved 'between the interests of landlords, including their entitlement to derive profit from their property, and the general interest of the community'. One of the dissenting judges did not accept that a landlord has a right to profit.

enactments over recent years giving leaseholders not only greater rights in relation to the management of the property, but even the right to acquire the freehold.[117]

In everyday usage, ownership carries a different meaning. Non-lawyers and non-theorists do not usually think in terms of bundles of rights in relation to things but have a much more instinctive understanding of what ownership is. Although it may be that this perception can be picked apart as unrefined, it is useful to think about leases in this light. The key distinction made is one between 'renting' and 'owning'. Few people would think of the weekly tenant as an owner, whereas most would readily describe the long residential leaseholder as owner.[118] Why?

In part, it may be to do with who has the ability to sell or create further interests in the property: the weekly tenant is unlikely to have significant powers to dispose of the tenancy whereas the long leaseholder will usually have full powers of alienation. More probably, however, it is to do with how the resources, in the sense of value, have been allocated between the landlord and tenant. The more resources that are retained by the landlord, the less like an owner the tenant looks. The long residential leaseholder has most of the 'resource' in the property, particularly at the outset of a long lease, whereas the weekly tenant has virtually no resource as all the capital value is in the landlord's reversion. The weekly tenant may enjoy very similar use-privileges to the leaseholder, and, if a social tenant with security of tenure, he may have an expectation of remaining in the property for a very long time. Even so, he would not be thought of as an owner because of the fact that he is making regular payments for the right to occupy. The long residential leaseholder looks like an owner because the lease has a capital value, and although there will be some kind of rent payment it will be relatively minor. He will be able to sell his interest in the property, usually without restriction, for a capital sum. When the lease is very long the landlord retains little, save possibly for the right to extract money in the form of management fees.

Ownership and renting may shade into one another. There are many leases that provide for medium term occupation, around 21 years, which will usually be at a market rent. Even so, tenants of these leases are still more usually thought of as renting rather than owning. The distinction – the sorting of ownership from renting – probably turns on where the capital value in the property lies. With medium term leases, the larger part of the capital value will typically remain in the freehold reversion.[119]

In the context of leases it appears, therefore, that the language of ownership is generally used for the interest that carries the major part the capital value, and the language of renting is used to describe a tenant who pays a rent to reflect the true value of the land and any buildings on it. With the exception of long residential leases and a few very long commercial leases, this will usually mean that the landlord is thought of as the owner of the property and the tenant as a 'mere' renter.

---

[117] See D Clarke, 'Long Residential Leases: Future Directions' in S Bright (ed), *Landlord and Tenant Law: Past, Present and Future* (Oxford, Hart, 2006); and ch 25.

[118] Blandy and Robinson write that housing discourse defines ownership by the method of access to property, to include all circumstances where it is acquired by payment of a sale price and makes no distinction between leaseholders and freeholders as both are owner-occupiers: S Blandy and D Robinson, 'Reforming Leasehold: Discursive Events and Outcomes, 1984–2000' (2001) 21 *JLS* 384, 393.

[119] D Clarke, 'Long Residential Leases: Future Directions' in S Bright (ed), *Landlord and Tenant Law. Past, Present and Future* (Oxford, Hart, 2006) 173.

2.9 Intervention in the Landlord and Tenant Relationship

2.9.1 Law and Policy

Much of the legislative intervention that is specifically directed at the leasehold sector stems from policy concerns that have a national economic and social impact. The earliest controls on private rented housing were closely linked to the severe social and political unrest amongst tenants faced with rising rents during World War I, threatening to unbalance what stability there was. The first major statutes regulating agricultural tenancies flowed from the economic imperative to give support to an agricultural industry struggling in the face of a succession of poor home harvests and growing international agricultural competition providing cheap imported crops.[120] The stimulus behind the first statutory regulation of commercial tenancies reflected a rather limited attempt to respond to the shortage of commercial property following World War I. Indeed, it is probably the case that most major reforms have followed from social and economic concerns that extend far beyond the leasehold relationship, the solution to these problems being seen to lie, in part, in reform of the process of letting land. This is equally true of many recent reforms. What is commonly described as the 'deregulation' of the private rental market by the Housing Act 1988 was in large part designed to encourage greater investment in private rental housing so as to stimulate supply. It is even true of some of the reforms that look much more like 'lawyer's law' than policy driven changes. In 1995, there was a major reform of the rules governing the enforcement of covenants contained in leases, a reform undoubtedly driven by the perceived adverse economic impact of what was known as 'original tenant liability'.[121]

Reform can also result from a concern to achieve an appropriate balance in the division of interest between landlord and tenant, and often to protect the tenant from a perceived inequality in the bargaining relationship. In considering this balance many questions have to be asked. Should a tenant be made responsible for the cost of maintaining the property if he has only a limited interest in it? Should a tenant have to pay for property which is not fit for the purpose? Should a tenant be able to remain in the property once the contractual term has expired, and, if so, on what terms? Should members of his family? Should a tenant who has signed up to a long interest be able to end the lease early, or pass it on to someone else, if his occupational needs change? Should a landlord be able to bring a lease to an end early because of some default by the tenant? If so, should this be allowed only if the tenant's behaviour will damage the landlord's reversionary interest? The law has responded to these, and other, questions variously by introducing schemes giving security of tenure, rights of succession, control of alienation rights, rights to compensation for improvements, relief from forfeiture, regulation of rent levels and landlord repairing obligations.

In its 1987 report on the reform of landlord and tenant law, the Law Commission summarised the case for intervention in each of the main sectors. It must be noted, however, that attitudes and policies have changed since, often dramatically:

---

[120] A Densham, 'Agricultural Tenancies. Past and Present' in S Bright (ed), *Landlord and Tenant Law. Past, Present and Future* (Oxford, Hart, 2006).

[121] See ch 18; see also S Bridge 'Commercial Leases Past and Present: The Contribution of the Law Commission' in S Bright (ed), *Landlord and Tenant Law. Past, Present and Future* (Oxford, Hart, 2006).

2.6 One major concern has been to protect tenants against the oppressive use of the landlord's power. This is a classic interference with apparent freedom of contract, in the belief that the position of the parties when they negotiate is so unequal that the freedom is illusory ...

Agricultural land

2.8 The problems of an agricultural tenant of arable land are unique in one way. Unless he is allowed to occupy the land let to him for long enough to harvest any crop he has sown, he may not be able to obtain any return at all from his use of the property. This is balanced by the fact that unless he observes the tenets of good husbandry, he can seriously prejudice the future productivity of the soil, and therefore the value of the land. Again, good farming may require the provision of permanent improvements, which will benefit the landlord after the tenancy ceases ... In agriculture, more than in any other field, landlord and tenant legislation emphasises the partnership between the two parties, each of whom should appropriately contribute to what is in a sense a joint enterprise.

2.9 Security of tenure was given to farm tenants to protect their farming business, and it is in effect conditional on their conducting that business properly. The influence of parallel legislation covering residential properties, where the motive is to provide tenants with a permanent home, led to an extension of the security of agricultural tenants, allowing members of the family to succeed them on death or retirement. Because this dramatically reduced the number of farms offered for letting, this policy was reversed.

Business property

2.10 Similar influences affected legislative intervention into the law governing commercial tenancies, although it came later. A business established on leasehold property can be put at risk when the lease expires, if the landlord does not wish to renew it or demands exorbitant terms. Also, a tenant may wish to make an improvement to increase the efficiency of the business. If there is residual value in that improvement when the lease ends, he might simply have provided a greater incentive to the landlord to decline to renew it.

2.11 ... In the first instance, the emphasis was on ensuring that tenants were not unjustly deprived of the residual value of improvements they had made: they were given the option of compensation or a new lease. Later, the emphasis was placed on renewal of the tenancy, and, with certain exceptions, tenants now have the right to a new lease when their current one ends.

Residential property

2.12 Three separate strands of policy can be detected in the considerable volume of legislation which has been passed to protect residential tenants. First, there is a desire to ensure that the properties they occupy are suitable, properly repaired and with reasonable facilities. Secondly, statute provides a guarantee that tenants can remain in their home indefinitely. Thirdly, tenants who paid a capital sum for a long lease are protected against the consequences of that lease expiring. These elements overlap ... [122]

2.9.2 Intervention – A Denial of Property Rights?

One of the key issues in landlord and tenant law is the extent to which it is proper for the state to intervene, whether it is being done to regulate the supply of decent affordable housing, to support economic and agricultural production, or to secure the tenant's interests,

---

[122] Law Commission, 'Landlord and Tenant: Reform of the Law' (Law Com No 162, 1987).

be they economic or social. Inevitably, statutory controls place restrictions on the ability of a landlord to do with his property as he wishes, and on such terms as he wishes. Legal challenges to the various legislative controls nowadays tend to be played out in the arena of human rights law (see chapter 10), but even before statutory law could be used to mount formal challenges, the powerful political and philosophical rhetoric of property was used to argue against intervention. Commenting on the early attempts to deal with overcrowded and insanitary housing, Gauldie writes:

> Private property stood as a defence between the state and the individual, giving the English the kind of strength which had in the past defeated attempts at despotic monarchy and ambitious parliaments. Thus the very idea of the creation of the inspectorate which would have been necessary to enforce building standards was interpreted as an intolerable attack on private property.[123]

Although not contained in any formal constitutional documents, a right to property has operated as a constraint on both Parliament and the Executive in law making and law enforcement. Allen writes:

> In its simplest form, a constitutional right to property recognises that the State has only limited power to take and regulate property. In the Middle Ages and later, most writers believed that a right to property formed part of the fundamental law of England. Fundamental law bound Parliament and the Crown, although the courts had only a limited power to enforce it against either body. In this sense, the constitution (in the broadest sense) included a right to property, despite the lack of a written constitution or a judicial power of review over legislation. [footnotes omitted][124]

These sentiments are echoed in other jurisdictions. Describing the approach towards regulation of landlord and tenant in France de Moor writes:

> The general law of landlord and tenant is contained in articles 1713 through 1779 of the French Civil Code. The underlying principle which gave birth to these articles almost two hundred years ago is the assumption that the right of the landlord over his property should be virtually absolute, and that the relationship between landlord and tenant should constitute a contract which is best left unconstrained by legislation.[125]

Notwithstanding the power of property rhetoric, in no sector is the landlord and tenant relationship left entirely to be negotiated between the parties; in each sector there has been some form of intervention. The importance attached to 'property', however, is such that any interference with it requires explanation and justification. Reich states:

> Property is a legal institution the essence of which is the creation and protection of certain private rights in wealth of any kind. The institution performs many different functions. One of these functions is to draw a boundary between public and private power. Property draws a circle around the activities of each private individual or organisation. Within that circle, the owner has a greater degree of freedom than without. Outside, he must justify or explain his actions, and show his authority. Within, he is master, and the state must explain and justify

---

[123] E Gauldie, *Cruel Habitations: A History of Working-Class Housing 1780–1918* (London, George Allen & Unwin Ltd, 1974) 117.
[124] T Allen, *Property and the Human Rights Act 1998* (Oxford, Hart, 2005) 8.
[125] A De Moor, 'Landlord and tenant in French law: a recent statute' (1983) 3 *OJLS* 425, 425.

any interference. It is as if property has shifted the burden of proof; outside, the individual has the burden; inside, the burden is on government to demonstrate that something the owner wishes to do should not be done.[126]

These sentiments are reflected in the common law:

According to Blackstone the absolute right inherent in every Englishman is that of property 'which consists of the free use, enjoyment and disposal of all his acquisitions, without any control or diminution save only by the laws of the land'. For this purpose property rights include the right of a person who is sui juris to manage and control his own property. Nourse J referred to,

'The general principle in our law that the rights of a person whom it regards as having the status to deal with them on his own behalf will not be overridden' (*Re Savoy Hotel Ltd* [1981] Ch 351 at 365).[127]

In the common law, property's elevated position is reflected in a principle of statutory interpretation by which there is a presumption against taking property without compensation:

[41] Hence it is a principle of statutory interpretation that by the exercise of state powers the property or economic interests of a person should not be taken away, impaired or endangered except under clear authority of the law. Where a statutory provision takes away a right which would have existed at common law, the provision is not to be enlarged more than the words clearly permit or require (per Sellers LJ in *Newtons of Wembly Ltd v Williams* [1965] 1 QB 560 at 574). Where property rights given at common law are curtailed by statute, the statutory conditions must be strictly complied with (Bennion on Statutory Interpretation (4th ed) at 725).[128]

The strength of this presumption has declined in recent years but it remains the position that the courts will be 'slow to impute to Parliament an intention to override property rights in the absence of plain words to that effect'.[129]

What Reich describes as the burden placed on government is now exemplified in the legislative protection to property rights contained in the ECHR. Article 1 of the First Protocol, protecting the right to the peaceful enjoyment of possessions, provides that there can be no deprivation of possessions unless this is in the public interest, and no control of the use of property unless this is in the general interest. This has been used by landlords to challenge laws giving tenants the right to buy their freeholds or to extend their leases compulsorily, as well to challenge rent controls. There are also increasing human rights challenges being made by tenants, relying both on the right to peaceful enjoyment of possessions, and the right to respect for the home contained in Article 8. The use of human rights law in the context of leasehold relationships is discussed in chapter 10.

---

[126] C Reich 'The New Property' (1964) 73 *Yale LJ* 733, 771.

[127] *Re The Landlords Association for Northern Ireland's Application for Leave to Apply for Judicial Review; Re Boyle, Greer, Jackson and Laird's Application for Judicial Review* [2005] NIQB 22 [40]; [2006] NI 16.

[128] *Re The Landlords Association for Northern Ireland's Application for Leave to Apply for Judicial Review; Re Boyle, Greer, Jackson and Laird's Application for Judicial Review* [2005] NIQB 22, [2006] NI 16.

[129] *Secretary of State for Defence v Guardian Newspapers Limited* [1985] AC 339 (HL) 362. See further the discussion in T Allen, *Property and the Human Rights Act 1998* (Oxford, Hart, 2005) 12–13.

2.9.3 The Limitations of Law in the Pursuit of Policy

The relationship between the landlord and tenant is influenced by many factors that are not strictly related to law. So, for example, the terms of a commercial tenancy will depend not only on the relative bargaining strength of the particular parties but also on the fiscal impact of particular forms of leasing, and current approaches to property development and financing. One of the aims of this book is to explain this wider context.

It is also important to appreciate that the law does not always achieve the desired objective, and other extra-legal factors will usually be at work alongside the law. Taking the private rental market as one example, it is frequently claimed that restrictive rent controls and security of tenure made investment in housing for rental unattractive and thereby caused the dramatic decline in the private rental sector during the last century. Indeed, one of the planks of the government reforms implemented in the Housing Act 1988 was to remove rent control from new lettings, enabling landlords to charge a market rent, in the hope that this would stimulate the revival of the private rental sector. This is, however, an oversimplistic analysis of the way that the housing market works. While protective legislation may have contributed to the decline, it is only one factor amongst many. Balchin identifies numerous factors that contributed to the decline in this sector: slum clearance; policies aimed at dealing with overcrowding; housing rehabilitation (with finance available for upgrading property, many were sold for owner occupation); the unattractiveness of investing in private rented housing (high construction costs and rent control); the cost of repairs and maintenance; the desire to own one's own house; and subsidies and tax allowances (favouring owner occupation and public housing).[130]

Indeed, legislative reform of landlord and tenant law is often accompanied by exaggerated claims about its expected impact. This is not to deny that some changes can have a substantial effect upon the pattern of housing provision, as for instance in the conferral of the Right to Buy on council tenants by the Housing Act 1980. Nevertheless, as Donnison and Ungerson have pointed out:

> ... [past] experience in the housing field – with the Rent Act 1957, the half-million housing programme of 1966 and the Housing Finance Act 1972, for example – suggests that the impact of new policies is rarely as dramatic as either their advocates hope or their critics fear.[131]

As Kemp notes:

> ... policy makers have tended to assume that private landlords, if not perfectly informed and economically rational investors, are at the least fairly knowledgeable and reasonably rational economic agents who will respond to market signals, economic incentives and changes in tenancy legislation. However, research indicates that a substantial minority of landlords scarcely conforms to this 'reasonably rational investor' image ...[132]

What is important to bear in mind, therefore, is that while the law is an important mechanism it will seldom, by itself, be pivotal to change. Instead, it should be seen as playing a part, alongside other economic and social factors, in the process of change. Indeed,

---

[130] P Balchin and M Rhoden, *Housing Policy: an Introduction* 4th edn (London, Routledge, 2002) 123–4.
[131] D Donnision and C Ungerson, *Housing Policy* (Harmondsworth, Penguin, 1982) 161.
[132] P Kemp, *Private Renting in Transition* (Coventry, Chartered Institute of Housing, 2004) 93.

only if the law is in tune with these wider dimensions is it likely to be successful in achieving its policy goals:

> Housing policies are clearly only one factor in shaping wider housing systems. The institutional, economic and social contexts ... [are] fundamental to shaping both policies and outcomes and ... policies are most successful when they follow the grain of economic and social change, and least successful when they do not.[133]

Just as there can be a gap between policy objectives and market reality, so too there are frequently gaps between the aim of legislation designed to influence the way in which individual landlords and tenants behave towards one another, and actual behaviour. Part of this gap is the result of ignorance. Detailed research into the commercial property market conducted by a team at the University of Reading has revealed a surprising level of ignorance about key features of the leasehold relationship, such as whether the lease is contracted out of the legislation that offers renewal rights to commercial tenants (Part II of the Landlord and Tenant Act 1954) or whether the tenant has a right to end the lease at particular points during its term by serving notice (exercising a break clause).[134] One of the considerations driving the Law Commission's reform proposals for rented homes is that many landlords and tenants are not aware of their rights and responsibilities. It is notable that not only are tenants ignorant of their rights; a surprising number of landlords also are unaware of their legal rights and obligations. A study of private landlords revealed that one in four did not know what sort of tenancy they had granted.[135] This ignorance has also been shown to cause some landlords to 'overstep legal boundaries', leading to harassment and unlawful eviction. This will in part be due to the complexity of the law, but will also reflect the fact that many private sector landlords are letting property as a sideline business, and few employ professional managers.[136]

The vulnerability of tenants further contributes to the gap between goals and reality. In a study of the private rental sector in six countries Harloe observed that:

> Each country had complex legal provisions which aimed to regulate landlord/tenant relations. These laws could, in principle, be analysed without too much difficulty. But in so personal a matter as the relationship between a landlord and a tenant, the ability of the law to govern actual conduct was severely limited. These limitations were probably most often experienced at the bottom end of the market ... [Landlords] were often able to pick and choose tenants and to control the terms of their tenancies in ways which had little regard to the law. Tenants who might protest at the unfair burdens which this placed on them knew that it could cost them their tenancy. In some cases disregard for the law was also the product of the widespread ignorance of its provisions which both landlords and tenants frequently displayed.[137]

---

[133] A Holmans, M Stephens and S Fitzpatrick, 'Housing Policy in England since 1975: An Introduction to the Special Issue' (2007) 22 *Housing Studies* 147, 159.

[134] N Crosby, C Hughes and S Murdoch, *Monitoring the 2002 Code of Practice for Commercial Leases* (ODPM, March 2005) 190–2.

[135] ADH Crook and P Kemp, 'Private Landlords in England' (Housing Research Summary, Number 54, DETR, 1996).

[136] ADH Crook and P Kemp, 'Private Landlords in England' (Housing Research Summary, Number 54, DETR, 1996); ADH Crook and others, 'Repair and Maintenance by Private Landlords' (Housing Research Summary Number 138, ODPM, 2000).

[137] M Harloe, *Private Rented Housing in the United States and Europe* (London, Croom Helm, 1985) 266.

The impact of vulnerability on 'gap' can also be seen in a survey of older people in the private rented sector. This found that although many suffered from abuse and harassment,[138] there was nonetheless a reluctance to challenge the landlord through fear of being evicted, even when living conditions were poor. The absence of long-term security in the private sector makes it very difficult for any tenant to exercise rights effectively: a 'complaining troublemaker' can simply – and usually lawfully – be served with notice to quit. Even when the tenant does enjoy some level of security of tenure, the study of older people revealed that, through ignorance of the law, many would unnecessarily vacate property when served with notice to quit, even though it might be unlikely that a court would have ordered eviction.

The situation is worsened by the generally poor level of provision of advisory services for tenants and lack of legal representation, due in part to the cost of seeking a court-based remedy and ignorance of the availability of legal aid. The Civil Justice Review in 1988 found a large unmet legal need in the housing field and found clear evidence of minimal take-up of legal remedies.[139] The Citizens Advice Bureau reports that there are housing advice deserts where people simply cannot find a lawyer.[140] This is part of a wider problem of access to justice. The problem of poor legal information is not confined to the housing sector. There is much less empirical work in the other sectors, but the University of Reading's research into commercial leases showed that small business tenants often enter into leases without receiving any professional advice, even though they usually have no previous experience of leasing, and are likely to take the lease on the first terms offered.[141]

The shortfall between legislative aims and practice is visible in several areas. One example is the Landlord and Tenant Act 1987 which was passed in order to cure some of the management problems that arise in private blocks of residential flats. The legislation aimed to strengthen tenants' powers in relation to management and to give them a right of pre-emption when a landlord decides to sell the reversion, thus enabling them to assume a management role themselves. However, a report published in 1991 showed that the Act's effectiveness in practice was seriously impaired. There was widescale ignorance of its provisions and the pursuit of the remedies made available was seen as costly, lengthy and restrictive.[142]

Similarly, a study conducted by Shelter into harassment and illegal eviction following the implementation of the Housing Act 1988 found widespread ignorance of the law by landlords, tenants and solicitors. But the efficacy of the law was also reduced in other ways. The effectiveness of the legislation as a deterrent depends upon the willingness of authorities to prosecute landlords acting improperly and on the willingness of tenants to bring civil proceedings. Shelter found, however, that tenant fear of reprisal made them reluctant to pursue landlords and made obtaining evidence difficult. On top of this, there were

---

[138] N Carlton and others, *The harassment and abuse of older people in the private rented sector* (Bristol, The Policy Press, 2003). It is not possible to quantify abuse and harassment because often there will not be formal complaints, and complaints made are not always recorded.

[139] Lord Chancellor's Department, 'Report of the Review Body on Civil Justice' (Cm 394, 1988) esp ch 10.

[140] Citizens Advice Bureau, 'Home Remedies: the challenges facing publicly funded housing advice, meeting the challenge of access to justice' (May 2004).

[141] N Crosby, C Hughes and S Murdoch, *Monitoring the 2002 Code of Practice for Commercial Leases* (ODPM, March 2005) 201. Twenty-five per cent of leases involved no negotiation over terms (this is for tenants of all sizes).

[142] A Thomas and others, 'The Landlord and Tenant Act 1987: Awareness, Experience and Impact' (DoE, 1991).

difficulties in obtaining legal aid to bring proceedings and those tenants not eligible for legal aid were concerned about the costs of going to court. Local authority response to harassment also varied a lot – with some authorities according very low priority to it – and there was a large gap between the number of cases of harassment reported and the number of prosecutions brought.[143] Commenting on a later study of unlawful eviction and harassment that he was involved in, Cowan writes:

> It is difficult to resist the conclusion that landlord-tenant relations, after the formalistic process of contract (if any), operate on the basis of superimposed informal understandings.[144]

The Law Commission is carrying out various projects that aim to address some of these issues in the area of housing. The belief underlying their approach is that tenants are generally not well informed about what is in their tenancy agreement (assuming that there is a written agreement in the first place). The Renting Homes project makes a written contract containing mandatory terms central to the landlord and tenant relationship in order to increase the awareness of both parties of their rights and responsibilities.[145] The Housing Disputes paper explores ways of improving the resolution of housing problems by focusing on the problems that people have with housing and asking how they can be solved, rather than by focusing narrowly on courts and tribunals as the mechanism for dispute resolution.[146] There are also tentative steps being taken towards a programme to encourage responsible renting, which more specifically addresses the gap between the legal rules and the reality.[147]

The problem of 'gap' discussed above has focussed on the (non) enforcement of rights within the private law relationship. There are inevitably gap problems also in areas affected by 'regulatory law'. Unless there is the political will, energy and resources for effective enforcement, many regulatory measures will fail to meet the planned goals. This has always been so. The early housing measures in the nineteenth century put in place a number of initiatives to deal with the housing problem but were effectively a dead letter as there was no real political will behind them.[148] The success of the scheme for licensing houses in multiple occupation introduced by the Housing Act 2004 will similarly turn largely on the will and ability of local authorities to chase non-compliant landlords.

2.9.4 Avoiding Statutory Control

In addition to the problems caused by ignorance and non-enforcement of legal remedies, it is not uncommon for landlords to arrange their affairs so as to escape effective regulation. The land owner may do this by structuring the occupation agreement in a way that avoids the legislative controls, for example, by entering into a partnership agreement with a farmer

---

[143] L Burrows and N Hunter, *Forced Out: A Report on the Harassment and Illegal Eviction of Private Tenants after the Housing Act 1988* (London, Shelter, 1990). See also ch 23.

[144] D Cowan, 'Harassment and unlawful eviction in the private rented sector – a study of in(-)action' [2001] *Conv* 249, 258.

[145] Law Commission, 'Renting Homes: The Final Report. Volume 1: Report' (Law Com No 297, 2006).

[146] Law Commission, 'Housing: Proportionate Dispute Resolution, An Issues Paper' (March 2006).

[147] Law Commission, 'Encouraging Responsible Letting' (Law Com CP No 181, 2007).

[148] E Gauldie, *Cruel Habitations* (London, George Allen & Unwin Ltd, 1974) ch 10.

rather than granting him a tenancy. He may also avoid legislative control by taking advantage of statutory exceptions, such as the ability to 'contract out' of the business tenancy legislation. The land owner may also seek to avoid controls artificially, for instance, granting licences rather than leases. The effectiveness of these various routes is discussed in the introduction to Part Three of this book.

2.10 Interpretation of Leases and Leasehold Notices[149]

Many legal issues that arise in the context of leases involve matters of interpretation. The leasehold contract itself will often be in writing and, particularly in the case of commercial and long residential leases, the contractual documentation may be substantial.[150] With long leases the agreement will often be the product of negotiations involving lawyers and other professional advisers. Shorter residential leases are less uniformly recorded in writing (although they will be if the Law Commission's proposals are enacted).[151] In practice, however, many leasehold disputes arise out of disagreements over the interpretation of leasehold provisions, perhaps where the lease is poorly drafted, or it is simply unclear how the wording used applies to the disputed situation. The courts have, therefore, had to address how the words in leases must be interpreted. Although interpretation will always depend on the particular wording that has been used (and therefore a result in a particular case may have little direct impact on subsequent cases), it is important to understand the approach that the courts take towards interpretation. The importance of contractual interpretation is particularly evident in the chapters on how to distinguish leases from licences, rent variation, and repair.

Similar issues arise in the context of exercising leasehold notices. Sometimes it will be the lease itself that contains a provision which is to be triggered by the service of a notice within a specified timescale, such as a break clause or rent review. In addition, many notices are required to be served under statutory provisions, such as when the tenant evinces his desire to acquire the freehold to the property by serving a specified form of notice. In practice, however, notices often contain errors in their wording or do not conform with the strict timetable required: should a relatively minor slip or error invalidate the notice?

In *Mannai Investments Co Ltd v Eagle Star life Assurance Co Ltd* Lord Hoffmann suggested that the rules for the construction of notices should be the same as those for the construction of contracts.[152] This proposition is not universally accepted. As Sir Christopher Staughton has pointed out, notices are quite different creatures from contracts: notices involve unilateral acts which do not require the consent of the other party, whereas a contract must reflect the common intention of all parties.[153] Although the degree of assimilation in approach may be in doubt, it is clear in the case of both contracts and notices that

---

[149] See generally K Lewison, *The Interpretation of Contracts* 3rd edn (London, Sweet & Maxwell, 2003).

[150] Or, as Hoffmann J said in *Norwich Union Insurance Society v British Railways Board* [1987] 2 EGLR 137 (Ch), the wording may be 'torrential'.

[151] Law Commission, 'Renting Homes: The Final Report. Volume 2: Draft Bill' (Law Com No 297, 2006).

[152] [1997] AC 749 (HL) 779.

[153] C Staughton, 'How do the Courts Interpret Commercial Contracts?' (1999) 58 *CLJ* 303, 309.

courts have generally become more willing to adopt a commercial approach that gives effect to what the parties would understand the contract or notice to mean.

2.10.1 Contractual Interpretation

In line with developments in contract law more generally, the last two decades have seen the law moving away from a literal and technical construction of the wording used in leases, towards adopting a commercially sensible interpretation as this is more likely to give effect to the intention of the parties. This can be seen particularly in the context of rent review provisions in commercial leases.[154]

Rent review clauses are a form of 'inflation proofing', enabling the rent to be adjusted to reflect current market conditions at periodic intervals during the life of a lease. This general aim is often achieved by providing that the rent will be reviewed by valuing what is known as the 'hypothetical lease' with the aim of adjusting the rent to take account of current property values. This will be based on the actual lease between the parties but will also make certain assumptions (such as that the tenant is not in breach of any obligations); and the detail of the 'assumptions' made has generated much litigation. Sometimes a strict or literal reading of the words used could lead to a bizarre result, unlikely to have been intended by the parties. During the 1980s, for example, there were several cases involving the assumption that on review the hypothetical lease would be on the same terms 'other than the rent hereby reserved'. This could be read to exclude *all* of the provisions relating to rent, including the fact that there would be future reviews of rent, and would have an inflationary effect on the rent.[155] Rather than adopt this interpretation, the courts accepted that the hypothetical lease would contain review provisions as it was important to have regard to the reality and commercial purpose of the contract. This approach is encapsulated in the remarks of Nicholls LJ in *Basingstoke BC v Host Group Ltd*:

> ... like all points of construction, the meaning of this rent review clause depends on the particular language used, interpreted having regard to the context provided by the whole document and the matrix of the material surrounding circumstances. We recognise, therefore, that the particular language used will always be of paramount importance. Nonetheless it is proper and only sensible, when construing a rent review clause, to have in mind what normally is the commercial purpose of such a clause.[156]

The context is relevant to interpretation. In a recent case involving a residential rent review provision, *White and White v Riverside Housing Association Ltd*, Lord Neuberger referred to the non-commercial context – the fact that the landlord was a publicly funded charity and the tenants unversed in construing legal documents – as relevant to the interpretation of the contractual wording, accepting that in a commercial context the wording may carry a different meaning.[157]

---

[154] Rent review is discussed in more detail in ch 16.

[155] A result described by Sir Browne-Wilkinson in *British Gas Corporation v Universities Superannuation Scheme Ltd* [1986] 1 WLR 398 (CA) as 'manifestly contrary to commercial common sense'.

[156] [1988] 1 WLR 348 (CA) 353. This pre-dates the 'restatement' of the principles of contractual interpretation in contractual documents set out by Lord Hoffmann in *Investors Compensation Scheme Ltd v West Bromwich Building Society* [1988] 1 WLR 896 (HL) 912–3, but reflects the same approach.

[157] [2007] UKHL 20.

Courts refer to the commercial purpose of a provision to guide issues of interpretation, not only in the context of rent review but also in other contexts, such as the interpretation of repair covenants.[158] Further, as the quotation from *Basingstoke BC v Host Group Ltd* shows, the courts will take account of the context or background, which will include:

> ... knowledge which would reasonably have been available to the parties in the situation in which they were at the time of the contract.[159]

In cases of ambiguity the courts can also have regard to the fact that the parties are unlikely to have agreed to unusual obligations[160] and will draw on the *contra preferentum* rule so that an ambiguity in a provision is interpreted against the party seeking to rely on it.[161] It is also important to bear in mind that the purposive approach does have limits: the courts cannot go against the natural meaning of the words. In *Hemingway Realty Ltd v Clothworkers Co* the rent could go up or down on review and, expecting a lower rent, the tenant wanted to initiate a rent review.[162] The judge accepted that the general purpose of a rent review clause is to enable the landlord to obtain the market rate for the time being. In this case, however, the question concerned not the purpose of the review but the machinery of review and the relevant clause had a 'plain and obvious meaning' which was that only the landlord could exercise the right to review.

2.10.2 Leasehold Notices

A similar progression has occurred in the context of leasehold notices. Statutory notices will usually have prescribed requirements for the effective service of notices, relating to the form of the notice, the content, and the timing. Functionally these rules can fulfil a number of different roles: not only do they indicate the notice-giver's intent but they may have an advisory role, informing the recipient of his rights, and contain information that the recipient needs in order to respond, and ensure that rights are exercised within prescribed time limits. Until the House of Lords decision in *Mannai Investments v Eagle Star*[163] in 1997, these rules had to be strictly complied with in order for the notice to be valid.[164] This had the advantage of certainty and promoting careful and accurate drafting. The problem was, however, that a simple, and unimportant, error could invalidate the notice.

In *Mannai Investments* there was a ten year lease 'from and including the 13th day of

---

[158] See the reference to 'businesslike arrangements' in *Credit Suisse v Beegas Nominees Ltd* [1994] 4 All ER 803 (Ch) 817.

[159] But the 'law excludes from the admissible background the previous negotiations of the parties and their declarations of subjective intent. They are admissible only in an action for rectification': *Investors Compensation Scheme Ltd v West Bromwich Building Society* [1988] 1 WLR 896 (HL) (Lord Hoffmann). Rectification is discussed in ch 4. Similarly, evidence of subsequent conduct is inadmissible, although in *AG Securities v Vaughan* [1990] 1 AC 417 (HL) 469 Lord Oliver said: 'though subsequent conduct is irrelevant as an aid to construction, it is certainly admissible as evidence on the question of whether the documents were or were not genuine documents giving effect to the parties' true intentions.'

[160] *Norwich Union Insurance Society v British Railways Board* [1987] 2 EGLR 137 (Ch).

[161] *Gilje v Charlgrove Securities Ltd* [2001] EWCA Civ 1777 [27]. Regulation 7 of the Unfair Terms in Consumer Contracts Regulations 1999 SI 1999/2083 has a similar effect: see ch 4.

[162] [2005] EWHC 299 (Ch).

[163] *Mannai Investments Co Ltd v Eagle Star Life Assurance Co Ltd* [1997] AC 749 (HL).

[164] *Hankey v Clavering* [1942] 2 KB 326 (CA).

January 1992' which included a tenant break clause enabling the tenant to end the lease by 'serving … notice to expire on the 3rd anniversary of the term'.[165] The House of Lords took this to require the notice to expire on 13 January 1995.[166] Instead, the tenant gave notice to 'determine the Lease on 12th January 1995'. By a majority of 3-2 the House of Lords held this to be effective to end the lease. According to Lord Steyn, the question is:

> … how a reasonable recipient would have understood the notices. And in considering this question the notices must be construed taking into account the relevant objective contextual scene.[167]

The test then becomes, as both Lord Steyn and Lord Hoffmann said, one of whether the reasonable recipient would have been misled. In answering this, the words used will be construed in the light of the background. In cases where the intent is ambiguous and unclear the notice will not be valid. In *Barclays Bank plc v Bee* two inconsistent notices (one was invalid, but the other was potentially valid) were served and as the 'reasonable recipient' would be left in doubt as to the landlord's intent the Court of Appeal held both notices to be ineffective.[168]

This 'reasonable recipient' approach has been applied not only in relation to contractual notices,[169] but also where notices are served in accordance with statutory provisions.[170] There are, however, considerable difficulties in applying *Mannai*, which tend to be heightened when *Mannai* is applied in a statutory context. In any context, one difficulty is the level of inaccuracy that is allowed. As Lord Goff (dissenting) predicted there will be cases on the borderline in which there is doubt as to whether the intention is sufficiently clear. In *Mannai* itself the two dates were contiguous and the House of Lords talked about there being an obvious slip or error. In other cases, where there is greater divergence, it may be more difficult to work out if the 'reasonable recipient' would have been misled. In both *Garston v Scottish Widows*[171] and *Peer Freeholds v Clean Wash*[172] there was a reasonable gap between the date given for termination in the break notice and the correct date for breaking the lease but in both cases the notice was held effective, the question being whether a reasonable landlord with knowledge of the leasehold terms would have been left in no doubt as to the tenant's intentions.

It can be difficult to work out if the formal requirements are mandatory: if they are then, notwithstanding *Mannai*, even a small departure from the prescribed form will be fatal, even if the purpose of the notice (such as indicating the notice-giver's intent) is still fulfilled.

---

[165] *Mannai Investments Co Ltd v Eagle Star Life Assurance Co Ltd* [1997] AC 749 (HL).
[166] But the correctness of this is questioned by M Robinson, 'Once Upon a Time' (1999) 115 *LQR* 389.
[167] [1997] AC 749 (HL) 761.
[168] [2001] EWCA Civ 1126; [2002] 1 WLR 332. The notices were served under the Landlord and Tenant Act 1954 s 25: one notice opposed a new tenancy, the other said that a new tenancy would not be opposed. For discussion of Part II of the Landlord and Tenant Act 1954, see ch 20.
[169] Schedule of dilapidations: *Westminster City Council v HSBC Bank Plc* [2003] EWHC 393 (TCC). Notice to quit: *Trafford MBC v Total Fitness (UK) Ltd* [2002] EWCA Civ 151 [3].
[170] Landlord and Tenant Act 1954: *Barclays Bank Plc v Bee* [2001] EWCA Civ 1126; Leasehold Reform Housing and Urban Development Act 1993: *Lay v Ackerman* [2004] EWCA Civ 184; Housing Act 1988 s 20: *Ravenseft Properties Ltd v Hall* [2001] EWCA Civ 2034; Leasehold Reform Act 1976: *Speedwell Estates Ltd v Dalziel* [2001] EWCA Civ 1277; Law of Property Act 1925 s 146: *Akici v LR Butlin Ltd* [2005] EWCA Civ 1296, [2006] 1 WLR 201.
[171] *Garston v Scottish Widows Fund & Life Assurance Society* [1998] 1 WLR 1583 (CA).
[172] *Peer Freeholds Ltd v Clean Wash International Ltd* [2005] EWHC 179 (Ch).

In some cases the statutory scheme, while prescribing the form to be used, also allows a form which is 'substantially to the same effect'. This is the case in relation to what were known as 'section 20 notices': before 1996 it was possible for landlords to avoid giving residential tenants security of tenure by serving a section 20 notice under the Housing Act 1988. A number of cases have involved defective section 20 notices, a common error being getting dates wrong. In *Ravenscroft Properties Ltd v Hall* the Court of Appeal took the approach that in order to see if the form was 'substantially' to the same effect it was necessary to work out what its purpose was.[173] The essential purpose of the section 20 notice was taken to be to inform the tenant that the tenancy was to be an assured shorthold tenancy (giving no security): provided the tenant would still understand the special nature of this tenancy, defects would not invalidate the notice.

In other cases the statutory form is taken to be prescriptive.[174] In *McDonald v Fernandez* the landlord served a notice requiring possession on '4th January 2003'.[175] The relevant statutory provision stated that the notice of not less than two months should give a date 'being the last day of a period of the tenancy'. Each monthly period ended on the 3rd of the month and so the notice should have referred to '3rd January'. In holding the notice to be invalid Hale LJ observed that it was not a matter of what a 'reasonable tenant' would have understood, or of whether the purpose was to give sufficient notice to enable the tenant to start making alternative plans, but what the statute requires. As Lord Hoffmann observed in *Mannai*:

> If the clause had said that the notice had to be on blue paper, it would have been no good serving a notice on pink paper.[176]

The ruling in *McDonald v Fernandez* reintroduces technicality and creates unnecessary traps.[177] It remains difficult to see exactly how much latitude there is for errors following *Mannai*, and the jurisprudence is not entirely clear. The starting point must be to see whether the particular statutory or contractual provisions sets out a mandatory procedure. If not, and there is not strict compliance with any requirements, the question will then be whether the 'reasonable recipient' would have been misled.

2.10.3 *The Loss of Certainty*

One of the criticisms levelled at the move towards purposive construction is that it generates uncertainty.[178] Undoubtedly it can make interpretation less predictable, but it does enable courts to reach more satisfactory outcomes in line with what the parties intended.

---

[173] [2001] EWCA Civ 2034.
[174] *Keepers and Governors of John Lyon Grammar School v Secchi* [1999] 3 EGLR 49 (CA) (tenant's notice to acquire new lease under the Leasehold Reform, Housing and Urban Development Act 1993); *Speedwell Estates Ltd v Dalziel* [2001] EWCA Civ 1277 (tenant's notice to acquire freehold under the Leasehold Reform Act 1967); *Burman v Mount Cook Land Ltd* [2001] EWCA Civ 1712, [2002] Ch 256 (tenant's notice to acquire new lease under the Leasehold Reform Act 1967).
[175] [2003] EWCA Civ 1219, [2004] 1 WLR 1027 [21] – [22].
[176] [1997] AC 749 (HL) 776.
[177] [2003] EWCA Civ 1219, [2004] 1 WLR 1027.
[178] See, for example, C Staughton, 'How do the Courts Interpret Commercial Contracts?' (1999) 58 *CLJ* 303.

PART TWO

ENTERING THE RELATIONSHIP

The two chapters in this part of the book are concerned with the very first stage of the landlord and tenant relationship. Chapter 3 looks at the legal principles used to determine whether an agreement conferring rights to occupy land amounts to a tenancy or some other relationship, as well as the situation where the occupier simply moves onto the land with the owner's consent but without a formal agreement. These principles are part of the common law, applicable to all types of agreement: residential, commercial and agricultural. Although the principles are the same across the sectors, their application may vary as the courts take account of the fact that statute confers rights to remain on certain types of tenancy. As Blandy and Hunter observe, application of the common law principles takes place 'in the shadow of the legislation which would otherwise apply' as judges are influenced 'by a common sense understanding of the policies which underlie the ... statutory regimes'.[1]

Chapter 4 looks at the process of entering a tenancy: how tenants (and landlords) are selected, what documentation is needed on entering into a lease, and what typical lease terms provide. Most of this material also applies across the differing sectors although, as will be seen, there are particular measures that apply only to residential tenancies.

---

[1] S Blandy and C Hunter, 'Judicial Directions in Landlord and Tenant Law' in S Bright (ed), *Landlord and Tenant Law. Past, Present and Future* (Oxford, Hart, 2006) 63 and 61.

3

IDENTIFYING LEASEHOLD RELATIONSHIPS

3.1	The essential elements of a lease
3.2	Different categories of occupation
3.3	Categorising a relationship

3.1 The Essential Elements of a Lease

3.1.1 Introduction

The focus of this chapter is on identifying when the relationship of landlord and tenant occurs. A variety of relationships can exist between an owner of property and someone renting or occupying it, and there are not precise boundaries between them. The case law does not always give much guidance on categorisation as it is often sufficient to dispose of a case to decide that the relationship is not, for example, a leasehold estate without having to decide exactly what it is. In general, the occupier will have greater legal protection if he is a tenant, although under the Law Commission's proposed Renting Homes scheme there would be no distinction between a licensee and a tenant in terms of the protection conferred by the housing legislation.[1] A further complication is that the language of 'tenancy' itself covers a number of situations, ranging from a relationship in which there is no leasehold estate and that can be ended at a moment's notice, to one that can last for many hundreds of years.

The issue of categorising an occupancy arrangement can arise in a variety of contexts. Historically, the distinction between leases and licences affected voting rights and taxation. Nowadays the question most frequently arises when an owner is trying to evict the occupier, as the occupier who is a tenant may have various legal rights that protect his right to occupation. If the occupier has a leasehold estate under section 1(1)(b) of the Law of Property Act 1925 he is potentially able to enforce his interest against third parties. Minimum notice periods apply to certain leases. Further, a tenant may have a statutory right to remain in the property after the contractually agreed period has come to an end. In the private residential sector the tenant's rights of security of tenure were especially strong under the Rent Act 1977, and many of the cases that are discussed below reflect the desire of owners to rent out property without the tenant acquiring these statutory rights. This can

---

[1] Law Commission, 'Renting Homes: The Final Report. Volume 1: Report' (Law Com No 297, 2006).

also be seen in cases involving business leases, especially where the parties are still negoti-ating a lease and the occupier, if held to have a tenancy, will effectively acquire a statutory right to stay. Eviction is not the only context in which categorisation arises. For example, in an important case which is discussed below, *Bruton v London and Quadrant Housing Trust*,[2] the occupier needed to show that he had a tenancy in order to benefit from a statutory repairing obligation.

There cannot be a tenancy if the grantor has no power to create a tenancy. Further, in order to have a leasehold estate[3] there must be an intention to create legal relations, exclusive possession and a term.[4] Identifying when these features exist will not always be straightforward. There are also some situations in which these three 'indicia' or 'hallmarks' of a tenancy do exist, and yet there is still no tenancy as their existence is explained by reference to some other legal relationship.

3.1.2 Intention to Create Legal Relations

It was not until the Court of Appeal decision in *Booker v Palmer* in 1942[5] that the judiciary began to talk about 'intention' as being relevant to classification. Although some of the cases refer to an 'intention to create a tenancy', it is clear that what is meant is that there cannot be a tenancy unless there is an 'intention to create a legal relationship'. This is not surprising: in most cases (if not all) the tenancy will be a contract,[6] implied if not express, and an intention to create legal relations is one of the requirements for a contract binding in law. Even the tenancy at will (which can be brought to an end at a moment's notice) is contractual.[7]

There will be cases, however, where what the parties intend is a 'gentleman's agreement', not a contract binding in law. *Booker v Palmer* was treated as this sort of case. The owner agreed with a friend that an evacuee could live rent free in a cottage on his land during the war.[8] When Lord Greene MR held the arrangement to be a licence because there was no intention to create the relationship of landlord and tenant he was referring to the fact that the parties did not intend the arrangement to be governed by the domain of law.[9] Many friendship cases are also treated in this way. In *Cobb v Lane* the owner's sister lived in a house rent free and Denning LJ emphasised the fact that she was only intended to have a 'personal privilege'.[10] Similarly in *Heslop v Burns*, where the owner allowed a couple with whom he had formed an emotional bond to live rent free in his house, the Court of Appeal said that there was no intention to create legal relations.[11]

---

[2] [2000] 1 AC 406 (HL).

[3] This 'term of years absolute' can be a legal or equitable estate: Law of Property Act 1925 s 1.

[4] In *Street v Mountford* [1985] 1 AC 809 (HL) Lord Templeman said that the three hallmarks of a lease are exclusive possession, rent and term. Although usual, rent is not necessary: Law of Property Act 1925 s 205(1)(xxvii).

[5] [1942] 2 All ER 674 (CA).

[6] Except the tenancy at sufferance (below), which is not a tenancy in any meaningful sense. It is possible to create a lease by deed. It is, however, hard to imagine the grant of a lease that is not contractual. See also ch 2.

[7] *Ley v Peter* (1858) 3 H&N 101; *Ramnarace v Lutchman* [2001] UKPC 25, [2001] 1 WLR 1651 [17].

[8] [1942] 2 All ER 674 (CA).

[9] The end result was not, however, what the owner wanted. He was happy to continue with the arrangement, but possession was successfully sought by a farmer who had been given a lease of the land (including the cottage) in order to cultivate the fields.

[10] [1952] 1 All ER 1199 (CA).

[11] [1974] 1 WLR 1241 (CA).

In all of the 'friendship' cases mentioned in the last paragraph, the accommodation was rent free. Although the explanation for there being no tenancy given by the courts was that there was no 'contractual intent' they can also be explained as non-contractual on the grounds that there was no rent, and therefore no consideration. The arrangements were not contracts because they were not 'bargains'. The simple fact of the relationship being made between friends, or family members, does not mean that there cannot be a tenancy. In cases where no rent is paid, however, this is a likely interpretation of events. In *Levy v Vesely* the Court of Appeal found an arrangement involving the payment of a contribution towards household expenses not to be a tenancy, Mummery LJ agreeing with counsel that:

> ... a rent-free arrangement for the exclusive use and occupation of premises would not create a tenancy, if the correct inference from the purpose of the arrangement and the surrounding circumstances was that there was no intention to create the landlord and tenant relationship between the parties.[12]

On the other hand, in cases where rent is agreed between them it may well be that there is a tenancy.[13] In *Ward v Warnke* a cottage was occupied by the daughter and son-in-law of the owner and Fox LJ said:

> I see no reason for saying that there was no intention of entering into legal relations. It was, of course, a transaction between members of a family. But this does not prevent the creation of a legal relationship. If the facts constitute a tenancy the relationship of the parties does not displace that.[14]

The problem with using the concept of 'intent' to distinguish between tenancies and licences is that it is extremely malleable. There are many occasions where it looks as though intent is used by courts to 'cloak policy decisions in the mantle of private contractual autonomy'.[15] In tenancy law courts may be reluctant to find a tenancy where the owner has acted with kindness towards an occupier (if the consequence of finding a tenancy is that security of tenure would follow). In *Marcroft Wagons Ltd v Smith* the Court of Appeal held that there was no tenancy when the owner's agent had allowed the tenant's daughter to remain in the property after the tenant's (her mother's) death.[16] Lord Evershed MR said:

> I should be extremely sorry if anything which fell from this court were to have the effect that a landlord could never grant to a person in the position of the defendant any kind of indulgence ... [17]

In *Street v Mountford* Lord Templeman explained the finding of no tenancy in *Marcroft Wagons* as being due to the fact that the parties did not intend to contract at all.[18] This looks very much like a policy decision cloaked in the language of contractual intent.

---

[12] [2007] EWCA Civ 367 [48].

[13] The presumption in contract law that parties to a domestic or family arrangement do not intend to create legal relations – stemming from the decision in *Balfour v Balfour* [1919] 2 KB 571 (CA) – seems inappropriate in a tenancy context. There should be no presumption, for or against, and the question of a tenancy will depend on whether there is a rent agreed, and on other indications as to whether legal relations are intended.

[14] *Ward v Warnke* (1990) 22 HLR 496 (CA) 500. See also *Nunn v Dalrymple* (1989) 21 HLR 569 (CA).

[15] BA Hepple, 'Intention to Create Legal Relations' (1970) 28 *CLJ* 122, 134.

[16] [1951] 2 KB 496 (CA).

[17] [1951] 2 KB 496 (CA) 501.

[18] [1985] 1 AC 809 (HL) 820.

The tolerated trespasser cases (discussed at 3.2.3 below) provide a further example. These cases concern residential tenants whose tenancies have been brought to an end by a possession order but who, nonetheless, have been allowed to stay in occupation. Doctrinally it could be argued that there is a new tenancy, but the courts have set their face against this analysis and held the former tenants to be 'tolerated trespassers'. The explanation given by Arden LJ in *Lambeth v O'Kane* as to why there is no new tenancy in this situation was based on the absence of an intention to create legal relations.[19] It is clear that policy underlies the development of the tolerated trespasser concept, in particular the concern that to find a new tenancy in this situation would discourage landlords from acting kindly towards former tenants,[20] and that contractual intent is the language used to dress the policy decision in.

3.1.3 Exclusive Possession

Exclusive possession is the legal right to exclude others from the property. It is this right to exclude, and the territorial control inherent in it, that distinguishes the lease from the licence. If the landlord has an unlimited right to enter the property, or to introduce other persons to share the property, this will prevent the occupier from being a tenant.[21] As Lord Templeman stated:

> A tenant armed with exclusive possession can keep out strangers and keep out the landlord unless the landlord is exercising limited rights reserved to him by the tenancy agreement to enter and view and repair.[22]

As Gray writes, 'excludability' is an essential quality of property.[23] This is why exclusive possession is the marker that divides leases from licences, the proprietary from the non-proprietary. A person with exclusive possession can be said to have a 'stake in the land'.[24] The importance of exclusive possession is emphasised in the following quotation from the Australian case of *Radiach v Smith*:

> What then is the fundamental right which a tenant has that distinguishes his position from that of a licensee? It is an interest in land as distinct from a personal permission to enter the land and use it for some stipulated purpose or purposes. And how is to be ascertained whether such an interest in land has been given? By seeing whether the grantee was given a *legal right of exclusive possession* of the land for a term or from year to year or for a life or lives. If he was, he is a tenant. And he cannot be other than a tenant, because a legal right of exclusive possession is a tenancy and the creation of such a right is a demise … A right of

---

[19] See *LB of Lambeth and Hyde Southbank Ltd v O'Kane; Helena Housing Ltd v Pinder* [2005] EWCA Civ 1010 [60], and S Bright, 'Tolerated Trespass or New Tenancy' (2006) 122 *LQR* 48.

[20] See *Burrows v Brent LBC* [1996] 1 WLR 1448 (HL) 1454. Most tenants of local authority housing are 'secure' tenants. They have a variety of statutory rights: the right to buy, succession rights, and security.

[21] Smith suggests an alternative: 'There is a strong argument that exclusive possession is based upon the right to prevent the owner from entering at will, rather than the owner's having no right to introduce other occupiers', RJ Smith, *Property Law* 5th edn (Harlow, Longman, 2006) 370. This is not consistent with Lord Oliver in *AG Securities v Vaughan; Antoniades v Villiers* [1990] 1 AC 417 (HL) 469 or Chadwick LJ in *Parkins v Westminster CC* [1998] 1 EGLR 22 (CA) 25.

[22] *Street v Mountford* [1985] 1 AC 809 (HL) 816.

[23] See K Gray, 'Property in Thin Air' (1991) 50 *CLJ* 252.

[24] The phrase 'stake in the room' was used by Lord Denning MR in *Marchant v Charters* [1977] 1 WLR 1181. 'Stake in the land' is now widely used to describe proprietary interests in land.

exclusive possession is secured by the right of a lessee to maintain ejectment and, after his entry, trespass. A reservation to the landlord, either by contract or statute, of a limited right of entry, as for example to view or repair, is, of course, not inconsistent with the grant of exclusive possession. Subject to such reservations, a tenant for a term or from year to year or for a life or lives can exclude his landlord as well as strangers from the demised premises. All this is long-established law: see Cole on *Ejectment* ((1857) pp.72, 73, 287, 485.[25]

It is important to distinguish exclusive possession, which is a legal concept, from a right to exclusive occupation which is simply descriptive of the fact that someone has the sole right to occupy property, but not a right which carries with it the right to exclude others from the property.[26] An example involving exclusive occupation is a lodging arrangement; the lodger 'cannot call the place his own' if the owner has unrestricted rights of access even if the lodger is be the only person living in the property.[27] In *Marchant v Charters*, a person lived alone in a bed-sit but as the owner cleaned the rooms daily and provided clean linen this meant that he did not have exclusive possession.[28]

Exclusory powers are not, however, necessarily absolute. An occupier may have the right to exclude some, but not all. Until recently it was widely thought that there could only be a lease if the occupier had possession to the exclusion of the whole world, including the power to exclude the true or superior owner.[29] The decision of the House of Lords in *Bruton v London and Quadrant Housing Trust*[30] suggests otherwise. In this case Lambeth Borough Council planned to redevelop a site and granted a licence to the London & Quadrant Housing Trust so that the property could be used for temporary housing in the interim. In turn the Trust purported to grant a 'weekly licence' to Mr Bruton. By the time the case reached the House of Lords, the planned development scheme had been abandoned and Mr Bruton had been living in the flat for ten years. The particular issue for decision was whether the Housing Trust was subject to the repairing obligations imposed upon landlords by section 11 of the Landlord and Tenant Act 1985, which applies only to 'leases'. The Housing Trust – having only a licence itself – could not, of course, grant the power to exclude the superior owner, the freeholder, because of the principle of *nemo dat quod non habet* – no one can convey what he does not own. The House of Lords held that Mr Bruton nonetheless had exclusive possession, and thus a tenancy. This means that it will be sufficient for a tenancy to show that the grantee has exclusive possession in the sense of having the legal right to exclude all, including the grantor, save for someone with a superior title.[31]

---

[25] (1959) 101 CLR 209 (HCA) 222 (Windeyer J), adopted by Lord Templeman in *Street v Mountford* [1985] 1 AC 809 (HL) 827.

[26] The distinction is not always kept clear, even by the senior judiciary: see, eg, *AG Securities v Vaughan; Antoniades v Villiers* [1990] 1 AC 417 (HL) (Lord Templeman); *Aslan v Murphy (Nos 1 and 2)* [1990] 1 WLR 766 (CA) (Lord Donaldson MR).

[27] See *Street v Mountford* [1985] 1 AC 809 (HL) 817–18; *Luganda v Service Hotels Ltd* [1969] 2 Ch 209 (CA) 219.

[28] [1977] 1 WLR 1181 (CA).

[29] See *Bruton v London and Quadrant Housing Trust* [1998] QB 834 (CA) 845 (Millett LJ).

[30] [2000] 1 AC 406 (HL). This case elicits a range of reactions: see S Bright, 'Leases, Exclusive Possession and Estates' (2000) 116 *LQR* 7; M Pawlowski, 'Occupational Rights in Leasehold Law: Time for Rationalisation?' [2002] *Conv* 550; P Routley, 'Tenancies and Estoppel – After Bruton v London & Quadrant Housing Trust' (2000) 63 *MLR* 424; M Dixon, 'The non-proprietary lease: the rise of the feudal phoenix' (2000) 59 *CLJ* 25; M Harwood, 'Leases: Are they still not Really Real?' (2000) 20 *LS* 503; JP Hinojosa, 'On Property Leases, Licenses, Horses and Carts: Revisiting *Bruton v London and Quadrant Housing Trust*' [2005] 69 *Conv* 114.

[31] See *Western Australia v Ward* [2002] HCA 28 [478].

The *Bruton* case raises difficult issues. An earlier Court of Appeal case, *Family Housing Association v Jones*,[32] had similarly involved the grant of 'short-life' accommodation by a housing association which had only a 'licence'. Although the Court of Appeal found the occupier to be a tenant, the lack of the grantor's title had not been argued in that case.[33] Until *Bruton* it had been widely assumed that all leases[34] were estates. This was a view with considerable judicial support. In *Milmo v Carreras* Lord Greene MR said:

> I myself find it impossible to conceive of a relationship of landlord and tenant that has not got that essential element of tenure in it, and that implies that the tenant holds of his landlord, and he can only do that if the landlord has a reversion. You cannot have a purely contractual tenure.[35]

If it is possible to have exclusive possession in the relational sense referred to by the House of Lords in *Bruton*, the tenancy resulting will not be an estate in land, as was accepted by Lord Hoffmann. This turns conventional understanding on its head and gives rise to a number of consequential questions that have yet to be addressed by the courts, such as whether formality provisions will apply to these non-estate leases.[36]

3.1.4 *Certainty of Term*

In order to be a lease, there must be a 'term certain', which means that the beginning, the duration and the end-date of the lease must be ascertainable as at the commencement of the lease. The need for certainty is long established in English law:

> ... every contract sufficient to make a lease for years ought to have certainty in three limitations, viz in the commencement of the term, in the continuance of it, and in the end of it: so that all three ought to be known at the commencement of the lease.[37]

This requirement was recently re-affirmed by the House of Lords in *Prudential Assurance v London Residuary Body*.[38] A strip of land adjoining a road was granted by the London County Council 'until the ... land is required for the purposes of the widening of Walworth Road and the street paving works rendered necessary thereby'. This was held void as a lease because it was uncertain.[39]

The rule requires that a lease must have both a certain beginning and a certain end. It is possible to have a lease that takes effect at a future date, known as a reversionary lease, but

---

[32] [1990] 1 WLR 779 (CA).

[33] Explained by Lord Hoffmann in *Bruton v London and Quadrant Housing Trust* [2000] 1 AC 406 (HL) 415 on the grounds that the lack of title was irrelevant.

[34] Except the tenancy at will and tenancy by estoppel, which have always been regarded as special exceptions.

[35] [1946] KB 306 (CA) 310.

[36] There is also the question as to whether the arrangement in *Prudential Assurance Co Ltd v London Residuary Body* [1992] 2 AC 386 (HL), discussed below, could have been upheld as a contractual lease if the certainty rules apply only to estate leases.

[37] *Say v Smith* (1530) 1 Plowden 269, 272. See also P Sparkes, 'Certainty of Leasehold Terms' (1993) 109 *LQR* 93 for an account of judicial support for this rule.

[38] *Prudential Assurance Co Ltd v London Residuary Body* [1992] 2 AC 386 (HL).

[39] *Prudential Assurance Co Ltd v London Residuary Body* [1992] 2 AC 386 (HL). See also *Lace v Chantler* [1944] KB 368 (CA).

by section 149(3) of the Law of Property Act 1925 the term cannot take effect more than 21 years after the grant.

3.1.4.1 Indeterminate Leases

It is in relation to the end-date that the greatest difficulties are found. There is no problem if the lease provides for an end-date but is capable of being brought to an end earlier, for example, by the landlord forfeiting the lease, or the tenant exercising a break clause.[40] Nor is there any difficulty if the lease is not for a continuous period. In *Cottage Holiday Associates Ltd v Customs and Excise Commissioners*, Woolf J accepted that a timeshare arrangement giving the right to exclusive possession for one week every year over an 80 year period was a tenancy.[41] Further, there are statutory provisions that operate on certain indeterminate leases to avoid the problems of uncertainty. Thus, the Law of Property Act 1925, section 149(6), converts a lease at a rent or for a premium which is granted for someone's life or until a person marries (or determinable on death or marriage) into a lease for ninety years. After the person's death or marriage, either party can end the lease by serving notice. Section 145 of the Law of Property Act 1922 converts a perpetually renewable lease into a lease for 2000 years (discussed further 3.2.7 below).

These statutory provisions do not save all leases, however. If it cannot be said when the lease is granted what the maximum duration is, then the lease will be void for uncertainty. The certainty required is not simply linguistic certainty (that is, a sufficiently clear definition of the end-date), but predictability (that is being able to predict when the end-date will occur). So, for example, in *Lace v Chantler* a lease for the duration of the war was held uncertain because when the lease began it could not be known how long the war would last.[42] It will remain uncertain even if there is a careful definition as to when the war will be taken to have ended (for example, the signing of a peace treaty).[43]

3.1.4.2 Justifying the Certainty Requirement

The explanation for the certainty requirement is sometimes said to rest in the fact that it serves to distinguish leases, as determinate interests, from freeholds, which are of uncertain duration (such as for life, indefinitely, or until the happening of some future event). There are, however, difficulties with accepting this as a continuing justification for the rule. As seen, statute clearly accepts the notion of a *lease for life* as it provides that it is to be converted into a fixed period lease determinable on death, and this makes it therefore difficult to argue that determinacy can tell us on which side of the line an interest falls. Further, there are usually other ways of knowing if an interest is freehold or leasehold, especially as it is common (though not universal) for a rent to be paid if there is a lease.[44] It has also been argued that the rule is simply part of the *numerus clausus* principle in land law (the idea that there is a

---

[40] Law of Property Act 1925 s 205(1)(xxvii) defines 'term of years absolute' as being for a 'term of years... either certain or liable to determination by notice, re-entry, operation of law...'.

[41] [1983] QB 735. See also: *Smallwood v Sheppards* [1895] 2 QB 627, upholding a lease for three successive bank holidays.

[42] [1944] KB 368 (CA).

[43] In *Eker v Becker* (1946) 174 LT 410 Charles J upheld a lease in these terms but this case is inconsistent with *Prudential Assurance Co Ltd v London Residuary Body* [1992] 2 AC 386 (HL).

[44] It has not been possible to attach a rent to a freehold since the Rentcharges Act 1977.

closed list of rights that can exist as property rights) and the certainty requirement draws a line which marks the boundary between property and contract rights.[45] At one level, this is clearly true but it does not tell why the line is drawn where it is. The rule has also been supported for promoting careful drafting,[46] but this would need only a rule requiring linguistic certainty.

None of these explanations provides a convincing justification for retaining a rule which strikes down otherwise good commercial arrangements. Why should a landlord not be able to agree with a tenant that he can occupy a workshop 'until planning permission is obtained to redevelop the site'? In *Prudential Assurance Co Ltd v London Residuary Body* Lord Browne-Wilkinson invited the Law Commission to review the basis of the rule:

> No one has produced any satisfactory rationale for the genesis of this rule. No one has ever been able to point to any useful purpose that it serves in the present day. [47]

This remark is, perhaps, too dismissive. Although not designed for this purpose, the rule can have the benefit of releasing a landlord from what turns out to have been an improvident bargain. The commercial intention behind the workshop example is that the tenant occupies the workshop as an interim measure. With careful drafting this result can already be achieved by using a lease; a lease for ten years determinable by the landlord in the event of obtaining planning permission would be a good lease.[48] The risk of the workshop example expressed as being 'until planning permission is obtained' is that it may become clear that planning permission will never be given, thereby creating a perpetual lease. The common law does not recognise 'a lease in perpetuity'.[49] This risk materialised in *Prudential Assurance* itself.[50] The lease was to end when the land was required for road widening. Circumstances changed, and the road was never widened. The 'lease' that had been intended to only be of short duration when granted in 1930 for a fixed rent of £30 per annum was still running in 1992, by which time the current rental value was in excess of £10,000 per annum. The fact that the letting was intended by the parties to be fairly short term and was drafted on that basis means that the arrangement, initially evenly balanced, became heavily slanted against the landlord over time.[51] By declaring the lease void the court opens up the relationship so that it can be renegotiated to reflect current property values; in *Prudential Assurance* the lease for the agreed term failed but the fact that the occupier went into possession and paid a yearly rent made him a yearly tenant, enabling the landlord to serve notice and renegotiate the terms.[52] But it is unlikely that the certainty rule was ever intended to facilitate contractual variation; and the problem remains that it strikes down not only leases that have become unfair over time, but all leases that have an unknown end-date.

---

[45] See TW Merrill and HE Smith, 'Optimal Standardization in the Law of Property: The Numerus Clausus Principle' (2000) 110 *Yale LJ* 1.

[46] See PF Smith, 'What is Wrong with Certainty in Leases?' [1993] *Conv* 461, who strongly defends the rule.

[47] [1992] 2 AC 386 (HL) 396.

[48] See *Prudential Assurance Co Ltd v London Residuary Body* [1992] 2 AC 386 (HL) 395.

[49] *Sevenoaks, Maidstone, and Tunbridge Railway Co v London, Chatham, and Dover Railway Co* (1879) 11 Ch D 625, 635–36.

[50] *Prudential Assurance Co Ltd v London Residuary Body* [1992] 2 AC 386 (HL)

[51] See further: S Bright, 'Uncertainty in Leases – Is it a Vice?' (1993) 13 *LS* 38.

[52] *Prudential Assurance Co Ltd v London Residuary Body* [1992] 2 AC 386 (HL) 392.

3.1.4.3 A Statutory Solution

There is a way to solve the problem of uncertainty. This is to follow the solution adopted to deal with the problem of war time leases: the Validation of War Time Leases Act 1944 converted leases for 'the war' into leases for ten years determinable upon the earlier ending of the war. Under such a scheme, a lease would be valid if the event upon which it is to end is adequately defined so as to be identifiable when it occurs (so complying with the need for linguistic certainty) provided that if that event does not occur within (say) ten years of the commencement of the lease, it will end on the tenth anniversary or on any later date specified in the lease (so meeting concerns over perpetuity).[53] This would enable the parties' bargain to be upheld whilst avoiding the risk of a perpetual lease.

3.1.4.4 Saving an Uncertain Lease as a Contractual Licence?

There is a further interesting and difficult question that arises with a lease for an agreed, but indeterminate, period. As seen above, the effect of the term being uncertain in *Prudential Assurance* was that the relationship was treated as a periodic tenancy, terminable on notice. The question is whether it could have been treated as a contractual licence 'until…',[54] and thus as binding in contract law.[55] In *Lace v Chantler* Lord Greene MR considers, but rejects this:

> The intention was to create a tenancy and nothing else. The law says that it is bad as a tenancy. The court is not then justified in treating the contract as something different from what the parties intended, and regarding it merely as a contract for the granting of a licence. That would be setting up a new bargain which neither of the parties ever intended to enter into. The relationship between the parties must be ascertained on the footing that the tenant was in occupation and was paying a weekly rent.[56]

This is not a convincing argument. Although the parties define their respective rights and obligations, they are not free to choose what their relationship is called, this depends upon the substance of the relationship.[57] In any event it may well have been more important to the parties in *Lace v Chantler* that the agreement run for the agreed period rather than that it created a tenancy. Megarry and Wade also reject the contractual licence route, on the grounds that 'the grant of exclusive possession of the land is the hallmark of a tenancy'.[58] This is also not a good reason for saying that there cannot be a licence; exclusive possession creates a lease, but only if the other 'indicia' of a lease are also present. If there is no certain term, exclusive possession cannot give rise to a tenancy but there is no reason why it cannot create a contractual licence. While courts lean strongly against a construction that could result in perpetuity, the principle of contracts of indefinite duration is accepted.[59] More particularly,

---

[53] Following a solution proposed in New Zealand: see H Wilkinson, 'Fresh Thoughts from Abroad' [1994] *Conv* 428.

[54] The licence point was not argued in *Prudential Assurance Co Ltd v London Residuary Body* [1992] 2 AC 386 (HL).

[55] Licences may be enforceable in specie against the grantor.

[56] [1944] KB 368 (CA) 372.

[57] *Street v Mountford* [1985] 1 AC 809 (HL).

[58] C Harpum (ed), *Megarry & Wade, The Law of Real Property* 6th edn (London, Sweet & Maxwell, 2000) 783.

[59] *Llanelly Rly & Dock Co v London & N W Rly Co* (1875) LR 7 HL 550. See: AR Carnegie, 'Terminability of Contracts of Unspecified Duration' (1960) 85 *LQR* 392.

the idea of a potentially perpetual licence has been accepted.[60] Although there have been no cases in which a lease void for uncertainty has been upheld as a contractual licence there is not a convincing reason as to why it could not be.

3.1.4.5 Certainty and Periodic Tenancies[61]

The discussion so far has focussed on leases where the parties have agreed that the lease is to run for a defined period. Many leases are periodic, that is, they run for a period and are automatically renewed unless ended by notice being served. Lord Templeman made clear in *Prudential Assurance* that the rule on certainty applies equally to periodic as to fixed term leases.[62] Nevertheless, it is not clear how (or why) the certainty rules apply to periodic tenancies. At the beginning of a periodic tenancy, it is not known what the maximum duration will be. As Russell LJ pointed out in *Re Midland Railway*:

> It cannot be predicated that in no circumstances will it exceed, for example, 50 years; there is no previously ascertained maximum duration for the term; its duration will depend on the time that will elapse before either party gives notice of determination. [63]

Yet the juristic nature and legal quality of periodic tenancies is not doubted. The most common explanation as to how they satisfy the requirements of certainty is that each separate period is of known maximum duration:

> A tenancy from year to year is saved from being uncertain because each party has power by notice to determine at the end of any year.[64]

But this is highly unsatisfactory as an explanation. It ignores the fact that periodic tenancies are not seen as a series of separate and new tenancies but as one continuing tenancy.[65]

A preferable approach would be to say that the rule on certainty does not apply to periodic tenancies. There is no reason why it should: it is not necessitated by the definition of 'term of years absolute' in section 205 of the Law of Property Act 1925 which refers to terms 'for a fraction of a year or from year to year' quite separately from the reference to certainty earlier in the definition. Nor are periodic tenancies objectionable in principle. Ability to predict the overall maximum duration is not important. They do not tend to perpetuity, in that they can be ended at any time on notice. The fairness of the bargain is achieved by the power to end the relationship – in effect, a renegotiation tool.

3.1.4.6 A Summary of the Certainty Rule

Given the difficulties in explaining how the certainty rule applies to periodic tenancies and the fact that a tenancy at will[66] is still a tenancy (but cannot be an estate), it is perhaps best to think of the 'term' requirement as shorthand. The full expression of this is that:

---

[60] *Winter Garden Theatre (London) Ltd v Millennium Productions Ltd* [1948] AC 173 (HL); *Re Spenborough UDC's Agreement* [1968] Ch 139 (Ch) 149–50.

[61] See also the discussion on repugnancy and periodic tenancies at 3.2.5.2.

[62] [1992] 2 AC 386 (HL).

[63] *In re Midland Railway Co's Agreement; Charles Clay & Sons Ltd v British Railways Board* [1971] Ch 725 (CA) 732.

[64] *Prudential Assurance Co Ltd v London Residuary Body* [1992] 2 AC 386 (HL) 394.

[65] *Hammersmith and Fulham LBC v Monk* [1992] 1 AC 478 (HL) 490.

[66] The tenancy at will can be brought to an end at any time; see 3.2.4 below.

... in order for a tenancy to come within the definition of a term of years absolute there must be a known maximum end date (even if it can be ended earlier) or be capable (either immediately or by some known point in the future) of being brought to an end by either party serving notice.

3.1.5 *Power to Grant a Tenancy*

In order for there to be a 'term of years', the parties must be legally competent to grant and receive an estate. Of course, in the light of *Bruton v London and Quadrant Housing Trust*[67] it has become apparent that it is still possible to have a 'lease' if exclusive possession is granted, without there being an estate.[68] Nonetheless, it remains the case that unless the grantor has an estate in the land, it cannot grant a leasehold estate.

It is not possible for a lease to be granted to a person under the age of 18 as by section 1(6) of the Law of Property Act 1925 they are unable to hold a legal estate in land. This has created difficulties particularly for social landlords seeking to grant tenancies to young persons leaving home. Under the Law Commission's Renting Home proposals, it will be possible for occupation contracts to be made with 16 and 17 year olds.[69]

Local authorities have various restrictions imposed on them. So, for example, the statutory provision in issue in *LB of Camden v Shortlife Community Housing* made it ultra vires for the Council was to grant a tenancy to a body other than an individual without the consent of the Secretary of State.[70]

It is not possible for a lease to be granted to an unincorporated association, as 'such a body has no legal status.'[71] Thus when an agreement was granted allowing club members for the time being to use the premises it could only be a licence, not a lease.[72]

Where the land is owned by joint tenants, all must participate in the grant in order for a lease (or licence) to be created that binds all co-owners.[73]

3.2 Different Categories of Occupation

3.2.1 *Non-consensual Occupation: Trespassers and Tenancy at Sufferance*

A broad distinction can be made between consensual and non-consensual occupation. Someone who occupies land without permission will be a trespasser. In *Westminster CC v Basson* someone who had shared with the tenant stayed on after the tenant left. When the

---

[67] *Bruton v London and Quadrant Housing Trust* [2000] 1 AC 406 (HL).

[68] See discussion at 3.1.3.

[69] Law Commission, 'Renting Homes: The Final Report. Volume 1: Report' (Law Com No 297, 2006) paras 3.10–3.12.

[70] (1992) 25 HLR 330 (Ch). This explains why housing trusts are granted only licences to provide temporary housing, as for example in *Bruton v London and Quadrant Housing Trust* [2000] 1 AC 406 (HL).

[71] *Camden v Shortlife Community Housing* (1992) 25 HLR 330 (Ch) 342. Although: 'in appropriate circumstances it may be possible, by a liberal construction, to save the grant by construing it as a grant to the persons who were the members of the association at the date of the grant.'

[72] *Onyx (UK) Ltd v Beard* [1996] EGCS 55 (Ch).

[73] For full discussion, see M Pawlowski, 'Unilateral Tenancies and Licences' (2005) 9 *Landlord & Tenant Rev* 161.

council discovered this they wrote to her, making clear that her occupation was unlawful and claiming for payment for use and occupation. [74] The Court of Appeal agreed that she was a trespasser as her occupation was non-consensual.

A trespasser is liable to pay 'mesne profits'[75] based on the 'user principle'. This means that the owner is entitled to recover a reasonable rent for the wrongful use of his property, even if there is no actual loss and even if the trespasser has not derived any actual benefit from the use.[76] Usually this will be based on the proper letting value of the property in the open market but this approach is not applied inflexibly. The guide is to do what is fair, and in assessing a reasonable rent the court can take account of the benefit received by the trespasser from the wrongful use.[77]

If the occupier is a tenant who holds over once his lease has ended 'without either the agreement or disagreement of the landlord'[78] and without paying rent (acceptance of rent would imply consent from the landlord), there is a tenancy at sufferance. This is not a tenancy in any meaningful sense and simply avoids the occupier being labelled a trespasser. The landlord is still able to sue for damages for use and occupation of the property.[79] Tenancies at sufferance are rare.

3.2.2 Licence

An occupier who is there with the owner's consent but who does not have a tenancy is likely to be a licensee.[80] If there is no contract between them then he will be a bare licensee, and can be turned out at any point in time; after he has had a reasonable time to leave he will become a trespasser. If, however, there is a contractual relationship he has a contractual entitlement to remain for the period promised,[81] and will often have agreed to pay a 'licence fee' for that period.

There is an important difference between the licence and the tenancy in terms of the rules on duration. As seen earlier, a lease must be for a 'certain' period, but there is no reason why there cannot be a licence for an uncertain period, such as 'until the land is required for road widening'. The contractual right to stay for an agreed period also marks a

---

[74] (1990) 62 P & CR 57 (CA).

[75] As observed in *Dean and Chapter of the Cathedral and Metropolitan Church of Christ Canterbury v Whitbread plc* [1995] 1 EGLR 82 (Ch) 84 the term 'mesne profits' is often used loosely (but wrongly) to include payment for consensual occupation.

[76] *Inverugie Investments v Hackett* [1995] 1 WLR 713 (PC) 718. In *Ministry of Defence v Asham* (1993) 66 P & CR 195 (CA) 201 Hoffman LJ said that the claimant had to choose, before judgment, between two alternative bases of claim: loss actually suffered (damages), and the value of the benefit to the occupier (restitutionary). Whilst some later cases have adopted this (see, eg, *Dean and Chapter of the Cathedral and Metropolitan Church of Christ Canterbury v Whitbread plc* [1995] 1 EGLR 82 (Ch)) Lord Lloyd said in *Inverugie* that the user principle 'need not be characterised as exclusively compensatory, or exclusively restitutionary; it combines element of both' (718). In *Attorney-General v Blake* [2001] 1 AC 268 (HL) Lord Nicholls accepts that these awards are not strictly compensatory and may be measured by benefit received but does not expressly describe them as restitutionary.

[77] *Kuwait Airways Corporation v Iraqi Airways Company* [2004] EWHC 2603 (Comm).

[78] *Wheeler v Mercer* [1957] AC 416 (HL) 426.

[79] *Bayley v Bradley* (1848) 5 CB 396.

[80] Unless he is a tolerated trespasser, see 3.2.3.

[81] Although the usual remedy for breach is damages, it may be possible to get in species protection by the award of an injunction: *Winter Garden Theatre (London) Ltd v Millennium Productions Ltd* [1948] AC 173 (HL); *Verrall v Great Yarmouth BC* [1981] QB 202 (CA).

distinction between the licensee and the tenant at will (who can be evicted on a moment's notice).

3.2.2.1 The Absence of Exclusive Possession

The key distinction between a licence and a tenancy lies in the concept of exclusive possession, the right to exclude others from the property. The licensee does not generally have exclusory powers in relation to the property. In distinguishing between a licence and a tenancy it is therefore crucial to ask whether the occupier has been granted exclusive possession; without that there cannot be a tenancy and the occupier will probably be a licensee.

Whether or not exclusive possession exists on the facts of any case will not always be easy to determine as it will depend upon whether the rights reserved to the owner are so extensive that the occupier is effectively denied the degree of territorial control necessary to the finding of a lease. As Lord Donaldson MR said in *Aslan v Murphy*:

> … there is a spectrum of exclusivity ranging from the occupier of a detached property under a full repairing lease, who is without doubt a tenant, to the overnight occupier of a hotel bedroom who, however up-market the hotel, is without doubt a lodger. The dividing line, the sorting of the forks from the spades, will not necessarily or even usually depend on a single factor, but on a combination of factors.[82]

An important consideration is whether the owner is allowed unrestricted access to the property. The retention of keys, by itself, reveals nothing; it is usual for a landlord to keep keys so that he can enter in an emergency or simply to check on the state of repair. But if keys are kept so that the owner can provide services, such as cleaning and changing the linen, then the occupier will only be a licensee. Further, what matters is the contractual position even if the parties do not keep to it strictly (subject to what is said below about 'pretence'). In *Huwyler v Ruddy* the licence fee included payment for cleaning and laundry.[83] Initially, the room was cleaned weekly and the linen was changed, but over time these services gradually stopped. Nonetheless, the Court of Appeal held this to be a lodging arrangement (a licence) rather than a lease because the occupier was still contractually entitled to the cleaning services.

Other factors that point away from there being exclusive possession are where the owner has a significant degree of supervisory control over the use of the property, and the right to move the occupier to another part of the property. In *Westminster CC v Clarke*[84] Mr Clarke was given accommodation in a hostel by the local authority 'designed to be a halfway house for rehabilitation and treatment en route to an independent home'. Under the 'licence' it was said that the accommodation allocated to him could be changed from time to time. Mr Clarke caused disturbance to the neighbours and the Council wanted to get possession quickly. If Mr Clarke had exclusive possession he would have security. The House of Lords paid particular attention to the council's object of providing 'temporary accommodation for vulnerable homeless persons' and its need to retain possession of every room. It was held that Mr Clarke did not have exclusive possession, Lord Templeman stating:

---

[82] *Aslan v Murphy (Nos 1 and 2)* [1990] 1 WLR 766 (CA) 770.
[83] (1995) 28 HLR 550 (CA).
[84] [1992] 2 AC 288 (HL).

By the terms of the licence to occupy Mr Clarke was not entitled to any particular room, he could be required to share with any other person as required by the council and he was only entitled to 'occupy accommodation in common with the Council whose representative may enter the accommodation at any time' … He was forbidden to entertain visitors without the approval of the council staff and was bound to comply with the council's warden or other staff in charge of the hostel. These limitations confirmed that the council retained possession of all the rooms of the hostel in order to supervise and control the activities of the occupiers, including Mr Clarke. Although Mr Clarke physically occupied room E he did not enjoy possession exclusively of the council.[85]

The retention of extensive supervisory control by the owner and the mobility clause show that Mr Clarke had only a licence as he could not be said to have a 'stake in the land'.

Similar examples can be found in a commercial context. In *Dresden Estates v Collinson* a workshop and store were occupied under an agreement called a licence which gave the licensor the right to require the licensee to move to other property owned by the licensor.[86] Glidewell LJ stated:

You cannot have a tenancy granting exclusive possession of particular premises, subject to a provision that the landlord can require the tenant to move to somewhere else.[87]

This kind of serviced accommodation arrangement is becoming more common, particularly with buildings intended to provide accommodation for small businesses at their start-up. The occupier takes space which may be serviced, for example with heating and secretarial help, and the owner retains considerable control over the use of the building. In *Regus v Epcot* it was assumed (without argument) that an agreement for serviced office accommodation did not create a tenancy: the agreement stated that it was the business equivalent of a hotel, and provided that the allocated accommodation could be changed.[88]

It can be a very difficult question to determine where a particular arrangement falls on the 'spectrum of exclusivity'. In *NCP v Trinity Development* the Court of Appeal had to decide if a 'licence' agreement to operate a car park was in fact a tenancy.[89] The question as to whether or not there was exclusive possession focussed on two particular clauses. One of these clauses provided that the licensee would allow entry to the licensor's employees in the exercise by them of the 'licensor's rights of possession' and give assistance to allow the licensor to carry out resurfacing; another allowed the licensor to have 40 car parking spaces. In deciding whether or not there was exclusive possession the Court of Appeal attached significance to the fact that the parties had expressed this agreement to be only a licence. While only a pointer, this could help the courts to work out what the substance was. The fact that the parties had called the agreement a licence was used to help the court decide

---

[85] [1992] 2 AC 288 (HL) 301.

[86] (1988) 55 P & CR 47 (CA).

[87] (1988) 55 P & CR 47 (CA) 53. For criticism see: PF Smith, 'A Dent in Street v Mountford' [1987] *Conv* 220; S Bridge, 'The Unusual Case of Sneyd Hill Pottery' (1987) 50 *MLR* 655. For an example of a mobility clause in an agricultural context see *McCarthy v Bence* [1990] 1 EGLR 1 (CA).

[88] *Regus (UK) Ltd v Epcot Solutions Ltd* [2007] EWCA 938 (Comm). Had it been a lease, the Unfair Contract Terms Act 1977 would not have applied: see ch 4.

[89] *National Car Parks Ltd v Trinity Development Company (Banbury) Ltd* [2001] EWCA Civ 1686.

that there was no exclusive possession, and therefore no tenancy, although courts would not necessarily use such reasoning in non-commercial cases.[90]

3.2.2.2 Parties Cannot Choose to Call a Tenancy a Licence

It is not open to the parties to avoid a tenancy simply by saying that they intended to create a licence. In *Street v Mountford* (discussed below) the House of Lords firmly stated in that if there was an agreement giving exclusive possession for a term this would create a tenancy and the parties were not free to attach their own label to the relationship.[91] Before *Street v Mountford* there had been several cases in which the courts had said that there was exclusive possession but no tenancy because the parties had intended only to create a personal privilege. In fact, most of these cases can be explained on the basis that there was in fact no exclusive possession, notwithstanding what is said in the judgements. So, for example, in *Shell-Mex v Manchester Garages* the licence agreement for a petrol station stated that the licensee had no right to impede the exercise by the owner of its rights of possession and was required to,

> ... give all reasonable assistance and facilities to ... [the licensor's agents] for the alteration at any time of the layout decorations or equipment of the premises.[92]

Although Lord Denning MR said that the question as to whether this was a lease or a licence did not depend on whether there was exclusive possession but on whether it was 'personal in its nature', what made it personal was the degree of control that the owner retained. There are several such cases in which the courts said that there was only an intention to create a personal interest and 'no intention to create a tenancy' and which are better explained as licences, not because this is what the parties wanted to call them, but because there is no exclusive possession.[93]

There are signs, however, of a retreat from the strictness of the position in *Street v Mountford*, especially in commercial cases. *NCP v Trinity Development* has already been discussed, in which the Court of Appeal took account of the label attached by the parties.[94] In that case, the reason why there was a licence was not because this is what the parties had called it, but because the label, considered along with the clauses giving the owner rights of access, showed that it was not intended to grant exclusive possession. In a more recent case, *Clear Channel UK Ltd v Manchester CC*, involving whether agreements involving the siting of advertising displays were licences or leases, the Court of Appeal makes clear that labels do sometimes matter:

> Where the contract ... negotiated [between two substantial parties of equal bargaining power and with the benefit of full legal advice] contains not merely a label but a clause which sets out in unequivocal terms the parties' intention as to its legal effect, I would ... have taken some persuading that its true effect was directly contrary to that expressed intention.[95]

---

[90] [2001] EWCA Civ 1686. Both Buxton LJ at [41] and Arden LJ at [29] referred to the fact that the parties were (presumably) given appropriate advice.

[91] [1985] 1 AC 809 (HL).

[92] [1971] 1 WLR 612 (CA).

[93] *Abbeyfield (Harpenden) Society Ltd v Woods* [1968] 1 WLR 374 (CA); *Heslop v Burns* [1974] 1 WLR 1241 (CA); *Marchant v Charters* [1977] 1 WLR 1181 (CA).

[94] *National Car Parks Ltd v Trinity Development Company (Banbury) Ltd* [2001] EWCA Civ 1686.

[95] [2005] EWCA Civ 1304 [29].

3.2.2.3 Exclusive Possession Referable to a Legal Relationship other than a Tenancy

There will not always be a tenancy even if there is exclusive possession. It may be that the possession is explicable by reference to some other legal relationship, such as an employment relationship,[96] or that there is not a term certain. These are sometimes described, following the approach of Lord Templeman in *Street v Mountford*,[97] as exceptions to the usual position in which exclusive possession means that there is a tenancy. There are a number other legal relationships that can explain exclusive possession.

a) Occupation Prior to Sale

A purchaser who is allowed into property before completion will not be a tenant because the exclusive possession is referable to the equitable interest which the purchaser has in the property pending completion. As Hoffman J explains in *Essex Plan Ltd v Broadminster*:

> [Counsel] drew attention to the fact that contracts for the sale of land commonly provide for the purchaser to be allowed into occupation as a licensee pending completion on terms that he is to pay all outgoings together with interest on the purchase money and is to keep the premises in good repair. The purchaser's possession is ancillary and referable to his interest in the land created by his contractual right to a conveyance and Lord Templeman acknowledges [in *Street v Mountford*] that such a relationship, although exhibiting the ordinary badges of a tenancy, does not create one.[98]

In *Essex Plan* the exception was extended to cover occupancy under a licence agreement pending the exercise of an option to take a long lease of the property:

> The option gave Essex Plan the right to call for the grant of the lease and therefore gave it in equity an immediate interest in the land. Its entry into occupation pending the exercise or expiry of the option was ancillary and referable to that interest. There is therefore no need to infer the creation of a tenancy which would give Essex Plan a different interest in the same land.[99]

It is important to understand that this exception is confined to cases where there is some other legal relationship between the parties. Thus the exception did not apply in *Bretherton v Paton* where the occupier was given exclusive possession of property on the understanding that she would do it up with a view to buying it when it was in good enough condition for her to be able to obtain mortgage finance.[100] There was no enforceable sale agreement and therefore no other interest in the land to which exclusive possession could be referred apart from a tenancy.

There are also several cases in which the occupier moves in and starts to pay rent whilst the parties are trying to agree the terms of a lease.[101] These cases can be difficult to

---

[96] Other examples of interests involving exclusive possession are the fee simple owner, the adverse possessor, and the mortgagee in possession. The text discusses only those most likely to be confused with the tenancy. See *Street v Mountford* [1985] 1 AC 809 (HL) 818E, 821B, 826H-827B.

[97] [1985] 1 AC 809 (HL).

[98] (1988) 56 P & CR 353 (Ch) 355–56. See also *Camden LBC v Shortlife Community Housing* (1993) 25 HLR 330 (Ch) 341.

[99] (1988) 56 P & CR 353 (Ch) 356.

[100] (1986) 18 HLR 257 (CA).

[101] See, eg, *Javad v Mohammed Aqil* [1999] 1 WLR 1007 (CA).

analyse and the outcome in most of the cases is to find that there is a tenancy at will (or licence) but not a periodic tenancy or fixed term lease. These are not examples falling within this exceptional category as the exclusive possession cannot be explained by pointing to some other relationship between the parties. The tendency of the courts in these cases is to refer to the fact that the parties did not intend to create a tenancy (with all the consequences that flow from that), but the better doctrinal explanation for why there is not a periodic tenancy lies, probably, in the absence of certainty of term. These cases are discussed 3.2.4 below.

b) Service Occupancy

Where an employee is required to occupy his employer's accommodation in order to better perform his duties, he will be a licensee and not a tenant.[102] What matters is that living there enables him to do the job better, the classic example being the caretaker. The test set out by Lord Reid in *Glasgow Corporation v Johnstone*[103] is whether it is *necessary or of material assistance* in carrying out his employment duties. Examples of licences include where a mechanic, also employed to drive coaches, was required to live at the premises so that he would be available in an emergency (*Norris v Checksfield*);[104] where a surgeon was required to live at the hospital (*Dobson v Jones*);[105] and where a hotel manager was required to live on the premises (*Carroll v Manek*).[106]

Service occupancy tends to focus on the residential accommodation of the employee, but questions as to status can also arise in relation to the business being run on the premises. Management agreements, under which someone enters into occupation of property in order to run a business, are fairly common. If the manager is running a business for the owner then the occupational rights will be those of a licensee. Even if there is exclusive possession, the arrangement will be like the master/servant exception recognised by Lord Templeman in *Street v Mountford*[107] as the occupation will be a necessary corollary to support the management relationship. If, however, the grantee is running his own business and has extensive control over the business and premises then even if it is dressed up to look like a management agreement, it is likely to be a tenancy.[108] In *Dellneed v Chin*[109] the lessee of a Chinese restaurant entered into a 'management agreement' with a newly formed company to run a business from the restaurant. Although it looked like a management agreement in certain respects, the grantor had not kept any keys and the grantee had an obligation to repair the property. These, and other features, showed that in reality the grantee had exclusive possession to run his own business, and thus there was a lease.

---

[102] *Norris v Checksfield* [1991] 1 WLR 1241 (CA).

[103] [1965] AC 609 (HL).

[104] [1991] 1 WLR 1241 (CA).

[105] (1844) 5 Man & G 112.

[106] *Carroll v Manek and Bank of India* (2000) 79 P & CR 173 (Ch).

[107] [1985] 1 AC 809 (HL) 818E, 821B.

[108] If a management agreement is in fact held to be lease this may have unanticipated consequences: if the grantor has a leasehold interest which prohibits further alienation there is the risk of forfeiture, there may be unintended security of tenure, and important fiscal consequences.

[109] (1987) 53 P & CR 172 (Ch). See further *Bon Apettito Ltd v Poon; Speedhold Ltd v Bon Apettito Ltd, Cuscani* (Newcastle Cty Ct) 18 January 2005, discussed at S Bright, 'Managing or Leasing' [2005] 69 *Conv* 352.

c) Occupation as a Beneficiary

In *Gray v Taylor* the trustees of a charity allowed Mrs Taylor to occupy an almshouse.[110] The Court of Appeal held that she was not a tenant, instead she was enjoying the occupation as a beneficiary:

> At the time when the trustees grant an almsperson a right of occupation there exists between them the relationship of trustee and beneficiary...[The] almsperson's occupation and his or her right to exclusive possession are referable to a legal relationship other than a tenancy.[111]

The Court of Appeal was influenced by the fact that finding a tenancy could 'fetter the performance by the trustees of their duty to provide accommodation for deserving persons' as it would make it difficult to recover possession if, for example, one of the occupiers became wealthy by receiving a substantial legacy.[112] Barr comments that the fact that the occupier is the beneficiary of a charity need not necessarily exclude the co-existence of a contractual agreement for occupation, but this possibility was not given any serious consideration in *Gray v Taylor*.[113]

It is difficult to know the width of this exception. A number of registered social landlords are established as charities to provide for particular categories of person, but there is little doubt that they grant tenancies to occupiers. Further, in *Bruton v London and Quadrant Housing Trust* Lord Hoffmann said that the fact that the trust was 'a responsible landlord performing socially valuable functions' could not make an 'agreement to grant exclusive possession something other than a tenancy'.[114]

d) Tolerated Trespass

The tolerated trespasser (discussed more fully at 3.2.3 below) is, broadly, a former residential tenant who is allowed to remain in possession even after the tenancy has come to an end as the result of a possession order. The working of the tolerated trespasser concept is hugely complicated.[115] In essence, there are some situations in which a former tenancy is treated as in a 'suspended' state and is liable to be revived upon court order.[116] If, during this period of 'limbo', the former tenant is allowed to stay in occupation, he is treated in law as a tolerated trespasser and not a tenant. The occupier has exclusive possession, pays rent, and appears to have a periodic term but there is no tenancy. A possible explanation as to how this result fits into the doctrinal picture is that the exclusive possession is referable to the 'limbo' tenancy and therefore there is no need to find a new tenancy to explain the occupation.[117]

---

[110] [1998] 1 WLR 1093 (CA).

[111] [1998] 1 WLR 1093 (CA) 1099.

[112] [1998] 1 WLR 1093 (CA) 1099.

[113] W Barr, 'Charitable Lettings and Their Legal Pitfalls' in E Cooke (ed), *Modern Studies in Property Law, Vol 1: Property* (Oxford, Hart, 2001) 247–9.

[114] [2000] 1 AC 406 (HL) 414.

[115] It is discussed more fully in ch 19.

[116] Under the Housing Act 1985 s 85(2) (local authority tenancy) or the Housing Act 1988 s 9(2) (private sector tenancy).

[117] There is some support for this in *Leadenhall Residential 2 Ltd v Stirling* [2001] EWCA Civ 1011, [2002] 1 WLR 499 [34]. But tolerated trespass status is undoubtedly policy driven and is difficult to explain doctrinally. The explanation given in the text here works, but it is not terribly convincing.

3.2.3 The Tolerated Trespasser[118]

The tolerated trespasser is, to quote Clarke LJ in *Pemberton v Southwark*, 'a recent, somewhat bizarre, addition to the dramatis personae of the law'.[119] It is not unusual for a local authority or housing association to obtain a possession order but not enforce it immediately, perhaps because it is being used as a management tool to assist with the recovery of rent arrears rather than primarily in order to recover possession.[120] The tenancy comes to end on the date given for possession by the court order.[121] The question then arises as to what the status of the occupier who remains in possession is. Often it is not simply a case of the occupier staying put but of being actively allowed to stay by the owner provided that she makes regular agreed payments for the accommodation.

The leading case is *Burrows v Brent* where an immediate order for possession had been granted against a secure tenant, Miss Burrows.[122] The local authority came to an arrangement with her in which she agreed to pay a 'rent charge' and an agreed amount towards the arrears, but she failed to keep up with these payments. More than two years later the local authority executed the warrant for possession. Miss Burrows argued that the agreement reached between her and the local authority made her a new tenant but the House of Lords disagreed. The agreement was simply one to 'forbear from executing the order'. Once the possession order ended the secure tenancy Miss Burrows became, in the words of Lord Browne-Wilkinson:

> … [a] trespasser whom the landlord has agreed not to evict – a 'tolerated trespasser' – pending either the revival of the old tenancy or the breach of the agreed conditions.[123]

Initially this concept appeared to be confined to public sector tenants, but the Court of Appeal has recently held, in *White v Knowsley Housing Trust*, that private sector tenants can also become tolerated trespassers.[124]

There are now hundreds of thousands of residential occupiers who have tolerated trespasser status.[125] They have no statutory rights, no security of tenure, and are unable to

---

[118] See: S Bright, 'The Concept of the Tolerated Trespasser: an Analysis' (2003) 119 *LQR* 495; I Loveland, 'Tolerated Trespass: a Very Peculiar Legal Creature' (2007) 123 *LQR* 455.

[119] *Pemberton v Southwark LBC* [2000] 1 WLR 1672 (CA) 1683.

[120] 98% of notices seeking possession taken out be social landlords are for rent arrears; only 4% of these result in evictions: H Pawson and others, 'The Use of Possession Actions and Evictions by Social Landlords' (ODPM, June 2005).

[121] Depending on the wording of the court order this could be any of: the date of breach of the conditions attached to the order, the date stated for possession in the order, or (with the modern wording used in the form N28A for possession of former secure tenancies) a date fixed by the court following application by the landlord once the conditions have been breached: see ch 19.

[122] *Burrows v Brent LBC* [1996] 1 WLR 1448 (HL). See also n 20. An immediate order is not made subject to conditions. In contrast, a 'suspended' possession order (now referred to as a 'postponed possession order', see ch 19) will be made subject to conditions and provided that the occupier complies with these the possession order will not be enforceable.

[123] *Burrows v Brent LBC* [1996] 1 WLR 1448 (HL) 1455. The former tenancy may be revived by court order under the Housing Act 1985 s 85.

[124] [2007] EWCA Civ 404.

[125] It has been estimated that there are in excess of 400,000 tolerated trespassers in local authority housing: T Horsley, 'Tolerated Trespass: latest court rulings and best practice' (Housing Quality Network, September 2006). A further one quarter of a million new tolerated trespassers were probably created when it was recognised that private

enforce any landlord covenants in the former tenancy. Strictly, a landlord should treat the tolerated trespasser differently from other tenants and be careful that correspondence distinguishes between the two statuses. Although some housing authorities, such as Greenwich, have carefully developed management policies that do this, many housing authorities do not keep such clear records. In many respects the occupier looks like a tenant: she has exclusive possession, and has often been encouraged to believe that she can stay for renewable periods so long as she pays for her occupation. She may even be treated by the housing authority in the same way that tenants are. Nonetheless, the approach of the courts in tolerated trespasser cases is to say that there will only be a new tenancy if *forced* to this result. In *Burrows v Brent* Lord Browne-Wilkinson said:

> It cannot be right to impute to the parties an intention to create a legal relationship such as a secure tenancy or licence unless the legal structures within which they made their agreement *force* that conclusion. (emphasis added)[126]

This dictum has been seized upon in later cases so that even action which suggests that the local authority is treating the occupier as a new tenant, such as sending out tenancy letters, new tenancy conditions or notices of rent increase will not create a tenancy.[127]

The reason why the occupier is labelled as a tolerated trespasser rather than a (new) tenant is undoubtedly policy led. The housing authority may be reluctant to accept an occupier with a bad payment record as a tenant, and the courts are fearful that housing authorities will seek to evict immediately if allowing a former tenant to stay in the property after the possession order risks creating a new tenancy.

Doctrinally, tolerated trespass status is hard to explain given that the indicia of a tenancy appear to be satisfied. It may be that there is no intention to create a contract,[128] but this is not very convincing as there often appear to be promises made by both parties. Nor does this explanation reflect the way that the courts usually approach cases. Alternatively it may be that the exclusive possession should be explained as being referable to the former tenancy that is now in 'limbo'.[129] The concept of the tenancy in limbo stems from the wording of section 85 of the Housing Act 1985.[130] This section confers wide discretionary powers upon the court to suspend, stay, postpone, rescind and discharge possession orders. As the court has power to postpone a possession date, it also is able to change 'the date on which the

---

sector tenants could become tolerated trespassers: *White v Knowsley Housing Trust* [2007] EWCA Civ 404. Previously it had been commonly thought that in the private sector they would remain as tenants until the possession order was executed and the tenant left the property. See further ch 19.

[126] *Burrows v Brent LBC* [1996] 1 WLR 1448 (HL) 1454.

[127] *LB of Newham v Hawkins* [2005] EWCA Civ 451; *LB of Lambeth and Hyde Southbank Ltd v O'Kane; Helena Housing Ltd v Pinder* [2005] EWCA Civ 1010. But the cases do not all go one way. In both *Leadenhall Residential 2 Ltd v Stirling* [2001] EWCA Civ 1011, [2002] 1 WLR 499 (private sector) and *Swindon BC v Aston* [2002] EWCA Civ 1850 there was a new tenancy.

[128] This was Arden LJ's suggestion in *LB of Lambeth and Hyde Southbank Ltd v O'Kane; Helena Housing Ltd v Pinder* [2005] EWCA Civ 1010. See 3.1.2 above.

[129] See text accompanying n 117.

[130] Housing Act 1985 s 85(2): 'On the making of an order for possession of such a dwelling-house...or *at any time before the execution of the order*, the court may – (a) stay or suspend the execution of the order, or (b) postpone the date of possession.' For the private sector, see Housing Act 1988 s 9(2).

tenancy is to come to an end, even after the tenancy has already determined'.[131] This means that:

> ... the court may revive or reinstate the existing secure tenancy which must thereafter be treated as having continued throughout without interruption.[132]

Consequently, it may be that the reason why the tolerated trespasser fails to acquire a new tenancy is because the exclusive possession is said to be explicable by reference to this suspended tenancy. The force of this as an explanation is somewhat diminished by the dual facts that the status appears to survive the transfer of the housing to a new landlord (even though it is not then possible for exactly the same tenancy to be revived) and that continuing 'revivability' is not treated as essential to the analysis.[133]

3.2.4 Tenancy at Will

A tenancy at will arises whenever a tenant, with the consent of the owner, occupies land as tenant 'at the will' of the landlord, that is, on terms that either party can bring the tenancy to an end at any time. It is a hybrid kind of interest: it is contractual,[134] and the occupier has exclusive possession but the fact that it can be brought to an end at any time means that there is no 'term of years'. For this reason it is not a legal estate:

> A tenancy at will, though called a tenancy, is unlike any other tenancy except a tenancy at sufferance, to which it is next-of-kin. It has been properly described as a personal relation between the landlord and his tenant: it is determined by the death of either of them or by any one of a variety of acts, even by an involuntary alienation, which would not affect the subsistence of any other tenancy.[135]

The personal nature of this interest means that the tenant cannot assign or sub-let his interest. Nor is it a tenancy that attracts statutory protection in most sectors, with the exception of the private residential sector where it is thought that the tenant at will probably does have protected status.[136] Nevertheless, as the tenant has 'possession' he is able to bring an action in trespass against a stranger. The tenancy at will can be created by express agreement,[137] but more usually arises by implication. If an attempt to create a fixed term lease fails, for example because the correct formalities have not been used or because the term is uncertain, then when the tenant is allowed into possession he will become a tenant at will.[138]

A tenancy at will commonly arises when an occupier moves into property whilst still negotiating the terms of a lease,[139] or holds over at the end of a tenancy whilst trying to

---

[131] *Greenwich LBC v Regan* (1996) 28 HLR 469 (CA) 475.

[132] *Greenwich LBC v Regan* (1996) 28 HLR 469 (CA) 475.

[133] *LB of Lambeth and Hyde Southbank Ltd v O'Kane; Helena Housing Ltd v Pinder* [2005] EWCA Civ 1010.

[134] *Ley v Peter* (1858) 3 H&N 101; *Ramnarace v Lutchman* [2001] UKPC 25, [2001] 1 WLR 1651 [17].

[135] *Wheeler v Mercer* [1957] AC 416 (HL) 427.

[136] *Francis Jackson Developments Ltd v Stemp* [1943] 2 All ER 601 (CA); a case on the Rent Restriction Acts but generally assumed to apply more widely.

[137] *Hagee (London) Ltd v A B Erikson and Larson* [1996] QB 209 (CA).

[138] *Braythwaite v Hitchcock* (1842) 10 M & W 494, 497. If rent is paid, it will become a periodic tenancy.

[139] See, eg, *Javad v Mohammed Aqil* [1999] 1 WLR 1007 (CA). In *Chamberlain v Farr* [1942] 2 All ER 567 (CA) the occupier was allowed in while work was finishing on another of the landlord's properties that he was buying, and was held to be a tenant at will.

reach agreement with the landlord as to the basis of the continuing occupation.[140] As such it is said that it serves 'one legal purpose, and that is to protect the interests of an occupier during a period of transition',[141] usually while trying to acquire a more permanent interest. Assuming that there is exclusive possession, it is often thought that a tenancy at will arises in these situations but that it is converted into a periodic tenancy upon the payment of rent. In fact, this is seldom the case. It is only if the payment of rent is unexplained that a periodic tenancy is presumed.[142] Usually, there is some explanation from the wider context and from what is said that explains the basis upon which the rent is being paid. If it is clear that the occupier can stay whilst the parties are trying to reach agreement but will be expected to leave if the negotiations breakdown, then the occupier is only in possession at the will of the owner and this cannot be a periodic tenancy. In *Javad v Mohammed Aqil*[143] the landlord allowed the business tenant into the premises because he had nowhere else to go and 'the landlord took pity on him'. The tenant paid £2,500 'as rent for three months in advance' but the plan was always to negotiate for the grant of a ten year lease. It was understood that the 'property was to be returned to the landlord if the parties were unable to agree terms'. Negotiations broke down. The Court of Appeal held the occupier to be a tenant at will. In the words of Nicholls LJ:

> ... when one party permits another to enter or remain on his land on payment of a sum of money, and that other has no statutory entitlement to be there, almost inevitably there will be some consensual relationship between them. It may be no more than a licence determinable at any time, or a tenancy at will. But when and so long as such parties are in the throes of negotiating larger terms, caution must be exercised before inferring or imputing to the parties an intention to give to the occupant more than a very limited interest, be it licence or tenancy. Otherwise the court would be in danger of inferring or imputing from conduct, such as payment of rent and the carrying out of repairs, whose explanation lies in the parties' expectation that they will be able to reach agreement on the larger terms, an intention to grant a lesser interest, such as a periodic tenancy, which the parties never had in contemplation at all.[144]

Similarly in *Cardiothoracic Institute v Shrewdcrest Ltd*[145] a business tenant occupied under a succession of leases. After the last lease expired the tenant remained while the parties were trying to agree the future terms, and Knox J held there to be a tenancy at will.

In a 'moving in' context the courts often have to determine whether the occupier has a periodic tenancy or a tenancy at will (or its close relation, the licence). In practice, how the arrangement is categorised is influenced by the statutory consequences that would follow, in particular whether secure status would result. The way that the courts tend to do this is by reference to the intention of the parties, recognising that in a negotiating situation they will seldom have intended a periodic tenancy, as this may well attract statutory protection.[146]

---

[140] See, eg, *Wheeler v Mercer* [1957] AC 416 (HL); *Cardiothoracic Institute v Shrewdcrest Ltd* [1986] 1 WLR 368 (Ch); *London Baggage Company v Railtrack plc* (2000) 80 P & CR D38 (Ch).

[141] *Heslop v Burns* [1974] 1 WLR 1241 (CA) 1253.

[142] *Doe d Lord v Crago* (1848) 6 CB 90; *Javad v Mohammed Aqil* [1999] 1 WLR 1007 (CA).

[143] [1999] 1 WLR 1007 (CA).

[144] [1999] 1 WLR 1007 (CA) 1013.

[145] [1986] 1 WLR 368 (Ch).

[146] See *Javad v Mohammed Aqil* [1999] 1 WLR 1007 (CA) 1012–3; *Cardiothoracic Institute v Shrewdcrest Ltd* [1986] 1 WLR 368 (Ch) 378.

Similarly, an arrangement that looks like a periodic tenancy or tenancy at will is sometimes categorised as a licence if the alternative would result in protected status.[147] In doctrinal terms, however, it is not what the parties intend to call the relationship that matters but whether the substantive requirements of a lease are present. Doctrinally, it will often be inappropriate to find a periodic tenancy in the negotiating situation because there is no certainty of term, and thus can be no periodic or fixed term lease. If the occupation is found to be 'at will' (that is, liable to be ended if negotiations break down) then choosing between a tenancy at will and a licence should depend on whether there is exclusive possession; if so, there will be a tenancy at will, and without exclusive possession there will be a licence.

During a tenancy at will, the rent will be the agreed rent. If nothing has been agreed then the basis of payment is the action for use and occupation. In holding over cases there is an evidential presumption that the rent continues at the old rate, but if it is clear that there is disagreement between the parties then the open market value will be used, as with mesne profits for trespass.[148]

3.2.5 Periodic Tenancy

A periodic tenancy is one which is for a period and which automatically continues from period to period until ended by the appropriate notice. A person could have, say, a weekly tenancy which continues week by week for fifty years. The law perceives periodic tenancies not to be a series of separate and new tenancies but as one continuing tenancy, 'not a reletting at the commencement of every year [week/month/quarter, *etc.*] but...a springing interest'.[149]

3.2.5.1 Implied Periodic Tenancies

Many periodic tenancies are created by express agreement between the parties. Most social housing rented from local authorities and housing associations will be let as periodic tenancies. As well as arising by express agreement, a periodic tenancy can arise informally where a person occupies land with consent and pays rent by reference to a certain period, for example, £200 monthly. Indeed, until recently it was commonly thought that there was a presumption that when someone entered into exclusive possession of property and started paying rent there would be a periodic tenancy. In *Doe d Lord v Crago*, Wilde CJ referred to:

---

[147] See *Sopwith v Stuchbury* (1983) 17 HLR 50 (CA); *Sharp v McArthur v Sharp* (1987) 19 HLR 364 (CA) (in this case, an agreement with all the indicia of a tenancy and a one month notice period was said to be a licence because of the 'exceptional circumstances' – which were not that exceptional). In *Isaac v Hotel de Paris Ltd* [1960] 1 WLR 239 (PC) a bar manager was held to be a licensee whilst the parties were trying to agree a formal contract. In *Street v Mountford* [1985] 1 AC 809 (HL) 823 Lord Templeman explains this as a case where there is no contractual intent. This is unlikely as an agreed rent was paid. It may be that there was no exclusive possession, but the case is not analysed in these terms by the Privy Council. Alternatively, it may be falsely labelled as the label was obiter, all that had to be decided was that there was not a periodic tenancy.

[148] *Dean and Chapter of the Cathedral and Metropolitan Church of Christ Canterbury v Whitbread plc* [1995] 1 EGLR 82 (Ch).

[149] *Gaudy v Jubber* (1865) 9 B & S 15. See also *Queen's Club Garden Estates v Bignell* [1924] 1 KB 117 (DC) 125 and 130.

... the principle, that, from the payment of rent, unexplained, the law will imply a tenancy from year to year, with the incidents attached to it, namely, the necessity of a regular notice to quit, before the defendant's possession could be disturbed.[150]

It is important to note that it is only where there is *unexplained* payment of rent that the periodic tenancy is presumed. Usually there will be some explanation as to the basis upon which the payment is being made that can be read from the parties' conduct and words. As Nicholls LJ noted in *Javad v Mohammed Aqil*, the presumption only applies where there is nothing more in the surrounding facts to indicate what the parties' intentions are:

> As with other consensually-based arrangements, parties frequently proceed with an arrange-ment whereby one person takes possession of another's land for payment without having agreed or directed their minds to one or more fundamental aspects of their transaction. In such cases the law, where appropriate, has to step in and fill the gaps in a way which is sensible and reasonable. The law will imply, from what was agreed and all the surrounding circum-stances, the terms the parties are to be taken to have intended to apply. Thus if one party permits another to go into possession of his land on payment of a rent of so much per week or month, failing more the inference sensibly and reasonably to be drawn is that the parties intended that there should be a weekly or monthly tenancy. Likewise, if one party permits another to remain in possession after the expiration of his tenancy. But I emphasise the quali-fication: "failing more". Frequently there will be more. Indeed, nowadays there normally will be other material surrounding circumstances. The simple situation is unlikely to arise often, not least because of the extent to which statute has intervened in landlord-tenant relationships. Where there is more than the simple situation, the inference sensibly and reasonably to be drawn will depend on a fair consideration of all the circumstances, of which the payment of rent on a periodical basis is only one, albeit a very important one.[151]

The courts refer to the 'intentions of the parties in all the circumstances'[152] in order to determine what kind of relationship exists, and, although there is conflicting authority on the issue, the better view is that intention is to be objectively assessed.[153] Nowadays the presumption of a periodic tenancy from possession and payment of rent is seldom used. Indeed, in *Javad v Mohammed Aqil* Nicholls LJ described it as an arid issue as to whether the 'so-called "old common law presumption"' no longer exists or is virtually never used in practice.[154]

There is a difficult issue hidden in this. According to *Street v Mountford* the question of how a relationship is labelled is a matter of law, not a matter for the parties to select. Lord Templeman also said that 'the Rent Acts must not be allowed to alter or influence the construction of an agreement'.[155] In cases where the courts have to determine whether it is correct to call the relationship a periodic tenancy or a tenancy at will or a licence it would therefore seem improper to refer to what the parties meant it to be, and to the statutory consequences of finding one way or another, and yet it is clear that these considerations do

---

[150] (1848) 6 CB 90, 99.
[151] *Javad v Mohammed Aqil* [1999] 1 WLR 1007 (CA) 1012.
[152] *Cardiothoracic Institute v Shrewdcrest Ltd* [1986] 1 WLR 368 (Ch) 378.
[153] *London Baggage Company v Railtrack plc* (2000) 80 P & CR D38 (Ch).
[154] *Javad v Mohammed Aqil* [1999] 1 WLR 1007 (CA) 1017.
[155] [1985] 1 AC 809 (HL) 825.

come into play. The courts recognise that the statutory consequences of finding a periodic tenancy will often mean that this result is unlikely to have been intended by the parties:

> Thus, in what used to be the ordinary case of a tenancy unaffected by statutory prolongation or protection coming to an end, and the parties giving and receiving rent but not expressly agreeing on the creation of a new tenancy, the preferred solution that the law has adopted is a periodic tenancy, on the footing that that is what the parties must have intended or be taken to have intended. Ultimately it is the intentions of the parties in all the circumstances that determines the result of the giving and acceptance of rent. Tenancies where there is no statutory protection of one sort or another are no longer the norm. Where statutory protection does exist that has been treated as a significant factor in evaluating the parties' intention in paying and receiving rent.[156]

Given that, according to *Street v Mountford*,[157] the parties' labelling choice is not meant to be relevant, a better way of explaining the cases that reject a periodic tenancy in favour of a tenancy at will (or licence) is to say that these are cases in which there is no agreed term because the parties intend for the occupier to be in possession 'at will' only (as discussed at 3.2.4 above). Only in those cases where the occupier moves into possession and pays rent and there is nothing to suggest that this is intended only to be a transitional or interim arrangement (an unexplained payment), will the correct inference be that the parties intend a periodic tenancy on a renewable basis. In *Javad v Aqil* the plan was always for the occupier to leave if the negotiations for a ten year lease fell through.[158] Hence, it would have been wrong to infer from the rental payment that they intended a periodic tenancy, as they clearly did not mean for the occupier to have the right to stay for successive periods subject only to notice to quit being served. Similarly in *Sopwith v Stuchbury* a person let into residential occupation pending agreement of the terms of a tenancy was held to be an (unprotected) licensee.[159] In all of these 'moving in' cases, no periodic tenancy is found because the parties are still trying to reach agreement and it is understood that if they do not reach agreement the occupier will have to leave.

A periodic tenancy can also arise if an agreement to create a fixed term lease fails. This can occur either if the term agreed is uncertain or if the incorrect formalities have been used.[160] Although the agreement to grant the land to the tenant until it was required for road widening failed to grant an estate in *Prudential Assurance*, the House of Lords nonetheless held that when the tenant,

> … entered into possession and paid the yearly rent of £30 reserved by the agreement…[it] became a yearly tenant holding on the terms of the agreement so far as those terms were consistent with the yearly tenancy.[161]

Where a periodic tenancy is implied, the period of the tenancy is calculated by reference not to how often the rent is paid but the period by reference to which it is calculated, for

---

[156] *Cardiothoracic Institute v Shrewdcrest Ltd* [1986] 1 WLR 368 (Ch) 378.
[157] [1985] 1 AC 809 (HL).
[158] *Javad v Mohammed Aqil* [1999] 1 WLR 1007 (CA).
[159] (1985) 17 HLR 50 (CA). As this was a private sector case, tenant at will status would have given protection. See also *Isaac v Hotel de Paris Ltd* [1960] 1 WLR 239 (PC).
[160] *Martin v Smith* (1874) LR 9 Ex 50.
[161] *Prudential Assurance Co Ltd v London Residuary Body* [1992] 2 AC 386 (HL) 392.

example, a rent of £12,000 per annum payable in £1,000 monthly instalments would be a yearly tenancy.[162]

3.2.5.2 *Periodic Tenancies, Certainty and Repugnancy*

Periodic tenancies continue until brought to an end by service of a notice to quit (the length of notice required is discussed in chapter 22). It is, therefore, of the essence of a periodic tenancy that either party is able to serve notice to end the relationship. For that reason it is said to be repugnant to the nature of the periodic tenancy if there is a restriction on terminating the tenancy. This is often discussed in the same context as the rule on certainty; as mentioned earlier there is a need for periodic tenancies to satisfy the rule that there must be a certain beginning, duration and end in order for there to be a tenancy. In the context of periodic tenancies this is a strange requirement but, in so far as it can be explained, it is said that periodic tenancies satisfy the rule because each party can end the tenancy and so the maximum duration is set by reference to the next period. Where the parties agree that one of them is unable to serve a notice to quit, this leads to both repugnancy and uncertainty.

Before *Prudential Assurance Co Ltd v London Residuary Body* it had been thought that one way around the certainty rule was to create periodic tenancies that contained a contractual fetter on the common law right to serve a notice to quit.[163] In both *Re Midland Railway*[164] and *Breams Property Investment Co Ltd v Strougler*[165] the Court of Appeal upheld periodic tenancies that contained provisos preventing the landlord from ending the tenancy unless the premises were required for the landlord's own use. Yet in other cases, the courts have said that restrictions on the right to determine the lease are repugnant to the nature of periodic tenancies. In *Cheshire Lines Committee v Lewis & Co* the Court of Appeal held a lease invalid where the landlord agreed not to serve a notice to quit until the landlord wanted the premises 'to pull them down'.[166] In *Centaploy v Matlodge* a tenancy of garages terminable only by the tenants was held void.[167] In *Prudential Assurance* the lease that had been agreed to last until the land was required for road widening was held to be void.[168] Lord Templeman considered the possibility that it nevertheless took effect as a yearly tenancy subject to a restriction that the landlord would not end the lease unless the property was required for the road widening. He firmly rejected this idea on the grounds that this:

> … would make a nonsense of the rule that a grant for an uncertain term does not create a lease and would make nonsense of the concept of a tenancy from year to year because it is of the essence of a tenancy from year to year that both the landlord and the tenant shall be entitled to give notice determining the tenancy.[169]

---

[162] *Adler v Blackman* [1953] 1 QB 146 (CA) 150. Contrast the statutory periodic tenancy arising at the expiry of a fixed term assured tenancy, which looks to the period which the last rental payment refers to: see ch 19.
[163] [1992] 2 AC 386 (HL).
[164] *In re Midland Railway Co's Agreement; Clay (Charles) & Sons Ltd v British Railways Board* [1971] Ch 725 (CA).
[165] [1948] 2 KB 1 (CA).
[166] (1880) 50 LJQB 121.
[167] [1974] Ch 1 (Ch).
[168] *Prudential Assurance Co Ltd v London Residuary Body* [1992] 2 AC 386 (HL).
[169] *Prudential Assurance Co Ltd v London Residuary Body* [1992] 2 AC 386 (HL) 392.

Re Midland Railway[170] was disapproved.

Following *Prudential Assurance*[171] it seems that a distinction needs to be drawn between three kinds of fetters:

(a) *total restrictions* (where one party has no right to end the lease, as in *Centaploy v Matlodge*):[172] the lease will be void.

(b) *partial restrictions* (where one party cannot end the lease 'unless a defined event happens', as in *Cheshire Lines Committee v Lewis & Co*):[173] such leases will also be invalid.[174]

(c) *restrictions limited to a fixed time* (where one party cannot end the lease for a set period 'unless a defined event happens', as in *Breams Property Investment Co Ltd v Strougler*[175] where the restriction on the landlord serving notice only applied for the first three years): these leases are valid. In *Prudential Assurance* Lord Templeman said that:

> ... [a] lease can be made from year to year subject to a fetter on the right of the landlord to determine the lease before the expiry of five years unless the war ends.[176]

In any of the cases where the lease is said to be invalid, it may still take effect as a periodic tenancy, but without the restriction.

3.2.6 Fixed Term Lease

This is a lease for a fixed period of time, and can be of any length provided that there is a known start date and a certain end (see 3.1.4 above). There are standard patterns used in the different sectors (see also chapter 1). A private residential tenancy which is for a fixed term (rather than periodic) is likely to be for six or twelve months. There is increasing diversity in the length of business tenancies but most will fall within the range of five to fifteen years.[177] Long residential leases tend to be for 99, 125 or 999 years. The fixed term will automatically end when the term finishes and there is no need to serve any notice to end the lease.

3.2.7 Perpetually Renewable Leases

A perpetually renewable lease is one for which the tenant can demand renewal on the same terms, that is, including the clause for renewal. These are converted by section 145 of (and Schedule 15 to) the Law of Property Act 1922 into leases for 2,000 years determinable earlier by the tenant but not by the landlord. Such a long lease is usually the last thing that either party would have intended and so the courts tend to lean against a construction that would

---

170 *In re Midland Railway Co's Agreement; Clay (Charles) & Sons Ltd v British Railways Board* [1971] Ch 725 (CA).
171 *Prudential Assurance Co Ltd v London Residuary Body* [1992] 2 AC 386 (HL).
172 [1974] Ch 1.
173 (1880) 50 LJQB 121.
174 But see D Wilde, 'Certainty of Leasehold Term' (1994) 57 *MLR* 117, who argues that these leases are not uncertain.
175 [1948] 2 KB 1 (CA).
176 *Prudential Assurance Co Ltd v London Residuary* Body [1992] 2 AC 386 (HL) 395.
177 N Crosby, C Hughes and S Murdoch, 'Monitoring the 2002 Code of Practice for Commercial Leases' (ODPM, March 2005) 85.

result in a perpetually renewable lease. Before the courts find a perpetually renewable lease they require very clear wording that the renewed lease was intended to include the right to renewal as well as all the other covenants. In *Marjorie Burnett Ltd v Barclay* a seven year lease contained a covenant for renewal for a further seven years, the renewed lease to 'contain a like covenant for renewal for a further term of seven years on the expiration of the term thereby granted'.[178] Nourse J held that this was not an obligation for perpetual renewal, only for double renewal. Nevertheless, the use of certain words has become a 'formula' for indicating a perpetually renewable lease. In *Caerphilly Concrete Products Ltd v Owen* this formula was used because the new lease was to contain 'the like covenants and provisos as are herein contained (including an option to renew such lease for the further term of five years at the expiration thereof)'.[179] Sachs LJ referred to the fact that the 2,000 year lease was at odds with the parties' intentions and referred to 'judicial unease' at this result. While the parties had been talking in terms of five year leases, it had become a lease for 2,000 years.

It may well be the case that the parties have not built into the lease the kinds of terms and conditions that one would normally expect to see in long leases, such as provision for rent increase, repair and decoration and so on. A result closer to the parties' expectations would be to permit only a limited number of renewals; although the number selected would be somewhat arbitrary, it would create less injustice. As Lord FitzGerald said in *Swinburne v Milburn*, only in cases where the parties have clearly intended a perpetual lease by using words such as 'for ever' or 'from time to time hereafter' should a 2,000 year lease be imposed.[180]

3.2.8 *Tenancy by Estoppel*[181]

The usual situation in which a tenancy by estoppel arises is where a grantor who does not have a legal title purports to grant (whether in writing or orally)[182] a lease to the grantee. The tenancy by estoppel is a creature of common law based on purported grant, there is no need to show 'reliance'. The parties will be 'estopped' from denying the title of the other, the grantor will be treated as a landlord and the occupier as a tenant:

> It is true that a title by estoppel is only good against the person estopped and imports from its very existence the idea of no real title at all, yet as against the person estopped it has all the elements of a real title.[183]

Any covenants agreed will bind the parties. In *Industrial Properties (Barton Hill) Ltd v Associated Electrical Industries Ltd* there was a tenancy by estoppel and the tenant could not get out of the obligation to repair by arguing that there was no lease; it had enjoyed the benefits of using the property and should therefore accept the responsibilities.[184] Successors

---

[178] [1981] 1 EGLR 41 (Ch).
[179] [1972] 1 WLR 372 (CA).
[180] (1884) 9 App Cas 844.
[181] See: AM Prichard, 'Tenancy by Estoppel' (1964) 80 *LQR* 370.
[182] *Edward H Lewis & Son v Morelli* [1948] 2 All ER 1021 (CA) 1024.
[183] *Bank of England v Cutler* [1908] 2 KB 208 (CA) 234.
[184] [1977] QB 580 (CA).

in title to the either party are also bound.[185] If the landlord later acquires a legal estate, this is said to 'feed the estoppel' and the tenant acquires a legal tenancy.[186]

Explaining the tenancy by estoppel has become more complicated following *Bruton v London and Quadrant Housing Trust*.[187] In *Bruton* the Housing Trust had purported to grant only a 'licence' to the occupier. The Court of Appeal held that this could not take effect as a tenancy by estoppel because there was no purported grant of a lease.[188] The House of Lords took a different approach, although what is said about tenancy by estoppel is obiter. Lord Hoffmann said that there was a tenancy because exclusive possession had been granted[189] and the parties are therefore estopped from denying any of the 'ordinary incidents or obligations of the tenancy on the ground that the landlord had no legal estate'.[190] The reasoning is strange: it is, in effect, saying that having entered into a lease, the parties cannot deny that there is a lease. But this is commonsense: having entered into any legal relationship the parties would surely be prevented from denying it. It is difficult to see what is added by talking of estoppel unless Lord Hoffman means that in cases where there is a non-estate tenancy the parties will nonetheless be able to exercise rights and remedies associated only with leasehold estates, such as the remedy of distress.[191] More fundamentally, it is difficult in the light of the finding that there was a tenancy in *Bruton* (albeit not a leasehold estate) to see when a tenancy by estoppel will now arise. The factual background in *Bruton* provides the classic situation in which a tenancy by estoppel would previously had been found, that is where a grantor without an estate then purports to grant a lease.

3.3 Categorising a Relationship

3.3.1 Putting a Label on the Relationship

The discussion above sets out not only the ways in which occupation of land can be categorised but also the principles that are used to distinguish the differing situations. There are three key questions that need to be asked: is there contractual intention, is there exclusive possession, and is there a certain term? This is illustrated in Figure 3.1.

Only if the answer to all three questions is yes can there be a leasehold estate. Since *Bruton* it has been recognised that it is possible for there to be a non-estate lease[192] if the landlord does not itself own an estate in the land but grants exclusive possession to the tenant. If only the certain term is missing there can be a tenancy at will. If there is no contract, there can be no tenancy.

These questions must be answered by reference to the intention of the parties. If there is

---

[185] *Cuthbertson v Irving* (1859) 4 H & N 742.
[186] *Rawlin's Case* (1587) Jenk 254.
[187] [2000] 1 AC 406 (HL).
[188] [1998] QB 834 (CA).
[189] This does, of course, depend upon accepting that exclusive possession is a relative concept (see discussion above at 3.1.3).
[190] *Bruton v London and Quadrant Housing* Trust [2000] 1 AC 406 (HL) 416
[191] A landlord under a tenancy by estoppel is able to distrain for rent: *Gouldsworth v Knights* (1843) 11 M & W 337. Distress is soon to be abolished: see ch 16.
[192] A contractual lease?

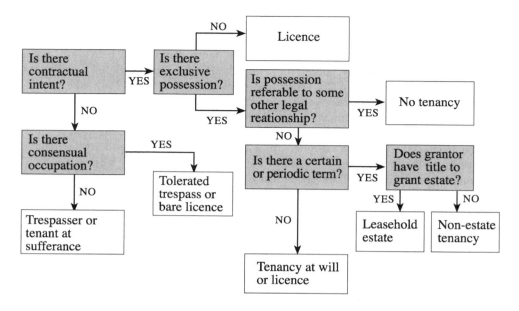

Figure 3.1: Key Questions in Categorising Single Occupancy

a written agreement, then the courts will look to this. In *Street v Mountford* the House of Lords held that where there is a written agreement between the owner and occupier which confers exclusive possession at a rent for a term, the parties cannot chose to call this a licence.[193] Mr Street granted Mrs Mountford the right to occupy rooms for a weekly rent, subject to termination by written notice. The terms were set out in a written agreement which was called a licence. It was conceded that Mrs Mountford had exclusive possession. The House of Lords held that this agreement was a tenancy: the parties were not free to attach their own label to the agreement. As Lord Templeman said:

> [If] the agreement satisfied all the requirements of a tenancy, then the agreement produced a tenancy and the parties cannot alter the effect of the agreement by insisting that they only created a licence.[194]

If the agreement is incomplete, or nothing much has been said, then the courts will have to fill in the gaps and answer the questions by gleaning what the intentions were from the wider circumstances.

There are two further questions that may need to be asked in order to put the correct label on the relationship. The first relates to cases involving multiple occupation as it appears that in order for there to be a lease to joint occupiers the 'four unities' required for co-ownership of land in the form of a joint tenancy must be satisfied (unity of time, title, interest and possession).[195] The second arises if there is a written agreement but this does

---

[193] [1985] 1 AC 809 (HL).
[194] [1985] 1 AC 809 (HL) 819.
[195] See: C Harpum (ed), *Megarry & Wade, The Law of Real Property* 6th edn (London, Sweet & Maxwell, 2000) 476–80.

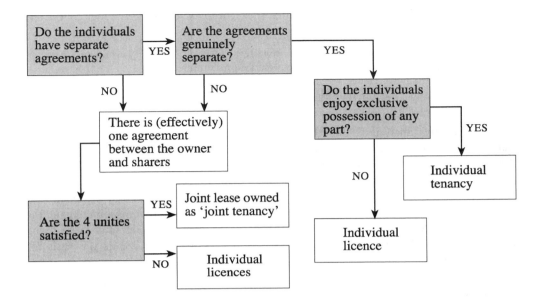

Figure 3.2: Multiple Occupation: Licences, Tenancies or Joint Tenancy?

not reflect the true relationship of the parties. The job of the courts is then to find the true agreement. These issues are often intertwined, as illustrated in Figure 3.2.

3.3.2 Multiple Occupation

In *Street v Mountford* there was only one occupier and the issue was the simple one of whether she was a licensee or a tenant. Lord Templeman did not address the difficulties that can arise in cases involving multiple occupation, perhaps a couple in a long term relationship, or a group of individuals, such as students, living together.

Where a property is occupied by more than one person the first question that must be asked is whether the arrangement is one made with a series of individuals, or if the arrangement is made to the occupiers as a collective. If it is a series of individual agreements, there are two ways that this can be analysed. First, if each individual has been given the right to exclusive possession of a part, for example their own room, then there will be individual leases.[196] Alternatively, the individuals may have only licences, with no right to exclusive possession. In the first of the co-joined appeals in *AG Securities v Vaughan* a flat had been 'let' to four occupiers who moved in at different times, paid different rents, and signed separate licence agreements denying exclusive possession.[197] As one left, the owner would find a replacement (with the agreement of the others). In practice, the occupiers also agreed amongst themselves who would have which room. The House of Lords held that

---

196 Even if they share facilities this can be an assured tenancy: Housing Act 1988 s 3.
197 *AG Securities v Vaughan; Antoniades v Villiers* [1990] 1 AC 417 (HL).

they were licensees; they had not been granted the right to exclude others, either collectively or individually. Lord Oliver puts this most clearly:

> None of them has individually nor have they collectively the right or power lawfully to exclude a further nominee of the licensor within the prescribed maximum ...
>
> The landlord is not excluded for he continues to enjoy the premises through his invitees, even though he may for the time being have precluded himself by contract with each from withdrawing the invitation.[198]

The alternative analysis is that there is one agreement with the collective group of sharers, in which case there will be a lease if the group has been granted exclusive possession of the property and they will own the lease as 'joint tenants'.[199] In accordance with land law principles there will be 'joint and several liability' which means that each member of the group will be liable, individually, for the whole of the obligations imposed by the tenancy.[200] The 'right of survivorship' will also apply so that on the death of one joint tenant the survivor takes over the whole interest in the property. This especially suits those living together on a long-term basis and for this reason it is recommended as the basis for allocation by housing authorities to such people:

> Where household members have long term commitments to the home, for example, when adults share accommodation as partners (including same sex partners), friends or unpaid live-in carers, housing authorities should normally grant a joint tenancy.[201]

There is, however, a further complication that can arise, particularly if there is intended to be a letting to a group as whole but it is entered into by a series of separate agreements.[202] The legal complication stems from the fact that it has been held that in order for there to be a joint lease the 'four unities' must be satisfied (unity of time, title, interest and possession).[203] It is not clear why, but the House of Lords assumed that this was required in *AG Securities v Vaughan*.[204] Similarly in *Mikeover Ltd v Brady* Slade LJ proceeds on this assumption.[205] The requirement to satisfy the 'four unities' has practical consequences. In *Mikeover v Brady* a couple signed two separate licence agreements, each containing an obligation to pay one half of the total rent for the flat.[206] Slade LJ accepted that there was 'a right of joint exclusive occupation of the property'.[207] Nonetheless, there was no lease simply because the absence of a joint monetary obligation meant that there could be no unity of

---

[198] *AG Securities v Vaughan; Antoniades v Villiers* [1990] 1 AC 417 (HL) 471.

[199] That is, a joint tenancy in the sense of being one of the two possible forms of co-ownership of land. It is confusing to use the word 'tenancy': in this context it is being used to represent co-ownership, and is nothing to do with leases. Might this ambiguity in the language explain some of the difficulties that have arisen in this area whereby it is said that a 'joint tenancy' [co-ownership] is needed for there to be a co-owned lease?

[200] If one of the joint tenants is called upon to pay the whole rent, he will have the right to claim reimbursement from his co-owners: *Chalmers, Guthrie and Co v Guthrie* (1923) LTJ 382.

[201] ODPM, 'Revision of the Code of Guidance on the Allocation of Accommodation' (November 2002) para 3.7.

[202] There may be a problem if these separate agreements have been used to disguise a collective agreement; this is discussed below under 'the pretence issue'.

[203] See n 195.

[204] [1990] 1 AC 417 (HL): see, for example, Lord Jauncey at 474.

[205] [1989] 3 All ER 618 (CA) 625. See also S Bright, 'Street v Mountford Revisited' in S Bright (ed), *Landlord and Tenant Law. Past, Present and Future* (Oxford, Hart, 2006).

[206] [1989] 3 All ER 618 (CA).

[207] [1989] 3 All ER 618 (CA) 625. He presumably meant exclusive possession.

interest.[208] This meant that the owner could evict the remaining occupier, as without a lease he did not have security of tenure.

There is another form of co-ownership of land apart from the joint tenancy, that is the tenancy in common. For this only unity of possession is required. The possibility that there might be a lease held as a tenancy in common was not considered in the cases discussed above, but provided that the sharers have the collective right to exclude others it could be argued that they co-own a lease as tenants in common. The downside of this analysis is that because the law imposes a trust of land in all cases of co-ownership they would in any event have to be treated as joint tenants, and thus jointly and severally liable, at law.[209] It would, however, at least enable the sharers to be treated as tenants.

3.3.3 The 'Pretence' Issue

In several cases the owner of property has tried to avoid the impact of statutory control by drafting agreements in such a way that the indicia of a tenancy are absent. There were a number of cases leading up to *Street v Mountford*[210] in which the owner did this by calling the agreement a licence. In *Somma v Hazelhurst*, for example, a single room with two beds was let to an unmarried couple by two separate agreements, which were described as licences.[211] The Court of Appeal looked to the fact that there were separate obligations in separate agreements and held that there was not a joint interest. In addition the owner had reserved the right to use the room in common with the couple and so they did not enjoy exclusive possession. They therefore had personal licences and not leases. The effect of this, and other cases was that owners could effectively opt out of statutory control by entering into licences rather than leases, even if the occupiers were in practice enjoying the substantive rights of a tenant.

In *Street v Mountford* the owner conceded that exclusive possession had been granted to Mrs Mountford and so the issue was simply one of attaching the wrong label to the relationship. Lord Templeman's remarks ranged much more widely, however, and have enabled later courts to tackle agreements which fail to reflect the reality of the relationship:

> Although the Rent Acts must not be allowed to alter or influence the construction of an agreement, the court should, in my opinion, be astute to detect and frustrate sham devices and artificial transactions whose only object is to disguise the grant of a tenancy and to evade the Rents Acts.[212]

Lord Templeman described the agreements in *Somma v Hazelhurst* as shams and held that

---

[208] Views differ as to whether unity of interest does require a joint monetary obligation. The requirement is supported by Sparkes and Thompson: P Sparkes, 'Co-Tenants, Joint Tenants and Tenants in Common' (1989) 18 *Anglo-American Law Review* 151, 152–3; MP Thompson, *Co-ownership* (London, Sweet & Maxwell, 1988) 63. Smith questions it: RJ Smith, *Property Law* 5th edn (Harlow, Longman, 2005) 369.

[209] There is no doubt that many long residential leases are jointly owned by tenants in common. Again, because of the statutory imposition of a trust by the Law of Property Act 1925 s 34, they will own the legal title as joint tenants on trusts for themselves in equity as tenants in common.

[210] [1985] 1 AC 809 (HL).

[211] [1978] 1 WLR 1014 (CA).

[212] [1985] 1 AC 809 (HL) 825.

the case had been wrongly decided. Following cases have developed this idea. In *AG Securities v Vaughan* Lord Templeman continued:

> Parties to an agreement cannot contract out of the Rent Acts; if they were able to do so the Acts would be a dead letter because in a state of housing shortage a person seeking residential accommodation may agree to anything to obtain shelter ... Since parties to an agreement cannot contract out of the Rent Acts, a document expressed in the language of a licence must nevertheless be examined and construed by the court in order to decide whether the rights and obligations enjoyed and imposed create a licence or a tenancy.[213]

There are a number of different ways in which 'devices' used to disguise the reality of the situation have been reviewed judicially: through the doctrines of 'sham', 'pretence', the artificial device doctrine developed in tax avoidance cases, statutory construction, and unlawful contracting out.[214] It is important to understand the correct limits of judicial intervention; parties are free to structure their affairs in a manner that avoids statutory control. Motive is irrelevant. If, however, the outward agreement does not represent the true agreement of the parties the courts will first have to discover the genuinely intended rights and obligations before considering the question of lease or licence. The agreement will not be genuine if the parties had no intention of honouring the rights and obligations set out in it. Unless the parties admit that the document was a 'pretence' (which is very unlikely) the courts will therefore have to look to the wider context to decide if the agreement is genuine or not. The facts that they look to include the pre-existing relationship between the occupiers, the negotiations, the fact that no attempt has been made to exercise the right[215] and the physical layout and size of the accommodation. There are several examples in the cases of non-genuine 'licences'.

In *Aslan v Murphy* there was a basement room measuring 4'3" by 12'6" occupied under an agreement which provided:

> ... the licensor is not willing to grant the licensee exclusive possession of any part of the room ... [and] the licensee is anxious to secure the use of the room notwithstanding that such use be in common with the licensor and such other licensees or invitees as the licensor may permit from time to time to use the said room.[216]

In addition, the agreement denied access to the room for 90 minutes daily. Lord Donaldson MR described these provisions as 'wholly unrealistic' and 'clearly pretences' with the result that the occupier had a lease. In *Antoniades v Villiers* a flat was rented to an unmarried couple by two identical 'licence' agreements which stated that the occupier may be required to share with someone of the landlord's choosing, and required the occupier to pay only a share of the rent.[217] The flat was totally unsuitable for two persons to live in unless they were 'a couple'.

---

[213] *AG Securities v Vaughan; Antoniades v Villiers* [1990] 1 AC 417 (HL) 458.

[214] For a full discussion of these see S Bright, 'Avoiding Tenancy Legislation: Sham and Contracting Out Revisited' (2002) 62 *CLJ* 146. See also: B McFarlane and E Simpson 'Tackling Avoidance' in J Getzler (ed), *Rationalising Property, Equity and Trusts* (London, LexisNexis UK, 2003) 135.

[215] '...though subsequent conduct is irrelevant as an aid to construction, it is certainly admissible as evidence on the question of whether the documents were or were not genuine documents giving effect to the parties' true intentions': *AG Securities v Vaughan; Antoniades v Villiers* [1990] 1 AC 417 (HL) 469.

[216] *Aslan v Murphy (Nos 1 and 2)* [1990] 1 WLR 766 (CA).

[217] *AG Securities v Vaughan; Antoniades v Villiers* [1990] 1 AC 417 (HL).

The House of Lords held that the sharing clause was a pretence and could be disregarded. In addition, there was a problem with the 'four unities' as the separate obligations to pay rent would prevent there being unity of interest. Again, the House of Lords took the view that it was unrealistic to see these as separate agreements. Instead they should be viewed as 'interdependent', and the problem with the four unities would then disappear. In the words of Lord Oliver:

> There is an air of total unreality about these documents read as separate and individual licences in the light of the circumstance that the appellants were together seeking a flat as a quasi-matrimonial home.[218]

Notwithstanding the fact that the agreements were called licences and denied exclusive possession, the House of Lords held that there was a joint tenancy.

The approach adopted by the courts to deal with these 'dressing up' cases throws up difficult issues, both doctrinally and practically. In *Street v Mountford* the House of Lords respected the contractual agreement reached but said that the parties could not attach their own label.[219] In the 'pretence' cases the courts have to tread carefully to ensure that they do not end up re-writing the parties' agreement. It is only legitimate to override the recorded agreement where the courts can be confident that this does not reflect the true agreement reached. There are also practical difficulties. How can a court be sure that the intention expressed in the agreement is not the true intention? Just because a provision has not been operated (yet) does not mean that it must be non-genuine. In *Mikeover Ltd v Brady* (where a couple had signed two separate licence agreements, each containing an obligation to pay one half of the total rent for the flat) the owner refused to accept the whole rent from the man after the woman had left.[220] In the light of this, it could hardly be said that it was a pretence to say that the obligations to pay were indeed separate. The absence of unity of interest meant, therefore, that the remaining occupier was indeed only a licensee. There was no material difference between *Antoniades v Villiers*[221] and *Mikeover v Brady*[222] except for the fact that one of the occupiers had later left in *Mikeover v Brady* and the landlord did not make the remaining occupier pay the entire rent. In *Antoniades v Villiers* this provision was never put to the test, so although it looked artificial (as it did in *Mikeover v Brady*) it may have been a genuine provision that never had to be called on. There is a risk that the courts could effectively re-write the parties' bargain. It is important, therefore, that the 'pretence' doctrine is restrictively used.

There is an interesting postscript to the *Antoniades v Villiers* story. The landlord applied to the European Commission on Human Rights, alleging that the House of Lords' ruling violated the right to peaceful enjoyment of possessions protected by Article 1 of the First Protocol to the European Convention for the Protection of Human Rights and Fundamental Freedoms (ECHR)(for a discussion of human rights law see chapter 10).[223] The application reveals that the couple occupying the flat, having as result of the judgment become Rent Act

---

[218] *AG Securities v Vaughan; Antoniades v Villiers* [1990] 1 AC 417 (HL) 467.
[219] [1985] 1 AC 809 (HL).
[220] [1989] 3 All ER 618 (CA).
[221] *AG Securities v Vaughan; Antoniades v Villiers* [1990] 1 AC 417 (HL).
[222] *Mikeover Ltd v Brady* [1989] 3 All ER 618 (CA).
[223] *Antoniades v United Kingdom* (App No 15434/89) ECHR 15 February 1990.

protected tenants, registered 'fair rents' (see chapter 15). Not only was the landlord unable to recover possession but his income was also reduced. Whereas the contractually agreed licence fee was £87 per month for each of the occupants (including rates, making £174 in total), the registered rent for the flat was £90 per month plus rates of £45 a month (£135 in total). The Commission held the complaint inadmissible: even if the judgment did amount to a 'control of the use of property' within Article 1 of the First Protocol (which the Commission did not decide), the rent legislation pursued a legitimate aim of social policy and the control was proportionate to this aim.

The whole pretence debate has been a judicial response to the attempts of landlords to avoid statutory protection. Yet, at the same time as the ability of courts to see beyond the form of words used to the genuine substance of the agreement was being affirmed, policy was moving on. In the residential sector there is now little need for landlords to dress up tenancies to look like licences; as will be seen in chapter 6, landlords can now easily rent out properties on leases without conferring security of tenure.

4

ENTERING THE TENANCY: ALLOCATION, FORMALITIES AND CONTENT

4.1	Allocation and choice
4.2	Formalities on entering into the landlord and tenant relationship
4.3	The effect of non-observance of the formality requirements
4.4	Vitiating factors and leases
4.5	Construction and rectification
4.6	Providing information to tenants
4.7	The structure of leases
4.8	Fairness and contract terms
4.9	The structure of commercial leases
4.10	The structure of residential leases
4.11	The variation of lease terms

4.1 Allocation and Choice

4.1.1 Selecting a Tenant

Landlords allocate accommodation by reference to three criteria: commercial matters, personal factors and formal/mechanical rules. It is only in the social sector, where there is a need to ensure that housing goes to those in greatest need, that allocation is heavily circumscribed by statute and regulatory requirements.[1] Apart from legislation to prevent unlawful discrimination (considered below) and the special rules that apply to social landlords, there are no formal obligations when allocating a lease. For all landlords, the ability of the prospective tenant to pay rent and to behave responsibly in the property will be important issues. Other factors will also come into play. In a shopping mall development, for example, tenant mix will be important to ensure that there is a variety of retailers to attract shoppers. Private landlords may target particular markets (such as the student market) or wish to avoid letting to certain groups (such as those in receipt of housing benefit). Registered Social Landlords (RSLs) may, in addition to any formal rules applying, be bound by provisions laid

---

[1] See ch 6.

down in their foundation instrument; many housing associations target particular groups, such as providing for the elderly or recently released prisoners.

Various statutory schemes make it unlawful for landlords (public and private) and agents to discriminate in the terms on which premises are offered or to refuse to let to a member of certain groups. Exception is usually made for resident landlords sharing premises that are not big enough for multiple households.[2] The Sex Discrimination Act 1975 prohibits discrimination on the grounds of sex.[3] The Disability Discrimination Act 1995 prohibits discrimination on the grounds of disability.[4] The Race Relations Act 1976 prohibits discrimination on the basis of race, and, following later amendments, on the grounds of ethnicity and national origins.[5] The Equality Act 2006 makes it unlawful to discriminate in the letting of premises on the basis of religion or belief.[6] While these various discrimination laws apply to all landlords, additional duties are placed on public authorities[7] to promote equality between different racial groups,[8] to promote equality of opportunity for disabled persons,[9] and to promote equality between men and women.[10]

In the case of private sector tenancies and commercial lettings, it is usual for a landlord to take up references on prospective tenants. In addition, the landlord may require a deposit to be provided, and seek guarantors.[11] In the US and Australia residential tenancy databases are frequently used to screen potential tenants. The information on the database is compiled from a variety of sources giving information about the reliability of the prospective tenant (such as court records and landlord complaints). These databases are, however, prone to error and abuse,[12] and a tenant who appears on one is, in effect, blacklisted.[13] In addition to recording quite legitimate concerns, such as past eviction for unpaid rent, they can list tenants for having brought litigation against the landlord (for instance, complaining about serious disrepair) or simply for making a late rent payment. Given the injustice that the databases can cause and the difficulty that they create for tenants in finding properties, a number of jurisdictions have legislated to regulate their use.[14]

---

[2] For example, the Equality Act 2006 s 48(1) provides that it is not unlawful to discriminate if the landlord or a near relative lives in the same premises and shares facilities such as a bathroom or kitchen.

[3] Ss 1, 2 and 30–32.

[4] Ss 22–24.

[5] Ss 1, 3 and 21(1); Race Relations Act (Amendments) Regulations 2003 SI 2003/1626.

[6] S 47.

[7] Although RSLs are not directly bound by this, they are brought within the scheme through regulation by the Housing Corporation.

[8] Race Relations Act 1976 s 71(1).

[9] Disability Discrimination Act 1995 s 49A.

[10] Sex Discrimination Act 1975 s 76A.

[11] See ch 16.

[12] R Kleysteuber, 'Tenant Screening Thirty Years Later: A Statutory Proposal To Protect Public Records' (2007) 116 *Yale LJ* 1344.

[13] M Neave, 'Recent Developments in Australian Residential Tenancies Laws' in S Bright (ed), *Landlord and Tenant Law. Past, Present and Future* (Oxford, Hart, 2006) 252–4.

[14] For Australian legislation, see M Neave, 'Recent Developments in Australian Residential Tenancies Laws' in S Bright (ed), *Landlord and Tenant Law. Past, Present and Future* (Oxford, Hart, 2006) 252–4; for different approaches in the US, see R Kleysteuber, 'Tenant Screening Thirty Years Later: A Statutory Proposal To Protect Public Records' (2007) 116 *Yale LJ* 1344, 1364–72.

4.1.2 Choosing a Property

The tenant is most likely to choose a property because of the characteristics of the property itself; availability, affordability, location, the standard of accommodation and service provision, and, increasingly in the case of major commercial tenants, the property's 'green' credentials.

Within the residential sector, the shortage of public sector and housing association accommodation means that many potential occupants are excluded from this sector and are forced into the lower end of the private residential sector (or onto the streets). For superior quality housing, the only option is the private sector. Choice-based letting is now being introduced in the social sector,[15] but until recently the person seeking social housing had no effective choice and simply had to accept whatever was offered, or risk getting nothing at all. Even under choice-based letting choice is still extremely limited. Other things being equal (such as price, location and quality), if there is real choice a tenant may make select between landlords on the basis of their reputation for fair treatment of tenants and quality of housing management services. Apart from the rent and length of tenancy being offered, the tenancy terms are unlikely to be taken into account.

In the commercial sector property related considerations tend to dominate the decision of which premises to take. Some commercial tenants will also take a keen interest in the terms of the lease being offered as these will impact upon the tenant's business and the ability to dispose of the lease during its life.[16] Although commercial landlords have historically tended rather complacently to offer leases on a 'take it or leave it' basis a number are now waking up to the commercial benefits of offering flexible leasing with different levels of servicing and seeing tenants as 'customers'(see 4.9.5 below).

4.2 Formalities on Entering into the Landlord and Tenant Relationship

4.2.1 To Create a Legal Lease

In order for there to be a legal lease the correct formalities must be used. This may, for example, require the lease to be granted by deed and to be registered at the Land Registry. There may be additional registration steps that can (or must) be taken in order to protect the priority of a lease in the event of a sale of the reversion but these do not affect the validity of the lease itself.[17] In the case of certain short leases it is possible to have a legal lease without any formalities being used (see below).

An outline of the various formality requirements is given in Table 4.1.

---

[15] See ch 6.

[16] Although a surprising number of commercial occupiers, particularly small business tenants, take no interest in the details of the lease: see 4.9.5 and ch 8.

[17] For details, the reader should refer to a land law text. In outline, a lease between 3 and 7 years can be protected by notice (Land Registration Act 2002 ss 32, 33). The grant of an easement to the tenant (such as a right of access) must be registered whatever the length of the lease in order to take effect at law: Land Registration Act 2002 s 27(1), (2)(d).

Table 4.1: Formalities and Registration Requirements for all Leases

Type of Lease	Formalities required
Lease for more than 7 years	Registration + Deed
Lease for 3 – 7 years	(Optional notice registration) + Deed
Lease for no more than 3 years taking effect in possession at market rent	No formalities
Reversionary leases taking effect in possession more than 3 months after grant	Registration + Deed
Discontinuous lease	Registration (see fn 28) + Deed[a]

[a]A discontinuous lease is unlikely to take effect in possession. Even if it does it is unlikely to come within the exemption as it will usually be granted for a premium.

4.2.1.1 When a Deed is Needed

The starting point is section 52 of the Law of Property Act 1925 which states that a deed is required in order to create a legal estate (including a lease). If no deed is used the conveyance 'is void for the purpose of ... creating a legal estate'. This then is the basic position, but there is an exception for certain short leases in section 54(2) of the Law of Property Act 1925. This provides that no formality is required for a lease which takes

> ... effect in possession for a term not exceeding three years ... at the best rent which can be reasonably obtained without taking a fine.

There are, therefore, three conditions that must be satisfied in order for the exception to apply:

(a)   the term must not exceed three years;
(b)   it must 'take effect in possession';
(c)   and it must be 'at the best rent which can be reasonably obtained without taking a fine'.

Each of these conditions merits further explanation.

Not exceed three years

A periodic tenancy, such as a weekly or monthly tenancy, counts as a lease not exceeding three years even though it may, in practice, continue for more than three years.[18] A lease which is initially for not more than three years will also be regarded as within section 54(2), even if it contains an option to renew beyond that period.[19] On the other hand, a lease for more than three years which can be determined earlier is not within the exception and will need to be created by deed.[20]

---

[18] *In re Knight, ex p Voisey* (1882) 21 Ch D 442.
[19] *Hand v Hall* (1877) 2 Ex D 355.
[20] *Kushner v Law Society* [1952] 1 KB 264 (Divisional Ct) 274.

Take effect in possession

The phrase 'in possession' is not the same as 'in occupation': it is possible to be 'in possession' without occupying the property. What is required is that the tenant has the present right to possession of the property, which can include the right to receive rents from it.[21] Reversionary leases, which take effect at some time in the future (even if this time is very soon), are not within this exception as they are not 'in possession'. In *Long v Tower Hamlets LBC* the commencement was three weeks away: this was held not to be in possession.[22] In *Northcote Laundry Ltd v Frederick Donelly Ltd* a six day interlude between the grant and the term commencement was held to make it a reversionary lease.[23] There is no logical cut off: unless the lease takes effect immediately in possession (presumably, on the same day) it must be made by deed if it is to be a legal estate.

At the best rent

Notwithstanding the wording of section 54(2), it is not necessary for the tenant to be paying *the best possible* rent. The exception covers leases for which the tenant is paying a rack rent and which have not been purchased by a capital premium.

The effect of these provisions is that any lease for more than three years must be created by deed in order to create a legal estate, whereas leases for three years or less (taking effect in possession at the best rent) can be created orally, by writing, or by deed.

In practice, very many short leases are entered into without a deed. In some cases there may be no formalities at all, as where an occupier simply moves into possession with the landlord's consent and starts paying rent. In this case, the exception applies because possession is immediate and there is likely to be a periodic tenancy or (if the parties intend only a temporary arrangement that can come to an end at any time) a tenancy at will.[24] But in many cases there will be a written agreement (which is not a deed) to take effect in the future, as is common with student agreements for housing which may be signed in March to take effect in September. In this case the exception will not apply and there will not be a legal lease. (The effect of such agreements is considered below but, in summary, the tenant will usually have an equitable lease.) A good case can be made for arguing that a written agreement should suffice for formalities purposes if the tenancy takes effect within a specified period, say six months. To require a deed seems an unnecessary formality.

Under the Law Commission's reform proposals for renting homes the contract is an essential plank of the consumer approach advocated; all agreements must be put in writing as this will set out the parties' respective rights and obligations and also provide evidence of the agreement.[25] Under the proposals it will not be necessary to have a deed or for the agreement itself to be in writing: it will be sufficient if a written statement is provided to the occupier within two weeks from the date that the occupier was entitled to take occupation. In order for the agreement to be a legal lease it will still need to comply with the requirements of section 52 the Law of Property Act 1925 discussed above.

---

[21] Law of Property Act 1925 s 205(xix).

[22] [1998] Ch 197 (Ch). Discussed at S Bright, 'Beware the informal lease: the (very) narrow scope of s 54(2) Law of Property Act 1925' [1998] *Conv* 229, also discussing the historic evolution of s 54(2).

[23] [1968] 1 WLR 562 (CA).

[24] See ch 3.

[25] Law Commission, 'Renting Homes: The Final Report. Volume 1: Report' (Law Com No 297, 2006) paras 3.34–3.35.

4.2.1.2 Registration Requirements

Under the Land Registration Act 2002, it is also necessary to register certain leases; failure to do so means that the transaction is ineffective at law.[26] Those leases requiring registration are: leases of more than seven years,[27] reversionary leases taking effect more than three months from the date of the grant; leases granted under the 'right to buy' provisions, and discontinuous leases (such as time share leases).[28]

The Land Registration Act 2002 reduced the term of a lease triggering compulsory registration from 21 to 7 years. This has dramatically increased the number of applications for registration,[29] and in an attempt to speed up the registration process, it is now necessary for an application for a lease granted out of registered land to be in the form of a 'prescribed clauses lease'.[30] In effect this requires a cover sheet to be produced in a land registry format that sets out the key terms of the agreement, including not only things such as the details of the parties and property but also details of any restrictive covenants or easements in the lease.[31]

After the lease has been formally completed, it may also be necessary to pay stamp duty land tax. The details on this are complicated[32] but what is especially relevant in terms of understanding the structure of leases is that the tax is calculated by reference to the premium paid, and also the rent passing under the lease throughout its life. This means that the length of the lease will affect the stamp duty land tax payable, and therefore fiscal considerations may be part of the context that explain the particular form that a lease takes.

4.2.2 Agreements for Lease

With long term leases, both commercial and residential, the lease is often the product of negotiations. The usual practice is for the landlord's solicitor to produce the first draft of the lease, which will then be amended by the tenant's solicitor, and so on until agreed upon. Once the parties have agreed upon the terms they may either proceed directly to the execution of the lease itself, or enter into a binding agreement to enter into a lease. Agreements for lease will be used, inter alia, when the tenant is undertaking a legal commitment to take a lease before the property is completed (in many major commercial developments such pre-lets are essential to the funding process).

In order to be an enforceable contract, the agreement must comply with all the usual requirements of contract law (such as offer, acceptance, and consideration), and also with

---

[26] Land Registration Act 2002 ss 7, 27.

[27] This period may be reduced in the future, most probably to three years.

[28] Land Registration Act 2002 ss 4, 27. If granted out of an unregistered estate a discontinuous lease needs registering only if the length of the separate periods is more than seven years.

[29] In 2005 the Land Registry stated that it received over 200,000 leasehold applications per year, a number likely to rise: Land Registry, 'Report on consultation July 2005: Presentation of prescribed information in registrable leases' (July 2005).

[30] Land Registration Rules 2003 r 58A. The initial proposal had been for a prescribed form of lease but this met with substantial opposition.

[31] This provides the essential information for registration which otherwise could be scattered throughout the lease.

[32] For a brief guide, see C Edwards and P Krendel, *Institutional Leases in the 21st Century* (London, EG Books, 2007) 122–27.

section 2 of the Law of Property (Miscellaneous Provisions) Act 1989. Section 2 requires that all of the terms of a contract to lease must be contained in a single signed written document (or in two documents that are exchanged):

Section 2

(1) A contract for the sale or other disposition of an interest in land can only be made in writing and only by incorporating all the terms which the parties have expressly agreed in one document or, where contracts are exchanged, in each.

(2) The terms may be incorporated in a document either by being set out in it or by reference to some other document.

(3) The document incorporating the terms or, where contracts are exchanged, one of the documents incorporating them (but not necessarily the same one) must be signed by or on behalf of each party to the contract.

Short leases (as referred to in section 54(2) of the Law of Property Act 1925) are exempted from these formalities requirements. This section applies to contracts entered into after 27 September 1989. For leases entered into before that date the relevant provision was section 40 of the Law of Property Act 1925.[33]

Often the agreement for lease is not being entered into in isolation. So, for example, in *BHP Petroleum Great Britain Ltd v Chesterfield Properties Ltd* a developer agreed to refurbish a substantial office building and to grant a 20 year lease of the greater part of the building to the tenant.[34] In other situations, an agreement for lease may form part of a larger commercial transaction, such as a company takeover, and may therefore be simply one aspect of a complex web of agreements. Great care must be taken to ensure that the resulting agreement still complies with the section 2 requirement for all the terms which the parties have agreed upon to be incorporated into one document. Where the parties do enter into an agreement for lease before the lease itself is completed, it is usual for the agreed form of lease to be annexed to the agreement so that there can be no dispute over the agreed terms of the lease.

If there is an enforceable agreement for lease and one party refuses to complete it, an action for breach can be brought. This could be either an action for damages or, more usefully, an action for specific performance. Specific performance is a discretionary remedy and will not be granted where, for example, the party seeking enforcement has behaved badly or where enforcement would cause intolerable hardship. If the agreement that is being enforced failed to specify the terms of the lease, the court will imply into the agreement a term that the lease will include the 'usual covenants and provisos'. What these are will be decided by reference to precedents, practice, type of property, the property location and its intended use. The usual covenants will include a covenant to pay rent, to pay rates and taxes, to keep and deliver up in repair, to allow the lessor to enter and view the state of repair, a covenant by the landlord for quiet enjoyment,[35] and a proviso for re-entry on non-payment of rent.[36] In addition, covenants that are in ordinary use for that kind of property, length of

---

[33] By s 40, oral contracts were valid but were unenforceable in proceedings in the absence of a written memorandum or a sufficient act of part performance.

[34] [2001] EWCA Civ 1797.

[35] *Hampshire v Wickens* (1878) 7 Ch D 555.

[36] *Hodgkinson v Crowe* (1875) 10 Ch App 622, 626.

lease, etc, may also be included as 'usual covenants'.[37] As practice changes, so may the usual covenants change.[38]

4.2.3 Estoppel

It may also be possible for a lease to arise notwithstanding the absence of the necessary formalities if an estoppel can be made out. Proprietary estoppel is to do with protecting reliance when one party has relied on assurances made by the other. The contexts in which this could arise with leases are where the prospective landlord has encouraged the prospective tenant to act to his detriment on the assurance that a lease would be granted, or where there is an agreement for lease in principle that has not yet been reduced to the correct formalities but which the prospective landlord says is safe for the prospective tenant to reply on. Estoppel then protects the prospective tenant's reasonable reliance. So, for example, in *Lloyd v Dugdale* B had spent considerable sums of money in reliance on A's assurance of a lease and it was a proportionate response to A's assurance and B's reliance to recognise that B had a lease on the agreed terms.[39]

4.3 The Effect of Non-observance of the Formality Requirements

This section is concerned with situations in which the parties have concluded any negotiations but have failed to record them in the correct form. There are two basic situations: where the parties have entered into an agreement to grant a lease in the future but no formal lease has yet been granted (that is, a further future document is intended), or where the parties have entered into a lease but used the wrong form. The well known case of *Walsh v Lonsdale* involved the former: the landlord had agreed to grant a lease of a mill for seven years and the tenant was let into possession without a formal lease being executed.[40] The case of *Martin v Smith* is an illustration of the latter: the parties entered into an agreement for a seven year lease but this was not by deed.[41] Although it might be argued that there is a distinction between these cases, the courts have treated cases in the latter group (failed legal leases) in the same manner as agreements for lease.[42]

   If the parties are still negotiating but the 'landlord' has allowed the 'tenant' to move in or spend money in reliance on the fact that a lease will be granted this will give rise either to an estoppel (see 4.2.3 above) or, once possession is taken, an implied periodic tenancy or tenancy at will (see chapter 3).

---

[37] *Flexman v Corbett* [1930] 1 Ch 672 (Ch); *Chester v Buckingham Travel Ltd* [1981] 1 WLR 96 (Ch).
[38] *Hampshire v Wickens* (1878) 7 Ch D 555, 561.
[39] [2002] 2 P & CR 13 (CA). In *JT Developments v Quinn* (1991) 62 P & CR 33 (CA) the landlord was bound to grant a renewed tenancy to the tenant on the basis of assurances made and relied upon. In *Habermann v Koehler* [2000] EGCS 125 (CA) estoppel gave rise to a lease for life at a peppercorn rent. In *Liverpool CC v Walton Group plc* [2002] 1 EGLR 149 (Ch) an agreement for a 999 year lease was held enforceable through estoppel. For further discussion, see S Bright and B McFarlane, 'Proprietary Estoppel and Property Rights' (2005) 64 *CLJ* 449.
[40] (1882) 21 Ch D 9.
[41] (1874) LR 9 Exch 50.
[42] *Parker v Taswell* (1858) 2 De G & J 559; *Industrial Properties (Barton Hill) v AEI* [1978] QB 580 (CA) 610.

If the parties fail to comply with the formality requirements, the agreed lease will not take effect as a legal estate in the agreed form. This does not mean, however, that it has no consequence: if possession is taken, this may generate an implied tenancy, and if there is an enforceable agreement, this may take effect as an equitable lease.

4.3.1 Tenancy Implied from Possession

When the tenant moves into occupation an implied tenancy will arise. If no rent is paid, this will take effect as a tenancy at will.[43] If the tenant starts paying rent, this may turn the tenancy at will into a periodic tenancy at law. Such a periodic tenancy will incorporate all of the terms of the abortive legal lease, so far as compatible with a periodic tenancy.[44]

4.3.2 Equitable Leases: Enforcing the Agreement for Lease

In equity, the effect of an informal lease may be much wider if there is an agreement for lease which is capable of specific performance. As equity looks on that as done which ought to be done, the tenant is regarded as having an equitable lease on the same terms as those in the 'abortive' legal lease. In *Parker v Taswell* the parties entered into a written agreement for renewal of a tenancy for a term of ten years, but there was no deed.[45] Although this meant that the lease was void at law, Lord Chelmsford LC said:

> … it would be too strong to say that because it is void at law as a lease, it cannot be used as an agreement enforceable in equity, the intention of the parties having been that there should be a lease, and the aid of equity being invoked only to carry that intention into effect.[46]

Nor did the fact that there was uncertainty in the terms of the agreement prevent specific performance, especially as the uncertainty related to 'subordinate matters' and the agreement had been partly executed by possession being taken under it: 'in such a case the Court will strain its power to enforce a complete performance'.[47] Further, although there were arguments that the tenant was in breach, only if breach was gross or wilful would this prevent specific performance.

In *Walsh v Lonsdale* the landlord granted a seven year lease in writing, one of the terms being that the tenant should pay the yearly rent in advance.[48] At law, because there was no deed, the tenant (in possession and paying rent) would be a periodic tenant. The tenant paid rent in arrears – which under a legal periodic tenancy he was entitled to do. If, however, the tenant was seen as having an equitable lease on the same terms as the defective

---

[43] Law of Property Act 1925 s 54(1). A tenancy at will will come within a legislative scheme offering security of tenure if it is a private residential tenancy, but not if a business tenancy or a residential letting from a local authority: see ch 6.

[44] *Martin v Smith* (1874) LR 9 Ex 50. If the agreed terms are inconsistent with a periodic tenancy this does suggest that the parties had some other intention, and modern courts may therefore be more reluctant to imply a periodic tenancy.

[45] (1858) 2 De G & J 559.

[46] (1858) 2 De G & J 559, 570–1.

[47] (1858) 2 De G & J 559, 571.

[48] (1882) 21 Ch D 9.

legal lease, he should pay rent in advance. The Court of Appeal decided that the rules of equity prevailed, Jessell MR stating that:

> ... there are not two estates as there were formerly, one estate at common law by reason of the payment of rent from year to year, and an estate in equity under the agreement. There is only one Court, and the equity rules prevail in it. The tenant holds under an agreement for a lease. He holds, therefore, under the same terms in equity as if a lease had been granted.[49]

The result was that the landlord was allowed to recover the rent in advance.

There are limitations on the ability of equity to 'save' informal leases. There can only be an equitable lease if the agreement is one capable of specific performance. So, for example, it will not be used to assist a tenant who is in breach of a covenant[50] or where specific performance would cause a breach, as in *Warmington v Miller* where granting the lease would cause the 'mesne landlord' to be in breach of a covenant against sub-letting in his own lease.[51] It is not *any* breach that will prevent specific performance: in *Parker v Taswell*, Lord Chelmsford LC suggested it was a breach that was gross or wilful. Sparkes has suggested that it depends on such a breach as would forfeit the lease.[52] A number of statutory provisions apply only to legal leases, such as paragraph 1 of Schedule 3 to the Land Registration Act 2002 by which legal leases up to seven years are interests that override.[53] Also, as the tenant of an equitable lease does not have a legal estate, there is no privity of estate and, so, the landlord will not be able to enforce leasehold covenants against successors in relation to leases entered into before 1996.[54]

4.4 Vitiating Factors and Leases

Leases may be set aside for the same reasons as other contracts. A lease can be rescinded for fraudulent misrepresentation.[55] In *Boustany v Piggott* the Privy Council set aside a lease on the grounds of 'unconscionability': the rent was one-sixth of the true value, fixed for ten years, with an option to renew for a further ten years at the same rent.[56] The Privy Council held that the tenant 'must have taken advantage' of the landlord. There is no reason why other contract doctrines should not also apply, such as *non est factum*, undue influence and duress.

---

[49] 1882) 21 Ch D 9, 14.

[50] As in *Coatsworth v Johnson* (1886) 55 LJQB 220 where the tenant was in breach of a covenant for cultivation.

[51] [1973] QB 877 (CA).

[52] P Sparkes, 'Forfeiture of Equitable Leases' (1987) 16 *Anglo-American L Rev* 160, 170.

[53] The wording does not expressly require the lease to be legal, but the use of the word 'granted' was held under the Land Registration Act 1925 to apply only to legal leases: *City Permanent Building Society v Miller* [1952] Ch 840 (CA). It is thought that the same would be true under the Land Registration Act 2002.

[54] See ch 18: the rules for enforcement of covenants changed in 1996, making the distinction between legal and equitable leases unimportant for leases entered into after that date.

[55] *Killick v Roberts* [1991] 1 WLR 1146 (CA).

[56] [1993] EGCS 85 (PC).

4.5 Construction and Rectification

Many leasehold disputes that come before the courts involve questions of interpretation of leasehold provisions, particularly in the context of rent review clauses, repair covenants, and break clauses. As with other contracts, there can be a fine line between interpretation, implication of terms and rectification. Very frequently a case is argued both on the grounds of construction arguments and rectification.

4.5.1 Principles of Construction in Contract Law

The principles of construction and interpretation of contracts are set out in Lord Hoffmann's five principles of construction in *Investors Compensation Scheme Ltd v West Bromwich Building Society*:

> The principles may be summarised as follows.
>
> (1) Interpretation is the ascertainment of the meaning which the document would convey to a reasonable person having all the background knowledge which would reasonably have been available to the parties in the situation in which they were at the time of the contract.
>
> (2) The background ... includes absolutely anything which would have affected the way in which the language of the document would have been understood by a reasonable man.
>
> (3) The law excludes from the admissible background the previous negotiations of the parties and their declarations of subjective intent. They are admissible only in an action for rectification. The law makes this distinction for reasons of practical policy and, in this respect only, legal interpretation differs from the way we would interpret utterances in ordinary life. The boundaries of this exception are in some respects unclear ...
>
> (4) The meaning which a document (or any other utterance) would convey to a reasonable man is not the same thing as the meaning of its words. The meaning of words is a matter of dictionaries and grammars; the meaning of the document is what the parties using those words against the relevant background would reasonably have been understood to mean. The background may not merely enable the reasonable man to choose between the possible meanings of words which are ambiguous but even (as occasionally happens in ordinary life) to conclude that the parties must, for whatever reason, have used the wrong words or syntax: see *Mannai Investments Co Ltd v Eagle Star Life Assurance Co Ltd* [1997] AC 749.
>
> (5) The 'rule' that words should be given their 'natural and ordinary meaning' reflects the common sense proposition that we do not easily accept that people have made linguistic mistakes, particularly in formal documents. On the other hand, if one would nevertheless conclude from the background that something must have gone wrong with the language, the law does not require judges to attribute to the parties an intention which they plainly could not have had.[57]

Traditionally, as Lord Hoffman states in the third principle, it has not been possible to allow evidence of prior negotiations or declarations of subjective intent as an aid to construction. Although the courts have been more willing to take account of a wider range of background matters in relation to construction in recent years, this exclusionary rule remains. A number of commentators are, however, calling for its abolition. Lord Nicholls has argued,

---

[57] [1998] 1 WLR 896 (HL) 912–3. See also Lord Bingham's principles in *The Starsin* [2003] UKHL 12, [2004] 1 AC 715 [9]–[13].

extra-judicially, for a relaxation of this exclusionary rule.[58] Others argue, however, that the rule promotes certainty:

> ... the admissible background should be limited to the sort of facts likely to be readily available to a lawyer asked to advise in circumstances in which a decision has to be taken without delay as to the course of action to be taken under the contract.[59]

In leasehold cases the courts have treated draft leases attached to earlier agreements as a legitimate part of the background in construction cases.[60]

Although the courts stress that their role is not to rewrite agreements reached by the parties they will often correct mistakes in the documentation. The conditions necessary for correcting mistakes are summarised by Brightman LJ in *East v Pantiles Plant Hire Ltd*:

> ... first there must be a clear mistake on the fact of the instrument; secondly it must be clear what correction ought to be made in order to cure the mistake.[61]

In *Janet Reger International Ltd v Tiree Ltd*, for example, the lease referred to a particular numbered clause which the judge said was obviously a mistaken reference to a different clause and that he would 'correct the mistake as a matter of construction'.[62] Similarly, in *Holding & Barnes plc v Hill House Hammond Ltd* surplus words were struck out that made no sense, the Court of Appeal referring to six other leases executed contemporaneously as part of the same overall transaction to show how the mistake had arisen and explain it.[63] In a bill of lading case, *The Starsin*, the House of Lords added seventeen words from a standard form; the wording showed that there was undoubtedly an omission and although this could have been corrected by the insertion of one word it was clear that what had in fact happened was that the wording of a standard precedent had been used and a string of words missed out.

Construction can therefore do far more than simply interpret the words used as it can be used to change, delete, or add words to a lease where there are obvious errors and it is clear what the correction should be. The courts are willing to look to the wording used in other relevant leases,[64] earlier drafts,[65] and standard precedents[66] as part of this process. Further, provided that 'gist' of the correction is clear, the precise wording does not matter.[67] If a correction is not possible on this basis, it is then either for the court to construe the

[58] D Nicholls, 'My Kingdom for a Horse: The Meaning of Words' (2005) 121 *LQR* 577 (based on a Chancery Bar Association lecture). Cited in *Proforce Recruit Ltd v The Rugby Group Ltd* [2006] EWCA Civ 69 [33] (Mummery LJ) and [57] (Arden LJ). See also G McMeel, 'Prior Negotiations and Subsequent Conduct – The Next Step Forward for Contractual Interpretation?' (2003) 119 *LQR* 272.

[59] A Berg, 'Thrashing through the Undergrowth' (2006) 122 *LQR* 354, 361.

[60] *Ladbroke Group plc v Bristol CC* [1998] 1 EGLR 126 (CA) 128–9; *KPMG LLP v Network Rail Infrastructure Ltd* [2007] EWCA Civ 363 [35]-[43].

[61] [1982] 2 EGLR 111 (CA) 112.

[62] [2006] EWHC 1743 (Ch) [84].

[63] [2001] EWCA Civ 1334. See ch 12.

[64] *Holding & Barnes plc v Hill House Hammond Ltd* [2001] EWCA Civ 1334.

[65] *KPMG LLP v Network Rail Infrastructure Ltd* [2007] EWCA Civ 363.

[66] *The Starsin* [2003] UKHL 12, [2004] 1 AC 715. This may be less useful in a leasehold context given the huge variety of precedents in circulation and the fact that many leases are 'tailor made'.

[67] In *The Starsin* [2003] UKHL 12, [2004] 1 AC 715 Lord Bingham suggested a high degree of certainty as to the error was needed for the court to correct a mistake, but Lord Millett said it was sufficient if the court 'knows their gist' [192]. In *KPMG LLP v Network Rail Infrastructure Ltd* [2007] EWCA Civ 363 the Court of Appeal followed Lord Millett's approach and was willing to look to the earlier agreement for lease even though some alterations had been made to the annexed draft lease.

uncorrected wording by some other process[68] or for the parties to proceed by seeking rectification of the document.

4.5.2 The Law on Rectification

Rectification can be given either for mutual mistake (where the contract does not reflect the
parties' joint agreement) or for unilateral mistake (where one party is mistaken and the other
knows and seeks to take advantage of this mistake). As pointed out by Lord Hoffmann in his
principles of construction, it is legitimate to refer to previous negotiations and declarations
of subjective intent in considering a case for rectification.

The requirements for rectification for mutual mistake are set out in the judgment of
Peter Gibson LJ in *Swainland Builders Ltd v Freehold Properties Ltd*:

> The party seeking rectification must show that:
> (1) the parties had a common continuing intention, whether or not amounting to an
>   agreement, in respect of a particular matter in the instrument to be rectified;
> (2) there was an outward expression of accord;
> (3) the intention continued at the time of the execution of the instrument sought to be
>   rectified;
> (4) by mistake, the instrument did not reflect that common intention.[69]

The requirements for rectification for unilateral mistake are set out by Buckley LJ in *Thomas
Bates & Sons Ltd v Wyndham's (Lingerie) Ltd*:

> I think it must be shown: first, that one party A erroneously believed that the document
> sought to be rectified contained a particular term or provision, or possibly did not contain a
> particular term or provision which, mistakenly, it did contain; secondly, that the other party B
> was aware of the omission or the inclusion and that it was due to a mistake on the part of A;
> thirdly, that B has omitted to draw the mistake to the notice of A. And I think there must be a
> fourth element involved, namely, that the mistake must be one calculated to benefit B. If these
> requirements are satisfied, the court may regard it as inequitable to allow B to resist rectifica-
> tion to give effect to A's intention on the ground that the mistake was not, at the time of
> execution of the document, a mutual mistake.[70]

Usually there will be rectification only if the recorded document does not reflect a prior
agreement, even in cases of unilateral mistake. In *Littman v Aspen Oil (Broking) Ltd*, however,
Jacobs LJ was prepared to rectify a lease even though there was no prior accord on the
point.[71]

4.5.3 Construction and Rectification in a Leasehold Context

In so far as the process of construction leads to the correcting of linguistic slips and mistakes

---

[68] In *KPMG LLP v Network Rail Infrastructure Ltd* [2007] EWCA Civ 363 Carnwath LJ pointed out that the
correction of obvious mistakes is simply one facet of construction: [47], [50].
[69] [2002] 2 EGLR 71 (CA) [33].
[70] [1981] 1 WLR 505 (CA) 516A-B.
[71] [2005] EWCA Civ 1579; Longmore LJ found it unnecessary to discuss this point, May LJ inclined to agree with
Jacobs LJ.

of expression it can do something similar to the equitable doctrine of rectification. In many cases, the courts begin by looking at construction matters first (for example, *Littman v Aspen Oil (Broking) Ltd*);[72] in some the courts have preferred to take rectification issues first (*KPMG LLP v Network Rail Infrastructure Ltd*).[73]

Construction and rectification of leases can be of enormous commercial significance. So, for example, in *KPMG LLP v Network Rail Infrastructure Ltd* the lease gave an opportunity to exercise a break clause.[74] In the earlier draft it was clear that the tenant was intended to have three opportunities to break, each dependent on there having been a rent review. The final wording contained some inelegant drafting and omitted wording that had been used in the earlier versions. One possible reading of the final wording, and the meaning argued for by the tenant, was that this gave a further two opportunities to exercise the break clause that were not dependent on rent review. As the current rent was higher than the market rent it was unlikely that the landlord would initiate a rent review, and the three opportunities reading could mean that the tenant was tied in until the end of the lease in 2029. On the tenant's reading, it would be able to exercise the break clause in 2008. The Court of Appeal held that the case for rectification had not been made out as, although there had been a common intention that was not reflected in the final lease, it was not proven that this had been the continuing intention of the parties (the tenant had had the change pointed out to it by its lawyer). As a matter of construction, however, Carnwarth LJ looked to the earlier drafts and held that it was clear that an error had been made and that the tenant was intended to have only three opportunities to break.

The Court of Appeal case of *Littman v Aspen Oil (Broking) Ltd* similarly involved a break clause.[75] Both parties had opportunities to exercise a break clause, but the clause said that *landlord* exercise was conditional on the tenant complying with all of the leasehold covenants. As will be seen in chapter 24, it is not unusual for the tenant to be required to have complied with all covenants in order to be allowed to exercise the break clause,[76] but the clause made no commercial sense in the form written whereby *landlord* exercise was conditional on tenant compliance. On the facts, the Court of Appeal unanimously agreed that as a matter of construction the word 'landlord' should be amended to 'tenant' as the wrong word had been used. Further, Jacobs LJ (with whom May LJ was inclined to agree) said that he would be willing to order rectification on the ground of unilateral mistake. This was not a case of mutual mistake as the tenant's solicitor had noticed the error, but it was inequitable for the tenant to rely on the mistake as his solicitor had deliberately chosen to keep quiet believing (wrongly in the event) that the mistake could only be to his client's advantage. The end result was that the tenant's exercise of the break clause was conditional on compliance, even though his solicitor would clearly not have agreed to this.

---

[72] [2005] EWCA Civ 1579.
[73] [2007] EWCA Civ 363.
[74] [2007] EWCA Civ 363.
[75] [2005] EWCA Civ 1579.
[76] No well-advised tenant should, however, agree to this.

4.6 Providing Information to Tenants

If a written lease has been entered into, the tenant is likely to have details of the terms of the tenancy (assuming that the tenant got a copy of the lease). However, as we have seen, there is no requirement for short leases to be in writing. Nor, even when the lease is in writing, will the tenant always have an adequate understanding of his position and rights. There are, therefore, various statutory provisions that are designed to provide information to tenants.

4.6.1 Information about the Terms of the Tenancy and the Identity of the Landlord

4.6.1.1 Weekly Residential Tenancies

In the case of weekly residential tenancies, section 4 of the Landlord and Tenant Act 1985 states that the landlord is under a duty to provide the tenant with a 'rent book', unless the rent includes a substantial sum for board. By section 4(3), this applies to both contractual licensees and tenants. The rent book must contain information prescribed by regulation[77] which includes the basic terms of the letting, such as the name and address of the landlord,[78] the address of the premises, the amount of rent payable, details of any other accommodation which the occupier has the right to share with other people, and a statement of the number of people permitted to use that dwelling.

The rent book thus performs an evidentiary role, witnessing the main terms of the letting. Nevertheless, the scope of the legislation has been criticised as being too narrow. The fact that it applies only to weekly tenancies is a major limitation. The Francis Committee considered that the duty to provide a rent book should not be confined to weekly tenancies but rather should apply to any residential letting where the rent is payable in intervals of not more than two months, and that the tenant should be entitled to keep the rent book so that she has a record of the basic terms (the existing duty is only to provide one). In addition, the Committee suggested that for furnished lettings the rent book should provide an inventory of the furniture supplied.[79] There have also been suggestions that the contents of the rent book should be more detailed:

> First, it is not made clear whether the stated rent is payable in advance or in arrear. Secondly, no statement is required concerning the nature of any services to be provided by the landlord at his own or at the tenant's expense. And thirdly, no reference is made to the landlord's responsibility for structural and external repairs in the case of short leases. [footnotes omitted][80]

An additional flaw is that many landlords simply do not provide a rent book; and even though section 7 of the Landlord and Tenant Act 1985 says that failure to do so constitutes a criminal offence, it does not prevent the landlord from recovering rent from the tenant.[81]

---

[77] Housing Act 1985 s 332, Housing (Prescribed Forms) Regulations 1990 SI 1990/447; Rent Book (Forms of Notice) Regulations 1982 SI 1982/1474, as amended by SI 1988/2198, SI 1990/1067 and SI 1993/656.

[78] Landlord and Tenant Act 1985 s 5(1).

[79] See Francis Committee, 'Report of the Committee on the Rent Acts' (Cmnd 4609, 1971) 226–227.

[80] D Hoath, 'Rent Books: The Law, Its Uses and Abuses' (1978–9) 1 *JSWL* 3, 12.

[81] *Shaw v Groom* [1970] 2 QB 504 (CA).

4.6.1.2 All Residential Tenants

For tenants of dwellings there is a right to request the landlord's identity in section 1 of the Landlord and Tenant Act 1985 which provides:

(1) If the tenant of premises occupied as a dwelling makes a written request for the landlord's name and address to –

(a) any person who demands, or the last person who received, rent payable under the tenancy, or

(b) any other person for the time being acting as agent for the landlord, in relation to the tenancy,

that person shall supply the tenant with a written statement of the landlord's name and address within the period of 21 days beginning with the day on which he receives the request.

Where the landlord is a body corporate, section 2 provides that the tenant can also request the name and address of every director and secretary of the landlord. These sections apply only to tenants, not licensees.

Failure to comply with the request is, by section 1(2), a criminal offence. The Nugee Report found that although few tenants had difficulties in identifying their landlord, it was 'a serious issue when it did arise'[82] and it considered that relatively few prosecutions were being brought under sections 121 and 122 of the Housing Act 1974 (the predecessor to section 1 of the Landlord and Tenant Act 1985). Accordingly, following the Nugee Report, further provisions were introduced to help the residential tenant communicate with his landlord. The provisions apply to residential tenancies which do not also include business use.[83] Section 47 of the Landlord and Tenant Act 1987 provides that all written demands for money due under the lease (whether rent, or service or administration charge), must contain the landlord's name and address; and if that address is outside the jurisdiction, an address for service in the jurisdiction must be given. Failure to include this results, by section 47(2), in the tenant not having to pay any service or administration charge element of the demand until the information is supplied. Section 48 requires the landlord to provide the tenant with an address within the jurisdiction for service of notices; failure to do so means that neither rent, nor service or administration charge shall be treated as being due. However, neither section relieves the tenant of making the relevant payment if a manager or receiver has been appointed to receive rents and service charges.[84]

In the case of public sector tenants, there is an additional requirement to keep tenants informed. Section 104 Housing Act 1985 provides:

(2) The landlord under a secure tenancy shall supply the tenant with ...

(b) a written statement of the terms of the tenancy, so far as they are neither expressed in the lease or written tenancy agreement (if any) nor implied by law;

and the statement required by paragraph (b) shall be supplied on the grant of the tenancy or as soon as practicable afterwards.

---

[82] Nugee Committee, 'Report of the Committee of Inquiry on the Management of Privately Owned Blocks of Flats' (1985) para 7.1.2.

[83] Landlord and Tenant Act 1987 s 46.

[84] Landlord and Tenant Act 1987 ss 47(3), 48(3).

The effect of section 104(2) is that even if the tenancy is made orally, the tenant should receive a written statement of the tenancy terms. It is now the norm for local authorities to issue written tenancy agreements.

4.6.2 Information about the Tenant's Rights

The Law Commission noted in the Renting Homes project that the early housing legislation often overwrote contractual provisions set out in tenancy agreements. The result was complexity and inaccessibility.[85] Existing legislative measures have gone some way to try to address these problems. First, there are the various duties to give tenants information about the identity of the landlord set out above. Second, there are some duties to give information not simply about the terms of the tenancy itself, but also about the tenant's rights. So, for example, where rent books are required by section 4 of the Landlord and Tenant Act 1985 for weekly residential tenancies, they must contain, in addition to information about the tenancy, information about the provisions on overcrowding contained in section 332 of the Housing Act 1985 and information about other potential rights, such as the possibility of claiming housing benefit and the fact that eviction without court order will be unlawful. In the public sector, the information to be supplied under section 104 of the Housing Act 1985 should include, in addition to the information on the terms of the tenancies, information about a landlord's repairing obligations and the rights given to public sector tenants.

Nonetheless, the result is that a tenant may have very patchy information about both the contractual terms of the tenancy and also his wider legal rights. The Law Commission's reform proposals applicable to residential tenancies regard the provision of information as central to the consumer approach. Under its proposals, whenever there is a contract for renting a home, the occupier must be provided with a written statement. This must contain information about:

(a)   key matters: the premises, the date on which occupation may begin, the rent, and the rental period;

(b)   fundamental terms: these will be mandatory statutory terms, and cover things such as the rules setting out the circumstances in which the landlord can go to court to seek an order for possession, repairing obligations and conduct that is prohibited by the contract.[86] These can be omitted or varied only if it works to the benefit of the occupier;

(c)   supplementary terms,[87] covering practical matters such as the obligation to pay rent and the obligation to use the home properly; and

(d)   additional terms.

---

[85] Law Commission, 'Renting Homes 1: Status and Security' (Law Com CP No 162, 2002) para 2.122.

[86] In its earlier report the Law Commission refereed to these as 'compulsory-minimum' terms and 'special' terms, language that better captures what they are about: Law Commission, 'Renting Homes' (Law Com No 284, 2003) para 3.29.

[87] The earlier Law Commission report referred to these as 'default' terms, again capturing the spirit more clearly: Law Commission, 'Renting Homes' (Law Com No 284, 2003) para 3.29.

4.6.3 *Commercial Leases*

There are no statutory duties for landlords to provide information to business tenants. The aim of the Business Lease Code 2007 (see 4.9.3 below) is, however, to make business tenants, particularly small businesses, more aware of the things to think about when entering into a lease.[88] There is considerable evidence that small business tenants tend to enter leases with an inadequate understanding of their commitments and that their leases do not sufficiently protect their commercial interests. A strong case can be made that rather than relying on landlords voluntarily complying with the Business Lease Code 2007 there should be some mandatory disclosure requirements prior to entering a lease, as is the case in some Australian states in relation to retail tenancies.[89]

4.7 The Structure of Leases

There is no such thing as a standard lease. Nevertheless, within each sector, it is possible to comment on the kind of things that tend to be covered by the lease and the patterns that leases commonly take. Residential tenancies will usually be fairly short, just a few pages long. In the commercial sector, however, leases are often heavily negotiated by the parties, their lawyers and surveyors. The result is a lease of considerable length, maybe 50 or more pages. It is also the case that long residential leases, purchased with a large capital sum, tend to be long documents.

A lease is generally divided into five parts:

The premises. These include details such as the date, details of the parties to the lease, a description of the property let (the parcels clause), the grant of the estate (the operative words), and any exceptions and reservations (for example, reserving a right of way for the landlord).

The habendum. This states the length of the term.

The reddendum. This reserves the rent.

The covenants. These are the obligations undertaken by the landlord and the tenant, and will often form a large part of the lease. The covenants may cover diverse matters, ranging from a covenant by the tenant to pay the rent, to a covenant 'each morning to empty any rubbish of the previous day suitably wrapped into the refuse receptacles or other means of refuse disposal provided by the landlord'. Covenants may be express (agreed between the parties) or implied (by statute or common law).

Provisos and options. The provisos will cover such things as what will happen if the rent is not paid on time; generally, this failure by the tenant would give the landlord the right to forfeit the lease (chapter 24). The options will, inter alia, state whether the tenant has the right to renew the lease.

---

[88] Joint Working Group on Commercial Leases, 'The Code for Leasing Business Premises in England and Wales 2007' (2007).

[89] See ch 8. See also S Bright, 'Protecting the Small Business Tenant' [2006] *Conv* 137; N Crosby, 'An Evaluation of the Policy Implications for the UK of the Approach to Small Business Tenant Legislation in Australia' (August 2006) available at www.rdg.ac.uk/rep/ausleaserpt.pdf.

4.7.1 Express Covenants

Leases will often contain covenants on the following matters:

(a) to pay rent (see chapters 14–16), service charges (see chapter 13), rates and taxes.

(b) user, regulating the manner in which the tenant can use the property (see chapter 13).

(c) repair, stating which party is responsible for the repairs and decorations (see chapter 12). It may well be that the landlord takes responsibility for external work, and the tenant for internal work. In addition, the clause may define the expected standard of work. An example of a decorating covenant in a commercial lease is for the tenant:

> As often as shall be necessary to maintain a high standard of decorative finish but not less than once in every five years and in the last year of the Term to decorate the Premises in a good and workmanlike manner and with appropriate materials of good quality the tints and colours and patterns of such decoration in the last year of the term to be approved by the Landlord such approval not to be unreasonably withheld or delayed.[90]

(d) alterations, stating whether or not the tenant is permitted to make any alterations to the premises (see chapter 12). Often, the tenant is not allowed to make any structural alterations, but is permitted to make internal, non-structural alterations with the landlord's consent, which the landlord agrees not to withhold unreasonably.

(e) alienation, stating whether or not the tenant is able to sell, sub-let, mortgage, etc, the leasehold interest (see chapter 17).

(f) insurance, stating which party is responsible for insuring the property (see chapter 13).

(g) quiet enjoyment, whereby the landlord covenants that the tenant 'shall peaceably hold and enjoy the Premises without any interruption by the landlord or any person claiming under or in trust for the landlord'. The covenant for quiet enjoyment has a fairly technical meaning, as will be discussed below.

4.7.2 Implied Covenants

In addition to the express covenants in the lease, there may be covenants that are implied by common law and statute. The main statutorily implied covenants relate to the state and condition of residential tenancies and are discussed in chapter 12. Covenants implied by common law fall into two categories: terms implied as a matter of law and terms implied in fact. Terms implied by law are implied as an incident of every contract of a particular kind. In relation to leases, there are two covenants implied by law into every leasehold relationship which are of great importance and of considerable antiquity: the covenant of quiet enjoyment and the duty not to derogate from grant. There is also a covenant not to disclaim the landlord's title, but this is of less significance. In the case of furnished residential lettings there is an implied warranty that the property is let in a habitable state,[91] and in the case of

---

[90] Clause taken from a 17 year lease of ground floor offices in London SW1 entered into between Friends' Provident Life Office and Internet Capital Group (Europe) Ltd dated 29 March 2000: available on www.contracts.onecle.com.

[91] *Smith v Marrable* (1843) 11 M & W 5.

with communal access the House of Lords has recognised 'an
ble care to keep in reasonable repair and usability' the access
venants, the courts are generally reluctant to imply terms; on the
is for the parties to negotiate the terms of the lease. Although, in
·act law, terms may be implied in fact if 'necessary' there are
terms are implied into leases on this basis. Most occur in the
ıssed in chapter 12.

, ,ʋı Quiet Enjoyment.

ıı the absence of an express covenant for quiet enjoyment, there will be a covenant for quiet
enjoyment implied from the landlord and tenant relationship. Historically the covenant was
solely concerned with protecting the tenant's title and possession of the property,[93] but the
scope has gradually been widened, first to include physical interference[94] and more recently
the courts have accepted that substantial interference with comfort, such as excessive noise,
may also constitute a breach.[95] The covenant has been held to have been breached when the
landlord removed doors and windows of the premises in order to force the tenant to leave;[96]
and when scaffolding was erected outside the tenant's shop, preventing the customers from
getting to the shop window.[97] Where the landlord is under an obligation to repair leasehold
property, he may need to take reasonable precautions (but not all possible precautions) when
carrying out repairs so as to avoid breaching the covenant for quiet enjoyment.[98] In *Kenny v
Preen*, Pearson LJ thought that there would be a breach if the tenant was persistently perse-
cuted and threatened with physical eviction.[99] Lord Hoffmann says that it is:

> … a covenant that the tenant's lawful possession of the land will not be substantially interfered
> with by the acts of the lessor or those lawfully claiming under him.[100]

This means it will be breached by a substantial interference either with title and possession or
with the tenant's ordinary lawful use of the property. Interference can occur not only by action,
but by inaction, effectively imposing a duty to act upon the landlord. So, for example, in
Chartered Trust plc v Davis it was recognised that the landlord may be under a duty to control
nuisance behaviour on the landlord's property that interferes with the tenant's enjoyment.[101] It
does, however, apply only to acts or omissions after the lease has been entered into, so if, for
example, flooding is caused by pre-existing defects there will be no breach.[102] The covenant

---

[92] [1977] AC 239 (HL) 256.
[93] *Dennett v Atherton* (1872) LR 7 QB 316, 326.
[94] *Browne v Flower* [1911] 1 Ch 219 (Ch) 228.
[95] *Southwark LBC v Tanner; Baxter v Camden LBC (No 2)* [2001] 1 AC 1 (HL).
[96] *Lavender v Betts* [1942] 2 All ER 72 (KB); this might also constitute the criminal offence of harassment, see ch 23.
[97] *Owen v Gadd* [1956] 2 QB 99 (CA).
[98] *Goldmile Properties Ltd v Lechouritis* [2003] EWCA Civ 49 [10]. Sedley LJ, giving judgment for the court,
accepted counsel's argument that the covenant for quiet enjoyment 'guarantees against disturbance of only that
which is demised, and the demise includes the lessor's obligation to use its reasonable endeavours to keep the
building in repair' [9].
[99] *Kenny v Preen* [1963] 1 QB 499 (CA) 513.
[100] *Southwark LBC v Tanner; Baxter v Camden LBC (No 2)* [2001] 1 AC 1 (HL) 10.
[101] *Chartered Trust plc v Davis* [1997] 2 EGLR 83 (CA).
[102] *Anderson v Oppenheimer* (1880) 5 QBD 602.

cannot be used, therefore, as a way of trying to get the landlord to improve the property or to bring it up to standard.[103]

4.7.2.2 Non-Derogation from Grant

The covenant not to derogate from grant is based on the principle that:

> … a grantor having given a thing with one hand is not to take away the means of enjoying it with the other.[104]

Applied to leases it means that the landlord should not at the same time as granting a lease to the tenant act in some way which effectively denies this lease to the tenant. It is described as 'a rule of common honesty', '… imposed in the interest of fair dealing'.[105] To work out the extent of the obligation it is, therefore, necessary to determine the extent of the grant which will include looking at the circumstances at the time of the grant, including the knowledge of the parties about their respective plans at the time of the grant and what was within the landlord's power to fulfil.

The covenant will be broken when the landlord, or someone claiming under him, does something which makes the premises materially less fit for the purpose of the lease; but, if that purpose is unusual, there will only be a breach if the landlord knew of the proposed use. In *Harmer v Jumbil* land was let specifically for the purpose of storing explosives.[106] The Court of Appeal held that the covenant against non-derogation was broken when buildings were erected on neighbouring land (by a later tenant of the landlord[107]) which prevented the tenant from legally using his land for storing explosives (because it amounted to a breach of the tenant's explosives licence). The Court of Appeal did not accept that the tenant should have obtained an express covenant from the landlord that the adjoining land would not be used in a way that threatened his licence.

In recent years, the courts have come to recognise that the covenant imposes not only the 'duty not to interfere' which the older cases focus on but that it can also lead to a duty to act, effectively imposing an obligation on the landlord which was not expressly bargained for. In addition, where the landlord has management responsibility of communal parts and the power to control other occupiers, such as other tenants of the landlord, the covenant can prove an effective tool to the tenant in requiring the landlord to take action. The first case to bring this application to prominence was *Chartered Trust plc v Davis*.[108] Here a tenant had been granted a lease of a retail unit in a shopping mall and was complaining about the way in which another tenant, a pawnbroker, was conducting business as it had the effect of deterring customers and eventually led to the collapse of the tenant's business. Given that the landlord retained the common parts of the mall and had reserved a service charge to cover management costs, the Court of Appeal held that the landlord should have done something to control the nuisance. There

---

103 *Southwark LBC v Tanner* [2001] 1 AC 1 (HL).
104 *Birmingham, Dudley and District Banking Co v Ross* (1888) 38 Ch D 295, 313 (Bowen LJ).
105 *Harmer v Jumbil (Nigeria) Tin Areas* [1921] 1 Ch 200 (CA) 225, 226 (Younger LJ).
106 *Harmer v Jumbil (Nigeria) Tin Areas* [1921] 1 Ch 200 (CA).
107 As the landlord was bound, so too was anyone claiming title under him.
108 [1997] 2 EGLR 83 (CA).

comes a point 'where the landlord becomes legally obliged to take action to protect that which he has granted to this tenant'.[109]

The covenant has also been used by courts in recent years to imply a term, in appropriate cases, that the landlord will not permit or operate a business that directly competes with the tenant's business where parties contemplated, at the time of the grant, that the tenant would have an exclusive right to use the premises for a particular purpose. In *Oceanic Village v Shirayama Shokusan Co Ltd* this approach was used to prevent the landlord from opening a kiosk near the tenant's shop that would sell aquarium-related products when the tenant had been granted a lease in order to run a gift shop for the London Aquarium.[110] This was, however, an unusual case and, as seen in chapter 13, a landlord is not generally prevented from allowing or conducting competing business use.

There is a large degree of overlap between the implied covenant not to derogate from grant and the implied covenant for quiet enjoyment, and judges seldom find it necessary to distinguish them.[111]

4.7.2.3 Disclaimer of Landlord's Title

This is a covenant not to deny the landlord's title or to act in a way inconsistent with the tenancy. In *W G Clark Ltd v Dupre Ltd*, disclaimer of title was likened to the tenant repudiating the lease:

> A tenant who repudiates the relationship of landlord and tenant should be in no different position from a party to a contract who repudiates or renounces it. It seems to me that the doctrine of disclaimer is analogous to the concept of repudiation of a contract … Hill and Redman's Law of Landlord and Tenant (18th ed, 1991) vol 1, para 2181 says:
>
> 'There is implied in every lease a condition that the lessee shall not do anything that may prejudice the title of the lessor; and that if this is done the lessor may re-enter for breach of this implied condition. The principle may be traced back to the reign of Henry II and appears to be founded on the oath of fealty given by a tenant of real property to his lord under the medieval system of tenure.'
>
> … Where the disclaimer is by words … then whether there has been a repudiation of the relationship is to be determined by looking at the words used in the context in which they were used. The court must decide whether those words in that context evinced an intention on the part of the tenant no longer to be bound by the relationship of landlord and tenant.[112]

4.8 Fairness and Contract Terms

The landlord and tenant have generally been left to negotiate their own leasehold terms. In so far as there have been certain fundamental responsibilities which they cannot avoid, these

---

[109] See also *Hilton v James Smith & Sons (Norwood) Ltd* (1979) 251 EG 1063 (CA) (the landlord should have controlled the blocking of a common access road); *Petra Investments Ltd v Jeffrey Rogers Plc* (2001) 81 P & CR 21 (Ch) (a shopping centre, although on the facts there was no actionable breach.)

[110] [2001] L & TR 35 (Ch).

[111] The difference between them is discussed in Hill & Redman's *Law of Landlord and Tenant* (Lexis-Nexis Butterworths) [6884].

[112] [1992] Ch 297 (Ch) 302–3.

were historically dealt with by the recognition of implied obligations. On the landlord's part, there are implied covenants of quiet enjoyment and the duty not to derogate from grant (discussed at 4.7.2 above). On the tenant's part there is a duty not to commit waste (altering the property). Although some statutory provisions are older it was during the twentieth century that increasing legislative provisions began to creep into the landlord and tenant relationship. Some of these would take the form of altering the meaning of agreed covenants as, for example, with a covenant not to assign without the landlord's consent which is statutorily subject to a proviso that consent is not to be unreasonably withheld.[113] Others are obligations implied into the tenancy, as with the statutory repairing obligation imposed on landlords of short residential leases.[114] All of these have been designed to deal with perceived issues specific to landlord and tenant relationships.

In addition, leasehold terms may be subject to tests of fairness or reasonableness by more general laws. Clauses restricting the way in which the tenant can use the property may be found to be anti-competitive or, although less likely, in restraint of trade (chapter 13). There are also two legislative provisions directed to unfair contract terms that must be considered: the Unfair Contract Terms Act 1977 and the Unfair Terms in Consumer Contracts Regulations 1999.[115]

4.8.1 *The Unfair Contract Terms Act 1977: Leases Excluded*

Notwithstanding its title, this Act does not tackle all unfair contract terms, but only those that attempt to exclude or restrict liability. Some such clauses are prohibited altogether; others are subject to a test of reasonableness. The main controls that might apply to leasehold terms are sections 2, 3, and 4, but Schedule 1 provides:

Sections 2 to 4 of this Act do not extend to –

(b)   any contract so far as it relates to the creation or transfer of an interest in land, or to the termination of such an interest, whether by extinction, merger, surrender, forfeiture or otherwise;

The grant of a lease is undoubtedly the creation of an interest in land, and its assignment is the transfer of an interest in land. The key question is whether it could be argued that the leasehold contract is a whole or whether there is a separable part that 'relates to the creation or transfer', leaving the remainder to be subject to the 1977 Act.

This issue arose in *Electricity Supply Nominees Ltd v IAF Group Ltd*.[116] The tenant in an action for arrears of service charge counterclaimed for breach of the repairing covenant by the landlord and sought to set this off against the landlord's claim. The lease, however, required the tenant 'to pay the rent and all other sums payable under this lease ... without any deduction or set-off whatsoever'. The tenant claimed that this was an unreasonable exclusion clause and so, by section 3 of the Unfair Contract Terms Act 1977, could not be relied on by the landlord. The judge decided that the lease should be seen as a composite

---

113 Landlord and Tenant Act 1927 s 19(1); see ch 17.
114 Landlord and Tenant Act 1985 s 11; see ch 12.
115 SI 1999/2083.
116 [1993] 1 WLR 1059 (QB). See also *Star Rider Ltd v Inntrepreneur Pub Co* [1998] 1 EGLR 53 (Ch).

contract and so all of the 'covenants that are integral to the lease which creates the interest in the land "relate to" the creation of that interest in land'. Therefore, none of the covenants in the lease were regulated by the Unfair Contracts Terms Act 1977.

The issue came before the court again in a tenant versus management company dispute in *Granby Village (Manchester) Management Co Ltd v Unchained Growth III plc*.[117] The context was again a claim that the prohibition on 'set off' was unreasonable but the Court of Appeal affirmed the earlier case law. In the words of Jonathan Parker J, the obligation to pay the service charge:

> ... is an integral part of the lease, providing the administrative mechanism for the enjoyment of the leasehold interest in common with, and for the benefit of, the other tenants of the development. To conclude that it did not 'relate to' the creation of the leasehold interest would ... be to lose sight of commercial reality.[118]

The 1977 Act does, however, apply to licence agreements. In *Regus (UK) Ltd v Epcot Solutions Ltd* a clause in an agreement for the provision of serviced office accommodation was held to be unreasonable within the Unfair Contract Terms Act 1977 as it deprived the occupier of any remedy at all for failure to provide air conditioning 'in what is the business equivalent of an hotel, not the lease of a flat'.[119] At one point the judge referred to Regus's customers as tenants[120] but although there was no argument on the point it is most likely that this particular arrangement was a licence.[121]

4.8.2 The Unfair Terms in Consumer Contracts Regulations 1999 (UTCCR)[122]

The UTCCR apply to contracts entered into on or after 1 October 1999. Regulation 4 provides that they apply 'to unfair terms in contracts concluded between a seller or a supplier and a consumer'. Considerable doubt was expressed by some as to whether the earlier version of the Regulations produced in 1994[123] were capable of applying to leases, but this doubt was largely put to rest by a change in wording introduced in 1999. Whereas the 1994 version of the Regulations (departing from the EC Directive[124] they were based on) limited their application to 'goods' and 'services' contracts, these restrictions were removed when the Regulations were revised in 1999. Since then it has been widely accepted that the UTCCR apply to leases, an understanding now confirmed by the Court of Appeal in *Khatun v Newham LBC*.[125]

---

[117] [2000] 1 WLR 739 (CA).

[118] [2000] 1 WLR 739 (CA) 749.

[119] [2007] EWHC 938 (Comm) [50].

[120] At [46].

[121] Few details are given about the particular agreement, but it listed the rooms *initially allocated* for the occupier's use and stated that the agreement 'is the commercial equivalent of an agreement for accommodation in a hotel. The whole of the business centre remains our property and in our possession and control…'

[122] SI 1999/2083.

[123] SI 1994/3159. These came into force on 1 July 1995. The author argued, however, that the earlier Regulations also applied to land contracts: Bright, S and Bright, C 'Unfair Terms in Land Contracts: Copy-out or Cop Out?' (1995) 111 *LQR* 655.

[124] Council Directive (EC) 93/13 of 5 April 1993 on Unfair Terms in Consumer Contracts [2003] OJ L95/29.

[125] [2004] EWCA Civ 55, [2005] QB 37.

Before turning to the detail of the UTCCR it is helpful to explain how they are enforced, and how they are used to shape contracts. The UTCCR can be used in individual litigation. If, for example, a landlord sues a tenant for unpaid charges and the tenant claims that he is exercising a right of set-off, even though the tenancy provides that no deduction by way of set off can be made, the tenant may argue that the prohibition on set off is unfair.[126] Far more significant, however, has been the adoption of an administrative model of enforcement, giving the Office of Fair Trading (OFT)[127] and certain other consumer bodies[128] the power to investigate complaints about unfair terms drawn up for 'general use'.[129] The OFT has seized this opportunity by not only looking into individual complaints but by seeking to influence the way that tenancy agreements are drafted. In the tenancy context, the OFT has issued Guidance setting out not only the kinds of terms that may be unfair, but also making suggestions on terms that would be acceptable.[130] Tenancies drafted with an eye on the OFT Guidance have not only different content but also a very different 'feel' to other tenancies. The Guidance is an important source of information. It illustrates the thinking of the OFT, even though, as OFT Guidance is careful to emphasise, it is the courts that have the final decision as to whether any term is unfair.[131]

4.8.2.1 *The Scope of the UTCCR*

The UTCCR apply to contracts concluded between a seller or a supplier and a consumer. These terms are defined in regulation 3:

> 'seller or supplier' means any natural or legal person who, in contracts covered by these Regulations, is acting for purposes relating to his trade, business or profession, whether publicly owned or privately owned;
> 'consumer' means any natural person who, in contracts covered by these Regulations, is acting for purposes which are outside his trade, business or profession;

This means that they do not apply to contracts entered into between two businesses (often referred to as B2B contracts), but in the context of leases they will apply to many residential tenancies, both short term periodic tenancies and long leases. In *Khatun v Newham LBC* the Court of Appeal confirmed that the UTCCR apply to local authority tenancies, and the same reasoning means that they apply also to lettings by housing associations.[132] They will not apply to business tenancies as the tenant, even if a natural person, will not be a 'consumer'.

---

[126] The OFT Guidance states: 'We are likely to object to terms that require rent to be paid clear or free of deductions because this has the effect of denying tenants their right of set-off': OFT, *Guidance on Unfair Terms in Tenancy Agreements* (OFT 356, September 2005) para 3.26.

[127] The OFT has a duty to investigate complaints unless they are frivolous or vexatious, or another qualifying body has chosen to investigate, in which case that body falls under a duty: regs 10 and 12. The duty was originally given to the Director General of Fair Trading but this was changed to the OFT when the office of DGFT was abolished by the Enterprise Act 2002.

[128] Under the 1994 Regulations only the DGFT had this power; it was extended to other qualifying bodies by the 1999 Regulations.

[129] Reg 10: that is, standard form contracts. For fuller discussion of this method of enforcement and how the OFT works, see S Bright, 'Winning the battle against unfair contract terms' (2000) 20 *LS* 331, 333–38.

[130] OFT, 'Guidance on Unfair Terms in Tenancy Agreements' (OFT 356, September 2005) (replacing earlier guidance issued in November 2001). This looks primarily at potential unfairness in assured and assured shorthold tenancies: para 1.3.

[131] OFT, 'Unfair Contract Terms Guidance' (OFT 311, February 2001) 1.

[132] [2004] EWCA Civ 55, [2005] QB 37.

4.8.2.2 Exclusions from the Scope of the UTCCR

The UTCCR apply only to contract terms that have not been individually negotiated. In addition, two categories of terms are excluded from review for fairness.

Mandatory Statutory Provisions
By regulation 4:

> (2) These Regulations do not apply to contractual terms which reflect-

> (a)   mandatory statutory or regulatory provisions (including such provisions under the law of any Member State or in Community legislation having effect in the United Kingdom without further enactment);

The reason that mandatory statutory provisions are excluded from review is that they 'are presumed not to contain unfair terms'.[133] The Law Commission suggests that this may apply to some of the requirements imposed on registered social landlords by the Housing Corporation, and to terms required of a private landlord by a local authority under a licensing scheme.[134]

'Core Terms'
Regulation 6 provides:

> (2) In so far as it is in plain intelligible language, the assessment of fairness of a term shall not relate-
> (a)   to the definition of the main subject matter of the contract, or
> (b)   to the adequacy of the price or remuneration, as against the goods or services supplied in exchange.

Terms relating to the 'main subject matter of the contract' and the 'adequacy of the price' will not be subjected to the test of fairness but must still be in 'plain intelligible language'. What constitutes a 'core term' in the context of leases may involve difficult questions, but the exemption will be narrowly construed. The OFT states:

> 2.3 Terms in a tenancy agreement stating the rent, the details of the property, and the length of the tenancy are likely to be considered core terms.[135]

It is only the amount of rent that is excluded from assessment for fairness; any provisions for rent review will still be subject to the test of fairness.

4.8.2.3 The Test of Fairness

By regulation 5 any contract term that has not been individually negotiated is subject to test of fairness.

> 5(1) A contractual term which has not been individually negotiated shall be regarded as unfair if, contrary to the requirement of good faith, it causes a significant imbalance in the parties' rights and obligations arising under the contract, to the detriment of the consumer.

---

[133] Law Commission, 'Renting Homes 1: Status and Security' (Law Com CP No 162, 2002) para 6.25.
[134] Law Commission, 'Renting Homes 1: Status and Security' (Law Com CP No 162, 2002) para 6.26. For licensing schemes, see ch 12.
[135] OFT, *Guidance on Unfair Terms in Tenancy Agreements* (OFT 356, September 2005).

(2) A term shall always be regarded as not having been individually negotiated where it has been drafted in advance and the consumer has therefore not been able to influence the substance of the term.

(3) Notwithstanding that a specific term or certain aspects of it in a contract has been individually negotiated, these Regulations shall apply to the rest of a contract if an overall assessment of it indicates that it is a pre-formulated standard contract.

(4) It shall be for any seller or supplier who claims that a term was individually negotiated to show that it was.

By regulation 8, any term that is unfair will not be binding on the consumer (the tenant). Although, even after many years of operation, the precise application of the test of fairness remains unclear,[136] both procedural matters (the presentation of the tenancy agreement – such as font size, clarity of expression – and the process by which the tenancy is entered into) and substantive matters (the content of the lease itself) should be considered in determining whether or not the term is unfair.

4.8.2.3 Plain, Intelligible Language

Regulation 7 states:

(1) A seller or supplier shall ensure that any written term of a contract is expressed in plain, intelligible language.

(2) If there is doubt about the meaning of a written term, the interpretation which is most favourable to the consumer shall prevail but this rule shall not apply in proceedings brought under regulation 12.

The OFT Guidance stresses that terms must be clear not only to lawyers, but also to consumers.

4.8.2.5 The Work of the OFT in relation to Tenancies

Schedule 2 of the UTCCR contains a non-exhaustive list of terms that are potentially unfair. This list is in general terms but is used as the classification by the OFT in its tenancy guidance to explain which tenancy terms are potentially unfair. Through this book references will be made to the views of the OFT as appropriate in relation to particular issues.

The OFT issues bulletins reporting on its work. Mostly, the OFT deals with potentially unfair terms by negotiation with the supplier, making suggestions as to how potentially unfair terms should be amended. This may result in leasehold terms being deleted,[137] or the wording being amended to remove any potential for unfairness and to make the meaning clearer. On other occasions, substantive changes are made to leasehold terms. So, for example, changes made to the standard assured shorthold tenancy used by the Letting Centre[138] include the amendment of the alienation clause; from one prohibiting the tenant from assigning or sub-letting the property (as is extremely common to see) to one

---

[136] See S Bright, 'Unfairness and the Consumer Contract Regulations' in A Burrows and E Peel (eds), *Contract Terms* (Oxford, OUP, 2007).

[137] See, for example, OFT, 'Unfair contract terms' Bulletins 27 and 28 (OFT 743, September 2004) 112 reporting on changes made to the tenancy used by Spelthorne Housing Association.

[138] OFT, 'Unfair contract terms' Bulletins 27 and 28 (OFT 743, September 2004) 53.

permitting assignment or sub-letting with the landlord's consent, not to be unreasonably withheld.

The investigations by the OFT in relation to tenancies appear to have been confined to short rental agreements.[139] There is no reason why the UTCCR would not equally apply to long residential leases as the leasehold contract will usually be between a 'seller or supplier' and a 'consumer' but there are no reported cases.[140] This is, perhaps, surprising as many of the detailed tenant covenants in residential leases may appear unreasonable (such as strict 'no pet' rules and strict rules about user, etc).

4.8.2.5 The Law Commission's Renting Homes Proposals

As seen, the UTCCR apply only if there is a seller or supplier acting for the purposes of his trade, business or profession. It is unclear how this might apply to hobby landlords who own one or two properties as a sideline. The Law Commission propose that the requirements of the Regulations should apply to all renting home contracts, whether or not the landlord and tenant come within the definitions of 'seller or supplier' or 'consumer', on the basis that housing contracts should be fair to all occupiers. It is also proposed to apply the Regulations to all terms, whether negotiated or not.[141]

Under the model contracts proposed (4.6.2 above), the UTCCR will not apply to key matters (because they are core terms) or fundamental terms (because they are mandatory statutory provisions). Nor will they apply to supplemental terms if they have been incorporated in unmodified form, but both modified supplemental terms and any additional terms will be subject to the UTCCR.

4.9 The Structure of Commercial Leases

4.9.1 The Dominance of the Institutional Lease

The pattern of occupational business leases has changed considerably in the last 20 years or so. During the 1980s the 25 year 'institutional lease' dominated the prime letting market. Institutional investors are adverse to risk and sought to place all uncertain costs associated with property management on tenants whilst receiving a secure long-term income stream. As Edwards and Krendel write, the institutional lease:

> … was as much a financial instrument as a contract for occupation. It offered the landlord a high-quality cashflow predicated on the following:

---

[139] It may be that long leases have not been investigated because there have been few complaints, but also because lawyers are more usually involved in the drafting (although this does not necessarily mean that the resulting terms are any more fair). A warning letter was sent to one landlord of a long residential lease but no further action taken: information supplied to author by Contract Regulation Unit, OFT.

[140] There is also a difficult question that could arise where there is a successor to the landlord or tenant: do the Regulations continue to apply even though the parties are no longer the original contracting parties? What if the status of the parties (seller, supplier, consumer) changes on assignment?

[141] Law Commission, 'Renting Homes' (Law Com No 284, 2003) Part IV; Law Commission, 'Renting Homes: The Final Report. Volume 1: Report' (Law Com No 297, 2006) paras 1.35–1.38.

— full repairing and insuring liability placed on the tenant
— upward-only rent reviews offered a certain, inflation-hedged income
— priority over most other creditors for recovery of rent
— long lease terms (20 years+) offered longevity of income
— privity of contract – commonly known as 'first tenant liablity' – enabled the landlord to pursue former tenants where the current one defaulted.[142]

Although the detailed wording of leases varied considerably, the 'clear lease' idea meant that a fairly standard model of leasing emerged, at least for prime properties. Its influence extended also to the secondary and tertiary markets, so that these main features of the institutional lease were reflected in large part in much of the commercial property market.

This institutional lease structure was also important to the way that new commercial developments were financed. Edwards and Krendel refer to two kinds of development finance.[143] The first depends on pre-lets, signing a tenant up before construction begins:

> Prelets, unsurprisingly, are usually on 'institutional' terms, either because the developer is itself an institution, or is being funded by one so must bow to that institution's requirements as to the form of lease.[144]

The second form is speculative development where the building is built before a tenant is lined up. With the strong economy and property market during the 1980s many new developments took this form, but the economic recession of the early 1990s and the collapse of the property market meant that there was suddenly a lot of surplus space.[145] Office rents fell dramatically: in the City of London rents had peaked in late 1989/early 1990 at around £70 per square foot, but then dropped by more than 50 per cent to around £30 per square foot. The over-supply, combined with a number of other features, contributed to the decline of the institutional lease. Tenants were placed in a stronger bargaining position than they had generally enjoyed previously. But even as confidence in the property market has recovered, the institutional lease has not regained its former dominance.

4.9.2 Forces for Change

Changing economic and market conditions help to explain why the institutional lease is no longer dominant, but many other factors have contributed to its decline. During the early 1990s two particular aspects of leases grew to be deeply unpopular amongst tenants: one a point of law, the other the consequence of standard drafting.

The first was 'original tenant liability'. Under ordinary rules of contract law the original tenant, and landlord, would remain liable on their contractual promises throughout the term of a lease, even if they no longer had an interest in the property. The full impact of this became apparent during the recession: many tenants became insolvent and, in a weak property market, it was commercially sensible for the landlord to look to a former tenant

---

[142] C Edwards and P Krendel, *Institutional Leases in the 21st Century* (London, EG Books, 2007) 5.
[143] For a more detailed explanation of financing property development, see A Millington, *Property Development* (London, Estates Gazette, 2000) esp ch 12.
[144] C Edwards and P Krendel, *Institutional Leases in the 21st Century* (London, EG Books, 2007) 9.
[145] For a summary of the main property cycles, and the crash of the early 1990s, see A Baum, *Commercial Real Estate Investment* (Oxford, Chandos Publishing (Oxford) Ltd, 2000) 34–45.

for payment under the lease rather than forfeit the lease and attempt to relet. This would be especially so if the rent under the lease was higher than current market rents (because of the impact of upward only rent review – UORR). The result was that former tenants could be hit, out of the blue, with massive claims for rent arrears. Pressure built for reform and in 1995 legislation was passed which abandoned original tenant liability (although a tenant may still have to guarantee his immediate successor, see chapter 18).

The second aspect of leases that became subject to a great deal of criticism was UORR. UORR was almost standard in commercial leases: the lease would contain provisions for periodic review of the rent to reflect current property values, but would provide only for uplift and in a falling market rents could not go down. Until the recession of the 1990s no-one had seen this as a serious issue as no-one really anticipated that rents would fall. An influential report by Burton in 1992 claimed that UORR presented a serious underlying problem for the retail sector of the British economy because of its inflationary effects.[146] Fearful of legislative intervention, the lobbying arm of the commercial property industry came to life and it was agreed in 1995 that there should be a voluntary code of practice addressing the particular issue of UORR but also more generally encouraging transparency and flexibility in the commercial property market.[147] Although this particular Code had little impact,[148] it marked the beginning of an era in which greater flexibility and choice in leasing practices was promoted by the government.

As already mentioned, the first edition of the Code of Practice was found to have had little influence on the letting market. The Code was re-issued in 2002[149] and a team at the University of Reading was commissioned by the Government to review its operation. In 2004 they issued an Interim Report,[150] and the Final Report was issued in 2005.[151] In assessing the effectiveness of the 2002 Code of Practice it was necessary to explain what the phrases flexibility and choice meant; although the government had used these terms, it had not defined them. The Interim Report treated flexibility as to do with outcome, whether or not the lease provides flexibility for the tenant to respond to its changing business needs. Choice is to do with process, whether or not a range of alternative leasehold terms is made available to the contracting tenant.

In addition to the findings on the effectiveness of the 2002 Code of Practice, these Reports contain a great deal of information about the operation of the commercial property leasehold market. One of the difficulties with much of the empirical evidence about the structure of commercial leases is that it tends to be weighted towards larger properties; certainly many of the fulsome documents prepared by the property industry in response to the various consultations on UORR were from bodies representing investors and larger landlords, and much of the statistical information is drawn from information

[146] J Burton, 'Retail Rents, Fair and Free Market?' (London, Adam Smith Research Trust, 1992), although the claims are controversial.

[147] RICS Commercial Leases Group, Commercial Property Leases in England and Wales, Code of Practice (London, Furnival Press, December 1995).

[148] DETR, 'Monitoring the Code of Practice for Commercial Leases' (April 2000).

[149] RICS Policy Unit, A Code of Practice for Commercial Leases in England and Wales 2nd ed (2002).

[150] N Crosby, C Hughes and S Murdoch, Monitoring the Code of Practice for Commercial Leases, Interim Report (ODPM, April 2004).

[151] N Crosby, C Hughes and S Murdoch, 'Monitoring the 2002 Code of Practice for Commercial Leases' (ODPM, March 2005).

on the Investment Property Databank (IPD) which covers only properties owned by major property companies and financial institutions, and occupied by major tenants. Although by no means comprehensive, the two reports by a team at the University of Reading on the operation of the 2002 Code of Practice draw on a wider spread of the market.[152]

Landlords have often sought to keep the details of deals confidential. This is now much more difficult. From 13 October 2005 any document on the Land Register will be open for public inspection. It is possible to apply for any provisions considered to be prejudicial to be designated as an exempt information document (EID) and to be hidden from public view but this is unlikely to cover much of the information that landlords have traditionally guarded, such as the passing rent.

The Interim Report on the Code of Practice explains the market, institutional and legal framework within which commercial leases operate, and shows how commercial leasing practices are responsive to factors both internal and external to the property market: general economic conditions (interest rates, demands for space, bankruptcy rates, employment levels, globalisation and inwards and outward investment flows), cycles in the property market (yields, property investment, construction levels), changing business needs for space and style of property, accounting practices, and the legal framework (the abolition of original tenant liability, and the related impact on alienation covenants, easier contracting out, registration of leases).[153] The Final Report comments on later developments that also impact, in particular changes to the taxation of leases.

A combination of these external factors but also changing tenant needs means that there is now much more variety in the pattern of commercial leases than previously. For tenants, flexibility has become key. Changes to the land registration rules (see 4.2.1.2 above), stamp duty land tax, and accountancy practices[154] have all tended to encourage tenants to want shorter leases. Business needs also mean that many tenants are now reluctant to commit to long term use of space, not only because it is difficult to predict business growth but also because the way that modern space is used is constantly changing. Of course, some businesses prefer longer leases, such as those that have very high fitting out costs, and major retailers for whom location is crucial for their commercial success.

4.9.3 The Codes of Practice

The second edition of the Code contained 23 recommendations. Ten were directed to negotiation of new leases; the remainder related to how the parties were to deal with each other during the life of the lease. Overall the parties were encouraged to deal with each other constructively, courteously, openly and honestly throughout the term of the lease and to carry out their respective obligations fully and on time.

The 2002 Code of Practice was directed to property advisers as well as tenants but although it was more widely known than the first Code, and may well have played a part in

---

[152] These reports draw on selective records from the Valuation Office Agency which covers the whole of the property market, as well as interview and questionnaire surveys.

[153] N Crosby, C Hughes and S Murdoch, *Monitoring the Code of Practice for Commercial Leases, Interim Report* (ODPM, April 2004) ch 2. This is updated in chapter 2 of the Final Report.

[154] See C Edwards and P Krendel, *Institutional Leases in the 21st Century* (London, EG Books, 2007) 127–32.

introducing greater flexibility into the market, it had very little direct impact on individual lease negotiations. It is important to realise that a wide range of factors shape the lease negotiated between the parties. Even though the Final Report concluded that the 2002 Code of Practice had little direct impact on individual leases, it played:

> … an important part in the general application of pressure for change in leasing practices and … both Codes have undoubtedly had some long-term effect on the increasing flexibility and choice in commercial property leases.[155]

Even where the Code is known about, it is not always easy to get the landlord to use it. The high street retailer WH Smith plc has more than 500 different landlords to deal with, but finds that even large landlords do not always follow the Code of Practice.[156]

The third edition of the Code of Practice was issued in 2007.[157] The 2007 Business Lease Code remains voluntary but there is a suspicion by some that if this self-regulation does not work, legislative intervention may follow. The Introduction states:

> We hope the code will help the industry in its quest to promote efficiency and fairness in landlord and tenant relationships.

The emphasis in the Code is on offering choice to tenants. The government press statement accompanying its release emphasises its user-friendly format for small businesses.[158] In addition to a reduced number of recommendations (ten) it is accompanied by a guide for occupiers (with 'tips' to ask the landlord about and to watch out for) and a 'heads of terms' checklist which encourages parties to discuss key issues at the outset of the transaction.

The property industry is now taking seriously the need to be more responsive to the needs of occupiers, and landlords are making greater effort to offer leases that provide flexibility. The BPF has launched a commercial landlord voluntary self-accreditation scheme, known as the Commercial Landlords Accreditation Scheme (CLAS) to encourage tenant-friendly leasing.[159] Under this, scheme members will need to abide by five rules, including a commitment to explain the risk involved in a lease to prospective small business occupiers, to comply with the 2007 Business Lease Code and to provide a written complaints procedure.

4.9.4 Patterns of Modern Commercial Leases

It is clear that the commercial letting market has become much more flexible in recent years:

> If it was the property boom of the 1980s which brought about that perfect investment vehicle – the institutional lease – it was the long and deep property recession, which started in 1989 and lasted until the mid-1990s, that brought about its decline. Although, during those years,

---

[155] N Crosby, C Hughes and S Murdoch, 'Monitoring the 2002 Code of Practice for Commercial Leases' (ODPM, March 2005) 316.

[156] G Hewitt, 'The Modern Lease' (Conference Paper, 41st Joint Oxford Study Weekend, 2007).

[157] Joint Working Group on Commercial Leases, 'The Code for Leasing Business Premises in England and Wales 2007' (2007). The Code is available at www.leasingbusinesspremises.co.uk.

[158] DCLG, 'Small businesses will get better deal from landlords says Cooper' Press Release 061 (23 March 2007).

[159] See www.clascheme.org.uk.

landlords under existing leases gained substantial protection from, in particular, upward only rent reviews and original tenant liability, existing tenants paid a heavy price and would not again readily be drawn into signing the old style of lease.[160]

A greater variety of leasehold packages has become available to tenants during the last fifteen years or so, especially when it comes to the length of leases. It is no longer the case that the most common form of lease is for 25 years; indeed the BPF/IPD annual lease review for 2004/05 shows that nearly two thirds of leases were for five years or less, and that the average length of new lettings is continuing to fall. This review considered 9,500 new leases granted in 2004/05 and only 6 per cent of these new leases were for more than 15 years. Letting practices do tend to vary with different segments of the market. Thus, newer properties and higher value properties will tend to have longer than average lease lengths, and retail leases also tend to be longer, with around one third of retail leases being for 15 years.[161] Break clauses (enabling the tenant to end the lease early) have also become more common, especially in the secondary and tertiary markets. They are also more frequent in the office than retail sector.[162] Further, although it is still usually the case that it is the tenant who bears the financial responsibility for repair, it is now becoming more common at the beginning of a lease for second-hand property to provide a schedule of dilapidations recording the current state of the property, which means that the tenant will not have to return 'new for old'.

Nonetheless, certain features have not changed. UORR remains 'virtually universal' in leases containing review provisions. On the other hand, over 50 per cent of leases have no rent review provisions,[163] presumably reflecting the fact that leases are generally shorter. Again, there is diversity between sectors, with retail leases the most likely to contain review provisions. Five yearly review is the norm in the institutional market, and three yearly reviews in the secondary and tertiary markets. There remains very little flexibility in relation to alienation. A significant number of small business tenants have no right to assign or sub-let at all,[164] and where assignment is allowed, it is 'almost universal' that the tenant will be required to guarantee his immediate successor (by entering into an 'authorised guarantee agreement' – AGA – see chapter 18). Many leases permit sub-letting only if the rent is no less than the passing rent of the head lease, making it difficult to sub-let unless the market is rising. However, in response to the government's expressed concern about the inflexibility of alienation provisions, a number of large institutional landlords and property companies have announced that they will permit, with existing as well as new leases, sub-letting at a market rent even if this is less than the rent payable under the head lease.

---

[160] S Murdoch, 'Commercial Leases: Future Directions' in S Bright (ed), *Landlord and Tenant Law. Past, Present and Future* (Oxford, Hart, 2006) 93.

[161] N Crosby, C Hughes and S Murdoch, 'Monitoring the 2002 Code of Practice for Commercial Leases' (ODPM, March 2005) 10.

[162] N Crosby, C Hughes and S Murdoch, 'Monitoring the 2002 Code of Practice for Commercial Leases', (ODPM, March 2005) 10.

[163] N Crosby, C Hughes and S Murdoch, 'Monitoring the 2002 Code of Practice for Commercial Leases' ODPM, March 2005, 10.

[164] N Crosby, C Hughes and S Murdoch, 'Monitoring the 2002 Code of Practice for Commercial Leases' (ODPM, March 2005) 303.

4.9.5 Flexibility and Choice in Commercial Leases?

It is clear that there is now much greater variety in leases than previously. This does not mean, however, that there is much greater flexibility and choice. What many tenants want is flexibility, greater cost certainty, and quality service provision. For retailing occupiers, unrestricted user clauses are important as they give the opportunity to innovate and respond to changes. For most the ability to choose when to exit a lease is key, yet as we have seen few leases contain generous alienation provisions. Service charges fluctuating with expenditure remain standard, making it difficult for tenants to budget expenditure.

Edwards and Krendel refer to the analysis that Boots, the retailer, has done of its leasing practices. It occupies over 1,400 stores in the UK and the Republic of Ireland. From this it found:

> ... from its perspective, it makes economic sense to pay up to 133% of the rent quoted for a 15 year lease to reduce the term to five years.

As Edwards and Krendel point out, the small business tenant will simply not have this kind of knowledge about valuation.

In relation to choice, the Final Report concludes:

> An explicit set of appropriately priced lease terms is not being offered to tenants at the commencement of negotiations; it happens very occasionally but it is not usual.[165]

Landlords tend to offer leases that can be negotiated around the edges but seldom are alternative packages put to the tenant. For major multiples with many outlets having to negotiate leases with different landlords is difficult; although the tenant is a major company, landlords are often small property companies and, as seen below, this can make it hard to negotiate flexible packages.[166] For small business tenants it is harder still. Small business tenants often enter into leases without receiving any professional advice, even though they usually have no previous experience of leasing, and are likely to take the lease on the first terms offered.[167] The tenant focuses on the headline rent but largely ignores other terms that will have a significant impact upon the future of the business (such as service charges, repairing obligations, alterations, and entry and exit). Unless offered choice, the small business tenant is unlikely to ask for it. Nor will it understand the commercial advantages that a flexible lease may bring.

Some landlords have, however, recognised that the ability to provide the flexibility that occupiers want gives a commercial opportunity. For many tenants, especially small businesses that are starting up and who are inexperienced in the rental market, what is needed is an easy way in to letting. Recognising this need, a British businessman set up a small business centre in Brussels in 1989, Regus, which has now grown into a major international company providing 'workplace outsourcing'. The idea is that the business can rent fully equipped and serviced office space for an 'all in' fee on flexible terms. Agreements can

---

[165] N Crosby, C Hughes and S Murdoch, 'Monitoring the 2002 Code of Practice for Commercial Leases' (ODPM, March 2005) 11.

[166] C Edwards and P Krendel, *Institutional Leases in the 21st Century* (London, EG Books, 2007) 139–141.

[167] N Crosby, C Hughes and S Murdoch, 'Monitoring the 2002 Code of Practice for Commercial Leases' (ODPM, March 2005) 201. Twenty-five per cent of leases involved no negotiation over terms (this is for tenants of all sizes).

be as short as one page, and deals are quickly done so that the business can move in the following day if required. In practice, these short term agreements for serviced work space will usually be licences rather than leases as the owner will retain extensive control over the premises and the agreements will commonly contain mobility clauses.[168] For occupiers with much larger space requirements Land Securities plc, one of the UK's leading property companies, has developed a product known as 'Landflex'. When space is offered to prospective tenants they are asked on what basis they would like to occupy. The lease is priced according to the package. Landflex leases do not contain rent reviews and the landlord provides all of the services for the building (including within the tenanted parts) under a core service agreement. There is one price to cover rent and servicing which is subject to annual indexation.

4.9.6 Flexibility and Valuation

The value placed on a landlord's interest in property is important: a higher capital value improves the balance sheet and this higher company worth provides more opportunities to raise and borrow money in the capital markets. Because valuation is more difficult when a property is let on non-standard terms, this has discouraged flexibility in the letting market. Putting a capital value on a building that is let on a long lease with a strong tenant covenant, guaranteed minimum rent, and all unknown costs being passed on to the tenant is relatively uncomplicated. If the lease is shorter, contains a break clause, and is for an all inclusive rental it is much harder to value the property. There is a tendency for valuers to work on the 'worst-case scenario', assuming both that the break clause is exercised (even though in practice most are not) and that a long void follows.[169] For this reason, it is easier for large landlords to lease on a flexible basis as risks can be spread across the portfolio. For a small landlord flexible leasing may not be financially feasible. As Edwards and Krendel write:

> If its tenant breaks [the lease] or becomes insolvent and there is a void, [the single-property-owning investor with debt finance] ... is in trouble with its lender.[170]

4.9.7 A Consumer Focus?

Amongst some landlords the approach to the business of leasing is changing. Landlords are beginning to talk of tenants as 'customers'. Glynne Anthony of Land Securities suggests that there has been a shift in mind set. Historically the landlord and tenant relationship was relatively adversarial in nature:

> The mentality of many landlords was to try to let buildings on as long a lease as possible and only engage with the tenant at the end of a lease or at rent review ... Relationships were not seen as important or necessary. It was purely about creating as much value as possible.[171]

---

[168] See text accompanying n 121.
[169] See C Edwards and P Krendel, *Institutional Leases in the 21st Century* (London, EG Books, 2007) 105, 142–44.
[170] C Edwards and P Krendel, *Institutional Leases in the 21st Century* (London, EG Books, 2007) 144.
[171] G Anthony, 'The Modern Lease' (Conference Paper, 41st Joint Oxford Study Weekend, 2007). Cf C Edwards and P Krendel, *Institutional Leases in the 21st Century* (London, EG Books, 2007) 155–56.

He continues by suggesting that this has changed over time and that landlords now have greater understanding of the value in providing what occupiers really want.

4.10 The Structure of Residential Leases

4.10.1 Residential Tenancies

In the private sector, the parties are free to negotiate their own terms, subject to a number of statutory rights that will be implied irrespective of their agreement, such as the landlord's statutory repairing obligation under the Landlord and Tenant Act 1985 section 11. In practice, most tenancies will be drawn up by the landlord (or his agent) and presented to the tenant on a 'take it or leave it' basis. Small-scale research by Lister confirms the view that tenants seldom negotiate or discuss the tenancy relationship.[172]

For social housing, it will always be the landlord who prepares the tenancy agreement. Again, there will be a number of statutory rights given to the tenant.

4.10.2 The Law Commission's Proposals on Rental Contracts

As mentioned above, the Law Commission has proposed that a fair and transparent contract should be at the heart of the consumer approach to protecting occupants of rented homes. To enable landlords to meet the statutory requirements, model contracts will be promoted containing the fundamental and supplementary terms (see 4.6.2 above). In so far as the parties have inserted additional terms or have modified the supplementary terms, they will be subject to the regime under the UTCCR (see 4.8.2 above). They will be easy to complete and the Law Commission expects that they would be widely used.[173]

4.10.3 Residential Leases

As long residential leases are mainly used for properties such as flats that have communal parts and where services are provided, the documentation needs to be drawn up carefully to make clear exactly what is let (where the demised property ends and the retained parts begin), what services are provided (and how), and how service charges are calculated and recovered. The result is that leases tend to be long and detailed documents agreed between lawyers. Again, the norm is for the lease to be on the terms proposed by the landlord and relatively few amendments are likely to be agreed.

There is a considerable amount of legislation applicable to long residential leases, particularly relating to management and repairing issues. This means that the lease itself tells the leaseholder only of part of his rights. There is, however, no move to standardise leases in the same manner as is being proposed for rental contracts.

---

[172] D Lister, 'The nature of tenancy relationships: landlords and young people' in S Lowe and D Hughes (eds), *The Private Rented Sector in a New Century: revival or false dawn?* (Bristol, The Policy Press, 2002) 98.

[173] Law Commission, 'Renting Homes: The Final Report. Volume 1: Report' (Law Com No 297, 2006) paras 3.34–3.54.

4.11 Variation of Lease Terms

Generally, the terms of a lease can only be varied by consent of both parties.

4.11.1 Secure Tenancies

In the public sector there is, however, a statutory procedure for varying the lease terms. This provides three methods of varying the terms of a secure tenancy. The first method is by agreement between the landlord and the tenant.[174] The second method applies only to a variation relating to 'rent or to payments in respect of rates or services' and enables them to be varied in accordance with any provision in the tenancy agreement.[175] The third method applies to periodic tenancies and enables the landlord to vary a tenancy by serving a notice on the tenant after first giving the opportunity to comment on the proposed variation.[176]

These statutory methods provide the *only* permitted ways of varying a secure tenancy. In *R (on the application of Kilby) v Basildon DC* the local authority had included a clause in the tenancy providing that variations could be made only with the agreement of a majority of the tenants' representatives (persons elected to represent tenants on the tenants' management board).[177] When the landlord proposed a variation without following this procedure it was challenged by judicial review but the Court of Appeal held that the clause was 'incompatible with the Council's statutory right and power to vary their tenancies unilaterally'.[178]

4.11.2 Long Residential Leases

Part IV of the Landlord and Tenant Act 1987 contains provisions to enable the landlord or tenant to apply to the Leasehold Valuation Tribunal for the variation of long leases of flats where the lease fails to make satisfactory provision for repair, maintenance, insurance and servicing of the property (see chapter 11).

---

[174] Housing Act 1985 s 102(1)(a).
[175] Housing Act 1985 s 102(1)(b).
[176] Housing Act 1985 s 103(2).
[177] [2007] EWCA Civ 479.
[178] [2007] EWCA Civ 479 [32]. Rix LJ added that although unnecessary to go into these public law doctrines, the clause was also a fetter on the Council's statutory power and a delegation to the tenants' representatives of its statutory power of variation by notice: [35].

PART THREE
REGULATING THE RELATIONSHIP

The Structure of Part Three

The chapters in Part 3 set out the legislative controls applicable in the different sectors (rented homes, long residential leases, business tenancies, and agricultural tenancies), charting the historic development of controls and taking account of the socio-economic and policy factors that have shaped the present laws.

The question of which statutory code applies depends on the purpose for which the property is used, as outlined in Figure P3.

In this part of the book, the discussion of the law is largely descriptive, laying the foundation for the analysis of the different kinds of protection which occurs in the subsequent parts of the book.

As the policy issues and the statutory codes differ between the sectors there is a chapter dedicated to each sector that intermingles the discussion of policy and legislation (except for renting homes where the policy issues are much more complex and have been given a separate chapter). Thus chapters 5 and 6 cover policy and law respectively in relation to renting homes, chapter 7 deals with long residential leases, chapter 8 discusses business tenancies and chapter 9 looks at agricultural tenancies.

The final chapter of Part 3, chapter 10, discusses human rights law. Arguments based upon human rights law are increasingly a feature of landlord and tenant disputes, and concern to respect these rights is also taken into account in shaping legislative and policy changes. Chapter 10 sets out the main aspects of human rights law that have the potential to impact on the landlord and tenant relationship, and throughout the book there are references to human rights arguments in relation to particular topics.

The Importance of Policy in the Wider Context

Learning only about the law of landlord and tenant does not provide a rounded understanding of the resulting legal relationship. Instead, it is necessary to step outside a narrowly legal perspective to see the wider context. Looking beyond the law can help to explain why it is that there are so many (or so few) leasehold relationships. So, for example, the dramatic decline in the number of homes rented from private landlords (from around 90 per cent before World War I, to around 10 per cent some 90 years later) needs to be considered in the light of policies promoting home ownership, the growth in social housing, and the impact of rent control and security of tenure. The wider perspective also helps to explain both the particular structure of the individual relationship, and why parties behave as they do within

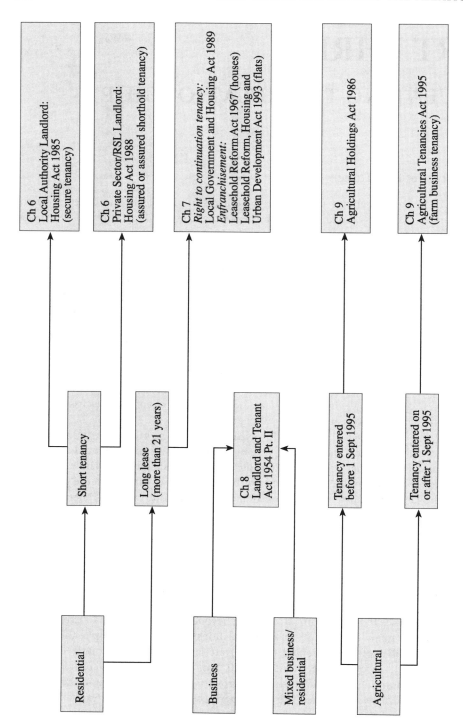

Figure P3: Which Statutory Code?

the relationship. Commercial leases are largely the product of negotiations between the landlord and the tenant, but the terms of the bargain will be affected by the attractiveness of the property, the state of the property market, the fiscal consequences of particular lease terms, whether professionals are involved in the negotiations, the relative strengths of the two parties, and so on. Further, a landlord acting from purely commercial motives is likely to have a different perception of its role and responsibilities as landlord than, say, a landlord providing social housing for vulnerable groups.

What is Policy?

Policy is often an important part of the wider context explaining tenancies. The discussion of policy in the following chapters is written for those with a background in legal analysis and who are not familiar with social science terminology or structure. This is not a book about policy, and the author is not a policy expert, but policy is discussed in so far as it aids an understanding of the law and the way that the legal relationship of landlord and tenant has been shaped, and is continuing to evolve. Establishing the links between policy, practice and the law requires novel frames of reference for lawyers. A preliminary question is, 'what is policy'? Policy is, broadly, the result of a decision taken as to how to achieve a particular objective. It could be narrow, as, for example, a decision about the particular approach to be taken towards the obligation to repair, or much wider, as, for example, the general attitude of government in encouraging owner-occupation over renting. It is this latter sense of policy that is focused upon in this part of the book.

At various times, it may be that there have been no clear objectives or policies identified, and the law has simply developed in a rather unguided manner. It is also the case that even once a broad objective is agreed upon, there may be alternative ways of moving towards it. If 'decent homes for all' is taken as an objective, there is a variety of policies that could be promoted for achieving this. It could be achieved through a policy of encouraging cheap owner-occupation through subsidies directed at the consumer in the form of tax relief on mortgage payments, or by allowing social landlords to build dwellings and then subsidising those landlords. The law can also play a critical role in the implementation of policy. So, for example, the objective of providing 'decent homes for all' is supported by a policy of mandatory licensing of landlords for certain kinds of property (see chapter 11).

It should also be noted that objectives are often phrased in very vague terms, making it difficult to assess with any precision how successful any implementation through specific policies has been. Further, there may well be a range of objectives, and their related policies may well conflict. So, for example:

A policy of housing those in most urgent need may conflict with a policy of replacing the worst houses, and both may conflict with a policy for stimulating demand through subsidies directed to those who are most likely to be persuaded by such help to build or buy homes for themselves: different people will benefit from the pursuit of each of these objectives … A policy designed to eliminate rent controls and create a 'free market' in housing may conflict with the need to avoid inflation of living costs and wages. Every country's housing policies contain the seeds of several such conflicts, for housing is so central a feature of the economy and the way of life it supports that many of the competing aspirations at work in a society gain some expression in this field.[1]

A major evaluation of housing policy over the period 1975-2000 commissioned by the Office of the Deputy Prime Minister (ODPM) found that:

> Few policies have been almost entirely unsuccessful. However, the evaluation found that while individual policy instruments are most successful when judged in their own terms, policies often had unintended, frequently undesirable, consequences. For example, Right to Buy raised the level of home ownership, the homelessness legislation provided a safety net for eligible families, and the planning system helps to protect the countryside. A series of policies reduced government funding and improved its targeting. Yet together with economic change and wider housing market restructuring, right to buy and the homelessness legislation contributed to the 'residualisation' of social rented housing which in turn created concentrations of poverty and exclusion. Targeting subsidies on the poorest tenants reduced incentives to work.
>   It was also clear that policies often presented trade-offs ... Transferring social rented housing to the housing association sector has brought in new investment, but has also fragmented management and increased costs of funding.[2]

One way to measure the success of policy and legislative measures is through surveys, empirical studies and collation of statistical information. Throughout the book reference is made to this kind of information in order to help in the process of evaluating the effectiveness of the law.

Avoiding Statutory Protection[3]

As the law imposes controls upon landlords in pursuit of policy, so landlords have sought, by various means, to avoid these controls. This was seen in chapter 3, for example, where owners sought to avoid the Rent Acts by using licences instead of leases. This is not something confined to the residential sector; there are also examples of attempts at avoidance in relation to long residential leases, business tenancies and agricultural tenancies. In some situations there are specific anti-avoidance measures that have been built into the legislation, but the courts have also developed judicial tools to distinguish between what is permissible and what is not. The legal principles used by judges to judge whether an avoidance measure is effective or not are considered here as they apply to all of the sectors discussed in the following chapters.

There are two broad avoidance techniques used by landlords. The first is to 're-route' the legal relationship so as to take it outside the remit of the protective legislation. Examples include the use of a licence instead of a lease (see chapter 3), letting a home to a company instead of an individual (see chapter 6), and entering into a farming partnership instead of an agricultural tenancy (see chapter 9). So long as the route chosen is genuine, then it will

---

[1] JB Cullingworth, *Problems of an Urban Society* (London, Allen and Unwin, 1973) Vol 2, 40.

[2] A Holmans, M Stephens and S Fitzpatrick, 'Housing Policy in England since 1975: An Introduction to the Special Issue' (2007) 22 *Housing Studies* 147, 158–9.

[3] The following arguments are more fully presented in S Bright, 'Avoiding Tenancy Legislation: Sham and Contracting Out Revisited' (2002) 61 *CLJ* 146.

be effective. The task of the courts at this stage is to determine if the agreement is genuine. Motive is irrelevant: the fact that a transaction has been structured in a particular way to avoid statutory controls, even if highly artificial, does not, by itself, make it unlawful.

The second avoidance technique is to include some provision within the tenancy agreement which seeks to avoid statutory control. An example is requiring an agricultural tenant protected by the Agricultural Holdings Act 1986 to agree not to serve a counter-notice in response to being served with a notice to quit, thereby effectively denying the tenant farmer any security.[4] The effectiveness of these techniques usually depends upon statutory construction, but public policy also plays a significant role.

Avoiding Statutory Protection by Re-routing

Usually a transaction will be taken at face value, and the question is the simple one of whether the agreement falls within, or outside, the statutory controls. Where, however, it is shown that some aspect of the agreement does not reflect the reality of what the parties have agreed, the courts will need to discover the true intention of the parties to see if the agreement attracts statutory control. In determining if the route is genuine, the courts have used the doctrines of labeling, sham and pretence.

Labelling is straightforward: it is what Lord Templeman was drawing on in *Street v Mountford* when he said that the effect of an agreement is a matter of law and does not depend on the label that the parties have attached to it.[5] In this case, it was agreed between the parties that Mrs Mountford had been granted exclusive possession for a term at a rent, and the question was simply whether the fact that the parties had called this a 'licence' was conclusive. The House of Lords held not: the agreement was a tenancy and the parties were not free to attach their own label to the agreement. As Lord Templeman said, if:

> … the agreement satisfied all the requirements of a tenancy, then the agreement produced a tenancy and the parties cannot alter the effect of the agreement by insisting that they only created a licence.[6]

Sham is essentially about saying one thing and doing another.[7] It is a narrow doctrine and occurs where the paperwork is a lie, intended to mislead a third party, and both parties know that the true position is otherwise. It occurred in *Bhopal v Walia* where the agreed rent was £300 per month but the paperwork showed it as £450 per month.[8]

Pretence is a wider doctrine, and will be found where there is no genuine intention to implement the agreement as it stands. To see if there is a pretence it is necessary to look at the content of the agreement, not only the label attached to it, to discover if the rights and obligations set out in the agreement are genuine. As Lord Donaldson MR said in *Aslan v Murphy*, it 'is the true rather than the apparent bargain which determines the question: tenant or lodger'.[9] This will depend on whether there was ever a real intention that both

---

[4] *Johnson v Moreton* (1980) AC 37 (HL)
[5] [1985] 1 AC 809 (HL). See further ch 3.
[6] [1985] 1 AC 809 (HL) 819.
[7] *Snook v London & West Riding Investments Ltd* [1967] 2 QB 786 (CA) 802.
[8] (1999) 32 HLR 302 (CA).
[9] *Aslan v Murphy, Wynne v Duke* (1990) 1 WLR 766 (CA) 776.

parties should honour the obligations and enjoy the rights expressed in the agreement. It is usually the occupier who will be seeking to argue that the agreement is non-genuine, and he will be able to rely upon external evidence, such as the physical layout, and post-agreement conduct, to prove that the formal agreement is a sham/non-genuine. In *Antoniades v Villiers*, an unmarried couple had signed two separate 'licence' agreements denying exclusive possession, and providing that the licensor could use the flat with the licensee.[10] The flat was suitable only for a single person or couple to live in. The House of Lords referred both to the physical impossibility of a third person living there, and that no attempts had been made to move anyone else in, to support the finding that the real transaction was a joint tenancy.

Avoiding Statutory Protection by Agreement

Some statutes contain specific provisions against contracting out.[11] Others contain general anti-avoidance measures.[12] The hardest cases are those where the statute is silent on the particular form of contracting out that has been used. The question is whether the courts are free to hold contracting out unlawful if it goes against the clear policy of the statute but the statute does not expressly prohibit it. The answer to this is, probably, no. A case that came close to doing this is *Johnson v Moreton*.[13] An agricultural tenant covenanted not to serve a counter-notice on the landlord if served with a notice to quit. As will be seen in chapter 9, by serving a counter-notice the tenant might have been able to challenge the landlord's notice to quit, and so stay on the farm. In practice, and notwithstanding the agreement, the tenant did serve a counter-notice. The House of Lords unanimously held that the tenant's covenant not to serve the counter-notice was invalid, but the ratio of the case is not clear. Lord Simon (with whom Lord Edmund Davies agreed) advocated a wide approach that might suggest that contracting out is not permissible when this would run against the mischief that the statute was designed to remedy:

> Where it appears that the mischief which Parliament is seeking to remedy is that a situation exists in which the relations of parties cannot properly be left to contractual regulation, and Parliament therefore provides for statutory regulation, a party cannot contract out of such statutory regulation (albeit exclusively in his own favour), because so to permit would be to reinstate the mischief which the statute was designed to remedy and to render the statutory provision a dead letter.[14]

Although all of the speeches emphasise the importance of policy and the public interest in supporting farming, statutory construction also plays a significant role in the reasoning.[15] Further, it is not possible to say if the wider remarks relating to the intention of Parliament and policy should be taken as applying in other contexts not involving the Agricultural Holdings Act 1986.

---

[10] *A G Securities v Vaughan; Antoniades v Villiers* (1990) 1 AC 417 (HL) 467–9. See further ch 3.
[11] For example, Agricultural Holdings Act 1986 s 5.
[12] For example, Landlord and Tenant (Covenants) Act 1995 s 25.
[13] *Johnson v Moreton* (1980) AC 37 (HL).
[14] *Johnson v Moreton* (1980) AC 37 (HL) 69.
[15] Especially Lords Salmon and Hailsham.

The Court of Appeal in *Bankway Properties Ltd v Pensfold-Densford* has, however, developed this wider approach.[16] This was not, strictly, a contracting out case as the tenants were not bargaining away any rights. The property was let on an assured tenancy within the Housing Act 1988 (which carried security rights) to tenants in receipt of housing benefit. The initial rent was £4,690 per annum but a review clause provided for the rent payable to be increased to £25,000 per annum, well above the market rent. It is clear that the landlord's plan was that when the rent was put up to £25,000, the tenants would either choose to leave the property because of the unaffordable rent or would fall into arrears with the rent, thus generating a mandatory ground for possession. There is no doubt that *Bankway Properties* involved a device intended to avoid the security of tenure provisions in the Housing Act 1988. The Court of Appeal held it ineffective and set aside the possession order. Arden LJ said there was 'in substance an unlawful contracting out or evasion of an Act of Parliament'.[17] Pill LJ said that there was 'inconsistency with the statutory purpose of the agreement'.[18] Given, however, that the Housing Act 1988 itself, allows the parties to agree both the initial rent and any provisions for reviewing it, it is hard to see how this was an unlawful contracting out. Arden LJ's reasoning was on the basis that it was not a payment for rent at all but really a basis for recovering possession.

If the approach in *Bankway Properties* is followed, then it may be that a much broader range of avoidance techniques will be held to be invalid than previously.[19] Rather than draw on such a broad and vague doctrine, courts may now prefer to invalidate unfair devices by using the Unfair Terms in Consumer Contract Regulations 1999,[20] although these Regulations apply only to contracts entered into with consumers.[21]

---

[16] *Bankway Properties Ltd v Pensfold-Dunsford* [2001] EWCA Civ 528, [2001] 1 WLR 169.

[17] *Bankway Properties Ltd v Pensfold-Dunsford* [2001] EWCA Civ 528, [2001] 1 WLR 169 [52].

[18] *Bankway Properties Ltd v Pensfold-Dunsford* [2001] EWCA Civ 528, [2001] 1 WLR 169 [68].

[19] For fuller discussion of this, see S Bright, 'Avoiding Tenancy Legislation: Sham and Contracting Out Revisited' (2002) 61 *CLJ* 146.

[20] SI 1999/2083. See ch 4.

[21] They were not in force at the relevant time for the facts involved in *Bankway Properties*.

5

RENTING HOMES: THE POLICY BACKGROUND

5.1   Introduction
5.2   Tenure division
5.3   Social renting and private renting
5.4   The period to 1980
5.5   From 1980 onwards
5.6   Current housing issues
5.7   Current issues and directions in the different tenures
5.8   Summary: rented housing in 2007

5.1 Introduction

Although this is a book about the law of landlord and tenant law an understanding of housing policy helps to explain how much property is rented, by whom, and to whom; how rent levels are set; the condition of rented property; the changing expectations of the landlord's managerial role; and the behaviour of both landlords and tenants. There is an extensive literature available on housing policy, but this chapter looks at housing policy only in so far as it impacts on rented homes.[1]

Housing policy has recently moved up the political agenda. For many years, it has been a Cinderella subject, with governments reacting to issues as they arose. But in March 2004, the Barker report was published, and considerable media coverage was given to its conclusion that the volatility of the housing market has had an adverse effect on the United Kingdom's economic and social success, and has exacerbated problems of macroeconomic instability.[2] The impact of the Barker review is that housing policy is now being taken seriously. During 2007, two major reviews of housing reported, both commissioned by the government. In February 2007, the Hills review was published with the aim of prompting a debate on the

---

[1] There is much more to 'housing' law and policy than is covered here. Housing law covers a morass of different areas of law; planning, mortgages, public health, welfare law, ownership, and compulsory purchase, as well as tenancy law.

[2] K Barker, 'Review of Housing Supply – Delivering Stability: Securing our Future Housing Needs' (HM Treasury and ODPM, March 2004). There was also a review of housing policy commissioned by the government which reported in 2005: M Stephens, C Whitehead and M Munro, 'Lessons from the Past, Challenges for the Future for Housing Policy: an Evaluation of English Housing Policy 1975 – 2000' (ODPM, 2005).

role that social housing can play in the twenty-first century.[3] In June 2007, the Cave Review reported on regulation of social housing.[4] Further, the Labour government's Green Paper on housing, published in July 2007, proposes an increase in new social housing for rent and, for the first time in more than two decades, accepts that local authorities can play a direct part as providers of new social housing.[5]

The mantra guiding housing policy is 'both simple and fundamental – to ensure a decent home for every individual in the country'.[6] Linked to this, and reflecting the growing concern about social exclusion, attention is also being turned to the importance of building 'truly sustainable communities', ones that contain the infrastructure, amenities and sense of place that are necessary to create communities where people will want to live and stay. The key issue dominating housing policy now is ensuring that there is an adequate supply of housing, in places where people want to live, that is of decent standard, and that is affordable. To achieve these goals, attention is being paid to the planning system, the release of land for building, and the financing of housing.

The approach to housing policy taken in this chapter is largely an historical one, looking at how policies have evolved and changed over the years. There will be particular emphasis on tenure (how much housing is provided through the rental market, and how much through home ownership), and on housing standards and management, as these aspects of housing policy impact most strongly on the law of landlord and tenant.

5.2 Tenure Division

Tenure describes the way in which housing is held, as freehold or leasehold. The commonly-used tenure division in housing policy is four-fold: owner-occupation, council renting, housing association renting and private renting. Housing policy writers are cautious of using housing tenure as an organisational tool, as it has 'great analytical limitations'.[7] The first is that 'each tenure is in fact far more heterogeneous than the labels imply'; a council tenant in a tower block on a run down estate is in a very different position from one in a stone cottage in a rural location. The second problem for housing policy writers is that 'tenure is a mere consumption label: it tells us something about the terms on which households occupy their homes', but there is no necessary link between tenure and housing finance or housing production.[8] Although this may be a drawback for policy focused analysis, it is helpful when policy is being used in order to illuminate the legal relation of landlord and tenant.

The last one hundred years or so has seen a dramatic reduction in the amount of housing that is privately rented (from around 90 per cent to just under 11 per cent),[9] the

---

[3] J Hills, 'Ends and means: The future roles of social housing in England' (CASE Report 34, February 2007).
[4] M Cave, 'Every Tenant Matters: A review of social housing regulation' (June 2007).
[5] DCLG, 'Homes for the future: more affordable, more sustainable' (Cm 7191, July 2007).
[6] HM Treasury and ODPM 'Housing policy: an overview' (July 2005) 1.1.
[7] P Malpass and A Murie, *Housing Policy and Practice* 5th edn (Basingstoke, Macmillan, 1999) 6.
[8] P Malpass and A Murie, *Housing Policy and Practice* 5th edn (Basingstoke, Macmillan, 1999) 7.
[9] Rising to more than 20% in inner London and some other areas: M Ball, 'Buy to Let. The Revolution – 10 Years On' (ARLA, September 2006) 4.

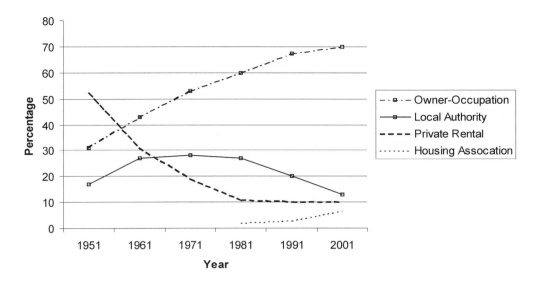

Figure 5.1: Trends in Housing Tenure

growth of a meaningful social rented sector, and rapid growth of owner-occupation (from around 10 per cent to 70 per cent). These trends are shown graphically in Figure 5.1.[10]

British governments have tended to focus on promoting particular forms of tenure rather than having a housing policy that is focused on ensuring an adequate supply of housing. The major problem has been, and remains, an inadequate supply of housing that is both affordable and decent. Even now that housing supply is acknowledged as a priority issue, housing policy is still very much driven by promoting a particular tenure form, namely, ownership, and as most households who can afford to buy into full ownership have already done so alternative models of shared ownership are now being pushed. It is this story that largely explains the shape and role of rented housing and for this reason tenure division provides the basis of the discussion in this chapter.

5.3 Social Renting and Private Renting

5.3.1 *Defining Social Renting*

Within the rental sector, it is usual to distinguish between renting according to landlord type. At several points in this book it is necessary to follow this pattern as the law similarly treats

---

[10] *Compiled from:* M Boddy, *Building Societies* (London, Macmillan, 1980) Figure 2.5, and S Wilcox, *UK Housing Review 2005/2006* (Coventry, Chartered Institute of Housing and London, Council of Mortgage Lenders, 2005). The percentages for the years before 1971 are for England and Wales; for 1971 onwards they are for England.

lettings by council landlords differently from lettings by housing association landlords, and from lettings by private landlords. In terms of understanding the landlord and tenant relationship in a wider sense it is helpful, however, to think in terms of there being a broad distinction that can be drawn between social renting and private (or market) renting.

This, of course, begs the question as to what is 'social renting'. In the Hills review, social housing is taken to mean 'housing provided, normally at sub-market rents, by not-for-profit landlords'.[11] As a working definition this provides the gist of what social housing is about, but even at this broad level it is not fully accurate as recent changes have meant that commercial bodies ('for profit' developers) are also involved in the provision of social housing (see text accompanying fn 87 below). Further, although the phrase social housing is now a normal part of the vocabulary of housing law and policy, Cowan and McDermont point out that:

> ... the conjunction of the words 'social' and 'housing' represents a relatively recent, and per-haps paradoxical truth-claim in the history of state involvement in the provision of housing in the United Kingdom. In the early 1990s, at a time when we questioned the existence of the social, or talked of its crisis, the term began to be applied to rented housing provided by local councils and housing associations in a rapidly demunicipalizing not-for-profit rented sector. It was in an attempt to recover both a distinctiveness and commonality of purpose in the face of fragmentation that the term 'social housing' belatedly came into currency.[12]

A United Nations European policy document identifies the following factors as indicators of what tends to make 'social housing' social:

(a)   financial support from the public sector, in the form of supply-side subsidies (such as financial aid for construction and major repair programmes);
(b)   rent policies designed to keep rents to below market levels;
(c)   allocation to tenants on the basis of some social criteria, usually related to income or housing need;
(d)   a restricted ownership, so that the government is able to ensure that the public support serves its housing policy aims;
(e)   better protection against eviction than residents in private rentals;
(f)   the involvement of residents in decision-making (known as tenant participation).[13]

Not all of these factors are necessarily present in any individual system of social housing. Further, missing from this list is the feature that Cowan and McDermont regard as central to an understanding of social housing, 'that it is first and foremost a site of *governance*'.[14] According to them, the conjunction of the words 'social' and 'housing' have enabled a space to be created within which it is possible to regulate in order to achieve certain ends,

---

[11] J Hills, 'Ends and means: The future roles of social housing in England' (CASE Report 34, February 2007) 13.

[12] D Cowan and M McDermont, *Regulating Social Housing, Governing Decline* (Abingdon, Routledge-Cavendish, 2006) 1–2.

[13] UN Economic Commission for Europe (UNECE), 'Guidelines on Social Housing' (draft) (2005) ch II. The final version of this document notes the difficulty in defining what social housing is about and is less specific in relation to the indicators of what 'social' is: UNECE, 'Guidelines on Social Housing: Principles and Examples' (April 2006) UN Doc ECE/HBP/137, ch II.

[14] D Cowan and M McDermont, *Regulating Social Housing, Governing Decline* (Abingdon, Routledge-Cavendish, 2006) 21.

including moral regulation ('responsible' tenants), a redistributive agenda (making good quality housing available to all regardless of income) and a social integrationist agenda.

While the idea of social housing is, therefore, a slippery concept, Fitzpatrick and Pawson suggest that:

> ... there is one indispensable characteristic common to all social housing – 'access' is determined on the basis of 'administrative criteria' rather than 'price rationing'.[15]

5.3.2 The Role of Social Housing

As will be seen, the role of social housing has changed enormously in England, at times representing a broad concept, where rented dwellings are provided for a wide segment of the population, and at other times a more narrow concept where housing is provided largely for those with particular needs (often referred to as a 'safety net' role).

The question of the role of social housing is, however, about far more than whom the housing is for. The Hills review implicitly accepts that social landlords should be model landlords, and that social housing has a role way beyond providing a simple roof over the head:

> ... arguments about higher quality than private landlords, avoiding discrimination, affordability, the avoidance of area polarisation, and avoidance of strong disincentives for tenants to work and save, are potentially all very powerful.[16]

In setting out the markers for a debate about the role of social housing, Hills suggests that social housing should be integrated into a far wider social agenda: a better quality of housing and housing management than exists in the private sector,[17] the promotion of sustainable mixed income communities, encouraging social mobility and opportunity (including labour mobility), and providing access to a wider range of responses to housing need (questioning, perhaps, the assumption that the solution to a housing problem is necessarily the grant of a secure tenancy for life). Against these measures, social housing is not currently achieving all that it could: levels of dissatisfaction with both accommodation and landlords are rising amongst social tenants, the geography and allocation of social housing drives area polarisation rather than solving it and rates of employment are disappointingly low.[18]

5.3.3 Distinctions in Law

When it comes to the legal framework that regulates rented housing there are two main statutory codes, but the line between them is not drawn on the basis of whether the housing

---

[15] S Fitzpatrick and H Pawson, 'Welfare Safety Net or Tenure of Choice? The Dilemma Facing Social Housing Policy in England' (2007) 22 *Housing Studies* 163, 164 referring to M Stephens, N Burns and L MacKay, 'The limits of housing reform: British social rented housing in a European context' (2003) 40 *Urban Studies* 767.

[16] J Hills, 'Ends and means: The future roles of social housing in England' (CASE Report 34, February 2007) 1.

[17] Why should it be *better* than the private sector? Should not private tenants also be able to expect high standards?

[18] One concern is that the difficulty of moving within the social sector means that tenants fail to pursue employment opportunities that would necessitate moving.

is social or private. Instead, it depends on the landlord type. Council housing is governed by the Housing Act 1980, but housing association lettings come within the Housing Act 1988 that applies to private landlords. In terms of the substantive rights enjoyed by tenants, however, housing association lettings are usually much closer to council lettings than other private landlords lettings. This is because housing associations choose to use the Housing Act 1988 and their contractual tenancies in a way that comes close to mirroring the rights enjoyed by council tenants. This is especially true in relation to security of tenure, that is, the expectation that tenants have of being able to remain in their home indefinitely. Indeed, the primary distinction drawn by the Law Commission in the renting homes project is between agreements that provide long term security of tenure, and those that have much less security of tenure:[19]

> 1.21 Social housing is designed to provide long-term housing for tenants who, for a variety of social and economic reasons, are particularly vulnerable within the housing market. The creation of sustainable communities relies on confidence by tenants that, if they keep to their terms of their agreement, they will keep their long term family homes …
>
> 1.23 In the private rented sector … the long-term social dimension is now less in evidence. Landlords are, in the main, providing accommodation to niche sectors of the market who in general fall outside the scope of social housing and many of whose tenants are not seeking to be housed on a long-term basis. The private sector now exists within a market framework.[20]

The degree of security available is not, however, a useful tool for distinguishing between social and private renting. Although the length of security enjoyed by tenants now broadly corresponds to landlord type, with social landlords providing long term security and private landlords not, this has not always been the case. In the past, under the former Rent Acts, private tenants also enjoyed long term security. Nor is it the case, contrary to what the Law Commission suggests, that the private sector is a 'niche market'. As seen in chapter 1, there are many 'sub-markets' within the private sector and while some landlords cater for young professionals, others are renting to tenants who may well have preferred to be in the social sector with 'tenure for life' but for some reason have not been able to access social housing.

5.3.4 A Working Definition

Within this book, social housing is taken to refer to council and housing association lettings which are entered into for social purposes, and private (or market) renting refers to lettings by private landlords (together with the occasional lettings by councils and housing associations that do not form part of their social lettings). The reason for classifying in this way is that although governed by different statutory codes there is a great similarity between housing association and council lettings. The approaches to rent setting, allocation, debt

---

[19] This division broadly corresponds to the secure tenancies available to council tenants under the Housing Act 1980, and the assured tenancies under the Housing Act 1988 (used by housing associations) that give long term security; and assured shorthold tenancies under the Housing Act 1988 (mainly used by private landlords) that give no long-term security

[20] Law Commission, 'Renting Homes 1: Status and Security' (Law Com CP No 162, 2002).

collection, the role and responsibilities of the landlord, tenant participation, and the level of security enjoyed have much in common.

5.4 The Period to 1980

5.4.1 The Birth of State Provision of Housing

The 'problem' of housing is not new. With rapid population growth[21] and the urbanisation of Britain in the early nineteenth century came problems of severe overcrowding and insanitary living conditions. The response was not to provide more houses, but to see housing as part of a public health problem.[22] In other words, the early response was to treat the symptoms, not the cause. Further, the public health response tended to worsen the problems of overcrowding, as improvement schemes involved slum clearance without the provision of new housing. During this period, most housing was rented from private landlords but renting became less economic for them as minimum standards in new dwellings began to be imposed through by-laws from the mid 1800s. No subsidy was provided to encourage the private landlords to build. By the turn of the century, it was clear that something needed to be done to ease the problems, but private landlords were not able, or willing, to expand to meet the housing need. 'Model housing companies', such as Peabody and Guiness were set up in 1862 and 1890 respectively, with the aim of showing that it was possible to maintain public health standards and prevent overcrowding while providing a five per cent return on investment. In practice, however, they still had to set rents that were too high for the poorest households.[23]

During the nineteenth century the question began to emerge as to whether there should be some state responsibility, either at the central or local level, for providing housing or at least dealing with slum clearance. There were some legislative measures giving powers to local bodies, but these were largely ineffective.[24] It was housing associations who were made the early executors of state policy through the Cross Act.[25] This provided for local authorities to acquire and clear slum sites, for selling or leasing to charities which would rebuild and let at five per cent on investment. The housing associations were not, however, able to do enough. They could neither build sufficient houses to meet the need, nor could they provide housing cheaply enough for the poorest of those looking for accommodation. Further, the early philanthropists tended to focus help on the 'deserving poor', with those

---

[21] The population of England and Wales doubled between 1801 and 1851: E Gauldie, *Cruel Habitations: A History of Working-Class Housing 1780–1918* (London, George Allen & Unwin Ltd, 1974) 91.

[22] See E Gauldie, *Cruel Habitations: A History of Working-Class Housing 1780–1918* (London, George Allen & Unwin Ltd, 1974) ch 6.

[23] P Kemp, 'The Origins of Council Housing' in J Goodwin and C Grant (eds), *Built to Last?* 2nd edn (London, ROOF, 1997) 49.

[24] For an overview of the early legislative measures, see WR Cornish and G de N Clark, *Law and Society in England 1750–1950* (London, Sweet & Maxwell, 1989) 180–84.

[25] Named after the reforming Tory home secretary who introduced it, but properly titled the Artisans' and Labourers' Dwellings Improvement Act 1875. For the early history of housing associations, see P Malpass, *Housing Associations and Housing Policy: A Historical Perspective* (Basingstoke, Macmillan, 2000), and J White, 'Business out of charity' in J Goodwin and C Grant (eds), *Built to Last?* 2nd edn (London, ROOF, 1997).

unwilling or unable to help themselves often ejected, again, adding to the problems of overcrowding. As was remarked in 1870:

> 'In helping those only who help themselves, or who can get others to help them, we have left unhelped those who need help' said a Member of Parliament ...[26]

This is one of the recurrent issues in housing: landlords, even those motivated by social concern, tend to prefer letting to safe, respectable tenants. In more recent times, the obligation to house those with the greatest housing need has been forced on local authorities, but as will be seen in chapter 6 allocation policies still permit exclusion of certain groups.

By the beginning of the twentieth century, it was clear that neither housing associations nor private landlords could supply adequate housing at affordable rents for all of the working class. The housing crisis deepened with the outbreak of World War I. The responses to this have had a lasting effect on the shape of English rented housing. Civil unrest led to the imposition of the first rent controls in the private sector, combined with security of tenure.[27] Intended as a temporary wartime measure to prevent landlords profiteering from the housing shortage, rent control became an almost permanent part of private tenancy laws throughout much of the twentieth century. The private rental sector began a decline, from which it has never recovered.

Attention shifted instead to local government to provide the much needed housing. Again, this has had a lasting impact: in Britain the rental sector divided into two distinct forms, public and private. There was a more diverse response in other European countries:

> Elsewhere in Europe ... a much more plural system of housing the working classes emerged at this time. It often incorporated private landlords as well as other agencies; trade unions, co-ops, housing associations, employers, local councils, the national state itself.[28]

In Britain, there was little expansion of housing associations from this point until the mid-1970s.[29]

As shown in Table 5.1 below, in 1914 council housing accounted for only one per cent of housing in Britain; by 1979, 32 per cent of housing stock was owned by local authorities. This rise began immediately after World War I. Lloyd George had famously promised 'homes for heroes' and there was a fear of revolution if proper homes were not provided for the returning soldiers.[30] The Addison Act in 1919[31] provided a very generous 'bricks and mortar' subsidy to local authorities for building new homes, which enabled them to keep rents below market levels. By the early 1920s the fear of civil unrest had diminished and the generous subsidies were axed.

---

[26] H Calvert, *Social Security Law* (London, Sweet & Maxwell, 1978) 4–5.
[27] Rent and Mortgage Interest (War Restrictions) Act 1915.
[28] S Lowe, 'Homes and Castles' in J Goodwin and C Grant (eds), *Built to Last?* 2nd edn (London, ROOF, 1997) 5.
[29] For an account of the role of housing associations between the Second World War and the 1970s, see P Malpass, 'The missing years' in J Goodwin and C Grant (eds), *Built to Last?* 2nd edn (London, ROOF, 1997) 125.
[30] M Swenarton, *Homes Fit for Heroes* (London, Heinemann Educational Books, 1981) 77–9.
[31] Known by the name of the minister responsible for steering it through Parliament. The proper title is the Housing and Town Planning Act 1919.

5.4.2 Central Control v Local Government Autonomy in Housing Supply

This began a cycle of changes to housing finance, again setting a pattern followed since, in which central government has used subsidy as a means of controlling local authorities. Government policy between the Wars varied between providing general subsidies and simply funding to allow slum clearance. In part the swings result from changing political approaches to the role of social housing: whether it is to provide general housing that is available widely, or whether it is 'safety net' housing for those unable to access other housing. Much of the early council housing was of good quality, and was desirable. On the whole local authorities tended to allocate not to the poorest members of society, but to the better-off working class, tenants with secure incomes who could pay the rent. A purely welfarist role has always been forced on local authorities through the subsidy regimes, rather than chosen. Harloe distinguishes between two social housing models: the mass model and the residual model. The mass model is characterised by large scale building of social rented housing, designed for occupation by a wide segment of the population. The residual model concentrates on small-scale construction programmes, focusing on the needs of the lowest income groups. Under the residual model, social housing tends to be occupied by those who are the most vulnerable and marginalised in society. In Britain, four periods can be identified:

> In two, a short period after the First World War and a much longer period after the Second World War, the mass model prevailed. In the other two periods, the later 1920s and 1930s and the years since the mid 1970s, the residual model has been dominant.[32]

The argument that Harloe develops is that the residual model is the normal form of social housing. The mass model is pursued only in 'abnormal' times:

> … that is, when varying combinations of social, economic and political circumstances limit the scope for private provision *and* when this limitation is of strategic significance for certain aspects of the maintenance and development of the capitalist social and economic system.[33]

This approach sees the variations in approach to housing as about more than political ideology. The mass building programme after World War I is explained by the fact that the housing need was accompanied by civil unrest, turning it into a strategically important housing need. The years immediately following World War II saw another period of growth in the public sector to cope with the loss of housing caused by the war. Indeed, most house building during this post war period was for public authorities.[34] However, notwithstanding the rapid expansion of council housing, even as late as 1951 the majority of people lived in privately rented accommodation (as Table 5.1 shows).

Legislation, as well as subsidy, has also had the effect of reducing local authority autonomy in housing. Sometimes this interference in the local decision making processes can be for welfare reasons rather than a desire to obtain greater influence over the implementation of housing policy. An illustration is the Housing (Homeless Persons) Act 1977

---

[32] M Harloe, *The People's Home? Social Rented Housing in Europe and America* (Oxford, Blackwell Publishers, 1995) 7.

[33] M Harloe, *The People's Home? Social Rented Housing in Europe and America* (Oxford, Blackwell Publishers, 1995) 7.

[34] 80% according to J English, 'Building for the masses' in J Goodwin and C Grant (eds), *Built to Last?* 2nd edn (London, ROOF, 1997) 92.

Table 5.1: Housing Stock by Tenure (as percentage of all housing)

	Owner-occupation	Local authority/ new town	Private rented/housing association	
1914	10	1	89	
1951	31	17	52	
1961	43	27	31	
1971	53	28	19	
1979	55	32	13	
			Private	Housing Association
1981	60	27	11	2
1986	64	23.5	10	2.5
1991	67.5	20	10	3
1996	68	17	10.5	4.5
2001	70	13	10	6.5
2004	71	11	10.5	7.5

Compiled from: M Boddy, *The Building Societies* (London, Macmillan, 1980) Figure 2.5, and S Wilcox, *UK Housing Review 2005/2006* (Coventry, Chartered Institute of Housing, and London, Council of Mortgage Lenders, 2005). For the years before 1971, the figures are for housing in England and Wales. For 1971 onwards, the figures are for housing in England.

under which local authorities were no longer free to allocate local housing according to their own criteria, but instead they were to take account of statutorily defined housing need in allocations. On the other hand, there was still an element of central government seeking to dictate local policies, as the reason why legislation imposed statutory duties (without any additional funding) was because many authorities were not following centrally recommended advice and guidance concerning homeless persons.

5.4.3 Expansion of Owner-Occupation

After the second World War, the speculative building industry was preparing itself to take over the lead role in construction and develop housing for owner-occupation, which it succeeded in doing by the early 1960s. Since then, owner-occupation has expanded, first at the expense of the private rented market and, when that had dwindled to a level where no further encroachment was possible, the public sector was eaten into. The goal of owner-occupation has been promoted by both of the main political parties for several decades, in large part, through the provision of fiscal incentives. Once the private suppliers of housing were ready, the Conservative government restricted growth in council house funding in order to let the private sector fill the gap thereby created. The almost full employment that existed in Britain during that period also helped the change of emphasis to owner-occupation. Thus times of economic prosperity would inevitably lead to the better-off opting to buy their homes; by the 1950s and 1960s, the government was providing additional incentives through generous tax concessions to people buying on a mortgage (MITR: mortgage interest tax relief).

5.4.4 Tenure Patterns at the end of the 1970s

The period up to 1979 saw ever increasing constraints on the public sector, especially in relation to housing finance. Up to 1979, though, there was no question but that council housing was seen by both parties as having a major role to play in housing provision. The 1971 White Paper on Local Government stated:

> One of the most important functions of local government is housing. The government believe that the accurate assessment of housing requirements and the provision of housing and housing advice to the individual is of such paramount importance that the service should be operated as close to the citizen as possible.[35]

Before 1960, public housing development was placed firmly in the hands of local authorities and new towns, despite initiatives in the Housing Acts 1935 and 1936 whereby the government made small grants to the National Federation of Housing Societies. Although some moves were made in the 1960s to encourage housing association activity, including the creation of the Housing Corporation in 1964 and a greater willingness on the part of councils to co-operate in renovations especially, it was the Housing Finance Act 1972 and the Housing Act 1974 which revitalised their efforts. Towards the end of the period to 1980, housing associations were beginning, slowly, to be resuscitated from a somewhat moribund state. It is not really until the next phase, post 1980, however, that housing associations have assumed a much more important role in the provision of housing.

By the end of the 1970s, the private rented sector was providing only 13 per cent of housing. The pattern of rent control and security of tenure that had been laid down in World War I had undoubtedly contributed to this decline. It was compounded by the absence of subsidy for private landlords, contrasting with the generous subsidies available (at times) to local authorities until the 1970s, and the growth of alternative investment outlets for private investors.[36] The sector had also been tarnished by the image of 'Rachmanism',[37] the letting of slum property to poor tenants by disreputable landlords. Council housing, on the other hand, was by far the most significant rental sector, and represented a relatively healthy sector with a reasonably good mix of family homes and smaller units. At this time, housing associations provided only a small fraction of rented housing. Things were set to change, however. The effect of public expenditure cuts in the 1970s was beginning to be felt, central government was tightening its control over local authorities, and the dominance of home ownership as the preferred tenure was to strengthen, with an impact on all rental tenures.

---

[35] DoE, 'Local Government in England: Government Proposals for Re-organisation' (Cmnd 4584, 1971) paras 2–3.

[36] For a fuller discussion of the causes of decline, see P Kemp, *Private Renting in Transition* (Coventry, Chartered Institute of Housing, 2004) ch 1.

[37] A phrase coined after Peter Rachman, a notorious landlord who bought up substandard properties in the Notting Hill area in the 1950s and 1960s. He evicted sitting tenants, often through intimidation, and let the houses, badly overcrowded, to immigrants, at exorbitant rents. His name came to light during the Profumo scandal, when Britain's Minister of War was forced to resign over a sex scandal and one of the call girls involved had earlier been Rachman's mistress.

5.5 From 1980 Onwards

5.5.1 The Changing Role of Local Authority Housing

The period from 1980 is marked by a reduction in the scale and scope of state involvement in housing, the continued expansion of owner occupation, the further erosion of local authority autonomy, and the revival of housing associations. The role of the local authority underwent a significant change in this period, often referred to as a change from provider to enabler, determining local policy and strategy, but not actually providing the homes. This shift in role is seen in the following policy statements taken from the 1987 White Paper on Housing:

> ... the Government will encourage local authorities to change and develop their housing role. Provision of housing by local authorities as landlords should gradually be diminished, and alternative forms of tenure and tenant choice should increase ... Local authorities should increasingly see themselves as enablers who ensure that everyone in their area is adequately housed; but not necessarily by them ...
>
> The future role of local authorities will essentially be a strategic one identifying housing needs and demands, encouraging innovative methods of provision by other bodies to meet such needs, maximizing the use of private finance, and encouraging the new interest in the revival of the independent rented sector. In order to fulfil this strategic role they will have to work closely with housing associations; private landlords; developers; and building societies and other providers of finance.[38]

Owner-occupation was promoted by all major political parties, and 1980s Thatcherism saw a 'property-owning democracy' as an article of faith. Various policies have supported this, but perhaps the most important in terms of explaining the contemporary role of local authority housing was the introduction of the Right to Buy (RTB) in 1980. Until then, it had been possible for councils to sell council housing to sitting tenants, but few had chosen to do so on a voluntary basis. The RTB gave secure (council) tenants of, then, three years standing the right to purchase their council property at a substantial discount. Furthermore, central government prohibited local authorities from using the capital receipts for new building. In 1982 alone the effect was to take over 200,000 council houses into the owner-occupied sector, without replacement. In total, more than 1.7 million homes have been bought through the RTB in England.[39] If a local authority attempted to restrict sales, possibly as part of an election commitment to reduce council house waiting lists or to ensure a sufficient supply for the elderly, the Secretary of State could intervene to force through RTB applications.[40]

This deconstruction of the council sector was not initially supported by the Labour Party, but before the 1987 election it came out in favour of the RTB simply because of the electoral damage its negative attitude was causing. Since 1987 policy differences between the main political parties have been minimal. RTB has had a marked impact, changing the profile of council tenants as wealthier tenants seized the opportunity to become

---

[38] DoE, 'Housing: The Government's Proposals' (Cm 214, 1987) para 1.16, and 14.

[39] S Wilcox, *UK Housing Review 2005/06* (Coventry, Chartered Institute of Housing and London, Council of Mortgage Lenders, 2005) Table 20a (the period 1980–2004). Across Britain, the number is almost 2.2 million (Table 20d).

[40] The power to intervene is now in the Housing Act 1985 ss 164–66.

owner-occupiers, as well as contributing to the undeniable shortage of social housing for rent. As seen at 5.6.2 below, there are now attempts to limit the uptake of RTB.

Around the same time as RTB was introduced, changes were made to housing finance and subsidy systems that made buying even more attractive, especially in the house price spiral of the 1980s. By the mid 1980s the level of subsidy to owner-occupiers was, for the first time, greater than that available to council tenants. Whereas in 1980/81 the total assistance with housing costs (including both general subsidies and means-tested assistance) available to council tenants was almost £3,000 million and that available to home-owners was the lesser amount of slightly under £2,000 million, by 1985/86 the position was reversed so that council tenants received subsidy of a little over £3,200 million, and home-owners received almost £5,000 million.[41] In addition, since the early 1970s central government subsidy had been used as a crude tool to influence local authority rents: rents were increased to cut central costs and to encourage council tenants to become owner-occupiers. For a while, rents rose faster than inflation. Many of those on good incomes preferred to pay for home ownership rather than rent. Those unable to pay the high rents were assisted by means-tested rent allowances. Whereas in 1975 most subsidy was on the supply side (80 per cent), by 2000 this had been reversed so that around 85 per cent of housing subsidies were demand sided. This rejigging of the subsidy system contributed to the residual model of social housing getting a firm hold, with council housing being seen as a social service for the poor.

The impact of the loss of council homes through RTB was worsened by the restriction placed on new building. Central government has used its subsidy leverage to control the quantity of local authority housing since 1919, but it had always been the case before the International Monetary Fund crisis in the mid-1970s that an increase in stock was to be expected. The financial cuts made to the housing budget again provide evidence of a concerted attempt to marginalise centrally funded housing. Since the late 1970s the amount of new public sector housing has plummeted; in 1970 there were 130,181 public sector[42] housing completions in England; by 1999 this dropped to the historically low number of 84![43]

In certain respects, the RTB was a remarkably successful policy in that, as intended, it did further increase home-ownership. By 2000, home ownership was around 70 per cent, up from 55 per cent in 1979 (see Table 5.1). The policy has enabled many householders to become home owners who could not otherwise have done so, or to become home owners sooner than would have otherwise been possible. It has also made it possible for them to become owners without having to move location, and in this way has contributed to a tenure mix on council estates. It has also had much less desirable, and unintended, consequences.

Inevitably, it was the better off tenants who were able to exercise the RTB. Further, it was the nicer stock, particularly the family homes, that was bought. The inability to reinvest the

---

[41] Source: Table 121a, S Wilcox, *UK Housing Review 2005/06* (Coventry, Chartered Institute of Housing and London, Council of Mortgage Lenders, 2005).

[42] This does not include, therefore, housing associations, but covers local authorities, government departments and new towns.

[43] Figures taken from Table 19b, S Wilcox, *UK Housing Review 2005/06* (Coventry, Chartered Institute of Housing and London, Council of Mortgage Lenders, 2005).

sale proceeds in new stock led to a diminishing stock of (less attractive) council housing, rented by the poorest members of society who were unable to jump onto the owner-occupier bandwagon. The long-term effect has been the residualisation[44] of council housing, and an increasing concentration of low income households – the unemployed, elderly, disabled and lone parents – in council stock. Ethnic minorities are disproportionately housed in the social rented sector.[45] This process of 'residualisation' of council housing has been exacerbated by the statutory obligation to house those in greatest need, contained in the Housing (Homeless Persons) Act 1977: in 1989/90, 59 per cent of council lettings in London were to homeless people.[46] The net effect of this was that council housing, by the end of the 1990s, provided only 13 per cent of all housing, and housed the most marginalised members of society. While 23 per cent of local authority households had no earning members in 1971, by 1995/6 this had risen to 62 per cent.[47] It has also caused spatial polarisation as most council housing was built as estates. Although there is now a degree of tenure mix in those estates that include houses (which have been bought under the RTB), those that are mainly flats (where RTB take up has been much lower) remain pre-dominantly occupied by social tenants (73 per cent).[48] Social housing in Britain has the role much more of a safety net than in many European countries; while social renters in France, Germany, the Netherlands, and Sweden have incomes at least 70 per cent of the average, British social renters have less than half.[49]

Residualisation is not, however, only the result of housing policy (or lack of); Malpass and Murie emphasise that it is more to do with changing patterns of poverty and social inequality. Housing policy itself contributes to:

> … the pattern of incentives and opportunities which are associated with the poverty trap, the work incentives trap and the savings trap through the operation of housing benefits and the interaction between housing finance and the social security system.[50]
> In addition, the very concentration of the 'marginalised poor' in run-down estates can contribute to the spiral of decline and the social and economic problems that stem from poverty.

The language of residualisation and marginalisation is now being replaced by that of 'social exclusion'. Problems of social exclusion are greatest in the social rented sector, particularly in local authority housing. It is not only about housing:

---

[44] 'Residualisation' is one of three terms used to describe the restructuring of housing in the latter parts of the twentieth century. It is described as 'a process embracing changes in the social composition of council housing as well as the related policy changes'. 'Marginalisation' refers to the emergence of a class of people who are unskilled, and living on occasional earnings and state benefits, turning to local authorities to provide housing as they are unable to access housing elsewhere. The final term, 'privatisation', refers not only to the transfer of ownership into the private sector, but also privatisation of housing management. See P Malpass and A Murie, *Housing Policy and Practice* 5th edn (Basingstoke, Macmillan, 1999) 17–18.

[45] J Hills, 'Ends and means: The future roles of social housing in England' (CASE Report 34, February 2007) 48.

[46] J Richards and J Goodwin, 'Changing Duties' in J Goodwin and C Grant (eds), *Built to Last?* 2nd edn (London, ROOF, 1997) 142.

[47] A Holmans, 'Housing and Housing Policy in England 1975–2002' (ODPM, January 2005) Chronology and Commentary, para 33.

[48] J Hills, 'Ends and means: The future roles of social housing in England' (CASE Report 34, February 2007) 89, Table 9.1.

[49] M Stephens, C Whitehead and M Munro, 'Lessons from the past, challenges for the future for housing policy' (ODPM, January 2005) para 1.50.

[50] P Malpass and A Murie, *Housing Policy and Practice* 5th edn (Basingstoke, Macmillan, 1999) 123–4.

> Social exclusion happens when people or places suffer from a series of problems such as unemployment, discrimination, poor skills, low incomes, poor housing, high crime, ill health and family breakdown. When such problems combine they can create a vicious cycle.[51]

Residualisation, and cuts in public spending, have had a detrimental impact on management of the council stock as a whole. Some areas became known as 'problem' estates. Harloe observes:

> A combination of bad design and location, a lack of maintenance and inadequate management plus the increasing concentration of low-income tenants in these projects resulted in a complex mixture of social, economic and physical difficulties. Problems such as crime, vandalism and the breakdown of the more settled social networks and structures which had existed on most social housing estates in earlier years added to the complex pathology of these areas.[52]

As will be discussed later, the resulting problems of social exclusion have led to changing expectations of the roles and responsibilities of landlords. When the Labour Government came to power in 1997 it adopted an agenda to tackle social exclusion, focusing on neighbourhoods with a high concentration of deprived households.[53] Social landlords are now expected to do much more than simply manage individual properties. It has also led to changes in the regulation of tenancies, emphasising the responsibilities that come with occupation. There are echoes here of the Victorian notions of the deserving and undeserving poor.

In line with Conservative policy throughout the 1980s, and as part of the move from provider to enabler, central government also promoted the 'privatisation' of housing (sometimes referred to as 'demunicipalisation'). This was achieved not only through the RTB, but also (following the Housing Act 1988) by providing for 'landlord choice' for all council tenants. The rhetoric of landlord choice was not matched by the reality. The idea was that tenants should be free to choose who their landlord was, but in practice the schemes on offer gave very little effective choice to tenants. Under 'tenants' choice' private landlords (in particular housing associations) could take over transferred council stock, subject to agreement of the tenants. Housing action trusts (HATs) were bodies with powers to take over areas of poor council housing, improve them, and then dispose of them to new owners, such as housing associations and private landlords. Neither tenants' choice nor HATs proved popular, but large-scale voluntary transfer (LSVT) has had (and continues to have) much more impact.[54] Under this, a council transfers some or all of the ownership and management of its stock to a housing association, usually one specifically set up for the purpose, after a ballot of its tenants in favour of a change of landlord. In 1996 a new category of public landlord was created, the registered social landlord (RSL). This includes housing associations, but also enabled 'local housing companies' to be formed. These are non-profit making bodies set up by local authorities to take over the council stock. Whereas

---

[51] As defined by the Social Exclusion Unit of ODPM.

[52] M Harloe, *The People's Home? Social Rented Housing in Europe and America* (Oxford, Blackwell Publishers, 1995) 434.

[53] D Mullins and A Murie, *Housing Policy in the UK* (Basingstoke, Palgrave Macmillan, 2006) ch 12.

[54] For discussion of the origins of this policy, see A Murie and B Nevin, 'New Labour Transfers' in D Cowan and A Marsh (eds), *Two Steps Forward* (Bristol, The Policy Press, 2001).

some tenants were wary of transfer to independent housing associations, local housing companies had local authority representation on their boards and were more acceptable as landlords to tenants. They are also able to compete alongside housing associations for public funds.

The first stock transfers took place during the late 1980s, but the rate accelerated in the late 1990s. More than one million homes have now been transferred under LSVT, representing about one quarter of the total 1988 local authority housing stock. For the local authority, stock transfer has provided a means of new private finance being accessed to renovate the sector as the RSL transferees are outside the public expenditure constraints. The price received by the local authority is used to repay housing debt, and the RSL can borrow from the private sector to improve the stock.

5.5.2 The Changing Role of Housing Associations

5.5.2.1 The Housing Corporation as Funder and Regulator

Housing associations provide the least amount of rental housing in England and Wales, and always have done, but their role is expanding. Having changed little during the first three quarters of the twentieth century, things began to change in 1974 when a new regulatory and financial system was introduced with the aim of giving housing associations a key role in inner-city renewal. The Housing Corporation had been set up in 1964, but in 1974 it assumed a more significant role as housing associations needed to register with it in order to receive public funds. This marked 'the start of the process through which successive governments have moulded the movement'.[55] As Table 5.1 shows, by 2004 they were not far behind either local authorities, or private landlords as providers of housing.

From its early start as a body concerned essentially with registration, and some financial monitoring, the Housing Corporation now performs an important auditing role in social housing. It not only deals with public funding and registration of housing associations, but it also acts as regulator. A housing association that wishes to access funding through the Housing Corporation has to comply with regulatory guidance issued by the Housing Corporation covering issues such as governance, rent setting, allocation policies, debt collection, and management issues.[56] The Audit Commission works alongside the Housing Corporation and conducts inspections to ensure that associations are delivering the required level of service to tenants. By 2005 the Housing Corporation was regulating around 2,000 associations, who managed more than two million homes.

5.5.2.2 The Expansion of the Sector

The new financial system introduced in 1974 enabled housing associations to access capital grants to fund new developments. Approved schemes were 100 per cent funded, removing any need to rely on private finance, and enabling risk-free expansion. The years to the late 1980s saw some expansion of the housing association sector, although cuts to the loan programme in 1980 meant that they did not grow at the rate that some had anticipated.

[55] P Malpass, *Housing Associations and Housing Policy: A Historical Perspective* (Basingstoke, Macmillan, 2000) 161.

[56] The power to issue this guidance is set out in the Housing Act 1996 s 36.

These were important years for showing that the housing associations could be trusted by lending institutions, ready for the next major step in their development which occurred after the Housing Act 1988.

5.5.2.3 Private Finance

By 1986 the government was looking for ways to reduce central government subsidy to associations, including encouraging private funding from financial institutions. The 1987 Housing White Paper[57] recommended that the public grant regime be replaced with one that mixed public and private finance. The Housing Act 1988, therefore, adopted an approach which changed the very nature of association lettings and was 'a defining moment in the history of housing associations'.[58]

From 15 January 1989, instead of being treated as part of the public sector, housing associations were moved firmly into the private sector. For tenants this meant that they would no longer be given the secure tenancies that local authority tenants enjoy, but would be granted 'assured tenancies', like other private sector tenants. This shift was accompanied by important changes to the financing of new builds by housing associations. Publicly provided housing grants were reduced, and housing associations were expected to raise money from private funders. Housing grants became payable up-front – rather than, as in the past, on completion – which meant that cost management was crucial as any over-run would have to be financed by the housing association (in effect, through rents). The use of assured tenancies meant that housing associations now became responsible for setting their own rents, not tied to government formulae or 'fair rents'; although there were still expectations that housing association rents would be affordable they would also need to be sufficient to meet the costs of loan repayments.

In combination, the Act provided the opportunity for expansion of the housing association sector, but the price was higher rents for tenants, many of whom were forced to rely on benefits. These were very significant changes, challenging the role and ethos of the housing association movement.

5.5.2.4 Stock Transfer

The nature of housing associations has also been affected by the stock transfer programme (5.5.1 above). Most of the transferees of local authority housing are newly created for the specific purpose of receiving this housing stock; relatively few transfers are to the traditionally established housing associations. This has ushered in a new era with a greater degree of professionalism in housing management and has contributed to the rapid growth in the size of the housing association sector in recent years.

5.5.2.5 The Right to Acquire

In 1996, housing association tenants were given the right to acquire (RTA), similar to the RTB of council tenants but with less generous discounts, and available only on new developments. Funding is available to compensate housing associations for the discounts

---

[57] DoE, 'Housing: The Government's Proposals' (Cm 214, 1987).

[58] J Blake, 'The New Providers' in J Goodwin and C Grant (eds), *Built to Last?* 2nd edn (London, ROOF, 1997) 177.

and administrative costs associated with sales and, unlike local authorities, housing associations have been able to use the capital receipts to finance new developments, recognizing the argument that sales deplete social housing stock and threaten the viability of housing associations.

5.5.2.6 A Wider Management Role

The expectation now is that RSLs will do far more than simply let and manage homes. What is described in the Cave Review as 'landlord plus' services[59] will include such things as being involved in neighbourhood projects promoting community cohesion, such as providing drop-in centres, or schemes to help tenants to find work. Interestingly, the Tenant Involvement Commission found that what tenants want first and foremost is a good landlord, and only if the housing association is doing this well should it branch out into wider community development projects.[60] What no-one seems to be asking is whether this is the appropriate role for a housing association, or is a task better left to other agencies.

5.5.2.7 The Impact of the Reforms

The changes brought about by these reforms, particularly those of 1988, have transformed the housing association sector. The sector has doubled in size since then, but there is great diversity. Some housing associations have remained small, and pursue goals related to the founding ethos. The main growth, however, has been in large associations, a growth 'shaped by government and fuelled by large amounts of public expenditure.'[61] The price paid for this growth has been a loss of autonomy and the pursuit of objectives set by the government. The housing association movement began life as voluntary, not-for-profit organisations, commonly motivated by religious and philanthropic ideals. Modern housing associations are much more business like. These heavily regulated associations are:

> … little more than agents of the state, and … the voluntary element has been reduced to only marginal and largely symbolic importance … [62]

5.5.3 Continued Expansion of Owner-Occupation

Throughout the 1980s and 1990s owner-occupation continued to be promoted, although the financial subsidies to owner-occupation were gradually withdrawn, something that had been called for by many commentators for some time in order to create more of a level playing field between the sectors. MITR began to be phased out after 1990, and was finally abolished in 2000. Renovation grants have been reduced, and the help with mortgage costs linked to income support has been cut back. Capital gains tax exemptions are still, however, available on sale of the home. The extent of these changes is shown in Table 5.2.

---

[59] The Cave Review of Social Housing Regulation, 'Independent review of regulation of social housing: A call for evidence' (DCLG, December 2006).

[60] Tenant Involvement Commission, 'What Tenants Want: Report of the Tenant Involvement Commission' (National Housing Federation, 2006).

[61] P Malpass, *Housing Associations and Housing Policy: A Historical Perspective* (Basingstoke, Macmillan, 2000) 19.

[62] P Malpass, *Housing Associations and Housing Policy: A Historical Perspective* (Basingstoke, Macmillan, 2000) 259. The final chapter of Malpass looks to the possible future direction for housing associations.

Table 5.2: Help with Housing Costs in all Tenures in Great Britain

	1990/91	2000/01	2003/04
£ million			
Social housing			
Council subsidy	1,217	−1,184[a]	209
Housing association grant	1,293	847	1,597
Housing benefit (council)	3,368	5,259	5,037
Housing benefit (associations)	391	2,967	4,285
Total	6,269	7,889	11,128
Private renting			
BES subsidies (business expansion schemes, see below)	105		
Renovation grants	26	17	18
Housing benefit	1,388	2,940	3,034
Total	1,519	2,957	3,052
Home owners			
MITR (mortgage interest tax relief)	7,600		
ISMI (income support mortgage interest)	539	490	306
Renovation grants	493	326	343
RTB discounts	542	250	0
LCHO (low cost home ownership)	92	106	289
Total	9,266	1,172	938
Total all tenures	17,054	12,018	15,118

Source: Table 122, S Wilcox, *UK Housing Review 2005/06* (Coventry, Chartered Institute of Housing, and London, Council of Mortgage Lenders, 2005)
[a]This figure reflects the fact that in some areas council rents were used to pay housing benefit costs and those transfer payments exceeded the 'basic' housing subsidy paid to a minority of councils.
Notes: Renovation grants figures are based on 95 per cent of total private sector grants; 5 per cent are apportioned to the private rented sector.
Costs of RTB discounts are assessed to be those in excess of 40 per cent of vacant possession value (this is the economic cost of RTB given that RTB sales are to sitting tenants; for fuller discussion see: S Wilcox, *UK Housing Review 2005/06* (Coventry, Chartered Institute of Housing, and London, Council of Mortgage Lenders, 2005) 79).

5.5.4 The Private Rented Sector

The continual decline of the private rental sector during the 1980s caused concern. The Conservative party recognised that there would always be a role for private rented housing; for the young, those unable to afford owner-occupation, and those preferring the mobility that renting gives.

The Housing Act 1988 marked a changed approach to regulation of this sector, often described as 'deregulating' the sector, in an attempt to boost supply. The changes mean that property can now be rented in a way that enables the landlord to recover possession at the end of the contractual tenancy, getting rid of the long term security of tenure that had dogged the sector for most of the twentieth century. The Act also enables landlords to rent at market rents. The Finance Act of the same year extended the 'Business Expansion Scheme' to residential properties; this provided tax benefits to individuals buying shares in companies investing in rental properties. The tax breaks were, however, limited to a five year period. Although they did bring some new property into the rental market,[63] the long-term impact has been minimal. The hope was that this package, deregulation and tax incentives, would revitalise the sector; encouraging more landlords to let, and also encouraging corporate investment.

There was some revival after 1988; the number of lettings in England increased by 25 per cent from 1988 to 1999 (from 1.8 million to 2.3 million dwellings),[64] assisted by the slump in the housing market which meant that many owners who were unable to sell when moving location ended up renting out the property. A further boost was given in 1996 when buy-to-let mortgages were introduced. While it had previously been possible to borrow in order to purchase for rental, the financial market was limited, and the rates were high. The main differences with a buy-to-let mortgage were that the lender was prepared to take into account not only the borrower's income in deciding whether or not to make a loan, but also the expected rental income, and rates were close to those paid by owner-occupiers. The take up of buy-to-let mortgages has been high.[65] It has also improved the image of landlordism and made investing in private rental respectable again.[66] Further it has been argued that without buy-to-let:

> ... there is a strong chance that the privately rented sector would not have expanded as it has and possibly even shrunk, as it had done for most of 80 years prior to 1990.[67]

Nonetheless, by European standards, the private rental sector remains very small; the European average is 23 per cent of housing stock being in the private rental sector, compared to around 11 per cent in Britain.[68]

5.6 Current Housing Issues

The remainder of this chapter will look at housing since 2000. The first section will look at the key challenges in housing now; the second section will discuss issues within the different

---

[63] 81,000 dwellings: ADH Crook, J Hughes and P Kemp, 'The Supply of Privately Rented Homes: Today and Tomorrow' (York, Joseph Rowntree Foundation, 1995).

[64] S Wilcox, *UK Housing Review 2005/06* (Coventry, Chartered Institute of Housing and London, Council of Mortgage Lenders, 2005) Table 54a.

[65] 58% of private rented residential properties result from investment in buy-to-let property: O Carey Hones, 'ARLA Members Survey, Source and Tenure of Property in the Residential Rental Market, First Quarter 2005' (Leeds, ARLA, March 2005).

[66] D Rhodes and M Bevan, 'Private Landlords and Buy to Let' (York, The Centre for Housing Policy, University of York, September 2003).

[67] M Ball, 'Buy to Let. The Revolution – 10 Years On' (ARLA, September 2006) 24.

[68] Shelter, 'Home truths: The reality behind our housing assumptions' (August 2005). In Switzerland almost 70% of homes are rented (85% of these are in the private sector), in Germany 57% are rented (with 51% of these in the private sector): M Hammar, 'Time to Unite' Private Renter Issue 4 in ROOF March/April 2006.

tenures. Since 2000 there has been much more attention turned to housing, and numerous policy documents.

5.6.1 Housing Conditions

The history of chronic underinvestment in housing since the 1970s and the controls on expenditure and rent have created a serious problem in relation to the condition of housing. By 1997 there was a reported £19 billion backlog of disrepair in local authority homes, and two million social homes failed to meet the decency standards (representing more than half of all social housing units). In 1996 the government announced a target for social housing; that by 2010 all social housing should meet the 'Decent Homes Standard' (DHS). A decent home is one that is warm, weatherproof, and has reasonably modern facilities and services. To meet the DHS it must comply with the minimum fitness standards (see chapter 12) and be in a reasonable state of repair. This target applies only to social housing. Conditions in the private sector, where disrepair is equally a serious issue, are being tackled through a different route. A scheme of compulsory licensing of landlords of houses in multiple occupation (HMOs) has been introduced as this is the sub-sector within private renting which tends to have the very worst conditions. New fitness standards have also been introduced which are applicable to all residential premises (see chapter 12). This will not achieve as much as the DHS, and not all properties will fall within the licensing regime. There is, however, a target that applies to 'vulnerable' people in the private sector;[69] and for these, seven out of ten should have decent homes by 2010.

There are three ways in which English local authorities can work to achieve the DHS:[70] by stock transfer, by setting up an ALMO (an arms length management organisation, which is a company owned by the local authority to manage its homes and make them decent, while the local authority retains ownership), or through private finance initiatives (PFI; the local authority retains ownership and management, but obtains financial support from the private sector). PFI has had little impact, but both ALMOs and stock transfer have been popular.[71] The clear thrust of policy is to encourage local authorities to move away from managing housing so that they can concentrate on a wider strategic role. Indeed, the government has refused to make funding available for the achievement of the DHS target if stock is retained under local authority management. This is so even though there is no clear evidence that transferring management necessarily leads to an improved service.[72] Further,

---

[69] That is, those in receipt of means tested or disability related benefits.

[70] Different approaches are being followed in Scotland and Wales. The English target did not include one of the targets in the Welsh Housing Quality Standard, that the house should be located in a safe and attractive environment.

[71] Since 1988, there have been more than 240 transfers. By May 2006, there were 52 ALMOs managing more than 800,000 homes: DCLG, 'Review of Arms Length Housing Management Organisations' (June 2006).

[72] 'We have not heard evidence that creating an ALMO per se enhances the achievement of Decent Homes, or indeed of tenant satisfaction': ODPM, Housing, Planning, Local Government and the Regions Committee, 'Decent Homes' Fifth Report HC (2003–04) 46–1 [139]; C Holmes, *A New Vision for Housing* (London, Routledge, 2006) 64. Notwithstanding these views, it is clear that ALMOs are delivering significant improvements to homes, with an 'impetus to provide the best homes and services for tenants and leaseholders': DCLG, 'Arms Length Management Organisations: Early impacts and process lessons from Rounds 1 to 3' (Housing Research Summary, Number 237, 2007). While it may be that the additional funding available to ALMOs explains this progress, it is likely that the structural change is also a factor. See also ch 11. For the impact of stock transfer, see also ch 17.

the results of inspections carried out by the Housing Inspectorate show that the best local authorities compare well with the best RSLs, and are able to combine their strategic and management roles successfully. The fourth option, with the local authority retaining both ownership and management, is available only if the local authority is able to achieve the DHS without any extra funding.[73] Since 2001 extra resources have been made available to assist with maintenance and repair, and the government says it will be 93 per cent of the way to meeting the Decent Homes target by 2010.[74] As Table 5.3 shows, there has already

Table 5.3 Housing Decency by Tenure

	1996		2001		2003	
	Decent	Non-decent	Decent	Non-decent	Decent	Non-decent
Owner-occupied	60.3	39.7	70.8	29.2	72.3	27.7
Private rented	37.6	62.4	49.3	50.7	52.5	47.5
LA	46.1	53.9	58.2	41.8	60.4	39.6
RSL	52.4	47.6	66.8	33.2	71.2	28.8

Source: English House Condition Survey, Key Findings for 2003 (ODPM, London 2005)

been considerable progress made; the percentage of non-decent social housing in 1996 was 52.6, but by 2003 this had fallen to 35.3 per cent.

The sector where most remains to be done is the private rental sector where almost half of all homes were still not meeting the decency standard in 2003. As well as having the highest proportion of non-decent housing, the level of disrepair is also worse than for other housing tenures:

> ... the *2001 English House Condition Survey* found that the mean 'basic standardised repair costs' was £38.62 per square metre for the privately rented sector compared with £18.66 for the stock as a whole. On average, privately rented dwellings required £2,500 urgent repair work compared with £1,300 for the housing stock as a whole ...[75]

5.6.2 Housing Supply

In 2000 attention was still focused on the poor state of repair of much social housing stock. The Green Paper of April 2000[76] and the subsequent policy statement[77] concentrated on the condition of the rented sector, especially social housing, and up-grading existing stock. At this point in time there was little mention of supply problems, that is, that there is not

---

[73] C Holmes, *A New Vision for Housing* (London, Routledge, 2006) 64.
[74] ODPM, 'HomeBuy-Expanding the Opportunity to Own, Government's Response to Consultation' (September 2005) 9.
[75] P Kemp, *Private Renting in Transition* (York, Chartered Institute of Housing, 2004) 84.
[76] DETR, 'Quality and Choice: A Decent Home for All, The Housing Green Paper' (April 2000).
[77] DETR, 'Quality and Choice: A Decent Home for All, The Way Forward' (December 2000).

enough affordable housing. Supply issues came into focus in February 2003 with the publication of 'Sustainable Communities: Building for the Future',[78] which included plans to
increase the supply of housing in high house price and shortage areas, and to tackle the
problems of low demand and abandoned housing in other regions (parts of the North and
Midlands). The seriousness of the problem was even more fully highlighted when the
independent review of housing by Kate Barker reported in March 2004.[79] This concluded
that the volatility of the housing market had a deleterious effect on the economy of the
United Kingdom. The evaluation of housing policy conducted for the ODPM found that the
key failure of housing policy was the inadequate supply of housing for rental.[80] In order to
improve affordability and increase access to housing, more housing has to be built.

The problem of inadequate supply stems from the decline in house building that has
occurred since the 1960s. In the mid 1960s over 300,000 units were completed annually; this
had fallen to just over 150,000 in 2004.[81] By far the largest decline has been in social
house-building. That there is a massive shortage of housing is beyond doubt but the overall
figures hide huge regional variations; the main shortfall of housing is in the South East
where house building has failed to keep pace with rates of household formation. In some
parts of the country, however, house building has outstripped household growth. The
impact of this shortage can be seen through the increased numbers of persons being housed
in temporary bed and breakfast accommodation, the number of households placed in
temporary housing has more than doubled since 1997.[82] The number of people on council
house waiting lists has doubled since 1997 to 1.6 million.

The government has accepted that the answer to the long-term problem of affordability
in housing is to increase the supply. Attempts are being made to do this through a wide
package of measures: reform of the planning system and increased investment in infrastructure to support housing, as well as building more homes. There is a commitment is to
increase the annual house build from 150,000 in 2004 to 240,000 by 2016, and the money
allocated for housing has been significantly increased.[83] A new homes agency is being
created to help deliver the housing objectives of increasing supply and regeneration of
disadvantaged areas.[84]

The government is also committed to a specific expansion of the social sector, where the
total stock of housing is still falling, notwithstanding a slight rise in new build since 2001. It
is planned to further increase new social house building so that 50,000 new social rented

[78] ODPM, 'Sustainable Communities: Building for the Future' (February 2003). See also G Bramley, 'The Sudden
Rediscovery of Housing Supply as a Key Policy Challenge' (2007) 2 *Housing Studies* 221.

[79] K Barker, 'Review of Housing Supply – Delivering Stability: Securing our Future Housing Needs' (HM Treasury
and ODPM, March 2004).

[80] M Stephens, C Whitehead and M Munro, 'Lessons from the Past, Challenges for the Future for Housing Policy:
an Evaluation of English Housing Policy 1975 – 2000' (ODPM, 2005).

[81] S Wilcox, *UK Housing Review 2005/06* (Coventry, Chartered Institute of Housing and London, Council of
Mortgage Lenders, 2005) 52.

[82] HM Treasury and ODPM, 'Housing policy: an overview' (July 2005) Chart 2.10, 31.

[83] DCLG, 'Homes for the future: more affordable, more sustainable' (Cm 7191, July 2007).

[84] This brings together English Partnerships, the Housing Corporation and certain delivery functions from the
DCLG: DCLG, 'Delivering Housing and Regeneration: Communities England and the future of social housing
regulation' (Consultation, June 2007). The new agency was initially to be called Communities England but this
name has been dropped and the new name is awaited.

homes will be provided annually.[85] This will reduce the level of shortage but by no means eradicate it.

The Housing Corporation manages most social house building. Amendments have been made to legislation to enable social housing grant[86] to be allocated not only to RSLs but also to 'for profit' developers.[87] Being non-registered, these bodies do not come within the regulatory regime of the Housing Corporation but the grant payments will be made subject to compliance with certain conditions in relation to the intended client group, and management by an accredited manager. There will also be control of rent levels and tenancy terms, and tenants will have the RTA. The aim is that private sector social housing will in substance be subject to the same regulatory requirements as RSL housing.

The shortage of social housing has been exacerbated by the fact that RTB and RTA have been taking more stock out than has been provided by new build. The government has now begun to restrict RTB, in part as a response to the lack of affordable housing,[88] but also to prevent perceived profiteering that has occurred in regeneration areas. In 2003, local authorities in particular areas of housing pressure had the maximum discount available under RTB reduced. The Housing Act 2004 introduced further restrictions on RTB, including extending the period of occupancy required to qualify. Social landlords have also been given a right of first refusal if the property is sold within ten years of exercising the RTB.

There are also new powers to deal with empty private sector property; the Housing Act 2004 introduced empty dwelling management orders (EDMO) which enables a local authority to secure the occupation and proper management of privately owned houses and flats that have been unoccupied for six months.

Notwithstanding these initiatives, the reality is that there is likely to be a housing shortage for some considerable time.

5.6.3 Affordability[89] and Choice

There has always been a difficulty in housing the poorest members of society: decent homes can not be built at a price that is supported by the rents that low income households can afford to pay. There must, therefore, be subsidy, either of construction costs or of rents.

As seen earlier, the approach until the mid-1950s was to subsidise supply, enabling rents for all social housing to be set at levels lower than for comparable private housing. It is still the case that social housing rents are set at 'sub-economic' levels, with council rents being the lowest, next housing association rents and then the highest rents are found in the private

---

[85] DCLG, 'Homes for the future: more affordable, more sustainable' (Cm 7191, July 2007).

[86] The capital grant provided by the Housing Corporation to fund development of social housing.

[87] Housing Act 1996 s 27A, introduced by the Housing Act 2004. The Housing Corporation launched a pilot scheme in 2005, known as the New Partnerships in Affordable Housing Programme, with £200 million of social housing grant from the 2005–6 programme being allocated to non-RSLs. The 2006–08 £3.9bn National Affordable Housing (NAH) programme aims to provide 84,000 new homes across England: The National Affordable Homes Agency and the Housing Corporation, 'Delivering affordable housing. Meeting the challenges of growth and efficiency' (July 2007). Of the 81 successful bidders to this programme in 2007, only seven were private developers. For the period 2008–11 the Housing Corporation will be working with 22 private developers.

[88] As many RTB owners in fact stay put after buying the home, it may be that RTB has not contributed significantly to the overall shortage.

[89] See also ch 15.

sector. Nonetheless, this does not necessarily mean that rents are affordable. During the 1980s and early 1990s housing policy drove up rents in the social sector. In a six year period following the Housing Act 1988, with the move to market rents for housing associations, rents rose by 80 per cent, compared to a Retail Price Index (RPI) increase of just 30 per cent.[90]

The response to affordability issues has been to provide demand sided subsidies to tenants in the form of housing benefit. The rapid rent rises of the 1980s and 1990s meant that more tenants, in all sectors, have been pushed into claiming housing benefit, and housing benefit bills have soared. In the period between 1989-90 and 1995-6 the cost of housing benefit trebled, from £1.4 billion to £5.4 billion. By 2004, the housing benefit cost was estimated as being £11.5 billion.[91] The dramatic growth in housing benefit bills, in all sectors, is shown in Table 5.2 above.

The problem created by this is not simply the cost to the public purse of housing benefit per se, but the housing benefit system itself has been riddled with difficulties since its inception. It is administratively complex, and changes in the claimant's financial situation necessitate the recalculation of benefit entitlement. Errors are not infrequent, and delays in payment are common, leading all too often to possession actions being brought for rent arrears.[92] The tapering system, whereby housing benefit reduces as income rises, is a disincentive to work and is described by Hills as a major contributor to the 'poverty trap', where people's net incomes rise by only a very small proportion of any rise in gross earnings.[93] The ODPM commissioned evaluation of housing policy found that there is also a real problem with affordability for private sector tenants who are on low incomes and yet do not qualify for housing benefit.[94]

Reform of the benefit system is currently underway, which will address some of the issues identified but by no means all. In place of a system that requires officers not only to assess the financial position of applicants but also to link benefit payments to the particular property be rented, a new kind of allowance, known as the Local Housing Allowance, is being piloted that pays out a flat rate allowance based on the financial needs and accommodation needs of the claimant. The claimant is then able to 'choose' how to spend this allowance on meeting their housing needs. The intention is that this will encourage tenants to shop around for cheaper housing as the allowance is based on local rent levels and the tenant is able to retain any surplus (subject to a cap). This pilot is to be rolled out nationally but the original plans to extend it to the social sector have been abandoned, for now at least.

These housing benefit reforms chime with a general movement towards respecting tenants as consumers and enabling them to have choices in relation to how their housing needs are met. This can also be seen in the introduction of choice based lettings (see

[90] P Malpass, *Housing Associations and Housing Policy: A Historical Perspective* (Basingstoke, Macmillan, 2000) 214.

[91] J Birch, '30:30 Vision' ROOF September/October 2005 36.

[92] See ch 19.

[93] J Hills, 'Ends and means: The future roles of social housing in England' (CASE Report 34, February 2007) 133. See also M Stephens, C Whitehead and M Munro, 'Lessons from the Past, Challenges for the Future for Housing Policy: an Evaluation of English Housing Policy 1975 – 2000' (ODPM, 2005) 44.

[94] M Stephens, C Whitehead and M Munro, 'Lessons from the Past, Challenges for the Future for Housing Policy: an Evaluation of English Housing Policy 1975 – 2000' (ODPM, 2005).

chapter 6), by which a prospective tenant is able to bid for a particular property rather than simply having to accept a property nominated to him.

The way in which social rents are set is also being changed. Historically there has been unevenness in rent levels: there has been no consistency in the approach to rent setting between properties, between local authorities, or between local authorities and housing associations. This means that two social tenants occupying very similar properties could be paying very different rents even though property values and economic conditions in the two areas are comparable. The government has therefore begun a rent restructuring programme, to be completed by 2012, under which all social landlords adopt a single approach to setting rents (see further chapter 15). This will be governed by a rent formula which is based on property size, the average earnings in the local area, and the size, location and condition of the property. The expressed aims are to achieve rents that are fairer and less confusing for tenants; a closer link between rents and the qualities that tenants value in properties; and the removal of differences between the rents set by local authorities and those set by RSLs. Unless rents reflect the value of a particular property the notion of choice based lettings will be undermined. It was also intended at one point to roll out the Local Housing Allowance to social tenants as well as private tenants and, again, this would make little sense if rents were fairly random. In the event, the plans to apply the Local Housing Allowance to the social sector have been abandoned for now.

5.6.4 Housing Management: Extent and Style[95]

Recent years have witnessed a change in what is expected of housing management, in part as a response to the problems of social exclusion and anti-social behaviour, especially in the social sector. There has been increasing recognition that there are pockets of deprivation, much of which is to be found in local authority housing,[96] caused in part by the residualisation and marginalisation processes discussed earlier:

> Over recent decades, as owner occupation has increased, social housing stock has declined in quantity and quality and priority has been given to housing the most vulnerable. As a result, many social housing estates have become concentrations of severe poverty, multiple depriva-tion and social exclusion … [T]hese places today have become detached from the economic mainstream.[97]

Employment rates of those in social housing are in the region of 30 per cent to 40 per cent compared to a national figure of 75 per cent. It is wrong, however, to see social exclusion as wholly tenure related; research for the Joseph Rowntree Foundation analysing patterns of deprivation in five localities found that, although disadvantage tended to be concentrated in council housing,

---

[95] See also ch 11.

[96] Nearly one half of all social housing is located in the most deprived fifth of neighbourhoods. 'In the areas origi-nally built as flatted council estates more than a fifth of social tenants report the presence of drug users or dealers as a serious problem; nearly a fifth the general level of crime, a fear of being burgled, vandalism and litter; and 18% that they feel unsafe alone even at home or outside in daylight. One in seven social tenants in these areas say they are *very* dissatisfied with their neighbourhood'. J Hills, 'Ends and means: The future roles of social housing in England' (CASE Report 34, February 2007) 99.

[97] HM Treasury and ODPM, 'Extending home ownership' (2005) 8–9.

... many of the most disadvantaged areas are areas of mixed tenure or tenures other than council housing. There are major differences in the spatial distribution of poverty and its relationship with housing tenure in different cities.[98]

The responses to the problems of social exclusion range far more widely than landlord and tenant law. Local authorities are charged with a responsibility in the Local Government Act 2000 to prepare 'community strategies' for promoting or improving the economic, social and environmental well-being of their areas. There are programmes for 'neighbourhood renewal' and 'sustainable communities'. Nevertheless, the polarisation of tenures into particular geographic areas is seen as contributing to the problems of social exclusion, and attention is increasingly being turned to ways, through the planning system and otherwise, to move to greater tenure integration:

The UK mixed communities demonstration projects will ... [involve] remodeling selected social housing estates through tenure diversification plus improved public services and local environments.[99]

Housing is part of the problem of social exclusion, and housing policy can both contribute to, and be used to alleviate, cycles of depravation. Malpass and Murie argue that:

... where people live is both a factor reflecting differences in opportunity and choice and a factor contributing to these – it is both a cause and consequence of exclusion. The persistence and extent of exclusion are affected by a range of factors including where people live and what opportunities and resources are available.

...

Addressing concentrations of poverty in the social rented sector requires more than changes to housing benefits, housing finance and improved housing management. As with mixed-tenure and other deprived areas it also requires concerted and sustained activity to increase employability and the skills needed to command well-paid jobs; and it requires attention to be paid to local service delivery to ensure that neighbourhoods provide opportunity rather than entrapment. But the agenda does not stop there. Addressing concentrations of poverty in the social rented sector also requires sustained action to renew and redevelop social rented housing whether in the council housing sector or other ownerships.[100]

It is important to be aware of these wider contemporary debates in order to have a full appreciation of the changing role of landlords. Although it is the case that social housing management has nearly always been involved with the control of tenants' conduct,[101] it has more visibly become an instrument of social control in recent years. Increasingly, social landlords are expected to do far more than the traditional management of individual properties (through rent setting, rent collection, allocation, repair and so on). They are now expected to get involved in much wider estate management, engaging with the local community and helping with projects such as the establishment of community centres, and so on.

Local authorities have a duty of 'best value' that applies to all local authority functions,

98 P Lee and A Murie, *Poverty, Housing Tenure and Social Exclusion* (Bristol, The Policy Press, 1997).

99 HM Treasury and ODPM, 'Extending home ownership' (2005) 9.

100 P Malpass and A Murie, *Housing Policy and Practice* 5th edn (Basingstoke, Macmillan, 1999) 129, 131.

101 E Burney, *Crime and Banishment: Nuisance and Exclusion in Social Housing* (Winchester, Waterside Press, 1999).

including housing. This requires them to secure continuous improvement in services, having regard to economy, efficiency and effectiveness. This impacts not only on the strategic role that local authorities play in housing, but also on the housing management functions in relation to its housing stock. The requirement to be responsive to the needs of users means that there is now greater emphasis on consultation of tenants, and also tenant participation. All local authorities are now required to have a 'Tenant Participation Compact' which enables tenants to participate in management of housing services. The Housing Corporation expects RSLs to apply similar principles, both in relation to best value and tenant participation.

Whilst at the strategic and collective level social landlords are now expected to engage positively with communities so as to enhance social inclusion, at an individual level within the landlord and tenant relationship there is arguably more emphasis on notions of 'responsible' and 'irresponsible' behaviour. There has, therefore, been a shift away from a dependency culture which conceptualises tenants as passive recipients towards a governance culture that promotes tenants as active agents, consumers with communitarian responsibilities towards other members of the neighbourhood.[102] This can be seen both in social housing and in private renting. Tenancy contracts are drawn up in a manner that emphasises the duty to behave. So, for example, it is usual for social tenants now to be granted introductory or probationary tenancies initially and they will only gain full 'security' after a trial period if they have shown good behaviour. Underlying the licensing scheme introduced for HMOs is a concern to deal with poor management by a minority of private landlords, and bad behaviour by a few tenants, drawing a crude distinction between good and bad landlords and tenants.

Private landlords are generally seen in a more positive light nowadays, having shaken off much of the negativity arising from the 'Rachman era'. It is becoming more common for local authorities to engage with local landlords, providing advice and assistance. Some local authorities have set up voluntary landlord accreditation schemes with criteria relating to property condition, management practice and to the landlord's past management record.[103] Letting agents are employed to handle at least some aspect of housing management in 58 per cent of lettings accessible to the public; and these tend to be the properties in a better state of repair, where inventories are used, and references taken up before moving into occupation.[104] Nonetheless, there are still rogue landlords, and recent initiatives, such as the scheme for mandatory HMO licensing and selective licensing in areas of low demand, are designed to tackle problems of inadequacy in management by requiring those involved in the management of the property to be competent and fit for such a role.[105]

---

[102] See J Flint, 'Reconfiguring Agency and Responsibility in the Governance of Social Housing in Scotland' (2004) 41 *Urban Studies* 151.

[103] There are more than 150 voluntary accreditation schemes. Many are based on the national framework code developed by the Accreditation's Network (www.anuk.org.uk).

[104] ODPM, 'English House Condition Survey 2001: Private Landlords Survey' (December 2003) 1.

[105] The Law Commission has suggested the adoption of a system of 'enhanced self regulation' throughout the private rented sector that would require all landlords to belong to an accreditation scheme or landlords' association, or to use a letting agent that belongs to a scheme: Law Commission, 'Encouraging Responsible Letting' (Law Com CP No 181, 2007).

The widening role of landlords is particularly evident in relation to their responsibilities to tackle anti-social behaviour. Anti-social behaviour is not primarily a housing issue, but the early legislative responses tended to see it as such and focused on the housing management powers of local authorities (discussed in chapter 11). Many of the powers designed to enable local authorities to deal with anti-social behaviour have since been rolled out to RSLs, but again this means that it tends to be seen as a problem to do with 'tenants', and that it is a responsibility of landlords to tackle it. The licensing scheme introduced by the Housing Act 2006 extends this responsibility of landlords to deal with anti-social behaviour to private landlords of HMOs.[106]

5.7 Current Issues and Directions in the Different Tenures

Rented housing accounts for around 30 per cent of housing nowadays. As Figure 5.2 shows, the sector growing most rapidly is the housing association sector, reflecting the transfer of property from council housing and fact that most new social housebuilding is by housing associations.

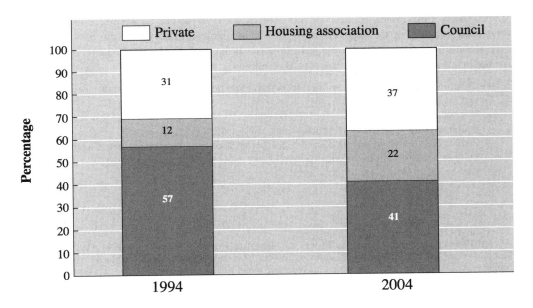

Figure 5.2: Rental Stock by Tenure. Source: Housing in England 2003/04, Part I: Trends in Tenure and Cross Tenure Topics (ODPM, April 2005)

---

[106] It is also proposed to give local authorities (and police) powers to temporarily close properties (including owner-occupied property) following significant and persistent anti-social behaviour: Home Office, 'New House Closure Powers for Neighbours from Hell' Press Release (30 May 2007).

5.7.1 Owner-Occupation

Even though the rate of owner occupation is already high in Britain (second only to Spain and Greece amongst countries in the European Union in 2002),[107] the government is committed to expanding home ownership yet further.

The five year plan published in January 2005 refers to a survey finding that nine out of ten households would prefer to own their own home if they could.[108] It is not a policy that is necessarily being pursued to meet the demand for accommodation, but, as Sternlieb and Hughes write (commenting on the American housing market) to protect 'the premier middle-class collectible'.[109] *Homes for All* states:

> 2.17 Homes are not just places to live – they are assets. And assets are important: research con-firms that those who own or have access to assets in their twenties have better outcomes later in life ...
>
> 2.19 Almost all homeowners benefit from a significant and growing asset which gives them – and their children – financial security, choice and opportunity.[110]

Owner-occupation in Britain has embedded itself in the popular culture as a goal for which to strive, almost as part of being British. Given affordability problems the government is introducing new ways to enable households to get on the housing ladder, planning for 100,000 new households to become homeowners by 2010. For first time buyers, shared ownership schemes (part buy, part rent) will be available, and social tenants will be able to buy through various 'Homebuy' schemes.[111] This is all part of the way to increase owner-occupation further, in pursuit of the following stated objectives:

— Creating mixed, sustainable communities, through a better balance of housing types, tenures and incomes ...
— Freeing up social housing ...
— Enabling more people to share in increasing asset wealth ...
— Reduce the number of people housed in temporary accommodation or classified as homeless,
— Increase reinvestment in the construction of more social homes for rent, and
— Free up social lettings for others in need.[112]

---

[107] ODPM, Live Tables on Stock, Table 114.

[108] ODPM, 'Sustainable Communities: Homes for All, A Five Year Plan from the Office of the Deputy Prime Minister' (Cm 6424, 2005) para 2.3. Research by Shelter, however, questions whether home ownership is what people really want. Their conclusion is that many people would prefer public money to be spent on tackling poor housing conditions, improving neighbourhoods, and building more affordable social housing, rather than helping people to become owner occupiers: Shelter, 'Home truths, The reality behind our housing aspirations' (August 2005) 4.

[109] G Sternlieb and J Hughes, *The Future of Rental Housing* (Piscataway NJ, Centre for Urban Policy Research, 1981) 1–2.

[110] ODPM, 'Sustainable Communities: Homes for All, A Five Year Plan from the Office of the Deputy Prime Minister' (Cm 6424, 2005) (footnotes omitted).

[111] For details, see ODPM, 'HomeBuy-Expanding the Opportunity to Own, Government's Response to Consulta-tion' (September 2005). By July 2007, Social Homebuy (enabling social tenants to buy a share in their existing home while paying rent on the part they do not own) was operated on a voluntary basis by 78 housing associations and 7 local authorities: DCLG, 'Homes for the future: more affordable, more sustainable' (Cm 7191, July 2007).

[112] ODPM, 'HomeBuy-Expanding the Opportunity to Own' Governments Response to Consultation (September 2005) 7.

Not all commentators would agree that this relentless push for further expansion of home ownership is a good idea. Also, notwithstanding the rhetoric about the dream of home ownership and the aspirations referred to in the five year plan, the Hills Review shows that many social tenants actively prefer to be social tenants, more than 40 per cent of social tenants would prefer social renting over owner occupation.[113]

5.7.2 Private Renting

There is now all party support for an expanded and diverse private rental sector but there has been no clear path charted as to how to achieve this. Having recognised for some time the desirability of encouraging greater corporate investment, a new investment vehicle, the REIT (real estate investment trust) was introduced in January 2007. Although it is hoped that this will boost the private rental market, it is likely to have only a relatively modest impact.[114] A REIT is an investment vehicle which individual investors can invest in. It is specially created to invest in property, and pays dividends from pre-tax profits, ensuring that returns are only taxed once. There were also much publicised plans to enable private investors to include residential property in SIPPS (self invested personal pensions). These were to be introduced in April 2006 but the level of interest fuelled fears that this might cause a surge of investment in buy-to-let properties, causing the price of property to escalate. This would enable wealthier people to invest and make significant tax savings, whilst pricing first time purchasers and key workers out of the market. Only months before their introduction there was a U-turn on this.

There remains little corporate investment in residential property. Indeed the sector is increasingly dominated by small-scale private landlords; levels of ownership by private individuals grew from 47 per cent in 1994 to 65 per cent in 2001.[115] Further, private landlords are increasingly small, 'sideline' or 'hobby' landlords; the average number of properties owned dropped from nine in 1994 to four in 2001, and the proportion letting only a single property grew from 24 per cent in 1994 to 30 per cent in 2001. The make up of landlords has an impact on regulation; the fact that most are non-professional means that there is little expertise, and increases the challenge of ensuring that regulation is complied with, something that is being taken up by the Law Commission.[116]

The private rented sector is diverse. Many properties are of very good quality, rented to young professionals who are not yet able to afford home ownership or for whom mobility is important. There are, however, many properties at the other end of the spectrum where conditions are poor, and those renting are doing so because they simply cannot afford to

---

[113] J Hills, 'Ends and means: The future roles of social housing in England' (CASE Report 34, February 2007) 70. By contrast, only 8% of private renters prefer this tenure; most want ownership but of the others more would chose social renting over private renting.

[114] A report commissioned by the Council of Mortgage Lenders (CML) estimates only 2–4% of the private rented market would be in these investment funds: M Ball and J Glascock, 'Property Investment Funds in the UK' (London, CML, 2005). This is because its nature, including the heavy expense of stock exchange listing, is not well-suited to mainstream residential accommodation: M Ball and JL Glascock, 'Property Investment Funds for the UK: Potential Impact on the Private Rental Market' (London, CML, 2005). See also British Property Federation, 'Letting in the Future, Housing Manifesto 2006'.

[115] ODPM, 'English House Condition Survey 2001: Private Landlords Survey' (December 2003) 1.

[116] Law Commission, 'Encouraging Responsible Letting' (Law Com CP No 181, 2007).

rent anything else and are unable to gain access to social housing. It was to deal with the problems at this end of the market that the mandatory and selective licensing scheme for HMOs was introduced in 2006.

5.7.3 Social Renting

There have been a number of successful recent initiatives in social housing that give greater responsibility to tenants; in particular, the introduction of choice based lettings (so that social tenants do not have to accept allocated accommodation on a take it or leave it basis), a restructuring of rents so that they better reflect the relative attractiveness of individual properties; and the reform of housing benefit so that all tenants bear the marginal cost of housing. There are also plans for tenants to have greater choice and more involvement in management.

Nonetheless, there are serious challenges ahead in this sector. One of the big issues is the problem of supply, highlighted by the Barker review. As seen earlier, there are plans to increase new social house building and new ways are being introduced for funding development (5.6.2 above), although the commitment to further expansion of home ownership reveals that social housing is seen as essentially the 'safety net' for those unable to opt into home ownership.

The Hills review suggests that focusing on new social housing and access routes into social housing is unbalanced and neglects the needs and lives of the nearly four million households already living in social housing. Issues that need addressing include the problem of area polarisation, the limited 'exit' power that dissatisfied tenants have, lack of responsive to tenant choice, and the severe constraints on mobility within social housing that limits job-related moves. The ideas mooted in the Review suggest a more diverse and complex role for social landlords in relation to community regeneration, greater diversification of their portfolios,[117] greater engagement with employment services, and a greater commitment to providing 'housing options' and advisory services.[118]

The Cave Review was established to investigate the question of whether the current regulatory framework is the most appropriate model to ensure that social housing residents receive high quality, value for money services and provide best use of public funding.[119] As is noted in the Call for Evidence, RSLs are unlikely to suffer meaningful sanctions for underperformance unless there is clear failure.[120] These questions are particularly apposite now that steps have been taken to expand social housing provision beyond the traditional

---

[117] Perhaps by selling a social housing unit when it becomes vacant and replacing it with a new unit from a different area, in an attempt to reduce spatial polarisation.

[118] For example, encouraging tenants to think about shared ownership.

[119] The Cave Review of Social Housing Regulation, 'Independent review of regulation of social housing: A call for evidence' (DCLG, December 2006).

[120] The Cave Review of Social Housing Regulation, 'Independent review of regulation of social housing: A call for evidence' (DCLG, December 2006) para 15. In the case of severe failure, the Housing Corporation is able to make appointments to the association's board, institute a statutory inquiry into its affairs and, as the ultimate sanction, transfer the assets to another RSL. In *R (on the application of Clays Lane Housing Cooperative Ltd) v Housing Corporation* [2004] EWCA Civ 1658 a RSL lost a judicial review application that alleged that the Housing Corporation's compulsory transfer of its housing to a particular RSL following maladministration violated its rights under Article 1 of the First Protocol for failing to take account of its preference that the compulsory transfer should be to a different RSL.

local authority and RSL providers. The Cave report concluded that the current regulatory regimes suffers from a number of drawbacks, including inadequate concern for tenant interests, over-regulation, and poor incentives for efficiency. It identified three principal objectives for the regulation of social housing:

— To ensure continued provision of high quality social housing
— To empower and protect tenants
— To expand the availability of choice of provider at all levels in the provision of social housing.

The government is consulting on the recommendation that a statutory independent regulatory body for social housing be created.[121]

Within the housing association sector, the majority of housing is let as 'social housing' but recent years have also seen housing associations increasingly involved in market rentals, generally aiming to fill gaps in provision such as student accommodation and key worker housing. Overall, however, it still accounts for only a small proportion of total housing association stock.[122] A study by Goodchild and Syms found that the reasons for housing associations diversifying in this way include:

(a)   generating cross-subsidies for social housing;
(b)   meeting a gap in the local housing market;
(c)   regenerating an area;
(d)   diversifying their activities away from social housing;
(e)   in some cases, to meet the wishes of a local authority; and
(f)   reducing the stigma associated with being tenants of a social housing landlord.[123]

If this is a model that is to be expanded, with housing associations helping to plug the gap in the supply of housing, then there may need to be further changes, as the research by Goodchild and Syms found that the regulatory model used by the Housing Corporation was a deterrent to expansion of market renting.

5.8 Summary: Rented Housing in 2007

For years, housing policy was largely neglected. It is now accepted that England is facing a housing crisis; much property does not meet modern standards of decency, and there is an insufficient supply of affordable housing in parts of the country. The need for a vibrant rented housing market is recognised, even though owner-occupation is still being promoted as the preferred tenure. The shrinkage of the private rental sector and council housing is,

---

[121] DCLG, 'Delivering Housing and Regeneration: Communities England and the future of social housing regulation' (Consultation, June 2007).

[122] Two per cent in 2005 was non-social housing: J Spenceley and C Whitehead, 'Housing Associations in 2005' (Cambridge, Dataspring, April 2006) 12. Non-social housing was defined as: 'housing developed without public subsidy to meet a broader range of needs than those that are intended to be met by the provision of core social housing.' This included shared ownership where the purchaser has not acquired 100% of the equity.

[123] B Goodchild and P Syms, 'Developing and managing market renting schemes by housing associations' (Joseph Rowntree Foundation, Findings, No 213, February 2003).

partly, the consequence of home ownership being promoted to the point where the rental sector was seen to be for those whose income cannot cover the cost of purchasing a home and for the main part has assumed a second class status. Yet, apart from needing to supply accommodation for those for whom owner-occupation is financially impossible, it is also necessary for other economic and social reasons, such as supporting labour mobility.

The most rapidly expanding rented sector is now housing associations, and RSLs are now the main provider of new rented housing. The dramatic decline of the private rental sector from the position almost a century ago has stopped, and seems to have reached a fairly steady state, with some predictions of moderate growth of around 2 per cent to 3 per cent a year for the next 15 years.[124] Council housing is still in decline, as RTB continues to remove dwellings from the stock and LSVTs move housing into the RSL sector. Its position as residual housing, providing for the most marginalised members of society has been confirmed.

---

[124] From 2006: M Ball, 'Buy to Let. The Revolution – 10 Years On' (ARLA, September 2006) 27.

6

RENTING HOMES: LEGISLATIVE CONTROLS

6.1   Introduction

6.2   Legislative history of housing law

6.3   Allocation of housing

6.4   The Housing Act 1988: the private rented sector

6.5   The Housing Act 1985: local authorities and the secure tenancy

6.6   The housing association sector

6.7   Statutory control of rented homes

6.8   Future directions

6.1 Introduction

This chapter traces the development of legislative controls in relation to rented housing, charting the principal approaches that have been adopted in so far as they relate to individual landlord and tenant relationships. The policy background against which these legislative measures should be considered has already been discussed in chapter 5. The aim of this chapter is fourfold: to set out the legislative history of the regulation of rented housing; to look at how housing is allocated to tenants, and any formal controls on this process; to describe the types of tenancy that attract statutory control in each sub-sector; and, finally, to provide a summary of the key statutory controls on the residential landlord and tenant relationship. The nature of the controls is set out in tabular form, leaving more detailed consideration of the regulatory provisions to later chapters. So, for example, the broad scheme of security of tenure is explained in this chapter but the detailed grounds for recovering possession and procedures that need to be followed are dealt with later. This chapter does not deal with what are sometimes referred to as 'collective rights' (such as participation rights), landlords' responsibilities in relation to wider estate management, or regulation of housing standards (such as licensing of HMOs); these issues are dealt with in Part Four. The chapter concludes with a look forward: the Law Commission's rented homes project proposes major reforms to the regulation of this sector, driven by the desire to simplify the law, and based on the twin objectives of 'landlord neutrality' and underpinning regulation with a 'consumer protection' approach.

6.2 Legislative History of Housing Law

6.2.1 Early Legislative Initiatives

Until the mid-nineteenth century, the residential tenant's only source of protection was through the common law and custom. The principles of freedom of contract and freedom of property were dominant and the government did not see it as its role, or as appropriate, to intervene in the landlord and tenant relationship. There were few contractual rights, the two most important ones being the implied covenants of quiet enjoyment and of non derogation from grant (see chapter 4). Most urban tenants moved frequently and had only short, weekly or monthly, tenancies.[1]

As mentioned in chapter 5, early controls in relation to housing focused on dealing with the public health concerns that emerged towards the end of the nineteenth century following the rapid urbanisation of England. Building regulations were introduced in the second half of the nineteenth century, controls were imposed on lodging houses, and measures were introduced that were designed to curb the worst nuisance behaviour and overcrowding. The benefits of these measures do not, however, appear to have been passed down to tenants.[2]

There were also a number of measures passed that more directly focused on the tenancy relationship. With the exception of the Small Tenements Recovery Act 1838, which provided a simpler process for recovering possession for landlords, most of these were broadly pro-tenant. Various changes were, for example, made to the law on distress exempting certain goods and regulating bailiffs.[3] What the common law had denied in 1843,[4] statute introduced in 1885: a condition to be implied into residential lettings to the 'working classes' that the house be fit for human habitation. This applied to lettings below a certain rental level, and for some years this was sufficient to cover most working class housing.[5] The aim was to address the twin evils of insanitary housing and overcrowding.[6] This provision is now, however, in effect, a dead letter; the rent level has not been raised since 1957 and is set at such a low level that virtually no rented housing is covered.

By the end of the nineteenth century the notion of landlord responsibility had begun to take hold: a contemporary writer noted that owners 'are now constantly reminded that property has other obligations than the mere collection of rents'.[7] This was, of course, all taking place in a context where more than 90 per cent of housing was privately rented.

---

[1] J Burnett, *A Social History of Housing 1815–1985* 2nd edn (London, Methuen, 1986) 64.

[2] R Rodger, *Housing in Urban Britain 1780–1914* (Cambridge, CUP, 1995) 49–51.

[3] The Metropolitan Police Courts Act 1839, Law of Distress Amendment Act 1888, Law of Distress Amendment Act 1895. On distress, see ch 16.

[4] *Hart v Windsor* (1844) 152 ER 1114. The court in this case rejected the idea that there was an implied warranty of habitability in residential tenancies.

[5] Housing of the Working Classes Act 1885 s 12.

[6] For full discussion of this, see Law Commission, 'Landlord and Tenant: Responsibility for State and Condition of Property' (Law Com No 238, 1996) paras 4.7–4.19.

[7] E Ellice-Clark, *Public Health Administration* (1874) 1, quoted in MJ Daunton, *House and Home in the Victorian City* (London, Edward Arnold, 1983) 152.

The next major step in tenant protection came with the introduction of security of tenure and rent control in 1915 for private sector tenants at the lower end of the market.[8] Tenant protection from this point diverged between the private and public sectors. As will be seen, housing association tenancies have at times fallen within the controls for the local authority sector, but currently come within the scheme applicable to private sector lettings.

6.2.2 The Private Rented Sector

6.2.2.1 Measures before the Housing Act 1988

The security of tenure and rent control measures that had been introduced in 1915 were intended to be temporary measures in response to the tenant unrest in areas important to the war effort. However, with rapid inflation post war and acute housing shortages it proved impossible to repeal them, and these features remained – in some form or other – part of the private rented sector landscape for most of the twentieth century. The precise details of the legislative controls have varied; the scope of the legislation has at times included most rented housing within its remit,[9] and at other times has moved certain categories of dwellings out of it.[10] Legislative controls have also sometimes focused on rentals that are intended to be long term rather than temporary. From an early stage, therefore, lettings that included payment for services or for the use of furniture have been excluded or enjoyed a lower level of protection. By the mid-1970s it was apparent, however, that increasing numbers of landlords were choosing to let property furnished, often poorly, so as to avoid regulation. This led to the introduction of full controls on furnished lettings in 1974.

During the 1950s the government began to deregulate the private rented sector but this soon led to problems with harassment of tenants. The 1957 Rent Act decontrol meant that landlords now had an incentive to get rid of sitting tenants, so that they could be replaced by tenants paying a higher rent. There were stories of intimidation and threats being made to tenants to 'persuade' them to leave. In response to these abuses, the Protection from Eviction Act 1964 made it an offence to evict a tenant without first obtaining a court order. In the following year, illegal eviction and harassment were made criminal offences. The idea that the tenant should not be forced out of accommodation without 'due process' is still an important feature of the law. A minimum notice period of four weeks was also introduced in 1965.

Whereas earlier rent control provisions had operated by freezing rents to historic levels with certain permitted increases (as under the 1915 provisions), the Rent Act 1965 moved to a different system of rent regulation. The objective was to prevent rents being forced up by housing shortage. The Act provided for rents to be set at a 'fair rent' level; this was intended to reflect the value of the property but to disregard the impact on rent of any scarcity in housing. Fair rents have always been considerably lower than market rents: a government

---

[8] The Rent and Mortgage Restriction Act 1915.

[9] By 1953 over 90% of dwelling houses in England and Wales were within the rateable value limits: M Partington and J Hill, *Housing Law: Cases, Materials and Commentary* (London, Sweet & Maxwell, 1991) 113.

[10] For example, the Rent and Mortgage Interest Restrictions (Amendment) Act 1933 and the Increase of Rent and Mortgage Interest (Restrictions) Act 1938 removed more valuable houses and prevented progressive decontrol of other less valuable ones.

committee in 1971 reported that on average the registered fair rent was about 20 per cent lower than related market rents;[11] in 2004/05 the average fair rent registered was £322 per month, whereas the average rent for an assured letting (with a market rent) was £522 per month.[12] Under both historic rent control and the 'fair rent' approach, the impact was inevitably to reduce the return to landlords on their investments and is said to be one of the factors that contributed to the decline of the private rental sector through the twentieth century.

In 1974, early steps were taken to try to make more rented housing available. A 'resident landlord' exception was introduced, to encourage owner occupiers to let part of their homes without the tenant gaining full protection. There was also some relaxation of the security of tenure provisions so that landlords who intended to rent a property only temporarily (such as for a winter letting of summer holiday accommodation, or to cover a temporary absence abroad) could make use of a mandatory ground for possession provided that the requisite notice was served in advance of the letting. In other respects, the climate became less attractive for landlords. The Rent Act of 1977 provided that there could be two successions following the death of the tenant, and succession could be either to the tenant's spouse or members of the tenant's family. Although a landlord could recover possession on certain grounds, in most cases a tenant could expect to enjoy long-term security in the property.

For the most part, the quality of housing conditions has been regulated through public measures, such as house building regulations and the powers of local authorities to enforce housing standards. There is still no minimum standard of habitability enforceable between the landlord and tenant (the statutory 'fitness' requirement introduced in 1885 does not bite), but there is a statutory obligation to repair placed upon landlords of leases for less than seven years which was first introduced in the Housing Act 1961 (see chapter 12).

As seen in chapter 5, there is no one factor that alone accounts for the decline in the private rental sector during the large part of the twentieth century, but the impact of rent regulation and security of tenure undoubtedly contributed to this. The restrictions imposed by the legislation also led landlords to find ways around it, including entering into 'licences' rather than leases. It is against this background that the lease/license cases leading up to and including *Street v Mountford*[13] emerged (see chapter 3).

When the Conservatives came to power in 1979, they sought to reverse the decline of the private rented sector. The fair rent concept was retained but new forms of letting were introduced in the Housing Act 1980. One of these, the 'shorthold' (then known as the protected shorthold) has since formed an important part of the private sector landscape, although the details of how it works have changed over time. The essential feature underlying the shorthold was that the landlord could enter into a tenancy for a fixed term and be sure of being able to regain possession at the end of that term. The shorthold was then hedged around with various restrictions; it could only be for a period of between one and five years, and a specific form of notice had to be served before the tenancy was entered into.

---

[11] Francis Committee, 'Report of the Committee on the Rent Acts' (Cmnd 4609, 1971) 62.
[12] DCLG, Live Tables on rents, lettings and tenancies, 'Table 731: Private tenancies and rents, by type of tenancy'. 'Assured' includes assured shorthold tenancies; these terms are explained later in this chapter.
[13] [1985] 1 AC 809 (HL).

These measures brought relatively little new property onto the market and in 1987 the government decided that a more radical approach was necessary. Rent control and security of tenure were together seen as having contributed to both a shortage of private rental housing and poor housing conditions:

> 1.3 Too much preoccupation since the War with controls in the private rented sector, and mass provision in the public rented sector, has resulted in substantial numbers of rented houses and flats which are badly designed and maintained and which failed to provide decent homes. The return to private sector landlords has been inadequate to persuade them to stay in the market or to keep property in repair …
>
> 1.8 Rent controls have prevented property owners from getting an adequate return on their investment. People who might have been prepared to grant a temporary letting have also been deterred by laws on security of tenure which make it impossible to regain their property when necessary. These factors have contributed to shortages of supply and poor maintenance.[14]

6.2.2.2 The Housing Act 1988

The Housing Act 1988 represented a marked change in direction. Rent control was all but removed so that tenancies could be at a market rent. Fears were expressed that the move to market rents would lead to a new wave of Rachmanism, with landlords trying to force out existing Rent Act protected tenants (paying a fair rent) in order to replace them with new market rent tenants. To meet these concerns, the Housing Act 1988 strengthened further the pre-existing laws on harassment and unlawful eviction.

A letting under the Housing Act 1988 will be either an 'assured shorthold' (with no effective security) or an 'assured tenancy' (with much greater security): see further 6.4 below. A landlord is unable to recover possession without obtaining a court order, and must prove to the court that a ground for possession exists. Some grounds are mandatory, and if proven the court must grant possession, others are discretionary and an order will only be given if the court considers it 'reasonable'. The Housing Act 1988 introduced new mandatory grounds for possession, making it easier for landlords to recover possession for their own management interests, and it was also made easier to recover possession from a bad tenant. An important new mandatory ground for possession was serious rent arrears (Ground 8). The shorthold concept was also extended, enabling it to be used for leases as short as six months with no maximum length. A paper only possession procedure (known as the accelerated possession procedure, and obviating the need for a court hearing in most cases) was introduced for assured shortholds in 1993. In 1997, there was further change, and the assured shorthold became, in effect, the default tenancy for new lettings. Until then, in order to create a shorthold a landlord had to serve a particular form of notice; after 1996, however, a tenancy was taken to be a shorthold unless the landlord served a notice to say that it was a assured tenancy.[15]

The assured shorthold has now become the main tenancy found in new private rental sector lettings, as the landlord effectively has the legal right to recover possession whether or not there is any tenant default. As is shown in Figure 6.1 (below at 6.4), almost 63 per cent of all private sector lettings are assured shortholds, only 10 per cent are assured tenancies,

---

[14] DoE, 'Housing: The Government's Proposals' (Cm 214, 1987).
[15] Housing Act 1988 s 19A, effective from 28 February 1997.

and 5 per cent are regulated (that is, governed by the Rent Act 1977).[16] If only market rentals available to members of the public are taken into account, then the proportion of assured shortholds is much higher. A survey conducted for ARLA and its panel of mortgage lenders found that 87 per cent of new tenancies were assured shortholds and 11 per cent were 'non Housing Act' tenancies (company lets).[17] The assured tenancy is now mainly used by Registered Social Landlords (RSLs). Most assured shorthold tenants stay in the same property for a relatively short period,[18] although 'many tenants live with reasonable security for a number of years under assured shorthold tenancies'.[19]

6.2.3 Social Renting

Until 1954, lettings by housing associations came within the Rent Acts. In 1954 some were removed,[20] and the Rent Act 1977 exempted housing association tenancies provided that the association was registered with the Housing Corporation. This meant that, as with local authority lettings (discussed below), exempted housing associations were left largely free to manage their tenancies as they wished. Non-exempt housing associations continued to fall within the private sector regime.

It was not until 1980 that council tenants acquired meaningful statutory rights. Before then, tenancies were governed by common law principles. Most were periodic and could be ended by a notice to quit. The local authority tenant enjoyed none of the statutory security of tenure offered to the private sector tenant. This is not to say that local authorities threw their tenants onto the street as the whim took them, but there was no statutory system of protection. Protection stemmed not from rules but from 'political pressure'[21] and the fact that local authorities 'could be expected to act responsibly'.[22] In the words of Lord Greene MR:

> They are subject to criticism by members of their own body, and by ratepayers outside .... They may be trusted, one would have thought, to exercise their powers in a public-spirited and fair way in the general public interest, and without any flavour of what, without offence, I may call profiteering.[23]

In 1980 the Tenants' Charter was introduced. For the most part, it merely codified existing practice and required a change in council procedures. In *Harrison v Hammersmith and Fulham LBC* Brandon LJ commented that, unlike in the private sector, this had not been

---

[16] DCLG, Live Tables on rents, lettings and tenancies, 'Table 731: Private tenancies and rents, by type of tenancy'.

[17] O Carey Jones, 'ARLA Members Survey, Source and Tenure of Property in the Residential Rental Market, First Quarter 2005' (Leeds, ARLA, March 2005): 2.2% were 'other'. Company lets are not regulated by the Housing Act 1988.

[18] More than three quarters of tenants (77%) remain in the same property for between 10 and 18 months: O Carey Jones, 'ARLA Members Survey, Source and Tenure of Property in the Residential Rental Market, First Quarter 2005' (Leeds, ARLA, March 2005).

[19] *Griffiths v St Helens MBC* [2006] EWCA Civ 160, [2006] 1 WLR 2233 [9].

[20] Housing Repairs and Rents Act 1954 s 33.

[21] *White v Knowsley Housing Trust* [2007] EWCA Civ 404 [8].

[22] *Banjo v Brent LBC* [2005] EWCA Civ 292, [2005] 1 WLR 2520, 2530. See also *White v Knowsley Housing Trust* [2007] EWCA Civ 404 [8].

[23] *Shelley v London CC* at the CA stage [1948] 1 KB 274, 283.

'enacted in order to meet any immediate or urgent crisis in housing accommodation'.[24] Instead, Brandon LJ continued,

> … its purpose was rather the social one of giving to tenants in the public housing sector, so far as reasonably practicable, the same kind of protection from being evicted from their homes without good and sufficient cause as had been enjoyed by tenants in the private housing sector for many decades under the Rent Acts. This assimilation of rights as between public and private sector tenants, though no doubt regarded as desirable in the general interests of social equality and non-discrimination, was not an urgent matter … In this connection it is to be observed that, for numerous years past, it had been thought safe and proper to give to local authority landlords a complete discretion with regard to the eviction of public sector tenants, and to rely on them to exercise such discretion fairly and wisely.[25]

The Tenants' Charter is now to be found in the Housing Act 1985. It gives protection to 'a secure tenant' (the tenant of a local authority, see further 6.5 below) who is accorded a variety of rights. As under the private sector regime, a tenant cannot be evicted other than by court order,[26] and, before a court order will be given, a ground for possession must be shown to exist.[27] Unlike the private sector, there are no mandatory grounds for possession, and discretionary grounds can be used only if shown to be 'reasonable'. In addition, the secure tenant may have the Right to Buy (RTB)[28] and the right of succession.[29] There is no statutory formula regulating rents between the landlord and tenant, although (as was seen in chapter 5) the rent policy of local authorities has always been influenced not only by local matters but also by central government policy. Even with the rent increases that have occurred in recent years, council rents remain considerably below market levels.[30]

The security of tenure rights were also made available to housing association tenants in 1980 provided that the housing association was registered, but for the purposes of rent regulation, the fair rent procedures of the Rent Acts continued to apply to all housing association tenancies. In 1988, as part of the move to enable housing associations to access private funding more easily, housing association lettings became part of the private sector controls. Since then housing associations have let property under the Housing Act 1988. Nonetheless, housing association tenants have on the whole enjoyed full security, as the Housing Corporation has encouraged housing associations to let under assured tenancies rather than shortholds. The grounds for possession relied on by housing associations are similar to those used in practice by local authorities for secure tenants. The fact that local authority tenants have secure tenancies but most housing associations tenants have assured tenancies means that a stock transfer will entail the change in the legal rights of the tenant.

There has also been concern in recent years to do something about 'bad' tenants. The

---

[24] [1981] 1 WLR 650 (CA).

[25] *Harrison v Hammersmith and Fulham LBC* [1981] 1 WLR 650, (CA) 661.

[26] Housing Act 1985 s 81.

[27] Housing Act 1985 s 84, Sch 2.

[28] See ch 25.

[29] See ch 17.

[30] In 2005/06 the mean monthly rent for a Council tenant was £265, for a housing association tenant £310, and for a market tenant £546: DCLG Live Tables, Chart 732: 'Private and local authority rents and tenures by tenancy type: 1995/96, 2004/05, 2005/06'. These figures are based on actual rents; the comparison is not one of 'like for like' and variations in size, location and condition will also impact on rents.

Housing Act 1996 introduced the concept of an 'introductory tenancy' which can be granted to new tenants for the first year. At the end of this they will automatically become secure tenants, but during this year a local authority can easily recover possession. The idea behind this has now, following the Anti-social Behaviour Act 2003, been extended to the secure tenancy itself; where there has been antisocial or nuisance behaviour the secure tenancy can be downgraded to a demoted tenancy. Again this will last for one year and can be easily brought to an end during this time. The tenor of these changes reflect the view that only 'good' tenants deserve secure housing. This approach is mirrored in the housing association sector, with assured shortholds being used as probationary tenancies, and assured tenancies being downgradable to demoted assured shorthold tenancies.

6.3 Allocation of Housing

How landlords allocate housing to tenants is important to a book on landlord and tenant law. As discussed in chapter 1, there are many different landlord types, and those renting for purely investment motives are likely to have a different approach to tenant selection than landlords planning to let a home in their house, or those driven by welfare considerations. Many landlords will prefer to let to 'good' tenants who have a secure income and good references that indicate that they will look after the property well, and not trouble the neighbours. That is, those tenants who will be easy to manage. Historically, this was as true of council lets as of private lets. In 1969, the Cullingworth Report noted that council tenancies tended to be given:

> … only to those who deserved them and that the most deserving should get the best houses. Thus unmarried mothers, cohabitees, 'dirty' families and 'transients' tended to be grouped together.[31]

In practice, however, landlords often let to those who do not conform to this 'model' tenant. There are many reasons why. Landlords may be motivated by more philanthropic concerns; keen to provide for the more vulnerable, and those who would be excluded from finding homes if only 'model tenants' were housed. For some housing associations, the type of tenant they are to choose is laid down in their foundation instrument; for example, they may only be able to let to single parents or recently released prisoners. Landlords may be letting property at the lower end of the market that is not attractive to 'model tenants' and may have little choice about whom they rent to. In addition, there may be legal (and non-legal) constraints on the landlord, that impact on both the questions of whom they must rent to, and of whom they can exclude from housing. In exploring allocation policies it is, therefore, important to consider not only who has priority for the grant of a lease, but also, conversely, which groups of applicant will, or can, be excluded, whether expressly or implicitly.

Most landlords will have both prejudices and preferences. The English House Condition Survey of 2001 found that 80 per cent of private landlords had preferred tenant types, most commonly young professionals or people in full-time work, and that 40 per cent of

---

[31] B Cullingworth, 'Council Housing Purposes, Procedures and Priorities' (DoE, 1969) 32–3.

landlords with more than one property were unwilling to let to tenants on housing benefit.[32]

As seen in chapter 4, there are various legislative provisions that make it unlawful to discriminate against members of particular groups; on the grounds of sex, disability, race, ethnicity, national origins or religious belief. Discrimination in housing is a very real problem. The website of the Commission for Racial Equality, for example, states:

> Research data and studies over recent years show that ethnic minorities have suffered severe discrimination in housing. This has operated in two ways:
>
> — It has denied them access to housing; for example, accommodation bureaux have received and acted upon instructions from landlords and landladies not to let property to anyone who is black.
> — Ethnic minorities have been discriminated against in the quality of accommodation they receive; for example, some local housing authorities have allocated poorer accommodation to ethnic minorities than to UK whites, even though their circumstances were similiar.

People from ethnic minority groups are around three times more likely than other households to be accepted as homeless without any fault on their part and in 'priority need'.[33]

There is a statutory code on race equality in housing that provides practical guidance to landlords to prevent unlawful racial discrimination or harassment, and to ensure equality of opportunity and good race relations in housing.[34] This does not have the force of law but will be used by courts and tribunals in considering questions arising under the Race Relations Act 1976.

Subject to these various statutory requirements that prohibit discrimination on certain specified grounds, landlords are free to choose who they wish to let to and so can take account of financial factors, behavioural issues (such as those with good character references, or non-smokers only), preferred family groupings (for example, not wanting tenants with children), and so on.

6.3.1 Allocation of Social Housing

6.3.1.1 Introduction

Until the late 1980s, central government did little to intervene in the allocation policies of local authorities. In the words of Lord Porter in *Shelley v LCC*, councils could 'pick and choose their tenants at will'.[35] When allocating housing, local authorities were under a general duty to give reasonable preference[36] to people living in insanitary or overcrowded housing or unsatisfactory housing conditions, but retained enormous discretion in the way tenants were selected. The most direct interference with local authority autonomy came with the Housing (Homeless Persons) Act 1977, passed to deal with the problem that local authorities were not, on the

---

[32] ODPM, 'English House Condition Survey 2001: Private Landlords Survey' (December 2003) para 3.3.2.

[33] DCLG, 'Homelessness Code of Guidance for Local Authorities' (July 2006) 14. For the meaning of priority need, see 6.3.1.2 below.

[34] Commission for Racial Equality, 'Statutory Code of Practice on Racial Equality in Housing' (2006).

[35] [1949] AC 56 (HL) 66.

[36] The requirement of showing 'reasonable preference' to certain categories of person was first introduced in 1924.

whole, taking measures to meet the needs of the homeless. This placed local authorities under an obligation to secure accommodation for those in statutorily defined classes of housing need, effectively setting boundaries to the local authorities' allocation policies. The 1985 Housing Act required local authorities to give 'reasonable preference' to those deemed homeless: how 'reasonable preference' was worked out varied between authorities, with some giving outright priority to the homeless and others using some kind of balancing mechanism. The problem then became that, with the housing stock shrinking following the introduction of the RTB, the decline in social house-building, and more latterly the large-scale stock transfers that have taken place, the obligations owed to the homeless made it increasingly difficult to make housing available to others. As Fitzpatrick and Pawson write:

> ... in high demand areas the rational course of action for households in housing need may well be to attempt to have themselves accepted as homeless if this is perceived to be their only realistic route to rehousing ... [Lettings] to the statutory homeless have accounted for between a quarter and a half of all local authority lettings over the past two decades, with a renewed rising trend since 1999 (since 1997 in London). This group has consistently absorbed more than half of all lets to new tenants made by London boroughs over the past decade; in many such authorities homeless lettings would have pre-empted virtually all lets of family sized accommodation during this period.[37]

A consultation paper issued in 1994 suggested that giving priority to homeless people in allocations had confused the safety net aspect of the legislation with a fast track to a Council tenancy.[38] Homelessness indicates a short-term crisis but not necessarily a long-term housing need. In fact:

> ... most homeless applicants were already on local authority waiting lists, but nevertheless, the notion that homeless people were 'queue jumpers' took hold and fuelled calls for new and more restrictive legislation.[39]

The Housing Act 1996 moved to a system whereby new allocations to council housing or local authority nominations to RSL housing were to be made through a housing register maintained by local authorities (but the duty to maintain a register has since been abolished).[40] The approach to homelessness was changed. The 'reasonable preference' category no longer included those to whom a duty was owed under the homelessness legislation. Nor could local authority or RSL housing be used to meet the homelessness duty for more than two years. Local authorities did not have a duty to house homeless people if suitable accommodation was available in the area, such as private rented housing. Asylum seekers were excluded from the homelessness duties. At the same time, local authorities were required to ensure the availability of advisory services to the homeless. When Labour came to power in 1997, those to whom the homelessness duty was owed were again given reasonable

---

[37] S Fitzpatrick and H Pawson, 'Welfare Safety Net or Tenure of Choice? The Dilemma Facing Social Housing Policy in England' (2007) 22 *Housing Studies* 163, 170.

[38] DoE, 'Access to Local Authority Housing: a Consultation Paper' (1994). See D Mullins and P Niner, 'A Prize of citizenship? Changing access to social housing' in A Marsh and D Mullins (eds), *Housing and Public Policy: Citizenship, Choice and Control* (Buckingham, Open University Press, 1998) 186.

[39] J Richards and J Goodwin, 'Changing duties' in J Goodwin and C Grant (eds), *Built to Last?* 2nd ed (London, ROOF, 1997) 143.

[40] Homelessness Act 2002 s 14.

preference in the allocations systems and any private sector accommodation offered would only be seen as suitable if it was available for at least two years.

At the same time as the changes in approach to homelessness, there has been a radical change in the way that local authority housing is allocated. Previous systems, based on bureaucratic mechanisms, are being replaced with systems designed around market place mechanisms involving choice.

The provisions relating to public sector housing allocation are now found in the Housing Act 1996, as amended by the Homelessness Act 2002: Part VI deals with allocation, and Part VII with homelessness duties.

6.3.1.2 Duties Owed to the Homeless

The law on homelessness is complex; what follows is an outline of the main obligations, but for details the reader should refer to a specialist text. The detail does not belong in a book on 'landlord and tenant law', but as the duties owed to certain categories of homeless persons can result in a tenancy it is important to understand that this can be one route into the leasehold relationship. It also has a knock-on effect on the availability of homes for other housing applicants, who are not homeless but who are waiting for local authority housing to become available.

The Homelessness Act 2002 introduced changes to require local authorities to adopt a more strategic approach to homelessness and to encourage co-operation with other bodies, such as the social services authority. Sections 1-3 place the local authority under an obligation to conduct a 'homelessness review' and publish a homelessness strategy which includes plans for the prevention of homelessness, ensuring that there is sufficient accommodation available for the homeless, and that there is satisfactory support provided.

Table 6.1 (overleaf) outlines the main obligations owed by local authorities under Part VII of the Housing Act 1985. All homeless persons are entitled to receive advice and assistance, but not all are entitled to housing. There are, however, certain categories of homeless persons who do become entitled to housing. The provider of the housing need not be the local authority; the homelessness duties in Part VII can lead to private sector tenancies or social tenancies. Nor are all homeless persons entitled to a 'permanent housing solution'; some are entitled only to accommodation to tide them over whilst they find somewhere else, but even where there is a full duty, this is often discharged by a series of temporary tenancies pending a settled solution being found. The statutory duties set out in the Housing Act 1996 are supplemented by a detailed Homelessness Code of Guidance (HCoG) issued by the ODPM and Department of Health.[41]

As can be seen from Table 6.1, there are two main routes into housing arising from the homelessness duties. One route is only to interim accommodation. The duty to secure that interim accommodation is available is owed only to the applicant who has a priority need and will last throughout the time that the local authority investigates his application. If the applicant is found to be intentionally homeless, this obligation to secure the availability of interim accommodation continues, but only for a short period; the idea is to give the

---

[41] DCLG, 'Homelessness Code of Guidance for Local Authorities' (July 2006). The Housing Act 1996 s 182(1) provides that a 'local housing authority ... shall have regard to such guidance'. This requires the local authority to take account of it and give clear reasons if they decide to depart from it: *Newham LB v Khatun, Zeb and Iqbal* [2004] EWCA Civ 55, [2005] 1 QB 37.

Table 6.1: Homelessness Duties

Applicant for housing	Local Authority Responsibility
All persons	*Advice and assistance* free of charge about homelessness and prevention of homelessness (HA 1996 s 179) Advice to be wide ranging on housing options but also on factors that contribute to homelessness (welfare, household budgets etc) (HCoG)
Enquiry stage Person *homeless or threatened with homelessness* applies to local authority for accommodation or help in finding accommodation (HA 1996 s 183)	Local authority must *enquire* whether the individual is entitled to assistance and, if so, the extent of the duty owed (HA 1996 s 184) If in *priority need*, there is an additional *interim duty to secure accommodation* pending the outcome of enquiries (HA 1996 s 188)
Post-Enquiry: eligible and homeless Applicant found to be '*intentionally homeless*' (defined in HA 1996 s 191)	Duty to provide *advice and assistance*, taking account of the applicant's housing needs, and giving advice about the likely availability of suitable housing, including location and sources (HA 1996 s 190) If in *priority need*, there is an additional *duty to secure interim accommodation* to enable applicant to find housing (HA 1996 s 190(2)(a)). Can be for only 28 days (HCoG). If children under 18 involved, social services must be informed (HCoG).
Applicant found to be '*unintentionally homeless*' (homeless through no fault of their own)	*No priority need*: duty to provide *advice and assistance*, taking account of the applicant's housing needs, and giving advice about the likely availability of suitable housing, including location and sources (HA 1996 s 192); power to secure accommodation (HA 1996 s 192(3)) *Priority need* (main homelessness duty): *duty to secure accommodation* (can be temporary, and subject to referral to other local authority which applicant has local connection with), duty continues until settled home found (or duty brought to an end by other circumstances) (HA 1996 s 193)

applicant time to find his own home. At this stage, the ODPM guidance suggests that 28 days may be enough. The other route is to settled housing. This results from what is known as the main homelessness duty, owed to persons who the local authority is satisfied are homeless, in priority need, and who are not intentionally homeless. No duties of housing assistance are owed to persons from abroad and subject to immigration control.[42] There is

---

[42] Housing Act 1996 s 185(1).

also an exception when the applicant has no local connection; the case may be referred to another authority in this situation if the applicant does have a local connection with the authority to which the case is referred; for example, where he was normally resident in the other authority.[43] Whenever there is a duty on the local authority to secure accommodation, this can be discharged either by providing that accommodation itself or securing it from some other person.[44]

There is a third possible route into housing if the local authority chooses to secure accommodation to a person without priority need who is not intentionally homeless, but there is no duty in this situation.[45]

The extent of the duties does, therefore, turn on some key phrases: 'homelessness', 'priority need' and 'intentionally homeless'. Homelessness does not only cover those who are literally without a roof over their heads. Homelessness and threatened homelessness are defined in section 175; broadly, a person is homeless if he has no accommodation which it is reasonable for him to continue to occupy, and he will be threatened with homelessness if it is likely that he will become homeless within 28 days. Intentional homelessness is loosely referred to in the HCoG as homelessness arising through his own fault; the statutory definition in section 191 refers to a deliberate act or failure to act in consequence of which a person ceases to occupy accommodation which is available and which it would have been reasonable for him to continue to occupy. This can include things such as failing to pay the rent if this is affordable, being evicted for anti-social behaviour, or simply leaving accommodation. It is accepted, however, that it is not reasonable to continue to occupy accommodation if it is probable that this would lead to domestic or other violence.[46] Those in priority need include pregnant women, persons with dependent children, persons vulnerable through age, mental illness or disability, and those who are homeless or threatened with homelessness as a result of emergencies.[47] It is for the local housing authority to be 'satisfied' or not as to these things, and any challenge to their decision has to be a public law challenge through judicial review.[48]

It is the main homelessness duty that will result in the applicant obtaining long term accommodation. Often this will be a secure or introductory tenancy allocated under the Part VI duties (or a nomination for a housing association assured tenancy). The offer of 'settled' accommodation will bring the main homelessness duty to an end, but it may be that before such an offer is made the applicant will have been given a series of temporary accommodations.[49] This means that the private sector is often used to fulfil the local authority's duties under Part VII: according to the ODPM, over half of all temporary accommodation is in the private rented sector. Constantly moving from one property to another is very disruptive to family life, and not having property that is self contained is especially difficult for families. Bed and breakfast accommodation should not, therefore, be

---

[43] Housing Act 1996 ss 198–201.
[44] Housing Act 1996 s 206(1)).
[45] Housing Act 1966 s 192 (3).
[46] Housing Act 1996 s 177.
[47] Housing Act 1996 s 189.
[48] *Crawley BC v B* (2000) 32 HLR 636 (CA).
[49] In 2007 the use of temporary accommodation was more than double what it was a decade earlier: J Hills, 'Ends and means: The future roles of social housing in England' (CASE Report 34, February 2007) 42.

used for those with family commitments (for discharging either the interim housing duties or the full duty) unless no other accommodation is available and it lasts for no more than six weeks.[50]

The main homelessness duty will be brought to an end in a number of situations: if the applicant accepts accommodation under Part VI or an assured tenancy from a private landlord and is no longer regarded as homeless;[51] if the applicant ceases to be eligible for assistance or becomes homeless intentionally,[52] or if 'the applicant has acted to frustrate the efforts of the local housing authority to overcome their homelessness'.[53] This will include turning down a suitable offer of housing having been informed of the consequences of turning it down; either a written offer of accommodation under Part VI which is termed a 'final offer',[54] or an offer of housing which the local authority regards as suitable for the applicant (provided that the applicant is told of his right to review of the decision as to suitability).[55]

It is clearly important to know what 'offers of accommodation' count. If, for example, the applicant is offered an assured shorthold tenancy by a private landlord (which gives no long term security) and turns it down, will this end the homelessness duty? Or if the applicant does not like the accommodation and turns it down, will this bring the duty to an end? Section 193(7F) provides that the local authority cannot make a 'final offer' of accommodation that will discharge its housing duty unless it is satisfied that the accommodation is suitable for the applicant and that is reasonable for him to accept the offer. This can include an offer of an assured shorthold tenancy, but only if the applicant chooses to accept it; while an applicant might choose to accept the offer of an assured shorthold tenancy as a discharge of the homelessness duty, there is no compulsion to do so, and the applicant must be given a written statement which explains that there is no obligation to accept the offer but that if it is accepted the local authority's duty will come to an end.[56] This is because assured shortholds offer no long term security; there is a minimum of six months security but an assured shorthold can be brought to an end thereafter on two months' notice unless a longer fixed term has been granted (although many continue beyond this in practice). Given that assured shortholds offer no long term security it may seem somewhat peculiar for the local authority duty ever to be discharged by the applicant accepting the offer of an assured shorthold. In *Griffiths v St Helens Council*,[57] Lloyd LJ explained the thinking behind this:

> ... assured shorthold tenancies from private landlords have their disadvantages — the rent is not controlled and the tenure is technically insecure – but ... some homeless applicants may reasonably prefer to accept the offer of such a tenancy, rather than remain in temporary accommodation for a long time until they may be offered secure accommodation under Part VI. Some homeless applicants may therefore be prepared to accept an offer of an assured shorthold tenancy from a private landlord as the permanent accommodation which in practice

[50] Homelessness (Suitability of Accommodation) (England) Order 2003 SI 2003/3326.
[51] Housing Act 1996 s 193(6).
[52] Housing Act 1996 s 193(6).
[53] *Griffiths v St Helens Council* [2006] EWCA Civ 160, [2006] 1 WLR 2233 [34].
[54] Housing Act 1996 s 193(7).
[55] Housing Act 1996 s 193(5).
[56] Housing Act 1996 s 193(7D).
[57] [2006] EWCA Civ 160, [2006] 1 WLR 2233.

it is often capable of being. But they must only do so with their eyes fully open, and the local housing authority must be satisfied that it is reasonable for the applicant to accept the offer. Applicants are entitled to reject the offer. But if they do accept it, the local housing authority's duty ceases.

> ... if the applicant accepts the offer and the accommodation subsequently ceases to be available, the authority's duty will have to be performed again, assuming that the applicant's circumstances have not otherwise relevantly changed.[58]

Interestingly, Lloyd LJ contrasts an assured shorthold with 'temporary' accommodation even though the shorthold may not provide a long-term solution.

6.3.1.3 Local Authority Allocation

How to allocate social housing is a difficult issue, particularly in a climate where there is generally not enough housing and where much of it is not desirable. In the early days of council housing, allocation was largely on the basis of date order rather than need.[59] After the Cullingworth Report, local authorities began to allocate more strictly on the basis of need.[60] Local authorities ran housing waiting lists, but there were problems with who should go on to this list and how those waiting for housing should be prioritised. Most local authorities adopted bureaucratic practices, with the aim of achieving fair and equal treatment, but Mullins and Niner describe how the rules and procedures adopted have in fact often been found to have direct and indirect discriminatory effect and have been informed by moral beliefs.[61] Further, using need as the basis of allocation, assumes a rationing approach to allocation:

> Rather than the notion of rights it is the notion of control of access (rationing) which has been in the forefront throughout most of the history of social housing provision in Britain particularly in relation to homelessness ... Debate about allocation policies usually appears to be concerned with bureaucratic or professional definitions of need and how these are operationalised (the use of, for example, merit, date order, point schemes, medical assessments).
>
> Access to social housing can be seen as a series of control processes ... control is exerted at various stages to determine who gets what, where and when. Legislation, regulation, eligibility, prioritisation, selection and offer policies all exemplify a rationing approach with control by providers, professionals and the State.[62]

This tells the story of how local authority housing was allocated in the past. During the 1990s, dissatisfaction grew with this bureaucratic system of allocation based on need; it gave rise to complex 'points systems' which were difficult to explain to applicants.[63] In line with more recent emphasis on choice and responsibility in housing, market-based mechanisms for

---

[58] *Griffiths v St Helens Council* [2006] EWCA Civ 160, [2006] 1 WLR 2233 [36], [38].

[59] P Somerville, 'Allocating housing – "letting" people choose?' in D Cowan and A Marsh (eds), *Two Steps Forward* (Bristol, The Policy Press, 2001) 114.

[60] B Cullingworth, 'Council Housing Purposes, Procedures and Priorities' (London, DoE, 1969).

[61] D Mullins and P Niner, 'A Prize of citizenship? Changing access to social housing' in A Marsh and D Mullins (eds), *Housing and Public Policy: Citizenship, Choice and Control* (Buckingham, Open University Press, 1998) 177–8.

[62] D Mullins and P Niner, 'A Prize of citizenship? Changing access to social housing' in A Marsh and D Mullins (eds), *Housing and Public Policy: Citizenship, Choice and Control* (Buckingham, Open University Press, 1998) 177–9.

[63] E Laurie, 'The Homelessness Act 2002 and Housing Allocations: All Change or Business As Usual?' (2004) 67 MLR 48.

allocation are now being adopted and promoted by the government. The Homelessness Act 2002 reflects this concern with both choice and responsibility.[64] It contains:

> ... provisions that allow the departure from a purely needs based allocation model to a more flexible system, which allows authorities on the one hand to give applicants greater input into the allocation process while, on the other hand, permitting authorities to take into account a broader range of factors in deciding who should receive housing ... [It also contains provisions] that allow authorities to take into account an applicant's behaviour in reaching an allocation decision.[65]

Local housing authorities are required to have a scheme for determining priorities in allocating housing[66] and are not able to allocate housing apart from in accordance with this scheme.[67] Section 167(2) requires that the scheme must include provisions to secure that 'reasonable preference' (giving much scope for discretion) is given to certain categories of people, including those who are homeless, living in unsatisfactory housing conditions, need to move for medical or welfare reasons, or who are moving into the district and would suffer hardship unless their housing needs are met.[68] The scheme may also be framed so as to give 'additional preference' to people within subsection (2) with urgent housing needs. The scheme may contain provision for determining priorities in allocating housing accommodation to people within subsection (2); factors which can be taken into account include (but are not limited to) the financial resources available to a person to meet his housing costs, any behaviour of a person (or of a member of his household) which affects his suitability to be a tenant, and any local connection which exists between a person and the authority's district.[69] RSLs have a duty under section 170 of the Housing Act 1996 to 'co-operate to such extent as is reasonable in the circumstances in offering accommodation to people with priority under the authority's allocation scheme.'

In contrast to the idea of giving preference to certain persons, it is permissible to exclude from these preference groups someone 'guilty of unacceptable behaviour serious enough to make him unsuitable to be a tenant' (or behaviour of a member of his household).[70] A survey conducted by Shelter during 2003 found that just over half of the 28 authorities evaluated planned to use this 'unacceptable behaviour' test as part of their allocation policies; and that where it would be applied to tenants with rent arrears the level of arrears likely to trigger the test was alarmingly low.[71]

Further, the scheme adopted for determining priorities must provide for the individual applicant to be able to obtain information about how his application is likely to be treated

---

[64] For a fuller discussion on the Homelessness Act 2002, see E Laurie, 'The Homelessness Act 2002 and Housing Allocations: All Change or Business As Usual?' (2004) 67 *MLR* 48.

[65] E Laurie, 'The Homelessness Act 2002 and Housing Allocations: All Change or Business As Usual?' (2004) 67 *MLR* 48, 56.

[66] Housing Act 1996 s 167(1).

[67] Housing Act 1996 s 167(8).

[68] A statutory code has been issued under the Housing Act 1996 s 169: ODPM, 'Revision of the Code of Guidance on the Allocation of Accommodation' (November 2002).

[69] Housing Act 1996 s 167(2)(A).

[70] Housing Act 1996 s 167(2C).

[71] S Credland, 'Local Authority Progress and Practice, Local authorities and the Homelessness Act 2002 – the first year' (London, Shelter, July 2003). Some use it at the stage of considering 'eligibility' (for meaning of this, see text around note 89), others in relation to 'reasonable preference' and some for both.

(particularly to find out if he is within one of the groups given preference), how likely it is that suitable accommodation will be available and how long this is likely to take.[72]

Subject to meeting the 'reasonable preference' duty, the scheme can also make provision for making allocations to a person making a specific application for a property and other descriptions of person.[73] This provision is key to moving away from bureaucratic needs based allocation systems to facilitate two approaches to lettings that have come of favour in recent years. The first reflects the move towards seeing tenants as consumers or customers, an approach that emphasises individual choice and responsibility in finding a property to live in. Thus the scheme can permit property to be allocated to a person who applies for it. 'Choice based letting' (CBL), defined by the government as 'a way of allocating social housing through giving tenants a greater say over where they live', is actively promoted by the government with funding available for piloting schemes. In line with this approach, applicants for housing are known as 'home seekers' and housing professionals talk of 'lettings' rather than allocations. Allowing seekers to bid for homes that are advertised will be an important element in any CBL scheme. The following quotations show how CBL schemes work.

> The schemes allow people to apply for advertised social housing vacancies – often in the local press or through an inter-active website. Applicants can see the full range of available properties and apply for any home to which they are matched. The successful applicant is the person with the highest priority for the property which they have bid for.[74]
>
> [Priority] will depend to a large extent upon the amount of currency [the household] … has been allocated … How the various components of need are weighted within the currency, or indeed whether some factors are included at all, is determined by local policy and practice.[75]

According to the government, CBL leads to 'more satisfied tenants, who stay longer, pay the rent and look after their homes. This in turn will ensure more stable, viable and inclusive communities.'[76] Although a degree of scepticism has been voiced about these claims, the early signs (albeit based on limited evidence) are that there is improved tenant satisfaction, if this is measured by tenancy sustainment (the length of time before tenancies are ended).[77]

Although there is no statutory obligation to run CBL, the whole tenor of recent developments has been to move strongly in this direction. Following the changes in 2002, the housing allocation scheme run by local authorities must include a statement of the policy on offering choice and the opportunity to express preferences about the housing accommodation to be allocated.[78] Research conducted by Shelter in February 2003 found that although 20 out of the 26 authorities surveyed were making changes to implement choice in the light of the 2002 reforms, only one third were introducing choice-based lettings schemes, and one-third who operated 'one offer' policies[79] had no plans to offer more

---

[72] Housing Act 1996 s 167(4A).

[73] Housing Act 1996 s 167(2E).

[74] ODPM, 'Sustainable Communities: Homes for All, A Strategy to Choice Based Lettings' (June 2005).

[75] D Cowan and A Marsh, 'From need to choice, welfarism to advanced liberalism? Problematics of social housing allocation' (2005) 25 *LS* 22, 45.

[76] ODPM, 'Sustainable Communities: Homes for All, A Strategy to Choice Based Lettings' (June 2005).

[77] DCLG, 'Monitoring the Longer-Term impact of choice-based letting' (Housing Research Summary, Number 231, 2006).

[78] Housing Act 1996 s 167(1A).

[79] In 2000, 75% of local authorities gave only one 'reasonable' offer to a homeless household (if that was turned down the local authority treated its duty as discharged): H Pawson and others, 'Local Authority Policy and Practice on Allocations, Transfers and Homelessness' (DETR, 2001).

choice to housing applicants.[80] The government plans that all authorities should be using CBL for at least part of their stock by 2010,[81] and a statutory code of guidance will be issued setting out factors which authorities should take account of in framing a CBL scheme.[82] Some authorities in areas of high housing demand were cautious about the amount of choice realistically available. Further, although the legal requirement to maintain a housing register had been abolished, nearly all (22 of the 25 replying) planned to retain a register.

Applicants for housing who are owed the main homelessness duty must also be supplied with a copy of the local authority's policy of offering choice to people allocated housing accommodation under Part VI of the Housing Act 1996.[83] The plan is to extend choice based lettings further with a nationwide system of choice being in place by 2010, so as to promote not only choice in local authority lettings, but to include other social and even private landlords in the scheme, to promote other housing options such as shared ownership and exchange, and to operate regionally, extending beyond local authority boundaries.

It is still early days in the assessment of the effectiveness of choice based letting. One fear is that 'increasing applicant choice would only mean that unequal outcomes would become more likely', the wealthier applicants are more likely to be able to wait for something good to come along, whereas the poorer and needier households more likely to accept whatever is available.[84] The DCLG research suggests that consumers have taken note of the fact that bidding for properties in the less popular neighbourhoods may enhance their prospects of success.[85] There were also early predictions that 'the system quite clearly will have little or no impact in high demand areas'.[86] Although government sponsored research into early choice based lettings pilots 'demonstrates that CBL can be implemented successfully in both high and low demand areas',[87] a survey by ROOF shows huge levels of demand for individual properties. For one council property in the London borough of Newham there were 1,035 bids, and for every social rented home that becomes available in Newham there is an average of more than 330 bidders.[88]

The second letting scheme permitted by section 167(2E) is one that gives priority to the needs of local communities, in line with the wider objective of promoting sustainable communities. Thus, housing could, for example, be allocated to 'key workers' or, in a more socially engineered manner, to ensure an appropriate mix of household sizes and make up.

[80] S Credland, 'Local Authority Progress and Practice, Local authorities and the Homelessness Act 2002 six months on' (London, Shelter, February 2003). More recent research conducted for the DCLG found that by 2005 more than one quarter of local authority landlords had adopted CBL, and two thirds of the remaining councils had firm plans to do so: DCLG, 'Monitoring the Longer-Term impact of choice-based lettings' (Housing Research Summary, Number 231, 2006).

[81] J Hills, 'Ends and means: The future roles of social housing in England' (CASE Report 34, February 2007) 163.

[82] The government has consulted on the draft code: DCLG, 'Allocation of Accommodation: Choice Based lettings. Code of Guidance for Local Housing Authorities' (January 2007).

[83] Housing Act 1996 s 193(2).

[84] P Somerville, 'Allocating housing – or 'letting' people choose? in D Cowan and A Marsh (eds), *Two Steps Forward* (Bristol, The Policy Press, 2001) 118.

[85] DCLG, 'Monitoring the Longer-Term Impact of Choice-Based Lettings' (Housing Research Summary, Number 231, 2006).

[86] D Cowan, 'From allocations to lettings: sea change or more of the same? in D Cowan and A Marsh (eds), *Two Steps Forward* (Bristol, The Policy Press, 2001) 140.

[87] ODPM, 'Piloting choice-based lettings: an evaluation' (Housing Research Summary, Number 208, 2004).

[88] E Hawkey, 'Bidding Wars' ROOF May/June 2007 20.

The discourse of choice is accompanied by one of 'responsibility'; local authorities are able to allocate only to 'eligible persons' and are able to treat an applicant as ineligible if the local authority is satisfied that, according to section 160A(7) of the Housing Act 1996:

(a)   he, or a member of his household, has been guilty of unacceptable behaviour serious enough to make him unsuitable to be a tenant of the authority; and

(b)   in the circumstances at the time his application is considered, he is unsuitable to be a tenant of the authority by reason of that behaviour.

For these purposes, unacceptable behaviour is behavior that would entitle the local authority to a possession order under Part 1 of Schedule 2 of the Housing Act 1985 (the discretionary grounds for possession).[89] A study by Hunter and others found that just over half of the local authorities operated exclusion policies, but the criteria for exclusion varied considerably.[90] More than half of local authorities in England exclude applicants who have been evicted for rent arrears (and most housing associations disqualify housing applicants who owe arrears from a former tenancy). Further, there is a growing trend for social landlords to exclude households on the grounds of antisocial behaviour. Some even exclude tenants if they have been suspected of not being able to abide by the tenancy agreement.[91]

6.3.1.4 RSLs and Allocation

In addition to the statutory duty to co-operate with the local authority mentioned above and any criteria in a RSL's founding instrument, RSLs also need to comply with the regulatory guidance issued by the Housing Corporation. This provides that RSLs must have letting policies that:

— are responsive to local authority housing duties;
— take account of the need to give reasonable priority to transfer applicants including applicants from other associations;
— are responsive to national, regional and local mobility and exchange schemes;
— are demonstrably fair and effectively controlled.[92]

6.3.2 Allocation in the Private Sector

In the private sector, the landlord is able to let to whomsoever he wishes so long as this is consistent with the non discrimination laws already discussed. The English House Condition Survey of 2001 notes how different landlord profiles can influence the choice of tenant:

... there is a strong preference for working tenants and particularly young professionals amongst landlords, but this preference is strongest amongst smaller landlords. Small landlords often use a combination of experience and 'judgement' or 'instinct' to find the right tenant but many have reported that these approaches were not always reliable. As a result, research

---

[89] Excluding Ground 8.

[90] C Hunter, J Nixon, and S Shayer 'Neighbour Nuisance, Social Landlords and the Law' (Coventry, Chartered Institute of Housing, 2000). This study was based on the law in s 160 of the Housing Act 1996, now replaced by s 160A.

[91] H Pawson and others, 'The Use of Possession Actions and Evictions by Social Landlords' (ODPM, June 2005) 20.

[92] Housing Corporation, 'The Regulatory Code and Guidance' (August 2005) para 3.6f.

has found, 'sideline' landlords have tended to be very conservative in their approach to select-ing tenants, relying on stereotypes to define their preferences. Those that let to groups generally conceived of as less desirable (e.g. students), are often operating in 'niche' markets and have devised letting and management practices particularly suited to a specific demand group.

The letting practices of small, sideline landlords, particularly those with a personal attach-ment to their property, it is suggested, are often driven by their concerns over damage to their property. Those with an investment approach to their properties are more concerned that their rent is paid. Many landlords hold negative views characterised by a stereotypical images of young people and people on housing benefit, and negative experiences with the administration of housing benefit have made many landlords unhappy about letting to households on hous-ing benefit …

[Some] landlords develop their lettings and management practices specifically to operate in … 'niche markets'. For example, whether property is let furnished or unfurnished can have a major influence on who the property is likely to be let to (unfurnished property is often tar-geted at young professionals and other households with sufficient income to have acquired and be able to transport their own furnishings). Amongst the business-oriented small land-lords there is evidence of more strategic targeting of certain tenant groups. Research conducted for Help the Aged identified landlords who took in or even targeted disadvantaged people such as ex-street homeless, prostitutes, alcoholics or drug abusers. For landlords in this group, housing benefit is often seen as one of the many business risks that needs to be actively managed (methods of managing these risks, however, can verge on being overly intrusive (for example 'helping' the tenant filling claim forms). [footnotes omitted][93]

The housing benefit rules impact not only on the letting decisions of landlords but also play a part in the properties which tenants chose to rent; although location and size are also important to tenants, those in receipt of housing benefit are influenced by whether housing benefit will cover the rent payable.[94]

In contrast to the social sector, private tenants usually have a degree of real choice over which property they rent. In the social sector, even with the move to CBL, a housing applicant is unlikely to have much choice as to where he lives. This may be one reason why some low income tenants prefer the private sector.

The private sector is also increasingly being used to house those who in earlier years would have been given permanent housing in the social sector. One obstacle to accessing private rental housing has been the widespread practice of landlords requiring rent deposits (required in more than four-fifths of lettings in 2000-2001).[95] A number of schemes are available that enable prospective tenants to overcome the difficulties of funding the necessary deposit (see chapter 16).[96] Local authorities are increasingly, both formally and informally, referring homeless households to the private sector and providing introductory services for landlords.

---

[93] ODPM, 'English House Condition Survey 2001: Private Landlords Survey' (December 2003) para 3.2.
[94] ODPM, 'Housing benefit and the private sector' (Housing Research Summary, Number 95, 1999).
[95] ODPM, 'English House Condition Survey 2001: Private Landlords Survey' (December 2003) para 3.3.4.
[96] These are seen as highly cost-effective as 'the savings in probable temporary accommodation expenditure outweigh the outlays involved in securing access to private tenancies (whether or not deposits are successfully recovered)': DCLG, 'Evaluating Homelessness Prevention' (Homelessness Research Summary, Number 3, 2006) 4.

6.4 The Housing Act 1988: The Private Rented Sector

The principal legislation governing private sector tenancies is now contained in the Housing Act 1988, which came into effect on 15 January 1989. Tenancies entered into before that date are still governed by the Rent Acts (and are known as 'regulated tenancies'), but these now form a very small portion of private sector lettings and are declining in number (see Figure 6.1).

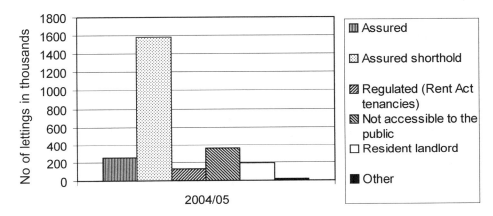

Figure 6.1: Private Rental Sector by Tenancy Type. Source: DCLG, Survey of English Housing, Live Tables, S510, 'Trends in Letting'.

As previously mentioned, there are two main types of tenancy: the assured tenancy and the assured shorthold. In essence, the assured tenancy is a tenancy of a home entered into between a private sector landlord and an individual. Nowadays, most new private sector tenancies are assured shortholds, a sub-set of the assured tenancy which offers no security beyond the contractual term.

6.4.1 Assured Shorthold Tenancies

The vast majority of new private sector lettings are assured shortholds (almost 90 per cent of private rented sector lettings available to members of the public).[97] The attraction of these to the landlord is that the tenant gains no long term security and the landlord is able to recover possession once the term has expired, provided this is at least six months after the beginning of the tenancy, and two months' notice has been given. This ensures that the assured shorthold tenant has a right to a minimum six months possession (labelled by the Law Commission as the six-month moratorium). For tenants this moratorium provides a measure of tenant protection, whereas landlords argue that it brings unwelcome inflexibility. The Law

---

[97] S Wilcox, *UK Housing Review 2005/06* (Coventry, Chartered Institute of Housing and London, Council of Mortgage Lenders, 2005) Table 54a.

Commission has recommended abolition of this moratorium to promote choice and flexibility; concerns that this might leave disadvantaged groups more vulnerable are, in its view, better addressed by other means.[98]

Before 1997, a specific form of notice had to be served prior to the commencement of the tenancy in order to create an assured shorthold tenancy (minor errors generating much case law),[99] but the assured shorthold is now the default tenancy,[100] and a landlord wishing to create an assured tenancy (as distinct from an assured shorthold) will need to serve notice to this effect before the tenancy.[101]

6.4.2 Assured Tenancies

In order to be an assured tenancy or an assured shorthold tenancy five conditions must be satisfied:

(a) there must be a tenancy;
(b) the dwelling house must be let as a separate dwelling;
(c) the tenant, or in the case of a joint tenancy, each of the tenants, must be an individual;
(d) the tenant, or at least one of the joint tenants, must occupy the dwelling house as his only or principal home; and
(e) the tenancy must not be within the list of those excluded by Schedule 1 of the Housing Act 1988.

6.4.2.1 Tenancy

Private sector regulation has only ever applied to tenancies, not licences. This would make sense if licences were only used for short-term arrangements that do not involve sole occupation but, as shown in chapter 3, there are many licence arrangements that look very much like leases and in which the occupier is the only person with a right to live in the accommodation. It is not evident why such a person should not enjoy statutory rights, and this is the view now being promoted by the Law Commission who propose that the statutory scheme should be based around a contract for the rent of a home:

> 9.39 Considerable conceptual difficulties are caused by the distinction between exclusive occupation and exclusive possession. It is not readily understandable by the public at large.
> 9.40 … we regard the contract between the landlord and the occupier as central to the operation of our scheme. We see no reason why any distinction should be drawn between a contract which comprises a lease and a contract which comprises a licence. This distinction is essential where the proprietary consequences of the contract are concerned, and should remain so, but it should not affect the statutory regulation of the contract as between the contracting parties themselves.[102]

---

[98] Law Commission, 'Renting Homes: The Final Report. Volume 1: Report' (Law Com No 297, 2006) paras 1.51–1.56.
[99] See ch 2.
[100] Housing Act 1988 s 19A.
[101] Housing Act 1988 Sch 2A.
[102] Law Commission, 'Renting Homes 1: Status and Security' (Law Com CP No 162, 2002). The Rented Homes Bill (if enacted) will apply to an occupation contract conferring the right to occupy premises as a home (Law Commission, 'Renting Homes: The Final Report. Volume 2: Draft Bill' (Law Com No 297, 2006) Rented Homes Bill cl 1).

For now, however, protection is available only to tenants. Under the Rent Acts, this was taken to include tenancies by estoppel,[103] tenants at will,[104] and even tenants at sufferance.[105] It is not evident why protection should be available to these categories (particularly the last two) given that it is not available to licensees who may have a much stronger connection with the property, and that the distinction between licences and tenancies at will is so fine. Although it is generally thought that the same approach will be followed under the Housing Act 1988, the authorities in this area are not conclusive[106] and it would be open to a later court to re-examine this issue.

6.4.2.2 A Separate Dwelling

The requirement that there be a 'separate dwelling' is not always easy to apply. A dwelling house can be a house or part of a house.[107] Flats clearly count as separate dwellings. The more difficult cases tend to involve occupation of rooms within a larger building, particularly if there is some sharing of facilities. Both 'dwelling' and 'separate' have been hard to define.

(i) Protection is only available if the property is let for the purpose of using it as *a single unit of habitation*. It will not cover the letting of a larger unit which is intended to be broken down into smaller units of occupation.[108] This interpretation promotes the purpose of providing protection to residential occupants and not, for example, to entrepreneurs who take a lease intending to profit from sub-letting parts.

(ii) There is longstanding authority that a single room may be a dwelling-house,[109] but for some time there was a view that it could only constitute a 'dwelling' if the tenant was able to carry on 'all the major activities of life, particularly sleeping, cooking and feeding' in it.[110] On this view, the absence of cooking facilities in a room meant that there could be no protected tenancy. In *Uratemp Ventures Ltd v Collins*, the House of Lords reviewed the law in this area and described this view as a heresy: the proper question was whether it was his 'home', 'the place where he lives and to which he returns and which forms the centre of his existence'.[111] In particular, it was quite possible to have an assured tenancy of a room even though there were no cooking facilities.

(iii) Sharing cases have created particular problems. Under the older Rent Acts (pre-1949) the view developed in case law was that even if an occupier had exclusive possession of one room, then the fact that there were shared 'living' facilities in other parts of the premises (such as a kitchen) would prevent there being a protected tenancy as the occupier's room formed only *part* of a dwelling.[112] It was this approach that, according to Lord Millett in *Uratemp Ventures Ltd v Collins*, fed the heresy discussed above relating to the

---

[103] *Stratford v Syrett* [1958] 1 QB 107 (CA), although obiter on this point.

[104] *Francis Jackson Developments Ltd v Stemp* [1943] 2 All ER 601 (CA). NB in the public sector the Court of Appeal has expressed doubt as to whether a tenancy at will can be a secure tenancy: *Banjo v Brent LBC* [2005] EWCA Civ 292, [2005] 1 WLR 2520.

[105] *Artizans, Labourers and General Dwellings Co v Whitaker* [1919] 2 KB 301 (KB).

[106] On tenants at will, see P Sparkes, 'Purchasers in Possession' [1987] *Conv* 278.

[107] Housing Act 1988 s 45(1).

[108] *St Catherine's College v Dorling* [1980] 1 WLR 66 (CA); *Horford Investments Ltd v Lambert* [1976] Ch 39 (CA).

[109] *Curl v Angelo* [1948] 2 All ER 189 (CA).

[110] *Wright v Howell* (1947) 204 LTJ 299 (CA) 300.

[111] [2001] UKHL 43, [2002] 1 AC 301 [31].

[112] *Neale v Del Soto* [1945] KB 144 (CA).

need for the dwelling to provide for all of the essentials of living.[113] The matter has now been settled by statute. Section 3 of the Housing Act 1988 provides that where a tenant has 'exclusive occupation of any accommodation' (separate accommodation) then even if there is also 'shared accommodation', the 'separate accommodation shall be deemed to be a dwelling-house let on an assured tenancy'. This does not, however, apply if the shared accommodation is shared with the landlord, Lord Millett explaining the thinking behind this exception:

> ... the right to occupy a living room in common with and at the same time as the landlord is such an invasion of his privacy that Parliament cannot be taken to have intended that the tenant should enjoy security of tenure. For this purpose a kitchen is a living room ... so that a right to occupy a kitchen ... in common with the landlord will take the tenancy out of the Acts.[114]

(iv) If the dwelling-house is let with other land, the entire letting can be protected provided that the 'main purpose of the letting is the provision of a home for the tenant'.[115]

(v) In order to be a dwelling there must be a degree of permanency in the siting of the structure, such as a home fixed to the ground or connected to services.[116] Mobile homes (now known as park homes) can fall within the Housing Act 1988 provided that the home is rented and there is the requisite degree of permanency in its siting. The majority of park homes, however, are not rented but owned, with the occupier renting the site only. Almost 70,000 households in England and Wales live in park homes.[117] Separate legislation regulates these. There is limited protection through the Caravan Sites Act 1968 which provides for there to be four weeks' notice to quit and for eviction to occur only after a court order. The Mobile Homes Act 1983, applying to persons who own the park home and rent the site, gives a greater degree of security, as well as the right to sell the home and to gift it.

6.4.2.3 The Tenant must be an Individual

The requirement for a tenant to be an individual means that lettings to companies are not assured tenancies, even if the company is being used as a device to route the tenancy through so as to avoid the legislative codes.[118]

6.4.2.4 Only or Principal Home

This condition is aimed at ensuring that an individual can only claim protection for one home; under the Rent Act 1977 there was no such provision and it was possible to claim protection for two homes.[119] The phrase 'principal home' is not defined. It is clear that temporary absences, such as holidays or short periods working away, will not affect assured tenancy status, but there can be difficulties with longer periods of absence, and in particular

---

[113] [2001] UKHL 43, [2002] 1 AC 301 [45].

[114] [2001] UKHL 43, [2002] 1 AC 301 [58].

[115] Housing Act 1988 s 2. Note, however, that mixed residential/business lettings are excluded from the Housing Act 1988 and governed by the business tenancy regime, see 6.4.2.6.

[116] *R v Rent Officer of Nottingham Registration Area, ex p Allen* (1985) 17 HLR 481 (QB).

[117] Berkeley Hanover Consulting, Davis Langdon Consulting and the University of Birmingham, 'Economics of the Park Homes Industry' (ODPM, October 2002) 7.

[118] *Hilton v Plustitle* [1988] 3 All ER 1053 (CA); *Kaye v Massbetter* [1991] 39 EG 129 (CA).

[119] *Langford Property Co Ltd v Tureman* [1949] 1 KB 29 (CA).

where someone else is allowed into occupation. In *Ujima Housing Association v Anash*[120] an assured tenant moved out for almost 18 months to protect his children from a neighbour's abuse, during which time he sub-let the premises (in breach of his own tenancy) on furnished assured shortholds. The judge at first instance had refused the possession order sought by the landlord housing association on the grounds that the tenant remained an assured tenant as he had retained the property as 'his only or principal home'. The Court of Appeal overturned his decision on the basis that the judge had been wrong to apply a subjective test of intention rather than an objective test. The proper approach to deciding whether or not the property remained his only or principal home was to ask whether there was a continuing intention to return to occupy the premises at some later date coupled with a sufficient physical sign of that intention. Factors that counted against finding it still to be his principal home were that he did not leave any personal possessions in the flat, and he made a profit out of the sub-letting. Although neither factor is conclusive, the Court of Appeal considered that viewed objectively it was no longer his principal home. It is interesting that the fact of sub-letting does not automatically prevent the property remaining as the principal home,[121] but it does shift the burden to the tenant to prove that it is.[122]

6.4.2.5 *If and so long as*

If any of the above conditions cease to exist, then the tenancy will cease to be assured.

6.4.2.6 *The Tenancy must not be Excluded*

Some tenancies are prevented from being assured tenancies even if the above conditions are met. Most of the exceptions are contained in Schedule 1 to the Housing Act 1988, and are set out below. References to paragraphs in the following section relate to Schedule 1.

(i) Pre-Housing Act 1988 tenancies and transitional cases (paragraphs 1 and 13): the 1988 Act applies only to tenancies entered into on or after 15 January 1989.

(ii) Tenancies of dwelling houses with high values (paragraph 2). Housing at the top end of the market (with rent of more than £25,000 a year[123]) is excluded from protection; tenants who can afford to rent more expensive housing are generally better able to negotiate their own terms, and there has not historically been the same pressing shortage of accommodation as for low rent housing.

(iii) Tenancies at a low rent. Paragraphs 3 and 3A-C exclude tenancies at no rent or at a low rent (less than £1,000 a year in Greater London or £250 elsewhere).[124] Unlike the Rent Act 1977, the Housing Act 1988 does not prohibit the taking of a premium on letting property. There is a risk therefore that landlords may seek to avoid regulation by charging the tenant a large sum on entering into the tenancy while reserving only a low rent. The courts have in the past looked to the substance of a payment rather than its form and, in *Samrose Properties Ltd v Gibbard*, treated a premium payment as commuted rent.[125]

---

[120] (1998) 30 HLR 831 (CA).
[121] In the public sector a sub-letting of the whole automatically removes secure status, and that status cannot be revived: Housing Act 1985 s 93(2).
[122] *Waltham Forest Community Based Housing Association v Fanning* [2001] L & TR 41 (QB).
[123] For tenancies entered into before 1 April 1990, exclusion is by reference to rateable value rather than rent.
[124] For tenancies entered into before 1 April 1990, exclusion is by reference to rateable value.
[125] [1958] 1 WLR 235 (CA).

(iv) Business tenancies. Historically, mixed use lettings fell within the Rent Acts,[126] but where any part of the premises is used for business purposes the letting will now come within Part II of the Landlord and Tenant Act 1954 and be excluded from the Housing Act 1988 (paragraph 4). This will be true even if the original letting was for residential purposes and the occupant later uses it for business purposes.[127]

(v) Licensed premises (paragraph 5).

(vi) Agricultural land. Tenancies which include agricultural land exceeding two acres with the dwelling (paragraph 6) and tenancies of dwellings occupied by the person responsible for the farming of an agricultural holding (paragraph 7) are excluded.

(vii) Lettings to students. A letting to a student 'who is pursuing or intends to pursue a course of study provided by a specified educational institution' (including universities) is exempt so long as the tenancy is granted by the educational institution itself and not, for example, by a private landlord (paragraph 8). If the educational institution has taken a lease from another landlord in order to provide student accommodation, that landlord will not be subject to the statutory repairing obligations usually imposed by section 11 of the Landlord and Tenant Act 1985.[128]

(viii) Holiday lets: where the tenant has the right to occupy for a holiday the tenancy is excluded (paragraph 9). There is no statutory definition of holiday. In *Buchmann v May* the Court of Appeal said that the dictionary definition of 'a period of cessation from work or a period of recreation' would be a workable definition provided the word recreation was not too narrowly construed.[129] This has, however, been criticised as it would appear to exclude, for example, working holidays; instead, it is argued, the emphasis should be on whether it is being used as a *home* or not.[130] In *Francke v Hackmi*, a wider view was taken:

> … a holiday is a temporary suspension of one's normal activity not necessarily implying a period of recreation. A temporary suspension involves such a period of time as would indicate that one intends to resume one's normal activity at its conclusion *and* that period is not so long as to imply that another activity had taken its place.[131]

The intention behind this exception is clearly to enable owners to let out properties for holidays without the risk of the occupants claiming that they have a right to remain at the end of the holiday.

In the past, the holiday let was frequently used by landlords as a means of avoiding the protective legislation.[132] An example is *R v Rent Officer for LB of Camden, ex p Plant* where the landlord let to student nurses whilst they were studying (knowing they were not really 'on holiday') but the tenancy stated that it was for the purpose of a holiday.[133] Although pre-dating *Street v Mountford*[134] Glidwell J approached the issue by looking for the real

---

[126] See the discussion in *Patel v Pirabakaran* [2006] EWCA Civ 658 [22]-[25], [2006] 4 All ER 506.
[127] *Cheryl Investments v Saldanha* [1978] 1 WLR 1329 (CA).
[128] Landlord and Tenant Act 1985 s 14(4).
[129] [1978] 2 All ER 993 (CA).
[130] TJ Lyons, 'The Meaning of "Holiday" under the Rent Acts' [1984] *Conv* 286.
[131] [1984] CLY 1906.
[132] Indeed, in 1982 the Labour Party announced that they would remove the holiday let exception as it was a loophole in the Rent Acts.
[133] [1981] EGLR 73 (QB).
[134] [1985] 1 AC 809 (HL).

purpose (if this differed from the stated purpose). Finding 'clear evidence that the purpose expressed in the tenancy agreement was not the true purpose of that agreement' it was not within the holiday let exception and the tenancy was protected.

(ix) Resident landlords. A letting by a landlord who shares with the tenant will not be an assured tenancy. There are complex provisions in paragraph 10 and Part III of Schedule 1 explaining when a landlord will be regarded as resident in the same building, but the gist is that it applies where the tenancy has been granted by a landlord who, at the time of the grant, and since, has had his or her only or principal home in the same building. The exception will not apply if the building is a purpose built block of flats, unless the landlord is sharing the actual flat. In *Bardrick v Haycock*, it was said that what constitutes a building is a question of fact for the trial judge.[135] In *Bardrick*, the landlord lived in an extension which had been built with its own entrance and he was held not to be a resident landlord.

Under the Rent Act 1977, resident landlord lettings were not capable of being protected tenancies[136] but were not totally exempt from control; they fell into the category known as 'restricted contracts',[137] which essentially meant there was some form of rent control but very limited security of tenure. Scarman LJ referred to the purpose behind this exception in *Bardrick*:

> … the mischief at which the section was aimed was the mischief of that sort of social embarrassment arising out of close proximity which the landlord had accepted in the belief that he could bring it to an end at any time allowed by the contract of tenancy.[138]

There is also a clear housing policy objective in encouraging home-owners to rent out spare rooms. Commenting on the resident landlord exemption in the Rent Act 1977, Hirst LJ stated in *Barnett v O'Sullivan*:

> The purpose of s12 is manifest, namely to encourage resident owners of houses with rooms to spare to let them, with the assurance that they will be able to recover possession at the end of the contractual tenancy (as they may very understandably wish to do so should the tenant prove incompatible), and also to enable them to sell what is probably their major asset with vacant possession.[139]

The 1988 Act aimed to remove all restrictions on resident landlords: not only is there no rent control or security of tenure, but the resident landlord does not have to serve four weeks' notice to quit under the Protection from Eviction Act 1977 to evict a tenant[140] or obtain a court order to recover possession.[141] To further promote the renting of spare rooms it is also possible for a resident landlord to claim a 'Rent a Room' allowance if he rents a furnished room, which means that rental income up to a specified sum will be tax free (usually, all rental income is taxable, subject to allowable deductions). Around seven per cent of all private sector lettings are resident landlord lets (see Figure 6.1).

---

[135] (1976) 31 P & CR 420 (CA).
[136] Rent Act 1977 s 12.
[137] Rent Act 1977 s 20.
[138] (1976) 31 P & CR 420 (CA), 424.
[139] [1995] 1 EGLR 93 (CA).
[140] Protection from Eviction Act 1977 s 5(1B).
[141] Protection from Eviction Act 1977 ss 3 and 3A.

(x) 'Public landlords'. Lettings by the Crown or a government department (paragraph 11) or certain local authority or other public bodies (paragraph 12) cannot be assured tenancies (but most of the latter will be secure tenancies governed by the Housing Act 1985). RSL lettings are, however, within the Housing Act 1988.

6.4.3 Security and Assured Tenancies

The landlord of an assured tenancy cannot bring the tenancy to an end without obtaining a court order, which will be given only if a statutory ground for possession exists.[142] The reason that a court order is required is to protect the tenant from simply leaving a property that he may well be entitled to stay in. In practice, however, in the vast majority of cases the tenant voluntarily leaves when the tenancy comes to an end without the landlord having to resort to court action.

In the case of a fixed term tenancy a statutory periodic assured tenancy will come into existence at the end of the fixed term.[143] The grounds on which possession may be given are set out in Schedule 2 to the 1988 Act. Part 1 contains a list of mandatory grounds; if proved, the court must grant an order for possession.[144] Part II lists the discretionary grounds for possession for which the court may only order possession where it considers it reasonable to do so.[145]

6.5 The Housing Act 1985: Local Authorities and the Secure Tenancy

In the public sector it is the 'secure tenant' who gains various statutory rights. The basic definition is contained in section 79(1) of the Housing Act 1985 which provides that:

> A tenancy under which a dwelling-house is let as a separate dwelling is a secure tenancy at any time when the conditions described in sections 80 and 81 as the landlord condition and the tenant condition are satisfied.

The words 'at any time' are significant as it has been held that the landlord and tenant conditions have an 'ambulatory' effect in that occupiers may pass in or out of 'secure' status, depending on either a change of landlord or a change in the tenant's own circumstances.[146] Broadly, in order to be secure, at any time, the following conditions must be met:

(a)   the dwelling house must be let as a separate dwelling (section 79);

(b)   there must be a tenancy (section 79), although this does (potentially) carry an unusual meaning;

(c)   the landlord condition must be satisfied (section 80);

---

[142] Housing Act 1988 s 5(1).
[143] Housing Act 1988 s 5(2).
[144] Housing Act 1988 s 7(3).
[145] Housing Act 1988 s 7(4).
[146] *Basingstoke & Deane BC v Paice* (1995) 27 HLR 433 (CA); *Crawley BC v Sawyer* (1987) 20 HLR 98 (CA); *Elvidge v Coventry City Council* (1993) 26 HLR 281 (CA).

(d) the tenant condition must be satisfied (section 81). This means that the tenant must be an individual, and the dwelling must be his only or principal home (similar to the requirements for an assured tenancy).

6.5.1 *The Dwelling House must be a Separate Dwelling*

A dwelling-house 'may be a house or a part of a house', and so will include not only houses but also flats and bungalows.[147] It will also include 'land let together with a dwelling-house' (except for agricultural land exceeding two acres).[148] As with the private sector, the Housing Act 1985 requires that the dwelling-house is let as a separate dwelling, but there is no equivalent to section 3 of the Housing Act 1988 that provides that if there is exclusive possession of part it can still be seen a home even though some other parts are shared. The difficulty with the case law prior to *Uratemp Ventures Ltd v Collins* in relation to the private sector,[149] may therefore still be relevant to the public sector. Before the *Uratemp* case, any sharing of 'living facilities', such as kitchens and living rooms, would prevent there being a letting of a separate dwelling. Although the House of Lords clearly decided that the absence of cooking facilities would not prevent the tenant occupying a 'dwelling', the House of Lords in that case did not have to deal with the particular issue of whether or not it could still be a 'separate' dwelling (section 3 of the Housing Act 1988 making this an irrelevant question). Nonetheless, it would be entirely consistent with the approach taken to say that a person who has exclusive possession of a room can occupy a 'separate dwelling' even though there is shared use of other facilities (and that, therefore, the absence of an equivalent to section 3 is unimportant).

6.5.2 *The Need for a Tenancy*

Section 79 appears to eschew the distinction between leases and licences adopted in the private sector as it applies not only to a lease, but subsection (3) states that it also applies 'to a licence to occupy a dwelling-house (whether or not granted for a consideration) as … in relation to a tenancy'. In fact, however, this adds little to the requirement of a tenancy as the House of Lords held in *Westminster CC v Clarke* that 'a licence can only create a secure tenancy if it confers exclusive possession of a dwelling house'.[150] As seen in chapter 3, most arrangements granting exclusive possession will be leases.

In *Westminster CC v Clarke* Mr Clarke was given a room with cooking facilities in a warden controlled hostel.[151] The Licence conditions included provision for the Council to change the room allocated without notice (a mobility clause), to require the sharing of rooms, not to have overnight visitors, and to ensure that all visitors leave by 11pm. In deciding whether or

---

[147] Housing Act 1985 s 112 (1).
[148] Housing Act 1985 s 112(2).
[149] [2001] UKHL 43, [2002] 1 AC 301, see above.
[150] [1992] AC 288 (HL) 300. The explanation is probably in the history of the case law on the lease/licence distinction. *Street v Mountford* was decided in May 1985, and the Housing Act was passed in October 1985. Prior to *Street v Mountford* it was possible to grant exclusive possession and still call the arrangement a licence (see ch 3). To catch all exclusive possession arrangements, therefore, the legislation would need to include these licences as well as tenancies.

not there was exclusive possession, Lord Templeman had regard to the social purpose of the housing provision:

> … the provision of temporary accommodation for vulnerable homeless persons, the necessity for the Council to retain possession of all the rooms in order to make and administer arrangements for the suitable accommodation of all the occupiers and the need for the Council to retain possession of every room not only in the interests of the Council as the owners of the hostel but also for the purpose of providing for the occupiers supervision and assistance.[152]

Policy was influential in the reasoning of Lord Templeman, but only to underline the fact that the denial of exclusive possession to Mr Clarke was genuine. As he did not enjoy exclusive possession, he could not be a secure tenant.

A tenancy at will is probably not capable of being a 'secure tenancy'. In *Banjo v Brent LBC*, Mr Banjo had been allowed to remain in premises rent free after the expiry of a long lease, becoming, according to the Court of Appeal, a tenant at will.[153] The particular point for decision related to security of tenure,[154] but Chadwick LJ also noted that a tenant at will has no rights of succession under sections 87 to 90, and doubted whether a tenancy at will can be a 'secure tenancy' even if the landlord and tenant conditions are satisfied. Buxton LJ comments that it is 'most unlikely' that the RTB was intended to extend to a 'relationship as fugitive as that of a tenant at will'.[155]

6.5.3 The Landlord Condition

The landlord condition in section 80(1) simply requires that the landlord be one of a number of specified bodies, but the main one for our purposes is the local authority.

6.5.4 The Tenant Condition

By section 81:

> The tenant condition is that the tenant is an individual and occupies the dwelling-house as his only or principal home; or, where the tenancy is a joint tenancy, that each of the joint tenants is an individual and at least one of them occupies the dwelling-house as his only or principal home.

6.5.4.1 The Tenant Must be an Individual

To qualify as secure, the tenant must be an individual or, in the case of joint tenants, several individuals. As *Camden LBC v Shortlife Community Housing Ltd* makes clear, a body corporate cannot be an individual.[156]

---

[151] [1992] AC 288 (HL).

[152] [1992] AC 288 (HL) 301.

[153] [2005] EWCA Civ 292, [2005] 1 WLR 2520.

[154] The Court of Appeal held that the tenancy at will could be brought to an end without court order as s 82 bit only on fixed or periodic tenancies.

[155] As was argued earlier, it is hard to understand why a tenant at will merits protection in either the private or public sectors.

[156] (1993) 25 HLR 330 (Ch).

6.5.4.2 *The Dwelling-House Must be the Only or Principal Home*

This is a question of fact. Where the tenant has two homes, it is still possible that the council dwelling will be his principal one. In *Governors of the Peabody Donation v Grant,* the daughter, seeking to succeed to the tenancy under what is now section 87 of the Housing Act 1985, proved that she resided at her father's flat because she spent a good proportion of every week living there and she kept clothes and books there, despite her father having filled in a census form which did not include her as resident.[157] On the other hand, in *R v Worthing BC, ex parte Bruce,* where the tenant at all material times had a bungalow adapted to his disability as well as his council flat, the Court of Appeal held that it was reasonable to conclude that the council flat was not his only or principal home, although the case turned on other matters and the issue was not directly addressed.[158]

The approach followed is the same as that for the private sector (see above); during periods of absence the question will be whether there is a continuing intention to occupy the premises as home together with sufficient physical sign of that intention.[159] In *Crawley BC v Sawyer* the tenant was largely absent for around 18 months while he was living with his girlfriend.[160] During this time, he continued to pay the rent and rates on his council property, visited about once a month, spent a week there at some point but he did also arrange for the electricity and gas supplies to be cut off. He was served with a notice to quit, but before it expired he had split up with his girlfriend and moved back to the house. On these facts, the Court of Appeal held that the property remained his principal home.

As with the assured tenancy, this intention to return must be objective, but the court 'will focus not on fleeting changes of mind but on the enduring intention of that person'.[161] This is particularly important in cases such as *LB of Hammersmith and Fulham v Clarke* where the secure tenant was elderly and was in and out of nursing homes with various illnesses, seemingly changing her mind as to where she wanted to stay permanently.[162] Absences may even be for a long period so long as there is this intention to return together with signs of occupation. In *Amoah v London Borough of Barking and Dagenham* a secure tenant sentenced to twelve years in prison for drug offences was able to resist a notice to quit on the grounds that he intended to return; during his absence his furniture and possessions remained, and his stepdaughter was living there and paying rent.[163]

In the cases considered above, it was found that there had remained a continuing intention to occupy the premises as home during the periods of absence. As the tenant condition has ambulatory effect it is even possible to resume secure status following a period of absence in which the tenant has a home elsewhere. So, in *Hussey v Camden LBC,* the Court of Appeal found the occupier was a secure tenant even though he had previously moved out and allowed someone else to live there (without formally sub-letting).[164] If,

---

[157] (1982) 6 HLR 43 (CA).
[158] (1993) 26 HLR 223 (CA).
[159] *Crawley BC v Sawyer* (1987) 20 HLR 98 (CA).
[160] (1987) 20 HLR 98 (CA).
[161] *LB of Hammersmith and Fulham v Clarke* (2001) 33 HLR 881 (CA).
[162] (2001) 33 HLR 881 (CA).
[163] (2001) 82 P & CR D12 (Ch).
[164] (1994) 27 HLR 5 (CA).

however, the tenant 'parts with possession', for example by sub-letting, this automatically (and for all time) ends the secure tenancy by virtue of the Housing Act 1985 section 93(2),[165] even if the tenant intends to return at a future date.

6.5.5 The Tenancy Must not be Excluded

Even if the tenant satisfies sections 79-81, he will still fail to be secure if one of the exclusionary paragraphs in Schedule 1 to the Housing Act 1985 is applicable.

6.5.5.1 Introductory and Demoted Tenancies (paragraphs 1A and 1B)

As part of the campaign against anti-social behaviour, and reflecting the policy that secure status is something to be 'earned', introductory and demoted tenancies can be used by local authorities and are excluded from being 'secure tenancies'.[166] If housing is offered, the local authority can elect to offer *all* new tenancies (but it cannot do so selectively) on an 'introductory' basis.[167] The idea is that the local authority has a year to see if the tenant is likely to be a good tenant; during the first year the tenancy can be ended for any reason so long as the correct procedure is followed, but at the end of this trial period it will become a secure tenancy.[168] More recently the local authority has been given power to apply for an extension of the introductory period by a further six months, provided that at least eight weeks' notice is given, reasons are given for the extension, and the tenant is informed of her right to have the decision to extend reviewed, and to take advice if help is needed.[169] Whereas the use of introductory tenancies is general, the extension of the 'trial' is on an individual basis.

During the introductory tenancy, the tenant enjoys some, but not all, of the rights enjoyed by secure tenants; there are rights of succession for introductory tenancies, and the right to be consulted on housing management issues, but there are no alienation rights, and no RTB (although the period of occupation can count towards the RTB).[170] The advantage to the landlord of using introductory tenancies is the ease with which they can be ended; a notice must be served setting out the landlord's reasons, and telling the tenant of her right to request a review of the decision, but if the landlord confirms the decision to evict and the case goes to court, the court must grant possession.

A demoted tenancy operates in a similar way. A demoted tenancy is one which used to be secure but for which the county court has made a 'demotion order' following the landlord's application.[171] This can be given if the tenant has been involved in anti-social behaviour or

---

[165] There is no equivalent statutory provision in the Housing Act 1988, so an assured tenant can retain the status even after sub-letting provided there is an objectively ascertainable intention to return.

[166] Housing Act 1985 Sch 1 paras 1A (introductory) and 1B (demoted).

[167] A survey based on figures for 1997/8 found that just under a third of local authorities were making use of introductory tenancies, but terminations of them were usually explained as being for rent arrears and only 1 in 5 was terminated for neighbour nuisance: C Hunter, J Nixon, and S Shayer 'Neighbour Nuisance, Social Landlords and the Law' (Coventry, Chartered Institute of Housing, 2000).

[168] Housing Act 1996 ss 124–130. Housing Action Trusts can also operate introductory tenancy regimes. The introductory tenancy regime has been unsuccessfully challenged on human rights grounds (see *R (on the application of McLellan) v Bracknell Forest BC* [2001] EWCA Civ 1510, [2001] 1 All ER 899) and on the grounds of illegality (*Manchester CC v Cochrane* [1999] 1 WLR 809 (CA)).

[169] Housing Act 1985 ss 125A and 125B (introduced by the Housing Act 2004).

[170] Housing Act 1996 ss 131–33.

[171] Housing Act 1985 s 82A; Housing Act 1996 s 143A-B (introduced by the Anti-social Behaviour Act 2003).

has used premises for unlawful purposes within the meaning of sections 153A or 153B of the Housing Act 1996, and the court considers it reasonable to grant the order. The secure tenancy ends from the date given in the order and the tenancy becomes a demoted tenancy. After one year, unless already ended, the demoted tenancy will return to being a secure tenancy. As with the introductory tenant, the demoted tenancy can be ended by the landlord serving notice giving its reasons for doing so and advising the tenant of his right to review. Again, the court has no option but to grant possession if these conditions are met.[172]

6.5.5.2 Long Leases (paragraph 1)

Long leases cannot be secure. Long leases are defined in section 115 to exclude leases for over 21 years (rare in the public sector) or those granted under the RTB, even if for a shorter period.

6.5.5.3 Employment Related Tenancies (paragraph 2)

The Housing Act 1985 does not give a secure tenancy to someone granted his lease as a result of his job with the local authority or other prescribed body if his 'contract of employment requires him to occupy the dwelling-house for the better performance of his duties'.[173] The usual category of employee-tenant who will be caught is the caretaker on the council estate or in the tower block who has been given his tenancy 'for the better performance of his duties'.

If a secure tenancy was originally granted and a subsequent change in employment status means that residence there became a term of his new contract of employment for the better performance of his duties, then the tenant loses his security.[174] On the other hand, if it is not an express term of the contract of employment that the tenant occupy the dwelling-house for the better performance of his duties, the House of Lords held in *Hughes v LB of Greenwich*, that there must be a compelling reason for deeming it to be implied.[175] In *Hughes*, a headmaster's contract did not require him to live in school-provided accommodation and it was not essential for the better performance of his duties; the school provided a facility, it did not impose an obligation, and so he was a secure tenant. Under paragraph 2(1) there are two steps: it must be a requirement of his contract of employment, express or implied, that he live there *and* it must be for the better performance of his duties.

6.5.5.4 Shortlife Tenancies of Properties Acquired for Development (paragraph 3)

Shortlife tenancies of properties acquired for development enable a local authority to let 'land which has been acquired for development ... as temporary housing accommodation' without the risk of creating secure tenancies. Local authorities will often compulsorily purchase land to enable public building projects, such as road schemes or schools, to go ahead. Rather than have properties stand empty, this exemption encourages efficient land use, as Fox LJ noted in *Hyde Housing Assocation Ltd v Harrison*:

> It is undesirable that land should be sterilised and removed from the housing stock pending

---

[172] Housing Act 1985 ss 143D–143G.
[173] In practice, service occupancies are usually licences and not leases (see ch 3) but as s 79(3) provides that licences can be secure tenancies, an employee who has exclusive possession would, but for the exception in para 2, be a secure tenant even if he is only a licensee.
[174] *Elvidge v Coventry CC* (1994) 26 HLR 281 (CA).
[175] (1994) 26 HLR 99 (HL).

development. It is desirable to encourage its use for housing, provided that does not impede the development.[176]

Further, it need not be the landlord itself that has acquired the land for development.[177]

6.5.5.5 Short Term Tenancies for Homeless Applicants (paragraph 4)

Local authorities often have to supply accommodation to homeless people while a decision is taken about their long term housing needs. A tenancy granted under the homelessness duties in Part VII of the Housing Act 1996 will not be a secure tenancy unless the local authority has notified the tenant that it is to be secure. Previously there was a time limit after which the tenant would automatically become secure; while this time limit has now been removed,[178] the local authority will usually give notice that the tenancy is secure once it has finished its enquiries and concludes that the tenant is entitled to an allocation.

6.5.5.6 Asylum-seekers (paragraph 4A)

Housing granted to an asylum seeker under section 4 or Part VI of the Immigration and Asylum Act 1999 will not be a secure tenancy unless the landlord notifies the tenant that it is secure.

6.5.5.7 Short Term Properties for Those Taking up Employment (paragraph 5)

Many local authorities have some property available for people newly moved into the area. If a local authority serves notice on granting a tenancy that it is subject to paragraph 5, then the tenancy will not be secure until the landlord notifies the tenant that it is secure. The aim is to assist those people moving into the area to take up employment.

6.5.5.8 Temporary Housing Leased from the Private Sector (paragraph 6)

Where the local authority takes a lease[179] of a dwelling-house 'for use as temporary housing accommodation' from a private landlord then such leases of the property as the local authority grants will not be secure. In practice, much of the temporary accommodation offered to homeless applicants is private sector leased accommodation, as Mann LJ noted in *Tower Hamlets LBC v Abdi*:

> [Private] leased accommodation … has to a great extent supplanted bed and breakfast accommodation as temporary accommodation for the homeless. It is a means by which local housing authorities can obtain the temporary use of private sector accommodation for the homeless.[180]

This has considerably reduced the number of households having to be placed in bed and breakfast accommodation; whereas 25 per cent of homeless households in temporary accommodation in England were placed in bed and breakfast accommodation in 1990, this had

---

[176] (1990) 23 HLR 57 (CA) 60.
[177] *Hyde Housing Association Ltd v Harrison* (1990) 23 HLR 57 (CA).
[178] By the Homelessness Act 2002.
[179] This has been held also to include licences: *Tower Hamlets LBC v Miah* [1992] QB 622 (CA).
[180] (1993) 25 HLR 80 (CA) 83.

reduced to 5 per cent by 2004, largely due to the use of private leased accommodation which now houses 45 per cent of those in temporary accommodation.[181]

In order for the tenancy to be exempted from the definition of a secure tenancy, the dwelling-house must have 'been leased to the landlord with vacant possession for use as temporary housing accommodation' (paragraph 6(a)), on terms which provide for the private sector landlord 'to obtain vacant possession from the landlord on the expiry of a specified period or when required' (paragraph (6)(b)). The detail of this is important. In *LB of Haringey v Hickey* the Court of Appeal held that the local authority was unable to recover possession from a tenant occupying property leased to the local authority for temporary housing because the lease between the local authority and the private landlord did not contain any provision for the private supplier to end the lease before the fixed term expired.[182] The Court of Appeal held that the wording of paragraph 6(b) meant that the private landlord must be able to recover vacant possession *either* on expiry of a specified period *or* when required by him. The reasoning used by Sir Martin Nourse is that this is the only way to make sense of the statutory wording (as all leases can be ended when the fixed term runs out part of the wording would be otiose if they did not *both* have to be satisfied), but it is an odd result in policy terms: the fact that the private landlord must be able to recover the property when required means that local authorities will have little certainty about how long the arrangement is likely to last.

6.5.5.9 Short Term Lets while Works are Effected (paragraph 7)

It will be rare for this provision to be used, for it only affects leases granted to persons while works are effected on their normal residences and such persons were not secure tenants in their normal residences.

6.5.5.10 Tenancies Relating to Specific Businesses

Where the lease is of premises used as either an agricultural holding or farm business tenancy (paragraph 8), or as licensed premises (paragraph 9), or as business premises within the 1954 Act (paragraph 11), then no secure tenancy is created.

6.5.5.11 Student Lets (paragraph 10)

The tenancy will not be secure if it 'is granted for the purpose of enabling the tenant to attend a designated course[183] at an educational establishment' and the student was notified in advance that the exception applies. It will become secure if the tenant remains for six months after the course finishes.

6.5.6 Security and the Secure Tenancy

A public sector landlord is only able to evict a secure tenant by first obtaining a court order.

---

[181] S Wilcox, *UK Housing Review 2005/06* (Coventry, Chartered Institute of Housing and London, Council of Mortgage Lenders, 2005) Table 91a.

[182] [2006] EWCA Civ 373.

[183] Such as a degree course: see Secure Tenancies (Designated Courses) Regulations 1980 SI 1980/1407; Secure Tenancies (Designated Courses) (Amendment) Regulations 1993 SI 1993/931.

In order to do so it will need to establish a ground for possession. These fall into three broad categories:

(a)   discretionary grounds: the court may order possession if it considers it reasonable to do so;

(b)   grounds on which the court may order possession if suitable alternative accommodation is available. This facilitates better estate management.

(c)   discretionary grounds on which the court may order possession if it considers it reasonable and suitable alternative accommodation is available.[184]

Unless an estate management reason exists, or for some reason the tenant is an unsatisfactory tenant (giving rise to a ground for possession), this means that most 'good' tenants can expect life-long security. One of the questions raised by the Hills review is whether it is always appropriate to give social housing for life:

> First, people's needs differ and their circumstances change over time. What may be the best solution at one moment may not be at another, and some might prefer support to come in a different form from others. Second, the 'standard' social housing offer is quite an expensive one. If some people do not need so much support, or if their circumstances improve later on, there might be savings from a less generous offer (for example … for a fixed period), allowing available resources to stretch further.[185]

6.6 The Housing Association Sector

Since the introduction of the Housing Act 1988, new housing association lettings have come within the assured tenancy regime of the 1988 Act rather than the secure tenancy regime reserved for council lettings. The Regulatory Code and Guidance issued by the Housing Corporation requires, however, that housing associations offer 'the most secure form of tenure compatible with the purpose of the housing and the sustainability of the community'.[186] In practice, most new housing association tenancies are what are known as 'starter' or 'probationary' tenancies, replicating the introductory tenancy regime introduced for council tenants which offer a trial period to see if the tenant will be a 'good' tenant before security is conferred. This is achieved in the housing association sector by granting a fixed term (usually twelve months) assured shorthold tenancy. If no action is taken by the housing association then this will automatically become an assured tenancy at the end of that period.

The assured tenancy regime offers considerable security to housing association tenants although the availability of possession under 'Ground 8' is controversial.[187] This ground gives the landlord a mandatory right to recover possession if the rent is in arrears for a specified period (see chapter 19; where rent is payable monthly, two months unpaid rent will trigger the ground). There is no equivalent to this for secure tenancies. The Antisocial

---

[184] Housing Act 1985 s 84(2).

[185] J Hills, 'Ends and means: The future roles of social housing in England' (CASE Report 34, February 2007) 193.

[186] Housing Corporation, 'The Regulatory Code and Guidance' (August 2005) para 3.5.2.

[187] For arguments for and against retention of this Ground, see Law Commission, 'Renting Homes 1: Status and Security' (Law Com CP No 162, 2002) paras 7.30–7.44. In the final report, possession for serious rent arrears is available only for 'standard contracts' (for the meaning of this, see below, 6.8).

Behaviour Act 2003 also introduced the concept of demoted assured shorthold tenancies that can be used by RSLs,[188] mirroring the demoted tenancy for council tenants. Again the idea is that the landlord is able to apply to the County Court for a demotion order where there has been antisocial behaviour, demoting the assured tenancy to the status of an assured shorthold tenancy for one year (giving much lesser security). The grounds for securing the demoted order are the same as for secure tenancies.

6.7 Statutory Control of Rented Homes

Having explained the main types of tenancies found in the residential sector by reference to the statutory codes applicable to tenancies entered into in the present day, it is useful to outline the major controls that apply to them. The details of these various provisions are dealt with in later chapters. The aim here is to provide an overview. The key provisions are set out below in tabular form.

6.7.1 Landlord's Obligation to Repair[189]

For all leases of dwellings for a term of less than seven years the landlord is under an obligation to keep in repair the structure and exterior of the dwelling, to keep in repair and proper working order the installations for the supply of water, gas and electricity and for sanitation, and to keep in repair and proper working order the installations for space heating and heating water.[190]

6.7.2 Minimum Notice Provisions[191]

With a few exceptions, the occupier of a dwelling is entitled to four weeks' written notice to quit.[192]

6.7.3 No Eviction without Court Order[193]

To ensure that a residential occupier does not unnecessarily vacate property when he may have a right to remain, it is not possible to evict the occupier (with a few exceptions) without a court order being obtained,[194] and without the occupier being given notice of the landlord's intention to recover possession.

---

[188] Housing Act 1988 s 20B.
[189] For details, see ch 12.
[190] Landlord and Tenant Act 1985 s 11.
[191] For details, see ch 22.
[192] Protection from Eviction Act 1977 s 5
[193] For details, see ch 22.
[194] Protection from Eviction Act 1977 s 3.

Table 6.2: Main Statutory Controls for Residential Tenancies

Applies to:	Control	Source
Lease of dwelling for less than 7 years (except lettings *to* local authorites, RSLs, educational institutions – Landlord and Tenant Act 1985 s 14(4))	Landlord obligation to repair structure and exterior, and installations for utilities	Landlord and Tenant Act 1985 s 11 *see* chapter 12
Lease of dwelling	No forfeiture by peaceable re-entry, court order necessary	Protection from Eviction Act 1977 s 2 *see* chapter 24
Licence or lease of dwelling (except resident landlord, holiday let, gratuitous let)	No eviction without court order	Protection from Eviction Act 1977 s 3 *see* chapter 22
Licence or lease of dwelling (except resident landlord, holiday let, gratuitous let)	Four weeks' written notice to quit	Protection from Eviction Act 1977 s 5 *see* chapter 22
Assured tenant (private sector landlords and RSLs)	No termination by landlord without court order; landlord must prove mandatory or discretionary ground for possession	Housing Act 1988 ss 5, 7, Sch 2 *see* chapter 19
	At end of fixed term, a statutory periodic tenancy will arise	Housing Act 1988 s 5 *see* chapter 19
Assured periodic tenant (private sector landlords and RSLs)	Rent: contractually agreed, with statutory or contractual review	Housing Act 1988 s 13 *see* chapter 16
	Tenant can assign or sub-let with landlord's consent, but landlord can withhold consent for any reason	Housing Act 1988 s 15 *see* chapter 17
	Succession (one only) to spouse/civil partner	Housing Act 1988 s 17 *see* chapter 17
Assured shorthold (private sector landlords and RSLs)	No termination by landlord in first six months; two months' notice must be given and fixed term must be at an end. Court order needed for possession	Housing Act 1988 s 21 *see* chapter 19
	At end of fixed term, a statutory periodic tenancy will arise	Housing Act 1988 s 5 *see* chapter 19
	Rent: contractually agreed, excessive rents referable to Rent Assessment Committee	Housing Act 1988 s 22 *see* chapter 16
Secure tenant (local authority landlord; NB. different for introductory and demoted tenancies)	No termination by landlord without court order; landlord must prove discretionary ground for possession	Housing Act 1985 ss 82, 84, Sch 2 *see* chapter 19
	Right to buy	Housing Act 1985 Part V *see* chapter 25
	Right to consultation on housing management	Housing Act 1985 s 105 *see* chapter 11
	Succession (one only) to tenant's spouse/civil partner or member of tenant's family living with tenant for twelve months	Housing Act 1985 s 87 *see* chapter 17
	Right to take in lodgers, and to sub-let with consent	Housing Act 1985 ss 93, 94 *see* chapter 17
	No general right to assign, except for exchange, court order under family jurisdiction, or to person with succession rights	Housing Act 1985 s 95 *see* chapter 17

6.7.4 Security of Tenure[195]

The private sector assured tenant and the secure tenant of council housing both enjoy aconsiderable degree of security. The landlord is unable to obtain possession without a court order, but in addition to this a court order will not be granted unless a ground for possession has been established. In the private sector both mandatory and discretionary grounds are available to the landlord. In the public sector, there are no mandatory grounds.

The assured shorthold tenant has no long term security and, once the initial six months have expired and the contractual term has come to an end, can be made to leave on two months' notice.

6.7.5 Rent Control[196]

In the past, rent control was an important plank of tenant protection in the private sector. Apart from the few remaining Rent Act protected tenancies, there is no effective rent control now in this sector.

6.7.6 The Tenant's Right to Transfer the Tenancy[197]

At common law the tenant is entitled to transfer his interest in the property by assignment or to create new sub interests by, for example, sub-letting the tenancy. In practice, however, this right will usually be restricted by the contractual terms. In relation to an assured periodic tenancy there is an implied right to assign or sub-let, but in practice this is illusory because the landlord is able to withhold consent for any reason. The secure tenant is given certain rights by the Housing Act 1985: to take in lodgers, to assign by way of exchange, to assign pursuant to a court order, and to assign to a limited class of people. There is a right to sub-let part of the premises, although the sub-letting of the whole will result in the tenancy ceasing to be secure.

6.7.7 Succession Rights[198]

Rights of succession are given to the spouse (or civil partner) of an assured periodic tenant and the secure tenant (and, in the case of the secure tenant, to members of the tenant's family who have been living with him for the preceding twelve months).

6.7.8 Right to Buy and Right to Acquire[199]

The secure tenant may have the right to buy the freehold (or long lease) of his property at a discount. No similar right exists in the private sector for tenants of short leases. Housing

---

[195] For details, see ch 19.
[196] For details, see ch 15.
[197] For details, see ch 17.
[198] For details, see ch 17.
[199] For details, see ch 25.

association tenants may have a 'preserved' RTB if the reversion has been transferred from a council landlord to the housing association after they moved in. There is also a 'right to acquire' (RTA) scheme for housing association tenants, which is similar to the RTB, but not all properties qualify and discounts are usually lower than for the RTB.

6.8 Future Directions

In 2006, the Law Commission published its final report on Renting Homes.[200] This follows an extensive consultation exercise, beginning with the publication of two consultation papers during 2002,[201] and the publication of a report setting out its policy conclusions in 2003.[202] The renting homes project has been driven by a desire to achieve simplification, increased comprehensibility, and flexibility. Two fundamental principles lie at the heart of their recommendations: landlord neutrality and a consumer protection approach.

> 1.4 First, we recommend the creation of a single social tenure. … Our recommendations are 'landlord neutral'. They enable social housing providers, referred to in the [draft] Bill as 'community landlords', and those private sector landlords who so wish to rent on identical terms. This has long been sought by local authorities and registered social landlords. This offers the prize of vastly increased flexibility both to policy makers and landlords in the provision and management of social housing.
>
> 1.5 Secondly, we recommend a new 'consumer protection' approach which focuses on the contract between the landlord and the occupier (the contract holder), incorporating consumer protection principles of fairness and transparency. Thus our recommended scheme does not depend on technical legal issues of whether or not there is a tenancy as opposed to a licence (as has usually been the case in the past). This ensures that both landlords and occupiers have a much clearer understanding of their rights and occupations.
>
> 1.6 The terms of the contract, underpinned by a statutory scheme, will be set out in model contracts that we anticipate will be free and easily downloadable. They will benefit landlords by explaining their rights and obligations, thus reducing the ignorance many landlords have had about their responsibilities. They will benefit occupiers who also have a clear statement of their rights and obligations, which sets out the basis on which they occupy accommodation, and the circumstances in which their rights to occupy may come to an end.

An important goal of the rented homes project is simplification. This means getting rid of the many different categories of rental agreements that can exist in the present law. Under their proposed scheme, there will be just two forms of occupation contract that can be used: the *secure* contract, akin to the present secure tenancy and giving substantial security of tenure; and the *standard* contract, akin to the assured shorthold tenancy, with the length of tenancy defined by the contract itself. (These labels may lead to confusion given that the protected council tenant is currently known as a secure tenant.) The occupation contract itself will be a contract that confers the right to occupy premises as a home which is made between a landlord and an individual. It can be either a tenancy or a licence. Most of the

---

[200] Law Commission, 'Renting Homes: The Final Report. Volume 1: Report' (Law Com No 297, 2006)
[201] Law Commission, 'Renting Homes 1: Status and Security' (Law Com CP No 162, 2002); Law Commission, 'Renting Homes 2: Co-occupation, Transfer and Succession' (Law Com CP No 168, 2002).
[202] Law Commission, 'Renting Homes' (Law Com No 284, 2003).

existing complexities in the definitions of the various protected tenancies will be done away with. The rental limits in the private rented sector will disappear. There will no longer be a requirement that the premises must be occupied as the only or principal home,[203] as the purpose of the scheme is to ensure that *all* contract holders are informed about their contractual rights and obligations. The Law Commission recommend that existing tenancy agreements and licences are converted into the new secure and standard contracts,[204] to avoid further complexity in the law.

Community (social) landlords will usually be required to enter into secure contracts as these reflect their social goals. There will, however, be various exceptions permitted. A community landlord will, for example, be able to enter a standard contract for a probationary period (similar to the introductory tenancy but on an individual basis rather than an 'all or nothing' approach). RSLs will be able to enter standard contracts for market rent lettings, as, for example, with housing provided for key workers.

The number of exceptions from the scheme will be reduced and will fall into three categories:

(a) those that can never be occupation contracts, mainly because they come within other regimes, such as business tenancies;

(b) those that are not occupation contracts unless the landlord elects to make it one and gives notice stating that the contract is an occupation contract. So, for example, accommodation shared with the landlord and rent free accommodation will usually fall outside the scheme, but the landlord is able to opt into it by serving notice.

(c) special cases: contracts providing accommodation for the homeless, and supported accommodation (where housing plus support services are provided).[205]

Transparency is also important under this scheme: both parties to the occupation contract should be fully aware of their contractual rights and obligations. A written statement of the contract is compulsory, and the content is partially prescribed. There will be key matters (which are the details particular to this contract, such as the description of the parties, the property, rent and so on) and also 'fundamental' terms that reflect statutory provisions and which cannot be omitted or altered (such as the proposed prohibited conduct term providing that the occupier may not use or threaten to use violence against a person lawfully living on the premises).[206] In addition there will be 'supplementary fundamental' terms that can be modified provided that the alteration gives greater protection to the occupier. To make things easier for the parties, model contracts will be made readily available, and it is expected that most landlords will opt to use these. To ensure fairness, it is recommended that the Unfair Terms in Consumer Contracts Regulations 1999[207] should apply to *all* occupation contracts (not only to those where the landlord is a 'supplier' and the tenant a 'consumer').

---

[203] Although it will still be possible for the landlord to require this contractually.

[204] With the exception of Rent Act protected tenancies, due to the high level of tenant resistance.

[205] The Law Commission state that one of the biggest challenges during the rented homes project was to create an appropriate legal regime for supported housing: Part 10 of the Final Report sets out their conclusions on this.

[206] Law Commission, 'Renting Homes: The Final Report. Volume 2: Draft Bill' (Law Com No 297, 2006) Rented Homes Bill cl 51.

[207] SI 1999/2083.

The aim is to provide a ready source of information to the contract-holder. Thus, the contract will, for example, set out clearly what rights the contract-holder has to transfer the contract and add new contract-holders. There are also number of substantive consumer protection measures that will be built into the detail of these contracts. One welcome (and long overdue) suggestion is that that should be a term that the accommodation meets certain minimum standards at the outset.[208]

These reform proposals have received widespread support. Many organisations have for some time been arguing that there should be a single form of tenancy available for all social lettings, irrespective of landlord type. Further, the emphasis placed on transparency and fairness through requiring a written contract which sets out the rights and obligations of both parties should help foster a 'mind-set' in which tenants are seen as consumers with rights and expectations, and landlords as service providers opting in to a regulated regime. Whether or not the proposals will progress to become law will depend, of course, on the political process. Legislation of this sort is complex and not politically eye-catching but it would be most unfortunate if these very welcome proposals never make it to the statute book.

---

[208] Achieved by reference to the category one hazard used by the new HHSR (Housing Health and Safety Rating) system introduced by the Housing Act 2004.

7

LONG RESIDENTIAL LEASES

7.1   The reasons for using long leases
7.2   Problems with long leasehold
7.3   The case for reform
7.4   Reform at last
7.5   An overview of legislative controls of residential long leases
7.6   The future?

7.1 The Reasons for Using Long Leases

The relationship between the landlord and tenant in a long residential lease differs significantly from that in a short term rental relationship. Most long residential leases are for fixed terms of 99/125 years or 999 years, although some such leases are sold for shorter terms. In broad terms, a long residential lease is generally one that is for more than 21 years, that has been purchased for a premium, and for which a ground rent (not a market rent) is payable.

A DETR paper published in 1998 estimated that there were around 900,000 leaseholders of houses in England and Wales, and over a million leaseholders of flats.[1] Of those leaseholders with flats, around 200,000 have local authority landlords,[2] and 152,500 have housing association landlords.[3]

Properties are sold nowadays on a long leasehold basis primarily to overcome the inability to enforce positive covenants between adjoining freehold owners. In the case of houses that are vertically divided, sales can be either on a freehold or leasehold basis, but it is simply not practically possible to sell a flat in a mansion block as a freehold because this would mean that the owner has only a freehold of a block of airspace (known as a 'flying freehold'). Financial institutions would not be willing to lend against the security of only a flying freehold. Without there being enforceable obligations of support and maintenance, the unit-holder is vulnerable to the behaviour of other unit-holders. From the perspective of the other unit-holders, there needs to be a way of ensuring that obligations (such as those to

---

[1] DETR, 'Residential Leasehold Reform in England and Wales: a Consultation Paper' (1998).
[2] M Davey, 'Long Residential Leases: Past and Present' in S Bright, *Landlord and Tenant Law. Past, Present and Future* (Oxford, Hart, 2006).
[3] P Robinson, *Leasehold Management: A Good Practice Guide* (Coventry, Chartered Institute of Housing, National Housing Federation and the Housing Corporation, 2003) 30.

repair, maintain, and contribute towards expenses) are enforceable not only against the current unit-holder but future unit-holders as well.

Given that the English common law has set its face against the enforceability of positive covenants in freehold land, there is no easy mechanism for ensuring a scheme of enforceable obligations. This is why conveyancers turned to the long leasehold as a device to provide for the sale and purchase of property for which a scheme of enforceability is necessary. Covenants contained in leases are enforceable whenever there is privity of estate (a relationship of landlord and tenant), and so the long leasehold has been used for the sale of residential flats. Historically, it has also been used in the sale of houses, partly because leasehold covenants could be used to retain strict control on the overall appearance of an area (for example, requiring all front doors to be painted the same colour), but also because it provided the freeholder with the opportunity to realise a fresh premium when the lease expired.[4]

There is a further reason why long leases have been used for selling property in the past: the lease can be a way of maintaining income from the land. In practice, the rental component is usually low, but money can be made through managing the property, for example, taking commissions on insurance premiums and making profits on management and administration.[5] As will be seen, it is no longer regarded as acceptable for the landlord to use leases in this way and legislative changes have reduced the opportunity for landlords to make money through management and through resale when the lease expires.

7.2 Problems with Long Leasehold

The long leasehold has never been an entirely satisfactory tool to use for long-term ownership.

For the leaseholder, the purchase of a long lease is usually a major financial commitment in which the leaseholder is effectively choosing to become an 'owner-occupier'. In law, however, the leaseholder is subject to a number of constraints that freeholder owners are free from: the terms on which the home is occupied are regulated by the leasehold contract, the lease can be forfeited if there is a breach of covenant by the tenant, there is a need for management of communal areas (particularly in flat sales) that means that decisions about maintenance are not in the control of the individual leaseholder, and the value of the lease diminishes as the term shortens and the lease becomes harder to sell. The reality of leasehold ownership comes as a surprise to many leaseholders who consider themselves owners: there can be a sense of 'powerlessness and exclusion from the norms of control and responsibility associated with home ownership'.[6] Many leaseholders appear not to have

---

[4] Some commercial developments are also sold on this basis where there are communal facilities shared amongst unit holders.

[5] D Clarke, 'Long Residential Leases: Future Directions' in S Bright (ed), *Landlord and Tenant Law. Past, Present and Future* (Oxford, Hart, 2006) 175–77.

[6] S Blandy and D Robinson, 'Reforming Leasehold: Discursive Events and Outcomes, 1984–2000' (2001) 28 *JLS* 384, 396, drawing on comments in a study by I Cole and others, 'The Impact of Leasehold Reform: Flat Dwellers' Experiences of Enfranchisement and Lease Renewal' (DETR, 1998).

understood, or appreciated the impact of, the 'wasting asset' problem, that is, the fact that as the lease shortens this can have a significant impact on its resale value.[7]

Problems with management are common. Whenever there is shared use of communal space within a building there will always be a need for regulations to govern the use of that space, and of the individual units where user of them can impact on adjoining owners. There is also a need for one body to be responsible for maintenance and repair of the structure of the building and for that body to be able to recover the costs of maintenance from individual unit holders. Many leases have been carefully drafted to ensure that management is appropriately provided for. Modern developments often provide for the management of the property to be transferred to a management company controlled by the leaseholders on completion. The lease is not, however, always so well designed. Part of the problem is that there is no such thing as a 'standard' form of lease, and leases are often put together from different precedents. In the course of 'tailor-making' the lease in this way, amendments can often be made to precedents which are not well thought through (or not made where they need to be). One example is illustrated in the case of *Holding & Barnes plc v Hill House Hammond Ltd* when the wording in the lease was appropriate for a letting of part of a building, but had in fact been used for a lease of a whole building and made no sense.[8] Further, responsibility for management is sometimes retained by the developer landlord and day to day management may be handed over to a managing agent. Some landlords may be disinterested in management, or may exploit leaseholders through excessive management charges. The result is that leaseholders can feel cut off from decisions that affect their daily lives closely as they have very little say in how the property is looked after, or how much they have to pay towards the management.

Legislation has been used to respond to these issues. The freeholder's possession rights have been altered by giving leaseholders the right to stay at the end of their leases, and by placing limitations on the right to forfeit for non-payment of service charges. Problems with management have been tackled by giving leaseholders various rights to take over the management of property, by providing for consultation, and restricting recovery of service charges to 'reasonable' sums. The problem of the 'wasting asset' (as well as management problems) has been dealt with through giving leaseholders the right to enfranchise (individually in the case of houses, and collectively in the case of flats) or extend their leases. The following section tells the story of the long battle for leasehold reform and how these measures came to be adopted.

7.3 The Case for Reform

The story of the long leasehold is one of struggle, showing that there has never been full acceptance of it as an appropriate means for owning property. It is also a story of resistance,

---

[7] A study confirmed that many flats dwellers thought that they owned their property in the same way as owners or buyers of freehold properties: I Cole and others, *The Impact of Leasehold Reform: Flat Dwellers' Experiences of Enfranchisement and Lease Renewal* (DETR, 1998).

[8] [2001] EWCA Civ 1334. See further ch 12.

with freeholders opposed to reform that threatens their property rights. Since Victorian times, 'leaseholders, social reformers, and politicians' have argued

> … that the law governing long residential leases was heavily biased in favour of landlords, and that this imbalance called out for statutory redress. The most radical demand was for enfranchisement, that is to say a power on the part of the leaseholder to compel the freeholder to transfer the freehold to the leaseholder at a price to be determined by agreement, or by an independent tribunal or court. [footnotes omitted][9]

Indeed, Davey writes that in the period between 1884 and 1925 there was a remarkable 143 Bills introduced on the issue of leasehold enfranchisement. It was not until the Leasehold Reform Act of 1967, however, that enfranchisement was finally introduced for some residential long leaseholders of houses.

Whilst there have been movements supporting enfranchisement for over a hundred years, the reasons given for justifying such radical intervention with freeholders' rights have been given differing emphasis at differing times.[10] By contrast, the grounds of opposition have been fairly consistently based on the interference with sanctity of contract, freedom of property, the impact upon estate management and fears of the break-up of the traditional estates. There have been essentially four major arguments used to support the call for enfranchisement. The early case for enfranchisement was heavily based upon the effect that the building lease had on housing standards and conditions. The Royal Commission on the Housing of Working Classes (1884-5) supported enfranchisement on the grounds that it would lead to an improvement in housing for the working classes. The building lease system was considered conducive to bad building and led to a deterioration in property towards the end of the lease due to lack of incentive for the occupier to keep it in repair. A few years later the Select Committee on Town Holdings (1889), while accepting these arguments, was against general enfranchisement for fear that it would discourage new development and so lead to a decline in housing provision for the working classes. The Select Committee was also concerned that it would make good estate management difficult, a view that has been repeated on many occasions since. During the first part of the twentieth century concern over housing conditions diminished as other mechanisms were put in place to monitor this, such as the development of planning and public health laws.

Around the middle of the twentieth century the case for enfranchisement shifted from one based on housing conditions (a public interest argument) to one of protecting tenants (the landlord now being seen as a man of property reaping where the tenant has sown). In 1950 the Leasehold Committee was not persuaded by this argument and did not accept that long leases were based on inequality and injustice, the focus at this stage still being on the building lease (rather than the quite different issues raised by leases of flats).[11] By 1953 the Government, without finally deciding the issue of principle, decided that the practical difficulties that would follow a scheme of enfranchisement (prohibitive costs to tenants, management of

---

[9] M Davey, 'Long Residential Leases: Past and Present' in S Bright, *Landlord and Tenant Law. Past, Present and Future* (Oxford, Hart, 2006) 148.

[10] The arguments used in the campaign for leasehold enfranchisement are fully explored in M Davey, 'Long Residential Leases: Past and Present' in S Bright, *Landlord and Tenant Law. Past, Present and Future* (Oxford, Hart, 2006).

[11] Leasehold Committee, 'Final Report' (Cmd 7982, 1950). The Minority Report did not agree. It felt that property carries obligations and that the extortion associated with building leases was abusing this social responsibility. Interference with freeholders' rights was therefore justifiable. See 'Minority Report', especially para 39.

large estates and so on) outweighed the possible gains.[12] What long leaseholders really needed was security of tenure rather than freehold ownership – it would therefore be sufficient to protect their right of occupation, rather than give a new right of ownership. In consequence, the Landlord and Tenant Act 1954, Part I conferred on tenants of long leases at a low rent a right to remain at the end of the contractual term and entitling them to a statutory tenancy within the Rent Acts.[13] It soon became apparent that this measure did not succeed in relieving the injustice to tenants at the expiry of their leases, given that the tenant had to pay freshly assessed (market) rents and often faced large claims for dilapidations.

7.4 Reform at Last

7.4.1 Enfranchisement of Houses

It was not until 1967 that rights to enfranchise were given in the Leasehold Reform Act 1967. The important idea underlying this was that 'the land belongs in equity to the landowner and the house belongs in equity to the occupying leaseholder'.[14] What made the issue particularly urgent was the fact that houses developed under the building lease system popular in late Victorian times were now nearing the end of their leases, heightening awareness of the lease as a diminishing asset.[15]

The Leasehold Reform Act 1967 gives the tenant of a house on a long lease at a low rent and within certain rateable value limits the right to acquire the freehold of the premises by enfranchisement or the right to an extended lease. Flats were not included in the scheme, allegedly because 'different considerations of equity apply and there would be many practical difficulties in providing for enfranchisement of flats'.[16] An equally significant factor was probably that enfranchisement of flats was not an issue on the political agenda as few flat leases were yet short enough to cause major concern. Concerns over the impact that enfranchisement would have upon estate management were met by the introduction of estate management schemes whereby the landlord could apply for a scheme to be established enabling him to retain powers of management over houses to be enfranchised.[17]

The premise underlying the legislation did not go without challenge. Many did not agree that the house belonged in equity to the tenant.[18] Moreover, this premise also shaped the price payable on enfranchisement. On enfranchisement the price payable was the open market value of the reversion on the assumption that the tenant has exercised his statutory right to extend the lease for fifty years and that the tenant was not the purchaser.[19] The overall effect was that the

---

[12] 'Government Policy on Leasehold Property in England and Wales' (Cmd 8713, 1953).

[13] See Landlord and Tenant Act 1954 Part I; ch 20.

[14] Ministry of Land and Natural Resources, 'Leasehold Reform in England and Wales' (Cmnd 2916, 1966) para 4.

[15] Ministry of Land and Natural Resources, 'Leasehold Reform in England and Wales' (Cmnd 2916, 1966): '… a great, many leasehold estates were built … when landowners used their *monopoly* power to prevent development taking place on other than leasehold terms … These leases are beginning to fall in and the leaseholders are now experiencing the full *harshness* of the leasehold system', para 3 (emphasis added). The problem was particularly prevalent in South Wales.

[16] Ministry of Land and Natural Resources, 'Leasehold Reform in England and Wales' (Cmnd 2916, 1966) para 8.

[17] Leasehold Reform Act 1967 s 19.

[18] See, for example, R Megarry and HWR Wade, *The Law of Real Property* 5th edn (London, Steven & Sons, 1984) 1172.

[19] Leasehold Reform Act 1967 s 9.

tenant was deemed to have already paid for the house and so only had to pay for the site value. In 1974 the scheme was extended to include some houses with a higher rateable value and a different basis of valuation was applied. The price payable was the amount that the freehold would fetch on the open market on the assumption that at the end of the tenancy the tenant had the right to remain in possession of the house under the 1954 Act. This was intended to give the landlord a more favourable figure based on the market value of the site and house and allowing him a part of the 'marriage value'. (The sum of the freeholder's interest – subject to the lease – and the leaseholder's interest is less than vacant possession value. Marriage value is the additional value released by the merger of the freeholder's and the leaseholder's interests.)[20]

7.4.2 Addressing the Problems of Leasehold Flats

The fact that the Leasehold Reform Act 1967 applied only to houses meant that the problems with long leaseholds still applied to flats. Enfranchisement of flats became a live issue during the 1980s as the mansion blocks built during the post-War years began to experience serious diffi-culties with repair and condition. The problems of management were highlighted by the Nugee Report in 1985[21] which found poor maintenance, excessive service charges, lack of consultation over works, not knowing who the landlord was, little contact between landlords and tenants, inadequate leases and lack of management expertise.

The problems with service charges and management have since been addressed on several occasions, adopting, as Davey notes, a 'consumer protection' approach.[22] To prevent freeholders exploiting leaseholders various measures have been passed to control excessive charging. The Landlord and Tenant Act 1985 requires that costs in service charges are 'reasonably incurred'[23] and that leaseholders are consulted before expensive works are carried out or long-term contracts entered into.[24] Leaseholders of houses are able to choose their own buildings insurance for the property rather than use an insurer nominated or approved by their landlord.[25] Leaseholders have also been given fuller rights to take charge of the overall management in certain situations. The first step towards this was taken by the Landlord and Tenant Act 1987 which gave leaseholders the right to apply to the court for the appointment of a manager where the landlord was in breach of his tenancy obligations, and to apply for compulsory acquisition of the freehold where there was a serious breach which was likely to continue (see chapter 25). The 1987 Act was notoriously badly drafted and had little impact. More recently, a 'no fault' right to manage has been given by the Commonhold and Leasehold Reform Act 2002 (see chapter 11).

None of these management solutions addressed the more fundamental problem with leasehold ownership; that the leasehold term eventually runs out. Returning to the 1980s, the pressure for change continued to build. The problem over leases as 'wasting assets'

---

[20] See further ch 25.

[21] Nugee Committee, 'Report of the Committee on the Management of Privately Owned Blocks of Flats' (London, 1985).

[22] M Davey, 'Long Residential Leases: Past and Present' in S Bright, *Landlord and Tenant Law. Past, Present and Future* (Oxford, Hart, 2006).

[23] Landlord and Tenant Act 1985 s 19.

[24] Landlord and Tenant Act 1985 s 20, as amended by the Commonhold and Leasehold Reform Act 2002.

[25] Commonhold and Leasehold Reform Act 2002 s 164.

became more noticeable as residential leaseholders found it difficult to sell leases with only 40-45 years remaining, especially as lenders were reluctant to lend on an asset with diminishing value.[26] Enfranchisement was also seen to fit with the government's plans to extend home-ownership. Eventually, the Leasehold Reform, Housing and Urban Development Act 1993 was passed, giving tenants of long leasehold flats the collective right to enfranchise at market value, or the individual right to extend their leases by 90 years at market value. The purchase price in the 1993 Act was based on normal valuation practice. The price of enfranchisement was the purchase of the freehold plus at least 50 per cent of the marriage value.[27] Since then, there have been various amendments to the details of enfranchisement to make it easier for leaseholders to exercise the right and to reduce the opportunity for landlords to block claims (see chapter 25).

7.4.3 Commonhold

In many respects, enfranchisement of flats, was perceived as a subsidiary issue to the commonhold proposals. The Department of Constitutional Affairs website describes commonhold thus:

> A commonhold consists of individually owned but interdependent freehold properties (known as units) and common parts. In a block of flats, for example, each flat would typically be a unit and the remainder, including the structure and exterior of the block, the stairs, hallway and grounds, would be common parts. Each unit is owned by a unit-holder. The common parts are owned and managed by a commonhold association, which is a limited company, of which only the unit-holders may be members. The members will have direct ownership of the unit they own and an interest in the ownership and management of the common parts through membership of the commonhold association.
>
> The commonhold is managed by the commonhold association in accordance with the rules of the commonhold community statement (CCS).

Throughout the 1990s, commonhold was seen as providing the answer to the problems of long leaseholds; it provides a system of freehold ownership which is specifically designed for buildings in multiple occupation. Indeed, in the 1987 Law Commission paper[28] commonhold was seen as a necessary forerunner to any form of leasehold enfranchisement for flats. The Commonhold Paper of the same year was directed at the technicalities of a scheme of commonhold.[29] A Consultation Paper issued in 1990 was similarly directed primarily towards commonhold, with leasehold enfranchisement mentioned only as a secondary issue which should not be introduced without commonhold.[30] In the end, commonhold did not arrive until the Commonhold and Leasehold Reform Act 2002, coming into effect in September 2004.

In practice, however, commonhold has not proven popular with developers (and unless developers choose commonhold, there are no units available to purchase). The way that the

---

[26] Building Societies Association, 'Leasehold – Time for a Change?' (London, 1984).

[27] It is now 50% of the marriage value, the reference to 'at least' was confusing and usually was 50% in practice.

[28] Law Commission, 'Landlord and Tenant: Reform of the Law' (Law Com No 162, 1987) para 4.37.

[29] Law Commission, 'Commonhold – Freehold Flats and Freehold Ownership of other Interdependent Buildings' (Cm 179, July 1987).

[30] Lord Chancellor's Department, 'Commonhold, A Consultation Paper' (Cm 1346, 1990).

legislation has been drafted means that lenders are cautious about lending on the security of a commonhold.[31] To date, very few commonholds have been sold.

7.5 An Overview of Legislative Controls of Residential Long Leases

There are now many measures that are designed to deal with abuses within the long leasehold relationship and to enable long leaseholders themselves, rather than outside investors, to be in control. Table 7.1 shows the major legislative controls within this sector, which are discussed in more detail in later chapters.

7.6 The Future?

The long leasehold story continues. The extremely poor take-up of commonhold to date means that most new developments continue to be marketed as long leaseholds. The right to enfranchise may remove some of the difficulties with leasehold but it requires a considerable degree of determination to go through with a collective enfranchisement claim and, as Davey writes, 'it remains a formidably complex and potentially expensive process'.[32] The tranche of what Davey describes as 'consumer protection' measures has made things better for leaseholders, albeit at the price of great complexity in the law.

Clarke has proposed a more radical change in approach. He argues that the division of interest in long leases of 99 or 125 years is 'rarely genuine' and is 'unacceptable'. [33] According to Clarke, the reason why a freeholder would choose to sell on this basis, rather than to sell on a 999 year lease which hands over the management to the leaseholders through a management company, is often to preserve the opportunity for a capital windfall through termination or to make money through management. In practice, it would be unusual for a landlord to receive a capital windfall through termination as forfeiture of long residential leases is not common. The more likely scenario is that the developer landlord hopes to receive further money if the lease-holders choose to enfranchise (see chapter 25). Nonetheless, the issue raised by Clarke is an important one: should landlords be free to sell on 99 or 125 years? His answer is 'no': Parliament has made clear through the various enfranchisement acts and the reforms to management that preserving the opportunity to make money through capital windfall and management is unacceptable. Clarke suggests a two-fold solution. First, to prevent the future creation of residential leases of more than 21 years and less than 999 years; any attempt to do so would be transformed into a term of 999 years.[34] Second, once the last unit of a development is sold, there would be a requirement that the freehold is transferred to a leaseholder controlled management company.

---

[31] D Clarke, 'Long Residential Leases: Future Directions' in S Bright, *Landlord and Tenant Law. Past, Present and Future* (Oxford, Hart, 2006) 180–6.

[32] M Davey, 'Long Residential Leases: Past and Present' in S Bright, *Landlord and Tenant Law. Past, Present and Future* (Oxford, Hart, 2006) 167.

[33] D Clarke, 'Long Residential Leases: Future Directions' in S Bright, *Landlord and Tenant Law. Past, Present and Future* (Oxford, Hart, 2006) 172.

[34] For similar views, see also the Leasehold Advisory Service, 'Chairman's Report' *Annual Report 2006* (London, 2006), and the web-site for the Campaign for the Abolition of Residential Leasehold (www.carl.org.uk).

Table 7.1: Outline of Statutory Controls for Long Residential Leases

Control	Applies to:	Source	Book chapter
Right to remain on expiry of lease at market rent ('continuation tenancy')	Long tenancy at low rent used as home	Landlord and Tenant Act 1954, Part 1; Local Government and Housing Act 1989 Schedule 10	20
Right to enfranchise or 50 year lease extension	Long tenant of house; tenant for last 2 years	Leasehold Reform Act 1967	25
Control of service charges	Tenants of dwellings	Landlord and Tenant Act 1985	13
Right of first refusal	Building at least 50 per cent residential; 2 or more flats with qualifying tenants; more than half of flats with qualifying tenants; supported by more than 50 per cent of the qualifying tenants	Landlord and Tenant Act 1987 Part I	25
Leasehold Valuation Tribunal (LVT) appointment of receiver/manager if management breach and just and convenient to make the order	Must be 2 or more flats (not on continuation tenancies)	Landlord and Tenant Act 1987 Part II	11
Right of Compulsory Acquisition	Failure in management of long leaseholds; at least 50 per cent residential; at least 2 qualifying tenants; supported by not less than 2/3 of qualifying tenants	Landlord and Tenant Act 1987 Part III	25
Collective right of enfranchisement of flats	Long lease; at least 2 flats held by qualifying tenants; no more than 25 per cent non-residential use; support from half of flats.	Leasehold Reform, Housing and Urban Development Act 1993 Part I, Chapter I	25
Lease extension of 90 years for flat	Long lease; tenant for last 2 years	Leasehold Reform, Housing and Urban Development Act 1993 Part I, Chapter II	25
'No fault' right to manage through RTM company	2/3 of flats held by long leasehold qualifying tenants; at least 2 flats held by qualifying tenants; no more than 25 per cent non-residential use; at least 50 per cent support from qualifying tenants	Commonhold and Leasehold Reform Act 2002 Part II, Chapter 1	11
Choice of insurer	Long lease of house	Commonhold and Leasehold Reform Act 2002 section 164	13
Controls on forfeiture	Long lease of dwelling	Commonhold and Leasehold Reform Act 2002 sections 167–171	24

It is, perhaps, improbable that such a radical solution will be pursued. More likely, again in the words of Clarke:

> There will be no new initiatives, either to develop commonhold or to streamline the format of long residential leases. So, new developments will continue as we have them now. Each standard lease will be different to those in any other development. There will be no guarantee that even the terms of each lease are the same in a single development. The full panoply of the landlord and tenant legislation, drafted on the basis that there was an outside landlord, will continue to apply to tenants' management companies.
>
> Is this desirable? It is a future of continued leasehold complaints; more problems with out-of-date lease terms; rising case loads for leasehold valuation tribunals; and, continued legislative tinkering.[35]

---

[35] D Clarke, 'Long Residential Leases. Future Directions' in S Bright, *Landlord and Tenant Law. Past, Present and Future* (Oxford, Hart, 2006) 189–90.

8

BUSINESS TENANCIES

8.1   Policy and legislative history in the commercial property sector
8.2   The operation of the Landlord and Tenant Act 1954, Part II
8.3   Tenancies to which Part II of the 1954 Act applies
8.4   Future directions

8.1 Policy and Legislative History in the Commercial Property Sector[1]

8.1.1 The Background to Part II of the Landlord and Tenant Act 1954

As with the private residential sector, commercial lettings were largely unregulated until the early part of the twentieth century. The primary focus of legislative control since then has been the protection of goodwill (either through providing compensation when goodwill is lost or through providing the right to remain in the business premises) and compensating the tenant for the cost of certain improvements that he has carried out on the premises.

The immediate impetus for the first major regulation was, as in the private residential sector, the shortage of premises following World War I. As there was a ready supply of new tenants when the lease came to an end, the landlord could force tenants to leave without giving them a chance to stay on fair terms, or put the rents of existing tenants up to unconscionable levels (which tenants would pay in order to be able to stay in the property).[2] While recognising the need for some tenant protection, a Select Committee reporting in 1920 noted that in order to avoid discouraging new building (which would be to the tenant's disadvantage in the long term), intervention should be kept to a minimum.[3]

The early legislation was contained in Part I of the Landlord and Tenant Act 1927.[4] Section 1 of the 1927 Act provided that tenants could get compensation for the cost of certain improvements they had made to the premises and, although little used, this right

---

[1] See also S Bridge, 'Commercial Leases Past and Present: The Contribution of the Law Commission' in S Bright (ed), *Landlord and Tenant Law. Past, Present and Future* (Oxford, Hart, 2006); S Murdoch, 'Commercial Leases: Future Directions' in S Bright (ed), *Landlord and Tenant Law. Past, Present and Future* (Oxford, Hart, 2006).

[2] Select Committee on Business Premises, 'Business Premises' HC (1920). Haley notes that the need for legislation to protect business tenants was accepted before the end of the nineteenth century: M Haley, 'The statutory regulation of business tenancies: private property, public interest and political compromise' (1999) 19 *LS* 207, 216.

[3] Select Committee on Business Premises, 'Business Premises' HC (1920).

[4] For a discussion of the background to this, see M Haley, 'The statutory regulation of business tenancies: private property, public interest and political compromise' (1999) 19 *LS* 207.

has been retained (see chapter 11). More successfully, section 19 of the Act (still in force, though now heavily amended) addressed the problem of landlords being able to hold tenants to ransom where consent for alienation, improvements or change of use was required under the terms of the lease. In the case of dealings and improvements it provided that consent could not be unreasonably withheld (see chapters 17 and 11, respectively). In relation to change of use it prevented the landlord from charging for the consent (see chapter 12).

The 1927 Landlord and Tenant Act also enabled a tenant to obtain compensation for the loss of goodwill at the end of its tenancy but, as will be seen, this proved inadequate to give business tenants the protection needed. The aim of the goodwill provisions was to prevent the landlord from unfairly profiting from the tenant's business. In the words of Lord Greene MR:

> ... the mischief at which this part of the Act [the goodwill provisions] was aimed, and that also is true of the part which deals with compensation for improvements, was to deal with the case of a landlord acquiring through the activities of his tenant, either by improving the property or by creating in the property, and adherent to the property, a goodwill of which the landlord would take the benefit when the lease came to an end. It was obviously thought unjust by the legislature that the landlord should obtain that type of unearned increment on the termination of a lease ...[5]

In practice, however, this was an extremely limited goal and offered very little tenant protection. It did not generally provide tenants with what they most wanted, security. In addition, the compensation provisions were limited – the calculation of goodwill reflecting not the potential loss to the tenant but the gain to the landlord from the tenant's use of the property.[6] Compensation for loss of goodwill was only available if the tenant could show that as a result of carrying on his business for at least five years he had increased the letting value of the premises. But this only gave the tenant compensation when he could show what became known as 'adherent goodwill', that is goodwill adhering to the premises rather than to the business. In the colourful language of Scrutton LJ, this is only one aspect of goodwill:

> A division of the elements of goodwill ... appears in Mr Merlin's book as the 'cat, rat and dog' basis. The cat prefers the old home to the person who keeps it, and stays in the old home though the person who has kept the house leaves. The cat represents that part of the customers who continue to go to the old shop, though the old shopkeeper has gone; the probability of their custom may be regarded as an additional value given to the premises by the tenant's trading. The dog represents that part of the customers who follow the person rather than the place; these the tenant may take away with him if he does not go too far. There remains a class of customer who may neither follow the place nor the person, but drift away elsewhere. They are neither a benefit to the landlord nor the tenant, and have been called the 'rat' for no particular reason except to keep the epigram in the animal kingdom ... It is obvious that the division of the customers into 'cat, rat and dog' must vary enormously in different cases and different circumstances. The 'dog' class will increase with the attractiveness and new accessibil-

---

[5] *Stuchbery v General Accident Fire and Life Assurance Corp Ltd* [1949] 2 KB 256 (CA) 264.

[6] See M Haley, 'The statutory regulation of business tenancies: private property, public interest and political compromise' (1999) 19 *LS* 207, 208.

ity of the tenant; the 'cat' class with the advantage of the site; all sorts of variations may affect the 'rat'.[7]

In order to be entitled to compensation on leaving, the tenant therefore had to show that the landlord's rent on the premises had increased beyond the mere site value, to include an amount for the 'cat' element of goodwill – the goodwill that would attach itself to any new business set up on the old premises. This would be difficult for the tenant to prove. In addition, he would be unable to claim compensation if the landlord was not going to gain from this adherent goodwill – if, for example, the landlord intended to demolish the property. However, *if* the tenant was able to prove adherent goodwill, he may also have been able to establish a case for renewal. If the compensation for loss of the adherent goodwill would not cover the actual loss of goodwill that he would suffer through removal (that is, if he could establish that he would lose 'the rats' as well as the 'cats'), *then* he may be able to claim a renewal of the lease for up to fourteen years.

When the Leasehold Committee reported in 1949 and 1950, it noted the unsatisfactory nature of these provisions. They were both unnecessarily complicated and failed to protect the tenant's primary concern, security. Although both the Interim Report in 1949 under the chairmanship of Lord Uthwatt and the Final Report in 1950 under the chairmanship of Jenkins LJ accepted the need for reform, the proposed solutions differed. The importance of security to the business tenant was noted in the Interim Report:

> A tenant with a flourishing business, or with a business which is only beginning to get on its feet, necessarily feels qualms about the results of moving. This is particularly true of retail and other traders, whose customers get used to shopping with them in a certain place but may well not all remain loyal to the extent of seeking them out in another street or even some distance away in the same street. But it applies with almost equal force to manufacturers and other businesses employing a skilled or trained labour force. Removal even within a relatively small area may involve losing valued workers, and consequent loss of production: it may interrupt carefully-organised arrangements for the supply of components, disposal of by-products, etc.[8]

Haley comments on the contrasting approaches of the two committees:

> The Interim Report based its recommendations upon the assumption that business tenants wanted security of tenure and the ability to carry on trade without interruption. Compensation was viewed as insufficient to achieve this stability. The Committee felt that there was an immediate need to secure the sitting tenant against the risk of unreasonable disturbance by the landlord. This enabled it to make the crucial leap and recommend that a general entitlement to security of tenure for existing tenants was the only way to ensure fair dealing …
>
> Jenkins LJ [in the Final Report] felt that the business tenant's predicament had been overstated in the Interim Report and did not justify placing drastic restrictions on the contractual rights of all landlords of commercial premises. Unlike the previous report, Jenkins LJ refused to accept that lessees had a specific and occupational interest in the premises which, outweighing that of their landlords (who were interested primarily in the financial return from the property), should be translated into tenants' rights. Instead, the extent of intervention was to

---

[7] *Whiteman Smith Motor Co v Chaplin* [1934] 2 KB 35 (CA) 42.

[8] Lord Uthwatt (Chair), 'Leasehold Committee: Interim Report on Tenure and Rents of Business Premises' (Cmd 7706, 1948–49) para 34.

be tempered by the fact that safeguards were necessary only for a minority of tenants who had to deal with a small class of unscrupulous landlords. [footnotes omitted][9]

In the Final Report, the Committee referred to the difficult exercise of balancing the tenant's security interests against management concerns of the landlord:

[The tenants] should not have such a degree of security as will protect the bad tenant or per-petuate the inefficient business; or will prevent the due expansion of existing businesses or the setting up of new ones; or will in other ways promote stagnation and interfere with redevelop-ment or other desirable change.[10]

The Committee then considered the principles that should guide legislative change in this area. The idea of retaining the principle of compensation but improving the formula for its assessment was rejected as it did not sufficiently protect the tenant's commercial interests; by having to move premises he may lose more than goodwill, as there are other inconve-niences and expenses involved in displacement. Preferring then to allow the tenant to claim renewal, the difficulty was to determine the basis of any renewal. The principle to guide renewal claims was:

... upon the broad ground that refusal to renew would cause a substantial diminution in the value of the business as a going concern instead of being confined to loss of goodwill, or –in the case of non-profit-making concerns – that it would cause a substantial increase in costs or loss of efficiency.

151. Security of tenure is not to be at the expense of the landlord and is not to subsidise the inefficient business. It follows that the terms of renewal, and particularly the rent, should not be out of line with those which other efficient businesses might be expected to pay for similar premises. The tenant entitled to renewal should therefore be required to pay a fair market rental.[11]

8.1.2 The Framework of Part II of the Landlord and Tenant Act 1954

No general legislation followed and three years later there was a further report. In this, the government accepted the approach of extending greater security to business tenants but rejected the details of the scheme that had been proposed earlier. The alternative scheme put forward formed the basis of the Landlord and Tenant Act 1954, Part II:

43. ... the landlord of business premises, when an existing tenancy comes to an end, should have the right to resume possession himself if he requires the premises for the purpose of his own business or for the purpose of a scheme of redevelopment. If, however, he does not require the premises for himself for one of these purposes, he is entitled as landlord to a fair contemporary market rent for the premises – neither more nor less: and if the sitting tenant is willing and able to pay that rent and to enter in to other reasonable terms of tenancy, then the sitting tenant has a greater right than any alternative tenant to the tenancy on those terms. Unless, therefore, he is in substantial breach of his covenants, or is otherwise an unsatisfactory tenant, or has declined an offer of suitable alternative accommodation, or has failed to exercise

---

[9] M Haley, 'The statutory regulation of business tenancies: private property, public interest and political compromise' (1999) 19 *LS* 207, 218–9.
[10] Lord Justice Jenkins (Chair), 'Leasehold Committee: Final Report' (Cmd 7982, 1950) para 143.
[11] Lord Justice Jenkins (Chair), 'Leasehold Committee: Final Report' (Cmd 7982, 1950) paras 150–1.

a reasonable contractual option for renewal of his tenancy, the sitting tenant ought to be entitled to obtain a renewed tenancy without proof of 'adherent goodwill'. (By 'sitting tenant' is meant a tenant who is in occupation. No special consideration is due at the end of his tenancy to a tenant who has sublet and does not occupy; in such a case, it is the occupying sub-tenant who should be able to look for security of tenure.)

44. ... Such a scheme would be in general conformity with the present normal practice of good landlords. The landlords' legitimate interests would be fully preserved, while the sitting tenant who wished to continue in the premises could not be forced to outbid the fair market rent as the price of doing so ...

49. The Government consider that the tenant is entitled to compensation only if his failure to obtain a renewal is in no way attributable to anything done or omitted to be done by himself. In other words, the right to compensation should be limited to those cases where the tenant has sought renewal but the landlord has succeeded in getting possession for the purposes of his own business or of redevelopment, and should not extend to cases where the tenant's failure to obtain renewal has been due to the fact that he is in breach of his covenants or is otherwise an unsatisfactory tenant, or has declined an offer of suitable alternative accommodation, or has failed to exercise a reasonable contractual option for renewal of his tenancy.[12]

This statement sets out the framework of Part II of the 1954 Act, although later amendments have made it easy to opt out of this scheme. When the tenant's lease comes to an end the tenant can continue to occupy unless the lease is terminated in accordance with the provisions of the Act. The tenant also has the right to renew his lease at a market rent unless he is a bad tenant, is offered suitable alternative accommodation or the premises are required for landlord estate management reasons. In the latter two situations the tenant should be compensated for his disturbance under a rough and ready measure of his loss of goodwill. The grounds on which the landlord can oppose renewal are along the same lines as those available for possession in the case of protected residential tenancies.

This basic structure has proven extraordinarily resilient although, as discussed below, some are beginning to question its future. Derek Wood writes:

The Act has achieved an almost impossible balance between giving security and continuity to business tenants and, by ensuring that lease renewals are always on market terms, maintaining reversionary values. It has not, because of section 30 (1)(f) [entitling the landlord to oppose renewal on redevelopment grounds], stood in the way of redevelopment.[13]

Some changes were made in 1969. The interim rent was introduced, enabling the landlord to receive a revised rent during the continuation tenancy, that is the tenancy enjoyed by the tenant after the termination of the contractual lease but before the new tenancy has been finalised. The 1969 amendments also enabled rent review provisions to be inserted into renewed leases.

8.1.3 Contracting Out

The major change was, however, the introduction of 'contracting out'. When the Act was first introduced, all lettings of fewer than three months were automatically excluded from Part II,

---

[12] Government Policy on Leasehold Property in England and Wales (Cmd 8713, 1953).

[13] D Wood, 'Mapping the Recent Past' in S Bright (ed), *Landlord and Tenant Law. Past, Present and Future* (Oxford, Hart, 2006) 10.

but other commercial lettings were covered. In 1969 the Law Commission took the view that this was unduly restrictive:

> There are many cases where the landlord would be willing to let on a temporary basis and a tenant would be willing to accept such a tenancy. This may happen, for example, when the landlord has obtained possession and intends to sell, demolish or reconstruct the property but is not ready to do so immediately ... The permissible period of three months as the maximum for tenancies outside the Act will often be too short to be of practical use ... We also accept that there may be cases where a tenant is willing, for good reasons, to accept a tenancy for more than six months without rights under the Act.[14]

As a result, the Act was amended so that lettings not exceeding six months were automatically excluded, but it was also made possible for the parties to obtain a court order excluding longer business tenancies from the Act. At the time, little attention was paid to these contracting out provisions; they were intended to be used to enable short term lettings of premises that would otherwise be unused and there was certainly no expectation that contracting out would become entirely standard.[15] The reality, however, is that contracting out is commonplace and quite unexceptional.

Contracting out was made possible by the parties making a joint application for a court order under section 38(4), the original intention being that the court could control the process as a safeguard to the tenant. In practice, however, the wording of section 38(4) did not dictate a rigorous examination of the facts of the case and it became little more than a rubber stamping exercise. As Lord Denning MR observed in *Hagee (London) Ltd v AB Erikson and Larson*:

> We are told that the court invariably approves such an agreement when it is made by business people, properly advised by their lawyers. The court has no materials on which to refuse it.[16]

Research found that fewer than four per cent of all contracting out applications failed, and the most common reason for failure was that the forms had not been correctly filled in and submitted.[17] Drawing on this research, the Office of the Deputy Prime Minister (ODPM) stated:

> ... the role of the judge is merely to check that the agreement is lawful and genuine, and that the tenant has had an opportunity to receive advice about the prospective loss of statutory rights. The judges are therefore performing an administrative rather than a judicial role, in some cases delegating scrutiny of applications to court officials.[18]

What was initially expected to be the exceptional route, with safeguards for the tenant, had therefore become quite normal, being used for leases of all lengths and with market forces effectively driving the question as to whether or not a lease was to be contracted out.

---

[14] Law Commission, 'Report on the Landlord and Tenant Act 1954, Part II' (Law Com No 17, 1969) paras 32–33.

[15] Law Commission, 'Landlord and Tenant: Report on the Landlord and Tenant Act 1954, Part II' (Law Com No 17, 1969) paras 32–33.

[16] [1976] QB 209 (CA) 215.

[17] D Cowan and others, 'Section 38 Landlord and Tenant Act 1954 – Failed Applications' Urban Research Summary No 9 (ODPM, 2003). A higher number failed on the initial application but were successful when resubmitted.

[18] Statement by the ODPM in relation to the Regulatory Reform (Business Tenancies) (England and Wales) Order 2003.

Recently, in 2003, there have been further reforms of the 1954 Act, although the process began some 20 years ago with a Department of the Environment consultation exercise. This was followed by a Law Commission working paper in 1985 and a Law Commission report in 1992[19] (both limited exercises concerned not to disturb the balance of the Act). There were further Department of Environment Transport and Regions consultations in 1996 and 2001[20] (both limited in scope to the more technical aspects of the working of the Act). The end result was the reform introduced by the new regulatory reform parliamentary procedure,[21] in the form of the Regulatory Reform (Business Tenancies) (England and Wales) Order 2003 (the 'RRO 2003').[22]

The RRO 2003 made a number of changes to the 1954 Act. The most fundamental to business tenants was the removal of the need for a court order in order to contract out, replacing it with a prior notice (health warning) procedure, 'intended primarily to assist small business occupiers, who may not be aware of the implications of excluding security of tenure'.[23]

The overall effect of these various changes has been that a scheme introduced in 1954 to apply to all business tenancies has become optional, not as result of deliberate policy choice but by the accident of parliamentary process. In the words of Murdoch:

> In most instances, landlords will be able to insist on a contracted out lease; only where location is particularly critical for tenants – notably in the retail and other locationally-dependent sectors – will tenants be able to hold out for security of tenure. This may, of course, be a perfect end result. It is always been arguable that the 1954 Act was too widely drawn and confers rights of renewal on those whose businesses are not vulnerable to any change of location. The real objection is that this is a sufficiently important matter to have been the subject of open public debate rather than sleight of hand.[24]

There are no reliable figures available on the extent of contracting out but it is thought to be widespread. Edwards and Krendel suggest that:

> … most leases, particularly of small properties, are outside the security of tenure provisions of the 1954 Act and the protection of the Act is usually restricted to the larger areas of space, perhaps 5,000 sq ft or more when relating this to office property and highly rented shops, perhaps with a passing rent of £20,000 or more.[25]

8.1.4 Supporting Choice and Flexiblity?

Apart from conferring statutory rights to renewal, the approach in the commercial property sector has been largely one of non-intervention, leaving things to market forces. The stated aim of government policy is to support choice and flexibility:

---

[19] Law Commission, 'Business Tenancies: A Periodic Review of the Landlord and Tenant Act 1954, Part II' (Law Com No 208, 1992).

[20] DETR, 'Business tenancies legislation in England and Wales: the Government's proposals for reform' (2001).

[21] This procedure can be used only to reduce burdens imposed on those carrying on a business.

[22] SI 2003/3096.

[23] DCLG, 'Landlord and Tenant Act 1954: Review of Impact of Procedural Reforms' (August 2006) para 15.

[24] S Murdoch, 'Reform of Part II of the Landlord and Tenant Act 1954: Silk Purse or Pig's Ear?' Conference Paper, Reading University Fifth Biennial Property Conference (March 2004).

[25] C Edwards and P Krendel, *Institutional Leases in the 21st Century* (London, EG Books, 2007) 115–6.

... the function of the property market is to provide business premises on terms that meet occupiers' needs, subject to market conditions.[26]

In practice, however, it is usually the landlord who has the upper hand in leasehold negotiations and the occupier will seldom be able to negotiate a package that is specifically geared to protecting its anticipated business needs. The generally non-interventionist policy was continued almost without question until the impact of the severe slump in the property market at the end of the 1980s and the beginning of the 1990s became apparent. The early 1990s was a time that marked a significant shift in leasing patterns. Until then, the institutional lease had been dominant,[27] the 25 year lease placing the burden of all variable costs (servicing) on the tenant, thus ensuring the landlord a net guaranteed rental income. Further, the lease provided for the rent to be reviewed at regular intervals, but only in an upward direction which meant that in a falling rental market the landlord was protected while the tenant could be left paying historically high rents. In addition, the original tenant would remain liable on the tenant covenants throughout the life of the lease even if there was a new tenant. In combination this gave the landlord a great deal of financial security and explains why investment in UK commercial property was such an attractive proposition. The potential unfairness of this to business tenants was, perhaps, hidden in a strong economic climate with rising property prices. However, the impact of this pattern of leasing on tenants was quite different as property prices fell in the late 1980s and early 1990s. With high numbers of business insolvencies, and falling rents, original tenants were frequently being pursued by landlords to pay rents which were now well above the market level, for properties that they may well have long ceased to occupy. During this period there was, therefore, increasing and mounting pressure for changes to be made.

For most of the 1990s and into the present century the focus was on upward only rent review (UORR) which was perceived by many to be unfair. A government consultation paper issued in 1993 questioned the use of UORR clauses.[28] Any suggestion, however, that UORR might be banned has always led to very active campaigning by the property industry who see upwards only review as crucial to the attractiveness of investing in UK commercial property. What followed from the early questioning about UORR was agreement by the property industry to adopt a voluntary code of practice. The first Code of Practice on commercial leases was produced in 1995 but had virtually no effect.[29] What did transpire at this time, however, was reform of the original tenant liability rules. The Landlord and Tenant (Covenants) Act 1995 introduced a fundamental change to tenant liability. For new lettings, no longer is the original tenant automatically liable throughout the life of the lease; following assignment the tenant can be required to guarantee performance only of its immediate successor (through the use of an authorised guarantee agreement – AGA) but will otherwise be released from future liability. Concern continued to be expressed, however, about the continued use of UORR. As the ineffectiveness of the voluntary code became

---

[26] ODPM, 'Commercial property leases: options for deterring or outlawing the use of upwards only rent review clauses' (May 2004) Appendix A [9].

[27] See chs 1 and 4.

[28] DoE, 'Consultation Paper on Commercial Property Leases' (27 May 1993).

[29] RICS Commercial Leases Group, *Commercial Property Leases in England and Wales, Code of Practice* (London, Furnival Press, December 1995).

known and the prospect of legislative intervention again loomed large, a new second edition of the Code of Practice was produced in 2002.[30]

The 2002 Code of Practice was intended to promote choice in leasehold terms, but again had limited effectiveness. The working of the 2002 Code of Practice has been subjected to a thorough review by a team based at the University of Reading. This research found that in practice the impact of the Code has been limited,[31] with landlords seldom offering alternate packages to tenants.[32] UORR continues to be almost universally found in leases containing rent review provisions. Further, the research revealed that the way that alienation provisions are used in leases makes it difficult for business tenants to have a flexible approach to business development. The successful tenant may wish to move to expand its business, or to remain in a good location at the expiry of its lease. A business tenant whose needs for space are contracting will need to be able to move to reduce expenditure, or to sub-let surplus space. But none of these things are easy in commercial leases. Not all leases permit alienation, and where they do an assignment is unlikely to release the tenant from financial liability as AGAs are 'almost universal'. In a weak property market, conditions attached to sub-letting (in particular, a requirement that the rent for the sub-lease is not less than the passing rent under the headlease) make sub-letting difficult. Break clauses, although more frequently being found in leases, are operated only in 15 per cent to 20 per cent of cases, as the timing and conditions attached to them will not always suit tenants.[33] Nor will the tenant who wants to stay necessarily be able to do so as the statutory right to renew is often excluded.

Although there may have been little change in the content of certain aspects of leases or much greater choice being offered to tenants, the letting market has become much more diverse. The 25 year institutional lease is no longer king. Leases have become much shorter, and with shorter leases the whole package tends to differ. So, for example, many short leases do not make any provision for rent review.

The 2002 Code of Practice has been replaced by the 2007 Business Lease Code (see chapter 4).[34] It remains to be seen if this will be any more effective in promoting choice and flexibility but there does appear to be a greater awareness amongst landlords, the big ones at least, of the need to be more responsive to the needs of tenants if further legislation is to be avoided. The government is not only keeping a watching eye on the use of UORR, but attention is now also turning to the restrictive nature of alienation provisions and the particular difficulties faced by small business tenants.

---

[30] RICS Policy Unit, *A Code of Practice for Commercial Leases in England and Wales* 2nd edn (2002)

[31] Only 22% of all respondents to the tenant survey were aware of the Code, and half of these simply knew of its existence rather than having knowledge as to its contents; very small businesses were even less likely to be aware of the Code: N Crosby, C Hughes and S Murdoch, 'Monitoring the 2002 Code of Practice for Commercial Leases' (ODPM, March 2005) 311.

[32] N Crosby, C Hughes and S Murdoch, 'Monitoring the 2002 Code of Practice for Commercial Leases' (ODPM, March 2005) 11.

[33] N Crosby, C Hughes and S Murdoch, 'Monitoring the 2002 Code of Practice for Commercial Leases' (ODPM, March 2005) 301.

[34] Joint Working Group on Commercial Leases, 'The Code for Leasing Business Premises in England and Wales' (2007).

8.2 The Operation of the Landlord and Tenant Act 1954, Part II

Lord Nicholls summarised the structure of Part II of the Landlord and Tenant Act 1954 in *Graysim Ltd v P & O Property Holdings Ltd*:

> Subject to some exceptions, a business tenancy ... does not come to an end unless terminated in accordance with the statutory provisions. A landlord may terminate a business tenancy by giving the tenant a section 25 notice. If the landlord has given the tenant such a notice, or if the tenant has served a section 26 notice requesting a new tenancy, the tenant[35] may apply to the court for a new tenancy.
>
> On an application for a new tenancy, if the landlord fails to establish any of the section 30 grounds of opposition the court is required to make an order for the grant of a new tenancy. The property comprised in the new tenancy, however, will not necessarily include all the property comprised in the business tenancy. The tenant is entitled only to a new tenancy of 'the holding': section 32(1). 'The holding' means, in short, all the property comprised in the business tenancy except any part not 'occupied' by the tenant or his employees: section 23(3).
>
> If the landlord makes good any of the section 30 grounds of opposition to the satisfaction of the court, the application for a new tenancy will be dismissed. If the tenant's application fails on some of the section 30 grounds, for instance, because the landlord intends to reconstruct the premises, then on quitting the holding the tenant is entitled to recover compensation from the landlord. The amount of the compensation is calculated according to a formula based on the rateable value of the holding: section 37.[36]

8.3 Tenancies to which Part II of the 1954 Act applies

8.3.1 The Statutory Criteria

Section 23 of the Landlord and Tenant Act 1954 provides:

> (1) ... this part of this Act applies to any tenancy where the property comprised in the tenancy is or includes premises which are occupied by the tenant and are so occupied for the purposes of a business carried on by him or for those and other purposes.
>
> (2) In this Part of this Act the expression 'business' includes a trade, profession or employment and includes any activity carried on by a body of persons, whether corporate or unincorporate.
>
> (3) ... the expression 'the holding', in relation to a tenancy to which this Part of this Act applies, means the property comprised in the tenancy, there being excluded any part thereof which is so occupied neither by the tenant nor by a person employed by the tenant and so employed for the purposes of a business by reason of which the tenancy is one to which this Part of this Act applies.
>
> (4) Where the tenant is carrying on a business, in all or any part of the property comprised in a tenancy, in breach of a prohibition (however expressed) of use for business purposes which subsists under the terms of the tenancy and extends to the whole of that property, this Part of this Act shall not apply to the tenancy unless the immediate landlord or his predecessor in title

---

35 Following the RRO, the landlord is also able to apply for a new tenancy, see ch 21.
36 [1996] AC 329 (HL) 334.

has consented to the breach or the immediate landlord has acquiesced therein.

In this subsection the reference to a prohibition of use for business purposes does not include a prohibition of use for the purposes of a specified business, or of use for purposes of any but a specified business, but save as aforesaid includes a prohibition of use for the purposes of some one or more only of the classes of business specified in the definition of that expression in subsection (2) of this section.

8.3.2 *There Must be a Tenancy*

As with private sector residential property, in order for the occupier to be protected there must be a tenancy. A tenancy by estoppel is protected.[37] Licences are excluded.[38] However, unlike the private residential sector, tenancies at will are not protected, whether created by operation of law[39] or by express agreement between the parties.[40] In *Wheeler v Mercer*, Lord Morton commented that it would be:

… surprising if the legislature had intended to bring within the scope of the Act a relationship so personal and so fleeting as a tenancy at will.[41]

As discussed in chapter 3, it can be difficult to determine whether a relationship is a periodic tenancy, a tenancy at will or a licence. In *Hagee (London) Ltd v AB Erikson and Larson* the Court of Appeal said that it would look closely at an agreement purporting to be a tenancy at will to see if it was a cloak for a periodic tenancy,[42] and in *Javad v Aqil*, Nicholls LJ commented:

Given that a periodic tenancy can exist where the period is very short indeed, a layman could be forgiven for being surprised to find that the distinction between a periodic tenancy and a tenancy at will can be all-important for the purposes of the statutory protection afforded to business tenancies.[43]

The Law Commission has considered, but dismissed, the idea that renewal rights should be extended to include licensees and tenants at will:

The temporary nature of the interest granted either by a tenancy at will or by a licence is not likely to satisfy someone wanting to occupy business premises for any length of time, and we consider that the differences between such an interest and an ordinary tenancy or lease will be readily apparent, so that a prospective tenant will not enter into such an arrangement inadvertently.

… The inclusion of tenancies at will and licences within the Act would clearly have a major effect on the balance between landlord and tenant which we wish to maintain as it is.[44]

If it is the temporary nature of such interests that explains the reason for their exclusion

---

[37] *Bell v General Accident Fire and Life Assurance Corporation Ltd* [1998] 1 EGLR 69 (CA).
[38] *Shell-Mex & BP Ltd v Manchester Garages* [1971] 1 WLR 612 (CA).
[39] *Wheeler v Mercer* [1957] AC 416 (HL).
[40] *Hagee (London) Ltd v AB Erikson and Larson* [1976] QB 209 (CA).
[41] *Wheeler v Mercer* [1957] AC 416 (HL) 428.
[42] [1976] QB 209 (CA) 215, 217.
[43] [1991] 1 WLR 1007 (CA) 1009.
[44] Law Commission, 'Business Tenancies, A Periodic Review of the Landlord and Tenant Act 1954 Part II' (Law Com No 208, 1992) paras 3.13–3.14.

then it is clearly right that a tenancy at will, which the parties only ever intend to be temporary, should be excluded. The same is not necessarily true, however, of licences, which are also excluded. Take, for example, the concessionaire operating under a licence arrangement within a department store or a kiosk in a hotel foyer; these traders will not usually have exclusive possession and, as they do not have leases, they are therefore unable to retain any goodwill built up even though the expectation may be that they are there for the long term.[45]

8.3.3 There Must be a Letting of Premises

'Premises' has been taken to include not only buildings but also land without buildings,[46] easements granted as appurtenant to the land and buildings and other incorporeal hereditaments which are the subject matter of the habendum.[47] The inclusion of incorporeal hereditaments reflects the fact that renewal of these rights can be just as important to protect the goodwill and future of the business as the renewal of estates in leasehold property.

8.3.4 The Tenant Must Occupy the Premises

The Act seeks to protect the tenant in his continuing use of the property for the purposes of some business activity by the tenant on the property in question.[48] Renewal is, therefore, available only to those occupying the premises and not, for example, to a tenant who has sub-let the property. The meaning of occupation is not, however, always straightforward.

8.3.4.1 Non-constant Use

Inevitably there are periods during a tenant's business in which the premises will not be in constant use. So, for example, the premises are likely not to be occupied for 24 hours a day, seven days a week, and there may be periods when they are closed for refurbishment or for holidays. In *Graysim Ltd v P & O Property Holdings Ltd*, Lord Nicholls said that:

> … the concept of occupation is not a legal term of art, with one single and precise legal meaning applicable in all circumstances … Like most ordinary English words 'occupied,' and corresponding expressions such as occupier and occupation, have different shades of meaning according to the context in which they are being used.[49]

In the context of section 23 the focus has been on whether during periods of absence there is, nonetheless, a 'thread of continuity':

> I think it is quite clear that a tenant does not lose the protection of Part 2 of the Landlord and Tenant Act, 1954, simply by ceasing physically to occupy the premises. They may well continue to be occupied for the purposes of the tenants business although they are de facto empty for

---

[45] In South Australia, the retail tenancy legislation applies to licences as well as to tenancies.

[46] *Bracey v Read* [1963] 1 Ch 88 (Ch).

[47] *Whitely v Stumbles* [1930] AC 554 (HL). Although said in relation to s 17 of the 1927 Act, the Court of Appeal has applied this to 'premises' in s 23 of the 1954 Act: *Pointon York Group plc v Poulton* [2006] EWCA Civ 1001 [24]-[25].

[48] *Graysim Ltd v P & O Property Holdings Ltd* [1996] AC 329 (HL).

[49] [1996] AC 329 (HL) 334.

some period of time. One example would be if there was a need for urgent structural repairs and the tenant had to go out of physical occupation in order to enable them to be effected. Another example is that which the Court of Appeal had to deal with in *Teasdale v Walker* [1958] 1 WLR 1076. There premises were only occupied during discontinuous periods: they were closed and empty in the winter and only used in the summer. On the other hand, as the Court of Appeal pointed out, a mere intention to resume occupation if a new tenancy is granted will not preserve the continuity of business user if the thread has once been definitely broken.[50]

The test for determining whether a closure destroys the continuity of business occupation is whether the event is, according to Simon Brown LJ in *Bacchiocchi v Academic Agency Ltd*,

> ... recognisable as an incident in the ordinary course of conduct of business life. By the same token that trading may have to cease mid-term for repairs, so also it may have to be delayed for the premises to be fitted out in the first place, or may have to end before the term of the lease expires so that the premises may be cleaned up and handed over with vacant possession on the due date.[51]

In *Pointon York Group plc v Poulton* Arden LJ agreed with Simon Brown and Ward LJJ's remarks that the interpretation of occupation in section 23 bears the same meaning as it was given in *Bacchiocchi v Academic Agency Ltd*[52] in relation to sections 37 and 38 (to do with the award of compensation for non-renewal). In Arden LJ's words, this meant that:

> ... a tenant need not be physically present in the premises if he is using them in some other way as an incident in the ordinary course or conduct of business life, provided that the premises are occupied by no other business occupier and are not used for any non-business purpose.[53]

The result was that the tenant in *Pointon York Group plc v Poulton* was found to occupy offices that it had sub-let but which it planned to use itself after the sub-lease ended, three days before its own lease was due to expire. The basis of the occupation of the offices was that workmen who were employed by the sub-tenant to put the offices back in shape at the end of the sub-lease were checked on by the tenant to make sure that the offices would be left in a suitable state for the tenant's intended use of them. This is, perhaps, a generous interpretation of the section as the tenant had not been using the offices for its own business, but was merely planning to.

8.3.4.2 Incorporeal Hereditaments

Occupation is not the same as user and this has created difficulties with incorporeal hereditaments. In *Land Reclamation Co v Basildon District Council*, a waste disposal company gained access to its depot along a road over which it had a right of way by lease but it was denied renewal rights under the 1954 Act on the grounds that enjoyment of this right was not occupation of premises.[54] More recently the Court of Appeal held in *Pointon York Group*

---

[50] *I & H Caplan Ltd v Caplan (No 2)* [1963] 1 WLR 1247 (Ch) 1260.
[51] *Bacchiocchi v Academic Agency Ltd* [1998] 1 WLR 1313 (CA) 1321.
[52] [1998] 1 WLR 1313 (CA).
[53] [2006] EWCA Civ 1001 [31].
[54] [1979] 1 WLR 767 (CA) 775.

plc v Poulton that where a tenant of office premises also used car parking spaces under a right to use them during normal business hours,[55] this was occupation for the purposes of section 23. The *Land Reclamation* case was distinguished on the basis that the:

> ... right to use a parking space is not like a right of way leading from one place to another which members of the public or persons other than the tenant might wish to use.[56]

8.3.4.3 Multiple Users

Often there will be more than one person using the premises. The tenant may not personally be on-site carrying out the business but may have employees and others doing so. Or the tenant may be generally supervising activities there. Or the business may consist of allowing others to use the property for their business purposes. Lord Nicholls provides two examples, at opposite ends of the spectrum: a hotel that allows an antique fair to use rooms and facilities once a month, and a tenant who sub-lets office accommodation. Who is in occupation is a question of fact and degree:

> The difference between the two extremes is a difference of degree, not of kind. When a landowner permits another to use his property for business purposes, the question whether the landowner is sufficiently excluded, and the other is sufficiently present, for the latter to be regarded as the occupier in place of the former is a question of degree. It is, moreover, a question of fact in the sense that the answer depends upon the facts of the particular case. The circumstances of two cases are never identical, and seldom close enough to make comparisons of much value. The types of property, and the possible uses of property, vary so widely that there can be no hard and fast rules. The degree of presence and exclusion required to constitute occupation, and the acts needed to evince presence and exclusion, must always depend upon the nature of the premises, the use to which they are being put, and the rights enjoyed or exercised by the persons in question.
>
> Since the question is one of degree, inevitably there will be doubt and difficulty over cases in the grey area.[57]

Where the landowner has granted a sub-lease, ordinarily it will be the sub-tenant who is the occupier,

> ... because he has a degree of sole use of the property sufficient to enable him to carry on his business there to the exclusion of everyone else.[58]

Further, there cannot be dual occupation; it is not possible for the individual traders to have protected sub-tenancies, and for the very same property also to remain part of the tenant's business tenancy.[59] This means that in a situation where a tenant has sub-let all of the independent units, and retained only the common parts, the tenant does not have renewal rights because the sub-tenants would themselves have protected sub-tenancies and

---

[55] [2006] EWCA Civ 1001.

[56] [2006] EWCA Civ 1001 [29]. There is some support for this ground of distinction in the *Land Reclamation* case itself as Buckley LJ suggests that the outcome might have been different if the right of way were exclusive.

[57] *Graysim Ltd v P & O Property Holdings Ltd* [1996] AC 329 (HL) 336.

[58] *Graysim Ltd v P & O Property Holdings Ltd* [1996] AC 329 (HL) 336.

[59] *Graysim Ltd v P & O Property Holdings Ltd* [1996] AC 329 (HL) 336–7.

if their leases are renewed by the head-landlord, there is no business of 'managing the units' left for the tenant.[60]

In *Graysim Holdings Ltd v P & O Property Holdings Ltd* the tenant was a market operator and had a lease of a market hall, fitted out with wooden stalls.[61] Each stallholder secured his own unit with a padlock and key. The tenant employed a superintendent who had an office in the hall and opened and closed the market, controlled the heating system and generally kept an eye on things. On the tenant's application for a new tenancy, the question arose as to whether the tenant occupied the market hall for the purposes of a business, even though individual traders had exclusive possession of their stalls. The House of Lords held not: the individual traders had business tenancies and when the reversion to these units vests in the freeholder, the tenant can no longer carry on its business of operating the market, for which it needs not only the retained parts but also the reversion to the traders' tenancies:

> The use of the parts retained by Graysim was ancillary to the traders' use of the sublet units, providing access and other facilities for the traders and their potential customers. Part II of the Act of 1954 is concerned to protect tenants in their occupation of property for the purposes of their business. But Graysim itself did nothing on the units. Graysim did not itself carry on business in the units. It let the units for others to do business there. Its income from Wallasey Market consisted solely of rentals from these lettings. The Act is not concerned to give protection to tenants in respect of such income. The Act looks through to the occupying tenants, here the traders, and affords them statutory protection, not their landlord. Intermediate landlords, not themselves in occupation, are not within the class of persons the Act was seeking to protect.[62]

8.3.4.4 *Occupation by Related Persons*

Businesses often operate flexibly; the legal person named as tenant is not always strictly the same person as the business operator. So, for example, an individual may have taken the lease in the name of his company but in fact carry on the business in his own name. Section 23(1A) accommodates these arrangements within the Act by providing that

> (1A) Occupation or the carrying on of a business—
>
> (a)   by a company in which the tenant has a controlling interest; or
> (b)   where the tenant is a company, by a person with a controlling interest in the company,
>
> shall be treated for the purposes of this section as equivalent to occupation or, as the case may be, the carrying on of a business by the tenant.

The Act also contains special provisions relating to occupation by beneficiaries, partnerships and companies. Where the property is let to trustees, occupation by beneficiaries of the trust will count as occupation by the trustees.[63] Similarly, it is not necessary for all members of a partnership who own the lease as joint tenants to occupy the premises for

---

[60] *Graysim Ltd v P & O Property Holdings Ltd* [1996] AC 329 (HL) 339–40, Lord Nicholls adopting the result in *Bagettes Ltd v GP Estates Co Ltd* [1956] Ch 290 (CA).

[61] [1996] AC 329 (HL).

[62] *Graysim Ltd v P & O Property Holdings Ltd* [1996] AC 329 (HL) 343. For a discussion of *Graysim*, see S Higgins, 'The Continuation Conundrum: Part II of the Landlord and Tenant Act' [1997] *Conv* 119, 127–131; M Haley, 'Business Tenancies: Parting with Occupation' [1997] *Conv* 139.

[63] Landlord and Tenant Act 1954 s 41.

business purposes in order for those who do so to have rights of renewal under the 1954 Act.[64] Occupation by members of the same group of companies as the tenant company will also suffice to give rights under the 1954 Act to the tenant company.[65]

8.3.5 Occupation Must be for Business Purposes

The word 'business' has a very wide meaning. It includes not only profit-making businesses and professions, but also organisations such as a lawn tennis club.[66] It can also include the letting of residential accommodation to students[67] and employees.[68]

8.3.6 The Tenancy Must not be Excluded

8.3.6.1 Excluded Classes of Tenancies

Some types of business tenancies are excluded from Part II by section 43:

(a)   agricultural holdings and farm business tenancies: these are covered by a separate code of protection.[69]

(b)   mining leases.[70]

(c)   (until 1989) tenancies of on-licensed premises. Leases of premises for the sale of intoxicating liquor to be consumed on the premises (public houses) were excluded from the Act until mid-1989 but are now included.[71] Even before this change, some on-licensed premises were included in the 1954 Act where a substantial proportion of the business consisted of something other than the sale of intoxicating liquor, for example, a hotel. The inclusion of public houses in the Act was part of a wider reform of the beer industry following a report of the Monopolies and Mergers Commission on beer supplies – taken together with other changes, it was intended to increase the tenant's independence from brewer landlords.

(d)   service tenancies – a tenancy granted by reason that the tenant was the holder of an office, appointment or employment from the grantor and lasting only so long as the office, appointment or employment continues.[72]

8.3.6.2 Short Term Tenancies

Section 43(3) excludes tenancies for a term certain not exceeding six months. If the tenancy itself permits renewal or extension beyond six months the tenancy will, however, be within the Act. Similarly, if the tenancy is for a fixed term of six months or less but the tenant (and/or a predecessor in business) has in fact occupied the premises for twelve months, the tenancy will again be protected. In *Cricket Ltd v Shaftesbury plc*, however, the tenant had

---

[64] Landlord and Tenant Act 1954 s 41A.
[65] Landlord and Tenant Act 1954 s 42.
[66] *Addiscombe Garden Estates Ltd v Crabbe* [1958] 1 QB 513 (CA).
[67] *Groveside Properties Ltd v Westminster Medical School* (1983) 47 P & CR 507 (CA).
[68] *Linden v Department of Health and Social Security* [1986] 1 WLR 164 (Ch).
[69] Landlord and Tenant Act 1954 s 43(1)(a) and (aa).
[70] Landlord and Tenant Act 1954 s 43(1)(b).
[71] Landlord and Tenant (Licensed Premises) Act 1990.
[72] Landlord and Tenant Act 1954 s 43(2).

occupied for more than twelve months but still was not protected as it had occupied under two fixed term tenancies for fewer than six months (which were, therefore, excluded tenancies), and then thereafter as a tenant at will (the tenancy at will not being protected).[73]

8.3.6.3 Mixed Residential/Business User

If the premises are used partly for residential and partly for business use, for example living accommodation over a shop, they will still be within Part II of the 1954 Act. Lord Denning provides useful illustrations in *Cheryl Investments v Saldanha*: in most cases business use will mean that the tenancy does fall within the 1954 Act but where the business use is purely incidental Part II of the 1954 Act will not apply to the tenancy. So, for example, it will not be a business tenancy if the tenant has business premises elsewhere but occasionally works at home:

> It is only if the [business] activity is part of the reason for, part of his aim and object in occupying the house that ... section [23] will apply.[74]

8.3.6.4 Contracting Out

As mentioned above, the RRO 2003 replaced the court based system of contracting out with a notice based 'health warning'. In order to contract out of the 1954 Act Part II:

(a)   the landlord must serve a notice on the tenant not less than 14 days before the tenancy is entered into or (if earlier) the tenant enters an agreement for lease. This notice is in a prescribed form that warns the tenant that there is no security of tenure and advises the tenant to obtain professional advice. In addition,

(b)   the tenant (or unauthorised agent) must, before the tenancy or agreement for lease, make a declaration in a prescribed form (or substantially the same form).

If it is not possible for the landlord to comply with this 14 day timetable, it is still possible to contract out provided that the landlord's notice is served before the tenancy or agreement for lease and the tenant (or agent) makes a statutory declaration in a prescribed form (or substantially the same form). Although the expectation was that the simple declaration would be the norm, it appears that the statutory declaration route is more commonly used,[75] either because the deal is being concluded in a hurry or because practitioners are worried that changes to the lease terms after the service of the health warning may affect the validity of the process.[76]

In each case, the agreement to exclude sections 24-28 of the 1954 Act, the landlord's notice, and the tenant's declaration must be contained in or endorsed on the tenancy agreement.[77]

---

[73] [1999] 3 All ER 283 (Ch).

[74] *Cheryl Investments v Saldanha* [1978] 1 WLR 1329 (CA) 1339; *Broadway Investments Hackney Ltd v Grant* [2006] EWCA Civ 1709, and see S Murdoch, 'Residential Use and the 1954 Act' (1 May 1993) *EG* 101.

[75] J Joyce, 'Analysing the Changes' (17 December 2006) *EG* 86.

[76] The latter fear is fuelled by the Court of Appeal decision in *Receiver for the Metropolitan Police District v Palacegate Properties Ltd* [2000] 13 *EGLR* 187 (CA) where it was suggested that substantial changes in the terms from those approved by the court in granting a s 38(4) order may nullify the order.

[77] Landlord and Tenant Act 1954 s 38(A); Regulatory Reform (Business Tenancies) (England and Wales) Order 2003 SI 2003/3096 Sch 1 and 2.

8.4 Future Directions

8.4.1 Retaining Renewal Rights

In some respects, it is surprising that there remains any statutory security in the commercial sector, given that it has gone from the private rented sector. Further, the fact that protection is now effectively optional has led some to question whether there remains a continuing justification for Part II.[78] The Government, however, remains committed to a scheme of protection giving statutory rights of renewal to business tenants while permitting contracting out:

> [The DCLG] is aware of views that business tenants should no longer enjoy statutory rights of security of tenure, particularly against a background of greater flexibility in the property market and shorter leases. It does not share these views, however, especially as abolition could be damaging to small business tenants who could lose their premises after establishing a viable business. It appreciates that security of tenure may be less important at the larger end of the market, but the 'contracting out' provisions provide the necessary flexibility.[79]

Even though some were concerned that the recent changes to the 1954 Act through the RRO may affect the level of contracting out, the early signs suggest that it has not had any impact:

> … there are no signs that the change in the procedures for agreements to exclude security of tenure has, of itself, increased the number or proportion of leases without security of tenure. While there are trends towards more contracting out, it is the market that has driven this rather than the procedures themselves.[80]

The focus of recent reviews of the Act is on technical issues rather than fundamental policy issues.[81] Thus consideration is being given to making it clear that changes to leasehold terms (even major ones) after the service of a contracting out warning notice will not invalidate the notice, and to permitting a single health warning to support leases between the same parties at a number of different premises (but a tenant declaration would still be required for each lease).[82]

8.4.2 Continuing Concern over Restrictive Alienation Provisions

Although the 1954 Act itself is not likely to undergo any significant changes, this does not mean that the law and practice of commercial leases will necessarily remain untouched.

---

[78] D Neuberger, 'Our Not so Flexible Friend' (30 September 2000) *EG* 139; S Bridge, 'Commercial Leases Past and Present: The Contribution of the Law Commission' in S Bright (ed), *Landlord and Tenant Law. Past, Present and Future* (Oxford, Hart, 2006) 70–1; S Murdoch, 'Commercial Leases: Future Directions' in S Bright (ed), *Landlord and Tenant Law. Past, Present d Future* (Oxford, Hart, 2006) 101. In contrast, Derek Wood suggests it will continue 'to act as a stabilising influence in the market': D Wood, 'Mapping the Recent Past' in S Bright (ed), *Landlord and Tenant Law. Past, Present and Future* (Oxford, Hart, 2006) 11.

[79] DCLG, 'Landlord and Tenant Act 1954: Review of Impact of Procedural Reforms' (August 2006) para 5.

[80] DCLG, 'Landlord and Tenant Act 1954: Review of Impact of Procedural Reforms' (August 2006) para 10.

[81] DCLG, 'Landlord and Tenant Act 1954: Review of Impact of Procedural Reforms' (August 2006) para 6.

[82] DCLG, 'Landlord and Tenant Act 1954: Review of Impact of Procedural Reforms' (August 2006).

Although the pressure for reform of UORR has reduced, the government is concerned about the difficulties that business tenants face.

It is not surprising that the market is not providing great flexibility and choice. The individuality of property is such that the decision to take a particular lease will usually focus more upon physical features of the property, such as location, design and repair, rather than the leasehold terms on offer. In so far as the terms of the letting are focused on, it is the rent and the length that will be the primary concern. Only the more sophisticated tenant with a strong market position and professional advisers, such as large retail outlets or other blue-chip tenants, will be in a position to negotiate over more detailed provisions.

Given the importance of commerce to the economy, and the fact that property costs are likely to be the second largest cost facing businesses,[83] the inflexibility and absence of effective choice do matter. Leases that are not well structured to support the tenant's business plans will impact on its success. The government's concern over UORR, perhaps somewhat overstated, led to an effective lobbying campaign by the property industry, leading to the issue of the first Code of Practice in 1995. More recently, expressing concern at the inflexibility of the commercial letting market (in particular in relation to alienation provisions and the failure of small business tenants to obtain advantageous letting terms) the government has announced that it will monitor the situation and conduct a review of the law on alienation.[84] Again, the property industry has reacted. The Business Lease Code 2007 has been issued to replace the 2002 Code of Practice,[85] and a number of larger landlords have announced that they will permit sub-lettings at market rent, even if this is below the rent in the head-lease. Whether these moves will be sufficient to deflect further legislation will depend in large part on the extent to which negotiations between landlords and tenants take account of the principles reflected in the Code.

8.4.3 Small Business Tenants

Inflexibility and absence of choice are particularly acute when it comes to small business tenants. Small business tenants are likely to have very short leases which are contracted out, and will often have no alienation rights.[86] Small business tenants often enter into leases without receiving any professional advice and are likely to take the lease on the first terms offered. [87] If there is negotiation this is likely to relate only to the rent and there is a surprising level of ignorance about key features of the leasehold relationship, such as whether the lease is contracted out of the 1954 Act with its renewal provisions or whether there is a break clause.[88] In the retail sector, it appears that there are high levels of tenant dissatisfaction,

---

[83] After salaries: R Bootle and S Kalyan, *Property in Business: A Waste of Space* (London, RICS, 2002) 31.

[84] ODPM, Hansard HC (series 6) vol 432 col 12WS (15 March 2005).

[85] Joint Working Group on Commercial Leases, 'The Code for Leasing Business Premises in England and Wales' (2007); see ch 4.

[86] N Crosby, C Hughes and S Murdoch, 'Monitoring the 2002 Code of Practice for Commercial Leases' (ODPM, March 2005) 303.

[87] N Crosby, C Hughes and S Murdoch, 'Monitoring the 2002 Code of Practice for Commercial Leases' (ODPM, March 2005) 197, 201.

[88] N Crosby, C Hughes and S Murdoch, 'Monitoring the 2002 Code of Practice for Commercial Leases' (ODPM, March 2005) 391–97.

particularly in relation to small independent retailers who are in a weak bargaining position.[89] In the light of this evidence, there is a strong case for extending greater protection to small business tenants.[90]

There are several ways in which the position of small business tenants could be improved. Procedural requirements could be beefed up by imposing a duty to disclose property-specific information to tenants (such as service charge estimates), and by requiring the lease to contain a 'health warning' referring tenants to the Business Lease Code 2007.[91] Tenants also need greater control over 'entry' and 'exit'; the fact that the 1954 renewal rights can be contracted out of mean that relatively few tenants have any real security of tenure, and the inflexibility of alienation clauses also makes it difficult for tenants to expand or contract their businesses without unnecessary financial cost. In addition to reform in discrete areas, there could be a more general power to intervene where terms of the lease are unfair, by bringing small business tenants within scheme of the Unfair Terms in Consumer Contracts Regulations 1999.[92]

The Law Commission's project on Renting Homes specifically aims to move the law on renting homes towards a consumer model.[93] There has been no voice to this effect in the commercial sector, yet a number of developments could be said to reflect this concern to emphasise the needs of the small business tenant as a consumer, or at least to redress the contractual imbalance that may result from the often unequal bargaining relationship. The primary motivation behind the Landlord and Tenant (Covenants) Act 1995 Act was arguably the perceived inequity of original tenant liability. In the important case of *Chartered Trust plc v Davies*, the Court of Appeal acknowledges both that a landlord may have obligations to protect the tenant's interest, even if not explicitly spelt out in the lease, and that the tenant can end the lease if there is a repudiatory breach by the landlord.[94] Arguably, the debate as to whether UORR should be prohibited is motivated not only by the perceived economic impact of rents being held above market levels in a falling market, but also by a sense of injustice, of tenants unable to negotiate for two-way review. The Landlord and Tenant Act 1988 was also concerned to strengthen the hand of the tenant against the landlord who was able to block attempts at alienation. Likewise, the Law Commission's proposals on termination of tenancies also proceed on the basis that the present law of

---

[89] Response of the British Retail Consortium to the 2004 consultation on UORR.

[90] Joint Working Group on Commercial Leases, 'The Code for Leasing Business Premises in England and Wales' (2007). For fuller argument, see S Bright, 'Protecting the Small Business Tenant' [2006] 70 *Conv* 137.

[91] In Australia most states have legislation regulating retail tenancies for small business tenancies. One aspect of this is 'information disclosure'. So, for example, in Victoria information (including disclosure of likely tenant expenses) must be disclosed to the tenant at least 7 days before the lease. For full discussion of the Australian position, see N Crosby, 'An Evaluation of the Policy Implications for the UK of the Approach to Small Business Tenant Legislation in Australia' (August 2006) available at www.rdg.ac.uk/rep/ausleaserpt.pdf.

[92] SI 1999/2083. The Law Commission has recommended the extension of the unfair terms regulations to small business contracts but has excluded land contracts from this: Law Commission, 'Unfair Terms in Contracts' (Law Com No 292, 2005). The reasons for the exclusion are unconvincing: S Bright, 'Protecting the Small Business Tenant' [2006] 70 *Conv* 137, 154–55.

[93] Law Commission, 'Renting Homes: The Final Report. Volume 1: Report' (Law Com No 297, 2006).

[94] (1998) 76 P & CR 396 (CA) (discussed in ch 4). But Lloyd LJ appears to question this in *Reichman v Beveridge* [2006] EWCA Civ 1659 as he remarks that there is no Court of Appeal decision confirming that a lease can be brought to an end by acceptance of a repudiatory breach: [10].

forfeiture is unjust. There is much diversity in the commercial lease market. As in contract law more generally, the big players need little protection: the market is able to regulate letting practices to achieve an appropriate balance in rights and responsibilities. At the lower end of the market, however, both landlords and tenants are commonly inexperienced and there is much to be said for adopting a model of consumer protection applicable to small businesses.

9

AGRICULTURAL TENANCIES

9.1 Policy and legislative history in the agricultural sector
9.2 Farm business tenancies
9.3 The impact of the ATA 1995
9.4 Future directions

9.1 Policy and Legislative History in the Agricultural Sector[1]

9.1.1 Introduction

There are now two separate bodies of statute law governing agricultural tenancies. They reflect very different philosophical approaches towards the sector and their application depends upon the date of creation of the tenancy. Agricultural tenancies created on or after 1 September 1995 are governed by the Agricultural Tenancies Act 1995 (ATA 1995), which is shaped around free market principles: the parties are free to negotiate most of the terms and there is no minimum length of term. This reflects a marked change of direction from earlier legislative controls which gave tenants long-term security in the land. Tenancies entered into before that date[2] come within the Agricultural Holdings Act 1986 (AHA 1986), which offers much more protection to tenants. The substantive law discussed in this book focuses on the ATA 1995, but the scheme of the earlier legislation is also set out in this chapter in order to illustrate the concerns that have influenced the legislative agenda in this area.

The history of regulation of agricultural tenancies is closely tied to wider policies towards farming and the appropriate use of rural land. Until the late nineteenth century, agricultural tenancies were governed largely by custom and common law. While, in general, this meant giving effect to the terms of the tenancy agreement, limited terms were implied imposing duties upon the tenant, such as a covenant 'to manage and cultivate the land in good and husband like manner'[3] and 'to keep the premises wind and watertight'.[4] The result was a situation in which a landlord had a number of remedies against the tenant but the tenant had very limited rights. Most tenancies were terminable by six months' notice, leaving the tenant in a precarious position. The problems generated by this are discussed by Atiyah:

---

[1] For a fuller discussion, see A Densham, 'Agricultural Tenancies: Past and Present' in S Bright (ed), *Landlord and Tenant Law. Past, Present and Future* (Oxford, Hart, 2006).

[2] Together with later succession tenancies entered into under the AHA 1986 regime, and tenancies inadvertently created under the doctrine of termination and regrant: see ATA 1995 s 4.

[3] *Powely v Walker* (1793) 5 Term Rep 373, 101 ER 208.

[4] *Auwoth v Johnson* (1832) 5 C & P 239, 172 ER 955.

... agricultural leases were usually annual leases so that the tenant had no security of tenure, nor had he any adequate incentive to invest in his farm. As an annual tenant he had no right, on termination of the lease, to compensation for improvements or fixtures, except in some places where certain customary rights were preserved. The tenant's legal position derived from the basic ideas of freedom of contract which had, by this time, become so firmly established. The landlord could not be made to pay compensation for improvements because he was under no obligation to pay for benefits conferred upon him without his consent. If the tenant chose to invest in the land, knowing of his limited security of tenure, it had to be 'assumed' that he knew what he was doing, and that he expected to derive an adequate return from the investment, even allowing for his limited tenure. There seems no doubt that during the last thirty years of the nineteenth century these factors were a serious inhibition on adequate investment in agriculture ... [5]

The tenant's position began to improve when the Agricultural Holdings (England) Act 1875 introduced a form of compensation on quitting and gave the tenant the right to remove fixtures in limited circumstances. There was also an extension of the notice period for an annual tenancy from six months to one year. This approach was strengthened in 1883, with a prohibition on contracting out of the compensation provisions. As Atiyah notes, this early legislation may well have been in response to the general agricultural depression of the 1880s caused by a series of bad harvests and cheap imports.[6] The position of the tenant gradually improved with a series of statutes in the early part of the twentieth century. In 1947 the tenant was, in effect, given lifetime security of tenure provided that the land was farmed efficiently.

9.1.2 The Agricultural Holdings Acts

The Agriculture Act 1947 marked a significant change to the agricultural tenancy regime which, together with other initiatives, such as the implementation of price support measures and improvement grants, aimed to encourage production, ensure profitability, and revitalise investment.[7] Not only was security of tenure introduced, but licences were also brought within the scheme.[8] The 1947 Act was soon re-enacted with further amendments as the Agricultural Holdings Act 1948. The rationale for such a fundamental change is explained by Lord Salmon in *Johnson v Moreton* as a response to the need to improve home food production during the World War II:

> The security of tenure which tenant farmers were accorded by the Act of 1947 was not only for their own protection as an important section of the public, nor only for the protection of the weak against the strong; it was for the protection of the nation itself.[9]

This scheme for security of tenure is carried through into the AHA 1986. The legislation applies to 'agricultural holdings',[10] agriculture being defined as including a number of listed

---

[5] PS Atiyah, *The Rise and Fall of Freedom of Contract* (Oxford, Clarendon Press, 1979) 634.

[6] PS Atiyah, *The Rise and Fall of Freedom of Contract* (Oxford, Clarendon Press, 1979) 746.

[7] R Gibbard and N Ravenscroft, 'The Reform of Agricultural Holdings Law' in P Jackson and D C Wilde (eds), *The Reform of Property Law* (Aldershot, Dartmouth, 1997) 114.

[8] Although as only licences giving exclusive occupation are within the scheme it is likely that these would in any event be held to be tenancies following *Street v Mountford* [1985] 1 AC 809 (HL).

[9] *Johnson v Moreton* [1980] AC 37 (HL) 52.

[10] AHA 1986 s 1.

farming activities, and permitting non-agricultural use provided that this does not substantially affect the character of the tenancy.[11] The whole scheme of security under the 1986 Act is based around the notion of a yearly tenancy, and security of tenure is provided by limiting the effectiveness of a notice to quit served to end the tenancy. Broadly, the Act operates to convert most tenancies into annual tenancies. Lettings for less than a year (periodic or fixed) are converted into yearly tenancies,[12] and fixed term leases of two years or more are continued as annual tenancies.[13] This system does not offer the tenant the kind of long term security that is available for other commercial leases through the right to renew for a term, but the limitations on the landlord's ability to serve a notice to quit (discussed below) mean that in practice agricultural tenants can end up staying for very long periods. The two main categories exempted from the security provisions are grazing and mowing agreements for a specified period of the year,[14] and fixed term lettings between 12 and 24 months (which have become known as *Gladstone v Bower* lettings.)[15]

The overall approach to security in the AHA 1986 is that the good tenant who is farming the land properly should have long term security (although there are some exceptions to this in which a landlord is able to end a tenancy even if the tenant is farming to high standards). The yearly tenancy is terminable by notice to quit but the tenant is given protection by being able to serve a counter notice challenging the notice to quit in certain cases. The details are complex but there are two broad approaches, depending on what basis the landlord is claiming possession. If the landlord's notice relies on one of the Cases in Part I of Schedule 3 (known as the 'Seven Deadly Sins'), the tenant is unable to serve a counter-notice[16] and the landlord's notice will bring the tenancy to an end (unless the tenant can show that the Case relied on is not made out).[17] Alternatively, if the landlord's notice to quit is unqualified (not relying on one of the Cases) then the tenant is able to serve a counter notice and the question of whether the notice is effective will turn on whether the Agricultural Land Tribunal is satisfied as to one or more of the matters mentioned in the AHA 1986 section 27(3). Even if it is so satisfied, it must still withhold consent to the notice to quit if the Tribunal considers that a fair and reasonable landlord would not insist on possession.[18]

The label of 'Seven Deadly Sins' is widely used, but is a misnomer as there are now not seven grounds, nor are they all based on tenant default.[19] In *Johnson v Moreton*, Lord Russell summarised the Seven Deadly Sins thus:

[11] AHA 1986 ss 1(2), 96.

[12] AHA 1986 s 2.

[13] AHA 1986 s 3.

[14] AHA 1986 s 3(a). Even lettings for 364 days avoid being converted into annual tenancies: *Reid v Dawson* [1955] 1 QB 214 (CA).

[15] In *Gladstone v Bower* [1960] 1 QB 170 (QB) Diplock J confirmed that these lettings fall outside the security provisions. The Court of Appeal affirmed his decision: [1960] 2 QB 384 (CA). Initially this was thought to be a Parliamentary oversight but later legislation failed to close the gap.

[16] AHA 1986 s 26(2).

[17] See AHA 1986 Sch 3, Part II.

[18] AHA 1986 s 27(2).

[19] The Cases are: A – Retirement of statutory smallholders; B – Land required for non-agricultural use; C – Certificate of bad husbandry; D – Remediable breach of tenancy, such as non-payment of rent; E – Irremediable breach of tenancy, such as assignment of the tenancy without the landlord's consent; F – Tenant insolvency; G – Death of tenant; H – Ministry certificate.

... [Stated] in very general terms they cover situations in which possession of the land is required by the landlord for a different permitted use, or the tenant has in some way misbehaved as such, and the relevant fact is asserted in the notice to quit.[20]

One important Case enables the landlord to end the tenancy if he has obtained planning permission for a non-agricultural use.[21] The assumption is that the opportunity to develop the land for non-agricultural use should belong to the landlord, and as planning law eases, freeing up vernacular buildings for non-agricultural use, many landlords have been able to secure very substantial development gains on traditionally low value agricultural land and buildings.[22] The tenant default grounds include bad husbandry, non-payment of rent and other unremedied breach.

Where the landlord is not relying on one of the Seven Deadly Sins, the notice will be effective only if one of the matters specified in section 27(3) exists. These grounds are based mainly around the proposed land use under the landlord's management. So, for example, one ground is that the 'carrying out of the purpose for which the landlord proposes to terminate the tenancy is desirable in the interests of good husbandry'.[23] There is also a very open-ended ground which places a wide degree of discretion in the Tribunal: 'that greater hardship would be caused by withholding than by giving consent to the operation of the notice'.[24]

At the same time that tenants were given security of tenure, a rent review procedure was also introduced in 1948. This was to be a fairly informal procedure, with the determination of the new rent to be referred to arbitration if the parties were unable to agree the new rent. Initially, the arbitrator was simply directed to determine the 'rent properly payable'. This produced considerable variation in the results and, in an attempt to introduce some consistency into awards, a market formula was adopted in 1958, the idea being that tenants should have security of tenure but not be shielded from paying market rents.

Under the agricultural holdings legislation, tenants are able to claim compensation on quitting the tenancy to compensate them for work done on the land for which they will not reap the benefit. In part, the compensation schemes provide an incentive for tenants to invest in the farm for the long term. Under the AHA 1986 compensation is available both for 'Tenant Right' (short term seasonal improvements, such as unharvested crops) and for improvements (subject to compliance with certain statutory requirements). To encourage good husbandry the tenant can also claim compensation for 'high farming' if the tenant has increased the value of the holding by adopting a more beneficial system of farming than is required by his tenancy agreement, or (if none is specified) than is practised on comparable holdings. Compensation is also available for disturbance if the tenant leaves after being given notice and is not in default.

The main features of protection for the agricultural tenant – security of tenure and compensation payments – were in place by the end of the 1940s. Although there have been numerous agricultural acts since, tinkering with the details of the regulation, the next major

---

[20] [1980] AC 37 (HL) 70.
[21] HA 1986 Sch 3 Part I, Case B.
[22] A Densham, 'Agricultural Tenancies: Past and Present' in S Bright (ed), *Landlord and Tenant Law. Past, Present and Future* (Oxford, Hart, 2006) 126.
[23] AHA 1986 s 27(3)(a).
[24] AHA 1986 s 27(3)(e).

change was not until 1976 with the introduction of succession rights, enabling close relatives of a deceased tenant to succeed to his tenancy so long as they are 'suitable' and 'eligible' to take on the tenancy. This could happen twice in relation to any tenancy.[25]

By the 1980s, the issues facing tenant farmers were very different from when security of tenure had been introduced. During World War II the concern had been to increase agricultural production, but by the 1980s over production was emerging as a problem. There were other difficulties. In 1979 the Northfield Committee report showed a decline in the amount of agricultural land available for letting, from 88 per cent in 1914 to around 35 per cent to 40 per cent in 1979.[26] This decline came about not only through landlords choosing not to relet land but also as the result of a trend 'for tenant farmers to buy their landlords' interest and become owner-occupiers themselves'.[27] The Northfield Committee, predicting further decline, considered it important to preserve the vibrancy of the tenanted sector. Succession rights had acted as a disincentive to landlords to let farmland and the Northfield Committee therefore recommended that there should be restrictions on the scheme. Further, when land became available for letting, there was strong competition for it and high rents could be commanded by landlords. This rent was unrelated to the true value of the land and the level of productivity that it could sustain. Inevitably, this also had an impact on the level of rent awarded by arbitrators on review. This caused great tenant dissatisfaction and led to a deal being made between the National Farmers Union (on behalf of tenants) and the Country Landowners' Association (on behalf of landlords), the former agreeing to accept the restrictions on succession rights in return for a new rent formula.

The new rent mechanism, introduced in 1984, excluded the reference to the 'open market' in an attempt to remove the 'scarcity' value from rent valuations (that is, the inflation of rent caused by there being a shortage of land available for renting).[28] Instead, the rent was to take account of the productive capacity of the farm and its profitability. Succession was restricted to 'one commercial unit' and tenant farmers were able to nominate someone to succeed on reaching 65, thus encouraging voluntary retirement. These amendments only apply to pre-July 1984 tenancies; succession rights were abolished altogether for most new tenancies after July 1984. A further change made in 1984 was to provide that fixed term tenancies between two and five years could be exempted from the security of tenure provisions with Ministry approval.

9.1.3 The Agricultural Tenancies Act 1995

Notwithstanding these changes, the decline in land available for letting continued. By 1994 only 24 per cent of agricultural holdings were tenanted and the transfer of land from the rented sector into owner occupation was continuing.[29] The nature of farming was also

---

[25] Cf succession rights under the Rent Act 1977.

[26] Northfield Committee, 'Report of the Committee of Inquiry into the Acquisition and Occupancy of Agricultural Land' (Cmnd 7599, 1979).

[27] R Gibbard and N Ravenscroft, 'The Reform of Agricultural Holdings Law' in P Jackson and D C Wilde (eds), *The Reform of Property Law* (Aldershot, Dartmouth, 1997) 115, referring to CS Orwin *A History of English Farming* (London, Nelson and Sons, 1949).

[28] For further discussion of scarcity, see ch 16.

[29] J Kerr, *Farm Business Tenancies: New Farms and Land 1995–97* (London, RICS, 1994) paras 2.1 and 5.2.

changing. There was less emphasis on production, growing recognition of the need for farmers to diversify in order to make a living and more focus on conservation. More radical changes were therefore put forward to revitalise this sector, which became law in the ATA 1995. The three guiding principles of the reform were to deregulate and simplify the existing legislation; to encourage letting of land; and to provide an enduring framework which can accommodate change. The details are discussed more fully below, but the main changes made were to remove security of tenure and to leave most of the details of the tenancy for agreement between the parties.

A tenancy governed by the ATA 1995 is known as a farm business tenancy (FBT). The only compulsory provisions are that there should be regular rent review and compensation for improvements upon quitting the tenancy. In the event of disputes, there is unilateral recourse to arbitration, a faster and simpler route than recourse to courts. There is also clear signposting of the end of tenancies, with at least a year's notice to be given when a tenancy is about to run out, anything less being considered inadequate for agricultural tenancies. There are no minimum notice provisions, however, for fixed term tenancies of two years or less or for periodic tenancies for periods of less than a year. In recognition of the changing nature of farming the 1995 Act also enables farmers to diversify without losing the protection of the 1995 Act. Changes were made at the same time to the inheritance tax regime (which had also acted as a disincentive to letting) so that the same level of relief was available for tenanted land as for owner occupied land.

9.1.4 Avoiding Statutory Protection[30]

Given the restrictions that the Agricultural Holdings legislation placed upon landlords, in particular the difficulty in recovering land, much farmland has been let in ways that avoid the statutory controls. A report in 1990 found that 25 per cent of tenanted agricultural land was farmed through 'unconventional tenancies'.[31] One way is to arrange for the land to be farmed without there being a tenancy at all. This can be done by entering into partnerships, share farming,[32] and other forms of joint venture. A further route is to take advantage of the 'get-outs' provided by the legislation itself. By far and away the most frequent unconventional tenancies found in the 1990 report were 'gentleman's agreements'[33] and 'grass keep'.[34]

More controversial routes have also been attempted in which there has clearly been a letting that falls within the legislative code but which have been structured to try to avoid the tenant being able to challenge the landlord's notice to quit. None of these attempts has been successful. In *Johnson v Moreton* the tenant covenanted not to serve a counter-notice upon the landlord if served with a notice to quit.[35] The inability to challenge the landlord's notice to quit would effectively mean that the tenant had no security. The House of Lords

---

[30] See S Bright, 'Avoiding Tenancy Legislation: Sham and Contracting Out Revisited' (2002) 61 *CLJ* 146.

[31] M Winter, *Agricultural Land Tenure in England and Wales* (London, RICS, 1990) 57. Unconventional tenancies included those with Ministry approval, *Gladstone v Bower* lets, farming through partnership, share farming, informal agreements, and cropping licences (permission to cultivate crops for a limited period of time).

[32] Where both the landowner and working farmer jointly farm the same land.

[33] Informal arrangements, concluded over a pint of beer and a handshake!

[34] This term is not defined in the report but is, presumably, referring to grazing agreements. 'Grass keep' is when grassland is let to a farmer for grazing livestock or cutting for winter forage, for less than a year.

[35] [1980] AC 37 (HL).

was unanimous in holding that the tenant's covenant was invalid. Although some of the Law Lords treated this as a matter of statutory construction, all of the speeches place importance on the public interest involved in farming. The later case of *Featherstone v Staples* involved a similar attempt, although in this case the tenant had agreed not to serve the counter-notice without the consent of a company which was controlled by the landlord.[36] The Court of Appeal upheld the validity of the counter-notice that was served by the tenant. In *Gisborne v Burton* the landowner granted a tenancy to his wife, who in turn sub-let the farm.[37] When the head-tenancy was terminated this would automatically bring any sub-letting to an end. As the wife would not contest the notice to quit, this would mean that the sub-tenant had no security. The Court of Appeal (by a 2-1 majority) held this device to be ineffective. The reality was that there was a letting to the tenant farmer.

In these cases the landlord has not be able to require the tenant to bargain away his statutory rights. In *Johnson v Moreton* Lord Simon stated:

> Where it appears that the mischief which Parliament is seeking to remedy is that a situation exists in which the relations of parties cannot properly be left to contractual regulation, and Parliament therefore provides for statutory regulation, a party cannot contract out of such statutory regulation (albeit exclusively in his own favour), because so to permit would be to reinstate the mischief which the statute was designed to remedy and to render the statutory provision a dead letter.[38]

Even where the 'escape route' chosen has not been expressly prohibited by Parliament the courts have nonetheless held the device ineffective by recourse either to principles of statutory construction,[39] or wider principles of public policy[40] and artificial devices.[41] Given the emphasis on contractual freedom under the ATA 1995 and the absence of long-term security for tenant farmers, these issues are unlikely to arise in new tenancies as landlords will not find it necessary to resort to avoidance measures.

9.2 Farm Business Tenancies

9.2.1 Lettings within the ATA 1995

Most new lettings entered into on or after 1 September 1995 will be FBTs governed by the ATA 1995. There are some exceptional categories of new lettings which will continue to be governed by the AHA 1986, in particular a tenancy entered into under the succession provisions of the AHA 1986, and a new tenancy that is created simply because of the operation of the doctrine of implied surrender and regrant.[42] There will, however, continue to be AHA holdings for some considerable time as the AHA 1986 gives both security and also succession

---

[36] [1986] 1 WLR 861 (CA).
[37] [1989] QB 390 (CA).
[38] [1980] AC 37 (HL), 69.
[39] Especially Lords Salmon and Hailsham in *Johnson v Moreton* [1980] AC 37 (HL).
[40] Especially Lords Russell, Simon and Edmund-Davies in *Johnson v Moreton* [1980] AC 37 (HL).
[41] *Gisborne v Burton* [1989] QB 390 (CA).
[42] ATA 1995 s 4. For the doctrine of implied surrender and regrant, see ch 24.

rights. The Department for Environment, Food and Rural Affairs (DEFRA) tenanted land survey in 2006 found approximately 3.7 million hectares of tenanted land in England of which the largest single category was that farmed under a full agricultural tenancy,[43] almost twice as much as that farmed under a FBT.[44]

The ATA 1995 provides that a tenancy is a 'farm business tenancy' if 'it meets the business conditions together with either the agricultural condition or the notice conditions'.[45] The business condition test requires that at least part of the land is (and has been since the start of the tenancy) farmed for the purposes of a trade or business.[46] In addition it must satisfy either the agriculture condition or the notice conditions. The agricultural condition is that 'the character of the land is primarily or wholly agricultural'.[47] It is likely that most lettings take advantage of the notice conditions; all this requires is that the specified notice is given before the tenancy by each of the landlord and the tenant, and that *at the beginning of the tenancy* the character of the tenancy was primarily or wholly agricultural.[48] The effect of this is that even if there is a substantial change in the land use after the commencement of the tenancy, it will remain a FBT so long only that part of the land is farmed commercially. Where no notice is served, however, the letting will only remain a FBT so long as the character of the tenancy is primarily or wholly agricultural. Later diversification in land use to more commercial and non-agricultural activity could result in a 'no-notice' letting becoming subject to Part II of the Landlord and Tenant Act 1954 with rights of renewal for the tenant.

The Act also provides that any breach of the user terms (without the landlord's consent) will not be taken account of in determining whether the tenancy meets the business conditions or the agricultural conditions.[49] This prevents the tenant trying to side step the ATA 1995, for example, by changing the user and so bringing the tenancy within the Landlord and Tenant Act 1954 (with its more favourable renewal rights).

'Agriculture' is defined by reference to a non-exclusive list of farming activities,[50] the same approach as adopted under the AHA 1986. During the passage of the Agricultural Tenancies Bill through Parliament some had sought to modernise this definition to refer specifically to contemporary land uses, such as arable land, and energy crops (such as miscanthus and biomass) but, given that the definition is non-exclusive, this was considered unnecessary.

There are no formality requirements for FBTs aside from the requirement to give notice in order to take advantage of the option of ensuring that the FBT will remain such notwithstanding any later change in use (the notice conditions). The lettings will be subject to the general formality requirements if the lease is for more than three years (see chapter 4) but, if

[44] This phrase is not defined in the statistics but presumably refers to tenancies governed by the Agricultural Holdings Act 1986.
[44] 49% under a full agricultural tenancy, 27% under a FBT (but those for less than 1 year are included in seasonally let land), 12% under a seasonal agreement (less than 1 year), 12% under some other agreement: DEFRA, 'Tenanted Land Survey – England 2006, Summary of Results' (15 March 2007).
[45] ATA 1995 s 1(a).
[46] ATA 1995 s 1(2).
[47] ATA 1995 s 1(3).
[48] ATA 1995 s 1(4).
[49] ATA 1995 s 1(8).
[50] ATA 1995 s 38(1).

for a shorter period, a written or oral lease is capable of being a FBT. There is no minimum length of tenancy but farm business tenants must be given at least twelve months' notice if the lease is an annual tenancy[51] or for more than two years.[52]

9.2.2 Rent

The rent under a FBT is left to free market negotiation. There is no control on initial rent fixing. The parties also have considerable freedom in agreeing the mechanism for rent review, provided that it is not upward only. They can:

(a)   agree that there is to be no review of rent,[53] or

(b)   agree a rent review mechanism by which the rent is to be varied by a specified amount or in accordance with an objective formula which does not preclude a reduction,[54] or

(c)   provide for the rent to be reviewed by an independent expert whose decision is final provided that this does not preclude a reduction.[55]

If there is no such rent review mechanism in the lease, either party can request the rent to be reviewed by arbitration at three yearly intervals,[56] unless the parties have expressly excluded this Part of the Act.[57] The arbitrator can increase or reduce the rent payable on an open market basis as between willing parties.[58] In determining the open market rent the arbitrator is to take account of the terms of tenancy but to disregard:

(a)   any increase in rental value due to tenant's improvements,[59]

(b)   the impact on rent of the fact that the tenant is already in occupation,[60]

(c)   and any lowering of rent caused by any dilapidation or deterioration caused or permitted by the tenant. [61]

9.2.3 Compensation for Improvements

The tenant will be entitled to compensation for improvements on quitting the holding, provided that the improvement is not removed from the holding (section 16) and that the landlord has given written consent to the improvement (section 17). The landlord's consent

---

[51] ATA 1995 s 6.
[52] ATA 1995 s 5.
[53] ATA 1995 s 9(a).
[54] ATA 1995 s 9(b).
[55] ATA 1995 s 9(c) (ii).
[56] ATA 1995 s 10.
[57] ATA 1995 s 9 (c) (i).
[58] ATA 1995 s 13(2).
[59] other than –
    (a) any tenant's improvement provided under an obligation which was imposed on the tenant by the terms of his tenancy or any previous tenancy and which arose on or before the beginning of the tenancy in question,
    (b) any tenant's improvement to the extent that any allowance or benefit has been made or given by the landlord in consideration of its provision, and
    (c) any tenant's improvement to the extent that the tenant has received any compensation from the landlord in respect of it (s 13(2)).
[60] ATA 1995 s 13(4)(a).
[61] ATA 1995 s 13(4)(b).

can be given either in response to an individual request or in the tenancy agreement itself. Although, therefore, there is no statutory right to compensation for tenant right matters (growing crops, etc), the landlord and the tenant may agree in a written tenancy agreement that there will be compensation for tenant right. During the tenancy there is no requirement for the landlord to give consent but the tenant is able to refer the issue to arbitration if the landlord refuses consent. The arbitrator:

> … shall consider whether, having regard to the terms of the tenancy and any other relevant circumstances (including the circumstances of the tenant and the landlord), it is reasonable for the tenant to provide the proposed tenant's improvement.[62]

Tenant's improvements include not only physical improvements made by the tenant's effort or at his own expense[63] but also intangible benefits.[64] These could include the holding of a milk quota, or goodwill, so long as the tenant has first obtained the landlord's written consent to this counting as an improvement. This means that a tenant farmer who has, for example, diversified into offering bed and breakfast accommodation can claim compensation on quitting for the goodwill attached to the commercial element, but only if he has obtained the landlord's consent to this 'improvement'. The amount of compensation is:

> … an amount equal to the increase attributable to the improvement in the value of the holding at the termination of the tenancy …[65]

with discount for any allowance made by the landlord to the tenant[66] and any public grant paid to the tenant.[67]

The idea underlying the compensation provisions is, as under the AHA 1986, that the tenant should receive compensation for value that he has added to the landlord's interest at his own expense or effort. The right to compensation provides the tenant with an incentive to make improvements to the land and the system under the ATA 1995 is simpler than under the AHA 1986. In addition, unlike the AHA 1986, these compensation provisions will override any agreement to the contrary[68] and so it will not be possible for the level of compensation to be written down. Nevertheless, there are concerns that landlords may unreasonably withhold consent to improvements. This is most likely to arise when the tenant is improving in order to diversify beyond traditional agricultural land use. Although it is always possible for the tenant to refer the refusal to arbitration, the costs of doing so may be prohibitive.

9.2.4 Compensation for Improvements Consisting of Planning Permission

There are special provisions that apply to planning permission obtained by the tenant farmer for development on the land. In order for the tenant to claim compensation the landlord must have given consent which is expressly stated to be for the purpose 'of enabling a

---

[62] ATA 1995 s 19(5)
[63] ATA 1995 s 15(a).
[64] ATA 1995 s 15 (b).
[65] ATA 1995 s 20(1).
[66] ATA 1995 s 20(2).
[67] ATA 1995 s 20(3).
[68] ATA 1995 s 26.

specified physical improvement ... to be provided by the tenant' or 'of enabling the tenant lawfully to effect a specified change of use'.[69] In addition, the planning permission must be 'unused' at the end of the tenancy, that is 'the specified physical improvement has not been completed or the specified change of use has not been effected'.[70] The availability of compensation in this situation reflects the tenant's effort in securing the planning permission, and the added value that an unused permission brings to the land. Unlike with other tenant improvements, the obtaining of the landlord's consent for the planning application cannot be referred to arbitration. The amount of compensation for an unimplemented planning permission is, subject to any upper limit agreed between the parties:

> ... an amount equal to the increase attributable to the fact that the relevant development is authorised by the planning permission in the value of the holding at the termination of the tenancy.[71]

9.2.5 Dispute Resolution

Disputes that arise in relation to FBTs can either be referred to a third party under a provision in the lease agreement or referred to an arbitrator.[72]

9.3 The Impact of the ATA 1995

It is difficult to assess what impact the ATA 1995 has had. Changes that were suggested by some of the very early surveys have not necessarily continued. A study by the University of Plymouth for DEFRA based on the first year's operation of the ATA 1995 found that only seven per cent of FBTs were to new entrants, and that as the market was highly competitive, rents were high.[73] Terms were also quite short: in England 55 per cent were for two years or less. It is still the case that rents under FBTs are higher than for agricultural holdings, but whereas rents for the latter are very slowly rising, FBT rents have fallen by significant amounts in recent years. As Table 16.1 in chapter 16 shows, in the five year period to 2006 average FBT rents fell by 17.5 per cent. The early indications that FBT terms would be very short have not necessarily been sustained: the Tenanted Farms Survey 2004 carried out by the Central Association of Agricultural Valuers (CAAV) reported that the average term for new FBTs was 7.2 years. There was also an early indication that the decline in the amount of tenanted land had been reversed; but by 2004 the CAAV survey showed a net loss (of 2.5 per cent) of agricultural land to the tenanted sector for the first time since 1996, and in the following year there was a further fall of 2.5 per cent.

What does seem to be the case is that the ATA 1995 is not bringing in many new entrants. Although renting land is less expensive for new entrants than having to buy farmland, it is still very difficult to finance: FBTs tend to have higher rents, the relatively

---

[69] ATA 1995 s 18(1)(a),(b).
[70] ATA 1995 s 18(1)(c).
[71] ATA 1995 s 21(1).
[72] ATA 1995 ss 28, 29.
[73] A Errington and others, 'Economic Evaluation of the Agricultural Tenancies Act 1995' (DEFRA, 2002).

short term nature can make borrowing difficult, and the economics of modern farming favours large holdings. Land that becomes available appears to be taken mainly by established farmers seeking to expand the size of their existing units rather than by new entrants to the industry.[74] Expansion of farm units may be necessary in order to be able to compete effectively in agricultural production,[75] but it does not help new entrants to farming. As Gibbard, Ravenscroft and Reeves comment, the ATA 1995 has provided a 'vehicle for expansionism' by existing farmers rather than an opening for new entrants.[76]

One of the concerns expressed with the move away from long-term security was that this might cause tenant farmers to farm without regard to the future. The importance of 'farming for the future' is illustrated by Lord Hailsham's remarks in *Johnson v Moreton*:

> Fertility is not something built up as the result of a mere six months' activity on the part of the cultivator … It takes years (sometimes generations) of patient and self-abnegating toil and investment to put heart into soil, to develop and gain the advantage of suitable rotations of crops, and to provide proper drains, hedges and ditches. [77]

Although FBT terms are relatively short compared to the long term security potentially available to AHA 1986 tenants, it must be remembered that the system of protection under the AHA 1986 was so unattractive to landowners that even before the 1995 legislation most were already entering into letting arrangements designed to avoid conferring security (through Ministry consent, *Gladstone v Bower* agreements and grazing agreements). Sixty-five per cent of lettings made in the year to 31 October 1993 were on short term lettings.[78]

As with so much of landlord and tenant law, it is too simplistic to attribute the decline of the tenanted sector to the impact of the restrictive hold of legislation, in this case the AHA 1986. This means that the move to free market principles in the ATA 1995 was also unlikely, by itself, to reverse this. Errington, Whitehead and Fellon comment on the variety of factors that have contributed to the decline of the tenanted sector during the twentieth century:

> … a myriad of other influences have shaped decision making of both landlord and tenant … For landlords, socio-economic factors such as the decimation of a generation of landowners through two world wars, increased returns from in-hand farming and differential taxation have all contributed to the process. For tenants, dramatic increases in land values, the vacant possession premium and the consequent attraction of buying out their landlord, technological advances in farming, the understandable preference amongst banks to lend to property owners

---

[74] A Errington and others, 'Economic Evaluation of the Agricultural Tenancies Act 1995' (DEFRA, 2002). Trends also found in B Ilbery and others, 'Research into the potential impacts of CAP reform on the diversification activities of tenant farmers in England – baseline study' (Coventry University and University of Hull, March 2006) passim.

[75] M Cardwell, 'Agricultural Tenancies: Future Directions' in S Bright (ed), *Landlord and Tenant Law. Past, Present and Future* (Oxford, Hart, 2006).

[76] R Gibbard, N Ravenscroft, and J Reeves, 'The Popular Culture of Agricultural Law Reform' (1999) 15 *J of Rural Studies* 269.

[77] [1980] AC 37 (HL) 59.

[78] J Kerr, *Farm Business Tenancies: New Farms and Land 1995–97* (London, RICS, 1994) para 5.2. This figure does not include grazing agreements, and so the percentage of short-term agreements is even higher than this.

rather than tenants and pressure to increase farm size have also been significant influences on the process.[79]

The recent drop in the amount of tenanted land has been blamed by some on the introduction of the Single Farm Payment following reform of the Common Agricultural Policy. In order to claim, it was necessary to be a farmer undertaking agricultural activity and holding a Single Payment Entitlement; these entitlements were allocated in 2005 and it is thought that some landowners took land into owner-occupation for this purpose.

9.4 Future Directions

Since the ATA 1995 there have been further reviews of the farming industry and tenanted land against the background that financial considerations are pushing farmers away from food production towards diversification and countryside stewardship.[80] More than two-thirds of farmers have diversified beyond traditional agriculture.[81] Private owners appear to form the largest landlord grouping, followed by landed estates and institutions (such as the Church, the National Trust, Royal Estates and local authorities).[82]

In May 2003 there was a report from the Tenancy Reform Industry Group (TRIG, a group set up by the government to investigate the health of the tenanted sector). This group first worked with the government to identify the government's objectives. In so far as they relate directly to tenancies, these objectives are:

— To ensure tenant farmers can:
  —diversify where this will improve the viability of their business;
  —and take steps to help enhance and protect the environment
  —without fear of losing their tenancy or jeopardizing succession rights.
— To ensure that holdings can be restructured without jeopardizing a tenant's rights.
— To maintain an appropriate balance between landlord and tenant interests.
— To ensure that a variety of sustainable entry routes are available which provide an opportunity for new entrants to join and progress within the farming industry.
— To maintain the area of let land.
— To increase the area of land let under whole farm agreements.
— To maintain and improve flexibility within the rental market.[83]

The focus of the TRIG recommendations is to promote flexibility and enable tenant

[79] A Errington and others, 'Economic Evaluation of the Agricultural Tenancies Act 1995' (DEFRA, 2002) [1.7].

[80] M Cardwell, 'Agricultural Tenancies: Future Directions' in S Bright (ed), *Landlord and Tenant Law. Past, Present and Future* (Oxford, Hart, 2006)

[81] 70.3% according to B Ilbery and others, 'Research into the potential impacts of CAP reform on the diversification activities of tenant farmers in England – baseline study' (Coventry University and University of Hull, March 2006) 8; 65.7% according to the Centre for Rural Research, 'Farm Diversification Activities: benchmarking study 2002. Final Report to DEFRA' (University of Exeter, 2002). These findings are indicative only as the samples are small. Also, definitions of diversification vary.

[82] The proportions were 46.2%, 18.5% and 12.8% respectively but the sample group was small, and not necessarily wholly representative: B Ilbery and others, 'Research into the potential impacts of CAP reform on the diversification activities of tenant farmers in England – baseline study' (Coventry University and University of Hull, March 2006).

[83] TRIG, 'Final Report' (DEFRA, 2003) 7.

farmers to diversify more easily and to adopt agri-environment schemes, without fear of losing their tenancy or losing any succession rights that they have. TRIG then identified four key principles to guide its report:

— tenancy legislation can directly affect, positively as well as negatively, the availability of land to let and the operation of the tenanted sector.
— where possible non-legislative measures should be used to maintain confidence in the framework of the legislation taking into account the long-term nature of rural land management.
— the long-term view requires the need to provide flexibility for circumstances as yet unforeseen which are generally best delivered by greater freedom of contract with appropriate legislative safeguards.
— there should be a level playing field between tenancies and other means for delivering land management and the tax system should treat them equally so that decisions can be taken on practical and not artificial grounds.[84]

Some of the changes recommended by TRIG have since been implemented. The survey carried out by the University of Plymouth has revealed poor levels of understanding about the 1995 Act[85] and it is now proposed to produce 'model' clauses that can be used to 'mirror' the terms of an AHA 1986 tenancy in a FBT to help tenants transfer between holdings.[86]

Following TRIG it is likely that regulation of agricultural tenancies will for some time continue to be based upon the principles of freedom of contract. Within this, Cardwell argues greater adjustment needs to be made for the broader European and world trade context within which the farming industry has to operate.[87] To illustrate this, he refers to the fact that payments made to farmers are subject to compliance with statutory management requirements in relation to such matters as animal welfare and the environment. Compliance with these requirements may, however, put at risk the status of a tenancy. By way of example, it is not necessary for land to be in agricultural production in order to comply with European criterion for the Single Farm Payment, and yet it is questionable whether non-production would qualify for either the 1986 or 1995 statutes. The earlier report by the University of Plymouth[88] had expressed similar concerns and suggested relaxing the agricultural requirement in FBTs and removing the business condition. In its report, TRIG considered this but thought the FBT did provide an appropriate mechanism, implying that few holdings would be converted to environmental use that did not involve agricultural management activity.[89] A wholly diversified enterprise would be better within the Landlord and Tenant Act 1954, Part II. What is clear is that within the broad approach of freedom of contract, it will remain necessary for the agriculture tenancy regime to accommodate, as Cardwell argues, 'both the status and the specific regulation of agriculture in European Community and world trade law'.[90]

---

[84] TRIG, 'Final Report' (DEFRA, 2003) 1–2.
[85] A Errington and others, 'Economic Evaluation of the Agricultural Tenancies Act 1995' (DEFRA, 2002).
[86] TRIG, 'Final Report' (DEFRA, 2003) 3.
[87] M Cardwell, 'Agricultural Tenancies: Future Directions' in S Bright (ed), *Landlord and Tenant Law. Past, Present and Future* (Oxford, Hart, 2006) 144; see also L Bodiguel and M Cardwell, 'Evolving Definitions of "Agriculture" for an Evolving Agriculture?' [2005] 69 *Conv* 419.
[88] A Errington and others, 'Economic Evaluation of the Agricultural Tenancies Act 1995' (DEFRA, 2002).
[89] TRIG, 'Final Report' (DEFRA, 2003) 10.
[90] M Cardwell, 'Agricultural Tenancies: Future Directions' in S Bright (ed), *Landlord and Tenant Law. Past, Present and Future* (Oxford, Hart, 2006) 145.

10

HUMAN RIGHTS IN LANDLORD AND TENANT LAW

10.1   Introduction: human rights
10.2   Human rights in domestic law
10.3   The meaning of public authority
10.4   Interpreting Convention rights
10.5   The Convention rights
10.6   Interpretation of legislation
10.7   International rights to housing

10.1 Introduction: Human Rights

In 1948 the United Nations (UN) adopted the Universal Declaration of Human Rights. This historic moment marked the first of many international statements on the importance of protecting fundamental rights. At least two of the Articles touch on issues that landlord and tenant law relates to. Article 25 declares that 'everyone has the right to a standard of living adequate for the health and well-being of himself and of his family, including … housing …', and Article 12 states that 'No one shall be subjected to arbitrary interference with his privacy, family, home or correspondence …'

The Universal Declaration of Human Rights made a powerful political and moral statement, but did not create enforceable legal rights. It was swiftly followed by the Council of Europe adopting the European Convention on Human Rights and Fundamental Freedoms (ECHR) in 1950. In addition to a reference to 'the home' in similar form to that in Article 12 of the Universal Declaration, a later Protocol to the Convention also recognises a right to the peaceful enjoyment of possessions. Although the UK ratified this Convention in 1951 and thereby came under an international obligation to conform, it was not until the enactment of the Human Rights Act 1998 (HRA 1998) that the rights enshrined in the Convention became directly enforceable in UK domestic law.

10.2 Human Rights in Domestic Law

Since the HRA 1998 came into force in October 2000 there have been numerous cases testing the extent to which human rights law impacts on the leasehold relationship. Although most of the challenges have occurred in the context of renting homes, it is clear that human rights arguments can reach far beyond this into long leasehold relationships[1] and even commercial tenancies.[2] Cases have raised issues on many different aspects of the landlord and tenant relationship: access,[3] security,[4] covenant enforcement,[5] forfeiture,[6] enfranchisement,[7] conditions[8] and management.[9] On the whole, however, human rights arguments have seldom led to effective legal remedies in the courts for tenants or landlords. Only in a few cases has there been a dramatic impact on the substantive outcome, notably in *Ghaidan v Godin-Mendoza* in which the House of Lords held that the law regulating the succession of tenancies breached Article 14 of the ECHR and should apply equally to homosexual couples living together as a family as to heterosexual couples.[10] In a Northern Irish case, *Re The Landlords Association for Northern Ireland's Application*,[11] a registration scheme for houses in multiple occupation (HMOs) was found to violate Convention rights as there was insufficient certainty on the scope of the scheme and a discriminatory fee structure.

Nonetheless, the impact of human rights law on landlord and tenant law is significant, and likely to expand. The reach of human rights law is not only seen in the case law, but in the context of the new human rights landscape new policies and legislative developments are now shaped so as to be human rights compliant.[12]

Under the ECHR states parties[13] are under an obligation to secure the various rights and freedoms to those within their jurisdiction.[14] Before the HRA 1998, however, an individual within the UK who wanted to challenge the UK government for not complying with this obligation had to take the case to the European Court of Human Rights (ECtHR) in Strasbourg, and could even then do so only after showing that there was no remedy in the UK courts. An example of that occurred in *James v United Kingdom* when the Duke of Westminster challenged the enfranchisement laws contained in the Leasehold Reform Act 1967 before the ECtHR.[15] These laws give tenants of houses held on long leases at a low rent the right to acquire the freehold of the premises compulsorily (see chapter 25). As the

---

[1] *DP v United Kingdom* (App No 11949/86) (1988) 10 EHRR 149 (usually referred to as *Di Palma v United Kingdom*)

[2] *PW & Co v Milton Gate Investments Ltd* (2003) EWHC 1994 (Ch), [2004] Ch 142 (Neuberger J stating obiter that s 3 of the HRA 1998 could affect the construction of ss 141 and 142 of the Law of Property Act 1925, in the context of commercial leases).

[3] *Appleby v United Kingdom* (App No 44306/98) (2003) 37 EHRR 38.

[4] *Kay v LB of Lambeth; Leeds CC v Price* [2006] UKHL 10, [2006] 2 AC 465.

[5] *PW & Co v Milton Gate Investments Ltd* (2003) EWHC 1994 (Ch), [2004] Ch 142.

[6] *Di Palma v United Kingdom* (App No 11949/86) (1988) 10 EHRR 149.

[7] *James v United Kingdom* (App No 8793/79) (1986) 8 EHRR 123.

[8] *Lee v Leeds CC; Ratcliffe v Sandwell MBC* [2002] EWCA Civ 6, [2001] 1 WLR 1488.

[9] *Re The Landlords Association for Northern Ireland's Application for Leave to Apply for Judicial Review; Re Boyle, Greer, Jackson and Laird's Application for Judicial Review* [2005] NIQB 22, [2006] NI 16.

[10] [2004] UKHL 30, [2004] 2 AC 557.

[11] *Re The Landlords Association for Northern Ireland's Application for Leave to Apply for Judicial Review; Re Boyle, Greer, Jackson and Laird's Application for Judicial Review* [2005] NIQB 22, [2006] NI 16.

[12] So, for example, one of the four principles expressly underpinning the Law Commission's Renting Home projects is compliance with human rights law: Law Commission, 'Renting Homes' (Law Com No 284, 2003) para 2.11. The HRA 1998 s 19 requires a statement of compatibility with human rights to be made by the Minister presenting a Bill to Parliament.

[13] That is, governments who have ratified the Convention.

[14] ECHR, Art 1.

[15] (App No 8793/79) (1986) 8 EHRR 123.

freeholder of extensive residential estates in London he argued that the legislation violated his right to the peaceful enjoyment of possessions. Although the ECtHR accepted that there had been an 'interference' with his property it held that the enfranchisement laws were in the 'public interest' and did not involve a disproportionate response to the perceived problems (see further at 10.5.5 below).

The HRA 1998 was intended to 'bring rights home', essentially making the ECHR rights enforceable in domestic courts and tribunals. It does this through two primary mechanisms:

(a) making it unlawful for a public authority to act incompatibly with Convention rights;[16] and

(b) requiring all legislation to be interpreted and given effect to as far as possible compatibly with Convention rights.[17]

The full impact of this on landlord and tenant law, indeed all areas of law, is still being worked out. The application to discrete areas of landlord and tenant law will be dealt with in successive chapters. In this chapter, an overview of the legal framework is provided.

10.3 The Meaning of Public Authority

Section 6 of the HRA 1998 provides:

(1) It is unlawful for a public authority to act in a way which is incompatible with a Convention right.

(2) ...

(3) In this section 'public authority' includes –

(a) the court or tribunal, and

(b) any person certain of whose functions are functions of a public nature,

but does not include either House of Parliament or a person exercising functions in connection with proceedings in Parliament.

(4) ...

(5) In relation to a particular act, a person is not a public authority by virtue only of subsection (3)(b) if the nature of the act is private.

(6) 'An act' includes a failure to act ...

The HRA 1998 has an obvious application where a landlord is a 'public authority' and will therefore be under a duty not to act in a way that is incompatible with any Convention rights. Importantly, the definition is further extended by section 6(3)(b) to include any person 'whose functions are functions of a public nature'. This means that it becomes necessary to look at the function being performed; a body that performs both public and non-public functions will be a public authority only if it is the public function in issue. There is no clear guide to what a public function is but according to Lord Nicholls in *Aston Cantlow* (in deciding whether a Parochial Church Council was a public authority):

---

[16] HRA 1998 s 6.
[17] HRA 1998 s 3.

Factors to be taken into account include the extent to which in carrying out the relevant function the body is publicly funded, or is exercising statutory powers, or is taking the place of
central government or local authorities, or is providing a public service.[18]

The effect is that not only will local authority landlords need to comply with the HRA
1988, but so too will any other landlords 'whose nature is governmental in a broad sense of
that expression'.[19] The position of registered social landlords (RSLs) is unclear. In *Poplar
Housing & Regeneration Community Association Ltd v Donoghue* the Court of Appeal held
that a RSL may be a 'public authority' for the purposes of section 6.[20] As seen in chapters 5
and 6, RSLs are in an unusual position. In certain respects they resemble private landlords
(and many of them began as privately endowed charitable institutions) and are treated as
such within housing legislation. In other respects they are more akin to public bodies, being
regulated by the Housing Corporation, receiving state funding, and assisting local authorities to fulfil many of the statutory housing duties. In recent years RSLs have also been
created in order to take over some of the housing stock of local authorities. Whether or not
a RSL is a public authority will depend on the context. In the words of Lord Woolf CJ:

> ... housing associations as a class are not standard public authorities. If they are to be a public
> authority this must be because a particular function performed by an individual RSL is a pub-
> lic as opposed to a private act. The RSL would then be a functional, or hybrid, public
> authority.[21]

This means that it will always be necessary to look at the particular function at issue to
determine if a RSL comes within section 6(3):

> Section 6(3) means that hybrid bodies, who have functions of a public and private nature are
> public authorities, but *not* in relation to acts which are of a private nature. The renting out of
> accommodation can certainly be of a private nature. The fact that through the act of renting
> by a private body a public authority may be fulfilling its public duty, does not automatically
> change into a public act what would otherwise be a private act ...[22]

In the particular case, the Poplar housing association had been created by a local
authority for the purpose of receiving a transfer of its housing stock. It was subject to local
authority guidance, and five of its board members were also members of the local authority.
On these facts the Court of Appeal held that Poplar was a public authority, using the
following principles:

> (i) While section 6 of the Human Rights Act 1998 requires a generous interpretation of who is
> a public authority, it is clearly inspired by the approach developed by the courts in identifying
> the bodies and activities subject to judicial review. The emphasis on public functions reflects
> the approach adopted in judicial review by the courts and textbooks since the decision of the

---

[18] *Aston Cantlow and Wilmcote with Billesley Parochial Church Council v Wallbank* [2003] UKHL 37, [2004] 1 AC
546 [12].
[19] *Aston Cantlow and Wilmcote with Billesley Parochial Church Council v Wallbank* [2003] UKHL 37, [2004] 1 AC
546 [7].
[20] [2001] EWCA Civ 595, [2002] QB 48.
[21] *Poplar Housing & Regeneration Community Association Ltd v Donoghue* [2001] EWCA Civ 595, [2002] QB 48
[68].
[22] *Poplar Housing & Regeneration Community Association Ltd v Donoghue* [2001] EWCA Civ 595, [2002] QB 48
[67].

Court of Appeal (the judgment of Lloyd LJ) in *R v Panel on Take-overs and Mergers, Ex p Datafin plc* [1987] QB 815.

(ii) Tower Hamlets, in transferring its housing stock to Poplar, does not transfer its primary public duties to Poplar. Poplar is no more than the means by which it seeks to perform those duties.

(iii) The act of providing accommodation to rent is not, without more, a public function for the purposes of section 6 of the Human Rights Act 1998. Furthermore, that is true irrespective of the section of society for whom the accommodation is provided.

(iv) The fact that a body is a charity or is conducted not for profit means that it is likely to be motivated in performing its activities by what it perceives to be the public interest. However, this does not point to the body being a public authority. In addition, even if such a body performs functions, that would be considered to be of a public nature if performed by a public body, nevertheless such acts may remain of a private nature for the purpose of sections 6(3)(b) and 6(5).

(v) What can make an act, which would otherwise be private, public is a feature or a combination of features which impose a public character or stamp on the act. Statutory authority for what is done can at least help to mark the act as being public; so can the extent of control over the function exercised by another body which is a public authority. The more closely the acts that could be of a private nature are enmeshed in the activities of a public body, the more likely they are to be public. However, the fact that the acts are supervised by a public regulatory body does not necessarily indicate that they are of a public nature. This is analogous to the position in judicial review, where a regulatory body may be deemed public but the activities of the body which is regulated may be categorised private.

(vi) The closeness of the relationship which exists between Tower Hamlets and Poplar. Poplar was created by Tower Hamlets to take a transfer of local authority housing stock; five of its board members are also members of Tower Hamlets; Poplar is subject to the guidance of Tower Hamlets as to the manner in which it acts towards the defendant.

(vii) The defendant, at the time of transfer, was a sitting tenant of Poplar and it was intended that she would be treated no better and no worse than if she remained a tenant of Tower Hamlets. While she remained a tenant, Poplar therefore stood in relation to her in very much the position previously occupied by Tower Hamlets.

While these are the most important factors in coming to our conclusion, it is desirable to step back and look at the situation as a whole. As is the position on applications for judicial review, there is no clear demarcation line which can be drawn between public and private bodies and functions. In a borderline case, such as this, the decision is very much one of fact and degree. Taking into account all the circumstances, we have come to the conclusion that while activities of housing associations need not involve the performance of public functions, in this case, in providing accommodation for the defendant and then seeking possession, the role of Poplar is so closely assimilated to that of Tower Hamlets that it was performing public and not private functions. ... We emphasise that this does not mean that all Poplar's functions are public. ... The activities of housing associations can be ambiguous. For example, their activities in raising private or public finance could be very different from those that are under consideration here. The raising of finance by Poplar could well be a private function.[23]

RSLs may therefore be public authorities for some purposes but not others. In *Poplar Housing v Donoghue* the closeness of the relationship between Poplar and the local authority

---

[23] *Poplar Housing & Regeneration Community Association Ltd v Donoghue* [2001] EWCA Civ 595, [2002] QB 48 [69]–[70].

appears to have been an especially important factor. Many commentators have been critical of this being treated as significant,[24] and in *YL v Birmingham City Council* Lord Mance (in the majority) and Baroness Hale (in the minority) commented that the Court of Appeal in *Poplar Housing v Donoghue* had placed too much reliance on the 'close historical and organisational assimilation of Poplar Housing with the local authority'.[25]

Cases since *Poplar Housing v Donoghue* have, instead, emphasised the importance of analysing the character of the function concerned. In *Aston Cantlow* Lord Hope stated that:

> ... [section 6(3)] requires a distinction to be drawn between functions which are public and those which are private. It has a much wider reach [than section 6(1)], and it is sensitive to the facts of each case. It is the function that the person is performing that is determinative of the question whether it is, for the purposes of that case, a 'hybrid' public authority. The question whether section 6(5) applies to a particular act depends on the nature of the act which is in question in each case.[26]

This approach was also applied by the House of Lords most recently in *YL v Birmingham City Council* in determining whether a private care home was a public authority for the purposes of the Human Rights Act 1998.[27] Although the home provided accommodation and care to residents pursuant to arrangements made with a local authority and, in many cases paid for by the local authority, it was held not to be a public authority. The care home was a private body providing care on a contractual basis, and the fact that the local authority pays fees for some of the residents did not turn this into a function of a public nature.[28]

In *YL v Birmingham City Council* Lord Mance referred to the suggested hallmarks of a public authority as being the existence of any special powers or duties, democratic account-ability, public funding in whole or in part, an obligation to act only in the public interest and a statutory constitution.[29] Some of these factors point in favour of RSLs being treated as public authorities, for example, the special powers that they have been given to take action in relation to anti-social behaviour (see chapter 11), and in relation to the allocation of housing (see chapter 6), as well as the level of public funding. There is no doubt that a private sector landlord is not a public authority for these purposes, and, as Lord Neuberger points out, the fact that tenants receive state housing benefit does not mean that a private landlord falls within section 6(3)(b). On the other hand, Lord Neuberger makes the intriguing comment that:

> ... it appears to me to be far easier to argue that section 6(3)(b) is engaged in relation to the provision of free housing by an entity all of whose activities are wholly funded by a local authority, than it is in relation to the provision of housing by an independently funded entity to impecunious tenants whose rent is paid by the local authority.[30]

---

[24] See, for example, K Markus, 'Leonard Cheshire Foundation: What is a Public Authority?' [2003] *EHRLR* 92; D Oliver, 'Functions of a Public Nature under the Human Rights Act' [2004] *PL* 329.

[25] [2007] UKHL 27 [105] and [61].

[26] *Aston Cantlow and Wilmcote with Billesley Parochial Church Council v Wallbank* [2003] UKHL 37, [2004] 1 AC 546 [41].

[27] [2007] UKHL 27.

[28] Lord Bingham and Baroness Hale issued strong dissents.

[29] [2007] UKHL 27, adopting the approach of Lord Nicholls in *Aston Cantlow and Wilmcote with Billesley Parochial Church Council v Wallbank* [2003] UKHL 37, [2004] 1 AC 546.

[30] [2007] UKHL 27 [165].

What kind of body he has in mind in the first part of this sentence is unclear.

Some have argued for a more expansive approach to the meaning of public authority. The Joint Committee of the House of Commons and House of Lords on Human Rights[31] (the 'Joint Committee') argued that a body should be seen as a functional public authority where:

> ... it exercises a function that had its origin in governmental responsibilities ... in such a way as to compel individuals to rely on that body for realisation of their Convention rights.[32]

Although this suggestion was said to be based on the functional approach put forward by Lord Hope in *Aston Cantlow*, the application of that test by the House of Lords in *YL v Birmingham City Council* shows that it does not extend as far as the Joint Committee suggests. The care home residents in that case were dependent on the care home for realization of their Convention rights but the body was not held to be a public authority. Therefore the fact that individuals have to rely on RSLs for realisation of their Article 8 rights does not, of itself, mean that the RSL will be a public authority.

Section 6 can also come into play even where there is a private landlord. This is because the court itself is a 'public authority', and cannot therefore act incompatibly with Convention rights. The question could, for example, arise if the court is asked to order repossession in favour of a private landlord. As Lord Nicholls observed in *Kay v LB of Lambeth; Leeds CC v Price*:

> Courts are bound to conduct their affairs in a way which is compatible with Convention rights. The court's own practice and procedures must be Convention-compliant. Whether, and in what circumstances, the court's section 6 obligation extends more widely than this, and affects the substantive law to be applied by the court when adjudicating upon disputes between private parties, still awaits authoritative decision.[33]

There is an extensive body of literature discussing this question.[34] It is clear that courts do accept that the HRA 1998 affects relationships between private individuals, although the extent to which it does remains uncertain.

10.4 Interpreting Convention Rights

The Convention rights of most direct relevance to the leasehold relationship are Article 3

---

[31] Joint Committee of the House of Commons and House of Lords on Human Rights, 'The Meaning of Public Authority under the Human Rights Act' (HL Paper 39, HC 282, 23 February 2004).

[32] Joint Committee of the House of Commons and House of Lords on Human Rights, 'The Meaning of Public Authority under the Human Rights Act' (HL Paper 39, HC 282, 23 February 2004) para 157.

[33] [2006] UKHL 10 [61], [2006] 2 AC 465.

[34] The debate is conducted in the language of vertical or horizontal impact. On vertical effect between public authorities and citizens: R Buxton, 'The Human Rights Act and Private Law' (2000) 116 *LQR* 48. Direct horizontal effect between individuals: W Wade, 'Horizons of Horizontality' (2000) 116 *LQR* 217. Indirect horizontal effect: M Hunt, 'The "Horizontal Effect" of the Human Rights Act' [1998] *PL* 423, N Bamforth, 'The Application of the Human Rights Act 1998 to Public Authorities and Private Bodies' (1999) 58 *CLJ* 159, N Bamforth, 'The True "Horizontal Effect" of the Human Rights Act' (2001) 117 *LQR* 34, G Phillipson, 'The Human Rights Act, "Horizontal Effect" and the Common Law: a Bang or a Whimper?' (1999) 62 *MLR* 824. Sophisticated form of horizontal effect: A Lester and D Pannick, 'The Impact of the Human Rights Act on Private Law: The Knight's Move' (2000) 116 *LQR* 380.

(prohibition of degrading treatment), Article 6 (right to a fair trial), Article 8 (right to respect for the home), Article 14 (prohibition of discrimination), and Article 1 of the First Protocol (right to peaceful enjoyment of possessions). These rights are discussed more fully in the next section as it is helpful first to look at two principles that courts have developed when interpreting Convention rights: the notion of there being a 'margin of appreciation' (or deference) and the doctrine of positive obligations.

10.4.1 Margin of Appreciation

At the international level, the ECtHR has allowed states a level of leeway in the manner in which human rights are protected, acknowledging that national courts may be in a better position to judge the situation in their country than the international court sitting in Strasbourg. This has become known as the 'margin of appreciation'. In addition, the ECtHR has developed the concept of 'proportionality'. Broadly, this means that the means chosen to promote the policy objective must not go further than is necessary. When the ECtHR is deciding whether an act interfering with Convention rights can be justified it must have regard:

> ... to the fair balance that has to be struck between the competing interests of the individual and of the community as a whole. In both contexts the State enjoys a certain margin of appreciation in determining the steps to be taken to ensure compliance with the Convention.[35]

English courts have adopted a similar approach under the HRA 1998, generally accepting that in the context of housing those more closely involved with policy implementation (generally local authorities) are better placed to decide the appropriate response that is 'necessary in a democratic society'.[36] Instead of the language of 'margin of appreciation', this discretion tends to be referred to in the domestic context as a form of 'deference' or a 'margin of discretion'.[37] Due regard will have to be had:

> ... to the needs and resources of the community and of individuals. And, in striking the balance between the resources of a local housing authority (and the need to meet other claims upon those resources) and the needs of the individual',[38]

the courts will be conscious of the need 'to show a proper sensitivity to the limits of permissible judicial creativity'.[39]

The courts are generally reluctant to second guess the decisions made by local authorities in relation to housing, taking the view that housing policy is 'very much a matter for the allocation of resources in accordance with democratically determined priorities.'[40] In *Ghaidan v Godin-Mendoza* Lord Nicholls said:

---

[35] *Hatton v United Kingdom* (36022/97) (2002) 34 EHRR 1 [96]. See also *Lee v Leeds CC; Ratcliffe v Sandwell* MBC [2002] EWCA Civ 6, [2001] 1 WLR 1488 [48].

[36] This is the wording used in Art 8.

[37] Although the language of 'margin of appreciation' is also sometimes used in the domestic context. For fuller discussion of 'proportionality' see J Rivers, 'Proportionality and Variable Intensity of Review' (2006) 65 *CLJ* 174.

[38] *Lee v Leeds CC; Ratcliffe v Sandwell* MBC [2002] EWCA Civ 6, [2001] 1 WLR 1488 [49].

[39] *Southwark LBC v Tanner; Baxter v Camden LBC (No 2)* [2001] 1 AC 1 (HL) 8.

[40] *Southwark LBC v Tanner; Baxter v Camden LBC (No 2)* [2001] 1 AC 1 (HL) 9–10. See also D Rook, 'Property Law and the Human Rights Act 1998: a Review of the First Year' [2002] *Conv* 316.

... the court will reach a different conclusion from the legislature only when it is apparent that the legislature has attached insufficient importance to a person's Convention rights. The readiness of the court to depart from the view of the legislature depends upon the subject matter of the legislation and of the complaint. National housing policy is a field where the court will be less ready to intervene. Parliament has to hold a fair balance between the competing interests of tenants and landlords, taking into account broad issues of social and economic policy.[41]

10.4.2 Positive Obligations[42]

The Convention rights are commonly thought of as 'freedoms from interference'. Convention jurisprudence recognises, however, that states may be under an obligation to 'take action', even when the right in question is framed negatively. As Professor Feldman has noted, the dynamic interpretation of the Convention has resulted in 'more extensive obligations on states than are immediately obvious from a superficial perusal of the text'.[43]

The jurisprudence of what are commonly referred to as the 'positive obligations' (duties to act) under the Convention is still developing. They have been used to ensure that Convention rights are 'practical and effective', not 'theoretical or illusory'.[44] The doctrine of positive obligations may prove to be especially important in protecting those most vulnerable within society who have no place to shelter: the Convention does not give a 'right to housing', but there may come such a level of deprivation of the basic necessities of life, such as housing, that some provision has to be made. This possibility can be seen in the discussion of Articles 3 and 8 below.

10.5 The Convention Rights

This section considers the Convention rights most likely to impact on leasehold relationships. There are, however, other rights that may also come into play. So, for example, Articles 10 and 11 (freedom of speech, and freedom of assembly and association) may be affected by restrictions on the use of property.[45]

10.5.1 Article 3

Article 3 provides that:

> No one shall be subjected to torture or to inhuman or degrading treatment or punishment.

What looks like a right to do with prisoners and the like, can in fact require the state to do something to assist those who are completely destitute. This was made clear in the important case of *R (Limbuela) v Secretary of State for the Home Department*.[46] The case

---

[41] [2004] UKHL 30, [2004] 2 AC 557 [19].
[42] See A Mowbray, *The Development of Positive Obligations under the European Convention on Human Rights by the European Court of Human Rights* (Oxford, Hart, 2004) ch 6.
[43] D Feldman, *Civil Liberties and Human Rights in England and Wales* 2nd edn (Oxford, OUP, 2002) 53.
[44] *Papamichalopoulos v Greece* (App No 14556/89) (1993) 16 EHRR 40 [42].
[45] See 'Controlling Access to Leasehold Property' in ch 11.
[46] [2005] UKHL 66, [2006] 1 AC 396.

involved the Nationality, Immigration and Asylum Act 2002. Section 55 allows all support (accommodation and support for other essential living needs) to be withdrawn from an asylum seeker who has not claimed asylum within a reasonable period of arrival in the UK. The House of Lords held that if this led to someone having to sleep rough it could amount to a violation of Article 3. In the words of Lord Bingham:

> Treatment is inhuman or degrading if, to a seriously detrimental extent, it denies the most basic needs of any human being. As in all article 3 cases, the treatment, to be proscribed, must achieve a minimum standard of severity, and I would accept that in a context such as this, not involving the deliberate infliction of pain or suffering, the threshold is a high one. A general public duty to house the homeless or provide for the destitute cannot be spelled out of article 3. But I have no doubt that the threshold may be crossed if a late applicant with no means and no alternative sources of support, unable to support himself, is, by the deliberate action of the state, denied shelter, food or the most basic necessities of life.[47]

In *O'Rourke v United Kingdom*[48] the applicant complained that eviction from local authority accommodation forced him to sleep rough for 14 months, and that this violated Article 3. Although the ECtHR said that the level of suffering did not engage Article 3, Lord Bingham has since commented that:

> ... had his predicament been the result of state action rather than his own volition [he had turned down offers of accommodation], and had he been ineligible for public support (which he was not), the court's conclusion that his suffering did not attain the requisite level of severity to engage article 3 would be very hard to accept.[49]

10.5.2 Article 6

Article 6, entitled 'right to a fair trial', is the key procedural provision in the Convention and provides that:

> 1. In the determination of his civil rights and obligations ... everyone is entitled to a fair and public hearing within a reasonable time by an independent and impartial tribunal established by law ...

This Article will have an impact not only in relation to how disputes are resolved judicially but also in relation to the review of certain administrative decisions. This can be important in housing law. The phrase 'civil rights and obligations' is treated 'as an autonomous concept, not dependent upon the domestic law classification of the right or obligation'[50] and

> ... the Strasbourg court has extended article 6 to cover a wide range of administrative decision-making on the ground that the decision determines or decisively affects rights or obligations in private law.[51]

---

[47] [2005] UKHL 66, [2006] 1 AC 396 [7].
[48] (App No 39022/97) ECHR 26 June 2001.
[49] *R (Limbuela) v Home Secretary* [2005] UKHL 66, [2006] 1 AC 396 [9].
[50] *Begum (FC) v Tower Hamlets LBC* [2003] UKHL 5, [2003] 2 AC 430 [29].
[51] *Begum (FC) v Tower Hamlets LBC* [2003] UKHL 5, [2003] 2 AC 430 [30].

Which kind of administrative decisions relate to 'civil rights and obligations' remains uncertain. In *Tsfayo v UK* the ECtHR held that the appeal procedure for review of housing benefit entitlement failed to comply with Article 6 because the review body was not independent from the executive.[52] It may well be that decisions relating to homelessness obligations (such as the suitability of offered accommodation)[53] and decisions taken to end introductory tenancies[54] will also come within Article 6.

Where a decision calls for review it is not, however, necessary for the reviewing body to conduct a full appeal on the merits. It appears that it will be sufficient if there is provision for internal review accompanied by the possibility of judicial review:

> [Strasbourg jurisprudence] has said, first, that an administrative decision within the extended scope of article 6 is a determination of civil rights and obligations and therefore prima facie has to be made by an independent tribunal. But, secondly, if the administrator is not independent (as will virtually by definition be the case) it is permissible to consider whether the composite procedure of administrative decision together with a right of appeal to a court is sufficient. Thirdly, it will be sufficient if the appellate (or reviewing) court has 'full jurisdiction' over the administrative decision. And fourthly ... 'full jurisdiction' does not necessarily mean jurisdiction to re-examine the merits of the case but ... 'jurisdiction to deal with the case as the nature of the decision requires'.[55]

10.5.3 Article 8

Article 8 provides:

> 1. Everyone has the right to respect for his private and family life, his home and his correspondence.
> 2. There shall be no interference by a public authority with the exercise of this right except such as is in accordance with the law and is necessary in a democratic society in the interests of national security, public safety or the economic well-being of the country, for the prevention of disorder or crime, for the protection of health or morals, or for the protection of the rights and freedoms of others.

Article 8 has generated a lot of case law in the housing context, although its scope extends also to business premises.[56] 'Home' has an autonomous meaning in the ECtHR jurisprudence:[57] it includes not only conventional living arrangements, but also gypsy caravan accommodation.[58] In order to be a 'home' the occupier must have 'sufficient and

---

[52] (App No 60860/00) ECHR 14 November 1996. The housing benefit appeal procedure has since changed.

[53] *Begum (FC) v Tower Hamlets LBC* [2003] UKHL 5, [2003] 2 AC 430: whether this decision was a determination of civil rights was left undecided in this case. See ch 6.

[54] *R (on the application of McLellan) v Bracknell Forest BC; Reigate and Banstead BC v Benfield* [2001] EWCA Civ 1510, [2002] QB 1129. See ch 19.

[55] *Begum (FC) v Tower Hamlets LBC* [2003] UKHL 5, [2003] 2 AC 430 [33].

[56] *Neimietz v Germany* (App No 13710/88) (1992) 16 EHRR 235 [31]: 'to interpret the words "private life" and "home" as including certain professional or business activities or premises would be consonant with the essential object and purpose of Article 8 (art. 8), namely to protect the individual against arbitrary interference by the public authorities'.

[57] *Buckley v United Kingdom* (App No 20348/92) (1996) 23 EHRR 101 [63]; *Harrow LBC v Qazi* [2003] UKHL 43, [2004] 1 AC 983 [9], [23], [61] and [95].

[58] *Buckley v United Kingdom* (App No 20348/92) (1996) 23 EHRR 101; *Connors v United Kingdom* (App No 66746/01) (2004) 40 EHRR 189.

continuous links',[59] so, for example, a gypsy family who had been on land for only two days had not made their 'home' there.[60] The fact that an occupier had no lawful right to enter onto land does not, however, prevent it from being 'home'.[61]

Article 8 gives a 'right to respect'. It is often spoken of as being 'engaged' when there has been an interference with the home, but its scope goes beyond active interference and Convention jurisprudence shows that positive obligations are 'inherent in effective respect for private or family life':

> ... although the object of Article 8 (art. 8) is essentially that of protecting the individual against arbitrary interference by the public authorities, it does not merely compel the State to abstain from such interference: in addition to this primarily negative undertaking, there may be positive obligations inherent in an effective respect for private or family life (see the Airey judgment of 9 October 1979, Series A no. 32, p. 17, para. 32). These obligations may involve the adoption of measures designed to secure respect for private life even in the sphere of the relations of individuals between themselves.[62]

The ECtHR found there to be a violation of Article 8 when a gypsy family was summarily evicted from a local authority site, recognising that the vulnerable position of gypsies as a minority led to there being,

> ... a positive obligation imposed on the Contracting States by virtue of article 8 to facilitate the gypsy way of life.[63]

In a similar vein, recognising that Article 8 rights may place restrictions on a local authority's eviction powers, the ECtHR in *Marzari v Italy* drew attention to the positive aspects of Article 8:

> ... although article 8 does not guarantee a right to have one's housing problems solved by the authorities, a refusal of the authorities to provide assistance in this respect to an individual suffering from a severe disease might in certain circumstances raise an issue under article 8 of the Convention because of the impact of such refusal on the private life of the individual. The court recalls in this respect that, while the essential object of article 8 is to protect the individual against arbitrary interference by public authorities, this provision does not merely compel the state to abstain from such interference: in addition to this negative undertaking, there may be positive obligations inherent in effective respect for private life. A state has obligations of this type where there is a direct and immediate link between the measures sought by an applicant and the latter's private life.[64]

On the particular facts, the eviction was found to be justified but mainly,

---

[59] *Harrow LBC v Qazi* [2003] UKHL 43, [2004] 1 AC 983 [9], [64] and [68].
[60] *Kay v LB of Lambeth; Leeds CC v Price* [2006] UKHL 10, [2006] 2 AC 465.
[61] *Harrow LBC v Qazi* [2003] UKHL 43, [2004] 1 AC 983.
[62] *X and Y v The Netherlands* (App No 8978/80) (1986) 8 EHRR 235 [23]. See also *Lopez Ostra v Spain* (16798/90) (1995) 20 EHRR 277 and *Guerra v Italy* (App No 14967/89) (1998) 26 EHRR 357: both cases involved pollution and the ECtHR required the public authority not merely to avoid interference with the exercise of the claimant's rights under Art 8 but to take positive steps to ensure effective respect for them.
[63] *Connors v United Kingdom* (App No 66746/01) (2004) 40 EHRR 189 [84].
[64] (36448/97) (1999) 28 EHRR 175 [179]-[80].

… because the applicant had been 'never co-operative' and had not 'use[d] the avenues which were available to him and which were even pointed out to him in order to avoid the eviction'.[65]

It is likely that the law on 'positive obligations' will continue to develop in a way that will impact significantly upon the obligations of landlords who can be classified as 'public authorities'. In *Moreno Gomez v Spain*[66] the ECtHR held there to be a violation of Article 8 when a local authority failed to take action to prevent night-time disturbance from noise. Similarly, in *Surugiu v Romania*[67] the ECtHR found a violation when the authorities had failed to stop various acts of harassment which included dumping several cartloads of manure in front of the applicant's door and under the windows of his house.

It is clear, however, that Article 8 does not,

… give a right to be provided with a home and does not guarantee the right to have one's housing problem solved by the authorities …[68]

In *Chapman v United Kingdom* the ECtHR said:

It is important to recall that article 8 does not in terms give a right to be provided with a home. Nor does any of the jurisprudence of the court acknowledge such a right. While it is clearly desirable that every human being has a place where he or she can live in dignity and which he or she can call home, there are unfortunately in the contracting states many persons who have no home. Whether the state provides funds to enable everyone to have a home is a matter of a political not judicial decision.[69]

It has been accepted that Article 8 may assist in an argument that the local authority is under an obligation to repair premises, but, if so, this will be only in the most extreme cases of disrepair.[70] As will be seen in later chapters, social landlords have increasing responsibility in relation to the management of 'bad' tenants. The Northern Ireland Court of Appeal found a violation of Article 8 in *Re Donnelly's Application for Judicial Review* when a landlord refused to take possession proceedings against a tenant, explaining the refusal on the grounds that proceedings could not be taken without serious risk to the personal safety of the landlord's staff.[71] In reaching its decision the court explicitly recognised that it was not negative obligations but positive obligations that were involved on the facts. In applying the test of fair balance Carswell LCJ said:

[10] … the failure of the Executive to exercise its power to seek possession of the Gambles' house has undoubtedly given rise to a substantial detriment to the enjoyment of their private and family life on the part of the appellant and the members of his family. The issue is whether … that failure is to be regarded as necessary under the terms of art 8(2) or, putting it the other way, the Executive failed to take reasonable and appropriate measures to secure the appellant's rights under art 8(1).

[65] *Kay v LB of Lambeth; Leeds CC v Price* [2006] UKHL 10, [2006] 2 AC 465 [155].
[66] (App No 4143/02) (2005) 41 EHRR 40.
[67] (App No 48995/99) ECHR 20 April 2004.
[68] *Kay v LB of Lambeth; Leeds CC v Price* [2006] UKHL 10, [2006] 2 AC 465) [90].
[69] (App No 27238/95) (2001) EHRR 399 [99].
[70] *Lee v Leeds CC; Ratcliffe v Sandwell MBC* [2002] EWCA Civ 6, [2001] 1 WLR 1488.
[71] [2003] NICA 55, [2004] NI 189.

Although the court accepted that the safety of staff was a relevant and material consideration, it nonetheless held that the landlord had not 'discharged its duty to take reasonable and appropriate measures to secure the appellant's rights'.

The bulk of cases have, however, concentrated on the 'negative' obligations inherent in Article 8. There has been a stream of cases challenging eviction actions (see chapter 19). Although a landlord's claim to possession will always bring Article 8 into play,[72] it is very important to understand that the 'right to respect' is not absolute and an interference with this right by a public authority will almost invariably be justified by reference to Article 8(2). Justification is often broken down into three limbs. The act must be in accordance with the law, in pursuit of a legitimate aim (in a leasehold context, 'public safety or the economic well-being of the country, for the prevention of disorder or crime, the protection of health or morals, or for the protection of the rights and freedoms of others'), and 'necessary in a democratic society'. In practice, the courts tend to exercise a low level of review. Provided that the relevant authority can show that it acted lawfully, the courts are likely to accept government assertions that that the act served a 'legitimate aim', such as regulating housing need or promoting social justice, without overly close scrutiny of the claim. It is the third limb, that of necessity, that provides the most stringent condition but again the courts have shown great deference to local housing authorities.

In the particular context of recovering possession, it is not only the position of the occupier that needs to be considered but the position of others, those hoping to gain access to the very limited supply of social housing, and in this context,

> … [satisfaction] of the housing needs of others is regarded as a legitimate aim … because it was intended to promote 'the economic well-being of the country' and 'the protection of the rights of … others': *Blecic v Croatia* (2004) 41 EHRR 185, para 58.[73]

Whether the recovery of possession is 'necessary' will depend on whether the interference is proportionate to the legitimate aim being pursued, bearing in mind that a 'margin of appreciation' is given. In the vast majority of cases, a landlord seeking to recover possession from an occupier who has no contractual or proprietary right to remain can do so without risk of violating Article 8.[74] But the method of doing so is also important:

> … the right to respect for a home has inherent in it the principle that procedural fairness will be observed before the home is taken away (see, for example, *Connors v United Kingdom* (2004) 40 EHRR 189, para 83).[75]

Further, where the tenant has been behaving badly, there is increasing recognition of the fact that it is not only the rights of the person against whom action is being brought that need to be taken account of, but also the rights of neighbours affected by the tenant's conduct.[76]

---

[72] *Kay v LB of Lambeth; Leeds CC v Price* [2006] UKHL 10, [2006] 2 AC 465.
[73] *Kay v LB of Lambeth; Leeds CC v Price* [2006] UKHL 10, [2006] 2 AC 465 [66].
[74] *Kay v LB of Lambeth; Leeds CC v Price* [2006] UKHL 10, [2006] 2 AC 465.
[75] *Moat Housing Group South Ltd Harris* [2005] EWCA Civ 287, [2006] QB 606 [102].
[76] See *Manchester CC v Romano and Samari* [2004] EWCA Civ 834, [2005] 1 WLR 2775; *Manchester CC v Higgins* [2005] EWCA Civ 1423, [2006] 1 All ER 841.

10.5.4 Article 14

Article 14 provides that there can be no discrimination in the enjoyment of Convention rights:

> The enjoyment of the rights and freedoms set forth in this Convention shall be secured without discrimination on any ground such as sex, race, colour, language, religion, political or other opinion, national or social origin, association with a national minority, property, birth or other status.

The phrase 'or other status' has been interpreted widely in Strasbourg to include, among other things, sexual orientation, marital status, and illegitimacy. Article 14 has been described by Lord Nicholls as 'an important article of the Convention'.[77] It is not, however, a freestanding right of non-discrimination; in order for it to be applicable, the facts must come within one or more of the other Convention rights. In relation to leases, it may well be very important. It has already been mentioned that in *Ghaidan v Godin-Mendoza* the House of Lords held that the succession provisions in the Rent Act 1977 treated homosexual partnerships less favourably than heterosexual partnerships and that this therefore breached Articles 8 and 14 (see chapter 17).[78] In *Re The Landlords Association for Northern Ireland's Application*,[79] the High Court of Northern Ireland found that a Fees Order was discriminatory under Article 14 as it exempted certain bodies from having to pay fees for the registration of HMOs, whereas other bodies including non institutional private landlords, did have to pay, and this differential treatment had not been justified. Similarly, in *Larkos v Cyprus*,[80] the ECtHR held that there had been a violation of Article 14 in conjunction with Article 8. The landlord in that case was the government and obtained an eviction order against the applicant. Had the applicant been the tenant of a private landlord he would have enjoyed a degree of security of tenure, but this protection did not extend to him as he occupied government owned property. The Court stated that:

> ... the legislation was intended as a measure of social protection for tenants living in particular areas of Cyprus. A decision not to extend that protection to government tenants living side by side with tenants in privately-owned dwellings requires specific justification ... However, the Government has not adduced any reasonable and objective justification for the distinction which meets the requirements of Article 14 of the Convention, even having regard to its margin of appreciation in the area of the control of property.

In the words of Baroness Hale in *Ghaidan v Godin-Mendoza*:

> The state's duty under article 14, to secure that [the rights and freedoms set out in the European Convention] are enjoyed without discrimination ... is fundamental to the scheme of the Convention as a whole. It would be a poor human rights instrument indeed if it obliged the state to respect the homes or private lives of one group of people but not the homes of private lives of another.[81]

---

[77] *Ghaidan v Godin-Mendoza* [2004] UKHL 30, [2004] 2 AC 557 [9].
[78] Legislation (the Civil Partnerships Act 2004) now achieves the same end.
[79] *Re The Landlords Association for Northern Ireland's Application for Leave to Apply for Judicial Review; Re Boyle, Greer, Jackson and Laird's Application for Judicial Review* [2005] NIQB 22, [2006] NI 16.
[80] (App No 29515/95) (1999) 30 EHRR 597.
[81] [2004] UKHL 30, [2004] 2 AC 557 [131].

10.5.5 *Article 1 of the First Protocol*[82]

Article 1 of the First Protocol, entitled 'protection of property' provides:

> Every natural or legal person is entitled to the peaceful enjoyment of his possessions. No one shall be deprived of his possessions except in the public interest and subject to the conditions provided for by law and by the general principles of international law.
>
> The preceding provisions shall not, however, in any way impair the right of a State to enforce such laws as it deems necessary to control the use of property in accordance with the general interest or to secure the payment of taxes or other contributions or penalties.

The text of Article 1 of the First Protocol is poorly worded, the result of a compromise when the Convention was negotiated. Indeed, as Allen charts, the right to property was so contentious that it was omitted from the Convention itself and left for insertion in a separate protocol that would be signed at a later date.

In *Sporrong and Lonnroth v Sweden*, the ECtHR stated that the Article contains three rules:

> The first rule, which is of a general nature, enounces the principle of peaceful enjoyment of property; it is set out in the first sentence of the first paragraph. The second rule covers deprivation of possessions and subjects it to certain conditions; it appears in the second sentence of the same paragraph. The third rule recognises that the States are entitled, amongst other things, to control the use of property in accordance with the general interest, by enforcing such laws as they deem necessary for the purpose; it is contained in the second paragraph.[83]

The word 'possessions' used in the first two rules has been taken to have an autonomous meaning (in the same way as 'home' in Article 8).[84]

The three rules are not distinct in the sense of being unconnected. In *James v United Kingdom* the ECtHR said:

> … the second and third rules are concerned with particular instances of interference with the right to peaceful enjoyment of property and should therefore be construed in the light of the general principle enunciated in the first rule.[85]

In *Sporrong and Lonnroth v Sweden* the Court nonetheless went on to say that categorising cases into the correct rule was important: the court should see if it falls within rules two and three before considering if the first rule was complied with. Nonetheless, Allen demonstrates that the court has not developed general principles on categorisation and, in practice, the 'fair balance/proportionality' test tends to apply similarly between them.[86] There has, however, been a narrow approach taken in relation to the scope of rules two and three. In *Iatridis v Greece* the applicant was evicted from his cinema premises. The Court said that this did not fall within rules two or three:

---

[82] For a thorough discussion, see T Allen, *Property and the Human Rights Act 1998* (Oxford, Hart, 2005).
[83] *Sporrong and Lonnroth v Sweden* (App No 7151/75 and 7152/75) (1983) 5 EHRR 35 [61].
[84] *Iatridis v Greece* (App No 31107/96) (2000) 30 EHRR 97 [54].
[85] (App No 8793/79) (1986) 8 EHRR 123 [37].
[86] See T Allen, *Property and the Human Rights Act 1998* (Oxford, Hart, 2005) 104–5, 121.

Since he holds only a lease of his business premises, this interference neither amounts to an expropriation nor is an instance of controlling the use of property but comes under the first sentence of the first paragraph of Article 1.[87]

Similarly, in *Mellacher v Austria*,[88] the ECtHR held that rent control laws which had dramatic effects on the economic value of the landlord's property did not amount to an expropriation within rule two although it was a control of the use of property falling within the second paragraph (rule three).

Article 1 of the First Protocol does not give an absolute guarantee of property. Although the principle of peaceful enjoyment of possessions is established, it is possible for there to be a deprivation if this is in the public interest and in accordance with the law. Further, the state is able to control the use of property in accordance with the general interest. In some factual situations Article 8 and Article 1 of the First Protocol will both be argued in the same case. In practice, the fair balance approach tends to be applied both under Article 8 and under Article 1 of First Protocol, and the intensity of review likewise tends to be low. Nonetheless, there are differences between them. Under Article 8, any interference is required to be 'necessary in a democratic society'. A 'deprivation' within Article 1 of the First Protocol is justified if it is 'in the public interest'; and control of 'the use of property' will be justifiable if 'in the general interest' (or a fiscal provision). In *James v United Kingdom* the ECtHR said that:

> ... the notion of 'public interest' is necessarily extensive. In particular ... the decision to enact laws expropriating property will commonly involve considerations of political, economic and social issues on which opinion within a democratic society may reasonably differ widely. The court, finding it natural that the margin of appreciation available to the legislature in implementing social and economic policies should be a wide one, will respect the legislature's judgment as to what is 'in the public interest' unless that judgment be manifestly without reasonable foundation.[89]

One of the arguments relied upon by the trustees to the Duke of Westminster to support their claim of a human rights violation was that the enfranchisement laws were not in the 'public interest' as the property was not to be used for the community generally but for an individual's private benefit. (For details of the enfranchisement laws, see chapter 25). Between April 1979 and November 1983, eighty tenants had enfranchised their interests, causing losses to the trustees of about £2.5 million. Further, several of these tenants later sold on the newly acquired freehold at a substantial profit. The ECtHR said that the phrase public interest could include transfer from one individual to another where it was in pursuance of legitimate social policies. The aim of eliminating what was perceived to be a social injustice in an area of prime social need (housing) was within this:

> The taking of property in pursuance of the policy calculated to enhance social justice within the community can properly be described as being 'in the public interest'. In particular, the fairness of the system of law governing the contractual or property rights of private parties is a matter of public concern and therefore legislative measures intended to bring about such

---

[87] (App No 31107/96) (2000) 30 EHRR 97 [55]. Nb: the Court does, however, appear to be dealing with a non-proprietary lease, see [53].
[88] (App No 10522/83, 11011/84 and 11070/84) (1990) 12 EHRR 391.
[89] (App No 8793/79) (1986) 8 EHRR 123 [46].

fairness are capable of being 'in the public interest', even if they involve the compulsory transfer of property from one individual to another.[90]

Under Article 1 of the First Protocol compensation may be relevant to the question of
the fairness of an intervention.[91] In *James v United Kingdom* the ECtHR accepted that:

> ... the taking of property without payment of an amount reasonably related to its value would
> normally constitute a disproportionate interference which could not be considered justifiable
> under article 1.[92]

On the facts, the landlords did not receive the full market value but the court noted that the
legislation was drafted on the principle that 'in equity the bricks and mortar belonged to the
qualified leaseholder' and, given the wide margin of appreciation, it had not been shown that
this was not a fair balance. It was also argued for the trustees that to apply a blanket solution
approach, applying the same rule to all cases, infringed the principle of proportionality. The
ECtHR observed that the compensation provisions could lead to anomalies, with tenants
who purchased end of term leases making windfall profits. Nonetheless, the principle of
enfranchisement and the compensation provisions were within the state's margin of appreciation.

In *Di Palma v United Kingdom* a long leaseholder whose lease had been forfeited because
she had failed to pay the service charge (because she was in a dispute with the landlord)
argued that she had been deprived of property unjustifiably and on unjust terms.[93] In her
case, there was a particular problem because she had been unable to claim relief from
forfeiture due to the limited jurisdiction of the County Court (which has since been
increased). The European Commission of Human Rights found there to be no violation of
Article 1 of the First Protocol, placing considerable weight upon the fact that what had
happened was not the result of the state interference but resulted from the private law
relationship between her and her landlord. Since then it has been said that the concept of
positive obligations applies to Article 1 of First Protocol:

> ... genuine, effective exercise of the right protected by that provision does not depend merely
> on the State's duty not to interfere, but may require positive measures of protection, particu-
> larly where there is a direct link between the measures which an applicant may legitimately
> expect from the authorities and his effective enjoyment of his possessions.[94]

This may mean that a different approach would be taken were facts similar to those of *Di
Palma v United Kingdom* arise now.

There have been several challenges before the ECtHR to the statutory control of leases
based on Article 1 of the First Protocol, but again the usual response is to find that the
controls fall within the margin of appreciation accorded to states. In *Mellacher v Austria*
various landlords alleged that the Austrian rent control laws (under which the tenants were

---

[90] (App No 8793/79) (1986) 8 EHRR 123 [41]. The United States Supreme Court has similarly found that 'public
use' under the 'Takings Clause' of the US Constitution ('private property [shall not]... be taken for public use,
without just compensation'), permits the compulsory taking of property from one private individual to another:
Kelo v City of New London 545 US 469, 125 S Ct 2655 (2005).

[91] See T Allen, *Property and the Human Rights Act 1998* (Oxford, Hart, 2005) ch 6.

[92] (App No 8793/79) (1986) 8 EHRR 123 [54].

[93] *Di Palma v United Kingdom* (App No 11949/86) (1988) 10 EHRR 149.

[94] *Oneryildiz v Turkey* (App No 48939/99) (2005) 41 EHRR 20 [134].

able to obtain considerable reductions to the contractually agreed rents – of 82.4 per cent, 80 per cent, and 22.1 per cent) amounted to an expropriation of the landlord's property without compensation.[95] (For discussion of rent control, see chapter 15.) The ECtHR did not accept that this was an expropriation, but did find that it was a control of the use of property within the second paragraph. It therefore had to be 'in accordance with the general interest'. On this the Court stated, drawing on the approach put forward in *James v United Kingdom*:

> Such laws are especially called for and usual in the field of housing, which in our modern societies is a central concern of social and economic policies.
>
>   In order to implement such policies, the legislature must have a wide margin of appreciation both as regards the existence of a problem of public concern warranting measures of control and as to the choice of the detailed rules for the implementation of such measures. The court will respect the legislature's judgment as to what is in the general interest unless that judgment be manifestly without reasonable foundation.[96]

By majority, the court held that there had been no breach. It accepted that the rent controls pursued a legitimate aim ('to reduce excessive and unjustified disparities between rents for equivalent apartments and to combat property speculation'), and that the interference achieved a fair balance between the demands of the general interest of the community and requirements of the protection of the individual's fundamental rights (satisfying the proportionality requirement).[97] The basis of the dissent was that the controls were disproportionate:

> The applicants bore an individual and excessive burden which was not legitimate in the circumstances, with an upsetting of the requisite fair balance which is to be struck between the demands of the general interest of the community and requirements of the protection of the individual applicants' fundamental rights.

This dissenting voice reflects the same kind of concerns that led the Irish Supreme Court to find that rent controls were unconstitutional in *Blake v Attorney General*.[98] The legislation at issue here not only placed restrictions on rents but also limited the landlord's rights to recover possession of dwellings at the end of the tenancy, and imposed repairing obligations on landlords. It applied only to dwellings below certain rateable values (a common feature of housing legislation). The legislation had a devastating impact on property values, in some cases almost eliminating any sale value. The Supreme Court noted that,

> … in this legislation rent control is applied only to some houses and dwellings and not others; that the basis for the selection is not related to the needs of the tenants, to the financial or economic resources of the landlords, or to any established social necessity; and that, since the legislation is now not limited in duration, it is not associated with any particular temporary or emergency situation …

---

[95] (App No 10522/83, 11011/84 and 11070/84) (1990) 12 EHRR 391.

[96] (App No 10522/83, 11011/84 and 11070/84) (1990) 12 EHRR 391 [45].

[97] The American Supreme Court has similarly affirmed the constitutionality in principle of rent controls: *Pennell v City of San Jose* 485 US 1, 108 S Ct 849 (1988). See also: *Spath Holme Ltd v United Kingdom* (App No 78031/01) ECHR 14 May 2002 in which the claim that the Rent Acts (Maximum Fair Rent) Order 1999 SI 1999/06 breached Article 1 of the First Protocol was ruled inadmissible as the Order was provided for by law and represented a legitimate aim of social policy.

[98] [1982] IR 117 (ISC).

In the opinion of the Court, [the rent restricting provisions] restrict the property rights of one group of citizens for the benefit of another group. This is done, without compensation and without regard to the financial capacity or the financial needs of either group, in legislation which provides no limitation of the period of restriction, gives no opportunity for review and allows no modification of the operation of the restriction. It is, therefore, both unfair and arbitrary. These provisions constitute an unjust attack on the property rights of landlords ...[99]

Excessive regulation has also been found to violate Article 1 of the First Protocol in another Northern Irish case, *Re The Landlords Association for Northern Ireland's Application*.[100] The Northern Ireland Housing Executive ('the Executive') introduced a scheme to regulate the duties of landlords in HMOs. Amongst the conditions of registration that could be imposed was one that could require the manager of the house to take,

... such steps as are reasonably practicable to prevent the existence of the house or the behaviour of the residents from adversely affecting the amenity of character of the area, or to reduce any such adverse effect.[101]

This was stated by the High Court of Northern Ireland to be so,

... vague and lacking in defined scope that it would ... fall foul of the principles of legal certainty required under Convention law [50].

Further, the width of the scheme and the way in which HMOs were defined was said to take the scheme:

[51] ... well beyond the social ill which the state considered existed in relation to HMOs and which was the underlying mischief to which the new legislation was directed. As formulated the scheme (which could have been restricted to certain categories of HMOs) produces a wholly disproportionate impact on houses occupied by three or more unrelated persons who may be closely associated in the one household ... Legislation of this nature has profound effects on property rights and has the potential capacity to deleteriously distort property developments. An ill formulated scheme may (inter alia) have the undesirable and unintended impact of reducing the number of HMOs available to provide accommodation to persons in need of it. It could dissuade owners from providing accommodation in circumstances where this may produce undesirable social results.

... [54] The consequence ... is that the scheme as a whole is effectively a bad scheme in that the Executive and Department failed to have regard to art 1 of First Protocol of the Convention.

Article 1 of the First Protocol has also been used more pro-actively, so as to generate a claim for damages when a promised lease failed to materialise. In an unusual case, *Stretch v United Kingdom,* the applicant had been granted a lease of land for 22 years that included an obligation to erect up to six buildings for industrial use, together with an option to renew for 21 years.[102] In fact, the district council had no statutory powers to grant the option. The applicant's argument was that:

---

[99] [1982] IR 117 (ISC) 138–40.
[100] *Re The Landlords Association for Northern Ireland's Application for Leave to Apply for Judicial Review; Re Boyle, Greer, Jackson and Laird's Application for Judicial Review* [2005] NIQB 22, [2006] NI 16.
[101] Housing (Northern Ireland) Order 1992 SI 1992/1725 Art 75G(1)
[102] (App No 44277/98) (2004) 38 EHRR 12.

[28] ... his contractual and property rights under the lease, namely his legal rights to part of the consideration for entering into the lease (which he lost) and the loss of value of his investment in his property (which he has partly lost) which together was his ability to enjoy his business assets as a whole, ... were 'possessions' within the meaning of Art 1 of Protocol No 1.

Further:

[29] He stated that the deprivation of his possessions which he has suffered is wholly disproportionate as the loss caused to him as a result of failure to grant or enforce the option outweighs any real or perceived benefit to the general interest in applying the *ultra vires* principle, and that of corporate incapacity, on the facts of this case. He points to the lack of any compensation payable and to the passing of legislation which now permits local authorities to grant such options.

The UK government argued that the option, as a legal nullity, could not be a 'possession'. The ECtHR held that the applicant had a 'legitimate expectation' of exercising the option to renew, which attached to his leasehold property rights, and that by refusing to renew the lease there was either an interference with or deprivation of the applicant's possessions. Even though the ultra vires doctrine provides an important safeguard against the abuse of power, in this case the interference did not represent a 'fair balance'. The Court did not, however, say that the Council had to grant the lease (or give its value in compensation). There was a violation but instead of a specific form of remedy, damages were awarded based on 'what the consideration was for the option to renew'.[103]

10.6 Interpretation of Legislation

Section 3 of the HRA 1998 provides that all legislation is to be interpreted, so far as it is possible to do so, in a manner that is consistent with the Convention rights:

Section 3
(1) So far as it is possible to do so, primary legislation and subordinate legislation must be read and given effect in a way which is compatible with the Convention rights.

(2) This section –

(a) applies to primary legislation and subordinate legislation whenever enacted;
(b) does not affect the validity, the continuing operation or enforcement of any incompatible primary legislation; and
(c) does not affect the validity, continuing operation or enforcement of any incompatible subordinate legislation if (disregarding any possibility of revocation) primary legislation prevents removal of the incompatibility.

As will be seen, courts have at times struggled with this, but regard their interpretive obligation under section 3 as very strong and far reaching. Exceptionally, however, when it is not possible to interpret legislation compatibly the courts come under a duty to declare the legislation incompatible under section 4 of the HRA 1998:

---

[103] *Stretch v United Kingdom* (App No 44277/98) (2004) 38 EHRR 12.

Section 4

(1) Subsection (2) applies in any proceedings in which a court determines whether a provision of primary legislation is compatible with a Convention right.

(2) If the court is satisfied that the provision is incompatible with a Convention right, it may make a declaration of that incompatibility.

(3) Subsection (4) applies in any proceedings in which a court determines whether a provision of subordinate legislation, made in the exercise of the power conferred by primary legislation, is compatible with a Convention right.

(4) If the court is satisfied –

(a)   that the provision is incompatible with a Convention right, and

(b)   that (disregarding any possibility of revocation) the primary legislation concerned prevents removal of the incompatibility,

it may make a declaration of that incompatibility.

(5) In this section 'court' means –

(a)   the House of Lords;

(b)   the Judicial Committee of the Privy Council;

(c)   ...

(d)   ...

(e)   in England and Wales or Northern Ireland, the High Court or the Court of Appeal.

(6) A declaration under this section ('a declaration of incompatibility') –

(a)   does not affect the validity, continuing operation or enforcement of the provision in respect of which it is given; and

(b)   is not binding on the parties to the proceedings in which it is made.

As many landlord and tenant cases, in particular housing cases, are heard in the County Court it is important to note that the County Court is unable to make a declaration of incompatibility.

The importance of the interpretive obligation can be seen in *Ghaidan v Godin-Mendoza*.[104] The Rent Act 1977 gave succession rights to the surviving spouse of a statutory tenant and provided that the person living with the tenant 'as his or her wife or husband' was also to be treated as the spouse of the tenant. On a literal reading of this, persons in a same-sex relationship were not included.[105] The House of Lords held, however, that this was discriminatory (under Article 14, as it affected Article 8 rights). Using the far reaching interpretive powers under section 3, the relevant statutory provision could, however, be read as extending to same-sex partners.

The jurisdiction given by section 3 is undoubtedly very wide. As Lord Steyn observed in *Ghaidan v Godin-Mendoza*, section 3 should be used even if there is no ambiguity in the legislative wording; the obligation goes beyond purposive interpretation; and is not restricted to requiring a 'reasonable interpretation'.[106] Further, in *PW & Co v Milton Gate Investments Ltd* Neuberger J took the view (obiter) that section 3 can be used even if it is a common law rule that causes the breach of a Convention right (in this case, an 'estoric'

---

[104] [2004] UKHL 30, [2004] 2 AC 557.

[105] *Fitzpatrick v Sterling Housing Association Ltd* [2001] 1 AC 27 (HL) (the tenant in this case had died several years before the implementation of the HRA 1998).

[106] [2004] UKHL 30, [2004] 2 AC 557 [44].

point that a sub-tenancy will end when a head-lease is ended by notice to quit; see chapter 24).[107] Section 3 cannot, however, be used to reach a result that is directly contrary to express statutory words. The courts have struggled to articulate the limits on when the section 3 interpretive obligation can be used, Lord Steyn remarking that:

> Like the proverbial elephant such a case ought generally to be easily identifiable. What is necessary, however, is to emphasise that interpretation under section 3(1) is the prime remedial remedy and that resort to section 4 must always be an exceptional course. In practical effect there is a strong rebuttable presumption in favour of an interpretation consistent with Convention rights.[108]

Lord Bingham in a later House of Lords case, *Sheldrake v DPP, Attorney General's Reference No 4 of 2004*, summarised what had been said in *Ghaidan v Godin-Mendoza* about the limit beyond which interpretation is not possible:

> … members of the committee used differing expressions: such an interpretation would be incompatible with the underlying thrust of the legislation, or would not go with the grain of it, or would call for legislative deliberation, or would change the substance of the provision completely, or would remove its pith and substance, or would violate a cardinal principle of the legislation (paras 33, 49, 110-113, 116).[109]

Although declarations of incompatibility are to be used only exceptionally, there are examples within housing law. In *R (Morris) v Westminster CC; R (Badu) v Lambeth LBC* the Court of Appeal declared section 185(4) of the Housing Act 1996 to be incompatible with Articles 8 and 14 as it denied the right to housing assistance to a British citizen on the basis of a dependent's immigration status.[110]

10.7 International Rights to Housing

This chapter has focused on the ECHR rights touching on property as these are now justiciable in the UK. There are, however, many other international conventions that recognise a right to housing in some form. The most important of these is the right contained in Article 11(1) of the International Covenant on Economic, Social and Cultural Rights (1966) (ICESCR):

> The States Parties to the present Covenant recognize the right of everyone to an adequate standard of living for himself and his family, including adequate food, clothing and housing, and to the continuous improvement of living conditions. The States Parties will take appropriate steps to ensure the realization of this right, recognizing to this effect the essential importance of international co-operation based on free consent.

The UK has ratified this Covenant, which means that the state is under an international obligation to comply with it, but it does not create rights that are directly enforceable by individual citizens. There is a draft optional protocol that will allow individuals to bring

---

[107] (2003) EWHC 1994 (Ch), [2004] Ch 142.
[108] *Ghaidan v Godin-Mendoza* [2004] UKHL 30, [2004] 2 AC 557 [50]. For further discussion of section 3, see A Kavanagh, 'The Elusive Divide between Interpretation and Legislation under the Human Rights Act 1998' (2004) 24 *OJLS* 259.
[109] [2004] UKHL 43, [2005] 1 AC 264 [28].
[110] [2005] EWCA Civ 1184, [2006] 1 WLR 505.

complaints about violations of their economic, social, and cultural rights to the attention of the UN Committee on Economic, Social & Cultural Rights (ICESCR) but this has not yet been adopted.[111]

What is of especial value in relation to this right is the adoption by the ICESCR of General Comment 4 on the Right to Adequate Housing.[112] This is the single most authoritative legal interpretation of what the right to housing means in legal terms under international law. It is quoted at some length below because it fleshes out what a right to housing entails and makes the point that for housing to be adequate it needs to be more than a roof over the head.

General Comment 4 on the Right to Adequate Housing

7. In the Committee's view, the right to housing should not be interpreted in a narrow or restrictive sense which equates it with, for example, the shelter provided by merely having a roof over one's head or views shelter exclusively as a commodity. Rather it should be seen as the right to live somewhere in security, peace and dignity. This is appropriate for at least two reasons. In the first place, the right to housing is integrally linked to other human rights and to the fundamental principles upon which the Covenant is premised. This 'the inherent dignity of the human person' from which the rights in the Covenant are said to derive requires that the term 'housing' be interpreted so as to take account of a variety of other considerations, most importantly that the right to housing should be ensured to all persons irrespective of income or access to economic resources. Secondly, the reference in article 11 (1) must be read as referring not just to housing but to adequate housing. As both the Commission on Human Settlements and the Global Strategy for Shelter to the Year 2000 have stated: 'Adequate shelter means … adequate privacy, adequate space, adequate security, adequate lighting and ventilation, adequate basic infrastructure and adequate location with regard to work and basic facilities – all at a reasonable cost'.

8. Thus the concept of adequacy is particularly significant in relation to the right to housing since it serves to underline a number of factors which must be taken into account in determining whether particular forms of shelter can be considered to constitute 'adequate housing' for the purposes of the Covenant. While adequacy is determined in part by social, economic, cultural, climatic, ecological and other factors, the Committee believes that it is nevertheless possible to identify certain aspects of the right that must be taken into account for this purpose in any particular context. They include the following:

(a) *Legal security of tenure* … Notwithstanding the type of tenure, all persons should possess a degree of security of tenure which guarantees legal protection against forced eviction, harassment and other threats …

(b) *Availability of services, materials, facilities and infrastructure* An adequate house must contain certain facilities essential for health, security, comfort and nutrition. All beneficiaries of the right to adequate housing should have sustainable access to natural and common resources, safe drinking water, energy for cooking, heating and lighting, sanitation and washing facilities, means of food storage, refuse disposal, site drainage and emergency services;

(c) *Affordability* Personal or household financial costs associated with housing should be at such a level that the attainment and satisfaction of other basic needs are not threatened or compromised. Steps should be taken by States parties to ensure that the percentage of hous-

---

[111] This is the Committee that monitors state compliance.

[112] CESCR, 'General Comment 4 on the Right to Adequate Housing (Art 11(1))' (United Nations, 13 December 1991).

ing-related costs is, in general, commensurate with income levels. States parties should establish housing subsidies for those unable to obtain affordable housing, as well as forms and levels of housing finance which adequately reflect housing needs. In accordance with the principle of affordability, tenants should be protected by appropriate means against unreasonable rent levels or rent increases ...

(d) *Habitability* Adequate housing must be habitable, in terms of providing the inhabitants with adequate space and protecting them from cold, damp, heat, rain, wind or other threats to health, structural hazards, and disease ...

(e) *Accessibility* Adequate housing must be accessible to those entitled to it. Disadvantaged groups must be accorded full and sustainable access to adequate housing resources. Thus, such disadvantaged groups as the elderly, children, the physically disabled, the terminally ill, HIV-positive individuals, persons with persistent medical problems, the mentally ill, victims of natural disasters, people living in disaster-prone areas and other groups should be ensured some degree of priority consideration in the housing sphere. Both housing law and policy should take fully into account the special housing needs of these groups ...

(f) *Location* Adequate housing must be in a location which allows access to employment options, health-care services, schools, child-care centres and other social facilities ...

(g) *Cultural adequacy* The way housing is constructed, the building materials used and the policies supporting these must appropriately enable the expression of cultural identity and diversity of housing ...

11. States parties must give due priority to those social groups living in unfavourable conditions by giving them particular consideration ...

In addition to the general right to adequate housing recognised by the ICESCR, a number of international treaties emphasise its importance to particular groups. All of those set out below have been ratified by the UK.

International Convention on the Elimination of All Forms of Racial Discrimination (1965), Article 5

... States Parties undertake to prohibit and to eliminate racial discrimination in all its forms and to guarantee the right of everyone, without distinction as to race, colour, or national or ethnic origin, to equality before the law, notably in the enjoyment of the following rights:

(e) Economic, social and cultural rights, in particular:...

(iii) The right to housing;...

Convention on the Elimination of All Forms of Discrimination against Women (1979) Article 14 (2)

States Parties shall take all appropriate measures to eliminate discrimination against women in rural areas in order to ensure, on a basis of equality of men and women, that they participate in and benefit from rural development and, in particular, shall ensure to such women the right:...

(h) To enjoy adequate living conditions, particularly in relation to housing, sanitation, electricity and water supply, transport and communications.

Convention on the Rights of the Child (1989) Article 27

1. States Parties recognize the right of every child to a standard of living adequate for the child's physical, mental, spiritual, moral and social development.

2. The parent(s) or others responsible for the child have the primary responsibility to secure, within their abilities and financial capacities, the conditions of living necessary for the child's development.

3. States Parties, in accordance with national conditions and within their means, shall take appropriate measures to assist parents and others responsible for the child to implement this right and shall in case of need provide material assistance and support programmes, particularly with regard to nutrition, clothing and housing.

Convention relating to the Status of Refugees (1951) Article 21
As regards housing, the Contracting States, in so far as the matter is regulated by laws or regulations or is subject to the control of public authorities, shall accord to refugees lawfully staying in their territory treatment as favourable as possible and, in any event, not less favourable than that accorded to aliens generally in the same circumstances.

There is an additional right to housing in Article 31 of the amended European Social Charter (1961)[113] but the revision that incorporates this right has not yet been ratified in the UK. It provides:

Article 31 – The Right to Housing
With a view to ensuring the effective exercise of the right to housing, the Parties undertake to take measures designed:

1.   to promote access to housing of an adequate standard;
2.   to prevent and reduce homelessness with a view to its gradual elimination;
3.   to make the price of housing accessible to those without adequate resources.

In the language of human rights a division is often made between civil and political rights on the one hand and socio-economic rights on the other. The right to housing is then placed in the category of socio-economic rights. Traditionally there has been a reluctance to make these kinds of rights judicially enforceable because of the complex resource implications. In some respects the division is artificial: it is hard for a person denied access to basic levels of human support to exercise civil and political rights. Further, the courts, as witnessed in the *Limbuela* judgment,[114] recognise that the failure to provide basic levels of support (effectively socio-economic rights) may reach such a level of deprivation that they are justiciable within the HRA 1998. In some jurisdictions socio-economic rights have been constitutionally protected. So, for example, in the South African constitution there is a recognised right of access to adequate housing,[115] and although in the *Grootboom* case the South African Constitutional Court accepted that this would not give a right to housing as such, it did find that the state's housing programme had failed to provide sufficient support for those in desperate need.[116] In the UK, the right to housing is something that is likely to be most effective at the political and policy level, the language of a right to housing has a rhetoric significance that is not translated into legal rights.

---

[113] The European Social Charter was adopted in Turin on 18 October 1961, revised and amended in 1996 to include Article 31 on the right to housing. State compliance with this Charter is monitored by the European Committee of Independent Experts.

[114] *R (Limbuela) v Secretary of State for the Home Department* [2005] UKHL 66, [2006] 1 AC 396.

[115] The Constitution of the Republic of South Africa Act 108 of 1996 s 26 provides that: '(1) Everyone has the right to have access to adequate housing. (2) The State must take reasonable legislative and other measures, within its available resources, to achieve the progressive realisation of this right. (3) No one may be evicted from their home, or have their home demolished, without an order of court made after considering all the relevant circumstances. No legislation may permit arbitrary evictions.'

[116] *Government of the Republic of South Africa v Grootboom* [2001] 1 SA 46 (CC).

PART FOUR

MANAGING THE RELATIONSHIP

Within the tenancy relationship, the way in which the property is managed will affect both parties to the relationship. For the tenant, property management will affect the manner in which the tenant is able to enjoy the property – whether as a home or as a business. Perhaps the most obvious aspect of property management is maintaining the condition of the property, but other things may be equally important to the tenant, particularly in a multi-occupied property. So, for example, the commercial success of a tenant of a retail unit in a shopping centre will be dependent upon good advertising of the centre, signposting, heating, cleaning, ensuring a good tenant mix, security and so on.

For the landlord, good property management is important to maintain rental income and increase the capital value of the reversion, especially in the commercial sector.

> Property management is very closely linked with property investment: it is very largely about the day-to-day administration of such investments, and is instrumental in realising the aspirations of the investor, ie, income growth, capital appreciation or the release of development potential.
>
> ...
>
> The best rents and rent increases will only be obtained if the tenants of the property are happy with the appearance and condition of the building, its location, and above all with the day-to-day running of the property.[1]

Rent-setting and rent-collection are important to property management; prompt and efficient rent collection may impact on the value of the reversionary interest. Good management is not only about economic returns, however. Residential landlords, particularly in the social sector, are involved not only in maintaining the value of the 'estate' but also in promoting safe and sustainable communities.

Not all aspects of property management are regulated by the tenancy agreement itself. Legislation (which includes more general legislative developments which impact upon leases, such as disability laws), and commercial and social concerns, will also influence behaviour and expectations. So, for example, ensuring that there is a good mix of tenants in a shopping centre is achieved primarily through matters external to the lease. The lease can set out what the tenant is allowed to use the property for, but the variety of tenants, the attractiveness of the tenants to the shopping public and the number of units occupied will be dependent upon the strength of the economy and property market at any time, and upon the allocation policy of the landlord.

---

[1] CJ Arnison, H Bibby and AD Mulquiney, *Commercial Property Management* (London, Shaw & Sons, 1990) xx and xxi.

The following six chapters address different aspects of management. Chapter 11 is concerned with broad issues of estate management and making management work. This is concerned not so much with the management of individual properties but with what might broadly be termed as collective management issues; involving tenants in management and protecting the wider environs in which an individual property is situate. This could mean managing shopping centres, looking after the shared areas of flats, and dealing with anti-social behaviour on housing estates. As will be seen, this raises a difficult, but crucial, question about the role of a landlord: to what extent can, and should, a landlord be required to carry any responsibility for the behaviour of its tenants? Chapter 12 looks at matters more traditionally associated with property management, especially looking after the physical state of the property. It considers who bears responsibility for carrying out the maintenance and repair of the property, who has to pay for the repair and maintenance, and what the required standard of repair is. The chapter additionally looks at the ability of a tenant to make physical changes to the property ('improvements'). The following chapter, chapter 13, covers how the property can be used, responsibility for insurance, and the recoverability of landlord costs through the service charge.

The final three chapters of this part all look at rent. Chapter 14 is a short chapter that introduces some of the issues relating to fixing the level of rent. In the commercial sector, rent setting has been left to the parties but in the rented homes sector there has been much regulation of rent setting in order to promote affordability. For this reason, chapter 15 looks only at issues that arise in relation to rents in the rented homes sector: the constraints that operate on a social landlord in setting rents, and tackling affordability issues through the imposition of rent controls and welfare payments. Chapter 16 looks at how leases provide for rents to be varied over time, and how landlords can protect against non-payment by taking rent deposits and guarantees.

11

MANAGING THE LEASEHOLD RELATIONSHIP

11.1   What is management?
11.2   Management and disability legislation
11.3   Leasehold estate management
11.4   Management and long residential leasehold
11.5   Managing anti-social behaviour
11.6   Landlords and third parties
11.7   Ensuring effective management
11.8   Disputes

11.1 What is Management?

11.1.1 Core Landlord Services

The phrase 'estate management' carries a variety of meanings. It can be used to refer to the management of an individual property, the 'core landlord functions', such as arranging maintenance and collecting rents. In this sense, all landlords are involved in leasehold management. In addition to management of individual properties, there are two further dimensions to 'estate management': looking after a bigger development, such as a shopping centre ('leasehold estate management'), and, in the context of social housing, having responsibility for the social environs in which the property is situated ('wider community management'). These are discussed further in the following sections.

The degree of the landlord's involvement in management will depend upon a number of factors. There will be very little management, for example, with a building lease sold for a capital sum. It is more usual, however, for the landlord to have some more active management role. Management begins with the selection of tenants for the property, taking up references, preparing tenancy agreements and receiving rental deposits (see chapter 16). Usually there will be a rent reserved under the lease, and collecting this will be one of the management functions. In addition, there is a day to day management role which will be concerned with ongoing repair and maintenance of the property, and, in the case of leasehold schemes, the provision of services, such as cleaning and security (see chapter 13). In longer leases, any alienation of the lease will usually require the landlord's consent to be given (see chapter 17).

Property also has to be managed when things go wrong, not only doing things such as fixing leaky pipes and so on, but also dealing with tenants who are in breach of their leasehold terms. Later chapters discuss in more detail the ability of landlords to end leases; but this chapter looks at how the power to evict tenants is used as a management tool.

The 'standard' of management will also vary. The landlord will be under certain legal obligations, set out in the contract and in statute. In addition to these legal duties, the landlord's approach to management will be influenced by his 'ethos' as a landlord and by financial considerations. With long residential and commercial property, management is likely to be at the tenant's expense as the lease will usually provide for the tenant to pay the costs of management in the form of a service charge, in addition to the rent. In contrast, as short residential tenancies do not usually contain service charge provisions any repairs etc will reduce the landlord's net income.

Both capital and income returns may be affected by the quality of management. High quality management is likely to increase the value of the landlord's reversion and may be reflected in higher rents where there is strong demand for property. In areas of low demand, however, the standard of management may have little impact on rents receivable as there may not be tenants willing (or able) to pay a higher rent.[1]

In recent years, a discourse has emerged in relation to the private rental sector that distinguishes between the 'many good and well-intentioned landlords' and 'a small minority of private landlords [who] set out to exploit their tenants and the community at large in flagrant disregard of the law'.[2] Cowan and McDermont argue that this:

> … dividing strategy has both moral and ethical overtones. The regulatory strategies proposed for each group diverge sharply. For the former [the 'good' landlords], the hallmarks of etho-politics – responsible self-government, community regulation and self-policing (voluntary licensing, accreditation, kite marks) – are appropriate. For the latter [the 'bad' landlords], an array of more intrusive, disciplinary regulation is prescribed – licensing, housing benefit restrictions, risk-based regulation of property quality.[3]

This discourse has undoubtedly influenced recent approaches to regulation of the private rental market. Not all of the 'intrusive' measures mentioned by Cowan and McDermont are, however, wholly 'disciplinary'. For example, there is now licensing of houses in multiple occupation (HMOs) but this is justified by reference to risk, rather than being a disciplinary measure for bad landlords only.[4]

11.1.2 Leasehold Estate Management

Perhaps the most common understanding of estate management in the landlord and tenant context relates to the management of an area let on individual leases that form part of a

---

[1] For discussion of the correlation between rents and management standards, see ch 12.

[2] DETR, *Quality and Choice: A Decent Home for All-The Housing Green Paper* (April 2000) para 5.4. See also D Cowan and M McDermont, *Regulating Social Housing, Governing Decline* (Abingdon, Routledge-Cavendish, 2006) 151–55; S Blandy, 'Housing standards in the private rented sector and the three Rs: regulation, responsibility and rights' in D Cowan and A Marsh (eds), *Two Steps Forward* (Bristol, The Policy Press, 2001).

[3] D Cowan and M McDermont, *Regulating Social Housing, Governing Decline* (Abingdon, Routledge-Cavendish, 2006) 152.

[4] See ch 12. But the selective licensing scheme is closer to a disciplinary model.

common scheme, and in which there is sharing of the common parts of the 'estate'. Typically, this would cover the renting of shopping malls, office blocks, industrial and retail parks, and residential blocks of flats. Historically, there were also large tracts of residential land on which leasehold houses were built, with the landlord undertaking to manage the estate and the communal facilities on payment of a service charge. With the enactment of enfranchisement laws (see chapter 25) this latter use has fallen away. In this chapter, estate management in this sense will, for convenience, be referred to as 'leasehold estate management'. The content of the landlord's responsibilities for leasehold estate management will be largely regulated by the terms of the leasehold contract negotiated between the landlord and the tenant.

11.1.3 Wider Community Management

The final dimension to estate management is somewhat more nebulous, and focuses upon the responsibilities of social landlords. While private landlords (commercial and residential) have largely been able to manage in a 'self interested' fashion, subject only to statutory and contractual obligations, the role of social landlords is more complex. Until the Housing Act 1980, there were few legal mechanisms controlling the exercise of local authorities housing management powers as it was widely thought that they could be 'trusted … to exercise their powers in a public spirited and fair way in the general public interest'.[5] In practice, the relative absence of tenant rights gave local authority landlords a fairly free hand to do as they wished in the name of the 'general public interest'. The main constraints stemmed from controls exercised by central government through the financial regime. As seen in earlier chapters, local authorities have often preferred to let to respectable working class families rather than the poorest and most vulnerable members of society, as this makes the job of management easier. A purely welfarist role was forced upon local authorities by central government control of subsidies. The legal framework changed with the introduction of security of tenure in 1980 which meant that decisions to evict needed to be justified before a court. Further, the residualisation of social housing and the declining quality of local authority housing stock has led to an expansion of the managerial role of social landlords and greater use of housing management to achieve social control. As Burney explains in *Crime and Banishment*, there has always been an element of social control in the management of social housing, both in relation to access to housing and in relation to the behaviour of tenants once housed.[6] The early philanthropists involved with the housing association movement often saw housing management as concerned with moral education and teaching occupiers how to be good tenants. Whilst it is not the case, therefore, that using housing management as a form of social control is new, there has been a change in the legal landscape so that what might have historically been a 'moral mission' is now embedded into the legal and regulatory framework. Further, it is no longer advice about how to manage a home and good housekeeping that is doled out, but social control has now become akin to 'crime control'.

There has also been a shift in thinking about management as primarily to do with

---

[5] *Shelley v London CC* [1948] 1 KB 274 (CA) 283.

[6] E Burney, *Crime and Banishment: Nuisance and Exclusion in Social Housing* (Winchester, Waterside Press, 1999), esp ch 2. See also D Cowan and M McDermont, *Regulating Social Housing, Governing Decline* (Abingdon, Routledge-Cavendish, 2006), passim.

looking after lettings and individual properties, to seeing management by social landlords as including the management of communities, what is referred to in the Cave Review as 'place-shaping'.[7] Concern over the decline in the quality of the environment in areas with significant amounts of social housing has led to both legal and political obligations being imposed, in particular on local authority landlords, to become involved with managing the wider neighbourhood. The width of responsibilities is shown by the 'key lines of enquiry' (KLE) used by the Housing Inspectorate (part of the Audit Commission) to carry out service inspections. In addition to the traditional role of tenancy management (such as lettings, tenancy sign up, rent collection and rent arrears, repairs and – more recently – tenant consultation) the KLE also cover 'estate' management, including ways of dealing with anti-social behaviour, caretaking of common areas, neighbourhood renewal, resident involvement, with the likely of addition of delivering 'respect' through housing management.[8]

This transformation of the role of social landlords (which is beginning to show some creepage also into the rented private sector) is significant on many levels. It expands what a landlord is required to do considerably beyond the maintenance of the built environment. The scope of management is no longer almost exclusively property centred: there is a responsibility in relation to people and communities as well as buildings. Nor is the source of responsibility primarily to be found in the contractual relationship between the leasehold parties (contrasting with the position in relation to commercial and agricultural tenancies, and to a lesser extent private sector tenancies). To some extent, this may have come about from the dual roles of local authorities as both landlord and a branch of local government. Under the Local Government Act 2000 local authorities have a duty to prepare 'community strategies' for promoting or improving the economic, social and environmental well-being of their areas.[9] There is also a duty – in partnership with the police and others – to produce and implement a strategy for the reduction of crime and disorder.[10] Both of these duties show that local authorities are expected to perform a strategic role in the functioning of communities. While these duties are placed on them qua local authorities, many more legal duties have been placed upon them specifically because they are landlords. The same kind of duties have also been rolled out into the housing association sector.

This expansion of management roles brings major challenges. Landlord and tenant law is no longer only concerned with the private law relationship between the landlord and tenant but, at least in the case of social housing, forms part of a much bigger legal canvas. Whilst the aim is to make the community a better place to live in, there is a risk that these wider management roles stretch landlords too far. A survey by the Tenant Involvement Commission into 'What Tenants Want' conducted for the National Housing Federation confirms that what housing association tenants want first and foremost is for landlords to 'get the basics right':

---

[7] M Cave, 'Every Tenant Matters: A review of social housing regulation' (June 2007). The earlier call for evidence referred to this wider role as 'landlord plus services': Cave Review of Social Housing Regulation, 'Independent review of regulation of social housing: A call for evidence' (DCLG, December 2006).

[8] As part of the Labour government's 'Respect' agenda. See ODPM, 'A Respect Standard for Housing Management: Consultation Paper' (April 2006).

[9] S 4.

[10] Crime and Disorder Act 1998 s 6.

Fundamentally, housing associations should provide a home fit to live in, collect rent and carry out maintenance work. Before considering broadening the scope beyond this, tenants say that housing associations must first do well at delivering core housing services ...

A good basic level of service is perceived as:

— commitment to delivering a quality service;
— competent and polite service from front-line delivery staff;
— speedy repairs completed to a high standard;
— listening to tenants;
— security;
— affordable rent.[11]

11.2 Management and Disability Legislation

The disability discrimination legislation has a considerable impact on the management of tenanted property. The Disability Discrimination Act 1995 has already been extensively amended since its initial enactment – there are numerous regulations relating to it, and codes of practice have been issued by the Disability Rights Commission. What follows is an outline of its impact but for detailed commentary the reader should refer to specialist texts.

Disability is not confined to mobility problems but by section 1 covers any:

... physical or mental impairment which has a substantial and long-term adverse effect on ... [a person's] ability to carry out normal day-to-day activities.

In terms of tenancy management the legislation can therefore affect not only things such as the installation of wheelchair ramps,[12] but clearer signage or removal of hazards for those with poor eyesight, and audible devices for the hard of hearing. It can also have a significant impact on eviction when a tenant is mentally impaired.

Under the Disability Discrimination Act 1995, sections 24C and D, landlords and managers of both commercial and residential property may be under a duty to tenants and other lawful occupiers of tenanted property who are disabled to 'provide an auxiliary aid or service' or to change a 'practice, policy or procedure' if, without that aid/service or change, it is 'impossible or unreasonably difficult' for the disabled person to take a letting of the property or to enjoy the premises or use a benefit or facility conferred with the lease. The duty is to 'take such steps as it is reasonable, in all the circumstances' to take, but does not extend to the removal or alteration of a physical feature.[13] The kind of changes that might be reasonable would be a clip-on receiver that vibrates when a doorbell rings that would assist a tenant with a hearing impediment, or allowing a tenant who has mobility difficulties to leave his rubbish somewhere other than the usual designated place if access is difficult. It remains unclear, however, exactly how far these positive duties go. In *Richmond Court (Swansea) Ltd v Williams*, a case decided on the old law (where there was a duty not to discriminate but no positive duties were placed on the controllers of premises) the Court of

---

[11] Tenant Involvement Commission, 'What Tenants Want: Report of the Tenant Involvement Commission' (National Housing Federation, 2006) ch 2.
[12] Physical adaptations are discussed in ch 12.
[13] Disability Discrimination Act 1995 s 24E.

Appeal held that there was no discrimination when the landlord refused to install a stair lift in the common parts for a mobility impaired leaseholder.[14] The cost of the installation would have been covered by a disability grant and the leaseholder offered that the premises would be reinstated when she left her flat. Whether the positive duty to provide auxiliary aids or services would now require the landlord to agree to a stair lift being installed in similar circumstances is unclear. As mentioned, the positive duty does not – at present – extend to the alteration or removal of a physical feature, and although there are Regulations[15] (and a Code of Practice) fleshing out what this means it is not clear whether the installation of a stair lift would be covered. The government proposes to clarify this in the case of residential lettings so that:

> Where a disabled person finds it impossible or unreasonably difficult to use the common parts of their let residential premises, the landlord should be under a duty to make a disability-related alteration to the common parts, where reasonable, and at the disabled person's expense (including any reasonable maintenance costs).[16]

These adjustments will only be necessary if the landlord or manager receives a request from the tenant or prospective tenant. They do not apply to premises which are, or have been at any time, the principal or only home of the landlord or manager[17] or if the property comes within the 'small premises' exemption.[18] When the duties do apply, failure to comply will be unlawful unless there is justification, which by section 24(K) means either that in the controller's reasonable opinion compliance would endanger the health or safety of any person, or that the disabled person is incapable of entering into an agreement or giving informed consent.

In practice, many social landlords make a wide range of adjustments for disabled tenants, beyond those required by the statutory duties. Fewer private sector residential landlords are aware of the disability legislation or consider it is likely to apply to them.[19]

Section 24F makes it unlawful to victimise the tenant, for example by evicting him or increasing his rent (but not the rent of others in comparable positions) because of costs incurred in connection with making any adjustments for the disability.

Public authorities are subject to additional duties that include the need to take steps to take account of disabled persons' disabilities, even where that involves treating disabled persons more favourably than other persons.[20] The meaning given to public authorities is very wide ('any person certain of whose functions are functions of a public nature')

---

[14] [2006] EWCA Civ 1719. As none of the reasons for refusing consent related to the tenant's disability there had been no act of discrimination against her. The tenant could not have been said to be have been treated any less favourably than any comparator is since it was clear that all tenants would have been treated in the same way.

[15] The Disability Discrimination (Premises) Regulations 2006 SI 2006/887.

[16] DCLG, 'Discrimination Law Review: A Framework for Fairness. Proposals for a Single Equality Bill for Great Britain' (Consultation paper, June 2007) para 13.2. This proposal is subject to views expressed in response to the consultation.

[17] Disability Discrimination Act 1995 s 24H.

[18] Disability Discrimination Act 1995 s 24B(3) and (4), 24H (3) and (4). Broadly, this is where the landlord or manager lives on the property and there are no more than six occupiers, or the premises do not contain accommodation was on to other households.

[19] J Aston, D Hill and C Williams, 'Landlords' responses to the Disability Discrimination Act' (DWP, Research Report 429, 2007).

[20] Disability Discrimination Act 1995 s 49A.

and, as well as local authority landlords, could include a number of non-local authority landlords.[21]

11.3 Leasehold Estate Management

11.3.1 The Importance of Good Leasehold Estate Management

A well drafted management scheme is important whenever there are shared facilities, to ensure that they are properly maintained and looked after. This includes not only horizontally divided property, such as residential blocks of flats and office blocks, but also where there are stand-alone units, such as industrial parks with landscaped areas and a shared access road. The scheme will need to make clear who has responsibility for cleaning and maintenance, and how the costs are to be paid for. In the case of serviced accommodation, the landlord may charge one fee to cover both the rental element and all maintenance costs. Commonly, however, there will be separate provision for payment of a variable service charge under which the landlord is able to recover the costs of servicing the leasehold units (see chapter 13).

In the context of commercial lettings, leasehold management goes well beyond selecting the tenant and responsibility for the fabric of the property. Good estate management is important for the prosperity of commercial developments, both for tenants and for landlords. A shopping mall, for example, will need to be proactively managed in order for the complex to continue to attract a large footfall.[22] As shopping trends change it may, for example, be necessary to refurbish and renovate the centre to remain popular with the shopping public. It will also be necessary to ensure that entrance ways are kept clear, external surfaces are not covered with posters and graffiti, and that access routes are clean and attractive. A well drafted lease will impose management obligations on the landlord but will also contain covenants to regulate tenant behaviour, such as:

> … not to affix upon any part of the exterior of the demised premises or in any windows a signboard, poster, facia, placard or advertisement except as may previously have been approved by the lessors.[23]

> … To keep the display windows, if any, of the demised unit dressed and illuminated in a suitable manner in keeping with a good class shopping centre unless prevented by matters or circumstances beyond the tenant's reasonable control and to keep the windows of those parts of the demised unit which are used for storage purposes obscured to the satisfaction of the landlord.[24]

In addition to specific leasehold covenants it is common to reserve general powers to

---

[21] Disability Discrimination Act 1995 s 49B; and The Disability Discrimination (Public Authorities) (Statutory Duties) Regulations 2005 SI 2005/2966. For the meaning of functions of a public nature in the context of human rights law, see ch 10.

[22] Footfall counts the number of pedestrians entering the space, and is used as a measure of the popularity of retail areas.

[23] As in *Bristol and West Building Society v Marks and Spencer plc* [1991] 2 EGLR 57 (Ch).

[24] As in *F W Woolworth plc v Charlwood Alliance Properties Ltd* [1987] 1 EGLR 53 (Ch).

make management regulations from time to time which can deal with every day matters of management, such as refuse collection.

Good estate management also requires a careful letting policy. It will be important to secure a good mix of tenants and to ensure that any voids are filled as quickly as possible. Surveys of shopping habits have found that the range of shops available within a shopping mall is a very important factor in determining where consumers choose to shop, second only to the importance of its location.[25] Critical to the success of most shopping complexes will be the presence of an anchor tenant – in *Transworld Land Co Ltd v J Sainsbury plc*, Sainsbury's was the anchor tenant in a shopping centre that was no longer a prime site.[26] When Sainsbury's closed its store, the trade of the other retail units in the centre fell off by up to 50 per cent. To secure the vitality the centre, it is common to impose a covenant requiring a tenant to keep the shop open during normal business hours.[27] This will be broken not only by a shop that does not stay open for these hours, but also if the shop ceases trading. What the landlord requires (as well as other tenants) is for the shop to remain open; in practice, however, securing this is very difficult if the tenant would prefer to close the shop down (see chapter 13).

11.3.2 Contractual Duties

The management obligations of the landlord or management company will be set out in the leasehold contract.[28] Frequently the landlord will covenant to 'use reasonable endeavours to provide' listed services 'in accordance with the principles of good estate management'. The services may cover such things as repair, cleaning, servicing of lifts, supply of utilities, the provision of signs, refuse collection, and the provision of security staff.

In addition to the express management obligations there may be an obligation to manage pro-actively that stems from the express or implied covenants of quiet enjoyment and non derogation from grant (see also chapter 4). Although historically used to restrain a landlord from doing anything that interfered with the grant to the tenant, it is now acknowledged that in certain situations these covenants may impose a duty to act on a landlord. This was seen in *Chartered Trust Plc v Davies*.[29] A small shopping mall of five units was marketed as being for 'high-class retail outlets', but was not a success. An empty unit was let as a pawn-broking business but this led to some undesirable people hanging around in the mall outside the claimant's shop. Eventually his business failed. The Court of Appeal held that the landlord was under a duty to control the nuisance caused by the pawnbroker's business, the source of the duty being found in the covenant not to derogate from grant.[30] In explaining the reason why the landlord had to act, Henry LJ states:

---

[25] M Ford, 'Breathing New Life into Ailing Shopping Centres' [1994] 4 *Property Rev* 116, 117.

[26] [1990] 2 EGLR 255 (Ch).

[27] This will not require it to keep open on a Sunday unless specifically required by the lease: Sunday Trading Act 1994 s 3.

[28] Sometimes a management company is included as a party to the lease and undertakes the obligations to provide services.

[29] (1998) 76 P & CR 396 (CA).

[30] As explained by Hart J in *Petra Investments Ltd v Jeffrey Rogers PLC* (2001) 81 P & CR 21 (Ch) [51].

... the nature of the grant to a large measure depended upon the proper management of the shopping mall, and the common parts thereof. This development was marketed as a shopping mall, was legally set up in a way which gave the landlord rule-making powers in relation to the development, and the tenants were charged a service charge to finance the necessary management. Proper management might, in appropriate cases, require the provision of security, whether men or cameras, to police the mall. Here it may be that determined use of the rule-making powers to preserve the shared rights of way over the common parts would have sufficed. Instead the landlords did nothing.

... There must come a point where the landlord becomes legally obliged to take action to protect that which he has granted to his tenant ... Where a landlord is granting leases in his shopping mall, over which he has maintained control, and charged a service charge therefor, it is simply no answer to say that a tenant's sole protection is his own ability and willingness to bring his individual action. Litigation is too expensive, too uncertain and offers no proper protection against, say, trespassing and threatening members of the public. The duty to act should lie with the landlord.

... the landlords could have acted to stop the pawnbroker's clientele queuing in the access and, if necessary, could have cleared the tables and chairs obstructing that access. Then the back shops might have had a chance. This could have been done either directly under the lease, enforcing the covenant against causing a nuisance, or by making rules ensuring that the passageway was kept clear. ... Instead, the landlords prevaricated and did nothing. They could have acted effectively and they should have done so. Instead they chose to do nothing, and thereby made the premises materially less fit for the purpose for which they were let. In failing to act to stop the nuisance, in my judgment, the landlords continued the nuisance and derogated from their grant.[31]

In *Petra Investments Ltd v Jeffrey Rogers PLC* Hart J began to explore the extent of this duty.[32] The complaint in this case again related to a shopping mall marketed as a speciality shopping centre. Again, the centre struggled and its character changed as Gap and, later, Virgin Megastore took large units, necessitating physical changes to be made to the centre. The defendant's business struggled and, in a claim for rent and service charge arrears, it counterclaimed that there had been a repudiatory breach based on the duty not to derogate from grant. Hart J accepted that this imposed limits on the extent to which the landlord could change the character of the mall but stated clearly that this did not mean that:

... the landlord had assumed a general responsibility not to do anything in the exercise of its reserved powers which might cause damage to the businesses of its tenants. To do so would not be to show proper respect for the complete absence of any such obligation in the express provisions of the lease entered into between parties of equal bargaining power.[33]

It did, however, mean that:

... the landlord was under a duty when exercising those rights and powers to take account of the expectations of its existing lessees.[34]

On the facts, while the changes made to the centre could possibly have amounted to a

[31] (1998) 76 P & CR 396 (CA) 408–9.
[32] (2001) 81 P & CR 21 (Ch).
[33] (2001) 81 P & CR 21 (Ch) [53].
[34] (2001) 81 P & CR 21 (Ch) [53].

derogation, the defendant had, with full knowledge of the proposed works, accepted a reduction in service charges in full and final settlement of any claim that they may have had in that respect.

In a much earlier Court of Appeal decision, *Malzy v Eicholz*, a landlord was held not liable to the complaining tenant for nuisance committed during the holding of mock auctions by the licensee of another tenant, even though the landlord had not taken reasonable steps to end the nuisance.[35] What distinguishes these cases is the managerial role expected of the landlord: in *Chartered Trust plc v Davies* Henry LJ had mentioned that the crucial factual distinction from *Malzy* was that in the case before him 'the nature of the grant to a large measure depended upon proper management of the shopping mall and the common parts thereof'.[36] For this reason, it is less likely that there will be a duty to act in lettings of single units where the landlord has no responsibility to manage common parts, even if the landlord does have power to act to stop the nuisance stemming from some capacity other than being the common landlord.[37] That is not to say that the landlord will *never* be found in breach of duty in such a case. In *Yankwood v Havering*, for example, land had been let by the Council for use as an Equestrian Centre and the lessees were also granted the right to use nearby bridle paths.[38] Various activities on adjoining Council land caused substantial interference with the Equestrian Centre and use of the bridle paths, leading Neuberger J to find that there had been a derogation from grant. In each case what needs to be determined is the nature of the grant to the tenant and what was contemplated by the parties at the time of the grant.

11.3.3 *Controlling Access to Leasehold Property*

It is common nowadays for large parts of town centres to be developed under a leasehold structure, perhaps with the local authority exercising compulsory purchase powers to acquire a large area of land which it then lets to a property developer for the construction of a shopping centre. The completed leasehold development will then be rented to individual retail units holders. In this manner, significant areas of 'public space' will in fact be privately owned even though they may contain public buildings, such as job centres and libraries. To date, the courts have maintained that as this is private land the owner is able to control access to it. Subject to complying with race relations legislation and disability laws, the landlord is entitled to exclude access to members of the public, as where the owner excluded an environmental group seeking signatures for a petition[39] and youths alleged to be a nuisance.[40]

---

[35] [1916] 2 KB 308 (CA).

[36] (1998) 76 P & CR 396 (CA) 409.

[37] A local authority landlord would, for example, have power to act against nuisance creators on a housing estate by issuing injunctions, etc, even though the landlord had no responsibility to manage 'common parts'.

[38] *Yankwood Ltd v London Borough of Havering* (Ch 6 May 1998).

[39] *Appleby v United Kingdom* (App No 44306/98) (2003) 37 EHRR 38.

[40] *CIN Properties Ltd v Rawlins* [1995] 2 EGLR 130 (CA). The excluded youths argued before the European Commission on Human Rights (in *Anderson v United Kingdom* (App No 44958/98) (1998) 25 EHRR CD 172) that this exclusion breached their right to peaceful assembly under Art 11. This was rejected. The youths had no history of using the centre for organised assembly, and Art 11 did not guarantee a right to pass and re-pass in public places, or to assemble for social purposes. Further, the Commission noted that Protocol No 4 to the ECHR, Art 2 of which guarantees the right to liberty of movement within a State, has not been ratified by the UK.

Members of the public have access to the shopping centre under an implied licence from the owner, but this can be revoked at will.[41]

In *Appleby v United Kingdom*[42] the environmental campaigners complained to the European Court of Human Rights (ECtHR) that their exclusion breached their rights to freedom of expression and freedom of peaceful assembly contained in Articles 10 and 11 of the European Convention for the Protection of Human Rights and Fundamental Freedoms (ECHR).[43] They argued that the State was directly responsible, as a public corporation had built the shopping centre and a minister had approved the transfer into private ownership, but the ECtHR did not accept that State responsibility arose from this. In addition, it was argued that the State had a positive obligation to secure the exercise of their rights. On the facts, the ECtHR took the view that as the campaigners had alternative outlets to exercise their rights, there was no violation. The outcome might be different if the 'entire municipality was controlled by a private body' as the ban would then prevent 'any effective exercise of freedom of expression'.[44] In applying the 'fair balance' approach the Court took account also of 'the property rights of the owner of the shopping centre under Article 1 of Protocol 1'.[45]

It may be that the extremity of this position will, over time, be eroded. In a partly dissenting opinion, Judge Maruste in *Appleby v United Kingdom* states:

> [The] area in its functional nature and essence is … 'quasi-public' … [The] applicants … had justified expectations of being able to use the area as a public gathering area … It is in the public interest to permit reasonable exercise of individual rights and freedoms, including the freedoms of speech and assembly on the property of a privately owned shopping centre, and not to make some public services and institutions inaccessible to the public and participants in demonstrations. The Court has consistently held that if there is a conflict between rights and freedoms, the freedom of expression takes precedence. But in this case it appears to be the other way round—property rights prevailed over freedom of speech.[46]

Of course, this dissent was couched in this way to reflect the particular rights being challenged. Given the approach taken by the ECtHR, it seems unlikely that a right of access will be found through human rights law. It may, however, be that the common law itself will be incrementally developed to curtail an owner's exclusory powers. The Court of Appeal accepted that this was a possibility in *Porter v Commissioner of Police of the Metropolis*,[47] referring to the argument by Gray and Gray that, in line with a trend in other common law jurisdictions, the law should be developed so that an owner of quasi-public space may exclude members of the public from those premises only on grounds which are objectively reasonable and rationally communicable.[48]

---

[41] *Appleby v United Kingdom* (App No 44306/98) (2003) 37 EHRR 38; *CIN Properties Ltd v Rawlins* [1995] 2 EGLR 130 (CA).

[42] (App No 44306/98) (2003) 37 EHRR 38.

[43] For a discussion of the law on human rights, see ch 10.

[44] (App no 44306/98) (2003) 37 EHRR 38 [47].

[45] (App no 44306/98) (2003) 37 EHRR 38 [43].

[46] (App no 44306/98) (2003) 37 EHRR 38.

[47] [1999] All ER (D) 1129 (CA).

[48] K Gray and S Gray, 'Civil Rights, Civil Wrongs and Quasi-Public Space' [1999] EHRLR 46. See also K Gray and S Gray, *Elements of Land Law* 4th edn (Oxford, OUP, 2005) 287–93; T Allen, *Property and the Human Rights Act 1998* (Oxford, Hart, 2005) 219–23. For a contrary view, see D Radlett and Y Luo, 'Hoodies out … or in?' (2006) 156 *NLJ* 1501.

This question as to whether there should be public access to 'quasi-public space' is not a matter confined to leasehold developments. Nonetheless, given that many modern retail areas will be developed on leasehold basis with shared access ways, the issue is most likely to arise in this context. Further, there are private law dimensions to this question which have not been explored in the case law. Roberts points out that tenants of retail units in a shopping centre will usually be granted an easement of access, for themselves and their invitees, and it is doubtful that the landlord, as owner of the servient tenement has the power to exclude visitors, at least without the consent of all tenants.[49] Thus, the law of easements may provide the opportunity for the incremental development of the common law hinted at in *Porter v Commissioner of Police of the Metropolis*.[50]

11.4 Management and Long Residential Leasehold

11.4.1 The Problems with Long Leaseholds

Managing property with multiple occupiers and shared facilities is seldom easy as occupiers may have differing requirements as to standards of management, and different financial resources available to them. The problems can, however, be particularly acute in the case of long residential leaseholds. It is not only 'private' leaseholders affected. Many council tenants living in flats who have exercised the right to buy (RTB) find themselves long leaseholders with a reluctant local authority as landlord.[51] Often these flats are situated in ageing tower blocks that require expensive repairs.

The lease is likely to be the leaseholder's main financial asset, as well as being 'home'. This means that leaseholders will care deeply about how it is managed. With modern leasehold developments, the freehold reversion is often transferred by the developer to a body controlled by the leaseholders, but even when management is in the hands of the lease-holders there can be bitter disputes. How frequently the windows are cleaned, or the colour the hallway is painted, can be very divisive issues, and ones upon which each leaseholder may wish to express an opinion. In developments where the freehold is retained by the developer landlord or sold to an outsider as an investment, management problems are common. Management is then outside the hands of the leaseholders, which not only reduces the extent to which they can have a say in decision-making but can also provide an opportunity for exploitation as the landlord seeks to make a profit through management. As Clarke writes, the potential abuses are well known:

> These may include: exorbitant fees for notices or services; excessive interest charges on ground rent arrears; insurance policies selected to maximise the commission payable to the freeholder;

---

[49] N Roberts, 'Access to Quasi-Public Spaces – Whose Visitor?' [2007] 71 *Conv* 235 who argues that: 'If some tenants refuse to revoke the implied licence to visit their units, then the Landlord would be entitled to apply to the court to order the owner of the unit to withhold his licence. The wishes of an individual tenant could be overruled only if reasonable cause were shown.' (237).

[50] [1999] All ER (D) 1129 (CA).

[51] Around 200,000 according to M Davey, 'Long Residential Leases: Past and Present' in S Bright (ed), *Landlord and Tenant Law. Past, Present and Future* (Oxford, Hart, 2006) 163.

repair and maintenance work being done (often at a shoddy standard) at high cost by firms that are part of (or intimately linked to) the freeholder's empire; and, the early recourse to forfeiture proceedings in the hope of getting one or two windfall terminations.[52]

There can be further difficulties caused by defective lease drafting, or by a landlord who simply aimed to make money from selling the leases but who has no continuing interest in managing the property. Problems in this sector highlighted by the Nugee Committee[53] included poor communications, lack of say in the appointment of managing agents, and inadequate provision of information. There have been several measures passed to try and tackle the problems.

11.4.2 The Landlord and Tenant Act 1987

The Landlord and Tenant Act 1987 contained various measures designed to help tackle management difficulties. First, where the premises contain two or more flats the tenant is able to apply to a leasehold valuation tribunal for the appointment of a manager where a landlord is in breach of a management obligation in the tenancy or has failed to comply with a prescribed code of management practice (see 11.7.1 below). A manager will be appointed if the tribunal considers it 'just and convenient to make the order in the circumstances of the case'.[54] In practice, a study reporting in 1991 found that the cost of obtaining an order was often prohibitive and the appointment of a manager was perceived as a mere stop-gap on the way to the tenants obtaining the freehold under the 1987 Act.[55] Second, Part III of the Act gives long leaseholders the right to acquire the landlord's interest when the appointment of a manager has not worked or there is a breach of the management obligation in the tenancy which is likely to continue.[56] Third, Part IV of the Act gives the court power to vary the provisions of a lease if 'the lease fails to make satisfactory provision with respect to' repair, maintenance, insurance or service charges.[57] The Act has not been effective. Davey writes:

> Unfortunately the Act, which passed into law after very little debate, has since become an object lesson in bad drafting, and has had severe critical comment showered on it by the courts and commentators. [For instance, see: *Belvedere Court Management Ltd v Frogmore Developments Ltd* [1997] QB 858 (CA)].
>
> The difficulties exposed by the Act were symptomatic of much of the regulatory framework designed to combat landlord abuse. Its provisions were weak, it contained insufficient

---

[52] D Clarke, 'Long Residential Leases: Future Directions' in S Bright (ed), *Landlord and Tenant Law. Past, Present and Future* (Oxford, Hart, 2006) 179. See also the stories reported in I Cole and D Robinson, 'Owners yet Tenants: The Position of Leaseholders in Flats in England and Wales' (2000) 15 *Housing Studies* 595.

[53] Nugee Committee, 'Report of the Committee of Enquiry on the Management of Privately Owned Blocks of Flats' (London, 1985).

[54] Landlord and Tenant Act 1987 ss 21 and 25. The initial wording, before amendment by the Housing Act 1996, applied only if the tenant could show that the breach was likely to continue. The 1996 Act also moved the jurisdiction from the court to the leasehold valuation tribunal, where costs tend to be lower.

[55] A Thomas and others, *The Landlord and Tenant Act 1987: Awareness, Experience and Impact* (DoE, 1991) para 4.8. This study was carried out before the 1996 amendments, transferring jurisdiction to the leasehold valuation tribunal.

[56] Landlord and Tenant Act 1987 s 29. See ch 25.

[57] S 35.

anti-avoidance measures, and the penalties for non-compliance were so weak that the Act was largely ignored by landlords.[58]

11.4.3 The Right to Manage (RTM)

The Commonhold and Leasehold Reform Act 2002 has made further changes, introducing a 'no fault' right to manage.[59] The rights under the Landlord and Tenant Act 1987 could be exercised only if the landlord was failing to exercise its management obligations properly. The RTM enables leaseholders to take over the 'management functions' of the property without any fault on the part of the landlord, and without payment of any compensation to the landlord. This is done through the vehicle of a RTM company (a company limited by guarantee)[60] and ownership of the reversionary title is unaffected (which means that the landlord is still entitled to the ground rent). The details of the statutory RTM are complex, and Davey observes that leaseholders will need 'to be well organised and professionally advised' in order to assume the RTM.[61] The RTM arises only if the premises qualify and if there is support from a sufficient number of tenants. A number of terms need further explanation.

11.4.3.1 The Premises

Section 72 provides:

> (1) This Chapter [the RTM] applies to premises if –
> (a) they consist of a self-contained building or part of a building,[62] with or without appurtenant property,
> (b) they contain two or more flats held by qualifying tenants, and
> (c) the total number of flats held by such tenants is not less than two-thirds of the total number of flats contained in the premises.

A tenant qualifies 'if he is tenant of the flat under a long lease', that is a lease 'granted for a term of years exceeding 21 years'.[63] The building is excluded if more than 25 per cent of the internal floor area is non-residential, or if there is a resident landlord and no more than four units, or if the local authority is the landlord 'of any of the qualifying tenants'.[64]

The effect of these various provisions is that the RTM applies only to buildings that are predominantly residential, with most of the flats being long leasehold, and with a private landlord. Although the focus is on predominantly residential property, a tenant does not have to be resident in order to qualify, nor is there any limit on the number of flats that an individual tenant can own.

---

[58] M Davey, 'Long Residential Leases: Past and Present' in S Bright (ed), *Landlord and Tenant Law. Past, Present and Future* (Oxford, Hart, 2006) 162.

[59] Commonhold and Leasehold Reform Act 2002 ss 71–113.

[60] Commonhold and Leasehold Reform Act 2002 s 73.

[61] M Davey, 'Long Residential Leases: Past and Present' in S Bright (ed), *Landlord and Tenant Law. Past, Present and Future* (Oxford, Hart, 2006) 168.

[62] Further defined in s 72(2)-(5).

[63] Ss 75(2) and 76(2). The meaning of 'long lease' is further defined in ss 76 and 77.

[64] Sch 6, paras 1, 3 and 4.

11.4.3.2 Sufficient Support

In order to exercise the RTM, 'not less than one-half of the total number' of qualifying tenants of flats must support the claim by joining the RTM company.[65]

11.4.3.3 Management Functions

There is a statutory procedure that has to be followed to get the RTM, but once acquired, the 'management functions' ('functions with respect to services, repairs, maintenance, improvements, insurance and management')[66] pass to the RTM company. The RTM company does not, however, acquire the right to manage the non-residential parts of the building or flats of non-qualifying tenants.[67] Nor is the RTM company able to exercise 'functions relating to re-entry or forfeiture'.[68] These are important qualifications and, where relevant, will add to the complexity of managing the building. The legislation makes no provision for how to deal with the problems that can arise from this. Further, some landlords have traditionally resorted to threats of forfeiture when service charges have not been paid, but as functions relating to forfeiture are not transferred to the RTM company the only remedies it will have for non-payment of the service charge will be the usual ones for recovery of debt (unless the landlord is willing to co-operate with the RTM company). (As the ability to use forfeiture for debt recovery is hard to defend more generally this particular limitation is entirely reasonable.)

11.4.4 Ongoing Problems

The problems of long leasehold management are fairly intractable. Notwithstanding the reforms that provide the opportunity for the leaseholders to take over the management of their homes, there will always be the potential for disagreement as to the quality of services that tenants wish to pay for. Managing property that has shared facilities is by no means an easy task, and can be complex, time-consuming, stressful and expensive. The LEASE website[69] cautions about the difficulties that can occur when tenants take over management, noting that in addition to the burdensome legal and accounting regimes, 'some leaseholders are irrational in their expectations', 'there may be difficult and sensitive issues in dealing with neighbours and fellow leaseholders' and 'leaseholders who routinely default on payment will prove a headache'.

11.4.5 The Introduction of Commonhold

The introduction of commonhold in September 2004 was intended to cure the perceived defects of leasehold ownership (see also chapter 7). Within a commonhold development

---

[65] S 79.
[66] S 96(5).
[67] S 96(6).
[68] S 96(b).
[69] The Leasehold Advisory Service provides free advice on the law affecting residential long leasehold property and commonhold (www.lease-advice.org).

the purchasers buy a freehold of the individual unit (the flat)[70] and the commonhold association[71] owns, and is responsible for, the management and upkeep of the common parts of the development.

Commonhold therefore provides the opportunity for freehold ownership of horizontally divided property without outside investment, giving control of management to the owners of the individual units. Further, there is no risk of forfeiture or of eviction at the end of a lease term. The problems of management are reduced by providing for a uniformity of structure and standardised documentation, which means that there will always be appropriately drafted rules for managing the property. It is possible to use commonhold for new developments but also for existing leaseholds to convert to commonhold. In practice, however, commonhold is virtually never used and the legislation introducing it, the Commonhold and Leasehold Reform Act 2002 is unsatisfactory. According to Clarke, the legislation:

> … contains some fundamental flaws that will prevent its widespread adoption for both large and mixed residential estates and developments. Indeed, these inadequacies are proving so fundamental to the key players (the developers and lenders) that the commonhold will possibly be consigned to the margins. There were, by 27 September 2005, only five commonholds registered a year after commonhold was brought into force, and they are all small homogenous developments [footnotes omitted].[72]

11.5 Managing Anti-social Behaviour

11.5.1 Anti-Social Behaviour

The aspect of wider estate management that has seen the greatest expansion in the powers and duties of social landlords in recent years is in relation to anti-social behaviour. Cowan (writing in 1999, since when there have been many further developments) stated that:

> … housing and its management has become a crucial part of the crime control industry; housing departments have become the intermediators in the new criminal justice system.[73]

This is so notwithstanding doubts as to the legitimacy of social landlords taking on this role, and difficulties in defining what anti-social behaviour is. There is no one accepted definition; the phrase is used variously to describe both relatively low-level nuisance behaviour (such as graffiti and poor garden maintenance) and criminal behaviour (such as assaults on housing staff). The Code of Guidance on anti-social behaviour policies issued by the ODPM gives a non-exhaustive list of anti-social behaviour including noise nuisance, intimidation and harassment, local environmental quality issues, aggressive and threatening

---

[70] Commonhold can also be used for industrial, or other, units.
[71] A limited company which has the unit-holders as members.
[72] D Clarke, 'Long Residential Leases: Future Directions' in S Bright (ed), *Landlord and Tenant Law. Past, Present and Future* (Oxford, Hart, 2006) 181. The flaws in the legislation are discussed in Clarke's chapter.
[73] D Cowan, *Housing Law and Policy* (Basingstoke, Macmillan, 1999) 492.

language and behaviour, violence, hate behaviour, and unlawful use of premises (such as drug dealing).[74]

11.5.2 Locating Anti-Social Behaviour

11.5.2.1 Problem Estates

The expanding role of housing management in social housing is partially a response to 'problem estates'. Papps explains how this term is variously understood:

> … [For] the general public such estates are areas they fear to enter because of the stories of crime, vandalism and general bad behaviour. For housing managers they are 'difficult to let' estates which because of poor housing conditions, high repair and maintenance costs, high void levels and high densities of vulnerable tenants are also very difficult to manage. For the tenants residing on these estates they are 'difficult to live in' and 'difficult to get out of' … They not only experience the consequences of the poor housing conditions and inadequate housing management but have to cope with high rates of crime, vandalism and anti-social behaviour and often appalling environmental conditions. The stigma attached to living on an estate labelled as problematic can lead to discrimination in obtaining, for example, employment and credit … [references omitted][75]

As Papps continues, there are many explanations offered for the existence of these problem estates – poor design, inadequate neighbourhood support networks, reputation and labelling (getting a bad name because of the area), the demographic profile of council tenants, and housing allocation and transfer policies. The effect of housing policy in the last 30 years or so has been to create a 'marginalised' group of council tenants, a problem exacerbated by the fact that there has been 'spatial' polarisation: two-thirds of social housing is located in areas originally built as council estates, and nearly half of social housing is located in the most deprived fifth of neighbourhoods.[76] Further, in any account of problem estates the residualisation and marginalisation impact of the RTB (discussed in chapters 5 and 25) also features strongly. By the late 1970s the housing management function itself was seen to be contributing to the problem, and so might also be part of the solution.

11.5.2.2 A Social Housing Problem

For many years dialogue concerning problems estates focused on social housing, in particular council housing. Although it is now increasingly recognised that there are also problem areas within the private rented sector, evidencing problems of 'poor management, poor housing conditions, incidences of antisocial behaviour and market instability', there has been an undoubted focus on anti-social behaviour as a social housing problem.[77]

Why is it that powers to deal with anti-social behaviour been concentrated on only *social* landlords, and why are only *social tenants* (and not also private tenants, owner occupiers

---

[74] ODPM, 'Anti-Social Behaviour: Policy and Procedure, Code of Guidance for local housing authorities and housing action trusts' (August 2004) 12.

[75] P Papps, 'Anti-Social Behaviour Strategies-Individualistic or Holistic?' (1998) 13 *Housing Studies* 639, 640.

[76] J Hills, 'Ends and means: The future roles of social housing in England' (CASE Report 34, February 2007) 4.

[77] DCLG, 'Dealing with "Problem" Private Rented Housing' (Housing Research Summary, Number 228, 2006).

and long leaseholders) subject to these controls?[78] In *Crime and Banishment*, Burney explores how (civil) social housing law has been seized upon as a tool for suppressing crime and disorder, noting that social tenants place:

> … themselves in a position where their past, present and possible future behaviour, and that of all household members, may be subject to scrutiny and may be used to deprive them of their home or even to bar them from further tenancies in the social sector. It is hard to think of any other group of citizens, outside institutional life, subject to the same level of governance in their daily lives.[79]

A number of factors contribute to explaining why it is that powers to tackle anti-social behaviour have been concentrated on social landlords. The impact of residualisation and the demographics of social housing mean that problems are often concentrated in areas with significant amounts of social housing:

> The British Crime Survey (BCS) shows that people within the local authority housing and low-income areas perceive the highest levels of antisocial behaviour.[80]

Housing managers spend a significant portion of time handling with complaints about anti-social behaviour,[81] and many of the early calls for increased powers to deal with anti-social behaviour came from local authority housing departments who were struggling with the problem of anti-social behaviour. Tenants also looked to their landlords to do something about the problem. There is a further explanation: the spotlight has been on social housing because it is in this sector that governance can occur. Private sector landlords are not readily identifiable, and the sector is less easy to govern.[82]

11.5.3 The Variety of Legal and Extra-legal Responses

Since 1996, there has been a flood of legal measures designed to deal with anti-social behaviour. Local authorities have been key players in this, with many of the powers being given to them qua landlord and housing manager.

Section 128A of the Housing Act 1996 requires social landlords (not just local authority landlords) to publish, and keep under review, anti-social behaviour policies and procedures directed at protecting their tenants.[83] The introduction of 'Best Value' in housing management (discussed below) and the need to improve service standards also requires that social landlords have clear policies to deal with anti-social behaviour.

---

[78] See, for example, A Arden and M Partington, 'Housing Law: Past and Present' in S Bright (ed), *Landlord and Tenant Law. Past, Present and Future* (Oxford, Hart, 2006) 204.

[79] E Burney, *Crime and Banishment: Nuisance and Exclusion in Social Housing* (Winchester, Waterside Press, 1999) 11 and 123.

[80] ODPM, 'Enabling local authorities to contract their Anti-Social Behaviour Order functions to organisations managing their housing stock, Consultation Paper' (November 2005). See also Home Office, 'Respect Action Plan' (10 January 2006) 27.

[81] P Papps, 'Anti-social Behaviour Strategies-Individualistic or Holistic?' (1998) 13 *Housing Studies* 639.

[82] See D Cowan and M McDermont, *Regulating Social Housing, Governing Decline* (Abingdon, Routledge-Cavendish, 2006).

[83] Added by the Anti-social Behaviour Act 2003 s 12. A code of guidance has been issued to assist local authorities with the preparation of guidance: ODPM, 'Anti-Social Behaviour: Policy and Procedure, Code of Guidance for local housing authorities and housing action trusts' (August 2004).

There is now a plethora of legal powers available to tackle anti-social behaviour. Several of these were initially introduced by the Housing Act 1996, but have since been extended by the Anti-social Behaviour Act 2003 and the Housing Act 2004. Social landlords now have powers to exclude anti-social persons from the allocation of social housing,[84] and to take account of behaviour in determining priority to be given to an application for housing[85] (see chapter 6). Around half of all social landlords have formal exclusion policies, many excluding tenants who have displayed 'unacceptable behaviour'.[86] If housing is offered, a local authority can elect to offer all new tenancies on an introductory basis, which is effectively a trial so that only 'good' tenants will gain security (see chapter 6).[87] Following the reforms in the Housing Act 2004, this probationary period can now be extended for a further six months where there are still doubts about the tenant.[88] RSLs can similarly offer probationary 'starter' tenancies using the assured shorthold tenancy. The Anti-social Behaviour Act 2003 also introduced provisions for social tenancies to be 'demoted' by court order to a non-secure status if there is anti-social behaviour or unlawful use of the premises, and the court considers it reasonable to order demotion[89] (see chapter 6). Together, these provisions represent a shift in the way that social housing is thought about. They carry echoes of the Victorian notions of the 'deserving' and the 'undeserving': only those who can prove themselves to be responsible tenants can enjoy the privilege of secure status.[90]

Local authorities are also making use of extra legal powers to tackle anti-social behaviour. There is increasingly a shift in thinking that emphasises prevention, support and rehabilitation rather than focusing on enforcement.[91] This can be seen in various social projects, such as the Dundee Families project which offers a programme of intensive support for anti-social families.[92] To 'encourage' greater take-up of such schemes the government is piloting schemes that will impose a housing benefit sanction for those evicted for anti-social behaviour who refuse offers of help.[93] Many alternative approaches are being used: mediation, problem solving meetings, reward schemes for good tenants, designing out crime, warning letters and 'abcs' (acceptable behaviour 'contracts').[94] Indeed,

---

[84] Housing Act 1996 s 160A.

[85] Housing Act 1996 s 160.

[86] C Hunter, J Nixon, and S Shayer, 'Neighbour Nuisance, Social Landlords and the Law' (Coventry, Chartered Institute of Housing, 2000) 102–05.

[87] Housing Act 1996 ss 124–5.

[88] Housing Act 1996 s 125B.

[89] Housing Act 1995 ss 82A, 143A; Housing Act 1988 ss 20A and B.

[90] Compare the language used by the DWP when consulting on housing benefit sanctions for anti-social behaviour: 'The rights we gain from civil society – including the right to financial support when we need it – should be balanced by responsibilities to behave responsibly towards our fellow citizens', DWP, 'Housing Benefit Sanctions and Antisocial Behaviour – a consultation paper' (May 2003) 1.

[91] The Policy Action Team, for example, recommended a three-pronged attack: prevention, enforcement and resettlement, 'National Strategy for Neighbourhood Renewal, Report of Policy Action Team 8: Anti-Social Behaviour' (March 2000). See also DTLR, 'Tackling Anti-Social Tenants, A Consultation Paper' (April 2002).

[92] E Hawkey, 'Intensive care' ROOF Jan/Feb 2002 32. This, and similar projects, report very high success rates and promote housing stability: Home Office, 'Respect Action Plan' (10 January 2006) ch 5; DCLG, 'Anti-social behaviour intensive family support projects' (Housing Research Summary, Number 230, 2006).

[93] Home Office, 'Respect Action Plan' (10 January 2006) ch 5; and DWP, 'Action to tackle nuisance neighbours' Press Release (5 June 2006). See s 130B of the Social Security Contributions and Benefits Act 1992, inserted by s 31 of the Welfare Reform Act 2007.

[94] These are voluntary non legally-binding contracts agreeing on the behaviour that will be avoided. Evidence suggests that they are popular with landlords as they are both inexpensive and often effective: H Pawson and others,

there is increasing emphasis being placed on a more 'joined up' response to nuisance behaviour, emphasising the need to develop multi-agency partnerships[95] and improve information sharing. Amendments made to the Anti-social Behaviour Act 2003 enable social landlords to apply for parenting orders where children have been involved in anti-social behaviour which 'directly or indirectly relates to or affects the housing management functions' of the landlord.[96]

Where the perpetrator suffers from a disability, which can include mental impairment, a landlord needs to be very careful when taking any action to deal with the anti-social behaviour. This is because the effect of section 22(3)(c) of the Disability Discrimination Act 1995 is that any act that discriminates against a disabled person by subjecting him to a detriment will be unlawful unless justified within the terms of the legislation, effectively requiring that in the reasonable opinion of the landlord the action 'is necessary in order not to endanger the health or safety of any person'.[97] Discrimination is given a very wide definition: it will be discrimination if the perpetrator is treated differently than someone who has not behaved anti-socially and it is 'irrelevant that the landlord would have reacted in the same way to anti-social behaviour that was not the result of a mental impairment'.[98] This means that applying for demotion, extending the period of an introductory tenancy, seeking an injunction or an Anti-Social Behaviour Order (ASBO) are all potentially unlawful and will require justification. In these cases, inter-agency work will be especially important. (For further discussion, see chapter 19.)

11.5.4 Housing Injunctions

In addition to the legal powers directed at ensuring that only 'good and responsible' tenants should have security, social landlords also have powers to deal with bad behaviour during the life of the tenancy, and to hasten its end.

Social landlords are able to apply to the High Court or County Court for injunctions in a variety of circumstances, although the granting of one is always at the discretion of the court. Injunctions have many advantages over other possible remedies; in particular they tend to provide swift 'justice', focus on changing behaviour and witness intimidation is less problematic as hearsay evidence can be used in affidavits. On the other hand, as will be seen, their modern manifestation gives rise to a number of civil liberties questions, particularly as

'The Use of Possession Actions and Evictions by Social Landlords' (ODPM, 2005) ch 6. Over 13,000 were issued between October 2003 and September 2005: Home Office, 'Tackling Anti-Social behaviour in 2005: summary of survey results' (10 January 2006).

[95] For example, DTLR, 'Tackling Anti-Social Tenants, A Consultation Paper' (April, 2000) 34; ODPM, 'Anti-Social Behaviour: Policy and Procedure, Code of Guidance for local housing authorities and housing action trusts' (August 2004) 17. RSLs tend to find it more difficult to become fully integrated into this kind of partnership working: DCLG, 'Priority review of the uptake by social landlords of legislative powers to tackle anti-social behaviour' (Housing Research Summary, Number 232, 2006).

[96] Ss 25A, B, and 26A in force on 29 June 2007. Amendments were made by the Police and Justice Act 2006.

[97] Disability Discrimination Act 1995 s 24(2) and (3).

[98] N Cobb, 'Patronising the mentally disordered? Social landlords and the control of "anti-social behaviour" under the Disability Discrimination Act 1995' (2006) 26 LS 238, 256.

an injunction may 'have the effect of excluding a person from his normal place of residence'.[99]

It has always been possible for an injunction to be obtained for breach of contract, but the modern statutory powers to apply for an injunction given to social landlords are much more extensive than this. Section 153D of the Housing Act 1996 enables social landlords[100] to apply for an injunction for breach of tenancy and it is now usual for 'good behaviour' requirements to be built into tenancy agreements. The landlord is able to apply for an injunction if there is a breach or anticipated breach of a tenancy agreement:

(1) ... on the grounds that the tenant –

(a) is engaging or threatening to engage in conduct that is capable of causing nuisance or annoyance to any person, or

(b) is allowing, inciting or encouraging any other person to engage or threaten to engage in such conduct.

If there is violence, or threatened violence, or a significant risk of harm then:

(3) The court may include in the injunction a provision prohibiting the person in respect of whom it is granted from entering or being in –

(a) any premises specified in the injunction;

(b) any area specified in the injunction.

(4) The court may attach a power of arrest to any provision of the injunction.

There is also power for social landlords[101] to apply for an 'Anti-Social Behaviour Injunction'; this is not specifically tied to the tenancy, but relates to the housing management functions of the landlord. Whereas the section 153D injunction can only be made against a tenant, the anti-social behaviour injunction can be made against anyone. By section 153A of the Housing Act 1996 an antisocial behaviour injunction can be granted that 'prohibits the person ... from engaging in housing related anti-social conduct of a kind specified in the injunction'. 'Housing related' means any conduct that directly or indirectly relates to the housing management functions of the landlord. It can be issued against a person who:

(3) ... is engaging, has engaged or threatens to engage in housing-related conduct capable of causing a nuisance or annoyance to –

(a) a person with a right (of whatever description) to reside in or occupy housing accommodation owned or managed by a relevant landlord,

(b) a person with a right (of whatever description) to reside in or occupy other housing accommodation in the neighbourhood of housing accommodation mentioned in paragraph (a),

(c) a person engaged in lawful activity in, or in the neighbourhood of, housing accommodation mentioned in paragraph (a), or

(d) a person employed (whether or not by a relevant landlord) in connection with the exercise of a relevant landlord's housing management functions.

---

[99] Housing Act 1996 s 153E.

[100] A housing action trust, local authority, registered social landlord or charitable housing trust: Housing Act 1996 s 153E(7), 153E(8).

[101] A housing action trust, local authority, or registered social landlord (but not a charitable housing trust): Housing Act 1996 s 153E(7).

The section therefore applies where the behaviour could cause nuisance or annoyance to other tenants, visitors, people living in the neighbourhood, or the housing management staff of the landlord, and it is immaterial where the conduct occurs. Further the prohibited behaviour need not be directed to a particular person: behaviour can be proscribed if it is capable of causing nuisance or annoyance to 'some' person.[102] The anti-social behaviour injunction can, for example, be used when threats are made to housing staff.

Section 153B enables a social landlord to apply for an injunction against the unlawful use of housing accommodation. With both sections 153A and 153B if there is violence or threatened violence, or a significant risk of harm, the court is able to attach a power of arrest and to exclude the person under injunction from entering particular premises (an ouster provision) or a specific area (an exclusion provision).[103]

The various housing injunctions can be made for a specific period (of any duration) or for an indefinite period.[104] In practice, many housing practitioners welcome the Anti-Social Behaviour Injunction as a way of protecting witnesses.[105]

The impact that these injunctions can have upon a family can be seen in the Court of Appeal case of *Moat Housing Group-South Ltd v Harris*.[106] Here an RSL was granted a 'without notice' injunction against a tenant which not only prohibited her from engaging in antisocial behaviour but also contained an ouster provision requiring her (and therefore her four children) to leave her home (immediately). The tenant had received no notice or other warning that her behaviour had put the family at risk of eviction. The injunction was served on her at 9 pm on a Friday evening, with a power of arrest attached. When the order was served, the family had nowhere else to go and the police were reluctant to enforce it. On their advice she contacted a solicitor and an order was obtained from a High Court judge at 1:30 am on the Saturday morning staying the effect of the ouster. When the matter came before the Court of Appeal they stressed that a without notice injunction should be an exceptional remedy, perhaps justified if there is a risk of significant harm if the order is not made immediately, but even so it must not be wider than necessary. On the facts, it was not necessary to make an ouster order or an exclusion order without notice, particularly as much of the evidence showed that the anti-social behaviour had in fact been committed by another family on the estate.

11.5.5 ASBOs

Social landlords[107] also have powers to apply to a magistrates court for the much publicised ASBOs. Section 1 of the Crime and Disorder Act 1998 provides that they can be applied for where it appears to the applicant that:

---

[102] S 153A(4). This was a change implemented in 2007, driven by the desire to protect the anonymity of witnesses.
[103] Housing Act 1996 s 153C.
[104] Housing Act 1996 s 153E(2)(a).
[105] See, for example, *Moat Housing Group-South Ltd v Harris* [2005] EWCA Civ 287, [2006] QB 606 [91-93]. Bill Pitt, Head of the Nuisance Strategy Group, Manchester City Council has also emphasised the value of injunctions and ASBOs (see below) in witness protection: 'Lost in Translation: Housing Management, Antisocial Behaviour and the Law' (conference at Oxford Brookes University, 22 September 2004).
[106] [2005] EWCA Civ 287, [2006] QB 606.
[107] A local authority, housing action trust or RSL: Crime and Disorder Act 1998 s 1(1A). There are plans to allow TMOs to apply for ASBOs: draft Local Authority (Contracting Out of ASB Order Functions) (England) (Order) 2007.

(a) that the person has acted … in an anti-social manner, that is to say, in a manner that caused or was likely to cause harassment, alarm or distress to one or more persons not of the same household as himself; and

(b) that such an order is necessary to protect relevant persons from further anti-social acts by him.

Although this would include criminal acts, its scope is much wider; it catches non-criminal acts which fail to show 'respect' to other members of the community.[108] This is significant because although an ASBO is a civil remedy, breach of an ASBO can lead to imprisonment and a fine.[109] A news item in Shelter's magazine, ROOF, mentions that a landlord with around 450 tenants had been served with an ASBO following threats to shoot a housing enforcement officer, and was later jailed for changing the locks on one of his properties while the tenant was out.[110]

According to Woolf LJ, the objective is the:

… protection of a selection of the public who would otherwise be likely to be subjected to conduct of a socially disruptive nature.[111]

ASBOs consist of those prohibitions 'necessary for the purpose of protecting persons … from further anti-social acts',[112] and often contain exclusion orders preventing the offender from entering a particular location. They last for a minimum of two years and have no maximum duration.[113] Although in many respects they are similar to Housing Act injunctions they are not formally linked to the housing management role of local authorities. County Courts are also able to make an ASBO in eviction proceedings related to anti-social behaviour.

ASBOs have received a mixed reaction. They make substantial inroads on civil liberties. Almost two-thirds of people against whom ASBOs are taken out have some 'mitigating factor', such as drugs or alcohol abuse or learning disabilities.[114] Many of the people against whom ASBOs are made are young.[115] The penalty for breach can be higher than the criminal sanction for the same 'offence', without offering any of the procedural safeguards available in a criminal prosecution. As Ashworth asks, 'does this not amount to a subversion of fundamental legal values?'[116] Many practitioners on the ground, however, claim that they are useful and effective weapons and some local authorities, notably Manchester, have made extensive use of them.[117]

---

[108] See P Ramsay, 'What is Anti-Social Behaviour?' [2004] *Crim LR* 908.

[109] Crime and Disorder Act 1998 s 1(10).

[110] ROOF May/June 2007 6.

[111] *R (McCann) v Manchester Crown Court* [2001] 1 WLR 358 (QB) [24].

[112] Crime and Disorder Act 1998 s 1(6).

[113] Crime and Disorder Act 1998 s 1(9). ASBOs issued to young people should be administratively reviewed after one year: Home Office, 'A guide to anti-social behaviour orders' (August 2006) 45.

[114] S Campbell, 'A Review of Anti-Social Behaviour Orders' (Home Office Research Study 236, 2002) 17–9.

[115] S Campbell, 'A Review of Anti-Social Behaviour Orders' (Home Office Research Study 236, 2002).

[116] A Ashworth, 'Social Control and "Anti-Social Behaviour": The Subversion of Human Rights' (2004) 120 *LQR* 263, 288.

[117] Across England, 7,356 ASBOs were issued between April 1999 and September 2005: www.crimereduction.gov.uk.

11.5.6 Using Eviction

Bad behaviour also enables the landlord to apply for eviction of the tenant – and it need not be the tenant himself who is a nuisance; other members of his household or even visitors who create trouble can also lead to the tenant being evicted (see chapter 19).[118] Indeed, Hunter and Nixon use case studies to show that there is a gender bias in that single woman are more likely to be the subject of complaints about anti-social behaviour than men or joint tenants, and in the majority of cases it is not their behaviour that is in issue but the behaviour of an 'unruly' son or boyfriend.[119] The details of the landlord's legal powers to evict are considered in chapter 19; here, the focus is on how eviction is used to help in the fight against anti-social behaviour.

Eviction should be the last resort;[120] the loss of the home has serious consequences but is also a somewhat peculiar response to bad behaviour, especially if the behaviour does not relate specifically to the use and occupation of the tenanted property. The ability to evict for anti-social behaviour outside the home means that social tenants who commit crimes (or even non-crimes) can be subjected to penalties which may be much more serious than a criminal sentence. As Burney writes:

> … eviction as a form of behaviour control raises important questions of principle. One is vicarious punishment: should everybody in the household suffer the loss of their home because of the conduct of perhaps only one member, or even of someone who is only a visitor? The other is double jeopardy: should somebody who has been convicted in the courts and punished by the sentence, be punished again (and other household members, vicariously punished) by having their home repossessed on grounds of that conviction?[121]

Eviction does not necessarily solve anything: evicted families will find it hard to be re-housed, and many evicted tenants end up living nearby with friends or in privately rented housing.[122] The decision to evict is taken against a complex background of legal, political and social considerations. Studies show that deciding to evict is not usually a decision that is taken lightly: many perpetrators are themselves vulnerable (two-thirds were described as having a particular problem or special needs), and there is usually multi-agency dialogue with conflicting opinions as to the appropriate response.[123] Nonetheless, recognising the devastation caused to 'victims', by the time a possession action reaches court the judiciary

---

[118] Housing Act 1985, Ground 2, Sch 2. RSLs and private landlords are also able to recover possession on these grounds: Housing Act 1988, Ground 14, Sch 2.

[119] C Hunter and J Nixon, 'Taking the blame and losing the home: women and antisocial behaviour' (2001) 23 *JSWFL* 395.

[120] Housing Corporation circular 07/04 requires RSLs to 'show a commitment to using the full range of tools now available to tackle ASB. Eviction should be considered only when other interventions have failed to protect the wider community' para 3.2.1.

[121] E Burney, *Crime and Banishment: Nuisance and Exclusion in Social Housing* (Winchester, Waterside Press, 1999) 102. See also A Ashworth, 'Social Control and "Anti-Social Behaviour": The Subversion of Human Rights' (2004) 120 *LQR* 263, 285; and the remarks of Sedley LJ in *Portsmouth CC v Bryant* (2000) 31 HLR 906 (CA) 917.

[122] C Hunter, J Nixon and S Shayer, 'Neighbour Nuisance, Social Landlords and the Law' (Coventry, Chartered Institute of Housing, 2000) 101.

[123] C Hunter, J Nixon and S Shayer, 'Neighbour Nuisance, Social Landlords and the Law' (Coventry, Chartered Institute of Housing, 2000) ch 5; H Pawson and others, 'The Use of Possession Actions and Evictions by Social Landlords' (ODPM, 2005) ch 6.

are likely to order possession where there is serious misbehaviour.[124] While a Notice Seeking Possession (NSP) served for rent arrears is often being used as a lever to 'encourage' payment, an NSP served for anti-social behaviour usually reflects a serious intention to evict; an NSP is four times more likely to lead to eviction when brought for anti-social behaviour than when being brought for rent arrears.[125]

Social landlords are under growing pressure from tenants to make more active use of possession powers in response to antisocial behaviour.[126] The need to give weight to the impact of bad behaviour on others can be seen in case law[127] but is now also reflected in statute. An amendment to the Housing Act 1985 introduced by the Anti-social Behaviour Act 2003 requires the court, when considering the reasonableness of a possession order in the context of anti-social behaviour, to consider 'in particular' the effect that the 'nuisance or annoyance' has had *on others*, continues to have, and is likely to have in the future.[128] The Court of Appeal has provided guidance on how courts are to approach the exercise of discretion in such cases. Discretion occurs at two stages: in deciding whether it is 'reasonable' to order possession, and, if so, whether possession should be immediate or suspended. In *Manchester CC v Higgins* it was the tenant's son who was engaged in anti-social behaviour.[129] An injunction had been tried, but failed, and an ASBO had been granted, but to no effect. The recorder ordered possession, but suspended it on the basis that there was still hope and it would not therefore be 'proportionate to exclude the family, given the multifarious problems they have, immediately'. The Court of Appeal disagreed; the time had come to order immediate possession. Ward LJ noted that each case must depend upon its own facts and circumstances, and that guidance is therefore inevitably going to be of a very general nature. Against that background, Ward LJ set out various principles. If the conduct is:

> ... serious and persistent enough to justify an ASBO then that will be strong but not conclusive evidence that the tenant will have forfeited his entitlement to retain possession.[130]

It is important to realise that the court's response sends a message to others; those who suffer need to see that something is being done. In deciding whether or not to suspend, the question requires one to look to the future. Ward LJ quoted Kay LJ in *Canterbury CC v Lowe*: 'There is no point suspending an order if the inevitable outcome is a breach'.[131] Ultimately, it is a question of proportionality: is an immediate order for possession necessary in order to meet the need to protect the rights and freedoms of others, the neighbours?

---

[124] C Hunter, J Nixon and S Shayer, 'Neighbour Nuisance, Social Landlords and the Law' (Coventry, Chartered Institute of Housing, 2000) ch 9.

[125] H Pawson and others, 'The Use of Possession Actions and Evictions by Social Landlords' (ODPM, 2005) para 3.3.

[126] H Pawson and others, 'The Use of Possession Actions and Evictions by Social Landlords' (ODPM, 2005) para 6.3.

[127] See, for example, the cases referred to in C Hunter and J Nixon, 'Taking the blame and losing the home: women and antisocial behaviour' (2001) 23 *JSWFL* 395, 405; and in A Arden and M Partington, 'Housing Law: Past and Present' in S Bright (ed), *Landlord and Tenant Law. Past, Present and Future* (Oxford, Hart, 2006) 205.

[128] Housing Act 1985 s 85A, being mirrored for assured tenancies in Housing Act 1988 s 9(A). In *Knowsley Housing Trust v McMullen* [2006] EWCA Civ 539 Neuberger LJ states that this merely codifies and mandates the already existing jurisprudence [4].

[129] [2005] EWCA Civ 1423, [2006] 1 All ER 431.

[130] *Manchester CC v Higgins* [2005] EWCA Civ 1423, [2006] 1 All ER 431 [36].

[131] (2001) 33 HLR 53 (CA).

Manchester CC v Higgins should be not taken to mean that immediate possession will be inevitable in anti-social behaviour cases.[132] A number of alternative measures had already been tried in that case, but failed. In contrast, in *Moat Housing Group South Ltd v Harris* a 'without notice' injunction had been served on an assured tenant, ordering immediate ouster and exclusion from the property.[133] This was followed by an immediate order for possession (partly on the grounds that it would be very difficult to find any witnesses prepared to give evidence of a breach of a suspended order for fear of retaliation). On these facts, the Court of Appeal considered that possession should have been suspended. The tenant had had no prior warning of possible eviction, and eviction was not being used as a last resort. Further, although the court is directed to look at the impact of the behaviour on others[134] it must not neglect the impact that the order will have upon the tenant and her family, especially as two of her children appeared relatively blameless. The fact that children are involved does require careful consideration to be given to the circumstances, Brooke LJ observing that:

> For a child, to become part of an 'intentionally homeless' family, with the bleak prospect of being allotted sub-standard accommodation with his/her parents or being taken into care, is such a serious prospect that every RSL should be alert to intervene creatively at a far earlier stage than occurred in the present case, in order to do everything possible to avert recourse to eviction. European Court of Human Rights jurisprudence, indeed, makes it clear that the right to respect for a home has inherent in it the principle that procedural fairness will be observed before the home is taken away (see, for example, *Connors v United Kingdom* (2004) 40 EHRR 189, para 83), so that an RSL should be slow to short-circuit its normal procedures in nuisance cases by proceeding straight to a notice seeking possession ('NSP') or an eviction without prior notice.[135]

Similarly, in *Knowsley Housing Trust v McMullen* a suspended possession order was upheld by the Court of Appeal even though there had been serious anti-social behaviour by the tenant's son.[136] Neuberger LJ agreed that the County Court judge had been right not to grant an outright possession order as the landlord was happy with a suspended order, the tenant was unable to control her son,[137] the tenant was disabled (which was highly material) and there had been no problems in recent times.

In combination these cases show that the guide that eviction should be seen as a last resort must be taken seriously. An NSP should not simply arrive 'out of the blue'. Public authorities bear responsibility towards tenants and their families under Article 8 of the ECHR to show respect for the home. This, and published ASB policies, mean that social landlords should try to tackle the anti-social behaviour in other ways before moving to possession. If other steps have failed, however, the balance appears to shift. If the tenant (or nuisance creator) persists in the bad behaviour having been given a chance, and some help, then the court must take the impact that this behaviour is having on others seriously. If there are real signs that things might change, supported by evidence, then it may well be

---

[132] [2005] EWCA Civ 1423, [2006] 1 All ER 431.
[133] [2005] EWCA Civ 287, [2006] QB 606.
[134] Housing Act 1985 s 85(A).
[135] *Moat Housing Group South Ltd v Harris* [2005] EWCA Civ 287, [2006] QB 606 [102].
[136] [2006] EWCA Civ 539.
[137] This factor goes both ways: see the discussion throughout the case.

appropriate to grant a suspended possession order. But if the culprit is 'unrepentantly' anti-social then, having regard to the Article 8 rights of others in the area, an immediate possession order may be necessary.

As will be seen in the next section, it can be very difficult for a victim of anti-social behaviour to get anything done about the problem if the landlord is reluctant to act. An interesting step has been taken in the Northern Territory in Australia. The Antisocial Behaviour (Miscellaneous Amendments) Act 2006 amends earlier residential tenancy legislation by providing that a person adversely affected by repeated nuisance behaviour, or whose reasonable peace and privacy has been repeatedly disturbed, can apply to the court for the eviction of the nuisance creator. The papers must also be served on the landlord and if there is an objection the court is only able to make the order in exceptional circumstances.

11.5.7 Using the Remedies

Research conducted for the DCLG found that social landlords find injunctions 'swift and easy to use'.[138] Eviction is also commonly used for anti-social behaviour. Demoted tenancies were much less frequently used, and many landlords considered them not to be very effective. ASBOs were seen as the most difficult powers to use. Landlords also expressed frustration at the time it takes for a case to go through the court and the perceived lack of consistency in the process and outcome.

11.5.8 Anti-social Behaviour and Private Rented Housing

While it remains the case that many of the legal powers to deal with anti-social behaviour are tenure specific, it is recognised that the problem is not confined to social housing. Anti-social behaviour measures are now being rolled out into wider society, even in relation to owner occupied homes.[139] There is a clear link with the housing environment, but not necessarily with tenure:

> … youth nuisance and antisocial behaviour are widespread problems which are frequently found in high density, low-income areas, many of which suffer from multiple deprivation including high levels of unemployment, family breakdown, high rates of social exclusion and benefit dependency, truancy, school exclusions, and alcohol and drug dependency. Typically such areas were characterized as being low demand estates containing a mixture of social housing, private rented and owner occupied dwellings.[140]

As the amount of social housing reduces, those unable to access it or excluded from it, have taken refuge in the private rental sector. There have always been particular safety concerns in relation to HMOs and for this reason licensing schemes have targeted this

---

[138] DCLG, 'Priority review of the uptake by social landlords of legislative powers to tackle anti-social behaviour' (Housing Research Summary Number 232, 2006).

[139] It is also proposed to give local authorities (and police) powers to temporarily close properties (including owner-occupied property) following significant and persistent anti-social behaviour: Home Office, 'New House Closure Powers for Neighbours from Hell' Press Release (30 May 2007).

[140] J Nixon and others, 'Tackling Antisocial Behaviour in Mixed Tenure Areas' (ODPM, March 2003) 8.

sub-sector. More recently, however, discourse about private landlords has become bifurcated; with talk of 'good' and 'bad' landlords. 'Bad' landlords often end up housing 'bad' tenants, a problem concentrated in areas of low housing demand:

> ... as prices fall and owner-occupiers find it difficult to sell their properties there is often an increase in the private rented sector as landlords see the opportunity to purchase properties cheaply and therefore receive a good return on their investment through renting.
>
>   As prices fall further the area may become more attractive to less scrupulous property investors, who are less interested in proper management of the properties and tenancies, as well as novice investors who do not have proper knowledge of their management responsibilities.[141]

In response to this, the Housing Act 2004 has given selective licensing powers to local authorities in these areas, designed partly to engage private landlords in dealing appropriately with anti-social behaviour (see chapter 12). It is claimed that:

> ... selective licensing will ensure that all landlords and managers of privately rented properties in a designated neighbourhood are identified to the local authority as 'fit and proper' persons and that satisfactory management standards are in place in the property. Licensing will enable local authorities to work with landlords to raise the standards of management in the properties, support them in tackling anti-social behaviour problems and engage them in the regeneration of the area.[142]

In addition to compulsory licensing, voluntary accreditation schemes have also been vigorously promoted in recent years with property condition and decent management practices at the heart of accreditation schemes.

11.6 Landlords and Third Parties

This section considers two related questions: first, whether a landlord is liable to others (including other tenants) for damage and nuisance caused by the landlord's tenant; and second, whether those others (victims) can compel a landlord to take action against a tenant who is committing a nuisance.[143] As seen already, the landlord has extensive powers to take action, the question here is whether a victim can force a landlord to do so. There are various potential sources of liability: tort law, contract law (through the lease), and, in the case of public authorities, public law (including human rights law).

11.6.1 Liability in Tort

It is very unlikely that a landlord could be held responsible through the duty of care concept. Not only have courts eschewed the notion that this duty attaches to

---

[141] Explanatory memorandum to The Licensing of Houses in Multiple Occupation (Prescribed Descriptions) (England) Order 2006 SI 2006/371 [20].

[142] Explanatory memorandum to The Licensing of Houses in Multiple Occupation (Prescribed Descriptions) (England) Order 2006 SI 2006/371 [32].

[143] On these questions, see also S Bright, 'Liability for the Bad Behaviour of Others' (2001) 21 *OJLS* 311; S Bright and C Bakalis, 'Anti-Social Behaviour: Local Authority Responsibility and the Voice of the Victim' (2003) 62 *CLJ* 305.

landowners,[144] but it is extremely difficult to claim negligent breach where there is a failure to act rather than misfeasance. Additionally, the courts are reluctant to impose duties of care upon public authorities which will make it even more difficult to succeed against a local authority landlord. In *Smith v Scott* it had been argued that Lewisham London Borough Council owed a duty of care to the Smith family which was breached when they housed the unruly Scott family next door.[145] Pennycuick VC rejected this. In *O'Leary v London Borough of Islington* the claim was brought by a council tenant trying to get the council to take action against her anti-social neighbour, also a council tenant.[146] The argument here was not that there had been a breach of duty in housing the disruptive tenant next door but that the Council owed a duty of care to enforce the leasehold covenant prohibiting nuisance type behaviour. Whereas *Smith* allegedly involved a negligent action, the duty of care was here being used to provoke action. The argument fared no better. Finally, in *Hussain v Lancaster City Council*, where there was severe racial harassment committed by tenants on a local authority estate against freeholders, it was argued that the local authority should have taken steps to stop the harassment, by obtaining injunctions or evicting the troublemakers.[147] Again, the Court of Appeal rejected that argument that there was a duty of care.[148]

There will also be difficulties in attaching liability through nuisance law. The general approach in nuisance law is that landowners can be held liable for nuisance acts committed by persons on their land if they are aware of the problem but fail to take reasonable steps to stop it within a reasonable time. The liability of landowners in nuisance law flows from the acceptance that an occupier of land is liable for the continuance of a nuisance created by others if he 'continues or adopts' it. In the words of Viscount Maugham in *Sedleigh-Denfield v O'Callaghan*:

> … an occupier of land 'continues' a nuisance if with knowledge or presumed knowledge he fails to take any reasonable means to bring it to an end …[149]

This means that generally a landowner can be held responsible for the nuisance behaviour of those on his land, even if he has not authorised the behaviour in any way, if the land is in his 'control and possession', the landowner is aware of the nuisance, has the ability to stop it, but fails to take reasonable steps to do so within a reasonable time.

A different principle is, however, applied to land that is leased. A landlord will be responsible for the nuisance behaviour of his tenant only if (a) he has in some manner licensed this behaviour and (b) there is a sufficient nexus between the tenant's behaviour and the tenant's land. There is a long line of authority illustrating the first point, that only if there is

---

[144] See *Smith v Scott* [1973] Ch 314 (Ch); *Hussain v Lancaster City Council* [2000] QB 1 (CA). For further discussion see S Bright, 'Liability for the Bad Behaviour of Others' (2001) 21 *OJLS* 311.

[145] [1973] Ch 314 (Ch).

[146] (1983) 9 HLR 83 (CA). The argument in tort was a subsidiary argument. The main argument was that there was an implied contractual term to take best endeavours to enforce the nuisance covenant, which was rightly rejected.

[147] [2000] QB 1 (CA).

[148] See fuller discussion and criticism of this in S Bright, 'Liability for the Bad Behaviour of Others' (2001) 21 *OJLS* 311.

[149] [1940] AC 880 (HL) 894.

express or implied authorisation of the nuisance will the landlord be liable.[150] Authorisation will be found only if the nuisance is 'certain to result from the purposes for which the property is let'.[151] The second point appears to be the only way to explain satisfactorily the decision in *Hussain v Lancaster*.[152] In this case there was a large gang of troublemakers, some of whom were tenants of the defendant authority, and they were involved in severe acts of harassment towards the Hussain family on the defendant council's housing estate. The Court of Appeal held that there was no act of nuisance in law because 'it did not involve the tenant's use of the tenant's land.' Whether the nexus has to be so close that it is only use of the tenanted land itself that can create an actionable nuisance is, perhaps, debatable[153] but there must clearly be some link.

This exemption from the landowner's nuisance liability in relation to misbehaviour by a tenant may not apply if there is a nuisance on retained land (land which remains in the control and possession of the landlord) that is, common parts such as walkways in tenanted shopping malls and shared access roads. So, for example, in *Hilton v James* the continuation test was used by the Court of Appeal to explain why the landlord was liable for the nuisance caused by the blockage of a shared access road used by his tenants.[154] Although explained as a 'continuation' case, however, the liability was in fact owed to a tenant, not to a member of the public. A better explanation of the decision is that landlord liability can arise in relation to misuse of common parts, but this will be a liability only to other tenants and only if the 'continuation' also amounts to a derogation from grant (see discussion above, at 11.3.2). A carefully worded passage in *Chartered Trust v Davies* supports this:

> ... in a landlord and tenant context, nuisances caused or continued by the landlord which interfere with the enjoyment of the demised land will usually also be conduct which renders the demised land unfit or materially less fit for the purpose for which the demise was made and so constitute a derogation from grant.[155]

An alternative argument has been put by Loveland, who says that a landlord can be liable to tenants for the nuisance behaviour of other tenants if there is a 'common scheme' and, knowing of breaches of a 'no-nuisance' covenant, he continues to receive rent from the misbehaving tenants.[156] Such a scheme could be found if a large scale landlord lets a building or estate on standard form contracts which include a 'no nuisance' clause, or if the landlord promotes a scheme which emphasises it will be managed with regard to each others' privacy or quiet enjoyment, or if it is an RSL (having regard to Housing Corporation guidance that RSLs must have anti-social behaviour strategies).

---

[150] *Malzy v Eicholz* [1916] 2 KB 308 (CA); *Southwark LBC v Tanner; Baxter v Camden LBC (No 2)* [2001] AC 1 (HL).

[151] [1973] Ch 314 (Ch) 321. See also *Rich v Basterfield* (1847) 4 CB 783. In *Smith v Scott* [1973] Ch 314 (Ch) Pennycuick VC also rejected the argument that there had been a breach of a duty of care.

[152] *Hussain v Lancaster City Council* [2000] QB 1 (CA).

[153] See *Lippiatt v South Gloucestershire Council* [2000] QB 51 (CA) 64–5; J Morgan, 'Nuisance and the unruly tenant' (2001) 60 *CLJ* 382, 397–400; M Davey, 'Neighbours in law' [2001] *Conv* 31, 55.

[154] *Hilton v James Smith & Sons (Norwood) Ltd* [1979] 2 EGLR 44 (CA). See also *Chartered Trust v Davies* [1997] 2 EGLR 83 (CA); *Mowan v Wandsworth* (2001) 33 HLR 56 (CA).

[155] [1997] 2 EGLR 83 (CA) 87.

[156] I Loveland, 'Fixing Landlords with Liability for the Anti-Social Behaviour of their Tenants' [2005] *J of Planning L* 273 and 405.

The general rule remains, however, that a landlord will not usually be liable for the nuisance of his tenant. No satisfactory explanation has been given in the case law as to why a landowner can be held responsible for acts of nuisance creators on his land, but not a landlord for acts of nuisance by his tenant. In law, the distinction lies in the 'possession and control' that is retained, as a landlord parts with 'possession' he is no longer liable (barring authorisation). Why this distinction matters is unclear. In *Winch v Mid Bedfordshire District Council*, counsel argued that the landlord principle (no liability) applied in relation to a gypsy site managed by a local authority on the grounds that, although there was no tenancy, there were nonetheless statutory powers that restrained the local authority when seeking repossession (four weeks notice, and a court order).[157] Astill J did not agree: the statutory provisions did not operate to prevent a local authority from recovering possession, but simply ensured that there was due process and appropriate notice given, and so the authority had not given away the 'right to possession' in the same way that a landlord does. The idea that the level of control somehow explains why landowners generally are liable, but not landlords, is not convincing; as already seen landlords, although they have parted with possession, have extensive powers to 'control' the tenant, including the power to evict.

If the grounds for distinction are unconvincing, this leads to the question as to whether or not all landowners (and landlords) should be held responsible for the acts of those on his land. On the one hand, it is generally going to be easier and more cost effective for the landowner to take steps to control the nuisance than for the victim to mount a successful legal action. Both Davey and Loveland argue for an extension of the general approach to tenancies, so that a landlord will be liable when it has the legal means to control a nuisance but takes no step to do so.[158] On the other hand, it can be argued that no landowner should be held responsible for the acts of autonomous third parties. As the Australian judge Dixon J said:

> ... the general rule is that one man is under no duty of controlling another to prevent his doing damage to a third.[159]

This liability has come about by the extension of a principle (the continuation of nuisance principle) developed in the quite different context of liability for nuisance caused by the physical state of land. It has been argued by this author that it should not apply to impose liability for the way that other people behave.[160]

11.6.2 Liability through the Leasehold Contract

Another potential source of liability, already discussed, is through the duty not to derogate from grant. The parties' expectations play a key part in defining the nature of the grant, and given that social landlords now publish anti-social behaviour policies, the expectations

---

[157] [2002] All ER (D) 380 (QB).

[158] M Davey, 'Neighbours in law' [2001] *Conv* 31; I Loveland, 'Fixing Landlords with Liability for the Anti-Social Behaviour of their Tenants' [2005] *J of Planning L* 273 and 405.

[159] *Smith v Leurs* (1945) 70 CLR 256 (HC Aust) 261.

[160] S Bright, 'Liability for the Bad Behaviour of Others' (2001) 21 *OJLS* 311. See also A Ashworth, 'Social Control and "Anti-Social Behaviour": The Subversion of Human Rights' (2004) 120 *LQR* 263, 270, who asks in relation to the social landlord: 'Is there sufficient justification for departing from the basic principle that we should not be treated as our fellow citizen's keeper?'

stemming from this will be material to the question as to whether the landlord is in breach of covenant in failing to control anti-social behaviour that affects a tenant. Apart from this, it is unlikely that there will be contractual routes to liability. One of the options considered by the Law Commission was to require social landlords to include,

> ... a term specifying that the landlord should take all reasonable steps to ensure that the occupier should be able to occupy the home unaffected by anti social behaviour by other occupants of other premises owned by the landlord.[161]

In view of the resource implications of this, it is not surprising that it has not been pursued.

11.6.3 Liability in Public Law

In *Mowan v London Borough of Wandsworth* a council leaseholder lived beneath another council tenant, Miss Abrahart, who was mentally disturbed. Mrs Mowan's flat was regularly flooded with sewage from the flat above, she suffered persistent noise, and a death threat was made against her.[162] In the course of dismissing her private law claim against the local authority for failing to do something, the Court of Appeal hinted that judicial review of the decision not to evict might be possible. The difficulty with this is that courts will not use public law to 'second guess' local authority action, but will intervene only on the grounds of legality, rationality and natural justice.[163] It is therefore unlikely that in a typical case any of the local authority's reasons for not dealing with the problem will be subject to a successful judicial review challenge, particularly given the difficult balancing questions involved in deciding the best and most appropriate response to anti-social behaviour. The decision whether or not to take legal action is not taken lightly and the local authority cannot simply look at the suffering of the victim, but will have to take account of the vulnerability of the perpetrator, and, where eviction is at issue, the concerns that legal action will simply displace the problem. In *Mowan*, for example, the Council took the view that the perpetrator, Miss Abrahart, should live in the community. Indeed, Peter Gibson LJ points out that the Council had earlier brought proceedings for possession against her but that these were suspended while she was sectioned and a decision was taken not to go ahead with the possession action following social services involvement and Miss Abrahart receiving treatment. It is not going to be 'irrelevant', 'irrational' or 'illegal' to take account of responsibilities that they have towards the perpetrator, of the resource implications of acting, or of any policy they may have in relation to anti-social behaviour.[164]

There is greater scope for liability in human rights law (see chapter 10). Although UK courts have shown a degree of reluctance to intervene in matters of housing policy, the development of positive obligations suggests that a local authority (or RSL, if performing a public function) may be in breach of Article 8 of the ECHR if it fails to protect a victim from serious anti-social behaviour. This is most likely if the conduct is so extreme that it threatens the Article 2 right to life, but there are now several cases that show that the ECtHR

---

[161] Law Commission, 'Renting Homes 1: Status and Security' (Law Com CP No 162, 2002).

[162] *Mowan v Wandsworth* (2001) 33 HLR 56 (CA).

[163] The classic exposition by Lord Diplock in *Council of Civil Service Unions and Others v Minister for Civil Service* [1985] AC 374 (HL) 410–11.

[164] See E Hawkey, 'Intensive care' ROOF Jan/Feb 2002 32.

will not be willing to condone inaction by a local authority where disturbances have a serious impact on the enjoyment of the home (even without any threat to personal security). In *Surugiu v Romania,* the ECtHR found the authorities to be liable for failing to take any steps to stop interferences with the applicant's land and home that had occurred over many years, which included acts such as dumping loads of manure, and threatening and insulting behaviour.[165] In *Moreno Gomez v Spain,* the applicant complained that the local authority had failed to put a stop to night-time disturbances stemming from noise from nightclubs.[166] The local authority here had declared the area to be an 'acoustically saturated zone', but even after resolutions not to permit any new nightclubs it granted a further licence for a discotheque. Eventually, having failed in her domestic remedies, the applicant complained to Strasbourg. The ECtHR upheld a complaint that there had been a violation of Article 8 and awarded pecuniary damages for the cost of installing double glazing, as well as non pecuniary damages and costs. The judgment of the Court could easily be applied to the problem of anti-social behaviour in England, particularly given that social landlords are under a duty to have procedures to deal with this in place. The Court held that:

> [53] … the individual has a right to respect for his home, meaning not just the right to the actual physical area, but also to the quiet enjoyment of that area. Breaches of the right to respect of the home are not confined to concrete or physical breaches, such as unauthorised entry into a person's home, but also include those that are not concrete or physical, such as noise, emissions, smells or other forms of interference. A serious breach may result in the breach of a person's right to respect for his home if it prevents him from enjoying the amenities of his home…

> [61] Although the Valencia City Council has used its powers in this sphere to adopt measures (such as the bylaw concerning noise and vibrations) which should in principle have been adequate to secure respect for the guaranteed rights, it tolerated, and thus contributed to, the repeated flouting of the rules which it itself had established during the period concerned. Regulations to protect guaranteed rights serve little purpose if they are not duly enforced and the Court must reiterate that the Convention is intended to protect effective rights, not illusory ones. The facts show that the applicant suffered a serious infringement of a right to respect for her home as a result of the authorities' failure to take action to deal with the night-time disturbances.

What remains unclear in relation to the Article 8 positive obligations, is the level of public authority involvement required in order for there to be a sufficient nexus between the State and the victim to support a direct action in human rights law. This gets little attention in academic commentary or case law, but it is worth noting that in the cases in which there has been held to be an Article 8 violation the public authority has not been an 'innocent onlooker'. The Grand Chamber in *Hatton v UK* notes that:

> Article 8 may apply in environmental cases whether the pollution is directly caused by the State or where the State responsibility arises from the failure properly to regulate private industry.[167]

---

[165] (App No 48995/99) ECHR 20 April 2004.
[166] (App No 4143/02) (2005) 41 EHRR 40.
[167] *Hatton v United Kingdom* (App No 36022/97) (2003) 37 EHRR 28 [98] (a case involving noise from night flights).

Elsewhere it refers to this as 'domestic irregularity'[168] and observes that in previous cases where environmental questions gave rise to Convention violations there was always some domestic irregularity.[169] In a Court of Appeal case on asylum seekers, *Ala Anufrijeva v Southwark*, Lord Woolf CJ states that before:

> ... inaction can amount to a lack of respect for private and family life, there must be some ground for criticising the failure to act. There must be an element of culpability. At the very least there must be knowledge that the claimant's private and family life were at risk.[170]

In anti-social behaviour cases, if a public authority has knowledge of the problem then the powers to act given to social landlords will probably suffice to put the authority under a positive obligation to act. In a Northern Irish case, *Re Donnelly's Application for Judicial Review*, it has been held that failing to take possession proceedings violated Article 8 (see discussion in chapter 10).[171] It could therefore be that in a case such as *Hussain v Lancaster CC*[172] (a striking out case) the victim would be more successful bringing an action against the local authority under the Human Rights Act 1998 than trying to sue the local authority as landlord of the perpetrators.[173] This was a case involving extreme racial harassment by a group of youths (many of whom were tenants of the local authority) directed at the Hussain family. The nuisance claim failed, according to Hirst LJ, because the nuisance was not committed by the youths from their land, and the local authority was not responsible for the nuisance acts of its tenants. As the local authority did, however, possess various powers to act, and was well aware of the severe interference with the Hussain family's Article 8 (and possibly Article 2)[174] rights, it may well be that this would place them under a positive obligation to protect the Hussain family.

Although it can be difficult to pursue an effective remedy against a local authority for failing to deal with complaints about anti-social behaviour, there is also the option of reporting a case to the Local Government Ombudsman (on the role of ombudsmen see 11.8.2.3 below). So, for example, in a complaint against Bristol City Council there was found to be maladministration because although the Council had a 'clear and robust policy for dealing with complaints about antisocial behaviour', a number of errors had been made in applying it because of a breakdown in communication and because the key officers were not sufficiently familiar with the policy.[175] Not only did the complaint lead to various procedural recommendations being made to the Council (including immediate investigation of the continuing problems experienced by the victim) but also compensation of £2,000 was recommended.[176]

---

[168] *Hatton v United Kingdom* (App No 36022/97) (2003) 37 EHRR 28 [120].

[169] In *Lopez Ostra v Spain* (App No 16798/90) (1995) 20 EHRR 277 the complaint related to factory pollution and the State had facilitated (possibly encouraged) the siting of the factory in the particular location, and stood by whilst it operated without the necessary license. In *Guerra v Italy* (App No 14967/89) (1998) 26 EHRR 357 the State had breached its own domestic laws in failing to supply information about the risk of toxic poison from a factory.

[170] *Anufrijeva v Southwark LBC* [2003] EWCA Civ 1406 [45].

[171] [2003] NICA 55, [2004] NI 189.

[172] [2000] QB 1 (CA).

[173] Not an option on the facts as the Human Rights Act 1998 was not in force at the relevant time.

[174] Article 2: Everyone's right to life shall be protected by law.

[175] Report on an investigation into complaint no 05/B/11750 against Bristol City Council (30 October 2006).

[176] See also complaint no 05/A/02280 against Milton Keynes Borough Council (8 January 2007) for a finding of maladministration for failing properly to deal with a complaint about anti-social behaviour and for failing to treat the associated application for transfer with sufficient urgency.

11.7 Ensuring Effective Management

11.7.1 The Role of Codes

A number of guides are available that aim to promote good management. In practice, however, they do not have a significant impact upon management as knowledge of their existence is very patchy, and they are not readily accessible to members of the public. The Business Lease Code 2007 is mostly directed to issues to be taken account of when negotiating the new lease and although there is some reference to ongoing management, it is not really a guide as to how to manage a property well.[177] There is a guide to good practice on service charges in commercial property (see chapter 13).[178] Codes have not been much used in the agricultural sector, although recently a code of practice for agri-environment schemes and diversification has been issued to provide a framework for landlords and tenants to use in agreeing what agri-environment and diversification schemes can be pursued under existing tenancy arrangements.

In the residential sector, management of social housing is steered through the extensive regulatory guides issued by government departments and the Housing Corporation. The Charter for Housing Association Applicants and Residents issued by the Housing Corporation specifies a number of management guides, such as the need for an effective complaints and compensation policy, consultation over major works and shaping services around customer needs.

In the private residential sector there is a statutory procedure for the approval of codes to 'promote desirable practices in relation to ... the management of residential property'. [179] Two such Codes, published by the Royal Institution of Chartered Surveyors, have been approved: the *Rent Only Residential Management Code*[180] (applicable to properties 'where only rent is payable to the landlord ... and the landlord is usually responsible for expenses of repairing and servicing the property'), and the *Service Charge Residential Management Code*[181] (for leaseholders who pay a service charge). They are addressed primarily to 'the manager' and cover issues relating to holding tenant's money, dealing with disputes, repairs, etc. Breach of the code does not of itself give rise to a cause of action, but the code may be put before any court as evidence of good practice, and (in the case of long leases) failure to comply with the code is one of the grounds for an application to the Leasehold Valuation Tribunal to appoint a new manager or to end the right to manage.[182] There is also an approved Code issued by the Association of Retirement Housing Managers which refers specifically to purpose-built retirement property.[183] It is intended that the codes will drive up standards of management and maintenance and encourage dialogue with tenants, but

---

[177] Joint Working Group on Commercial Leases, 'The Code for Leasing Business Premises in England and Wales 2007' (2007).

[178] RICS Code of Practice, *Service Charges in Commercial Property* (June 2006).

[179] The Leasehold Reform, Housing and Urban Development Act 1993 s 87.

[180] 2nd edn (Coventry, RICS, 2002).

[181] (Coventry, RICS, 1997).

[182] The Leasehold Reform, Housing and Urban Development Act 1993 s 87(7).

[183] Association of Retirement Housing Managers, 'Code of Practice' (2006).

given how poorly they are publicised they are unlikely to reach private landlords who do not already employ managing agents.

The Housing Act 2004 also gives power to the Secretary of State to approve codes for managing houses that have been exempted from the definition of HMOs; and codes of practice for student accommodation let from university landlords have been adopted.[184]

11.7.2 Consultation and Involving Tenants in Management

11.7.2.1 Communication and Tenant Satisfaction

Tenant satisfaction may be influenced by the degree to which tenants are consulted in relation to matters that affect them. It is clearly good practice for landlords and tenants to keep each other abreast of proposed future activities. Indeed, the Royal Institution of Chartered Surveyors' James Report, annexed to the Nugee Report,[185] stated that where there was good communication, there tended to be fewer management difficulties in relation to long residential leases.

Surveys in the residential tenancy sector show that more than 80 per cent of tenants regard the landlord as very good or fairly good at keeping them informed of things that affect them as tenants.[186] In contrast, tenant satisfaction levels in the commercial property sector are very low, with tenants complaining of poor communication, adversarial stances, and slow response times to problems.[187]

11.7.2.2 Consultation Rights in the Social Sector

It is only in the social housing sector that there are legal rights to consultation. In the social sector, tenant 'voice power' in the form of representation and participation in management is also perceived as a way of addressing the fact that there is no effective market in social housing; through this tenants are able to be part of the regulatory mechanism in place to ensure that social landlords deliver quality services.[188] Even before the introduction of legal rights, however, a number of local authorities had already set up formal schemes for involving tenants in management decisions.[189] Legal rights to information and consultation

---

[184] Universities UK/SCOP 'Code of Practice for the Management of Student Housing' (20 February 2006); The Accreditation Network UK, 'Code of Standards for Larger Developments for Student Accommodation Managed and Controlled by Educational Establishments' (2007); The Accreditation Network UK, 'Code of Standards for Larger Developments for Student Accommodation Not Managed and Controlled by Educational Establishments' (2007).

[185] Nugee Committee, 'Report of the Committee of Enquiry on the Management of Privately Owned Blocks of Flats' (London, 1985).

[186] DCLG, Live Tables, Chart S807, 'How good landlord is at keeping residents informed of things that affect them as tenants'.

[187] RICS, 'Tenant Satisfaction Index: Tune into Tenants' (2005).

[188] The Cave Review of Social Housing Regulation, 'Independent review of regulation of social housing: A call for evidence' (DCLG, December 2006) 9; J Hills, 'Ends and means: The future roles of social housing in England' (CASE Report 34, February 2007) 21. The Cave Review recommended that a 'national tenant voice' be established with a remit over the entire social housing domain: M Cave, 'Every Tenant Matters: A review of social housing regulation' (June 2007). The government's consultation in response to this suggests that it might have a focus on an advocacy role as there are other national bodies already representing tenants: DCLG, 'Tenant Empowerment: A consultation paper' (June 2007) 24.

[189] R Goodland, 'Developments in tenant participation: accounting for growth' in D Cowan and A Marsh (eds), Two Steps Forward (Bristol, The Policy Press, 2001) 188–89.

were first introduced for council tenants by the Housing Act 1980. Section 105 requires a local authority landlord to inform secure tenants of housing management proposals that are likely to affect them substantially, and to give the tenants an opportunity to 'make their views known' and to consider any resulting representations made. This duty is, however, very subjectively worded: the local authority is only required to maintain such arrangements as *it considers appropriate* to provide the information, the duty relates to matters which *in the opinion of the local authority* relate to housing management, and it is left to the local authority to decide if these matters are likely substantially to affect the secure tenants or a group of them. The National Consumer Council was 'dismayed' at the weakness of this because of the discretion given to landlords.[190]

In *R (on the application of Beale) v Camden LB* a group campaigning against Camden's proposal to set up an ALMO to manage its housing stock objected that in consulting its tenants Camden had not set out the case against the proposal.[191] Munby J held that it was not under a legal obligation to do so and that the court could not intervene if a reasonable authority could have concluded that the consultation exercise would enable Camden's 'tenants and leaseholders to be reasonably informed as to the nature of, the reasons for and the implications of, its ALMO proposals'.[192] Although the duty in section 105 does not include a requirement to consult on rents or service charges, a significant number of local authorities do so.[193]

Section 106A, together with Schedule 3A, require consultation prior to a stock transfer (indeed, if a majority of tenants oppose the proposal, then the transfer cannot go ahead; see chapter 25).

11.7.2.3 Residential Tenant Involvement in Management

More recently, there has been a move towards not merely consultation but active tenant participation in management, at least in relation to residential tenants. The rights of long leaseholders were discussed earlier in the chapter (see 11.4 above). In the local authority sector tenants have had a statutory right to manage their homes through Tenant Management Organisations (TMOs) since 1994.[194] RSL tenants do not have a similar right to manage, partly for the reason that while many local authority tenants live on estates, RSL stock has historically tended to be more spatially dispersed.[195] Although the government has no plans to extend the statutory right to manage to RSL tenants,[196] it is proposing that in all social housing there should be a voluntary route to tenant management.[197]

---

[190] J Birchall, 'Council Tenants – Sovereign Consumers or Pawns in the Game?' in J Birchall, *Housing Policy in the 1990s* (London, Routledge, 1992) 172.

[191] [2004] EWHC 6 (Admin).

[192] [2004] EWHC 6 (Admin) [34] and [35].

[193] R Goodland, 'Developments in tenant participation: accounting for growth' in D Cowan and A Marsh (eds), *Two Steps Forward* (Bristol, The Policy Press, 2001) 189.

[194] TMOs are tenant organisations which take on the responsibility for management with the local authority retaining ownership of the stock. A tenant-led TMO can enter into management contracts with the landlord. They must comply with certain statutory conditions. Some TMOs manage a few properties, others manage thousands.

[195] DCLG, 'Tenant Empowerment: A consultation paper' (June 2007) 18.

[196] As it does not wish to increase regulatory burdens, cause a loss in lender confidence, or threaten the private sector classification of RSLs: DCLG, 'Tenant Empowerment: A consultation paper' (June 2007) 19.

[197] DCLG, 'Tenant Empowerment: A consultation paper' (June 2007).

Even when there is not a full transfer of management powers to tenants, as with TMOs, tenants can be involved with management in other ways. Consultation was discussed in the previous section. Involvement in decision making is also promoted through 'tenant participation'. The first collective rights to tenant participation followed from the introduction of compulsory Tenant Participation Compacts (TPCs) in April 2000.[198] These compacts, or agreements, between local authorities and tenants explain how tenants can get involved collectively in local decisions on housing matters. The Housing Corporation requires RSLs to follow a similar approach. Social landlords are also encouraged to involve tenants in governance. Although the primary objective of Arms Length Management Organisations (ALMOs)[199] is to deliver decent homes, they are also promoted as a means of increasing tenant participation in management; the governance model used for ALMOs requires a minimum of one third of the board of management comprising tenants. It is also likely that 'tenant-led' ALMOs will be developed.[200] The Tenant Involvement Commission proposed a Customer First Plan for housing associations to adopt, emphasising the need for housing associations to listen to tenants and to involve tenants in the management of their homes.[201] It is the norm for stock transfer housing associations to have tenants as board members, and from April 2008, the Housing Corporation will require large housing associations to have at least one resident board member.[202] While tenant involvement at board level may be seen as good governance, the irony is that tenants (who perceive themselves as the voice of the residents) are legally obliged to act neutrally in the interests not of the tenant body but of the organsiation.[203]

There are different objectives underlying the moves to greater tenant involvement in management: it can be about sharing in a partnership with the landlord, giving real power to tenants, or to do with accountability.[204] Certainly, it is portrayed by government as being to do with empowering tenants, in line with a consumerist approach. The Best Value in Housing and Homelessness framework (BVHH) states that:

> Tenant Empowerment is at the heart of the government's drive to ensure that decent homes are available to all those renting from social housing landlords. Ministers expect tenants to have meaningful opportunities to participate in the day-to-day management of their properties, as well as to be involved in their landlords' strategic decision-making processes.

[198] See ODPM, 'National Framework for Tenant Participation Compacts' (March 2005).

[199] At present, ALMOs are companies set up by the local authority to manage and improve its housing stock, whilst the local authority retains ownership. See ch 5 and 11.7.3.2.

[200] DCLG, 'Tenant Empowerment: A consultation paper' (June 2007) 32. These would differ from existing ALMOs in that they would be tenant owned. As well as managing properties there may also be a transfer of the ownership of housing assets to the ALMO.

[201] Tenant Involvement Commission, 'What Tenants Want: Report of the Tenant Involvement Commission' (National Housing Federation, 2006).

[202] This applies to all housing associations owning 250 or more units of social housing; for those with more than 1000 units there must be a higher level of resident involvement: The Housing Corporation, 'Housing Corporation requirements in relation to resident involvement' (Circular, May 2007). The Tenant Involvement Commission proposed that at least one quarter of board membership should be open to tenants.

[203] Audit Commission and Housing Corporation, 'Housing: Improving services through resident involvement' (June 2004).

[204] See generally M Riseborough, 'More control and choice for users? Involving tenants in social housing management' in A Marsh and D Mullins, *Housing and Public Policy: Citizenship, Choice and Control* (Buckingham, Open University Press, 1998).

A number of assumptions underpin these objectives. First, that tenant participation will improve the quality of management. That it does so is asserted clearly by the government; in the forward to the National Framework for Tenant Participation Compacts (2005) the Minister for Housing, Keith Hill, states that:

> ... there is clear evidence that good quality tenant involvement delivers better, more effective and efficient services. At the estate and neighbourhood levels, local approaches to housing management in which tenants play a key role can help to sustain local communities and turn around deprived neighbourhoods.

Research shows that TPCs appear to have made local authorities more customer focused, but whether they have had an impact on housing service delivery is very difficult to assess.[205] TMOs, which take tenant involvement much further, are also said to be effective, often more so than landlord management.[206] Second, tenant involvement fits with the policy thrust of treating tenants as consumers, and the Tenant Involvement Commission found that tenants want the relationship to go beyond customer service to become one of partnership. A number of commentators see tenant participation as reflecting a new approach to governing, in which the individual is made active in their self government.[207] In social housing terms, the tenant is no longer a 'passive welfare recipient' but an 'autonomous, empowered and responsible individual' and:

> ... the empowerment of tenants is given an explicit moral worth as, through participating in the management of their housing, their conduct is aligned with the normalised acts of consumption and socially beneficial self-regulation ascribed to owner occupiers.[208]

A third assumption, that tenants want to be involved in management, is more doubtful. Whilst it is undoubtedly the case that tenants wish to know 'what is happening' and be consulted, it is less obvious that they would wish to devote time and energy to involvement in the management process.[209] The Tenant Involvement Commission found a huge appetite amongst tenants for *choice*, from choosing the look of a new kitchen to whether new community buildings should be built.[210] Choice (or voice) is, however, quite different from involvement in management. Although there was support for tenant involvement through board representation (but much less for TMOs), there was a strong sense that what tenants really want it to be consulted and listened to without having to carry the responsibility of management.[211] Inevitably, only a small selection of tenants choose to become involved in

---

[205] Aldbourne Associates and IRIS Consulting, 'Interim Evaluation of Tenant Participation Compacts' (ODPM, October 2003) 17, 20–22.

[206] DCLG, 'Tenant Empowerment: A consultation paper' (June 2007) para 3.9.

[207] This argument is developed strongly by D Cowan and M McDermont, *Regulating Social Housing, Governing Decline* (Abingdon, Routledge-Cavendish, 2006).

[208] J Flint, 'ReConfiguring Agency and Responsibility in the Governance of Social Housing in Scotland' (2004) 41 *Urban Studies* 151, 153.

[209] See also M Riseborough, 'More control and choice for users? Involving tenants in social housing management' in A Marsh and D Mullins, *Housing and Public Policy: Citizenship, Choice and Control* (Buckingham, Open University Press, 1998) 224.

[210] Tenant Involvement Commission, 'What Tenants Want: Report of the Tenant Involvement Commission' (National Housing Federation, 2006) ch 4.

[211] Tenant Involvement Commission, 'What Tenants Want: Report of the Tenant Involvement Commission' (National Housing Federation, 2006) ch 5.

this manner and Carr and others suggest that tenant participation can in fact 'further marginalise those who, for a variety of reasons find it difficult to express their views'.[212] Early evidence supports this. Research for the ODPM suggests that TPCs, while strengthening the hand of tenants' representatives, have not broadened participation and, indeed, there is a degree of concern that tenant activists are not representative.[213] This research also found that most local authorities had focused on developing an authority wide TPC and only 35 per cent had developed issue based or local compacts, despite earlier research that showed tenants were most interested in local issues.[214]

Tenant involvement in housing is generally regarded as a 'good thing' but there are serious questions that remain about its utility and content. The question also arises, as with anti-social behaviour:

> ... why have social housing tenants been singled out for special attention?
>
>   So far the evidence suggests that social landlords have been directed and pressured to 'do tenant involvement' as a result of central control through regulation and funding ... It ... suggests that social tenants are somehow seen to need to be involved more than those in other tenures. Does this mean that social tenants are perceived as a social problem or are they seen as the victims of structural and pervasive inequality which results in many of them being socially and economically excluded? Either way the implication is that social control is a paramount function of involvement, although the analysis of the issue is different. Conse-quently, tenants are cast in the role of the oppressed who need to be empowered, are seen as useful unpaid actors who can help solve social problems or are given walk on parts as consumers.[215]

11.7.3 Delivery of Management Services: Delegation and Best Value

11.7.3.1 Landlord or Agent Management?

A landlord will often use an agent to manage property. In the commercial sector, particu-larly where the landlord lets more than one property in the locality, it is usual for the landlord to employ a professional management company to look after the landlords' properties.

In the private rented sector, landlords often find management difficult: in the five-year period prior to the 2001 English House Condition Survey the landlords of 44 per cent of properties had had problems dealing with difficult tenants,[216] although a later survey shows

---

[212] H Carr, D Sefton-Green and D Tissier, 'Two steps forward for tenants?' in D Cowan and A Marsh (eds), *Two Steps Forward* (Bristol, The Policy Press, 2001) 165. This view is supported by the research conducted by M Riseborough, 'More control and choice for users? Involving tenants in social housing management' in A Marsh and D Mullins, *Housing and Public Policy: Citizenship, Choice and Control* (Buckingham, Open University Press, 1998).

[213] Aldbourne Associates and IRIS Consulting, 'Interim Evaluation of Tenant Participation Compacts' (ODPM, October 2003) 17.

[214] Aldbourne Associates and IRIS Consulting, 'Interim Evaluation of Tenant Participation Compacts' (ODPM, October 2003) 5–6.

[215] M Riseborough, 'More control and choice for users? Involving tenants in social housing management' in A Marsh and D Mullins, *Housing and Public Policy: Citizenship, Choice and Control* (Buckingham, Open University Press, 1998) 239.

[216] ODPM, 'English House Condition Survey 2001: Private Landlords Survey' (December 2003) 20.

that few management problems are serious.[217] More than half of landlords manage properties themselves.[218] Properties let or managed by agents tend to be the better quality properties, and better business practices are used more frequently when agents are involved (such as requiring references, supplying written contracts, inspecting and taking deposits). Given the assumption made in government policy documents that the majority of landlords are well-intentioned but lacking in experience, a growing number of support and advice initiatives are being developed by local authorities to assist with landlord management, such as 'kite marking' schemes and landlord forums. To deal with 'bad landlords' the Housing Act 2004 (as mentioned earlier) enables local authorities to introduce selective licensing: complementing these powers, it is also possible for a local authority to take over the management of individual properties if there are significant anti-social behaviour problems which the landlord is failing to tackle.[219]

Given the difficulties with managing blocks of flats, a surprising number of long lease-holders manage the property themselves: nearly 40 per cent manage without any professional help, and 47 per cent employ managing agents (two thirds of these are appointed by landlords, one third by the leaseholders' own management company).[220]

11.7.3.2 Local Authority Delegation of Management

Local authorities are also able to delegate management functions, in line with the government drive to separate the housing management functions of local authorities from their strategic role.[221] Delegation of management functions will involve entering into a management agreement under section 27 of the Housing Act 1985, which requires the consent of the Secretary of State as well as consultation with tenants under section 105 of the Housing Act 1985. Delegation can occur in one of four ways, to:

(a)   ALMOs;

(b)   TMOs;[222]

(c)   bodies managing housing as part of private finance initiative schemes (PFI can be used only for part of the local authority's housing stock, the local authority retains ownership, typical PFI contracts last for about 30 years and management is often sub-contracted to a housing association); and

(d)   RSLs.[223]

---

217 ODPM, 'English House Condition Survey 2003: Private Landlords Survey' (April 2006) ch 6.

218 Agents are responsible for day to day management in 48% of 'open market' dwellings: ODPM, 'English House Condition Survey 2003: Private Landlords Survey' (April 2006) 36.

219 The Housing (Interim Management Orders) (Prescribed Circumstances) (England) Order 2006 SI 2006/369.

220 P Robinson, *Leasehold Management: A Good Practice Guide* (Coventry, Chartered Institute of Housing, National Housing Federation and the Housing Corporation, 2003) 3.

221 Some doubt whether there is evidence that this leads to a better service: C Holmes, *A New Vision for Housing* (London, Routledge, 2006) 64.

222 The Housing (Right to Manage) Regulations 1994 SI 1994/627. In 2002 there were 202 TMOs in England (and 81 in development), covering 84,000 homes – a fraction of the homes managed by ALMOs. They mostly perform better than their host local authority: ODPM, 'Tenants Managing: Evaluation of Tenant Management Organisations in England' (Research Summary 174, 2002). The government proposes to make it easier for tenants to set up TMOs: DCLG, 'Tenant Empowerment: A consultation paper' (June 2007).

223 See ODPM, 'Enabling local authorities to contract their Antisocial Behaviour Order functions to organisations managing their housing stock, Consultation paper' (November 2005).

ALMOs have proved the most popular route: almost one half of council homes are managed by them. The Cave Review advocates greater diversity in providers of management to social housing so that, for example, an RSL should be able to contract with an ALMO for the latter to undertake management.[224]

Since 2000 local authorities have had to carry out all local authority functions (including housing management) with regard to a duty of Best Value, requiring them:

> ... to secure continuous improvement in the way in which [their] ... functions are exercised, having regard to a combination of economy, efficiency and effectiveness.[225]

This means that local authority housing services must be responsive to the needs of users, of a high quality and cost effective, and fair and accessible to all who need them. Although this duty does not strictly apply to RSLs, the Housing Corporation expects them to apply a similar approach.

11.7.4 Ensuring Compliance

As noted in the Cave Review, there is a particular need for strong regulation of social housing because the shortage of affordable housing has created a system:

> ... in which tenants cannot switch and are put at risk of poor treatment by providers, which face limited pressures to offer good service and choice, or even to operate efficiently. Not all providers will behave in this way. But when they do, the error will not be self-correcting, as it is in other market contexts. This is not a standard market failure but a consequence of the objective of delivering housing at affordable rather than market prices.[226]

Consequently, social housing providers are heavily regulated. Both local authorities and housing associations are subject to best value and inspection by the Audit Commission. In order to qualify for the funding available to ALMOs to help bring homes up to the decent home standard, they need to obtain a top star rating from the Housing Inspectorate. The Housing Corporation acts as regulator of RSLs. The Cave Review has recommended that the regulation of social housing be changed by the creation of a single independent regulatory body for all social housing providers.[227]

Attention is now turning to compliance in the private sector. Letting associations have promoted various self-regulation schemes but there is a perception that in practice the law has little impact on how the landlord and tenant behave. There is thought to be widespread non-compliance: a lack of knowledge about the law, and a reluctance to invoke the law. High levels of ignorance reflect the amateurish nature of private landlordism. The absence of security means that tenants seldom complain about their landlord's behaviour; landlords may shortcut legal processes because of the delays and frustrations in

---

[224] M Cave, 'Every Tenant Matters: A review of social housing regulation' (June 2007).

[225] Local Government Act 1999 s 3. See 'Best Value in Housing and Homelessness Framework' (BVHH). The duty of Best Value replaced Compulsory Competitive Tendering.

[226] M Cave, 'Every Tenant Matters: A review of social housing regulation' (June 2007) 12.

[227] The government supports this for RSLs and for 'for profit' providers but wishes to consult further on the issue of whether it should also be the regulatory body for local authority landlords: DCLG, 'Delivering Housing and Regeneration: Communities England and the future of social housing regulation' (Consultation, June 2007) paras 7.25–7.29.

waiting for the full process. This has generated discussion on how to improve 'compliance'. The Law Commission is considering how better to promote responsible behaviour by landlords.[228] Its consultation paper considers, but rejects, licensing and voluntary self-registration as the way forward. Instead, it proposes a scheme of 'enforced self-regulation' that would require landlords to join an accreditation scheme or landlords' association, or to use a letting agent which is a member of a professional body. A central regulator would approve and regulate the schemes, associations and professional bodies.

There is, however, little hard data on the size of the 'compliance problem'. When referring to the 'good and well-intentioned landlords' the Housing Green Paper of 2000 implicitly accepts that there is non-compliance through inadvertence and amateurism (as well as the more deliberate and exploitative breaches by a 'small minority' of bad landlords).[229] Even the Law Commission paper has no evidence as to whether the compliance problem occurs throughout the private rented sector or is focussed on the worst properties rented out by bad landlords. Regulation, particularly if it increases costs and 'red tape', can act as a disincentive to landlords entering or remaining in the market; any steps taken in this direction must, therefore, be taken cautiously.

11.8 Disputes

A variety of dispute resolution mechanisms are available to respond to disagreements between landlord and tenant. Where a point of law or statutory interpretation is at issue, the courts will usually be the most appropriate forum for this to be decided in. Judicial proceedings can, however, be protracted and expensive. Further, they will not always be appropriate; the outcome will involve there being a winner and a loser, whereas sometimes the parties want to achieve something else, particularly if they are in an ongoing relationship. There are several alternative mechanisms for dispute resolution in the landlord and tenant relationship that may provide not only quicker and cheaper resolution, but also a more effective outcome for both parties.

11.8.1 Commercial and Agricultural

In the commercial sector, the lease may contain provisions for dispute resolution. It is common to provide that disputes, particularly in relation to rent review, can either be referred to arbitration or to an independent expert. The benefits of appointing an arbitrator or expert are that they are usually property professionals who will have expert knowledge of the problem before them, such as the proper value of a commercial lease in a particular area. The authority and jurisdiction of an independent expert depends on the terms of the lease, whereas disputes referred to arbitration are subject to the provisions of the Arbitration Act 1996.[230] There are a number of detailed differences between referral to an arbitrator and to an independent expert.[231]

---

[228] Law Commission, 'Encouraging Responsible Letting' (Law Com CP No 181, 2007).
[229] DETR, 'Quality and Choice: A Decent Home for All – The Housing Green Paper' (April 2000).
[230] Or, in the case of older leases, the earlier Arbitration Acts of 1950 and 1979.
[231] For a summary of these in tabular form, see C Edwards and P Krendel, *Institutional Leases in the 21st Century* (London, EG Books, 2007) 88–9.

The aim of these alternative dispute resolution routes is to enable disputes to be resolved in a fair and impartial manner, without delay and expense, and in a private arena.

Both experts and arbitrators can refer not only to the law but can also take account of other considerations (for example, common business practice).[232] Although it is possible to appeal to court from an arbitrator's decision, the grounds are very limited. There is no right of appeal from an expert's determinations. Arbitration can prove to be cheaper than taking a matter to court, but this will not necessarily be the case as, particularly in the larger commercial disputes, both parties are still likely to have legal representation.

Arbitration is also used in the agricultural sector, although the approach adopted by the Agricultural Tenancies Act 1995 is to encourage alternative dispute resolution, with arbitration being used as a fallback.[233]

There is a recognised need for more effective dispute resolution that is quick, effective and inexpensive. The British Retail Consortium notes that the tenant unreasonably refused consent to assign will usually find that the deal has fallen through by the time he has been able to challenge the refusal. Further, there was initial outcry from the property industry when the Law Commission proposed the abolition of the 'self-help' remedy of forfeiture by physical re-entry[234] as this would lead to unacceptable delays in the recovery of possession. Following the civil justice reforms stemming from the Woolf reforms[235] ADR (alternative dispute resolution, or, sometimes, *appropriate* dispute resolution) is actively encouraged as part of active case management, in accordance with the 'overriding objective' to 'deal with cases justly'. Nonetheless, it remains difficult to obtain speedy remedies.

11.8.2 Residential

11.8.2.1 Infrequent Use of Judicial Action

In the residential sector, there are a number of alternatives already available besides court resolution. In fact, compared to the number of complaints that there are about housing law, relatively few end up in court. This is not surprising. Obtaining legal advice in the first place can be difficult; not only is the legal aid budget severely limited so that few tenants can access paid legal advice, but there are 'housing advice deserts' in which there are simply no legal advisers with the relevant expertise.[236] Further, most consumers prefer to deal with matters informally,[237] or not at all, rather than pursue complaints by formal legal mechanisms in which the costs of litigation (financial, emotional and health-wise) are often perceived to

---

[232] An arbitrator, however, acts only on evidence submitted to him, but is able to draw the parties' attention to matters that they may not be aware of.

[233] Agricultural Tenancies Act 1995 ss 28–30.

[234] Law Commission, 'Report on the Forfeiture of Tenancies' (Law Com No 142, 1985). See ch 24.

[235] See Lord Woolf, 'Access to Justice: Final Report to the Lord Chancellor on the civil justice system in England and Wales' (London, July 1996).

[236] Citizens Advice Bureau, 'Home Remedies: The challenges facing publicly funded housing advice, meeting the challenge of access to justice' (May 2004) para 31.

[237] National Consumer Council, *Seeking Civil Justice – A Survey of People's Needs and Experiences* (1995), referred to in H Collins, *Regulating Contracts* (Oxford, OUP, 1999) 87; H Genn, *Paths to Justice: What People do and think about going to law* (Oxford, Hart, 1999) especially ch 3.

exceed the benefits that stand to be achieved. Social landlords are expected to set out complaints procedures that aggrieved tenants should pursue.[238]

A survey conducted in the context of long leaseholds found that tenants would not use the courts because of the effort involved, the delays in getting a decision and, overwhelmingly, the cost of proceedings.[239] Landlords have expressed similar frustrations with the court system.

11.8.2.2 Mediation

There is also increasing use being made of meditation. This can be particularly appropriate to housing disputes where the parties remain in the landlord-tenant relationship after the dispute is over. Many social landlords publicise the availability of local mediation schemes, and the Civil Procedure Rules also require courts to consider the potential use of mediation.[240] Mediation is not, however, suitable for all disputes: in many cases there is no happy middle ground to work towards, as for example, if the landlord is seeking possession for serious tenant default. Mediation can also work against tenants if there is no 'equality of arms' between the landlord and the tenant.

11.8.2.3 Ombudsmen Schemes

If an issue remains unresolved, the complainant can take the matter further either by referral to an Ombudsman service or by court action.

Complaints about local authorities are made to the Local Government Ombudsman (LGO), who is able to investigate allegations of maladministration. By way of illustration, in a complaint against Oxford City Council a council tenant in sheltered accommodation complained to the LGO that the council had wrongly applied its rent charging system because his home had not been modernised. The LGO made a finding of maladministration causing injustice and recommended that he was paid £1000 for his time, trouble and frustration in pursuing his complaint, and a further sum of around £3600 representing a refund of rent plus interest. In addition, the council agreed to provide appropriate refunds to other tenants who had similarly suffered.[241]

Although the LGO has no jurisdiction to investigate when a remedy is available through a court or tribunal, there is a discretion to admit complaints when satisfied that it is not reasonable for the complainant to pursue the judicial route, and the courts have shown a willingness to allow the LGO to look into complaints where this can provide a just remedy which a court might not be able to.[242]

Complaints about RSLs can be made to the Independent Housing Ombudsman Scheme

---

[238] In the year to March 2006 the most common cause of reference to the IHOS was about the way that landlords handled tenants' complaints: IHOS, 'Housing Ombudsman Service Annual Report and Accounts' (2006) 3.

[239] A Thomas and others, *The Landlord and Tenant Act 1987: Awareness, Experience and Impact* (DoE, 1991) 82 *et seq.*

[240] Civil Procedure Rules 1998 SI 1998/3132.

[241] Complaint 03/B/13806 against Oxford City Council (2006). See also complaint 04/C/17184 against Macclesfield BC (29 August 2006) where the Local Government Ombudsman recommended that the council pay the difference between the price paid to purchase under the RTB and the lower price that the tenant would have paid had she been given the correct advice some years earlier.

[242] *R v Local Commissioner for Local Government for North and North-east England, ex p Liverpool City Council* [2001] 1 All ER 462 (CA).

(IHOS); all RSLs must be members of this scheme, and other private landlords can join on a voluntary basis. The Ombudsman has powers to investigate cases involving maladministration but also, more widely, to investigate any unresolved dispute and his obligation is to make determinations by reference to what, in the opinion of the Ombudsman, is fair in all the circumstances of the case.

Access to Ombudsmen is free, but before making a complaint the applicant must usually have exhausted internal complaint procedures.[243] Housing complaints form the largest single category under the LGO scheme, even excluding housing benefit problems.[244] Under both schemes, many of the complaints made relate to repairs and anti-social behaviour.[245] Ombudsmen are able to make a variety of recommendations, including financial redress, apologies, and procedural reviews, and although there are no direct enforcement mechanisms for these recommendations they carry a 'moral authority' which leads to compliance in practice. Referral to Ombudsmen is probably not appropriate when complex points of law are involved.

The case loads of the Ombudsmen have grown considerably in recent years. Further, as the Law Commission notes, whereas their traditional domain was in citizen and state matters (challenging decisions taken by agents of the State) there has been creepage into party-party matters (disputes between parties to the leasehold relationship), which gives rise to questions as to whether the working methods and enforcement mechanisms are always appropriate.[246] The Cave Review recommends that Ombudsmen services should be unified across the social housing sector.[247]

11.8.3.4 Public Law Remedies

Party-party disputes are the traditional substance of private law suits. Given that local authority landlords are also public bodies, there can be an uncomfortable division between public law and private law remedies for tenants. It is also possible that RSLs, at least when exercising 'public functions', may be vulnerable to public law challenges.[248] For some time following the House of Lords decision in *O'Reilly v Mackman*,[249] the view was that if a public law remedy was available, then an aggrieved person should bring a judicial review action rather than a private law action. This might prove to be limiting in the landlord and tenant context, and, of course, judicial review is not generally an appealing action; it must be brought within a strict three month time limit of the decision being taken and the court is

---

[243] This may change in the case of the LGO: see Cabinet Office, 'Reform of Public Sector Ombudsmen Services in England, Consultation Paper' (August 2005).

[244] LGO Annual Report 2004/05 states that 24% of complaints related to housing (plus a further 8% relating to housing benefit).

[245] Apart from housing benefit complaints, repairs formed by far the biggest category of complaints to the LGO in 2004/05 (26% of housing complaints) (LGO Annual Report 2004/05). Until 2006, repairs were the largest source of complaints to the IHOS (25% of complaints in 2005); in the year ending March 2006, repairs were second to complaints about complaint handling, followed by complaints about anti-social behaviour (IHOS, 'Housing Ombudsman Service Annual Report and Accounts' (2006) 30).

[246] Law Commission, 'Housing: Proportionate Dispute Resolution, An Issues Paper' (March 2006) ch 6.

[247] M Cave, 'Every Tenant Matters: A review of social housing regulation' (June 2007). The Law Commission is also looking at the role of Ombudsmen as part of its project on remedies against public bodies.

[248] Although the law relating to bodies liable to judicial review challenges is different from the law defining public authority for the purposes of the Human Rights Act 1988, similar principles tend to be followed. See ch 10.

[249] [1983] 2 AC 237 (HL).

concerned only with the process of the decision making, to see if the public authority has acted in a manner that is lawful, rational and consistent with natural justice. There has, however, been a relaxation of *O'Reilly* so that is now possible to bring a private law action even if this raises a question as to the validity of a public law decision, and, in defending a private law action, to raise a public law issue.[250] So, for example, in *Wandsworth LBC v Winder*[251] the local authority had issued notices of rent increases which the tenant had felt were excessive and so he had continued to pay the old rent. Wandsworth LBC sued for possession and for the arrears. Winder's defence was that he was not liable for arrears since the rent increases were *ultra vires* and counterclaimed for a declaration to that effect. At first instance the counterclaim and defence were struck out as an abuse of process since a challenge to the council's policies should be initiated by judicial review. The judgment, however, was reversed by the Court of Appeal and the House of Lords. Lord Fraser held that a local authority could be challenged on its policies in a private, as opposed to public, action, at least by way of defence where there is 'a pre-existing private law right'.[252]

In theory, the availability of public law remedies may widen the opportunity for challenge by a tenant. As mentioned above, the Court of Appeal in *Mowan v Wandsworth*[253] hinted that Mrs Mowan might have been able to challenge the landlord's decision not to evict her unruly neighbour by bringing a judicial review action. In practice, however, even if procedurally possible (and not, for example, barred for being out of time), the courts show such a degree of deference to public authority decision making in the context of housing that it will only be in rare cases that a public law challenge is likely to succeed.

11.8.3.5 Courts and Tribunals

In an attempt both to reduce costs and make use of specialisation, a number of housing disputes are now dealt with not in court but before a tribunal, under the umbrella organisation of the Residential Property Tribunal Service (RPTS). This includes Rent Assessment Committees (that deal with disputes about fair and market rents), Leasehold Valuation Tribunals (that deal with leasehold property, for example, disputes over the price to be paid to enfranchise, or liability to pay a service charge), and Residential Property Tribunals (that deal with appeals against denial of the Right to Buy). These tribunals tend to be chaired by a lawyer with expertise and training in housing law, but with expert advice from non-lawyers, including valuers. This offers a considerable advantage over the court system; housing disputes often involve complex points of law and many judges have little knowledge of housing law prior to taking up judicial office.[254] Indeed, the Law Commission is consulting on whether a specialised tribunal should be established to resolve housing disputes.[255] This would incorporate the current RPTS tribunals as well as having jurisdiction to deal with possession and disrepair claims.

---

[250] For fuller discussion, see P Craig, *Administrative Law*, 5th edn (London, Sweet & Maxwell, 2003) 792–805.

[251] [1985] 1 AC 461 (HL).

[252] [1985] 1 AC 461 (HL) 508.

[253] (2001) 33 HLR 56 (CA).

[254] Law Commission, 'Housing: Proportionate Dispute Resolution, An Issues Paper' (March 2006) para 8.17.

[255] Law Commission, 'Housing: Proportionate Dispute Resolution – the Role of Tribunals' (Law Com CP No 180, 2007).

11.8.2.6 Law Commission Consultation on Dispute Resolution

The Law Commission is now conducting a wide ranging consultation exercise to consider how 'a more "holistic approach" for the "proportionate" resolution of housing problems and disputes can be developed'.[256] In this they are concerned to look not only at the narrow question of how justiciable disputes are adjudicated, but to conduct a much broader enquiry as to how to help people who suffer 'housing unhappiness'. This covers how people access housing advice and are supported and guided through a complaint process, as well as the more traditionally legal questions of process that focus on dispute resolution. Further, it acknowledges that a proportionate response may require a balancing of competing values (time, expense, accuracy, fairness, equality of arms and so on) and that it may be appropriate to deal with underlying issues rather than the presenting problem. So, for example, while a possession action may come about because of rent arrears, the cause of this could be anything from problems with housing benefit administration (a very common problem), a dispute with the landlord over the standard of repair, or simple disorganisation.

The Law Commission suggests that a proportionate system could comprise three principal elements: 'triage plus' (advice, diagnosis, oversight and intelligence gathering), non-court/tribunal processes and court/tribunal processes. Triage plus should not simply be reactive but should reach out to make the public aware of its services. One method of doing this would be to adopt the model agreements in the Renting Homes report[257] which will provide information about triage plus. As the Law Commission points out, this model would not be revolutionary but evolutionary, building on processes that are already in place.

---

[256] Law Commission, 'Housing: Proportionate Dispute Resolution, An Issues Paper' (March 2006) para 1.3.
[257] Law Commission, 'Renting Homes: The Final Report. Volume 1: Report' (Law Com No 297, 2006).

12

REPAIR AND MAINTENANCE

12.1   Introduction: standards and repair
12.2   The state of tenanted housing
12.3   Ensuring good standards in rented property
12.4   The duty to repair
12.5   Regulatory controls
12.6   Beyond landlord and tenant law
12.7   Enforcing repairing obligations
12.8   Landlord's remedies for breach of tenant's repairing covenant
12.9   Tenant's remedies for breach of landlord's repairing covenant
12.10   Improvements and alterations

12.1 Introduction: Standards and Repair

There is a degree of overlap between the issues raised in the previous chapter and this chapter, particularly in relation to properties with multiple users and the problems associated with management, but the focus of this chapter is on the physical condition of individual properties. The previous chapter addressed issues relating to wider estate management and collective management issues.

The quality of the built environment will be affected both by initial standards and by the level of maintenance. It is important to appreciate the distinction between standards and maintenance in order to understand the obligations imposed by leasehold agreements. Initial standards will reflect the level of amenities provided, design, construction methods and the quality of materials used when building the property. Repair is to do with maintaining the pre-existing condition of the property rather than ensuring fitness or a good condition.

Although a somewhat broad generalisation, the lease itself seldom has any influence on initial standards; there are virtually no obligations to let a property 'fit for purpose'. Rather, standards tend to be influenced by commercial, social and policy considerations. Building and planning controls will apply on the initial construction. The quality of the build and specification will also be influenced by commercial considerations. For example, a developer landlord of a commercial property may consider it worthwhile investing heavily in completing a building to a high finish in order to secure a good rental income and long term capital growth. Further a number of regulatory controls, such as environmental health laws and mandatory licensing schemes for houses in multiple occupation (HMOs), have a significant impact upon the way that a landlord must behave, particularly in the residential sector.

With regards to maintenance, the lease may provide for things such as the allocation of responsibility for doing repairs, the standard of repair and the question of who has to pay for them. In the residential sector, there are also statutorily implied covenants.

12.2 The State of Tenanted Housing

12.2.1 The Decent Homes Standard

It is only in the residential sector that detailed information is available about standards and repair. Writing in 1991, Luba stated that:

> The state of Britain's housing stock is nothing short of a national scandal. The scale of unfitness and serious disrepair in the homes of this country is now such that present housing policies are completely unable to halt the present rapid decline in standards.[1]

When the Labour government came to power in 1997 it identified a £19 billion backlog in disrepair to local authority housing stock, and more than two million social homes falling below basic decency standards. In 2000 the government set a 'Decent Homes Standard' (DHS) with the target of bringing all social housing up to a decent standard by 2010[2] and for 70 per cent of vulnerable[3] households living in private homes (including owner-occupied) to be in decent homes by 2010. Given the profile of tenants, this means that the decent homes programme should reach those households which are most disadvantaged in society: the majority of lone parents, the poorest fifth of households and workless households, and the majority of households that include anyone who is long-term ill or disabled or elderly (aged 75 or more).[4]

The DHS defines decent homes by reference to four criteria:

(a)   the current minimum standard for housing;[5]
(b)   whether it is in a reasonable state of repair;
(c)   whether it has reasonably modern facilities and services; and
(d)   whether it provides a reasonable degree of thermal comfort (effective insulation and efficient heating).

Against these measures, the number of rented homes failing to meet basic decency standards has fallen significantly since 1996, as shown in the following Table 12.1. The measure of

---

[1] J Luba, *Repairs: Tenants' Rights* 2nd edn (London, Legal Action Group, 1991) 1.

[2] There are three ways in which local authorities can obtain funding to help reach this goal: though stock transfer, creating an Arms Length Management Order (ALMO), or the Private Finance Initiative (PFI) (see ch 5).

[3] Defined as households in receipt of at least one of the principal means tested or disability related benefits: see ODPM, 'A Decent Home – the definition and guidance for implementation' (February 2004).

[4] ODPM, 'English House Condition Survey 2003: Annual Report' (March 2006) para 8.10.

[5] From April 2006, this means the Housing Health and Safety Rating System (HHSRS) introduced by the Housing Act 2004. Prior to that date, standards were referenced to the fitness standard as defined in the Housing Act 1985 s 604. See 12.5.1

Table 12.1: Non-decent Homes by Tenure

% within tenure

	Private rented	RSL[a]	Local Authority	All social
1996	62.4	47.6	53.9	52.6
2005	40.6	23.8	33.7	27.5

Source: DCLG, 'English House Condition Survey 2005' Headline Report (January 2007) Table 1, 3. This survey takes the fitness standard from the Housing Act 1985 as the minimum standard of fitness as the new HHSRS was not in force during the survey period.
[a]Registered Social Landlord.

'decency' includes repair, so the figures given below will reflect not only issues to do with 'initial standards' but also levels of maintenance.

Similar progress has been made in reducing the proportion of vulnerable households living in non-decent homes, as shown in Table 12.2.

Table 12.2: Vulnerable Households

% of vulnerable households in non-decent homes

	Private rented	All Social
1996	72	52.6
2003	54.7	34.3
2005	48.3	Figures not available

Source: ODPM, 'English House Condition Survey 2003: Annual Report' (March 2006) Table 3.2, 67 and DCLG, 'English House Condition Survey 2005' Headline Report (January 2007) Table 4, 7.

Moving towards this decent homes target has been a central aspect of housing management for social landlords in recent years; chapter 5 discusses the ways in which local authorities can choose to deliver the necessary standards. Although it is clear that substantial progress is being made towards improving housing conditions generally, it must not be forgotten that these figures show that significant numbers of households are still living in non-decent homes. In absolute numbers, almost one million private rented homes were non-decent in 2004, and more than 1.2 million social homes. Almost one million vulnerable households were living in non-decent social homes in 2003, and 335,000 in privately rented homes.

The English House Condition Survey 2003 contains a detailed statistical analysis.[6] The most common reason for failing to meet the decency standard is the thermal comfort criterion, although this is where most progress has been made since 1996.[7] What is more

---

[6] ODPM, 'English House Condition Survey 2003: Annual Report' (March 2006).

[7] ODPM, 'English House Condition Survey 2003: Annual Report' (March 2006) paras 2.4 and 2.8.

disappointing is the lack of progress in relation to repair. Almost 9 per cent of homes (including owner occupied) fail on this ground.[8] There has been no significant progress on this measure since 2001. The privately rented sector has the most serious problems; homes with very high levels of disrepair are disproportionately concentrated among the privately rented stock.[9] Around half of privately rented non-decent homes fail because of the repair, fitness or modernisation criteria (compared to a third of the non-decent RSL homes).[10] The costs necessary to reach the thermal comfort standard tend to be lower than other repair costs; this partly explains why privately rented homes are on average more expensive to make decent. The profile of the housing stock also indicates why problems tend to be greatest in the private rented sector. Forty five per cent of privately rented homes were built before 1919 (where repair costs are likely to be higher), with significantly lower percentages of old homes in the social sector (less than ten per cent of local authority homes).[11] There is also a variation between different landlords. Crook comments that landlords who see letting the property as an investment tend to own the properties in the worst condition whereas those in the best condition are more likely to be owned by those who do not have investment motives (such as landlords providing housing for employees).[12] This is, however, only a generalisation: there will also be many investor landlords who rent out properties maintained to a high standard.

12.2.2 Liveability

The English House Condition Survey also tracks wider environmental considerations beyond matters pertaining to the individual property, described as 'liveability'. 'Poor quality environments' are grouped into three main types: those experiencing 'upkeep' problems (rubbish, graffiti, vandalism, general neglect and so on), those with traffic problems (air quality and noise), and those with 'utilisation' problems (derelict properties, intrusive industry). This chapter of the survey does not distinguish between privately owned homes and privately rented homes and the statistics are, therefore, perhaps less useful for our purposes. Nonetheless, it reports that households living on local authority built estates are most likely to have poor quality environments, and particularly, upkeep problems. Further, a significant proportion of households with liveability problems also live in non-decent homes.[13] This has significance in relation to local authority management, both in relation to the repair issues discussed in this chapter and also the general estate management issues discussed in the previous chapter.

---

[8] ODPM, 'English House Condition Survey 2003: Annual Report' (March 2006) paras 2.6.

[9] ODPM, 'English House Condition Survey 2003: Annual Report' (March 2006) para 4.17.

[10] ODPM, 'English House Condition Survey 2003: Annual Report' (March 2006) para 2.14.

[11] ODPM, 'English House Condition Survey 2003: Annual Report' (March 2006) Figure 1.1.

[12] ADH Crook, 'Housing conditions in the private rented sector within a market framework' in S Lowe and D Hughes (eds), *The Private Rented Sector in a New Century: revival or false dawn?* (Bristol, The Policy Press, 2002) 162.

[13] Around 1.2 million households living in poor quality environments also live in non-decent homes. Of these 290,000 (24%) are social sector tenants and 230,000 (19%) are vulnerable private sector households: DCLG, 'English House Condition Survey 2005' Headline Report (January 2007) 10.

12.2.3 Houses in Multiple Occupation

Some of the worst conditions are found in HMOs. HMOs can be variously defined (the definition used in the Housing Act 2004 is considered below); for present purposes an HMO can be loosely understood to refer to premises lived in by more than one household where there is some sharing of amenities. So, for example, it would include a house with a number of bedsits and shared use of the kitchen and bathroom. The greatest risks are associated with what are sometimes referred to as 'traditional HMOs'; typically pre-1919 houses with three or more storeys and five or more habitable rooms. The age of the property, the standard of conversion for multiple use, poor maintenance, the way in which the property is used, and the kind of tenants who often live in HMOs all tend to contribute to the level of risk. Not only is there a concern with the general fitness level, but it is these properties that have the most serious fire records. The OPDM Regulatory Impact Assessment on licensing in the private rented sector explains why these HMOs are subjected to a mandatory licensing scheme under the Housing Act 2004.

> 34. These HMOs have been chosen on the basis of risk. Research indicates that certain types of HMOs present significantly greater health and safety risks to tenants than comparable single occupancy dwellings. Risk assessment carried out by ENTEC for the Department of Environment, Transport and the Regions on fire safety in HMOs [DETR 'Fire Risk in Houses in Multiple Occupation: Research Report' (1998)] concluded that in all houses converted into bedsits, the annual risk of death per person is one in 50,000 (six times higher than in comparable single occupancy houses). In the case of bedsit houses comprising three or more storeys the risk is one in 18,600 (16 times higher).

> 35. In addition to the risk of fire, people living in HMOs may face increased levels of risk in other areas ... [In] HMOs there are ... likely to be significantly increased risks associated with hazards from damp and mould and those associated with intruders. Other hazards such as those associated with hot surfaces, electrical hazards, lead, carbon monoxide, crowding and noise, waste and food safety are also increased in HMOs.[14]

The report also states that poor management and unscrupulous landlords can increase these health and safety risks even if the property is in an acceptable state of repair. Further, occupancy profiles associated with HMO use can also increase the risks (a number of tenants have alcohol or drug dependencies and mental health problems).

12.2.4 Overcrowding

Overcrowding presents a further housing problem. In 2006, the Government estimated that between 350,000 and 410,000 households with dependent children live in overcrowded housing,[15] with the rate of overcrowding highest in the social rented sector.[16] This impacts upon the landlord-tenant relationship in various ways: local authorities possess various

---

[14] ODPM, 'Licensing in the Private Rented Sector. Consultation on the Implementation of HMO Licensing, Regulatory Impact Assessment, Housing Bill, Part 2' (November 2004) 24–5.

[15] DCLG, 'Tackling Overcrowding in England: A Discussion Paper' (July 2006) para 1.2.

[16] In London, 11% of social rented households are overcrowded (rising to 28% and 29% for black African and Bangladeshi households): J Hills, 'Ends and means: The future roles of social housing in England' (CASE Report 34, February 2007) 34.

enforcement powers to deal with overcrowded premises; overcrowding is one of the hazards covered by the Housing Health and Safety Rating System (HHSRS) introduced in the Housing Act 2004, and will be factored into the licensing of HMOs (for details of both, see 12.5 below). Overcrowding also provides one of the grounds that triggers the duty to give 'reasonable preference' in relation to the allocation of social housing (see chapter 6).

12.2.5 The Cost of Repair

How much it costs a landlord to look after a residential property should not be underestimated. Figures on the cost for social housing are given in the Hills review:

> By 2005–06, a total of £34 per week was being spent on supervision, management and regular repair of each council property, with a further £11 per week allowed for major repairs in the subsidy system, and around £10 per week covering interest on borrowing undertaken to improve the housing or build it in the first place, compared with just under £52 per week collected in gross rents (with the difference between rents and spending mainly met by a small net contribution from central government subsidy).[17]

12.2.6 The Private Rented Sector

In the long term, the rental tenure with the most significant problem with housing conditions will be the private sector housing non-vulnerable households. These tend to be older properties with poor amenities and high levels of disrepair. There is no effective obligation placed on a landlord to ensure that the property is habitable when let (although the HHSRS may have some impact on this), and the repairing covenants do not touch these more fundamental issues. Where the property is an HMO, the licensing regime will have some impact, but other properties, not falling with the targets for the Decent Homes Standard or the HMO regime, are likely to continue to be used for sub-standard housing for some time yet.

In purely financial terms there is little short term incentive for landlords to improve the quality of housing. Drawing on evidence from three research projects with which he had been involved, Crook notes that:

> … the worst conditions tend to be in shared dwellings, in urban areas, and occupied by tenants on low incomes, out of work, and in receipt of housing benefit. The dwellings owned in the worst conditions also tend to be owned by landlords who regard them as investments while those in better condition are regarded for non-commercial reasons.[18]

The available evidence on the correlation between investment returns and the state of a property presents a complex picture. Crook uses data from the English House Condition Surveys of 1991 and 1996, and a later survey of landlords,[19] to investigate

---

[17] J Hills, 'Ends and means: The future roles of social housing in England' (CASE Report 34, February 2007) 57. The figures for RSLs are in the region of £40 per week for each property for management, maintenance, major repairs and depreciation, against a rent of £56 per week.

[18] ADH Crook, 'Housing conditions in the private rented sector within a market framework' in S Lowe and D Hughes (eds), *The Private Rented Sector in a New Century: revival or false dawn?* (Bristol, The Policy Press, 2002) 164.

[19] ADH Crook and others, 'Repairs and Maintenance by Private Landlords' (Housing Research Summary, Number 138, DETR, 2000).

this.[20] In doing so, he draws a distinction between condition or fitness, and repair. As seen above, the state of repair is only one aspect contributing to the fitness of property. Crook shows that there is only a weak negative association between rents and outstanding comprehensive repair costs (that is, properties in bad repair suffer only relatively small drops in the rental income), and no association between rents and the level of fitness. When the overall rental rates of return are looked at, the rate of return is generally higher for poorer condition properties. This is because more money is spent on the better condition properties but this expenditure is not fully reflected in the rents receivable: in pure rental investment terms, the landlord is better off not spending money on maintaining and improving the property. However, once the impact on capital values is taken account of the picture changes. Well-repaired dwellings do have higher capital values. In addition, properties in the poorest condition tend to have higher voids (periods during which they are untenanted) and arrears.

The lack of any significant relationship between rents and condition is, perhaps, surprising. One explanation is that tenants are more concerned about superficial aspects of a property (for example its décor) and its location than structural and repair conditions. Given that many tenants have relatively short term commitments to properties this is not an irrational approach. These findings have implications for policy.

> ... [It] suggests that the owners of the worst property were, in effect, 'milking' them for their rental income. Because neither rents and capital values are likely to increase commensurately with improvement works, it may thus not be economically rational, even though it is socially desirable, for landlords of the worst property to undertake such action.
>
> These findings imply that the market is not providing rational investors with sufficient incentives to undertake the work that is needed on the worst properties. In other words, this appears to be a case of market failure. It raises the question of whether an intervention by central or local government could be effective in improving the condition of the worst property. This could involve enforcement action or financial assistance.[21]

Further, to the extent that rents set do reflect conditions, tenants may nonetheless prefer to pay a low rent for poor condition property rather than a higher rent for better property.[22]

12.3 Ensuring Good Standards in Rented Property

The following sections will look at ways of ensuring that the property is in good condition at the start of the letting and kept in good condition throughout the lease. This can be through a mix of public law controls, such as the licensing of HMOs, planning laws and building regulations (that play a part in ensuring that new buildings, in all sectors and all tenures, are built to satisfactory standards), as well as through the leasehold relationship. As between the landlord and tenant, claims can arise in a variety of contexts. In cases of serious disrepair, the

---

[20] ADH Crook, 'Housing conditions in the private rented sector within a market framework' in S Lowe and D Hughes (eds), *The Private Rented Sector in a New Century: revival or false dawn?* (Bristol, The Policy Press, 2002).

[21] ADH Crook, 'Housing conditions in the private rented sector within a market framework' in S Lowe and D Hughes (eds), *The Private Rented Sector in a New Century: revival or false dawn?* (Bristol, The Policy Press, 2002) 172.

[22] J B Cullingworth, *Housing in Transition* (London, Heineman, 1963).

tenant may be forced to move out, or refuse to pay the rent because of the condition of the property, and the issue comes before court in the landlord's action to recover unpaid rent. Other claims involve the tenant bringing an action against the landlord, trying to get him to put the property into a decent condition and, perhaps, seeking damages from the landlord for loss of income (in commercial cases), damage to the tenant's property and general inconvenience.

12.3.1 Repairs and Standards in a Leasehold Context

As will be seen, the law on fitness and repair is not satisfactory. The Law Commission issued a consultation paper in 1992 identifying various defects with the law. The recommendations in the subsequent report issued in 1996 remain unimplemented, although those affecting residential leases, are taken up by the more recent Law Commission report on renting homes. Before considering the details of the law, a number of factors should be highlighted.

12.3.1.1 Fitness for Purpose

With one exception in the case of furnished residential property, there is no requirement that premises should meet any particular standard at the time of letting. The approach in the common law has been one of caveat emptor, and this still governs in the commercial sector. In the residential sector, as will be seen below, as long ago as 1885 this was not considered acceptable and a statutory fitness obligation was introduced. In practice, however, this has been effectively a dead letter for some time and so the practical reality is that even in the residential sector there is no effective minimum standard required when letting property.

The cost implications of imposing a fitness requirement could be considerable. No figures are available on the commercial sector. The English House Condition Survey shows that the cost of making non-decent homes decent (in the private and social rented sectors) would be in the region of almost £14 billion.[23] In *Southwark LBC v Tanner*, Lord Millett noted that the cost of putting sound insulation into all the local authority flats in the borough of Southwark alone would be £37 million.[24] Further, the imposition of legal responsibilities on social landlords is often resisted on the grounds that this will affect their strategic priorities; while they may strive to ensure satisfactory standards, they wish to set their own priorities rather than divert energies and resources to individual claims.

12.3.1.2 Who Should Bear Responsibility for the Condition of Rented Property?

The question as to whether it should be the landlord or the tenant who is responsible for the looking after the property is complex. It will be affected by practical considerations (who is most conveniently placed to remedy problems), economic factors (who can afford to carry the cost, and who has an economic incentive to do so), the relative bargaining strengths of the parties to the lease and policy concerns (a wider public interest in ensuring well maintained properties for reasons of economic prosperity and public health). The answer will vary according to whether the property is designed for commercial or residential use, and

---

[23] Based on figures in Tables 2.4 and 2.5; ODPM, 'English House Condition Survey 2003: Annual Report' (March 2006).

[24] *Southwark LBC v Tanner; Baxter v Camden LBC (No 2)* [2001] 1 AC 1 (HL) 26.

on the length of the lease. Further, and perhaps surprisingly, there is no legal requirement that responsibility for repair is actually dealt with in the lease; with the result that neither party may be responsible.[25]

Part of the difficulty is that the division of interest between landlord and tenant also dilutes the incentive to repair:

> A rational actor puts more effort into looking after something he owns than something he rents because when he owns it he reaps the full benefit of his investment … Splitting ownership from occupancy brings costs to both sides: the benefit of upkeep is split, so neither side is prepared to invest the full amount; the tenant has less incentive to act on problems early, when they are cheaper to fix; and the landlord must spend additional effort monitoring the behaviour of the tenant. The result is that both may invest less time and effort in property maintenance compared to the efficient level.[26]

The tenant will be keenly interested in the standard of amenity and repair as he has day-to-day use of the property; its condition will affect his comfort and, in the case of commercial lettings, the success of his business. On the other hand, the wasting nature of leases provides little incentive for tenants to undertake long term repairs and improvements to rented property as the beneficiary of such works will be the landlord.

For the landlord, there may be little correlation between the standard of repair and the rent receivable (as seen above in relation to residential lettings). On the other hand, the condition of the property is likely to impact on long term investment values. Of course, if the landlord is able to pass on the cost of all repair to the tenant (as is the norm in commercial lettings), the landlord has every incentive to keep the property to a high standard. It is not uncommon, particularly in large commercial developments and blocks of long leasehold flats, for the obligation to repair, maintain and service the property to be placed upon a third party, usually a management company, that will also be made a party to the lease.

There is also a wider public interest argument as the state of rented property affects all aspects of modern society and the economy. Further, poor maintenance feeds into the problem of general neighbourhood decline, something very much at the centre of government concerns nowadays. Maxwell refers to the 'broken window' theory of crime:

> [It] emphasises the signalling function of neighbourhood characteristics: if one window is left broken, passers-by will assume that no one cares about the building, and soon it will have no windows. Those who live and work in the area withdraw as they begin to feel more vulnerable, and become less willing to intervene to maintain public order or to address visible signs of deterioration. The reverse could also be true: a fresh coat of paint on a house, pot plants or a new front door can all give the impression of pride in the local area.[27]

The Law Commission's report on the state and condition of property accepted that different approaches should be taken to commercial and residential lettings. In relation to

---

[25] Law Commission, 'Landlord and Tenant: Responsibility for State and Condition of Property' (Law Com No 238, 1996) para 1.9.

[26] D Maxwell, *Shifting Foundations: Home Ownership and Government Objectives* (London, Institute for Public Policy Research, 2005) 11.

[27] D Maxwell, *Shifting Foundations: Home Ownership and Government Objectives* (London, Institute for Public Policy Research, 2005) 11.

commercial lettings, parties should, so far as possible, be free to make their own bargains. This reflects current law. In practice, this bargain almost invariably results in the commercial tenant bearing responsibility for the cost of repairs. Where, unusually, the tenant is responsible only for internal repairs and the cost of external repairs is borne by the landlord, the landlord will expect a rent that is 2.5 per cent to 10 per cent higher.[28] However, the norm is for all repairing obligations to be placed on the tenant through the FRI lease (Full Repairing and Insuring Lease). In practice, where the property is not a stand-alone property and forms part of a larger unit such as a shopping mall or an office block the landlord (or a management company) will usually be responsible for actually doing the repairs but a proportionate cost will be passed on to the tenant through the service charge (Full Recovery Lease). For the landlord, the FRI and Full Recovery lease means that all the uncertain costs are imposed on the tenant so that the rent provides a 'clear' return. An unusually onerous repairing obligation is likely, however, to have an impact on the rent: in *Norwich Union Life Insurance Soc v British Railways Board* the repairing covenant in a 150 year lease included an obligation to rebuild the premises at the end of their natural life and this led to the rent being discounted by 27.5 per cent on review.[29] Even with the greater flexibility now being seen in the commercial lease market, the FRI and Full Recovery leases are still the norm (and there is little evidence of dissatisfaction with this), although in the case of stand-alone second-hand property it is often tempered by a schedule of condition attached to the lease.[30] The schedule will record the condition of the property at the commencement of the lease; where used, the tenant will not be required to put the property into a better condition than it was at the start.

In relation to residential tenancies, the Law Commission accepted that a distinction should be made based on the length of the lease. Short term tenants, particularly those who hold periodic tenancies, deserve protection; this is currently provided through the statutory repairing obligation implied by section 11 of the Landlord and Tenant Act 1985 (discussed in more detail below). This was first introduced in 1961 in order to prevent the imposition of 'unreasonable repairing obligations' on tenants and to ensure that 'necessary repairs get done'.[31] On the other hand, residential leaseholders who hold a lease which, at least when it was granted, had a clear capital value should not expect their landlords to repair or maintain the fitness of property in the absence of an express agreement between the parties. Persons who have a significant financial stake in the property ought to take responsibility for it.[32] As most of these leases tend to be in developments with communal facilities it is in practice necessary for the landlord or a management company to be responsible for actually doing much of the repair and maintenance, at the expense of the leaseholders; as seen in the previous chapter and further below, this can create enormous difficulties in terms of getting the work done to an acceptable standard at a reasonable cost.

[28] C Edwards and P Krendel, *Institutional Leases in the 21st Century* (London, EG Books, 2007) 30.
[29] [1987] 2 EGLR 137 (Ch).
[30] N Crosby, C Hughes and S Murdoch, 'Monitoring the 2002 Code of Practice for Commercial Leases' (ODPM, March 2005) 303.
[31] Law Commission, 'Landlord and Tenant: Responsibility for State and Condition of Property' (Law Com No 238, 1996) para 5.11.
[32] Law Commission, 'Landlord and Tenant: Responsibility for State and Condition of Property' (Law Com No 238, 1996) paras 1.27 and 8.16.

In the agricultural sector, model repairing clauses are read into leases falling within the Agricultural Holdings Act 1986. Although there is provision for the parties to contract out of these, the idea is that they simply fill a vacuum. They prescribe terms as to the maintenance, repair and insurance of 'fixed equipment', including an obligation on the landlord for structural repairs. Repair issues are left entirely to agreement between the parties under the farm business tenancy regime.

12.3.1.3 Civil Remedies and Regulatory Controls

In the residential sector standards can be and, to some extent are, regulated by public law controls. The Law Commission make the case however, for tenants also having civil remedies against landlords. Public law remedies are not intended for the vindication of individual rights and compensation is not normally available (whether for loss flowing from the state of the property or for the cost of remedying defects). Nor do public law remedies necessarily compel the landlord to get the work done.[33] Civil remedies may stem not only from contractual obligations (express or implied) but also from tortious rules. Private law remedies do, however, also suffer from limitations. Tenants are often reluctant to initiate legal action because of ignorance, cost and effort. In the private sector the absence of long term security means that there is usually very little incentive to bring legal action, and it is not uncommon for landlords to respond to tenant complaints by issuing them with a notice to quit.

12.3.1.4 Statutory Responsibilities

In addition to any contractual leasehold obligations there are several statutory measures that place obligations and responsibilities, often onerous, on owners and occupiers of premises. The burden may fall on the landlord or tenant or both, in their capacity as owner, occupier, employer, employee, person 'in control of premises', or as a 'service provider'. Thus, for example, the Regulatory Reform (Fire Safety) Order 2005 requires the 'responsible person' to carry out thorough risk assessments and to take any necessary steps. In the case of multi-occupied property both the landlord and the tenant may have to assume responsibilities under this Order. The Factories Act 1961 (with obligations that affect the construction of common parts, and the provision of drinking water and sanitary facilities) and the Offices, Shops and Railway Premises Act 1963 (with obligations relating to temperature, ventilation, lighting, and sanitary facilities as well as structural matters) both place obligations on the owner and the occupier. Again, the Health and Safety at Work Act 1974 and the Electricity at Work Regulations 1989 will affect both employer and employee. The details of these various statutory obligations are beyond the scope of this book. As it is usual for a commercial tenant to covenant to comply with all statutory requirements, breach of one of these statutory obligations may well lead to liability under the lease.

Residential landlords are under a statutory duty to ensure that all gas appliances are safely maintained, and before the tenant takes up occupation of the property the landlord must provide him with a copy of the gas safety record and ensure that there is an annual gas

---

[33] Law Commission, 'Landlord and Tenant: Responsibility for State and Condition of Property' (Law Com No 238, 1996) para 8.12.

safety check.[34] Non-compliance is a criminal offence. Furniture and soft furnishings supplied by the landlord must also meet fire safety requirements.[35] Similarly, although there is no requirement for safety testing, all electrical equipment supplied must be safe to use.[36]

12.3.1.5 Multiple Occupation

Things become much more complicated when there is multiple occupation. Repair and maintenance of the exterior, structure and communal parts needs to be carried out by one person and the costs of this will usually be passed on to the various tenants. There is multiple occupation in every sector: with shopping malls and office blocks in the commercial sector, HMOs and flats in the rented housing sector, and flats (and, rarely) houses in the long leasehold sector. Repairing obligations will need to be very carefully drafted to make clear where tenant responsibility for the interior of the demised premises ends, and landlord or management company responsibility for the exterior begins. As seen in the previous chapter, there can also be problems getting management companies to do the necessary maintenance and work and there are many disputes over what needs to be done and how much it costs.

12.3.2 Implied Covenants of Fitness

12.3.2.1 No Warranty of Fitness in Most Tenancies

Until the 18th century the tendency of the courts was to apply the maxim caveat emptor to all types of contract, but during that century the idea grew that warranties could be implied.[37]

By the nineteenth century it was becoming usual to imply terms as to quality and fitness for purpose into commercial contracts unless the parties agreed express terms excluding them. There were early signs that this approach might also be adopted for tenancies. The tenant in *Smith v Marrable* (decided in 1843) took a short lease of a furnished house but left within a few days because it was infested with bugs.[38] The landlord's action to recover the balance of rent due under the lease failed as the tenant was held entitled to leave; there was 'an implied condition of law, that … [the landlord] undertakes to let … [the premises] in a habitable state'.[39] Later the same year, however, further cases showed the limited nature of this ruling and set the shape of the modern law on implied covenants in leases. In *Sutton v Temple* the tenant of pasturing land ceased to use it after several of his cattle had died from a poisonous paint substance found buried in the manure heap.[40] The court, including three of the same judges as in *Smith v Marrable*, held the tenant liable for the rent, notwithstanding that the land was not usable for the intended purpose. *Smith v Marrable* was distinguished on the grounds that it involved the letting of a furnished house. Closer to *Smith v Marrable*, the tenant in *Hart v Windsor* again abandoned a house which he had

---

[34] The Gas Safety (Installation and Use) Regulations 1998 SI 1998/2451.
[35] The Furniture and Furnishings (Fire) (Safety) Regulations 1988 SI 1988/1324.
[36] The Electrical Equipment (Safety) Regulations 1994 SI 1994/3260; Plugs and Sockets (Safety) Regulations 1994 SI 1994/1768.
[37] *Wettern Electric Ltd v Welsh Development Agency* [1983] QB 796 (QB) 804.
[38] (1843) 11 M & W 5.
[39] (1843) 11 M & W 5, 8.
[40] (1843) 12 M & W 52.

taken a three year lease of because it was infested with bugs.[41] Parke B, involved in all three cases, explained that there was no warranty that the property would be fit for occupation as the lease was a contract 'for real estate merely' and the only implied warranties related to this estate and its continuance. *Smith v Marrable* was distinguished on the grounds that it had been for a furnished letting, the 'bargain is not so much for the house as the furniture' (even though in *Smith v Marrable* itself only one judge had mentioned – in passing – the fact that a furnished let was involved). Later that century the same laissez-faire approach was applied to a commercial letting. In *Manchester Bonded Warehouse Co v Carr* the floor of a warehouse collapsed and it was again held that there was no implied warranty 'that the building was fit for the purpose for which it was to be used'. [42] More recently, this approach was confirmed in *Post Office v Aquarius Properties Ltd* where the basement of an almost new office building let in water up to ankle-deep for several years; the Court of Appeal held that there was no implied covenant that the premises would be let in 'a satisfactory state for their intended purpose'.[43]

Thus, in each sector – commercial, agricultural and residential – there is no implied warranty at common law as to fitness for purpose, or safety of the premises. Lord Hoffmann has described the absence of any warranty of fitness as 'a fundamental principle of the English law of landlord and tenant'.[44] The explanation given for this stance in *Hart v Windsor*, that the lease is for an estate only, fitted in an economy in which agrarian leases were the main form of leases found and the land itself was the main object of the contract. This would explain why a different approach could be adopted in *Smith v Marrable* as the furnished nature of the premises indicated that the contract was not only for the 'land for a time'. The nature of letting has, however, changed significantly in subsequent years. Many leases now include substantial 'servicing' elements; the tenant is contracting for far more than the 'land for a time'. In addition, it is unrealistic, and often impossible, for a prospective tenant to inspect the structure of the property before committing to a tenancy. In *Cruse v Mount* Maugham J appeared keen to allow an implied covenant in relation to a residential flat on the basis that a flat has a 'special character' as the tenant has no opportunity to examine the structure of the building (of which the flat forms part) before moving in, but felt bound by authority to hold otherwise.[45]

12.3.2.2 Implied Warranties in the US

Recognition of changing nature of leases has led the US courts to adopt a different approach. In the seminal case of *Javins v First National Realty Corporation*[46] the District of Columbia Court of Appeals held that a warranty of habitability should be implied into leases of urban dwellings, and the premises should both be habitable at the outset and maintained in habitable condition. The reasoning of Judge Skelly Wright explains the need for 'the rigid doctrines of real property law' to be adapted to reflect modern housing conditions:

---

[41] (1843) 12 M & W 68.

[42] 5 CPD 507.

[43] [1987] 1 All ER 1055 (CA) 1063.

[44] *Southwark LBC v Tanner; Baxter v Camden LBC (No 2)* [2001] 1 AC 1 (HL) 7.

[45] [1933] Ch 278 (Ch).

[46] 428 F 2d 1071 (DC Cir 1970). This was not the first case to impose a warranty of habitability (see *Delameter v Foreman* 239 NW 148 (Minn 1931) 149; *Pines v Perssion* 14 Wis 2d 590 (1961)) but it was the most influential.

In our judgment the common law itself must recognise the landlord's obligation to keep his premises in a habitable condition ...

The old common law rule absolving the lessor of all obligation to repair originated in the early Middle Ages. Such a rule was perhaps well-suited to an agrarian economy; the land was more important than whatever small living structure was included in the leasehold, and the tenant farmer was fully capable of making repairs himself. These historical facts were the basis on which the common law constructed its rule; they also provided the necessary prerequisites for its application ...

Today's urban tenants, the vast majority of whom live in multiple dwelling houses, are interested, not in the land, but solely in a 'house suitable for occupation'. Furthermore, today's city dweller usually has a single specialized skill unrelated to maintenance work; he is unable to make repairs like the 'jack-of-all-trades' farmer who was the common law's model of the lessee ... In addition, the increasing complexity of today's dwellings renders them much more difficult to repair than the structures of earlier times. In a multiple dwelling repair may require access to equipment and areas in the control of the landlord ...

Our approach to the common law of landlord and tenant ought to be aided by principles derived from the consumer protection cases ... In a lease contract, a tenant seeks to purchase from his landlord shelter for a specified period of time. The landlord sells housing as a commercial business-man and has much greater opportunity, incentive and capacity to inspect and maintain the condition of his building. Moreover, the tenant must rely upon the skill and *bona fides* of his landlord ...

... Contract principles established in other areas of the law provide a ... framework for the apportionment of landlord-tenant responsibilities; they strongly suggest that a warranty of habitability be implied into all contracts for urban dwellings. [footnotes omitted][47]

Many of the US jurisdictions now give private law rights and remedies to tenants whose homes do not meet minimum standards of habitability.

The reasons underpinning the adoption of this warranty of habitability – no opportunity to inspect, inadequate knowledge of building safety and design, unequal bargaining relationship, lack of incentive to repair given the shortness of leases – will also sometimes be found in commercial situations, especially with 'small businesses' taking space in larger units. Some US courts have extended the idea of a warranty of fitness for purpose to commercial leases, albeit that there is great divergence in the approach taken in commercial cases. In *Davidow v Inwood North Professional Group* the Supreme Court of Texas held that a commercial lease included an implied warranty that the premises were suitable for their intended commercial purpose, and that the tenant's obligation to pay rent was dependent on the landlord's compliance with this warranty. Referring to the reasoning used in the residential cases, Spears J stated:

It cannot be assumed that a commercial tenant is more knowledgeable about the quality of the structure than a residential tenant. A businessman cannot be expected to possess the expertise necessary to adequately inspect and repair the premises, and many commercial tenants lack the financial resources to hire inspectors and repairmen to assure the suitability of the premises ... Additionally, because commercial tenants often enter into short-term leases, the tenants have limited economic incentive to make any extensive repair to their premises ...

Although minor distinctions can be drawn between residential and commercial tenants,

---

[47] 428 F 2d 1071 (DC Cir 1970) 1075–1079.

those differences do not justify limiting the warranty to residential leaseholds. Therefore, we hold there is an implied warranty of suitability by the landlord in a commercial lease that the premises are suitable for their intended commercial purpose.[48]

Recent evidence bears out this notion that commercial tenants are often ill-informed about the nature of the obligations that they are taking on. A report on 'Pubco'[49] tenants showed that many of them failed to get a survey of the public house before signing the lease, even though they covenanted to repair.[50]

12.3.2.3 Assessing the Common Law Position

English judges have been much more conservative than their US counterparts; the common law still maintains the position that there is no implied covenant of fitness for purpose, save in the exceptional cases of furnished lettings. The assumption made by Maugham J in *Cruse v Mount*, that the rent will reflect the poor state of a house let in a tumble down state,[51] is not borne out by Crook's research, which shows that there is often little (if any) correlation between rent and the condition of the property.[52] The effect of saying that there is no implied warranty is that even though the tenant has no real opportunity to inspect the property for structural soundness before entering the tenancy, he will remain liable to pay the rent even if the premises are not usable. The unconvincing nature of the common law position is revealed by contrasting it with the approach adopted in relation to licences. In *Wettern Electric Ltd v Welsh Development Agency*[53] a manufacturing company took a lease of a factory. As the business was expanding it was agreed to extend the factory, and while the work was being done the landlords granted a 12 month licence to the company of a different factory unit. (The law report states that the licence was on similar terms to the lease, but no details are given as to why the agreement was a licence rather than a lease.) The factory premises became unsafe, forcing the licensee to move out. The licensee successfully claimed damages for breach of an implied term that the unit was of good construction and would be reasonably suitable for the intended purposes. The term was implied using the 'business efficacy' test propounded in *The Moorcock*[54] (that is, to give effect to the presumed intention of the parties in order to make the contract work). The reason why this approach could be adopted here, even though the case involved a contract for the hire of land, was because a licence does not involve the grant of an estate and thus could be distinguished from the 'no warranty' cases involving leases.

12.3.2.4 Ineffective Statutory Warranty

The unsatisfactory position of the common law has been long recognised, at least in relation to rented housing. In order to deal with the twin evils of insanitary conditions and

---

[48] 747 SW 2d 373 (Tex 1988) 376–7.
[49] That is pub companies, companies with no brewing dimension who lease out their public house properties. They developed in response to concerns over the competition aspects of ties in leases from large brewer landlords.
[50] Trade and Industry Committee, 'Pub Companies' HC (2004–05) 128–1.
[51] [1933] Ch 278 (Ch).
[52] ADH Crook, 'Housing conditions in the private rented sector within a market framework' in S Lowe and D Hughes (eds), *The Private Rented Sector in a New Century: revival or false dawn?* (Bristol, The Policy Press, 2002).
[53] [1983] QB 796 (QB).
[54] (1889) 14 PD 64.

overcrowded housing, and to correct the anomaly that an implied fitness obligation applies to furnished but not unfurnished premises,[55] the Housing and Working Classes Act 1885 implied a covenant of fitness for human habitation into lettings for 'habitation by persons of the working classes'. At the time of its enactment a substantial proportion of leased housing came within its jurisdiction. The provision is now contained in section 8 of the Landlord and Tenant Act 1985, but it applies only to lettings below specified rent levels that have not been increased since 1957 and are now so low that the covenant is effectively a dead letter.[56] Section 8 provides:

> (1) In a contract to which this section applies for the letting of a house [or part thereof] for human habitation there is implied, notwithstanding any stipulation to the contrary –
>
> (a)   a condition that the house is fit for human habitation at the commencement of the tenancy, and
>
> (b)   an undertaking that the house will be kept by the landlord fit for human habitation during the tenancy.
>
> …
>
> (5) This section does not apply where a house is let for a term of three years or more … upon terms that the tenant puts the premises into a condition reasonably fit for human habitation.

A landlord will not be liable for breach under section 8 unless the defect is brought to his notice.[57]

It is not clear why the rent levels have not been raised to give the section some bite, although the Law Commission suggest that the existence of an implied statutory repairing obligation (in section 11 of the Landlord and Tenant Act 1985; see 12.4.4.3 below) may have led to the view that unfitness could be dealt with through the repairing obligations.[58] The Court of Appeal decision in 1985, *Quick v Taff Ely Borough Council* showed that this can not be relied on.[59] In this case, a house had been badly designed and built, to the point where the levels of condensation made the house, according to Dillon LJ, 'virtually unfit for human habitation'. The problem, however, was not one of 'disrepair'. Lawton LJ states that repair is to do with fixing something that 'is in a condition worse than it was at some time earlier'. The result is that even though a statutory repairing obligation exists, it does not mean that landlords have to ensure that property is fit for habitation.

Apart from the absurdly low rent level, there are other criticisms of section 8. The standard of fitness is set out in section 10 of the Landlord and Tenant Act 1985, which is not the same as the much more precise and rigorous test of habitability found in public health legislation (formerly, Housing Act 1985 section 604(1), and now the HHSRS of the Housing Act 2004; see 12.5.1 below). Section 10 provides that:

---

[55] See Law Commission, 'Landlord and Tenant: Responsibility for State and Condition of Property' (Law Com No 238, 1996) paras 4.8–4.9 and 4.18.

[56] For lettings on or after 6 July 1957 the rental limit is £80 per annum in London and £52 per annum elsewhere.

[57] *McCarrick v Liverpool Corporation* [1947] AC 219 (HL), using the same approach as was then applied to breach of the repair covenant.

[58] See Law Commission, 'Landlord and Tenant: Responsibility for State and Condition of Property' (Law Com No 238, 1996) para 4.14.

[59] [1986] QB 809 (CA).

regard shall be had to its condition in respect of the following matters -

— repair,
— stability,
— freedom from damp,
— internal arrangement,
— natural lighting,
— ventilation,
— water supply,
— drainage and sanitary conveniences,
— facilities for the preparation and cooking of food and for the disposal of waste water;

and the house shall be regarded as unfit for human habitation if, and only if, it is so far defective in one or more of those matters that it is not reasonably suitable for occupation in that condition.

While it is relatively obvious to see what section 8 covers, described by Atkin LJ in *Morgan v Liverpool Corporation*,[60] as a condition threatening the life, limb or health of the occupier, the fitness test applies only to the demised premises, and not to any common parts. Dangerous stairs that are used by all the tenants to get to their respective flats will not be covered by section 8. A further constraint on the effectiveness of section 8 is the decision in *Buswell v Goodwin*, which held that the obligation is subject to the premises being capable of being made fit at a reasonable expense to the landlord.[61] The consequence seems to be, anomalous as it might appear, that if the landlord allows the premises to reach a level of unfitness that would require major expense to rectify, then the property can be let, or continue to be let, without regard to section 8.

Although section 8 is for all intents and purposes redundant, the existence of this statutory covenant has had an impact on the judiciary. In *McNerny v Lambeth LBC*, the Court of Appeal declined to imply a fitness term into the letting of unfurnished property because of the existence of the implied statutory term.[62] Parliament had 'conspicuously refrained from updating the [rent] limits' and any extension of the implied covenant was for Parliament and not the court.[63] In the words of Lord Millett:

These cases raise issues of priority in the allocation of resources. Such issues must be resolved by the democratic process, national and local. The judges are not equipped to resolve them.[64]

12.3.2.5 *Reform*

In its 1992 consultation paper one of the reform options suggested by the Law Commission was to impose a duty on the landlord (transferable to the tenant by agreement, with certain exceptions):

… to put and keep the demised property, and all parts of it, in such state and condition that it may safely, hygienically and satisfactorily be used, and continue in the immediate future to be

---

[60] [1927] 2 KB 131 (CA).
[61] [1971] 1 WLR 92 (CA).
[62] [1989] 1 EGLR 81 (CA).
[63] [1989] 1 EGLR 81 (CA) 84.
[64] *Southwark LBC v Tanner; Baxter v Camden LBC (No 2)* [2001] 1 AC 1 (HL) 26.

used, for its intended purpose with an appropriate degree of convenience and comfort for the occupants.[65]

This would have applied to commercial and residential tenancies. The final report rejected such a wide duty of fitness for purpose in the light of objections from respondents on the grounds, inter alia, of cost, the impact on the investment market, and the inappropriateness of such an intrusion into the relations of landlord and tenant.[66] It did, however, recommend that:

> ... there should be implied into a lease of a dwelling house which is for a term of less than seven years a covenant by the lessor –
>
> (a)   that the dwelling house is fit for human habitation at the commencement of the lease; and
> (b)   that the lessor will keep it fit for human habitation during the lease.[67]

Some of the limitations found in the current section 8 would be retained, so the landlord would be under no liability for loss caused by unfitness of which he has no notice, and his liability would be limited to cases where the premises could be made fit at a reasonable expense. The recommendation has been taken up by the Law Commission in its Renting Homes final report where it recommends that one of the fundamental terms of the occupation contract would require landlords to ensure that there is no 'category 1 hazard' on the premises (hazard rating, introduced by the Housing Act 2004, replaces the definition of fitness found in the Housing Act 1985; see 12.5.1 below).[68] There is some doubt as to how this welcome, but long overdue, suggestion would work in the private rented sector. Given that assured shorthold tenants have no security beyond their term (which is likely to be periodic or for six months), there is little to stop a landlord getting rid of a complaining tenant at the first opportunity.[69]

12.4   The Duty to Repair

12.4.1   The Meaning of 'Repair'

This section considers the meaning of repair when there is a repairing obligation on one of the parties. It may be the landlord or the tenant who has the obligation to repair, and this section therefore refers simply to the covenantor as the person carrying the responsibility. The extent of the repairing obligation will depend upon the wording used when there is an express covenant. The obligation to repair has limited usefulness in relation to ensuring

---

[65] Law Commission, 'Landlord and Tenant: Responsibility for State and Condition of Property' (Law Com CP No 123, 1992) para 5.7.

[66] Law Commission, 'Landlord and Tenant: Responsibility for State and Condition of Property' (Law Com No 238, 1996) para 1.20. For criticism of the proposal, see PF Smith, 'Repairing Obligations: A Case Against Radical Reform' [1994] *Conv* 186.

[67] Law Commission, 'Landlord and Tenant: Responsibility for State and Condition of Property' (Law Com No 238, 1996) ch 8.

[68] Law Commission, 'Renting Homes' (Law Com No 284, 2003) Part 8.

[69] See S Bridge, 'Putting it Right? The Law Commission and the Condition of Tenanted Property' [1996] *Conv* 342, 350–1.

minimum standards because repair is to do with fixing something if it goes wrong; there is an idea that at some time in the past the premises were in a better state of repair and that they have since deteriorated.

> A landlord's obligation to repair arises when the subject matter of the covenant … has deteriorated from a previous condition so that it has fallen below the standard which a reasonably minded tenant would expect under the lease. It will only be in a state of disrepair if one can point to a previous time at which the [subject matter of the covenant] … was in a better condition so that one can say there has been deterioration.[70]

In the words of Dillon LJ in *Quick v Taff Ely BC*, disrepair is not to do with 'lack of amenity or inefficiency'.[71] A design defect may render property unusable but unless there is deterioration from a pre-existing standard, the repair obligation will not be triggered. In *Post Office v Aquarius Properties Ltd* weak areas of concrete allowed water into the basement to a depth of about six inches, but, perhaps surprisingly, no damage resulted. The Court of Appeal held that remedying this defect would not amount to a repair because there was no damage; there had been no deterioration from a previously better condition.[72]

There are a number of principles elaborating the meaning of 'repair'.

12.4.1.1 'Repair' is not 'Renewal'

If there is only an obligation to 'repair', it may be necessary to distinguish between repair and renewal. The question will be important either if one party is trying to get the other to do something which it is argued is so extensive that it goes beyond the contractual obligation, or if the landlord wants to do something that the tenant does not want to have to pay for. *Minja Properties Ltd v Cussins Property Group plc* shows the context in which these disputes can occur.[73] Under the lease of a commercial building the landlord had responsibility to 'maintain and keep in good and tenantable repair, inter alia, the window frames (excluding glass)'. The tenant had to keep the glass in repair, to allow the landlord access for repair, and to pay for the cost of the landlord's repairs through the service charge. The landlord wanted to repair the corroded steel frames by replacing the single pane windows with double-glazed aluminium windows. Two of the tenant occupiers objected as their leases were running out fairly soon and as they had no intention of staying they did not want to pay for this. Accordingly, they refused the landlord access. Harman J said that repair could involve more than 'patching up' provided that it is not the whole structure of the building that is being renewed in this way. There was no doubt that the frames had to be replaced and as the difference between single and double glazing replacements was a 'comparatively trivial amount' it was

---

[70] *Janet Reger International Ltd v Tiree Ltd* [2006] EWHC 1743 (Ch) [61]. See also Lord Hoffmann in *Southwark LBC v Tanner; Baxter v Camden LBC (No 2)* [2001] 1 AC 1 (HL) 8 (in relation to the implied statutory repairing covenant, Landlord and Tenant Act 1985 s 11): 'the landlord is obliged only to restore the house to its previous condition. He does not have to make it a better house than it originally was'.

[71] [1986] QB 809 (CA) 818.

[72] [1987] 1 All ER 1055 (CA) 1063–5. For a more recent application, see *Janet Reger International Ltd v Tiree Ltd* [2006] EWHC 1743 (Ch). Commenting on the *Post Office* case in *Minja Properties Ltd v Cussins Property Ltd* [1998] 2 EGLR 52 (Ch) 55, Harman J remarked that the Court of Appeal has perhaps allowed 'intellect to take precedence over any other processes'.

[73] [1998] 2 EGLR 52 (Ch).

held to come within the covenant to repair and not amount to renewal. Thus the tenants had to allow access.

The distinction between repair and renewal turns, according to Buckely LJ in *Lurcott v Wakely and Wheeler,* on the extent of the work required:

> Repair is restoration by renewal or replacement of subsidiary parts of a whole. Renewal, as distinguished from repair, is reconstruction of the entirety, meaning by the entirety not necessarily the whole, but substantially the whole.[74]

On the other hand, renewal of different subsidiary parts during the course of the lease may amount to an effective reconstruction of the entirety. In *Brew Bros v Snax*, Sachs LJ noted the difficulty in defining whether or not something was a repair or went beyond this, and emphasised that it was in every case a matter of degree, requiring one:

> … to look at the particular building, to look at the state which it is in *at the date of the lease*, to look at the precise terms of the lease, and then come to a conclusion as to whether, on a fair interpretation of those terms in relation to that state, the requisite work can fairly be termed repair.[75]

The cost of the work was a factor which the Court of Appeal took into account in *Brew Bros*. In holding that the required work went beyond repair the Court of Appeal noted that the cost of remedial work was almost equal to the cost of the complete rebuilding of the premises.[76] Similarly in *Scottish Mutual v Jardine Public Relations*, in deciding that the works that the landlord had effected to fix a flat roof went beyond repair, the judge took account of the fact that it was only a short three year lease with no renewal rights:

> … this lease does not entitle the landlord to charge to the tenant the cost of carrying out works suitable for the performance of his obligations over a period of twenty or more years when such works are not necessary for the fulfilment of those obligations over the actual period to which they relate.

Where the lease calls for 'renewal', as opposed to just repair, then the obligation is wider. In *Credit Suisse v Beegas Nominees Ltd* the lease required the landlord to

> … maintain, repair, amend, renew, cleanse, repaint and redecorate and otherwise keep in good and tenantable condition the structure of the building and in particular the roof, foundation and walls thereof … [77]

Under the lease the tenant was liable for a proportionate share of all the landlord's costs associated with performance of that obligation. The aluminium cladding on the walls had always leaked and had been a bone of contention throughout the lease. The necessary work went beyond mere repair, and the question was whether the duty to 'renew' meant that the landlord was nevertheless obliged to fix this defect. Lindsay J held that each word had to be given its full meaning and, thus, the landlord was bound to fix the defect. Similarly, in *New*

---

[74] [1911] KB 905 (CA) 924.

[75] [1970] 1 QB 612 (CA) 640.

[76] Contrast *Elite Investments v TI Silencers* [1986] 2 EGLR 43 (Ch) where His Honour Judge Paul Baker QC found that replacing a roof was a 'repair' and not 'renewal' by comparing the cost of replacing the roof with the cost of a completely new building.

[77] [1994] 4 All ER 803 (Ch) 810; J Morgan, 'Repairing the Breach: Proudfoot v Hart Revisited' [1994] *Conv* 145.

England Properties plc v Portsmouth New Shops Ltd, a badly designed roof had to be completely replaced.[78] The court was prepared to hold that the landlord's express obligation in the lease to renew would have given rise to liability if it had not already found that the replacement of the roof was a repair within the traditional test.

12.4.1.2 'Repair' is not 'Improvement'

> As a matter of principle, someone who has a duty to repair property is not obliged to improve it. Accordingly, a landlord who covenanted to repair a house, the outside walls of which had no damp proof course, was not obliged to insert one – *Pembery v Lamdin* [1940] 2 All ER 434.[79]

In practice, however, is often difficult to distinguish repair from improvement, especially where an improvement would also deal with the damage arising from the defect:

> … it is always a question of degree whether that which the tenant is being asked to do can properly be described as repair, or whether on the contrary it would involve giving back to the landlord a wholly different thing from that which he demised.
>
>   In deciding this question, the proportion which the cost of the disputed work bears to the value or cost of the whole premises, may sometimes be helpful as a guide.[80]

12.4.1.3 'Repair' and 'Inherent Defects'

An especial difficulty arises where the damage is caused by an inherent defect, especially as they tend to be expensive to remedy when compared to the usual day-to-day maintenance costs. The covenant to repair does not, of itself, require inherent defects to be remedied. Thus, in *Quick v Taff Ely BC* discussed above, the condensation problem had been caused by defective design and there was no disrepair.[81] Notwithstanding the landlord being under a statutory repairing obligation, the tenant was left living in miserable conditions without there being any breach on the landlord's part. If an inherent defect causes no damage, then there is no responsibility to remedy it at all. In *Post Office v Aquarius Properties* the Court of Appeal said:

> It is not possible to hold that the wetting of the basement floor, or the presence of the water on the floor, coupled with the inconvenience caused thereby to the tenant, constitutes damage to the premises demised. There is, accordingly, no disrepair proved in this case and therefore no liability under the tenant's covenant to repair has arisen.[82]

Where an inherent defect in the premises gives rise to damage, the covenantor may have to repair the damage but not remedy the inherent defect, because that would go beyond putting right deterioration that arose after the granting of the lease.[83] Of course, if the inherent defect that causes the damage is not remedied, then the damage will recur and the covenantor will be constantly carrying out short-term repairs. In some cases, however,

---

[78] [1993] 1 EGLR 84 (Ch).
[79] Law Commission, 'Landlord and Tenant: Responsibility for State and Condition of Property' (Law Com CP No 123, 1992) para 2.22.
[80] *Ravenseft Properties Ltd v Davstone (Holdings) Ltd* [1980] QB 12 (QB) 21–22.
[81] [1986] QB 809 (CA).
[82] [1987] 1 All ER 1055 (CA) 1063.
[83] *Lister v Lane and Nesham* [1893] 2 QB 212 (CA) 216.

remedying the inherent defect is the sole means of effecting the 'repair' to the damage, and the covenantor may be obliged to deal with the root cause of the problem.[84] In the words of Chadwick LJ the cases,

> ... show that, where there is a need to repair damage to the structure, the due performance of the obligation to repair may require the landlord to remedy the design defect which is the cause of the damage. They do not support the proposition that the obligation to repair will require the landlord to remedy a design defect which has not been the cause of damage to the structure; notwithstanding that the defect may make the premises unsuitable for occupation or unfit for human habitation.[85]

In *Ravenseft Properties Ltd v Davstone (Holdings) Ltd* the tenant had to spend £55,000 replacing external cladding to remedy the inherent defect in the original fixing system: Forbes J held that in certain circumstances remedying an inherent defect could fall within a tenant's repairing obligation, but that each case must be viewed on its facts since it is a question of degree as to whether what the tenant is being obliged to do or fund 'can properly be described as a repair'.[86]

Where the obligation to repair does mean that an inherent defect has to be remedied it may be possible to bring an action against the building contractor and professional team involved in the design and construction of the building (architect, structural engineer, mechanical and electrical engineer and quantity surveyor). Assuming that the building has not changed hands, the landlord may have a contractual remedy. Tenants may also insist on being able to enter into 'collateral warranties' with the contractor and others as a condition of taking a lease; in the event that the tenant is required by the lease to remedy inherent defects it may then have a contractual claim against those responsible for the problem.

12.4.1.4 The Importance of the Words Used in the Covenant

Repairing obligations frequently contain reference to other terms beyond simple 'repair', as in *Credit Suisse v Beegas* where Lindsay J said that even when a torrential style of drafting has been used,[87] each stream of this should be taken to add to the meaning.[88] In *Credit Suisse* Lindsay J thought that there was an important difference between an obligation simply to repair and one to keep in good and tenantable condition. In *Credit Suisse* the covenant imposed an obligation on the landlord in the following terms:

> To maintain repair amend renew cleanse repaint and redecorate and otherwise keep in good and tenantable condition:
>
> (1) the structure of the Building and in particular the roof's foundations and walls thereof but excluding nevertheless therefrom ... (ii) the internal faces of boundary walls that enclose the demised premises ...
>
> (2) the boundary walls ... of and in the curtilage of the Building ...

---

[84] *Quick v Taff Ely BC* [1986] QB 809 (CA).
[85] *Lee v Leeds CC; Ratcliffe v Sandwell MBC* [2002] EWCA Civ 6, [2001] 1 WLR 1488 [13]
[86] *Ravenseft Properties Ltd v Davstone (Holdings) Ltd* [1980] QB 12 (QB) 21.
[87] An expression used by Hoffmann J in *Norwich Union Life Insurance Society v British Railways Board* [1987] 2 EGLR 137 (Ch) 138, and often repeated.
[88] [1994] 4 All ER 803 (Ch).

The property was a high-class commercial building but the cladding was defective and leaked. Although the work required to fix the problem went beyond 'repair' (and involved considerable cost) it was covered by this covenant as the wording would also require the landlord to amend and renew and, additionally, the reference was to 'good and tenantable condition' rather than just repair. In *Welsh v Greenwich LBC*[89] this form of wording led to a local authority being responsible for issues arising from condensation and damp problems, in contrast to the result that had been reached in *Quick v Taff Ely BC*[90] and other cases. The covenant in the local authority tenancy contained an obligation 'to maintain the dwelling in good condition and repair'. Although there had been no structural damage, the landlord was nonetheless found to be in breach by failing to provide thermal insulation or dry lining for the external walls. Latham LJ remarked:

> As far as the phrase 'good condition' is concerned, it seems to me to concentrate the mind on the state of the dwelling, whereas 'repair' is looking at the matter more from the perspective of the need to do particular repairing work.
> ... this is a contract between a local authority, as the provider of social housing, and a tenant in circumstances where one would not expect the tenant to be taking legal advice. I therefore consider that such a term should be approached on the basis that one should, so far as possible, give to it the meaning that the ordinary person in the street would accept as being the sensible construction of the phrase. It seems to me that the judge approached it properly in that regard and has produced a solution to the meaning of the clause which will accord with the ordinary person's understanding of the phrase and also the ordinary person's sense of fairness.[91]

Similarly, as seen earlier in *Norwich Union v British Railways*, a covenant may even require property to be rebuilt.[92]

Although there are broad principles used in the construction of repairing covenants, the particular wording of covenants is crucial to their meaning; this is especially important in commercial cases where it is usual for there to be a detailed repairing covenant. Further, Robert Walker LJ notes that:

> ... a decision on the language of one clause is never decisive, and may sometimes not even be helpful, as to the meaning of another clause, even though it uses some of the same words.[93]

Drafting of repair, maintenance and servicing obligations can be very difficult. Care has to be taken to ensure that the scope of the repairing obligations is carefully defined and that the end result is a clearly worded covenant that reflects the wishes of the parties. Much case law is generated over the meaning and interpretation of covenants to repair. One illustration is the case of *Holding & Barnes plc v Hill House Hammond Ltd*.[94] The tenant covenanted to keep 'the property' in good internal repair. The landlord covenanted:

> TO keep the foundations and the roof in good and tenantable repair and condition and to

---

[89] (2001) 33 HLR 40 (CA).
[90] [1986] QB 809 (CA).
[91] *Welsh v Greenwich LBC* (2001) 33 HLR 40 (CA) [32]–[33].
[92] *Norwich Union Life Insurance Society v British Railways Board* [1987] 2 EGLR 137 (Ch).
[93] *Welsh v Greenwich LBC* (2001) 33 HLR 40 (CA) [25]
[94] [2001] EWCA Civ 1334. For an example of careless drafting of a repairing covenant in an under-lease, see *Delgable Ltd v Perinpanathan* [2005] EWCA Civ 1724.

keep the structure and the exterior of the Building (other than those parts comprised in the property) in good and tenantable repair and condition.

As the 'property' included the whole building the words in brackets in the landlord's covenant appeared to strike out the immediately preceding obligation. According to Clarke LJ this would make no sense. In approaching the question of construction, Clarke LJ (and Peter Gibson LJ) applied the approaches advocated in *Mannai Investments Co Ltd v Eagle Star Life Assurance Co Ltd*[95] and *Investors Compensation Scheme Ltd v West Bromwich Building Society*.[96] This meant that,

> ... the question is what a reasonable person would understand the parties to mean by the words of the contract to be construed. It is important to note that that the reasonable person must be taken to have knowledge of the surrounding circumstances or factual matrix.[97]

The context of the case was that this lease formed part of a larger transaction involving the grant of several leases of parts of buildings, and one other lease of a whole building. The wording used in the contested lease followed the wording appropriate for a lease of part, as it then made sense for the landlord to repair the exterior of the building, and the tenant the (smaller) demised part. Accordingly, the words in brackets should be struck. Sir Martin Nourse preferred to say that he was following a classical approach to construction and simply correcting a clerical error.[98]

Where a tenant is responsible for repairs (or for maintaining fittings) it is common for there to be an exception for 'fair wear and tear'. So, for example, the tenant in *Barrett v Lounova (1982) Ltd* covenanted:

> To do all inside repairs (if any) now required and to keep and at the expiration of the tenancy to leave the inside of the said premises and fixtures in good repair order and condition but fair wear and tear to be allowed at the end of the tenancy.[99]

There is no fixed definition of what this phrase means, but it essentially excuses the tenant from disrepair that results simply from ordinary and reasonable use of the property.[100] Even if there is no express covenant to repair placed on the tenant, the implied obligation to use premises in a tenant like manner (see 12.4.4.2 below) probably requires a tenant to:

> Restore ... [the premises] to the state they would be in if he had committed no waste,[101] or deliver up premises as they were demised to him, fair wear and tear excepted. But at any rate he must deliver up premises of the same character as those which were demised to him.[102]

12.4.1.5 Summary

The meaning of repairs is not straightforward. Further, a repairing obligation may not fully reflect the desires of either the landlord or tenant as to maintaining the condition of the

---

[95] [1997] AC 749 (HL).
[96] [1998] 1 WLR 896 (HL).
[97] [2001] EWCA Civ 1334 [18].
[98] For the principles of interpretation, see ch 2.
[99] [1990] 1 QB 348 (CA).
[100] See *Terrell v Murray* (1901) 45 Sol Jo 579 (DC); *Regis Property Co Ltd v Dudley* [1958] 1 QB 346 (CA).
[101] See below for meaning of waste.
[102] *Marsden v Edward Heyes Ltd* [1927] 2 KB 1 (CA) 6.

premises. In practical terms it is not sensible that the party under a repairing obligation has no duty to fix an inherent defect and that 'patching up' damage caused by this defect is an adequate response. Indeed, as *Post Office v Aquarius* and *Quick v Taff Ely* illustrate, unless there is damage to the structure or fabric of the premises there is no duty to do anything.

12.4.2 What is the Standard of Repair?

The question of what is a repair is bound up with the question of the standard of any repair.

> A covenant to 'keep' the premises in good repair imposes a double requirement. First, the covenantor must put the premises into repair even if, at the commencement of the term, they are in a state of disrepair [subject to the above discussion, that repair does not require the covenantor to make the property better than it ever was]. Secondly, he must ensure that they should not at any stage fall into disrepair [footnotes omitted].[103]

> A covenant that requires a tenant merely 'to repair' the property is satisfied by keeping it in substantial repair, that is 'as nearly as may be in the state in which it was at the time of the demise by the timely expenditure of money and care'. Covenants that require a tenant to keep the premises in 'good', 'habitable' or 'tenantable' repair have the same meaning, namely, [per Lopes LJ in *Proudfoot v Hart* (1890) 25 QBD 42, 55]

> 'such repair as, having regard to the age, character, and locality of the house, would make it reasonably fit for the occupation of a reasonably minded tenant of the class who would be likely to take it.'[104]

Although the quotation from *Proudfoot v Hart* refers to a house, the same approach is applied in commercial cases. In determining the appropriate standard, the courts are to have regard to the 'age, character and locality' of the property. However, while an old and dilapidated building will not generally merit as extensive repairs as other premises, a repairing obligation is never redundant or obsolete. In the words of Fletcher Moulton LJ:

> We must bear in mind that while the age and the nature of the building can qualify the meaning of the covenant, they can never relieve the [tenant] from his obligation. If he chooses to undertake to keep in good condition an old house, he is bound to do it, whatever be the means necessary for him to employ in so doing. He can never say: 'The house was old, so old that it relieved me from my covenant to keep it in good condition'.[105]

The standard as set out in *Proudfoot v Hart* has regard to several variable factors which may or may not be relevant to any given letting or to any particular type of lease.

When carrying out a repair, the landlord may have to take reasonable precautions to minimise disturbance so as not to breach the covenant of quiet enjoyment.[106]

---

[103] Law Commission, 'Landlord and Tenant: Responsibility for State and Condition of Property' (Law Com No 238, 1996) para 2.9.

[104] Law Commission, 'Landlord and Tenant: Responsibility for State and Condition of Property' (Law Com No 238, 1996) para 2.8.

[105] *Lurcott v Wakely and Wheeler* [1911] 1 KB 905 (CA) 916.

[106] *Goldmile Properties Ltd v Lechouritis* [2003] EWCA Civ 49 [10].

12.4.3 Notification of Disrepair

A Court of Appeal decision in 1996, *British Telecommunications plc v Sun Life Assurance Society plc*, confirmed, after some doubt in earlier cases, that the general rule is that where there is a covenant to 'keep in repair' there will be a breach from the moment of disrepair. According to Nourse LJ:

> The general rule is that a covenant to keep premises in repair obliges the covenantor to keep them in repair at all times, so that there is a breach of the obligation immediately a defect occurs.[107]

On the facts, a bulge appeared in the brick cladding on the external wall of the let premises in September 1986. The landlord had covenanted to 'keep in complete good and substantial repair and condition' the premises, and the remedial works were begun in February 1988. It was held that liability for the breach arose as soon as the bulge appeared. This rule would, however, be unreasonable where the landlord is responsible for repair but the disrepair is within the demised premises and he has no knowledge of it. Accordingly:

> There is an exception where the obligation is the landlord's and the defect occurs in the demised premises themselves, in which case he is in breach of his obligation only when he has information about the existence of the defect such as would put a reasonable landlord on inquiry as to whether works of repair are needed and he has failed to carry out the necessary works with reasonable expedition thereafter.[108]

Where the disrepair is within the demised premises this means that the landlord's liability does not commence until he is notified of the disrepair and a reasonable time must be allowed for the landlord to deal with the problem. This is likely to include time to find out what is wrong, to take advice, to prepare specifications, to find a contractor and, where the cost is to be covered through service charges, time may also need to be allowed for any statutory consultation periods (see chapter 13).[109]

Nourse LJ left open two points. First, where the damage is caused by something wholly outside the landlord's control, such as a neighbour's tree falling. He was inclined to think that this should also be made an exception to the general rule, but did not decide the point.[110] He also left open the position where the covenant was simply 'to repair' rather than 'to keep in repair', observing that this was 'a rarity in modern leases and tenancy agreements'.

12.4.4 Implied Repair and Maintenance Obligations

As already mentioned, not all leases are drafted so as to allocate repairing obligations to one or other of the parties. The question then arises as to whether it is possible to imply such obligations. Terms may be implied at common law, or by statute.

---

[107] [1996] Ch 69 (CA) 78–9.
[108] [1996] Ch 69 (CA) 79.
[109] *Earle v Charalambous* [2006] EWCA Civ 1090.
[110] It is difficult to see why this should be an exception: HW Wilkinson, 'Landlords' repair covenants – when is the breach?' (1995) 145 *NLJ* 1793, 1794.

12.4.4.1 Implied Terms at Common Law

In accordance with general contractual principles, terms may be implied by law or on the basis of the specific facts. The distinction is that a term implied by law is not dependent on the presumed intent of the parties but is implied whenever there is a contract of a defined type, whereas if it is to be implied on the facts then it must be one that both parties would have agreed to at the time of the contract on the basis that without it the contract will not work – the latter is sometimes known as the business efficacy or officious bystander test.[111] In *Liverpool CC v Irwin*[112] tenants of a maisonette on the ninth and tenth floors of a 15 storey tower block withheld rent as a protest against conditions. The judge accepted that there were:

> … defects in the common parts, which may be summarised as continual failure of the lifts, sometimes of both at one time, lack of lighting on the stairs, dangerous condition of the staircase with unguarded holes giving access to the rubbish chutes and frequent blockage of the chutes.

There was no bilateral written contract; the tenants had signed 'tenancy conditions' but the landlord had signed nothing. Was there any implied term relating to the maintenance of the common parts? As Lord Wilberforce noted, this involved a somewhat different situation from the usual one of implying terms into apparently complete bilateral contracts, as here the court has to establish what the contract is. There would clearly need to be an easement for the tenants to use the staircase, lifts and rubbish chutes, and the obligation accompanying these easements should be determined by a test of necessity, not one of reasonableness. The House of Lords held that it was a legal incident of this kind of contract (landlord and tenant in a multi-occupational dwelling) that the landlord is under 'an obligation to take reasonable care to keep in reasonable repair and usability' the access ways.[113] On the facts of the particular case, however, the tenants had not proven a breach of this obligation.

As a consequence of *Liverpool CC v Irwin* there are now two situations in which the law will imply terms as an incident of the type of contract; a term of fitness for human habitation in lettings of furnished dwellings,[114] and an obligation to take reasonable care to maintain common parts retained by the landlord over which tenants have essential rights of user or access in the case of multi-occupied dwellings. This latter principle was applied in *King v South Northamptonshire DC* to imply an obligation to maintain the rear access to a house on a local authority housing estate where the estate had been designed in a way that the houses 'could not be enjoyed or function in accord with their design without the rear access'.[115]

Outside of these categories, terms can be implied only in accordance with the 'business efficacy' test, and the degree of strictness of this implication 'seems to vary with the current legal trend'.[116] The general rule is that:

---

[111] *The Moorcock* (1889) 14 PD 64.
[112] [1977] AC 239 (HL).
[113] [1977] AC 239 (HL) 256.
[114] See 12.3.2.1
[115] (1992) 64 P & CR 35 (CA).
[116] *Liverpool CC v Irwin* [1977] AC 239 (HL) 253.

... it has never been held in any general way that it is necessary to imply a repairing covenant on the part of the landlord.[117]

In *Duke of Westminster v Guild* a tenant of commercial premises sought to argue that there was an obligation on the landlord to maintain a drain.[118] This was, however, distinguished from *Liverpool CC v Irwin* on the grounds both that there was in *Guild* an apparently complete bargain between the parties,[119] and it was not a contract of a special type such as the multi-occupied dwelling in *Irwin*. The appropriate test was therefore the 'business efficacy' one, and on this basis there could be no such term implied. The lease already contained detailed repair provisions:

> If it had been intended that other contractual obligations relating to repair should be placed on the landlords themselves, one would prima facie have expected this particular lease to say so.[120]

Further, the lease set out a perfectly workable scheme without this term. In *Barrett v Lounova (1982) Ltd*[121] (a case which has 'attracted both praise and criticism')[122] the Court of Appeal was prepared to hold that where the lease imposes an express obligation on the tenant to keep the interior in repair, it was proper to imply a similar obligation on the landlord in relation to the exterior; indeed, it was the only option that made business sense as without such an obligation on the landlord, the tenant was unable to perform his obligation.[123] In reaching this decision he drew on the remarks of Slade LJ in *Duke of Westminster v Guild* that:

> ... in some instances it will be proper for the court to imply an obligation against a landlord, on whom an obligation is not in terms imposed by the relevant lease, to match a correlative obligation thereby expressly imposed on the other party.[124]

The Law Commission summarise further judicial principles used in correlative obligation cases:

(i)   Where there is an unqualified obligation to pay a specified amount in respect of repairs or maintenance, a court will readily imply an obligation on the part of the landlord to carry out such work [cf *Barnes v City of London Real Property Co* [1918] 2 Ch 18, 32–33].

---

[117] *Tennant Radiant Heat Ltd v Warrington Development Corporation* [1988] 1 EGLR 41 (CA) 43.

[118] [1985] QB 688 (CA).

[119] See also *Hannon v 169 Queen's Gate Ltd* [2000] 1 EGLR 40 (Ch) 41: '... the courts are reluctant to imply a term where ... there is a long and complex legal document drawn up by the lawyers in which the parties have crystallised the terms of their relationship'.

[120] [1985] QB 688 (CA) 700. See also *Hafton Properties Ltd v Camp* [1994] 1 EGLR 67 (QB) 69.

[121] [1990] 1 QB 348 (CA).

[122] Law Commission, 'Landlord and Tenant: Responsibility for State and Condition of Property' (Law Com No 238, 1996) para 3.16. Kerr LJ gave two reasons for his decision. The first, that at some point the tenant would not be able to repair the interior unless the outside had been maintained, is less controversial than the second, that the obligation must be imposed on someone. In fact, courts have accepted that the repairing obligation may rest with no-one: *Demetriou v Robert Andrews (Estate Agencies) Ltd* (1990) 62 P & CR 536 (CA) 544–5; *Sleafer v Lambeth Borough Council* [1960] 1 QB 43 (CA).

[123] In *Lee v Leeds CC; Ratcliffe v Sandwell MBC* [2001] EWCA Civ 6, [2002] 1 WLR 1488 the tenant unsuccessfully argued that an obligation to remedy defects which make the premises unfit for human habitation was a necessary correlative to the obligation on the tenant to reside there, and that an obligation to remedy design defects which led to excessive condensation and mould was a necessary correlative to the tenant's obligations in respect of internal decorative repair: [67].

[124] *Duke of Westminster v Guild* [1985] QB 688 (CA) 697.

(ii) The same may be true where the tenant is obliged to pay the cost of carrying out a particular work at specified intervals. [See *Edmonton Corporation v W M Knowles & Son Ltd* (1961) 60 LGR 124 (obligation on landlord implied from the tenant's covenant to pay the cost of painting the exterior of the premises every third year of the term)].

(iii) The position is less clear when the tenant's obligation of payment is conditional on the performance of the service whether that service is provided at his request or otherwise. [See *Duke of Westminster v Guild* [1985] QB 688, 697].

(iv) The mere fact that the landlord reserved the right to enter to inspect the state of repair of the premises or does in practice carry out any repairs does not mean that an obligation will be implied that he *must* carry out such repairs. [*Sleafer v Lambeth Borough Council* [1960] 1 QB 43; *Duke of Westminster v Guild*, above, at p 697. The existence of such right may carry with it certain obligations as to repair however] (footnotes from the Law Commission Report contained in square brackets).[125]

In the absence of specific contractual allocation of the repairing responsibility there may well be no provision for repair; the common law's approach to the implication of such terms is limited and cautious. The Law Commission conclude:

> The state of the present law as to when a court will imply an obligation in a lease to carry out repairs is thoroughly unsatisfactory. There is a presumption against implication of a repairing obligation in a lease because it is not considered to be necessary to give business efficacy to the agreement. The corollary of this is that it is quite possible for there to be a lease which does not allocate responsibility for some repairs to either party.[126]

12.4.4.2 Implied Obligations on the Tenant[127]

There are certain, albeit limited, obligations on the tenant that impact on the condition of the property. It is most unlikely that they impose any obligation to repair on the tenant, rather what they do to is to make the tenant liable where he causes harm to the property.

In any sector, a tenant for a term of years or a periodic tenant[128] may be liable for the tort of voluntary waste if he causes damage by 'an act which alters the nature of the thing demised'.[129] Voluntary waste occurs where the tenant acts to destroy the property (or part of it) in any way or even to make alterations to the property (such as changing the method of cultivation). Where, however, the act of waste improves the value of the property it is known as ameliorating waste and the tenant will not be liable. The fact that waste is tortious means that the right to sue for it cannot be assigned and will not pass with an assignment of the landlord's reversion. It also means that the tenant is liable not only for his own acts but also for those of others. There are very few actions brought involving waste and so this area of law is shrouded with uncertainties. One of the very few (relatively) recent cases, *Mancetter Development Ltd v Garmanson Ltd*, left open whether

---

[125] Law Commission, 'Landlord and Tenant: Responsibility for State and Condition of Property' (Law Com No 238, 1996) para 3.15.

[126] Law Commission, 'Landlord and Tenant: Responsibility for State and Condition of Property' (Law Com No 238, 1996) para 3.17.

[127] For a full discussion, see Law Commission, 'Landlord and Tenant: Responsibility for State and Condition of Property' (Law Com No 238, 1996) Part X.

[128] The position in relation to tenants at will and tenants at sufferance is less clear, see Law Commission, 'Landlord and Tenant: Responsibility for State and Condition of Property' (Law Com No 238, 1996) paras 10.23–24.

[129] *West Ham Central Charity Board v East London Waterworks Co* [1900] 1 Ch 624 (Ch) 635.

an action will lie in the tort of waste if the landlord has the option of suing in contract under a relevant covenant.[130]

There is also a tort of permissive waste (which involves omission, as where a property is allowed to fall into disrepair). It is, however, doubtful if the tenant can be liable for permissive waste in the absence of an obligation to repair, as the effect would be to impose a positive obligation on a tenant, something that the law is most unlikely to do.[131] Further, the Law Commission observed that there are very few examples of permissive waste.

Close to this doctrine of waste is an implied obligation placed on tenants to use property in a 'husbandlike' or 'tenant like' manner and, if the lease is for one year or greater duration, it has sometimes been said that he must keep the premises wind and watertight.[132] In *Warren v Keen* Denning LJ considered that this latter expression was of doubtful value and best avoided. Instead, it is better to refer to the simple obligation 'to use the premises in a tenantlike manner', and what this meant is best explained by reference to examples:

> The tenant must take proper care of the place. He must, if he is going away for the winter, turn off the water and empty the boiler. He must clean the chimneys, when necessary, and also the windows. He must unstop the sink when it is blocked by his waste. In short, he must do the little jobs about the place which a reasonable tenant would do. In addition, he must, of course, not damage the house, wilfully or negligently; and must see that his family and guests do not damage it: and if they do, he must repair it. But apart from such things, if the house falls into disrepair through fair wear and tear or lapse of time, or for any reason not caused by him, then the tenant is not liable to repair it.[133]

The Law Commission is critical of the uncertainty surrounding both the law of waste and the implied obligation of tenant like user. It is not clear which relationships these obligations apply to, and the content of them is unclear. Accordingly, it has recommended that the law of waste applicable to tenancies and licences be abolished, as well as the covenant of tenant like user. In place of these doctrines, the 1996 Repair report recommended the

> … creation of an implied obligation on the part of tenants and licensees to take reasonable care of the property which they occupy.[134]

This implied covenant or statutory duty would, as well as requiring the tenant to take proper care of the premises, require him to make good any damage wilfully done or caused to the premises by him or others occupying or visiting the premises, and not to alter the premises (or part) in any way which destroys or alters their character or causes detriment to the landlord's interest. This would apply to all tenancies and licences, whether created formally or informally, the objective being:

---

[130] [1986] QB 1212 (CA) 1223.
[131] *Herne v Bembow* (1913) 128 ER 531.
[132] *Wedd v Porter* [1916] 2 KB 91 (CA) 100.
[133] [1954] 1 QB 15 (CA) 20.
[134] Law Commission, 'Landlord and Tenant: Responsibility for State and Condition of Property' (Law Com No 238, 1996) para 10.34.

... to ensure that a person who is in lawful possession of occupation of property assumes certain very basic responsibilities for the reasonable care of it.[135]

The duty would be excludable by express agreement.

The draft bill in the Law Commission's Renting Homes report provides that the common law principles of waste and tenant like user do not apply to occupation contracts, and they propose as a supplementary (default) term that the tenant must take care of the premises and fix any damage as a result of the tenant's, or occupier's, lack of care.[136] Occupiers of HMOs are already placed under a duty to 'take reasonable care to avoid causing damage to anything which the manager is under a duty to supply, maintain or repair' and to store litter in the manner proposed by the manager.[137]

12.4.4.3 Statutorily Implied Terms

The major source of intervention in leases in relation to repairs has come from statute.

(i) Landlord and Tenant Act 1985

In the residential sector, the Landlord and Tenant Act 1985 (as amended) creates duties for the landlord whether the landlord be a local authority, a housing association or from the private sector. Section 11 applies to a lease of a dwelling house for a term of less than seven years.[138]

This section has been of immense importance to tenants. It provides:

Section 11

(1) In a lease to which this section applies ... there is implied a covenant by the lessor –

(a) to keep in repair the structure and exterior of the dwelling-house (including drains, gutters and external pipes),

(b) to keep in repair and proper working order the installations in the dwelling-house for the supply of water, gas and electricity and for sanitation (including basins, sinks, baths and sanitary conveniences, but not other fixtures, fittings and appliances for making use of the supply of water, gas or electricity), and

(c) to keep in repair and proper working order the installations in the dwelling-house for space heating and heating water.

...

(6) In a case in which the lessor's repairing covenant is implied there is also implied a covenant by the lessee that the lessor, or any person authorised by him in writing, may at reasonable times of the day and on giving 24 hours' notice in writing to the occupier, enter the premises comprised in the lease for the purpose of viewing their condition and state of repair.

It was the application of section 11 that was in issue in *Bruton v London and Quadrant*

---

[135] Law Commission, 'Landlord and Tenant: Responsibility for State and Condition of Property' (Law Com No 238, 1996) para 10.40.

[136] Law Commission, 'Renting Homes: The Final Report. Volume 1: Report' (Law Com No 297, 2006) para 8.16, and Appendix A.

[137] The Management of Houses in Multiple Occupation (England) Regulations 2006 SI 2006/372. This applies to all HMOs falling within the general definition in s 254 of the Housing Act 2004 and is not limited to those that are subjected to the mandatory licensing scheme. Failure to comply with the regulations is an offence, but it will be a defence to show 'reasonable excuse'. Presumably, good tenancy agreements will include these provisions.

[138] Landlord and Tenant Act 1985 s 13.

Housing Trust where Mr Bruton, who had been living in the flat for ten years by the time the case came before the House of Lords, argued that the Housing Trust was in breach of the statutory implied repairing obligation. The House of Lords held that section 11 did apply to the agreement conferring exclusive occupation on Mr Bruton even though the grantor did not itself have a legal estate.[139] Contracting out of section 11 obligations is prohibited,[140] and any covenant that seeks to impose repair obligations on the tenant (or the cost of them)[141] that are placed on the landlord by the Act will be ineffective.[142]

Section 11 requires the landlord 'to keep in repair the structure and exterior of the dwelling-house'. Under the doctrine in *Proudfoot v Hart*[143] the landlord is, thus, under an obligation to put the premises into repair if they are not so at the commencement of the lease. It has been held that wallplaster is part of the exterior and structure,[144] as are windows,[145] and partition walls in converted flats:

> The external parts of premises are those which form the inclosure of them, and beyond which no part of them extends: and it is immaterial whether those parts are exposed to the atmosphere, or rest upon and adjoin some other building which forms no part of the premises let.[146]

Paths providing access to the dwelling-house which are within the demise form part of the exterior,[147] but not paving slabs in the back yard[148] or steps in the back garden.[149] Installations, as opposed to the structure and exterior, have to be kept in repair and proper working order. Where a house had no working space heaters at the commencement of the lease, *Hussein v Mehlman* held that the landlord was in breach of section 11(1)(c) until some were installed.[150] So, even though there is no 'disrepair' in the technical sense and the problem is caused by a design fault, the landlord may have to do work to put an installation into proper working order.[151] A landlord is not obliged to take preventative measures, such as lagging pipes and insulating lofts,[152] although any damage caused to the structure, the exterior or an installation by reason of failure to take preventative measures will give rise to liability on the part of the landlord under section 11.

Section 11 does not make the landlord liable to rebuild the premises if they are destroyed by fire etc, or to repair tenant's fixtures.[153]

Prior to amendment in 1988, the Act did not work satisfactorily where the tenant rented a flat in a dwelling in multiple occupation, especially so if it was in a tower block. The

---

[139] *Bruton v London and Quadrant Housing Trust* [2000] 1 AC 406 (HL). See ch 3.

[140] S 12, although the County Court with the consent of both parties can exclude or modify the terms implied by s 11 (s 12(2)) – to do this would be most unusual.

[141] S 11(5).

[142] S 11(4).

[143] (1890) 25 QBD 42.

[144] *Hussein v Mehlman* [1992] 2 EGLR 87 (Cty Ct).

[145] *Boswell v Crucible Steel of America* [1925] 1 KB 119 (CA); *Hastie v City of Edinburgh* 1981 SLT 61.

[146] *Green v Eales* (1841) 2 QB 225, 237.

[147] *Brown v Liverpool Corporation* [1969] 3 All ER 1345 (CA) (necessary as a means of access).

[148] *Hopwood v Cannock Chase DC* [1975] 1 WLR 373 (CA) (not necessary as a means of access).

[149] *McAuley v Bristol CC* [1992] QB 134 (CA).

[150] [1992] 2 EGLR 87 (Cty Ct).

[151] *O'Connor v Old Etonian Housing Association Ltd* [2002] EWCA Civ 150, [2002] Ch 295 [15]-[16].

[152] *Wycombe Area Health Authority v Barnett* (1982) 5 HLR 84 (CA).

[153] S 11(2)(b) and (c).

problem was that the Act was held to apply solely to the structure, exterior and installations of that particular flat. Thus, in *Campden Hill Towers v Gardner*[154] the tenant of a flat in the middle of a tower block could not complain if the roof leaked causing damage to the interior decoration of his flat or if the communal central heating boiler situated outside his own flat broke down. For tenancies starting on or after 15 January 1989, however, section 11 has been amended. Under section 11(1A) and (1B), where the enjoyment of a flat in a dwelling in multiple occupation is affected by disrepair or failure to maintain an installation in proper working order, it is of no consequence that the disrepair is to another part or that the installation is situated in another part of the building in which the landlord has an interest or estate. The landlord is liable to the tenant so long as the effect is felt in the tenant's demise. If the landlord does not have a right to enter the part of the building or to access the installation to carry out the required repairs then it is a defence in any proceedings relating to a failure to comply to show that 'he used all reasonable endeavours to obtain' the necessary access rights.[155] Leases created on or after 15 January 1989 also oblige the landlord to keep the common parts in good repair.

The Act does not permit the tenant to be a bad tenant. By section 11(2)(a) the landlord is not required to carry out repairs:

> … for which the lessee is liable by virtue of his duty to use the premises in a tenant-like manner, or would be so liable but for an express covenant on his part.

The meaning of 'tenant like' user is linked to how a reasonable tenant would behave in the circumstances. In *Wycombe Area Health Authority v Barnett* the tenant had not failed to act in a 'tenant like' manner when she left her home for a couple of days during cold weather without draining the water system or turning off the stop-cock, leading to the unlagged water pipes bursting.[156]

The standard of repair required reflects that at common law, although account is also take of the life of the building, which means that the landlord's obligations are waived if the cost is too high in relation to the value of the building:[157]

Section 11
(3) In determining the standard of repair required by the lessor's repairing covenant, regard shall be had to the age, character and prospective life of the dwelling-house and the locality in which it is situated.

The Landlord and Tenant Act 1985 is subject to several exceptions. The obligation will only arise when the landlord knows of the need to repair and a reasonable time must have elapsed since the landlord acquired such knowledge so that he can set any repairs in motion.[158] There is no need for the landlord to have been informed by the tenant: the fact that a council worker, not even from the housing department, knew of the disrepair was sufficient to impute notice to the local authority landlord in *Dinefwr BC v Jones*.[159] The only

---

[154] [1977] QB 823 (CA).
[155] S 11(3)(A).
[156] (1982) 5 HLR 84 (CA).
[157] *Patel v Newham LB* (1978) 13 HLR 77 (CA).
[158] *Morris v Liverpool CC* (1988) 20 HLR 498 (CA) and *Hughes v Liverpool CC* The Times 30 March 1988 (CA).
[159] (1987) 19 HLR 445 (CA).

exception to the rule that the landlord has to be given notice of the disrepair is where that disrepair is to part of the premises retained by the landlord, such as common areas, for example, stairs or communal basements. Section 11 does not affect commercial or agricultural tenancies,[160] and section 14(5) exempts the Crown as landlord from section 11 liabilities. Finally, section 14(4) excludes certain types of tenant from protection, including educational institutions, the aim being to confine the obligations to those landlords with tenants who are individuals rather than institutions.

Although of tremendous importance, the section does not ensure that living conditions will be satisfactory; as seen in *Quick v Taff Ely BC*,[161] it is only triggered if there is disrepair and the landlord may not be required to fix problems that stem from design faults. The Law Commission is rightly critical of this limitation as the policy justifications for imposing the section 11 repairing obligation on the landlord apply with just as much force to unfitness that is caused by inherent defects.[162] Of course, if the Law Commission's proposed covenant of fitness for human habitation is implemented then this would deal with the problem as it would require fitness not only at the time of the letting but throughout it. In its Renting Homes report, the Law Commission proposes that a modern form of section 11 is included as a fundamental term which would apply to all occupation contracts, thus applying to licences as well as leases.[163]

(ii) Duty of Care and the Defective Premises Act 1972[164]

In practice the landlord may come under an obligation to repair if he owes a duty of care to the tenant (and others). At common law there was no such duty.[165] This has now been altered by statute; by section 4 of the Defective Premises Act 1972 where the landlord has an obligation to repair and maintain the premises, there is a duty to take reasonable care to see that the tenant and visitors are safe from injury. This is a duty owed whenever there is 'right to occupation given by contract' and is not confined to tenancies.[166] Section 4(1) provides that:

> Where the premises are let under a tenancy which puts on the landlord an obligation to the tenant for the maintenance or repair of the premises, the landlord owes to all persons who might reasonably be expected to be affected by defects in the state of the premises a duty to take such care as is reasonable in all the circumstances to see that they are reasonably safe from personal injury or from damage to their property caused by a relevant defect.

This duty of care will arise whether the obligation is express, implied by statute[167] or is an implied term at common law.[168] The duty is owed if the landlord:

---

[160] Ss 32(2) and 14(3)

[161] [1986] QB 809 (CA).

[162] Law Commission, 'Landlord and Tenant: Responsibility for State and Condition of Property' (Law Com No 238, 1996) para 5.16.

[163] Law Commission, 'Renting Homes: The Final Report. Volume 1: Report' (Law Com No 297, 2006).

[164] For critical commentary, see JR Spencer, 'The Defective Premises Act 1972 – Defective Law and Defective Law Reform, Part III' (1975) 34 *CLJ* 48, 62–78.

[165] *Cavalier v Pope* [1906] AC 428 (HL). For criticism, see PF Smith, 'Confined to the Contract' [1989] *Conv* 216. If the landlord was also the builder, there may be tortious liability for negligent design and construction: *Rimmer v Liverpool City Council* [1985] QB 1 (CA).

[166] S 4(6).

[167] S 4(5).

[168] *McAuley v Bristol CC* [1992] QB 134 (CA).

... knows (whether as a result of being notified by the tenant or otherwise) or if he ought in all the circumstances to have known of the relevant defect (section 4(2)).

A relevant defect is one which is:

... a defect in the state of the premises ... arising from, or continuing because of, an act or omission by the landlord which constitutes or would if he had had notice of the defect, have constituted a failure by him to carry out his obligation to the tenant for the maintenance or repair of the premises (section 4(3))

and which exists at the earlier of the time when the tenancy begins, the agreement is entered into or when the tenant moves into possession (section 4(3)).

While this looks as though it would not impose any greater responsibility than that already placed on the landlord by the lease (expressly or by implication), it does have the effect of widening his responsibility. First, this is a duty owed not only to the tenant but to all persons who could be affected by the defects. Second, it applies not only where the landlord knows of the defect but where he ought to have known (whereas the statutory obligation in section 11 requires notice and a reasonable time to take action). Third, the impact of section 4 is considerably extended by subsection (4) that provides that where the landlord has the *right* to enter premises to repair, he is deemed to owe a duty of care, even if he is not under a leasehold (express or implied) *obligation* to repair:

(4) Where premises are let under a tenancy which expressly or impliedly gives the landlord the right to enter the premises to carry out any description of maintenance or repair of the premises, then, as from the time when he first is, or by notice or otherwise can put himself, in a position to exercise the right and so long as he is or can put himself in that position, he shall be treated for the purposes of subsections (1) to (3) above (but for no other purpose) as if he were under an obligation to the tenant for that description of maintenance or repair of the premises; but the landlord shall not owe the tenant any duty by virtue of this subsection in respect of any defect in the state of the premises arising from, or continuing because of, a failure to carry out an obligation expressly imposed on the tenant by the tenancy.

In *Smith v Bradford Metropolitan Council*[169] a council tenant broke his leg when the concrete in a back patio crumbled; under the tenancy the council had the right to enter to maintain, but the statutory implied repairing obligation[170] did not extend to the patio. Nonetheless, the council was held liable by virtue of section 4(4). For the purposes of section 4(4), 'premises' means all of the property let, both land and buildings.[171] In *Boldack v East Lindsey District Council* it was held not to make the local authority landlord liable for having failed to remove a heavy concrete slab from the garden when this fell and injured the tenant's son, as removing the slab was neither 'repair' nor 'maintenance'.[172] Nor can section 4(4) be used to address design defects which have led to serious condensation problems, as the remedial works necessary to remedy these defects are not within the expression 'any description of maintenance or repair of the premises'.[173] Similarly, it does not include a duty

---

[169] (1982) 44 P & CR 171 (CA).
[170] S 32(1) of the Housing Act 1961, the precursor to s 11 of the Landlord and Tenant Act 1985.
[171] *Smith v Bradford Metropolitan Council* (1982) 44 P & CR 171 (CA) 176.
[172] (1999) 31 HLR 41 (CA).
[173] *Lee v Leeds CC; Ratcliffe v Sandwell MBC* [2001] EWCA Civ 6, [2002] 1 WLR 1488.

to 'make safe', so in *Alker v Collingwood Housing Association* a tenant was unable to claim damages for personal injury which had been caused by putting her arm through her front door which did not contain safety glass.[174] Although it was recognised that this kind of glass posed a safety hazard it had satisfied building standards at the time of construction.

(iii) Agricultural Leases

In relation to agricultural holdings falling within the Agricultural Holdings Act 1986, model clauses are inserted into leases by statutory instrument which allocate responsibility for the repair, insurance and maintenance of fixed equipment. Fixed equipment is defined by section 96 of the Act to include 'any building or structure affixed to the land and any works on, in or under the land'; it also includes things grown for reasons other than to use after severance from the land, such as, for example, a line of trees planted to protect crops or buildings. The most important aspect of fixed equipment with respect to repairing obligations, however, is in relation to buildings provided for the tenant to live in and those provided to do with the running of the farm, such as a milking shed.

The model clauses impose an obligation on the landlord for structural repairs, subject in some cases to the landlord being able to seek a contribution from the tenant of one half of the costs. In turn, the tenant is under a duty, inter alia, to keep in repair non-structural features of the fixed property within the demise. The landlord and tenant are free to contract out of these model clauses, although one party can then refer the issue to arbitration to see if the lease should be varied to bring it back in line with the model clauses.[175]

Under the new farm business tenancy regime there are no model clauses as to repair. The allocation of liability for repair is left to contractual agreement between the parties.

12.4.5 Reform

The Law Commission regards it as unsatisfactory that there may be no one responsible for the state and condition of rented property; it is in the public interest that rented stock is properly maintained. Nor is it desirable that in the absence of express contractual provision it is necessary to go to court to see if there is an implied repairing obligation. With the exception of short residential leases, which would be adequately provided by the fitness covenant and section 11, they propose reform in accordance with the following objectives:

> 7.4 First, when parties are negotiating a lease, they should be obliged to address the issue of responsibility for repairs ... [In] every lease, either the landlord or the tenant should be responsible for the repair of –
>
> (i)   the premises let;
> (ii) any common parts; and
> (iii) any other premises owned by the landlord that may impinge on the enjoyment of the property leased;

---

[174] [2007] EWCA Civ 343.
[175] Agricultural Holdings Act 1986 ss 7 and 8.

unless parties have expressly decided that this should not be so … [It] should no longer be possible for the situation to arise in which neither party is responsible for repairing some part of the property due to an oversight, but only as a result of a conscious decision.

7.5 Secondly, the repairing obligations in every lease should be certain. The possibility that there may be an implied term as to repair to give business efficacy to the lease or because the property let is of a particular kind (such as the letting of furnished accommodation), should be excluded. Any reform should seek to obviate the need to take court proceedings to determine whether there is an implied repairing obligation.

7.6. Thirdly, the parties should be free either to allocate the responsibility for repairs between themselves or (if they so choose) to exclude it in whole or part … [Although] we are anxious to encourage repair, we acknowledge that there may be cases where the parties quite reasonably decide that neither of them shall have repairing obligations in respect of all or part of the property. It may be, for example, that the landlord intends to redevelop the premises on the termination of the lease [footnotes omitted].[176]

These principles would be reflected in an implied covenant that the landlord shall keep (and put) the premises and common parts in repair. This would be a default covenant, and would apply unless the parties have made alternative provision for repair, have expressly excluded the covenant or if there is a statutory repairing obligation. The expectation is that in most commercial cases the covenant will be expressly excluded. The default covenant would not apply to short residential tenancies, agricultural holdings, farm business tenancies or oral leases.

12.5 Regulatory Controls

For more than 100 years, local authorities have possessed various powers to tackle bad housing standards. Most of these powers are not specific to rental properties, and therefore this section will provide only an outline of these. Two of the main powers have been the ability to deal with 'unfitness' under the Housing Act 1985 and statutory nuisance under the Environment Protection Act 1990. Mandatory licensing of HMOs has been introduced recently, and this is given more detailed discussion even though the complexity of the legislation is such that specialist texts will need to be referred to for comprehensive coverage.

12.5.1 Unfitness and HHSRS

The definition of unfitness in section 604 of the Housing Act 1985 gave a local authority the power to deal both with lack of repair and lack of amenities. If the house was unfit for human habitation then the local authority was able to respond by serving a repairs notice (requiring specified works to be carried out), a closing or demolition order, or a deferred action notice (giving an opportunity to remedy the problems before more serious enforcement measures are taken). This notice would be served on the 'person having control

---

[176] Law Commission, 'Landlord and Tenant: Responsibility for State and Condition of Property' (Law Com No 238, 1996).

of the premises' (which included a landlord receiving a rack rent).[177] Failure to comply with the notices would generally constitute a criminal offence. One of the main criticisms of the system was that the fitness standard did not deal with many of the conditions that threaten the health and safety of users, such as fire safety and poor energy efficiency.

The unfitness provisions have now been replaced by the Housing Health and Safety Rating System (HHSRS) introduced under the Housing Act 2004. By section 3 the local housing authority is required to 'keep the housing conditions in their area under review with a view to identifying any action that may need to be taken by them'. Section 4 requires them to decide when it is appropriate to inspect individual dwellings, and imposes a duty to inspect following an 'official complaint' from a justice of the peace or parochial or community council. This enables local authorities to determine whether a hazard exists at residential premises which may cause harm to the health or safety of an occupier. Where there is such a hazard the local authority is able to take enforcement measures, such as serving a hazard awareness notice, an improvement notice (which requires work to remove or reduce the hazard) or a prohibition order (restricting the use of the property), in addition to certain emergency measures. Again, the notice is to be served on the person having control of the premises.[178] Under the HHSRS, categories of hazard are identified and there is a method for calculating the seriousness of these hazards.[179] If the most serious, category one, hazard is found then the local authority will be under a duty to take action. It is estimated that category one hazards are present in about 1.6 million dwellings (as compared to 880,000 dwellings that are unfit according to the section 604 definition).[180]

A problem with both the unfitness provisions and most of the provisions of the environmental legislation (below) is that they are enforced by the local authority; this prevents their use in favour of council tenants where the dwelling is within the local authority landlord's area. In *R v Cardiff CC, ex p Cross* the Court of Appeal held that a local authority cannot be compelled to apply enforcement provisions to itself.[181] This remains the case under the HHSRS, although the Decent Homes Standard[182] will require the social housing stock to be free of category one hazards.

The effectiveness of the HHSRS will undoubtedly depend upon the ability of local authorities to carry out inspections and bring enforcement actions: under the old fitness regime lack of resources contributed to its limited effect in tackling poor conditions.[183] Further, enforcement action is essentially arbitrary in the sense that it does not necessarily reflect strategic decisions by enforcement bodies related to the degree of disrepair present.[184]

---

[177] Housing Act 1985 s 207. In the case of the closing or demolition order the notice also had to be served an 'owner' (Housing Act 1985 s 268).

[178] Housing Act 2004 Sch 1. Where the property is licensed, the notice is to be served on the license holder.

[179] The Housing Health and Safety Rating System (England) Regulations 2005 SI 2005/3208. These came into force on 6 April 2006.

[180] Explanatory Memorandum to The Housing Health and Safety Rating System (England) Regulations 2005 SI 2005/3208 para 7.6.

[181] (1982) 6 HLR 1 (CA).

[182] See 12.2.1.

[183] S Blandy, 'Housing standards in the private rented sector and the three Rs: regulation, responsibility and rights' in D Cowan and A Marsh (eds), *Two Steps Forward* (Bristol, The Policy Press, 2001) 81–3.

[184] Law Commission, 'Encouraging Responsible Letting' (Law Com CP No 181, 2007) Part 4.

12.5.2 Public Health Powers

Environmental health legislation has existed in some form since 1846 and controls 'statutory nuisances'. A statutory nuisance is defined by section 79 of the Environmental Protection Act 1990 and includes 'premises in such a state as to be prejudicial to health or a nuisance', applying to both residential and commercial premises. If a property is found to violate section 79, then the local authority shall serve an abatement notice under section 80, requiring the nuisance to be abated and any necessary works to be executed or steps to be taken.

Further, there is a means by which a tenant (even a council tenant) can directly enforce public health standards as section 82 of the Environmental Protection Act 1990 allows anyone aggrieved by a statutory nuisance to go to the Magistrates' Court for an abatement order. The order will prevent any future repetition of this nuisance and will require the person responsible, which might be a local authority, to do any necessary work. Such work can be extensive, as was seen in *Birmingham DC v Kelly*,[185] where the landlord had to re-wire the house, install gas central heating and secondary double glazing, insulate the roof and fill the cavity walls. The court can also fine the perpetrator of the nuisance and can order compensation to be paid to the aggrieved party. The Environmental Protection Act 1990 cannot, however, be used to support a civil action.[186]

Whilst useful, this section is unable to address many of the problems associated with poor housing. The section has been given a narrow meaning by the courts, unwilling to apply the wording to deal with problems arising from the absence of certain amenities or poor design. In *Birmingham City Council v Oakley* a council tenant complained to the magistrates court that the absence of a washbasin in a lavatory created a 'statutory nuisance'.[187] Although the House of Lords accepted that this created a hygiene risk, it held (by majority of 3-2) that the section was designed to deal with 'noxious matters' and that the absence of a washbasin was not a statutory nuisance.[188] Having regard to the statutory history of the section, Lord Slynn stated that section 79 was:

> ... directed to the presence in the house of some feature which in itself is prejudicial to health in that it is a source of possible infection or disease or illness such as dampness, mould, dirt or evil-smelling accumulations or the presence of rats. The state of the house must in itself have been prejudicial to health.[189]

Lord Clyde, in the minority, differed, preferring to give the section a modern meaning to fulfil 'the basic purpose of ensuring that people may live and work in hygienic and sanitary conditions and that the risks of disease and ill-health may be minimized'.[190] As in many of the cases in which the courts have declined to give tenants remedies to address problems of poor design, the House of Lords considered that the allocation of large sums of public money

---

[185] (1985) 17 HLR 572 (DC).
[186] *Issa v Hackney BC* [1997] 1 WLR 956 (CA).
[187] [2001] 1 AC 617 (HL).
[188] Nor was a steep staircase in *R v Bristol CC, ex p Everett* [1999] 2 All ER 193 (CA) or inadequate sound insulation in *R (on the application of Vella) v Lambeth LBC* [2005] EWHC 2473 (Admin).
[189] [2001] 1 AC 617 (HL) 627.
[190] [2001] 1 AC 617 (HL) 635–5.

was something to be addressed specifically by Parliament rather than by judicial development.[191]

Further, the section is limited to what would be either a public or private nuisance at common law.[192] This means that where the problem exists in the tenant's own dwelling, he cannot complain of the nuisance – it must emanate from some external source.

These public health remedies provide a useful supplement to repairing obligations when coupled with the HHSRS (although they are of more limited value to council tenants). Indeed it has been argued that as leasehold repairing covenants fail to prevent serious deterioration, public remedies are superior.[193]

12.5.3 HMO Licensing

In recognition of the higher level of risk in HMOs many local housing authorities voluntarily ran HMO registration schemes under section 346 of the Housing Act 1985. There was, however, no obligation to do so and there was a plethora of schemes across the country applying different standards. The focus of the schemes was the health and safety of occupiers. In 1996, amendments to the Housing Act 1985[194] made it possible to include 'special control provisions' which permitted the inclusion of controls to prevent HMOs 'by reason of their existence or the behaviour of their residents from adversely affecting the amenity or character of the area in which they are situated'. It appears that few local authorities used these provisions.[195]

Part 2 of the Housing Act 2004 introduces a mandatory national scheme of licensing for HMOs. It applies to HMOs of three storeys or more with five or more occupants living there[196] as their only or main residence in two or more single households[197] and sharing basic amenities.[198] The aim is to ensure that those HMOs which present the most serious risks come to the attention of the local authority. Licensing is intended to ensure that:

— Landlords of HMOs are fit and proper persons or employ agents who are.
— The standards of tenancy relations management and property management employed by a landlord or agent are adequate.
— High risk HMOs and their landlords are identified, so that health and safety measures … can be targeted on the worst cases.

---

[191] See, for example, Lord Hoffmann at 628; Poole J in *R (on the application of Vella) v Lambeth LBC* [2005] EWHC 2473 (Admin) [70]-[71].

[192] *NCB v Neath BC* [1976] 2 All ER 478 (HL).

[193] D Tiplady, 'Recent Developments in the Law of Landlord and Tenant: The American Experience' (1981) 44 *MLR* 129, 140.

[194] S 348B-F.

[195] H Carr, D Cowan and C Hunter, 'Policing the Housing Crisis' (2007) 27 *Critical Social Policy* 100.

[196] Not necessarily as tenants. Licensees are also included.

[197] Family members constitute a single household: Housing Act 2004 s 258. The Licensing and Management of Houses in Multiple Occupation and Other Houses (Miscellaneous Provisions) (England) Regulations 2006 SI 2006/373 set out what a 'household' is in more detail, covering employees and carers, and govern administrative aspects of the licensing scheme.

[198] Or the living accommodation must be lacking in one or more basic amenities. The Licensing of Houses in Multiple Occupation (Prescribed Descriptions) (England) Order 2006 SI 2006/371. See A Dymond, 'Houses in Multiple Occupation – The New Definition' [2006] *J of Housing L* 50.

— Where landlords refuse to meet the required criteria, authorities can step in to manage proper-
  ties.
— Vulnerable tenants can be protected.
— HMOs are not occupied by excessive numbers of people.
— Local authorities can identify landlords and support them in participating in working to regen-
  erate rundown areas or to tackle problems of antisocial behaviour.[199]

It is, therefore, not only the problems of individual property management (repair and
condition) that licensing is intended to help with but also the wider goals referred to in the
previous chapter, of engaging:

> … private landlords in the renewal of areas of low housing demand and engaging private
> landlords in a duty to deal appropriately with anti-social tenants.[200]

The details of the HMO licensing are complex, and beyond the scope of this book; there
are five sections which deal with the definition of HMOs, supplemented by Regulations.[201]

In addition to the mandatory licensing, section 56 of the Housing Act 2004 makes
provision for additional licensing by giving local authorities a discretionary power to apply
licensing to a particular area and to particular categories of HMO where the local authority
considers:

> … that a significant proportion of the HMOs of that description in the area are being man-
> aged sufficiently ineffectively as to give rise, or to be likely to give rise, to one or more
> particular problems either for those occupying the HMOs or for members of the public.[202]

This is intended to be used for areas in which there is a significant number of HMOs not
falling within the mandatory scheme but which give rise to particular problems of
management or anti-social behaviour; generally expected to be in areas of low housing
demand. Nottingham City Council has, for example, declared the whole of the area within
the city of Nottingham to be an area subject to additional licensing.

Part 3 of the Housing Act 2004 also provides for selective licensing (not confined to
HMOs), intended primarily to be used in areas of low housing demand where there have
been particular problems of poor management and anti-social behaviour. At first blush it
seems strange that the problems are most acute in areas of low housing demand as it might
be thought that landlords would then have to try harder to attract tenants. The explanation,
however, is that as property prices fall they become attractive to less scrupulous investors
who are not good managers and who wish to make a good return on their investment
without putting money into repair and management. In addition, where properties are
difficult to let landlords may not be able to let to desirable tenants and problems of
anti-social behaviour tend to occur. There are a number of limitations on when selective

---

[199] ODPM, 'Licensing in the Private Rented Sector. Consultation on the Implementation of HMO Licensing,
Regulatory Impact Assessment, Housing Bill, Part 2' (November 2004) Part 2, para 29.
[200] Explanatory Memorandum to the Licensing of Houses in Multiple Occupation (Prescribed Descriptions)
(England) Order 2006 SI 2006/371, para 13.
[201] Housing Act 2004 ss 77, 254–259. In addition to Part Two of the Housing Act 2004 numerous statutory instruments implement the scheme. The Management of Houses in Multiple Occupation (England) Regulations 2006 SI
2006/372 set out management regulations for all HMOs. Student accommodation owned and managed by educational establishments which have signed up to a Code of Practice are not classified as HMOs.
[202] Housing Act 2004 s 56 (2).

licensing can be introduced to ensure that this cannot become licensing of the entire private rented sector by the back door.[203] By section 80, a local housing authority can designate an area subject to selective licensing if either it is an area of low housing demand[204] and licensing will 'contribute to the improvement of the social or economic conditions in the area'[205] or the area suffers from significant and persistent anti-social behaviour and some private sector landlords are failing to take action to combat the problem and the designation will lead to a reduction in, or elimination of, the problem.[206]

Both additional licensing and selective licensing can be introduced only if this is consistent with the authority's overall housing strategy[207] and must be coordinated with its approach in connection with homelessness, empty properties and anti-social behaviour[208] and it must have considered whether other courses of action would have proven effective and then decided that the designation will 'significantly assist them to deal with the problem or problems (whether or not they take any other course of action as well)'.[209] Designation must be confirmed by the appropriate national authority.[210]

Where licensing is required, the application for a licence must be made to the local housing authority which must satisfy itself as to the following matters before granting the licence:

Section 64

(3) The matters are –

(a)   that the house is reasonably suitable for occupation by not more than the maximum number of households or persons [specified in the application or decided by the authority]…

(b)   that the proposed licence holder –
       (i)   is a fit and proper person[211] to be the licence holder …

(d)   that the proposed manager of the house is a fit and proper person to be the manager of the house; and

(e)   that the proposed management arrangements for the house are otherwise satisfactory.[212]

In reaching the decision as to suitable occupancy numbers the authority will have regard to prescribed standards of amenities and facilities.[213] Licences will also be granted subject to conditions relating both to the 'management, use and occupation' of the house, and its

---

[203] The Selective Licensing of Houses (Specified Exemptions) (England) Order 2006 SI 2006/370 excepts certain tenancies from the remit of selective licensing, such as owner-occupied long leaseholds (lettings by RSLs are exempt under s 79(3) of the Housing Act 2004).

[204] Determined by reference to Housing Act 2004 s 80(4).

[205] Housing Act 2004 s 80(3).

[206] Housing Act 2004 s 80(6). The appropriate national authority may provide for additional conditions (Housing Act 2004 s 80(7)).

[207] Housing Act 2004 ss 57(2) and 81(2).

[208] Housing Act 2004 ss 57(3) and 81(3).

[209] Housing Act 2004 ss 57(4) and 81(4).

[210] Housing Act 2004 ss 58(1) and 82(1).

[211] 'Fit and proper' is decided by reference to the matters in Housing Act 2004 s 66, and includes whether there has been any contravention of landlord and tenant law.

[212] For selective licensing, see Housing Act 2004 s 88(3), similar to those in s 64 minus the reference to the maximum number of occupiers.

[213] Housing Act 2004 s 65, and The Licensing and Management of Houses in Multiple Occupation and Other Houses (Miscellaneous Provisions) (England) Regulations 2006 SI 2006/373.

'condition and contents'.[214] There are some compulsory conditions listed in Schedule 4, such as a requirement that smoke alarms are installed and kept in proper working order, and conditions as to gas and electrical safety. In addition, the licence is also able to include much broader conditions, for example, requiring steps to prevent or reduce anti-social behavior by those occupying or visiting the house or attendance at training courses in relation to applicable codes of practice. Failure to obtain a licence, or allowing the HMO to be occupied by more than the specified number of people, will be a criminal offence punishable by fines up to £20,000.[215] There may also be a 'rent penalty' for a landlord who receives rent while operating unlicensed property.[216] In addition, a breach of any the licensing conditions will be a criminal offence with a fine of up to £5,000.

Landlords of HMOs falling within the licensing regime are subject to a strict regulatory regime. In relation to management, for example, there is a duty in relation to the common parts which is considerably more extensive than the duty in section 11 of the Landlord and Tenant Act 1985, as it requires the manager to ensure that all common parts are maintained in good and clean decorative repair, maintained in a safe and working condition, and kept reasonably clear from obstruction.[217]

Finally, Part 4 (Chapter 1) of the Housing Act 2004 enables local authorities to take over the management of private rented properties in certain situations, including where it is necessary to protect the health and safety of tenants, or where the landlord is failing to deal with persistent anti-social behaviour.[218] Perhaps most controversially, there are also powers in Part 4 (Chapter 2) to take over empty dwellings, those that have been unoccupied for at least six months and where making an empty dwelling management order gives a reasonable prospect that the dwelling will be occupied.[219] These powers are subject to exceptions and require authorisation from the Residential Property Tribunal but have been described in somewhat extreme terms by the press as 'the most pernicious assault on individual freedom and property rights ever attempted by a peacetime government in this country'.[220]

It is recognised by the government that HMOs provide a vital role in making affordable housing available to some of the most vulnerable and disadvantaged groups in society. The intention behind these various licensing schemes is undoubtedly good, intending to drive up standards of management and to ensure safety for the occupiers of HMOs. In practice, responsible landlords will register. It is the 'bad' landlords with rundown properties who are most likely to ignore the requirement to register, and yet these are the very landlords that the legislation is most designed to tackle. Again, the effectiveness of the legislation will

---

[214] See Housing Act 2004 ss 66 and 67 and (for selective licensing) ss 89 and 90. See also The Management of Houses in Multiple Occupation (England) Regulations 2006 SI 2006/372.

[215] Housing Act 2004 s 72.

[216] Housing Act 2004 s 73. Also, s 75 provides that a landlord cannot serve a s 21 notice on a shorthold tenant if the property is unlicensed (but should be).

[217] The Management of Houses in Multiple Occupation (England) Regulations 2006 SI 2006/372. See also the Licensing and Management of Houses in Multiple Occupation (Additional Provisions) (England) Regulations 2007 SI 2007/1903.

[218] Housing Act 2004 ss 101–131; The Housing (Management Orders and Empty Dwelling Management Orders) (Supplemental Provisions) (England) Regulations 2006 SI 2006/368. The Housing (Interim Management Orders) (Prescribed Circumstances) (England) Order 2006 SI 2006/369.

[219] Housing Act 2004 ss 101–131; The Housing (Empty Dwelling Management Orders) (Prescribed Exceptions and Requirements) (England) Order 2006 SI 2006/367.

[220] M Hall, 'Labour's great homes robbery is straight out of the Stalin textbook' The Express 13 July 2006 10.

depend upon the ability of local authorities to detect unregistered HMOs. Currie refers to earlier research of his that shows that the success of discretionary licensing of HMOs in Scotland (prior to the introduction of mandatory licensing in 2000) was limited by inadequate resources to implement it and low priority being given to HMO work. Further, licensed owners believed schemes were failing because the worst HMO owners were avoiding licensing;[221] and early evidence following the introduction of mandatory licensing in Scotland shows that significant numbers of HMO landlords had failed to register.[222] The complexity of HMO licensing under the Housing Act 2004 also means that it will not be easy to operate. Additionally, there are fears that the cost to landlords of applying for registration (which vary from a couple of hundred pounds to £1,000), bringing the property up to standard, and dealing with the paperwork may deter landlords from entering or remaining in the HMO market. In addition, some of the works necessary to conform to HMO standards may detrimentally affect the capital value of the property on resale, again making investment in HMOs unattractive to landlords. A survey in 2000[223] (before the details of the new scheme were known) suggested that HMO licensing is likely to reduce the supply of HMOs, that some HMO landlords will raise rents in order to fund higher repairs expenditure, some would not convert into HMOs, and some would convert HMOs into self-contained flats.[224] Crook suggests that tougher enforcement measures (including licensing) will 'not, of themselves, address the fundamental economic and financial barriers to improvements and might lead to a reduction in overall supply'.[225] The licensing provisions came into force in April 2006 and it is too early to assess their impact yet.

In Northern Ireland a HMO registration scheme was successfully challenged in judicial review proceedings in *Re Landlord's Association for Northern Ireland* on the ground that it lacked certainty and was disproportionate, offending the principles of legal certainty and proportionality required under the European Convention for the Protection of Human Rights and Fundamental Freedoms (ECHR).[226] The provisions causing difficulties were the very broad definition of HMOs (applying to all houses with a capacity to hold ten people provided three non family members lived there) which made it a disproportionate measure, and the 'special control' provisions in paragraph 10.4 of the scheme:

> … it is a condition of registration that the person having control of the house, or the person managing the house, shall take such steps as are reasonably practicable to prevent the existence of the house or the behaviour of its residents from adversely affecting the amenity or character of the area in which the house is situated, or to reduce any such adverse effect.

---

[221] H Currie, 'The Scottish System of Licensing Houses in Multiple Occupation' in S Lowe and D Hughes (eds), *The Private Rented Sector in a New Century: revival or false dawn?* (Bristol, The Policy Press, 2002) 90.

[222] See studies referred to in H Carr and others, *The Housing Act 2004. A Practical Guide* (Bristol, Jordans, 2005) para 3.33.

[223] ADH Crook and others, 'Repairs and Maintenance by Private Landlords' (Housing Research Summary, Number 138, DETR, 2000).

[224] The application of the HMO scheme to self contained flats and converted buildings is far from clear: see Housing Act 2004 ss 254 and 257; Houses in Multiple Occupation (Certain Converted Blocks of Flats) (Modifications to the Housing Act 2004 and Transitional Provisions for section 257 HMOs) (England) Regulations 2007 SI 2007/1904.

[225] ADH Crook, 'Housing conditions in the private rented sector within a market framework' in S Lowe and D Hughes (eds), *The Private Rented Sector in a New Century: revival or false dawn?* (Bristol, The Policy Press, 2002) 172.

[226] [2005] NIQB 22, [2006] NI 16 [49] and [52].

The effect of this was to create uncertainty as the property owner would not know with reasonable clarity what he could or could not do, and it did not necessarily require a close nexus between the tenanted property and the problem behaviour.

The details of the Northern Irish scheme differ significantly from the HMO licensing scheme introduced by the Housing Act 2004, but two points of general interest emerge. First, Judge Girvan drew attention to the risk that such a broad regulatory regime might cause landlords to leave the market:

> ... legislation of this nature has profound effect on property rights and has the potential capacity to deleteriously distort property developments. An ill formulated scheme may (inter alia) have the undesirable and unintended impact of reducing the number of HMOs available to provide accommodation for persons in need of it. It could dissuade owners from providing accommodation in circumstances where this may produce undesirable social results.[227]

Second, commenting on the case, Carr and others remark how HMO licensing has been used not simply as a tool to ensure good standards but as a crime control mechanism. Commenting on the HMO in Northern Ireland, they state it was hijacked:

> ... for the purpose of dealing with criminality. All the policy literature has concerned the safety of HMOs – they are risky buildings, which therefore require competent management. Here, though, the scheme was being used explicitly as a crime control mechanism ...

Further, as licences can be revoked where criminality results from the property:

> ... the license-holder becomes responsibilised into the obligation of ensuring the maintenance of civility in their properties by their residents and guests. The license-holder occupies an intermediate role between the state and the occupier, responsible for crime control.[228]

Although it is too early to assess the impact of HMO licensing in England and Wales, the risk that Judge Girvan referred to, of landlords being deterred from renting out rooms in HMOs, also exists here even with a less intrusive licensing scheme. It is also clear that the English licensing scheme shares the mixed objectives: is not only about housing conditions and safety but also about controlling behaviour.

12.6 Beyond Landlord and Tenant Law

As the Law Commission points out, the law relating to the repair of rented property is far from satisfactory. A number of their recommendations for reform have been referred to in this chapter. In the residential sector it is shocking that notwithstanding various civil rights given to tenants and public law measures to deal with poor housing, there continues, in the words of Brooke LJ in *Issa v Hackney BC* '... to be a class of case where a serious wrong continues to be without a remedy in the civil courts'. [229] Tenants are unable to force their landlords to do anything about dwellings that are in appalling condition through damp

---

227 [2005] NIQB 22, [2006] NI 16 [50].
228 H Carr, D Cowan and C Hunter, 'Policing the Housing Crisis' (2007) 27 *Critical Social Policy* 100, 117 and 119.
229 [1997] 1 WLR 956 (CA) 965.

mould and condensation,[230] although a remedy may be available through the statutory nuisance route. Nor can anything be done about premises that are noisy because of inadequate sound installation (as in *Southwark v Tanner*[231] and *Vella v Lambeth LBC*).[232]

Given that the remedies designed for tenants often do not work, attempts have been made to use more generalised laws to deal with the problem. In *Lee v Leeds CC* tenants argued that the Human Rights Act 1998 provided a way through the difficulties.[233] This was a further case involving condensation and damp caused by the way in which the house was constructed. It was argued that section 6 imposed on the:

> ... local authority landlord an obligation to take steps to ensure that the condition of ... [the] dwelling house which it has let for social housing is such that the tenant's convention right under article 8 is not infringed.

Addressing this argument, Chadwick LJ noted the need to balance the resources of the local housing authority against the needs of the individual tenant and concluded that there was not a 'general and unqualified obligation on local authorities in relation to the condition of their housing stock'.[234] He left open the possibility that there may be cases in which the condition of the house may involve a breach of the positive duty inherent in Article 8, but on the particular facts it had not been proven that the breach was sufficiently serious.

In *Southwark v Tanner* local authority tenants sought to draw on 'two ancient common law actions'[235] (the covenant for quiet enjoyment and the law of nuisance) to deal with inadequate sound insulation in their flats. As with attempts to argue for implied terms and expansive interpretations of statutory provisions the House of Lords made clear that the allocation of responsibility for standards and repairs is a matter for Parliament, not for judicial creativity, Lord Hoffmann famously stating that:

> ... in a field such as housing law, which is very much a matter for the allocation of resources in accordance with democratically determined priorities, the development of the common law should not get out of step with legislative policy.[236]

The action on the covenant for quiet enjoyment failed. It is a,

> ... covenant that the tenant's lawful possession of the land will not be substantially interfered with by the acts of the lessor or those lawfully claiming under him.[237]

Although this can be breached by regular excessive noise, it is 'prospective in its nature' and applies only to things done after the grant. The tenant takes the property in the physical condition in which he finds it:

> In the grant of a tenancy it is fundamental to the common understanding of the parties, objectively determined, that the landlord gives no implied warranty as to the condition or

---

[230] As in *Quick v Taff Ely BC* [1986] QB 809 (CA) and *Lee v Leeds CC; Ratcliffe v Sandwell MBC* [2001] EWCA Civ 6, [2002] 1 WLR 1488.
[231] *Southwark LBC v Tanner; Baxter v Camden LBC (No 2)* [2001] 1 AC 1 (HL) 9.
[232] *R (on the application of Vella) v Lambeth LBC* [2005] EWHC 2473 (Admin).
[233] *Lee v Leeds CC; Ratcliffe v Sandwell MBC* [2002] EWCA Civ 6, [2001] 1 WLR 1488.
[234] *Lee v Leeds CC; Ratcliffe v Sandwell MBC* [2002] EWCA Civ 6, [2001] 1 WLR 1488 [49].
[235] *Southwark LBC v Tanner; Baxter v Camden LBC (No 2)* [2001] 1 AC 1 (HL) 9.
[236] *Southwark LBC v Tanner; Baxter v Camden LBC (No 2)* [2001] 1 AC 1 (HL) 9–10.

fitness of the premises. Caveat lessee. It would be entirely inconsistent with this common understanding if the covenant for quiet enjoyment were interpreted to create liability for disturbance or inconvenience or any other damage attributable to the condition of the premises.[238]

The claim in nuisance was more swiftly dismissed. Nuisance involves unreasonable interference. Here the interference was caused by neighbours using their flats in entirely reasonable ways. Lord Hoffmann concluded:

> If the neighbours are not committing a nuisance, the councils cannot be liable for authorising them to commit one … Once again, it all comes down to a complaint about the inherent defects in the construction of the building. The appellants say that the ordinary use of the flats by their neighbours would not have caused them inconvenience if they had been differently built. But that, as I have said more than once, is a matter of which a tenant cannot complain.[239]

An attempt was made in *Dunn v Bradford MDC; Marston v Leeds CC*[240] to argue that letting property not fit for habitation, again because of damp and mould, was in breach of section 13 of the Supply of Goods and Services Act 1982 which provides that:

> In a contract for the supply of a service where the supplier is acting in the course of business, there is an implied term that the supplier will carry out the service with reasonable care and skill.

Not surprisingly, the Court of Appeal was not willing to find that this statutory provision applied to landlords renting out residential property. As Chadwick LJ comments, 'it would be bizarre' to find the obligation imposed through this indirect route when Parliament had not imposed such an obligation directly. He did not accept that the landlord was, simply by letting the property as against later carrying out particular services such as repair and maintenance, providing a service:

> A contract of tenancy creates an estate or interest in the demised premises. The tenant is entitled to occupy the demised premises by virtue of the right of possession which is an incident of that estate or interest. In recognising the tenant's right to occupy the demised premises the landlord is doing no more than giving effect to his grant; the landlord is not carrying out a service; he is not carrying out any activity; he is simply respecting existing property rights. Even if it can be said that, in granting tenancies in respect of its housing stock, a local authority is carrying out a service—rather than, or as well as, fulfilling a statutory function—that service ends when the tenancy is granted.[241]

Notwithstanding the inventive arguments relied upon by various counsel to overcome the limitations of statute, courts have clearly set their face against achieving by development of the common law or statutory interpretation what Parliament has declined to confer directly

---

[237] *Southwark LBC v Tanner; Baxter v Camden LBC (No 2)* [2001] 1 AC 1 (HL) 10.

[238] *Southwark LBC v Tanner; Baxter v Camden LBC (No 2)* [2001] 1 AC 1 (HL) 12.

[239] *Southwark LBC v Tanner; Baxter v Camden LBC (No 2)* [2001] 1 AC 1 (HL) 16.

[240] [2002] EWCA Civ 1137.

[241] [2002] EWCA Civ 1137 [52]. He gave little attention to the (briefly reported) case of *Camden LBC v McBride* [1999] CLY 3737 (Cty Ct) that had held that a tenancy was a service for the purposes of the Unfair Terms in Consumer Contracts Regulations 1994 SI 1994/3159 (UTCCR). Given the different statutory contexts and, in particular, the European origin of the UTCCR this is not surprising. For the approach to the UTCCR, see ch 4.

on residential tenants, an enforceable right to accommodation that is fit for purpose. The solution lies in adoption of the Law Commission's recommendations.

12.7 Enforcing Repairing Obligations

Even if one of the parties is subject to an express or implied repairing obligation, there is still the question of how this can be enforced and what remedies are available for breach. Of course, the ideal position is that if there is a problem with repair it is simply sorted out without resort to legal remedies once it is brought to the attention of the party responsible for repair. In the residential sector, 71 per cent of private renters are satisfied with the way that the landlord deals with repairs, compared to 59 per cent of council tenants.[242] If this fails, it may be necessary to resort to the law. The remedies differ depending on whether the complainant is the landlord or the tenant. Where the landlord is suing the tenant for breach of a repairing covenant he may seek specific performance, damages or, if a right of re-entry has been reserved, he may seek to evict the tenant, subject to various statutory controls. The landlord's ability to 'forfeit' or end the tenancy because of breach of the repairing covenant is discussed in chapter 24. Where the tenant is suing the landlord, once again damages and specific performance may be available, but the tenant might also be able to appoint a manager or receiver, and may even be able to simply walk away from the property if there has been a repudiatory breach.

12.8 Landlord's Remedies for Breach of Tenant's Repairing Covenant

12.8.1 Doing the Work Himself: Rights of Entry

If the lease contains an express covenant imposing the repairing obligation on the tenant, it is usual for the lease also to give the landlord the right to enter the demised premises to view the state of repair and to give written notice to the tenant of any defects found. The tenant will then usually have a period of time in which to make good the defects, and in default the landlord has the right to go onto the premises to do the work itself and recover the costs from the tenant on demand. Even in this situation, however, the landlord's ability to enter to carry out repairs is not guaranteed. In *Hammersmith and Fulham LBC v Creska Ltd* the Council, as tenant of commercial premises, was in breach of its covenant to repair the underfloor heating.[243] The Council accepted that it would have to repair at the end of the lease but in the meantime it preferred to pay damages as the room was used for computing equipment which needed to be kept cool and any repair work would also be highly disruptive. In the circumstances the court thought that an injunction would be disproportionate.

---

[242] DCLG, 'Housing in England 2004/05' (October 2006) 127. The Hills Review, referring to the British Social Attitudes Survey 2005/06, table 3.9, suggests a quite different picture, with 51% of council tenants thinking that their landlord type 'nearly always or often' provides a good standard of repair and maintenance compared to 34% of private renters.

[243] (1999) 78 P & CR D 46 (Ch).

It is important to understand that where the landlord does carry out works then his claim against the tenant is one that sounds in debt and not in damages. As a claim in debt it avoids the restrictions placed on landlords by the Leasehold (Property) (Repairs) Act 1938 which is discussed in the next section

In the absence of an express right of entry the landlord will not have a right to enter to do the repairs. The Law Commission notes that such a right is unlikely to be implied unless the landlord has an obligation to do repairs.[244]

12.8.2 Damages

As with contract law more generally, the principle underlying the award of damages is to put the landlord in the position he would have been in had there been no breach by the tenant. There are, however, various statutory provisions that place limitations on the landlord's recovery of damages for breach of the repairing covenant.

12.8.2.1 The Leasehold Property (Repairs) Act 1938: No Recovery in Long Leases without Leave

Under the Leasehold Property (Repairs) Act 1938 the landlord is unable to recover damages for breach of a tenant's repairing covenant in relation to certain leases (or to forfeit for such a breach) without leave of the court. The Act applies where there is a lease of seven years or more with at least three years still remaining. Originally it applied only to leases of small houses but it has since been extended to apply to long leases generally, both residential and commercial. It does not apply to agricultural leases.[245] The idea behind it is to prevent landlords from using dilapidation claims or threats of forfeiture for non repair as a tool to get tenants to leave so that the landlord can realise the vacant possession value of the property, without ever having a serious intention of doing the property up with the tenant in place. The Act does not apply to a tenant covenant to put the premises in repair on taking possession of the premises or within a reasonable time thereafter.[246]

The mischief at which the Act is generally understood to have been directed is described by Vinelott J in *Hamilton v Martell Securities Ltd* (drawing on Lord Denning MR's remarks in *Sidnell v Wilson* [1966] 2 QB 67, 76) as being that:

> ... an unscrupulous landlord would buy the reversion of a lease which had little value as a reversion and harass the tenant with schedules of dilapidations not with a view to ensuring that the property was kept in proper repair for the protection of the reversion, but to put pressure on the tenant, who might be a person of limited means, and who might not be in a position to obtain or accustomed to obtaining proper advice as to his liabilities, to the point at which he would accept an offer for the surrender of his lease.
>
> An unscrupulous landlord who takes that course does not need to put his hand into his pocket to carry out the repairs which he seeks to compel the tenant to carry out, and indeed

---

[244] Law Commission, 'Landlord and Tenant: Responsibility for State and Condition of Property' (Law Com No 238, 1996) para 9.5, referring to *Edmonton Corporation v W M Knowles & Sons Ltd* (1961) 60 LGR 124 (QB) 127.

[245] That is, agricultural holdings within the Agricultural Holdings Act 1986 and farm business tenancies within the Agricultural Tenancies Act 1995: Leasehold Property (Repairs) Act 1938 s 7(1).

[246] Leasehold Property (Repairs) Act 1938 s 3.

in the case of a long lease, he might have no real interest in ensuring that those repairs are carried out.[247]

The 1938 Act prevents a landlord from enforcing a right to damages for breach of a tenant's repairing covenant when three or more years of the term are unexpired unless, at least one month before the commencement of the action, a notice is served under section 146 of the Law of Property Act 1925 containing prescribed information and indicating the breach. This notice also gives the tenant 28 days to serve a counter-notice, the effect of which is that the landlord must then seek leave to continue his action for damages (or re-entry or forfeiture). Section 1(5) of the Leasehold Property (Repairs) Act 1938 states that leave will be given only if the landlord proves, on the balance of probabilities,[248] one of five grounds:

(i)   that the immediate effecting of the repair is necessary to prevent a substantial dimi-nution in the value of the reversion or such diminution has already occurred;

(ii)   that immediate repairs are needed to comply with any statute, court order or require-ment of any authority established by statute;

(iii)   where the tenant is not in occupation of the whole of the premises, that remedying the defect is necessary in the interests of the occupier;

(iv)   that current costs would be relatively small by comparison with the costs if there were to be a delay; or

(v)   it is otherwise just and equitable in the circumstances.

An important limitation on this is that the 1938 Act applies only where the landlord is seeking to recover damages from the tenant. If the landlord has exercised a right of entry to effect the repairs itself and is seeking to recover the cost of this from the tenant then this will be an action in debt and not one for damages, and therefore will not be caught by the Act. This was confirmed by the Court Of Appeal in *Jervis v Harris*,[249] Millett LJ referring again to Vinelott J's comments in *Hamilton v Martell Securities Ltd*:

> It is not to my mind obvious that the presumed legislative purpose of countering [the] ... mischief [the Act was intended to remedy] should be extended so as to fetter a lessor's right to recover moneys which he has actually spent.[250]

In *Jervis v Harris* the tenant had refused to allow the landlord to enter the property to do repairs, and the landlord sought an injunction to restrain the tenant from denying him access. The question was whether the landlord was entitled to enter, repair and claim the cost from the tenant without obtaining the leave of the court under section 1 of the 1938 Act. Millett LJ said that the Act simply did not apply as this would be for a claim in debt; unlike a claim for damages the landlord had to show only that he had incurred the expense, and there is no need to prove loss.

---

[247] [1984] Ch 266 (Ch), 278.
[248] *Associated British Ports v C.H. Bailey plc* [1990] 2 AC 703 (HL).
[249] [1996] Ch 195 (CA).
[250] [1996] Ch 195 (CA) 205, referring to [1984] Ch 266 (Ch) 278.

12.8.2.2 Measure of Damages

Where damages are recoverable, how is the loss to be measured? There are different measures that could be used. First, the cost of putting the property into a state of repair so that it meets the standard referred to by Lord Evershed MR in *Proudfoot v Hart*, that is to 'make it reasonably fit for the occupation of a tenant of the class who would be likely to take it'.[251] Second, actual costs spent. Third, the amount by which the landlord's reversionary interest is damaged by the disrepair.[252] *Jaquin v Holland* provides an illustration of the potential qualitative difference between these tests.[253] The tenant was in breach of a covenant to keep the interior of the premises in good repair. When she left at the end of the tenancy the landlord spent £19.10 on repairs (remember, this was at 1960 values) and then, because the market was strong, was able to re-let the premises. The costs necessary to meet the *Proudfoot v Hart* standard would have been in the region of £90–£100; and the diminution in value[254] was £50. On the facts, the Court of Appeal accepted that the guide was the amount necessary to put the property into the *Proudfoot v Hart* condition (although, for reasons discussed below, this was subject to a cap based on the diminution in value).[255]

The cost of repair is, however, only a guide. The principle that the courts apply in calculating the 'the damage which the covenantee has sustained by the breach of covenant'[256] is that damages should be assessed according to the diminution in the value of the landlord's reversion.[257] There are various ways in which diminution in value can be established.[258] Where the claim is being brought at the end of the lease, however, the cost of carrying out the repairs is often taken as the appropriate guide to use.[259] Usually, therefore, a claim for dilapidations at termination of the lease is based on the actual cost if the repair is carried out.[260] If, however, the repairs are not carried out this may suggest that they are not reasonably necessary and, perhaps, that there is no diminution in value.[261]

On any approach, there is a maximum amount recoverable based on the diminution in value of the landlord's reversion. Section 18(1) of the Landlord and Tenant Act 1927, applicable to all leases, places a cap on the amount recoverable and provides that damages:

> … shall in no case exceed the amount (if any) by which the value of the reversion (whether immediate or not) in the premises is diminished owing to the breach of such covenant.

---

[251] (1890) 25 QBD 584.

[252] That is, the difference in value between the value of the reversion with the premises in disrepair and that which it would have been had there been no breach by the tenant.

[253] [1960] 1 WLR 258 (CA).

[254] That is, the reduction in value of the landlord's reversion.

[255] [1960] 1 WLR 258 (CA) 263–4,

[256] *Conquest v Ebbetts* [1896] AC 490 (HL) 494.

[257] *Joyner v Weeks* [1891] 2 QB 31 (CA); *Conquest v Ebbetts* [1896] AC 490 (HL) 494; *Jervis v Harris* [1996] Ch 195 (CA).

[258] *Latimer v Carney* [2006] EWCA Civ 1417 [29]–[46].

[259] *Hanson v Newman* [1934] Ch 298 (CA) 300.

[260] *Haviland v Long* [1952] 2 QB 80 (CA). See also Law Commission, 'Landlord and Tenant: Responsibility for State and Condition of Property' (Law Com No 238, 1996) para 9.36 and DN Clarke, 'Tenant's Liability for Non-Repair' (1998) 104 *LQR* 372.

[261] *Latimer v Carney* [2006] EWCA Civ 1417 [24]. Arden LJ also accepted, however, that the repairs may not be done for other reasons, for example if the landlord cannot afford them: [46]–[48].

Thus in *Jaquin v Holland* the landlord was restricted to damages of £50.[262] If the landlord wishes to occupy the premises for its own purposes at the end of the lease, this cap can operate unfairly as the landlord will, in effect, be forced to pay for repairs that the tenant should have done.[263]

Section 18(1) contains a further limitation that:

> … no damage shall be recovered for a breach of any such covenant … to leave or put premises in repair at the termination of a lease, if it is shown that the premises, in whatever state of repair they might be, would at or shortly after the termination of the tenancy have been or be pulled down, or such structural alterations made therein as would render valueless the repairs covered by the covenant.

The effect of section 18 and the 1938 Act is that, during the life of the lease, it is often preferable for the landlord to exercise the right to enter and do the works itself, recovering the cost from the tenant as a debt, rather than attempt to claim damages. This illustrates the importance of careful drafting of the lease as the right to enter must be expressly included.

Claims for damages for dilapidations at the end of the lease (known as terminal dilapidations claims) generate a lot of work for property professionals and not infrequently lead to litigation. A pre-action protocol has been developed by the Property Litigation Association which aims to improve pre-action communication between the landlord and tenant.[264]

12.8.3 Specific Performance

In *Rainbow Estates Ltd v Tokenhold Ltd* Lawrence Collins QC noted that:

> Until relatively recently it was generally accepted that repairing covenants could not be specifically enforced, whether they were landlord's covenants or tenant's covenants. The decision on which that view rested was the decision of Lord Eldon L.C. in *Hill v. Barclay* (1810) 16 Ves. 402.[265]

Reporting in 1996, the Law Commission was critical of this. They saw no good reason in logic or policy for denying specific performance for breach of repairing obligations. Permitting specific performance would serve the public interest in securing the proper repair and maintenance of tenanted property as it would, unlike damages, secure the timely repair of the premises.[266] Sitting as a deputy High Court judge, Lawrence Collins QC in *Rainbow Estates* held that given the way that the law had developed since *Hill v Barclay* specific performance was now a possible remedy for breach of a landlord or tenant repairing covenant in appropriate cases. Subsequent cases (outside the leasehold context) adopt the more flexible approach towards specific performance that was set out in *Rainbow Estates*.

---

[262] [1960] 1 WLR 258 (CA).

[263] HH Judge Marshall argues that there should be a discretion for the court, in appropriate cases, to order damages based on the costs of carrying out the works even if it exceeds the notional diminution to the value of the premises: Interview of HH Judge Marshall (14 April 2007) *EG* 138.

[264] It is likely to be adopted by RICS as part of their Dilapidations Guidance Note. For comment, see R White, 'A storm is brewing in the fraternity' (12 April 2007) *EG* 188.

[265] [1999] Ch 64 (Ch) 68.

[266] Law Commission, 'Landlord and Tenant: Responsibility for State and Condition of Property' (Law Com No 238, 1996) Part IX.

There were three perceived problems with specific performance as a remedy. The ⟨first⟩ was the absence of mutuality: it was assumed that the tenant's repairing covenant could not be enforced by specific performance and thus, because there was no mutuality, neither could the landlord's covenant be enforced by specific performance. Second, there was a concern that the works required could not be adequately defined, as is required for specific performance. And last, it was thought that effective compliance would require constant supervision by the court. Lawrence Collins QC rejected each of these reasons. Mutuality is a discretionary and not an absolute bar to specific performance. Further, although precision is important, he cited Lord Hoffmann's speech in *Co-operative Insurance Society Ltd v Argyll Stores (Holdings) Ltd*[267] as authority for the courts accepting a 'certain degree of imprecision in cases of orders requiring the achievement of a result in which the plaintiffs' merits appeared strong'. In relation to the need for constant supervision, he again cited Lord Hoffmann where he drew a distinction between the conduct of activities and the achievement of results. Where an order is to achieve results the court 'if called upon to rule, only has to examine the finished work and say whether it complies with the order'.[268] Further, the law since *Hill v Barclay* has evolved to accept that specific performance can be awarded of an agreement to build provided that the building work is sufficiently defined by the contract (for example, by reference to detailed plans), damages would not compensate the complainant for the defendant's failure to build, and the defendant is in possession of the land so that the complainant cannot employ another person to build without committing a trespass.[269] In *Jeune v Queen's Cross Ltd* the analogy between agreements to build and repairing covenants was noted and Sir John Pennycuick VC granted specific performance of a landlord's repairing covenant.[270]

Given these various developments, Lawrence Collins QC concluded that:

> A modern law of remedies requires specific performance of a tenant's repairing covenant to be available in appropriate circumstances … and there are no constraints of principle or binding authority against the availability of the remedy …
>
> Subject to the overriding need to avoid injustice or oppression, the remedy should be available when damages are not an adequate remedy or, in the more modern formulation, when specific performance is the appropriate remedy. This will be particularly important if there is substantial difficulty in the way of the landlord effecting repairs: the landlord may not have a right of access to the property to effect necessary repairs, since (in the absence of contrary agreement) a landlord has no right to enter the premises, and the condition of the premises may be deteriorating.[271]

It would, however, be 'a rare case' in which specific performance of the tenant's repairing covenant is appropriate; in commercial leases the landlord will usually have the right to forfeit or to enter to do the repairs at the tenant's expense, and in residential cases there will also normally be a right to forfeit. Nonetheless, on the unusual facts in *Rainbow Estates*, specific performance was ordered. There was no adequate alternative remedy as the leases

---

[267] [1998] AC 1 (HL) 14.
[268] [1998] AC 1 (HL) 13.
[269] *Wolverhampton Corporation v Emmons* [1901] 1 QB 515 (CA) 524–5.
[270] [1974] Ch 97 (Ch).
[271] *Rainbow Estates Ltd v Tokenhold Ltd* [1999] Ch 64 (Ch) 72–3.

ure clauses or provisions for the landlord to enter and do the repairs
ld not be adequate as one tenant was a £100 company[272] and the other
ith unknown means. The level of disrepair was serious and the works
iently clearly defined to be capable of enforcement. It was also argued
se in which damages would not be available unless the requirements of
met, it would also not be appropriate to order specific performance as
mventing the provisions of the legislation. This argument was rejected,
although the judge accepted that a court will need to be mindful to ensure that the landlord
is not seeking a decree simply in order to harass the tenant (the mischief the 1938 Act is
designed to cure), and that a court may therefore take into account considerations similar to
those required under the 1938 Act. On the facts, however, even if these grounds were looked
to, several of them could be met here: there was a substantial diminution in value,
enforcement notices had been served under the environmental legislation, and the cost of
the works would be increased by delay.

12.9 Tenant's Remedies for Breach of Landlord's Repairing Covenant

12.9.1 Damages

A tenant may claim damages from the landlord for breach of its repairing obligation and:

> ... in the context of the breach of an obligation to repair property let to another, the purpose
> of the award of damages, so far as an award of money can do so, is to place the tenant in the
> position he or she would have been in if the obligation to repair had been properly per-
> formed.[273]

How this translates into figures will always depend upon the facts of the particular case. It
can include compensation for discomfort and inconvenience, loss of enjoyment and consequential damages. Assessing the appropriate amount:

> ... inevitably involves a comparison of the property as it was for the period when the landlord
> was in breach of his obligation with what it would have been if the obligation had been per-
> formed ...[For] periods when the tenant remained in occupation of the property,
> notwithstanding the breach of the obligation to repair, the loss to him requiring compensation
> is the loss of comfort and convenience that results from living in a property that was not in
> the state of repair it ought to have been in if the landlord had performed his obligation ... [If]
> the tenant does not remain in occupation, but, being entitled to do so, is forced by the land-
> lord's failure to repair to sell or sublet the property, he may recover for the diminution of the
> price or recoverable rent occasioned by the landlord's failure to perform his covenant to
> repair.[274]

The last principle mentioned in this quotation will cover the situation where a tenant has
purchased the leasehold interest as an investment, perhaps for onward sale, rather than for

---

[272] That is, the liability of the company is limited to £100.
[273] *Wallace v Manchester CC* [1998] 3 EGLR 38 (CA) 40.
[274] *Wallace v Manchester CC* [1998] 3 EGLR 38 (CA) 42.

personal occupation. Where the tenant has remained in occupation, discomfort and inconvenience can be measured in a number of different ways which can include a notional reduction in rent, but the actual figure is always a matter for the judge at first instance. Where the landlord's breach has the effect of depriving the tenant of enjoyment of his property, a notional reduction in the rental value of the premises is likely to be the most appropriate starting point for assessing damages.[275]

12.9.2 Specific Performance

As seen above, it was accepted in *Jeune v Queen's Cross Ltd* that the tenant could, in an appropriate case, obtain specific performance of a landlord's repairing covenant.[276] Further, in the case of dwellings, there is now a statutory jurisdiction to order specific performance.

Section 17 Landlord and Tenant Act 1985 provides:

(1) In proceedings in which a tenant of a dwelling alleges a breach on the part of his landlord of a repairing covenant relating to any part of the premises in which the dwelling is comprised, the court may order specific performance of the covenant whether or not the breach relates to a part of the premises let to the tenant and notwithstanding any equitable rule restricting the scope of the remedy, whether on the basis of a lack of mutuality or otherwise …

(2) …

(c) 'landlord', in relation to a tenant, includes any person against whom the tenant has a right to enforce the repairing covenant, and

(d) 'repairing covenant' means a covenant to repair, maintain, renew, construct or replace any property.

Under section 17, a tenant can obtain specific performance for the landlord to carry out repairs to the common parts of the building, not just to his own premises.

12.9.3 Council Tenants: Right to Repair

The Right to Repair is a scheme designed to ensure that secure and introductory tenants can get urgent repairs (which might affect their health, safety or security) done quickly and easily.[277] It applies to repairs which will not cost more than £250 to carry out and which fall within a prescribed description, known as 'qualifying repairs', such as unsafe electrics, a loss of water supply, blocked flues, and leaking drains and soil pipes.[278] Where the landlord is notified of a qualifying repair it will arrange for a contractor to do the work within a specified time period. If it is not done within this period, then the tenant can claim compensation for the delay from the landlord, although the landlord is able to set off compensation against any monies owed to it by the tenant, for example, rent arrears.

---

[275] *Earle v Charalambous* [2006] EWCA Civ 1090 [32].
[276] [1974] Ch 97 (Ch).
[277] Provided by the Housing Act 1985 s 96.
[278] Listed in the Schedule to the Secure Tenants of Local Housing Authorities (Right to Repair) Regulations 1994 SI 1994/133.

12.9.4 Appointment of a Receiver or Manager

In certain cases the tenant can also apply to the court for the appointment of a receiver or manager. Under section 37(1) of the Supreme Court Act 1981, an application can be made to the courts for the appointment of a receiver, where it is just and convenient so to do, to carry out some of the functions of a landlord. It can be used where the landlord's repairing obligations have not been fulfilled. Receivers can collect rents and service charges and apply them to the carrying out of repairs where the landlord is not traceable or where he has persistently failed to carry out repairing obligations and resists the application.[279] The remedy is available in the agricultural and commercial sectors and in the residential sector except with respect to local authority landlords.[280] As section 21 of the Housing Act 1985 vests all management functions in the local authority it is not appropriate for the court to appoint a receiver under the Supreme Court Act 1981.

The difficulties that can occur with the management of long residential leaseholds have already been discussed in chapter 11. As explained there, the tenant may be able to apply to a court for the appointment of a manager if the landlord is not carrying out its management functions properly. There is also a 'no fault Right to Manage', although exercising this right will not be straightforward.

12.9.5 Repudiation

In extreme cases, disrepair can give a right to end the lease if the breach is sufficiently fundamental so as to amount to a repudiatory breach. In *Hussein v Mehlman* the landlord had consistently failed to comply with the statutory repairing obligation set out in section 11 of the Landlord and Tenant Act 1985: there was no heating, the ceiling of one bedroom had collapsed, water pipes had burst, the flat roof extension was leaking and there was damp in the hall.[281] Stephen Sedley QC, sitting as an assistant recorder in the County Court, held that the landlord's conduct constituted a repudiatory breach which the tenant could accept by vacating the premises and returning the keys without incurring further rent liability. Although the idea that a lease can be brought to an end by repudiation was relatively novel, later courts have accepted this principle (albeit not in cases involving breach of a repair covenant).[282]

12.9.6 Alternative Remedies

At the end of 2003, a pre-action protocol for housing disrepair cases was introduced. The aim is to encourage an early exchange of information relating to the claim and, where possible, to avoid litigation by agreement between the parties. Failure to follow the protocol can lead to costs, and other, sanctions.

---

[279] *Hart v Emelkirk Ltd* [1983] 1 WLR 1289 (Ch); *Blawdziewicz v Diodon Establishment* [1988] 2 EGLR 52 (Ch).
[280] *Parker v Camden LBC* [1985] 2 All ER 141 (CA).
[281] [1992] 2 EGLR 87 (Cty Ct). See S Bright, 'Repudiating a lease – contract rules' [1993] *Conv* 71; C Harpum, 'Leases as Contracts' (1993) 52 *CLJ* 212.
[282] *Chartered Trust Plc v Davies* (1998) 76 P & CR 396 (CA); *Nynehead Developments Ltd v RH Fibreboard Containers Ltd* [1999] 1 EGLR 7 (Ch); *Petra Investments Ltd v Jeffrey Rogers plc* [2000] 3 EGLR 120 (Ch). In *Reichman v Beveridge* [2006] EWCA Civ 1659, however, Lloyd LJ is more doubtful: see ch 24.

Alternative routes to resolving the dispute are encouraged, such as using mediation or the Independent Housing Ombudsman (IHO). In practice, complaints about repairs have constituted a significant proportion of all complaints made to both the Local Government Ombudsman (LGO) and the IHO.[283] The effectiveness of referral to an Ombudsman can be seen in a complaint made against Basildon DC. Council tenants moved into a bungalow that needed repair to the roof and windows. These repairs were not completed for 19 months (after complaint to the LGO), and the resulting cold and damp worsened the arthritis suffered by one of the tenants. The LGO found that the delays were unacceptable; the Council agreed to complete the repairs and also to pay £1,000 for the injustice caused by having to live in unsatisfactory housing conditions.[284]

12.9.7 'Self-help' Remedies: Withholding Rent

As the tenant's principal aim is to have the landlord fulfil his repairing obligation, specific performance or the appointment of a receiver or manager are more useful than a mere claim for damages. Specific performance and the appointment of a receiver or manager, though, require the tenant to go to court. There are some things which the tenant can do, short of initiating court action, that may serve to get the repairs done. What a tenant cannot do, however, is simply withhold rent if the landlord fails to fulfil his repairing obligations.[285] Nonetheless, it is not uncommon for tenants to do this and although there is no guarantee that the landlord will effect the repair just because the tenant stops paying rent, it does put him under an awful lot of pressure. It is, however, a risky approach. A rent strike may be construed as a repudiatory breach by the tenant which may, subject to how statutory protections interrelate with this common law remedy,[286] entitle the landlord to end the tenancy. In addition, rent arrears are likely to provide a landlord with a ground for possession and although the landlord's breach of repairing covenant may mean that possession is not given, there is always the risk that it will not be accepted that the tenant has a good case.

It is possible, however, for a tenant to carry out repairs himself and set off the cost of this against future payments. In addition, the tenant may be able to set off a damages claim against the landlord if an action is brought to recover rent due.

12.9.7.1 Common Law Right of Recoupment

Although sometimes described as set off, the common law right of recoupment is 'an ancient common law right' that was given modern recognition by the decision of Goff J in *Lee-Parker v Izzet*.[287] Forbes J summarised when the right arises in *British Anzani (Felixstowe) Ltd v International Marine Management (UK) Ltd*:

---

283 See ch 11.
284 Report on an investigation into complaint no 06/A/13667 against Basildon DC (19 April 2007). See also Report on an investigation into complaint no 05/C/02965 against Nottingham CC (19 April 2007) in which the Council was ordered to apologise, pay £2,450 in compensation, do necessary repairs, and review its approach to allocation of unsuitable properties to homeless applicants.
285 *Camden Nominees v Forcey* [1940] Ch 352 (Ch); *R v Parnell* (1881) 14 Cox CC 508.
286 Which is not straightforward: see ch 24.
287 [1971] 1 WLR 1688 (Ch).

... where the tenant expends money on repairs to the demised premises which the landlord has covenanted to carry out, but in breach has failed to do so (at any rate where the breach significantly affects the use of the premises) ... To this proposition there must be added two riders. First, that as the landlord's obligation to repair premises demised does not arise until the tenant has notified him of want of repair,[288] such notification must have been given before the set off can arise; and secondly that the set off must be for a sum which is ... a sum certain which has actually been paid and in addition its quantum has either been acknowledged by the landlord or in some other way can no longer be disputed by him, as for instance, if it is the subject of an award on a submission to arbitration.[289]

In practice, it is sensible for tenants to make sure that the landlord knows about the breach and has had time to sort it out. If the work is not done by the landlord, the tenant should tell the landlord that he plans to do it himself, and give estimates of the costs to the landlord before the work is done. If the tenant then withholds rent to recoup the repair costs and the landlord seeks to forfeit the lease in order to recover the shortfall in rent, the tenant will have a good defence – the monies were expended in performing the landlord's own repairing obligations which the rent is, in part, supposed to cover.

12.9.7.2 Equitable Set-Off[290]

Not all tenants will be able to afford to pay for repairs and then reclaim the cost out of future of rent. In equity, it is possible for a tenant to set off a claim for damages for breach of the repairing covenant against the landlord's claim for unpaid rent. There is no need in a set off claim for the sum to be certain (liquidated). In *Muscat v Smith* Sedley LJ summarised the principles involved in recoupment and set off:

> ... money expended by a tenant on discharging his landlord's covenants will in appropriate circumstances operate as a partial or a complete discharge so as to furnish a defence at law to a claim for unpaid rent; and where the tenant has suffered damage by the breach rather than paid money to repair it, an equitable set off is in appropriate circumstances available. Appropriate circumstances in the latter case include ... any close reciprocity in the subject matter of the cross-claims. It is accepted that damages for breach of a repairing covenant and rent payable under the same agreement are an instance of such reciprocity.[291]

If the landlord seeks to distrain for the arrears accumulated while the tenant is 'saving' to pay for the repairs, *Eller v Grovecrest Investments Ltd* holds that set-off is also a good defence against distraint.[292] However, it would be wise to separate out the rent payments saved from any general household monies, lest the court find the claim for a set-off is not justified and the tenant then has to pay off the arrears.[293]

---

[288] This notice requirement depends on whether the disrepair is within the demised premises or not: see 12.4.3
[289] [1980] QB 137 (QB) 147–8. Forbes J says the sum must have been either unchallenged or unchallengeable before it could be regarded as deductible.
[290] For discussion of equitable set off as a self help remedy, see R Derham, 'Equitable Set-Off: A Critique of Muscat v Smith' (2006) 122 *LQR* 469, 473–4.
[291] [2003] EWCA Civ 962 [9], [2003] 1 WLR 2853.
[292] [1994] 4 All ER 845 (CA).
[293] *Haringey LBC v Stewart* (1991) 23 HLR 557 (CA).

12.9.7.3 Excluding the Rights to Set-off and Recoupment

It is possible to exclude the tenant's right to set-off and recoupment by using clear wording in the lease.[294] Most modern commercial leases do so. A commonly used form of wording is to say that the rent should be paid 'without any deduction or set-off whatsoever';[295] this will exclude the right to set-off. If the term simply says 'without deduction' then this will neither exclude the equitable right to set off[296] or the right to recoupment.[297] In the case of residential leases coming within the scope of the Unfair Terms in Consumer Contracts Regulations 1999,[298] such terms are likely to be held unfair as the costs, delays and uncertainties involved in requiring a tenant to go to court to obtain redress may, in practice, force them to give up their claim and deprive them of their rights.[299] It is also been argued that clauses excluding the right of set-off are unreasonable within the Unfair Contract Terms Act 1977, but the Court of Appeal in *Unchained Growth III plc v Granbyvillage (Manchester) Management Co Ltd* has held that the relevant provisions of the Act do not apply as contracts that relate 'to the creation … of an interest in land' are excluded by paragraph 1 of Schedule 1 and:

> … the obligation to pay a service charge [but the same would apply to rent payments] … is a provision which 'relates to' the creation of the leasehold interest. It is an integral part of the lease, providing the administrative mechanism for the enjoyment of the leasehold interest in common with, and for the benefit of, the other tenants of the development. [300]

12.9.8 The Tolerated Trespasser

The law surrounding the tolerated trespasser is complicated. The question of when a tenant loses the status of tenant and becomes a tolerated trespasser is discussed in chapters 3 and 19 but, in outline, it occurs when the (former) residential tenant stays in occupation of a property with the landlord's consent even though the tenancy has been brought to an end by the landlord obtaining a possession order. Much of the case law in this area has involved the occupier seeking to obtain a remedy for non-repair; and given that there are now hundreds of thousands of tolerated trespassers this is a crucial issue for social landlords.[301] As the tenancy

---

[294] *Gilbert-Ash (Northern) Ltd v Modern Engineering (Bristol)* [1974] AC 689 (HL); *Connaught Restaurants Ltd v Indoor Leisure Ltd* [1994] 1 WLR 501 (CA).

[295] As in *Electricity Supply Nominees Ltd v IAF Group Ltd* [1993] 1 WLR 1059 (QB) and *Star Rider Ltd v Inntrepreneur Pub Co* [1998] 1 EGLR 53 (Ch).

[296] *Connaught Restaurants Ltd v Indoor Leisure Ltd* [1994] 1 WLR 501 (CA).

[297] AJ Waite, 'Repairs and Deduction from Rent' [1981] *Conv* 199, 210–11.

[298] SI 1999/2083. For the scope of these Regulations, see ch 4.

[299] OFT, 'Guidance on unfair terms in tenancy agreements' (OFT 356, September 2005) paras 3.26–3.27. Such a clause was held unfair in *Cody v Philips* (unreported), discussed in *Private Renter* Issue 4 March 2006 in ROOF March/April 2006.

[300] [2000] 1 WLR 739 (CA) 749 (set off against service charge payment in relation to alleged overpayments of maintenance charges), agreeing with the first instance judgments in *Electricity Supply Nominees Ltd v IAF Group Ltd* [1993] 1 WLR 1059 (QB) (set off against service charge payment in relation to damages for breach of repairing covenant) and *Star Rider Ltd v Inntrepreneur Pub Co* [1998] 1 EGLR 53 (Ch) (set off against licence fees in respect of damages claim for alleged anti-competitive beer tie).

[301] It is very unlikely that there would be a tolerated trespasser with a private sector landlord, but following the Court of Appeal decision in *White v Knowsley Housing Trust* [2007] EWCA Civ 404 it is clear that tenants of RSLs can become tolerated trespassers.

has come to an end, none of the covenants contained in the former tenancy can be relied upon.[302] Nor does the tolerated trespasser have the benefit of the Defective Premises Act 1972. It is, however, possible for the tenancy to 'revive' in certain circumstances (for example, if the court postpones the date for possession), and if this occurs, the effect will be to 'retrospectively revive the old secure tenancy, together with its covenants'.[303]

In *Lambeth v Rogers* the principles set out by Lord Browne-Wilkinson were taken to the seemingly inevitable conclusion; upon revival of the tenancy, the tenant was able to recover damages for non-repair that had occurred during the limbo period.[304]

As the law relating to tolerated trespassers is developing there are some strange results. During the 'limbo period' (that is, after the tenancy has ended but whilst it is still possible that it might be revived) the 'landlord' is not subject to a repairing covenant, nor the statutory obligation to repair; yet if the tenancy is later revived, the tenant is able to recover damages for non-repair at a time when the 'landlord' was under no obligation. Furthermore, in *Pemberton v Southwark* the Court of Appeal held that a tolerated trespasser did have a sufficient interest in the property in order to bring a nuisance action against the local authority to deal with a cockroach infestation.[305]

The end result of these cases is that a 'landlord' can no longer safely assume that it owes no repairing obligation to a tolerated trespasser.

12.10 Improvements and Alterations

12.10.1 The Tenant's Right to Improve

As seen above (12.4.1.2), the contractual obligation to repair does not include an obligation to improve, save in the case of building leases. The tenant has a limited interest in the property and, even if there is an obligation on the tenant to repair, he only has to return what has been given, not something better. However, where the tenant has a long term interest in a property, either through a long lease or through security of tenure guarantees, then he may be willing to invest in order to improve the property and, concomitantly, his own experience of living in or working there. The question then is whether the tenant is allowed to make improvements.

Most leases will restrict the tenant's right to improve or alter the property. Even in the absence of express prohibition, the law on waste makes it a tort to alter the property (although, as seen earlier, the extent of this tort is uncertain).

---

[302] *Burrows v Brent LBC* [1996] 1 WLR 1448 (HL) 1454–5 (Lord Browne-Wilkinson); see also *Lambeth LBC v Rogers* (2000) 32 HLR 361 (CA) 367 (Mummery LJ).

[303] *Burrows v Brent LBC* [1996] 1 WLR 1448 (HL) 1455 (Lord Browne-Wilkinson); see also *Greenwich LBC v Regan* (1996) 28 HLR 469 (CA) 475–6 (Millett LJ); *Lambeth LBC v Rogers* (2000) 32 HLR 361 (CA) 367 (Mummery LJ).

[304] *Lambeth LBC v Rogers* (2000) 32 HLR 361 (CA). In *Southwark LBC v Edem* [1999] CLY 3713 the possession date was postponed when the occupier was in substantial compliance with the terms of the suspended possession order, the court recognising that this would enable the disrepair claim to be pursued.

[305] *Pemberton v Southwark LBC* [2000] 1 WLR 1672 (CA).

12.10.1.1 Fully Qualified Covenants

The prohibition on alterations may be absolute. Where there is a 'qualified' right to make improvements (that is, improvements are allowed with the landlord's permission), section 19(2) of the Landlord and Tenant Act 1927, which applies to all but agricultural leases, states that consent must not be unreasonably withheld (a 'fully qualified' covenant). McKinnon LJ explains the 'mischief' which the Act is designed to cure:

> The mischief aimed at by this s. 19, sub-s. 2, is obviously the power of the landlord to exact arbitrary payment – not to use a harsher word – from a tenant as the price of his consent. The remedy is the enforced addition to the covenant that consent is not to be unreasonably withheld.[306]

It is for the tenant to prove that the consent was unreasonably withheld.[307] The landlord is able to protect its interests as section 19(2) continues:

> … but this proviso shall not preclude the right to require as a condition of such [permission] the payment of a reasonable sum in respect of any damage to or diminution in the value of the premises or any neighbouring premises belonging to the landlord, and of any legal or other expenses properly incurred in connection with such [permission] nor, in the case of an improvement which does not add to the letting value of the holding, does it preclude the right to require as a condition of such [permission], where such a requirement would be reasonable, an undertaking on the part of the tenant to reinstate the premises in the condition in which they were before the improvement was executed.

If the landlord asks for a sum by way of compensation for damage or diminution in value and the tenant thinks this is unreasonable, it is for the tenant to prove unreasonableness and if he is unable to do so the landlord will be taken to have acted reasonably.[308] Where permission is sought under a commercial lease, the tenant's improvement might only be appropriate for the type of business carried on by that tenant and, thus, the second limb of the proviso to section 19(2) may apply, requiring the tenant to reinstate the premises at the end of the tenancy.

The effect of section 19(2) is therefore that where a lease provides that the tenant cannot make improvements without the landlord's consent, the landlord is only able to refuse this consent if there are reasonable grounds.

In considering whether or not the refusal of consent is reasonable, Peter Gibson LJ in *Iqbal v Thakrar* adapted the principles that Balcombe LJ distilled in *International Drilling Fluids Ltd v Louiseville Investments (Uxbridge) Ltd*:[309]

> (1) The purpose of the consent is to protect the landlord from the tenant effecting alterations and additions which damage the property interests of the landlord.

> (2) A landlord is not entitled to refuse consent on grounds which have nothing to do with his property interests.

> (3) It is for the tenant to show that the landlord has unreasonably withheld his consent to the

---

[306] *FW Woolworth and Co Ltd v Lambert* [1938] Ch 883 (CA) 908–09.
[307] *FW Woolworth and Co Ltd v Lambert* [1938] Ch 883 (CA) 906.
[308] [1938] Ch 883 (CA).
[309] [1986] Ch 513 (CA). This case is discussed in ch 17.

proposals which the tenant has put forward. Implicit in that is the necessity for the tenant to make sufficiently clear what his proposals are, so that the landlord knows whether he should refuse or give consent to the alterations or additions.

(4) It is not necessary for the landlord to prove that the conclusions which led him to refuse consent were justified, if they were conclusions which might be reached by a reasonable landlord in the particular circumstances.

(5) It may be reasonable for the landlord to refuse consent to an alteration or addition to be made for the purpose of converting the premises for a proposed use even if not forbidden by the lease. But whether such refusal is reasonable or unreasonable depends on all the circumstances. For example, it may be unreasonable if the proposed use was a permitted use and the intention of the tenant in acquiring the premises to use them for that purpose was known to the freeholder when the freeholder acquired the freehold.

(6) While a landlord need usually only consider his own interests, there may be cases where it would be disproportionate for a landlord to refuse consent having regard to the effects on himself and on the tenant respectively.

(7) Consent cannot be refused on grounds of pecuniary loss alone. The proper course for the landlord to adopt in such circumstances is to ask for a compensatory payment.[310]

(8) In each case it is a question of fact depending on all the circumstances whether the landlord, having regard to the actual reasons which impelled him to refuse consent, acted unreasonably.[311]

In *Iqbal v Thakrar* it was held reasonable to refuse consent to alterations because the tenant had not supplied sufficiently detailed plans showing what would be done if it emerged that the alterations affected load-bearing parts of the premises.[312]

Most leases do contain some kind of restriction on altering the premises but the wording will usually refer to 'alterations' or 'additions' rather than 'improvements'. An example is found in the leading case of *FW Woolworth and Co Ltd v Lambert* where the tenant covenanted:

> ... not without the previous consent of the lessors to erect or suffer to be erected any other building upon the said demised premises nor to make or suffer to be made any structural alterations in or additions to the demised premises.[313]

The lease in this case was a 42 year lease of a shop. The tenants also rented adjoining premises and wanted to knock down most of the rear wall to join up the two properties. This would also involve removing the staircase from the demised property, as well as other works. They offered to reinstate the premises at the end of the tenancy and to pay any associated costs that the landlord incurred in connection with the request, and provided security for such costs. The landlord refused consent. The tenant covenant did not expressly refer to 'improvements' but the Court of Appeal held this immaterial: the covenant would still become a fully qualified one by virtue of section 19(2) if the alterations were in fact 'improvements'. The landlord argued that they could not be improvements as they would detrimentally affect the

---

[310] This proposition is new, reflecting the impact of *v FW Woolworth & Co Ltd v Lambert* [1938] Ch 883 (CA), see below.
[311] [2004] EWCA Civ 592 [26].
[312] [2004] EWCA Civ 592.
[313] [1938] Ch 883 (CA).

value of the reversion. The Court of Appeal disagreed. The wording of the proviso to section 19(2) shows that improvements do not necessarily increase the value of the premises. Further, the mischief the Act was directed to also suggests a wide meaning should be given to improvements. Whether an alteration is an improvement must be regarded from the point of view of the tenant. On the facts, the alterations were improvements. Also, the landlord had unreasonably withheld consent: while 'many considerations, aesthetic, historic or even personal, may be relied upon as yielding reasonable grounds for refusing consent'[314] the only reason the landlord had given here was the damage to the value of the reversion, but the landlord could have protected this by claiming compensation under the proviso.

Provisions similar to section 19(2) apply to secure tenants. By section 97 of the Housing Act 1985 it is a 'term of every secure tenancy that the tenant will not make any improvement without the written consent of the landlord'. This consent is not be unreasonably withheld and if the question arises as to reasonableness, it is for the landlord to show it was reasonable.[315] If the question of reasonableness is referred to a court, it will have regard to the extent to which the improvement has made the premises less safe, increased the landlord's expenditure, or reduced the open market or letting value of the property.[316] Similarly, if conditions are imposed by the landlord, these too must be reasonable.[317] Failure to comply with a reasonable condition will be treated as a breach of tenancy. In the Law Commission's Renting Homes Final Report it is stated that the local authority tenant's right to improve has not worked well in practice, but no details are given.[318]

Although this will only apply to a small number of situations, there is a right under section 610 of the Housing Act 1985 to apply to the court for a variation of a lease which restricts the conversion of a dwelling-house into flats. This will apply only where the character of the neighbourhood has changed so that a property which is difficult to let as a single dwelling will be easier to let as smaller dwelling units, and planning permission has already been obtained for this change.

As noted above, section 19(2) does not apply to agricultural leases. In practice, the issue of consenting to improvements by tenant farmers is wrapped up with the question of compensation for improvements considered at 12.10.2.1 below.

12.10.1.2 Disability Legislation and Improvement of Tenanted Premises

The Disability Discrimination Act 1995 contains extensive provisions relating to the letting of premises, with the aim of not only protecting disabled tenants and occupiers but also ensuring that premises used by the public are reasonably accessible to the disabled. Although a landlord or manager of tenanted property may come under various duties to provide auxiliary aids and services or to amend management procedures to accommodate the needs of disabled persons (these are discussed in chapter 11), section 24E states that these do not extend to a requirement to remove or alter physical features.

A duty to adjust physical features may, however, arise where services and goods are supplied to the public. This could apply both to a landlord, for example in relation to

---

[314] [1938] Ch 883 (CA) 906.
[315] Housing Act 1985 s 98(1).
[316] Housing Act 1985 s 98(2).
[317] Housing Act 1985 s 99.
[318] Law Commission, 'Renting Homes: The Final Report. Volume 1: Report' (Law Com No 297, 2006) para 8.17.

common parts in a shopping mall, and to tenants. Section 21 of the Disability Discrimination Act 1995 imposes a duty to take reasonable steps to remove or alter, or provide a
reasonable means of avoiding, a physical feature which 'makes it impossible or unreasonably
difficult for disabled persons to make use of the service provided'. This could cover things
such as providing ramps, handrails and clear signage. A wide range of businesses such as
shops, offices and leisure facilities are covered by this. If the tenant is not permitted by the
lease to make the necessary adjustments, section 18A provides that the lease will take effect
as if it provided for the tenant to make a written application for consent to the alteration
and that the landlord is not permitted to unreasonably withhold such consent or to impose
unreasonable conditions. The Disability Rights Commission has issued a detailed code of
practice outlining the duties under the legislation and also providing practical guidance on
how to prevent discrimination.[319]

The legislation also regulates, in section 49G, the giving of consent to the improvement
of residential premises in order to accommodate disabilities. This does not apply to secure
tenants, as it is similar to sections 97 and 98 of the Housing Act 1985 discussed above. It
applies where the tenanted property is the tenant's only or principal home and it is lawfully
occupied by a disabled person. If the tenancy prohibits tenant improvements, then the
tenant can apply for an adjustment of the terms of a letting under section 24D.[320] If the
tenancy provides that the tenant may make improvements with the landlord's consent and
the tenant applies for consent to an improvement that is likely to facilitate the disabled
person's enjoyment of the premises (such as installing a grab rail), section 49G of the
Disability Discrimination Act 1995 provides that:

(2) If the consent of the landlord is unreasonably withheld it must be taken to have been given;

(3) Where the tenant applies in writing for the consent-

(a) if the landlord refuses to give consent, he must give the tenant a written statement of the
     reason why the consent was withheld;

(b) if the landlord neither gives nor refuses to give consent within a reasonable time, consent
     must be taken to have been withheld.

(4) If the landlord gives consent to the making of an improvement subject to a condition
which is unreasonable, the consent must be taken to have been unreasonably withheld.

(5) In any question as to whether –

(a) the consent of the landlord was unreasonably withheld, or

(b) a condition imposed by the landlord is unreasonable,

it is for the landlord to show that it was not.

Further, the Disability Rights Commission is able to make arrangements to provide conciliation services in relation to disputes relating to the improvement of premises.[321]

---

[319] Disability Rights Commission, 'Code of Practice – Rights of Access: services to the public, public authority
functions, private clubs and premises' (2006).
[320] The Explanatory Note to the Disability Discrimination Act 2005 states that the government intends to make
regulations setting out the circumstances in which it is reasonable for a landlord to have to modify or waive a term
in a lease prohibiting the making of alterations to a let dwelling house [150]. S 24D would not have helped the
tenant in *Richmond Court (Swansea) Ltd v Williams* [2006] EWCA Civ 1719 who wanted to install a stair lift as the
installation was in the common parts (see ch 11).
[321] Disability Discrimination Act 1995 s 49H.

12.10.2 The Right to Compensation for Improvements

Given that an improvement may be carried out by the tenant, the question arises as to compensation for that work. It may be seen as a matter of fairness that tenants who spend money improving the landlord's property should be given some kind of compensation when the lease comes to an end.[322]

12.10.2.1 Agricultural Leases

Entitlement to statutory compensation for improvements was first introduced in 1875 in the agricultural sector, recognising that tenant farmers with only limited tenure needed incentives to invest in the land.[323] Since then, compensation on quitting has been an important feature of agricultural leasehold law (see also chapter 9), and remains so even in the deregulated regime under the Agricultural Tenancies Act 1995 (ATA 1995). Under this Act the tenant is entitled to compensation for tenant's improvements on quitting the holding provided that the improvement is not removed from the holding and that the landlord has given written consent to the improvement.[324] The landlord's consent can be given either in response to an individual request or in the tenancy agreement itself. For these purposes, tenant's improvements are defined as including physical improvements made on the holding, or intangible advantages that become attached to the holding (such as planning permission and quotas).[325] Under the Agricultural Holdings Act 1986 (AHA 1986), tenant farmers were also entitled to compensation for 'tenant right matters' (such as crops still to be harvested and acts of husbandry, such as sowing seeds) and 'high farming' (where the tenant has increased the value of the holding by adopting a more beneficial system of farming than required by his tenancy agreement or — if there is no agreement — than is practised on comparable holdings). In the ATA 1995 there is no statutory right to compensation for these matters, although the parties are free to agree compensation rights in the contract.

During the tenancy there is no requirement for the landlord to give consent to improvements, but the tenant is able to refer the issue to arbitration if the landlord refuses consent and the arbitrator:

> … shall consider whether, having regard to the terms of the tenancy and any other relevant circumstances (including the circumstances of the tenant and the landlord), it is reasonable for the tenant to provide the tenant's improvement.[326]

The amount of compensation is:

> … an amount equal to the increase attributable to the improvement in the value of the holding at the termination of the tenancy as land comprised in a tenancy,

with a discount for any allowance made by the landlord to the tenant and any public grant

---

[322] See, for example, PS Atiyah, *The Rise and Fall of Freedom of Contract* (Oxford, Clarendon Press, 1979) 636 for how this argument relates to tenant farmers.
[323] Agricultural Holdings (England) Act 1875.
[324] Agricultural Tenancies Act 1995 ss 16 and 17.
[325] Agricultural Tenancies Act 1995 s15.
[326] Agricultural Tenancies Act 1995 s 19(5).

paid to the tenant.[327] An amendment in 2006 enables the parties to agree a different rate of compensation.[328]

There are special provisions that apply to planning permission obtained by the tenant farmer for development on the land which, in outline, give the tenant a right to compensation for unimplemented planning permission.[329]

The idea underlying these compensation provisions is that the tenant should receive compensation for value that he has added to the landlord's interest at his own expense or effort. The right to compensation provides the tenant with an incentive to make improvements to the land and the system under the ATA 1995 is much simpler than the predecessor AHA 1986. The absence of any right to make improvements, or requirement that the landlord must not unreasonably withhold consent, may, however, make it difficult for some improvements be made, particularly if they involve diversification activities which the landlord resists. Although there is the right to refer the matter to arbitration, the costs of this may deter tenants.

12.10.2.2 Commercial Tenancies

Section 1 of the Landlord and Tenant Act 1927 provides that given that certain requirements are met, commercial tenants[330] are entitled to compensation at the termination of the lease. The idea underlying this is that it is unfair if the tenant spends money on improving the property in ways that will accrue to the benefit of the landlord at the end of the lease without receiving any compensation. As Ormrod LJ said in *Pelosi v Newcastle Arms Brewery (Nottingham) Ltd*:

> Parliament intended that a landlord whose property had been improved by a tenant so that its letting value at the end of the tenancy had been increased, should pay compensation for the benefit he had received.[331]

In order to be entitled to this compensation, section 3 provides that the tenant must first have served notice on the landlord, with a specification and plan of the proposed works. Improvements made less than three years before the end of the tenancy do not give the right to compensation.[332] The amount of compensation is not to exceed the addition to the value of the holding resulting from the improvement or the reasonable cost of carrying out the improvement at the end of the tenancy.[333]

Haley describes the procedure for claiming compensation as unwieldy, difficult to operate and in urgent need of simplification.[334] The Law Commission recommended the

---

[327] Agricultural Tenancies Act 1995 s 20.

[328] Agricultural Tenancies Act 1995 s 20(4).

[329] Agricultural Tenancies Act 1995 ss 18 and 21.

[330] But not tenants with agricultural holdings or farm business tenancies: Landlord and Tenant Act 1927 s 17(1).

[331] (1982) 43 P & CR 18 (CA) 22.

[332] Landlord and Tenant Act 1927 s (2)(1)(c).

[333] Landlord and Tenant Act 1927 s 1(b), subject to any deductions necessary to put the improvement into a reasonable state of repair.

[334] M Haley, 'The statutory regulation of business tenancies: private property, public interest and political compromise' (1999) 19 *LS* 207, 216.

abolition of this little used right to compensation in 1989 but no repeal has yet been passed.[335]

Tenants' improvements are generally to be ignored on rent review, although the law surrounding this common sense attitude is complex.[336]

12.10.2.3 Secure Tenancies

If a secure tenant carries out improvements with the landlord's consent (or deemed consent) that increase the open market or letting value of the property the local authority has the power (but no obligation) to compensate the tenant under section 100 of the Housing Act 1985. In addition, for certain 'qualifying' improvements begun after 1 April 1994 (such as installation of toilets, loft insulation and double glazing) there are regulations that give tenants the right to compensation at the end of the tenancy[337] based on a statutory formula.[338] Council tenants are also protected under the Housing Act 1985 from rent increases on account of the increase in value of the property resulting from an improvement effected by the tenant at his own full or partial cost.[339]

12.10.3 Tenant's Fixtures

At the end of the lease the tenant must remove his chattels, that is the things that belong to him that are tangible and moveable. If the chattel has become 'annexed' to the land it may be regarded as a fixture. There are two broad tests used to decide whether something is a fixture or an asset: the method and degree of annexation, and the object and purpose of annexation. So, the courts will look at questions such as whether the thing can be removed without causing serious damage (which makes it more like a chattel), and whether it was fixed with a view to being a permanent and lasting improvement.

In relation to fixtures, a tenant is allowed to take away trade fixtures at the end of the lease,[340] although he will not be obliged to do so unless there is a specific covenant in the lease requiring their removal. If he does remove them, he must make good any damage.[341]

---

[335] Law Commission, 'Compensation for Tenants' Improvements' (Law Com No 178, 1989) and M Haley, 'Compensation for Tenants' Improvements' (1991) 11 *LS* 119.

[336] See ch 16.

[337] With some exceptions, for example where a possession order is made based on tenant default.

[338] Secure Tenants of Local Authorities (Compensation for Improvements) Regulations 1994 SI 1994/613.

[339] Housing Act 1985 s 101(2).

[340] *Elitestone v Morris* [1997] 1 WLR 687 (HL).

[341] *Mancetter Ltd v Garmanson Ltd* [1986] QB 1212 (CA).

13

USING, INSURING AND SERVICING TENANTED PROPERTY

13.1   Introduction
13.2   User
13.3   Insurance
13.4   Service charges

13.1 Introduction

This chapter discusses three aspects of managing leasehold property: regulating how it can be used, making appropriate insurance arrangements, and recovery of the cost of servicing the property.

In the case of short residential tenancies, these matters will usually be fairly straight-forward. In a typical tenancy, the landlord will assume responsibility for insuring the structure and exterior of the property, and any costs associated with servicing the property (including the cost of insurance) will be borne by the landlord; the tenant will not usually be required to pay any sums to the landlord to cover these items, in addition to the rent. The tenancy agreement will generally provide that the tenant can use the property only as her only or main home (secure tenancies) or as a single private residential dwelling. With long residential leases and commercial leases the contractual arrangements for user, insurance and paying for services can be much more complex.

13.2 User

13.2.1 User Restrictions

As part of the general management of the property, it is usual to have some kind of restriction in the lease on what the tenant is allowed to use the premises for. Independently of this restriction, there will be other factors that affect the way in which the premises can be used: planning restrictions, the law on nuisance and restrictions in any superior title. Most leases contain general prohibitions on use for 'immoral or illegal purposes', or use that causes a nuisance, annoyance or disturbance to neighbours. With residential property it is also common for the lease to state that the property can be used 'as a single private dwelling only'.

With commercial leases of individual properties, the user clauses will be directed to protecting the landlord's financial interest in the property. Where the lease is of one unit in a larger development, the user provisions will also be designed to secure that the development as a whole works efficiently. In a shopping complex, for example, both the landlord and the tenant will normally wish to ensure that the centre attracts shoppers; this may mean that there needs to be a variety of outlets with no competing businesses or, if it is a specialist centre, that there are complementary stores. Either way, the user covenant in the lease is the way to control permitted use.

13.2.2 Tenants and Competition

It is important to some commercial tenants, particularly in the retail sector, that there are no competitors in the immediate vicinity. Where the landlord also owns other property in the area (as, for example, with a shopping centre) the tenant may be able to negotiate for the lease to contain a clause preventing the landlord from using adjoining premises for a competing purpose. To be effective this should also provide that conveyances or leases that the landlord enters into in relation to adjoining property will contain a similar restriction (and the landlord should promise the tenant to enforce these restrictions).[1]

The importance of non-competing user to tenants can be seen in a number of cases where the tenant has sought to prevent the landlord from letting nearby property to a competing business. The difficulty for the tenants in these cases was that their leases did not contain any terms expressly prohibiting the landlord's action and they had to argue for some kind of implied prohibition. For many years the case of *Port v Griffith* has been the leading authority.[2] This established that even,

> ... if premises are let for a particular trade, there is nothing to prevent the landlord from leasing an adjoining shop for the same purpose.

In *Romulus Trading Co Ltd v Comet Properties Ltd* it was argued that letting nearby premises for a similar purpose breached both the express covenant to administer the building in accordance with good estate management and the implied covenant not to derogate from grant.[3] Both arguments were unsuccessful.

In recent years, the strictness of this approach has been challenged. In *Petra Investments Ltd v Jeffrey Rogers plc* Hart J accepted that the approach of *Port v Griffith* and *Romulus Trading* may require qualification, given that the doctrine of non-derogation from grant:

> ... 'involves identifying what obligations, if any, on the part of the operator can fairly be regarded as necessarily implicit, having regard to the particular purpose of the transaction when considered at the time the transaction was entered into.'[4] ...
>
> [In] a case involving a letting in a purpose-built centre ... it is not so obviously unreasonable to suppose that the parties contemplated that the landlord was to be subject to

---

[1] The precise wording will be important. For illustrations see M Ross, *Commercial Leases* (London, Butterworths, 1998) K [166].

[2] [1938] 1 All ER 295 (Ch).

[3] [1996] 2 EGLR 70 (QB).

[4] Hart J was citing Nicholls LJ in *Johnston & Sons Ltd v Holland* [1988] 1 EGLR 264 (CA) 268.

obligations that had not been expressly bargained for, but that were implicit in the use for which the landlord had designed the centre and for which the defendant had taken the lease of its unit.[5]

This might mean that the landlord is:

… under a duty, when exercising [rights over unlet parts or its powers under other leases] … to take account of the expectations of its existing lessees.[6]

In *Oceanic Village v Shirayama Shokusan Co Ltd*, Mr Nicholas Warren QC, sitting as a deputy judge of the High Court, developed this line of reasoning and held that the doctrine of non-derogation from grant could operate to restrict the landlord from permitting a competing business.[7] In this case, the tenant had been granted a lease with the specific purpose of being a gift shop for the London Aquarium. In addition to the tenant user covenant, the landlord covenanted not to permit any other gift shop to be operated in the same building. The landlord later proposed to operate a gift shop selling aquarium products on an external walkway, something that was not prohibited by the wording of the express covenant. On these facts, it was held that at the time of the grant of the lease it would have been in the reasonable contemplation of the parties that the landlord would not operate a gift shop selling aquarium related products. What made the difference between this and the earlier cases (in addition to an expanding approach to the doctrine of non-derogation from grant, see chapter 4) was the particular purpose for which the land had been let to the tenant, namely running a gift shop which carried with it an exclusivity over the sales of aquarium related products. The principle established by *Port v Griffith* remains, so that a 'mere' covenant restricting the tenant's user (not giving exclusive user rights) will not prevent the landlord from authorising a competing use.

The problem with the *Oceanic Village* decision is that it may create uncertainty. *Port v Griffith* still establishes the general principle and it appears to have been the specificity with which the purpose was defined in *Oceanic Village* which took it away from the general principle. The principle of non-derogation from grant turns on what is in the reasonable contemplation of the parties at the time of the grant, and was effectively used in *Oceanic Village* to create implied terms. Although the landlord's proposed action in this case would undermine the tenant's business, it would have been much more straightforward to stick to a rule that a tenant who wishes to prevent competing businesses must expressly bargain for such a restriction.

13.2.3 *Width and Variation of User Clauses*

If the user clause is narrowly drawn, permitting a very limited range of uses of the property, this will enable the landlord to exercise tight management control over the premises. In a shopping complex, for example, the landlord may need to narrowly restrict user clauses so that he can ensure that all of the shoppers' needs are met. For instance, the shopper may expect a grocer, newsagent, DVD store, clothing outlet, sports retailer and so on. In other

---

[5] [2000] 3 EGLR 120 (Ch) 126–7.
[6] [2000] 3 EGLR 120 (Ch) 128.
[7] [2001] L & TR 35 (Ch).

situations, the landlord may be seeking to develop a specialist mall, with similar retail outlets attracting the same customer profile. Unless the tenant is confined to a particular use there is a risk that these aims will be defeated, and a tenant may simply abandon a low profit use in favour of a more profitable one. A narrow clause will, however, have an adverse effect upon the rent which the landlord is able to receive upon review (unless there is a wider hypothetical user clause assumed for the purposes of reviewing the rent; see chapter 16): in *Plinth Property Investments Ltd v Mott, Hay and Anderson*, for example, the rent was £89,200 per annum with user limited to civil engineering business, but would be £130,455 per annum without such a restriction.[8] From the tenant's point of view, a wide user clause is advantageous in that it gives him a range of permitted uses (which may be important as his business develops) and will make the lease easier to assign. It will also, however, generally result in higher levels of rent being awarded on review.

There are several situations in which a tenant may wish to change the user clause – for example, if his own business interests change so that they would no longer be within the permitted use, or if he wishes to assign the lease to a tenant intending to use the premises for different purposes. Whether he is able to do so will depend upon the wording of the leasehold covenant relating to user. Recommendation 8 of the Business Lease Code 2007 states:

> Landlords' control over ... changes of use should not be more restrictive than is necessary to protect the value ... of the premises and any adjoining or neighbouring premises of the landlord.[9]

In *Sportoffer Ltd v Erewash BC*, for example, the landlord refused consent for a change of use on the grounds that the proposed user would compete with its own business and also would generate traffic that would discourage potential customers of its facilities (and this was held to be reasonable).[10]

13.2.3.1 Absolute and Qualified Covenants

There are various ways in which the user clause may be drafted. It may be absolute, making no provision for the user clause to be changed in the future, for example, 'not to use the premises otherwise than as a single private dwelling-house'. In 1985, the Law Commission accepted that landlords might have legitimate management reasons for imposing absolute covenants.[11] Alternatively, the user covenant may be qualified, for example, 'not to use the premises otherwise than as an office without the consent of the landlord'. With a qualified covenant the landlord can refuse consent on any ground. This differs from the approach with both alienation and improvement clauses where statute provides that in the case of a qualified covenant 'consent is not to be unreasonably withheld'.[12] In relation to user clauses, the only statutory provision is contained in section 19(3) of the Landlord and Tenant Act

---

[8] (1978) 38 P & CR 361 (CA).
[9] Joint Working Group on Commercial Leases, 'The Code for Leasing Business Premises in England and Wales 2007' (2007).
[10] [1999] 3 EGLR 136 (Ch). For fuller discussion, see 13.2.3.2 below.
[11] Law Commission, 'Covenants Restricting Dispositions, Alterations and Change of User' (Law Com No 141, 1985) esp para 4.44.
[12] Landlord and Tenant Act 1927 s 19(1)(a), (2).

1927 which provides that no money can be required as a condition of giving consent, subject to a proviso that the landlord can require compensation:

> ... of a reasonable sum in respect of any damage to or diminution in the value of the premises or any neighbouring premises belonging to him and of any legal or other expenses incurred in connection with such licence or consent.[13]

The effect is that, in the case of qualified covenants, the landlord has no incentive to consent to a request for a change of use – he is under no legal obligation to act reasonably, and has no commercial incentive to consent as he cannot charge a premium or a higher rent for doing so, even though the change in use might actually make the lease more valuable to the tenant. If the tenant is also seeking consent for alterations, as will frequently happen when he is seeking to change the use of the premises, then the restriction in section 19(3) on asking for money from the tenant does not apply. Qualified covenants can be misleading: the reference to consent suggests that consent can be obtained, yet consent does not have to be given. The Law Commission recommended in 1985 that it should no longer be possible to have qualified user covenants (the covenant must be either absolute or provide that consent will not be unreasonably refused),[14] but this recommendation has not been implemented.[15]

13.2.3.2 Fully Qualified Covenants and Reasonableness

A user covenant may be 'fully qualified', requiring the tenant to obtain consent for a change of use but also providing that the landlord may not withhold his consent unreasonably. An example is that used in *Sportoffer Ltd v Erewash BC* where the tenant covenanted to use the demised premises:

> ... as and for a squash club, but not for any other purpose, except with the previous consent in writing of the landlord, such consent not to be unreasonably withheld.

In determining whether a landlord's refusal of consent, or any condition attached to his consent, is reasonable or not, the courts have used as a guide the principles referred to by Balcombe LJ in the leading case on fully qualified covenants against assignment, *International Drilling Fluids Ltd v Louiseville Investments (Uxbridge) Ltd*[16](discussed in chapter 17). Indeed, many of the cases litigated involve both an application for consent to assignment and change of use. A particular issue in some of these cases is whether the fact that the assignee proposes a use which may breach one of the tenant's covenants in the lease makes it reasonable for the landlord to refuse consent to the assignment itself. In *Ashworth Frazer Ltd v Gloucester CC* (a case on assignment) the House of Lords held (obiter) that it may well be reasonable for a landlord to withhold consent to the assignment because of concerns about probable future user.[17] This is discussed more fully in chapter 17.

---

[13] This section does not apply to agricultural holdings or farm business tenancies: Landlord and Tenant Act 1927 s 19(4).

[14] That is, a 'fully qualified' covenant.

[15] Law Commission, 'Covenants Restricting Dispositions, Alterations and Change of User' (Law Com No 141, 1985).

[16] [1986] Ch 513 (CA).

[17] [2001] UKHL 59, [2002] 1 WLR 2180. Of course, if the landlord does consent to the assignment, the assignee will still be bound by the terms of the user covenant and so the landlord can bring an action for breach if the assignee uses the premises inconsistently with the lease.

The onus of proving that consent has been unreasonably withheld is on the tenant.[18] Reasonableness is to be considered by reference to the reasons given by the landlord at the time as well as any unexpressed reasons which influenced the landlord's decision.[19] A refusal will be reasonable if the conclusions were such that a reasonable man might have reached them in the circumstances.[20] In contrast to the position in relation to applications to assign,[21] there is no statutory duty on the landlord to deal with requests for consent within a reasonable time or to show that a refusal was reasonable.

Although the principles set out by Balcombe LJ in *International Drilling Fluids* are frequently referred to as the starting point of any analysis of reasonableness, Lord Bingham in *Ashworth Frazer* emphasised three overriding principles:

> The first, as expressed by Balcombe LJ in *International Drilling Fluids Ltd v Louisville Investments (Uxbridge) Ltd* [1986] 1 All ER 321 at 325, [1986] Ch 513 at 520 is that –
>
> 'a landlord is not entitled to refuse his consent to an assignment on grounds which have nothing whatever to do with the relationship of landlord and tenant in regard to the subject matter of the lease.'
>
> Secondly, in any case where the requirements of the first principle are met, the question whether the landlord's conduct was reasonable or unreasonable will be one of fact to be decided by the tribunal of fact ...
>
> Thirdly, the landlord's obligation is to show that his conduct was reasonable, not that it was right or justifiable. As Danckwerts LJ held in the *Pimms'* case [1964] 2 All ER 145 at 151, [1964] 2 QB 547 at 564:
>
> '... it is not necessary for the landlords to prove that the conclusions which led them to refuse consent were justified, if they were conclusions which might be reached by a reasonable man in the circumstances ...'
>
> Subject always to the first principle outlined above, I would respectfully endorse the observation of Viscount Dunedin in *Viscount Tredegar v Harwood* [1929] AC 72 at 78, [1928] All ER Rep 11 at 14 that one 'should read reasonableness in the general sense'. There are few expressions more routinely used by British lawyers than 'reasonable', and the expression should be given a broad, commonsense meaning in this context as in others.[22]

In practice, therefore, the courts are to approach the question of reasonableness afresh in each case and should not be constrained by any strict rules.[23] Further, although it is nearly always emphasised that the landlord cannot refuse consent on grounds that have nothing to do with the relationship of landlord and tenant in regard to the subject matter of the lease, it has been held that a landlord can 'reasonably take into account the circumstances of other property of his own',[24] including any 'perceived damage to his trading interests in adjoining or neighbouring property'.[25] Whilst it may be entirely reasonable and natural for landlord to

---

[18] *Sportoffer Ltd v Erewash BC* [1999] 3 EGLR 136 (Ch); *London & Argyll Developments v Mount Cook Land Ltd* [2003] EWHC 1404 (Ch) [20].

[19] *London & Argyll Developments v Mount Cook Land Ltd* [2003] EWHC 1404 (Ch) [20]

[20] *London & Argyll Developments v Mount Cook Land Ltd* [2003] EWHC 1404 (Ch) [21].

[21] See ch 17.

[22] *Ashworth Frazer Ltd v Gloucester CC* [2001] UKHL 59, [2002] 1 WLR 2180 [3]-[5].

[23] *Bickel v Duke of Westminster* [1977] QB 571 (CA) 524, and approved in *Ashworth Frazer Ltd v Gloucester CC* [2001] UKHL 59, [2002] 1 WLR 2180.

[24] *Sportoffer Ltd v Erewash BC* [1999] 3 EGLR 136 (Ch) 142.

[25] *Sargeant v Macepark (Whittlebury) Ltd* [2004] EWHC 1333 (Ch), [2004] 4 All ER 662 [55].

take these matters into consideration, is hard to see how the landlord's own business interests in nearby property have anything to do with the relationship of landlord and tenant.

Several cases illustrate that it is legitimate for the landlord to take account of its own commercial interests. In *Sportoffer Ltd v Erewash BC* the local authority landlord was able to refuse consent for a proposed change of use linked to an assignment on the grounds that a change of use from a squash club to a more general health and fitness club would compete with two nearby leisure facilities owned and operated by the local authority.[26] In support of this approach Lloyd J drew on an earlier case (pre-dating *International Drilling Fluids*), *Whiteminster Estates Ltd v Hodges Menswear Ltd,* where refusal of consent to assign to a competing menswear business was upheld as reasonable and Pennycuick VC had expressly said that 'a landlord was entitled to take into account his own interests as well as his interest as a landlord'.[27] In *Sportoffer Ltd v Erewash BC* the impact of refusal on the tenant was likely to be considerable; the premises were let on a 99 year building lease and the club was struggling as the popularity of squash had declined considerably since the lease was granted. The landlord did not, however, have to take account of the impact of a refusal of consent on the tenant unless, exceptionally, it would have 'disproportionately adverse consequences for the tenant'. There was talk of the club having to close unless the assignment went ahead (which would happen only if the change of user was consented to). Nonetheless, it was held that there was no 'clear evidence' of disproportionate impact on the tenant as there may have been other opportunities for the tenant to dispose of its interest had the lease been actively marketed. In a similar vein, Lewison J accepted in *Sargeant v Macepark (Whittlebury) Ltd* that, in principle, a landlord could make consent to change of use conditional on the new use being limited to activities that did not directly compete with the landlord's own business.[28]

13.2.3.3 Obsolete Covenants

There is power under section 84 of the Law of Property Act 1925 to apply to the Lands Tribunal for an obsolete restrictive covenant to be modified when the original lease was for more than 40 years and at least 25 years of the term have expired. The covenant can be discharged or modified where, inter alia, the covenant has been made obsolete by changes in the character of the property, the neighbourhood, or other circumstances.

13.2.4 User Clauses Restricting Trade

Certain industries have the practice of using 'tied' leases. Leases of public houses may contain a tie requiring the tenant to purchase specified beers and drinks from the landlord or a nominated supplier. Similarly, leases of service stations may require the tenant to purchase petrol supplies from the landlord. In the case of tied leases, at least historically, the landlord has been involved in the tenancy relationship primarily as a means of securing outlets for its

---

[26] [1999] 3 EGLR 136 (Ch).
[27] (1974) 232 EG 715 (Ch).
[28] [2004] EWHC 1333 (Ch), [2004] 4 All ER 662. On the facts the condition set by the landlord was unreasonably restrictive, but a wider form of wording protecting the landlord's business interests would have been acceptable.

products. This kind of arrangement may well be advantageous to a tenant. The idea is that the tenant will usually pay a lower rent for the property itself than a tenant of a 'free' property would be paying and the landlord's return on the property investment is obtained not only through rent, but also through the product sales, such as the number of barrels sold. In *Caerns Motor Services Ltd v Texaco Ltd, Geddes v Texaco Ltd*, a case involving leases of petrol stations with solus agreements for the tenants to sell only petroleum products and fuel supplied by the landlord, evidence was given as to the difference in rental income with and without the tie.[29] The lease of one site was at a rent of £12,000 per annum, the rental value without the tie was £63,500 per annum. In practice, however, there is evidence to suggest that tenants do not always get a good deal from this kind of arrangement.[30] So, for example, in *Crehan v Inntrepreneur Pub Company* Park J at first instance found that the property rental element in a tied pub lease was in fact the same as the whole rent that a free house operator would have been paying, and on top of this the tenant was paying a higher sum for beer purchase than a free tenant would be able to negotiate with suppliers.[31]

There is a chance that these provisions may be found to be in restraint of trade; if so, they will be illegal and unenforceable, although they will generally be severable from the rest of the lease. There is some uncertainty as to whether or not the doctrine of restraint of trade applies to trading restrictions in leases. The House of Lords, in *Esso Petroleum Co Ltd v Harper's Garage (Stourport) Ltd*, stated that the doctrine does not apply to restrictive covenants in leases, on the grounds that the tenant is not giving up a previously enjoyed freedom and, so, is not being restrained:

> A person buying or leasing land had no previous right to be there at all, let alone to trade there and when he takes possession of that land subject to a negative restrictive covenant, he gives up no right or freedom which he previously had ...[32]

Given that the doctrine is based on protecting the public interest, it is hard to accept that the restraint of trade doctrine is incapable of applying to leases.[33] If the doctrine does apply, then whether a covenant is in restraint of trade will depend on whether the restraint is reasonable as between the parties and with reference to the public interest.[34] In the case of leases, most restrictions are likely to be found to be reasonable.

There is also a risk that user clauses restricting competing businesses, or restricting the tenant's ability to deal with the landlord's competitors, might offend European Community and UK competition rules where the effect of the clause, taken together with similar clauses in other leases from the same landlord, is to affect trade between Member States[35] or within the UK.[36] The details of competition law are complex, and for full explanation the reader should refer to a specialist text. In practice, however, it is unlikely that a provision in an

---

[29] [1994] 1 WLR 1249 (Ch).

[30] Trade and Industry Committee, 'Pub Companies' HC (2004–05) 128–1.

[31] [2003] EWHC 1510 (Ch) [138] – [141].

[32] [1968] AC 269 (HL) (Lord Reid) 298; see also Lord Pearce at 325, Lord Wilberforce at 333.

[33] See GH Treitel, *The Law of Contract* 11th ed (London, Sweet & Maxwell, 2003) 472–3.

[34] *Nordenfelt v Maxim Nordenfelt Guns and Ammunition Co* [1894] AC 535 (HL); *Lobb (Alec) (Garages) Ltd v Total Oil GB Ltd* [1985] 1 WLR 173 (CA).

[35] EC Treaty (Treaty of Rome, as amended), Arts 81 (anti-competitive agreement) and 82 (abuse of dominant position).

[36] Competition Act 1998.

individual lease will have sufficient effect on trade to offend these competition rules. In *P &
S Amusements Ltd v Valley House Leisure Ltd* the tenant, in breach of a beer tie, changed
supplier from the one nominated by the landlord.[37] In an action seeking an injunction
against the tenant, Sir Andrew Morritt summarily dismissed the tenant's defences based on
the Competition Act 1998 as the tenant had not shown that the beer tie had any appreciable
effect on the bar trade in Blackpool, nor was the landlord dominant in the market.

'Land agreements' are excluded from the Competition Act 1998, but the exclusion only
applies to obligations or restrictions which are either accepted in, or for the benefit of, an
undertaking's capacity as holder of an interest in land.[38] Where the restriction relates instead
to the business interests of the landlord it does not come within the exclusion. Guidelines
from the Office of Fair Trading give the example of a lease which requires the tenant of a
petrol station to buy the petrol he sells only from the landlord – this would not be covered
by the exclusion.[39] Further, although restrictions can be placed on activities, for example,
limiting the range of goods that the tenant may be able to sell on the premises, the exclusion
does not cover restrictions that affect the sources of goods sold.

The issue normally arises in the context of a network of similar agreements, such as
'standard' leases from a brewery landlord. Practices in relation to pub leases changed
following the 1989 report of the Monopolies and Mergers Commission (MMC) on the
supply of beer which led to controls on tied leases of public houses and allowed only partial
ties.[40] Before then, breweries commonly let pubs on short tied leases with reasonable/low
rents. Following the MMC report, and subsequent Beer Orders, most breweries sold off the
majority of their pubs. In place of this, pubcos (specialist pub management companies)
emerged and rents for pubs rose. Pubcos tend to grant standardised (non-negotiable) leases.
The typical lease used by Inntrepreneur, for example, is for a term of 25 years, with five
yearly upward only rent review, tenant responsibility for repairs and a beer tie requiring the
tenant to purchase a minimum quantity of beer from Inntrepreneur or its nominated
supplier. These leases have created a large body of dissatisfied tenants, and there have been
numerous judicial challenges, especially to the beer ties. In the most recent case, *Crehan v
Inntrepreneur Pub Co*, the House of Lords affirmed the finding of the first instance judge
that the relevant Inntrepreneur beer tie arrangements did not offend Article 81 of the EC
Treaty.[41]

13.2.5 Covenants to Keep Open

To secure the vitality of a shopping centre, it is common to impose a covenant specifying the
hours during which the shop must be open for trading, particularly in the case of a 'magnet'

---

[37] [2006] EWHC 1510 (Ch).

[38] Competition Act 1998 (Land Agreements Exclusion and Revocation) Order 2004 SI 2004/1260.

[39] OFT, 'Land agreements: Understanding Competition Law' (December 2004).

[40] Monopolies and Mergers Commission, 'The Supply of Beer: A Report on the Supply of Beer for Retail Sale in the
United Kingdom' (Cm 651, 1989); Supply of Beer (Loan Ties, Licensed Premises and Wholesale Prices) Order 1989 SI
1989/2558; Supply of Beer (Tied Estate) Order 1989 SI 1989/2390. The 1989 Beer Orders have since been repealed:
Supply of Beer (Tied Estate) Revocation Order 2002 SI 2002/3204; Supply of Beer (Loan Licensed Premises and
Wholesale Prices) (Revocation) Order 2003 SI 2003/52.

[41] [2006] UKHL 38, [2007] 1 AC 333.

or 'anchor' tenant. In the leading case of *Co-operative Insurance v Argyll* the tenant covenanted:

> To keep the demised premises open for retail trade during the usual hours of business in the localities and the display windows properly dressed in a suitable manner in keeping with a good class parade of shops ...[42]

The presence of an anchor tenant is often crucial to the success of a development – it will act as a draw to shoppers and in turn this will help the other retail outlets and impact on the rent receivable. For the landlord, therefore, this is an important obligation undertaken by the tenant. For the tenant this can prove burdensome.

A covenant to keep open will be broken not only by the store failing to keep the usual hours, but also by closing down altogether. Closure of a store in breach of this covenant may have a substantial impact on a development. This is shown by the findings in *Costain Property Developments Ltd v Finlay & Co Ltd*.[43] Finlays, a 'well known multiple retailer of confectionery, newspapers and journals, stationery and (at that time) tobacco', closed. After its closure the reversioners tried to sell the reversionary interests in the whole development:

(a)   The fact that the Finlays shop was closed had a detrimental effect upon the attractiveness of the Centre in the eyes of shoppers, of prospective assignees of shops, and of investors ...

(d)   The fact that the shop was closed greatly reduced, and perhaps eliminated, for the vendors the possibility that an institution would bid.

(e)   The fact that the shop was closed also reduced the attractiveness of the freehold investment to a property company.

(f)   It is more likely than not that if the shop had been open, a bid higher than £4.35 million [the price paid] would have been received from GPE [the purchaser of the reversionary interests] or from some other property company or from an institution.[44]

During the marketing of the Centre to potential investors there were a number of other stores also on the market, but, even so, the drop in the value of the reversionary interests caused by the closure of the Finlays store alone was found to be £180,000. The landlord may also suffer non-financial loss if a large store closes; in *Braddon Towers v International Stores Ltd*, it was accepted that the landlord would suffer damage to its reputation as a developer/landlord by having an unsuccessful centre in its portfolio.[45]

It is not only the landlord who will suffer loss from the closure of an anchor store. Smaller retailers in the precinct may be heavily dependent for their customers on shoppers drawn into the centre by the anchor store. Local residents will also be affected, as in *Braddon Towers*, where they signed a petition to try to stop the shop being closed.

Although a store that closes will remain liable for rent even in the absence of a keep open covenant, the advantage of the keep open covenant is that the landlord may be able to claim damages for breach, in addition to the rent. Damages awarded can include a sum for the diminution in the value of the landlord's reversion, as in *Costain Property Developments Ltd v Finlay & Co Ltd*,[46] and for rent losses caused by concessions granted to other traders

---

[42] *Co-operative Insurance Society Ltd v Argyll Stores (Holdings) Ltd* [1998] AC 1 (HL).
[43] (1988) 57 P & CR 345 (QB).
[44] (1988) 57 P & CR 345 (QB) 353.
[45] [1987] 1 EGLR 209 (Ch) 211.
[46] (1988) 57 P & CR 345 (QB).

following the closure of an anchor store, as in *Transworld Land Co Ltd v J Sainsbury plc*.[47] In a recent Scottish case, *Douglas Shelf Seven Ltd v Co-Operative Wholesale Society Ltd & Kwik Save Group Plc*, the Outer House of the Court of Session awarded damages for both the capital and revenue loss, coming to almost £600,000.[48] Even though the value of the shopping centre was already depressed because of its poor location, design defects, and years of neglect, the closure of the anchor tenant's supermarket premises was held to have a significant effect on the value of the Centre. Damages were:

> ... based upon a comparison of the capital value of the Centre as it is and as it would have been if the keep-open clause had been performed, together with accrued revenue losses.[49]

When an anchor store threatens to close, the landlord (and also other tenants and local residents) may want an injunction to stop the store from closing, rather than damages. However, even if the closure will be a clear breach of the lease, the House of Lords has confirmed that courts will not usually grant an injunction or order specific performance.

In *Co-operative Insurance v Argyll*, Safeways was the anchor tenant in the Hillsborough Shopping Centre and had a 35 year lease from 1979. In the trading year ending May 1995 it made a loss of £70,300.[50] So, with 19 years still to run on the lease, it closed the store and stripped out the premises. To continue to trade in this location would mean pouring money into a loss-making enterprise. The landlord sought specific performance of the covenant. Previous authority, especially *Braddon Towers v International Stores Ltd,* had held that even where the proposed closure is in clear breach of the lease, it was 'settled and invariable practice ... never to grant mandatory injunctions requiring persons to carry on business' but instead to award damages.[51] The Court of Appeal in *Co-operative Insurance v Argyll* granted specific performance, noting in particular the difficulty in assessing the landlord's damages and the impact that closure would have on other traders.[52] When the case came before the House of Lords, the orthodox position was restored and specific performance refused.

Lord Hoffmann gave various reasons as to why an order to carry on a business is not a suitable remedy. One difficulty is that of enforcement, the only means available being the quasi-criminal procedure of punishment for contempt and it is 'no way to run a business' with this threat hanging over a defendant. In addition, there would be 'imprecision in the terms of the order'; how can it be known if the tenant is doing enough to comply? Also, the loss that the defendant may suffer from having to run a business at a loss indefinitely may be far greater than the loss caused by the breach of contract. Finally, it is not in the public interest for the courts to require a business to be conducted at a loss if there is some alternative by which the other party can be compensated: 'it is not only a waste of resources but yokes the parties together in a continuing hostile relationship'.

The Court of Appeal had been influenced by the 'commercial cynicism' of the

---

[48] [1990] 2 EGLR 255 (Ch).
[48] [2007] CSOH 53.
[49] [2007] CSOH 53 [604].
[50] *Co-operative Insurance Society Ltd v Argyll Stores (Holdings) Ltd* [1998] AC 1 (HL). See A Tettenborn, 'Absolving the Undeserving: Shopping Centres, Specific Performance and the Law of Contract' [1998] *Conv* 23; A Phang, 'Specific Performance-Exploring the Roots of "Settled Practice"' (1998) 61 *MLR* 421.
[51] [1987] 1 EGLR 209 (Ch) 213.
[52] [1996] Ch 286 (CA).

defendant's breach and, indeed, the effect of the House of Lords' decision does appear to undermine the significance of a promise. Nonetheless, the covenant is not without effect. Even if specific enforcement is most unlikely, a tenant who closes a store in breach of a keep open covenant is likely to face a significant damages claim. There are also further practical steps in drafting the lease that a landlord can take to lessen the impact: it may be, for example, that in the event of store closure the rent will increase,[53] and/or the landlord could reserve a right to display goods in the windows (making the centre more attractive).

13.2.6 Enforcing User Covenants

It is not only the landlord who may want to enforce a user covenant; tenants may well wish either directly or via the landlord to enforce user covenants in the leases of neighbouring tenants. Issues relating to enforcement are considered in chapter 18.

13.3 Insurance

13.3.1 Contractual Provisions for Insurance

In the case of short, rack rent leases it is the landlord who will invariably insure the property because of what he stands to lose if there is no insurance. The lease may make no reference to insurance. With longer leases, the lease will normally include complex provisions relating to insurance. If the property is destroyed, both the landlord and the tenant potentially lose something of value. The lease will, therefore, need to state who is responsible for taking out insurance on the property. These provisions will need to cover such things as how much the property is to be insured for (market value, or the cost of rebuilding with modern materials, or the cost of exact reinstatement), which insurance companies may be used, what risks are to be insured against (fire, storm, flood, etc), and, if the lease provides for rent to be suspended should the building become uninhabitable, insurance for the loss of rent. In addition, the lease should make provision for several other related issues that will be important should the property in fact be damaged or destroyed, such as who is liable to rebuild the property and whether the tenant continues to be liable for rent during the period for which the property is unusable.

Insurance provisions have been a cause of considerable tenant dissatisfaction, particularly in relation to the level of premiums charged. There is no regulation in the commercial sector, although the Business Lease Code 2007 contains recommendations[54] and the RICS is likely to issue a code of guidance on insurance in the near future. In the residential sector various statutory provisions give tenants rights in relation to inspection of the insurance policy, control over excessive premiums and (for long leaseholders) a choice of insurer. These are summarised in Table 13.1 and discussed more fully in the text below.

---

[53] P Luxton, 'Are You Being Served? Enforcing Keep-Open Covenants in Leases' [1998] *Conv* 396, subject to caution in relation to the rule on penalties.

[54] Joint Working Group on Commercial Leases, 'The Code for Leasing Business Premises in England and Wales 2007' (2007).

Table 13.1: Controls on Insurance Charges

Residential		Commercial
Control:	Applies to:	
If tenant contributes to insurance, right to written summary of policy and inspection of policy	Tenancies of dwellings (except short local authority tenancies): LTA 1985 Sch	Depends on contractual wording Business Lease Code 2007 provides terms should be 'fair and reasonable' and represent 'value for money', commission should be disclosed, and insurance details given on request
If tenant has to insure with landlord's nominated/approved insurer, can apply for determination as to whether insurance satisfactory or premiums excessive	Tenancies of dwellings (except short local authority tenancies): LTA 1985 Sch	
If tenant has to insure with landlord's nominated/approved insurer, right to insure with any 'authorised' insurer	Long lease of 'house': CLRA 2002 s 164	

13.3.2 Responsibility and Liability for Insurance

The question of who should insure the property involves two separate issues: who is responsible for effecting the insurance, and who pays for the cost of the insurance (liability).

13.3.2.1 Cost and Choice of Insurer

With 'clear' commercial leases, the cost of the insurance is borne by the tenant, either by the tenant taking out the insurance (a full repairing and insuring lease) or, more usually, by the landlord insuring the property and recouping the cost of doing so from the tenant via the service charge (a full recovery lease).

The cost of insurance has proven controversial when it is the tenant who has to pay. In the case of long residential leaseholds there is evidence that some landlords charge heavily inflated fees for insurance, up to five times the cost of the insurance premium, and that this is hidden in the service charge.[55] Similarly, many commercial landlords and agents fail to obtain competitive quotes and inflate the charges passed on to tenants by adding 'commissions' of 40 per cent to 80 per cent.[56] Commercial tenants, especially large companies, may be able to obtain better rates for their properties than their landlords. Where it is the landlord who effects the insurance at the tenant's expense, there is, however, no obligation to 'shop around' for the cheapest insurance[57] and courts have rejected arguments that terms

---

[55] L Barnard, 'No premium put on transparency' (10 June 2006) *EG* 61. For a discussion of the costs of placing insurance: see J Purvis, 'A mandate for disclosure' (17 March 2007) *EG* 152.

[56] Editorial (31 March 2007) *EG* 29.

should be implied that insurance premiums must be 'reasonable' or that the tenant should 'not be required to pay a substantially higher sum than he could himself arrange with an insurance office of repute'.[58] In *Havenridge Ltd v Boston Dyers Ltd* the Court of Appeal rejected the argument that reimbursement of insurance premiums 'properly expend[ed]' in 'some insurance office of repute' was limited to the amount of 'reasonable premiums':

> The suggested implication of 'reasonably' or 'reasonable' is neither necessary nor was it clearly intended, though left unexpressed, by the parties to these contracts.[59]

Nevertheless, the Court of Appeal did accept that the tenant would be protected from having to pay wholly extravagant or outlandish claims. Whilst the landlord did not have to show that the amount claimed was 'reasonable', the tenant only had to reimburse the landlord for premiums which reflected the 'going rate' in the market place:

> The limitation [on the tenant's obligation to indemnify the landlord] … can best be expressed by saying that the landlord cannot recover in excess of the premium which he has paid and agreed to pay in the ordinary course of business as between the insurer and himself. If the transaction was arranged otherwise than in the normal course of business, for whatever reason, then it can be said that the premium was not properly paid, having regard to the commercial nature of the leases in question, or, equally, it can be supposed that the both parties would have agreed with the officious bystander that the tenant should not be liable for a premium which had not been arranged in that way.[60]

Recommendation 9 of the Business Lease Code 2007 provides that:

> Where landlords are insuring the landlord's property, the insurance policy terms should be fair and reasonable and represent value for money, and be placed with reputable insurers.
>
> Landlords must always disclose any commission they are receiving and must provide full insurance details on request.[61]

In the case of long residential leases of houses,[62] where the tenant is required to insure with an insurer nominated or approved by the landlord, the tenant now has a statutory right under section 164 of the Commonhold and Leasehold Reform Act 2002 to effect insurance with any 'authorised insurer' subject to complying with the statutory requirements of notification and coverage.

13.3.2.2 Who Insures, and Protecting the Other Party

In addition to issues surrounding how much is paid for insurance, there are related insurance issues that need to be covered: who should effect the insurance, how the other party can find out details of what is covered, and how the other party can ensure that their interests in the

---

[57] *Bandar Property Holdings Ltd v J S Darwen (Successors) Ltd* [1968] 2 All ER 305 (QB); *Havenridge Ltd v Boston Dyers Ltd* [1994] 2 EGLR 73 (CA).

[58] *Berrycroft Management Company Ltd and Girling v Sinclair Gardens Investments (Kensington) Ltd* (1998) 75 P & CR 210 (CA).

[59] [1994] 2 EGLR 73 (CA) 75.

[60] [1994] 2 EGLR 73 (CA) 75.

[61] Joint Working Group on Commercial Leases, 'The Code for Leasing Business Premises in England and Wales 2007' (2007).

[62] Broadly, leases for more than 21 years: Commonhold and Leasehold Reform Act 2002 ss 76 and 77.

building are sufficiently protected. Landlords normally retain the right to select the insurer used. Where the tenant has a lease of part of a building, the insurance will be taken out by the landlord as it is impractical for individual tenants to take out buildings insurance for only part of a building, and it would also mean that common parts and unlet units are not insured. In these multi-occupied buildings, the landlord will also usually be the person responsible for repairs. In this way, responsibility for insurance mirrors the provisions for repair – the landlord will be responsible for external and structural repairs, and will also be the party who insures the building against the risk of damage. The *cost* of both items will, however, generally be shared amongst all the tenants of the building.

The issue is not so straightforward with leases of an entire building. Often, the lease will make the tenant liable to repair the building and, it can be argued, the responsibility for insurance should follow the responsibility for repair. If the building is destroyed by fire, the tenant is liable to rebuild under the repairing covenant and so needs to be sure that there will be insurance monies available for this purpose. On the other hand, the landlord may feel it unwise to rely simply upon the covenant of the tenant, and likewise may desire the comfort of being in control of the insurance and making sure that the monies will in fact be available. Irrespective of the merits of the tenant's case for effecting the insurance, the norm, in practice, is now for the landlord to take control of insuring the property.

A simple landlord covenant to insure the building (without providing what is to happen in the event of damage, etc) offers little protection to a tenant. In *Lambert v Keymood Ltd* the landlord covenanted to insure at its own expense.[63] When the buildings were damaged by fire caused by the tenant's negligence, the insurers (exercising the landlord's right to sue through the doctrine of subrogation)[64] were able to sue the tenant; the covenant to insure was relatively meaningless from the tenant's perspective.

There are ways in which the tenant can seek to secure better protection, to make sure that the insurance is, in fact, taken out and that any proceeds are, if appropriate, spent on reinstatement. If the lease requires the insurance to be taken out in the 'joint names' of the landlord and tenant, then both parties will be notified when the policy is due for renewal, and any insurance monies paid out will be paid into the joint names of the landlord and tenant, giving the tenant a say in the reinstatement of the building. Further, joint names insurance will prevent the insurers from exercising rights of subrogation against the tenant where the tenant has caused the damage. Even where the insurance is in the landlord's name alone, it was held in *Mark Rowlands Ltd v Berni Inns Ltd* that insurers may not be able to exercise rights of subrogation against the tenant when he has contributed to the premium.[65] Joint names insurance is not possible in the case of a multi-tenanted building, nor will the landlord always agree to it even if the lease is of an entire building. In this event, the tenant can still ask for his name to be noted on the policy. The effect of being noted on the policy is, again, that the insurers cannot sue the tenant by subrogation[66] and should also mean that if the policy does lapse then the tenant will be notified.

Tenants of dwellings (including local authority tenants with long leases but excluding

---

[63] [1997] 2 EGLR 70 (QB).

[64] Subrogation is where the insurer who pays out money is able to step into the shoes of the claimant to bring an action against the person responsible for the loss.

[65] [1986] QB 211 (CA).

[66] *Petrofina (UK) Ltd v Magnaload Ltd* [1984] 1 QB 127 (QB).

other local authority tenants)[67] who pay a service charge which includes an element for insurance have a right to require the landlord to supply a written summary of the insurance and to inspect the relevant policy.[68] Where the tenant is required to effect the insurance with an insurer nominated or approved by the landlord, he is able to apply to the County Court or leasehold valuation tribunal for determination as to whether the insurance is unsatisfactory or the premiums are excessive.[69] In view of the statutory right now contained in section 164 of the 2002 Act for leaseholders this provision is only likely to be used by tenants with short leases (see 13.3.2.1 above).

13.3.3 Application of the Insurance Proceeds

In the event of the building being damaged by any of the insured risks, the insurance monies will normally be spent on reinstating the premises. If, however, they are not so spent for some reason, several difficult issues arise, especially where the insurance is not in joint names and so the tenant does not automatically receive any of the insurance proceeds.

When insurance is the responsibility of the landlord, a well drafted lease will usually provide that the landlord must spend the insurance proceeds on reinstating the building. What happens if there is no such covenant in the lease? This occurred in *Mumford Hotels Ltd v Wheler*.[70] The lease provided that the landlord was to insure the property and the tenant was to pay the cost of insurance to the landlord. The leased hotel was destroyed by fire and the insurance monies were paid to the landlord, but the landlord refused to reinstate the hotel and was not under a contractual obligation to do so. The tenant succeeded in its claim that the insurance proceeds must be spent on reinstating the property. Harman LJ rejected the idea that such a reinstatement obligation could be contractually implied but, rather, based his decision on the idea that where a tenant is paying for the insurance, the landlord has some kind of quasi-fiduciary obligation:

> … Mrs. Wheler's [the landlord's] obligation to insure, done as it was at the tenant's expense, was an obligation intended to ensure for the benefit of both parties, and … Mrs. Wheler cannot simply put the money in her pocket and disregard the company's [the tenant's] claim.[71]

Later, in *Vural Ltd v Security Archives Ltd*, Knox J implied that this obligation could arise equally from an implied contractual obligation as from a proprietary obligation, but again reached the view that rights under the insurance policy must be exercised 'in such a way as to preserve the tenant's interest in what he has paid for'.[72]

The tenant may also have rights under section 83 of the Fires Prevention (Metropolis) Act 1774. Notwithstanding the title of the Act, it applies throughout England and Wales. Section 83 provides that 'any person or persons' 'interested in' a building can request the insurance company to 'cause the insurance money to be laid out and expended, as far as the same will go, towards rebuilding, reinstating, or rebuilding' the property. The Act is fairly

---

[67] Landlord and Tenant Act 1985 Sch para 9.
[68] Landlord and Tenant Act 1985 Sch paras 2 and 3.
[69] Landlord and Tenant Act 1985 Sch para 8.
[70] [1964] 1 Ch 117 (Ch).
[71] [1964] 1 Ch 117 (Ch) 126–7.
[72] (1989) 60 P & CR 258 (Ch) 273.

limited in its application, for example, covering only fire insurance and not other insured risks, but, when applicable, will enable the tenant (or landlord) to ask for the insurance monies to be spent on rebuilding.

Rebuilding is not always possible; the issue then is who is entitled to the insurance proceeds. In *Re King, decd*, it was not possible to rebuild after a fire, initially because of building restrictions and later because the land was compulsorily purchased.[73] The insurance had been taken out by the tenant in the joint names of the landlord and tenant and the proceeds were paid into a joint account. The Court of Appeal held that the proceeds belonged solely to the tenant. However, Lord Denning MR's dissent on this point is more generally regarded as correct. Lord Denning MR placed great weight on the insurance being in joint names, and felt that the money 'should be divided proportionately to the interests of landlord and tenant in the property'.[74] Proportionate division was ordered in *Beacon Carpets Ltd v Kirby*, where the parties had both accepted that the premises would not be rebuilt as the tenants had found new premises.[75] The Court of Appeal held that the monies were to be shared between landlord and tenant in proportions that reflected their respective interests in the building immediately before it was destroyed. *Re King* was distinguished on the grounds that rebuilding had in that case been made impossible and that in *Re King* the repairing obligation had been the tenant's, whereas in *Beacon Carpets* it was the landlord who had an obligation to reinstate.[76] Neither of these distinguishing features is persuasive. While each case turns on its own particular facts, the trend of these cases is that where the tenant has borne the cost of insurance both parties should be seen as having some interest in the proceeds.

13.3.4 The Problem of Uninsured Risk[77]

Insurance does not cover all risks. Following the IRA bombings in the City of London in the early 1990s insurers withdrew cover for terrorism.[78] It is also becoming difficult to get coverage for flooding in certain parts of the country. In the past, where damage resulted from uninsured risks, the landlord would typically not be under an obligation to reinstate the premises, but rent would still be payable, and the tenant might even be liable for rebuilding under the repair obligation in the lease.

In modern commercial leases, it is now likely that the landlord will bear the risk of uninsured damage. The tenant is likely to remain liable to pay the rent for a period after damage to the property, say 12 months, but thereafter rent will be suspended. The landlord will usually have an option to rebuild. The Business Lease Code 2007 provides that:

---

[73] [1963] Ch 459 (CA).

[74] [1963] Ch 459 (CA) 486.

[75] (1984) 48 P & CR 445 (CA).

[76] (1984) 48 P & CR 445 (CA) 454.

[77] G Dale, 'Landlords, tenants and the changing world of insurance' (23 September 2006) *EG* 190; C Edwards and P Krendel, *Institutional Leases in the 21st Century* (London, EG Books, 2007) 100–4.

[78] In response to the problem of terrorism being uninsured, Pool Re was set up by the Government in 1993 to ensure that terrorism insurance for commercial property would continue to be available. HM Treasury is the reinsurer of last resort for Pool Re, protecting it in the event that it exhausts all its financial resources following claim payments. See M Ross, *Commercial Leases* (London, Butterworths, 1998) L [117]–[166].

If the whole of the premises are damaged by an uninsured risk as to prevent occupation, tenants should be allowed to terminate their leases unless landlords agree to rebuild at their own cost.[79]

In a lease with a 'consumer', a term that requires the tenant to continue to pay rent if the building is uninhabitable is likely to be held unfair.[80]

13.4 Service Charges

13.4.1 The Aim of Service Charges

The lease will often provide that the landlord is able to recover the costs of servicing tenanted property from the tenants through a service charge. It may be that even if there is no contractual provision for a service charge, the service provider will be able to recover payment from the tenant on the basis of restitution,[81] but these cases will be the exception. In most cases, the reservation of a service charge payment is expressly provided by the lease, and the tenant's obligation to pay is often expressed to be 'additional rent'.[82] Depending on the contractual wording, this may cover not only repairing costs but other management costs, such as cleaning and heating of common parts, external decoration, the employment of managing agents and caretakers, and the cost of buildings insurance. In a full recovery (clear) lease, the aim of the service charge provisions will be to ensure that the costs of property management are passed onto the tenant so that the landlord receives a 'clear rent'. Service charges are used in commercial lettings where the landlord has property management costs; such as multi-tenanted office blocks, shopping centres and business parks. Even if the units are freestanding they may share common services such as landscaping of the grounds, lighting and maintenance of communal roads. Service charges may also be used in residential lettings, particularly with flats which share common parts, whether rented or sold on long leases. The service charge cannot, however, include the recovery of costs in respect of items for which the landlord has been made responsible by statute.[83]

As greater flexibility is emerging in leasehold structures in the commercial sector, there is a trend to offer serviced office suites, where units are let on an all-inclusive rental basis.[84] The advantage to the tenant is that it has cost certainty. So, for example, the 'Landflex' product offered by one of the UK's leading commercial landlords, Land Securities plc, is

---

[79] Joint Working Group on Commercial Leases, 'The Code for Leasing Business Premises in England and Wales 2007' (2007) Recommendation 9.

[80] OFT, 'Guidance on unfair terms in tenancy agreements' (OFT 356, September 2005) para 3.128.

[81] This was implicitly accepted in *R (on the application of Rowe) v Vale of White Horse DC* [2003] EWHC 388 (Admin), although on the facts the conditions for restitution were not made out.

[82] Expressed as rent, this enables the remedy of distress to be used for non-payment, and avoids the need to serve a s 146 notice before forfeiture: Law of Property Act 1925 s 146(11); see ch 24. If there is a *covenant* to pay service charge the s 146 procedure must be followed: see M Ross, *Commercial Leases* (London, Butterworths, 1998) M [165]. Under the Tribunal, Courts, and Enforcement Act 2007 the remedy of distress will be abolished and the CRAR (commercial rent arrears recovery) will not be available for service charge arrears. The date for commencement of this Act is not yet known.

[83] *Campden Hill Towers Ltd v Gardner* [1977] QB 823 (CA) 832.

[84] M Ross, *Commercial Leases* (London, Butterworths, 1998) M [2].

marketed on the basis that there is an all inclusive accommodation charge that covers rents, core services (such as cleaning, maintenance etc), plus the option of additional servicing, such as the provision of furnishings.

The service charge provisions will need to set out what services the landlord can recover payment for, how each tenant's share of the total cost is to be allocated, and provide a mechanism for establishing the sum due, usually involving certification by a third-party.[85] The clause may either state in general terms that the tenant is to pay a *fair proportion* of the landlord's expenditure, or set out a formula for working out that share. The formula might, for example, provide for the tenant to pay a fixed percentage of the total expenditure, the percentage being based on the proportion that the floor area let to the tenant bears in relation to the floor area of the whole development.[86] The service charge will often provide for a 'sinking' (or reserve) fund to cover the costs of major items of expenditure that will be needed at irregular intervals, such as the cost of re-roofing or replacing boilers and lifts. The landlord may even be building up a fund for eventual replacement of the building itself. The idea of the sinking fund is that the landlord anticipates future expense and, through the service charge, builds up a reserve to draw on, spreading the cost of major capital items over a number of years.[87]

13.4.2 Service Charges as a Cause of Disputes

There are frequent disputes as to the correct interpretation of service charge provisions and cases usually turn not on general principles of law but on the proper construction of the particular wording found in the lease. As with covenants for repair, it is important to define carefully which parts of the building are covered by the clause. There may also be questions as to whether the service charge is intended for running costs only, or also includes capital items, the standard of repair to be adopted, and whether any contractual (or statutory) process and consultation measures have been followed. So, for example, in *Northway Flats Management Co (Camden) Ltd v Wimpey Pension Trustees* the landlord was unable to recover the cost of works as he had failed, as required by the lease, to obtain estimates for the tenant's approval before carrying out the work.[88]

The problem lies not only in badly drafted leases but also in low standards of management, poor communication and a common failure to act responsibly in taking decisions about spending someone else's money. The following remarks of Jonathan Gaunt QC at first instance in *Princes House Ltd v Distinctive Clubs Ltd* reveal the sorry story of many service charge disputes:

---

[85] M Ross, *Commercial Leases* (London, Butterworths, 1998) M ch 5.

[86] In a surprising decision, *Pole Properties Ltd v Feinberg* (1981) 43 P & CR 121 (CA) the Court of Appeal varied the fixed proportion that a tenant was liable to pay after the acquisition of further property by the landlord meant the tenant's fixed share was no longer a 'fair and reasonable' proportion. For more details on methods of apportionment, see M Ross, *Commercial Leases* (London, Butterworths, 1998) M ch 5.

[87] M Ross, *Commercial Leases* (London, Butterworths, 1998) M ch 9. For further discussion of the things that a tenant should consider in negotiating a service charge clause, see C Edwards and P Krendel, *Institutional Leases in the 21st Century* (London, EG Books, 2007) ch 2.

[88] [1992] 2 EGLR 42 (CA).

… this case contains many of the typical elements which cause and exacerbate disputes of this kind: first, a managing agent who did not regard it as part of his job to read the lease or give any consideration to whether the items, a contribution to the cost of which he was invoicing, properly fell within the service charge; secondly, a landlord who, despite earlier misgivings, appears to have decided to include all the costs of his project in the claim for service charges irrespective of the propriety of doing so, placing on his tenants the onus of challenging his demands if they were able to discover and disentangle the calculations on which they had been based; thirdly, a situation where the tenant had been led to expect a certain level of charge and then found himself being charged four times as much with no explanation being offered as to how this state of affairs had come about; leading, fourthly, to the tenant becoming so frustrated and alarmed that he dug in his heels, refused to pay and resolved to take every point going, good or bad, with a view to resisting what he regarded as his landlord's patently unjustified behaviour. A more potent recipe for expensive and unproductive litigation it would be difficult to devise. Tenants who agree to service charge clauses under which they contract to pay against a surveyor's estimate or an accountant's certificate rely upon the professional people involved performing their roles with professional scrupulousness, diligence, integrity and independence and not in a partisan spirit, supposing their only task to be to recover as much money as they can for the landlord. Experience teaches that such reliance can be misplaced.[89]

Service charges are contentious in both the residential and commercial sectors. As will be seen below, the residential sector is now heavily regulated by statute, to the point where management of residential properties is extremely difficult. In addition to specific legislation directed at service charges, it has also been accepted by the Lands Tribunal that leasehold terms relating to service charges can be challenged under the Unfair Terms in Consumer Contracts Regulations 1999 where there is a contract between a seller/supplier and a consumer.[90] On the particular facts in *Canary Riverside PTE Ltd v Schilling* the clause was not found to cause a significant imbalance to the detriment of the consumer.[91]

The commercial sector remains unregulated but the launch of a new Code relating to Service Charges by the RICS (the RICS Service Charge Code 2006, discussed at 13.4.5 below)[92] reflects an attempt to tackle some very serious failings in relation to service charges. If self-regulation fails, it may be that statutory intervention will follow.

A summary of the controls that apply to service charges is given in Table 13.2, with fuller discussion in the text following.

13.4.3 Controlling the Level of Service Charges

The division between responsibility for property management and liability for the costs of property management frequently creates tensions. One area of contention lies in the fact that although the tenant is frequently obliged to pay for all services provided, there is often no corresponding obligation on the landlord to provide anything beyond essential services. Frequently the lease will impose an obligation on the landlord to provide certain essential services, with an option (but no obligation) to provide other services – beyond essential services the landlord wishes to be free to choose what work is needed and when it should be

---

[89] [2006] All ER (D) 117 (Sep) (Ch) [113]. NB. This case was later heard before the Court of Appeal.
[90] SI 1999/2083: see ch 4.
[91] [2006] Lands Tribunal LRX/65/2005.
[92] RICS Code of Practice, *Service Charges in Commercial Property* (Coventry, RICS Books, 2006).

Table 13.2: Controls on Service Charges

Residential		Commercial (Service Charge Code)
Control	Applies to:	
Unfair term not binding on consumer	Tenancy between supplier/seller and consumer: UTCCR 1999	
Consultation with recognised tenants' association on appointment of managing agent	Tenancies of dwellings: LTA 1985 s 30B	Management service to be regularly tendered or benchmarked against the market
Right to written summary of costs	Tenancies of dwellings: LTA 1985 s 21	Summary of expenditure to be provided Tenants should have annual report of outcome against budget and an explanation of variances
Right to inspect accounts and supporting vouchers	Tenancies of dwellings: LTA 1985 s 22	Landlord to deal with reasonable enquiries
Right to management audit (if 2/3 of qualifying tenants require)	Long leases of dwellings: LRHUDA 1993 s 76	Accounts to be certified and, if required by tenant, audited at tenant's cost
Consultation requirements: need to consult with tenants and any recognised tenants' association (s 29 LTA 1985) - on qualifying works (which require contribution of more than £250 from a tenant) - on qualifying long term agreement (lasting more than 12 months and tenant contribution of more than £100)	Tenancies of dwellings: LTA 1985 s 20	No equivalent but Code requires communication and consultation to be timely
Landlord can only recover costs 'reasonably incurred' and for services of 'reasonable standard'	Tenancies of dwellings (except short local authority tenancies): LTA 1985 s 19(1)	Costs must be properly incurred; maintenance, repair and replacement costs must be 'reasonable'; must be 'value for money' Management fees cannot be based on % of spend
Sums payable before costs incurred must be reasonable	Tenancies of dwellings (except short local authority tenancies): LTA 1985 ss 19(2), 26	Interim payments to be based on budget estimate of annual cost
Tenant not liable to pay 'old' costs (incurred more than 18 months ago), unless given written notification	Tenancies of dwellings: LTA 1985 s 20B	Tenants must receive budgets at least one month prior to commencement of service charge year. Accounts must be issued within 4 months of year end
Service charge must be held on trust	Tenancies of dwellings (except exempt landlords – local authorities and RSLs, s 58): LTA 1987 s 42	Reserve, sinking and replacement funds to be held on trust and interest to accrue (less tax)
'Administration' charges must be reasonable	Tenancies of dwellings: CLRA 2002 s 158, Sch 11	
No right to forfeit for non-payment of service/administration charge unless agreed or LVT determine it payable	Tenancies of dwellings: HA 1996 s 81	
No right to forfeit for non-payment of sums less than £350 unless outstanding more than 3 years	Long leases of dwellings: CLRA 2002 s 167	

done. The courts will not generally be willing to impose a contractual obligation on the landlord to perform the services, even if the lease provides for the tenant to pay the landlord's expenses in performing these additional services.[93] In some cases this can lead to the landlord not providing an adequate range of services. In other situations it can lead to 'over-servicing'.

A further question relates to how much the landlord can charge for services. As the landlord has control of property management, there is a danger that he will provide a very high level of services, using highly priced contractors who have to be paid for by the tenants. In the commercial sector, it is the contractual terms that set out what can be charged for, the principle to guide apportionment between tenants,[94] and so on (but, as seen below, a new Code of Guidance issued by RICS seeks to promote 'best practice' in the form of value for money).[95] The tenants will generally be liable for all costs incurred by the landlord in the provision of services, unless they can negotiate for them to be 'reasonable costs' for 'reasonably required' services. Nevertheless, in *Finchbourne v Rodrigues* (a residential case), the Court of Appeal was prepared to imply a term that the service charges must be 'fair and reasonable':

> It cannot be supposed that the plaintiffs were entitled to be as extravagant as they chose in the standards of repair, the appointment of porters etc … [T]he parties cannot have intended that the landlords should have an unfettered discretion to adopt the highest conceivable standard and to charge the tenant with it.[96]

This is an unusual decision. As seen in the discussion of insurance costs, the courts are reluctant to imply terms requiring costs to be 'reasonable'. In shorter commercial leases tenants are sometimes able to negotiate for service charges to be fixed or capped.[97]

The Confederation of British Industry response to the consultation on upward only rent review mentioned service charges as an area of concern, referring to high charges and the fact that tenants have little control over expenditure and value. A study of UK office service charges suggested that tenants are potentially paying £942 million more service charge per year than is necessary.[98] Part of the difficulty faced by tenants is budgeting. Although the 2002 Code of Practice on Commercial Leases[99] contained a recommendation (3) that 'landlords should provide estimates of any service charges and other outgoings' a study of service charges found that in office buildings service charge budgets tend to be poor estimates of

---

[93] *Sleafer v Lambeth Borough Council* [1960] 1 QB 43 (CA); *Duke of Westminster v Guild* [1985] QB 688 (CA). Exceptionally they may do so: *Barnes v City of London Real Property Co* [1918] 2 Ch 18 (Ch); *Edmonton Corpn v W M Knowles & Son Ltd* (1961) 60 LGR 124 (QB).

[94] A common apportionment method is based on lettable floor area but the RICS Code refers also to using: fixed amounts, rateable value, weighted floor area (recognising the different costs in servicing different sized units), or a fair and reasonable proportion.

[95] RICS Code of Practice, *Service Charges in Commercial Property* (Coventry, RICS Books, 2006).

[96] [1976] 3 All ER 581 (CA) 587.

[97] M Ross, *Commercial Leases* (London, Butterworths, 1998) M [2].

[98] Service Charge Study by Loughborough University Business School, referred to in D Barrass, 'Cost-efficient measures' (30 September 2006) *EG* 180, 181. Office tenants alone paid £4.41billion in service charges in 2005.

[99] RICS Policy Unit, 'A Code of Practice for Commercial Leases in England and Wales' 2nd edn (2002).

[100] No budgets arrived more than three months ahead, at least 45% arrived after the start of the period in question, and at least 13% arrived more than one year late: JR Calvert, 'Service Charge Study Update' (Loughborough University Enterprises Ltd, November 2005).

actual costs and many arrive very late in the year, making financial planning difficult for tenants.[100]

13.4.3.1 Statutory Control in relation to Dwellings

In the residential sector there are statutory controls that apply to service charges, relating to process, the amount that can be recovered and providing for consultation. Any service charge demand in relation to a dwelling must give the name and address of the landlord, an address for service, and must be accompanied by a summary of the rights and obligations of the tenant.[101] Failure to do this will result in the charge being treated 'as not being due from the tenant to the landlord at any time before that information is furnished'.[102]

Section 19 of the Landlord and Tenant Act 1985,[103] originally limited to flats but extended to 'dwellings' by the Landlord and Tenant Act 1987,[104] limits service charge recovery to costs that are 'reasonably incurred' and the amount can be challenged before the leasehold valuation tribunal.[105] This does not apply to local authority tenants unless the tenancy is a long tenancy.[106]

Section 19

(1) Relevant costs shall be taken into account in determining the amount of a service charge payable for a period –

(a)   only to the extent that they are reasonably incurred, and

(b)   where they are incurred on the provision of services or the carrying out of works, only if the services or works are of a reasonable standard;

and the amount payable shall be limited accordingly.

(2) Where a service charge is payable before the relevant costs are incurred, no greater amount than is reasonable is so payable, and after the relevant costs have been incurred any necessary adjustment shall be made by repayment, reduction or subsequent charges or otherwise.

'Relevant costs' and 'service charge' are defined in section 18:

Section 18

(1) ... 'service charge' means an amount payable by a tenant of a dwelling as part of or in addition to the rent –

(a)   which is payable, directly or indirectly, for services, repairs, maintenance, improvements[107] or insurance or the landlord's costs of management, and

---

[100] Landlord and Tenant Act 1985 s 21B, which comes into force on 1 October 2007. The summary must be in a particular form: The Service Charges (Summary of Rights and Obligations, and Transitional Provision) (England) Regulations 2007 SI 2007/1257.

[102] Landlord and Tenant Act 1987 s 47.

[103] Amended by the Landlord and Tenant Act 1987 SI 1988/1285, and the Commonhold and Leasehold Reform Act 2002.

[104] In *Oakfern Properties Ltd v Ruddy* [2006] EWCA Civ 1389, [2006] All ER 337 this was held to apply where a tenant had more than one dwelling, and thus on the facts to a property management company which was the mesne landlord and sublet the 24 flats. In reaching this decision, Jonathan Parker LJ was influenced not only by the statutory wording but also by the policy of providing the tenant 'with a way of challenging unreasonable charges sought to be levied by his landlord' [78].

[105] Landlord and Tenant Act 1985 s 27A.

[106] Landlord and Tenant Act 1985 s 26.

[107] The earlier wording of s 18 did not include improvements: see *Sutton (Hastoe) Housing Association v Williams* (1988) 20 HLR 321 (CA).

(b)   the whole or part of which varies or may vary according to the relevant costs.

(2) The relevant costs are the costs or estimated costs incurred or to be incurred by or on behalf of the landlord, or a superior landlord, in connection with the matters for which the service charge is payable.

(3) For this purpose –

(a)   'costs' includes overheads, and

(b)   costs are relevant costs in relation to a service charge whether they are incurred, or to be incurred, in the period for which the service charge is payable or in an earlier or later period.

In *Continental Property Ventures Inc v White* costs were held not to have been 'reasonably incurred' when the works could have been done under guarantee.[108]

By section 42 of the Landlord and Tenant Act 1987 any service charge paid by two or more tenants of dwellings must be held on trust (which will provide protection in the event of insolvency), and in the future funds will be required to be held in a designated trust account.[109]

The Housing Corporation has issued good practice guidance on service charges taking account of 'what customers want'.[110] This goes beyond the legal requirements and suggests that tenants should be given different options for making payment, there should be greater consultation with residents, and a greater level of sophistication in testing value for money. There is also a *Service Charge Residential Management Code* that applies to leasehold service charges, but it is not well publicised.[111]

Where the tenant has acquired a long leasehold of a flat under the Right to Buy, the lease may require the tenant 'to bear a reasonable part of the costs incurred by the landlord' in repairing, servicing, and insuring the building.[112] During the first five years after the exercise of the Right to Buy the amount that the landlord is able to recover is limited by reference to estimated costs that were set out in the landlord's notice served under section 125 of the Housing Act 1985 (see further, chapter 25).

13.4.4 Consultation In Relation To Service Charges

Another difficulty stemming from the division of responsibility and liability is that tenants feel excluded from management decisions.

13.4.4.1 Consultation of Residential Tenants

The Landlord and Tenant Act 1985 went some way towards redressing this in the residential context (both social and private) by introducing a consultation procedure. Following amendment in 1987 and 2002, section 20 now provides that a tenant must be consulted before the landlord/manager carries out works above a certain value (which will result in a

---

[108] [2006] 1 EGLR 85 (Lands Tribunal).
[109] Landlord and Tenant Act 1987 ss 42A and 42B, not yet in force.
[110] Housing Corporation, 'Service Charges: value for money?' (March 2007).
[111] Published by RICS and approved under s 87 of the Leasehold Reform, Housing and Urban Development Act 1993; see ch 11.
[112] Housing Act 1985 Sch 6 para 16A.

contribution from any tenant of more than £250) or enters into a long-term agreement for the provision of services (which will result in a contribution from any tenant of more than £100 over twelve months).[113] The process includes not only notifying tenants, and any recognised tenants' association, of the landlord's proposals but giving tenants the opportunity to nominate a person from whom the manager should obtain an estimate, and the opportunity to make observations on the proposals. The landlord must obtain at least two estimates, one of which must be from a person wholly unconnected with the landlord, and give reasons for the particular choice of contractor (unless this is the tenant's nominee). In the case of emergency works a leasehold valuation tribunal can dispense with the consultation requirements 'if satisfied that it is reasonable' to do so.[114]

The statutory consultation procedure is detailed, complex, time consuming and administratively burdensome. It will apply equally to the arm's length landlord as to where tenants are in charge of management, whether through a Right to Enfranchise Company,[115] a Right to Manage company,[116] or other tenant management company. Arguably, this is unnecessarily complex. It makes the whole process of leaseholders managing their own blocks of flats even more burdensome, and provides ammunition for the difficult leaseholder.[117] The penalty for not complying is that the landlord/manager is unable to recover service charges above a statutory minimum amount of £100 per tenant per year in respect of a long term contract or £250 per tenant for works to the building. This can have devastating consequences, potentially making a management company insolvent.

In addition, the tenant is entitled to a written summary of the costs[118] and to inspect accounts and supporting vouchers.[119] Failure to comply with these sections is a criminal offence.[120]

The Commonhold and Leasehold Reform Act 2002 also introduced controls on 'administration charges' for tenants of dwellings.[121] This covers charges made by the landlord for obtaining consents required by the lease, providing information, and costs in connection with unpaid rent or breach of covenant. Such charges are required to be 'reasonable'.

To prevent abuse of the right to forfeit, forfeiture proceedings in relation to dwellings cannot be brought for failure to pay a service or administration charge unless a leasehold valuation tribunal[122] has determined that the charge is payable or the tenant admits it is

---

[113] Service Charges (Consultation Requirements) (England) Regulations 2003 SI 2003/1987. Very large contracts may also come within EU procurement rules.

[114] Landlord and Tenant Act 1985, ss 20(1), 20(ZA).

[115] See ch 25.

[116] See ch 11.

[117] See M Davey, 'Long Residential Leases: Past and Present' and D Clarke in S Bright (ed), *Landlord and Tenant Law. Past, Present and Future* (Oxford, Hart, 2006) 163, 179 respectively.

[118] Landlord and Tenant Act 1985 s 21. A new s 21 has been substituted by the Commonhold and Leasehold Reform Act 2002, but the date for commencement is not yet appointed. Under this section, the landlord will be required to issue an annual summary of account (without the need for the tenant to request this) and where he fails to do so the tenant will have a statutory right under s 21A to withhold the service charge.

[119] Landlord and Tenant Act 1985 s 22. A new s 22 will come into force on the same date as the new s 21. It will provide that the tenant's request to inspect documents must be received within 6 months from the receipt of the service charge summary.

[120] Landlord and Tenant Act 1985 s 25.

[121] Commonhold and Leasehold Reform Act 2002 s 158 and Sch 11.

[122] Or a court or arbitral tribunal.

payable.[123] In relation to long leases of dwellings, the landlord is unable to exercise the right to forfeit for non-payment of sums less than £350, unless outstanding for more than three years.[124]

13.4.4.2 Consultation and Commercial Tenants.

In commercial leases there is usually provision for certification of accounts by an accountant or surveyor, but there is seldom any formal requirement for consultation with the tenants.

13.4.5 The RICS Service Charge Code 2006 for Commercial Property[125]

For some years there has been a guide to good practice on service charges for commercial properties. The impact has been relatively small but the code was reissued in June 2006, to take effect on 1 April 2007.[126]

The Code is designed to set out 'best practice' and cater for large properties.[127] It is targeted at managers of commercial property, and when new leases are drafted they will need to take account of the Code. Poor communication is often a major source of conflict between managers and tenants and the key goal of the Code is to ensure transparency and good communication. An important aspect of this is to provide for proper forecasting and budgeting. It states that the owner should provide 'an estimate of likely service charge expenditure and appropriate explanatory commentary' one month before the commencement of the next service charge year[128] (but although it encourages more communication and a better information flow, it does not provide for consultation or give tenants the opportunity to challenge budget plans).

In relation to costs it promotes a principle of 'not for profit, not for loss'. It accepts that managers and suppliers of services can expect to make a reasonable profit on the services provided but all costs should be made transparent, and all services should be procured on a value for money basis. Fees should not be charged on a percentage basis (thereby removing a possible incentive to 'over-service'). Parties are encouraged to use ADR to resolve service charge disputes.

Although the Code is not mandatory, it has the status of 'guidance.' It states that it will be of use in professional negligence claims, the interpretation of leases, and applications for a new tenancy. The interaction of the Code with established principles of law suggests, however, that these claims may be over-ambitious, and it has been described as a 'toothless tiger'.[129] A surveyor would be potentially negligent if it followed the Code in preference to furthering the landlord's best leasehold interests. Further, although the Code can be used as

---

[123] Housing Act 1996 s 81 (dwellings). See further ch 24.

[124] Commonhold and Leasehold Reform Act 2002 s 167; Rights of Re-entry and Forfeiture (Prescribed Sum and Period) (England) Regulations 2004 SI 2004/3086.

[125] RICS Code of Practice, *Service Charges in Commercial Property* (Coventry, RICS Books, 2006).

[126] RICS Code of Practice, *Service Charges in Commercial Property* (Coventry, RICS Books, 2006)

[127] The Opening states: 'its application to smaller properties therefore requires both managers and occupiers to apply common sense as to the scale and applicability of the Code'.

[128] A study by Loughborough University Business school found that 63% of budgets arrive after the beginning of the year to which they relate, with 20% arriving more than one year late: D Barrass, 'It's the devil's own job' (16 September 2006) *EG* 190.

[129] S Jourdan, 'All bark and no bite' (7 April 2007) *EG* 98.

the basis for drafting new leases, with existing leases it is the wording used that must be followed. As Jourdan writes:

> English law contains no principle under which advice on best practice issued by a professional body can be taken into account when interpreting lease terms.[130]

In relation to lease renewal, it is not clear how easy it will be to get the principles of the Code incorporated into the new tenancy. Given that many leases coming up for renewal will be around 25 years in length, and that service charge standards have changed considerably in recent years, the extent of change sought on renewal may be considerable. Section 35 of the Landlord and Tenant Act 1954 states that on lease renewal the terms of the new lease are to be agreed between the landlord and tenant or settled by the court.[131] The starting point is to have regard to the terms of the current tenancy. The leading decision is *O'May v City of London Real Property Co Ltd*,[132] sometimes perceived as a case that makes if difficult to modernise leases on renewal. Indeed, in *O'May* itself it was the service charge provisions that were in issue. Under the original lease the landlord was responsible for most of the servicing costs but sought on renewal for the costs to be transferred to the tenant under a clear lease, in return for a reduction in rent. Before the House of Lords it was the transfer of risk from landlord to tenant that prevented the landlord from persuading the court to agree to the change. *O'May* does, however, permit change – even in the absence of agreement – if the party proposing the change is able to justify it as fair and reasonable. Given that the tenor of the Service Charge Code is to promote best practice, it is may be that the courts will be sympathetic to updating leases on renewal to accommodate the principles underlying the Code in appropriate circumstances. This is, perhaps, most likely if the changes sought relate to process rather than the basis of charging itself.[133]

The Code is not designed for small properties. It is especially important for the small business tenant to be aware of likely running costs before committing to a lease. As seen various legislative controls apply to residential leases, limiting recovery to costs reasonably incurred and requiring consultation before substantial expenditure, but there are no controls that apply to business tenancies, even though very similar issues will arise.[134] It is assumed that tenants will negotiate 'reasonableness' and 'economy' into the leasehold terms but there is in fact virtually no negotiation of service charge provisions, particularly by small business tenants.

13.4.6 Mixed Use Premises

It is not unusual for buildings to be part commercial and part residential, as for example, with a row of high street shops that have residential flats above. In this situation, a landlord

---

[130] S Jourdan, 'All bark and no bite' (7 April 2007) *EG* 98.

[131] See ch 21.

[132] [1983] 2 AC 726 (HL).

[133] Commentators express differing views. Jourdan suggests it may be easier for a tenant to argue for change than the landlord: S Jourdan, 'All bark and no bite' (7 April 2007) *EG* 98. By contrast, Freedman has suggested that it will be harder for tenants to achieve change, and a landlord seeking a change that is not to the disadvantage of the tenant may succeed: P Freedman, 'Service Charges' (Conference Paper, 41st Joint Oxford Study Weekend, 2007).

[134] Many Australian states regulate service charges in retail tenancies, limiting the kind of items that can be included as 'operating expenses' and limiting recovery of capital expenditure.

will have to apply all relevant residential statutory rules if there are any service charge expenses that the residential tenants contribute to, even if he perceives of himself as a commercial landlord. This is so even if, as in *Oakfern Properties Ltd v Ruddy*,[135] the residential accommodation is let on a headlease to a mesne landlord who in turn sub-lets it as 24 residential flats.

[135] [2006] EWCA Civ 1389, [2006] 1 All ER 337.

14

RENT

14.1   Introduction
14.2   Setting the rent
14.3   Fixing initial rent levels

14.1 Introduction

The material on rent is divided between three chapters. This chapter introduces the general concept of rent and discusses the many factors that explain how the landlord and tenant go about fixing the contractual rent. The main focus of the following chapter, chapter 15, is on what can broadly be called ensuring affordability in the residential sector. For most of the last century this was achieved in the social sector largely through the housing finance system enabling rents to be set at affordable levels and in the private sector by having a system of rent control. Latterly, as residential rents have risen, affordability issues have been addressed primarily through personal welfare subsidies. The final chapter on rent, chapter 16, looks at how rents in commercial and residential leases can be increased during the currency of a tenancy, and at various ways in which landlords try to protect rent payment and recover arrears.

14.2 Setting the Rent

Although the reservation of rent is not essential to create a lease,[1] most leases will include an obligation to pay rent. Rent is properly called 'rent-service', terminology which illustrates the fact that landlord and tenant law has feudal origins. Thus, the payment of rent was the form of service which the tenant owed to his feudal lord and payment for use of the land could take a variety of forms, not only monetary, such as:

> ... in delivery of hens, capons, roses, spurres, bowes, shafts, horses, hawks, pepper, comine, wheat or other profit that lyeth in render, office, attendance, and such like.[2]

Nowadays, however, as Lord Diplock stated in *United Scientific Holdings Ltd v Burnley Borough Council*:

---

[1] *Ashburn Anstalt v Arnold* [1989] Ch 1 (CA).
[2] E Coke, *The first part of the Institutes of the laws of England, or, A Commentary upon Littleton* 19th edn (London, J & WT Clarke and others, 1832) Ch 12, Sect 213, 142a.

… the medieval concept of rent as a service rendered by the tenant to the landlord has been displaced by the modern concept of a payment which a tenant is bound by his contract to pay to the landlord for the use of his land.[3]

The amount of rent payable will be affected by a large number of factors. In some cases, as with many modern occupational business leases and private sector residential tenancies, it will be largely the outworking of market forces, reflecting the price that the particular property can command in the market place based on making periodic payments. Where, however, the interest in the property has been paid for by a large 'up front' capital payment, as with many long residential leases, the rent is likely to be a relatively small sum payable annually (known as a 'ground rent'). In each of these cases, the figure is fixed by contractual agreement. The parties are not always free, however, to set the rent by reference to market considerations alone. In the social housing sector, the government has influenced rent setting through a variety of mechanisms with the somewhat mixed goals of ensuring that social housing is affordable whilst at the same time controlling public spending. Nor has it always been the case that the private residential sector has been left to market forces; indeed, throughout most of the twentieth century some form of rent control was in place.

In this section of the book addressing rent issues, as throughout the book, the primary focus is on the law as it applies to tenancies entered into at present. In order to understand the role of rent within the landlord and tenant relationship it is, however, necessary to review the history of controls on rent setting, particularly in the residential sectors, as this has played an important part in housing policy as part of the attempt to ensure an adequate supply of affordable housing. In the commercial sector, too, the fixing of rent levels is highly significant. For a considerable period during the 1990s and into the present century, the threat of government intervention in the form of banning upward only review clauses has had a considerable impact on commercial letting practices in an attempt to forestall legislative action. Much of the debate generated by the proposed ban focussed on the impact that interfering with commercial rent setting could have on the attractiveness of UK commercial property as an investment vehicle.

Rent setting is not, therefore, something that relates simply to the contractual relationship between the landlord and tenant, but can have far wider economic and political significance in all sectors. Given that rent also represents the primary reason for much landlord investment it is also seen as an essential aspect of 'property ownership', and external controls on rent levels may meet resistance on the grounds that this is an undue interference with property.

14.3 Fixing Initial Rent Levels

Even in the absence of external regulatory controls, landlords are not always motivated to set the highest rent achievable for a property. Nonetheless, this will be the broad approach of many landlords in both the commercial and private rented sectors.[4] The rent obtainable will

---

[3] [1978] AC 904 (HL) 935.

[4] 72% of private individual residential sector landlords see the property as an investment or pension, with income being the most common (45%) form of return sought: ODPM, 'English House Condition Survey 2003: Private Landlords Survey' (April 2006) 27.

depend on the strength of the property market, local economic factors (including wage levels), the demand for property of the particular type, the desirability of the location, the standard of amenities and so on. The rate of return is especially important when the property has been purchased as an investment. The landlord may be relying on the income not only to cover the property costs, including the financing of the purchase price as well as ongoing maintenance and management fees, but also to produce a net profit.

Investment is not, however, simply about income; capital growth is usually important as well. In the commercial sector, the capital value of an investment property will be related to the rental stream. As Brett explains:

> The capital value of land or property (which is just another way of saying 'the price') is … generally related to the income it produces or could produce (we will ignore housing for the moment, where the considerations are rather different). The buyer of a revenue-producing property investment – a tenanted office block, say – is effectively paying a capital sum today in return for the right to receive a stream of income in the future.
>
> If the property is freehold, he has the right to the income in perpetuity, though it will not necessarily remain the same. The investor hopes the income will increase, though at some point the building may become obsolete and the income will decrease or cease altogether as tenants choose more modern properties instead. At this point the owner will need to lay out further funds to refurbish or redevelop it so that he still has a building for which a tenant is prepared to pay rent.
>
> The yield on a property is usually defined as the initial return – in the form of income – that an investor receives on the money he lays out to buy a property …
>
> Why should an investor accept a return of only 6% on the property even at times when he might get a perfectly safe return of, say, 10% on a fixed-interest government stock: a gilt-edged security
>
> The answer, of course, is that he expects the rental income from the property to grow as the general level of rents rises, whereas the interest income from the gilt-edged security will remain exactly the same throughout its life. It is worth accepting a lower yield today in return for the expectation of a rising income in the future
>
> But the income is not the whole of the story. If the rents from the office block rise, not only does the owner get a higher income. The capital value of his investment (the price somebody would be prepared to pay for it in the market) should rise as well.[5]

In the residential sector many landlords see property investment as part of their pension planning and so long as there is no revenue loss many are content to invest in order to realise long term capital growth.[6]

Although slightly dated now, a table produced by Rhodes and Kemp indicates the variety in rates of return within both the residential and commercial markets (see Table 14.1). Rates do, of course, change dramatically according to the state of the property market but for the year shown in the table, the capital growth component of the total return was greater than the income return throughout the residential sector, whereas the relative rates of income and capital return vary considerably according to the particular property type in the commercial sector.

---

[5] M Brett, *Property and Money* 2nd edn (London, Estates Gazette, 1997) 11–12.
[6] One quarter of dwellings are owned by landlords who seek only a capital return on their investment: ODPM, 'English House Condition Survey 2003: Private Landlords Survey' (April 2006) 27.

Table 14.1: Annualised Total Rates of Return in Great Britain, 2000

	Net yield/income return (%)	Capital growth (%)	Total return (%)
Residential lettings, University of York Index GB Valuations Index[a]			
Detached houses (4 beds)	4.1	5.9	10.0
Semi-detached houses (3 beds)	4.8	7.6	12.4
Terraced houses (2 beds)	6.0	8.6	14.6
Flats (2 beds)	6.9	8.2	15.1
Flats (1 bed)	7.2	8.8	16.0
All	5.7	8.1	13.8
Commercial property, IPD UK annual index			
Retail	6.2	0.4	6.6
Office	7.4	8.1	15.5
Industrial	8.4	5.4	13.8
All	6.9	3.5	10.4
Other assets			
Equities (all share)	2.1	−8.0	−5.9
Gilts (long dated)	5.2	4.0	9.2
Cash (Treasury bills)	6.2	—	6.2

Source: D Rhodes and P Kemp, 'Rents and returns in the residential lettings market' in S Lowe and D Hughes (eds), *The Private Rented Sector in a New Century: revival or false dawn?* (Bristol, Policy Press, 2002) 51.
[a]NB. This Index is no longer produced.

Commercial rents vary enormously, according not only to location, but also property type (retail, office, industrial or other), the standard of the property build and its fitting out, as well as wider economic factors. Table 14.2 gives an indication of the great variety that there is in rent levels.

In a weak property market landlords are often reluctant to drop the 'headline rent' on a new letting and may prefer to offer a range of incentives to prospective tenants. These can include rent-free periods (the tenant not having to pay any rent for, say, the first year of the lease), the landlord carrying out the initial fitting out works at its own cost (that is, fitting out the property with partitions and so on for the tenant's particular requirements), and agreeing to break clauses which only the tenant is able to trigger (giving the tenant the option to end the lease before the expiry of the fixed term). In return, landlords may require confidentiality clauses whereby the tenant agrees not to disclose the details of the deal; this means that it avoids becoming public knowledge and will not affect the level of comparables for rent review purposes (see further chapter 16).

In the residential sector, as seen in chapter 1, landlords can be quite differently motivated; those primarily renting property as an investment will be concerned to achieve a

Table 14.2: Range of Commercial Rents mid 2006

Property type	Lower level rents (£ per sq m per annum)	Higher level rents (£ per sq m per annum)
Prime Office Grade A space	Plymouth £153.40	London (City) £592
Prime New-Build Industrial/Distribution Premises	Black Country £56.50	Heathrow £161.50
Retail (in town, Zone A rents)	Yeovil £968.80	London Oxford St West £5382.00
Retail (out of town, average rent for gross internal area	Barnstaple Retail Park £121.10	Bournemouth Castle Point Retail Park £672.80

Source: Collated from information from website of UK Property Consultants King Sturge (rental data pages).

good rate of return whereas others may be less concerned with making money. So, for example, as is discussed further in chapter 15, social landlords have historically looked to cover their costs when setting the rent level rather than to maximise profits (but now are moving to more standardised rent setting driven by government formulae). Resident landlords are also likely to be less concerned with profit margins; what is crucial for them is whether they will get on with the tenants that they are sharing with.

The problem with a free market approach to rent setting is that some potential tenants (and even existing ones on renewal) may be priced out of the market. The problems in the commercial sector are less acute than the residential sector; to some extent most business tenants should be able to pass through rent rises in the pricing of their goods and services. In addition, although businesses are crucial to the UK economy, the ability to rent decent business premises is a less basic need than the need to rent a home.

There are two ways of addressing the affordability problem for residential tenants: to contain rents to affordable levels, or to provide assistance with payment through the welfare system. In the case of social housing, rents were largely kept to affordable levels for most of the last century by the generous bricks and mortar subsidies available to landlords. As rents have risen dramatically since 1980 with the withdrawal of housing subsidy, affordability issues have been addressed instead through increasing housing benefit payments (personal subsidies). In the private sector, from World War I until the passage of the Housing Act 1988 rent levels were subject to artificial constraints through rent control measures. Following the removal of rent control on new lettings in 1988, welfare payments to private sector tenants have also increased. These points are discussed more fully in the next chapter.

15

RESIDENTIAL RENTS

15.1   Setting rents in the social sector
15.2   Rent control
15.3   Ensuring affordability through welfare payments
15.4   The tolerated trespasser and payment for occupation

15.1 Setting Rents in the Social Sector[1]

15.1.1 Historic Approach to Social Rent Setting

For social landlords rent setting is not about maximising the return on property. Instead, rent is best seen as a way of being able to cover the costs of providing and maintaining the housing stock.

15.1.1.1 Local Authority Rents

The level at which social rents are fixed is intimately connected with matters of housing policy and, particularly, the housing finance system.

The basic principle is that rents need to be set at a level that will enable the books to be balanced. Since 1935 local authorities have been required to run Housing Revenue Accounts (HRAs), into which all housing related income is paid (subsidies and rents), and out of which all housing expenditure is to be paid (loan repayments, management and maintenance costs). Central government makes assumptions about housing income and spending for each local authority (creating a 'notional HRA'), and if the assumed spend is greater than the assumed income, HRA subsidy is payable to make up the difference. Through this system, central government has been able to influence, in a broad way, the level at which rents are set by controlling the level of housing subsidy. Subject to balancing the books, however, the setting of rents for individual properties has been left to local authorities.

Immediately after World War I and throughout the 1920s at least, council housing was of a significantly higher standard than that previously available to the working classes. The housing built following World War II was even more spacious. Given the high standard of housing, local authorities felt justified in charging high rents based on pooled, historic costs, but using central subsidies to reduce those rents generally, leaving council housing accessible

---

[1] Much of the following discussion draws on the Social Housing Finance chapter in D Mullins and A Murie, *Housing Policy in the UK* (Basingstoke, Palgrove Macmillan, 2006).

only to the better-off members of the working class. Although the poorest members of society could not generally afford council housing, the impact of subsidy meant that council rents were still considerably lower than rents for equivalent properties in the private sector.

By the 1960s, however, there were serious questions being asked about this approach to financing public housing. The subsidy levels meant that the financial cost of council housing was high. In addition, there was no link between rents and the local market, which meant that householders' decisions about housing tenure were distorted. Further, the fact that rents were linked to historic subsidies – which would vary tremendously between authorities – meant that there were significant variations between different local authorities for similar properties, and little or no correlation with market conditions.

In 1972 there was a shift in approach heralded by the Housing Finance Act 1972. Means-tested rent rebates were made compulsory. Further, there was to be a uniform system of fair rents and a reduction in the amount of central housing subsidy. Local authority discretion in rent setting was effectively removed, and the overall impact of the changes was that council rents were to be forced up by significant amounts. There was considerable opposition to this, both at the national and local level. The most famous act of resistance was by Clay Cross whose councillors were prosecuted for refusing to implement the Act.[2] The particular legislation was repealed by the incoming Labour government in 1974, ending the idea of a uniform rent standard. Nonetheless, the 1972 legislation had marked a turning point, and since then housing supply subsidies have withered.

As the amount of subsidy dropped dramatically during the 1980s, the effect was that rents had to rise. Average council rents rose in England during the 1980s by 53 per cent; but in one London Borough it went up by 123 per cent.[3] Of course, as rents rose, local authorities became less dependent on central government. This led, in 1989, to further change as central government sought to reassert financial control over local authority housing. Amongst these changes housing benefit subsidy was linked to the subsidy system. This, again, was a controversial step. Housing benefit is part of the social welfare system, and arguably the cost should not be met by rent. The end result of the change, however, was that rents for those tenants not reliant on housing benefit rose again, partly funding the benefit payments for other tenants. As a proportion of average earnings, council rents rose between 1980 and 1997 from 7 per cent to 11 per cent.[4]

Notwithstanding these various changes and attempts by central government to influence rent levels, rent setting remained very much up to the discretion of local authorities. The Housing Act 1985 refers only to local authorities setting such 'reasonable charges' as they determine, to be reviewed 'from time to time'.[5] The need to 'balance the books' showed the overall amount that had to be received in rent, but did not dictate how rents for individual properties were set. The methods commonly adopted gave some recognition to the amenity levels of differing properties but there was little consistency between different authorities.

[2] P Malpass, 'The road from Clay Cross' in J Goodwin and C Grant (eds), *Built to Last?* 2nd edn (London, ROOF, 1997).

[3] HRH Duke of Edinburgh (Chair), *Inquiry into British Housing* (London, National Federation of Housing Associations, 1985) 47.

[4] S Wilcox, *UK Housing Review 2006/07* (Coventry, Chartered Institute of Housing and London, Council of Mortgage Lenders, 2006) Table 72.

[5] Housing Act 1985 s 24.

The effect was that rent differentials bore little relation to the differing market worth of individual properties even within housing authorities, but were even more random between authorities. This remained so even after central government attempted to influence the way that local authorities set relevant rents by amending the Housing Act 1985 in 1989 to provide that local authorities:

> ... shall have regard in particular to the principle that the rents of houses of any class or description should bear broadly the same proportion to private sector rents as the rents of houses of any other class or description.[6]

In practice, however, few authorities paid close attention to this section.[7]

15.1.1.2 Housing Association Rents

In the housing association sector, the major change in relation to rents occurred after the passage of the Housing Act 1988, with the move into the private sector and much reduced levels of public grants. Until then, housing associations had been in a similar position to local authorities. The Housing Finance Act 1972 had applied fair rents (that is, generally, rents significantly lower than market rents) to housing associations' properties; and the charging of fair rents was made financially possible by the generous subsidy system established by the Housing Act 1974. The major element in this subsidy system was Housing Association Grant (HAG), a capital grant to cover building and conversion costs which meant that rents did not have to finance much of the new building costs. With the reduction in public subsidy and the expectation that housing associations would turn to the private sector for (at least, partial) funding of new construction following the 1988 Act, housing association rents needed to be set at a level that would meet their various financial obligations, which included repayments to private funders on commercial loans. Registered social landlord (RSL) rent levels are, however, also influenced by the regulatory hand of the Housing Corporation which urges associations to set rents at affordable levels and provides funding for schemes which meet this criterion. Nonetheless, the overall effect of these various changes has been a significant increase in housing association rents. As a proportion of average earnings, housing association rents rose between 1989 and 1997 from 10 per cent to 14 per cent.[8]

15.1.1.3 Residential Rent Levels

The end result of this rather complicated story of how rents are fixed in the residential sector is that there is a spectrum of rent levels. At the lowest end are rents in the local authority sector, next come housing association rents, and at the top end are rents in the private sector. This is illustrated in the following table, although the figures must be treated cautiously as some of the difference may be accounted for by the properties actually having different market worth because of the condition of the property, its location, level of amenities and so on.

---

[6] S 24(3); this now applies only in Wales as rent restructuring is being implemented in England and s 24(3) might conflict with this.

[7] A Marsh, 'Restructuring social housing rents' in D Cowan and A Marsh (eds), *Two Steps Forward* (Bristol, The Policy Press, 2001) 289.

[8] S Wilcox, *UK Housing Review 2006/07* (Coventry, Chartered Institute of Housing and London, Council of Mortgage Lenders, 2006) Table 72.

Table 15.1 Mean Weekly Rent in £, Net of Services

Type of Tenancy	2004/05
Council	59
Housing Association	68
Assured	108
Assured Shorthold	122

Source: DCLG Survey of English Housing

15.1.2 Restructuring Social Rents

It is difficult to progress a choice-based letting system if rents do not reflect market conditions and are not set on any consistent basis relating the rent for a specific property to the worth of that particular property. As housing association rents are generally higher than council rents, and private sector rents higher still, a home seeker has a financial incentive to prefer local authority housing. Similarly, if there is not a significant rent premium attached to larger, better quality, more desirable properties, there is again little incentive for a tenant to choose a less desirable property or to downsize if his occupational needs change.

The government's response to these concerns was to introduce rent restructuring for social housing in 2002.[9] There are four stated objectives:

(a)   to ensure that social rents remain affordable and well below those in the private sector;

(b)   to ensure that social rents are fairer and less confusing for tenants;

(c)   to provide a closer link between rents and the qualities which tenants value in properties; and

(d)   to remove unjustifiable differences between the rents set by local authorities and RSLs. Social rents should not depend on the identity of the landlord.

The intention is to harmonise rents, so that similar properties in the same area have similar rents. According to Hills:

> This was seen to be a good thing in itself, but also as a necessary prior step towards the long-term possibility of replacing the current Housing Benefit system in the social sector with some form of Local Housing Allowance. [see 15.3.2 below][10]

The effect will be to remove local authority autonomy in rent setting. All councils and RSLs are expected to move towards 'formula rents' over a ten year period to 2012,[11] although to ensure that there are no excessive increases annual rises are capped by reference to an inflation linked formula (which means that some landlords may take longer to reach the formula rent). The formulae take account of local earnings (to ensure that rents reflect local

---

[9] ODPM, 'A Guide to Social Rent Reforms in the Local Authority Sector' (February 2003).

[10] J Hills, 'Ends and means: The future roles of social housing in England' (CASE Report 34, February 2007) 82.

[11] Achieved not through statutory duties but 'through guidance backed up by annual performance monitoring, and modifications to the subsidy systems': D Cowan and M McDermont, *Regulating Social Housing, Governing Decline* (Abingdon, Routledge-Cavendish, 2006) 95.

incomes and remain affordable), property location and condition (reflecting the relative attractiveness of the property) and property size (to provide a differential between properties with different numbers of bedrooms). To ensure consistency and equitability between different landlords, properties are valued by reference to the national average value of a council property as at January 1999.

It is as yet too early to assess the effectiveness of restructuring but it is likely to achieve the goal of bringing rents for similar properties into line, irrespective of landlord type. There may, however, be other consequences. It is likely to result in rent increases for many council tenants, yet there is little indication that tenants will move from their existing home simply because other properties may cost less. Research produced in 2000 indicated that:

> ... most tenants are more likely to trade-up to a better standard of accommodation, but are unwilling to consider trading down, especially if this means moving to a less desirable area.[12]

Further, as rents can no longer be adjusted to take account of the financial commitments of the landlord, there is a danger that some landlords may run into deficit. For local authorities, this is not a serious risk as the HRA housing subsidy system has also been adjusted to take account of rent restructuring. Rent restructuring may, however, leave some housing associations exposed to financial risk, and to reduce this possibility there are signs that some are reducing investment in major repair programmes and new construction, thereby undermining other of the government's policy objectives.[13]

15.2 Rent Control

15.2.1 Introduction

Given that there is a finite amount of land available, and that the natural supply of land and property is further limited by other policies, in particular the restrictions placed on new development by planning controls, rent levels do not necessarily rise strictly in line with general inflation. In times of particular shortage, tenants are vulnerable to steep rent increases. In all sectors, rising rent levels are problematic. In the residential sector, those on low incomes may be left unable to afford decent homes. In the commercial sector, high rents can dampen business expansion and discourage entrepreneurs. Seen in this light, rent control, in the sense of setting an artificial (non-market) limit on rents, may appear to be the obvious way forward.

There is an extensive literature on rent control.[14] It commonly speaks of two kinds of control, referred to as first generation and second generation controls. First generation controls tend to be imposed in crisis situations (particularly war) and are intended as

---

[12] B Walker and others, 'Social housing tenants' attitudes and reactions to rent levels and rent differentials' (DETR, 2000).

[13] See D Mullins and A Murie, *Housing Policy in the UK* (Basingstoke, Palgrave Macmillan, 2006) 172–3 and research discussed there.

[14] Much of this paragraph is drawn from an unpublished paper by R Lee, 'The Private Sector: The Regulatory Landscape' presented at a workshop in London on Ensuring Responsible Renting organised by the Law Commission on 23 March 2006.

temporary measures, operating as rent freezes. These tend to be followed by decontrol measures (although decontrol occurs over very long periods of time), either by decontrol of large geographic areas which are free of housing crisis or by exempting higher value properties. A third approach to decontrol is sometimes adopted, which is to remove property from control when vacant possession is given, but this discourages tenants from moving and can also incite landlords to 'encourage' tenants to move. The second generation controls tend to be more sophisticated and are based not on historic rents but rent regulation, such as the fair rent system adopted in England and Wales in 1965, and discussed below.

For most of the twentieth century some form of rent control was in place in the private residential sector in this country and even, for a very short period, in the commercial sector. Although control in the commercial sector is less common, one example can be seen in recent legislation in Hawaii where rents of petrol stations have been capped by linking the rent receivable to a maximum specified percentage of profits from sales.

In this country, rent control has now been largely abandoned. It is problematic on a number of levels: it has not achieved the objective of ensuring affordable properties for rental; it is vulnerable to constitutional challenge; it may be unfair to landlords; and the particular regulatory measure applied in the 'fair rent' scheme proved difficult to apply. Each of these problems will now be looked at.

15.2.2 The Effects of Rent Control

The primary justification for any form of rent control is to ensure the affordability of rental property, and particularly to protect the vulnerable. There are serious doubts as to whether rent control can deliver these expectations.

Although there are different perspectives on the impact of rent control, most economists are highly critical of the economic effects of rent control.[15] The principal arguments against rent control follow.

1. Rent control has an adverse effect on the quantity of housing stock available for renting. In terms of new stock, as it is uneconomic to build only to receive a controlled rent, rent control can be effective only if coupled with a commitment from central government to underwrite building costs in order to encourage house building. Subsidy of private house building has not, however, been part of UK government policy. Further, with existing stock the low yield from residential property encourages landlords to disinvest, and rent control is undoubtedly one of the factors that contributed to the decline of the private rented sector through most of the twentieth century.[16]

2. Rent control has an adverse effect on the condition of the housing stock. Balchin refers to this process of deterioration noted by economists:

---

[15] For more detailed criticism of the economic effects of rent control see FA Hayek and others, *Verdict on Rent Control* (London, Institute of Economic Affairs, 1972); FA Hayek and others, *Rent Control, A Popular Paradox* (Vancouver, Fraser Institute, 1975); R Albon and DC Stafford, *Rent Control* (London, Croom Helm, 1987); R Lee, 'Rent Control – The Economic Impact of Social Legislation' (1992) 12 *OJLS* 543. For a contrary view see Anon, 'Reassessing Rent Control: Its Economic Impact in a Gentrifying Housing Market' (1988) 101 *Harvard L Rev* 1835.

[16] See P Kemp, *Private Renting in Transition* (Coventry, Chartered Institute of Housing, 2004) esp 35–7.

> Rented housing … consists of a combination of services. It is not just accommodation, but includes such items as repairs and maintenance, decoration, and possibly cleaning, lighting and heating – all being supplied at a price which in total constitutes rent. When rents are controlled below their market level, landlords' profits will be reduced or eliminated if they continue to provide services in full. They will consequently reduce the supply of services in an attempt to maintain profitability.[17]

Of course, it is not always the case that rent covers servicing; there is sometimes a separate charge made for servicing. In the case of residential tenancies, however, rent will usually be all inclusive and the effect of statutory obligations is that landlords cannot pass the cost of certain items onto tenants. Because of this effect of rent control, some jurisdictions permit landlords to charge higher rents if they can show that their properties are properly maintained. So, for example, many of the American second generation controls have allowed certain 'cost pass-throughs' to reflect increasing maintenance costs, provided that the property substantially complies with the building codes.

3. Rent control encourages 'winkling' (the payment of cash sums to 'encourage' tenants paying controlled rents to vacate) and harassment, so that the property can then be sold with vacant possession (for controls on this, see chapter 23).

4. Rent control leads to an excessive demand for housing with the result that, as price cannot be used as the basis for allocating property, other discriminatory allocation practices may be used.

5. Rent control discourages mobility of labour. Those living in secure low-cost accommodation are reluctant to give it up, even if this means losing employment opportunities available elsewhere.

6. Rent control encourages landlords to find ways to evade control.

15.2.3 Rent Control and Constitutional Challenges

In several jurisdictions, rent control measures have been challenged on the ground that that they violate the landlord's property rights. Although the challenge is dressed in different language according to the particular constitutional provisions being relied on, the legal issues usually revolve around the questions of whether the restrictions are justified in the general public interest, and whether they are proportionate to this goal. In most cases, the issues are finely balanced.

In Europe, any challenge is likely to be based upon Article 1 of the First Protocol European Convention for the Protection of Human Rights and Fundamental Freedoms (ECHR) which provides:

> Every natural or legal person is entitled to the peaceful enjoyment of his possessions. No one shall be deprived of his possessions except in the public interest and subject to the conditions provided for by law and by the general principles of international law.
>
> The preceding provisions shall not, however, in any way impair the right of a State to

---

[17] P Balchin and M Rhoden, *Housing Policy* 4th edn (London, Routledge, 2002) 129, referring to the views of M Frankena, 'Alternative Models of Rent Control' (1975) 12 *Urban Studies* 303; and JC Moorhouse, 'Optimal Housing Maintenance under Rent Control' (1972) 39 *Southern Economics J* 93.

enforce such laws as it deems necessary to control the use of property in accordance with the general interest or to secure the payment of taxes or other contributions or penalties.

In the recent case of *Hutten-Czapska v Poland* the Grand Chamber of the European Court of Human Rights (ECtHR) found that Polish tenancy laws violated this Article.[18] These laws included not only rent control measures but also placed maintenance obligations on landlords and imposed severe restrictions on the termination of leases. The particular measures were extreme. The first wave of rent controls introduced in 1994 obliged landlords to carry out costly maintenance works and prevented them from charging rents which covered even these costs: rents covered only 60 per cent of average maintenance costs, and the position was worse if major repairs were required. Although the strictness of these measures was reduced over a number of years, the replacement provisions similarly contained highly restrictive controls.

In *Hutten-Czapska v Poland* the applicant argued that her right of property was impaired because she was unable to derive any income from her property but also could not regain possession and use of the property. The Grand Chamber did not accept the argument that there was an expropriation falling within the first paragraph of Article 1: as she retained the ability to sell the property and ownership had not been transferred, her property rights had not been extinguished by the controls. This still left the second paragraph of Article 1 that entails consideration of two issues: whether the measures 'pursue a legitimate aim in the general interest', and whether the measures strike a fair balance between the general interest of the community and the applicant's right to peaceful enjoyment. The tenancy laws have to be understood against the particular housing background in Poland; there was a serious housing shortage during the transition period from communism to a free market system, with many people living below the poverty line. The Grand Chamber agreed with the finding of the Chamber that:

> ... the rent-control scheme in Poland originated in the continued shortage of dwellings, the low supply of flats for rent on the lease market and the high costs of acquiring a flat. It was implemented with a view to securing the social protection of tenants and ensuring – especially in respect of tenants in a poor financial situation – the gradual transition from State-controlled rent to a fully negotiated contractual rent during the fundamental reform of the country following the collapse of the communist regime ...[19]

In the light of this evidence, the Grand Chamber accepted that the legislation did have a legitimate aim in the general interest. Nonetheless, it failed to reach a fair balance due to the extremity of the measures. It is clear that in the sphere of housing, which plays a central role in welfare and economic policy, States enjoy a wide margin of appreciation enabling them to regulate to secure the housing needs of their citizens. This regulation can include rent control

---

[18] (App No 35014/97) (2006) BHRC 493. Further, it held that there was a systemic failure as the rent control scheme affected 100,000 landlords and from 600,000 to 900,000 tenants. Using the 'pilot judgment procedure' the Grand Chamber held that Poland had to put in place general measures in its domestic legal order to secure a fair balance between the interests of landlords, including their entitlement to derive profit from their property, and the general interest of the community – including the availability of sufficient accommodation for the less well-off – in accordance with the principles of the protection of property rights under the Convention: [239] NB: one partially dissenting judge disagreed with using the pilot judgement procedure (Judge Zagrebelsky) and a different partially dissenting judge did not accept that a landlord has a human right to derive profit from property (Judge Zapančič).

[19] (App No 35014/97) (2006) BHRC 493 [178].

measures, even if, as with the Austrian rent control laws (which were found not to violate Article 1 in *Mellacher and others v Austria*)[20] the effect is to dramatically lower rent levels. It was the unusual severity of the measures in *Hutten-Czapska v Poland* that explains why Article 1 was held to have been violated: the suppression of rent levels, the fact that there was no mechanism for recovering the costs of maintaining the property,[21] the absence of any state assistance or subsidy with maintenance, the allocation of the flat not by freely negotiated lease but by administrative act of the State, and the limits on landlords recovering possession. In combination, the laws 'impaired the very essence of the applicant's right of property'.[22]

The Grand Chamber agreed that this violated Article 1 and adopted the following conclusions of the Court:

185. As the Court has already stated on many occasions, in spheres such as housing of the population, States necessarily enjoy a wide margin of appreciation not only in regard to the existence of the problem of general concern warranting measures for control of individual property but also to the choice of the measures and their implementation. The State control over levels of rent is one of such measures and its application may often cause significant reductions in the amount of rent chargeable (see, in particular, *Mellacher and Others v Austria* [(App Nos 10522/83, 11011/84 and 11070/84) (1990) 12 EHRR 391 [45]]).

Also, in situations where, as in the present case, the operation of the rent-control legislation involves wide-reaching consequences for numerous individuals and has significant economic and social consequences for the country as a whole, the authorities must have considerable discretion not only in choosing the form and deciding on the extent of control over the use of property but also in deciding on the appropriate timing for the enforcement of the relevant laws. Nevertheless, that discretion, however considerable, is not unlimited and its exercise, even in the context of the most complex reform of the State, cannot entail consequences at variance with the Convention standards (see *Broniowski v Poland* [(App No 31443/96) (2006) 43 EHRR 1 [182]]).

186. The Court once again acknowledges that the difficult housing situation in Poland, in particular an acute shortage of dwellings and the high cost of acquiring flats on the market, and the need to transform the extremely rigid system of distribution of dwellings inherited from the communist regime, justified not only the introduction of remedial legislation protecting tenants during the period of the fundamental reform of the country's political, economic and legal system but also the setting of a low rent, at a level beneath the market value ... Yet it finds no justification for the State's continued failure to secure to the applicant and other landlords throughout the entire period under consideration the sums necessary to cover maintenance costs, not to mention even a minimum profit from the lease of flats.

...

188. Having regard to all the foregoing circumstances and, more particularly, to the consequences which the operation of the rent-control scheme entailed for the exercise of the applicant's right to the peaceful enjoyment of her possessions, the Court holds that the authorities imposed a disproportionate and excessive burden on her, which cannot be justified by any legitimate interest of the community pursued by them ...[23]

---

[20] (App Nos 10522/83, 11011/84 and 11070/84) (1990) 12 EHRR 391.

[21] The Grand Chamber notes that in *Mellacher and Others* the levels of rent were not set below the costs of maintenance and landlords were able to increase the rent in order to cover the necessary maintenance expenses: [224].

[22] (App No 35014/97) (2006) BHRC 493 [203].

[23] (App No 35014/97) (2006) 42 EHRR 15 cited at [223] of the Grand Chamber judgement.

In any constitutional challenge the courts tend to show a high degree of deference to the executive, generally taking the view that the courts are ill placed to second guess the advisability of regulatory housing measures. The facts of the Polish case were highly unusual. More surprisingly, less extreme measures were held by the Irish Supreme Court to be unconstitutional in *Blake v The Attorney General*.[24] The particular legislation had a devastating effect on property values; in one instance the sale value was almost eliminated, and in others it was severely reduced. The landlords argued that it was an unjust attack on their property rights, not justified by principles of social justice and the exigencies of the common good, and, therefore, that it violated the provisions of the Constitution. In finding the legislation to be unconstitutional, the Supreme Court referred to the fact that it did not apply to all residential lettings, was unrelated to either the financial needs and resources of the tenants or of the landlords, was not justified by there being an emergency situation, and provided no compensation.[25]

In the United States, rent control measures can, in theory, be challenged either under the 'takings' clause or the 'due process' clause of the Constitution.

The due process clause provides that no person can be deprived of property without due process of law. This provides a low level of review: a measure will not violate the due process clause if the legislature rationally believed that the measure would advance a legitimate state interest. A measure that violates the due process clause will be invalid. Rent controls challenged on this ground have been upheld, in the early days on the grounds that they were only temporary emergency measures,[26] and latterly on grounds that the continuing housing shortages meant that the regulations are rationally related to legitimate state goals and are therefore constitutional.[27]

The takings clause (also known as the just compensation clause) provides that private property shall not 'be taken for public use, without just compensation'.[28] This has been understood by the Supreme Court to mean that government cannot force 'some people alone to bear public burdens which, in all fairness and justice, should be borne by the public as a whole'.[29] Further, takings can involve not only physical takings (direct appropriation of property or title) but also 'regulatory takings', so that if the regulation goes too far this can be seen as a taking. If there is a taking, then compensation must be given.

Prior to the Supreme Court decision in *Lingle v Chevron USA Inc*[30] there were some cases that supported the view that there would be a regulatory taking if it could not be shown that a regulatory measure (such as rent control) substantially advanced a legitimate state interest. Relying on this understanding of what constituted a regulatory taking, Chevron argued in *Lingle v Chevron USA Inc* that the rent control measure applying to petrol station rents (limiting the rent that the oil company could charge dealers to 15 per cent of gross profits from gasoline sales plus 15 per cent of gross sales of products other than gasoline) did not substantially advance any legitimate government interest as there was no evidence

---

[24] [1982] IR 117 (ISC).
[25] See [1982] IR 117 (ISC) 138–140 (O'Higgins CJ).
[26] *Block v Hirsch* 256 US 135, 41 S Ct 458 (1921).
[27] See *Hutton Park Gardens v Town Council* 68 NJ 543, 350 A2d 1 (1975) (New Jersey SC).
[28] The Constitution of the United States 1776, Amendment v (1791).
[29] *Armstrong v United States* 364 US 40, 80 S Ct 1563 (1960) 49.
[30] 544 US 528, 125 S Ct 2074 (2005).

that it would reduce retail petrol prices. The argument was that the absence of proven reduction in petrol prices meant that the rent control was unconstitutional. Delivering the opinion of the Supreme Court, Justice O'Connor said that the test of whether or not there was a 'taking' was not whether the measure 'substantially advances' a legitimate state interest. Instead, to determine if there is a taking requiring compensation, it is necessary to look not to the purpose of the control but at the extent of the burden imposed on private property rights. Only if the burden it imposes on the individual property owner is severe, in the words of Justice O'Connor, functionally equivalent to a direct appropriation or ousting, will there be a taking requiring just compensation. Where the regulation falls short of physical invasion or complete deprivation of the economic use of the property, the test of whether it is 'too far' will depend on factors such as the magnitude of its economic impact and the extent to which it interferes with investment backed expectations.[31] In effect, to prove a taking it will be necessary to show that the economic impact of the measure is the functional equivalent of dispossession. On the facts, as Chevron had not proven that it suffered a serious burden on its property rights the Supreme Court could not find a regulatory taking.

Following *Lingle*, rent control measures are unlikely to be struck down as unconstitutional under the American constitution, unless severe. Some argue that the rent controls operating on mobile homes may meet this standard. Mobile home parks represent an important sector of the American housing market, particularly within certain States. Mobile home owners are, however, particularly vulnerable. Homes are generally owned by the occupants on a pitch rented from the park owner. While in theory 'mobile', the homes are, practically speaking, immobile. The body deteriorates so that movement becomes risky and expensive. In addition, tight planning controls mean that few sites are available for rent. In recent years, a number of States have found it necessary to enact legislation to protect the home owners. In *Yee v City of Escondido, California*[32] the Supreme Court rejected an argument that a mobile home rent control measure involved a 'taking'. The case had, however, been argued as a 'physical' taking and the Court seemed open to the possibility that there might be a 'regulatory' taking (although this was, of course, decided before the important *Lingle* decision). The impact of rent control in a mobile home context is to increase the capital value of the home, effectively transferring wealth from the landlord to the person who is home owner at the time of the imposition of control. These factors are peculiar to mobile homes – in the usual housing situation the tenant has no capital value in the home and the wealth transfer in terms of income is from landlord to the incumbent tenant and all future tenants. It is sometimes argued that this 'premium' taken from the park owner is a ·sufficient burden to constitute a regulatory taking, but there must be some doubts as to whether such an argument would succeed.

Although rent control is, therefore, vulnerable to the argument that it violates fundamental property rights, stripping away a landlord's ability to profit from his property, in all jurisdictions it is only in the most extreme cases that it is likely to be found unconstitutional.

---

[31] *Penn Central Transport Co v New York City* 438 US 104, 98 S Ct 2646 (1978).
[32] 503 US 519, 112 S Ct 1522 (1992).

15.2.4 The Fairness of Rent Controls

On a more abstract level, it is argued that rent control is unfair in that it involves a haphazard redistribution of wealth: there is no evidence that in general tenants are poor and landlords rich. Further, there is no reason why the cost of housing subsidy should be placed on landlords rather than taxpayers as a whole.

This argument may form one plank in a constitutional challenge. In *Hutten-Czapska v Poland* the unfairness of placing the burden of remedying the social housing problems on the landlords alone, rather than spreading the burden across society more generally, contributed to the finding that there was not a fair balance.[33] Singling out particular property owners to bear a social cost that should be borne by the wider community forms has also featured as a concern in American regulatory takings jurisprudence. So, for example, one form of rent control adopted in New Jersey exempting senior citizens on low incomes from rent increases was held by the Supreme Court of New Jersey in *Helmsley v Ft Lee* to be unconstitutional on the grounds that landlords and other tenants should not be forced to subsidise senior citizens.[34] These constitutional arguments tend to be finely balanced: a similar rent control ordinance was upheld in *Parrino v Lindsay* by the New York Court of Appeals on the basis that the exemption was a:

> Classification … [having] substantial relation to a legitimate public purpose, … the prevention of severe hardship to aging needy citizens resulting from shortage of low and moderately priced housing accommodations.[35]

15.2.5 Residential Rent Control in England

Rent control in the private residential sector began in 1915 in response to the political necessity of preventing landlords from exploiting the wartime shortages. Although initially intended as only a temporary measure,[36] rent control was retained in some form throughout most of the twentieth century.

The 1915 control was unsophisticated: rents for most houses were frozen at the level operative at the outbreak of war. The basic approach of controlling rents by reference to historic figures was continued until 1965, although a number of amendments were made, allowing increases to reflect higher maintenance costs and excluding more expensive properties. The result was that there was no systematic consistency as to the level of rents payable for similar properties.[37]

In 1965 there was a change in approach from one of control to regulation, with the introduction of the concept of 'fair rents'. Although 'fair rents' are commonly perceived as a way of keeping rent levels down, many rents did in fact rise very substantially after the

---

[33] (App no 35014/97) (2006) BHRC 493.

[34] 78 NJ 200, 394 A 2d 65 (1978) (NJ SC). NB. this case was appealed to the USSC and dismissed for want of a 'federal question' 440 US 978, 99 S Ct 182 (1979).

[35] 29 NY 2d 30, 323 NYS2d 689 (1971) (NYCA) 35.

[36] The Rent and Mortgage Interest (War Restrictions) Act 1915 was due to expire six months after the end of the war.

[37] FW Paish, 'Essay 4: The Economics of Rent Restriction' (first published 1950), in FA Hayek and others, *Verdict on Rent Control* (London, Institute of Economic Affairs, 1972) 48.

implementation of the 1965 legislation. After all, the previous control had artificially held rents at historic rent levels.[38]

Given that so few properties are still regulated by these fair rent provisions (as rent control does not apply to post 1988 lettings),[39] this section will focus not on the details of the law but on the principles adopted and the difficulties that this generated.

15.2.5.1 Fair Rents and Scarcity

Notwithstanding the language used, 'fairness' is not to do with affordability and abstract notions of justice and reasonableness,[40] but has a specific meaning based on the market rent for a property disregarding any impact that a local housing shortage has on rents, known as the scarcity factor, as defined in section 70 of the Rent Act 1977.[41] Section 70(2) requires it to be assumed that the number of persons seeking to become tenants of similar dwellings in the locality is not substantially greater than the number of such dwellings available for letting. Locality, however, is a difficult concept to apply in the context of property markets. Some parts of the country are more popular than others, some parts of a town more attractive than others, and property markets can be even more localised with particular neighbourhoods, or even individual streets, being especially sought after. How does 'scarcity' operate in this context?

In *Metropolitan Property Holdings Ltd v Finegold*[42] Lord Widgery CJ distinguishes local factors which affect the amenity value of the property and which can properly be taken into account in assessing a fair rent, such as the proximity of the property to the American school in the *Finegold* case itself, and wider market considerations which indicate that there is a scarcity of properties in the region leading to an excess of demand over supply and which must be discounted when determining the fair rent. This shortage must be judged in relation to 'a really large area'. The distinction between local amenity-based distortions and more wide-ranging scarcity is not clear cut and, according to Richards J in *Queensway Housing Association v Chairman of the Chilterns, Thames and Eastern Rent Assessment Committee*, the assessor has to determine if there are reasonable alternatives available to the potential tenant in the wider area in which the potential tenant could be expected to live.[43]

It will not always be easy to know whether or not there *is* a scarcity of housing. It is not simply a question of asking how many properties are available for renting; it is important to take account of the quality of the properties, of how comparable they are, of how quickly properties let, of how many people are actively seeking private sector accommodation (a more specific question than asking about the length of council and housing association waiting lists), and on what terms bargains are concluded (which is not necessarily the same

---

[38] DV Donnison, *The Government of Housing* (Harmondsworth, Penguin, 1967) 266–7.

[39] In 2004/05 5% of private sector tenancies were regulated, and fewer than half of these had registered rents.

[40] Although this has been argued: see A Prichard, 'Fair Rents and Market Rents' (1992) 142 *NLJ* 965; *Aspley Hall Estate Ltd v Nottingham Rent Officers* [1992] 2 EGLR 187 (Rent Assessment Com).

[41] *Curtis v London Rent Assessment Committee* [1999] QB 92 (CA). See also *Spath Holme Ltd v Chairman of the Greater Manchester and Lancashire Rent Assessment Committee* (1995) 28 HLR 107 (CA) where Morritt LJ stated that it is wrong to equate fair with reasonable.

[42] [1975] 1 WLR 349 (CA) 352.

[43] (1999) 31 HLR 945 (QB).

as the advertised terms).[44] Even if scarcity can be proven, it remains a difficult task to know what portion of a rent is attributable to this somewhat nebulous 'scarcity factor'. In practice, Rent Officers often rely on their own opinions and local knowledge rather than any 'hard and fast' evidence submitted to them,[45] although case law does stress the need for Rent Assessment Committees (the appeal body from Rent Officers) to give reasons for their decisions and to give some indication of how they have arrived at the deductions made for scarcity.[46]

In practice, the Rent Officer has considerable latitude in determining a fair rent. Until free market rents for new lettings were ushered in by the Housing Act 1988, there were so few market rentals that, as Lord Reid observed in *Mason v Skilling*, the 'most obvious and direct method [of determining the fair rent] is to have regard to registered rents of comparable houses in the area'.[47] The result was that, over time, there was little linkage between fair rents and 'market rents less scarcity'. Instead, fair rents were set mainly by reference to other registered rents, and so tended to be artificially depressed; perhaps fuelling the notion that they were to do with affordability and fairness to tenants but not to do with a fair return for the landlord.

The move to market rents brought in by the Housing Act 1988, brought new difficulties as the discrepancy between fair rents and market rents became apparent. Further, case law made clear that where market rent comparables are available these should be used as evidence in preference to registered fair rent comparables.[48] The effect was a dramatic rise in the level of fair rents, with increases of almost 20 per cent being typical, but far greater increases, of up to 250 per cent, being asked for by some landlords. In 1990, the mean weekly rent (net of services) for a regulated tenancy with a registered rent was £24, lower than both for other regulated tenancies (£33) and assured shortholds (£63).[49] By 1997, the registered rent had undergone more than a 100 per cent increase to £50 whereas the assured shorthold figure had risen by 40 per cent to £89.[50] The scale of these increases led to further intervention, ostensibly motivated by concern over the affordability of these fair rents for tenants who, as a group, are largely elderly and living on pensions,[51] but covertly by anxiety to contain the soaring housing benefit bill.[52] The Rent Acts (Maximum Fair Rent) Order 1999 imposed an artificial constraint on the amount by which a fair rent could go up by placing a cap on

---

[44] See Institute of Rent Officers and Rental Valuers, 'A Report on Good Practice in Assessing and Registering Fair Rents' (Southampton, 1998).

[45] See the Francis Committee, 'Report of the Committee on the Rent Acts' (Cmnd 4609, 1971) 57–61; see also P Watchman, 'Fair Rents and Market Scarcity' [1985] *Conv* 199.

[46] *Curtis v London Rent Assessment Committee* [1999] QB 92 (CA).

[47] [1974] 1 WLR 1437 (HL) 1439. See also M Davey, 'A Farewell to Fair Rents?' (1992) 14 *JSWFL* 497, 502.

[48] See, especially, the Court of Appeal in *Spath Holme Ltd v Chairman of the Greater Manchester and Lancashire Rent Assessment Committee* (1995) 28 HLR 107 (CA) and *Curtis v London Rent Assessment Committee* [1999] QB 92 (CA). Rodgers is critical of this approach for ignoring the social policy of objectives of the Rent Act 1977, giving insufficient weight to s 70(1), and for using as 'comparables' market rents which are drawn from tenancies governed by materially different statutory regimes: CP Rodgers, 'Fair rents and the market: judicial attitudes to rent control legislation' [1999] *Conv* 201.

[49] DCLG, Live Tables, Private Renters, S547 'Weekly mean and median rents net of services by type of letting'.

[50] DCLG, Live Tables, Private Renters, S547 'Weekly mean and median rents net of services by type of letting'.

[51] In 1996/97 over 60% of regulated private tenants with registered rents were retired, DETR, 'Limiting Fair Rent Increases: A Consultation Paper' (May 1998).

[52] See PN di C Willan, 'Fair rents or unfair rents?' (1995) 145 *NLJ* 348, CP Rodgers, 'Fair rents and the market: judicial attitudes to rent control legislation' [1999] *Conv* 201, 228.

increases, albeit above the level of general inflation.[53] Landlord objections to capping were dismissed on the basis that they had generally bought properties subject to regulated tenancies at a significant discount[54] in anticipation of future capital gains when the tenancies end but in the full knowledge that rental yields are lower than those from assured tenancies.

Research for the College of Estate Management has argued that the scarcity provision should be abandoned and rent increases controlled under the Fair Rents Order alone, as 'scarcity' is ill-understood and poorly applied:

> Scarcity is the most difficult factor to assess and the least well understood. The concept is insufficiently grounded in theory and the absence of defined criteria has led to practices that are confused and in some cases misguided.
>
> Valuation practice is being applied incorrectly and irrationally to valuing fair rents and practices vary in different parts of the country.[55]

The notion of scarcity has also been used in the rent review provisions for agricultural holdings, but has similarly been difficult to apply. Under the Agricultural Holdings Act 1986, in calculating the 'rent properly payable', the arbitrator had to take into account the rent payable on 'comparable lettings' but disregard, inter alia, any element of the rents due to an 'appreciable scarcity of comparable holdings available for letting' on similar terms to the subject holding, comparable with the number of persons seeking to become tenants of such holdings.[56] The concern underlying this provision was that the shortage of agricultural land available for renting was forcing the rent of new lettings above the level the land could support.

The guidance given to agricultural valuers on comparables shows what a slippery concept scarcity is:

> 3.1.12 'appreciable scarcity' – the disregard only has to be quantified if there is 'appreciable scarcity'. The word 'appreciable' must mean that the scarcity is capable of being appreciated, that is identified and therefore valued. It is not enough that the valuer has a vague notion that supply and demand are in balance or imbalance.
>
> 3.1.13 'scarcity' – this may have to be distinguished from rarity. Thus there will be always a shortage of Grade 1 arable farms or of well-equipped dairy farms with above average milk quota. This is rarity and is a very different matter from scarcity.
>
> 3.1.14 In quantifying the amount of the scarcity disregard the valuer must decide as a matter of skill and judgement what rent the comparable would command if there was a balance between supply and demand. The difference between that figure and the passing rent is the amount of the disregard.[57]

---

[53] SI 1999/6. The maximum registered fair rent for a property is now the existing rent increased in line with inflation since the last registration, plus an additional 7.5% at the first application, and 5% for subsequent applications. If improvements have been made to the property by the landlord so that the previous rent would increase by at least 15%, the restrictions in the Order do not apply.

[54] 30% to 40% below vacant possession value: DETR, 'Limiting Fair Rent Increases: A Consultation Paper' (May 1998) para 2.5. The formula can still produce large rent increases: see P Kenny, 'Fair Rents – Fair to Whom?' [1999] *Conv* 169.

[55] The College of Estate Management, 'Valuing for fair rents: the law and valuation of regulated residential tenancies' (2001).

[56] Agricultural Holdings Act 1986 Sch 2 para 1(3)(a).

[57] RICS, 'Guidance Notes for Valuers Acting in reviews of Rent at Arbitration under the Agricultural Holdings Act' (1986).

15.2.5.2 Avoiding Rent Control

Whenever rent control places a ceiling on rents receivable there will be landlords who, in a strong market, seek to avoid it. One way is, of course, to avoid the grant of a protected tenancy. This is what the owner attempted in *Antoniades v Villiers*, by granting two identical licence agreements to a couple occupying a flat.[58] As seen in chapter 3, this was unsuccessful and was held by the House of Lords to create a tenancy. The occupiers then applied to have a fair rent registered, which led to a reduction from £174 for the flat (including rates) to £135 (including rates). The landlord argued that this breached his rights under Article 1 of the First Protocol of the ECHR (protection of property), on the basis that the rent bore no relation to the market letting value of the flat or to the capital investment involved. The European Commission disagreed, stating that the fair rent regime pursued a legitimate social policy 'in that it seeks to protect the interests of tenants in a situation of a shortage of expensive housing' and was not disproportionate.[59]

An alternative way to try to avoid the controls is to seek the payment of 'key money', that is a lump sum paid at the beginning of the tenancy, in addition to the permitted rent. Such premiums were therefore prohibited under the Rent Act 1977 section 119. The Act also prohibited other avoidance devices such as payment of an excessive price for furniture,[60] payments on assignment[61] and substantial pre-payments of rent.[62]

15.2.5.3 Abandoning Private Residential Rent Control

Since the introduction of the Housing Act 1988 there has been no significant regulation of rents for new lettings in the private residential sector.[63] The belief of the government when implementing the Act was that deregulation was necessary in order to revitalise the private sector and encourage more investment. In relation to assured tenancies, there is no external control over rent levels. The only external influence is through the section 13 review procedure (see chapter 16), but the aim of this is not to limit rents, but instead to enable rents to be set at a market level.

In relation to assured shortholds, there is some form of control but this is extremely limited in its impact. With certain exceptions, an assured shorthold tenant may, during the first six months of the tenancy, apply to the Rent Assessment Committee (RAC) to determine the rent 'which, in the committee's opinion, the landlord might reasonably be expected to obtain'.[64] By section 22(3) the RAC cannot make a determination unless they consider that:

(a)   there is a sufficient number of similar dwelling-houses in the locality let on assured tenancies (whether shorthold or not); and

---

[58] *AG Securities v Vaughan; Antoniades v Villiers* [1990] 1 AC 417 (HL).
[59] *Antoniades v United Kingdom* (App No 15434/89) ECHR 15 February 1990.
[60] Rent Act 1977 s 123.
[61] Rent Act 1977 s 120.
[62] Rent Act 1977 s 126.
[63] In relation to tenancies entered into before 1 January 1989, and governed by the Rent Act 1977, the fair rent regime continues to apply.
[64] Housing Act 1988 s 22. No application can be made if the assured shorthold tenancy was granted on, or after, 28 February 1997 and more than six months have elapsed since the beginning of the tenancy: see s 22(2) for further exceptions.

(b) that the rent payable under the assured shorthold tenancy in question is *significantly higher* than the rent which the landlord might reasonably be expected to obtain under the tenancy, having regard to the level of rents payable [for similar tenancies in the locality].

Few applications are made: shorthold tenants do not have security beyond the fixed term and this may deter them from risking upsetting the landlord. Even if they do apply, it will take a lot to convince the RAC that the rent is significantly higher than market rents, and the landlord can always point to the fact that the tenant was willing to pay as a sign that this was a market rent:

> Ironically there is some evidence that tenants who do apply have been encouraged to do so by their landlord because the tenant is in receipt of housing benefit and the local authority are refusing to pay benefit above the rent officer's determination of a market rent ... In other words, the section 22 mechanism is being used as an informal appeal against the rent officer's determination of market rent for housing benefit subsidy purposes.[65]

15.2.6 Rent Control and the Commercial Sector in England

In relation to the commercial property sector, there has always been a policy of non-intervention in rents.[66] If controls were introduced, they would have the effect of keeping rents artificially low and distorting the market, thus discouraging any new property investment and creating a shortage of business premises. In addition, there is not the same 'affordability problem' with commercial tenants as with residential tenants; rent increases (so long as not way out of line) can always be passed on to the consumer through pricing of the business's goods and services.

The ability of the 'price mechanism' to control the market efficiently, and the ability of commercial tenants to pay, has, however, been questioned. An influential study by Professor Burton argued that rents under the standard system of review are 'impervious to market forces'. This study argued not for rent control (which would 'simply ape the disease') but for a more effective market, with greater transparency, triggering the long debate about the acceptability of upward only rent review clauses (discussed in chapter 16).[67]

15.3 Ensuring Affordability through Welfare Payments

It is the poorer members of the community who suffer most from high housing costs. Since the 1930s, means tested rent rebates have been encouraged by central government. Nevertheless, only 40 per cent of local authorities had rebate schemes in place by 1964. It was the Housing Finance Act of 1972 that made such rebates compulsory through a national scheme, but the numbers claiming were relatively low for many years – fewer than 10 per cent of council tenants.[68]

---

[65] M Davey, 'A Farewell to Fair Rents?' (1992) 14 *JSWFL* 497, 508.

[66] Apart from a rent freeze imposed for two and a half years in the early 1970s as part of the government's counter-inflationary measures: Counter-Inflation Act 1973 s 11.

[67] J Burton, *Retail Rents, Fair and Free Market?* (London, Adam Smith Research Trust 1992) 82–3.

[68] J Neuberger and G Long, 'Policy Briefing: Housing Benefit' (Shelter, August 2005) 2. Housing benefit was introduced in 1982.

15.3.1 The Housing Benefit System

The picture is now very different. As rents in both the social sector and the private sector have been driven upwards, so the housing benefit bill and the numbers of tenants receiving benefit have soared. The most dramatic rise followed the Housing Act 1988: between 1988/89 and 1996/7, there was a fivefold increase in rent allowances paid to housing association and private tenants,[69] with housing benefit in Great Britain now costing over £13 billion. Almost two-thirds of social renters are now in receipt of housing benefit, and slightly over one-fifth of private sector tenants.[70]

The housing benefit system is riddled with problems. Housing benefit is a means-tested payment. The regulations are detailed, administration of benefit claims is slow both for initial claims[71] and in response to changing personal circumstances, and payment errors are common. The benefit system also creates a poverty trap, providing little incentive for claimants to find work because of the impact that a rise in income has on the welfare payment.[72] The complexity of benefit regulations and other social factors, means that not all eligible persons claim housing benefit: it is estimated that around 15 per cent of those potentially eligible for housing benefit do not claim it.[73]

In response to the spiralling costs of housing benefit, 1996 saw the introduction of various controls in the private sector to limit the amount of benefit paid, in particular the Single Room Rent (SRR, see below) and the capping of payments by reference to the Local Reference Rent (LRR, the average rent for other similar dwellings in the area). The aim is to ensure that benefit is not being claimed for 'inappropriate' accommodation, by officers making a judgement both about whether the claimant needs to have a property of that size and whether the rent for the property is set too high. The result is that there is frequently a shortfall between the rent deemed eligible for housing benefit and the contractually agreed rent. Although the eligible rent for housing benefit purposes is prima facie the rent paid to the landlord, it will be reduced (and often is) if it is out-of-line for similar properties in the locality, or if the property is larger than necessary for the claimant's family. The Regulations require there to be a determination of what would be an appropriate rent for the property, taking account of average local rents, whether this particular property is necessary for the claimant, and whether (even if the rent is appropriate for the property) it is simply too high to expect the taxpayer to fund. It was hoped that these various restrictions would encourage claimants to live in cheaper accommodation of an appropriate size and encourage them to

---

[69] See P Kemp, *Housing Benefit: Time for Reform* (York, Joseph Rowntree Foundation, 1998).

[70] The number of private sector claimants has fallen since the mid-1990s. The spiralling housing benefit bill led to new restrictions on the levels of rent that would be covered by benefit, including the Single Room Rent and Local Reference Rent discussed below.

[71] The average time to process a new claim is 33 days, but some authorities take more than 100 working days: J Neuberger and G Long, 'Policy Briefing: Housing Benefit' (Shelter, August 2005) 2. Since this briefing paper, delays have been reducing, particularly in the poorest performing authorities: DWP, 'A new deal for welfare: Empowering people to work' (Cm 6730, 2006) 83–4.

[72] See the illustration given in J Neuberger and G Long, 'Policy Briefing: Housing Benefit' (Shelter, August 2005) 10. Changes have recently been made to make the transition to work easier: DWP, 'A new deal for welfare: Empowering people to work' (Cm 6730, 2006) 84.

[73] S Wilcox, *UK Housing Review 2006/07* (Coventry, Chartered Institute of Housing and London, Council of Mortgage Lenders, 2006) Table 117a.

bargain rents down.[74] Evidence suggests, however, that this does not happen, and the reality is that the restrictions tend to increase social exclusion by creating concentrations of poverty.[75] In addition, the system distorts access to housing as many landlords refuse to rent to benefit claimants (partly through concern that benefit will not cover the whole rent). To help avoid the shortfall trap, tenants are able to apply for a pre-tenancy determination to find out how much housing benefit will be payable for a particular property;[76] the difficulty, however, is that often a prospective tenant cannot wait for the outcome before deciding whether or not to take the accommodation as it may be snapped up by someone else. Following the changes in 1996, the number of households receiving benefit in the private rented sector did decline, not exclusively as a result of the changes but also because of a drop in unemployment numbers.[77]

Young people, especially, are constrained in their housing choices by the SRR which has been extremely controversial since its introduction in October 1996. The effect is that for people under 25 living in private sector accommodation, housing benefit will be based on rents for shared accommodation, such as rooms in shared houses with shared facilities. Young people taking accommodation which does not fit this description are likely to find that their housing benefit falls short of the rent payable. The problem is that it is difficult to find accommodation that meets the SRR criteria as there is a shortage of this type of accommodation, and many landlords now refuse to let to young people.[78] Almost 90 per cent of SRR claimants face significant shortfalls between their benefit entitlement and the contractual rent.[79] Many housing commentators are now calling for the abolition of the SRR.[80]

It is not altogether surprising that many landlords are unwilling to let to benefit claimants. It is difficult for many claimants to raise the money necessary for a deposit, as this is not covered by housing benefit. There is no assurance that the full rent will be covered by housing benefit, and many claimants will find it difficult to make up the shortfall from their meagre resources. Most landlords want rent paid in advance, but housing benefit is paid four weeks in arrears. There is often considerable further delay caused by poor administration: delays in settling housing benefit were thought to account for 10 per cent of

---

[74] 'It is clear that if there were no limit as to the amount of rent allowance, a person who was entitled to rent allowance in respect of 100% of his rent would be less inclined to bargain with his landlord for a lower rent than would the rest of the population who have to meet their rent bills out of their own pocket.' *R v Housing Benefit Review Board of the London Borough of Brent, ex p Connery* [1990] 2 All ER 353 (QB) 355 (Schiemann J). See also the comments of Sir Thomas Bingham MR in *R v Housing Benefit Review Board for East Devon DC, ex p Gibson and Gibson* (1993) 25 HLR 487 (CA).

[75] Citizens Advice Bureau, 'Falling short, the CAB case for housing benefit reform' (June 1999) para 3.11.

[76] Housing Act 1966 s 122.

[77] S Wilcox, *UK Housing Review 2006/07* (Coventry, Chartered Institute of Housing and London, Council of Mortgage Lenders, 2006) 79–80.

[78] Following the introduction of the SRR there was a 17% drop in private landlords renting to benefit claimants, mainly due to ceasing to let to young people: see Citizens Advice Bureau, 'Falling short, the CAB case for housing benefit reform' (June 1999) para 3.53, and see para 3.18. For analysis of the impact of the SRR, see Joseph Rowntree Foundation, 'The impact of housing benefit changes on help to secure private rented accommodation' (Housing Research Findings No 213, June 1997); P Kemp and J Rugg, *The Single Room Rent: Its Impact on Young People* (Centre for Housing Policy, University of York, 1998); J Harvey and D Houston, 'Research into the Single Room Rent Restrictions' (DWP, 2005).

[79] J Harvey and D Houston, 'Research into the Single Room Rent Restrictions' (DWP, 2005).

[80] Eg, S Ellery, 'Decade of Discrimination' ROOF November/December 2006 20.

rent arrears in 2000/01,[81] and as shown in chapter 19 tenants in both the public and private sectors are frequently evicted for rent arrears caused by delays in benefit payment. There are signs of a bifurcated private sector market evolving, with the housing available to housing benefit claimants decreasing in quality and additional burdens being imposed upon housing benefit tenants.[82]

Benefit payments are made directly to social landlords. In the private sector there is less consistency: between 40 per cent and 80 per cent of cases involve direct payment to landlords.

15.3.2 *Reform of the Housing Benefit System*

The shortcomings of the housing benefit system have long been recognised. In 2002 a radical system of reform was announced, the objectives being:

— to reduce barriers to work;
— to ensure affordability of decent homes to those on low incomes;
— to give tenants choice;
— to extend personal responsibility;
— to reduce administrative costs and complexity; and
— to reduce fraud.[83]

Under the new scheme, housing benefit is to be based on the 'Local Housing Allowance' (LHA), a flat rate allowance that is based on average rents for the area for a property deemed to be a suitable size for the claimant's needs. Initially introduced into nine 'pathfinder' areas, the intention is to roll the scheme out nationally to all private sector claimants.[84]

The LHA is paid direct to the claimant rather than the landlord.[85] The intention is that this will encourage claimants to focus on how much property costs: if they choose to go somewhere less good they can keep the surplus (subject to a cap),[86] if they go somewhere more expensive they will have to pay the difference. This fits with the move to choice-based lettings. The SRR has been replaced by a shared room rent that is slightly more generous.[87]

---

[81] Audit Commission, 'Local Authority housing rent income: Rent collection and arrears management by local authorities in England and Wales' (June 2003).

[82] See Citizens Advice Bureau, 'Falling short, the CAB case for housing benefit reform' (June 1999) paras 3.19 and 3.27.

[83] DWP, 'Building Choice and Responsibility: a radical agenda for Housing Benefit' (October 2002).

[84] It has already been extended to 18 areas and the intention is to roll it out nationally in 2008 but, for now, only to new claimants: DWP, 'A new deal for welfare: empowering people to work: consultation report' (Cm 6859, 2006). Power to do a national roll out is provided for in s 130A of the Social Security Contributions and Benefits Act 1992, inserted by the Welfare Reform Act 2007 s 30.

[85] With some exceptions for vulnerable claims or those with significant rent arrears.

[86] A cap of £15 per week was announced in DWP, 'A new deal for welfare: empowering people to work: consultation report' (Cm 6859, 2006). The cap was introduced following the study of implementation of LHA in the Pathfinder areas, where the excess was found to be over £100 per week in 30% of cases: British Property Foundation, 'Letting in the Future, Housing Manifesto 2006'.

[87] But there are still significant shortfalls.

Early evaluation of these reforms in the pathfinder areas is mixed. Fewer tenants had rent shortfalls,[88] but there is little sign that tenants are assuming greater personal responsibility and exercising greater choice. Further, although there have been some administrative benefits, they are not substantial.[89] Almost one-half of landlords appear less likely to let to someone on benefit following the move to LHA (the main reason being because of direct payment to tenants, but also because of concern about arrears), although the generally buoyant market meant that supply was still marginally increased overall.[90] Research by Shelter showed that just 8 per cent of more than 13,000 advertised rentals were available to benefit claimants.[91] The fears of increased arrears may be unfounded; as yet, there are no signs of it causing a significant increase in arrears, although direct payment to tenants creates difficulty as many poor claimants simply do not have bank accounts and find it difficult to manage money. It has also been suggested that one of the reasons for the relatively easy implementation of LHA in the pathfinder areas was that generous support was made available to provide advice during the transition, and if this success is to be maintained when the scheme is rolled out nationally then a similarly high level of support will need to be made available.[92]

The initial plan was to extend LHA into the social sector, even though there are important differences between the sectors and most housing benefit is paid direct to social landlords at present. The RSL sector in particular feared that LHA would affect cash-flow, and increase arrears and collection costs, all of which would jeopardise the financing structures that they rely on. The fact is that private funders have lent money to RSLs on the assumption that loans will be paid, taking account of the availability of benefit to social tenants. As Cowan writes, this:

> … illustrates the impotence now inherent in housing policy … It simply is not possible to withdraw this personal subsidy (because private lenders will exit the sector and there will be no new private money for building) … Indeed, tinkering with the system- to provide incentives for tenants to 'trade down' into housing they can afford- endangers continued rental income (more expensive housing would become vacant) and therefore the ability of associations to meet their loan repayments.[93]

The government has now announced that there will be no roll out into the social sector.[94]

Commentators have also expressed concern about the potential exclusory impact of the dual reform of rent restructuring and housing benefit:

---

[88] J Birch, 'Lessons Learnt' ROOF January/February 2007 29: the proportion with shortfalls fell from 58% to 39% in pathfinders but from 60% to 53% in control areas.

[89] DWP, 'Local Housing Allowance Evaluation 10, Local Housing Allowance Final Evaluation: Implementation and Delivery in the Nine Pathfinder Areas' (October 2006).

[90] DWP, 'Local Housing Allowance Evaluation 11, Local Housing Allowance Final Evaluation: The survey evidence of landlords and agents experience in the Nine Pathfinder Areas' (October 2006).

[91] J Birch, 'Lessons Learnt' ROOF January/February 2007 29: only one-third of properties advertised were within the maximum amount of housing benefit, one-third specifically barred claimants, and only 1 in 6 of the remaining landlords would accept a claimant.

[92] R Rafferty, 'Benefit of the Doubt' ROOF November/December 2005 17.

[93] D Cowan and M McDermont, *Regulating Social Housing, Governing Decline* (Abingdon, Routledge-Cavendish, 2006) 94.

[94] DWP, 'A new deal for welfare: empowering people to work: consultation report' (Cm 6859, 2006).

Taken together the rent restructuring initiative and the Housing Benefit reform experiment are intended to increase the use of price signals in the social rented sector and eventually enable tenants to respond directly to those signals. Whether social sector tenants will be willing and able to exercise choice in high-demand areas remains to be seen. If they respond to price differentials in the way intended, those who value and can afford better and/or larger properties will secure them, and those who do not value or cannot afford them will move to lower-quality and/or smaller dwellings. This may replicate 'efficient private market patterns', but at the risk of greater social exclusion and segregation. It also runs contrary to the view the social housing should meet the needs of those for whom market-like solutions are inappropriate.[95]

15.4 The Tolerated Trespasser and Payment for Occupation

Rent is the contractual payment for occupation during a lease, whereas the payments made for occupation by a tolerated trespasser are treated by statute[96] and by the courts as 'mesne profits'. Given that the tolerated trespasser concept is a somewhat strange doctrinal beast, it is not surprising that the categorisation of payments made is also difficult. Although the courts happily talk about the payment as mesne profits, and even that the 'landlord' can increase the amount of mesne profits,[97] mesne profits are not usually seen as consensual payments but as payments due to an owner for the wrongful use of the land (see chapter 3). In practice, social landlords tend to treat the payment due from tolerated trespassers in the same way as rents payable by tenants, and increases occur on the same basis.

---

[95] D Mullins and A Murie, *Housing Policy in the UK* (Basingstoke, Palgrove Macmillan, 2006) 177. See also J Neuberger and G Long, 'Policy Briefing: Housing Benefit' (Shelter, August 2005).
[96] Both s 85(3)(a) of the Housing Act 1985 and s 9(3) of the Housing Act 1988 refer to payments in respect of occupation after the termination of the tenancy as mesne profits.
[97] *LB of Lambeth and Hyde Southbank Ltd v O'Kane; Helena Housing Ltd v Pinder* [2005] EWCA Civ 1010 [46]. One of the unsuccessful arguments was that increasing the payments meant that there was a new tenancy.

16

VARYING THE RENT AND ENSURING PAYMENT

16.1   Introduction
16.2   Variation of the rent during a tenancy
16.3   Overpaying the rent
16.4   Ensuring payment
16.5   Remedies for non-payment
16.6   Cesser of rent

16.1 Introduction

Given that leases may last for a considerable time, it is common for there to be some method for the landlord to increase the rent. In the social sector, many tenancies are 'lifetime' tenancies and will often be subject to annual rent increases. In the case of commercial leases, rent review clauses are common, although the period of review will seldom be as frequent as an annual review. Formal review clauses are less common in the private (non-social) residential sector as tenancies tend to be relatively short. The first part of this chapter looks at the variety of methods that can be used for rent review, and some of the problems that arise, particularly matters of contractual interpretation. The remainder of the chapter looks at ways in which the landlord can try to improve the probability of rent payment, through taking guarantees and rent deposits, but also at the remedies available to recover rent arrears.

16.2 Variation of the Rent during a Tenancy[1]

Over the term of a lease, the economic value of the land will usually change. This can happen because the land value itself is diminished, for example, through the extraction of minerals. More commonly, it will change due to the effects of inflation. In addition to this general change in monetary values, there may well be changes more specific to the property. Property values as a whole may rise or fall independently of general monetary trends, and there may

---

[1] Generally on rent review, see the excellent book by DN Clarke and JE Adams, *Rent Reviews and Variable Rents* 3rd edn (London, Longman, 1990), and R Bernstein and K Reynolds, *Handbook of Rent Review* (London, Sweet & Maxwell, 1981).

be factors peculiar to the particular property that mean its value changes out-of-line with other properties. The opening of a shopping centre next to the let premises may, for example, cause its value to rise dramatically. Conversely, the closure of an adjacent car park or the opening a shopping complex at the other side of town may cause the value of the property to plummet. More usually, rents go up and it is common for a landlord to seek an increase in the rent at regular intervals by including a rent review clause in the lease. As will be seen, it is the norm, in commercial tenancies at least, for the rent review clause to be 'upward only' so that even in a falling market the rent will not go down.

Most parts of the residential sector will have no, or simple, rent review provisions. In the local authority sector the review clause is likely to be straightforward, providing simply that the rent can be changed from time to time.[2] In the private sector, fixed term tenancies for no more than one year will not usually contain review provisions because if the tenant stays beyond the year the new rent will be agreed on renewal of the lease. Tenancy agreements made with registered social landlords (RSLs) may have more detailed provisions for rent increases. This is because RSLs do not 'enjoy' the same statutory licence to make increases as is available to local authority landlords through the Housing Act 1985 section 24, and yet they expect their tenants to have long term security with periodic tenancies.[3] It is in the commercial sector, however, that review clauses tend to be most complex as the parties seek to agree a formulation that will ensure that the property is rented at a rack rent throughout the term.

Where the lease does provide for rent variation, there are a number of general questions that need to be asked about the objectives of the rent review:

(a)   Should the variation in rent be related to general changes in the purchasing power of money, or tied more specifically to fluctuations in the property market or, more specifically still, related to the particular property?

(b)   Should the aim of rent variation be to maximise the landlord's profits from the land or to enable both parties to share the risk of changes in value? The answer to this will affect whether rent can go down on review or only be increased.

(c)   Should the objective on variation of rent be the same as for the fixing of the initial rent, or should regard be had to the fact that the tenant already has an estate in the property? Should the tenant be given the advantage of rent concessions that would be available on a new letting, or the landlord the advantage of any premium that would be paid on a new letting?

There are many different approaches to rent review that could be adopted. In this country, the most common method of rent variation in commercial leases is to provide for revaluation of the let property at periodic intervals, the valuation being referred to an independent third party in the event of disagreement (see further 16.2.2 below). The object of this is to provide a periodic change in the rent to reflect not general monetary trends but the current market rent for the particular property. The sophistication of these rent review clauses, and the expense of operating them, makes them unsuitable for general use in

---

[2] The Manchester City Council tenancy agreement, for example, states: 'the rent may be increased or decreased from time to time – usually once a year. You will be told in writing at least four weeks before any rent change.'

[3] See *Riverside Housing Association Ltd v White* [2007] UKHL 20 [9] for an example.

residential leases where simpler methods of review are used. It is interesting, however, that these kinds of clauses are not popular in commercial property markets elsewhere. Outside the United Kingdom, other forms of review, in particular indexation, are much more commonly used. The explanation for the popularity of the market rent review here lies in the historic dominance of institutional landlords in the United Kingdom commercial property market and their concern with certain long term income growth.[4]

Before considering the market rent review clause in more detail we shall look at some alternative methods of rent review.

16.2.1 Methods of Rent Review

16.2.1.1 Step-up or Differential Rents

The lease may provide for a simple and pre-determined rent revision at periodic intervals. This form of rent increase is not very popular as there is no flexibility built into it; it is a very crude attempt to provide for increases and ignores the effects of changes in the pace of inflation or factors peculiar to the let property. Nevertheless, it is a relatively simple and inexpensive method of rent review. It may therefore be chosen where the annual rental of the premises is a low ground rent, for example, in a 99 year lease purchased with a substantial capital sum the initial rent may be £100 per annum, to be increased at 33 year intervals by a further £100.

16.2.1.2 Turnover or Equity Rents[5]

When the rent is based on turnover, it varies in line with the income from the let premises, either by reference to the tenant's business turnover at the premises (the turnover rent) or by reference to the rents received by the tenant in subletting the property (the equity rent). Turnover and equity rents are clearly appropriate in different situations. The turnover rent is most often found in relation to retail outlets where the rent is related to the level of sales made by the tenant. Equity rents might be used where the property is an investment and the freeholder has shared in the development process, for example, where the freeholder is a local authority which has helped in assembling land together for commercial development and receives a share of the rents received by the tenant developer. An example of an equity rent can be seen in *Ashworth Frazer v Gloucester CC*, where the developer was to be paid eight per cent of the rents 'receivable by the Lessee'.[6] In relation to agricultural land, there may be a sharecropping agreement whereby the tenant farmer agrees to pay for his use of the land by

---

[4] For a comparative study of rent provisions internationally, see RICS, 'International Leasing Structures' (Paper Number 26, May 1993) and A Hurndall (ed), *Property in Europe* (London, Butterworths, 1998).

[5] For problems with turnover rents, see NS Hecht, 'Variable Rental Provision in Long Term Ground Leases' (1972) 72 *Columbia L Rev* 625, 665–70. See further on the American aspects: DH Gross, 'Calculation of rental under commercial percentage lease' (1974) 58 ALR 3d 384; Anon, 'The Percentage Lease – Its Functions and Drafting Problems' (1948) 61 *Harvard L Rev* 317. Generally, see DN Clarke and JE Adams, *Rent Reviews and Variable Rents* 3rd edn (London, Longman, 1990) ch 21; H Willett, 'Turnover Rents – Coming out of Recession' (1997) 1 *Landlord & Tenant Rev* 90.

[6] *Ashworth Frazer Ltd v Gloucester CC* [1997] 1 EGLR 104 (CA). In this case, a difficulty arose in the interpretation of 'receivable' as the original lessee had assigned, and not sub-let, parts of the property. Adopting a 'commercial' approach, the Court of Appeal thought that 'receivable' should include notionally received rents.

giving the landowner a percentage of the profits of the harvest. The focus of our discussion will be upon turnover rents, as these relate to the occupational tenant.

Early provisions for rent variation were based upon the same kind of ideas as the turnover rent and took the form of 'produce rents', where the rent was dependent on the value of produce yielded from the land. In *Walsh v Lonsdale*,[7] there was a variable rent of thirty shillings per loom run in a weaving mill; the tenant had to run at least 540 looms (thus ensuring the landlord a minimum guaranteed rent) and the rent would increase with every additional loom to reflect the increase in output. Nowadays the turnover rent will usually be based upon the gross sales or takings of the tenant, but may also be coupled with a minimum base rent figure representing a portion of the market rent of the premises.[8] Thus, a lease of a retail unit in a shopping complex might provide that the tenant has to pay a fixed rent, representing 80 per cent of the market rent, plus 3 per cent of gross profits. A landlord who finds a property hard to let may agree to put more emphasis on the profit element and demand less of a base rent figure; the landlord of an easy to let complex may seek base rental figures approaching 100 per cent of the market rent.

Turnover rents lend themselves to developments where some kind of partnership exists between the landlord and tenant. For the landlord, the fact that he will share in the tenant's business fortunes (both successes and slumps) will be an incentive to promote the tenant's business actively. In a shopping centre, the landlord will therefore benefit from adopting high management standards, refurbishing the centre when it becomes out-dated, promoting the complex widely and ensuring a good tenant mix. The landlord's management policies will therefore contribute to the returns he receives on the property let. He will also be able to get a more immediate return on investment than is available from rent variation based on periodic revaluation, where it may be several years before the next review date. The tenant, too, will clearly benefit from a well-managed environment. In addition, the linkage between rent payable and turnover means that the tenant is sheltered during times of recession; if business is poor, the rent will be correspondingly lower. Conversely, during times of good trading conditions, the rent payable will be high.

Turnover rents have not, however, proved popular in this country although they are increasingly being used in major shopping centres such as Bluewater and Lakeside.[9] There are certain problems inherent to turnover rents (see below), but the fundamental constraint has been the reluctance of institutional investors to depart from the notion of upward only reviews or to share in the risk of the enterprise.[10]

Turnover rent provisions require careful drafting. While it might be agreed in principle that the tenant has to pay, say, 3 per cent of gross takings, this does need to be much more carefully defined when it comes to the documentation. What items will count as takings? The kind of difficulties that arise include how to treat refunds made to customers, inter-branch stock transfers, taxes paid by customers (such as value added tax), discounts given to staff, and so on. Even with careful drafting of the inclusion and exclusion provisions, it will be difficult to anticipate all potential difficulties. An illustration is provided by

---

[7] (1882) 21 Ch D 9.

[8] For an example, see *Debenhams Retail Plc v Sun Alliance & London Assurance Co Ltd* [2005] EWCA Civ 868 [4].

[9] R Bootle and S Kalyan, *Property in Business – A Waste of Space?* (London, RICS, 2002).

[10] See B Walsh, 'Shopping centres: why are turnover rents not more popular?' (2 April 1988) *EG* 20; H Hawkings, 'Shopping centres – turnover rents on the increase' (22 September 1990) *EG* 28.

Debenhams Retail Plc v Sun Alliance & London Assurance Co Ltd.[11] The lease contained a turnover rent (plus a base rent) but had been drafted before the introduction of VAT; the issue was whether the tenant's turnover should be calculated to include VAT paid by customers or not. On the facts, as a matter of construction, the Court of Appeal held that it should, although most modern leases would exclude VAT from turnover. Whereas in England these matters are for the parties to negotiate, in some jurisdictions there has been statutory intervention. So, for example, in Victoria, Australia, the Retail Tenancies Act 1986 lists a number of items that cannot constitute 'turnover', including, inter alia, discounts reasonably and properly allowed to any customer in the usual course of business, the value of trade-ins purchased from customers, uncollected credit accounts written off by the tenant, refunds on the return of merchandise, delivery charges and taxes on the purchase price of goods and services.

Where a turnover rent is used, there may be other changes to the lease structure[12] in order to shelter the landlord from an 'under-performing' tenant. So, for example, leases may be shorter and excluded from the renewal provisions of the Landlord and Tenant Act 1954. The landlord may also wish to prohibit sub-letting and impose restrictions on assignment. In America, the courts have held that the tenant is under an implied covenant to occupy the premises and use best efforts in the operation of his business.[13] It would clearly be unjust if the tenant were able to leave the premises vacant or to convert the premises to non-income producing activities, such as storage, and thus deprive the landlord of rent. As well as affecting the rent receivable from the particular tenant, vacant or under-used units could also have an adverse effect on trading within the complex as a whole. A well drafted lease would normally contain express use and occupancy covenants requiring the tenant to occupy the premises and to carry on the specified business throughout the agreed term.[14]

There is also the problem of accounting and honesty. For the tenant, the provision of detailed accounts will be burdensome and may also generate concerns lest the accounts should fall into the hands of competitors.[15] For the landlord, it is clearly critical to have an accurate record of the tenant's trading levels; a task becoming easier, though still burdensome, with the growth in electronic check outs and computing. Usually a clause will provide for periodic accounting.

16.2.1.3 *Sliding Scale Rent (Indexation)*

This is where the rent varies by reference to an independent index, normally a consumer price index (such as Retail Prices Index (RPI)).[16] Many of the early attempts at rent variation were done on this basis. Indexation has certain advantages: the rent can be increased at regular intervals (potentially at every payment date); indexation of rents is fairly easy to operate and is far cheaper than review based on revaluation as indexation does not entail the expense of referring determination of the rent to a third party.

---

[11] [2005] EWCA Civ 868.

[12] See, for example, M Heighton, 'Turn over the issues' (3 February 2002) *EG* 214.

[13] See, for example, *Stoddard v Illinois Improvement & Ballast Co* 113 NE 913, 275 Ill 199 (1916) (SC Ill).

[14] In this country, there would be difficulties in obtaining specific performance of this type of covenant following the House of Lords decision in *Co-operative Insurance Society Ltd v Argyll Stores (Holdings) Ltd* [1998] AC 1 (HL).

[15] The tenant may therefore insist on a confidentiality clause.

[16] In *Riverside Housing Association Ltd v White* [2007] UKHL 20 two indices were referred to, the RPI but also the Index of Average Earnings (as published by HMSO).

Nevertheless, there are drawbacks. The major disadvantage is the lack of suitable indices to be used as the base. Consumer price indices do not reflect fluctuations in the value of real property, only general monetary trends. In times of a buoyant property market this means that the landlord will be under-compensated for the use of the land; in times of recession in property values, the tenant may be paying well over the market rent.[17] A tenant paying rent above the market level will find it difficult to assign the lease other than by paying a reverse premium (a capital sum paid by the tenant to the assignee, reflecting the fact that the assignee is taking on a commitment to pay rent above the market level). There are, however, no suitable property-based indices to be used as an alternative. Further, indexation ignores any local factors, such as the decrease in a retail unit's value caused by the opening of a rival store or the introduction of a one-way traffic system. A variation on standard indexation is to link the review to items that are perceived to reflect changes in business costs, such as labour costs.[18]

Indexation is not commonly used in this country but is used more frequently in other jurisdictions, such as some of the American States (where it is known as linkage rent) and on the Continent. In Italy, for example, rents are typically reviewed annually by reference to an index (not to exceed 75 per cent of the corresponding increase in the Italian consumer price index). In Portugal, rent reviews are conducted by reference to a government cost of living index. In France, indexation operates as a ceiling on the permitted level of increase: landlords are entitled to review the rent at three year intervals, with a maximum increase calculated by reference to the official index of construction costs (unless the landlord can prove an increase of more than 10 per cent in the value of the leased property since the last review). In Belgium, the rent in a commercial lease is usually linked to an inflation index and, if the rent passing differs from the open market rental by more than 15 per cent, the landlord can apply for the rent to be revised by a judge. In these jurisdictions occupational leases are often short, generally being for periods of up to ten years maximum, and often much shorter.[19]

16.2.1.4 Unilateral Increase

A simple form of rent review is for the lease to provide for the rent to be unilaterally increased by the landlord serving a notice stating what the new rent will be. Although this is clearly a very simple and inexpensive form of rent review, it could easily be exploited by landlords in the absence of any ceiling on rent levels. In one case, Glidewell LJ felt that such a provision would not be valid: 'The tenancy agreement itself cannot give a landlord the power to alter a rent unilaterally'.[20] No explanation was given for this comment, however, and it is

---

[17] Indexation may therefore be used in conjunction with market rent review by having an annual RPI review and a five yearly market revaluation: EJS, 'The formula for success' [2006] 70 *Conv* 9.

[18] See the American cases of *Rich v Don-Ron Trousers Corp* 74 Misc 2d 259, 343 NYS 2d 684 (1973) (NYC Civ Ct) where a clause linked to the increased wages of elevator operators was upheld; and *Pittsburgh Allied Fabricators, Inc v Haber* 440 Pa 545, 271 A 2d 217 (1970) (SC Pa) where an option to renew at the same rental subject to 'adjustment for increase in taxes, water, sewage and/or maintenance costs' was held enforceable.

[19] Generally on European lease structures, see S Shone, 'EC leasehold regimes: a comparison' (21 March 1992) *EG* 92; DS Ryland, 'EC Leasing practices: Germany, France, Netherlands and Belgium' (4 July 1992) *EG* 110; RICS, 'International Leasing Structures' (Paper Number 26, May 1993); A Hurndall (ed), *Property in Europe* (London, Butterworths, 1998).

[20] *Dresden Estates Ltd v Collinson* (1988) 55 P & CR 47 (CA) 53.

hard to see what the doctrinal basis for the comment was. Indeed, in the case of *Greater London Council v Connolly*,[21] this kind of clause was upheld. In this case the terms of local authority tenancies provided that the rent was 'liable to be increased or decreased on notice being given'. The provision in the Greater London Council lease reflected a power granted by Parliament in statute.[22] The landlords needed the power to vary the rent in case the level of central government subsidy changed. The tenants were given three months notice of an increase in rent. The Court of Appeal saw no objection to this provision, so long as 'reasonable notice' of the increase was given (as it was on the facts):

> ... this rent was sufficiently certain, even though the amount of it was dependent, in a sense, on the whim of the landlords.[23]

In the *Connolly* case the tenant's main argument centred on claims that the provisions were 'uncertain'. An alternative ground upon which to challenge these clauses could be unconscionability. In an American case, the challenge was presented on this basis, but the clause was still upheld as there was a ceiling on the permissible increase. In *Witmer v Exxon Corp*,[24] a clause in leases of petrol stations provided that landlord could increase the rent by no more than one cent per gallon (rent was based on the number of gallons delivered) and if the tenant objected he could end the lease. The tenants argued, *inter alia*, that the provision was 'unconscionable'. Kaufmann J did not think that the terms were unreasonably favourable to the landlord:

> Exxon was not free under the clause to raise appellants' rents at its whim, but could do so only once during the lease term and to a maximum of one cent per gallon. Appellants were thus assured of a maximum rental for their lease terms.[25]

The fact that there was a ceiling on the increase in *Witmer* was, therefore, important in upholding the clause.

For residential tenancies, such a provision is now likely to be seen as unfair within the Unfair Terms in Consumer Contracts Regulations 1999.[26]

16.2.2 The Modern Rent Review Clause in Commercial Leases

Until the 1950s, commercial property investment was seen as providing fixed interest security. Leases were very long with fixed rents; only 5 per cent had rent reviews, and even then the rental change was usually pre-determined.[27] With the growth in inflation, the idea of rent review began to be explored by investors. By the 1970s the picture had changed completely; most commercial leases, at least of prime property, were for 20–25 years and provided for five yearly upward only review to a market rent. This remained the norm until

---

[21] [1970] 2 QB 100 (CA).

[22] Then, Housing Act 1957 ss 111 and 113; now see Housing Act 1985 s 24.

[23] [1970] 2 QB 100 (CA) 109.

[24] 495 Pa 540, 434 A 2d 1222 (1981) (SC Pa).

[25] 495 Pa 540, 434 A 2d 1222 (1981) (SC Pa) 1228.

[26] SI 1999/2083. OFT, 'Guidance on unfair terms in tenancy agreements' (OFT 356, September 2005) para 3.101. On the Regulations, see ch 4.

[27] S Murdoch, 'Commercial Leases: Future Directions' in S Bright (ed), *Landlord and Tenant Law. Past, Present and Future* (Oxford, Hart, 2006) 84.

the 1990s. The slump in the property market at the beginning of the 1990s gave tenants the opportunity to negotiate the leasehold package on offer, and the 'institutional FRI lease' lost its position of dominance. The reduction in the length of commercial leases seen in the last decade or so has been accompanied by a reduction in the number of leases containing review clauses.[28] Where the lease does provide for review a variety of methods are found. So, for example, turnover rents may be found in retail outlets. But by far the most common approach is, however, still to reset the rent at periodic intervals throughout the lease to a level that reflects market rents current at the time of review.

Although this form of rent review has become the norm, it does have disadvantages. The procedure is time-consuming and may be expensive. Parties will often need to appoint professionals to assist in the valuation exercise and if the review cannot be settled by agreement, and frequently it cannot, the costs will increase still further with the reference to a third party.

16.2.2.1 Principles Underlying the Modern Rent Review Clause

Although review clauses vary enormously in detail, it is possible to identify common features.

Periods of Review

Early clauses tended to contain provision for review every seven, ten or fourteen years. The standard review period is now five years for the institutional market, with three yearly review being more common in the secondary and tertiary markets with shorter leases.[29]

Machinery for Review

A common pattern gives the parties the opportunity to agree the new rent between themselves and, failing agreement, for the matter to be referred to an independent person acting as either an arbitrator or an expert. The expert gives his opinion qua expert in that field, which means that he not only listens to the evidence presented but also has a duty to make his own investigations to determine the appropriate rent. His decision binds the parties contractually and there is no right to appeal. The arbitrator seeks to resolve the dispute by judicial enquiry governed by the Arbitration Act 1996 and there is a right of appeal from his 'award' on limited grounds.[30] Resolution by an expert tends to be quicker and simpler, and may therefore be most appropriate for lower value properties.

Formula for Review

It is usual for rent to be reviewed by reference to an 'open market rent formula', that is the best annual rent reasonably obtainable for the demised premises if let on the open market with vacant possession by a willing landlord to a willing tenant for a specified term.[31] The idea behind this approach is to restore the original bargain between the parties to the lease,

---

[28] The survey of commercial leases by the University of Reading found that over 50% of leases had no rent review: N Crosby, C Hughes and S Murdoch, 'Monitoring the 2002 Code of Practice for Commercial Leases' (ODPM, March 2005) 13.

[29] N Crosby, C Hughes and S Murdoch, 'Monitoring the 2002 Code of Practice for Commercial Leases' (ODPM, March 2005) 13.

[30] For a fuller discussion of this distinction, see M Ross, *Commercial Leases* (London, Butterworths, 1998) G ch 8.

[31] Cf Housing Act 1988 s 14, see below; Landlord and Tenant Act 1954 s 34 (the formula for setting rent on a tenancy renewed under the Act, but note the s 34 wording is not entirely satisfactory, see DN Clarke and JE Adams, *Rent Reviews and Variable Rents* 3rd edn (London, Longman, 1990) 391–2).

taking account not only of inflation but also of matters peculiar to this tenancy of this property:

> The objective of variable rents can be more precisely identified as a method to maintain so far as possible the original bargain struck between the parties, a bargain that would otherwise be radically transformed by the impact of inflation …

If a periodic attempt is made to maintain and restore the original bargain between lessor and lessee it is not only the fall in the value of money by inflation that can be taken into account, for the bargain was made in relation to a particular property, the intrinsic value of which might also have altered and fluctuations in its market value may differ from the rate of inflation.[32]

For the tenant, the inclusion of rent review provisions enables him to negotiate for a longer lease than would otherwise have been possible, as Lord Salmon observed in *United Scientific Holdings Ltd v Burnley BC*:

> Tenants who are anxious for security of tenure require a term of reasonable duration, often two years or more. Landlords, on the other hand, are unwilling to grant such leases unless they contain rent revision clauses which will enable the rent to be raised at regular intervals to what is then the fair market rent of the property demised. Accordingly, it has become the practice for all long leases to contain a rent revision clause providing for a revision of the rent every so many years … Both the landlord and the tenant recognise the obvious, viz. that such clauses are fair and reasonable for each of them … It is for the benefit of the tenant because without such a clause he would never get the long lease which he requires … It is for the benefit of the landlord because it ensures that for the duration of the lease he will receive a fair rent instead of a rent far below the market value of the property which he demises.[33]

As these quotations show, the objective is to restore the original bargain by providing the landlord with a fair rent for the property, not one considerably below the market value, which it would be if left unadjusted. In effect, the review process is intended to restore the original contractual balance. In practice, however, the standard clause often fails to fulfil these objectives. Instead of restoring the original bargain and restoring 'fairness', the clause tends to overcompensate the landlord. This result is not a necessary consequence of this approach to rent review but reflects the negotiating strength often enjoyed by institutional landlords.

The Hypothetical Lease

Whilst the general objective of review clauses can be briefly stated, it is necessary to make detailed provision in the lease as to how this will be implemented. The parties are seeking to agree on a market rent, but of what? Of the property? But then what sort of lease would the property be let on? The assumptions made about the terms of the lease will clearly affect the level of the market rent:

> Although, generally, a particular property has a market value, it does not have a market rent. What does have a market rent is *a leasehold interest in that property*, the duration, terms and conditions of which are defined. The most common type of rent review clause therefore

---

[32] DN Clarke and JE Adams, *Rent Reviews and Variable Rents* 3rd edn (London, Longman, 1990) 6–7.
[33] [1978] AC 904 (HL) 948.

requires the parties to assume that certain property (usually the property which is the subject of the existing lease) is being let in the open market on a particular date (usually referred to as the review date), on a lease for a specified duration and containing specified terms and conditions (usually bearing some relationship to the duration, and terms and conditions, of the existing lease).[34]

As can be seen from this extract, the rent will not necessarily be fixed with reference to the particular lease of the particular property. In addition, it is normal for a review to take certain factors into account (the 'assumptions') and to discount other factors (the 'disregards'). The disregards are primarily concerned to avoid the tenant having to pay an increased rent for benefits that he has brought to the premises. Some of these assumptions and disregards will be artificial and will not reflect the actual lease under review. As Harman J observed in *Sterling Land Office Developments Ltd v Lloyds Bank plc*:

> Any person practising nowadays in the field of landlord and tenant will at once think of a number of questions as to the meaning of these artless phrases [market rent for the demised premises with vacant possession]; for example; in what state are the premises assumed to stand – as they in fact are at the date of review, in proper repair, or in some other, and what, state? For what term are the premises assumed to be available – for 21 years or some other term? On what conditions are the premises offered for letting ... on the 'usual' covenants, on the covenants in the Underlease, or on some other, and if so, what covenants?[35]

The following clause, taken from a precedent supplied by the solicitors Slaughter & May, shows the kinds of assumptions and disregards commonly found in a commercial lease when setting out the basis of reviewing the rent:

> ... 'the open market rental value' means the best[36] annual rent at which the Property could reasonably be expected to be let as a whole or the aggregate of the best annual rents at which the constituent parts of the Property could reasonably be expected to be let (whichever is the greater) on the open market at the relevant review date by a willing landlord to a willing tenant assuming that at that date:
>
> (i)   the Property is fully carpeted and fitted out and equipped for the immediate occupation and use of the hypothetical tenant and all services are available;
>
> (ii)   any rent free period which might be given to the hypothetical tenant on a new letting for fitting out has been given and has expired and no reduction is to be made to take account of it;[37]
>
> (iii) no work has been carried out to the Property or its services which has diminished its rental value;
>
> (iv)   if the Property or its services have been damaged they have been fully rebuilt and reinstated;[38]

---

[34] M Ross, *Commercial Leases* (London, Butterworths, 1998) G ch 1 [2].

[35] [1984] 2 EGLR 135 (Ch) 136.

[36] Often the reference will be to the open market rent rather than the 'best' rent. They may lead to the same result but if it can be shown that some tenants would have been willing to pay over the odds, the best rent may be higher.

[37] On a new letting a tenant may be able to negotiate a reduced rent during the time necessary to get the premises ready for its use. This is to be ignored on review seeing as the tenant is already using the premises.

[38] Usually if the premises are not usable the tenant will not have to pay rent because of a cesser of rent clause (see below) and so this clause is not unfair to the tenant. There may, however, be circumstances when the premises cannot be used yet the rent is not suspended; in this situation this assumption could be hard on the tenant. Tenants may try to amend this so that it only applies if the tenant is in breach.

(v) if access to the Property has been destroyed or damaged it has been fully restored;

(vi) the benefit of all rights or other matters appurtenant to the Property, all Consents and all licences, consents or permissions granted by the Landlord or its predecessors current at the relevant review date are freely available for the hypothetical tenant, its undertenants and their respective successors;

(vii) the Property is available to let for a period of ten years commencing on the relevant review date[39] with vacant possession without a premium[40] but subject to the provisions of this Lease (other than the amount of the principal yearly rent but including the provisions for review)[41]...;

(viii) the Property and its services are in good repair and condition and the covenants in this Lease have been fully performed and observed;[42] and

(ix) the hypothetical tenant can recover all VAT paid in respect of rent as input tax whether as a VAT credit or as a deduction from output tax[43] there being disregarded:

(x) any goodwill attached to the Property by reason of the carrying on there of business by the Tenant; [44]

(xi) any improvement for which the Landlord is not required to pay compensation and which was carried out during the term by the Tenant less than fourteen years before the relevant review date with the consent of the Landlord otherwise than in pursuance of an obligation to the Landlord; [45]

(xii) any effect on rent of the cost of complying with the tenant covenants as to reinstatement in this Lease;

(xiii) any adverse circumstances existing at the relevant review date which might reasonably be regarded as temporary or transient; and

(xiv) so far as may be permitted by law all Statutes which would otherwise restrict or reduce the amount of rent payable;

All assumptions and disregards are false to the extent that they require the parties to imagine something on rent review which is not the case in reality and it can be very hard to predict the valuation consequences of certain assumptions. The difficulties are illustrated in *Dukeminster v Somerfield*.[46] Here, the lease was of a 'mega-warehouse' with an area of 250,000 square feet, an unusually large size which would have no reliable comparables. To deal with this the lease provided that on review the rent would be based on the rent per square foot of a more common size of warehouse, 50,000 square feet. Again there was a problem; in the immediate vicinity, Ross-on-Wye, there were no comparable warehouses of even this smaller type. The lease therefore provided that the notional premises should be

---

[39] See below for discussion of assumptions made about term of hypothetical lease.

[40] This could be a premium payable by the tenant, or one paid by the landlord to the tenant (a reverse premium). Both are to be ignored.

[41] See below: less well worded clauses have created difficulties, excluding not only the actual rent but also the provisions for review.

[42] If the tenant is, for example, in breach of a repairing covenant this would have a negative impact on the market rent. The tenant should not be able to benefit from this.

[43] VAT can have a significant impact on lettings and review clauses will often make provision for this. There may well be an assumption about the VAT status of the landlord.

[44] It is unfair for the landlord to get a higher rent because of the success of the particular tenant.

[45] If the tenant improves the property at its cost, this will put the rent up and it is unfair for the tenant to have to pay more as a result. As to whether improvements made in accordance with duties under the Disability Discrimination Act 1995 should be disregarded, see the discussion in C Edwards and P Krendel, *Institutional Leases in the 21st Century* (London, EG Books, 2007) 74.

[46] *Dukeminster (Ebbgate House One) Ltd v Somerfield Property Co Ltd* (1997) 75 P & CR 154 (CA).

within a 35 mile radius of Ross-on-Wye. At review, a problem arose as to the interpretation of this provision; could the landlord select the North Bristol area, the most expensive letting area within a 35 mile radius, for the siting of the notional premises? The Court of Appeal, rejecting this interpretation in favour of a 'commercial solution' that would operate reasonably, held that the notional premises must be in a location comparable to the site of the actual premises.

Due to the uncertain economic and valuation consequences of assumptions and disregards, the general rule is that it is inadvisable for the hypothetical lease to differ from the actual lease more than is necessary. In the words of Hoffmann J:

> … there is, I think, a presumption that the hypothesis upon which the rent should be fixed upon a review should bear as close a resemblance to reality as possible.[47]

An additional reason for the hypothetical lease to mirror as closely as possible the actual lease (and for assumptions and disregards to be kept to a minimum) is that, if the aim is to restore the initial bargain, and thus fairness, then the tenant should pay the rent on the basis of what he actually has. This raises a further issue. At the time of review, the tenant will have a shorter lease than was initially granted. This will have valuation consequences, and the parties will have to negotiate what assumptions are to be made about the length of lease at each review, drawing on the advice of professional valuers. Rather than assume a lease for the original term, or the unexpired residue of the actual lease, a compromise may well be adopted, such as assuming that the term is the longer of ten years or the unexpired residue.

It is, therefore, often difficult to see what assumptions and disregards should be made in order to restore the contractual balance. Additionally, landlords often seek to 'improve' the terms of a hypothetical lease, that is, to build in assumptions that do not reflect the actual terms and that will lead to a higher rent being payable. 'Improvements' are often made in relation to the user assumptions. If the lease contains a narrow user clause ('to be used only as a grocers'), this will lower the rent as fewer tenants will want the property and those who do will want an allowance for the restricted use clause. Conversely, generous use provisions ('to be used for retail purposes'), will raise the rent and make the property more easy to let. In practice, therefore, a landlord may try to put an onerous clause into the lease, but to assume a more generous one on review. This can make a big valuation difference: in *Plinth Property Investments Ltd v Mott, Hay and Anderson*,[48] the full market rent was £130,455 without any use restriction, but limited to office use it was £89,200. Is it fair to assume a wider user clause on review than is found in the actual lease?

Upward Only Review
The idea of restoring the original contractual balance, of reflecting the market value at review, suggests that the rent should be capable of going up or down. In practice, rent reviews are upward only, so the rent will never fall below that being paid already. This means that if rental values have in fact fallen between the date of the last review and the date of the present

---

[47] *Norwich Union Life Insurance Society v Trustee Savings Bank Central Board* [1986] 1 EGLR 136 (Ch) 137.
[48] (1979) 38 P & CR 361 (CA).

review, the tenant is left paying historically high rents which do not reflect current economic conditions.

For more than a decade from the mid 1990s, upward only rent review (UORR) clauses were on the verge of being banned by the government. The focus on UORR was triggered by the impact of the severe property slump in the late 1980s and early 1990s, leaving many properties 'overrented' (with the tenant paying more than the current market rent because of upward only review).[49] High levels of tenant insolvency coupled with original tenant liability (the first tenant remaining contractually liable even after assignment) meant that many tenants had to pay more than the market rate for properties they no longer occupied. In 1993 a report by Professor Burton argued that UORR was inflationary and presented a serious underlying problem for the British economy in general, and the retail sector in particular.[50] In the same year the Department of the Environment issued a consultation paper on three aspects of commercial leases that were causing concern: UORR, confidentiality clauses and dispute resolution procedures.[51] In a couple of cases around this time dealing with renewal under the 1954 Landlord and Tenant Act, judges allowed upwards and downwards clauses to be inserted into the renewed lease on the grounds of 'fairness', Judge Thompson explaining in *Boots the Chemists Ltd v Pinkland Ltd*:

> If it be the case that we are now in the incipient stages of a prolonged bear market then present-day rents will seem exorbitant later in this decade and in the beginning of the next century. As a consequence, fixed rents, or rents which can only be revised upwards, will wreak the same sort of injustice upon tenants as that which has been suffered by landlords in previous decades when leases contained no provision for rent review at all.[52]

It was in response to government concern over UORR that the first voluntary code of practice for commercial leases was launched in 1995 with the stated objective of encouraging transparency and flexibility in the commercial property market (the '1995 Code of Practice').[53] Although the argument from 'fairness' has a clear logic to it, it overlooks the importance of the UORR to the commercial property market. In various responses to the consultation that continued over the next few years, it was argued that banning UORR would have a serious negative impact on the attractiveness of commercial property as an investment,[54] a point recognised in the following remark of Judge Diamond QC in *Blythewood Plant Hire Ltd v Spiers Ltd* when refusing to insert a two-way clause:

---

[49] By the end of 1992 virtually all investment office properties in Central London (of those included in the property assets measured by the IDP) were either vacant or overrented: Investment Property Forum, 'Response to the DoE consultation paper on Commercial Leases' (London, IPF and Association of British Insurers, 1993).

[50] J Burton, *Retail Rents, Fair and Free Market?* (London, Adam Smith Research Trust, 1992). The report revealed that the rise in rents of retail outlets between 1984 and 1988 was more than double the increase in retail sales and consumer expenditure, crippling many businesses and contributing to the failure of others.

[51] DoE, 'Consultation Paper on Commercial Property Leases' (27 May 1993).

[52] [1992] 28 EG 118 (Cty Ct) 119. See also (the earlier case of) *Janes (Gowns) Ltd v Harlow Development Corporation* [1980] 1 EGLR 52 (Ch) and *Forbouys plc v Newport Borough Council* [1994] 1 EGLR 138 (Cty Ct), where two-way clauses were inserted (in order to be 'fair to both parties', Judge Morgan in *Forbouys*). There was also an unsuccessful private member's bill seeking to outlaw UORR: Upwards-only Rent Review Clauses (Abolition) HC Bill (1993–94) [198].

[53] RICS Commercial Leases Group, *Commercial Property Leases in England and Wales, Code of Practice* (London, Furnival Press, December 1995).

[54] An extract from the RICS response to the government consultation on banning UORR (see n 57) dated 30 Sept 2004, states: 'It is probable that there will be unexpected consequences flowing from the introduction of legislation

A clause in this form would have the result that the landlord's interest would become more difficult to market. It would therefore have an immediate impact on the value of the landlord's interest. On the other hand, the evidence suggested that a tenant would not pay substantially more rent for an upward/downward clause as such a clause is likely to be of little immediate benefit to the tenant.[55]

When in *Abdul Amarjee v Barrowfen Properties Ltd*,[56] an upward/downward clause was inserted into a new tenancy under the Landlord and Tenant Act 1954, the judge also increased the passing rent to reflect the advantage given to the tenant.

Notwithstanding continuing government concern,[57] UORR remains lawful and the pressure for banning it seems to have weakened a little, albeit not disappeared altogether.[58] Even though the reports on the operation of the 2002 Code of Practice (which replaced the 1995 Code of Practice) found that there was greater flexibility and choice in commercial leases generally, UORR stubbornly remained 'virtually universal' in leases with review provisions.[59] This was so notwithstanding the recommendation in the 2002 Code of Practice that landlords should offer alternatives to upward only review.

The persistence of UORR reveals its importance to landlords and the fact that they often have the upper hand in negotiations; a survey carried out by the British Retail Consortium in response to the 2004 consultation found that 88 per cent of retailers wanted UORR banned. Notwithstanding these voices of protest, however, the University of Reading's report on the operation of the 2002 Code of Practice found that most tenants do not ask for an alternative form of review when negotiating and would not, if offered one, pay extra for the benefit.[60] The Business Lease Code 2007 says that the landlord should offer alternative rent review on request 'on a risk-adjusted basis', perhaps allowing up/down reviews with a minimum of the initial rent.[61] Whether this will change current practice is doubtful.

Comparability

The aim on review is to assess the market rent for the hypothetical lease. In standard economic market analysis this would mean looking at the excess of demand or supply and

prohibiting UORRs that would not be conducive to tenant interests or the interests of competitiveness. For example, higher costs of financing property or a restriction in the supply and investment in new property, or of overseas investment in commercial property. This may act to constrain supply and thus undermine choice in the market. There has also been speculation that initial rents might increase in order to protect capital values.'

[55] [1992] 2 EGLR 103 (Cty Ct).

[56] [1993] 2 EGLR 133 (Cty Ct).

[57] The Labour Party Business Manifesto in 2001 described UORR as a 'source of grievance to many in the business community'. In September 2004 the government issued a further consultation paper focusing on UORR which, although presenting a range of alternatives, was perceived to be pushing towards legislative intervention: ODPM, 'Commercial property leases: options for deterring or outlawing the use of upward only rent review clauses' (May 2004).

[58] In March 2005 the government announced that it remained concerned about areas of inflexibility in the commercial property market, in particular in relation to alienation provisions and UORR, but that it had no immediate plans to legislate against UORR.

[59] N Crosby, C Hughes and S Murdoch, 'Monitoring the 2002 Code of Practice for Commercial Leases' (ODPM, March 2005) 13 but the growth in the number of shorter leases has led to fewer leases providing for any rent review.

[60] N Crosby, C Hughes and S Murdoch, 'Monitoring the 2002 Code of Practice for Commercial Leases' (ODPM, March 2005) 307.

[61] Joint Working Group on Commercial Leases, 'The Code for Leasing Business Premises in England and Wales 2007' (2007) para 4.

expected future inflation over the period of review. In practice, surveyors and valuers have assessed market value by looking to 'comparables': recent open market lettings, rent reviews and lease renewals of similar properties in the area let on similar terms. This is a highly subjective process as no two properties are identical. In addition, this method does not take account of zero rents from empty and unlet premises.

Adopting the yardstick of comparability also assumes the existence of an effective market, but for this to exist there needs to be full information on the market. Often confidentiality clauses are used to hide the details of transactions, a practice acknowledged by the 2002 Code of Practice while urging parties to avoid 'unnecessary secrecy'. The Business Lease Code 2007 is silent on this.

16.2.2.2 Principles of Construction

The drafting of rent review clauses to reflect the principles of rent review is difficult. Large valuation differences can turn on seemingly very small points of construction. It can also be difficult to predict the valuation consequences of the various assumptions and disregards made on review. Given the vast amounts of money often at stake, disputes are relatively frequent. In *Secretary of State for the Environment v Associated Newspapers Holdings Ltd*,[62] for example, the tenant's interpretation of the clause would lead to a rent of £530,000 per annum and the landlord's to a rent of £1,575,000 per annum. Judges have emphasised that 'when it comes to construction of rent review clauses in commercial leases "there are no special rules".[63] It is necessary to interpret the particular wording used in the context of the lease as a whole and having regard to relevant circumstances known to both parties. The guidance given by Nicholls LJ in *Basingstoke and Deane v Host Group Ltd* provides the key:

> ... it is axiomatic that what the court is seeking to identify and declare is the intention of the parties to the lease expressed in that clause. Thus, like all points of construction, the meaning of this rent review clause depends on the particular language used interpreted having regard to the context provided by the whole document and the matrix of the material surrounding circumstances. We recognise therefore that the particular language used will always be of paramount importance. Nonetheless, it is proper and only sensible, when construing a rent review clause, to have in mind what is normally the commercial purpose of the clause.[64]

Although it is accepted that interpretation is always a matter of construing the particular words in context, this is by no means a straightforward exercise. As Hoffmann LJ remarked in *Co-operative Wholesale Society Ltd v National Westminster Bank plc*, 'language is a very flexible instrument'.[65] For this reason, courts have often adopted various aids to interpretation. Chief amongst these is to adopt an interpretation that gives effect to the 'commercial purpose' of the agreement. The judgment of Nicholls LJ in *British Gas Corporation v Universities Superannuation Scheme Ltd* sets out this approach:

---

[62] (1996) 72 P & CR 395 (CA).

[63] *Canary Wharf Investments (Three) v Telegraph Group Ltd* [2003] EWHC 1575 (Ch) [10], Neuberger J referring to Hoffmann LJ in *Co-Operative Wholesale Society Ltd v National Westminster Bank plc* [1995] 1 EGLR 99 (CA).

[64] [1988] 1 WLR 348 (CA) 353.

[65] *Co-operative Wholesale Society Ltd v National Westminster Bank plc; Scottish Amicable Life Assurance Society v Middleton Potts; Broadgate Square plc v Lehman Brothers Ltd; Prudential Nominees Ltd v Greenham Trading Ltd* [1995] 1 EGLR 97 (CA)

There is really no dispute that the general purpose of a provision for rent review is to enable the landlord to obtain from time to time the market rental which the premises would command if let on the same terms on the open market at the review dates. The purpose is to reflect the changes in the value of money and real increases in the value of property during a long term. Such being the purpose, in the absence of special circumstances it would in my judgment be wayward to impute to the parties an intention that the landlord should get a rent which was additionally inflated by a factor which had no reference either to changes in the value of money or in the value of property ... Of course, the lease may be expressed in words so clear that there is no room for giving effect to such underlying purpose. Again, there may be special surrounding circumstances which indicate that the parties did intend to reach such an unusual bargain. But in the absence of such clear words or surrounding circumstances, in my judgment the lease should be construed so as to give effect to the basic purpose of the rent review clause and not to confer on the landlord a windfall benefit which he could never obtain on the market if he were actually letting the premises at the review date ...[66]

Although there is general agreement that the correct approach is to interpret the meaning of the particular words used in context having regard to the commercial purpose of the review provisions, there is considerable divergence as to how this plays out in practice. There has been a tendency to refer to various presumptions to give further assistance. The danger is that these presumptions tend to distract from the need to construe the particular words in the particular case. The tension between the need for guiding principles and the need to look at each case individually is revealed in the following quotations. In the first, Sir Browne-Wilkinson VC issues a plea for guidance from the Court of Appeal:

... there is an urgent need to produce certainty in this field. Every year, thousands of rents are coming up for review on the basis of clauses such as the one before me – witness the growing tide of litigation raising the point. Landlords, tenants, and their valuers need to know what is the right basis of valuation without recourse to lawyers, let alone to the courts. The question cannot be left to turn on the terms of each lease without the basic approach being certain.[67]

In the next, Dillon LJ emphasises that construction must turn on the particular wording:

... however valuable guidelines are, the function of the court in each particular case is to construe the particular rent review clause which is in issue in that case.[68]

The Presumption of Reality

In a number of cases, courts have referred to a 'presumption of reality' described by Nicholls LJ in *Basingstoke and Deane v Host Group Ltd*:

Of course rent review clauses may, and often do, require a valuer to make his valuation on a basis which departs in one or more respects from the subsisting terms of the actual existing lease. But if and in so far as a rent review clause does not so require, either expressly or by necessary implication, it seems to us that in general, and subject to a special context indicating otherwise in a particular case, the parties are to be taken as having intended that the notional letting postulated by their rent review clause is to be a letting on the same terms (other than as to quantum of rent) as those still subsisting between the parties in the actual existing lease.

---

[66] [1986] 1 WLR 398 (Ch) 401.
[67] *British Gas Corporation v Universities Superannuation Scheme Ltd* [1986] 1 WLR 398 (Ch) 403.
[68] *Equity & Law Life Assurance Society Plc v Bodfield Ltd* (1987) 54 P & CR 290 (CA).

The parties are to be taken as having so intended, because that would accord with, and give effect to, the general intention underlying the incorporation by them of a rent review clause into their lease.[69]

It is, however, only a presumption and the weight given to it varies according to the context in which it is being used, and, possibly, depending on which party it is most likely to benefit (the courts being, perhaps, more reluctant to apply it where it would favour the landlord).[70]

The Duration of the Hypothetical Term

A review clause will often provide that the hypothetical lease is to be for the same duration as the original term without making it clear whether the assumption is for a lease of the original duration running from the original term commencement (the unexpired portion) or running from the review date (the full original term). The length of the hypothetical lease will affect the level of rent, although whether a shorter lease favours the landlord or tenant will vary according to the facts and market conditions.[71]

There have been several cases in which the courts have referred to the presumption of reality and taken the unexpired portion of the term as the relevant period: *Norwich Union Life Insurance Society v Trustee Savings Bank Central Board*,[72] *Ritz Hotel (London) Ltd v Ritz Casino Ltd* [73] and *St Martins Property Investments Ltd v CIB Properties Ltd*.[74] In the latter case, Aldous LJ said that unless the wording clearly required otherwise, the assumption should reflect the 'real position'. On the facts, the hypothetical lease was to be for 'a term equal in duration to the original term hereby granted' and the Court of Appeal said that review should be based upon the unexpired portion of the actual term which commenced in 1986.

More recently, in *Canary Wharf Investments (Three) v Telegraph Group Ltd*, Neuberger J cautioned against the danger of turning the presumption into a mechanistic rule.[75] In the case before him he held that the hypothetical term of 25 years was to run from the relevant review date, not the date that the original term began. This was the 'natural meaning' of the words used, a 'fair and sensible reading of the relevant provisions of the lease'. He also suggests that the strength of the presumption will depend upon the context in which it is being used, and whether it favours the landlord or tenant (see previous heading).[76]

Provisions About Rent Review

In the 1980s, there were a number of cases in which it was argued that the wording of the review clause required an assumption to be made upon review that there would be no further reviews, even though the leases did in fact provide for future reviews. The leases in issue

---

[69] [1988] 1 WLR 348 (CA) 354.

[70] See *Canary Wharf Investments (Three) v Telegraph Group Ltd* [2003] EWHC 1575 (Ch) [30]-[31]. Neuberger J comments that not relying on the presumption on the facts before him would be unfair (only) to the landlord; contrasting it with other cases in which the presumption may be relied where it would otherwise favour the landlord.

[71] *Canary Wharf Investments (Three) v Telegraph Group Ltd* [2003] EWHC 1575 (Ch).

[72] [1986] 1 EGLR 136 (Ch).

[73] [1989] 2 EGLR 135 (CA).

[74] [1999] 1 L & T R 1 (CA); discussed in PF Smith, 'Presuming Reality or Not Seeking Ambiguities' [1999] *Conv* 346.

[75] [2003] EWHC 1575 (Ch).

[76] [30]–[31].

contained assumptions that the hypothetical lease was on the same terms as the actual lease with an exception for rent; for example, it would state, 'other than the rent'. The question was whether this excluded not only the amount of the current rent but *all* provisions relating to rent (including that there would be a future review). This could make a significant valuation difference as a tenant will have to pay a higher rent for a lease with a fixed rent than one subject to periodic uplift.

Although some judges had adopted literal constructions of these clauses, such as Walton J in *National Westminster Bank plc v Arthur Young McClelland Moores & Co*,[77] Sir Browne-Wilkinson VC rejected an approach that would offend common sense and emphasised the need to have regard to the commercial purpose of the review provisions. This meant that usually it would be correct to assume that there would be future reviews when determining the market rent on review:

> In my judgment the correct approach is as follows: (a) words in a rent exclusion provision which require *all* provisions as to rent to be disregarded produce a result so manifestly contrary to commercial common sense that they cannot be given literal effect; (b) other clear words which require the rent review provision (as opposed to all provisions as to rent) to be disregarded (such as those in the *Pugh* case 264 EG 823) must be given effect to, however wayward the result; (c) subject to (b), in the absence of special circumstances it is proper to give effect to the underlying commercial purpose of a rent review clause and to construe the words so as to give effect to that purpose by requiring future rent reviews to be taken into account in fixing the open market rental under the hypothetical letting.[78]

Although the Vice Chancellor spoke in terms of giving effect to the commercial purpose, in *Canary Wharf Investments (Three) v Telegraph Group Ltd* Neuberger J treated it as an example of an (appropriate) application of the presumption of reality:

> … the presumption [in this kind of case] must apply with particular force. Not only would a valuation based on a hypothetical lease with no reviews be manifestly unfair, but it could only operate in favour of one party – namely the landlord – and it could prevent [sic] very serious valuation difficulties …[79]

Time of the Essence

Review clauses set out the procedure to be followed. Formalistic clauses setting out strict timetables for the service of notices and counter-notices are commonly found in older leases, but led to a rash of cases which had to deal with the question of what happens if one of the parties fails to trigger the review process or serve a required notice within the specified time. As nearly all review clauses are upward, it is the landlord who loses out if the failure to meet a timetable strictly means that there can be no review until the next review date; but there can be other procedural 'misses' that are disadvantageous to a tenant, such as a failure to serve a timely counter-notice challenging the landlord's proposed revised rent. To minimise these problems, modern leases are usually informal and do not set out strict timetables.

Prior to the leading case, *United Scientific Holdings Ltd v Burnley BC*, there had been a number of cases in which the outcome turned on fine distinctions. Eschewing these, the

---

[77] [1985] 1 EGLR 61 (Ch).
[78] *British Gas Corporation v Universities Superannuation Scheme Ltd* [1986] 1 WLR 398 (Ch) 403.
[79] [2003] EWHC 1575 (Ch) [30].

House of Lords held that the presumption is that time is not of the essence in relation to the procedural steps for rent review. In the words of Lord Diplock:

> ... the timetable specified in a rent review clause for completion of the various steps for determining the rent payable in respect of the period following the review date is not of the essence of a contract.[80]

Nevertheless, this presumption will give way to 'clear and explicit'[81] contra-indications in the wording or in how this provision interacts with other provisions in the lease or in the surrounding circumstances. Where there are such contra-indications time is of the essence.[82]

The sort of clause that can rebut the presumption is a deeming provision, as in *Starmark Enterprises Ltd v CPL Distribution Ltd* where the Court of Appeal held that time was of the essence where the lease provided:

> If the lessees shall fail to serve a counter-notice within the period aforesaid they shall be deemed to have agreed to pay the increased rent specified in the rent notice.[83]

The landlord had served a notice proposing a new annual rent of £84,800. The tenant served its counter-notice, proposing that the new rent should be £52,725, more than two months later, where the lease had required the counter-notice to be served within one month. The effect of the deeming provision was therefore that the landlord's proposed rent became the new rent.

In *First Property Growth Partnership Ltd v Royal and Sun Alliance Property Services Ltd* the review clause required the landlord's trigger notice to be served by a specified time and 'not at any other time'; a notice served one day late was held to be invalid as the wording made time of the essence.[84]

As Ross notes,

> ... the plethora of largely irreconcilable cases suggest that it is essential, where the parties intend that time should *not* be of the essence, that this should be specifically stated.[85]

Headline Rents and Incentives

On a new letting, a landlord may offer various incentives to attract a new tenant. These incentives can include the grant of rent free periods. Rent free periods may be given to reflect the time that it will take the tenant to fit out the premises for occupation, or for finding sub-tenants if the intention is to sub-let. A quite different reason for a rent free period is as an

---

[80] [1978] AC 904 (HL) 930.

[81] Lord Diplock had referred to 'contra-indications' but Neill LJ in *Bickenhall Engineering Co Ltd v Grant Met Restaurants Ltd* [1995] 1 EGLR 110 (CA) said that they must be clear and explicit.

[82] For the interrelationship between rent review and break clauses and time being of the essence, see *Central Estates Ltd v Secretary of State for the Environment* [1997] 1 EGLR 239 (CA) (it was held that time was of the essence for the rent review as the parties intended that the tenant should be able to consider whether to exercise the break once it knew that the rent was to be reviewed). There are other procedural defects that can occur. For problems with notices, see *Norwich Union Life Insurance Society v Sketchley plc* [1988] 2 EGLR 126 (Ch); *Commission for New Towns v R Levy & Co Ltd* [1990] 2 EGLR 121 (Ch). For the validity of the tenant's counter-notice, see *Nunes v Davies Laing & Dick Ltd* [1986] 1 EGLR 127 (Ch).

[83] [2001] EWCA Civ 1252, [2002] Ch 306.

[84] [2002] EWCA Civ 1687, [2003] 1 All ER 533.

[85] M Ross, *Commercial Leases* (London, Butterworths, 1998) G ch 2 [83].

inducement to enter the lease; here the length of the rent free period is unrelated to the time required to fit out the premises and is simply part of the deal. A landlord may well prefer to have a rent free period of, say, one year, and a rental of £20,000 per annum thereafter until review than, say, a rental of £16,000 per annum from day one, even though the actual income over the first five year period is the same. The longer rent free period produces a higher 'headline rent' which can be advantageous to the landlord as a basis for future review (especially if there is an upward only clause), and as a basis for comparability, as well increasing the capital value of the reversion.[86]

Whereas there is a degree of consensus that it may be fair on review to disregard the effect of rent free periods given for genuine fitting out of the premises before a tenant can move in[87] (a fitting out period being inappropriate as the tenant is already occupying at the review date), there is much less agreement about whether rent free periods used as inducements (and other incentives) ought to be disregarded. The point is that these inducements are part of the overall package, the going rate for the property, and to look only to the headline rent falsely inflates the letting value of the premises. The differences are significant; in one of the cases heard as part of the *Co-operative Wholesale v National Westminster* appeal, *Broadgate Square v Lehman Brothers Ltd*, the headline rent would be a little over £7 million, while a rent adjusted to take into account the inducement element of the rent free period would be just short of £5.3 million. In his judgment, Hoffmann LJ stated that:

> ... a clause which deems the market rent to be the headline rent obtainable after a rent-free period granted simply to disguise the fall in the rental value of the property is not in accordance with the basic purpose of a rent review clause. It enables a landlord to obtain an increase in rent without any rise in property values or fall in the value of money, but simply by reason of changes in the way the market is choosing to structure the financial packaging of the deal.[88]

In the absence of clear and unambiguous language, a court will not, therefore, be ready to construe a review clause as having the effect of looking to the headline rent only.

16.2.3 Rent Review in the Residential Sector

16.2.3.1 Private Sector

Until 1988 most residential lettings were regulated by the Rent Act 1977 with its system of 'fair rents' (see chapter 15). There was, therefore, very little scope for the parties to agree contractually how the rent would be varied as any such provisions could effectively be avoided by a regulated tenant applying for registration of a fair rent. Since the introduction of the Housing Act 1988, however, it has been possible for the parties to include rent review

---

[86] For an explanation of the relationship between headline rents and capital values, see M Brett, *Property and Money* 2nd edn (London, Estates Gazette, 1997) ch 50.

[87] In *99 Bishopsgate v Prudential Assurance* (1985) 273 EG 984 (CA) the Court of Appeal allowed, on the construction of the review clause, a significant reduction in rent for a fitting out period. This was widely perceived as inequitable to the landlord and clauses are now usually drafted to disregard fitting out periods that would be granted to new tenants.

[88] *Co-operative Wholesale Society Ltd v National Westminster Bank plc; Scottish Amicable Life Assurance Society v Middleton Potts; Broadgate Square plc v Lehman Brothers Ltd; Prudential Nominees Ltd v Greenham Trading Ltd* [1995] 1 EGLR 97 (CA) 99.

provisions within the lease. Even in the absence of such contractual agreement, there is a statutory procedure for rent variation aimed at enabling the landlord to recover the market rental for the premises.

The policy underlying the Housing Act 1988 is to permit the parties to agree the rent and any provision for reviewing it. Exactly how the provisions operate depends on the kind of tenancy involved.

In relation to periodic assured tenancies (including periodic shortholds), any rent review mechanism built into the lease – whether providing for fixed uplift or simply the machinery for reviewing the rent[89] – will govern all rent variations (subject to the Court of Appeal decision in *Bankway Properties Ltd v Pensfold-Dunsford*):[90] see Figure 16.1.

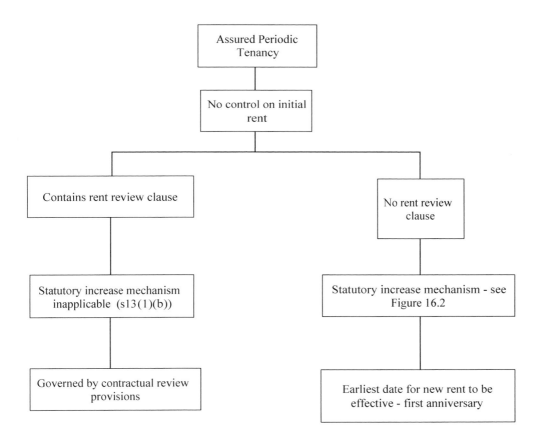

Figure 16.1: Rent Review in Assured Periodic Tenancy

---

[89] *Contour Homes Ltd v Rowen*, [2007] EWCA Civ 842.
[90] [2001] EWCA Civ 528, [2001] 1 WLR 169.

In *Bankway Properties* the tenancy provided for an initial rent of £4,690 per annum, with a review clause that provided for the rent payable to be increased to £25,000 per annum, well above the market rent and well beyond the means of the tenants, who were on housing benefit. It was clear that the review clause was invoked as a means of recovering possession and Arden LJ held it to be ineffective as it was 'in substance an unlawful contracting out or evasion of an Act of Parliament'.[91]

If there is no contractual provision for changing the rent level, the landlord can take advantage of the statutory increase mechanism set out in the Housing Act 1988 section 13. Figure 16.2 shows how this mechanism works.

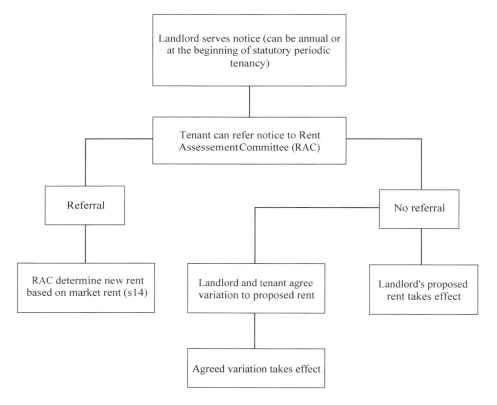

Figure 16.2: Statutory Increase Mechanism for Periodic Tenancy, Housing Act 1988 sections 13 and 14

The process is triggered when the landlord proposes an increased rent by serving notice in a prescribed form. This notice must state the date that the new rent is to take effect, which by section 13(3) must as a minimum be a period beginning not earlier than:

---

[91] For fuller discussion of the 'contracting out' ideas developed in *Bankway Properties*, see S Bright, 'Avoiding Tenancy Legislation: Sham and Contracting Out Revisited' (2002) 62 *CLJ* 146.

(a)   in the case of a yearly tenancy, six months;

(b)   in the case of a tenancy where the period is less than a month, one month; and

(c)   in any other case, a period equal to the period of the tenancy.

The parties are given the option of agreeing the rent increase between themselves, either by the tenant accepting the landlord's proposals as to the new rent or by reaching mutual agreement. Failing this, the tenant can refer the notice to a Rent Assessment Committee (RAC) which must consider the rent at which the 'dwelling-house concerned might reasonably be expected to be let in the open market by a willing landlord under an assured tenancy'.[92] In reaching its decision the RAC must take account of the period of the tenancy, the terms of the tenancy and the level of security the tenant has.[93] It must also disregard:

(a)   the effect of any improvements carried out by the tenant,

(b)   the fact that there is a sitting tenant, and

(c)   any reductions in value due to breaches by the tenant.

In effect, this formula is seeking a market rent in a similar way to that common in commercial rent reviews.

During a fixed term assured tenancy, the statutory mechanism for changing the rent level cannot operate, the only way that the rent can be varied during the fixed term is by the inclusion of rent review provisions within the tenancy agreement. This is shown by Figure 16.3. At the expiry of the fixed term, a statutory periodic tenancy arises under the Housing Act 1988 section 5(2) and the section 13 statutory increase mechanism can be invoked.[94]

The thrust of the Housing Act 1988 is, therefore, to encourage the parties either to include review procedures within the letting agreement or to use the statutory mechanism for increase. Either way, rents are likely to follow market rents closely. The Housing Act 1988 represents a marked change in the attitude towards private sector tenancies. Before the Act, review clauses were exceptional in this sector.

What method of review will be appropriate for residential lettings? It is clear that the periodic revaluation method used in commercial lettings is inappropriate: it is expensive to operate, too slow to respond to market changes (important in the shorter lets found in the residential sector) and too complex. Review procedures need to be far simpler and cheaper to operate in the residential sector. Various forms of clause have been proposed, of varying complexity: indexation linked to the Retail Prices Index;[95] agreement between the parties, failing which the issue is referred to a valuer;[96] and a landlord's unilateral notice of

---

[92] Housing Act 1988 s 14(1).

[93] That is, whether a notice has been served under any of Grounds 1 to 5 of Sch 2 of the Housing Act 1988.

[94] If there was a review provision in the fixed term tenancy it is arguable that this should continue to apply, to the exclusion of the statutory increase mechanism, because s 5(3)(e) of the Housing Act 1988 provides that the terms of the statutory periodic tenancy are to be the same as those of the fixed term tenancy (with an exception for termination provisions). It may be that the timing provided for by the contractual review would be inconsistent with the term of the statutory periodic tenancy. S 13(1)(a) states, however, that the statutory mechanism applies to the statutory periodic tenancy and the exclusion of tenancies that contain review provisions is in s 13(1)(b) and applies only to 'other' periodic tenancies.

[95] See EH SCammell (ed), *Precedents for the Conveyancer* (London, Sweet & Maxwell, 1970–) Vol 1, 5–99.

[96] See EH SCammell (ed), *Precedents for the Conveyancer* (London, Sweet & Maxwell, 1970–) Vol 1, 5–100 and 5–104.

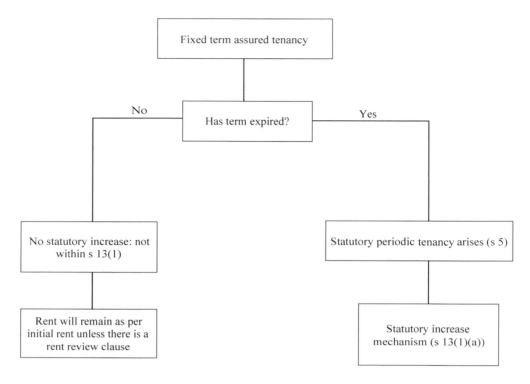

Figure 16.3: Rent Review for Fixed Term and Statutory Assured Tenancy

increase.[97] The guidance from the Office of Fair Trading (OFT) on the application of the Unfair Terms in Consumer Contract Regulations 1999 to tenancies suggests that rent variations clauses are most likely to be fair if:

(a)   they specify the amount and timing of any rent increases (they will probably then be regarded as 'core' terms); or

(b)   they permit increases linked to an index outside the landlord's control, such as the retail price index; or

(c)   they allow for objective review by a person unconnected with the landlord.

A fair term should also give the tenant sufficient notice of increase so that he can choose to leave before the increase is effective if it is not acceptable.[98]

As housing association lettings are now within the private sector, their rent review provisions need to follow the Housing Act 1988.

---

[97] See EH Scammell (ed), *Precedents for the Conveyancer* (London, Sweet & Maxwell, 1970–) Vol 1, 5–103; see further DN Clarke and JE Adams, *Rent Reviews and Variable Rents* 3rd edn (London, Longman, 1990) ch 17; D Clarke, 'Rent Reviews in Residential Tenancies' [1989] *Conv* 111.

[98] OFT, 'Guidance on unfair terms in tenancy agreements' (OFT 356, September 2005) paras 3.102–3.103.

The first House of Lord's case involving interpretation of a review clause in a residential tenancy suggests that a quite different approach is adopted than for commercial rent review provisions. In *White and White v Riverside Housing Association Ltd* the housing association tenancy provided for an annual rent increase by reference to indices on the first Monday in June on 28 days' notice.[99] When the landlord sought possession from the tenants on the grounds of rent arrears, they challenged possession on the basis that the rent had not been increased in accordance with the terms of the tenancy agreement. In 2000 there was no rent increase but the landlord, after consultation with a tenants' association, decided to increase the rent in April 2001. Thereafter April became the date for the annual rent increase; this was a better time of year for the landlord to operate the rent increases. For the tenants, the impact was, in effect, to have deferred the June increases by ten months. The change was therefore advantageous to the tenants. Notwithstanding the fact that the consequences to the landlord were, in Sir Peter Gibson's words, 'very serious', the Court of Appeal had held that the rent increases in 2001 and subsequent years were invalid. The presumption that time was not of the essence did not assist the landlord here because what was in issue was the date for the rent increase itself rather than the review process. The House of Lords took a different approach. Lord Neuberger noted that the question as to whether time was of the essence would be relevant only if the contract meant that the landlord could increase the rent only on the first Monday in June.[100] However, as a matter of interpretation, this was not what the tenancy agreement provided: it enabled the landlord to increase the rent once in any year from the first Monday in June on any date from and including the first Monday in June provided it gives 28 days' prior notice.

Although the outcome turns on the particular wording in the tenancy agreement what is especially interesting is the emphasis placed by Lord Neuberger on the differences between this kind of case and the commercial rent review clauses with which courts have become much more familiar. He noted that in a commercial context, the interpretation is more likely to be that the landlord can increase the rent in any year only on the first Monday in June, but that the requirement of 28 days' notice is not essential and so the landlord can give a late notice to increase the rent from that date. He identified three features which distinguish this case:

(a) The non-commercial context: the landlord was a publicly funded charity and the tenants have little experience of interpreting legal documents. This meant that an interpretation giving a moveable review date was sensible and fair.

(b) The rent was reviewed by reference to a 'cost of living' increase, rather than the commercial lease norm of valuation at the review date (which makes the particular review date important).

(c) The drafting of the clauses relating to the rent review was 'quite different from that which one would expect to find in any commercial lease'.

The end result is very welcome; it would have been most unfortunate and unjust to the landlord if the rent increases were not effective. Further, although the actual result in this case

---

[99] [2007] UKHL 20.

[100] But the presumption would not then assist on these facts: it does not enable a court to rewrite a tenancy agreement which provides for a rent increase on a specific date: [2007] UKHL 20 [25].

depended not on general presumptions but on the particular wording used, it is in line with the outcomes in many commercial cases where time is presumed not to be of the essence.

16.2.3.2 Local Authority Sector

Rent setting in the local authority sector has already been discussed and rents are now being adjusted in line with the new rent restructuring policy. There are, of course, general financial controls on the behaviour of local authorities through the auditing powers of the Audit Commission. In practice it is difficult and unusual for an individual tenant to mount a legal challenge in relation to the amount of rent set. Any challenge would be through public law: a judicial review application, or, if it is alleged that there has been maladministration, an application to the Local Government Ombudsman.[101] It is only if a decision to raise rents is *Wednesbury* unreasonable that a judicial review application would succeed.[102] In effect this means that the courts remain outside the political arena and allow local authorities a broad discretion in the setting and raising of rents, intervening only if the local authority's decision is so unreasonable that no reasonable authority could have come to it, or if it is ultra vires or absurd. An extreme example is *Backhouse v Lambeth LBC* where the local authority passed a resolution under the Housing Act 1957 section 111(1) increasing the rent of an unoccupied and unfit house by £18,000 a week.[103] The increase was made so that the local authority could find a way around the Housing Finance Act 1972 which required the local authority to raise 'average' rents. It was held to be ultra vires as being unreasonable and irrational.

16.2.4 Rent Review in Agricultural Leases

With agricultural tenancies falling under the Agricultural Holdings Act 1986 (AHA 1986), the parties are able to refer the rent payable from the next termination date to arbitration. If the arbitrator is involved the statutory formula requires him to take account of the productive and earning capacity of the holding, and to have regard to the current level of rents for comparable lettings, but in doing so he is directed to disregard the impact of scarcity value.[104] In so far as this represents an attempt to break the link between rent reviews and the free market, the agricultural review machinery under the AHA 1986 is perhaps more appropriately considered as a form of rent control rather than market based review.

The farm business tenancy (FBT) regime under the Agricultural Tenancies Act 1995 (ATA 1995) moves away from rent control. The provisions in the AHA1986 were thought by many to be overly complex and, in place of them, parties to a FBT are free to agree their own rent review mechanisms within the lease. In the early years of the FBT regime, rents under FBTs were significantly higher than those under the AHA regime. Recently, these rents have come closer together, although it is still the case that FBT rents are generally at a higher level, as seen in Table 16.1. There is no control on initial rent fixing. The parties can agree that there is to be no review of rent[105] or agree a rent review mechanism by which the

---

[101] In complaint 03/B/13806 against *Oxford City Council* (2006) the LGO made a finding of maladministration where a council had overcharged the tenant for more than a decade and ordered a refund of around £3,600 plus £1,000 for his time, trouble, and frustration in pursuing the complaint.

[102] *Associated Provincial Picture Houses, Ld v Wednesbury Corporation* [1948] 1 KB 223 (CA).

[103] (1972) 116 Sol Jo 802 (QB).

[104] Agricultural Holdings Act 1986 s 12 and Sch 2. Cf the notion of scarcity in the residential sector, see ch 15.

Table 16.1: Average Rents (£ per Hectare) 2001–06

Type of holding	Full Agricultural Tenancy[a]		Farm Business Tenancy[b]		Change 2001–6	
	2001	2006	2001	2006	FAT	FBT
Cereal	124.39	127.65	182.30	148.73		
General cropping	140.66	137.85	214.78	167.20		
Dairy	137.61	134.41	173.06	168.33		
Cattle and sheep (less favoured area)	31.42	38.69	52.90	42.09		
Cattle and sheep (lowland)	102.37	107.94	112.41	88.99		
All	**111.33**	**113.98**	**161.33**	**133.21**	**+2.4%**	**−17.5%**

Source: Compiled from DEFRA, Tenanted Land Survey – England 2006, Summary of Results
[a]Not defined by DEFRA but presumably referring to tenancies within the AHA 1986
[b]Of one year or more

rent is to be varied by a specified amount or in accordance with an objective formula which does not preclude a reduction,[106] or agree that the rent (which can go up or down) is to be referred to an independent expert whose decision is final.[107] This prevents an upward only review clause from being effective.

If there is no such rent review mechanism in the lease, either party can request the rent to be reviewed by arbitration at three yearly intervals.[108] The arbitrator can increase or reduce the rent payable on an open market basis as between willing parties according to the ATA 1995 section 13(2):

> … the rent properly payable in respect of a holding is the rent at which the holding might reasonably be expected to be let on the open market by a willing landlord to a willing tenant, taking into account (subject to subsections (3) and (4) below) all relevant factors, including (in every case) the terms of the tenancy (including … [review dates] but not those which (apart from this section) preclude a reduction in the rent during the tenancy).

Subsections 13 (3) and (4) state that in determining the open market rent the arbitrator is to disregard:

(a) any increase in rental value due to tenant's improvements,[109]
(b) the impact on rent of the fact that the tenant is already in occupation,[110]

---

[105] ATA 1995 s 9(a).
[106] ATA 1995 s 9(b).
[107] ATA 1995 s 9(c).
[108] ATA 1995 s 10.
[109] other than –
    (a) any tenant's improvement provided under an obligation which was imposed on the tenant by the terms of his tenancy or any previous tenancy and which arose on or before the beginning of the tenancy in question,
    (b) any tenant's improvement to the extent that any allowance or benefit has been made or given by the landlord in consideration of its provision, and
    (c) any tenant's improvement to the extent that the tenant has received any compensation from the landlord in respect of it (ATA 1995 s 13(2)).

(c)   and any lowering of rent caused by any dilapidation or deterioration caused or
      permitted by the tenant. [111]

As shown in the Table 16.1, the average rents for agricultural holdings and farm business
tenancies differ. Average rents also differ according to the use of the land. Further, in the
period 2001-06 average rents for FBTs fell by more than 17 per cent whereas those for
agricultural holdings rose by more than 2 per cent.

16.2.5 Judicial Variation of Leasehold Terms?

In the absence of any provision for an increase in rent, is there anything a landlord can do if
he is locked into a lease with a rent now considerably below market rent? With an assured
periodic letting in the residential sector, the landlord can now invoke the statutory increase
mechanism in Housing Act 1988 section 13. There is no comparable statutory provision for
commercial lettings. Imagine a 99 year lease entered into in 1920 (when rent review clauses
were exceptional) and which provided for an annual rental of £3,000. Given the huge
increases in rental figures since then, the true market level would now be many times greater.
To restrict the landlord to recovering rent at 1920 levels seems unfair as the landlord is being
under-compensated for the use of his land at great advantage to the tenant.

    From time to time it has been argued that courts do (or at least should) have power to
alter contract terms when there has been such a change in circumstances that the strict
terms operate harshly. Support for this approach can be drawn from the cases of
Staffordshire Area Health Authority v South Staffordshire Waterworks Co[112] and *Pole Properties
v Feinberg.*[113] Neither case involved rent revision in leases. In the *Pole Properties* case, a lease
provided for the tenant to pay two-sevenths of the cost of fuel, a rate calculated by reference
to the floor area of the tenant's flat in relation to the whole building. When an additional
building was added the tenant argued that two-sevenths was now a disproportionate share
of the total cost and the Court of Appeal agreed with this; Lord Denning MR saying that as
the situation had radically changed, the terms of the lease no longer applied and the court
would do what was fair and reasonable in the all the circumstances.

    It is, however, very unlikely that a landlord would be able to get a revision of the rent
payable in a lease in the circumstances envisaged earlier; the courts have repeatedly stressed
that frustration cannot be used to strike down an improvident bargain. Nor have the courts
been willing to develop other ways to re-open long term contracts that have become
imbalanced over time. In *British Movietonews Ltd v London and District Cinemas*, Lord
Simon said:

> The parties to an executory contract are often faced, in the course of carrying it out, with a
> turn of events which they did not at all anticipate – a wholly abnormal rise or fall in prices, a

---

[110] ATA 1995 s 13(4)(a).
[111] ATA 1995 s 13(4)(b).
[112] [1978] 1 WLR 1387 (CA). In this case, the Court of Appeal held that a company was able to terminate an
agreement to supply water at a fixed price on 'reasonable notice'; even though the agreement was expressed to be
binding 'at all times hereafter'. The cost of supply had risen to over eighteen times the contract price.
[113] (1982) 43 P & CR 121 (CA).

sudden depreciation of currency, an unexpected obstacle to the execution, or the like. Yet this does not in itself affect the bargain which they have made.[114]

Frustration has been argued in a case analogous to long term leases with no rent review provisions, namely where the original lease was granted for a fixed rent and contained an option to renew. In *Bracknell Development Corporation v Greenlees Lennerds Ltd*, the original 21 year lease contained an option to renew 'at a full and fair market rent'.[115] Counsel for the landlord argued that the new lease should contain provisions for periodic review of the rent, the effect of inflation making a fixed rent so unfair that the doctrine of frustration would apply. This was rejected. However unfair the lease may be over time it is, therefore, very unlikely that the landlord will be able to obtain any relief.

16.3 Overpaying the Rent

If, by mistake, the tenant makes an overpayment of rent (or service charge), it may well be possible to recover the excess in the law of restitution. Where the mistake is one of fact, recovery has long been possible, but it is only following the House of Lords' decision in *Kleinwort Benson v Lincoln CC* that recovery has been possible where the tenant has paid under a mistaken view of the law.[116] In *Nurdin & Peacock v Ramsden* the tenant overpaid several instalments of rent.[117] Some of these were paid under a mistake of fact. The later overpayments were made after the tenant had become aware of a possible overpayment but on the advice of its lawyers who had said that if it turned out to be an overpayment it would be recoverable, and that it was better to pay the disputed rent than risk forfeiture of the lease. Neuberger J, applying *Kleinwort Benson*, held that the tenant was entitled to recover.

16.4 Ensuring Payment

Tenants have a contractual duty to pay rent. In the event of default, the landlord will usually have not only the right to recover the debt but the right to terminate the tenancy and repossess the property (although if the tenancy is statutorily protected this right may be heavily qualified). Eviction should, however, be a last resort. In the residential sector there are huge social and economic costs associated with eviction[118] which are not balanced by any guaranteed benefit as there is nothing to say that the next tenant will be any better positioned to pay the rent. In the commercial sector, eviction is unlikely to lead to the arrears being paid and the loss of business premises may lead the tenant into bankruptcy or receivership, where the landlord will be just another unsecured creditor.

Thus, alternatives have been adopted which seek to guarantee the recovery of the arrears. This section looks at things that the landlord can do to try to ensure that payments are

---

[114] [1952] AC 166 (HL) 185.
[115] [1981] 2 EGLR 105 (Ch).
[116] *Kleinwort Benson Ltd v Lincoln City Council* [1999] 2 AC 349 (HL).
[117] *Nurdin & Peacock plc v DB Ramsden & Co Ltd* [1999] 1 WLR 1249 (Ch).
[118] The housing charity, Shelter, estimates that the typical cost of evicting a tenant for rent arrears is £1,900–£3,200: DCLG, 'Guide on Effective Rent Arrears Management' (August 2006).

made; the next section looks at remedies for default, with the exception of eviction which is discussed in chapters 19 and 20.

16.4.1 References

It is standard practice in both the commercial property sector and the private residential sector for the landlord to take up references on the tenant prior to the letting. The reference will seek information on the financial standing of the tenant and on whether he is likely to be a good and reliable tenant in other ways.

16.4.2 Guarantees

The landlord may require a guarantor to join in the lease so as to guarantee the due performance of the tenant's obligations. This is most likely to occur with commercial lettings, but may also be required in the case of residential lettings.

In a commercial setting, a guarantor is likely to be required if the tenant is an individual, a newly formed company, does not have a large paid up capital or a track record of operating at a sufficiently high level of profit to give adequate cover for the rent, or if it is an overseas company. In practice, the guarantor is often the parent company or an associated company.

The extent of the guarantor's liability will depend upon when the lease is entered into.[119] If it is an 'old lease', entered into before 1996, the obligations of a guarantor will last throughout the term of the lease – so, unless the guarantee is expressly limited, it will not only apply to cover the original tenant (with whom he presumably has some kind of relationship), but will apply to any assignees who may be totally unknown to the guarantor.[120] In *Junction Estate Ltd v Cope*, for example, the guarantors were the directors of T1 but could still be required to make payments on the default of T2.[121] On the facts, however, the only rent default occurred when T2 stayed in possession after the expiry of the contractual lease and the guarantor's liability did not extend that far: unless it is clear in the wording of the guarantee that the parties intend liability to continue beyond the contractual lease (for example, to cover a renewed lease) the guarantor's liability ends with the contractual lease.[122]

The Landlord and Tenant (Covenants) Act 1995 has made a number of changes that assist guarantors (generally on this, see chapter 18). Before a guarantor can be sued he must be served with a section 17 problem notice,[123] and he will also have a right to apply for an overriding lease in accordance with section 19 if he pays the sums claimed in the section 17 notice. By section 18 he will not be liable for charges stemming from post-1995 variations to

---

[119] See generally on the guarantor's liability, ch 18.

[120] Eg *Cheverell Estates Ltd v Harris* [1998] 1 EGLR 27 (QB).

[121] (1974) 27 P & CR 482 (QB).

[122] And in the event of ambiguity the guarantee will be construed against the landlord. See *Junction Estate Ltd v Cope* (1974) 27 P & CR 482 (QB); *A Plesser & Co Ltd v Davis* [1983] 2 EGLR 70 (QB).

[123] It is not necessary for the landlord also to serve a problem notice on the tenant in order to preserve the right to sue the guarantor: *Cheverell Estates Ltd v Harris* [1998] 1 EGLR 27 (QB).

the lease. In the case of a lease entered into after 1995, the guarantor will be released from liability when the lease is assigned by the tenant.

The guarantor is liable not only to pay the initial rent reserved, but also for any increased rent payable as a result of rent review. For example, in *Torminster Properties Ltd v Green*, property was let to C Ltd at a rent of £7,100 per annum, with G and K acting as guarantors.[124] The rent review date was 24 June 1978. C Ltd was wound up in November 1978 and the lease was surrendered in April 1979. The amount of the new rent was not settled at £13,500 per annum until January 1980, but G and K were nonetheless held liable to pay this substantially increased amount of rent between the time when C Ltd stopped paying and surrender (a guarantor's liability ending on surrender as to future liabilities).

16.4.3 Security Deposits

It is common in both the residential and commercial sectors for the landlord to require a deposit to be paid at the beginning of the tenancy: deposits are taken in 82 per cent of assured shorthold tenancies.[125] The deposit provides security to the landlord to cover possible default by the tenant, and can be drawn against to cover things such as non-payment of rent, breakages and so on. The security deposit is to be distinguished from a holding deposit which is sometimes required by residential landlords in order to reserve a property and which serves a quite different function.

16.4.3.1 Commercial Deposits

With commercial lettings, the deposit will often cover three to six months rent and it is common to enter into some form of rent deposit deed to formalise the terms of the payment. It will, for example, set out how the money is held (for example, in a joint names interest bearing bank account) and the circumstances in which the landlord can draw on the account. The Occupier Guide attached to the Business Lease Code 2007 suggests that the deposit should be held in an account that belongs to the tenant (escrow or stakeholder account) in case the landlord becomes insolvent, and that interest accrues to the tenant.[126]

16.4.3.2 Residential Deposits

In the residential sector the taking of deposits is often an area of contention between the landlord and tenant but until recently there has been no regulation of deposit taking. The two biggest problems are the impact that it has upon access, and disputes that arise over returning deposits.

Deposits and Access

For those on low incomes the requirement to pay a deposit before the tenancy begins can make it very difficult to access property, especially as the private sector is increasingly being used to solve the problems of housing shortage and welfare payments do not include a sum for deposits. In relation to Rent Act 1977 regulated tenancies, landlords could only require

---

124 [1983] 1 WLR 676 (CA).
125 PKF Consultants, 'Tenancy Deposits Implementation. Scoping Study Report' (ODPM, August 2005).
126 Joint Working Group on Commercial Leases, 'The Code for Leasing Business Premises in England and Wales 2007' (2007), Occupier Guide Tip 6.

the payment of a deposit representing one-sixth of the annual rental and it had to be reasonable in relation to the potential liability in respect of which it was paid.[127] Under the Housing Act 1988 there is no such limitation, although it is usual to require only the payment of four weeks' rent as a deposit. Many landlords are already reluctant to take on tenants in receipt of housing benefit because of the delays that are commonplace in its payment, and the tenant's inability to put up a deposit makes it even harder to find accommodation. For this reason, a number of deposit guarantee schemes have been established by local groups, which often work by offering loans to prospective tenants who are in receipt of welfare benefit. Until 2006 there was also a national charity, the National Rent Deposit Forum (NRDF) that supported local rent deposit schemes and encouraged new schemes to develop. According to the Housing Minister, Yvette Cooper,

> … the number of rent deposit schemes has increased and been mainstreamed within housing advice and homelessness prevention. Recent local authority homelessness survey returns summarised in Survey of English Local Authorities About Homelessness Policy Briefing 13 which is available on the ODPM website showed that 87 per cent. of responding local authorities have established rent deposit/bond schemes as part of their homelessness prevention services.[128]

Regulating Deposits

Problems also arise at the end of the tenancy. Landlords have a reputation for not returning deposits quickly (if at all) to tenants. This reputation is not totally unfounded as surveys have shown variously that between 17 per cent and 30 per cent of private tenants do have difficulties in getting their money back.[129] Of course, it may be that the landlord has a good reason for withholding the deposit; the most common reasons given for not handing it back (in whole or in part) are because it is needed to pay for cleaning or to cover damage to the property.[130] Indeed, many tenants now anticipate these difficulties and deal with it by withholding the last month's rent payment. The student letting market presents a particular concern. In the past, students have often found it particularly difficult to recover rent deposits, but also tend to be culprits when it comes to leaving the property in a bad state, not paying the last rental due and then simply disappearing. The result is unsatisfactory both for landlords and tenants. For landlords, this means that the deposit is used to cover the last rental payment and if there is any damage to the property it is often difficult in practice to pursue a claim for contractual damages against the departed tenant. For tenants who do pay the rent, the failure to get back the deposit can create very real hardship and poverty, and may well mean that they are unable to raise a deposit for a new tenancy.

In order to address these difficulties the Housing Act 2004 (sections 212–215 and Schedule 10) has introduced regulation of deposit taking in relation to assured shorthold tenancies. Pilot schemes run by the Independent Housing Ombudsman led to the conclusion that 'systems for independently and fairly adjudicating tenancy deposit

---

[127] Rent Act 1977 s 128(1)(c), introduced by Housing Act 1980, s 79.
[128] Hansard HC vol 443 col 2584W (17 March 2006).
[129] National Centre for Social Research and ODPM, 'Survey of English Housing, 2003–2004' (SN 5506, October 2006) (17%); Office of National Statistics, Survey Division, 'Omnibus Survey' (SN 4145, March 1998) (30%).
[130] DCLG, 'Housing in England 2004/05' (October 2006) 131.

disputes could be made to work efficiently and effectively', but not if left to voluntary opt in.[131]

The provisions came into force on 6 April 2007. The idea behind regulation is that all deposits will be held in accordance with an accredited scheme with the twin aims of safeguarding tenants deposits and facilitating the resolution of disputes arising in connection with such deposits.

The landlord[132] of an assured shorthold tenancy is required to apply any tenancy deposit in accordance with an authorised scheme within 14 days of receiving it.[133] The tenancy deposit is defined for these purposes by section 212 (8) as meaning:

… any money intended to be held (by the landlord or otherwise) as security for-

(a) the performance of any obligations of the tenant, or

(b) the discharge of any liability of his,

arising under or in connection with the tenancy.[134]

The landlord must also let the tenant know within 14 days which scheme has been used and show that he has complied with it by using a prescribed form.[135] There are two types of scheme: a custodial scheme[136] (where deposits are paid into and held in a separate account managed by the scheme) and an insurance-based scheme[137] (where the landlord or agent will hold the deposit and any failure on his/her part to repay it to the tenant will be covered by the scheme's insurance arrangements). The custodial scheme is free to users: interest earned on the deposit money is paid to tenants at a prescribed rate and the surplus interest covers the costs of running the scheme. At the end of the tenancy, the deposit must be paid out by the scheme administrator within ten days of receiving notification from the landlord and tenant that they have agreed how the deposit should be returned. If they cannot reach agreement the deposit is kept until a court order is obtained specifying how the deposit should be paid out.[138] With the insurance scheme, as the landlord (or his agent) retains the deposit, it is the landlord who gets the interest from the deposit money but he may have to pay a fee in order to use the scheme. If the deposit is not returned to the tenant within ten days of him requesting the landlord to do so, the tenant can notify the scheme administrator who will direct the landlord to pay the disputed sum into the scheme within ten days. The insurance component is to cover the scheme having to pay tenants because the landlord fails to pay the money when directed. Again, if the parties cannot agree on how the money is to be paid out it may be necessary to obtain a court order.[139] Both types of scheme must provide an alternative dispute resolution service for settling tenancy disputes without

---

[131] M Biles, 'Tenancy Deposit Schemes' (2005) 9 *Landlord & Tenant Rev* 165.

[132] This includes 'a person or persons acting on his … behalf in relation to the tenancy', Housing Act 2004 s 212(9).

[133] This requirement applies 'despite any agreement to the contrary': Housing Act 2004 s 213(9).

[134] It does not matter, therefore, if the parties do not label it a deposit; it is the use of it that matters.

[135] Housing Act 2004 s 213(5) and (6) (or a form substantially to the same effect).

[136] Sch 10 paras 3 and 4.

[137] Sch 10 paras 5 and 6.

[138] Housing Act 2004 Sch 10 para 4.

[139] Housing Act 2004 Sch 10 paras 6 and 7.

recourse to litigation.[140] The dispute resolution service will be free to use (for both landlord and tenant) but cannot be made compulsory.

There are heavy sanctions for failing to use the scheme. If the tenant obtains an order from the County Court under section 214 confirming that the landlord has not applied the deposit in accordance with one of the authorised schemes, in addition to an order requiring the deposit be either repaid to the tenant or paid into a scheme, the court is also required by subsection (4) to:

> … order the landlord to pay to the applicant a sum of money equal to three times the amount of the deposit within the period of 14 days beginning with the date of the making of the order.

The landlord is also unable to serve a section 21 notice for recovery of possession on termination of the assured shorthold tenancy if the deposit is not being applied in accordance with an authorised scheme or if he has failed to provide the tenant with the prescribed information.

Although the regulation of deposits is to be welcomed in view of the problems that there have been in the past, it does, of course, place yet another regulatory burden on landlords.[141] It is also unclear quite what effect will it have on the 'naughtier' landlords and tenants. Some respondents to the ODPM's consultation paper, 'Tenancy Deposit Protection: Consultation on Secondary Legislation'[142] thought that rogue landlords will simply avoid the requirements, thus further marginalising tenants at the lower end of the market.[143] In addition, rent arrears and abandonment were thought likely to continue to be serious issues.

16.4.4 Late Payment Charges

Commercial leases generally provide for interest to be payable by the tenant if any rent, or other sums due under the lease, are paid late. This provides the tenant with an incentive to make prompt payment, and compensates the landlord for loss of use of the money if payment is late.

16.4.5 Rent Collection

Rent collection and arrears is an important aspect of tenancy management. As at March 2002, local authorities in England and Wales were owed £647 million in rent by current and

---

[140] Housing Act 2004 Sch 10 para 10. Deposit schemes in Australia and New Zealand report 2%–3% of disputes are taken to a tribunal: ODPM, 'Tenancy Money, Probity and Protection' (Consultation Paper, November 2002) Annex 6, para 18.

[141] Mike Stimpson (chair of the National Federation of Residential Landlords), for example, writes that the legislation is unbalanced and gives landlords no confidence that the government has acted in a proportionate manner towards landlords. He notes that if tenants withhold rent and abandon the premises there are no penalties for the tenant and the landlord, in order to recover 'his own money' in the custodial scheme, will need to apply to court (this aspect of the legislation is to be amended): M Stimpson, 'A step too far' Private Renter Issue 7 September 2006 in ROOF September/October 2006.

[142] ODPM, 'Tenancy Deposit Protection: Consultation on Secondary Legislation' (June 2006).

[143] ROOF reports a scheme that is being used as a 'dodge' to get round the deposit scheme at 'Homefront: Deposit Dodge' ROOF May/June 2007 6.

former tenants, with an average of more than £2 million for each authority.[144] Around 10 per cent of social renters claimed to have been in arrears at some point in 2004/05.[145] In the social sector, rent management is a key performance indicator and assumptions are made about the proportion of rent collected in determining subsidy levels for local authorities. Nonetheless housing inspectors for the Audit Commission have judged local authorities' rent arrears services to be weak in relation to other housing services.[146] In the housing association sector, high collection rates are necessary to service loan repayments.

The dramatic rise in residential possession levels between 1994 and 2001 (see chapter 19) led to a reappraisal of rent management, as possession action had effectively become a usual course of action to deal with arrears. Since then, social landlords have been making greater use of alternative ways of chasing arrears,[147] taking a more pro-active stance to prevent arrears arising and having early personal contact with tenants in arrears, and treating eviction as a last resort. DCLG guidance, supported by the Housing Corporation, emphasises that social landlords should seek to maintain and sustain tenancies,[148] an approach that is enhanced by the pre-action protocol for possession claims by social landlords that encourages greater pre-action contact between landlords and tenants. Prevention begins early: new tenants should be met and given information that will help them to pay the rent on time and to claim any benefits that they are entitled to. The result in the local authority sector has been that 'serious arrears' (rent arrears of more than 26 weeks) have been brought under control, and the drop in the number of tenants with serious arrears is reflected in the drop in possession actions.[149]

In the commercial sector, default rates are around 1.6 per cent of rent passing.[150]

16.5 Remedies for Non-payment

As mentioned above, non-payment will frequently lead to the tenant being evicted by the landlord exercising a right to forfeit or by bringing a periodic tenancy to an end (which, in the residential sector, will usually require a court order). Termination of tenancies is discussed in later chapters. Whether or not the tenancy comes to an end because of the default, there is still the matter of the landlord recovering arrears, either by bringing an action for debt or by exercising the right to distress.

With long residential leases, section 166 of the Commonhold and Leasehold Reform Act 2002 states that the tenant is not liable to make a rent payment unless he has been served

---

[144] Audit Commission, 'Local Authority housing rent income: Rent collection and arrears management by local authorities in England and Wales' (June 2003).

[145] DCLG, 'Housing in England 2004/05' (October 2006) 89.

[146] Audit Commission, 'Local Authority housing rent income: Rent collection and arrears management by local authorities in England and Wales' (June 2003).

[147] To good effect: see M Delargy, 'Tackling rent arrears' ROOF September/October 2004 25, M Delargy, 'Show me the money' ROOF September/October 2004 26, M Barry, 'Engaged tone' ROOF September/October 2004 28 and 'What works elsewhere' ROOF September/October 2004 28.

[148] See DCLG, 'Guide on Effective Rent Arrears Management' (August 2006).

[149] S Wilcox, *UK Housing Review 2005/06* (Coventry, Chartered Institute of Housing, and London, Council of Mortgage Lenders, 2005) 25–7.

[150] The Strutt & Parker IPD Lease Events Review 2006. Default is defined to mean loss of four quarters rent. Default rates were highest in the retail sector and lowest in the office sector.

with a prescribed notice[151] between 30 and 60 days before the payment is due stating the amount payable.

16.5.1 Recovery of Rent

To recover arrears, the landlord is able to bring an action for debt based on the express or implied covenant to pay rent.

16.5.1.1 Abandonment and Rent Arrears

The interrelationship between this action for debt and contractual claims for damages has not been explored much in English case law, even though it may be especially important to landlords and tenants in cases where the tenant has abandoned the premises.

If the tenant leaves the premises empty with no future use for them and stops paying rent there are usually two courses of action open to the landlord: to end the lease (which brings to an end the right to rent),[152] or to treat the lease as continuing and sue for rent as it falls due. There may be a third possibility – to relet the premises on the tenant's account, entering into possession on that basis and suing the tenant for any difference in rent[153] – but in *Reichman v Beveridge* Lloyd LJ was surprised at this possibility and thought that the English authority for it was weak.[154] Choosing between the first two will mainly depend on the state of the property market (how easy it will be to relet the premises, and at what rent). In a rising market with easy to let premises, the landlord will probably prefer to end the lease and relet at a higher rent; in a weak market the landlord may prefer to continue the lease and claim the rent due from the tenant. From the tenant's perspective the choice of options makes a big difference: continuing the lease means continuing tenant liability; ending the lease brings the tenant's liability to an end. In other jurisdictions these choices are portrayed as stemming from a property law approach and, by adopting what is said to be a contractual approach, a further (fourth) option is available to landlords, namely, to treat the lease as at an end while giving notice of an intention to claim damages. This approach has not been followed here.

Continuing the Lease Means Continuing Tenant Liability
If the tenant abandons premises part way through a fixed term (or without giving notice to quit under a periodic tenancy) it has been questioned from the perspective of both policy and principle whether the landlord should be able simply to sit back and recover the rent as it falls due.[155] In terms of policy, it is argued that it is economically inefficient for the premises to be left empty; in the Canadian case of *Globe Convestra v Vucetic* Taliano J said,

---

[151] Landlord and Tenant (Notice of Rent) (England) Regulations 2004 SI 2004/3096.
[152] *Reichman v Beveridge* [2006] EWCA Civ 1659.
[153] Referred to by Laskin J in the Canadian case of *Highway Properties Ltd v Kelly, Douglas & Co Ltd* (1971) 17 DLR (3d) 710 (SCC) 716.
[154] [2006] EWCA Civ 1659 [22]–[25].
[155] In other jurisdictions, see S Sternberg, 'The Commercial Landlord's Duty to Mitigate upon a Tenant's Abandonment of the Premises' (1984–85) 5 *Adv Q* 385; A Bradbrook, 'The Application of the Principle of Mitigation of Damages to Landlord-Tenant Law' (1976) 8 *Sydney L Rev* 15.

... it is difficult to accept, in this day and age, the continuing accuracy of a proposition that permits a landlord to sit back and do nothing to mitigate a loss occasioned by a forfeiting tenant.[156]

In terms of principle, it is said that in line with other areas of contract law the landlord should be under a duty to mitigate, which will generally mean that he ought to try to re-let the premises.

These issues were raised before the Court of Appeal in *Reichman v Beveridge*.[157] The tenants under a five-year lease stopped using the property just over two years into the lease and shortly thereafter ceased to pay any further rent. When the landlord sued for arrears, the defence was based on the argument that the landlord should have mitigated its loss by re-letting the premises. This defence was mounted on the basis of both policy (to discourage premises being left empty) and principle (the growing recognition of the contractual basis of leases making it appropriate to apply contract rules to breach of leases).

In rejecting the tenant's defence in *Reichman* Lloyd LJ rightly points out that this is not strictly a case concerning the duty to mitigate, as this duty applies only if the claim is one of damages.[158] A claim for rent is one of debt, so bringing it within the contractual principles set out in *White and Carter (Councils) Ltd v McGregor*.[159] In this case the House of Lords affirmed, by majority, that an innocent contractual party faced with a repudiation of the contract has the choice of either accepting the repudiatory breach and suing for damages or treating the contract as continuing, subject to the qualification mentioned by Lord Reid that where the innocent party has no legitimate interest, financial or otherwise, in performing rather than claiming damages, he ought not to be allowed to saddle the other party with the burden of performance.[160] As developed in charterparty cases this qualification has been taken to mean that the innocent party may have to accept the repudiatory breach in extreme cases where damages would be an adequate remedy and the decision to treat the contract as alive would be wholly unreasonable.[161] It therefore fell to the Court of Appeal in *Reichman* to consider if damages would be an adequate remedy, and if the decision to treat the lease as continuing would be wholly unreasonable.

Would damages be an adequate alternative? If the landlord accepts the lease as ended, and relets the premises but for a lower rent, can he claim the difference as contractual damages? The ancient case of *Walls v Atcheson* is authority for the proposition that the landlord cannot recover damages from the tenant for future loss of rent after he has re-entered so as to bring the lease to an end (although this case was not decided on the basis of tenant repudiation and damages for breach).[162] The Court of Appeal took this to represent the state of current English law. In this respect then, leases are treated differently from other contracts. Lloyd LJ acknowledges this after referring to the fact that in *White and*

---

[156] (1991) 15 RPR (2d) 200 (Onto CJ) [51].

[157] [2006] EWCA Civ 1659.

[158] See *Jervis v Harris* [1996] Ch 195 (CA) 202–3.

[159] [1962] AC 413 (HL). In the Australian case *J and S Chan Pty Ltd v McKenzie and McKenzie* [1994] ANZ Conv Rep 610 (ACTSC) the court similarly took the view that applying *White & Carter* meant that the landlord was not under a duty to mitigate.

[160] [1962] AC 413 (HL) 431.

[161] *Reichman v Beveridge* [2006] EWCA Civ 1659 [17].

[162] (1826) 11 Moore CP and Exch Rep 379.

Carter, and in the charterparty cases, the innocent party would have been able to sue for future losses if they had accepted the repudiatory breach:

> It may be a logical development to hold that a landlord, having forfeited the lease, can recover damages for the loss of future rent, at least if the breach which led to the forfeiture was fundamental and repudiatory, but it does not seem to me that English law has yet reached that stage.[163]

Other common law jurisdictions have gone further in assimilating leasehold law to contract law. In the Canadian case of *Highway Properties Ltd v Kelly, Douglas & Co Ltd*, a major tenant in an unsuccessful shopping centre moved out of its supermarket premises and later wrote repudiating the lease.[164] The tenant's departure had an adverse effect on the whole centre and other tenants moved out. The landlord in *Highway Properties* took possession but gave notice that it would look to the tenant for damages suffered as a result of the wrongful repudiation. Until *Highway Properties*, it had not been accepted that a landlord could obtain damages for post-repudiation losses but the Supreme Court held that damages for prospective losses were available:

> It is no longer sensible to pretend that a commercial lease, such as the one before this Court, is simply a conveyance and not also a contract. It is equally untenable to persist in denying resort to the full armoury of remedies ordinarily available to redress repudiation of covenants, merely because the covenants may be associated with an estate in land.[165]

The result of *Highway Properties* is that the landlord has not only the options of doing nothing and suing for rent, ending the lease and suing for accrued arrears, or reletting on the tenant's account but also the option of ending the lease and giving notice that damages will be claimed for losing the benefit of the lease for the remainder of the term. These damages can include the present value of the unpaid future rent or the loss resulting from repudiation.[166]

Australian cases have also permitted landlords to recover damages post tenant repudiation: in *Progressive Mailing House Pty Ltd v Tabali Pty Ltd* the damages awarded to the landlord included the cost of delay in reletting following a repudiatory breach,[167] and in *Wood Factory Pty Ltd v Kiritos Pty Ltd* damages included the net loss of rent on reletting.[168]

Lloyd LJ did not, however, accept it as possible in English law to claim damages post repudiation of a lease. The fact that damages for future loss are not available, or at least doubt on this point, means that one of the conditions necessary if the landlord is not to be allowed to treat the lease as continuing (that damages are an adequate alternative) does not exist. Further, the non-availability of damages following repudiation also means that it is not unreasonable for the landlord to treat the lease as continuing. As a matter of legal

---

[163] *Reichman v Beveridge* [2006] EWCA Civ 1659 [27].

[164] (1971) 17 DLR (3d) 710 (SCCA).

[165] (1971) 17 DLR (3d) 710 (SCCA) 721. Some later cases have distinguished *Highway Properties* on the basis that the lease imposed a 'continuous use' obligation on the tenant, and that the landlord had given notice of the claim for prospective damages.

[166] See *Grouse Mechanical Co v Griffith* (1990) 14 RPR (2d) 233 (BCSC) [39].

[167] (1985) 57 ALR 609.

[168] For criticism of the *Wood Factory* case, see J Effron, 'The Contractualisation of the Law of Leasehold' (1988) 14 *Monash U L Rev* 83, 96–8.

principle, therefore, Lloyd LJ considered that in line with *White & Carter* the landlord was free to elect to treat a lease as continuing and did not have to accept the repudiatory breach.

The policy argument, that it is economically inefficient for the landlord to be able to sit back and claim rent rather than reduce his losses,[169] was dismissed by Lloyd LJ in the following terms:

> ... if there is enough demand for the space, the market rent may exceed that payable under the lease in which case the landlord will no doubt terminate the lease and re-let at a profit. Equally, the tenant can attempt to find an assignee or sub-tenant to use the premises; it is not only the landlord who can take steps to fill the space.[170]

The consequence of holding that the landlord is not under a duty to mitigate means that the most prudent course of action for the landlord is to treat the lease as continuing, assuming of course that the tenant is likely to be good for the rent.

In other jurisdictions that have recognised Laskin J's fourth option (the right of the landlord to treat the lease as at an end while giving notice of his intention to claim prospective damages) there is also a duty to mitigate. Bollen J in the Supreme Court of South Australia in *Vickers v Stichtenoth Investments Pty Ltd*, referred to by counsel in *Reichman*, expressly supports the argument that a landlord should fall under a duty to mitigate.[171] Further, several United States jurisdictions have imposed a statutory duty to mitigate on landlords, both residential and commercial.[172] Leases may also contain terms imposing an express duty to mitigate on the landlord. So, for example, the Canadian case of *Vinland Holdings Ltd v Wisniowski* concerned a residential tenancy containing the following clause:

> If the tenant abandons the premises or terminates the tenancy otherwise than in the manner permitted, the landlord shall mitigate any damages that may be caused by the abandonment or termination to the extent that a party to a contract is required by law to mitigate damages.[173]

Although the point does seem to be moot in some jurisdictions, it is usually the case that the duty to mitigate will arise only if the landlord has chosen to go down the contractual route, electing to end the lease and claim damages. The option of pursuing what is described as a property perspective is still open to the landlord.[174] The landlord can, therefore, choose to treat the lease as continuing and sue for rent as it falls due. In the words of Taylor JA in *Transco Mills Ltd v Percan Enterprises Ltd*:

> There is no basis on which a landlord of commercial premises can be required to mitigate its loss where it maintains the lease in existence and claims for rent due.[175]

---

[169] An argument discussed by A Bradbrook, 'The Application of the Principle of Mitigation of Damages to Landlord-Tenant Law' (1976) 8 *Sydney L Rev* 15, 17.

[170] *Reichman v Beveridge* [2006] EWCA Civ 1659 [39].

[171] (1989) 52 SASR 90 (SASC) 100, referred to in *Reichman* at [6] but dismissed by Lloyd LJ at [32]–[33] as unsound for failing to take account of the points in *White and Carter (Councils) Ltd v McGregor* [1962] AC 413 (HL).

[172] For example, in Texas the Property Code chapter 91 section 91.006 states that a landlord has a duty to mitigate damages if a tenant abandons the leased premises in violation of the lease.

[173] (1990) 9 RPR (2d) 194 (SCNS).

[174] *607190 Ontario Inc v First Consolidate Holdings Corp* (1992) 26 RPR (2d) 298 (ODC).

[175] (1993) 100 DLR (4th) 359 (BCCA) [38].

In the Australian case of *Tall-Bennett & Co Pty Ltd v Sadot Holdings Pty Ltd* Justice Young similarly saw nothing unreasonable in the landlord treating the lease as continuing:

> I can see nothing unreasonable about a landlord insisting that he retain the comfortable legal position that the granting of the lease has put him in and I can see nothing unreasonable about the landlord being reluctant to assume the trouble of expending money and preparing a new lease and suing the tenant afterwards. I can see nothing particularly grotesque about the situation of putting it at the feet of the tenant who wishes to abandon his lease to go to the trouble to obtain a new tenant. If the landlord is unreasonable about consenting to the person who is to take the tenancy, then normally there can be a sub-letting or assignment without consent.[176]

It is presumably recognition of the fourth option that has led to the incorporation of leasehold clauses in other jurisdictions that set out in some detail what the landlord's rights are in the event of the tenancy ending early. So, for example, in the Canadian case of *Globe Convestra v Vucetic* Taliano J describes one of the clauses in the commercial lease:

> It provides that if the landlord elects to re-enter or take possession pursuant to legal proceedings, it may either terminate the lease or it may, without terminating the lease, make alterations and repairs as may be necessary in order to relet the premises. Upon reletting, all rentals received are to be applied first to the tenant's indebtedness, second to the payment of any costs and expenses of subletting, and the residue is to be applied to payment of future rent with the tenant remaining responsible for any deficiency. It goes on to say that no such re-entry or taking possession shall be construed as an election on its part to terminate the lease unless a written notice of such intention is given to the tenant. It goes on to provide that should the landlord at any time terminate the lease for any breach, it may recover from the tenant all damages it may incur by reason of such breach, including the cost of recovering the leased premises, reasonable solicitor's fees and the net worth, at the time, of the future value of the rental payments secured by the lease.[177]

It would be highly unusual to find a clause of this nature in an English lease.

Ending the Lease Means Ending the Tenant's Liability

In English law, if the landlord accepts that the lease as at an end when the tenant abandons the property, this ends the tenant's future liability to the landlord: the tenant is liable neither for the future rent that would have been payable had the lease continued, nor to pay damages to the landlord. The problem with this approach is that it provides no incentive for the landlord to try to make some use of the premises: assuming that the tenant is financially sound, the landlord will be better off if he treats the lease as continuing and thus retains the right to sue for rent.

Reletting the premises

In practice, what may often happen is that the landlord will try to relet the premises if the tenant vacates early. Unless the landlord formally acknowledges that the lease is ended, he can continue to recover rent from the tenant until the premises are relet, and the relet operates as

---

[176] (1988) NSW Conv Rep 57, 881.
[177] (1990) 15 RPR (2d) 220 (Onto CJ) [5].

a surrender by operation of law. This occurred in *Boyer v Warbey*.[178] The tenant had to give three months' notice but left without serving a notice to quit. The landlord relet the property but successfully sued the tenant for the rent due up to the date of the reletting (around three months). In the words of Denning LJ:

> He [the tenant] went out of possession, it is true, and thereupon the landlords would have been entitled to recover possession if they had so wished. But they did not so wish. They were not bound to accept possession whenever the tenant chose to offer it. They were entitled to hold him to the tenancy until he gave a valid three months' notice to quit. Very sensibly they did try to re-let; and as soon as they re-let the statutory tenancy came to an end by surrender by operation of law. But until it came to an end by valid notice to quit or by surrender they were entitled to hold the tenant liable for rent.[179]

16.5.2 Set Off

The tenant may be able to 'set off' (or deduct) sums from the rent. The main situation in which this will occur is when the landlord is in breach of its repairing obligation and the tenant sets off the costs of repair or damages for breach against the rent claim, but it could also occur in respect of damages for breach of the covenant of quiet enjoyment. The right of set-off is discussed in more detail in chapter 12.

16.5.3 Distress for Rent and Commercial Rent Arrears Recovery

The remedy of distress for rent is an ancient common law remedy that has been extended and modified by statute over time. In essence, it gives the landlord the right to enter the demised premises if rent is overdue and seize (and sell) goods found there. Unlike many other creditors, the landlord cannot simply withdraw the supply as a response to non-payment – it takes time and expense to recover possession and distress provides a fast and efficient remedy. In recent years it has, however, been subjected to heavy criticism and is shortly to be abolished by section 71 of the Tribunals, Courts and Enforcement Act 2007.[180] In its place will be the commercial rent arrears recovery (CRAR)[181] but there will be no equivalent to distress for the residential sector.

16.5.3.1 The Problems with Distress for Rent

The use of the distress remedy is governed by a set of complex and anachronistic rules. It can, for example, only be carried out between sunrise and sunset, and there are rules governing which goods can be taken and which are privileged.[182] It is also subject to set-off: in *Eller v Grovecrest*,[183] it was held that the tenant could set off potential damages for nuisance and

---

[178] [1953] 1 QB 234 (CA).
[179] [1953] 1 QB 234 (CA) 244–5.
[180] There is no commencement date for the relevant provisions yet.
[181] Tribunals, Courts and Enforcement Act 2007 s 72 and Sch 12.
[182] For further detail, see Law Commission, 'Landlord and Tenant: Distress for Rent' (Law Com No 194, 1991) Part II and App D.
[183] *Eller v Grovecrest Investments Ltd* [1995] QB 272 (CA).

breach of the covenant for quiet enjoyment against a claim for distress for rent withheld in protest at the landlord's breaches.

In the private residential sector distress is of little practical use: in the case of a dwelling-house let on an assured tenancy the leave of the County Court is required before distress can be levied.[184] The landlord will just as soon seek a possession order as a warrant for distress. It has, however, been used more commonly in the commercial sector and also in the public residential sector, although its popularity as a remedy has tended to wax and wane. For landlords, distress is often seen as an attractive remedy. It is quick and cheap, and in most cases the mere threat of distress is sufficient to induce payment of the arrears: the Certificated Bailiffs' Association for England and Wales gave evidence to the Law Commission that only 2 per cent of warrants actually lead to removal and sale, and the Chartered Institute of Public Finance and Accountancy said that the threat of distress alone is sufficient to make tenants pay in about 90 per cent of cases of arrears where local authorities use distress.[185] Consumer and housing groups, though, have pointed out that this simply increases other forms of indebtedness. It is not usually a case of tenants not being willing to pay, but of genuine financial hardship. Paying the arrears is simply at the price of greater indebtedness to other creditors.

There have been questions as to whether distress is human rights compliant. Even stripping aside human rights concerns, the Law Commission recommended the abolition of distress as a remedy:

> 3.2 We see distress for rent as wrong in principle because it offers an extra-judicial debt enforcement remedy in circumstances which are, because of its intrinsic nature, the way in which it arises and the manner of its exercise, unjust to the debtors, to other creditors and to third parties. The characteristics of distress for rent which contribute to this are –
>
> a)   priority given to landlords over other creditors;
> b)   vulnerability of third parties' goods;
> c)   harshness which is caused by the limited opportunity for the tenant to challenge the landlord's claim, the scope for the rules of distress to be abused, the unexpected intrusion into the tenant's property and the possibility of the sale of the goods at an undervalue;
> d)   disregard of the tenant's circumstances which demonstrates its general lack of recognition of a modern approach to debt enforcement.[186]

These objections were considered to apply to all sectors, notwithstanding arguments that the democratic controls on local authorities make them exercise distress responsibly, and that the humiliation suffered from the intrusion is far less for commercial tenants than residential tenants.

16.5.3.2 The Abolition of Distress/Introduction of CRAR

Following the Law Commission's recommendations and as part of a wider review of enforcement, the government consulted on distress for rent and found considerable support for retaining a modified procedure in the case of commercial property as it was said to be an

---

[184] Housing Act 1988 s 19 (this includes the assured shorthold). There are similar restrictions under the Rent Act 1977 s 147.

[185] See Law Commission, 'Landlord and Tenant: Distress for Rent' (Law Com No 194, 1991).

[186] Law Commission, 'Landlord and Tenant: Distress for Rent' (Law Com No 194, 1991).

effective remedy for landlords.[187] The outcome is that distress is to be abolished for residential premises,[188] but replaced by CRAR for commercial premises.

In many respects, CRAR will be like distress in that it allows the landlord to enter the demised premises in order to take goods belonging to the tenant, sell them, and recover rent arrears from the sale proceeds. It will, however, be available only to commercial landlords[189] and only if the arrears exceed a specified minimum level once any set-offs etc permissible under the common law have been deducted.[190] The procedure is set out in Schedule 11 of the Tribunals, Courts and Enforcement Bill. Mixed use premises where part is required to be used as a dwelling will not be covered by CRAR. Only rent arrears will be recoverable this way, that is money payable for the use and possession of premises, and so, for example, service charges will not be recoverable by CRAR even if they are defined in the lease as 'rent'.[191] There will be some procedural protection as the tenant will need to be served with notice of an intention to take action and then has the opportunity to apply to the court to set aside the notice.[192]

16.6 Cesser of Rent

The lease may contain a clause suspending the tenant's obligation to pay rent if the premises become unusable (or the premises are part of a larger property which is damaged in such a way that the tenant cannot use its property for the intended purpose). Such a clause is common in commercial leases and will need to cover such things as how long the rent is suspended for, and whether the suspension operates only if the property is damaged by an insured risk. It is unusual for the landlord to agree for an indefinite suspension of rent. In the absence of such a clause, the tenant may seek to argue that the rent liability ends due to frustration if the premises become unusable but, as seen in chapter 24, it is only in the most extreme situations that a lease is likely to be ended by frustration.

---

[187] *Lord Chancellor's Department, 'Enforcement Review Consultation Paper 5: Distress for Rent' (May 2001).*
[188] Tribunals, Courts and Enforcement Act 2007 s 71.
[189] Tribunals, Courts and Enforcement Act 2007 s 75. This includes agricultural holdings, with some modifications: s 80.
[190] The amount is to be prescribed in regulations.
[191] Tribunals, Courts and Enforcement Act 2007 ss 76, 77.
[192] Tribunals, Courts and Enforcement Act 2007 s 78.

PART FIVE

CHANGING THE PARTIES TO THE RELATIONSHIP

The next two chapters look at the related issues of a change in the identity of the landlord or tenant, and the impact that this has on liability under the leasehold covenants.

Not all forms of alienation will result in a change of parties to the particular leasehold relationship: it is possible for the tenant to allow others into occupation of the property whilst remaining a tenant himself. This can be done by granting a licence, or by carving a further leasehold interest out of the tenant's leasehold estate (sub-letting). Usually, there will be a covenant in the lease (known as an alienation covenant) that places restrictions on the tenant's ability to create further interests. A change of parties occurs only if there is an assignment of the reversion or the leasehold interest, either through voluntary assignment or through exercising a statutory right, such as where a member of the tenant's family is given a statutory right to succeed to the tenancy following the tenant's death. As any assignment of the lease will result in a new tenant, it is usual for the lease to contain an alienation covenant placing controls on the ability of the tenant to assign the lease so that the landlord can be sure that the new tenant is able to perform the leasehold obligations.

Chapter 17 looks at the forms of alienation covenants commonly used in practice, and the legislative controls that have been introduced in order to ensure that the tenant's rights are real, effective rights. It is highly unusual for the tenant to have any similar power to control assignment by the landlord,[1] although in the case of long residential leases lease-holders have been given rights of pre-emption that are discussed in chapter 25. Chapter 17 also looks at the succession rights that have been given to residential tenants. The focus of chapter 18 is on the legal rules governing the enforcement of covenants in the lease when there has been a change of landlord or tenant, including covenants entered into by guarantors. It considers both whether the original landlord and tenant remain liable following an assignment, and also the position of the assignee.

---

[1] Presumably because of their generally weaker negotiating position, but also because the identity of the landlord is generally less crucial to the tenant than vice versa as landlords undertake fewer ongoing obligations than tenants.

17

ALIENATION, TRANSFER AND SUCCESSION

17.1   General introduction
17.2   Change of tenant
17.3   Obtaining consent
17.4   Covenants against alienation
17.5   Alienation covenants in particular sectors
17.6   Disposition in breach of an alienation clause
17.7   Formalities and alienation
17.8   The position of sub-tenants
17.9   Statutory succession on death
17.10   Change of landlord
17.11   Transfer of local authority housing to new social landlords

17.1 General Introduction

Both the leasehold estate of the tenant and the reversionary estate of the landlord can be transferred to new owners. As will be seen, however, it is common for the tenant's rights to dispose of his interest, or to create new lesser interests, to be constrained by the terms of the lease. In some cases the lease may completely prohibit any such dealings, but more commonly the lease will permit some forms of dealing provided that the tenant obtains the landlord's consent. By way of contrast, it would be highly unusual for there to be any restrictions on the landlord's ability to deal with its reversionary interest.

17.2 Change of Tenant

17.2.1 Introduction

As a leasehold estate, the lease is freely alienable; it can be assigned or carved up into lesser interests by sub-letting or creating licences. In practice, however, the right of alienability is often cut down by the terms of the lease, and may be altogether proscribed. The landlord will have carefully chosen the first tenant taking account of his ability to meet the financial and other obligations in the lease and will generally wish to have a say on who can be tenant and who can occupy the property. On the other hand, it will also be important to tenants (particularly those who have long term leases with a capital value and to business tenants whose commercial needs fluctuate over time), that they should be able to move to other premises and be released from the leasehold obligations. Chapter 18 looks at the question of enforcement of leasehold covenants after assignment. This chapter looks at the law relating to alienation provisions.

Although there is much variation, the norm is for long leases to be freely assignable. Short residential tenancies and agricultural lettings are usually personal and cannot be assigned. Commercial leases are often assignable with the landlord's consent, and statute then provides that the consent cannot be unreasonably withheld. The practice and law relating to each sector is discussed in more detail below.

17.2.2 Assignment

This is where the tenant transfers his leasehold interest to a new tenant. Following assignment the tenant ceases to have a proprietary interest in the premises. The assignment may involve the payment of a premium from the assignee to the tenant – this will be usual for long residential leases where only a low rent is paid and long leases may change hands for sums close to freehold values. It can also occur with commercial leases if the property is 'underrented' (that is, market values have risen since the rent was agreed either on the initial let or on review). Conversely, in a falling property market it may be that the passing rent is higher than the current market value (the property will then be 'overrented') and the tenant may need to pay a 'reverse premium' to an assignee in order to be able to dispose of the lease.

The form that alienation covenants take in practice is influenced by the rules on the liability of tenants post assignment (which is discussed in chapter 18). Prior to the implementation of the Landlord and Tenant (Covenants) Act 1995 in 1996, the original tenant remained liable to the landlord throughout the life of the lease, even after assignment. A landlord could, therefore, perhaps be more relaxed towards allowing assignments knowing that the original tenant could still be sued should the assignee fall into arrears. This has changed for new leases entered into on or after 1 January 1996. The starting point now is that tenants are released from liability on assignment. As will be seen, the loss of original tenant liability was accompanied by reform giving landlords greater ability to set conditions on assignment.

17.2.3 Sub-letting

This entails the tenant granting a sub-lease (or underlease) to the sub-tenant (or underlessee) for a term shorter than his own lease, and becoming a mesne landlord. In effect, the tenant carves a further proprietary interest for the sub-tenant out of his own estate. The tenant continues to have a leasehold estate in the property and to be liable to the landlord under the headlease; as the tenant remains directly liable to the landlord, the landlord may be less concerned about controlling sub-letting than controlling assignments. The sub-tenant is liable to his own landlord (the tenant/mesne landlord), not to the head landlord. If the tenant attempts to sub-let the entire premises for the entire unexpired term of his own lease, this will count as an assignment.[1]

Sub-letting and underletting are the same thing, but there is a tendency to refer to 'underletting' more in the context of business tenancies (perhaps because the statutory provisions in the Landlord and Tenant Act 1927 refer to underletting). This chapter uses the language of sub-letting (and its associated phrases) but nothing turns on this.

17.2.4 Taking in a lodger/licensee

Lodgers have only a licence[2] and as with sub-letting, taking in a lodger does not result in a change of tenant.

17.3 Obtaining Consent

As will be seen, in most situations where dealing with the lease is permitted the tenant is first required to obtain the landlord's consent. The landlord is entitled to ask for information about the proposed dealing and the strength of the proposed disponee.[3]

17.3.1 Cannot Charge a Premium

By the Law of Property Act 1925 section 144, the landlord is not permitted to charge a premium as the price for giving consent to a disposition, unless the lease expressly gives such a right, but he can require the payment of a reasonable sum in respect of legal and related expenses.[4] Section 144 does not apply to leases containing absolute prohibitions on alienation. With absolute covenants the landlord is therefore free to withhold consent or to charge a premium for granting consent. In relation to qualified and fully qualified covenants (that permit alienation with the landlord's consent), the combined effect of section 144 and of section 19 of the Landlord and Tenant Act 1927, discussed below, is that the landlord cannot charge a premium for giving consent and cannot unreasonably withhold consent.

17.3.2 Must Not Act in a Discriminatory Manner

It is unlawful to withhold consent on the grounds of colour, race, nationality, ethnic or national origins.[5] There is one minor exception in the case of 'small premises' where the

---

[1] *Langford v Selmes* (1857) 3 K & J 220; *Milmo v Carreras* [1946] KB 306 (CA) 310.

[2] *Street v Mountford* [1985] 1 AC 809 (HL).

[3] *Norwich Union Life Insurance Society v Shopmoor Ltd* [1999] 1 WLR 531 (Ch) 542. He is entitled to see a proposed sub-lease (and linked documents – *Allied Dunbar Assurance plc v Homebase Ltd* [2002] EWCA Civ 666), but not the details of a proposed assignment, *Kened Ltd v Connie Investments Ltd* (1995) 70 P & CR 370 (CA).

[4] S 144 may be unnecessary as charging a premium would probably be construed as unreasonably withholding consent: see Law Commission, 'Covenants Restricting Dispositions, Alterations and Change of User' (Law Com No 141, 1985) para 3.9; *Greene v Church Commissioners* [1974] 1 Ch 467 (CA) 477 (Lord Denning MR) and 479 (Sir Eric Sachs).

[5] Race Relations Act 1976 s 24.

disponee would be in close contact with the landlord or a near relative of his. Similar restrictions exist for discrimination on the grounds of sex[6] and of disability.[7]

17.3.3 Must Act Reasonably

With the exception of agricultural tenancies, if the lease provides that the landlord's consent is required for alienation, the landlord cannot withhold consent unreasonably. The law relating to reasonableness is discussed above.

17.3.4 Duty to Decide Within Reasonable Time and to Give Written Reasons

Before the Landlord and Tenant Act 1988 landlords undoubtedly held the upper hand when tenants applied for consent to assignment or sub-letting. The problems before the Act are described by Peter Smith J in *Design Progression Ltd v Thurloe Properties Ltd*:

> [1] The qualified covenant against assigning is a powerful weapon in the hands of unscrupulous landlords. The need to obtain licence to assign from a landlord has been regularly exploited by unscrupulous landlords for their own devices. The ability to delay a transaction, and thus to cause it to go off, was regularly abused by landlords if they desired to obtain possession of premises, or desired to extract collateral advantages for their own benefit unrelated to the considerations that were properly relevant to the granting of a licence to assign. The landlords were able to exploit this because, prior to the Landlord and Tenant Act 1988, the only remedy available to a tenant was either to call the landlord's bluff and assign, or to seek proceedings for a declaration that the landlord had unreasonably refused licence to assign. Despite the elaborate case law designed to assist tenants in this area, culminating in the leading case of *International Drilling Fluids Ltd v Louisville Investments (Uxbridge) Ltd* [1986] Ch 513, neither remedy was particularly effective for the tenant.
>
> [2] The former required the prospective assignee to be confident that there were no reasonable grounds, and to complete the transaction with the risk that the landlord might establish a breach and place the assignment in jeopardy. The latter remedy was unsatisfactory for two reasons. First, obtaining the necessary declaration in court took time and, second, there was no provision whereby the tenant could be compensated for any loss or inconvenience caused by the unreasonable stance of the landlord.
>
> [3] The Landlord and Tenant Act 1988 introduced a regime that was designed to address these deficiencies.[8]

With the exception of secure and introductory tenancies, the Landlord and Tenant Act 1988 applies to tenancies containing alienation clauses which provide that the landlord's consent is not to be unreasonably withheld (whether by express wording or by statute).[9]

When the tenant makes a written application for consent, the landlord owes a duty to the tenant within a reasonable time[10] (a) to give consent, except in a case where it is reasonable

---

[6] Sex Discrimination Act 1975 s 31.

[7] Disability Discrimination Act 1995 s 22(4).

[8] [2004] EWHC 324 (Ch), [2005] 1 WLR 1.

[9] Landlord and Tenant Act 1988 s 5(3).

[10] Time may start to run as soon as the application is made even if the tenant has not, when requested, given an undertaking to pay the landlord's reasonable costs: *Aubergine Enterprises Ltd v Lakewood International Ltd* [2002]

not to give consent, and (b) to serve on the tenant written notice of his decision whether or not to give consent.[11] In addition, the decision notice must specify any conditions which the consent is subject to and, if consent is withheld, the reasons for withholding it.[12] The Act has also reversed the common law burden of proof in that it is the landlord who must prove that it was reasonable not to give consent, that the decision was given within a reasonable time, and that any conditions are reasonable.[13]

The Act has strengthened the position of tenants, and is being strictly construed by the judiciary. If the landlord needs more information from the tenant then he must request it.[14] What is a reasonable time will depend on all the circumstances of the particular case,[15] but will be lengthened if the tenant takes an undue length of time to deal with reasonable requests for information from the landlord.[16] In *Blockbuster Entertainment Ltd v Barnsdale Properties Ltd* it was said that the landlord should have given consent within one week.[17] With more complex transactions longer may be needed; in *NCR Ltd v Riverland Portfolio No 1 Ltd* the Court of Appeal considered that the three week period taken was not inherently unreasonable.[18] When the landlord serves a written notice giving an answer to the tenant, this shows that he does not need any further time – if he asks for any longer this will be treated as unreasonable.[19] A landlord is not allowed to rely on reasons or events that emerge after the reasonable time for deciding has expired,[20] or on reasons that he held but which were not put forward in writing within a reasonable time.[21] The duty to give reasons does not require the landlord to justify as a matter of fact the matters upon which he relies.[22]

The landlord is also under a duty to pass on the request to any other person whose consent must be given, such as a superior or inferior landlord.[23] Similar provisions apply where the tenant has sub-let the property and his sub-tenant is seeking consent but also needs the consent of the tenant's landlord.[24]

By section 4, breach of duty can lead to a claim in tort for breach of statutory duty.[25] In

---

EWCA Civ 177, [2002] 1 WLR 2149. Cf *Dong Bang Minerva (UK) Ltd v Davina Ltd* [1996] 2 EGLR 31 (CA). For discussion see M Ross, *Commercial Leases* (London, Butterworths, 1998) H [28].

[11] Landlord and Tenant Act 1988 s 1(3).

[12] Landlord and Tenant Act 1988 s 1(3)(b).

[13] Landlord and Tenant Act 1988 s 1(6).

[14] *Norwich Union Linked Life Assurance Co Ltd v Mercantile Credit Co Ltd* [2003] EWHC 3064 (Ch).

[15] *Go West Ltd v Spigarolo* [2003] EWCA Civ 17, [2003] QB 1140 [35]; *Mount Eden Land Ltd v Folia Ltd, Prohibition London Ltd* [2003] EWHC 1815 (Ch) [68].

[16] *Go West Ltd v Spigarolo* [2003] EWCA Civ 17, [2003] QB 1140 [36].

[17] [2003] EWHC 2912 (Ch) [23].

[18] [2005] EWCA Civ 312.

[19] *Go West Ltd v Spigarolo* [2003] EWCA Civ 17, [2003] QB 1140 [40].

[20] *CIN Properties Ltd v Gill* [1993] 2 EGLR 97 (QB); *Norwich Union Life Insurance Society v Shopmoor Ltd* [1999] 1 WLR 531 (Ch) 545.

[21] *Footwear Corp Ltd v Amplight Properties Ltd* [1999] 1 WLR 551 (Ch) 559; *Go West Ltd v Spigarolo* [2003] EWCA Civ 17, [2003] QB 1140 [22]. This was a much more difficult issue under the common law. In *Bromley Park Garden Estates Ltd v Moss* [1982] 1 WLR 1019 (CA) it was assumed (without deciding) that when considering reasonableness a landlord could rely on reasons that actually influenced him even if they were not expressly put forward prior to the refusal.

[22] *Air India v Balabel* [1993] 2 EGLR 66 (CA).

[23] Landlord and Tenant Act 1988 s 2(1).

[24] Landlord and Tenant Act 1988 s 3.

[25] In *Blockbuster Entertainment Ltd v Barnsdale Properties Ltd* [2003] EWHC 2912 damages of £70,000 were awarded.

Design Progression Ltd v Thurloe Properties Ltd Peter Smith J did not disguise his contempt for the way in which the landlord had behaved and awarded both ordinary damages and exemplary damages.[26] The premises were under-rented and the tenant found an assignee who was willing to pay a premium of £75,000 for the lease. The landlord adopted a 'deliberately obstructive policy'[27] in the hope that the assignment would not go ahead, thus forcing the tenant to surrender the lease, and enabling the landlord to let to the property at a market rent. In addition to compensatory damages of £160,000 (which included a sum representing the loss of the premium), exemplary damages of £25,000 were awarded in order to punish the defendant for his conduct.

17.4 Covenants against Alienation

17.4.1 The Form of Alienation Covenants: Restricting Dealings

Under the common law, if there is no provision to the contrary in the lease, the tenant is able to dispose of his interest in any way or carve new interests out of his own. In practice, however, this right is often restricted by leasehold alienation covenants and by statute.

When construing an alienation covenant it is important to look at both the types of dealings that are controlled and the form of control (such as whether there is a total prohibition or whether a dealing is permitted with consent). It is also possible for the landlord to limit the situations in which consent can be refused. In *Moat v Martin*, for example, the lease provided that 'consent will not be withheld in the case of a respectable and responsible person'.[28] It was held that if the proposed assignee was respectable and responsible, consent could not be withheld even though there might be other good reasons for refusing consent.

Alienation covenants may be concerned only with preventing one particular form of alienation. It may be, for example, that the landlord only wishes to protect the relationship of privity with this particular tenant and is not concerned about who is in occupation of the property. If so, the covenant would only restrict assignment, whilst permitting sub-letting and other forms of sharing occupation. Often, however, the prohibition is more extensive and places some form of restriction on assignment, sub-letting and sharing or parting with possession or occupation. A restriction on 'possession' is interpreted strictly to refer to the legally understood concept of 'possession', and the phrase 'parting with possession' will normally include an assignment.[29] In *Akici v LR Butlin Ltd* the Court of Appeal held that 'sharing possession' does not prevent sharing occupation.[30] The covenant against sharing possession was, however, broken on the facts as the tenant (an individual) seldom visited the property which was used by a pizza company[31] that had considerable control over the property and employed all the staff working on the property.

---

[26] [2004] EWHC 324 (Ch).
[27] [2004] EWHC 324 (Ch) [124].
[28] [1950] 1 KB 175 (CA).
[29] *Marks v Warren* [1979] 1 All ER 29 (Ch).
[30] [2005] EWCA Civ 1296, [2006] 1 WLR 201.
[31] In which the tenant was the sole director.

If the covenant applies to dealings with the *whole*, it will not be breached by a disposition of only *part* of the premises. If it is desired to restrict dealings with *part* as well, the clause must, therefore, specifically state this. It is unusual for a landlord to permit an *assignment* of part only of the premises, as this would result in the landlord having to deal with several tenants and, as a general rule, the greater the number of interests in the property, the greater the administrative and management burdens. There may be fewer objections to a sub-letting of part of the premises, particularly if the premises can be readily divided into separate parts. In a retail centre, for example, a major retailer may take a letting of two units which are joined to form a larger store. Should the tenant later want to sub-let, there is unlikely to be any objection to it being restored to the original two separate units. Where sub-letting of part is permitted, it is often specified in the lease which particular parts can be sub-let. In an office block, for example, sub-letting of whole floors may be allowed, but not sub-lettings of part of a floor.

The restrictions may be absolute, prohibiting any kind of dealing with the leasehold interest, or qualified. Qualified covenants may require the tenant to obtain the landlord's consent prior to dealing or impose a condition precedent.

17.4.2 Absolute Covenants

Whereas the law generally dislikes alienation of freeholds being prohibited, no similar antipathy is shown towards leases.[32] Indeed, it is quite possible for a lease to prohibit any form of alienation, although this may make it a commercially unacceptable product. Historically, it appears that absolute covenants against assignment were once usual,[33] but nowadays they are unusual (except in short lettings of secondary property).[34]

The Law Commission has not always been comfortable with absolute covenants. In its 1985 report on Covenants Restricting Dispositions it stated:

> [We] start from the position that a basic incident of the tenant's rights of property is that he should be able to dispose of property by assignment, subletting or otherwise. When he is prohibited or restricted from so doing, whether by statute or by the terms of the tenancy, an inroad is made on what would otherwise be his common law right. In the final analysis, therefore, it is the landlord's freedom to impose such a prohibition or restriction which has to be justified ...[35]

The Law Commission recommended that absolute covenants should, with certain exceptions, no longer be allowed.[36] This is a very pro-tenant perspective. Commenting on this proposal, Stuart Bridge asks:

---

[32] L Crabb, 'Restrictions on Assignment of Commercial Leases: A Comparative Perspective' (2006) 35 *Common L World Rev* 93, 93–4.

[33] T Fancourt, 'Licences to Assign: Another Turn of the Screw?' [2006] 70 *Conv* 37, 40.

[34] N Crosby, C Hughes and S Murdoch, 'Monitoring the 2002 Code of Practice for Commercial Leases' (ODPM, March 2005) 303.

[35] Law Commission, 'Covenants Restricting Dispositions, Alterations and Change of User' (Law Com No 141, 1985) para 4.6.

[36] For discussion of this proposal, see L Crabb, 'Restrictions on Assignment of Commercial Leases: A Comparative Perspective' (2006) 35 *Common L World Rev* 93, 97.

'What about the landlord's interests?' It is the landlord who has granted a tenancy. Doing so was a voluntary disposition of property by the landlord. Surely, it is up to the landlord to dispose of that property on whatever lawful terms he or she wants. It is not only the tenant who has rights of property (consequential upon the term), so also has the landlord (consequential upon the reversion).[37]

In the event, the Law Commission's recommendation was not implemented. Shortly afterwards, however, the pro-tenant reforms contained in the Landlord and Tenant Act 1988 were introduced (discussed above). This profoundly changed the way in which applications for consent are dealt with.

17.4.3 Qualified Covenants

A qualified covenant is one which permits alienation with the consent of the landlord. Before the Landlord and Tenant Act 1927, if the covenant simply said that consent must be obtained, without any specification about the circumstances in which consent must be given, it was possible for the landlord to withhold consent for any (or no) reason. It was to all intents and purposes like an absolute covenant, and therefore could be quite misleading as the tenant may well have assumed that consent would be given to a reasonable request.[38] Statute does, therefore, convert most qualified covenants into fully qualified covenants, so that consent cannot be unreasonably withheld.[39] Section 19(1) of the Landlord and Tenant Act 1927 provides that covenants against 'assigning, under-letting, charging or parting with the possession of demised premises or any part thereof without licence or consent' are deemed to be subject 'to a proviso to the effect that such licence or consent is not to be unreasonably withheld'.[40] This section does not, however, apply to agricultural holdings or farm business tenancies.[41]

17.4.4 Fully Qualified Covenants and Reasonableness

Most alienation covenants, at least in relation to leases entered into before 1 January 1996,[42] are fully qualified (either expressly or by statute), providing that the landlord's consent

---

[37] S Bridge, 'Commercial Leases Past and Present' in S Bright (ed), *Landlord and Tenant Law. Past, Present and Future* (Oxford, Hart, 2006) 73.

[38] Crabb says that qualified covenants 'lack transparency': L Crabb, 'Restrictions on Assignment of Commercial Leases: A Comparative Perspective' (2006) 35 *Common L World Rev* 93, 118. In the US this has led some (minority) judges in states where there is no legislation on this issue, to treat such clauses as ambiguous and imply a qualification that the landlord's refusal must be reasonable: see cases referred to by Crabb at 100–103.

[39] Assignment of leases was regulated in 1892, 1925 and 1927: T Fancourt, 'Licences to Assign: Another Turn of the Screw?' [2006] 70 *Conv* 37, 40.

[40] Landlord and Tenant Act 1927 s 19(1)(a), but this proviso does not preclude the right of the landlord to require payment of a reasonable sum in respect of any legal or other expenses incurred in connection with such licence or consent.

[41] Landlord and Tenant Act 1927 s 19(4). There is also a proviso that in building leases for more than 40 years no consent is required for an alienation which takes place more than seven years before the end of the lease provided that written notice is given within six months of the transaction, see s 19(1)(b). This building lease proviso does not, however, apply in relation to assignment of non-residential leases entered into after 1 January 1996 (s 19(1D)) or to mining leases.

[42] The date that the Landlord and Tenant (Covenants) Act 1995 came into force.

cannot be unreasonably withheld. If the landlord seeks to impose any condition as part of his consent, this will also need to satisfy the reasonableness test. In the public sector, consent to a sub-letting of part cannot be made subject to conditions.[43]

This section looks at the principles used to guide whether a refusal of consent is reasonable. There are, however, two important limitations on the scope of the reasonableness requirement.

17.4.4.1 Conditional Alienation

First, it has been held that the requirement of reasonableness does not apply where the lease imposes 'pre-conditions' to a dealing and those pre-conditions are not satisfied. The lease in *Crestfort Ltd v Tesco Stores Ltd* illustrates a common form of tenant covenant:

> … not to assign underlet or part with or share the possession of the whole of the demised premises without the previous consent in writing of the landlord (which consent shall not be unreasonably withheld) PROVIDED ALWAYS that: –
> … (d) any permitted underlease shall be granted subject to like covenants and conditions as are herein contained except as to the rent thereby reserved and the length of the term thereby granted.[44]

As Lightman J observes, this can be read in two ways. First it may be a precondition in the sense:

> … that it sets out the agreement of the parties as to what alienations are not absolutely prohibited and can be made with consent and accordingly restricts the circumstances in which a tenant can properly apply for consent to an underletting.

Alternatively:

> … it sets out conditions which the landlord can impose for giving consent or sets out circumstances in which the landlord's refusal of consent to underletting is to be deemed to be reasonable.[45]

Read in the second sense it would be unlawful, and Lightman J commented that the court should be slow to reach this interpretation given that these clauses are in common commercial use and this reading would make it legally ineffective. Although the point has never been thoroughly argued in a higher court, the tenant's concession in *Allied Dunbar Assurance plc v Homebase Ltd*[46] that it was a precondition was accepted by the Court of Appeal in that case as properly made, a view that Lightman J also supported in *Crestfort Ltd v Tesco Stores Ltd*.[47]

It is, therefore, now generally accepted that the landlord is able to set conditions for a dealing which will not be subjected to a test of reasonableness. This considerably weakens the impact of section 19. Given the policy reasons as to why alienability should be facilitated, it is perhaps surprising that the alternative reading has not found favour. To describe the requirements as 'pre-conditions' is necessary to the logic of the argument, yet the reality

---

43 Housing Act 1985 s 94(5).
44 [2005] EWHC 805 (Ch).
45 [2005] EWHC 805 (Ch) [42].
46 [2002] EWCA Civ 666 [3], [16] and [42].
47 [2005] EWHC 805 (Ch).

is that consent is being sought for a disposition on particular terms; the terms do not pre-exist the application for consent. In the case of a proposed sub-letting, the sub-lease will result from the consent and requiring it to be in a particular form, however the alienation covenant is worded, is simply a 'condition' of consent and should be subjected to reasonableness. Further, if it is possible to set (pre)conditions that are not subjected to the reasonableness test, the so-called major 'reform' in section 19(1A) (discussed immediately below) is far less radical than billed.

17.4.4.2 Section 19(1A): New Leases and Agreed Circumstances and Conditions

The statutory provisions applying to the assignment (not sub-letting) of non-residential leases entered into on or after 1 January 1996 changed following the implementation of the Landlord and Tenant (Covenants) Act 1995. The abandonment of original tenant liability created serious concerns for landlords as they would lose the comfort of being able to sue the original tenant should an assignee fail to meet its obligations under the lease. As part of a rather messy and hastily put together political compromise, landlords of non-residential leases were given the opportunity to have greater control on assignment by amendments made to section 19(1) of the Landlord and Tenant Act 1927 in return for the loss of original tenant liability.[48] As this is restricted to non-residential leases, it is discussed below under 'Alienation Covenants in Commercial Leases'. In outline, the changes mean that the landlord will not be acting unreasonably if he withholds consent to a proposed assignment on the grounds that circumstances exist which the parties had previously agreed would be a reason for withholding consent or if he imposes conditions that it has been previously agreed can be imposed as a condition of consent.[49]

17.4.4.3 Reasonableness

Subject to the above, where reasonableness is the applicable test it is treated as a question of fact, depending on the particular circumstances.

A number of principles were set out by Balcombe LJ in *International Drilling Fluids Ltd v Louisville Investments (Uxbridge) Ltd*:[50]

(1) The purpose of a covenant against assignment without the consent of the landlord, such consent not to be unreasonably withheld, is to protect the lessor from having his premises used or occupied in an undesirable way, or by an undesirable tenant or assignee: *per* Smith LJ in *Bates v Donaldson* [1896] 2 QB 241 at 247, approved by all the members of the Court of Appeal in *Houlder Brothers & Co Ltd v Gibbs* [1925] Ch 575.

(2) As a corollary to the first proposition, a landlord is not entitled to refuse his consent to an assignment on grounds which have nothing whatever to do with the relationship of landlord and tenant in regard to the subject matter of the lease: see *Houlder Brothers & Co Ltd v Gibbs*, a decision which (despite some criticism) is binding on this court: *Bickel v Duke of Westminster* [1977] QB 517. A recent example of a case where the landlord's consent was unreasonably

---

[48] Landlord and Tenant Act 1927 s 19(1)(A-E), introduced by Landlord and Tenant (Covenants) Act 1995 s 22. On the 'political process' leading to this reform, see C Harpum, 'The Law Commission and Land Law' in S Bright and J Dewar (eds), *Land Law. Themes and Perspectives* (Oxford, OUP, 1998) 159–62; S Bridge, 'Former Tenants, Future Liabilities and the Privity of Contract Principle' (1996) 55 *CLJ* 313, 328–31.
[49] Landlord and Tenant Act 1927 s 19(1A).
[50] [1986] 1 Ch 513 (CA) 519–21.

withheld because the refusal was designed to achieve a collateral purpose unconnected with the terms of the lease is *Bromley Park Garden Estates Ltd v Moss* [1982] 1 WLR 1019. [In this case there were separate lettings of a restaurant and a flat above it. The landlord refused consent to assign the flat as he wanted the tenant to leave so that he could relet both as a single unit. This was held unreasonable – although it made sense in estate management terms, the single letting was not an object which the covenant had been designed to achieve.]

(3) The onus of proving that consent has been unreasonably withheld is on the tenant: see *Shanly v Ward* (1913) 29 TLR 714 and *Pimms Ltd v Tallow Chandlers Company* [1964] 2 QB 547 at 564.

[This is no longer the case: see section 1(6)(c) Landlord and Tenant Act 1988, 17.3.4 above.]

(4) It is not necessary for the landlord to prove that the conclusions which led him to refuse consent were justified, if they were conclusions which might be reached by a reasonable man in the circumstances: *Pimms Ltd v Tallow Chandlers Company, op.cit.*

(5) It may be reasonable for the landlord to refuse his consent to an assignment on the ground of the purpose for which the proposed assignee intends to use the premises, even though that purpose is not forbidden by the lease: see *Bates v Donaldson, op.cit.*, at 244.

(6) There is a divergence of authority on the question, in considering whether the landlord's refusal of consent is reasonable, whether it is permissible to have regard to the consequences to the tenant if consent to the proposed assignment is withheld …
[After reviewing the authorities Balcombe LJ concluded that] while a landlord need usually only consider his own relevant interests, there may be cases where there is such a disproportion between the benefit to the landlord and the detriment to the tenant if the landlord withholds his consent to an assignment that it is unreasonable for the landlord to refuse consent.

(7) Subject to the propositions set out above, it is in each case a question of fact, depending upon all the circumstances, whether the landlord's consent to an assignment is being unreasonably withheld: see *Bickel v Duke of Westminster, op.cit.*, at 524 and *West Layton Ltd v Ford* [1979] QB 593 at 604, 606-607.

Two further propositions were added by Phillips LJ in *Mount Eden Land Ltd v Straudley Investments Ltd,*[51] a case involved with a request for sub-letting:

(1) It will normally be reasonable for a landlord to refuse consent or impose a condition if this is necessary to prevent his contractual rights under the headlease from being prejudiced by the proposed assignment or sublease.

(2) It will not normally be reasonable for a landlord to seek to impose a condition which is designed to increase or enhance the rights that he enjoys under the headlease.

The principles distilled by Balcombe LJ have been frequently referred to in later cases. Nonetheless, it has been stressed that a judge must always decide reasonableness on the particular facts of each case rather than being bound by strict rules.[52] In *Ashworth Frazer Ltd v Gloucester CC* Lord Bingham said that effect must be given to three overriding principles:

---

[51] (1997) 74 P & CR 306 (CA) 310.
[52] *Bickel v Duke of Westminster* [1977] QB 571 (CA) 524, and approved in *Ashworth Frazer Ltd v Gloucester CC* [2001] UKHL 59, [2001] 1 WLR 2180.

The first, as expressed by Balcombe LJ in *International Drilling Fluids Ltd v Louisville Investments (Uxbridge) Ltd* [1986] 1 All ER 321 at 325, [1986] Ch 513 at 520 is that –

'a landlord is not entitled to refuse his consent to an assignment on grounds which have nothing whatever to do with the relationship of landlord and tenant in regard to the subject matter of the lease.'

Secondly, in any case where the requirements of the first principle are met, the question whether the landlord's conduct was reasonable or unreasonable will be one of fact to be decided by the tribunal of fact …

Thirdly, the landlord's obligation is to show that his conduct was reasonable, not that it was right or justifiable.[53]

Numerous examples can be given of when it may be reasonable to refuse consent, and when it has been held to be unreasonable.

Reasonable refusal
— when the references of the proposed assignee are unsatisfactory.[54]
— when the assignee would acquire statutory protection under the Rent Acts,[55] or a statutory right under the Leasehold Reform Act,[56] which the assignor could not claim or did not want.
— when the proposal was to reassign the lease to the original tenant in order that it could exercise a personal break clause that the current tenant could not, and so bring the lease to an end, causing substantial loss in the value of the landlord's reversion.[57]
— when the assignment will necessarily, or is likely to, lead to a breach of covenant.

This has most commonly arisen where the proposed assignee intends to use the premises inconsistently with the user covenant. Before *Ashworth Frazer Ltd v Gloucester CC*[58] a distinction had developed between necessary breach (where refusal would be reasonable) and likely breach (where refusal would be unreasonable). The explanation was that if breach was not inevitable, a landlord would be in no worse position with an assignee who proposed a change of use than an existing tenant. In *Ashworth Frazer Ltd v Gloucester CC* the House of Lords rejected this distinction (albeit obiter),[59] and accepted that in some cases it may be reasonable to refuse consent even if breach is not certain to follow. As Lord Rodger observed, a landlord faced with the prospect that the assignment of the lease is likely to result in a breach of a user covenant could well decide, reasonably, to withhold consent: an assignee who plans to challenge the user provisions will cause inconvenience and cost to the landlord.[60]

The effect of likely breach by the disponee also arose in *Woolworth v Charlwood*,[61] when the assignee clearly intended to disregard a keep open covenant in the lease: given the

---

[53] *Ashworth Frazer Ltd v Gloucester CC* [2001] UKHL 59, [2001] 1 WLR 2180 [3]-[5].
[54] *Shanly v Ward*, (1913) 29 TLR 714 (CA).
[55] *Lee v K Carter Ltd* [1949] 1 KB 85 (CA); *Swanson v Forton* [1949] Ch 143 (CA); *Dollar v Winston* [1950] Ch 236; *Brann v Westminster Anglo-Continental Investment Co Ltd* [1976] 2 EGLR 72 (CA).
[56] *Norfolk Capital Group Ltd v Kitway* [1977] QB 506 (CA); *Bickel v Duke of Westminster* [1977] QB 571 (CA).
[57] *Olympia & York Canary Wharf Ltd v Oil Property Investments Ltd* [1994] 2 EGLR 48 (CA).
[58] [2001] UKHL 59, [2001] 1 WLR 2180.
[59] On the majority's view of the construction of the lease the point did not arise.
[60] [2001] UKHL 59, [2001] 1 WLR 2180 [68]-[71].
[61] *Woolworth (FW) plc v Charlwood Alliance Properties Ltd* [1987] 1 EGLR 53 (Ch).

weakness of alternative remedies available to the landlord (see chapter 13), it was held reasonable to refuse consent.

— where the assignment itself will be a breach of the alienation covenant. This is the seeming meaning of the strangely worded section 1(5) of the Landlord and Tenant Act 1988. This section states:

> For the purposes of this Act it is reasonable for a person not to give consent to a proposed transaction only in a case where, if he withheld consent and the tenant completed the transaction, the tenant would be in breach of a covenant.

In *Moat v Martin* the lease provided that consent would not be withheld if the proposed assignment was to a respectable and responsible person.[62] If the proposed assignment is to a respectable person, but in some other respects is unsuitable, it will nevertheless be an unreasonable refusal if the landlord withholds consent, as the actual assignment would not put the tenant in breach of covenant. This is the understanding given to section 1(5) by Aldridge and Ross (drawing on the Law Commission paper that made the proposal);[63] some commentators skirt over it as it is very difficult to be sure exactly what meaning the section is meant to carry. It is certainly did not meant to change the law on reasonableness generally; if refusal of consent to a proposed assignment would be unreasonable under the pre-1988 Act principles, it remain unreasonable post 1988.

— if there are breaches of a repairing covenant which are more than minimal, unless the proposed assignee will remedy them.[64]

Unreasonable Refusal
— when the landlord wanted to recover the premises for himself.[65]
— when the would-be assignee was a tenant of other property of the landlord and planned to vacate the other property which would be hard to re-let.[66]
— when the landlord said he would consent to a sub-letting only if the proposed sub-tenant made a direct covenant with the head landlord to pay him rent under the head tenancy (which was greater than the rent under the sub-tenancy).[67]

Although the first two of Balcombe LJ's principles suggest that a landlord can refuse consent only if the proposed assignee is for some reason unacceptable, in practice good reasons for refusal are not limited to matters that are wholly concerned with the assignee's ability to be a good tenant. So, for example, in *Sportoffer Ltd v Erewash BC* the landlord was able to refuse consent to assignment and change of use on the grounds that the proposed use by the assignee would compete with its own commercial interests.[68] For the tenant this assignment was very important: its business was close to failure and the assignment would

---

[62] [1950] 1 KB 175 (CA).
[63] T Aldridge, 'Consent to assignment and underletting – plus ça change' (1989) 133 *SJ* 1277; M Ross, *Commercial Leases* (London, Butterworths, 1998) H [27].
[64] *Orlando Investments Ltd v Grosvenor Estate Belgravia* [1989] 2 EGLR 74 (CA) 77; *Crestfort Ltd v Tesco Stores Ltd* [2005] EWHC 805 (Ch) [51].
[65] *Bates v Donaldson* [1896] 2 QB 241 (CA).
[66] *Houlder Brothers & Co Ltd v Gibbs*, [1925] Ch 575 (CA).
[67] *Balfour v Kensington Gardens Mansions Ltd* (1932) 49 TLR 29 (KB).
[68] [1999] 3 EGLR 136 (Ch).

carry a significant capital premium. Some jurisdictions adopt a stricter approach. Crabb notes that:

> In Victoria the landlord can only withhold consent where the assignee proposes a non-permitted use, the landlord considers that the proposed assignee does not have sufficient financial resources or business experience to meet the obligations under the lease or the assignor has not made statutory disclosure. [footnotes omitted][69]

17.5 Alienation Covenants in Particular Sectors

17.5.1 Alienation Clauses in Commercial Leases

The particular form that an alienation clause takes will depend upon a variety of factors: the length of the lease (the longer it is, the more powers to dispose of the lease the tenant will want); the type of premises (how easily they can be sub-divided, etc); and the relative bargaining powers of the parties. The form of the alienation covenant will also be affected by its interrelationship with the rent review provisions within the lease; although tight control over alienation might appear attractive to landlords, this could have an adverse impact upon the rent levels set at review and for this reason landlords are likely to eschew overly restrictive provisions.

As seen earlier, the reasonableness requirement in section 19 of the Landlord and Tenant Act 1927 has been held not to apply to preconditions to a dealing. It has become common, therefore, for alienation covenants to contain preconditions for both assignment and sub-letting.

17.5.1.1 Assignment

There is an important difference between leases entered into before 1 January 1996 ('old leases') and those entered into on or after that date ('new leases'). If the landlord imposes a condition as part of the consent to assignment for an old lease, the condition itself must be reasonable in order to satisfy the 1927 Act (unless it is a pre-set condition, in which case the courts may take the view that the reasonableness test is not triggered if those pre-conditions are not satisfied, see 17.4.4.1 above).

With the changes brought by the amendment to section 19(1) of the Landlord and Tenant Act 1927, landlords of new leases are able to impose conditions on assignments of non-residential leases entered into on or after 1 January 1996 which are not subject to a test of reasonableness. In practice, in a lease that contains rent review provisions, the landlord has a commercial interest to stick only to reasonable conditions. Section 19(1A) provides:

> Where the landlord and the tenant under a qualifying lease [a non-residential new lease] have entered into an agreement specifying for the purposes of this subsection –
>
> (a) any circumstances in which the landlord may withhold his licence or consent to an assignment of the demised premises or any part of them, or

[69] L Crabb, 'Restrictions on Assignment of Commercial Leases: A Comparative Perspective' (2006) 35 *Common L World Rev* 93, 111.

(b) any conditions subject to which any such licence or consent may be granted,

then the landlord –

(i) shall not be regarded as unreasonably withholding his licence or consent to any such assignment if he withholds it on the ground (and it is the case) that any such circumstances exist, and

(ii) if he gives any such licence or consent subject to any such conditions, shall not be regarded as giving it subject to unreasonable conditions;

and section 1 of the Landlord and Tenant Act 1988 (qualified duty to consent to assignment etc) shall have effect subject to the provisions of this subsection.

Although this agreement will usually be part of the lease itself, it need not be; it can be entered into simultaneously with the lease yet be a separate document, or can be entered into at a later stage (so long as it is before the tenant applies for consent to assign).[70] The agreement can require an assignee to meet certain objectively defined criteria and can confer a limited degree of discretion upon a landlord, so long as either (a) that discretion is required to be exercised reasonably or (b) the tenant can require that discretion to be reviewed by an independent third party whose decision is conclusive.[71]

It has become usual for landlords to require the assignor tenant to enter into an authorised guarantee agreement (AGA) on assignment, that is a guarantee that covers default by the tenant's immediate assignee but not later tenants.[72] There may also be requirements in relation to the proposed assignee, such as that it meets specified financial criteria.[73] There is always a need for caution, however, in that the more restrictive the provisions, the harder it will be for the tenant to assign the lease and the greater the impact on rent review.[74]

17.5.1.2 Sub-letting

The ability to sub-let may be very important to a tenant; it may be, for example, that the tenant only wishes to move out of the property temporarily, or that a purchaser can only be found for an interest that is shorter than the entire remainder of the term. Further, if the property is over-rented, making assignment difficult, the tenant will be able to reduce its loss by sub-letting at a lower rent.

The lease will often contain provisions requiring sub-lettings to take a particular form. Although the tenant will remain liable to the landlord after a sub-letting, there are several situations in which the tenant may drop out of the picture leaving the sub-tenant as the

---

[70] Landlord and Tenant Act 1927 s 19(1B).

[71] Landlord and Tenant Act 1927 s 19(1C).

[72] S 16 of the Landlord and Tenant (Covenants) Act 1995. No further liability is permitted by the Landlord and Tenant (Covenants) Act 1995, see ch 18. See further, 17.5.1.4 below.

[73] The Association of British Insurers produced a report on the Landlord and Tenant (Covenants) Act 1995 containing model clauses, see 'Report of the ABI Working Party on the Landlord and Tenant (Covenants) Act 1995' (January 1996).

[74] It has been suggested that landlords can retain original tenant liability by prohibiting assignment but permitting sub-letting of the whole. There is doubt as to whether this is legally effective: see P Walter, 'Landlord and Tenant (Covenants) Act 1995: A Legislative Folly?' [1996] *Conv* 432, who was advised by the Lord Chancellor's Department that a sub-letting of the whole for virtually the whole of the remaining term would be a sham agreement, and liable to be struck down within Landlord and Tenant (Covenants) Act 1995 s 25. More importantly, the rent review implications mean that it is unlikely to be tried in practice.

direct tenant of the landlord. This will happen, for example, if the headlease is forfeited but the sub-tenant is granted relief against forfeiture. In this situation the landlord will care very much about the terms of the sub-lease. It has, therefore, become common for landlords to insist that there can be no sub-letting unless a number of conditions are met. The lease is likely to require any sub-tenant to enter into a direct covenant with the landlord (which will enable the landlord to take speedy enforcement action for breach of the sub-lease, rather than having to rely on the tenant to do so), that the sub-lease will contain covenants in the same form on the sub-tenant's part as the tenant's covenants in the headlease, that the rent payable under the sub-lease is the greater of the open market rent or the rent then passing in the headlease, and that any sub-lease must be contracted out of the rights of renewal under the Landlord and Tenant Act 1954. As 'pre-conditions', they avoid the 1927 Act reasonableness requirement (see 17.4.4.1 above).

These conditions can make it difficult for tenants to sub-let in a poor property market, especially if the lease is over-rented. Tenants have, therefore, tried to find ways around this. One attempt was for there to be a conforming sub-lease, accompanied by a collateral agreement in which the mesne landlord promised to reimburse the sub-tenant for the difference between the leasehold obligations and the lesser amount that it was commercially willing to pay. In *Allied Dunbar Assurance plc v Homebase Ltd* the tenant found a potential sub-tenant for its retail warehouse, but the sub-tenant was only prepared to pay a rent substantially below the passing rent, and as the property was out of repair it was not willing to assume repairing obligations as onerous as those in the head-lease.[75] They proposed to enter into two documents: a sub-lease complying with the terms of the head-lease and a collateral deed by which the tenant promised to indemnify the sub-tenant. The Court of Appeal read these two documents as interdependent and held that they did not satisfy the requirements of the head-lease. Chadwick LJ recognised that a landlord has a commercial interest in the terms of the sub-lease.[76] Although this particular route was unsuccessful, Lightman J suggested in *Crestfort Ltd v Tesco Stores Ltd* (obiter) that an indemnity given by a third party might work.[77] The explanation given for the difference between these two cases is that where the indemnity is provided by the mesne landlord the indemnity would provide a 'full and complete answer to any claim by the [mesne] landlord' and so it is 'unreal' to suggest that the sub-tenant has assumed the full obligation. Where, however, the indemnity is provided by a third party the position is 'totally different' as 'the obligation assumed by the tenant under the underlease is absolute and unlimited'.[78] It has also been held that a sub-lease can be coupled with the payment of a reverse premium (a sum paid by the tenant to the sub-tenant in recognition of the fact that the rent obligation in the lease is higher than the current market rent). In *NCR Ltd v Riverland No 1 Ltd*, again a case involving an overrented property, Peter Smith J held that an agreement that the tenant would pay a reverse premium of £3 million to the sub-tenant did not prevent the sub-lease complying with the terms of the head lease.[79]

---

[75] [2002] EWCA Civ 666.
[76] [2002] EWCA Civ 666 [38].
[77] [2005] EWHC 805 (Ch) [78].
[78] [2005] EWHC 805 (Ch) [78]
[79] [2004] EWHC 921 (Ch).

17.5.1.3 Surrender Back Clauses

If the rental payable under the lease is less than the current market rent for the premises, the assignor may require a premium from the assignee. If the landlord wishes to realise this premium value for itself, a surrender-back clause may be included in the lease. This works by requiring the tenant to offer to surrender the lease to the landlord prior to any assignment and only if the landlord refuses the offer can the tenant then proceed to dispose of the lease.

These clauses have generated difficulty with protected business leases: an agreement to surrender is void under section 38(1) of the Landlord and Tenant Act 1954 as it, in effect, prevents the 'tenant from making an application or request' for renewal under the Act. The tenant may therefore be left in a position where the agreement[80] to surrender is void and yet the tenant is still not free to dispose of the premises in any other way.[81]

17.5.1.4 Alienation Clauses in Practice

For tenants, the terms of alienation clauses are very important as they provide flexibility to respond to changing business needs. Indeed, a survey by Crosby and others showed that the inability to manage entry and exit strategies was a major concern of occupying tenants.[82] In addition to alienation a tenant may be able to move by simply exercising a break clause to end the lease (see chapter 24), but although break clauses have become more common in recent years, half of all leases still do not contain break clauses and even where they exist they are not often used because the conditions for their operation tend to be restrictive and will seldom enable the tenant to end the lease exactly when it wants to.[83] This means that the alienation provisions are crucial.

The University of Reading's Report on the Operation of the 2002 Code of Practice on Commercial Leases found that a significant number of small business tenants have no right to assign or sub-let at all.[84] The Business Lease Code 2007 says that leases should allow assignment subject to the landlord's consent not to be unreasonably withheld. Where assignment is allowed, it is 'almost universal' that the tenant will be required to enter into an AGA as a condition of consent[85] (despite the 2002 Code of Practice recommending that an AGA should be used only where the assignee is of lower financial standing than the assignor at the date of assignment, a recommendation also found in the 2007 Code).[86] This

---

[80] But not an executed surrender.

[81] See *Allnatt London Properties Ltd v Newton* [1984] 1 All ER 423 (CA).

[82] N Crosby, V Gibson and S Murdoch, 'UK Commercial Property Lease Structures: Landlord and Tenant Mismatch' (2003) 40 *Urban Studies* 1487. This was based on large corporate occupiers and did not address the needs of small business tenants. The fact that small business tenants tend to have shorter leases may suggest that the problem would be less acute, although it is probably also the case that they have a greater need for flexibility.

[83] N Crosby, C Hughes and S Murdoch, 'Monitoring the 2002 Code of Practice for Commercial Leases' (ODPM, 2005) 312.

[84] N Crosby, C Hughes and S Murdoch, 'Monitoring the 2002 Code of Practice for Commercial Leases' (ODPM, 2005) 303.

[85] This is based on the tenant surveys, and so reflects what they think the position is (a relatively high number simply did not know): N Crosby, C Hughes and S Murdoch, 'Monitoring the 2002 Code of Practice for Commercial Leases' (ODPM, 2005) 303.

[86] The 2007 Code also suggests that for a smaller tenant, a rent deposit should be acceptable as an alternative: Joint Working Group on Commercial Leases, 'The Code for Leasing Business Premises in England and Wales 2007' (2007) para 5.

undermines much of the intent behind the Landlord and Tenant (Covenants) Act 1995 as the tenant will remain at a financial risk in relation to premises that it no longer occupies. If sub-letting is allowed, it is usual to require the sub-lease to be at the higher of either the passing rent or market rent which, in times of falling rents, makes it almost impossible to sub-let in practice.[87]

The British Property Federation (BPF) issued a Declaration on Sub-letting on 20 April 2005 that future occupational leases will permit sub-lettings at the market rent at the time of the sub-letting.[88] A number of landlords (especially larger ones) support this policy.[89] This declaration followed the government announcing, on the publication of the Report on the Operation of the Commercial Leases Code,[90] that it remained concerned about inflexibility in the market and, in particular, alienation provisions.[91] Further legislation on this remains a possibility and some see the BPF declaration as a cynical exercise to deflect further government action. The 2007 Business Leases Code follows the BPF declaration by stating that if 'subletting is allowed, the sublease rent should be the market rent at the time of subletting'.

17.5.2 Alienation and Residential Tenancies

As will be seen, there are differences between public and private sector tenancy rules. As part of its review of Renting Homes the Law Commission has made various recommendations for future changes. Driving their proposals is recognition of the need for the scheme:

> … to reflect the varieties of ways in which people actually live their lives. It needs to recognise the realities resulting from the formation and break down of relationships. The contract-holder may want to bring a new person into the agreement. People may want companionship, or someone to help pay the rent, so may want to share their accommodation with others, or take in a lodger. People may want to move around the country and exchange the premises where they currently live for another. At the same time … landlords must be able to retain a sensible degree of control over the property they are letting.[92]

A landlord who is able to end a tenancy on notice, as with most periodic private sector tenancies, has a high degree of control. Social landlords renting with longer term security face different issues, as the Law Commission notes:

> … they must be able to ensure that the people living in their accommodation have the requisite degree of housing need. At the same time, contract-holders under secure contracts must have an appropriate degree of autonomy in their use of the accommodation.[93]

---

[87] This is standard 'at the bigger end of the market': N Crosby, C Hughes and S Murdoch, 'Monitoring the 2002 Code of Practice for Commercial Leases' (ODPM, 2005). It is unclear what the position is in relation to small business tenants.

[88] British Property Federation, 'Declaration on Sub-letting' (20 April 2005).

[89] Initially, 36 but towards the end of 2006 numbers had increased to 46.

[90] N Crosby, C Hughes and S Murdoch, 'Monitoring the 2002 Code of Practice for Commercial Leases' (ODPM, March 2005).

[91] ODPM, Hansard HC vol 432 col 12WS (15 March 2005).

[92] Law Commission, 'Renting Homes: The Final Report. Volume 1: Report' (Law Com No 297, 2006) para 6.1.

[93] Law Commission, 'Renting Homes: The Final Report. Volume 1: Report' (Law Com No 297, 2006) para 6.2.

17.5.2.1 Public Sector Tenancies

Public sector tenants have only limited rights of alienation, reflecting the fact that local authorities need to be able to allocate housing to those most in need.

General Rule: No Assignment

Neither a secure tenant[94] nor an introductory tenant[95] can assign the tenancy. Even if the tenancy agreement purports to permit assignment, this is overridden by the statutory prohibition.[96] The only exceptions to this, discussed below, are:

(a)   where the assignment is an exchange by a secure tenant;[97]
(b)   where the assignment is made pursuant to family legislation;[98] or
(c)   the assignment is to someone who would have had a statutory right of succession had the tenant died immediately before the assignment.[99]

The fact that a secure tenancy is non-assignable (subject to the exceptions) led the Court of Appeal in *City of London Corporation v Bown* to classify it, at least during statutory continuation under section 86, as a personal right and not a right of property.[100]

Permitted Assignment (1): The Right to Exchange

There may be reasons for a public sector tenant to move from one local authority property to another. A tenant may want to move to be closer to a job or to be nearer family. Section 92 of the Housing Act 1985 gives a statutory right to exchange, subject to obtaining the landlord's consent. An exchange, in essence, involves swapping with another tenant. Schedule 3 sets out situations in which the landlord can refuse consent. Apart from the obvious, such as that either tenant has lost or is about to lose possession of his dwelling following a court order, consent can be refused if the exchange would lead to undercrowding or overcrowding, or to a person without special needs ending up in accommodation designed for people with special needs. It is probable that even if a Schedule 3 ground for refusal exists, it can be relied on only if reasonable.[101] Consent cannot be refused for any other reason, such as a previous bad record as a tenant, no matter how reasonable; if withheld on other grounds it is to be treated as given.[102] The landlord has 42 days from the tenant's application to rely on a Schedule 3 ground.[103] The only condition permissible to attach to a consent is that the tenant should first remedy any breach.[104]

---

[94] Housing Act 1985 s 91(1). Different rules apply to fixed-term secure tenancies granted before 5 November 1982: Housing Act 1985 s 91(2).

[95] Housing Act 1996 s 134.

[96] *City of London Corporation v Bown* (1989) 22 HLR 32 (CA) 37.

[97] Housing Act 1985 s 91(3)(a).

[98] That is, property adjustment orders under the matrimonial and civil partnership legislation, and property transfers under the Children Act 1989: Housing Act 1985 s 91(3)(b) (secure tenants); Housing Act 1996 s 134(2)(a) (introductory tenants).

[99] Housing Act 1985 s 91(3)(c) (secure tenants); Housing Act 1996 s 134(2)(b) (introductory tenants).

[100] (1989) 22 HLR 32 (CA).

[101] Law Commission, 'Renting Homes 2: Co-occupation, Transfer and Succession' (Law Com CP No 168, 2002) para 6.30.

[102] Housing Act 1985 s 92(3).

[103] Housing Act 1985 s 92(4).

[104] Housing Act 1985 s 92(5)–(6).

A council tenant can effect an exchange with any other tenant, whether in the same local authority or outside it, and even with a housing association tenant. As exchange must always be with another social housing tenant, it does not disrupt the allocation of housing to those in need. It is a frequently used right.

Permitted Assignment (2): Assignment under Family Legislation
This is discussed below; see 17.5.2.3.

Permitted Assignment (3): Transfer to a Potential Successor
The right to succeed is explained below, see 17.9.1 below. As the Law Commission explains, the right to assign to a potential successor:

> … does not prejudice the landlord as they would have exactly the same people as tenants as they would have had after the operation of the right of succession after the original tenant died; but it allows tenants to set their affairs in order before they die.[105]

Transfer
A secure or introductory tenant who is not able to arrange an exchange may ask for a simple transfer to a new property. The allocation scheme adopted by the local authority for determining priorities in allocating housing under Part VI of the Housing Act 1996 will then apply. The Code of Guidance issued under section 169 provides:

> 3.6 Those applying for a transfer must be treated on the same basis as other applicants in accordance with the provisions set out in the housing authority's allocation scheme, which should reflect a sensible balance between meeting the housing needs of existing tenants and new applicants, whilst ensuring the efficient use of stock. Transfers that the housing authority initiate for management purposes do not fall within Part 6. These would include a temporary decant to allow repairs to a property to be carried out.

The effect is that unless tenants come within the 'reasonable preference' categories, their 'chances of moving may be severely restricted, particularly in areas of high demand'.[106] This has a severe impact on tenant mobility, making it difficult, for example, to take up job opportunities.

Sub-letting
The right to sub-let is also restricted for secure tenants. Sub-letting of the whole or parting with possession will result in the tenancy ceasing to be secure, and it cannot again become secure.[107] There is a right, however, subject to consent from the local authority landlord, to sub-let part only of the premises.[108] Consent to a sub-letting of part cannot be unreasonably withheld and the burden of proof is on the local authority landlord to prove that the withholding is reasonable.[109] Consent cannot be given subject to a condition.[110] If the tenant

---

[105] Law Commission, 'Renting Homes 2: Co-occupation, Transfer and Succession' (Law Com CP No 168, 2002) para 6.43.
[106] J Hills, 'Ends and means: The future roles of social housing in England' (CASE Report 34, February 2007) 21.
[107] Housing Act 1985 s 93(2).
[108] Housing Act 1985 s 93(1)(b).
[109] Housing Act 1985 s 94(2).
[110] Housing Act 1985 s 94(5).

applied in writing for consent, the reasons for a refusal must also be in writing.[111] If no reply is given within a reasonable time consent is deemed to have been withheld.[112]

There are no statutory limitations on sub-letting introductory tenancies, although a sub-letting of the whole will mean a loss of the tenant's introductory status as the tenant condition will no longer be satisfied.

Similar restrictions on assignment and sub-letting relate to public sector tenancies which are not secure because the tenant condition is not satisfied – the aim being to prevent tenants not in occupation, and hence not secure, from assigning etc to persons who might become secure tenants.[113]

The Right to Take in Lodgers

Secure tenants have the right under section 93(1)(a) of the Housing Act 1985 to take in lodgers regardless of the local authority landlord's views, although the premises must not become overcrowded.

17.5.2.2 Private Sector Tenancies

It is not unusual for private sector tenancies to include an absolute prohibition on assignment or sub-letting. The Office of Fair Trading (OFT) considers, however, that it may be unfair for a tenant to be held to a fixed term tenancy without the option of either surrendering the lease to the landlord, or assigning or sub-letting the property.[114]

If an assured periodic tenancy contains an alienation clause, this will govern[115] (and if it is a qualified covenant, it will be converted into a fully qualified one by Landlord and Tenant Act 1927 section 19(1)). In the absence of an express alienation clause, section 15(1) of the Housing Act 1988 implies a term that the tenant can not assign, sub-let or part with possession of the whole or part without the consent of the landlord.[116] Surprisingly, section 19 of the Landlord and Tenant Act 1927 is excluded[117] (and, therefore, the Landlord and Tenant Act 1988 will also not apply), which means that the landlord can unreasonably withhold consent.

17.5.2.3 Premises as the Family Home

Family breakdown raises difficult issues in tenancy law. Often the factual context is complex, with the parties moving between properties, perhaps in breach of the alienation provisions, without observing any requisite formalities and without keeping the landlord informed.[118] The departing tenant may also be under pressure to serve a notice to quit in order to be considered for rehousing by the local authority; if he does so, this will end the right of the remaining occupier to stay in the home. This is discussed in more detail in chapter 22; here the focus is on rights to transfer a tenancy to another family member.

---

[111] Housing Act 1985 s 94(6)(a).
[112] Housing Act 1985 s 94(6)(b).
[113] Housing Act 1985 s 95.
[114] OFT, 'Guidance on unfair terms in tenancy agreements' (OFT 356, September 2005) paras 4.22–4.28.
[115] Housing Act 1988 s 15(3)(a).
[116] Unless a premium is to be paid on the grant or renewal of the tenancy: Housing Act 1988 s 15(3)(b).
[117] Housing Act 1988 s 15(2).
[118] See, for example, the facts of *City of Westminster v Peart* (1992) 24 HLR 389 (CA).

Occupation Rights

In the case of a joint tenancy, if one tenant leaves the other will still be able to occupy the property and both tenants remain liable for payment of rent, etc. The departure of one tenant will not affect the protected status of a tenancy so long as the remaining joint tenant occupies the dwelling-house as his only or principal home.

If it is a sole tenant who leaves, however, things are more complicated. There will no longer be a protected tenancy as the tenant no longer occupies the house 'as his only or principal home' (as required for protection in both the public and private sectors) and the landlord may be able to end the tenancy without needing to prove a statutory ground for possession. Where the parties are in a legally recognised relationship (marriage or civil partnership) the remaining occupier is an a much stronger position. Under section 30 of the Family Law Act 1996, the remaining spouse/civil partner has a statutory right of occupation which can be treated as being occupation by the tenant[119] and a right to pay rent, etc, as if it were being paid by the tenant,[120] provided that the property has been, or was intended to be, used as the matrimonial/civil partnership home.[121] This means that if a spouse/civil partner with family home rights remains in occupation, then s/he cannot be evicted so long as the marriage/civil partnership exists unless there is a statutory ground for possession. The court is also able to make an occupation order under section 35 for a former spouse/civil partner, and under section 36 for cohabitants, but the order 'must be limited so as to have effect for a specified period not exceeding six months' (extendable on one or more occasions for a further six months).

Transferring the Tenancy

None of the above results in a 'change of tenant'. It may be, however, that the departing tenant is willing to transfer the tenancy to the remaining occupier. The ability of the parties to assign the tenancy will depend, in the private sector, upon the terms of any alienation covenant in the lease and, if none, upon getting the landlord to consent. In the public sector, a secure or introductory tenancy can be assigned under the potential successor rules to a spouse or civil partner who was living with the tenant for twelve months ending on the assignment and occupying the house as the principal home.[122] In practice, however, if the departing tenant has already left, there will be no secure or introductory tenancy left to assign.

A transfer can be made to the remaining occupier by court order, even against the will of the departing tenant, under family law legislation.

The Family Law Act 1996, section 53 and Schedule 7, gives the court powers to order a transfer of a tenancy on relationship breakdown. In the case of a married couple this means divorce, nullity or judicial separation, and for civil partners it means dissolution, nullity or a separation order. The powers can also be exercised if unmarried cohabitants cease to live together as husband and wife, provided that they have lived together in the property as husband and wife. The court can order a transfer of a tenancy if it is a secure, assured, or

---

[119] Family Law Act 1996 s 30(4).
[120] Family Law Act 1996 s 30(3).
[121] Family Law Act 1996 s 30(7).
[122] Housing Act 1985 s 91(3)(c) and s 87.

introductory tenancy[123] so long as the property has at some time been the couple's home[124] (and where relevant, the spouse/civil partner seeking the transfer has not remarried/formed a civil partnership). If it is the tenant partner who has moved out, this can create difficulties as there will then be no relevant tenancy to transfer (the tenant no longer living in the property as his only or principal home). The only option then is to apply for an occupation order under sections 30, 35 or 36.[125] Further, there cannot be a transfer if the tenant partner is a joint tenant with someone other than the transferee, as this would force the non-transferring joint tenant into a joint tenancy relationship with the transferee.[126]

When there is a transfer of the tenancy, the transferor will, in the absence of a court order directing otherwise, cease to be liable on the tenancy covenants from the date of the order.[127] The Family Law Act 1996 also gives the court power to order the payment of compensation to the transferor;[128] although compensation orders are not likely to be common, they could be used, for example, to cover removal expenses or to compensate for a secure tenant's loss of the right to buy. In considering whether or not to order a transfer, the courts are directed to have regard to 'all the circumstances', including the circumstances in which the tenancy was granted; the housing needs and resources of each of the parties and any child living with one or both of them (or any other child that the court considers relevant); the financial resources of each party; the likely effect that making or refusing the order will have on the health, safety or well-being of any relevant child; and the suitability of the parties as tenants. In addition, in the case of cohabitants where only one of them is entitled to occupy the house by virtue of the tenancy, consideration must be given to the nature of the relationship; the length of time that they have lived together as man and wife; whether they have any children or have parental responsibility for any children; and the length of time that has elapsed since they lived together.[129]

Both the power to order a transfer in respect of cohabitants and the statutory criteria were introduced in 1996, following the recommendations of the Law Commission which were concerned to remove discrimination against cohabitants and ensure that children are properly housed.[130] The intention underlying Schedule 7 is clearly to enable the 'deserted and deserving' partner to remain in the family home following a relationship breakdown.

A similar, but not identical, jurisdiction exists to transfer 'property' on divorce, etc, in the Matrimonial Causes Act 1973, sections 24 and 25.[131] There is an argument that tenancies can only be transferred by section 24 if there is no contractual or statutory restriction on

---

[123] Statutory tenancies within the Rent (Agriculture) Act 1976 and protected and statutory tenancies under the Rent Act 1977 are also covered, Sch 7 para 1. Given that most private sector tenancies are now shortholds, and carry no security, transfer of these is not going to provide a long-term solution to the housing needs.

[124] Family Law Act 1996 Sch 7 para 4; *Hall v King* (1987) 19 HLR 440 (CA).

[125] *Gay v Sheeran* [2000] 1 WLR 673 (CA).

[126] *Gay v Sheeran* [2000] 1 WLR 673 (CA).

[127] Family Law Act 1996 Sch 8 paras 7(2) and 11.

[128] Family Law Act 1996 Sch 7 para 10.

[129] Family Law Act 1996 Sch 7 para 5 and cross referring to ss 33 and 36.

[130] Law Commission, 'Domestic Violence and Occupation of the Family Home' (Law Com No 207, 1992) paras 6.2–6.12.

[131] In deciding whether to order a transfer, the court can take account of the interaction of its decision and the likely exercise by the local authority of its rehousing obligations, see *Jones v Jones* (1997) 29 HLR 561 (CA).

transfer by the tenant;[132] if correct this may limit the courts powers to deal with many private sector tenancies. Secure and introductory tenancies can be transferred this way as there is express provision in the Housing Act 1985 section 91(1)(b).

The problem with these various statutory powers is that they can be easily defeated by a departing tenant (whether sole or joint) serving notice on the landlord[133] or surrendering the tenancy[134] before the application for transfer has been made.

A court may also order a transfer of a tenancy where children are involved. This power is contained in the Children Act 1989, Schedule 1, paragraph 1(2)(d) and (e). The court can make an 'order requiring either parent to transfer [property] to the other parent for the benefit of the child'. Benefit has been interpreted widely and will extend beyond the financial benefit of the child to include *welfare* benefit.[135] The criteria which the court is to use in the exercise of its discretion are set out in the Children Act 1989, Schedule 1, paragraph 4(1), and include the financial resources and earning capacity of the parent and of the child, the financial needs of the parent and of the child, and any disability of the child. In *K v K* the power was used to order the father to transfer his rights in a joint tenancy of council property to the mother. It may be that the power cannot be used if the proposed transfer is not a permitted assignment within the tenancy,[136] although it could also be argued that the specific statutory power should be taken to override any limitations in the lease so as not to defeat the statutory objective.

17.5.2.4 Reform of Alienation and Residential Tenancies

The Law Commission has given much consideration to dealing with residential tenancies. It identifies a number of areas in which the law currently fails to take sufficient account of the way in which people live their lives nowadays. Whether or not these proposals will be adopted by the government is unclear.

New joint occupiers

At present, a new joint tenant can only be brought into the agreement by assignment, or by surrender followed by a new grant. The draft Rented Homes Bill provides that a contract holder may (more easily and with the consent of the landlord which is not to be unreasonably withheld) add another person to the contract.[137]

The Right to Take in Lodgers

The Law Commission recommends that the right to take in lodgers, without the need for consent, be extended to all secure contracts (secure as defined by the Rented Homes Bill).[138]

---

[132] See the remarks of Megaw LJ in *Hale v Hale* [1975] 1 WLR 931 (CA), but note this was a case where there was no such restriction on transfer.

[133] *Newlon Housing Trust v Al-Sulaimen* [1999] 1 AC 313 (HL).

[134] *Sanctuary Housing Association v Campbell* [1999] 3 All ER 460 (CA), decided under the Matrimonial Homes Act 1983 (which the Family Law Act 1996 replaced, with changes).

[135] *K v K* [1992] 1 WLR 530 (CA).

[136] Law Commission, 'Domestic Violence and Occupation of the Family Home' (Law Com No 207, 1992) para 6.5.

[137] Law Commission, 'Renting Homes: The Final Report. Volume 2: Draft Bill' (Law Com No 297, 2006) Rented Homes Bill cl 108.

[138] For an explanation of the Law Commission's meaning of secure and standard, see ch 6.

For standard contracts, there should be a supplementary term giving this right subject to consent not to be unreasonably withheld.[139]

Sub-letting (referred to as 'sub-occupation' by the Law Commission given the break with property law concepts).
The Law Commission is not prescriptive on this but suggests there could be a supplementary term for all occupation contracts allowing sub-occupation with consent. Consent would not be subject to a reasonableness test, thus giving the landlord a right of veto so that the landlord is able to control who finally ends up in possession of the property.[140]

The Right to Exchange
Under the present law an exchange can take place only if there is 'mutuality', that is there will be no void properties at the end of the chain. The Law Commission recommends a relaxation of this, to fit with the desires of social landlords, so that there can be a simple chain of transfers even if there is a potentially a void at both ends. This will encourage mobility and choice based letting. Further, the right to exchange with consent should extend to all secure contracts made by community landlords, provided that both contract-holders hold secure contracts from a community landlord. [141]

Transfer to a Potential Successor
The right to transfer to a person who would have the statutory right to succeed if the current occupier died should be given, subject to the landlord's consent not to be unreasonably withheld,[142] to any sole contract-holder with a secure contract.

Impact on Landlord
The current law is unclear as to the effect on the landlord of unauthorised dealings by the tenant. Under the Law Commission's proposed scheme the landlord will not be bound if the contract-holder deals with the occupation contract in a way not permitted by the contract or in accordance with a family property order.[143] Any non permitted dealing will be a breach of contract which will expose the contract-holder to the risk of possession proceedings.

17.5.2.5 Alienation and Long Residential Leases

Lessees who have paid significant sums to buy a lease will be reluctant to agree any restraint on their ability to deal with their interest. It is unusual, therefore, for there to be strict controls on alienation of long leaseholds. Nevertheless, it is not uncommon to find some

---

[139] Law Commission, 'Renting Homes: The Final Report. Volume 1: Report' (Law Com No 297, 2006) paras 6.9–6.12.

[140] Law Commission, 'Renting Homes: The Final Report. Volume 1: Report' (Law Com No 297, 2006) paras 6.13–6.20.

[141] Law Commission, 'Renting Homes: The Final Report. Volume 1: Report' (Law Com No 297, 2006) paras 6.46–48.

[142] The landlord should also be able to impose a condition that the potential successor is to be treated as a priority successor or reserve successor, thus precluding the possibility of a further right of succession on the potential successor's death: Law Commission, 'Renting Homes: The Final Report. Volume 1: Report' (Law Com No 297, 2006) para 6.74.

[143] Law Commission, 'Renting Homes: The Final Report. Volume 2: Draft Bill' (Law Com No 297, 2006) Rented Homes Bill cl 120(3).

restrictions, such as a requirement that prior to any assignment the assignee must enter into a direct covenant with the landlord. The lease may also contain a fully qualified covenant against sub-letting the whole; in practice, if the tenant is buying the property as an investment and plans to rent it out on short tenancies, such a wide restriction (rather than one, perhaps, applying only to sub-leases of a more than a certain period) will be inconvenient and it is hard to see why the landlord needs to protect its interest.

17.5.2.6 Alienation and Agricultural Leases

In agricultural leases, it is usual for the tenant to have limited ability to alienate. It should also be noted that section 19(1) of the Landlord and Tenant Act 1927 does not apply to agricultural leases. The reason why agricultural leases have tended to be treated differently is because of the 'importance to the landlord of the character and ability of the tenant'.[144] The Law Commission felt that qualified covenants in agricultural leases should be fully qualified but that there was still a case for permitting absolute covenants.

17.6 Disposition in Breach of an Alienation Clause

17.6.1 Common Law

If the tenant alienates without obtaining necessary consent, he will be in breach of covenant, even if consent could not have been reasonably withheld.[145] The transaction itself will, however, still be valid.[146] If the tenant does dispose in breach of covenant, the landlord can claim for damages to his reversion and (assuming the lease contains a forfeiture clause and that the breach has not been waived) bring an action for forfeiture. Where there has been an assignment in breach of a covenant against assignment the section 146 notice must be served on the assignee, not the assignor.[147]

The landlord may also have a remedy against the sub-tenant if there has been a sub-letting in breach of the lease. In *Crestfort Ltd v Tesco Stores Ltd* the tenant, Tesco, anxious to reduce the burden of meeting its obligations under the lease, proceeded to sub-let to a newish company, Magspeed, without finalising the landlord's consent.[148] Negotiations had gone on for some time but there were outstanding issues relating to compliance with the insurance and repair obligations in the lease. The landlord did not want to forfeit the lease but did want to end the sub-lease, and sought an injunction

---

[144] Law Commission, 'Covenants Restricting Dispositions, Alterations and Change of User' (Law Com No 141, 1985) para 6.6.

[145] *Eastern Telegraph Co v Dent* [1899] 1 QB 835 (CA); *Barrow v Isaacs & Son* [1891] 1 QB 417 (CA); *Creery v Summersell and Flowerdew & Co Ltd* [1949] Ch 751.

[146] *Old Grovebury Manor Farm Ltd v W Seymour Plant Sales and Hire Ltd (No 2)* [1979] 1 WLR 1397 (CA) (covenant not to assign business premises without landlord's consent); *Peabody Donation Fund Governors v Higgins* [1983] 1 WLR 1091 (CA) (assignment of secure tenancy; the lease, pre-dating the Housing Act 1980, contained a total prohibition on assignment).

[147] *Old Grovebury Manor Farm Ltd v W Seymour Plant Sales and Hire Ltd (No 2)* [1979] 1 WLR 1397 (CA). On forfeiture, see ch 24.

[148] [2005] EWHC 805 (Ch).

ordering the surrender of the sub-lease. In order to succeed it would need to show a cause of action not only against Tesco, but also against Magspeed. It was argued that Magspeed was liable on the principle that the alienation covenant in the headlease was a restrictive covenant that bound the sub-tenant. There were two problems with this argument: first, there is some doubt as to whether a 'restrictive' covenant covers anything other than covenants restrictive of the user of land; and second, the:

> ... covenant (even if it bound Magspeed) only bound Magspeed not to underlet. It did not bind Magspeed before it took the underlease not to accept an underlease.[149]

Magspeed was, however, found liable in tort for inducing or aiding a breach of contract. An earlier case, *Hemingway Securities Ltd v Dunraven Ltd*, had similarly held a sub-tenant liable on this basis.[150] It is necessary to show actual knowledge of the breach (knowledge that sub-letting without consent, or in the *Hemingway* case without the sub-tenant entering into a direct covenant with the landlord, is in breach of the headlease) and an intention that the breach be committed, and that damage is caused. In *Crestfort Ltd v Tesco* damage could be shown as it was recognised that landlords have a commercial interest in the form of a sub-lease,[151] and the wrongful grant 'deprived the landlords of the opportunity to require payment of a premium as the price for giving consent to such grant'.[152] Finding Magspeed liable meant that both the tenant and sub-tenant were liable in damages in respect of the sum that the landlord might reasonably have demanded for relaxing the covenant against sub-letting, but also led to an order for the surrender of the sub-lease.

17.6.2 Residential Tenancies

If the tenancy is assured, the landlord has a discretionary ground for possession if the tenant has broken an obligation of the tenancy.[153]

In the public sector also, unlawful disposition will lead to the landlord being entitled to recover possession: the idea underlying controls on dispositions in the public sector is to ensure that it is the local authority that remains in control of allocating housing, and this goal cannot be circumvented by tenant dispositions. If a secure or introductory tenant sub-lets the whole or parts with possession, the tenancy will cease to be secure/introductory and cannot later recover its status.[154] In the case of a sub-letting of part without the landlord's consent, this will entail a breach of the tenancy giving the landlord a discretionary ground for possession.[155] In the case of a purported assignment not within any of

---

[149] [2005] EWHC 805 (Ch) [59].

[150] (1996) 71 P & CR 30 (Ch).

[151] Drawing on *Allied Dunbar Assurance plc v Homebase Ltd* [2002] EWCA Civ 666.

[152] [2005] EWHC 805 (Ch) [67].

[153] Housing Act 1988 Ground 12 Sch 2. With dealings other than assignment this means that the landlord can seek a court order for possession against the tenant. There appear to be no reported cases on the position post-assignment. Under the common law, the assignment is effective and the assignee will, therefore, be the tenant. Following the reasoning in *Crestfort Ltd v Tesco* [2005] EWHC 805 (Ch) the assignee is not in breach and although intuitively it seems right that the landlord can obtain possession it is difficult to see what ground could be used.

[154] Housing Act 1985 s 93(2); Housing Act 1996 s 125(5a), (6).

[155] Ground 1 Part 1 Sch 2 of the Housing Act 1985.

the permitted exceptions, the assignment is ineffectual – the assignor tenant ceases to be a secure tenant as he will no longer satisfy the tenant condition (not being in occupation) and the new occupier has no tenancy.[156]

The Law Commission regards this as unnecessarily complex. Under its proposals:

> The landlord is not bound by any purported transfer or other dealing by a contract-holder which required, but did not have, the landlord's consent. The landlord can take proceedings against a purported transferee who will have no legal entitlement to occupy the premises as against the landlord.[157]

17.7 Formalities and Alienation

In order for a lease to be validly assigned, the assignment must be by deed.[158] This is so even if the lease is for not more than three years and can be created orally.[159] Although there is no obligation at common law to inform the landlord of the assignment, there is usually a contractual obligation to do so even in leases where there are no restrictions on alienation.

In addition, where the leasehold title is registered, the assignment will be complete only when registered, and the assignment of an unregistered legal lease with more than seven years left to run must be registered.[160] This can have important and unexpected consequences. In *Brown & Root*, although a licence to assign was completed and the assignee was treated as the new tenant and was paying rent, the transfer was never registered at HM Land Registry because of an unresolved stamp duty problem.[161] The original tenant then sought to exercise a break clause that was personal to the original tenant and that would 'cease to have effect upon the assignment of the lease'. The Court of Appeal held that as there had been no assignment of the legal estate,[162] the exercise of the break clause was effective. This is an inconvenient result; registration has to be effected by the assignee and there is nothing more that the landlord or the assignor can do to transfer the legal estate. In this case, the outcome was that the break clause was unexpectedly exercisable, and there are undoubtedly other consequences to be discovered in future cases.

If there is no deed but the purported assignment is in writing signed by both parties and containing all the terms, as required by section 2 of the Law of Property (Miscellaneous) Provisions Act 1989, then it may take effect as an equitable assignment. The word

---

[156] *City of London Corporation v Bown* (1990) 22 HLR 32 (CA) 38–9.

[157] Law Commission, 'Renting Homes: The Final Report. Volume 1: Report' (Law Com No 297, 2006) para 6.57.

[158] Law of Property Act 1925 s 52(1). An assignment that takes effect by operation of law need not by deed: s 52(2)(g) and s 53(1)(a) of the Law of Property Act 1925. This would include a purported sub-lease for a period not less than the remaining term of the lease and within the Law of Property Act 1925 s 54(2): see *Milmo v Carreras* [1946] KB 306 (CA); *Parc Battersea Ltd v Hutchinson* [1999] L & TR 554 (Ch).

[159] *Crago v Julian* [1992] 1 WLR 372 (CA).

[160] Land Registration Act 2002 ss 4 and 27.

[161] *Brown & Root Technology Ltd v Sun Alliance & London Assurance Co Ltd* [2001] Ch 733 (CA).

[162] Had this been unregistered land, the legal title would have passed on completion of the assignment. In *Gentle v Faulkner* [1900] 2 QB 267 (CA), the Court of Appeal held that 'assignment' means assignment of the legal estate (and did not include a declaration of trust, as occurred in that case). Perhaps the better outcome in *Brown & Root Technology Ltd v Sun Alliance & London Assurance Co Ltd* [2001] Ch 733 (CA) would have been to distinguish *Gentle v Faulkner* and hold that 'assignment' in the break clause included an equitable assignment.

'assignment' can bear different meanings in different contexts, so that for some purposes a legal assignment is required but for others an equitable assignment will suffice.[163]

In order to create a sub-lease, the same rules apply as for the creation of the head-lease (see chapter 4).

Under the Law Commission's Renting Homes scheme the formality requirements are relaxed. The Rented Homes Bill provides that there is no need for a deed and an occupation contract can be transferred in writing signed by both parties.

17.8 The Position of Sub-tenants

17.8.1 Protected Status

In this section, the term 'head-tenancy' will be used to refer to the lease between the landlord and the tenant, and 'sub-tenancy' to the lease between the tenant and the sub-tenant. If there is a sub-letting, the sub-tenant may have protected status depending upon the general rules applicable to that sector.

In the public sector, a sub-tenant cannot be a secure tenant as the landlord condition is not satisfied.[164] The head tenancy will cease to be a secure tenancy if there is a sub-letting of the whole.[165]

In the private residential sector, on a sub-letting of the whole, the head-tenancy will not be assured as the tenant will not be in occupation.[166] The sub-tenant may, however, be an 'assured tenant' so long as the conditions in section 1 are met.[167] If there is a sub-letting of part, the sub-tenant will not be an assured tenant if there is a resident landlord.[168] The tenant is not prevented from being an assured tenant simply because he has granted rights to others to share some of the accommodation.[169]

In the commercial sector, if there is a lawful sub-letting of the whole of business premises, the tenant will not have renewal rights under the Landlord and Tenant Act 1954 as he is no longer in occupation of the premises.[170] However, the sub-tenant may have renewal

---

163 Under the Landlord and Tenant (Covenants) Act 1995, 'assignment' includes equitable assignment: s 28. Given Mummery LJ's observation in *Brown & Root Technology Ltd v Sun Alliance & London Assurance Co Ltd* [2001] Ch 733 (CA) that equitable title is 'capable of passing by virtue of a specifically enforceable contract to assign the lease', this raises interesting questions, in conjunction with the Landlord and Tenant (Covenants) Act 1995, about when an assignee becomes liable on the tenant's covenants in situations where an agreement to purchase is entered into prior to the actual assignment. See also the *obiter* remarks of Sir Christopher Slade in *City of Westminster v Peart* (1991) 24 HLR 389 (CA), where he held that for the purposes of the Housing Act 1985 s 87 assignment includes equitable assignment: '... it seems to me improbable that the legislature would have intended that parties who wished to take advantage of s 91(3)(c) [which permits assignments] would find themselves obliged to undertake the formality and expense of executing a deed (which would probably require legal assistance) ...' Although the relevant assignment was oral in this case, it could be effective as it predated the Law Reform (Miscellaneous) Provisions Act 1989.
164 Housing Act 1985 s 80(1).
165 Housing Act 1985 s 93(2).
166 Housing Act 1988 s 1.
167 'Tenancy' and 'tenant' include 'sub-tenancy' and 'sub-tenant', Housing Act 1988 s 45.
168 Housing Act 1988 Sch 1 para 10.
169 Housing Act 1988 s 4.
170 Landlord and Tenant Act 1954 s 23(1).

rights if the conditions in section 23 are satisfied,[171] although many sub-tenancies in practice have these rights excluded.[172] On a sub-letting of part, both the tenant and sub-tenant can have rights of renewal in relation to the part they occupy.

17.8.2 Liability[173]

As the sub-tenant is in a contractual relationship with the tenant, all covenants in the sub-lease will be enforceable between these parties. Where the sub-tenant has been required to enter into a direct covenant with the head-landlord (as is usual), the sub-tenant will also be liable to the head-landlord while a sub-tenant.[174] Even in the absence of such a direct covenant, the sub-tenant will be bound by all restrictive covenants in the head-lease, such as the user covenant.[175]

The sub-tenant may also be able to enforce covenants against the landlord if they touch and concern the land, but only in relation to tenancies entered into before 1 January 1996.[176]

17.9 Statutory Succession on Death

As an estate in land, a lease will pass on the death of the tenant.[177] In the case of a long leasehold, this can be a valuable inheritance.

17.9.1 Residential Tenancies

With short term residential leases, as the contractual tenancy can generally be terminated on notice, the transmission on death of a bare contractual tenancy is of little importance. Instead, what is important is to determine the effect of the tenant's death on the protected status of periodic tenancies.

In practice, succession to protected residential tenancies is governed by statute that, broadly, gives the right to succeed to certain categories of person. Where there are no succession rights, the landlord is usually able to recover possession. As will be seen, there are differences between the public and private sector in relation to who is given the right to succeed, differences that are difficult to explain in policy terms and that may be more the

---

[171] 'Tenancy' includes a 'sub-tenancy': Landlord and Tenant Act 1954 s 69.

[172] Landlord and Tenant Act 1954 Part II s 38(4) and 38(A).

[173] See generally ch 18.

[174] For leases entered into before 1 January 1996, the duration of any direct contractual liability of the sub-tenant will turn on the wording but may extend to the duration of the lease.

[175] *Tulk v Moxhay* (1848) 2 Ph 774; Landlord and Tenant (Covenants) Act 1995 s 3(5).

[176] Law of Property Act 1925 s 78; *Caerns Motor Services Ltd v Texaco Ltd* [1994] 1 WLR 1249 (Ch). S 78 does not apply to tenancies entered into on or after 1 January 1996: Landlord and Tenant (Covenants) Act 1995 s 30(4). The sub-tenant may also be able to enforce a head-landlord covenant by using the Contract (Rights of Third Parties) Act 1999 if the term 'purports to confer a benefit on him' (or he is given express rights to enforce). In practice, the 1999 Act will usually be expressly excluded.

[177] The Law Commission recommend that if there is no right of survivorship under a joint tenancy or statutory succession, a periodic residential occupation contract will terminate automatically following the tenant's death: Law Commission, 'Renting Homes: The Final Report. Volume 2: Draft Bill' (Law Com No 297, 2006) Rented Homes Bill cl 159.

result of historic accident than design. Further, although the Civil Partnership Act 2004 has recently extended succession rights to same-sex couples,[178] the debate generated by the previous exclusion of same-sex couples has disclosed other categories of person who arguably should be granted succession rights.

17.9.1.1 Private Sector

Under the Housing Act 1988, succession rights are given to the (sexual) partner of an assured periodic tenant. Section 17 provides that where a sole tenant of an assured periodic tenancy dies and, immediately before the death, the tenant's spouse or civil partner was occupying the dwelling-house as his or her only or principal home, the tenancy will vest in the spouse or civil partner, and not devolve under the tenant's will or intestacy. Cohabitants also have succession rights, provided they were living with the tenant as his or her wife or husband or as if they were civil partners.[179] There can be only one succession;[180] and where the survivor of a joint tenancy becomes sole tenant by survivorship this counts as succession.[181] Where there is no-one with succession rights an assured tenancy will pass to the tenant's estate, but to prevent a periodic tenancy continuing indefinitely, the landlord has the right to end a periodic tenancy within twelve months of the tenant's death when the tenancy has devolved in this way, and the acceptance of rent from a new tenant does not by itself create a new tenancy.[182]

17.9.1.2 Public Sector

In the public sector, a broader range of persons is given succession rights. In addition to (sexual) partners, family members may also be able to succeed to a secure tenancy. By the Housing Act 1985 section 87 a person is entitled to succeed if he occupies the house as his only or principal home at the time of the tenant's death and is either the tenant's spouse or civil partner, or another member of the tenant's family who lived with the tenant throughout the twelve month period ending with his death.[183] It is not necessary for the twelve month residency to have been in the particular council property; in *Waltham Forest LBC v Thomas* the tenant's brother was able to succeed even though they had only moved to this particular house from another council home ten days before the tenant died.[184] If there is more than one potential successor, preference is given to the spouse or civil partner over other family members.[185]

In the public sector, cohabitants (living together as husband and wife or as civil partners) are treated in the same way as other 'family' and so will need to satisfy the twelve month

---

[178] Before that, succession rights in the private sector were different for those living together as husband and wife, and others. In *Ghaidan v Godin-Mendoza* [2004] UKHL 30, [2004] 2 AC 557 the House of Lords held that this infringed the human rights of homosexual couples, and the Human Rights Act 1998 s 3 was used to read the relevant legislation as extending to same sex couples so as to eliminate its discriminatory effect.

[179] Housing Act 1988 s 17(4).

[180] Whether by statute, testamentary succession or by joint tenancy survivorship: Housing Act 1988 s 17(1), (2) and (3).

[181] Housing Act 1988 s 17(2)(b).

[182] Housing Act 1988 Sch 2 Ground 7.

[183] The twelve month period can be interrupted temporarily: *Camden LBC v Goldenberg* (1996) 28 HLR 727 (CA).

[184] [1992] 2 AC 198 (HL).

[185] Housing Act 1985 s 89(2).

residency requirement. The concept of family is not open-ended for these purposes[186] but is defined by section 113 to be (in addition to cohabitants): parent, grandparent, child, grandchild, brother, sister, uncle, aunt, nephew and niece. It includes relationships by marriage or civil partnership, half-blood, step-relationships, and illegitimate children are to be treated as the legitimate child of the mother and the reputed father. The Court of Appeal has held that a minor child can succeed to a secure tenancy (although this may give rise to practical difficulties).[187]

In *Wandsworth LBC v Michalak*, this restricted meaning of family was challenged by a distant relative of the deceased secure tenant who had lived in the tenant's flat for several years.[188] His claim that the list in section 113 was not intended to be exhaustive was rejected, the Court of Appeal confirming that section 113 provides a deliberately closed list of family in the interests of certainty.[189] He also argued that there had been unlawful discrimination, in breach of his human rights protected by Article 14 (non-discrimination) and Article 8 (right to respect for the home). Although the Court of Appeal accepted that there was discrimination, in that a closer relative coming within section 113 would have been entitled to succeed,[190] the difference in treatment had an 'objective and reasonable justification'. In the words of Brooke LJ:

> It appears to me that this is pre-eminently a field in which the courts should defer to the decisions taken by a democratically-elected Parliament, which has determined the manner in which public resources should be allocated for local authority housing on preferential terms … It is understandable why Parliament wished a home not to be broken up on the death of a secure tenant when his wife or other very close relative was living with him as a member of his family at that time. It is equally understandable why Parliament decided that this privilege should not be extended to a more distant relative like Mr Michalak who was living at the secure tenant's home at the time of his death.[191]

The secure tenancy will pass with all concomitant rights, including the Right to Buy.[192] As the death of a tenant may lead to under-occupation of a dwelling, the Housing Act 1985 enables the landlord to re-house the successor if there is suitable alternative accommodation (unless the successor is the tenant's spouse)[193] if the court considers it reasonable, provided that proceedings are taken between six and twelve months after the tenant's death.[194]

---

[186] In *Wandsworth LBC v Michalak* [2002] EWCA Civ 271, [2003] 1 WLR 617 [14] and [41].

[187] *Kingston v Prince* [1999] 1 FLT 539 (CA). As a legal estate cannot be held by an infant (Law of Property Act 1925 s 1(6)) the minor will become a tenant in equity. In *Kingston*, the child's mother was also living in the house but had not been there long enough to have a right to succeed. The Law Commission recommend that a child under 16 cannot be a successor: Law Commission, 'Renting Homes: The Final Report. Volume 1: Report' (Law Com No 297, 2006) para 7.26.

[188] [2002] EWCA Civ 271, [2003] 1 WLR 617.

[189] [2002] EWCA Civ 271, [2003] 1 WLR 617 [14] and [41].

[190] An alternative comparator put forward in *Michalak* was based on the wider meaning of family under the Rent Act 1977. The Court of Appeal rejected this both on the basis that even the Rent Act understanding would not have extended to the distant relationship involved in *Michalak* and also the differences between the public and private sector regimes were too great to make it a relevant comparator.

[191] [2002] EWCA Civ 271, [2003] 1 WLR 617 [41].

[192] *Harrow LBC v Tonge* (1992) 25 HLR 99 (CA).

[193] And, probably, civil partner. The exception in Sch 2 Ground 16 refers to 'members of family other than spouse' but the subsection cross-referred to is s 87(b), and 87(a) refers to both spouse and civil partner.

[194] Housing Act 1985 Sch 2 Ground 16.

As in the private sector, there can be only a single succession; and succession includes becoming tenant by assignment as well as becoming the sole tenant by virtue of survivorship (as will be common with a couple living together).[195] In *R (on the application of Gangera) v Hounslow LBC* the son of secure tenants was unable to succeed to the secure tenancy on the death of his mother as she had already been a successor under the survivorship doctrine.[196] As in *Wandsworth LBC v Michalak*,[197] the son argued that this breached his human rights by treating him in a discriminatory manner.[198] Moses J noted that his counsel was not arguing that the scheme allowing only one statutory succession was itself a disproportionate interference with the Article 8 right to respect for the home. Such an argument would not be tenable, as the balance between the allocation of limited housing resources and security of tenure was determined by Parliament, and the court,

> … should respect the legislative judgment as to what is in the general interest unless that judgment was manifestly without reasonable foundation.[199]

Instead, the son argued that there had been unlawful discrimination. By pointing to other persons who would have been able to succeed, such as the son of a sole tenant, he claimed that his Article 14 right of non-discrimination was breached when read with Article 8. Moses J held, however, there was no discrimination, as the claimant had not been treated differently from other persons. It was not the status of the claimant that meant that he could not succeed, but the fact that there had already been one succession.

Further, and obiter, even if there had been discrimination it had objective and reasonable justification and pursued a legitimate aim.

If there is no-one with succession rights the secure tenancy (whether periodic or for a fixed term) ends when the tenancy vests in the tenant's estate following his death.[200]

17.9.1.3 Comparing the Public and Private Sector Rules on Succession

The differences in the categories of person given succession rights between the public and private sector[201] are hard to explain in terms of policy, even accepting that there are significant differences between the statutory schemes protecting tenants in the public and private sectors. It may be that the perceived interference with property rights explains a narrow group in the private sector, but then why is 12 months residency required for cohabitants in the public sector but not in the private sector? Under the Law Commission's proposed Rented Homes scheme, the same succession rights will apply to all periodic occupation contracts. Nor is it that obvious why in the public sector there can not be two successions (to the surviving partner, and then a child) assuming that the successor has a strong

---

[195] See the full list in Housing Act 1985 s 88(1).

[196] [2003] EWHC 794 (Admin).

[197] [2002] EWCA Civ 271, [2003] 1 WLR 617.

[198] He also argued (unsuccessfully) that it was disproportionate and irrational given that at the time of the eviction his needs had not been assessed under the National Assistance Act 1948.

[199] [2003] EWHC 794 (Admin) [23].

[200] Unless the tenancy vests pursuant to a court order under the family legislation: Housing Act 1985 ss 89(3) and 90(3).

[201] For a list, see Law Commission, 'Renting Homes 2: Co-occupation, Transfer and Succession' (Law Com CP No 168, 2002) para 7.49.

housing need.[202] Further, Davis and Hughes suggest that succession rights should be based around the stability of a relationship rather than its sexual or familial context, although they do recognise that there will be difficulties in definition.[203] Is there, they question, 'any inherent logic in prioritising those partners who do have a sexual relationship'?[204] In neither sector are long-term cohabiting friends or carers given succession rights.[205] In *Fitzpatrick v Sterling Housing Association Ltd* Lord Hobhouse remarked that an argument could be made for sympathetic treatment not only for homosexual couples (at issue in the case) but also for other classes, such as

> ... devoted and caring friends who have lived for a long time with the tenant in the premises but have never engaged in sexual relations with the tenant.[206]

The absence of succession rights for particular people can be partially gotten around if long-term sharers each become joint tenants. The guidance given to local authorities encourages the use of joint tenancies:

> ... where household members have long-term commitments to the home, for example when adults share accommodation as partners (including same-sex partners), friends or un-paid live-in carers ...[207]

This is, however, only a partial solution. It is guidance and applies only to the local authority sector. The Law Commission's proposal to give tenants the right to add another person to a joint tenancy would also help ameliorate the limitations of succession rights, but again will be dependent upon the parties being sufficiently aware to foresee potential problems on death. The guidance given to local authorities also suggests that where a tenant dies and another household member has been living with the tenant for a year and either providing care or accepting responsibility for the tenant's dependants, the authority should consider granting a tenancy to the remaining person either in the same home or suitable alternative accommodation.[208] The recommendation is, however, subject to there being 'no adverse indications for the good use of the housing stock' and that person having 'sufficient priority under the allocation scheme'.

The Law Commission's Renting Homes scheme proposes a rationalisation of the approach to succession in an attempt to balance the importance of security in the home[209] against the needs of landlords to manage their housing stock. Under their proposals, there

---

[202] See M Davis and D Hughes, 'What's Sex got to do with it?' [2005] 69 *Conv* 318, 320. Under the Rent Act 1977, two successions are possible, although the second succession will be to a Housing Act assured tenancy rather than a Rent Act statutory tenancy: Rent Act 1977 Sch 1 para 6.

[203] M Davis and D Hughes, 'What's Sex got to do with it?' [2005] 69 *Conv* 318, 339–40.

[204] M Davis and D Hughes, 'What's Sex got to do with it?' [2005] 69 *Conv* 318, 341.

[205] *Carega Properties SA v Sharratt* [1979] 1 WLR 928 (HL).

[206] [2001] 1 AC 27 (HL) 67. Lord Hobhouse was dissenting on the question as to whether the survivor of a homosexual couple could succeed under the Rent Act 1977, which required the couple to be living together as husband and wife. This has since been amended to apply also to civil partners: Rent Act 1977 Sch 1 para 2.

[207] DCLG, 'Revision of the Code of Guidance on the Allocation of Accommodation' (November 2002) para 3.7.

[208] DCLG, 'Revision of the Code of Guidance on the Allocation of Accommodation' (November 2002) para 3.10.

[209] Law Commission, 'Renting Homes 2: Co-occupation, Transfer and Succession' (Law Com CP No 168, 2002) para 7.42 states: 'The home ... is the centre of a life. It is where families are raised, and from where social circles are developed. The home is, for many people, the core of their existence.'

are potentially two successions if the first succession is to a (sexual) partner. Succession can be not only to surviving partners but also to family members (defined as in section 113 of the Housing Act 1985)[210] who have lived with the tenant for the 12 months preceding the tenant's death. In addition, and meeting many of the criticisms of the existing law, carers who satisfy a 12 month residency condition will also be given succession rights (but not long term friends). In view of the needs of social landlords to 'use their housing stock efficiently and for the social purposes for which it was provided'[211] social landlords will be able to recover possession if there is under occupation, provided that suitable alternative accommodation is available.

17.9.2 Agricultural Leases

Before 1984, any consideration of statutory succession would have spent some time looking at the position in the agricultural sector, where two successions upon death were permitted to properly qualified successors. This was a highly developed system reflecting the fact that the lease was not simply a means of providing a dwelling for the tenant, but also the tenant's business. Thus, a lease granted before 12 July 1984 could (and still can), be passed on upon the retirement of the tenant at 65 to, inter alia, a close relative who has made his livelihood out of farming the holding for the past seven years. However, the Agricultural Holdings Act 1984 abolished all succession rights for new leases created after 11 July 1984. The right to succeed on retirement reflected the way of life of the farming community but was also regarded as a disincentive to landlords. The abolition of succession rights may discourage long term planning by an older farmer and the involvement of families in the farming business; the reform has ensured that the 'family farm' will be confined to the owner-occupied sector. The right to two statutory successions was probably excessive, but it may be that the baby was thrown out with the bath water.

17.10 Change of Landlord

17.10.1 Introduction

Just as the tenant may wish to dispose of his interest in the property, so the landlord may wish to sell his reversion, or there may be an involuntary disposition on his death or insolvency. However, whereas the landlord will normally restrict the tenant's power to alienate the property, in particular to provide the landlord with a way of vetting the assignee, it is unusual for the tenant to have any control over a disposition by a landlord. In the public sector, however, there may be a bulk disposition of the housing stock to a new landlord with consultation procedures to be followed to take account of tenants' views.

---

[210] Law Commission, 'Renting Homes: The Final Report. Volume 2: Draft Bill' (Law Com No 297, 2006) Rented Homes Bill cl 230.
[211] Law Commission, 'Renting Homes: The Final Report. Volume 1: Report' (Law Com No 297, 2006) 7.34.

552   ALIENATION, TRANSFER AND SUCCESSION

17.10.2 *Formalities on a Change of Landlord*

17.10.2.1 *Property Law Requirements: Deeds and Registration*

By section 52 of the Law of Property Act 1925, any assignment of the reversion needs to be by deed in order to convey the legal estate. In addition, it will be necessary to complete the transaction by registration. If the reversion is unregistered, then section 4(1)(a) of the Land Registration Act 2002 requires first registration of the title if the transfer is of a freehold or lease with more than seven years to run and is made for valuable or other consideration, by way of gift or in pursuance of an order of any court. In addition, if the reversion is being transferred as part of a local authority stock transfer (see 17.11 below), section 4(1)(b) requires it to be registered as part of the means by which the tenant's right to buy is preserved. It is not necessary to register if the transfer is by operation of law, for example, if the landlord's estate vests in his executors. Registration must occur within two months of the date of transfer, failing which the transfer 'becomes void as regards the transfer… of a legal estate'.[212] If title is already registered, section 27 of the 2002 Act requires the transfer to be registered and it will 'not operate at law' until registered.[213]

17.10.2.2 *Notifying Residential Tenants*

Where the property assigned includes a dwelling, section 3 of the Landlord and Tenant Act 1985 requires the new landlord to give written notice to the tenant of the assignment and of his name and address. This notice must be given:

> … not later than the next day on which rent is payable under the tenancy or, if that is within two months of the assignment, the end of that period of two months.

Failure to give this notice without reasonable excuse is a criminal offence.[214] The assignor landlord is also given an incentive to ensure that notice is given, either by the new landlord or by himself, as until written notice is given, the assignor landlord:

> (3A) … shall be liable to the tenant in respect of any breach of any covenant, condition or agreement under the tenancy … in like manner as if the interest assigned were still vested in him; and where the new landlord is also liable to the tenant in respect of any such breach occurring within that period, he and the old landlord shall be jointly and severally liable in respect of it.

17.11 Transfer of Local Authority Housing to New Social Landlords

17.11.1 *The Background to Voluntary Transfer*

Before 1988 there had been a few voluntary transfers of housing from local authorities to other social landlords, but the big change followed the Housing Act 1988. This Act

---

[212] Land Registration Act 2002 ss 6 and 7.
[213] There are exceptions provided by s 27(5) that include: a transfer on death or bankruptcy of an individual proprietor; and a transfer on the dissolution of a corporate proprietor.
[214] Landlord and Tenant Act 1985 s 3(3).

established the principle that a transfer could be forced on local authorities through Housing Action Trusts (HATs)[215] and the inaccurately named Tenants' Choice.[216] Neither of these took off,[217] but the process for voluntary transfer whereby local authority stock can be transferred to a housing association (or private sector landlord) has become very popular and has had a marked impact on the shape and ownership of social housing in the United Kingdom.[218] Through voluntary transfer local authorities have been able to transfer part or the whole of their housing stock, which has become known as large scale voluntary transfer (LSVT). For tenants, stock transfer means ceasing to be a secure tenant and coming within the private sector regulatory regime: see 17.11.4 below.

In essence, through LSVT local authorities sell their housing stock to housing associations which are able to use private finance to buy and renovate the local authority housing. The local authority is able to use the receipts to pay off its housing debts and any levy due to the government.[219] Any surplus can be used against other council debt, and the balance left can be used as capital investment. Not all transfers produce a surplus; if the receipt is less than the housing debt central government will pay off any outstanding debt. The main reason for using LSVT has been to finance the investment necessary to improve the housing stock. As insufficient public funding has been available for this, transfer has enabled access to private sector finance in order to improve and repair the housing stock. Other reasons given for promoting LSVT include increasing tenant choice and participation, and separating local authority landlord and strategic functions, enabling them to focus on the latter. How successful LSVT has been measured against these aims is considered below.

There have been three main stages in the transfer story to date. As Pawson records, at the outset voluntary transfer was just that, local authorities choosing to go down the route of transfer, perhaps:

... seeking to protect social housing from perceived threats to its existence and/or generate capital receipts sought to make creative use of an essentially permissive legal framework.

A shift came in 1993 when a national programme was introduced, with annual bids from authorities wishing to participate and size limits imposed to avoid the creation of monopolies. Since 1997, and particularly since 2000, the transfer process has become much more government led. It:

... is now very largely driven by the need for all local authorities to ensure that their housing stock meets the Government's Decent Homes Standard (DHS) by 2012. To this end, the 2000 Housing Green Paper announced a target to transfer 200,000 homes annually – a highly ambitious objective given the historic volume of transfer activity.[220]

[215] Housing could be compulsorily transferred to a HAT at the instigation of the Secretary of State.

[216] Whereby tenants can vote for a new landlord. It is a misnomer in the sense that an acquiring landlord must be approved, and it is the approved landlord that makes the application for transfer, subject to tenant approval.

[217] Tenants' Choice was repealed by the Housing Act 1966. Only six HATs were established, for renovating housing in the most deprived areas; several have now completed their work and been wound up.

[218] In practice, virtually all transfers are to RSLs. Transfer cannot take place if a majority of tenants do not want the disposal to proceed.

[219] The levy was introduced in 1993 by the Leasehold Reform, Housing and Urban Development Act 1993 which imposed a 20% levy on receipts net of council housing debts. There was a levy 'holiday' from March 1996 to November 1999.

[220] H Pawson, 'Reviewing Stock Transfer', paper delivered to the Housing Studies Association Spring Conference 2004.

17.11.2 *The Amount of Stock Transferred and the New Landlords*

Since 1998, 172 authorities have completed 241 transfers. More than 1 million homes have been transferred, representing almost 25 per cent of the 1988 local authority housing stock. The largest transfer was Sunderland City Council's transfer of 36,356 homes in 2001 (and the largest rejection of transfer by tenant ballot – see below- was in relation to Birmingham's proposed transfer of 88,000 homes in 2002). Only 50 per cent of local authorities now retain ownership of their housing stock.

Early transfers were most likely to be whole stock transfers in Southern non-metropolitan district councils with better stock (thus carrying a positive transfer value). Post 1997, partial transfers in more difficult urban areas became more common. The pace of transfer has increased in recent years: almost half of all transfers have occurred in the last six years.[221]

The vast majority of the new landlords are organisations that have been created from the transferor's housing department to receive the stock, rather than established housing associations, reflecting a local authority preference for bodies configured to retain some vestige of local accountability.[222] Only 5 per cent of transfers have been to existing housing associations.[223]

17.11.3 *The Process of Transfer and Tenant Consultation*

Local authorities are not automatically able to transfer housing stock in this way. A local authority that wishes to do so (or to create an ALMO, see chapter 5) must apply to the Secretary of State setting out the nature of the proposed transfer and the government then announces an annual stock transfer program. The details given must include the valuation of the properties, which is based on the 'Tenanted Market Value', a figure lower than market value, and which reflects the future continued use of properties for social housing. Under section 106A of the Housing Act 1985, special consultation duties are imposed on local authorities if they are to obtain ministerial consent. Since the new landlord will not satisfy the 'landlord condition' of sections 79 and 80 Housing Act 1985, the tenants will lose their 'secure' status, although the Right to Buy is preserved under sections 171A to 171H (PRTB). Their views have to be considered carefully and Schedule 3A refers to the need for tenants to be given details of the proposed transfer; paragraph 3 requiring the tenant to be given written information about the identity of the proposed new landlord, the likely consequences for the tenant, information about the PRTB and told of his right to make representations to the local authority. In *R v Secretary of State for the Environment, ex p Walters*, Schiemann LJ said:

---

[221] DCLG, Housing Statistics, Completed LSVTs (updated 3 April 2007).

[222] H Pawson, 'Reviewing Stock Transfer', paper delivered to the Housing Studies Association Spring Conference 2004, referring to P Malpass, *Housing Associations and Housing Policy: A Historical Perspective* (Basingstoke, Macmillan, 2000).

[223] H Pawson, 'Reviewing Stock Transfer', paper delivered to the Housing Studies Association Spring Conference 2004.

The whole purpose of the consultation requirement is to enable a tenant to have his say about the likely consequences of the disposal on him before he is placed in a position which he might regard as being worse off than his present one.[224]

By paragraph 5 the Secretary of State is unable to give consent 'if it appears that a majority of the tenants of the dwelling-houses to which the application relates do not wish the disposal to proceed'.[225] In practice, this consultation exercise will include a formal ballot to find out the views of tenants. Non-compliance with the consultation requirements does not, however, invalidate the Secretary of State's consent.[226]

In addition to the views of tenants, the Secretary of State will also look at whether the terms of transfer are acceptable, and whether the public expenditure represents value for money. Where the disposal receives approval, the purchaser will become landlord of all the properties, even of those properties for which the tenants wished to remain with the local authority.

17.11.4 *The Impact of Transfer on Tenants*

Post transfer, tenants will no longer have the same landlord. This means that they will not be secure tenants, but will instead be assured tenants within the Housing Act 1988. Legally this means that different grounds for possession exist, and, in particular, the new landlord is able to use the controversial Ground 8, the mandatory rent arrears ground (although many RSLs agree not to use this ground, see chapter 10). Given that their legal position is less protected, why would tenants consent to a transfer?

The main argument for transfer is that this will enable the money to be raised that is necessary to bring the housing up to the Decent Homes Standard (DHS).[227] As part of the consultation exercise, the local authority explains to its tenants what transfer will mean and makes various 'transfer promises' to them, typically giving a specified time frame for a repair and improvement programme (often going beyond the DHS), and offering a 'rent guarantee'.[228] By way of example, the following is an extract of what was sent to tenants of

---

[224] (1998) 30 HLR 328 (CA) 341.

[225] Leaseholders are not referred to in the statutory duties but statements of policy contained in the Housing Transfer Manual 2005 Programme (ODPM, October 2004) give 'rise to an obligation on the Secretary of State not to be oblivious of the view of the leaseholders': *Secretary of State for Communities and Local Government v Swords* [2007] EWCA Civ 795 [49]). In *Secretary of State for Communities and Local Government v Swords* this meant that 'the legal obligation … was either to take account of the views of the leaseholders, as expressed primarily in the ballot but also in the petitions and the template letters, or clearly to explain why [the Secretary of State] … was not doing so' [49].

[226] Housing Act 1985 Sch 3A para 6. But consent given on a misunderstanding of the law does give a court the ability to quash the Secretary of State's consent. This is a discretionary power and in *R v Secretary of State for the Environment, ex p Walters* (1998) 30 HLR 328 (CA) the Court of Appeal declined to quash the consent as most tenants wanted the transfer to take place and undertakings could be given to secure that the complaining tenant was not disadvantaged. The Secretary of State is not under a duty to carry out an independent assessment of the adequacy of the consultation exercise: *Swords v Secretary of State for Communities and Local Government and others* [2007] EWHC 771 (Admin).

[227] On the DHS, see chs 5 and 12.

[228] According to Pawson, these are generally limited to Retail Price Index plus 1% or sometimes even a cash freeze. Under rent re-structuring (see ch 15) increases should be not more than RPI plus 0.5%, creating difficulties for transfer housing associations that have business plans built on a higher level of increase: H Pawson, 'Reviewing Stock Transfer', paper delivered to the Housing Studies Association Spring Conference 2004. The campaigning group, Defend Council Housing, states that these guarantees are limited to five years, and 17% are broken.

Liverpool City Council in connection with its ballot in March 2007 about the proposed transfer to Liverpool Mutual Homes:

> This document contains plans for the future of homes if tenants vote to transfer. It explains how Liverpool Mutual Homes will bring a better housing service, more repairs, improvements such as central heating, double glazing, new kitchens and bathrooms as well as environmental work like fencing repairs which tenants have said they want.[229]

In addition, the rights of an assured tenant are often 'topped up' to match the stronger rights that a secure tenant has.[230]

The claims made in favour of transfer are often contested. An active campaigning group, Defend Council Housing (DCH), states:

> Transfer threatens tenants' rights. The transfer of council housing to a Registered Social Landlord (a housing association or similar company) means higher rents, more evictions, a less democratic housing service, and big pay rises for senior managers. Most importantly, it means that our homes will be privatised – transferred into the private sector where banks and building societies are in control, into a consumerist and market-driven world.[231]

As the pace of transfer has picked up, so too there have been some notable 'no' votes in the tenants' ballots. In fact, in one quarter of ballots, transfer is rejected. However, notwithstanding the voices raised against stock transfer and claims of empty promises, it does appear to be largely delivering on its aims. A report by the National Audit Office in 2003[232] found that most stock transfer promises have been kept. Research commissioned by the government also confirms that transfers usually deliver on repair and improvement targets.[233] There is also higher tenant satisfaction post transfer than with the local authority landlord.[234] Transfer associations usually also have a higher level of tenant participation and involvement at board level than traditional housing associations.[235] Further, Pawson shows that eviction rates are in fact lower amongst transfer associations than both traditional housing associations and local authorities. Tenant choice is, however, largely illusory: they can stop a transfer happening, but they have little say over who the new landlord is (although since 2001 local authorities have been required to involve tenants in the selection of the new landlord).[236] Indeed, some argue that the language of choice is highly misleading: there is, in effect, the choice of staying with the local authority with its under-investment in repair, or moving to a new landlord with the promise of improvements in the condition of housing. Mullen comments:

---

[229] Taken from the City of Liverpool website.

[230] H Pawson, 'Reviewing Stock Transfer', paper delivered to the Housing Studies Association Spring Conference 2004.

[231] Taken from the Defend Council Housing website.

[232] National Audit Office, 'Improving social housing through transfer' (HC 496, 19 March 2003).

[233] DETR, 'Views on the large scale voluntary transfer process' (Housing Research Summary, Number 110, 2000).

[234] DETR, 'Views on the large scale voluntary transfer process' (Housing Research Summary, Number 110, 2000).

[235] DETR, 'Views on the large scale voluntary transfer process' (Housing Research Summary, Number 110, 2000). H Pawson and C Fancie, *Maturing assets: The evolution of stock transfer housing associations* (Bristol, Policy Press in association with the Joseph Rowntree Foundation, 2003).

[236] Pawson notes that as a 'no' vote incurs a heavy financial penalty (no access to capital investment), it is 'hard to argue with the Defend Council Housing portrayal of stock transfer ballots as tantamount to "blackmail"': H Pawson, 'Reviewing Stock Transfer', paper delivered to the Housing Studies Association Spring Conference 2004.

If the rights of tenants collectively to make choices about their future housing is really valued then the 'choices' made available to tenants should not be artificially constrained. There is little point in using the rhetoric of choice if the only change from that status quo that is acceptable is the government's preferred option. To date, the formal legal framework for securing tenant consent to transfer has operated as a legitimating device in a descriptive rather than a normative sense.[237]

Although the major reason for transfer is improvement of housing, the cost to the taxpayer of the transfer is in fact greater than the cost would be of simply paying for the local authority to renovate properties according to the National Audit Office.[238] This cost has delivered:

> ... non quantifiable benefits such as earlier improvement of poor condition social housing, community regeneration and increased tenant participation, and achieved risk transfer, including risks relating to income and cost, maintenance and risks arising from shortfalls in demand ... [The] programme has been largely successful in delivering improvements in services to tenants and in transferring the financial risks in holding properties for letting.[239]

Things are not always easy for the transfer association. Pawson and Fancie note that high debt levels and 'transfer promises' often make the post-transfer period difficult: nearly one-fifth of transfer associations gave rise to serious concerns in respect of financial viability or governance.[240]

---

[237] T Mullen, 'Stock Transfer' in D Cowan and A Marsh (eds), *Two Steps Forward* (Bristol, The Policy Press, 2001) 53.

[238] Because of the availability of lower loan rates.

[239] National Audit Office, 'Improving social housing through transfer' (HC 496, 19 March 2003) 5.

[240] H Pawson and C Fancie, *Maturing assets: The evolution of stock transfer housing associations* (Bristol, Policy Press in association with the Joseph Rowntree Foundation, 2003).

18

ENFORCING LEASEHOLD COVENANTS

18.1	Introduction
18.2	The problem of continuing liability
18.3	New and old leases
18.4	Anti-avoidance
18.5	Liability of the original tenant under old (pre-1996) leases
18.6	Liability of the original tenant under new (post-1995) leases
18.7	The position of the assignee tenant under old (pre-1996) leases
18.8	The position of the assignee tenant under new (post-1995) leases
18.9	The position of the original landlord in old (pre-1996) leases
18.10	The position of the original landlord in new (post-1995) leases
18.11	The position of the new reversioner in old (pre-1996) leases
18.12	The position of the new reversioner in new (post-1995) leases
18.13	The new reversioner and pre-assignment breaches
18.14	The position of guarantors
18.15	The impact of the 1995 Act
18.16	Enforcement of covenants by and against management companies under new (post-1995) leases
18.17	The position of the superior landlord
18.18	Enforcing covenants between tenants?
18.19	The effect of disclaimer upon liability

18.1 Introduction

This chapter considers the ability of the landlord and tenant to enforce the leasehold covenants. The original landlord and tenant are liable to each other in contract law but unless leasehold covenants are also enforceable against successive owners of the lease and of the reversion, the long term lease would not be a marketable product. A landlord would not, for example, permit assignment if the assignee could not be made liable to pay the rent.

The focus of this chapter is on landlord and tenant liability after there has been an assignment of the leasehold interest or of the reversion, looking both at the liability of the new tenant (and/or landlord) and at the liability of the original party (which in some circumstances will continue even after an assignment). The chapter also discusses the liability of guarantors, the enforcement of covenants by third parties and enforceability between a sub-tenant and the superior landlord. Reference will occasionally be made to T1 and L1 (as the original tenant and the original landlord respectively), and T2 and L2 etc will refer to their respective assignees.

Prior to the passage of the Landlord and Tenant (Covenants) Act 1995, the position was, broadly speaking, that the original parties would remain contractually liable on the leasehold covenants throughout the lease, even after they ceased to have a proprietary interest in the premises. This meant that the landlord could sue the original tenant in relation to a breach committed by a later assignee, perhaps many years after the original tenant had assigned the lease. It was also common for T2 to be required to enter into a direct covenant with the landlord as a condition of consent to the assignment of the lease to T2; the effect being that T2 would remain liable after further assignment to T3. In this way, the original tenant and other former tenants may all bear a continuing liability to the landlord for the performance of the tenant covenants. Under the doctrine known as 'privity of estate' the current landlord and tenant would also always be liable on, and benefit from, the leasehold covenants.

The 1995 Act brought a major change in relation to leases entered into after 1995 with the abandonment of continuing liability for the original tenant. The 1995 Act supports the idea that liability should be co-terminus with possession of the lease or the reversion, but in practice this principle is applied neither to the landlord nor the tenant will full force. The tenant will usually be required to guarantee performance by its immediate successor, and the landlord will remain liable after assignment unless a release from liability is given.

18.2 The Problem of Continuing Liability

The old position (which will still be relevant for many years as it applies to all pre-1996 leases) reflects both the contractual and proprietary aspects of leases, but in a rather unsatisfactory manner. There need to be ways of ensuring that the new parties assume liability for, and take the benefit of, leasehold covenants, otherwise leases would never be both granted for long periods and freely assignable. The common law therefore evolved so that whenever there is privity of estate, that is the legal relationship of landlord and tenant, covenants which relate to the land are enforceable by and against the landlord and tenant for the time being, even though there may be no relationship of contract between these parties.[1] In this manner, leases are treated differently from other contracts, for which it is possible to assign the benefit, but not the burden, of the contract. Leasehold law achieves this by annexing covenants which touch and concern the land to the leasehold estate.[2] Yet, although this acknowledges the need for there to be special rules for leases to accommodate their proprietary base and to facilitate transmissibility of interests, the common law fails to make any adjustments to the contractual rules in recognition of this special status. By virtue of contract law, the original parties to the lease remain liable on these covenants for

---

[1] *Spencer's Case* (1583) 5 Co Rep 16a.
[2] See *City of London Corporation v Fell* [1994] 1 AC 458 (HL) 465.

the duration of the leasehold contract, even when they no longer retain an interest in the property, have ceased to benefit from the contract, and have no control over the current use of the property. This continuing liability of the original parties is popularly known as 'privity of contract', but is more accurately described as original tenant or original landlord liability, or continuing liability.[3]

Although continuing liability affects both parties, the burden of it falls more heavily on the original tenant than the original landlord as it is the tenant who will generally carry more onerous obligations within the lease. During the late 1980s and early 1990s the unfairness of continuing liability came to the fore as economic recession brought a higher rate of insolvency. In a strong property market, if the current tenant falls into serious arrears, the landlord may elect to forfeit and relet; in a weak property market it may be difficult to relet the premises and suing former tenants is a more attractive option, especially if the rental payable by the tenant is higher than the current rental value of the property. Demands against former tenants were not infrequent, and elicited much criticism, as noted by Lord Nicholls in *Hindcastle v Barbara Attenborough Associates Ltd*:

> Sometimes, in post-assignment cases, the landlord's protection may be achieved at an unreasonably high price to others. The insolvency may occur many years after the lease was granted, long after the original tenant parts with his interest in the lease. He paid the rent until he left, and then took on the responsibility of other premises. A person of modest means is understandably shocked when out of the blue he receives a rent demand from the landlord of the property he once leased. Unlike the landlord, he has no control over the identity of assignees down the line. He had no opportunity to reject them as financially unsound. He is even more horrified when he discovers that the rent demanded exceeds the current rental value of the property.[4]

In 1986, the Law Commission examined continuing liability and set out some of the arguments for and against:

> 3.1 Some people see the continuing liability of the privity of contract principle as intrinsically unfair. They regard the contractual obligations undertaken in a lease as only properly regulating the terms on which the owner for the time being of a property permits the tenant for the time being to occupy and use it, or as the case may be, to sublet and profit from it. They see no reason why responsibility should last longer than ownership of the particular interest in the property. Furthermore, as the facts seem to indicate that the continuing responsibility in practice falls more on tenants than on landlords, those of this view see the principle as operating in an unfair way, being biased against tenants …
>
> 3.3 The contrary view is that the obligations contained in a lease are freely entered into, and if the parties wish to limit their liability in any particular way, they are perfectly at liberty to do so. Freedom of contract is a basic principle of our law, and it should only be modified when it can be demonstrated that it is important or necessary to do so.[5]

---

[3] Strictly speaking, privity of contract is the contractual doctrine whereby non-parties to the contract cannot benefit from, or be burdened by, the contract. In leasehold law, non-contractual parties *are* bound to perform these contractual promises by privity of estate and so it is highly misleading to explain continuing liability as 'privity of contract'.

[4] [1997] AC 70 (HL) 83. See also *London Diocesan Fund v Phithwa* [2005] UKHL 70, [2005] 1 WLR 413 [11].

[5] Law Commission, 'Landlord and Tenant Law: Privity of Contract and Estate: Duration of Liability of Parties to Leases' (Law Com CP No 95, 1986).

Two years later the Law Commission proposed reform prefaced on the principle that:

… a landlord or a tenant of property should not continue to enjoy rights nor be under any obligations arising from a lease once he has parted with all interest in the property.[6]

Threat of the loss of continuing liability caused alarm to many landlords who argued that it was a crucial element in the attractiveness of commercial property as an investment medium; a strong original tenant covenant effectively guaranteed a secure income flow throughout the length of the lease. As will be seen, the principle put forward by the Law Commission was not fully translated into the Landlord and Tenant (Covenants) Act 1995 as a landlord will usually remain liable after an assignment of the reversion, and a tenant may be required to guarantee its immediate successor. The strong landlord lobby also ensured that the eventual reform applied only to future leases and not to leases already entered into at the commencement of the Act.[7] The 1995 Act began as a Private Member's Bill and was adopted by the Government late into the Parliamentary session after a complicated compromise between the British Property Federation (reflecting landlord interests) and the British Retail Corporation (reflecting tenant interests). The gist of the compromise was that landlords would not oppose the abandonment of original tenant liability for future leases, provided that the control they could exercise over assignment of the lease was strengthened by amendment of section 19 of the Landlord and Tenant Act 1927. While the haste of adoption of the reform resulted in some less than satisfactory drafting,[8] the 1995 Act marks a welcome break from a principle of landlord and tenant law that was hard to defend.[9]

18.3 New and Old Leases

The 1995 Act draws a basic distinction between 'new' tenancies and 'other' (existing) tenancies. A new tenancy is one entered into after the commencement of the Act (1 January 1996).[10] Although the Act does not use the terminology of 'old' leases, this label will be used here to refer to those leases entered into before 1 January 1996.

---

[6] Law Commission, 'Landlord and Tenant: Privity of Contract and Estate' (Law Com No 174, 1988) para 4.1.

[7] The Law Commission intended the reform to apply to existing as well as new leases: Law Commission, 'Landlord and Tenant Law: Privity of Contract and Estate: Duration of Liability of Parties to Leases' (Law Com CP No 95, 1986) para 4.59; *London Diocesan Fund v Phithwa* [2005] UKHL 70, [2005] 1 WLR 413 [38].

[8] In *First Penthouse Ltd v Channel Hotels and Properties (UK) Ltd* [2003] EWHC 2713 (Ch) [43] Lightman J said 'The 1995 Act is the product of rushed drafting, and its provisions create exceptional difficulties.'

[9] For further accounts of the Landlord and Tenant (Covenants) Act 1995 and its background, see C Harpum, 'The Law Commission and Land Law' in S Bright and J Dewar (eds), *Land Law: Themes and Perspectives* (Oxford, OUP, 1998) 159–162; S Bridge, 'Former Tenants, Future Liabilities and the Privity of Contract Principle: The Landlord and Tenant (Covenants) Act 1995' (1996) 55 *CLJ* 313; M Davey, 'Privity of Contract and Leases – Reform at Last' (1996) 59 *MLR* 78.

[10] A tenancy will also be an old tenancy if it was entered into pursuant to an agreement entered into before 1 January 1996. Therefore, a tenancy entered into pursuant to a contract for lease, option or right of pre-emption granted before 1 January 1996 will count as an old tenancy. A deemed surrender and re-grant after 1995 will lead to a 'new' tenancy.

18.4 Anti-avoidance

Section 25 of the Landlord and Tenant (Covenants) Act 1995 makes void any agreement that attempts to avoid the effect of the Act, and is to be 'interpreted generously, so as to ensure that the operation of the Act is not frustrated, either directly or indirectly':[11]

> **Section 25**
>
> (1) Any agreement relating to a tenancy is void to the extent that –
>
> (a) it would apart from this section have effect to exclude, modify or otherwise frustrate the operation of any provision of this Act, or
>
> (b) it provides for –
>
>   (i) the termination or surrender of the tenancy, or
>
>   (ii) the imposition on the tenant of any penalty, disability or liability,
>
> in the event of the operation of any provision of this Act …

18.5 Liability of the Original Tenant under Old (Pre-1996) Leases

18.5.1 Original Tenant Liability

The liability of the original parties to old leases is governed by contract law and so they will remain liable for performance of the leasehold covenants throughout the term of the lease, unless this liability has been limited by the contract itself. The effect of original liability is that even after the original tenant has assigned the lease and no longer has any interest in the property, he will be liable for breach of any covenants by the assignee. In practice, with a rack rent lease, it is the liability for rent that tends to be most commonly enforced against the original tenant. Although original liability exists with leases in all sectors, it is in relation to commercial leases that original tenants are most often sued for the default of later tenants. Short residential tenancies are seldom assigned, and, if they are, the landlord will usually end the lease if the rent is not being paid by the assignee. With long residential leases, original liability may be a problem but, as the rent is generally only a ground rent, it is only in the case of major repairs that it will be worth pursuing the original tenant. With commercial leases, however, there is no incentive for the landlord to forfeit the lease if the property market is weak (and the passing rent is higher than current market rents); it is easier to look to the original tenant for payment. Furthermore, the original tenant's liability is direct and primary and the landlord does not have to exhaust possible remedies against other persons before claiming from the original tenant.[12] The only defences available to the tenant are that he has already performed, that another person has performed, or that some operation of law, such as surrender, has put an end to the contractual obligations under the lease.[13] The tenant has an implied right of indemnity against his assignee[14] and a quasi-contractual right to be

---

[11] *London Diocesan Fund v Phithwa* [2005] UKHL 70, [2005] 1 WLR 413 [18].

[12] *Baynton v Morgan* (1888) 22 QBD 74; *Norwich Union Life Insurance Ltd v Low Profile Fashions Ltd* (1991) 64 P & CR 187 (CA).

[13] *Allied London Investments Ltd v Hambro Life Assurance Ltd* (1985) 50 P & CR 207 (CA).

[14] Unregistered land – Law of Property Act 1925 s 77(1)(c), but only if the assignment is for valuable consideration; registered land – Land Registration Act 1925 s 24(1)(b), replaced by Land Registration Act 2002 s 134(2),

re-imbursed by the defaulting tenant.[15] In addition, the tenant may have taken an express indemnity in the assignment deed. In practice, however, the indemnity is often worthless as the very time that the landlord will seek recovery from the original tenant is when the current tenant is insolvent.

18.5.2 Limitations on Original Tenant Liability

18.5.2.1 At Common Law

(a) Contractual Limitations

In theory, the original tenant's liability could be limited by contract to the period for which the original tenant has an estate in the property but, in practice, it was relatively unusual for this to be agreed to by the landlord. Even during the recession, with property hard to let, landlords were reluctant to agree to such limitations and preferred to offer other induce-ments to tenants to encourage them to take leases, such as rent-free periods, break clauses or shorter leases.

(b) Variations to the Lease

Where the lease is varied after an assignment, this may affect the liability of former tenants. Some variations may cause a deemed surrender and regrant; if this occurs all former tenants and guarantors will be released from future liability.[16] Alternatively, a variation may increase T2's obligations without triggering a surrender and regrant. In *Friends' Provident Life Office v British Railways Board*,[17] for example, a variation was agreed between the landlord and T2 that altered the alienation and user clauses and, to reflect the higher value of the lease, the rent was increased from £12,000 per annum payable quarterly in arrear to £35,000 per annum payable in advance. The Court of Appeal held that T1 (and other former tenants liable in contract) will be liable only to the extent of their own contractual promises and will not have to bear responsibility for increased liability resulting from variations to the lease.[18] The former tenant is not discharged by the variation but remains liable only for his promises

---

Sch 12 para 20. These sections have been repealed for new leases but still apply to old leases: Landlord and Tenant (Covenants) Act 1995 s 30. The s 24 indemnity includes 'all actions, expenses, and claims on account of the non-payment of the … rent or any part thereof, or the breach of the … covenants or conditions or any of them.' This has been held to apply to all 'fairly and reasonably' incurred expenses paid by the assignor, whether or not the assignor is legally liable to make the payments: *Scottish & Newcastle plc v Raguz* [2007] EWCA Civ 150, [2007] 2 All ER 871.

[15] 'Where one person is compelled to pay damages by the legal default of another, he is entitled to recover from the person by whose default the damage was occasioned the sum so paid', *Moule v Garret* (1872) LR 7 Ex 101, 104 (Cockburn CJ). See also S Bridge, 'Former Tenants, Future Liabilities and the Privity of Contract Principle: The Landlord and Tenant (Covenants) Act 1995' (1996) 55 *CLJ* 313, 325–6.

[16] See ch 24; and see S Bright, 'Variation of Leases and Tenant Liability' in P Jackson and DC Wilde (eds), *The Reform of Property Law* (Aldershot, Dartmouth, 1997) 73.

[17] [1996] 1 All ER 336 (CA).

[18] See Sir Christopher Slade at 351, Beldam LJ at 348. Earlier cases mistakenly held the original tenant liable for increased liability stemming from post-assignment variations on the flawed view that by assigning the lease the former tenants authorised all later acts by assignees; for analysis of these cases, see S Bright, 'Variation of Leases and Tenant Liability' in P Jackson and DC Wilde (eds), *The Reform of Property Law* (Aldershot, Dartmouth, 1997) 80–85.

and for adjustments made pursuant to these, such as rent increases agreed pursuant to the review mechanism in the lease,[19] and will not be liable for increases attributable to variations to the lease.

Section 18 of the Landlord and Tenant (Covenants) Act 1995, discussed at 18.5.2.2 below, received Royal Assent only days after the judgment in the *Friends' Provident* case, and is effectively made redundant by this decision.

(c) Release

Even if the original tenant is unable to negotiate for his liability to be limited by the original lease, he may be able to negotiate for the landlord to release him upon assignment, especially if T2 is of equal or greater financial strength.

A further way in which the original tenant may be released is when there is an agreement reached about payment between T2 and the landlord. In this situation, there is a crucial, but narrow, distinction between an agreement not to sue the later assignee and an agreement to release him, which will also release all other contractually liable tenants. This is illustrated in *Deanplan Ltd v Mahmoud* where the landlord agreed that the assignee could surrender the lease in consideration of the landlord accepting the assignee's goods 'in full and final settlement'.[20] The landlord maintained that he did not intend also to release the earlier tenant from liability but Judge Baker QC held this to be the effect of their agreement, there was 'accord and satisfaction'.[21] Discussing this decision in *Burford Midland Properties Ltd v Marley Extrusions Ltd* Cooke J stressed that not everything that discharges a debt meets the criteria of an accord and satisfaction; it is important to distinguish between an undertaking not to sue a particular individual and a release.[22]

(d) No Liability During Statutory Continuation

Unless the period of liability is extended by the wording of the lease, the original tenant's liability will cease when the contractual tenancy comes to an end.[23] In *City of London Corporation v Fell*, the original tenant, a large firm of solicitors, had assigned a ten-year lease to a company which later became insolvent. The landlord sought to argue that the original tenant remained liable even during the statutory continuation of the tenancy by section 24 of the Landlord and Tenant Act 1954, but the House of Lords firmly rejected this.[24]

In *City of London Corporation v Fell* the term of the lease was defined as being for a set period (ten years). In some leases, however, the term will be defined to include the original

---

[19] There is a potential complication if the lease itself contemplates the possibility of future variations, such as a user clause which prohibits a change of use without the consent of the landlord. It is submitted that the former tenant will not be liable if, under the lease, the landlord is able to refuse consent for any reason (either an absolute or qualified covenant). For further discussion, see S Bright, 'Variation of Leases and Tenant Liability' in P Jackson and DC Wilde (eds), *The Reform of Property Law* (Aldershot, Dartmouth, 1997) 82–3. See also *Metropolitan Properties Company (Regis) Ltd v Bartholomew and Dillon* (1996) 72 P & CR 380 (CA) for the impact of a personal concession contained in a licence to assign on the liability of the assignor and its sureties.

[20] [1993] Ch 151.

[21] [1993] Ch 151, 178.

[22] [1995] 2 EGLR 15 (Ch) 20. For more detailed discussion of release, see S Bridge, 'Former Tenants, Future Liabilities and the Privity of Contract Principle: The Landlord and Tenant (Covenants) Act 1995' (1996) 55 *CLJ* 313, 320–322.

[23] *City of London Corporation v Fell* [1994] 1 AC 458 (HL).

[24] *City of London Corporation v Fell* [1994] 1 AC 458 (HL).

grant plus any continuation or extension of it and, in this event, the contractual liability of the original tenant will extend to the statutory continuation.[25]

18.5.2.2 By Statute

The foregoing limitations on the original tenant's liability pre-date the Landlord and Tenant (Covenants) Act 1995. As part of the industry compromise reached on reform further concessions were made to alleviate the hardship caused to original tenants by continuing liability, applicable to both old and new tenancies.

(e) Notification of Arrears as a Condition for Claim against Former Tenant (section 17)
In order for the landlord to be able to claim arrears from a former tenant, he must serve the former tenant with notice of all 'fixed charge' arrears within six months of payment being due (a 'problem notice'). The notice must specify the amount due and state that the landlord intends to recover the sum due from the former tenant, and, if seeking interest, must give the basis of calculating the interest.[26] Fixed charge arrears will usually be rent and service charges, but may include other liquidated payments. This covers all categories of former tenants who remain liable: those liable under continuing liability in old leases, tenants of new leases liable under an authorised guarantee agreement, and those remaining liable following an excluded assignment (see 18.6 below).

The aim of this change is to protect tenants from receiving unexpected demands for long-standing arrears and to give tenants a chance to make necessary budgetary adjustments to cover the contingent liability. A fresh notice will need to be served each time a fixed charge payment becomes due. Thus, to preserve a right to sue a former tenant for ongoing rent default, the landlord will need to serve a problem notice each time the rent falls due and is not paid. For all of the notices that have to be served under the 1995 Act, there is a prescribed statutory form.[27]

A problem has arisen, not anticipated by the legislation, in relation to the position where rent reviews are outstanding. In *Scottish & Newcastle plc v Raguz* the rent review dates for two under-leases were 1995 and 1996.[28] The actual reviews were not settled until 2000 and 2001, but the new rent then became payable retrospectively from the review dates. Until 1999 the 'old' rents were paid, but in 1999 the then tenant went into administrative receivership. The question arose whether, in order to preserve the option to sue the former tenant for the increased rent now due from the review dates until 1999, the landlord should have served section 17 notices within six months of each rent payment date even though the 'old' rent was being paid and there was no default (described by Lloyd LJ as an 'advance protective notice'). As Rix LJ observed, to require this would be an 'uncommercial burden' for landlords'. Nevertheless, the Court of Appeal held that it was necessary to do so. Lloyd LJ considered this to be consistent with the policy:

---

[25] *City of London Corporation v Fell; Herbert Duncan Ltd v Cluttons* [1993] 2 All ER 449 (CA).
[26] Minor errors in the notice will not invalidate it: *Commercial Union Life Assurance Co Ltd v Moustafa* [1999] 2 EGLR 44 (QB).
[27] See Landlord and Tenant (Covenants) Act 1995 (Notices) Regulations 1995 SI 1995/2964.
[28] [2007] EWCA Civ 150.

... to ensure that original tenants get prior notice of the possibility that they will be looked to for the recovery of rent under a lease which they may have assigned many years before.[29]

Rix LJ perceived the policy differently: the tenant has sufficient notice of this possibility by having signed up to a lease with known review dates. The policy of section 17 was somewhat different:

The real purpose of the section 17(2) notice, as it seems to me, is to enable the former tenant to know that the current tenant is in default and *to act* in response to that knowledge. Thus the statute provides by section 19 that the former tenant can, after paying the amount notified, then take an overriding lease, in order to have control over the current tenant and the situation in general. In contrast, there is nothing the former tenant can do to influence a rent review.[30]

On his view, therefore, the outcome, although required by the statutory wording, did not serve any purpose, and may end up intimidating the former tenant unnecessarily.

In practical terms, the result creates a potential management headache: whenever there is an outstanding rent review and the landlord wishes to reserve the right to sue former tenants (even though the current tenant is not in default) a section 17 notice must be served on the former tenants within six months of each rent payment date.

(f) Restriction of Liability of Former Tenant Where Lease Varied (section 18)

Where the lease has been varied after assignment, the former tenant (and his guarantor, if any)[31] will not be liable to pay any sums referable to the variation, so long as the variation was one which the landlord had the absolute right to refuse when it was made and the variation was made on or after 1 January 1996.[32] This means that the landlord will be unable to recover from a former tenant charges that result from alterations to the premises, variations to user, extra space for an increased rent and so on, unless these were changes envisaged within the lease and which the landlord could not reasonably refuse. The landlord will be able to recover increases of rent following a rent review except to the extent that the increase reflects variations not part of the original review provisions. The Court of Appeal decision in *Friends' Provident*[33] (discussed at 18.5.2.1 above) renders section 18 unnecessary.[34] More importantly, the case goes further than section 18 as it would apply to variations whenever made, not simply those made after the commencement of the Act.

(g) Right to Overriding Lease (sections 19 and 20)

A former tenant who is called upon to pay the assignee's arrears has the right to call for an overriding lease within twelve months of paying the arrears.[35] In effect, if he elects to do this, the former tenant will become an intermediate landlord between the landlord and the

---

[29] *Scottish & Newcastle plc v Raguz* [2007] EWCA Civ 150, [2007] 2 All ER 871 [35].
[30] *Scottish & Newcastle plc v Raguz* [2007] EWCA Civ 150, [2007] 2 All ER 871 [69].
[31] Landlord and Tenant (Covenants) Act 1995 s 18(3).
[32] Landlord and Tenant (Covenants) Act 1995 s 18.
[33] *Friends' Provident Life Office v British Railways Board* [1996] 1 All ER 336 (CA).
[34] S 18 also applies to guarantees; although *Friends' Provident* does not do so expressly the principles applied would similarly apply to guarantors.
[35] Landlord and Tenant (Covenants) Act 1995 ss 19 and 20.

defaulting assignee tenant. The overriding lease will usually be three days longer than the defaulting tenant's lease[36] (the 'overridden' lease).

Landlord and Tenant (Covenants) Act 1995 section 19

(1) Where in respect of any tenancy ('the relevant tenancy') any person ('the claimant') makes full payment of an amount which he has been duly required to pay in accordance with section 17, together with any interest payable, he shall be entitled (subject to and in accordance with this section) to have the landlord under that tenancy grant him an overriding lease of the premises demised by the tenancy.

(2) For the purposes of this section 'overriding lease' means a tenancy of the reversion expectant on the relevant tenancy which—

(a) is granted for a term equal to the remainder of the term of the relevant tenancy plus three days or the longest period (less than three days) that will not wholly displace the landlord's reversionary interest expectant on the relevant tenancy, as the case may require; and

(b) (subject to subsections (3) and (4) and to any modifications agreed to by the claimant and the landlord) otherwise contains the same covenants as the relevant tenancy, as they have effect immediately before the grant of the lease.

Taking an overriding lease will enable the former tenant to have more control: he will be able to pursue remedies directly against the defaulting tenant (if still in occupation) or to regain possession of the property and make use of it personally. If the former tenant elects to take an overriding lease, this will be a lease on the same terms as the overridden tenancy with the exception of purely personal covenants and spent covenants, will include any variations that have been made, and, even though entered into after 1995, will be a 'new' tenancy only if the overridden lease is a new tenancy. If the lease has been varied, this will mean that the former tenant may have a difficult choice: if he does not take an overriding lease, he will not be liable for charges arising from variations to the lease (section 18, and *Friends' Provident*);[37] if he does take the overriding lease he will assume liability for these variations.

18.6 Liability of the Original Tenant under New (Post-1995) Leases

The most significant change introduced by the Landlord and Tenant (Covenants) Act 1995 was to abandon original tenant liability. For new leases a tenant will, by statute, be released on assignment from future liability but not from liability for breaches occurring before assignment.

Section 5

(2) If the tenant assigns the whole of the premises demised to him, he—

(a) is released from the tenant covenants of the tenancy, and

(b) ceases to be entitled to the benefit of the landlord covenants of the tenancy,

as from the assignment.

---

[36] Landlord and Tenant (Covenants) Act 1995 s 19(2)(a).
[37] [1996] 1 All ER 336 (CA).

All guarantors of the tenant will also be released.[38] The assignor will not be released if there is an 'excluded assignment', defined by section 11(1) as 'assignments in breach of a covenant ... or assignments by operation of law' (such as to personal representatives on the death of the tenant).

There is, however, an important qualification to this principle of automatic release. If the lease contains any restrictions on assignment (which is usual), the landlord may be able to require a guarantee from the assignor tenant (an 'authorised guarantee agreement', AGA),[39] but this guarantee can only make the tenant guarantee performance by the immediate successor. The AGA can also include a requirement that in the event of the lease being disclaimed following the insolvency of the assignee, the former tenant will enter into a lease for the non-expired residue on terms that are no more onerous.[40]

Landlord and Tenant (Covenants) Act 1995 section 16

(2) For the purposes of this section an agreement is an authorised guarantee agreement if –

(a)   under it the tenant guarantees the performance of the relevant covenant to any extent by the assignee; and

(b)   it is entered into in the circumstances set out in subsection (3); and

(c)   its provisions conform with subsections (4) and (5).

(3) Those circumstances are as follows –

(a)   by virtue of a covenant against assignment (whether absolute or qualified) the assignment cannot be effected without the consent of the landlord under the tenancy or some other person;

(b)   any such consent is given subject to a condition (lawfully imposed) that the tenant is to enter into an agreement guaranteeing the performance of the covenant by the assignee; and

(c)   the agreement is entered into by the tenant in pursuance of that condition.

(4) An agreement is not an authorised guarantee agreement to the extent that it purports –

(a)   to impose on the tenant any requirement to guarantee in any way the performance of the relevant covenant by any person other than the assignee; or

(b)   to impose on the tenant any liability, restriction or other requirement (of whatever nature) in relation to any time after the assignee is released from that covenant by virtue of this Act.

(5) Subject to subsection (4), an authorised guarantee agreement may –

(a)   impose on the tenant any liability as sole or principal debtor in respect of any obligation owed by the assignee under the relevant covenant;

(b)   impose on the tenant liabilities as guarantor in respect of the assignee's performance of that covenant which are no more onerous than those to which he would be subject in the event of his being liable as sole or principal debtor in respect of any obligation owed by the assignee under that covenant;

(c)   require the tenant, in the event of the tenancy assigned by him being disclaimed, to enter into a new tenancy of the premises comprised in the assignment –

(i)   whose term expires not later than the term of the tenancy assigned by the tenant, and

(ii)   whose tenant covenants are no more onerous than those of that tenancy;

---

[38] Landlord and Tenant (Covenants) Act 1995 s 24(2); see 18.14.3.
[39] Landlord and Tenant (Covenants) Act 1995 s 16.
[40] Landlord and Tenant (Covenants) Act 1995 s 16(5)(c).

(d) make provision incidental or supplementary to any provision made by virtue of any of
     paragraphs (a) to (c).

As part of the industry compromise, section 19 of the Landlord and Tenant Act 1927
(which provides that consent to assignment under qualified covenants cannot be unreasonably withheld) was amended by the insertion of section 19(1A) to enable landlords to set
conditions in new tenancies subject to which consent to assignment can be given (and
which would not be subjected to the test of reasonableness).[41] It is now the norm to require
an AGA automatically as a condition of assignment in new leases (and irrespective of
reasonableness).

In the absence of any alienation restrictions in the lease, the tenant is free to assign and
will be released from future liability upon assignment.

The effect of section 5, coupled with the way that AGAs are used in practice, is that a
tenant will usually remain liable after assignment, but only for so long as his immediate
assignee holds the lease in the premises. There is no statutory right to an indemnity in
respect of this liability,[42] and so T1 will have to rely either upon a contractual indemnity
from T2 or upon restitutionary action. An original tenant liable under an AGA will benefit
from sections 17–20, discussed at 18.5.2.2 above.

18.7 The Position of the Assignee Tenant under Old (Pre-1996) Leases

18.7.1 Privity of Estate – Liability While a Tenant

Under the doctrine of privity of estate leasehold covenants can be enforced by and against the
persons who are landlord and tenant for the time being even though they are not in a
contractual relationship. This is explained by Lord Templeman in *City of London Corporation
v Fell*:

> Common law, and statute following the common law, were faced with the problem of render-
> ing effective the obligations under a lease which might endure for a period of 999 years or
> more beyond the control of any covenantor. The solution was to annex to the term and the
> reversion the benefit and burden of covenants which touch and concern the land. The cove-
> nants having been annexed, every legal owner of the term granted by the lease and every legal
> owner of the reversion from time to time holds his estate with the benefit of and subject to
> the covenants which touch and concern the land. The system of leasehold tenure requires that
> the obligations in the lease shall be enforceable throughout the term, whether those obliga-
> tions are affirmative or negative. The owner of a reversion must be able to enforce the positive
> covenants to pay rent and keep in repair against an assignee who in turn must be able to
> enforce any positive covenants entered into by the original landlord ...
>
>   The effect of common law and statute on a lease is to create rights and obligations which
> are independent of the parallel rights and obligations of the original human covenantor who
> and whose heirs may fail or the parallel rights and obligations of a corporate covenantor

---

[41] This does not apply to residential leases. On assignment generally, see ch 17.
[42] Landlord and Tenant (Covenants) Act 1995 s 14 abolished the indemnity covenants implied by the Law of
Property Act 1925 s 77, and by the Land Registration Act 1925 s 24 for new tenancies.

which may be dissolved. Common law and statute achieve that effect by annexing those rights and obligations so far as they touch and concern the land to the term and to the reversion. Nourse LJ neatly summarised the position when he said in an impeccable judgment ([1993] 2 All ER 449 at 454 … :

'The contractual obligations which touch and concern the land having become imprinted on the estate, the tenancy is capable of existence as a species of property independently of the contract.' [43]

The rules for enforcement of covenants post-assignment are set out in *Spencer's Case*.[44] In order for covenants to be enforceable there must be privity of estate, that is, the legal relationship of landlord and tenant, and the covenant must touch and concern the land. Provided that these two conditions are satisfied, an assignee tenant will both be liable to have covenants enforced against it by the current landlord and able to enforce the benefit of any covenants against the current landlord. Under *Spencer's Case*, T2 becomes liable only when the assignment to him is executed and he will not be liable for breaches committed before he became a tenant.[45]

18.7.1.1 Requirements of Spencer's Case: Legal Relationships

The application of *Spencer's Case* is said to depend upon there being a legal relationship between the landlord and tenant. This would mean that the rules do not apply where either there is an assignment of an equitable lease or a purported assignment of a legal lease by writing but not by deed. The position with equitable leases is discussed at 18.7.3 below.

18.7.1.2 Requirements of Spencer's Case: Covenants Which Touch and Concern the Land

It is only covenants which 'touch and concern' the land which can be enforced under *Spencer's Case*. In practice, most leasehold covenants do satisfy this requirement. So, for example, the landlord can enforce rent covenants and decorating covenants against the assignee tenant, and the assignee tenant can enforce a covenant to insure against the landlord. It is only personal or collateral contracts that are likely not to be covered, such as a covenant to clean the landlord's premises or a covenant requiring payment of an annual sum to a third party.[46] In *Hua Chiao Commercial Bank Ltd v Chiaphua Industries Ltd* the Privy Council held that a landlord's covenant to return the tenant's deposit was a merely personal obligation and did not have reference to the subject matter of the lease.[47] The case itself involved a change of landlord, not tenant, but the principle applies equally in the converse situation.

In *P & A Swift Investments v Combined English Stores*, Lord Oliver put forward a working test for when the covenant touches and concerns the land:

(1) The covenant benefits only the reversioner for the time being, and if separated from the reversion ceases to be of benefit to the covenantee. (2) The covenant affects the nature, quality, mode of user or value of the land of the reversioner. (3) The covenant is not expressed to be personal (that is to say neither being given only to a specific reversioner nor in respect of the

---

[43] *City of London Corporation v Fell* [1994] 1 AC 458 (HL) 464–5.
[44] (1583) 5 Co Rep 16a.
[45] See R Thornton, 'Enforceability of Leasehold Covenants' (1991) 11 *LS* 47, 53 and cases referred to there.
[46] *Mayho v Buckhurst* (1617) Cro Jac 438.
[47] [1987] AC 99 (PC).

obligations only of a specific tenant). (4) The fact that a covenant is to pay a sum of money will not prevent it from touching and concerning the land so long as the three foregoing conditions are satisfied and the covenant is connected with something to be done on, to or in relation to the land.[48]

18.7.2 Liability Following Further Assignment

Unless T2 has entered into a direct covenant with the landlord, he will not be liable for any breaches that occur after he has parted with his interest in the property (or for any breaches which occurred before he acquired an interest).

In old leases it was, however, fairly common for a landlord to require an assignee to enter into a direct covenant with him as a condition of his consent to the assignment and, depending on the actual wording of the covenant, the assignee (T2) may well remain contractually liable even after he has assigned the lease to T3. In *Estates Gazette v Benjamin Restaurants*, the assignee (T2) had entered into a standard form of covenant:

> ... to pay the rents reserved by the lease at the time and in the manner provided for and to observe and perform the covenants on the lessee's part and the conditions contained therein.[49]

A surety also covenanted that the assignee would perform these obligations. After a further assignment, T2 sought to argue that it was no longer liable. The Court of Appeal rejected this, both T2 and the surety were liable on the covenants for the remainder of the term. In practice, when there is this contractual liability, the position of T2 is much the same as it is for the original tenant (T1) after assignment, and many of the comments made earlier in relation to the original tenant apply equally.

Since the Landlord and Tenant (Covenants) Act 1995, there are various further protections available to a former tenant (such as T2) who is called upon to pay the arrears of a later tenant, whether or not the lease is a new lease. Thus, a landlord will need to serve a problem notice under section 17 to preserve a right to sue the former tenant,[50] the former tenant will have the right to claim an overriding lease under sections 19 and 20, and by section 18 the former tenant will not be liable for sums attributable to variations to the lease. It may be that a landlord serves problem notices upon a number of persons – the original tenant (T1), all later assignees (T2, T3 etc), and guarantors. A person who has made full payment of the sums shown in the problem notices and all interest, is entitled to call for an overriding lease, and there are provisions within section 19 dealing with the question as to who has priority to the overriding lease when there is more than one request.[51]

---

[48] *P & A Swift Investments v Combined English Stores Group plc* [1989] 1 AC 632 (HL) 642.

[49] *Estates Gazette Ltd v Benjamin Restaurants Ltd* [1994] 1 WLR 1528 (CA).

[50] If T2 pays arrears and seeks to recover them from T3, there is no need for T2 to serve a s 17 notice: see D Stevens, 'Covenants and the chain of indemnity' (22 May 1999) *EG* 152.

[51] The first request in time has priority and where they are received on the same day, a former tenant has priority over a guarantor and an earlier tenant has priority over a later tenant, Landlord and Tenant (Covenants) Act 1995 s 19(8).

18.7.3 Equitable Leases (Agreements for Lease)

As the rule in *Spencer's Case* depends upon there being privity of estate, there may be problems enforcing covenants against successor tenants where there is only an equitable relationship between the landlord and the tenant. This could be either because there was only ever an agreement for lease (but no lease) or because the lease only takes effect in equity because the formalities rules for legal leases have not been complied with.[52] There will be no difficulty with the assignee tenant being able to enforce covenants against the landlord.[53] This ties in with general contract law, under which the *benefit* of a contract can be assigned. An equitable assignment will thus pass the benefit of all covenants to the assignee.

The problem lies with the burden, that is, the liability of the assignee tenant to be sued by the landlord. The case of *Purchase v Lichfield Brewery*[54] has generated much difficulty. In this case, Purchase had entered into an agreement for lease with the tenant. This equitable lease was then assigned to Lichfield by way of mortgage. The issue in the case was whether Lichfield could be held liable for non-payment of rent. Lush J held it could not. The implication of this decision is that an assignee of an equitable lease cannot be sued on covenants in the lease.

There are, however, various ways of challenging this result. First, it may be that *Purchase v Lichfield Brewery* is not of general application and is confined to its special facts, in particular, that the assignee was a mortgagee and had not entered into possession. Second, it is felt to be wrong in principle that the assignee tenant can sue the landlord but cannot be sued by the landlord. Smith suggests that the assignee tenant might be liable under the doctrine of mutual benefit and burden.[55] Third, in *Boyer v Warby*, Denning LJ mounted a brave argument that *Purchase v Lichfield Brewery* was simply wrong and that the rules should be the same in equity as at law.[56] Gray and Gray comment that this is generally felt to be a maverick view.[57] The Judicature Act 1873 fused the administration of law and equity but not the rules themselves. Fourth, Smith suggests that when the assignee tenant enters possession and starts to pay rent, there should be an implied contract between the assignee and the landlord which will be upon essentially the same terms as the assignor's lease.[58]

The decision in *Purchase v Lichfield Brewery* will not affect the running of negative covenants under the doctrine in *Tulk v Moxhay*.[59] So, for example, an equitable assignee will be bound by the user covenant in the lease. Often, however, it is the positive covenants to pay rent, etc, that will be in issue.

---

[52] See ch 4.

[53] *Manchester Brewery v Coombs* [1901] 2 Ch 608 (Ch).

[54] [1915] 1 KB 184 (KB).

[55] See R Smith, 'The Running of Covenants in Equitable Leases and Equitable Assignments of Legal Leases' (1978) 37 *CLJ* 98, 110 and 118.

[56] [1953] 1 QB 234 (CA).

[57] K Gray and S Gray, *Elements of Land Law* 4th edn (Oxford, OUP, 2005) 1585 and 1586.

[58] R Smith, 'The Running of Covenants in Equitable Leases and Equitable Assignments of Legal Leases' (1978) 37 *CLJ* 98, 105–8 and 117–18.

[59] (1848) 2 Ph 774.

Whichever approach is adopted, there can be little doubt that, in principle, the assignee tenant should be bound by the covenants in the lease.[60]

18.7.4 *Equitable Assignments of Legal Leases*

It is similarly the case that an assignee is not liable on positive covenants following an equitable assignment of a legal lease,[61] as where the assignment was not by deed.[62] If there is a forfeiture provision, the fact that a right of entry is a property right capable of running with the land[63] means that the lease may be forfeited for breach, in effect encouraging the assignee tenant to perform the covenants.[64] Again, it is hard to defend the position of non-liability.[65]

18.8 The Position of the Assignee Tenant under New (Post-1995) Leases

For new tenancies, the complex common law rules (*Spencer's Case* and the difficulties with equitable leases) are abandoned. Instead there is a simple statutory code, the basic principle of which is that the benefit and burden of all landlord and tenant covenants of a new tenancy[66] are annexed to the whole and each and every part of the lease and will pass on an assignment of the lease. The Landlord and Tenant (Covenants) Act 1995 provides as follows:

Section 3

(1) The benefit and burden of all landlord and tenant covenants of a tenancy –

(a)   shall be annexed and incident to the whole, and to each and every part, of the premises demised by the tenancy and of the reversion in them, and

(b)   shall in accordance with this section pass on an assignment of the whole or any part of those premises or of the reversion in them.

(2) Where the assignment is by the tenant under the tenancy, then as from the assignment the assignee –

(a)   becomes bound by the tenant covenants of the tenancy except to the extent that –
    (i)   immediately before the assignment they did not bind the assignor, or
    (ii) they fall to be complied with in relation to any demised premises not comprised in the assignment; and

(b)   becomes entitled to the benefit of the landlord covenants of the tenancy except to the extent that they fall to be complied with in relation to any such premises.

---

[60] For further discussion on the enforceability of covenants after assignment, see R Smith, 'The Running of Covenants in Equitable Leases and Equitable Assignments of Legal Leases' (1978) 37 *CLJ* 98; D Gordon, 'The Burden and Benefit of the Rules of Assignment' [1987] *Conv* 103; R Thornton, 'Enforceability of Leasehold Covenants' (1991) 11 *LS* 47.

[61] *Cox v Bishop* (1857) 8 De GM & G 815, 822–5.

[62] There must be a deed for a legal assignment: see ch 4.

[63] Law of Property Act 1925 s 1(2).

[64] RJ Smith, *Property Law* 5th edn (Harlow, Longman, 2006) 448; K Gray and S Gray, *Elements of Land Law* 4th ed (Oxford, OUP, 2005) 1585.

[65] But it is harder to argue that the existing law supports liability following equitable assignment of a legal lease than it is for liability following assignment of an equitable lease: RJ Smith, *Property Law* 5th edn (Harlow, Longman, 2006) 453.

[66] This will include covenants contained in any agreements collateral to the tenancy, such as an agreement for lease or a licence; see definitions of 'covenant' and 'collateral agreement' in Landlord and Tenant (Covenants) Act 1995 s 28.

This applies to equitable as well as legal relationships of landlord and tenant. It also makes no distinction between those covenants which touch and concern the land and those that do not;[67] although it will still be possible for the parties to a lease expressly to provide for covenants to be purely personal so that the benefit and burden of personal covenants will not pass on assignment.[68] The effect is that the assignee will be liable for all tenant covenants, unless they have been released or waived by the landlord, and has the benefit of all landlord covenants.

An assignee will not be liable in respect of breaches occurring before the assignment of the lease to him (unless an express contrary agreement is reached).

If the assignee tenant in turn assigns the tenancy, he will be statutorily released from liability by section 5[69] and, in the same way as for the original tenant, may be required to enter into an AGA depending upon the terms of the alienation covenant and the reasonableness of this (see discussion at 18.6 above in relation to the original tenant). If T2, etc, remain liable after assignment under any AGA entered into the protections in sections 17-20 will again be available (right to a problem notice, release if lease is varied, and the right to an overriding lease).

Annexation of covenants to each and every part ensures that on an assignment of part, all covenants are enforceable by and against the assignee although there is an exception to the extent that the covenant falls to be complied with in relation to the part not assigned (an 'attributable covenant').[70] An example given during Parliamentary debate relates to a lease of a house and a field which contains a covenant to repair. If the field alone is assigned, to which the repair covenant does not relate, the assignee will not be bound by that particular covenant. Similarly, the assignor tenant is released from liability in respect of covenants attributable to the part assigned.[71]

Where, as with most, the covenant cannot be attributed to a distinct part, the assignor and assignee will both be jointly and severally liable,[72] with a right of contribution between them[73] unless the parties agree an apportionment of liability between them. Sections 9 and 10 provide a procedure whereby the assigning parties can apply for an agreed apportionment to be binding on the other party to the lease.

18.9 The Position of the Original Landlord in Old (Pre-1996) Leases

18.9.1 Original Landlord Liability

As with tenants in old leases, the position of the original landlord is governed by contractual rules, the effect of which is that even after the landlord has assigned the reversion and no

---

[67] Landlord and Tenant (Covenants) Act 1995 s 2(a).

[68] Landlord and Tenant (Covenants) Act 1995 s 3(6)(a).

[69] It has been said to be arguable that s 5 only releases T1 because only he has 'premises demised to him', S Fogel and T Moross, 'Landlord and Tenant (Covenants) Act 1995: How has Practice been Affected?' Blundell Memorial Lecture (1996) but this is clearly not the policy underlying the statute.

[70] Landlord and Tenant (Covenants) Act 1995 ss 3(2) and 28(2).

[71] Landlord and Tenant (Covenants) Act 1995 s 5(3).

[72] Landlord and Tenant (Covenants) Act 1995 s 13(1).

[73] Landlord and Tenant (Covenants) Act 1995 s 13(3).

longer has any interest in the property, he will be liable for breach of any covenants by the new reversioner. There is no statutory indemnity from the new reversioner when a landlord assigns the reversion and, accordingly, the landlord should take an express indemnity for his own protection (in contrast to the position for tenants, see 18.5.1 above).

In practice, original landlord liability presents few problems and certainly does not generate the same claims of injustice as original tenant liability. In part, this is because landlords generally undertake far fewer obligations than the tenant and it is rare for a landlord to be sued by the tenant for post assignment breaches.[74]

18.9.2 Limitations on Original Landlord Liability

As with original tenant liability, it is possible to limit the liability of the original landlord by the terms of the contract. So a landlord may restrict its liability either by the terms of the covenant (so that it is liable only so long as it is landlord) or by getting the tenant to release it from liability on assignment.[75] As Lord Nicholls observes in *London Diocesan Fund v Phithwa*, 'this was legally possible, if seldom met in practice'.[76]

18.10 The Position of the Original Landlord in New (Post-1995) Leases

The reform of original landlord liability was far less radical than that for tenants. Because the tenant does not have the right to give or withhold consent on an assignment of the landlord's reversion, it was said that the proposals for landlord liability could not mirror those adopted for tenant liability. The starting point could not be to discharge the landlord's liability upon assignment because the tenant would never be able to ensure that in appropriate cases the landlord would remain liable under some kind of guarantee arrangement.[77] Instead, there is no automatic release of the landlord from future liability upon assignment of the reversion and, in order to be released, he must serve a notice on the tenant either before the assignment or within four weeks of the assignment requesting a release.[78] A former landlord who has not previously been released from liability can also apply for release on a later assignment.[79] The tenant then has four weeks to object to the proposed release. If there is no objection, the landlord is released as from the date of the assignment. However, if the tenant does object to the landlord being released from liability, the landlord will have to apply to the court and establish that it is reasonable for him to be released.

The landlord will, however, be released only from 'landlord covenants', not from personal obligations. In *BHP Petroleum GB Ltd v Chesterfield Properties Ltd*, for example, there was an agreement by which L1 (the developer) agreed to refurbish office premises and grant T a twenty year lease. This agreement contained obligations on the part of L1 to make good

---

[74] See Law Commission, 'Privity of Contract and Estate' (Law Com No 174, 1988) para 4.16.

[75] J Spencer-Silver, 'Landlord's continuing liability' (14 August 1993) *EG* 69.

[76] [2005] UKHL 70, [2005] 1 WLR 3956 [1].

[77] In contrast to the landlord's position on tenant assignment.

[78] Landlord and Tenant (Covenants) Act 1995 ss 6 and 8. In practice, requests for release are relatively unusual: PJG Williams, 'The tenant's lot is a happier one' (11 February 2006) *EG* 160, 162.

[79] Landlord and Tenant (Covenants) Act 1995 ss 7 and 8.

building works defects.[80] These were expressed to be 'personal obligations of the Landlord'. The lease was entered into three months later, and two years after that, when the reversion was assigned, L1 served a notice pursuant to section 8 applying to be released from its obligations under the lease. No counter notice was served by the tenant. Various defects developed and when the tenant brought an action against L1, it argued that it had been released from its obligations. The argument for L1 was that this was a landlord covenant, the burden of which passed to the new reversioner, and which L1 had been released from by virtue of the section 8 notice. The Court of Appeal disagreed. Reading together the definitions of 'landlord' and 'landlord covenant' in section 28, a landlord covenant is:

> ... an obligation 'falling to be complied with by [the person who may from time to time be entitled to the reversion on the tenancy].' An obligation which (that is to say, the burden of which) is personal to the original landlord is, by definition, not such an obligation, since it does not fall to be performed by the person who may from time to time be entitled to the reversion on the tenancy.[81]

L1 was not, therefore, released from its obligations.

If the landlord is not released, he remains liable throughout the remainder of the term, not just until the next assignment (although the landlord can apply again for a release on a later assignment). A landlord cannot, however, apply for release if the assignment is an excluded assignment.[82]

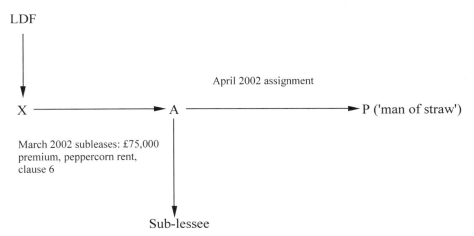

Clause 6: Landlord covenanted to pay rent in headlease, '(but not, in the case of Avonridge Property Co Ltd only, so as to be liable after the landlord has disposed of its interest in the property)...'

Figure 18.1: The Facts in London Diocesan Fund v Phithwa

---

[80] [2001] EWCA Civ 1797, [2002] Ch 194.
[81] [2001] EWCA Civ 1797, [2002] Ch 194 [59].
[82] Landlord and Tenant (Covenants) Act 1995 s 11(3).

It remains possible, however, for the landlord to limit its liability by the terms of the lease. In *London Diocesan Fund v Phithwa* the House of Lords decided, overturning the Court of Appeal decision, that the 1995 Act did not preclude such a limitation of liability.[83] The point arose in the context of what was clearly a scam. As shown in Figure 18.1, at the beginning of the story the head-lease was between the London Diocesan Fund (LDF) and the Avonridge Property Co Ltd (A) (the tenant by assignment). Subleases were granted by A for substantial premiums (totalling £458,500). In clause 6 of the sub-lease the (mesne) landlord (A) covenanted to pay the rent under the head-lease, but limited its liability to the period for which it was landlord. In other words, if A's interest in the sub-lease changed hands, A would no longer be contractually bound to pay rent under the head-lease to the LDF. Shortly afterwards, the reversion to the sub-leases was assigned to a 'man of straw'. The new landlord, P, did not pay the head-lease rent and the head-lease was forfeited. However, the sub-lessees were granted relief against forfeiture on condition that they took new leases at a rent equal to the apportioned part of the rent passing under the (forfeited) head-lease (the amount that A originally was paying to LDF). The effect was that the sub-lessees who had paid substantial sums for 'peppercorn' rents[84] ended up having to pay rent to the head-landlord (LDF).[85] The sub-lessees brought an action against A for breach of clause 6, arguing that the limitation on A's liability was made void by section 25 as it frustrated the purpose of the 1995 Act. Lord Nicholls wryly observed that A's case was not 'overburdened with merit'. Nonetheless, the limitation in clause 6 was held by the House of Lords to be effective.[86] The purpose of the Act was to *provide* exit routes from future liabilities; it did not intend to close *other* exit routes. Therefore, A had, by contract, successfully managed to limit its liability as landlord to the period during which it held the reversion to the subleases. As Dixon comments, the impact of *Phitwa* is to enable landlords, by careful drafting, to render sections 6-8 of the 1995 Act completely without effect.[87]

18.11 The Position of the New Reversioner in Old (Pre-1996) Leases

18.11.1 Legal Leases

In the case of an assignment of the reversion of an old lease, there are statutory rules laid down in sections 141 and 142 of the Law of Property Act 1925 relating to the passing of covenants. The effect of these sections is that the new reversioner is able to enforce all tenant covenants (section 141), and is bound by all landlord covenants (section 142), so long as they have 'reference to the subject matter of the lease'.

---

[83] [2005] UKHL 70, [2005] 1 WLR 3956.

[84] That is, nominal rents.

[85] From the perspective of the sub-tenants, these were very unwise transactions to enter. If they were professionally advised they should have been told not to proceed, as from the very start it was in A's power to put them in jeopardy of forfeiture. As Lord Nicholls comments, the risks were not obscure or concealed, they were evident in the text of the subleases: [2005] UKHL 70, [2005] 1 WLR 3956 [20].

[86] Lord Walker dissented on the grounds that s 8 provides the only route for a landlord to escape liability on landlord covenants.

[87] M Dixon, 'A Failure of Statutory Purpose or a Failure of Professional Advice?' [2006] 70 *Conv* 79, 83.

Law of Property Act 1925 section 141 (benefit of lessee's covenants)

(1) Rent reserved by a lease, and the benefit of every covenant or provision therein contained, having reference to the subject-matter thereof, and on the lessee's part to be observed or performed, and every condition of re-entry and other condition therein contained, shall be annexed and incident to and shall go with the reversionary estate in the land, or in any part thereof, immediately expectant on the term granted by the lease, notwithstanding severance of that reversionary estate, and without prejudice to any liability affecting a covenantor or his estate.

Section 142 (burden of lessor's covenants)

(1) The obligation under a condition or of a covenant entered into by a lessor with reference to the subject-matter of the lease shall, if and as far as the lessor has power to bind the reversionary estate immediately expectant on the term granted by the lease, be annexed and incident to and shall go with that reversionary estate, or the several parts thereof, notwithstanding severance of that reversionary estate, and may be taken advantage of and enforced by the person in whom the term is from time to time vested by conveyance, devolution in law, or otherwise; and, if and as far as the lessor has power to bind the person from time to time entitled to that reversionary estate, the obligation aforesaid may be taken advantage of and entered against any person so entitled.

The phrase 'having reference to the subject matter of the lease' is construed in the same manner as the reference to covenants which 'touch and concern' the land, discussed above at 18.7.1.2, although the covenant need not be contained in the lease itself.[88] On the landlord's part, covenants to insure, repair and give quiet enjoyment all touch and concern the land. However, in *Hua Chiao Commercial Bank Ltd v Chiaphua Industries Ltd*, the Privy Council held that a landlord's covenant to return the tenant's deposit was a merely personal obligation and did not have reference to the subject matter of the lease.[89] The effect in this case was that the tenant was unable to get the deposit returned: the new reversioner was not bound by the covenant to return it and the old landlord was insolvent. In *Caerns Motor Services v Texaco*, the reversions of petrol station leases were assigned and the tenants argued that the new landlord could not enforce the covenants requiring the tenants exclusively to buy petroleum products and motor fuel from the landlord.[90] Part of their argument was that these were personal covenants, to which the identity of the landlord was of vital importance. Judge Paul Baker QC noted that various factors supported this view:

The success of the entire business depends on marketability of products, an intensely competitive business. There is a commercial relationship with the landlord here which depends on their acting with integrity and fair play. It is important, thirdly, that Texaco [the original landlord] are not a one-man band, but a large organisation and so their standard terms will not be oppressive. Fourthly, there is no covenant by the landlords that their products are of good quality so the tenant is left to rely on the integrity of Texaco. Fifthly, there is no power to select which products the tenant takes so long as the landlord markets the products. They have to take their whole supply from the landlord and they have to stay open 24 hours a day. When you put all that together, it shows that the supplier has powers of life and death over the tenant.[91]

---

[88] 'The term "covenant" in this context is not confined to a contract under seal, but applies to a contract under hand and the covenant need not be contained in the lease provided that it touches and concerns the demised premises', *Lotteryking Ltd v AMEC Properties Ltd* [1995] 2 EGLR 13 (Ch) 15 (Lightman J).

[89] [1987] AC 99 (PC)

[90] *Caerns Motor Services Ltd v Texaco Ltd; Geedes v Texaco Ltd* [1994] 1 WLR 1249 (Ch).

[91] [1994] 1 WLR 1249 (Ch) 1264.

Nevertheless, the judge was influenced by an earlier case involving a brewery tie, *Clegg v Hands*, in which the Court of Appeal had found that a tie in a lease of a public house did 'touch and concern the land':

> It relates to the mode of enjoyment of a public house. The thing demised is a public-house, and the covenant compels the covenantee to buy the beer of the covenantor and his assigns.
>   In my opinion, it touches and concerns the demised premises; it affects the mode of enjoyment of the premises, and therefore it runs with the reversion.[92]

In *Caerns Motors*, the solus agreements were similarly held to be enforceable by the new landlord.

L2 will cease to be liable on further assignment. If, however, there is an assignment of a tenancy of premises that include a dwelling, the assignor will remain liable on leasehold covenants until written notice of the assignment and details of the new landlord are given to the tenant in accordance with section 3 of the Landlord and Tenant Act 1985.[93]

18.11.2 *Equitable Leases and Equitable Assignments of Old (Pre-1996) Legal Leases*

As mentioned earlier there may be difficulties in enforcing a covenant against an equitable assignee on a change of tenant. These problems do not arise with a change of landlord. Both sections 141 and 142 Law of Property Act 1925 apply equally to equitable leases as legal leases,[94] and so the rules discussed earlier will mean that the new reversioner is both subject to, and takes the benefit of, all covenants which have reference to the subject matter of the lease.

18.12 The Position of the New Reversioner in New (Post-1995) Leases

In relation to new leases, section 3 of the Landlord and Tenant (Covenants) Act 1995 provides that the benefit and burden of all landlord and tenant covenants of a new tenancy[95] are annexed to the whole and each and every part of the reversion. As from the assignment, L2 will be bound by landlord covenants[96] and benefit from tenant covenants.[97] There is no distinction drawn between those covenants which have reference to the subject matter of the tenancy and those that do not,[98] or between equitable and legal leases. Again, it will be possible for the parties to a lease to provide for covenants to be purely personal so that the benefit and burden do not pass on assignment.[99] With leasehold developments it is common

---

[92] (1890) 44 Ch D 503 (CA) 523.

[93] Landlord and Tenant Act 1985 s 3A.

[94] *Cole v Kelly* [1920] 2 KB 106 (CA) (written agreement for lease); *Scribes West Ltd v Relsa Anstalt (No 3)* [2004] EWCA Civ 1744, [2005] 1 WLR 1847 (CA) (transfer of legal title before registration).

[95] See s 3 at 18.8 above. This will include covenants contained in any agreements collateral to the tenancy, such as an agreement for lease or a licence; see definitions of 'covenant' and 'collateral agreement' in the Landlord and Tenant (Covenants) Act 1995 s 28.

[96] Except those that did not bind the assignor or relate to premises not comprised in the assignment.

[97] Except any that relate to premises not comprised in the assignment.

[98] Landlord and Tenant (Covenants) Act 1995 s 2(1)(a).

[99] Landlord and Tenant (Covenants) Act 1995 s 3(6)(a). See, for example, *BHP Petroleum GB Ltd v Chesterfield Properties Ltd* [2001] EWCA Civ 1797, [2002] Ch 194, text accompanying n 80.

for the developer landlord to assume responsibility for building defects, a responsibility that new reversioners will not want to take on. In this situation, therefore, it is important that the relevant covenants are expressed to be personal.

On a further assignment to L3, L2 is able to apply for release in the same manner as L1; if there is no release, then it seems that he will remain liable (in addition to L3 – and L1 if he has not been released) even in respect of future breaches, which is a wider liability than existed under the Law of Property Act 1925, section 142.

The effect is that the new reversioner can sue, and be sued upon, all covenants in the lease. Similar principles about attributable and non-attributable covenants apply to the position of the landlord on an assignment of part of the reversion as were discussed in relation to assignee tenants (see example given in text accompanying n 70 at 18.8 above).[100]

By section 15, the enforceability of covenants by and against landlords is also extended to certain other persons, such as a mortgagee in possession of the reversion.[101]

18.13 The New Reversioner and Pre-assignment Breaches

The position of L2 in relation to breaches that occurred before the assignment of the reversion, especially in relation to 'old leases', is complex. The two broad questions that arise in relation to breaches that took place before the assignment are: can L2 sue T1, and can T1 sue L2?

18.13.1 Can L2 sue T1?

By section 141(2) and (3) of the Law of Property Act 1925, L2 is able to sue the tenant for breaches that occurred prior to the assignment.[102] When the new reversioner (L2) acquires the benefit of the covenants, the old landlord (L1) loses any rights of action, even if the breaches were committed before the assignment.[103] As pointed out by Upjohn LJ in *Re King*, the fact that there is an unperformed but enforceable covenant will be reflected in the price negotiated for the sale of the reversion.[104]

For new leases (that is, post-1995 leases), L2 is not generally able to sue for past tenant breaches, although the parties are able to assign the right expressly:

Landlord and Tenant (Covenants) Act 1995 section 23
(1) Where as a result of an assignment a person becomes, by virtue of this Act, bound by or entitled to the benefit of a covenant, he shall not be virtue of this Act have any liability or rights under the covenant in relation to any time falling before the assignment.

---

[100] Landlord and Tenant (Covenants) Act 1995 s 6(3).

[101] Landlord and Tenant (Covenants) Act 1995 s 15(1) provides that 'Where any tenant covenant of a tenancy, or any right of re-entry contained in a tenancy, is enforceable by the reversioner in respect of any premises demised by the tenancy, it shall also be so enforceable by (a) any person (other than the reversioner) who, as the holder of the immediate reversion in those premises, is for the time being entitled to the rents and profits under the tenancy in respect of those premises, or (b) any mortgagee in possession of the reversion in those premises who is so entitled'.

[102] *In re King* [1963] Ch 459 (CA) (covenant to repair and reinstate); *London & County (A & D) Ltd v Wilfred Sportsman Ltd* [1971] Ch 764 (CA) (rent arrears).

[103] *In re King* [1963] Ch 459 (CA) 497.

[104] *In re King* [1963] Ch 459 (CA) 488 and 497.

(2) Subsection (1) does not preclude any such rights being expressly assigned to the person in question.

By section 23(3), where L2 acquires a right of re-entry, this right to forfeit can be exercised in relation to pre-assignment breaches, unless there was a waiver or release before the assignment.

18.13.2 Can L2 be sued by T1 for Breaches by L1?

In relation to old leases (that is pre-1996 leases), T1 is unable to sue L2 for breaches committed by L1.[105] This is because section 142 of the Law of Property Act 1925 does not transfer the burden of past breaches.[106] Coupled with the fact that L2 is able to sue T1 for past (pre-assignment) rent arrears, this could create an unjust effect; as Sedley LJ points out in *Muscat v Smith* it could mean that L1 could sell the reversion at close to vacant possession value (because L2 can recover the rent arrears in full and, if they are substantial, obtain a possession order on the strength of them) even though there is an outstanding serious breach by L1. This potential injustice is mitigated by the fact that T1 can rely on the defence of the common law of recoupment[107] or (as decided in *Muscat v Smith*) equitable set-off in any rent action for pre-assignment arrears brought by L2.[108] In *Muscat v Smith* L1 was in breach of his repairing obligation for a number of years and T began withholding rent. Following assignment of the reversion, L2 brought a claim for rent arrears and possession. The Court of Appeal held that T was able to set off the claim for damages for breach of the repairing obligation by L1 against L2's claim for rent arrears.[109]

By contrast, where L2 is claiming rent for the period post assignment, the Court of Appeal has held that no such right of set off is available.[110] Thus, in *Edlington Properties v Fenner & Co Ltd* the Court of Appeal held the tenant could not set off a damages claim against L1 for defective construction (a claim in the region of £52 million) against rent payments due to the assignee of the reversion in respect of post-assignment rent.[111]

---

[105] L1 remains liable to the tenant (*Stuart v Joy* [1904] 1 KB 362 (CA)), even after the tenant has assigned the lease (*City and Metropolitan Properties Ltd v Greycroft Ltd* [1987] 1 WLR 1085 (Ch)).

[106] *Duncliffe v Caerfelin Properties Ltd* [1989] 2 EGLR 38 (Ch), accepted by the Court of Appeal in *Muscat v Smith* [2003] EWCA Civ 962, [2003] 1 WLR 2853 [28] and [41]. Smith is critical of the inconsistency between allowing L2 to sue for pre-assignment tenant breaches, but not allowing T1 to sue L2 for pre-assignment landlord breaches: RJ Smith, *Property Law* 5th edn (Harlow, Longman, 2006) 439–40.

[107] That is, abatement of rent to reflect the money T1 has spent on repairs that should have been done by L1: *Muscat v Smith* [2003] EWCA Civ 962, [2003] 1 WLR 2853 [16]. On recoupment and set off, see ch 12.

[108] Sedley LJ's judgment goes further and appears to accept that the right to set off extends to post-assignment arrears, but in *Edlington Properties v Fenner & Co Ltd* [2006] EWCA Civ 403, [2006] 1 WLR 1583 Neuberger LJ (with whom the other members of the Court of Appeal agreed) says that Buxton LJ's judgment is to be preferred [36].

[109] The basis for this was that the assignee takes subject to equities. Derham rejects this as the appropriate basis. Instead, he says that the result in *Muscat v Smith* could be supported on the basis that L2 should not take the benefit of the lease for the period before the purchase by claiming unpaid rent without being subject to the claim based upon breach of the repairing covenant for that period: R Derham, 'Equitable Set-Off: A Critique of Muscat v Smith' (2006) 122 *LQR* 469, 491.

[110] Any seeming inconsistency between *Muscat v Smith* and *Edlington Properties v Fenner* is explained by the fact that, according to Neuberger LJ in the latter case: 'The right to recover the accrued rent … is a chose in action, whereas the right to recover future rent is not: it is simply an incident of the reversion' [47]. Contrast R Derham, 'Equitable Set-Off: A Critique of Muscat v Smith' (2006) 122 *LQR* 469, 489.

[111] [2006] EWCA Civ 403, [2006] 1 WLR 1583.

According to Neuberger LJ, the tenant's right to claim damages was a personal right and not an interest in land.[112] The case is complicated by the fact that the relevant obligation was in any event not contained in the lease itself, but in a separate building contract,[113] but Neuberger LJ's reasoning was not dependent on this fact.

This rather complex common law position can be made clear by careful drafting in the lease. The parties are able, for example, to state exactly what is being assigned (the right to sue for arrears, or not) and to specify when the right of set off will be available. In *Edlington Properties v Fenner & Co Ltd*, for example, Neuberger LJ says that the lease could have contained a term which provided T with a right of set-off against the landlord for the time being.

For new leases, the approach of the 1995 Act is to set out the principle that liability follows possession of the reversion. Consistently with this, section 23 provides that an assignee is not liable for pre-assignment breaches, although the parties are able to vary this contractually (for wording of section 23 see 18.13.1 above).

As L2 has no statutory right to sue for past rent arrears in relation to new tenancies, the equitable right to set off will not be available (unless there has been an express assignment by section 136 of the Law of Property Act 1925 in which event the assignment takes effect subject to equities, including the equitable right to set off).[114]

18.14 The Position of Guarantors

18.14.1 Guarantors of Former Tenants under Old (Pre-1996) Leases – Liability to the Contracting Landlord

It is common for landlords to require a guarantor to guarantee performance of the tenant's covenants, both in relation to the original tenant and later assignees. Any such guarantor will be in a contractual relationship with the landlord and will be subject to continuing liability, in the same manner as the original tenant under old leases, unless the covenant has been specifically worded so that liability will end upon an assignment by the original tenant. Under the general law, the guarantor is, however, discharged if any variations are agreed to the lease without his consent[115] (unless the variations are unsubstantial or cannot be

---

[112] [2006] EWCA Civ 403, [2006] 1 WLR 1583 [17]–[21]. Dixon disagrees with this, 'because the lease is proprietary and if the liability under leasehold covenants pass, so ... should the consequences of the enforcement of that liability': M Dixon, 'Leasehold Covenants and Equitable Set-Off' [2006] 70 *Conv* 460, 464.

[113] And so, as M Dixon notes, 'it is difficult to see what the fuss was about'. Neuberger LJ recognises [at 19] that the breach was not of a leasehold covenant but of an obligation in the building contract preceding the lease but does not consider this makes any difference. Dixon considers this makes all the difference as takes it outside the proprietary relationship: M Dixon, 'Leasehold Covenants and Equitable Set-Off' [2006] 70 *Conv* 460, 462.

[114] *Muscat v Smith* [2003] EWCA Civ 962, [2003] 1 WLR 2853.

[115] *Holme v Brunskill* (1878) 3 QBD 495. This may also include variations made in, for example, licences to assign; *West Horndon Industrial Park Ltd v Pheonix Timber Group plc* [1995] 1 EGLR 137 (Ch); *Howard de Waldon Estates Ltd v Pasta Place Ltd* [1995] 1 EGLR 79 (Ch). Compare the original tenant who will not be liable for increased liability stemming from variations, but remains liable on his original promises and is not discharged by the variations.

otherwise than beneficial to the surety).[116] In practice, however, many guarantee covenants are drafted so that liability will continue in this event.

Guarantors now benefit also from the various amendments that were introduced by the Landlord and Tenant (Covenants) Act 1995 to assist former tenants. Thus, before a guarantor can be sued he must be served with a section 17 problem notice,[117] he will not be liable for charges stemming from post-1995 variations to the lease (section 18), and he will be able to apply for an overriding lease if he pays the sums claimed in the section 17 notice (sections 19 and 20).

18.14.2 Guarantors of Former Tenants under Old (Pre-1996) Leases – Liability to New Reversioners

In relation to old leases, the liability of the guarantor to an assignee landlord (with whom there is no contractual relationship) is not straightforward. The Law of Property Act 1925, section 141, does not cover this situation as it annexes only covenants 'on the lessee's part to be observed and performed', not third party promises.[118] It is possible for the landlord expressly to assign the benefit of the guarantee to the new reversioner, but this does not always happen. In *P & A Swift Investments v Combined English Stores* the House of Lords held that the new reversioner was, in any event, able to enforce the guarantee.[119] They reached this result by relying on the common law rule under which the benefit of a covenant will run with the land if the assignee has a legal estate and the covenant is one which touches and concerns the land. The House of Lords rejected the argument that a surety covenant is 'purely collateral' and does not affect the value of the land. Adopting the view of Sir Browne-Wilkinson VC in *Kumar v Dunning*,[120] Lord Oliver said:

> It has been said that the surety's obligation is simply that of paying money and, of course, in a sense that is true if one looks only at the remedy which the landlord has against him in the event of default by the tenant. But ... I do not think that this is a complete analysis. The tenant covenants that he will do or refrain from doing certain things which undoubtedly touch and concern the land. A surety covenants that those things shall be done or not done as the case may be ... The content of the primary obligation is, as it seems to me, exactly the same and if that of the tenant touches and concerns the land that of the surety must, as it seems to me, equally do so.[121]

Similarly, in *Coronation Street Industrial Properties Ltd v Ingall Industries plc*, a guarantor had covenanted that if the tenant went into liquidation and the lease was disclaimed the surety would 'accept from the Lessor a Lease of the Demised Premises' for the unexpired residue and on the same terms and conditions as the tenant's lease.[122] The House of Lords

---

[116] *Holme v Brunskill* (1878) 3 QBD 495, 505.
[117] It is not necessary for the landlord also to serve a problem notice on the tenant in order to preserve the right to sue the guarantor: *Cheverell Estates Ltd v Harris* [1998] 1 EGLR (QB).
[118] *P & A Swift Investments v Combined English Stores* [1989] 1 AC 632 (HL).
[119] *P & A Swift Investments v Combined English Stores* [1989] 1 AC 632 (HL).
[120] [1989] QB 193 (CA).
[121] *P & A Swift Investments v Combined English Stores* [1989] 1 AC 632 (HL) 642.
[122] [1989] 1 WLR 304 (HL).

held that this was a covenant which ran with the land and was enforceable by the new reversioner.

18.14.3 Guarantors of Former Tenants under New (Post-1995) Leases

By the Landlord and Tenant (Covenants) Act 1995, section 24(2), the release of the tenant upon an assignment will also release any guarantor of that tenant.

Section 24

(2) Where –

(a) by virtue of this Act a tenant is released from a tenant covenant of a tenancy, and

(b) immediately before the release another person is bound by a covenant of the tenancy imposing any liability or penalty in the event of a failure to comply with that tenant covenant,

then, as from the release of the tenant, that other person is released from the covenant mentioned in paragraph (b) to the same extent as the tenant is released from that tenant covenant.

In practice, guarantees are often extremely important to landlords and a landlord will be unhappy with the prospect of losing the benefit of such guarantees upon assignment. There has been considerable debate as to whether an obligation by T1's guarantor to guarantee an AGA entered into by T1 on assignment to T2 can be enforced, or whether it would be struck down by the anti-avoidance provisions of section 25. The lease may, for example, provide that upon any assignment the guarantor will guarantee the tenant's AGA, but there is considerable doubt as to whether this is permitted or whether it offends the anti-avoidance provisions in section 25.[123] One way around this would be to insist upon the guarantor being a party to the lease (a joint tenant) and not merely a guarantor.

18.15 The Impact of the 1995 Act

Notwithstanding the concessions offered to tenants as part of the 1995 reform (particularly the overriding lease provisions, and section 17 notices), a truncated form of continuing tenant liability still exists even for new leases. Of course, the harshness of continuing liability has also been mitigated by the wider changes in the letting market. As commercial leases have become shorter so the impact of continuing liability has diminished, but it can still be substantial. The original reform proposals were to apply to all leases; the fact that the new release provisions apply only to new leases means that for many tenants continuing

---

[123] In support of the view that a guarantor can be required to enter into a fresh guarantee, see S Fogel and E Slessenger, 'Must a Surety Guarantee an AGA?' (8 August 1996) *EG* 59; J Adams, 'Another View of AGAs' (10 August 1996) *EG* 68; S Fogel, 'Blundell Memorial Lecture: Landlord and tenant reform – I' (10 August 1996) *EG* 64; M Dowden, 'Guaranteed to cause disputes' (20 July 1998) *EG* 162. Against this view, see S Bridge, 'Former Tenants, Future Liabilities and the Privity of Contract Principle: The Landlord and Tenant (Covenants) Act 1995' (1996) 55 *CLJ* 313, 340; S Cullen and R Potterton, 'Must a Surety Guarantee an AGA?' (11 May 1996) *EG* 118. For a general discussion of options, see AG Walker, 'Landlord and Tenant (Covenants) Act 1995: Sureties for tenants and assignees' (1998) 2 *Landlord & Tenant Rev* 124; E Slessenger and S Cullen, 'Is the guarantor on the hook?' (25 July 1998) *EG* 102.

liability still produces a big sting. In *Scottish & Newcastle plc v Raguz,* Hart J at first instance described the original tenant as facing a 'horrid' situation: as a major quoted company giving a 'blue chip' covenant it was unlikely that the landlord would bring things to an end by forfeiting the lease and the original tenant would remain liable until 2062.[124]

The 1995 Act has made a difference and improved the position that existed at common law but, as with many landlord and tenant reforms, the impact has not been as significant as some hoped for, and others feared. As Edwards and Krendal note, before the changes it was anticipated that a two tier market would emerge, with new leases commanding higher rents because of the release mechanism, and old leases would have improved investment values because of the more secure income stream.[125] Both predictions turned out to be groundless.

18.16 Enforcement of Covenants by and against Management Companies under New (Post-1995) Leases

Special provisions were introduced to cover the case of covenants that have been entered into by or with a management company, for example, where in a letting of an industrial unit a management company is a party to the lease and undertakes to perform the repair and maintenance obligations. The effect is to ensure that the benefit and burden of covenants with the management company will pass and the provisions for release on assignment will operate as with other parties to the lease.[126]

18.17 The Position of the Superior Landlord

The superior landlord does not enjoy a relationship of privity of estate with a sub-tenant. Nor are the benefits of the sub-tenant's covenants given to him under Landlord and Tenant (Covenants) Act 1995. The one exception to this is contained in section 3(5) of the Landlord and Tenant (Covenants) Act 1995, which provides that covenants which are 'restrictive of the user of the land' can be enforced against any person 'who is the owner or occupier of any demised premises to which the covenant relates'.

It is, however, usual for a sub-tenant to be required (as a condition of consent to an under-letting) to enter into a direct covenant with the superior landlord to observe the covenants in the underlease. This then gives the superior landlord a contractual right against the sub-tenant, but with new tenancies even a direct covenant will be enforceable only whilst the sub-tenant holds the sub-lease and the sub-tenant will be released from liability by a lawful assignment.[127]

Absent such a direct covenant (and user covenants apart) are there any other ways of arguing that the superior landlord can enforce covenants against a sub-tenant? In *Amsprop*

---

[124] [2006] EWHC 821 (Ch).

[125] C Edwards and P Krendel, *Institutional Leases in the 21st Century* (London, EG Books, 2007) 47.

[126] Landlord and Tenant (Covenants) Act 1995 s 12.

[127] This is not completely free of doubt but it is probably the case for two reasons. First, the direct covenant appears to come within the s 28 definition of tenant covenant. Second, for liability to continue beyond assignment would frustrate the operation of s 5 and thus be struck down by the anti-avoidance provisions in s 25: see S Fogel and others, *Leasehold Liability* (Bristol, Jordans, 2000) ch 2.

Trading Ltd v Harris Distribution,[128] the superior landlord argued that because the underlease referred to the superior landlord ('to permit the superior landlord to enter to view the state of repair', etc), this enabled it to enforce by virtue of section 56 of the Law of Property Act 1925.[129] Neuberger J rejected this argument, preferring the view that section 56 does not allow a third party to sue merely because the contract is made for his benefit; it must purport to be made with him.

There is more scope for arguing for enforceability by relying on the Contracts (Rights of Third Parties) Act 1999, unless the parties have excluded its operation. This applies to all contracts entered into after 11 May 2000. Under this Act, non-contracting parties are given the right to enforce a term of a contract in two situations, the two limbs of enforceability. The first limb, in section 1(1)(a), will given the third party a right to enforce a term of the contract if the contract expressly provides that he may. Such an express right would be unusual in a lease. The second limb, in section 1(1)(b), applies when the term of the contract 'purports to confer a benefit on him'. This is subject to an important proviso in section 1(2), whereby it will 'not apply if on a proper construction of the contract it appears that the parties did not intend the term to be enforceable by the third party'. In practice it is commonplace to exclude the Act from commercial leases. Where the Act is not excluded, whether or not the superior landlord is able to enforce covenants against a sub-tenant will therefore (unless there is a direct covenant or an express right of enforcement) depend on whether the relevant clauses can be said to 'confer a benefit' on the superior landlord. The kinds of clauses likely to be in issue are of two types:

(a)   a covenant (as in *Amsprop Trading*) that gives the superior landlord rights to enter and effect repairs at the under-tenant's expense;
(b)   a covenant prohibiting alienation without the consent of the superior landlord.

Although it remains unclear how widely the courts will construe the phrase 'confer a benefit',[130] it is likely that these covenants will be said to confer a benefit on the superior landlord and, therefore, they will be enforceable against the sub-tenant.

18.18 Enforcing Covenants between Tenants?

A tenant may wish to bring an action directly against another tenant rather than relying on the landlord to do so. Whether or not he is able to do so will depend upon the wording of the lease. An example of how it might be important can be illustrated by taking a shopping mall in which the tenants have covenanted with the landlord to keep open the premises during usual shopping hours. If the anchor tenant closes in breach of the covenant, the landlord is able to claim damages for breach, which can include loss of revenue to cover lower rents receivable from other units (see chapter 13). But the closure will also cause loss to other

---

[128] *Amsprop Trading Ltd v Harris Distribution Ltd* [1997] 1 WLR 1025 (Ch).

[129] S 56(1): 'A person may take an immediate or other interest in land or other property, or the benefit of any condition, right of entry, covenant or agreement over or respecting land or other property, although he may not be named as a party to the conveyance or other instrument'.

[130] A commercial case, *Nisshin Shipping Co Ltd v Cleaves & Co Ltd* [2003] EWHC 2602 (Comm), [2004] 1 All ER (Comm) 481 suggests that it will be given a wide interpretation.

tenants, and the question is whether they might be able to sue the anchor tenant for their losses. The answer will depend upon the applicability of the Contracts (Rights of Third Parties) Act 1999 to this situation (see 18.17 above). Clearly, if the lease of each unit expressly provides that other tenants can enforce the covenants then mutual enforceability is possible under the first limb in section 1(1)(a). This form of drafting is, however, unlikely to appeal to tenants: the ability to sue other tenants will also make the tenant vulnerable to claims from those other tenants. This means that the answer will depend on whether such covenants can be said to 'confer a benefit' on the tenant under the second limb in section 1(1)(b), subject of course to the Act not having been excluded from the lease.

Where the obligation in issue is 'restrictive' or 'negative' (broadly, an obligation 'not to') it may be possible to argue that there is mutual enforceability between tenants on the basis of a 'building scheme'. This is more conventionally thought of as enabling enforcement between freehold purchasers on an estate development but there is no reason in principle why it could not, in appropriate circumstances, be used to enable tenants to enforce restrictive covenants, such as user covenants, against other tenants. Gray and Gray suggest that the modern requirements of a scheme can be reduced to two essential requirements: an identifiable 'scheme' (the development of a defined area) and a mutually perceived common intention (purchasers bought on the common footing that all would be mutually bound by, and mutually entitled to enforce, a defined set of restrictions).[131] In *Williams v Kiley (t/a CK Supermarkets Ltd)* the Court of Appeal confirmed that tenants could enforce restrictive user covenants against other tenants within the same letting development in this way.[132] The claimant ran a shop as newsagent, confectioner and tobacconist under a lease that restricted use to those trades. The defendants ran a supermarket business from the adjoining premises under leases that excluded the business of 'newsagents, sugar confectioners, tobacconists', but in practice they sold tobacco, confectionary and stationery items. The claimants sought an injunction and damages against the defendant without the intervention of the common landlord, the local authority. Although the Court of Appeal noted the absence of reported cases relating to business leases,[133] it saw no reason why the principles applicable to 'building schemes' in the case of freehold sales should not also apply to leasehold schemes. On the facts, the Court of Appeal agreed with the first instance judge that the leases provided clear evidence of the intention to create 'reciprocity of obligation':

> It is not simply that the covenants are identical in form; each is carefully constructed, as a combination of requirements and exclusions, to dovetail with the other leases in the group of five shops. Each lessee not only has a positive obligation to carry on a particular business, but is protected against competition in that business from his neighbours. It is impossible, in my view, to see them as directed simply to protecting the interests of the council as lessors.[134]

This was reinforced by the fact that the common landlord had not retained the ability to vary the user clauses. There may be cases, however, where a scheme cannot be found because, for

---

[131] K Gray and S Gray, *Elements of Land Law* 4th edn (Oxford, OUP, 2005) 1384–91.

[132] [2002] EWCA Civ 1645.

[133] Apart from Canadian cases referred to by counsel. The Court of Appeal suggests that the explanation for the lack of authority is that action is normally brought by the landlord, whereas this option is usually not available in a freehold context as the original vendor will usually have dropped out of the picture once the development is fully sold.

[134] [2002] EWCA Civ 1645 [21].

example, the landlord has reserved the right to consent to changes in the user provisions (and this would by implication negate the implication that there is meant to be a scheme mutually enforceable by the tenants).[135]

As to the argument that the impact of this decision could have a 'freezing' effect, crystallising the permitted use for the length of the leases irrespective of the changing nature of retail trading, the Court of Appeal noted that the Lands Tribunal has powers to remove or modify restrictions in long leases after 25 years (the Law of Property Act 1925 section 84(12)), and, in extreme cases, the restraint of trade doctrine might have a role to play.[136]

18.19 The Effect of Disclaimer upon Liability[137]

When a tenant becomes insolvent and the lease vests in the tenant's liquidator (if the tenant is a company; a trustee in bankruptcy if the tenant is an individual), the liquidator has power to disclaim the lease as 'onerous property'.[138] The effect of a disclaimer will be to end the lease and thus to put an end to the rights and liabilities of the insolvent tenant.[139] This does not, however, affect the rights and liabilities of others:

> … when the lease is disclaimed it is determined and the reversion accelerated but the rights and liabilities of others, such as guarantors and original tenants, are to remain as though the lease had continued and not been determined. In this way the determination of the lease is not permitted to affect the rights or liabilities of other persons. Statute has so provided.[140]

If the insolvent tenant is the original tenant and there are no guarantors, the lease is put to an end and there is no further liability. Any guarantor – of the original tenant or of an assignee – will, however, remain liable, for as Lord Nicholls observed in *Hindcastle Ltd v Barbara Attenborough Associates Ltd*, the 'very object of giving and taking a guarantee would be defeated if the position were otherwise'.[141] Although the guarantor loses the right to indemnity from the insolvent tenant, he does have a statutory right to prove as a creditor from the insolvent tenant's estate. If the insolvent tenant is an assignee, the original tenant

---

[135] See discussion at [2002] EWCA Civ 1645 [10].

[136] [2002] EWCA Civ 1645 [28].

[137] See also ch 24.

[138] See Insolvency Act 1986 ss 178–182 (companies); Insolvency Act 1986 ss 315–321 (individuals).

[139] For the effect of disclaimer on sub-tenants, see *Hindcastle Ltd v Barbara Attenborough Associates Ltd* [1997] AC 70 (HL) 89 where Lord Nicholls states that the subtenant's interest continues, 'If he pays the rent and performs the tenant covenants in the disclaimed lease, the landlord cannot eject him. If he does not, the landlord can distrain upon his goods for the rent reserved by the disclaimed lease or bring forfeiture proceedings.' For a general discussion of *Hindcastle*, and this particular point, see T Tayleur, 'The Effect of Disclaimer: A Tale of Two Cases' [1997] *Conv* 24.

[140] *Hindcastle Ltd v Barbara Attenborough Associates Ltd* [1997] AC 70 (HL) 89. The relevant statutory provision is the Insolvency Act 1986, s 178(4) which provides: 'A disclaimer under this section – (a) operates so as to determine, as from the date of the disclaimer, the rights, interests and liabilities of the company in or in respect of the property disclaimed; but (b) does not, except so far as is necessary for the purpose of releasing the company from any liability, affect the rights or liabilities of any other person'. Similar provisions exist in relation to disclaimer by trustees in bankruptcy.

[141] *Hindcastle Ltd v Barbara Attenborough Associates Ltd* [1997] AC 70 (HL) 94. In reaching this result the House of Lords overruled the Court of Appeal decision in *Stacey v Hill* [1901] 1 KB 660 (CA) a case involving the guarantor of the original tenant.

and other former tenants who are contractually liable will also remain liable even after disclaimer.[142] All of these persons – original tenants, former tenants, guarantors – will have a right to apply for an overriding lease under section 19 of the Landlord and Tenant (Covenants) Act 1995[143] or a vesting order under the insolvency legislation.[144] In practice, many leases require the guarantor to enter into a lease with the landlord when there is a disclaimer.

Although Lord Nicholls stated in *Hindcastle Ltd v Barbara Attenborough Associates Ltd* that this issue will not arise in the case of new leases because the tenant is released on assignment, it could arise in the case of a tenant who has entered into an AGA, and liability will then remain under this guarantee even if the lease is disclaimed.

---

[142] *Hill v East and West India Dock Co* (1884) 9 App Cas 448, affirmed in *Hindcastle Ltd v Barbara Attenborough Associates Ltd* [1997] AC 70 (HL).

[143] Although Lord Nicholls accepts this as a possibility in *Hindcastle Ltd v Barbara Attenborough Associates Ltd* [1997] AC 70 (HL) 94, there is some doubt as to whether it is possible to claim an overriding lease when the overridden lease has been disclaimed, see T Tayleur, 'The Effect of Disclaimer: A Tale of Two Cases' [1997] *Conv* 24, 33.

[144] Insolvency Act 1986 ss 181 and 320.

PART SIX

CONTINUING THE RELATIONSHIP

The Right to Stay

Parts Six and Seven are to do with what happens at the end of a tenancy. There is an overlap between them: the broad distinction is that Part Seven covers situations in which the leasehold relationship is brought to an end, whereas Part Six looks at the situations in which the tenant has some protected status that either gives the tenant rights to continue the leasehold relationship or limits the ability of the landlord to bring the relationship to an end. Thus, Part Six covers what might loosely be called 'security of tenure'. The level of security available to tenants has varied over the years, reflecting the complex interplay of economic, social and political interests. The reason why there is so much overlap between Parts Six and Seven is that security of tenure is often provided by placing restrictions on rights that the landlord would otherwise have at common law to end the relationship. Some limited security is sometimes given to tenants by imposing minimum requirements on the length of notice that the landlord has to give if wanting to end the relationship; this can occur at both common law and by statute but is discussed in this book in Part Seven as the aim of minimum notice periods is not to significantly extend the relationship but to smooth the transition to ending it.

Why is Security Important?

In all sectors the ability to remain in a property may be important to the occupying tenant. For the residential tenant, the property is 'home'. More than a simple roof over the head it is the place around which personal and social lives are built and a person can find his place in the wider community.[1] Not only is a move time consuming and expensive, but it can lead to the break up of these very important social and community bonds, a factor important not only to the individual and his family but also to wider society, as is evident from the problems associated with social exclusion. Fox draws on studies in other disciplines to show how the concept of home represents social, psychological and cultural values:

> These feelings about home can be grouped into four main clusters of value-types: *home as a physical structure* offers material shelter; *home as a territory* offers security and control, a locus

---

[1] On the importance of 'home' see: L Fox, 'The Meaning of Home: a Chimeral Concept or a Legal Challenge?' (2002) 29 *J of L and Society* 580; T Honore, *The Quest for Security: Employees, Tenants, Wives* (London, Stevens, 1982) 36; Law Commission, 'Renting Homes 2: Co-occupation, Transfer and Succession' (Law Com CP No 168, 2002) para 7.42.

in space, permanence and continuity and privacy; *home as a centre for self-identity* offers a reflection of one's ideas and values, and acts as an indicator a personal status; and *home as a social and cultural unit* acts as the locus for relationships with family and friends, and as a centre of activities.[2]

Further, she shows that although some research has found that home ownership provides greater ontological security for occupiers than renting, other research shows that where people *choose* to rent they do not generally feel any less 'at home' than owner occupiers. Indeed, the factors that appear to promote a more meaningful home experience – security, continuity, control and freedom – are factors that governments could build into rental laws, 'thus ensuring that these characteristics of home could be experienced in the same way by renters'. Little work has, however, been done linking concepts of home with security of tenure, even though greater security may well be found to have positive impacts in relation to social inclusion and sustainable communities, both very much a key aspect of the government's programme for renewal and regeneration. Research for Shelter shows that tenants in the private rented sector (the sector with little effective security) have much lower 'social capital' scores than those in other tenure groups:

> ... a quarter of all private tenants say that they do not know anyone in their neighbourhood – more than four times the average across all tenures. The scores for privately renting households are particularly low on other factors relating to neighbourliness, such as talking to and looking out for those who live nearby.[3]

Indeed, on each measure used (influence on local decision-making, acting to solve local problems, speaking to neighbours, knowing neighbours, neighbours helping each other, satisfactory friendship network, satisfactory relatives network and being a victim of crime) private renters scored worse than social renters.

Unsurprisingly, eviction has a considerable emotional impact on tenants and their families and can have serious social and personal consequences.[4]

A forced move will also be disruptive and expensive for businesses, and for those for which the particular location is critical it could be economically disastrous. In the agricultural context, security can be important to encourage long term efficiency and cultivation in farming.

Against these factors that support security as a social and economic good, must be weighed the landlord's interests: his economic interest in the reversion, the need to be able to rid himself of bad tenants and manage his properties, and his freedom to let and recover property on terms of its choosing. Linked to this is the wider public policy in ensuring that there is a good supply of property for renting: severe restrictions on the ability to recover leased property are likely to discourage an active investment market.

---

[2] L Fox, 'The Meaning of Home: a Chimeral Concept or a Legal Challenge?' (2002) 29 *J of L and Society* 580, 590–1, 606.

[3] L Reynolds, *Safe and Secure? The private rented sector and security of tenure* (Shelter, 2005) 25.

[4] H Pawson and others, 'The Use of Possession Actions and Evictions by Social Landlords' (ODPM, June 2005) 11 and 21.

Trends in Security

Apart from the social sector, there has been a marked reduction in security for tenants in the last 20 years. In the agricultural and residential sectors this reflects concerns that high levels of security were strangling the tenanted sector. In the commercial sector the relaxation did not reflect a deliberate shift in policy but has resulted from what was perceived as merely a procedural change. In each sector, the buzz word has become 'flexibility'. Nonetheless, some security of tenure does remain for some tenants.

In Part Six the protection available to residential tenants, leaseholders (tenants of long residential leases) and business tenants is discussed in separate chapters (19, residential tenancies; 20, long residential leases; and 21, business tenancies). There are differences as to both the method of conferring security and in the details of the grounds on which the landlord is able to resist the tenant's claim to security. In broad terms, security in the residential short-term rental sectors is now provided by requiring a court order before the landlord can recover possession, and to obtain this order the landlord is required to prove that certain facts exist, loosely based around estate management grounds or the tenant's behaviour. Neither the introductory tenant in the public sector, nor the assured shorthold tenant in the private sector has much security; whereas the secure tenant in the public sector and the private sector assured tenant enjoy considerable security. The long residential lease-holder is given a right to stay in the property when the lease expires, but will probably have to start paying a market rent (whereas he may previously have been paying a relatively small ground rent). In the business sector, the protected tenant can apply to renew the tenancy at the end of the fixed term (although contracting out is commonplace). The landlord is able to resist this application on specified statutory grounds, again based on tenant default, and the landlord's estate management interests.

The advent of the Agricultural Tenancies Act 1995 means that there is no security now for tenant farmers with tenancies entered into after 1 September 1995. Those governed by the Agricultural Holdings Act 1986 continue to enjoy security of tenure under the scheme outlined in chapter 9. The grounds for recovering these agricultural leases reflect not only the kind of estate management and tenant quality issues seen in the other sectors but also factors more specific to farming. So, for example, it could be relevant that the landlord is able to show that he would make a better job of running the farmland,[5] and practices that promote environmental protection can also be factored in.[6] Given that new farm business tenancies do not enjoy security of tenure beyond the contractual term, this Part of the book does not include a chapter on agricultural leases.

The width of the grounds available to the landlord clearly impacts on the degree of security that a tenant enjoys. Few would doubt that a landlord should be able to recover possession from a bad tenant (although understandings of what is 'bad' may vary, and may reflect political mores), but there is probably less agreement on the extent to which the landlord's own interests and preferences should permit recovery. Should a landlord be able to recover property because he wishes to use it himself, and/or because he wants to develop its economic potential? Is the balance different if it is only the tenant's economic interests at

---

[5] Agricultural Holdings Act 1986 s 27(3)(a); *Davies v Price* [1958] 1 WLR 434 (CA).
[6] Agricultural Holdings Act 1986 Sch 3 Part II para 9.

stake as against the ontological security associated with 'home'? To what extent should landlords be required (or merely able) to evict someone as part of the fight against anti-social behaviour? Should a tenant's rights be dependent not only upon his performing property based obligations but also upon the 'proper' exercise of his responsibilities to the wider community? These questions are seldom made explicit in legal or policy discussions, but as the law relating to security of tenure is explained in the following chapters it is worth considering how satisfactorily the law currently balances the interests of the landlord, the tenant, and the wider community.

19

SECURITY AND RESIDENTIAL TENANCIES

19.1   Introduction
19.2   Scheme of protection
19.3   Grounds for possession

19.1 Introduction

In the past, tenants in both the public and private sector have enjoyed considerable security. Although public sector tenants did not have statutory rights until the Housing Act of 1980, in practice a responsible tenant could expect to remain for a long time. For most of the twentieth century private sector tenants had security, although the precise details and scope of the statutory protection varied with changing policy (see chapter 6).

For public sector tenants, the Housing Act 1980 introduced the 'secure tenancy' which, as the name implies, offered statutory security. The picture was largely unchanged until the introductory tenancy was introduced in 1996;[1] conceived as part of the drive to tackle anti-social behaviour, it in effect enables local authorities to test out a tenant for a year before they acquire security. This idea was expanded when demoted tenancies were introduced by the Anti-social Behaviour Act 2003;[2] the court can order a secure tenancy to be demoted on the grounds of anti-social behaviour, and during the one year period for which it is a demoted tenancy the landlord can end the tenancy without having to prove a ground for possession so long as the correct procedure is followed. Introductory and demoted tenancies are discussed further in chapter 6.

In the private sector, the big change came in 1988 with the launch of the assured shorthold through the Housing Act 1988. Although assured tenants retain security, the assured shorthold tenant has only a minimum of six months to rely on (or the contractual term, if longer). Almost 90 per cent of new private rented sector lettings available to members of the public are assured shortholds.[3]

The 1988 Act also placed housing associations firmly in the private sector. This, coupled with the transfer of much of the local authority housing stock to registered social landlords

---

[1] Housing Act 1985 Sch 1 para 1A.
[2] Housing Act 1985 Sch 1 para 1B.
[3] S Wilcox, *UK Housing Review 2005/06* (Coventry, Chartered Institute of Housing and London, Council of Mortgage Lenders, 2005) Table 54a.

(RSLs), means that many 'social' tenants do not have statutory security, although in practice RSLs tend to mirror the commitment to long term housing that is found with the secure tenancy by granting assured tenancies rather than assured shortholds.

19.2 Scheme of Protection

19.2.1 The Tenancy can be Ended only if there is a Statutory Ground for Possession

Security of tenure works in the residential sector by restricting the landlord's ability to end a tenancy. At common law, a periodic tenancy is ended by service of a notice to quit, and a fixed term expires by effluxion of time unless ended by an earlier forfeiture. These rules are modified for protected residential tenancies so that a court order is always needed to end the tenancy to ensure that tenants do not unwittingly give up valuable rights or get forced to move when they have the right to stay.

In the case of secure and assured periodic tenancies,[4] the landlord can only end the tenancy by court order,[5] which cannot be granted unless a statutory ground for possession exists. In the case of secure tenants, possession can be given only if the court considers it reasonable or on certain estate management grounds provided that suitable alternative accommodation (SAA) is available (for some grounds both reasonableness and SAA are required).[6] With assured tenancies there are, in addition to discretionary grounds which turn on reasonableness, some mandatory grounds which, if established, require the court to make an order for possession.[7] An order for possession will be given for an assured shorthold tenancy provided that the tenancy has come to an end (subject to a six month minimum) and the tenant has at least two months' notice.[8]

With fixed term tenancies, instead of expiring by effluxion of time, a periodic tenancy comes into existence at the end of the tenancy (known in the private sector as a statutory periodic assured tenancy). The parties and terms will be the same as those of the expired fixed term tenancy[9] and the period of the tenancy will be the same as that for which rent was last payable under the fixed term tenancy.[10] Both regimes enable these terms to be varied. With the statutory periodic assured tenancy, either party may serve a notice on the other proposing different terms and a variation in the rent to take account of these different terms within 12 months of the fixed term tenancy expiring.[11] There is also provision for the notice to be referred to a rent assessment committee if the parties are unable to agree on the proposed terms. The terms of the periodic tenancy arising at the end of the fixed term

---

[4] The meaning of these terms is discussed in ch 6.

[5] Housing Act 1985 s 82 (secure tenancy); Housing Act 1988 s 5 (assured tenancy).

[6] Housing Act 1985 s 84(1). See tables 19.1 and 19.2 below.

[7] Housing Act 1988 s 7. See tables 19.1 and 19.2 below.

[8] Housing Act 1988 s 21.

[9] Housing Act 1985 s 86(2)(b) (secure tenancies); Housing Act 1988 s 5(3).

[10] Housing Act 1985 s 86(2)(a)(secure tenancies); Housing Act 1988 s 5(3)(d), (e) (assured tenancies). In *Church Commissioners for England v Meya* [2006] EWCA Civ 821 this was taken to refer the frequency of payment. So, for example, a tenancy with a rent of '£x per year' payable monthly will lead to a monthly tenancy under the legislation, rather than, as at common law, an annual tenancy.

[11] Housing Act 1988 s 6.

secure tenancy can be varied by the procedure set out in sections 102 and 103 of the Housing Act 1985 (see chapter 4). The resulting periodic tenancy can, in both sectors, then only be ended in the same way as other protected periodic tenancies.

This process would be defeated if a landlord is able to forfeit a tenancy for grounds different to the statutory grounds for possession. Both regimes in effect provide that the right to forfeit can be used to end the lease only if a statutory ground for possession exists.[12] A fixed term assured tenancy can be ended during the term only if the lease itself permits this and only for Grounds 2 (mortgagees' repossession) and 8 (rent arrears) or a discretionary ground (apart from Grounds 9 (suitable alternative accommodation) and 16 (employment related)).[13]

In practice, many tenancies end without going to court. The tenant may be the one seeking to move, but even if the landlord seeks to end the tenancy the tenant will often move on quietly. For tenants hoping to be rehoused by the council it is necessary to stay put as they risk being deemed intentionally homeless (and thus not coming within the main homelessness duty) if they leave before a court order has been obtained.[14]

In 1993, an accelerated possession procedure was introduced, enabling a private landlord seeking possession to obtain an order for possession by paper without the parties having to attend court.[15] Initially this process was available for certain mandatory grounds for possession as well as the assured shorthold, but it is now confined to the latter.[16] It can only be used to recover possession and not, for example, to also recover rent arrears. In practice, however, research conducted in 1995/96 found that many landlords were using the accelerated possession procedure even when there were rent arrears, recognising that it was very unlikely the arrears would in any event be paid and that this provided the quickest way to cut their losses.[17]

Where possession is based on rent arrears it is now possible to commence an action online.[18]

19.2.2 Notice Seeking Possession

Due process is enhanced by notice requirements. In both the private sector and the public sector the landlord must serve a 'notice seeking possession' (NSP) before he can obtain a court order, unless the court 'considers it just and equitable to dispense' with the notice.[19]

---

[12] Housing Act 1985 ss 82(3) and 86 (secure tenancies); Housing Act 1988 s 5(2) and 7(6) (assured tenancies).

[13] The grounds are in Sch 2 of the Housing Act 1988.

[14] See also the discussion at ch 23.

[15] Described as 'another ... nail in the coffin of private tenants' rights' by Sue Waller, Camden Federation of Private Tenants, quoted in P Jew, *Law and Order in Private Rented Housing: Tackling Harassment and Illegal Eviction* (London, Campaign for Bedsit Rights, 1994) 6.

[16] When available on other grounds, 98% of cases were in any event to recover assured shortholds: D Levison, J Barelli and G Lawton, 'The Accelerated Possession Procedure: the Experience of Landlords and Tenants' (DETR, 1998).

[17] D Levison, J Barelli and G Lawton, 'The Accelerated Possession Procedure: the Experience of Landlords and Tenants' (DETR, 1998).

[18] www.possessionclaim.gov.uk

[19] Housing Act 1985 s 83; Housing Act 1988 s 8 (in the case of Ground 8 the court does not have power to dispense with the notice requirement). There are additional notice requirements where recovery is for domestic violence.

This must be in a prescribed form (or 'substantially to the same effect')[20] stating the ground(s) for possession. There must also be a delay between serving the notice and beginning proceedings, the extent of notice required varies according to the ground of recovery. Only with nuisance can proceedings begin immediately, and even then there must be a four week delay in the public sector (with no obvious reason for this differential treatment).

What is important about these notices is that they can provide advice to the tenant about his position and about any rights that he might have. The Law Commission sees the notice requirement as serving two functions:

> First is the need for clarity. There must be a clear warning that the home may be lost (together with an idea of what, if anything, can be done to lift the threat). Second, occupiers – taken as a whole – are less likely to take up their rights to challenge evictions than might be expected. One key reason is their lack of knowledge of their rights. There therefore needs to be a clear statement to the occupier that they may be able to challenge the possession proceedings and that they should seek advice quickly.[21]

So long as the notice served is in substance the same as the prescribed notice, it will be effective. Minor errors that will not mislead will not invalidate the notice,[22] but it is important that the notice is:

> … adequate to achieve the legislative purpose of the provision. That purpose, in my judgment, is to give to the tenant the information which the provision requires to be given in the notice to enable the tenant to consider what she should do and, with or without advice, to do that which is in her power and which will best protect her against the loss of her home.[23]

In *Mountain v Hastings*, the section 8 notice listed the grounds relied on, but did not give the full text of each ground as was required by the prescribed form of notice.[24] The relevant ground (Ground 8) would only lead to recovery of possession if the rent was unpaid at the date of service of the notice *and* at the date of the hearing. As this was not mentioned in the section 8 notice it was held to be defective for failing to convey the substance of one of the grounds relied on.[25]

Often the NSP is used by landlords not as reflecting a genuine desire to recover possession but as a tool for recovering rent arrears, to scare the tenant into paying. Although around 550,000 NSPs are served by social landlords each year (representing about 13 per cent of their housing stock), only one in four leads to court action (and an even smaller number, 26,000, lead to eviction). There is a 12 month time limit after serving a NSP within which any proceedings must be brought,[26] but on the basis of a 'use it or lose it' model the Law Commission recommends that this should be reduced to six months.[27]

---

[20] Secure Tenancies (Notices) Regulations 1987 SI 1987/755; Assured Tenancies and Agricultural Occupancies (Forms) Regulations 1977 SI 1977/194.

[21] Law Commission, 'Renting Homes 1: Status and Security' (Law Com CP No 162, 2002) para 10.8.

[22] *Dudley MBC v Bailey* (1990) 22 HLR 424 (CA) 431.

[23] *Mountain v Hastings* (1993) 25 HLR 427 (CA) 433.

[24] (1993) 25 HLR 427 (CA).

[25] For public sector examples see *Torridge District Council v Jones* (1985) 18 HLR 107 (CA) 113 and 114; *Slough BC v Robbins* [1996] 12 CL 353 (Cty Ct).

[26] Housing Act 1985 s 83(3)(b), (4)(b); Housing Act 1988 s 8(3)(c).

[27] Law Commission, 'Renting Homes: The Final Report. Volume 1: Report' (Law Com No 297, 2006) para 4.66.

19.2.3 Grounds for Possession (in outline)

The court is unable to order possession except for one of the grounds specified in the relevant statute. There is considerable overlap between the grounds in the public and private sectors.

The grounds for possession can be thought of as falling under three broad headings (although not grouped this way in the legislation): occupier default, social policy (anti-social behaviour, domestic violence, false statements), and estate management.[28] In the public sector, there are no mandatory grounds for possession. Possession can be granted for Grounds 1–8 only if the court considers it reasonable to make the order, for Grounds 9–11 only if the court is satisfied that suitable accommodation will be available for the tenant when the order takes effect, and for Grounds 12–16 only if the court both considers it reasonable to make the order and is satisfied that suitable accommodation will be available for the tenant when the order takes effect.[29] In the private residential sector, Grounds 1–8 are mandatory and Grounds 9–17 can be relied on only if the court considers it reasonable.[30] Many of the mandatory private sector grounds are designed to enable a landlord to enter into a letting with the certainty of being to recover possession when the property is needed for the landlord's purposes – these ends can now also be achieved by using the assured shorthold tenancy, lessening the need for such an eclectic list.

Tables 19.1 and 19.2 summarise the main grounds on which possession is available; the grounds are discussed in more detail below.

19.2.3.1 Reasonableness

Reasonableness confers a wide discretion on the trial judge.[31] In construing earlier statutory language to the same effect, Lord Greene MR said in *Cumming v Danson*:

> In considering reasonableness … it is … perfectly clear that the duty of the judge is to take into account all relevant circumstances as they exist at the date of the hearing. That he must do in what I venture to call a broad, common-sense way as a man of the world, and come to his conclusion giving such weight as he thinks right to the various factors in the situation. Some factors may have little or no weight, others may be decisive, but it is quite wrong for him to exclude from his consideration matters which he ought to take into account.[32]

Where reasonableness is in issue, the court must look at the case as a whole, including matters not directly to do with the grounds for eviction. This will include, for example, giving 'proper weight' to the impact that mental disability may have upon the tenant and whether it is susceptible to treatment.[33] Failure to consider reasonableness will invalidate the possession order.[34] The court should also bear in mind that,

---

[28] Law Commission, 'Renting Homes 1: Status and Security' (Law Com CP No 162, 2002) para 7.59.

[29] Housing Act 1985 s 84(2). Sch 2 Part IV has effect for determining whether suitable accommodation will be available for a tenant.

[30] Housing Act 1988 s 7. Sub-section (5A) restricts the grounds available to the landlord of a periodic tenancy arising at the end of a long residential lease under Schedule 10 to the Local Government and Housing Act 1989. Sub-section (6) restricts the right of the landlord to forfeit during a fixed term lease so that forfeiture is only possible on certain grounds.

[31] *Bell London and Provincial Properties Ltd v Reuben* [1946] 2 All ER 547 (CA).

[32] [1942] 2 All ER 653 (CA) 655.

[33] *Croydon LBC v Moody* (1998) 31 HLR 738 (CA).

[34] *Shrimpton v Rabbits* (1924) 131 LT 478 (KB); *Hounslow LBC v McBride* (1999) 31 HLR 143 (CA).

Table 19.1: (Public Sector) Secure Tenancies: Grounds For Possession, Housing Act 1985 Schedule 2

Ground No	Part I: If Reasonable	Ground No	Part II: SAA Available	Ground No	Part III: SAA and Reasonable
1	Rent arrears or breach of tenancy	9	Overcrowding	12	Employment related accommodation required for another
2	Nuisance, illegal use	10	Demolition or reconstruction	13	Specially designed accommodation
2A	Domestic violence	10A	Redevelopment scheme	14	Specialist housing association or trust
3	Deterioration of the premises	11	Conflict with objects of charity	15	Special needs
4	Ill treatment of furniture			16	'Under-crowding' following tenants death
5	False statement inducing tenancy				
6	Premium paid on exchange				
7	Unsuitable conduct in job-related accommodation				
8	Temporary accommodation during works on other property				

Table 19.2: (Private sector and RSL) Assured Tenancies: Grounds For Possession, Housing Act 1988 Schedule 2

Ground No	Part I: Mandatory Grounds	Ground No	Part II: If Reasonable
1	Owner-occupiers	9	Suitable alternative accommodation
2	Mortgagee repossession	10	Rent arrears
3	Out of season let of holiday home	11	Persistent delay in paying rent
4	Educational institutions' vacation lettings	12	Other breach of tenancy
5	Minister of religion	13	Deterioration of the premises
6	Demolition or reconstruction	14	Nuisance, illegal use
7	Periodic tenancy recently inherited	14A	(RSLs only) Domestic violence
8	Rent arrears (8 weeks if weekly/ monthly; 3 months if quarterly/yearly)	15	Ill-treatment of furniture
		16	Employment related accommodation required for another
		17	False statement inducing tenancy

... if a possession order is made, the date of possession can be postponed, or the execution of the order stayed or suspended, on such conditions as the court thinks fit.[35] (see below)

This might, for example, mean that the court can suspend a possession order on terms that give the tenant the time and opportunity to remedy a complaint. As will be seen, it is much more usual for a possession order to be made subject to conditions rather than ordering outright possession. These conditional orders have usually been referred to as suspended possession orders, although following procedural changes in 2006 (to do with the concept of the tolerated trespasser, discussed below at 19.25) they are now better described as postponed possession orders. Under a postponed possession order, conditions are set for continuing occupation and if there is breach the landlord is able to apply to the court for a date for possession.

19.2.3.2 The Exercise of Discretion

Whatever the theory about reasonableness, it is also important to understand the context in which possession orders are made. The next two sections look at the range and impact of possession orders; here the process is mentioned in order to see how this can impact upon the exercise of judicial discretion. Possession hearings tend to be very brief; there are sometimes 40–50 cases in a morning, leaving judges on average fewer than five minutes to reach a decision.[36] Inevitably this means that the district judge does not have much time to consider the circumstances of a particular case. A landlord will often appear before the court with a 'pre-agreed' deal in which the parties have met and decided how to proceed and there is a perception held by some that judges simply rubber-stamp the landlord's action,[37] a perception supported by research showing that some judges appear to show 'enormous respect' for 'pre-agreements', while others are more willing to reopen them.[38] In fact, however, it has long been recognised that merely 'rubber stamping' a consent order drafted by the parties is not a proper discharge of the judicial functions in this context;[39] the court must be satisfied that it has jurisdiction to make the order sought.[40]

Further, although there has been considerable improvement in the levels of tenant participation in the hearing during the last decade, it is still the case that in a majority of cases (55 per cent) there is no participation at all by the tenant in the hearing[41] even though attendance does influence outcomes (usually, but not always, in the tenant's favour).[42] Representation, by a solicitor or duty desk, does have a positive influence for the tenant: those represented are the least likely to get outright possession orders and the most likely to obtain an adjournment. A study by Nixon and others in 1996 found that when

---

[35] *Norwich City Council v Famuyiwa* [2004] EWCA Civ 1770 [23].

[36] C Hunter and others, 'The exercise of judicial discretion in rent arrears cases' DCA Research Series 6/05 (October 2005) 10 and 106.

[37] H Pawson and others, 'The Use of Possession Actions and Evictions by Social Landlords' (ODPM, June 2005) 34.

[38] D Cowan and others, 'District Judges and Possession Proceedings' (2006) 33 *J of L and Society* 547.

[39] Law Commission 'Renting Homes 1: Status and Security' (Law Com CP No 162, 2002) para 12.12.

[40] *LB of Hounslow v McBride* (1999) 31 HLR 143 (CA); *Chinwe Gil v Baygreen Properties Limited* [2002] EWCA Civ 1340.

[41] C Hunter and others, 'The exercise of judicial discretion in rent arrears cases' DCA Research Series 6/05 (October 2005) 17, Table 4.

[42] C Hunter and others, 'The exercise of judicial discretion in rent arrears cases' DCA Research Series 6/05 (October 2005) 56, 71.

tenants did not attend the hearing and were not represented they were more than three times as likely to be placed under the threat of eviction.[43]

There appears to be wide variation in the practice of different courts and different judges. The individual judge injects his or her own view of a case depending on things such as constructed models of worthiness (the worthy tenant being one who can't pay rather than won't pay, and who 'bothers' to attend the hearing),[44] perceptions as to whether the cause of arrears is a systemic failure or individual failure, whether the problem is perceived as a social welfare problem or a simple contractual debt, and the judge's perception of the judging role.[45] In arrears cases, attendance at the court, payment history, and the level of arrears have been shown to be important factors in the exercise of discretion, as has knowledge about the tenant's personal circumstances (such as dependant children, old age, and mental health issues).[46]

The Law Commission in its Renting Homes work noted widespread concerns about inconsistency in how judges exercise their discretion[47] and have recommended the adoption of a more structured discretion. This would require the court to take into account, amongst other things, general relevant circumstances (for example, the frequency and seriousness of a breach and the contract holder's responsibility for the breach), the effect that a possession order would have on the private and family life of the occupiers, the likelihood of complying with conditions attached to a possession order, and the effect of not making an order on the landlord's interests (including its ability to fulfil its housing functions).[48] Although some have expressed doubt as to whether this kind of structuring of the discretion involved in reasonableness would have the effect of reducing the 'lottery' of possession proceedings,[49] the Law Commission's proposals would, in requiring a judge to address the listed factors, ensure that a more considered and reasoned approach is adopted in these cases.

19.2.4 The Range of Possession Orders

There are a number of possible responses when a landlord goes to court seeking possession. Although in many respects these seem like detailed procedural points, they do have very important substantive consequences.

19.2.4.1 Mandatory Grounds for Possession

Where the landlord is relying on a non-discretionary ground for possession (Grounds 9–11 in the public sector; Part I, Schedule 2 to the Housing Act 1988 and assured shorthold

---

[43] J Nixon and others 'Housing Cases in County Courts' (The Policy Press in association with the Joseph Rowntree Foundation, 1996).

[44] D Cowan and E Hitchings, '"Pretty boring stuff": District Judges and Housing Possession Proceedings' (2007) 16 *Social & Legal Studies* 363.

[45] D Cowan and others, 'District Judges and Possession Proceedings' (2006) 33 *J of L and Society* 547.

[46] C Hunter and others, 'The exercise of judicial discretion in rent arrears cases' DCA Research Series 6/05 (October 2005).

[47] Law Commission, 'Renting Homes 1: Status and Security' (Law Com CP No 162, 2002) 12.11–12.16; Law Commission, 'Renting Homes' (Law Com No 284, 2003) para 9.83.

[48] Law Commission, 'Renting Homes: The Final Report. Volume 1: Report' (Law Com No 297, 2006) paras 5.31–5.42.

[49] D Cowan and others, 'District Judges and Possession Proceedings' (2006) 33 *J of L and Society* 547.

tenancies in the private sector), the court will grant an absolute order for possession if the ground is established. The order for possession can be postponed, but only for a short period:

Housing Act 1980 section 89

... the giving up of possession shall not be postponed (whether by the order or any variation, suspension or stay of execution) to a date later than fourteen days after the making of the order, unless it appears to the court that exceptional hardship would be caused by requiring possession to be given up by that date; and shall not in any event be postponed to a date later than six weeks after the making of the order.[50]

19.2.4.2 Discretionary Grounds for Possession

In relation to secure and assured tenancies where possession requires reasonableness, the court, if it considers it reasonable to make a possession order, can make an outright possession order, a postponed possession order, adjourn proceedings, or (rarely) dismiss the claim for possession. In practice, the usual questions that the judge must ask are, first, whether it is reasonable to make a possession order and, if so, whether it is reasonable to suspend that order.

It is this discretion available to a court to suspend etc a possession order that has led to the development of the tolerated trespasser concept. The power to suspend exists both in the public sector and the private sector where the ground for possession requires the court to be satisfied as to its reasonableness. The relevant powers for the public sector are contained in section 85 of the Housing Act 1985:

(1) Where proceedings are brought for possession of a dwelling-house let under a secure tenancy on any of the grounds set out in Part I or Part III of Schedule 2 (grounds 1 to 8 and 12 to 16: cases in which the court must be satisfied that it is reasonable to make a possession order), the court may adjourn the proceedings for such period or periods as it thinks fit.

(2) On the making of an order for possession of such a dwelling-house on any of those grounds, or at any time before the execution of the order, the court may –

(a)   stay or suspend the execution of the order, or
(b)   postpone the date of possession,

for such period or periods as the court thinks fit.

(3) On such an adjournment, stay, suspension or postponement the court –

(a)   shall impose conditions with respect to the payment by the tenant of arrears of rent (if any) and rent or payments in respect of occupation after the termination of the tenancy (mesne profits), unless it considers that to do so would cause exceptional hardship to the tenant or would otherwise be unreasonable, and
(b)   may impose such other conditions as it thinks fit.

(4) If the conditions are complied with, the court may, if it thinks fit, discharge or rescind the order for possession.

---

[50] In *Bain & Co v Church Commissioners* (1988) 21 HLR 29 (Ch) Harman J stated that he found this restriction 'astonishing' and held that s 89 only applied to the County Court, not to the High Court or Court of Appeal. In *Hackney LBC v Side by Side (Kids) Ltd* [2003] EWHC 1813 (QB), [2004] 1 WLR 363 Stanley Burnton J said that Harman J had been wrong [26].

Where discretionary grounds for possession are involved in the private sector, similar powers are contained in the Housing Act 1988 section 9(2)–(4).

The adjournment 'has come to be used as a standard order for many judges in rent arrears cases',[51] particularly as a way of trying to deal with the fact that so many arrears cases are attributed to benefit problems (see 19.3.1.3 below). When a possession order is made in circumstances where a court has discretion, suspended/postponed possession orders are much more common than outright orders: in the social housing sector there were 56,833 suspended possession orders and 29,088 outright orders made in 2005.[52] When a suspended order is granted, conditions will be attached such as a requirement that the tenant pays the current rent and an agreed periodic payment towards the arrears. The conditions may also relate to behavioural issues. So, for example, in *Knowsley Housing Trust v McMullen* the Court of Appeal upheld a possession order that had been suspended so long as neither the tenant nor anyone living with her cause a nuisance or annoyance to anyone residing in or visiting the vicinity.[53]

Research by Cowan and others, suggests that the different styles of judging adopted by different district judges will affect the likelihood of a particular order. For example, those typified by them as adopting a 'liberal' style tended to be animated by social justice and unlikely to make an outright possession order.[54]

As Table 19.3 shows, nearly all possession cases involve rent arrears. This is true for introductory tenancies as well as secure tenancies.

Table 19.3: Actions Entered in Court and Evictions by Local Authorities and Housing Associations in 2002/03: Breakdown by Reason for Action

	Rent arrears	Anti-Social Behaviour (ASB)	Rent arrears and ASB	Other	
	%	%	%	%	As % of stock
NSPs	97.93	1.46	0.25	0.35	13.4
Actions entered in court	97.75	1.41	0.35	0.50	3.8
Evictions implemented	92.57	5.56	0.72	1.15	0.63

Source: H Pawson and others, 'The Use of Possession Actions and Evictions by Social Landlords' (ODPM, June 2005) Table 3.3

---

[51] C Hunter and others, 'The exercise of judicial discretion in rent arrears cases' DCA Research Series 6/05 (October 2005) 18.

[52] Department for Constitutional Affairs, 'Judicial Statistics England and Wales for the Year 2005 (revised)' (Cm 6903, August 2006) Table 4.6. In the private sector a much higher proportion of outright orders are made given that the majority of possession actions will be for mandatory grounds: 2,212 suspended orders and 9,821 outright orders.

[53] [2006] EWCA Civ 539.

[54] D Cowan and others, 'District Judges and Possession Proceedings' (2006) 33 *J of L and Society* 547.

By no means do all NSPs end in eviction; indeed only around one in every 20 does so.[55]

19.2.5 When, and after, the Tenancy Ends

19.2.5.1 Secure Tenancies

By section 82(2) of the Housing Act 1985 a secure 'tenancy ends on the date on which the tenant is to give up possession in pursuance of the order'. In the case of an outright order, the tenancy will end on the date for possession given in the order.

Possession orders which are conditional raise more difficult issues.[56] The Court of Appeal held in *Thompson v Elmbridge BC* that the tenancy comes to an end as soon as the conditions attached to it are breached by the tenant.[57] It was commonly assumed after this case that with all suspended possession orders, therefore, the tenancy would continue so long as the tenant complied with the conditions. More recently, however, and against most expectations, the Court of Appeal held in *Harlow District Council v Hall* that the court form in then current use[58] had the effect of ending the tenancy on the date for possession, even if the occupier had complied with the conditions set.[59] In a blow this removed secure tenancy status from many occupiers. The principle from *Thompson v Elmbridge BC* was not, therefore, of general application. Instead, the date when the tenancy comes to an end will always turn on the precise wording of the court order itself. Since then, the Court of Appeal in *Bristol City Council v Hassan; Bristol City Council v Glastonbury* has approved a form of wording that will allow the tenancy to continue for as long as the conditions attached to the suspension are complied with.[60] This kind of order is referred to as a postponed possession order.

Once the tenancy has come to an end, the occupier may nonetheless remain in the property for some time. The question then is what status the occupier has during this period after the tenancy has ended and yet before a warrant for possession has been executed. It is further complicated by the fact that a landlord may well be quite happy for this position to continue as long as the occupier is broadly keeping up with payments for the occupation. Often the landlord does more than simply tolerate this situation; it may well accept the continuing occupation not only by consenting to it, but also by increasing the payments for occupation in line with the increases being made for tenants.

---

[55] H Pawson and others, 'The Use of Possession Actions and Evictions by Social Landlords' (ODPM, June 2005) 39.

[56] I Loveland, 'Tolerated Trespass: a Very Peculiar Legal Creature' (2007) 123 *LQR* 455.

[57] *Thompson v Elmbridge BC* [1987] 1 WLR 1425 (CA).

[58] The form of N28 used in this case had been introduced in October 2001.

[59] [2006] EWCA Civ 156, [2006] 1 WLR 2116. Although this would end the tenancy, the order for possession would not be enforceable if the occupier had complied with the conditions attached to the order.

[60] [2006] EWCA Civ 656, [2006] 1 WLR 2582. The DCA also responded rapidly to *Harlow District Council v Hall* [2006] EWCA Civ 156, [2006] 1 WLR 2116 by issuing a new form N28. Following *Bristol City Council v Hassan* yet another form N28A was issued. Under the new procedure, breaching the terms attached to the possession order will not automatically end the tenancy and the landlord will need to go back to court for a possession date to be fixed. The intention is for this to be a simple and quick procedure, but in one County Court case evidence was heard over two days before a date for possession was fixed: *Merton LBC v Cook* (Croydon Cty Ct, December 2006) (mentioned in J Holbrook and N Billingham, 'Rethinking possession orders' (2007) 157 *NLJ* 506). Articles by Latham anticipated these changes: R Latham, 'Tolerated Trespassers, the Problem and the Solution' (2006) *Legal Action* 35 (May); R Latham, 'Tolerated Trespassers, the Interim Solution' (2006) *Legal Action* 32 (May).

In the public sector, the court has wide powers under section 85(2) of the Housing Act 1985 to suspend, etc, possession. These powers can be exercised even after the tenancy has ended, giving rise to the prospect that a dead tenancy may nonetheless be revived in the future, even after a transfer of local authority housing to a RSL (in which case the revived tenancy will be an assured tenancy).[61] According to Millett LJ in *Greenwich v Regan*:

> ... the court may revive or reinstate the existing secure tenancy which must thereafter be treated as having continued throughout without interruption.[62]

There is no automatic revival of the secure tenancy if the conditions are fully complied with; a court order is always necessary.[63] Further, and counter-intuitively, if a tenant clears the outstanding arrears before making a section 85 application for revival, etc, he will have no standing to reinstate the tenancy.[64] As Chadwick LJ observed in *London & Quadrant Housing Trust v Ansell*, this creates a 'trap for former tenants and their advisers' because the tolerated trespasser who pays off the arrears will not be able to become a secure tenant again through revival, and will thus effectively be left occupying at the whim of the former landlord.[65]

During the period after the end of the tenancy but while the possibility of revival remains, the former tenant is often described as being in 'statutory limbo' and was described by Lord Browne-Wilkinson in *Burrows v Brent* as a tolerated trespasser:

> I think it is fair to characterise the former tenant as a trespasser whom the landlord has agreed not to evict – a 'tolerated trespasser' – pending either the revival of the old tenancy or the breach of the agreed conditions. [66]

There are hundreds of thousands of occupiers of local authority property who have this status: in Lambeth alone, there are around five thousand tolerated trespassers. They have no statutory rights,[67] no security of tenure, and are unable to enforce any landlord covenants in the former tenancy.[68] Further, this status may well continue for many years.

The situations in which tolerated trespasser status can arise are shown in Table 19.4.

The tolerated trespasser concept has been much criticised. It leads to some highly unsatisfactory outcomes. One illustration is given by the case of *London & Quadrant Housing Trust v Ansell*.[69] The tenant had paid off all arrears due under a suspended possession order (but was nonetheless a tolerated trespasser as she had breached the terms of the possession order). The effect was both that the order ceased to be enforceable but also that the court was no longer able to exercise any of the powers in section 85. The tenant had argued that the landlord could seek possession only by issuing a warrant under the possession order, but

---

[61] *London Borough of Lambeth and Hyde Southbank Ltd v O'Kane; Helena Housing Ltd v Pinder* [2005] EWCA Civ 1010.

[62] *Greenwich v Regan* (1996) 28 HLR 469 (CA) 475.

[63] *Marshall v Bradford Metropolitan DC* [2001] EWCA Civ 595. *London Borough of Lambeth and Hyde Southbank Ltd v O'Kane; Helena Housing Ltd v Pinder* [2005] EWCA Civ 1010.

[64] *Marshall v Bradford Metropolitan DC* [2001] EWCA Civ 595; *Swindon BC v Aston* [2002] EWCA Civ 1850 [20].

[65] [2007] EWCA Civ 326 [52].

[66] *Burrows v Brent LBC* [1996] 1 WLR 1448 (HL) 1455.

[67] No right to succession: *Brent LBC v Knightley* (1997) 29 HLR 857 (CA). No right to buy.

[68] *Burrows v Brent LBC* [1996] 1 WLR 1448 (HL) 1455; *Lambeth LBC v Rogers* (2000) 32 HLR 361 (CA) 367.

[69] [2007] EWCA Civ 326. This case involved a secure tenancy with an RSL as it had been entered into before 1989.

Table 19.4: After the Tenancy: Trespasser or Tolerated Trespasser?

Mandatory Ground	Discretionary Ground
When does the tenancy end?	
On date for possession (s 82(2) HA 1985; s 7(7) HA 1988; s 21 (3) HA 1988)	*Outright order:* on date for possession (secure tenancy, s 82(2) HA 1985; private sector, *Artesian Residential Development Ltd v Beck* [2000] 1 QB 541 (CA) 549)
	Possession orders subject to conditions: on date for possession (secure tenancy, s 82(2) HA 1985; private sector, *White v Knowsley Housing Trust* [2007] EWCA Civ 404)
	For court orders, post 2001 and pre-*Hassan* (*Bristol CC v Hassan* [2006] EWCA Civ 656) this was likely to be the date stated in the order, even if conditions complied with
	Post *Hassan* with correct wording, no date for possession is set and landlord can apply for fixing of date if there is breach
Is there a possibility that tenancy may be revived?	
No: No power to postpone possession beyond 14 days (other than exceptional hardship): s 89 HA 1980	Yes, unless all arrears have been cleared: Power to stay, suspend, postpone possession: s 85(2) HA 1985; ss 9(2) HA 1988
What is the status of the occupier once the tenancy ends?	
Trespasser (no possibility of revival)	Tolerated trespasser (former secure tenant, *Burrows v Brent LBC* [1996] 1 WLR 1448 (HL); former assured tenant, *White v Knowsley Housing Trust* [2007] EWCA Civ 404)

NB. As to when allowing former tenant to remain may lead to new tenancy, see chapter 3

as this was not possible her argument, if correct, would effectively make her irremovable. The only alternative was that the landlord was free to bring new proceedings on the basis that she was no longer a tenant (and no new tenancy had been granted). As Stanley Burnton, J put it:

> Legislation and authority compelled the stark and unsatisfactory choice between perpetual irremovability and unqualified insecurity. I do not think that that was what Parliament would or should have intended.[70]

19.2.5.2 Assured Tenancies

The Court of Appeal has recently held, in *White v Knowsley Housing Trust,* that an assured tenancy will end on the date for possession given in the court order and that the tolerated

---

[70] [2007] EWCA Civ 326 [62].

trespasser concept can therefore apply also in a private sector setting.[71] Although the Housing Act 1988 does not have an equivalent to section 82(2) of the Housing Act 1985 (giving statutory guidance on when a secure tenancy ends), the Court of Appeal considered that the 'natural' effect of the suspended possession order was to end the tenancy on the date given for possession.[72] In practice, many housing associations appear to have proceded on this basis in any event, assuming that any breach of the terms of a suspended order brings the tenancy to an end.[73]

19.2.5.3 Reform

This whole area of law relating to the tolerated trespasser is deeply unsatisfactory both in terms of doctrine[74] and policy. The tolerated trespass concept will disappear if the Law Commission's proposals are implemented as an occupation contract will end not when the date for possession passes but either when the occupier gives up possession or (if later) when the order is executed.[75]

19.2.6 Executing the Possession Order

Once the tenancy has come to an end, the landlord can apply for a warrant of possession, usually without giving any further notification to the occupier.[76] Although reasonableness may have to be proved at the time of obtaining a possession order, there is therefore no requirement on the landlord to prove that it is reasonable to execute the order. In *St Brice v LB of Southwark* a secure tenant who had breached the terms of a suspended possession order claimed that evicting him without notice under a warrant violated his human rights. The Court of Appeal disagreed, Kennedy LJ commenting that:

> … proportionality was considered, and by statute had to be considered, when the order for possession was made. Thereafter there was on any view non-compliance with the terms of suspension, and the arrears grew to a figure in excess of £4,000. For the local authority to then seek eviction cannot be regarded as a disproportionate response, given that the tenant knew what was being done, and had the right to seek assistance of the court under section 85.[77]

---

[71] [2007] EWCA Civ 404. In *Sherrin v Brand* [1956] 1 QB 403 (CA) it had been held that a Rent Act tenancy continued until the possession order was executed even if there had been breach of a suspended possession order. Because of this it was thought by many that private sector tenants could not become tolerated trespassers but would remain as tenants even after a possession order. In *White v Knowsley Housing Trust*, Buxton LJ distinguished *Sherrin v Brand* on the basis that under the Rent Acts, the tenant has a statutory tenancy, a creature of statute, whereas the assured tenancy is a contractual tenancy and the Housing Act 1988 restricts the landlord's freedom to end it.

[72] [2007] EWCA Civ 404 [55] (Longmore LJ). Buxton LJ refers to two further arguments. First, following the order the occupier does not have a 'right to exclusive possession' but only a right to remain provided she complies with the terms of the order and: 'That is significantly different from the right to possession of the premises that is the essence of a tenancy' [37]. Second, it is implicit in the wording of s 9(3) of the 1988 Act that the occupier remains in occupation *after termination* of the tenancy [38].

[73] C Hunter and others, 'The exercise of judicial discretion in rent arrears cases' DCA Research Series 6/05 (October 2005) 8.

[74] S Bright, 'The Concept of the Tolerated Trespasser: an Analysis' (2003) 119 *LQR* 495.

[75] Law Commission, 'Renting Homes: The Final Report. Volume 1: Report' (Law Com No 297, 2006) paras 4.54–4.56.

[76] That is, for execution of the order, by which a bailiff evicts anyone on the premises. After the warrant is passed to the bailiffs they will inform the occupier of the date for eviction and will visit the property to execute the warrant.

[77] [2001] EWCA Civ 1138, [2002] 1 WLR 1527 [6].

In some situations, however, the facts of a case will require that the landlord should have to apply to the court for permission before applying for a warrant for possession. In *Knowsley Housing Trust v McMullen*, for example, the Court of Appeal said that the possession order granted by the County Court should have contained a term requiring the landlord to apply to the court and give notice to the tenant before executing the possession order.[78] There was a greater risk of unfairness than usual in executing the order in this case because the tenant was disabled. Further, the problem was caused by her son (who she found difficult to control) and as an ASBO had been made against him this created the possibility that the problem may be resolved without having to enforce the possession order.

The occupier is able to apply for a hearing to set aside a warrant. Deciding whether to grant or dismiss this application is a very difficult decision for district judges:

> ... being acutely aware that their decision would have an immediate impact on the tenant's life, and that of any family members.[79]

It appears that there are significant differences in approach between judges on this issue in rent arrears cases, which to some extent turn on whether the judge approaches the case from a contractual perspective or is prepared to exercise discretion on social welfare grounds.[80]

Once the possession order is executed it can only be set aside if there is evidence of abuse of process or oppression. On the facts in *Circle 33 Housing Trust Ltd v Ellis* the Court of Appeal, stressing the need for finality, overturned the decision that there had been oppression because the housing association had not done enough to liaise with the local authority to sort out housing benefit arrears before executing the possession order.[81]

Oppression is not to do with the impact on the individual but 'the unfair use of court procedures':

> What is required before the court can intervene following eviction is that the court's process has been misused, so that the tenant has been evicted without having been afforded the protection which Parliament intended that he should have.[82]

19.2.7 The Use of Possession Actions by Social Landlords

In the decade to 2003 the number of possession actions by social landlords more than doubled.[83] There has been serious concern about the rising number, highlighted in a campaign run by the housing and homelessness charity, Shelter. Research commissioned by the ODPM suggests that much of this rise is, in fact, accounted for by rising eviction rates

---

[78] [2006] EWCA Civ 539.

[79] C Hunter and others, 'The exercise of judicial discretion in rent arrears cases' DCA Research Series 6/05 (October 2005) 101.

[80] C Hunter and others, 'The exercise of judicial discretion in rent arrears cases' DCA Research Series 6/05 (October 2005) 94.

[81] [2005] EWCA Civ 1233.

[82] *Circle 33 Housing Trust Ltd v Ellis* [2005] EWCA Civ 1233 [40].

[83] H Pawson and others, 'The Use of Possession Actions and Evictions by Social Landlords' (ODPM, June 2005) 39.

in the Midlands and North. Explanations for this are obscure, but it is thought to be attributable to the state of the housing market (in areas of low demand, tenants may be more relaxed about letting arrears mount up as they expect to find alternative housing easily) and, somewhat paradoxically, improving employment conditions (employment which is erratic and poorly paid makes household budgeting harder, especially given the unresponsive housing benefit system, than when receiving a steady state housing benefit, and therefore makes arrears more likely).[84]

The number of tenants actually evicted, as against being served with NSPs, and even having possession orders made against them, is much smaller: around 26,000 tenants. Although good practice guidance emphasises that eviction should be used as a last resort, in the case of rent arrears NSPs are often used at an early stage for debt recovery. This would explain why NSPs for anti-social behaviour are four times more likely to lead to actual eviction than in the case of rent arrears.[85]

Although the number of possession orders made appears to have peaked in 2002,[86] there has remained an upward trend in the number of evictions implemented.[87]

19.2.8 Resisting Possession on Human Rights Grounds

There have been many cases in which occupiers have argued that evicting them would involve a violation of the right to respect for private and family life and home, rights secured by Article 8 of the European Convention for the Protection of Human Rights and Fundamental Freedoms (ECHR). This right is not absolute: Article 8 (2) provides that there:

> … shall be no interference by a public authority with the exercise of this right except such as is in accordance with the law and is necessary in a democratic society in the interests of … public safety or the economic well-being of the country, the prevention of disorder or crime, for the protection of health or morals, or for the protection of the rights and freedoms of others.

Challenges have been brought when possession has been sought following the termination of assured shortholds (*Poplar Housing and Regeneration Community Association Ltd v Donghue*),[88] introductory tenancies (*R (Mclellan) v Bracknell Forest BC*),[89] non-secure local authority tenancies (*Sheffield CC v Smart*),[90] tenancies ended by notice to quit (*Harrow LBC v Qazi*),[91] and by 'mere occupiers' (*Kay v Lambeth LBC; Leeds CC v Price*).[92]

---

[84] H Pawson and others, 'The Use of Possession Actions and Evictions by Social Landlords' (ODPM, June 2005) 47.

[85] H Pawson and others, 'The Use of Possession Actions and Evictions by Social Landlords' (ODPM, June 2005) 41.

[86] Department for Constitutional Affairs, 'Statistics on Mortgage and Landlord Possession Actions in the County Court' Third-quarter 2006 Table 1b.

[87] H Pawson and others, 'The Use of Possession Actions and Evictions by Social Landlords' (ODPM, June 2005) 8.

[88] [2001] EWCA Civ 595, [2002] QB 48.

[89] [2001] EWCA Civ 1510, [2002] QB 1129.

[90] [2002] EWCA Civ 04.

[91] [2003] UKHL 43, [2004] 1 AC 983.

[92] [2006] UKHL 10, [2006] 2 AC 465.

The principles to be applied have most recently been set out by the House of Lords in *Kay v Lambeth*.[93] In this case there were seven Law Lords, each giving a speech, and giving different emphasis within them to the Article 8 claims. Nonetheless, it was unanimously accepted that possession actions do involve an interference with the home (in *Qazi*, Lord Scott – but not the other Law Lords – had taken a different position) but that a local authority bringing a possession action does not have to prove justification in every case. Any other result would be impractical, as Lord Nicholls put it:

> Day in, day out, possession orders are routinely made in county courts all over the country after comparatively brief hearings. The hearings are mostly brief because the time needed to dispose fairly of the formalities and also of questions of reasonableness, where they arise, is usually short. This will no longer be the position if, as has been contended, local authorities must now plead and prove in every case that domestic law meets the requirements of Article 8.[94]

Where possession is sought on a discretionary ground, the court will in any event be conducting a balancing act based on reasonableness. But even in cases involving mandatory right grounds and recovery based on termination at common law, Lord Bingham makes clear that an Article 8 challenge will succeed only in highly exceptional circumstances:

> [34] Under some statutory regimes, as where discretionary grounds are relied on to terminate a secure tenancy under the Housing Act 1985, the court may make an order for possession only where, other conditions for making such an order being met, the court thinks it reasonable to do so. This enables the court to take account of all circumstances which it judges to be relevant. If, in any case covered by such a regime, the statutory conditions are satisfied and the court does, on consideration of all the circumstances, think it reasonable to make a possession order, the court will in effect have undertaken the very assessment which article 8(2) requires. In such a situation article 8(2) adds nothing of substance to the protection which the occupier already enjoys.
> [35] Under some statutory regimes the court may be required to make an order for possession if certain prescribed conditions are met and there is no overriding requirement that the court considers it reasonable or just to make such an order. The statutory scheme is nonetheless likely to satisfy the article 8(2) requirement of proportionality if it is clear that the statutory scheme represents a democratic solution to the problems inherent in housing allocation. Thus in *Poplar Housing and Regeneration Community Association Limited v Donoghue* [2001] EWCA Civ 595, [2002] QB 48, the Court of Appeal found no breach of article 8(2) in the use of section 21(4) of the Housing Act 1988, as amended, to gain possession of an assured shorthold tenancy granted to a person who had been intentionally homeless, because (para 69) Parliament had intended to give preference to the needs of those dependent on social housing as a whole over those who, like the tenant, had been intentionally homeless. Similarly, in *R (McLellan) v Bracknell Forest Borough Council* [2001] EWCA Civ 1510, [2002] QB 1129, the Court of Appeal found no breach of article 8 where a housing authority determined the introductory tenancies of tenants whose rent was in arrears under section 127(2) of the Housing Act 1996, since (para 63) Parliament had decided that it was necessary in the interest of

---

[93] [2006] UKHL 10, [2006] 2 AC 465. See S Bright, 'Article 8 again in the House of Lords: Kay v Lambeth LBC; Leeds CC v Price' [2006] 70 *Conv* 294; A Goymour, 'Proprietary Claims and Human Rights – A "Reservoir of Entitlement"?' (2006) 65 *CLJ* 696; D Hughes and M Davis, 'Human rights and the triumph of property' [2006] 70 *Conv* 526.
[94] [2006] UKHL 10, [2006] 2 AC 465 [54].

tenants generally and the local authorities to have a scheme whereby, during the first twelve months, tenants were on probation and could be evicted without long battles in the county court, there being (it was held) adequate procedural safeguards. The Court of Appeal took a similar approach when holding, in *Sheffield City Council v Smart* [2002] EWCA Civ 4, [2002] HLR 639, para 37, that Parliament clearly enacted the relevant statutory provisions upon the premise that while a tenant is housed as a homeless person he enjoys no security of tenure. See also *Wandsworth London Borough Council v Michalak* [2002] EWCA Civ 271, [2003] 1 WLR 617, paras 63, 78. Where a statutory scheme covers the case of an occupier, and conditions are prescribed for obtaining possession, and those conditions are met, it will only be in highly exceptional circumstances that the occupier will gain additional protection from article 8.

[36] There are of course some cases (of which the present cases are examples) in which the relationship between public authority owner or landlord and individual tenant or occupier is not governed by any statutory scheme. But possession may be sought on expiry of the period for which the right to occupy was granted, or because the notice required by domestic property law to bring that term to an end has been given, or because one or more of the conditions on which the right to occupy was granted has been broken. It cannot be said that the relationship between the parties in such cases is the subject of a balance struck by Parliament, but it is not unrealistic to regard the general law as striking such a balance. The public authority owner or landlord has, broadly speaking, a right to manage and control its property within bounds set by statute. The occupier acquires a right, but only a limited right, to occupy. On due determination of that interest, a claim for possession must ordinarily succeed, since any indulgence to the occupier necessarily derogates from the property right of the public authority, whose rights are also entitled to respect. It is not therefore surprising that in *P v United Kingdom* (Application No 14751/89), 12 December 1990, and *Ure v United Kingdom* (Application No 28027/95), unreported, 27 November 1996, the occupiers' complaints were held to be inadmissible because the public authority's interference or assumed interference was held to be clearly justified. It would, again, require highly exceptional circumstances before article 8 would avail the occupiers.[95]

Where the occupier has no contractual or proprietary right to remain, an Article 8(2) defence will not succeed in the vast majority of cases. The issue giving rise to different opinions in *Kay v Lambeth* relates to the circumstances in which it is possible to run an Article 8(2) defence: the majority (Lords Hope, Scott and Brown and Baroness Hale) considered that it can be raised only if it is the law or the absence of procedural safeguards that is said to be non Article 8 compliant. This view of the majority is summarised by the Court of Appeal in the later case of *Birmingham CC v Doherty*:

> There are only two possible 'gateways' (our term) for a successful defence to summary judgment in such cases: (a) a seriously arguable challenge under Article 8 to the law under which the possession order is made, but only where it is possible (with the interpretative aids of the Human Rights Act) to adapt the domestic law to make it more compliant; (b) a seriously arguable challenge on conventional judicial review grounds (rather than under the Human Rights Act) to the authority's decision to recover possession.[96]

---

[95] [2006] UKHL 10, [2006] 2 AC 465.
[96] [2006] EWCA Civ 1739 [22].

The minority (Lords Bingham, Nicholls and Walker) accepted that other (and personal) circumstances can also be relied to show that the interference was not 'necessary in a democratic society'. [97]All agreed, however, that this would be the exception; in the usual case an Article 8(2) defence will go nowhere.

Commentators have noted how little scope remains after this judgment for injecting human rights concepts into housing law. In the words of Hughes and Davis:

> … the decisions in *Kay* and *Leeds* only serve to confirm how profoundly that body of law remains a bastion of the rights of the freeholder. A public sector dwelling is, of course, the tenant's 'home', but it is also the landlord's 'house', and 'house' rights generally trump 'home' rights.[98]

19.3 Grounds for Possession

In this section, the grounds for possession are considered in more detail. There are differences between the public and private sectors (see Tables 19.1 and 19.2) but here, where possible, the grounds are grouped together under themes, following (broadly) the order laid down in the Housing Act 1985.

19.3.1 Rent Arrears and Delays

Given that rent is such a fundamental element of every lease, it is not surprising that non payment gives a ground for possession. As has been seen, the vast majority of possession actions are based on rent arrears. In the public sector, there is only one rent arrears ground, and this is a discretionary ground based on non-payment. In the private sector, there are two discretionary grounds; one of these is based on non payment, but the other is based on persistent late payment. The most controversial ground is the mandatory Ground 8 of the 1988 Act where possession can be recovered without any need to prove reasonableness. In practice, the private sector landlord seeking possession may well refer to all three grounds in the NSP.

19.3.1.1 Discretionary Grounds for Possession based on Rent

Housing Act 1985 Schedule 2 Ground 1 [subject to reasonableness]
Rent lawfully due from the tenant has not been paid…

Housing Act 1988 Schedule 2 Ground 10 [subject to reasonableness]
Some rent lawfully due from the tenant –

(a) is unpaid on the date on which the proceedings for possession are begun; and
(b) except where subsection (1)(b) of section 8 of this Act applies, was in arrears at the date of the service of the notice under that section relating to those proceedings.

---

[97] NB. the Court of Appeal in *Birmingham CC v Doherty* [2006] EWCA Civ 1739 comments that it would have been helpful for there to have been a single majority judgment in *Kay* and *Leeds*, noting also extra-judicial comments of Lord Bingham regarding the need for accessibility and clarity in the law!
[98] D Hughes and M Davis, 'Human Rights and the Triumph of Property' [2006] 70 *Conv* 526, 550.

[section 8 (1)(b) deals with the case where it is just and equitable to dispense with the service of notice]

Housing Act 1988 Schedule 2 Ground 11 [subject to reasonableness]
Whether or not any rent is in arrears on the date on which proceedings for possession are begun, the tenant has persistently delayed paying rent which has become lawfully due.

At common law, the rule in *Bird v Hildage* means that if the tenant pays off the arrears before the hearing then the court cannot issue an order for possession.[99] It is likely that even if the tenant only pays off the arrears during the course of the hearing, it would be 'section 84(2) unreasonable' to order the tenant's eviction. Other factors going to reasonableness with respect to rent arrears would be, according to *Woodspring DC v Taylor*, the tenant's previous record of rent payments and the cause of the arrears.[100]

At common law, persistent late payment is not a ground for eviction. This is offset in the private sector by Ground 11, which allows a private sector landlord to seek possession on the ground of persistently late payment.

19.3.1.2 The Mandatory Ground 8

Housing Act 1988 Schedule 2 Ground 8 [mandatory]
Both at the date of the service of the notice under section 8 of this Act relating to the proceedings for possession and at the date of the hearing –

(a) if rent is payable weekly or fortnightly, at least eight weeks' rent is unpaid;
(b) if rent is payable monthly, at least two months' rent is unpaid;
(c) if rent is payable quarterly, at least one quarter's rent is more than three months in arrears; and
(d) if rent is payable yearly, at least three months' rent is more than three months in arrears;

and for the purpose of this ground 'rent' means rent lawfully due from the tenant.

Ground 8 has been controversial, especially when used by RSLs. When the ground was first introduced, the Housing Corporation recommended that housing associations should not use it. By 1994, this guidance had changed and the approach now taken is that although RSLs should first pursue all other reasonable alternatives to recover the debt, Ground 8 can be used as part of an arrears and eviction policy where tenants have been fully consulted. The study by Pawson and others found that about one-third of housing associations, and one-half of London based housing associations, were making some use of Ground 8.[101]

When relied on, the court has no discretion if the ground is proven. As will be seen below, rent is sometimes unpaid for reasons completely outside of the tenant's control, in particular, because of problems with the administration of housing benefit. Even in these circumstances, and however unreasonable possession may appear on the facts of the particular case, possession must be ordered if the requisite amount of arrears exists. Further, with weekly and fortnightly tenancies, the ground, as originally enacted, required 13 weeks' unpaid rent but this was reduced to eight weeks by the Housing Act 1996.

---

[99] [1948] 1 KB 91 (CA).
[100] (1982) 4 HLR 95 (CA).
[101] H Pawson and others, 'The Use of Possession Actions and Evictions by Social Landlords' (ODPM, June 2005) ch 5.

The DCA research into the exercise of judicial discretion in rent arrears cases found that most district judges disliked Ground 8.[102] Further, in practice, it was operating in a far from mandatory way.[103] Some judges showed an inclination to adjourn cases, particularly where the problems were caused by delays in housing benefit payments. Since this research, however, the Court of Appeal has made clear in *North British Housing Association Ltd v Matthews* that adjournment should be used only in exceptional cases (for example, if the tenant is robbed of the arrears on his way to court).[104] Dyson LJ shows how Parliament intended Ground 8 to be used strictly:

[32] … the power to adjourn a hearing date for the purpose of enabling a tenant to reduce the arrears to below the ground 8 threshold may only be exercised in exceptional circumstances…. [The] fact that the arrears are attributable to maladministration on the part of the housing benefit authority is not an exceptional circumstance. It is a sad feature of contemporary life that housing benefit problems are widespread. To a substantial extent, these are no doubt the product of lack of resources. But we do not consider that the non-receipt of housing benefit can, of itself, amount to exceptional circumstances which would justify the exercise of the power to adjourn so as to enable the tenant to defeat the claim.

[33] We acknowledge that this conclusion will lead to tenants who are in receipt of housing benefit having no defence to a claim for possession in circumstances where they are not at fault. The statutory scheme is, therefore, potentially draconian in its application.

[34] Parliament could have alleviated the position of tenants in a number of ways. Instead, in the Housing Act 1996 it reduced the threshold period for ground 8 from 13 weeks to eight weeks and did not mitigate the consequences of that reduction by making any special provision to deal with the particular and well-known problems occasioned by non-payment of housing benefit. It is of interest that during the debate on the Housing Bill on 30 April 1996 (Hansard (HC Debates), cols 982–984), Mr Simon Hughes MP proposed an amendment to clause 88 that there be added at the end of ground 8 a proviso that no order for possession should be made under that ground if the court was satisfied that prior to the date of the hearing the tenant had made a claim for housing benefit in respect of the period to which the arrears relate which had not been finally determined by the local housing authority. The minister responded that the local housing authorities were under a statutory duty to process claims within 14 days and rejected the proposal.

19.3.1.3 Issues Surrounding Rent and Eviction

As seen above, the number of evictions has increased in recent years. Given that nearly all possession actions involve rent arrears it is worth asking why there has been this increase. Unsurprisingly, the major factor behind rent arrears has been found to be poverty, and in the social rented sector growing levels of arrears have been attributed to the ongoing residualisation of social housing and the housing of greater numbers of

---

[102] C Hunter and others, 'The exercise of judicial discretion in rent arrears cases' DCA Research Series 6/05 (October 2005) 90.

[103] C Hunter and others, 'The exercise of judicial discretion in rent arrears cases' DCA Research Series 6/05 (October 2005) 89. There is no option of a postponed possession order in Ground 8 cases, and the study found that judges sometimes granted adjournments. As seen in the text below, the Court of Appeal has (since the research was conducted) stated that cases should only exceptionally be adjourned; this means that Ground 8 will have become more mandatory.

[104] [2004] EWCA Civ 1736, [2005] 1 WLR 3133.

vulnerable tenants who find it difficult to negotiate their way through the housing benefit claim procedures.[105]

Around 60 per cent of all social renters, and between 20 per cent and 30 per cent of private renters,[106] are in receipt of housing benefit. This means that prompt and accurate payment of housing benefit is crucial for the prompt payment of rent for many tenants, but in practice the administration of the benefit system is notoriously complex and slow.

Research for the ODPM found that a number of features of the housing benefit system were contributing to rent arrears:

(a)   processing delays (some claims sometimes taking three-four months);

(b)   lost claims;

(c)   the recovery of 'over-payments' (there is often a time lag between the changing financial circumstances of claimants and the payments made to them, frequently leading to serious arrears);

(d)   incorrect assessments (the system is very complex and research shows tenants facing eviction due to housing benefit mistakes);

(e)   non-dependent deductions (that is, contributions to rent assumed to be made by adult household members such as sons and daughters of the tenant which in practice parents do not require their children to pay).[107]

In addition to the problems caused by poverty and housing benefit delays, the growing professionalism of housing management may also be contributing to the rise in the number of possession actions for rent arrears. Rent collection is increasingly dealt with by specialist staff[108] and a firmer approach is being taken towards arrears as rent collection and arrears statistics are key indicators of management performance.[109]

Using NSPs as tools for debt collection is frowned upon by many.[110] Increasingly, there is emphasis being placed on managing rent arrears at an early stage so as to avoid serious arrears building up, and also to ensure that possession proceedings are genuinely only used as a last resort. The DCA has recently issued a protocol for possession claims by social landlords based on rent arrears to encourage more pre-action contact between landlords and tenants and to enable court time to be used more effectively.

---

[105] H Pawson and others, 'The Use of Possession Actions and Evictions by Social Landlords' (ODPM, June 2005) 24.

[106] DCLG, Survey of English Housing, Live Tables: Table S405 'Tenants in receipt of housing benefit' (social renters figures for 2005/06); DCLG, Survey of English Housing, Live Tables: Table S505 'Percentage of tenants receiving housing benefit by letting type' (assured and assured shortholds figures for 2004/05). For regulated tenancies (private), a much higher figure of 40%–50% receive housing benefit.

[107] H Pawson and others, 'The Use of Possession Actions and Evictions by Social Landlords' (ODPM, June 2005) 27–9.

[108] H Pawson and others, 'The Use of Possession Actions and Evictions by Social Landlords' (ODPM, June 2005) 9.

[109] H Pawson and others, 'The Use of Possession Actions and Evictions by Social Landlords' (ODPM, June 2005) 32–3, ch 5 (this contains a more detailed discussion of landlord's attitudes to rent collection policies).

[110] In its 36th session, the United Nations Committee on Economic, Social and Cultural Rights expressed concern with the many evictions in Canada on account of minimal rent arrears, without due consideration to the state party's obligations under the International Convention on Economic, Social and Cultural Rights: CESCR, 'Concluding Observations of the Committee on Economic, Social and Cultural Rights: Canada' (22 May 2006) UN Doc E/C.12/CAN/CO/4 – E/C.12/CAN/CO/5 para 29.

19.3.2 Nuisance, Annoyance and Breach of Tenancy

Both private and public residential sector laws allow, in very similar terms, for eviction for nuisance or illegal activity, nowadays swept together under the label of 'anti-social behaviour'.

Housing Act 1985 Schedule 2 Ground 2 [subject to reasonableness]
The tenant or a person residing in or visiting the dwelling-house –

(a) has been guilty of conduct causing or likely to cause a nuisance or annoyance to a person residing, visiting or otherwise engaging in a lawful activity in the locality, or
(b) has been convicted of –
   (i) using the dwelling-house or allowing it to be used for immoral or illegal purposes, or
   (ii) an indictable offence committed in, or in the locality of, the dwelling-house.

Housing Act 1985 section 85A cases involving anti-social behaviour (identical provisions in Housing Act 1988 section 9A)
(1) This section applies if the court is considering under section 84(2)(a) whether it is reasonable to make an order for possession on ground 2 set out in Part 1 of Schedule 2 (conduct of tenant or other person).

(2) The court must consider, in particular –

(a) the effect that the nuisance or annoyance has had on persons other than the person against whom the order is sought;
(b) any continuing effect the nuisance or annoyance is likely to have on such persons;
(c) the effect that the nuisance or annoyance would be likely to have on such persons if the conduct is repeated.

Housing Act 1988 Schedule 2 Ground 14 [subject to reasonableness]
The tenant or a person residing in or visiting the dwelling-house –

(a) has been guilty of conduct causing or likely to cause a nuisance or annoyance to a person residing, visiting or otherwise engaging in a lawful activity in the locality, or
(b) has been convicted of –
   (i) using the dwelling-house or allowing it to be used for immoral or illegal purposes, or
   (ii) an indictable offence committed in, or in the locality of, the dwelling-house.

In addition to these specific grounds, it is also a possible to bring a tenancy to an end where there has been breach of the tenancy agreement.

Housing Act 1985 Schedule 2 Ground 1 [subject to reasonableness]
… an obligation of the tenancy has been broken or not performed.

Housing Act 1988 Schedule 2 Ground 12 [subject to reasonableness]
Any obligation of the tenancy (other than one related to the payment of rent) has been broken or not performed.

It is commonplace to insert 'good behaviour' covenants into tenancy agreements, such as express tenant promises not to harass others, not to vandalise public property, not to make loud noises, and to exercise proper control over children and young people living in the home. A breach of any of these terms will provide a ground for eviction, subject to the landlord needing to prove that possession is reasonable (and subject also to any unfair terms being unenforceable under the Unfair Terms in Consumer Contracts Regulations 1999).[111]

19.3.2.1 The Width of Nuisance Grounds

The nuisance and annoyance ground has been strengthened considerably in recent years. A number of amendments were made in 1996. Originally it was limited to actual 'nuisance or annoyance', but in 1996 the wording was amended to include conduct '*likely to cause* a nuisance or annoyance'.[112] Initially it also covered only bad behaviour by occupiers, but now extends to bad behaviour by the tenant's visitors as well. As Cowan observes, this enhances both the sense that tenants are being 'responsibilised' and that rental housing has become a site of governance with not only landlords being used as governors, but tenants also being required to govern those who use rented housing.[113] Further, the grounds used to be limited to annoyance to 'adjoining occupiers' (private sector, Housing Act 1988) or 'neighbours' (public sector, Housing Act 1985).[114] The wording now has a much wider geographic spread ('the locality') so potential 'victims' are not restricted to local residents but can also include other visitors to the area. Finally, in addition to covering situations where the tenant has been convicted of using the dwelling itself for immoral or illegal purposes, it also applies where he has been convicted of indictable offences committed in the locality.

These changes make clear that the ground is not limited to conduct connected with the demised premises itself but protects the:

> … legitimate interest the landlords have in requiring their tenants to respect the neighbour-hood in which they live and the quiet enjoyment of their homes by those who live there.[115]

Since then, there have been yet further changes. The Anti-social Behaviour Act 2003 introduced a new section 85A to the Housing Act 1985 (mirrored in the private sector by section 9A of the Housing Act 1988). This specifically directs a court, when considering the 'reasonableness' of granting a possession order, to consider 'in particular' the effect that the bad behaviour has had *on others*, continues to have, and is likely to have in the future.

19.3.2.2 Type of Possession Order Appropriate

Judges have had great difficulties in these cases in deciding what type of possession order to make even when they have reached the decision that it is reasonable to grant a possession order. The difficulties are illustrated in the case of *Manchester CC v Higgins*.[116] The main problem in this case was the behaviour of the tenant's son who had engaged in a campaign of

---

[111] SI 1999/2083.

[112] The explanation put for this change was 'to enable third-party witnesses to give evidence (for example a local authority officer) so as to overcome the problem of intimidation of potential witnesses, especially the victims of the behaviour': Standing Committee G (Housing Bill) Hansard HC V cols 382–387 (27 February 1996).

[113] H Carr, D Cowan and C Hunter, 'Policing the Housing Crisis' (2007) 27 *Critical Social Policy* 100.

[114] Even under this wording, the courts did not adopt a narrow view of geography. In *Cobstone Investments Ltd v Maxim* [1985] QB 140 (CA) Wood J said that 'adjoining' (a private sector case) did not mean contiguous but 'whether the relevant premises are sufficiently close or related, so that the behaviour or conduct of the tenant of the one affects the access to, or occupation or enjoyment of the other by its occupier' (151). In *Northampton BC v Lovatt* [1998] 2 FCR 177 (CA) a wide view was taken of 'neighbours' so as to encompass the unruly behaviour of the tenant's children on the wider estate.

[115] *Northampton BC v Lovatt* [1998] 2 FCR 177 (CA).

[116] [2005] EWCA Civ 1423, [2006] 1 All ER 841.

anti-social behaviour. A number of agencies had been involved in trying to deal with the problem – housing services, the police, welfare services, youth offending teams and youth support teams. The trial judge noted that the tenant had shown 'belle indifference' to controlling her son and that a possession order was clearly reasonable on the facts. Nonetheless, he took the view that there was still some hope, and as the tenant was now receiving help with her parenting skills it would not be 'proportionate to exclude the family, given the multifarious problems they have, immediately'. The Court of Appeal noted that there was a high hurdle to overcome to appeal the exercise of the recorder's discretion but held here that the recorder had been wrong to suspend the order. Stressing that each case must turn on its own facts and circumstances, and that any guidance was therefore of a very general nature, Ward LJ nonetheless set out certain principles to be used in these cases. First, if the conduct is serious enough to justify an ASBO then 'that will be strong but not conclusive evidence that the tenant will have forfeited his entitlement to retain possession'.[117] Second, in deciding whether or not to suspend, the question requires one to look to the future – there is no point suspending an order if breach is inevitable. Ultimately, it is a question of proportionality: is an immediate order necessary in order to meet the need to protect the rights and freedoms of others (the neighbours)?

This case shows that once a serious level of antisocial behaviour is proven the spotlight turns to looking at the likely future impact on others in deciding whether or not to make a possession order, and whether to make it immediately. If there is little chance of reform, and neighbours are likely to continue to suffer, then immediate possession should be given. The reference to forfeiting the right to possess suggests that the Article 8 balance has shifted; it is no longer the tenant's Article 8 right to respect to his home that is paramount, but that of the neighbours, to whom the public authority also owes duties, whether or not they are tenants. In the Irish case of *Re Donnelly's Application for Judicial Review*, the landlord had failed to evict an anti-social tenant because the proceedings could not be taken without a serious risk to the personal safety of the housing officers.[118] The Irish Court of Appeal held that this inaction breached the Article 8 rights of the victim (see further, chapters 10 and 11).

This is not to say that even in cases of bad behaviour an immediate order for possession will always be the appropriate action. In *Moat Housing Group South Ltd v Harris* an immediate possession order was given but in this case the Court of Appeal held that it should have been suspended.[119] In part, this was because the evidence had not been well presented but, more importantly, the landlord was not really using eviction as a last resort. The tenant had had no prior warning that her family was at risk of eviction, and the housing association had not used the full range of tools available to it to tackle the anti-social behaviour. As seen in chapter 11, there are a number of other options that a social landlord can pursue before eviction: injunctions, demotion, ASBOs and, importantly, engagement with other social services. Further, the court must not neglect the impact that a possession order has on the family, particularly if there are children involved:

---

[117] [2005] EWCA Civ 1423, [2006] 1 All ER 841 [36].
[118] [2003] NICA 55, [2004] NI 189.
[119] [2005] EWCA Civ 287, [2006] QB 606.

For a child, to become part of an 'intentionally homeless' family, with the bleak prospect of being allotted sub-standard accommodation with his/her parents or being taken into care, is such a serious prospect that every RSL should be alert to intervene creatively at a far earlier stage than occurred in the present case, in order to do everything possible to avert recourse to eviction. European Court of Human Rights jurisprudence, indeed, makes it clear that the right to respect for a home has inherent in it the principle that procedural fairness will be observed before the home is taken away (see, for example, *Connors v United Kingdom* (2004) 40 EHRR 189, para 83), so that an RSL should be slow to short circuit its normal procedures in nuisance cases by proceeding straight to a notice seeking possession ... or an eviction without prior notice.[120]

What is common to both of these cases, and many others, is that the tenant is a single mother who finds it difficult to control her children. Hunter and Nixon have argued (albeit on research that is now slightly dated given the pace of policy change in this field) that the response of landlords and, in turn, courts has been to problematise women; women are more likely than male or joint tenants to be the subject of complaints about anti-social behaviour despite the fact that in the majority of cases the behaviour is committed by men.[121] Eviction is then seen as both a gendered and punitive response. Given that the nine out of ten lone parent families are headed by a woman, and that half of lone mothers with dependent children live in social sector housing, these findings are not surprising, but the question that they raise is whether eviction is appropriate as a response to the problem of anti-social behaviour. The answer turns on whether eviction can be justified as a risk management tool alone, or whether a degree of personal moral blame is also necessary to justify the loss of a home (and, if so, the extent to which lack of parental control can be seen as morally blameworthy).

The recent case law confirms that although anti-social behaviour does need to be taken seriously, eviction should be seen as a last resort. Social landlords must tackle anti-social behaviour in other ways before moving to possession. If, however, other steps have failed, the balance shifts and the court must take the impact that this behaviour is having on others seriously. If the culprit is unrepentantly anti-social then, having regard to the Article 8 rights of others in the area, an immediate possession order may be necessary.

19.3.2.3 Disability and Bad Behaviour

Anti-social behaviour is often disability related, the study by Hunter and others reporting in 2000 found that of the households involved in anti-social behaviour that they investigated, 18 per cent of the cases involved mental disability and 9 per cent physical disability.[122] Where this is the case, the landlord's decision to evict or not becomes especially hard, particularly in the light of its responsibilities under the Disability Discrimination Act 1995. Both mental and physical disabilities come within this legislation. The meaning of 'discrimination' is complex: to avoid discriminating it is not enough to show that there has been equal treatment. The statute provides that there will be discrimination if:

---

[120] [2005] EWCA Civ 287 [102].

[121] C Hunter and J Nixon, 'Taking the blame and losing the home: women and anti-social behaviour' (2001) 23 *JSWFL* 395.

[122] C Hunter, J Nixon and S Shayer, 'Neighbour Nuisance, Social Landlords and the Law' (Coventry, Chartered Institute of Housing, 2000) 18–19.

... for a reason which relates to the disabled person's disability, [the landlord] ... treats [a disabled person] ... less favourably than he treats or would treat others to whom that reason does not or would not apply and he cannot show that the treatment is justified.

This has been given a very broad definition by the Court of Appeal in *Clark v Novacold Ltd*.[123] The impact of this decision in the area of housing is summarised by Cobb:

... any prohibited act by a social landlord in response to conduct related to a relevant mental impairment ... whether or not it is aware of that impairment, will always amount to prima facie discrimination.[124]

By section 22(3)(c) of the Disability Discrimination Act 1995, issuing possession proceedings is capable of being a discriminatory act. The effect is that any discriminatory act (here, possession proceedings) will need to be justified under section 24, by showing that in the landlord's opinion it is 'necessary in order not to endanger the health or safety of any person.' This opinion must be both actually held and reasonable.

The effect of this, confirmed by the Court of Appeal in *Manchester CC v Romano* is that where a landlord is seeking possession for a reason that relates to the tenant's disability, it is not only the 'reasonableness' test under the housing legislation that must be satisfied in the opinion of the court, but the landlord itself must also believe that the eviction is necessary in order not to endanger the health or safety of others.[125] According to Brooke LJ, the question that the court must ask, taking account also of the impact of section 3 of the Human Rights Act 1998, is:

(1) Did the landlord hold the opinion that it was necessary to serve a notice seeking possession and/or to bring possession proceedings in order that the health of A (an identified person or persons) would not be put at risk? (2) Was that opinion objectively justified? ... Trivial risks to a person's health should be disregarded.[126]

Brooke LJ did, however, adopt a wide definition of health that goes beyond physical integrity, thereby making it easier for a landlord to justify the action on the grounds that to allow the behaviour to continue would cause distress to others:

The World Health Organisation has since 1948 adopted the following definition of the word 'health': 'Health is a state of complete physical, mental and social well-being and not merely the absence of disease or infirmity.'[127]

The width of this definition means that it is not only extreme forms of anti-social behaviour, but also lower level anti-social behaviour that can have sufficient impact on others to justify eviction. Manchester CC had been granted possession orders in respect of two secure tenants, Ms Romano and Ms Samari, on the basis of Ground 2. On the facts, both possession orders were upheld, but the Court of Appeal judgment illustrates the care that must be taken in disability cases:

---

[123] [1999] 2 All ER 977 (CA).

[124] N Cobb, 'Patronising the mentally disordered? Social landlords and the control of "anti-social behaviour" under the Disability Discrimination Act 1995' (2006) 26 *LS* 238, 256.

[125] *Manchester CC v Romano; Manchester CC v Samari* [2004] EWCA Civ 834, [2005] 1 WLR 2775.

[126] *Manchester CC v Romano; Manchester CC v Samari* [2004] EWCA Civ 834, [2005] 1 WLR 2775 [75].

[127] *Manchester CC v Romano; Manchester CC v Samari* [2004] EWCA Civ 834, [2005] 1 WLR 2775 [69].

This judgment shows that landlords whose tenants hold secure or assured tenancies must consider the position carefully before they decide to serve a notice seeking possession or to embark on possession proceedings against a tenant who is or might be mentally impaired. This is likely to compel a local housing authority to liaise more closely with the local social services authority at an earlier stage of their consideration of a problem that might lead to an eviction than appears to be the case with many authorities, to judge from some of the papers the DRC placed before the court. To remove someone from their home may be a traumatic thing to do in the case of many who are not mentally impaired. It may be even more traumatic for the mentally impaired.[128]

In the course of his judgment, Brooke LJ is extremely critical of how the disability legislation interacts with housing law and the difficulty that it places landlords in.

In addition to the difficulties that the disability legislation creates for landlords in relation to cases involving anti-social behaviour, Brooke LJ drew attention to other potential problems:

… further difficulty arises from the fact that a tenant could assert that his landlord could not recover possession for non-payment of rent because the reason why he could not manage his financial affairs efficiently relates to his mental disability.[[129]] Another difficulty lies in the fact that a private landlord who does not have to establish a 'reasonableness' ground for possession may nevertheless be confronted by an assertion that he has caused detriment to a disabled tenant by selecting him for eviction.[130]

As Cobb points out, the housing and disability legislation operate on different models of responsibility.[131] In the housing sphere, entitlement to social housing is conditional on responsible occupation. There are two rationalities used to explain the departure from the principle of welfarism (housing based on need) when a tenant is evicted for anti-social behaviour. First, exclusion is necessary in order to manage risk. Second, those who fail to meet accepted standards of behaviour are characterised as morally irresponsible and personally blameworthy. By contrast, in the medical world treatment of disability encourages risk reduction through inclusion, treatment and support, which applied to the housing context would suggest that disabled persons are best treated in a secure and stable setting. Further, the mentally disordered are treated as incapable of responsible agency and therefore blameless for their actions. Instead of anti-social disabled persons being seen as morally irresponsible, they are viewed as non-responsible. As Cobb shows, this medical model is contested. Not all mentally impaired persons are 'non-responsible', some are aware of the impact of their actions upon others and are capable of exercising self-control. However, the effect of the Disability Discrimination Act 1995, as interpreted by the courts, is

---

[128] *Manchester CC v Romano; Manchester CC v Samari* [2004] EWCA Civ 834, [2005] 1 WLR 2775 [117].

[129] Cobb notes that *Liverpool CC v Slavin* 29 April 2005 Legal Action (July 2005) accepted the argument that eviction for rent arrears may be prevented where the inability to pay is related to mental impairment unless there is an economic justification for this less favourable treatment: N Cobb, 'Patronising the mentally disordered? Social landlords and the control of "anti-social behaviour" under the Disability Discrimination Act 1995' (2006) 26 *LS* 238, 257.

[130] *Manchester CC v Romano; Manchester CC v Samari* [2004] EWCA Civ 834, [2005] 1 WLR 2775 [67]. See also ch 22.

[131] N Cobb, 'Patronising the mentally disordered? Social landlords and the control of "anti-social behaviour" under the Disability Discrimination Act 1995' (2006) 26 *LS* 238.

that a landlord cannot evict a disabled person where there is no risk to the health or safety of others even when that individual may be morally responsible.

19.3.3 Domestic Violence

In 1996 a new ground for possession was added where a partner had been forced out of the home because of domestic violence. In this situation it is often the victim (and any dependents) who leaves and finds herself in need of rehousing, while the violent partner remains a secure tenant, often under-occupying the property. This ground, available only to social landlords, enables the landlord to recover the tenancy but only where the victim is unlikely to return to the property.

Housing Act 1985 Schedule 2 Ground 2A [subject to reasonableness]
The dwelling-house was occupied (whether alone or with others) by a married couple, a couple who are civil partners of each other, a couple living together as husband and wife or a couple living together as if they were civil partners and –

(a)   one or both of the partners is a tenant of the dwelling-house,
(b)   one partner has left because of violence or threats of violence by the other towards –
  (i)   that partner, or
  (ii) a member of the family of that partner who was residing with that partner immediately before the partner left, and
(c)   the court is satisfied that the partner who has left is unlikely to return.

Housing Act 1988 Schedule 2 Ground 14A [subject to reasonableness, and RSLs only]
The dwelling-house was occupied (whether alone or with others) by a married couple, a couple who are civil partners of each other, a couple living together as husband and wife or a couple living together as if they were civil partners and –

(a)   one or both of the partners is a tenant of the dwelling-house,
(b)   the landlord who is seeking possession is a registered social landlord or a charitable housing trust,
(c)   one partner has left the dwelling-house because of violence or threats of violence by the other towards –
  (i)   that partner, or
  (ii) a member of the family of that partner who was residing with that partner immediately before the partner left, and
(d)   the court is satisfied that the partner who has left is unlikely to return.

For the purposes of this ground 'registered social landlord' and 'member of the family' have the same meaning as in Part I of the Housing Act 1996 and 'charitable housing trust' means a housing trust, within the meaning of the Housing Associations Act 1985, which is a charity within the meaning of the Charities Act 1993.

19.3.4 Deterioration in Condition

Both sectors provide grounds for possession where the property deteriorates during the tenancy as a result of the tenant's acts or omissions. The 1985 and 1988 Acts are similar in their wording.

Housing Act 1985 Schedule 2 Ground 3 [subject to reasonableness]
The condition of the dwelling-house or of any of the common parts has deteriorated owing to acts of waste by, or the neglect or default of, the tenant or a person residing in the dwelling-house and, in the case of an act of waste by, or the neglect or default of, a person lodging with the tenant or a sub-tenant of his, the tenant has not taken such steps as he ought reasonably to have taken for the removal of the lodger or sub-tenant.

Housing Act 1985 Schedule 2 Ground 4 [subject to reasonableness]
The condition of furniture provided by the landlord for use under the tenancy, or for use in the common parts, has deteriorated owing to ill-treatment by the tenant or a person residing in the dwelling-house and, in the case of ill-treatment by a person lodging with the tenant or a sub-tenant of his, the tenant has not taken such steps as he ought reasonably to have taken for the removal of the lodger or sub-tenant.

Housing Act 1988 Schedule 2 Ground 13 [subject to reasonableness]
The condition of the dwelling-house or any of the common parts has deteriorated owing to acts of waste by, or the neglect or default of, the tenant or any other person residing in the dwelling-house and, in the case of an act of waste by, or the neglect or default of, a person lodging with the tenant or a sub-tenant of his, the tenant has not taken such steps as he ought reasonably to have taken for the removal of the lodger or sub-tenant.

For the purposes of this ground, 'common parts' means any part of a building comprising the dwelling-house and any other premises which the tenant is entitled under the terms of the tenancy to use in common with the occupiers of other dwelling-houses in which the landlord has an estate or interest.

Housing Act 1988 Schedule 2 Ground 15 [subject to reasonableness]
The condition of any furniture provided for use under the tenancy has, in the opinion of the court, deteriorated owing to ill-treatment by the tenant or any other person residing in the dwelling-house and, in the case of ill-treatment by a person lodging with the tenant or by a sub-tenant of his, the tenant has not taken such steps as he ought reasonably to have taken for the removal of the lodger or sub-tenant.

Apart from the fact that Ground 13 refers to damage to the common parts as well as to the dwelling, the 1988 Act mirrors the provisions of the Rent Act 1977. Under the Rent Acts it was held that an order for possession can be made even if the deterioration stems only from neglect and not from breach of a contractual or common law duty, and even if no warning has been given that possession would be sought on this ground.[132]

19.3.5 Tenancy Induced by False Statements

Given that allocation of social housing is based around housing need, the information provided by the tenant is an important part of allocating property. If wrong information is supplied, knowingly or recklessly (but not innocently or negligently), the landlord can use this as a ground for recovering possession. So, for example, in *LB of Islington v Uckac*,[133] a husband and wife falsely claimed in their homelessness application that they were living in overcrowded accommodation and had been given notice to leave. The landlord sought to

---

[132] *Lowe v Lendrum* (1950) 159 EG 423 (CA).
[133] [2006] EWCA Civ 340, [2006] 1 WLR 1303.

recover possession on this basis. As RSLs now form part of the private sector, a 'false state-ment' ground was introduced into the Housing Act 1988 in 1996 (although, unlike the domestic violence ground, it is not confined to RSLs).

Housing Act 1985 Schedule 2 Ground 5 [subject to reasonableness]

The tenant is the person, or one of the persons, to whom the tenancy was granted and the landlord was induced to grant the tenancy by a false statement made knowingly or recklessly by –

(a)   the tenant, or
(b)   a person acting at the tenant's instigation.[134]

Housing Act 1988 Schedule 2 Ground 17 [subject to reasonableness]

The tenant is the person, or one of the persons, to whom the tenancy was granted and the landlord was induced to grant the tenancy by a false statement made knowingly or recklessly by –

(a)   the tenant, or
(b)   a person acting at the tenant's instigation.

LB of Islington v Uckac revealed a lacuna in the wording of the legislation.[135] The secure tenancy had initially been granted to the husband but was later assigned to his wife. This meant that Ground 5 could not be used as the Court of Appeal held that it permitted recovery only against the original tenant for misrepresentation by the original tenant ('the tenant *is* the person … *to whom the tenancy was granted*'). Nor could the common law of rescission be used: section 82 provides that a landlord can *only* bring a secure tenancy to an end by obtaining a court order for possession and the landlord cannot bring it to an end in any other way, for example, by rescission.[136] While the wording of section 5 of the Housing Act 1988 differs in certain respects from section 82 of the Housing Act 1985, the effect is the same as it provides that an assured tenancy cannot be brought to an end except by obtaining a court order. In the earlier case of *Killick v Roberts* the Court of Appeal allowed rescission on the basis of fraudulent misrepresentation,[137] but this was decided under the Rent Act 1977 which (unlike the 1985 and 1988 Acts) 'does not identify the method by which or the circumstances in which the landlord may terminate the protected tenancy'.[138]

19.3.6 Premiums

Housing Act 1985 Schedule 2 Ground 6 [subject to reasonableness]

The tenancy was assigned to the tenant, or to a predecessor in title of his who is a member of his family and is residing in the dwelling-house, by an assignment made by virtue of section 92 (assignments by way of exchange) and a premium was paid either in connection with that assignment or the assignment which the tenant or predecessor himself made by virtue of that section.

---

[134] NB. It is also an offence under Housing Act 1996 s 171 to knowingly/recklessly make a false statement in connection with a local housing authority function.
[135] [2006] EWCA Civ 340, [2006] 1 WLR 1303.
[136] *LB of Islington v Uckac* [2006] EWCA Civ 340, [2006] 1 WLR 1303.
[137] [1991] 1 WLR 1146 (CA).
[138] *LB of Islington v Uckac* [2006] EWCA Civ 340, [2006] 1 WLR 1303 [17].

In this paragraph 'premium' means any fine or other like sum and any other pecuniary consideration in addition to rent.

This provision is peculiar to the 1985 Act. The tenant can be evicted whether he paid or received the premium and regardless of who proposed its payment, but Ground 6 is subject to the reasonableness test.

19.3.7 Employment Related Tenancies

The Housing Acts 1985 and 1988 provide special rules for the case where the lease is related to the tenant's, or prospective tenant's, employment.

Housing Act 1985 Schedule 2 Ground 7 [subject to reasonableness]
The dwelling-house forms part of, or is within the curtilage of, a building which, or so much of it as is held by the landlord, is held mainly for purposes other than housing purposes and consists mainly of accommodation other than housing accommodation, and –

(a)   the dwelling-house was let to the tenant or a predecessor in title of his in consequence of the tenant or predecessor being in the employment of the landlord, or of –
>   a local authority,
>   a new town corporation,
>   a housing action trust
>   an urban development corporation, or
>   the governors of an aided school,

and

(b)   the tenant or a person residing in the dwelling-house has been guilty of conduct such that, having regard to the purpose for which the building is used, it would not be right for him to continue in occupation of the dwelling-house.

Housing Act 1985 Schedule 2 Ground 12 [subject to reasonableness and suitable alternative accommodation]
The dwelling-house forms part of, or is within the curtilage of, a building which, or so much of it as is held by the landlord, is held mainly for purposes other than housing purposes and consists mainly of accommodation other than housing accommodation, or is situated in a cemetery, and –

(a)   the dwelling-house was let to the tenant or a predecessor in title of his in consequence of the tenant or predecessor being in the employment of the landlord or of –
>   a local authority,
>   a new town corporation,
>   a housing action trust
>   an urban development corporation, or
>   the governors of an aided school,

and that employment has ceased, and

(b)   the landlord reasonably requires the dwelling-house for occupation as a residence for some person either engaged in the employment of the landlord, or of such a body, or with whom a contract for such employment has been entered into conditional on housing being provided.

Housing Act 1988 Schedule 2 Ground 16 [subject to reasonableness]

The dwelling-house was let to the tenant in consequence of his employment by the landlord seeking possession or a previous landlord under the tenancy and the tenant has ceased to be in that employment.

For the purposes of this ground, at a time when the landlord is or was the Secretary of State, employment by a health service body, as defined in section 60(7) of the National Health Service and Community Care Act 1990, or by a Local Health Board shall be regarded as employment by the Secretary of State.

The 1988 Act also has a very specific ground for properties used by ministers of religion.

Housing Act 1988 Schedule 2 Ground 5 [mandatory]

The dwelling-house is held for the purpose of being available for occupation by a minister of religion as a residence from which to perform the duties of his office and –

(a) not later than the beginning of the tenancy the landlord gave notice in writing to the tenant that possession might be recovered on this ground; and

(b) the court is satisfied that the dwelling-house is required for occupation by a minister of religion as such a residence.

In the public sector both grounds are subject to reasonableness, but Ground 12 (which is not based on tenant default) also requires there to be suitable alternative accommodation (SAA, discussed below at 19.3.8.1 below).

Ground 7 allows for eviction where the tenant's property is part of a building or is within the curtilage of a building used principally for non-housing purposes, the tenant obtained the lease in consequence of his employment by the landlord and he has now behaved in a manner inconsistent with the purpose for which the building as a whole is principally used. Since the building as a whole is to be used mainly for non-housing purposes, then this Ground could be used against a school caretaker but has no application to caretakers of blocks of flats. In most cases the question is what sort of conduct is going to be inappropriate to the main purpose of the building. Furthermore, since there has to be a *building* used for non-housing purposes, it would not apply to a cemetery worker with a property in the grounds, nor a park keeper. In such a case, Ground 12 would be the only means of obtaining possession. Once again there must be a building which is used for non-housing purposes or, to deal with the problem indicated above, the property must be in a cemetery. Eviction is possible under Ground 12 if the tenant or predecessor in title obtained the lease through his employment by the landlord, that employment has ceased and the new, replacement employee's contract states that his new job is conditional on housing being provided.

Ground 16 of the Housing Act 1988 is of a more general nature. The tenancy must have been let originally in consequence of the tenant being employed by the landlord or his predecessor in title and that employment has now ceased. There are no rules about the nature of the property, nor about the landlord needing the property for a new employee. Nevertheless, the court has a discretion as to whether to grant possession, and, therefore, the eviction must be reasonable. Ground 5, on the other hand, is mandatory if the tenant has been given notice in advance of the tenancy that the property may be necessary to house a minister of religion.

19.3.8 Estate Management Grounds

In both sectors there are grounds which recognise the need for landlords to make reasonable changes to their property. In the public sector, the Law Commission describe the approach as being to,

> … balance the social landlord's need for efficient use of their stock against the need to provide security and respect for home and family life, as well as avoiding disrupting the sustainability of communities by unnecessarily moving those who have created an established community.[139]

This is achieved by enabling the landlord to recover possession on estate management grounds on any one of nine separate grounds, but only if suitable alternative accommodation is available. The one exception is where the secure tenant has been put into temporary accommodation while the original home is being repaired or improved; it is then (though still subject to reasonableness) possible to return the tenant to the original home.

In the private sector, there are only two estate management grounds. One is a very general suitable alternative accommodation ground which is discretionary, the other is a complex ground relating to redevelopment.

19.3.8.1 Suitable Alternative Accommodation (SAA)

Only in the private sector is SAA a sufficient ground for possession (subject to reasonableness); in the public sector there must additionally to SAA also be a ground based on specific circumstances (these grounds are considered below).

Housing Act 1988 Schedule 2 Ground 9 [subject to reasonableness]
Suitable alternative accommodation is available for the tenant or will be available for him when the order for possession takes effect.

If possession is ordered on this ground, the landlord must also meet the tenant's reasonable removal expenses.[140]

The meaning of SAA is important in both sectors. It is defined in Part IV of Schedule 2 to the Housing Act 1985 for the public sector and in Part III of Schedule 2 Housing Act 1988 for the private sector. In outline, in order to be suitable property must be offered with a tenancy that offers a similar level of security to the existing tenancy, which means that it must be an assured tenancy to which none of Grounds 1–5 of the Housing Act 1988 apply and not an assured shorthold tenancy, or, additionally, in the public sector it can be a secure tenancy. The SAA need not be in the local authority sector, even if the current tenancy is. The accommodation must also, in the opinion of the court, be 'reasonably suitable to the needs of the tenant and his family'. The factors listed as relevant to this differ slightly between the public and private sectors. In the public sector, this will take account of the kind of accommodation that it is the landlord's practice to allocate to those with similar needs, the distance from work and school, the distance from family members who rely on the tenant for their well-being, the means of the tenant, and the size of the accommodation.

---

[139] Law Commission, 'Renting Homes' (Law Com No 284, 2003) para 9.34.
[140] Housing Act 1988 s 11.

In the private sector, it will again take account of the type of accommodation granted by the local housing authority to those with similar needs and refers to suitability 'as regards extent and character' taking account of the means and needs of the tenant and his family, but there is no specific reference to distance from other social bases. A certificate from the local housing authority that suitable alternative accommodation is available is conclusive evidence of suitability in the private sector.

Perhaps not surprisingly, suitability has often been contested. The fact that the new accommodation would not take the tenant's furniture was held to render it unsuitable in *McIntyre v Hardcastle*,[141] and where the tenant had children, the absence of a garden was similarly fatal to the landlord's claim in *De Markozoff v Craig*.[142] Matters of 'character' and 'environment' can be especially difficult. In *Dawncar Investments Ltd v Plews*, the Court of Appeal, somewhat surprisingly, upheld the judge's decision that to move from 'leafy' Hampstead Heath in London to Kilburn was not 'suitable' within the Housing Act 1988:

> I would be very unhappy for a woman like Miss Plews, having to live in 42 Iverson Road because of the noise, traffic, heavy lorries, proximity of railway lines, general roughness of the area and of the inhabitants.[143]

On the other hand, *Siddiqui v Rashid*, held that a loss of 'culture' could not be taken into account.[144] In *Armit Holdings Co Ltd v Shahbakhti (Feraidoun)* the issue was one of 'availability'.[145] The tenant here had other investment properties and the landlord was trying to recover a Rent Act protected flat (with a regulated rent) by arguing that it was reasonable and suitable for the tenant to move into another of his properties. Although the tenant would have been able to recover possession as he let on assured shortholds, the Court of Appeal did not accept this as SAA. It is not only the physical characteristics of a property that matter, but the fact that the tenant would incur expense and trouble, and the loss of investment income, made it unreasonable to see this as SAA.

19.3.8.2 Temporary Accommodation During Repairs

This is the only estate management ground that does not refer to SAA but given that this ground is all about evicting the tenant so that he can return to his original home it also effectively carries this requirement.

Housing Act 1985 Schedule 2 Ground 8 [subject to reasonableness]
The dwelling-house was made available for occupation by the tenant (or a predecessor in title of his) while works were carried out on the dwelling-house which he previously occupied as his only or principal home and –

(a) the tenant (or predecessor) was a secure tenant of the other dwelling-house at the time when he ceased to occupy it as his home,

(b) the tenant (or predecessor) accepted the tenancy of the dwelling-house of which possession is sought on the understanding that he would give up occupation when, on completion of

---

[141] [1948] 2 KB 82 (CA).
[142] (1949) 93 Sol Jo 693 (CA).
[143] (1993) 25 HLR 639 (CA) 640.
[144] [1980] 3 All ER 184 (CA).
[145] [2005] EWCA Civ 339.

the works, the other dwelling-house was again available for occupation by him under a secure tenancy, and

(c)   the works have been completed and the other dwelling-house is so available.

This ground is available to local authorities but not other social landlords, although they may be able to achieve the same end by using Ground 9 of the 1988 Act (see 19.3.8.1 above) and providing suitable alternative accommodation on an assured shorthold tenancy.

19.3.8.3 Overcrowding

Housing Act 1985 Schedule 2 Ground 9 [subject to SAA]
The dwelling-house is overcrowded, within the meaning of Part X, in such circumstances as to render the occupier guilty of an offence.

Reasonableness is not an issue under Ground 9. In deciding what is suitable, regard should be had to Part IV, Schedule 2 to the Housing Act 1985:

3. Where possession of a dwelling-house is sought on ground 9 (overcrowding such as to render occupier guilty of offence), other accommodation may be reasonably suitable to the needs of the tenant and his family notwithstanding that the permitted number of persons for that accommodation, as defined in section 326(3) (overcrowding: the space standard), is less than the number of persons living in the dwelling-house of which possession is sought.

The underlying purpose of paragraph 3 is to make sure that the new accommodation does not have to accommodate any lodgers or sub-tenants from the original dwelling. The local authority only has to provide SAA for the tenant and his family, as defined in section 113.

19.3.8.4 Under-crowding

The shortage of housing means that it is inefficient to leave a large family property under-occupied. Ground 16 allows the local authority to move the secure tenant into SAA where it is reasonable to do so and then allocate the property to an applicant needing a property of that size. Nevertheless, efficient use of property is given a lower priority than protecting the original tenant's interest in his home and the emotional attachment of the spouse on that tenant's death. Thus, this Ground can not be used against the original tenant, nor against the spouse of the original tenant who statutorily succeeded to the secure tenancy on the spouse's death.[146] Even other members of the family might not be evicted where their age, length of residence or support to the deceased original tenant would render it unreasonable; and the local authority only has a limited period of time during which it can serve the section 83 notice. To that extent, Ground 16 recognises that the lease provides more than merely four walls and a roof and that the tenant might have a psychological attachment to the dwelling which overrides the need for efficient allocation procedures.

Housing Act 1985 Schedule 2 Ground 16 [subject to reasonableness and SAA]
The accommodation afforded by the dwelling-house is more extensive than is reasonably required by the tenant and –

---

[146] This probably also covers civil partners. Although the exception in Ground 16 refers only to 'spouse' the subsection cross-referred to is s 87(b), which refers to family members other than those in s 87(a) which in turn refers to both spouse and civil partner.

(a) the tenancy vested in the tenant by virtue of section 89 (succession to periodic tenancy), the tenant being qualified to succeed by virtue of section 87(b) (members of family other than spouse), and

(b) notice of the proceedings for possession was served under section 83 (or, where no such notice was served, the proceedings for possession were begun) more than six months but less than twelve months after the date of the previous tenant's death.

The matters to be taken into account by the court in determining whether it is reasonable to make an order on this ground include –

(a) the age of the tenant,

(b) the period during which the tenant has occupied the dwelling-house as his only or principal home, and

(c) any financial or other support given by the tenant to the previous tenant.

19.3.8.5 Demolition, Reconstruction and Works

A local authority is able to recover possession where this is necessary in order to do construction works, but only if SAA is available. Under Ground 10 it must be able to show at the date of the hearing that it has a 'settled and clearly defined intention'[147] to demolish or carry out the construction works within a reasonable time of obtaining possession and that it could not do the works without obtaining possession. Ground 10A is appropriate where the local authority is going to sell the dwelling-house to a private firm for the latter to demolish or carry out the works.

Housing Act 1985 Schedule 2 Part II Ground 10 [subject to SAA]

The landlord intends, within a reasonable time of obtaining possession of the dwelling-house

(a) to demolish or reconstruct the building or part of the building comprising the dwelling-house, or

(b) to carry out work on that building or on land let together with, and thus treated as part of, the dwelling-house,

and cannot reasonably do so without obtaining possession of the dwelling-house.

Housing Act 1985 Schedule 2 Ground 10A [subject to SAA]

The dwelling-house is in an area which is the subject of a redevelopment scheme approved by the Secretary of State or the Housing Corporation or Scottish Homes in accordance with Part V of this Schedule and the landlord intends within a reasonable time of obtaining possession to dispose of the dwelling-house in accordance with the scheme.

or

Part of the dwelling-house is in such an area and the landlord intends within a reasonable time of obtaining possession to dispose of that part in accordance with the scheme and for that purpose reasonably requires possession of the dwelling-house.

The redevelopment scheme referred to in Ground 10A must be approved by the Secretary of State and the developer must consult with affected secure tenants and take into account their views before applying to the Secretary of State for approval. The Secretary of State must have regard to the following matters:

---

[147] *Wansbeck DC v Marley* (1988) 20 HLR 247 (CA). In the commercial sector, there is a similar ground in s 30(1)(f) of the Landlord and Tenant Act 1954, and much case law on the meaning of 'intention', see ch 21.

Housing Act 1985 Schedule 2 Part V

3 (1) In considering whether to give his approval to a scheme or variation the Secretary of State shall take into account, in particular –

(a)   the effect of the scheme on the extent and character of housing accommodation in the neighbourhood,

(b)   over what period of time it is proposed that the disposal and redevelopment will take place in accordance with the scheme, and

(c)   to what extent the scheme includes provision for housing provided under the scheme to be sold or let to existing tenants or persons nominated by the landlord;

and he shall take into account any representations made to him and, so far as they are brought to his notice, any representations made to the landlord.

If a tenant is evicted under Ground 10 or 10A, he is entitled to compensation under section 29 of the Land Compensation Act 1973 for loss of his home. Even if the tenant leaves voluntarily in circumstances where Grounds 10 or 10A might apply, then the local authority has a discretion as to whether to grant a compensation payment.[148]

In the private sector, the need to repossess in order to carry out construction works is a mandatory ground. Paragraph (b) of Ground 6 prevents the landlord relying on this Ground if he has acquired the freehold after the tenancy was created, but this exception has no application to a landlord who acquired the reversion either by will or intestacy or where no consideration passed. The aim is presumably to prevent tenanted property being bought by landlords who simply want to redevelop the site.

As is the case with other grounds that do not involve tenant default, Ground 6 can only be used against a periodic tenant.[149] The assured fixed term tenant can remain in the property until the expiry of the lease. A landlord forcing a tenant to move under Ground 6 may have to pay the tenant's reasonable expenses.[150]

Housing Act 1988 Schedule 2 Ground 6 [mandatory]

The landlord who is seeking possession or, if that landlord is a registered social landlord or charitable housing trust, a superior landlord intends to demolish or reconstruct the whole or a substantial part of the dwelling-house or to carry out substantial works on the dwelling-house or any part thereof or any building of which it forms part and the following conditions are fulfilled –

(a)   the intended work cannot reasonably be carried out without the tenant giving up possession of the dwelling-house because –

(i)   the tenant is not willing to agree to such a variation of the terms of the tenancy as would give such access and other facilities as would permit the intended work to be carried out, or

(ii)   the nature of the intended work is such that no such variation is practicable, or

(iii) the tenant is not willing to accept an assured tenancy of such part only of the dwelling-house (in this sub-paragraph referred to as 'the reduced part') as would leave in the possession of his landlord so much of the dwelling-house as would be reasonable to enable the intended work to be carried out and, where appropriate, as would give

---

[148] Land Compensation Act 1973 s 32(7B).
[149] Housing Act 1988 s 7(6).
[150] Housing Act 1988 s 11.

       such access and other facilities over the reduced part as would permit the intended
       work to be carried out, or

    (iv) the nature of the intended work is such that such a tenancy is not practicable; and

(b) either the landlord seeking possession acquired his interest in the dwelling-house before the
grant of the tenancy or that interest was in existence at the time of that grant and neither
that landlord (or, in the case of joint landlords, any of them) nor any other person who,
alone or jointly with others, has acquired that interest since that time acquired it for money
or money's worth; and

(c) the assured tenancy on which the dwelling-house is let did not come into being by virtue of
any provision of Schedule 1 to the Rent Act 1977, as amended by Part I of Schedule 4 to this
Act or, as the case may be, section 4 of the Rent (Agriculture) Act 1976, as amended by Part
II of that Schedule.

For the purposes of this ground, if, immediately before the grant of the tenancy, the tenant to
whom it was granted or, if it was granted to joint tenants, any of them was the tenant or one
of the joint tenants of the dwelling-house concerned under an earlier assured tenancy or, as
the case may be, under a tenancy to which Schedule 10 to the Local Government and Housing
Act 1989 applied, any reference in paragraph (b) above to the grant of the tenancy is a reference to the grant of that earlier assured tenancy or, as the case may be, to the grant of the
tenancy to which the said Schedule 10 applied.

For the purposes of this ground 'registered social landlord' has the same meaning as in the
Housing Act 1985 (see section 5(4) and (5) of that Act) and 'charitable housing trust' means a
housing trust, within the meaning of the Housing Associations Act 1985, which is a charity,
within the meaning of the Charities Act 1993 …

19.3.8.6 *Allocation and Management of Special Needs Housing*

For social landlords, the dearth of specialised housing for people with special needs means
that whatever exists cannot be wasted. Therefore, Schedule 2 to the Housing Act 1985 enables
local authorities to evict tenants for the better use of such housing by people with special
needs. RSLs have no need for special statutory authority as SAA is a stand-alone ground for
possession in the private sector (subject to reasonableness).

Housing Act 1985 Schedule 2 Ground 13 [subject to reasonableness and SAA]
The dwelling-house has features which are substantially different from those of ordinary
dwelling-houses and which are designed to make it suitable for occupation by a physically disabled person who requires accommodation of a kind provided by the dwelling-house and –

(a) there is no longer such a person residing in the dwelling-house, and
(b) the landlord requires it for occupation (whether alone or with members of his family) by
such a person.

Housing Act 1985 Schedule 2 Ground 15 [subject to reasonableness and SAA]
The dwelling-house is one of a group of dwelling-houses which it is the practice of the landlord to let for occupation by persons with special needs and –

(a) a social service or special facility is provided in close proximity to the group of
dwelling-houses in order to assist persons with those special needs,
(b) there is no longer a person with those special needs residing in the dwelling-house, and
(c) the landlord requires the dwelling-house for occupation (whether alone or with members
of his family) by a person who has those special needs.

Ground 13 relates specifically to housing for physically disabled people. The differences between this dwelling house and the general local authority housing have to be substantial and they have to have been designed for their purpose. A feature which would prove to be useful but which was not 'designed', would not meet this test. Ground 15 is aimed at sheltered accommodation with a warden or other form of social service. If there is no longer a person in the dwelling house with special needs and, as with Ground 13, there is a person with those needs requiring the premises, the local authority can evict the present incumbent.

19.3.8.7 Owner-Occupation

In the private sector, a landlord may have a mandatory ground for possession for owner-occupation.

> **Housing Act 1988 Schedule 2 Ground 1 [mandatory]**
> Not later than the beginning of the tenancy the landlord gave notice in writing to the tenant that possession might be recovered on this ground or the court is of the opinion that it is just and equitable to dispense with the requirement of notice and (in either case)
>
> (a) at some time before the beginning of the tenancy, the landlord who is seeking possession or, in the case of joint landlords seeking possession, at least one of them occupied the dwelling-house as his only or principal home; or
> (b) the landlord who is seeking possession or, in the case of joint landlords seeking possession, at least one of them requires the dwelling-house as his, his spouse's or his civil partner's only or principal home and neither the landlord (or, in the case of joint landlords, any one of them) nor any other person who, as landlord, derived title under the landlord who gave the notice mentioned above acquired the reversion on the tenancy for money or money's worth.

This ground can be used not only by the landlord who wishes to recover possession in order to occupy the property himself, as in *Lohan v Hilton*[151] (or his spouse/civil partner, paragraph (b)), but also by the landlord who used to live in the property and now wishes to sell it, as in *Lipton v Whitworth*[152] (paragraph (a)).

Notice of possible Ground 1 repossession must have been given by a landlord in writing before the tenancy began, unless the court feels it just and equitable to dispense with notice.

19.3.8.8 Death of the Tenant

Under section 17 of the Housing Act 1988, discussed in chapter 17, the tenant's (sexual) partner has a right to succeed to a periodic tenancy. If there is no such person, then it may devolve by will or intestacy but the mandatory Ground 7 is available to the landlord.

> **Housing Act 1988 Schedule 2 Ground 7 [mandatory]**
> The tenancy is a periodic tenancy (including a statutory periodic tenancy) which has devolved under the will or intestacy of the former tenant and the proceedings for the recovery of possession are begun not later than twelve months after the death of the former tenant or, if the court so directs, after the date on which, in the opinion of the court, the landlord or, in the case of joint landlords, any one of them became aware of the former tenant's death.

---

[151] [1994] EGCS 83 (CA).
[152] (1994) 26 HLR 293 (CA).

For the purposes of this ground, the acceptance by the landlord of rent from a new tenant after the death of the former tenant shall not be regarded as creating a new periodic tenancy, unless the landlord agrees in writing to a change (as compared with the tenancy before the death) in the amount of the rent, the period of the tenancy, the premises which are let or any other term of the tenancy.

The special rule about acceptance of rent from the inheriting tenant is to prevent any implied grant of tenancy.

19.3.8.9 Winter Lets

Ground 3 enables private sector landlords of holiday properties to let the premises out during the winter but then be secure in the knowledge that the tenant can be evicted before the lucrative holiday season starts.

Housing Act 1988 Schedule 2 Ground 3 [mandatory]
The tenancy is a fixed term tenancy for a term not exceeding eight months and –

(a) not later than the beginning of the tenancy the landlord gave notice in writing to the tenant that possession might be recovered on this ground; and

(b) at some time within the period of twelve months ending with the beginning of the tenancy, the dwelling-house was occupied under a right to occupy it for a holiday.

19.3.8.10 Vacation Lets of Student Accommodation

This ground allows educational institutions to let out student accommodation on a short term basis, for example, during the summer vacation.

Housing Act 1988 Schedule 2 Ground 4 [mandatory]
The tenancy is a fixed term tenancy for a term not exceeding twelve months and –

(a) not later than the beginning of the tenancy the landlord gave notice in writing to the tenant that possession might be recovered on this ground; and

(b) at some time within the period of twelve months ending with the beginning of the tenancy, the dwelling-house was let on a tenancy falling within paragraph 8 of Schedule 1 to this Act.

(Paragraph 8 of Schedule 1 exempts specified student lettings from the definition of assured tenancy, see chapter 6).

19.3.9 Mortgagor Arrears

Ground 2 enables a private sector property to be recovered where a mortgagee is exercising a power of sale.

Housing Act 1988 Schedule 2 Ground 2 [mandatory]
The dwelling-house is subject to a mortgage granted before the beginning of the tenancy and

(a) the mortgagee is entitled to exercise a power of sale conferred on him by the mortgage or by section 101 of the Law of Property Act 1925; and

(b) the mortgagee requires possession of the dwelling-house for the purpose of disposing of it with vacant possession in exercise of that power; and

(c) either notice was given as mentioned in Ground 1 above or the court is satisfied that it is just and equitable to dispense with the requirement of notice;

and for the purposes of this ground 'mortgage' includes a charge and 'mortgagee' shall be construed accordingly.

This ground will apply only where the tenancy was granted after the creation of the mortgage and with the consent of the lender. Without this ground, before the assured shorthold emerged, a mortgagee would be unlikely to consent to a tenancy being granted for fear of being stuck with a long-term tenant.[153] It is, however, only available to landlords who have served the 'owner-occupier' notice and cannot, therefore, be available to RSLs.

19.3.10 Assured Shorthold Tenancies

The grounds for possession discussed above apply to few private sector lettings. As already seen, the vast majority of new tenancies in the private sector that are accessible to members of the public are assured shortholds. Before the Housing Act 1996 was implemented, assured shortholds were subject to a number of limitations, in particular the need to serve a prescribed form of notice before the tenancy was entered into,[154] but since 28 February 1997, they have been the default tenancy for the private sector. There are some exceptions listed in Schedule 2A. For example, where a secure tenancy ends following stock transfer the new assured tenancy will not be a shorthold.

The landlord is able to end a shorthold tenancy on giving two months' notice, provided that the contractual term has come to an end,[155] the notice does not take effect earlier than six months after the beginning of the tenancy,[156] and (if periodic) the requisite period has been given for the notice to quit.[157] The notice can be served before the contractual term has ended, but a court order cannot be made until the contractual term has come to an end. If the tenant refuses to give up possession after that date, the landlord can apply for possession under the accelerated possession procedure.

The notice provisions as applied to periodic tenancies can trap a landlord. They have come before the Court of Appeal on several occasions. The difficulty is the strict meaning of the wording in section 21(4):

> (4) … a court shall make an order for possession of a dwelling-house let on an assured shorthold tenancy which is a periodic tenancy if the court is satisfied—
>
> (a) that the landlord or, in the case of joint landlords, at least one of them has given to the tenant a notice in writing stating that, after a date specified in the notice, being the last day of a period of the tenancy and not earlier than two months after the date the notice was given, possession of the dwelling-house is required by virtue of this section; and

---

[153] If the tenancy pre-dates the mortgage, then the mortgagee will usually take subject to the tenancy (but the mortgagee may require the tenant to waive his priority as a condition of its loan to the landlord). If the mortgage predates the tenancy but the tenancy is granted without the lender's consent (which is usually required by the mortgage) then the mortgagee has priority, even if vis-à-vis the landlord the tenant has a protected status: *Britannia Building Society v Earl* [1990] 2 All ER 469 (CA).

[154] Housing Act 1988 s 20. A number of cases arose in relation to these notice provisions: *Panayi & Pyrkos v Roberts* (1993) 25 HLR 421 (CA); *York v Casey* (1999) 31 HLR 209 (CA).

[155] Housing Act 1988 s 21(1).

[156] Housing Act 1988 s 21(5) (for post 28 February 1997 tenancies; tenancies before that date would be shortholds only if granted for a fixed term of not less than six months; s 20).

[157] Housing Act 1988 s 21(4).

(b) that the date specified in the notice under paragraph (a) above is not earlier than the earliest
     day on which, apart from section 5(1) above, the tenancy could be brought to an end by a
     notice to quit given by the landlord on the same date as the notice under paragraph (a)
     above.

In *Fernandez v McDonald* the section 21 notice gave as the date for possession the day after
the last day of the tenancy.[158] Section 21 itself requires that the date specified is *the last day of
a period of the tenancy*, and the Court of Appeal held that the day after will not do and so the
notice was invalid and the order for possession set aside (see also chapter 2). A more general
form of wording was approved by the Court of Appeal in *Lower Street Properties Ltd v Jones*:

> ... [this] notice will expire at the end of the period of your tenancy that will end after the
> expiry of two months from the service of this notice upon you.[159]

Although this is less of a trap for the landlord, it is also much less clear for the tenant as there
is no particular date specified on which he has to leave.

An RSL assured tenancy that is demoted will become an assured shorthold tenancy.[160]

The impact of the assured shorthold has been considerable. Coupled with the
liberalisation of the financial services market through buy-to-let, it has halted the decline of
private renting. At the same time, however, it has removed the hope of long term secure
housing in the private sector for many households and, given the difficulties in accessing
secure social housing, this has considerable social impact. A report by Shelter notes that:

> — the vast majority of assured shortholds tenancies (around 80 per cent) agreed in the preceding
>   three years provided security of tenure for less than twelve months. Although no figures were
>   available it was reasonable to assume that most were in fact for six months.
> — the ending of assured shorthold tenancies causes a disproportionately high amount of statutory
>   homelessness.
> — insecure tenancies may be driving a 'revolving door' effect in parts of the private rented sector.
> — one of the reasons for the low level of social capital held by private renters may be the increasing
>   rate of households moving between properties in the sector (over 40 per cent of those with
>   assured shorthold agreements moved in 2002/3).[161]

This report followed the Law Commission's consultation on Renting Homes that opened
the question as to whether even the 'six month moratorium' should be abandoned (that is,
whether there should continue to be a ban on a landlord being able to end an assured
shorthold tenancy within the first six months).[162] Some respondents, such as Shelter,
campaigned to have the moratorium extended to twelve months, and the issue deeply
divided consultees. The Law Commission's draft Rented Homes Bill does not retain the
moratorium, as it was not persuaded that any real benefit stemmed from the 'six month

---

[158] [2003] EWCA Civ 1219, [2004] 1 WLR 1027.

[159] (1996) 28 HLR 877 (CA). See also *Notting Hill Housing Trust v Roomus* [2006] EWCA Civ 407, [2006] 1 WLR
1375; *Church Commissioners for England v Meya* [2006] EWCA Civ 821. For a discussion of these cases, see A
Williams, 'Terminating Assured Shorthold Tenancies' (2006) 156 *NLJ* 1550.

[160] Housing Act 1988 ss 6A, 20B. See ch 6.

[161] L Reynolds, *Safe and Secure? The private rented sector and security of tenure* (Shelter, 2005) 11, 16–19, 18 and 6.
See also DCLG, 'Housing in England 2004/05' (October 2006) 13: 'The private sector is characterised by much
higher turnover than the social sector, with 41 per cent of private renters having lived in their current accommodation for less than a year'.

[162] Law Commission, 'Renting Homes 1: Status and Security' (Law Com CP No 162, 2002) paras 8.15–8.29.

moratorium', while to retain it would add considerable complexity to its proposed scheme of reform.[163] Under the draft Rented Homes Bill, the standard contract can be simply ended on two months' notice.

The low level of security under the assured shorthold tenancy also makes it difficult for tenants to assert other rights; a complaining tenant can simply, and lawfully, be evicted by the landlord complying with the two months' notice requirement. Writing in ROOF, a housing worker comments:

> ... we've heard many unscrupulous landlords exploiting section 21 of the Act and serving notice on tenants who make complaints to avoid the cost of vital repairs.
>
> Sometimes the eviction of a 'troublesome' tenant is enough to silence others in the same block. Fear renders tenants powerless; the threat of homelessness is far worse than the misery of living in a filthy, cold or unsafe environment.[164]

In response to these problems it has been recommended that a landlord should not be able to use a section 21 notice to evict a tenant if the tenant has recently taken steps to enfoce their statutory rights on disrepair or health and safety.[165]

19.3.11 Reform

The Law Commission has proposed a very different system for security.[166] It is built around the ideas of simplification and landlord neutrality. There will be two types of occupation contract: the secure and the standard. Although the contract types are landlord-neutral, the social landlord (called a 'community landlord' by the Law Commission in its Final Report on Renting Homes) will be required to use the secure contract (with some listed exceptions) as only this will offer long-term security.

With the secure contract there will be no mandatory grounds for possession. Discretionary grounds for possession will fall into two broad classes:

(a)   a general ground, for breach of any of the terms or conditions of the agreement; and
(b)   'estate management grounds' where, in addition to establishing that it is reasonable for a court to make the order, the landlord has to show that other suitable accommo-dation will be available to the occupier. These are grouped into three categories: redevelopment grounds, special accommodation grounds, and under-occupation grounds. There is also a general 'sweeping up' provision available where there is a 'substantial estate management reason' for possession.

With the standard contract, there will be two additional, mandatory grounds for possession:

---

[163] Law Commission, 'Renting Homes' (Law Com No 284, 2003) paras 6.3–6.16.

[164] D Crew, 'Put up or Get Out' ROOF March/April 2007 46. In a survey of environmental health and tenancy relations officers nearly half said that in their experience, people were often put off using the help they offer because they don't want to put their tenancy in jeopardy; 98% of those questioned said they agreed that legislative changes concerning s 21 needed to be made: D Crew, 'The Tenant's Dilemma' (CAB, June 2007).

[165] D Crew, 'The Tenant's Dilemma' (CAB, June 2007). Similar provisions, known as retaliatory eviction laws, exist in other jurisdictions.

[166] Law Commission, 'Renting Homes: The Final Report. Volume 1: Report' (Law Com No 297, 2006).

(a)   a notice only ground (cf the assured shorthold); and
(b)   serious rent arrears (cf Ground 8).

The Law Commission proceeded on the basis that the balance between landlord and tenant should remain broadly as at present, accepting that while social housing should continue to provide long term security, many tenants in the private rented sector are not seeking to be housed on a long-term basis.[167] To question whether long term security should be available within the private sector would have been beyond the Law Commission's remit. The private rented market is, however, by no means uniform. As well as providing for the niche executive market and young households who value mobility, the private rented housing is being used to assist local authorities discharge their homelessness duties and to provide housing for those unable to access social housing. The Shelter report mentioned in the preceding section shows the negative impact that short term tenancies can have for those after a long term home.

Greater security of tenure need not mean a return to the days of full Rent Act protection with the associated risk of disinvestment in private rented housing. So, for example, Parkinson has argued for a model of intermediate security along the lines of the system recently introduced in Ireland.[168] Under this, tenants are not protected during the first six months of their tenancy (cf the introductory tenancy) but thereafter have security for a further 3.5 years. During this period the landlord can gain possession only on certain grounds, for example, owner occupation, sale, change of use, or major refurbishment. During this period the tenant is able to serve a notice to quit.

If it is accepted that residential security is important for personal well-being and social inclusion, then housing policy and law ought also to attach a value to it. It should be possible for the government to plot a course that acknowledges the psychological value attached to the home whilst not discouraging investment in housing. Some local authorities are already managing to do this by having private leasing schemes under which private landlords lease their properties to local authorities for, typically, three or five years. The advantage to the private landlord of this arrangement is that it reduces the risk of voids. The British Property Federation has recently argued for a debate on intermediate tenancies which could be promoted by, for example, offering a fiscal incentive in the form of tax benefits or rental guarantees to landlords willing to offer rented housing on a long term basis to good tenants.[169]

---

[167] Law Commission, 'Renting Homes 1: Status and Security' (Law Com CP No 162, 2002) paras 1.19–1.23.
[168] N Parkinson, 'Securing the Future' ROOF Nov/Dec 2006 44.
[169] British Property Federation, 'Letting in the Future, Housing Manifesto 2006'.

20

SECURITY AND LONG RESIDENTIAL LEASES

20.1   Continuing rights of occupation for long leaseholders
20.2   Qualifying for protection
20.3   Continuing or ending the tenancy

20.1 Continuing Rights of Occupation for Long Leaseholders

As seen in chapter 7, long residential leasehold has never been an entirely satisfactory method of land-holding. One set of problems with long leases stemmed from the fact that they were often badly drafted, and the property badly managed, which led to problems in relation to repair and servicing. A different set of issues related to the claims of injustice and the 'wasting asset' problem. Until 1954, tenants of long leases would face the loss of their home at the end of the lease as they had no right to remain. In addition, they would often be faced with expensive claims for dilapidations to put the house back into repair. One possible solution to this was to give leaseholders enfranchisement rights but this was highly controversial, and also bedeviled by technical arguments about the difficulty of the exercise.

By the middle of the twentieth century concern over the position of the tenant on the expiry of his lease came to the fore. Rather than giving full enfranchisement rights it was considered that what long leaseholders really needed was security of tenure. Accordingly, it was thought to be sufficient to protect their right of occupation, rather than give a new right of ownership.[1] In consequence, the Landlord and Tenant Act 1954 was passed. Part I of the 1954 Act created a right to remain at the end of the contractual term and an entitlement to a statutory tenancy within the Rent Acts. These new rights applied to tenants of dwellings with 'long leases' at a 'low rent'. The 1954 Act has been phased out and replaced by Schedule 10 to the Local Government and Housing Act 1989.[2] The approach followed under the 1989 Act is essentially the same as the earlier legislation but, reflecting the new legislative code applicable to private sector tenancies, the tenant acquires an assured monthly periodic tenancy on expiry of the long lease rather than a statutory tenancy.

This right to remain proved insufficient to meet the needs of leaseholders, and since this right was conferred, the stronger rights of enfranchisement and of lease extension have been given to some long leaseholders (see chapter 25). Extension or enfranchisement rights will

---

[1] Government Policy on Leasehold Property in England and Wales (Cmd 8713, 1953).
[2] Local Government and Housing Act 1989 s 186.

usually be more attractive as they give much greater security: continuation on an assured tenancy basis can be brought to an end if the landlord is able to prove a ground for possession. The continuation tenancy will also be at a market rent. On the other hand, the stronger rights to extension and enfranchisement require capital expenditure. The continuation tenancy is discussed in this chapter as it is mainly to do with providing security to the former leaseholder; the extension and enfranchisement rights are discussed in chapter 25 as although they also provide security they are more to do with reinforcing the position of the leaseholder as owner-occupier.

20.2 Qualifying for Protection

In relation to tenancies entered into from 1 April 1990 the following conditions have to be met in order to qualify for protection.[3]

20.2.1 There Must Be a Long Tenancy

In order to be a long tenancy it must have been granted for a term of years exceeding twenty-one years.[4] Twenty-one years is taken as the basic guide to what is a long lease for most enfranchisement laws, not just the 1954 Act. The significance of this period is that it has developed into the standard legislative length of term to distinguish between a person who is simply renting property and one who has purchased a 'major interest' in the property.[5] The Act will also apply to another tenancy at a low rent if it follows on from a tenancy which was a long tenancy.[6]

20.2.2 The Tenancy Must Be at a Low Rent[7]

The aim was that the 1954 Act would apply to tenancies which would otherwise be within the statutory protection afforded by the Rent Acts, but were excluded because they were at a low rent. To be a low rent, it must be at no rent, or £1,000 or less a year in Greater London (or £250 or less a year elsewhere). 'High value' properties are excluded, defined by reference to a formula set out in paragraph 1(2A) of Schedule 10.

---

[3] For those entered into before this date, the lease would need to be a 'long tenancy at a low rent' as defined by Part I of the Landlord and Tenant Act 1954; although the scheme of protection is broadly the same, the details differ.

[4] Local Government and Housing Act 1989 Sch 10 para 2. It will not be a long lease if the 'tenancy is, or may become, terminable before the end of the term by notice given to the tenant'.

[5] Whether the legislative adoption of the 21 year limit was an example of law following practice, or vice versa, it does now clearly mark the point where there is a significant legal consequence to being on one side of the line or the other.

[6] Local Government and Housing Act 1989 Sch 10 para 16.

[7] Local Government and Housing Act 1989 Sch 10 para 2(4).

20.2.3 The Tenant Must Satisfy the 'Qualifying Condition'

The qualifying condition is set by reference to what is necessary for protection as an 'assured tenancy' under the Housing Act 1988 (minus the rent qualification).[8] This means that the house must be let as a separate dwelling to an individual (or individuals) as his only or principal home.

The intention behind this was referred to by Lord Denning MR in *Herbert v Byrne*:

> You are to look at the position at the end of the lease, and ask yourself whether the lease-holder would have been protected if it had not been a long lease at a low rent, but a short lease at a rack rent. If the leaseholder would have qualified under the old Rent Acts for protection on the expiry of such a short lease, he qualifies now, under the Act of 1954, for protection on the expiry of the long lease. There is, however, this difference – in determining whether he qualifies or not, you do not look at the terms of the old long lease itself as you would look at the terms of a short lease ... but you look at the state of affairs as it actually existed at the end of the long lease. That is made clear by section 22(3) of the Act of 1954.[9]

20.3 Continuing or Ending the Tenancy

If the tenancy comes within the Landlord and Tenant Act 1954 Part I and the tenant wants to end the tenancy, he can do so by serving one month's notice, which can end on or after the term date.[10] If the tenant does not end the tenancy, it will simply continue on the same terms and at the same rent until the landlord takes some action to end the tenancy.[11]

The landlord can end the tenancy either on the term date or at a later date by giving not more than twelve nor less than six months' notice.[12] The landlord can either seek to end the relationship if a ground for possession can be established, or create an assured periodic tenancy at market rent. The available grounds for possession are set out by reference to the discretionary grounds for possession under Part II, Schedule 2 to the Housing Act 1988 (except for the employment related ground), plus the redevelopment ground (Ground 6) in Schedule 1 to the Housing Act 1988.[13] Broadly, these are based on tenant default (apart from where suitable alternative accommodation is available or the redevelopment ground is relied on). There is an additional ground if the landlord proposes to demolish or recon-struct the whole or a substantial part of the premises for the purposes of redevelopment and the landlord is one of certain public bodies.[14]

Where the landlord is proposing an assured monthly periodic tenancy, the landlord's notice must propose a rent for the tenancy.[15] Unless the landlord proposes different terms,

---

[8] Local Government and Housing Act 1989 Sch 10 para 1. This means that there is an exclusion when the landlord is a local authority (Housing Act 1988 Sch 1 para 12) but tenancies with the Crown are expressly included by the Local Government and Housing Act 1989 Sch 10 para 22.

[9] [1964] 1 WLR 519 (CA) 525. The reference now would be to the Local Government and Housing Act 1989 Sch 10 para 1(7).

[10] Local Government and Housing Act 1989 Sch 10 para 8.

[11] Local Government and Housing Act 1989 Sch 10 para 3.

[12] Local Government and Housing Act 1989 Sch 10 para 4.

[13] Local Government and Housing Act 1989 Sch 10 para 5. See ch 19.

[14] Local Government and Housing Act 1989 Sch 10 para 5 (1)(b), (4).

[15] Local Government and Housing Act 1989 Sch 10 paras 4(5), (6), 9 and 10.

the terms implied will be the same as those of the long residential tenancy. The tenant is able to serve a notice suggesting a different rent and different terms and if the parties are unable to agree the terms or rent they can be settled by referral to a rent assessment committee. In settling the rent, the committee shall determine the monthly rent on an open market basis for an assured tenancy for that property. In determining the terms, it is to look to the terms that 'might reasonably be expected to be found in an assured monthly periodic tenancy' of the property.

The provisions of Schedule 10 have effect notwithstanding any agreement to the contrary, but they do not prevent the surrender of the tenancy.[16]

---

[16] Local Government and Housing Act 1989 s 186(4).

21

SECURITY AND BUSINESS LEASES

21.1   Introduction
21.2   Obtaining information
21.3   The end of the contractual term
21.4   Agreeing a new tenancy
21.5   Applying for an interim rent
21.6   Applying to court
21.7   Opposing a new tenancy
21.8   Compensation for non-renewal
12.9   The terms of the new tenancy

21.1 Introduction

The Landlord and Tenant Act 1954 (LTA 1954) sets out the scheme for providing security of tenure to business tenants in Part II. The approach of the legislation is to ensure that a protected tenancy cannot be ended without giving an opportunity for the tenant to obtain a new tenancy.[1] The landlord may be able to successfully oppose this if certain grounds can be made out (and may, on certain grounds, have to pay compensation), but failing this the tenant who wants to stay can do so.

When introduced, the scheme was to apply to all business tenancies with few exceptions. As discussed in chapter 8, the introduction and ease of contracting out means that this scheme is now effectively optional. The scale of contracting out is not known, but may be significant, somewhat undermining the government's stated policy that 'business tenants should normally have a statutory right to renew their tenancies'.[2]

21.2 Obtaining Information

In order to exercise rights under the legislation, it is necessary to serve statutory notices. Where there are only two parties, landlord and tenant, knowing who to serve a notice on is clearly straightforward but in many situations the leasehold set up is more complex and there

---

[1] Ch 8 explains when there will be a protected business tenancy.
[2] DCLG, 'Landlord and Tenant Act 1954: Review of Impact of Procedural Reforms' (August 2006) para 4.

may be a number of tenancies and sub-tenancies carved out of the freehold. Section 44 of the LTA 1954 contains provisions explaining who the relevant landlord is for the purposes of serving notices. If, for example, there is an intermediate lease that ends within 14 months the freeholder may be the relevant landlord for these purposes even though there is an intermediate landlord. A landlord will need to know the identities of any sub-tenants who may be able to assert their own rights under the Act. Section 40 accordingly places a duty on landlords and tenants to provide information to the other party when requested within a two year period before the lease comes to an end.

21.3 The End of the Contractual Term

If the tenancy is one to which the LTA 1954 Part II applies, section 24 provides that the tenancy cannot be ended other than in accordance with the provisions of the Act.[3] The provisions are complex, and timetables are strict. Table 21.1 gives an outline of the choices available to the tenant as the end of the lease approaches; the details are discussed in the text following.

Table 21.1: Tenant Options as End of Lease Approaches

Tenant wants to leave	Tenant wants to stay
Fixed Term Lease Move out before contractual term date (s 27(1A)), or Serve s 27 notice at least 3 months before the term date *Periodic Tenancy* Serve notice to quit	Do nothing — continuation tenancy (s 24) *12-6 months before contractual term:* Landlord serves s 25 notice: tenant can apply to court for new tenancy before tenancy expires (s 24) Tenant with fixed term of more than one year can serve s 26 notice requesting a new tenancy (landlord has 2 months to state if it opposes; thereafter tenant can apply to court for new tenancy)

21.3.1 Continuing the Tenancy

If neither party takes action to end the tenancy in accordance with the Act, there will be what is known as a 'continuation' tenancy when the contractual tenancy ends.[4] During this tenancy the terms will remain the same as for the contractual tenancy, save that there is provision for either party to apply for an interim rent (see 21.5 below).

Although the tenant remains liable on the leasehold covenants during the continuation tenancy, in the usual case guarantors and others will be released from liability. For pre-1996 tenancies,[5] the original tenant will therefore not be liable during the continuation tenancy

---

[3] The landlord can still, however, end the lease by forfeiture.
[4] Landlord and Tenant Act 1954 s 24.
[5] That is, leases entered into before the Landlord and Tenant (Covenants) Act 1995 came into force. For later tenancies, the tenant is released on assignment unless required to enter an AGA (see ch 18).

unless the leasehold contract was expressly drafted to include any statutory extension of the term,[6] and even if it is so drafted the original tenant's liability will extend only to the contractual rent and not to any increased interim rent.[7] Similarly, the liability of any guarantor will relate only to the tenant liability during the contractual term unless there is clear wording to show that it extends to any continuation.[8]

21.3.2 Ending the Tenancy

21.3.2.1 Termination by the Tenant

If the tenant wishes to bring the tenancy to an end, he can do so by serving a notice to quit if it is a periodic tenancy.[9] If it is a fixed term tenancy then, in accordance with section 27 of the LTA 1954, the tenant must serve a written notice on the immediate landlord,

> ... not later than three months before the date on which apart from this Act the tenancy would come to an end by effluxion of time, ... [stating] that the tenant does not desire the tenancy to be continued.[10]

Failure to serve such notice will mean that a continuation tenancy will arise at the end of the fixed term. If a continuation tenancy has already arisen at the end of a fixed term tenancy, section 27(2) provides that the tenancy,

> ... shall not come to an end by reason only of the tenant ceasing to occupy the property comprised in the tenancy but may be brought to an end on any . . . day by not less than three months' notice in writing given by the tenant to the immediate landlord, whether the notice is given . . . after the date on which apart from this Act the tenancy would have come to an end or before that date, but not before the tenant has been in occupation in right of the tenancy for one month.

The combined effect of these provisions is that if a protected business tenant does not wish to continue a fixed term tenancy then it must serve a notice on the landlord at least three months before the term is due to expire; failure to do so means that a continuation tenancy will automatically arise which can then be ended only by serving three months' written notice in accordance with section 27(2).

These provisions apply only if the tenancy is one to which the Act currently applies. If the tenant ceases to occupy the premises for business purposes before the end of the contractual tenancy (and so is no longer a protected business tenancy within section 23) then these provisions do not apply, reflecting the fact that the aim of the legislation is to protect not the tenant per se but the tenant's business.[11] Section 27(1A) states:

---

6 *City of London Corporation v Fell* [1994] AC 458 (HL).
7 *City of London Corporation v Fell; Herbert Duncan Ltd v Cluttons* [1993] 2 WLR 710 (CA).
8 *Junction Estates Ltd v Cope* (1974) 27 P & CR 482 (QB).
9 Landlord and Tenant Act 1954 s 24(2).
10 But a continuation tenancy will still arise if the notice is given before the tenant has been in occupation in right of the tenancy for one month.
11 M Haley, 'The Landlord and Tenant Act 1954: The Need for Continuing Occupation' [1998] *Conv* 218, 223.

Section 24 of this Act shall not have effect in relation to a tenancy for a term of years certain where the tenant is not in occupation of the property comprised in the tenancy at the time when, apart from this Act, the tenancy would come to an end by effluxion of time.

Section 27(1A) was an amendment to the legislation reflecting the Court of Appeal decision in *Esselte AB v Pearl Assurance plc.*[12] The tenant had two five-year leases[13] expiring on 14 February 1993. It served written notice on the landlords on 16 November and 24 December 1992 purporting to end the leases on 14 February and 31 March 1993 respectively. These notices were ineffective as they did not give the requisite three months' notice required under section 27(1). On 6 December 1992 the tenant ceased to occupy the property for business purposes. It then served notices ending the leases on 24 June 1993, which did comply with the requirements of section 27(2). The issue was whether the tenant was liable for rent between February (the end of the contractual term) and June (the end date of the effective notices) and this turned on whether the fact that the tenant had already vacated by February 1993 meant that section 24 with its restriction on the method of ending tenancies still applied. The Court of Appeal held not,[14] a result now confirmed by the statutory amendment in section 27(1A). As to the argument that this construction would leave a landlord at the mercy of its tenant, not knowing whether the tenant planned to stay or leave (as the tenant would not need to serve a notice), Morritt LJ said:

> I do not accept that a landlord must find himself in that position. If the tenant is in occupa-tion for the statutory purposes the landlord may serve a notice under section 25(1) to determine the tenancy at the term date. If the landlord is doubtful whether or not the tenant is in occupation for the statutory purposes then I see no reason why ... he should not serve a notice under section 25(1) without prejudice to his principal contention that as the tenant is not in occupation no such notice is required.[15]

21.3.2.2 *Termination by the Landlord*

If the landlord wishes to bring the tenancy to an end, section 29(2) enables it to apply to the court for an order ending the tenancy.

In order to make this application, either the landlord must have served a (hostile) notice under section 25 of the Act or it must have replied to a section 26 request from the tenant for a new tenancy opposing the grant (see below). The more usual route is for the landlord to serve a section 25 notice.

The service of a section 25 notice is strictly regulated. The notice must be in a prescribed form.[16] The landlord must give 'not more than twelve nor less than six months' notice,[17] and the notice must state the date on which the tenancy is to end. This date must be not earlier than the date on which the tenancy could be ended at common law by the effluxion

---

[12] [1997] 1 WLR 891 (CA).

[13] One was an underlease.

[14] In reaching this result the Court of Appeal explained why it did not follow the most recent Court of Appeal precedent. Might tenants, who vacated without serving s 27 notices before the *Esselte* decision and paid rent from the contractual end date until the (late) s 27 notice expired, be entitled to claim rent back by arguing it was payment under a mistake of law following *Kleinwort Benson Ltd v Lincoln City Council* [1999] 2 AC 349 (HL)?

[15] [1997] 1 WLR 891 (CA) 898.

[16] Landlord and Tenant Act 1954, Part 2 (Notices) Regulations 2004 SI 2004/1005 Form 2 Sch 2.

[17] Landlord and Tenant Act 1954 s 25(2).

of time (the contractual term date with a fixed term tenancy)[18] or by notice to quit (in the case of a periodic tenancy).[19] The notice must also state whether the landlord opposes the grant of a new tenancy[20] and, if so, the grounds of opposition.[21] (The landlord can also trigger the process for the renewal of a tenancy by serving a section 25 notice, but this is dealt with below).

Until the Regulatory Reform (Business Tenancies) (England and Wales) Order 2003 (RRO 2003),[22] the tenant who wished to stay in possession but who had been served with a section 25 notice had to serve a counter-notice and apply to the court within strict time limits. This proved a trap for many tenants and advisers, fuelling numerous negligence claims against advisers who forgot to serve the notices in time. Further, as there was nothing to be lost by serving a counter-notice and making the court application, they came to be done as a matter of routine to keep the tenant's options open.[23] Following the RRO 2003 the need for a counter-notice has been removed,[24] but the consequence for the landlord is that the tenant does not now have to indicate whether it wishes to renew the tenancy.

If the tenant wants to remain, he can apply to the court for a new tenancy under section 24(1) and must do so by the date specified in the section 25 notice for termination of the tenancy (unless the parties have agreed in writing to extend the deadline).[25] If the landlord does not want to wait this long to find out whether the tenant wants to stay or not, it may have to apply under section 29(1) for termination in order to flush out the tenant's intentions.

As is seen frequently in landlord and tenant law, it is very important to make sure that notices are served correctly and on time. Although minor inaccuracies that will not mislead the tenant will not prevent there being a valid notice,[26] it is important, in accordance with the House of Lords' ruling in *Mannai Investments*,[27] that the reasonable recipient would have understood the notice. The potential problems are illustrated by the facts of *Barclays Bank plc v Bee*.[28] Altogether, the landlord served three section 25 notices. Notice A and Notice B were served at the same time. Notice A stated that the landlord would oppose the grant of the new tenancy and, although following the prescribed form, it did not list the grounds of opposition. It was, therefore, invalid. Notice B stated that the landlord would not oppose the new tenancy. Notice C served later stated that the landlord would oppose the grant of the new tenancy and listed the grounds of opposition. If Notice B was valid, then Notice C would be ineffective as it is not possible to withdraw or amend a section 25 notice once served. In the event, the Court of Appeal held that neither Notice A nor Notice B was valid: applying the approach from *Mannai Investments*, the reasonable recipient would have

---

[18] Landlord and Tenant Act 1954 s 25(4).

[19] S 25(3). Where, unusually, more than six months' notice would be required at common law the date for termination must not be a date which makes the period between it and the giving of the notice more than six months longer than the common law notice to quit period: s 25(3)(b).

[20] Landlord and Tenant Act 1954 s 25(6).

[21] Landlord and Tenant Act 1954 s 26(7).

[22] SI 2003/3096.

[23] In most cases the parties agreed the new tenancy without the involvement of the court; in only around one fifth of court applications did the court end up ordering the grant of the new tenancy.

[24] This is controversial: see J Joyce, 'Analysing the changes' (17 December 2005) *EG* 86.

[25] Landlord and Tenant Act 1954 ss 29A and B.

[26] *Tegerdine v Brooks* [1977] 36 P & CR 261 (CA) 266; *Morrow v Nadeem* [1986] 1 WLR 1381 (CA).

[27] *Mannai Investments Co Ltd v Eagle Star Life Assurance Co Ltd* [1997] AC 749 (HL), see ch 2.

[28] [2001] EWCA Civ 1126, [2002] 1 WLR 332.

been unclear as to whether or not the landlord intended to oppose a new tenancy having received both notices at the same time. Notice C was therefore the effective notice.[29]

21.4 Agreeing a New Tenancy

Although either party is able to apply to the court for a new tenancy,[30] the parties may be able to agree terms without going to court. The process is initiated either by the landlord serving a section 25 notice or by the tenant's section 26 notice.

If the landlord is willing to grant a new tenancy it can serve a section 25 notice in accordance with the time limits described above (unless the tenant has already served a section 26 notice) and in a prescribed form[31] setting out the landlord's proposals for the new tenancy (the extent of the property, the rent, and other terms).[32] This serves as a basis for future negotiations as to the terms of the new tenancy. If the tenant informs the court that it does not want a new tenancy, the landlord's application for a new tenancy will be dismissed.[33]

Alternatively, if the tenant wants a new tenancy it can start the ball rolling by serving a section 26 notice (unless the landlord has already served a section 25 notice). To minimise the risk of duplicate applications to court, section 24(2A) provides that no application can be made if the other party has made and served an application.

By section 26(1) the tenant can only initiate renewal if it holds:

> … a term of years certain exceeding one year, whether or not continued by section twenty-four of this Act, or granted for a term of years certain and thereafter from year to year.

The reason why a periodic tenant is unable to serve a request is because most periodic tenancies are short term and temporary and it would be inappropriate for the tenant to be able to apply for a longer-term interest. In any event, as the Law Commission noted in 1969:

> … a periodic tenancy of its nature continues indefinitely until it is terminated. If the landlord serves notice under section 25 to terminate the tenancy, a weekly or monthly tenant has the same right as other tenants under section 24(1)(a) to apply for a new tenancy.[34]

In practice, a tenant who has not been served with a section 25 notice may well be content simply to continue to occupy under the terms of the old lease (particularly if this is at a favourable rent), but there may be reasons why the tenant would wish to apply for a new tenancy. This could be where the tenant wishes to have more security for his business interests than he has under a continuation tenancy.

Again there are strict requirements regulating the service of the tenant's notice. It must be in a prescribed form[35] and ask for the new tenancy to begin not more than twelve nor less

---

[29] It has been argued that this outcome condones careless drafting and that the doubt should have been resolved in the tenant's favour: M Haley, 'Section 25 Notices: A Tenant Confused?' [2002] *Conv* 292, 299.

[30] Landlord and Tenant Act 1954 s 24(1).

[31] Landlord and Tenant Act 1954, Part 2 (Notices) Regulations 2004 SI 2004/1005 Form 1 Sch 2.

[32] Landlord and Tenant Act 1954 s 25(8).

[33] Landlord and Tenant Act 1954 s 29(5).

[34] Law Commission, 'Landlord and Tenant: Report on the Landlord and Tenant Act 1954, Part II' (Law Com No 17, 1969) para 53.

[35] Landlord and Tenant Act 1954 s 26(3); Landlord and Tenant Act 1954, Part 2 (Notices) Regulations 2004 SI 2004/1005 Form 3 Sch 2.

than six months from the making of the request.[36] The request cannot be for the tenancy to begin before the current tenancy is set to expire,[37] and the request must set out the tenant's proposals for terms of the new tenancy (the extent of the property, the rent, and other terms).[38] If the landlord is not willing to grant a new tenancy section 26(6) requires it to give written notice to the tenant within two months of the tenant's request, stating that it opposes the application and giving the grounds of opposition; if it fails to do so within this timescale, it loses the right to oppose renewal of the lease. If the landlord is willing to grant a new tenancy it need do nothing at this stage. The purpose behind the landlord's counter-notice is to enable the tenant to know his position. Where the tenant serves a notice requesting a new tenancy, the current tenancy will end (subject to the provisions on continuation tenancies) on the date immediately before that given for the commencement of the new tenancy.[39]

Where the parties agree the terms of the new tenancy, section 28 provides that the current tenancy will end on the date agreed for the start of the new tenancy.

21.5 Applying for an Interim Rent

After the service of a section 25 or 26 notice, either the landlord or the tenant is able to apply to the court under section 24A for an interim rent to be payable during the continuation tenancy. The RRO 2003 has made a number of changes to the interim rent provisions. The previous wording allowed only the landlord to apply for an interim rent, the assumption being that there would be a rising property market and the landlord should be able to have the rent increased whilst waiting for the new tenancy to be granted (or for the tenant to leave). In a falling property market it would, however, be the tenant who wishes for a rental adjustment; hence the change to allow the tenant also to apply for an interim rent. The interim rent is payable from the earliest date for renewal of the tenancy which could have been specified in the statutory notice served by the landlord or tenant.[40]

There have also been changes made to the way that the interim rent is to be assessed. The previous wording gave a level of cushioning between the previous contractual rent and the rent payable under the new tenancy. Under the new wording, where the grant of a new lease of the whole of the property comprised in the property is unopposed, the amount of the interim rent will usually be the same as the rent for the new tenancy, that is a market rent, but with provision to adjust this if market conditions change significantly during the continuation tenancy or if the terms of the new lease are significantly different from the old lease in a way that would affect the rent.[41]

Where the grant of a new lease is opposed the interim rent is likely to be lower than the rent that will be payable under a new tenancy. Section 24D provides that the interim rent is the rent which it is 'reasonable for the tenant to pay' during the continuation tenancy and

[36] Landlord and Tenant Act 1954 s 26(2).
[37] Landlord and Tenant Act 1954 s 26(2). The tenant cannot, by exercising a break clause end a tenancy and yet still claim a right to renewal of the tenancy by serving a s 26 notice: *Garston v Scottish Widows' Fund and Life Assurance Society* [1998] 3 All ER 596 (CA).
[38] Landlord and Tenant Act 1954 s 26(3).
[39] Landlord and Tenant Act 1954 s 26(5).
[40] Landlord and Tenant Act 1954 s 24B.
[41] Landlord and Tenant Act 1954 s 24C.

although this is to be based on the market rent formula in section 34 that is used for a new tenancy, the court must also take account of the previous contractual rent and assume a yearly tenancy. In practice, this means that in a rising property market – both because of the reference to a yearly tenancy and also because of the comparison with the existing rent – the rent is likely to be discounted from a full market rent.

The application for an interim rent must be made no more than six months after the termination of the relevant tenancy.[42]

21.6 Applying to Court

Most tenancies are renewed by negotiation but it may be necessary for the court to settle the terms if the parties are unable to do so. It is important to realise that there are strict deadlines for applying to court, and the parties will lose the right to apply if the deadline passes without the parties having agreed an extension. Provided the application is made by the deadline the tenancy continues while the application is being considered; if not, the tenancy ends when the deadline for making an application passes.

Where the tenant requests a new tenancy following a section 26 notice, the application to court must be made during the period ending 'immediately before the date specified in his request' for the new tenancy to begin[43] but not during the first two months after serving the section 26 notice (unless the landlord has served notice opposing the grant of the tenancy).[44] Where the new tenancy is requested following a section 25 notice the application must be made during the period ending with the date on which the section 25 specified the tenancy was to end.[45] As Hill & Redman note:

> This … gives rise to a potential trap for tenants: an application made on the date specified in an s 25 notice is in time, but application made on the date specified in a s 26 request is too late.[46]

Following the RRO 2003, section 29B makes it possible for the parties to agree in writing[47] to extend these time limits, a power that is being widely used but is also said then to create more time traps for tenants.[48]

21.7 Opposing a New Tenancy

There are seven grounds upon which the landlord can oppose a new tenancy.[49] The grounds that the landlord intends to rely on must be stated in the section 25 or section 26(6) notice. If

---

[42] Landlord and Tenant Act 1954 s 24A(3).
[43] Landlord and Tenant Act 1954 s 29A(2)(b).
[44] Landlord and Tenant Act 1954 s 29A(3).
[45] Landlord and Tenant Act 1954 ss 24 and 29A(2)(a).
[46] Hill & Redman's *Law of Landlord and Tenant* (Lexis-Nexis Butterworths) B [62].
[47] Landlord and Tenant Act 1954 s 69(2).
[48] A survey conducted by Lovells on behalf of the Property Litigation Association found between one and five extensions common, the average length of time for an extension being between one and two months: J Joyce, 'Analysing the changes' (17 December 2005) *EG* 86.
[49] Landlord and Tenant Act 1954 s 30(1) (a)-(g). A new ground of opposition to renewal is being mooted for public bodies where possession is required for redevelopment or to enable a third party to carry out a specific

the landlord is able to establish any of these grounds 'to the satisfaction of the court, the court shall not make an order for the grant of a new tenancy'.[50] The mandatory aspect of this section is balanced by the fact that within some of the grounds there is an element of discretion. So, for the tenant default and uneconomic subletting grounds, the landlord can oppose an application only if the tenant 'ought not to be granted a new tenancy'.[51] Where renewal is opposed on any of the estate management grounds, compensation may also be payable under section 38 (see 21.8 below).

21.7.1 Tenant Default Grounds

21.7.1.1 Breach of Repairing Obligations

Landlord and Tenant Act 1954 section 30

(1) The grounds on which a landlord may oppose an application … are …

(a) where under the current tenancy the tenant has any obligations as respects the repair and maintenance of the holding, that the tenant ought not to be granted a new tenancy in view of the state of repair of the holding, being a state resulting from the tenant's failure to comply with the said obligations;

21.7.1.2 Persistent Delay in Paying Rent

Landlord and Tenant Act 1954 section 30

(1) The grounds on which a landlord may oppose an application … are …

(b) that the tenant ought not to be granted a new tenancy in view of his persistent delay in paying rent which has become due;

'Persistent' has been taken to refer to the frequency and duration of earlier delays in the payment of rent and the difficulty the landlord faced in obtaining the arrears.[52] The reason for the delay and the likelihood of it recurring will also be factors that the court can take account of.

21.7.1.3 Breach of Tenancy Obligations

Landlord and Tenant Act 1954 section 30

(1) The grounds on which a landlord may oppose an application … are …

(c) that the tenant ought not to be granted a new tenancy in view of other substantial breaches by him of his obligations under the current tenancy, or for any other reason connected with the tenant's use or management of the holding;

---

function for the public body (and the repeal of Landlord and Tenant Act 1954 s 57 which allows public bodies who are landlords to regain possession for their own purposes): DCLG, 'Landlord and Tenant Act 1954: Section 57' (Consultation Paper, February 2007).

[50] Landlord and Tenant Act 1954 s 31(1).
[51] See *Betty's Cafes Ltd v Phillips Furnishing Stores Ltd* [1959] AC 20 (HL); *Hurstfell v Leicester Square Property Co* [1988] 2 EGLR 105 (CA).
[52] *Hopcutt v Carver* (1969) 209 EG 1069 (CA).

21.7.2 Suitable alternative accommodation

Landlord and Tenant Act 1954 section 30

(1) The grounds on which a landlord may oppose an application … are …

(d) that the landlord has offered and is willing to provide or secure the provision of alternative accommodation for the tenant, that the terms on which the alternative accommodation is available are reasonable having regard to the terms of the current tenancy and to all other relevant circumstances, and that the accommodation and the time at which it will be available are suitable for the tenant's requirements (including the requirement to preserve goodwill) having regard to the nature and class of his business and to the situation and extent of, and facilities afforded by, the holding;

The landlord is able to oppose the grant of the new tenancy by offering the tenant suitable alternative accommodation (SAA). In deciding suitability account is taken not only of the physical amenities but also the terms on which it is being offered, and the preservation of the goodwill of the present business is also a relevant factor. Such SAA may simply amount to a smaller part of the original premises.[53] In most cases, the new accommodation should be close to the old premises and should try to maintain the situation, extent of, and facilities afforded by those original premises. The tenant is not entitled to any expenses or compensation when the failure to renew is for ground (d) (contrast the private residential tenant). It might be arguable that the expenses of moving would be 'other relevant circumstances' to be taken into account in considering whether the alternative accommodation is suitable, but there are no cases on this point. The explanation as to why compensation is not available in this instance but is for non-renewal on some other grounds seems to be that compensation should not be given where there is tenant default – and failure to take up other accommodation is associated with fault.[54] Unless relocation and removal expenses are taken account of in determining whether the alternative accommodation is suitable then it seems wrong to deny compensation and against the spirit of the legislation.

21.7.3 Estate Management Grounds

21.7.3.1 Uneconomic Subletting

Section 30(1)(e) of the Landlord and Tenant Act 1954 allows for non-renewal in limited circumstances where the landlord could make greater profits.

Landlord and Tenant Act 1954 section 30

(1) The grounds on which a landlord may oppose an application … are …

(e) where the current tenancy was created by the sub-letting of part only of the property comprised in a superior tenancy and the landlord is the owner of an interest in reversion expectant on the termination of that superior tenancy, that the aggregate of the rents reasonably obtainable on separate lettings of the holding and the remainder of that property would be substantially less than the rent reasonably obtainable on a letting of that property as a whole, that on the termination of the current tenancy the landlord requires possession

---

[53] *Lawrence v Carter* (1956) 167 EG 222 (Cty Ct).
[54] See Government Policy on Leasehold Property in England and Wales (Cmd 8713, 1953) para 49.

of the holding for the purpose of letting or otherwise disposing of the said property as a whole, and that in view thereof the tenant ought not to be granted a new tenancy;

The provision is very narrowly drafted and is difficult to prove,[55] and consequently little used. It allows a superior landlord, at the discretion of the court, to refuse renewal of a lease of part of the holding to a sub-tenant. However, the superior landlord has to prove that the rental value of the separate sub-leases is less than the return available if the property was let as a whole and it is only the return on rent, and no other matter under the lease, that is relevant. Nevertheless, if the superior landlord can prove this ground, then there is nothing to stop him selling the property rather than re-letting it.

21.7.3.2 Demolition and Reconstruction and Works

Landlord and Tenant Act 1954 section 30

(1) The grounds on which a landlord may oppose an application … are …

(f)   that on the termination of the current tenancy the landlord intends to demolish or recon-struct the premises comprised in the holding or a substantial part of those premises or to carry out substantial work of construction on the holding or part thereof and that he could not reasonably do so without obtaining possession of the holding;

Commercial landlords, like their residential counterparts, need to be able to manage the holding. In some cases this will entail demolition or major works being carried out. This is a frequently used ground and there is a significant amount of case law on its meaning. The ground requires not only that the landlord needs physical possession of the property but legal possession, the point being that the landlord may have sufficient access rights under the existing lease to do the work without bringing the tenant's legal rights of possession to an end.[56] The ground is qualified by section 31A[57] by which a tenant may be able to frustrate the landlord's aim of not renewing the lease by agreeing that a new lease will give the landlord the level of access necessary to do the works. Section 31A only applies where the landlord makes out his case under section 30(1)(f).[58] In the words of Charles J:

… a first stage in the consideration of whether the landlord can reasonably carry out the work intended without obtaining possession is to consider what parts of the work the landlord can carry out pursuant to the terms of the existing lease and the new lease containing those terms and the terms of access and other facilities the tenant agrees should be included therein for carrying out the work intended.[59]

Further, the tenant may still be able to get a new lease if he is willing to accept a tenancy of an economically separable part of the holding which would afford the landlord sufficient access to carry out the works.[60] In deciding what is economically separable, section 31A(2) provides that account is taken of the aggregate rents which the landlord would be able to

---

[55] M Ross, *Commercial Leases* (London, Butterworths, 1998) P [294].

[56] *Heath v Drown* [1973] AC 498 (HL).

[57] Inserted by the Law of Property Act 1969 s 7.

[58] This section was 'passed for the protection of tenants', *Heath v Drown* [1973] AC 498 (HL); *Redfern v Reeves* [1978] 2 EGLR 52 (CA).

[59] *Pumperninks of Piccadilly Ltd v Land Securities plc* [2002] EWCA Civ 621, [2002] Ch 332 [32].

[60] S 31A(1)(b).

receive after completion of the work with a separate letting of that part as against the rent that would be receivable for a letting of the whole.

Ground (f) requires a settled intention to do the works. In *Betty's Cafés Ltd v Phillips Furnishings Stores Ltd* the House of Lords said that intention requires not only a desire that the demolition or works would be effected, but also that there was a reasonable prospect of them actually being carried out.[61] Further, they said that this intention must be established at the time of the hearing. According to Asquith LJ in *Cunliffe v Goodman*, the project must have,

> ... moved out of the zone of contemplation – out of the sphere of the tentative, the provisional and the exploratory – into the valley of decision.[62]

Thus, it will be necessary to show that adequate funds are available for the enterprise[63] and where planning permission is required the landlord ought to have obtained it by the date of the hearing, or show that there is a reasonable prospect that it will be granted.[64] Intention can be proven if the landlord shows that he intends to re-let the premises on a building lease.[65] However, the landlord's motive for carrying out the works of construction is irrelevant,[66] even if it intends to occupy the property itself once the work is done.

In addition to case law exploring the meaning of 'intention', there are many cases in which the extent of the work that the landlord intends to do is discussed. Demolition speaks for itself, but reconstruction implies, in some sense, rebuilding, possibly after a partial demolition: construction means that something new is being built for the first time or something is being added on to a pre-existing structure.[67] Mere refurbishment may not suffice, therefore. Moreover, the demolition, reconstruction or works must, under the LTA 1954, be carried out on the holding itself. As Ross points out, this may (unsatisfactorily) make it difficult to establish the ground if the tenancy is of part of a building and, whilst substantial works are being carried out to the building as a whole, only trivial works are required on this holding.[68] At the end of the day, it is always a question of fact and degree:

> ... cases on the meaning of 'demolish' or 'reconstruct' for the purposes of section 30(1)(f) of the 1954 Act turn on the particular facts. In each case the relevant questions are: (i) what are the physical features of the property comprised in the tenancy; (ii) what, amongst those features, is capable of being demolished and reconstructed; (iii) is what is being done to those features which are capable of being demolished and reconstructed, taken as a whole, properly to be described as demolition or reconstruction of those features or a substantial part of them?[69]

---

[61] [1959] AC 20 (HL).

[62] [1950] 2 KB 237 (CA) 254.

[63] *DAF Motoring Centre (Gosport) Ltd v Hatfield and Wheeler Ltd* [1982] 2 EGLR 59 (CA).

[64] *Gregson v Cyril Lord* [1963] 1 WLR 41 (CA). For a case with no reasonable prospect (and thus the ground not made out) see *Coppen v Bruce-Smith* (1988) 77 P & CR 239 (CA).

[65] *Reohorn v Barry Corporation* [1956] 2 All ER 742 (CA), *Spook Erection Ltd v British Railways Board* [1988] 1 EGLR 76 (CA).

[66] *Turner v Wandsworth LBC* (1995) 69 P & CR 433 (CA).

[67] *Cook v Mott* (1961) 178 EG 637 (CA).

[68] M Ross, *Commercial Leases* (London, Butterworths, 1998) P [299] n 2.

[69] *Pumperninks of Piccadilly Ltd v Land Securities plc* [2002] EWCA Civ 621, [2002] Ch 332 [86].

In the case of an 'eggshell tenancy', where only the internal skin of a building is let, the ground has been held to be satisfied even though only internal partitions which are not load-bearing will be demolished.[70]

This is one of the heads for which compensation is available to the tenant in recognition of the loss of goodwill and expense of moving (see 21.8 below).

21.7.3.3 The Landlord's Own Need To Occupy the Property

Landlord and Tenant Act 1954 section 30

(1) The grounds on which a landlord may oppose an application … are …

(g) subject as hereinafter provided, that on the termination of the current tenancy the landlord intends to occupy the holding for the purposes, or partly for the purposes, of a business to be carried on by him therein, or as his residence.

Paragraph (g) requires that the landlord has an intention to occupy the premises to carry on a business or to reside there. Intention here bears the same meaning as under paragraph (f), that is, that there is not only a desire to occupy, but that there is a reasonable likelihood that it will come to fruition in the form of the landlord carrying on a business or, in the alternative, residing there. Again, intention must be established at the time of the hearing. Letting a manager run the business may be sufficient: in *Skeet v Powell-Sneddon* the ground was held satisfied where the landlord planned to run the business in partnership with her husband and daughter, even though the effective management would be by her husband,[71] but in *Zafiris v Liu* the Court of Appeal upheld the judge's refusal to find ground (g) satisfied when the property was to be run as a Chinese restaurant by the landlord's wife.[72] A business carried on by a company in which the landlord has a controlling interest or, where the landlord is a company, a business carried on by a person with a controlling interest in the company is enough to satisfy this ground.[73] By section 42(3), where the landlord is member of a group of companies, intended occupation by any other member of that group will also satisfy (g).

Following *Willis v Association of the Universities of the British Commonwealth*, the landlord must probably intend to occupy for more than a *de minimis* period, but six months might suffice.[74]

The landlord cannot rely on ground (g) where it has recently acquired its interest. Sub-section (2) prevents the landlord from using paragraph (g) to oppose renewal where his interest was created or was purchased by him within the five years preceding the termination of the current business tenancy.[75] A similar limitation applies where the person planning to use the property has acquired its controlling interest in the landlord in the last five years.[76] Thus, the landlord who purchases the reversion within the last five years of the tenancy cannot justify non-renewal on the basis that he wishes to occupy the premises to

---

[70] *Ivorygrove Ltd v Global Grange Ltd* [2003] EWHC 1409 (Ch), [2003] 1 WLR 2090. See also *Pumerpninks Ltd v Land Securities plc* [2002] EWCA Civ 621, [2002] Ch 332.

[71] [1988] 2 EGLR 112 (CA).

[72] [2005] EWCA Civ 1698 (the landlord had argued that the two of them planned to run it as a partnership).

[73] Landlord and Tenant Act 1954 s 30(1A), (1B).

[74] [1965] 1 QB 140 (CA) 152.

[75] *Artemiou v Procopiou* [1966] 1 QB 878 (CA).

[76] Landlord and Tenant Act 1954 s 30(2A).

carry on his own business. This provision may be unduly restrictive for the good of business. Where there is a takeover of a business, the purchaser may intend to expand the business in to the premises let, but would not be able to oppose renewal under section 30(2).

Compensation for disturbance is available to a tenant where renewal is opposed on this ground (see 21.8 below).

21.8 Compensation for Non-renewal

If the tenancy is not renewed, section 37 provides that the tenant will be entitled to compensation for disturbance on quitting[77] unless the landlord successfully opposed the grant of a new tenancy on the grounds of tenant default or the offer of suitable alternative accommodation. Lord Reid observed in *Cramas Properties v Connaught Fur*, that 'the Act of 1954 for the first time introduced for business what is in effect compensation for disturbance'.[78]

The level of compensation is not, however, linked to the tenant's own disturbance. The reasons for this are set out in the Government Report of 1953:

> 48. [Compensation] based on disturbance or the totality of the loss which the tenant might conceivably attribute to his failure to obtain a renewal (including removal expenses and potential diminution of trading profits in alternative premises) would be very difficult to evaluate justly, would probably lead to much uncertainty and litigation, and would sometimes be an inequitably onerous burden on the landlord.
>
> 50. As for the amount of compensation, it is highly desirable to provide a formula which is both simple and certain in its operation, so that both parties know that, when compensation becomes payable, there need be no dispute about the amount due under statute; it is also an advantage if, when the lease is entered into, both parties know, at any rate within broad limits, what is the probable order of magnitude of any compensation which may become due on the expiry of the lease … The Government therefore propose that the compensation, where payable, should be a sum equal to the rateable value of the premises in question where the tenant has been in occupation for not more than 14 years, and to a sum equal to twice that value when the tenant has been in occupation for more than 14 years.[79]

Although the details are more complex than this quotation suggests, the principle is that the level of compensation is based on the rateable value of the premises and, if the tenant and any predecessor in business have been in occupation throughout the previous fourteen years, the level of compensation is doubled. Following the RRO 2003 it is now also possible for the tenant to get compensation if he is induced not to apply to court, or to withdraw an application for renewal, because of a misrepresentation.[80] In *Sun Life Assurance plc v Thales Tracs Ltd* the tenant put in a section 26 notice even though it had no intention of entering a

---

[77] By an amendment made to s 37 in 1969 it was made clear that the tenant does not have to 'lose' in court in order to be entitled to compensation; a tenant who does not go to court is still entitled to compensation (an amendment designed to avoid unnecessary and cumbersome court applications): *Sight & Sound Education Ltd v Books etc Ltd* [1999] 3 EGLR 45 (Ch).

[78] [1965] 1 WLR 892 (HL) 898.

[79] Government Policy on Leasehold Property in England and Wales (Cmd 8713, 1953).

[80] Landlord and Tenant Act 1954 s 37A.

new lease (as it had bought alternative premises) so that it could preserve its entitlement to compensation; the Court of Appeal held the tenant's motive behind a section 26 notice is irrelevant, and the tenant was entitled to compensation.[81]

If the tenant has occupied the premises for the purposes of his business 'during the whole of the five years immediately preceding the date on which the tenant … is to quit the holding' (or, if there has been a change of occupier within those five years, he and his predecessor have so used the premises), section 38(2) provides that any agreement which purports to exclude or reduce the compensation payable under section 37 will be void. For this prohibition on contracting out of compensation to bite, occupation does not have to be constant and continue until the bitter end of the tenancy. In *Bacchiocchi v Academic Agency*, the tenancy ended on 11 August, but the tenant moved out (after a slight misunderstanding) on 23 July, finally clearing out of the premises on 29 July.[82] In the lease the tenant had contracted out of the right to compensation under section 37. If section 38(2) applied, this clause would be ineffective and the tenant would be entitled to £15,030 under the statutory provisions. The Court of Appeal held that the 12 day period during which the property was empty did not stop the occupation falling within section 38(2):

> … whenever business premises are empty for only a short period, whether mid-term or before or after trading at either end of the lease, I would be disinclined to find that the business occupancy has ceased (or not started) for that period provided always that during it there exists no rival for the role of business occupant and that the premises are not being used for some other, non-business purpose … [This recognises] that the tenant's business interests will not invariably require permanent physical possession throughout the whole term of the lease and he ought not to have to resort to devices like storage of goods or token visits to satisfy the statutory requirements of continuing occupation. If, of course, premises are left vacant for a matter of months, the court would be ready to conclude that the thread of continuity has been broken.[83]

Nonetheless, the question of when occupation ends and the tenant thereby becomes disentitled to compensation is sometimes difficult. In *Sight & Sound Education Ltd v Books etc Ltd* the landlord had served a section 25 notice ending the tenancy on 25 February 1998.[84] The tenant had been in the property for more than 14 years and was seeking to be paid twice the rateable value as compensation. It vacated the property in September 1997, shortly before the contractual end date for the tenancy. Applying the *Esselte* decision, moving out meant that the tenancy did in fact end in September. The difficulty for the tenant was that in order to be entitled to the higher rate of compensation section 37 (3) requires the tenant to have occupied the property 'during the whole of the 14 years immediately preceding the termination of the current tenancy' and section 37(7) defines the current tenancy for these purposes as 'the date of termination' specified in the landlord's section 25 notice or the date for the beginning of the new tenancy in a section 26 notice (here, February). Of course, this is quite different from *Bacchiocchi v Academic Agency* in which what was in issue was a few days at the end of the tenancy. The argument for the tenant was

---

[81] [2001] EWCA Civ 704, [2002] 1 WLR 1562.
[82] [1998] 1 WLR 1313 (CA).
[83] *Bacchiocchi v Academic Agency Ltd* [1998] 1 WLR 1313 (CA) 1322.
[84] [1999] 3 EGLR 45 (Ch).

that the legislative intention was that tenants should be able to organise their affairs sensibly, and where the tenant has been in occupation for 14 years the tenant ought to get its compensation. Nonetheless, although recognising the consequences could be awkward for the tenant (requiring it to stay to get its compensation) the judge considered that the wording was clear and the tenant was not entitled to the compensation.

In addition to compensation under the LTA 1954, the tenant of business premises may be entitled to compensation for improvements under the 1927 Landlord and Tenant Act, Part I. This is discussed in chapter 12.

21.9 The Terms of the New Tenancy

If the landlord does not oppose a new lease or if the court does not uphold the landlord's ground(s) of opposition, the tenant is entitled to a new lease. In practice, the terms of the new lease will usually be agreed between the parties, and by section 28 the new lease takes effect from the date agreed.

Failing agreement, the court determines the terms of the new tenancy, in accordance with section 35 of the LTA 1954, having regard to the terms of the current tenancy and all relevant circumstances:

Section 35

(1) The terms of a tenancy granted by order of the court under this Part of this Act (other than terms as to the duration thereof and as to the rent payable thereunder), including, where different persons own interests which fulfil the conditions specified in section 44(1) of this Act in different parts of it, terms as to the apportionment of the rent, shall be such as may be agreed between the landlord and the tenant or as, in default of such agreement, may be determined by the court; and in determining those terms the court shall have regard to the terms of the current tenancy and to all relevant circumstances.

(2) In subsection (1) of this section the reference to all relevant circumstances includes (without prejudice to the generality of that reference) a reference to the operation of the provisions of the Landlord and Tenant (Covenants) Act 1995.

This gives the court a very wide discretion. As Ross notes, the court can take account of the duration of the old lease, the length of time that the tenant has occupied for under the old rent, the tenant's business needs and personal circumstances, the landlord's own intentions as to occupation and the relative hardship between the parties.[85]

There are specific provisions in relation to the duration and rent. The duration of the new lease will be such as the court considers reasonable in all the circumstances, up to a maximum of fifteen years:

Section 33

Where on an application under this Part of this Act the court makes an order for the grant of a new tenancy, the new tenancy shall be such tenancy as may be agreed between the landlord and the tenant, or, in default of such an agreement, shall be such a tenancy as may be determined by the court to be reasonable in all the circumstances, being, if it is a tenancy for a

---

[85] M Ross, *Commercial Leases* (London, Butterworths, 1998) P [475].

term of years certain, a tenancy for a term not exceeding fifteen years,[86] and shall begin on the coming to an end of the current tenancy.

By consent, the court can order a longer term such as the twenty year term ordered in *Janes (Gowns) Ltd v Harlow Development Corporation.*[87]

The rent for the new tenancy is to be based on open market rental values as set out in section 34:

Section 34

(1) The rent payable under a tenancy granted by order of the court under this Part of this Act shall be such as may be agreed between the landlord and the tenant or as, in default of such agreement, may be determined by the court to be that at which, having regard to the terms of the tenancy (other than those relating to rent), the holding might reasonably be expected to be let in the open market by a willing lessor, there being disregarded –

(a) any effect on rent of the fact that the tenant has or his predecessors in title have been in occupation of the holding,

(b) any goodwill attached to the holding by reason of the carrying on thereat of the business of the tenant (whether by him or by a predecessor of his in that business),

(c) any effect on rent of an improvement to which this paragraph applies,

(d) in the case of a holding comprising licensed premises, any addition to its value attributable to the licence, if it appears to the court that having regard to the terms of the current tenancy and any other relevant circumstances the benefit of the licence belongs to the tenant.

(2) Paragraph (c) of the foregoing subsection applies to any improvement carried out by a person who at the time it was carried out was the tenant, but only if it was carried out otherwise than in pursuance of an obligation to his immediate landlord, and either it was carried out during the current tenancy or the following conditions are satisfied, that is to say, –

(a) that it was completed not more than twenty-one years before the application to the court was made; and

(b) that the holding or any part of it affected by the improvement has at all times since the completion of the improvement been comprised in tenancies of the description specified in section 23(1) of this Act; and

(c) that at the termination of each of those tenancies the tenant did not quit.

...

(3) Where the rent is determined by the court the court may, if it thinks fit, further determine that the terms of the tenancy shall include such provision for varying the rent as may be specified in the determination.

(4) It is hereby declared that the matters which are to be taken into account by the court in determining the rent include any effect on rent of the operation of the provisions of the Landlord and Tenant (Covenants) Act 1995.

The intention of section 34 is that the court should decide what is the open market rent for the particular premises, but disregard factors that are personal to the tenant that would inflate that figure. So, for example, the fact that the particular tenant already in occupation would pay more than other tenants in order to avoid being disturbed and losing the goodwill that it has

---

[86] This was increased from 14 by RRO 2003 to reflect modern rent review patterns.

[87] (1979) 253 EG 799 (Ch).

built up there would be ignored. It is also possible for the court to include a rent review clause in the new lease – until this was permitted by an amendment in 1969, the tendency was for courts to grant renewals only for short terms in order to avoid hardship to the landlords.

In the usual case, the tenant is entitled to a new tenancy only of that part of the property that was being occupied for its business:

Section 32

(1) Subject to the following provisions of this section, an order under section twenty-nine of this Act for the grant of a new tenancy shall be an order for the grant of a new tenancy of the holding; and in the absence of agreement between the landlord and the tenant as to the property which constitutes the holding the court shall in the order designate that property by reference to the circumstances existing at the date of the order.

What constitutes 'the holding' is set out in section 23:

Section 23

(3) In the following provisions of this Part of this Act the expression 'the holding', in relation to a tenancy to which this Part of this Act applies, means the property comprised in the tenancy, there being excluded any part thereof which is occupied neither by the tenant nor by a person employed by the tenant and so employed for the purposes of a business by reason of which the tenancy is one to which this Part of this Act applies.

There are some exceptions to this basic rule, for example, where the tenant is willing to accept a tenancy of part only in order to accommodate works access needed by the landlord.

Where the holding is only part of the property in the tenancy, the landlord may require the tenant to take a new tenancy of the whole:

Section 32

(2) The foregoing provisions of this section shall not apply in a case where the property comprised in the current tenancy includes other property besides the holding and the landlord requires any new tenancy ordered to be granted under section twenty-nine of this Act to be a tenancy of the whole of the property comprised in the current tenancy; but in any such case –

(a) any order under the said section twenty-nine for the grant of a new tenancy shall be an order for the grant of a new tenancy of the whole of the property comprised in the current tenancy, and

(b) references in the following provisions of this Part of this Act to the holding shall be construed as references to the whole of that property.

Where the tenancy includes other rights, such as rights of way, these rights will also be included in the new tenancy:

Section 32

(3) Where the current tenancy includes rights enjoyed by the tenant in connection with the holding, those rights shall be included in a tenancy ordered to be granted under section twenty-nine of this Act except as otherwise agreed between the landlord and the tenant or, in default of such agreement, determined by the court.

In *Re No 1 Albemarle Street* Upjohn J held that this did not apply to a licence within the lease for the tenant to put up advertising hoardings on the outside of the building which contained the demised premises, on the basis that this right to exhibit signs could not be described as part of the demised premises or as part of the holding.[88] Nonetheless, he held that he had a discretion to include such a term using the wider powers under section 35 (and did so). More recently, in *G Orlik (Meat Products) Ltd v Hastings and Thanet BS* the Court of Appeal refused to include a term permitting the tenant to park cars on the landlord's land.[89] This case is quite different from *Re No 1 Albemarle Street* as the tenant had failed to establish that it already had such a right exercisable against the current landlord (the disputed right had been agreed with a previous landlord).

Apart from these specific provisions, the courts, as required by section 35, determine the terms by reference to the current tenancy and all the relevant circumstances.

In deciding the new terms the courts have been anxious not to allow the tenant's business interests to be worsened. This is illustrated in *Gold v Brighton Corporation*, where the landlord was seeking on renewal to prevent the tenant from selling second-hand clothes without the landlord's consent.[90] The Court of Appeal refused this as it would damage the tenant's existing business. According to Denning LJ:

> The Landlord and Tenant Act 1954 plainly intends to protect the tenant in respect of his business … In as much as the tenant is to be protected in respect of his business, the terms of the new tenancy should be such as to enable him to carry on his business as it is. They should not prevent him from carrying on an important part of it. At any rate, if he is to be prevented from using the premises in the future in a way in which he has used them in the past, it is for the landlord to justify the restriction and there ought to be strong and cogent evidence for this purpose.[91]

As for the tenant's argument that the user clause should be the same as that in the former lease (wider than the tenant's actual business), Denning LJ rejected this, stating:

> The object of the Act is to protect a tenant in respect of his business, and not to put a saleable asset into his hands.[92]

A more difficult and controversial issue has been the extent to which the landlord should be able to 'modernise' the lease, where the changes have no direct effect upon the tenant's business. The aim of the legislation is not to protect the tenant from market forces, but to protect the tenant's business. As has been seen, the form of commercial leases changes over time. The question is the extent to which on renewal a landlord (or tenant) can seek changes to the original tenancy in order to bring the lease into conformity with modern letting practices.

This arose in *O'May v City of London Real Property Co Ltd*, where the landlord argued that the new lease should be a 'clear lease'.[93] Under the old tenancy, the landlord bore the cost of servicing the building. The landlord's proposal was that the fixed rental be reduced in return for the tenant accepting the risk of fluctuation in service charge costs. The tenant preferred to have a higher, but certain, fixed rent. Under both proposals the landlord would be responsible for carrying out maintenance, repairs and running the building, but under

---

[88] [1959] Ch 531 (Ch) 539.
[89] (1974) 29 P & CR 126 (CA).
[90] [1956] 3 All ER 442 (CA).
[91] [1956] 3 All ER 442 (CA) 443.
[92] [1956] 3 All ER 442 (CA) 444.
[93] [1983] 2 AC 726 (HL).

the clear lease proposal the cost of these services would be borne by the tenant. If the landlord succeeded, and the leases of all tenants in the building were similarly revised, the value of the landlord's interest in the building would rise by between £1 million and £2 million. Lord Hailsham stated the principle upon which the court was to determine the new terms:

> I do believe that the court must begin by considering the terms of the current tenancy, that the burden of persuading the court to impose a change in those terms against the will of either party must rest on the party proposing the change, and that the change proposed must, in the circumstances of the case, be fair and reasonable, and should take into account, amongst other things, the comparatively weak negotiating position of a sitting tenant requiring renewal, particularly in conditions of scarcity, and the general purpose of the Act which is to protect the business interests of the tenant so far as they are affected … by the approaching termination of the current lease, in particular as regards his security of tenure …
>
> There must, in my view, be a good reason based in the absence of agreement on essential fairness for the court to impose a new term not in the current lease by either party on the other against his will.[94]

This did not, however, mean that it would never be possible to update a lease:

> The words 'have regard to' [in section 35] … impose an onus upon a party seeking to introduce new, or substituted, or modified terms, to justify the change, with reasons appearing sufficient to the court … If such reasons are shown, then the court … may consider giving effect to them: there is certainly no intention … to freeze, or … to 'petrify' the terms of the lease. In some cases, especially where the lease is an old one, many of its terms will be out of date, or unsuitable in relation to the new term to be granted.[95]

On the facts, the landlord was unable to obtain a 'clear lease'. Indeed, the remarks of Lord Wilberforce, while directed to the issue of renewal, do seem to challenge more widely the fairness of the 'net rent' or clear concept of institutional leases:

> The character of the two parties' interests in the land – the landlord's an indefinite one by freehold, the tenants' a limited one over a comparatively short period, even though capable of renewal if the tenant so wishes, is such as to call for the assumption of long term risks by the former … Transference of these rights to the leaseholders, accompanied, as is inevitable, by separation of control, creates a risk disproportionate to their interest. If it is reasonable for the landlord to wish to get rid of these risks in exchange for a fixed payment (reduction in rent) it must be equally, or indeed more, reasonable for the tenants to wish, against receipt of that reduction, to avoid assuming it. The tenants are being asked to bear all the risks of property management, a business which they have not chosen, being management by others in the interests of those others.[96]

The particular lease at issue in *O'May* was for only five years, as against what was then the institutional norm of 25 years; this may explain the outcome in the particular case, the shortness of the lease making it inappropriate for the tenant to bear an unpredictable liability for services. The wider comments are, however, especially pertinent for the contemporary commercial property market where shorter leases are usual.

---

[94] [1983] 2 AC 726 (HL) 740–1.
[95] [1983] 2 AC 726 (HL) 747 (Lord Wilberforce).
[96] [1983] 2 AC 726 (HL) 749.

The Landlord and Tenant (Covenants) Act 1995 has also had an impact on letting practices, and section 35(2) of the LTA 1954 specifically refers to this as one of the relevant circumstances that the court should take account of in settling the terms of the new tenancy. The first case to consider its impact on the alienation clause on renewal was *Wallis Fashion Group Ltd v CGU Life Assurance Ltd*.[97] The original tenancy contained an alienation clause providing that the landlord's consent was required on assignment and requiring an assignee to enter into a direct covenant with the landlord to undertake all leasehold covenants for the remainder of the term. The lease fell for renewal after the 1995 Act came into effect. Under the 1995 Act a tenant is released from liability on assignment, but the landlord may require the outgoing tenant to enter into an authorised guarantee agreement (AGA) guaranteeing the performance of the immediate assignee's covenants (see chapter 19). The effect of the 1995 Act was that it was not possible to include the original alienation covenant in the new tenancy because it imposed liability on an assignee for the remainder of the term. The landlord sought an alienation covenant that provided that an AGA would automatically be required on assignment; the tenant argued that the clause should provide that an AGA could be required only 'if reasonable'. The research conducted into the operation of the 2002 Code of Practice on Commercial Leases[98] has revealed that it is 'almost universal' to require an AGA on assignment,[99] and the landlord's proposed covenant therefore more closely reflects both modern letting practices and the original lease. Nonetheless, Neuberger J said that the clause should be qualified, to require an AGA only if reasonable. Although at the time of the case the evidence about AGAs being almost standard was not available, Neuberger J would have been aware of this being a usual letting practice. The landlord had argued not only that an automatic AGA was closer to the original lease but also that a 'reasonableness' condition might provoke disputes (an argument rightly dismissed by Neuberger J) and would promote better estate management as other leases in the shopping centre contained similar alienation clauses providing for automatic AGAs. Instead of deferring to these arguments and normal letting practice, Neuberger J drew on the intention underlying the 1995 Act:

> The 1995 Act represents a sea change in the law relating to a tenant's liability after he assigns the lease, and it also alters the law relating to the landlord's power to impose terms on assigning the lease. It does not merely represent a sea change in what had been common practice, but in what a landlord can lawfully require, both in terms of what is to be included in the lease initially and what he can demand on an assignment.[100]

The exercise of the section 35 discretion should not run contrary to the apparent intention of the legislation.

The *Wallis Fashion* case reveals the difficulties that judges face in determining the terms of renewed leases. If the aim of the Act is to provide the tenant with security without otherwise protecting him from market forces, it seems to follow that the landlord should be

---

[97] [2000] 2 EGLR 49 (Ch). M Haley, 'Business Tenancies: Renewal and Authorised Guarantee Agreements' [2000] *Conv* 566.

[98] RICS Policy Unit, *A Code of Practice for Commercial Leases in England and Wales* 2nd edn (2002).

[99] N Crosby, C Hughes and S Murdoch, 'Monitoring the 2002 Code of Practice for Commercial Leases' (ODPM, March 2005) 303.

[100] [2000] 2 EGLR 49 (Ch) 52.

able to obtain a lease conforming with contemporary market practice. This would probably have led to a different outcome in the *Wallis Fashion* case; on the other hand, the aim of the 1995 Act was to provide that tenants should be released from liability on assignment.

Sections 32–35 have been criticised by Haley as leaving too much freedom to the judges to determine the new terms:

> The current provisions are too uncertain, poorly drafted and lack sufficient detail. The inconvenient absence of guidance, coupled with the high degree of discretion foisted upon the courts, produces a system that defies coherency and predictability.[101]

There is little evidence, however, to support that this view is shared within the business community and, on the whole, the Act is felt to be satisfactory.

---

[101] M Haley, 'Business tenancies and interventionism: the relegation of policy?' (1993) 13 *LS* 225, 240.

PART SEVEN
ENDING THE RELATIONSHIP

This part of the book looks at the ways in which the landlord and tenant relationship can be brought to an end. These fall into three broad categories.

The first is when the lease terminates at the end of its term. This can be either through non-renewal of a periodic tenancy or effluxion of time in the case of a fixed term. There may be a limited amount of security given in the form of requiring, for example, minimum notice periods to be given for periodic tenancies. The 'stronger' statutory rights to security of tenure that protected tenants have were discussed in Part Six. Chapter 22 looks at the methods of ending a lease where there is no such statutory security of tenure. Chapter 23 then looks at the controls that exist to discourage landlords from 'taking the law into their own hands' and getting rid of tenants without following due process.

The second kind of case is when the lease is ended early. This can be either consensual (for example, by an agreement to surrender or by the exercise a contractual break clause) or the result of breach by one of the parties. It is common for there to be a right to forfeit on tenant default, and both common law and statute regulate the exercise of this right to ensure that it is not abused and that the tenant's interests are sufficiently protected. The various ways by which a lease can be ended early are discussed in chapter 24.

Finally, the lease may end because it is transformed into a different relationship. This could occur through the exercise of a contractual right (such as the exercise of a tenant's option to buy the freehold) or of a statutory right (such as the Right to Buy or the enfranchisement laws). Chapter 25 explores the latter; the various statutory rights that have been given to residential tenants and leaseholders to buy the freehold (or a longer lease).

22

ENDING A LEASE

22.1   Introduction
22.2   Periodic tenancies
22.3   Fixed term leases
22.4   Statutory requirements for residential tenants
22.5   Other landlord remedies if the tenant refuses to leave

22.1 Introduction

This chapter discusses the rules relating to the termination of leases at the end of the term. The basic position at common law is that a periodic tenancy is ended by serving a notice to quit, and a fixed term lease comes to an end by the expiry of time. The common law rules about serving notice have, in the residential sector, been augmented by statutory rules that prescribe the amount of notice that must be given. In some situations, if the tenant is in breach of the tenancy, the landlord may wish to end the tenancy early; there are special rules that then apply and these are discussed in chapter 24. Further, as already seen, tenancies may come within a statutory scheme that gives rights to tenants to remain in the property even after the contractual term has come to an end. This chapter looks at the more straightforward situation of the lease coming to an end.

22.2 Periodic Tenancies

22.2.1 The Notice to Quit

At common law, a periodic tenancy is ended by serving a notice to quit. The length of notice needed depends upon the period of the tenancy (and any relevant statutory provisions). Ignoring statutory requirements, the length of notice required will usually be the period of the tenancy, given so as to expire at the end of a completed period.[1] So, for example, a quarterly tenancy will be ended by one quarter's notice, ending at the end of a completed quarter. Yearly tenancies are treated differently, requiring only a half year's notice, but this must end at the end of a completed year. So, for example, if a lease ends on 31 December then

---

[1] But see E Cooke, 'Notices to Quit for the Monthly Tenant' [1992] *Conv* 263 where it is argued that a lunar month should suffice for a monthly tenancy even though the period of the tenancy is a calendar month.

unless notice is served before 1 July in any year, the lease will run until the end of the current calendar year and the whole of the following year. These notice provisions can be varied by contract.

22.2.1.1 *Joint Tenancies and Notice to Quit*

In the case of a joint periodic tenancy, the House of Lords confirmed in *Hammersmith and Fulham LBC v Monk* that an effective notice to quit can be served by only one of the joint tenants.[2] The explanation for this is that a periodic tenancy is a contract for a period that is constantly being renewed. The service of a notice to quit does not end the tenancy as such, but indicates that the tenant does not wish to renew the tenancy. In order to renew a contract, all contracting parties need to consent, but the service of notice shows that one of the parties is not willing to contract again.

In *Hounslow LBC v Pilling* one of two joint weekly tenants served a notice to quit on the local authority landlord to take immediate effect.[3] This was construed by the Court of Appeal as being not the purported exercise of a notice to quit, but the operation of a break clause (because it purported to operate immediately and not on the expiry of a notice period). As such, unlike in *Hammersmith and Fulham LBC v Monk*,[4] the issue was not non-renewal but early termination, which could not be effective unless both joint tenants were party to the notice.

22.2.1.2 *Relationship Breakdown*

The result in *Hammersmith v Monk,* while entirely defensible doctrinally, has created problems in the social sector on relationship breakdown. In many cases to come before the courts, the female partner has left the property formerly occupied by a couple, and has served a notice to quit to end the tenancy. Although the facts vary between the cases, she is often encouraged to do this by the local authority so that she can be re-housed. The remaining occupier is usually not told about the notice to quit, and not given any opportunity to make representations as to why he should be able to stay in the house. The notice to quit ends his right to remain. This is so both if his ex-partner was a sole tenant (as in *Newham LBC v Kibata*)[5] and, by operation of the rule in *Hammersmith v Monk*, if they were joint tenants (as in *Harrow LBC v Qazi*,[6] and the joint appeals of *Bradney v Birmingham CC* and *Birmingham CC v McCann*).[7]

Notwithstanding ingenious arguments that have been raised for the remaining joint tenant to stay in possession, such a notice has always been held to be effective. In *Crawley BC v Ure*,[8] it was argued that by serving the notice without consulting her husband, the wife had acted in breach of trust and that the council had assisted in this; the Court of Appeal did not, however, find that there had been a breach of trust. In *Harrow v Johnstone*,[9] the

---

[2] *Hammersmith and Fulham LBC v Monk* [1992] 1 AC 478 (HL); and see ch 2.
[3] [1993] 1 WLR 1242 (CA).
[4] [1992] 1 AC 478 (HL).
[5] [2003] EWCA Civ 1785.
[6] [2003] UKHL 43, [2004] 1 AC 983.
[7] [2003] EWCA Civ 1783.
[8] [1996] QB 13 (CA).
[9] *Harrow London BC v Johnstone* [1997] 1 WLR 459 (HL).

husband had obtained an anti-molestation order against his wife preventing her, inter alia, from excluding him from their council home. When he was later informed that his wife had served a notice to quit on the local authority landlord, he argued that the notice violated this injunction and that the council, by encouraging her, had aided and abetted the breach. The House of Lords found that the injunction was to do with enabling the husband to exercise his existing rights as a joint tenant and avoid molestation; it was not to do with keeping those rights in being. Nor did the House of Lords accept the argument that the council had committed contempt. Yet a further argument was raised in *Newlon Housing Trust v Alsulaimen*,[10] when the husband sought to resist a possession application on the ground that he proposed to make an application under the Matrimonial Causes Act 1973, section 24 for a transfer of the tenancy. He could only do this if the notice to quit that the wife had served counted as a 'reviewable disposition' within section 37 of that Act but Lord Hoffman, with whom the other Law Lords agreed, stated that there had not been a disposition of property by the wife.[11]

The local authority's involvement, in procuring the service of the notice to quit and bringing possession proceedings against the remaining occupier, has also been challenged in public law, again without success. In the conjoined appeal in *Bradney v Birmingham CC* Mummery LJ commented that the council had acted within its powers and there was no breach of public law duties.[12] More specific public law points were argued when the *McCann* case returned to the Administrative court as *McCann v Birmingham CC*, but again without success.[13]

In *Harrow LBC v Qazi* Mr Qazi opposed the local authority's possession proceedings on the grounds that this violated his Article 8 of the European Convention for the Protection of Human Rights and Fundamental Freedoms (ECHR) right to respect for the home.[14] The fact that Mr Qazi lost shows that only in exceptional circumstances will it be possible to mount a successful human rights challenge when the local authority has, in property law, the right to possess.[15] (Human rights arguments are also discussed below in the context of the local authority's role in encouraging the departing joint tenant to serve a notice to quit.)

The deserted occupier is, therefore, left in a vulnerable position as a result of these cases. It may well be that the dispossessed occupier in turn becomes an applicant for housing, but this will only help him if he has priority under the homelessness legislation. The nub of the problem here is not that the local authority's right to possession cannot be questioned following *Qazi*, but that the notice to quit can be used in this way. The departing tenant

---

[10] [1999] AC 313 (HL).

[11] '[A] life interest in a property is an item of property with a temporal dimension, ceasing to exist on the death of the tenant for life. When that event happens, no property passes from the tenant for life to the remainderman. The latter's interest falls into possession but he becomes entitled to possession by virtue of his own interest and not by having acquired that of the tenant for life. The same is true when a lease for a term of years terminates by effluxion of time. The tenant does not dispose of his interest. At the moment when it expires, he has no property of which he can dispose. It ceases to exist and the landlord's reversion falls into possession': *Newlon Housing Trust v Alsulaimen* [1999] AC 313 (HL) 317.

[12] [2003] EWCA Civ 1783 [28] and [30]. The point had not, however, been argued in public law terms,

[13] [2004] EWHC 2156 (Admin).

[14] *Harrow LBC v Qazi* [2003] UKHL 43, [2004] 1 AC 983.

[15] [2003] UKHL 43, [2004] 1 AC 983. Although the majority of the House of Lords held that Art 8 would never prevail in this situation, the impact of *Kay v Lambeth LBC; Leeds CC v Price* [2006] UKHL 10, [2006] 2 AC 465 is that this now needs to be read as 'hardly ever': see ch 10.

does not usually understand the impact of serving the notice. In *Bradney*, for example, the female partner was asked by the council to sign a notice to quit; on her part she:

> ... wished to bring her own personal liability under the tenancy to an end, while safeguarding the position of [her former partner] as a tenant.[16]

In *McCann* the wife signed the notice to quit at the council's instigation but without understanding what it meant for Mr McCann, and she later tried – ineffectually – to retract or cancel the notice.

It is understandable that a local authority may seek to re-house the applicant in a smaller unit and recover an under-occupied family home, but to do so without regard to the position of the dispossessed occupier is at odds with the philosophy of social housing and respect for human rights. The reality is that the local authority is using the notice to quit in order to get around the security of tenure legislation. Unless the tenancy is ended, the local authority would only be able to recover the former family home on proof of a ground for possession and, usually, proof of 'reasonableness'. Instead, with the tenancy ended by notice, possession can be recovered without any consideration of factors that might make the remaining occupier's case for staying quite reasonable; as in *Qazi* where Mr Qazi had lived in the property for some time and there was no under-occupation as he now lived in it with his new wife and children. In addition, the remaining occupier is not usually told or forewarned in any way. If he knew of the plan then he could apply to have the tenancy transferred to him under the Family Law Act 1996, section 53 and Schedule 7 (although practically speaking, the timing of this would be difficult).[17] If there is a sole tenancy and the couple are married (as in *Kibata*) there may be a right to assign the tenancy under the Housing Act 1985, section 91(3). Such concerns clearly troubled the first instance judge in *Kibata* as he denied the possession action on the basis that the council had not acted fairly towards Mr Kibata.

It must be questionable whether the housing authority, by encouraging the departing joint tenant to serve a notice to quit without giving full consideration to the situation of the remaining joint tenant, is showing respect for the occupier's right to respect for his home under Article 8 of the ECHR. This is different from the argument rejected in *Qazi* because it takes into account the local authority's role as an allocator of public housing and focuses on the local authority's involvement at the earlier stage of procuring the notice to quit, rather than on property law rights once the tenancy has ended.[18] Nevertheless, an argument along these lines was unsuccessful in *Ure v United Kingdom*.[19] The husband claimed that the local authority, by advising his wife to end the tenancy and later bringing possession proceedings, had breached his right to respect for the home under Article 8 of the ECHR and the right to peaceful enjoyment of possessions under Article 1 of the First Protocol. The European

---

[16] [2003] EWCA Civ 1783 [9].

[17] See ch 17.

[18] Loveland makes a similar argument through using the developing concept of legitimate expectation in public law. He has argued that the *Monk* rule should be modified to make it Art 8 compliant through the recognition of a procedural legitimate expectation that would require a local authority landlord to notify the remaining occupier of the notice to quit: I Loveland, 'Rethinking the rule in Hammersmith v Monk from a human rights perspective' [2002] *EHRLR* 327. See also M Iller, 'Leeds CC v Price' (2006) (150) *SJ* 464 and M Iller, 'Joint Tenancies and Notices to Quite after Leeds City Council v Price' (2006) 36 *Family L* 877.

[19] (App No 28027/95) ECHR 27 November 1996.

Commission ruled this claim to be inadmissible on the grounds that any such interference was justifiable. It noted that the nature of a joint tenancy was that there was no right to sole occupation of the premises. Further, there had been no unreasonable treatment on the particular facts:

> ... it does not appear that the manner in which the authorities balanced the various interests involved, such as the interest of the leaving co-tenant, of those in need of accommodation, and of the applicant, was arbitrary or unreasonable. Thus, the applicant's housing need apparently changed as he was not living with his wife and child any more. Moreover, replacement housing accommodation had been obtained for the applicant.[20]

The combined effect of the rejection of the private law, public law and human rights arguments means that there is little possibility of the remaining joint tenant having a good legal ground to challenge the effectiveness of the notice to quit.

Under present law, the position of a remaining occupier is no different whether the basis of sharing the property was as joint tenants or the departing occupier was a single tenant. Either way, a notice to quit brings the tenancy to an end. In practice, however, a remaining (former) joint tenant may now do better when it comes to being able to stay. In 2002, a revised Code of Guidance on the allocation of accommodation was issued to Local Authorities under section 196 of the Housing Act 1996. This provides that:

> 3.9. Where a joint tenant serves notice to quit, housing authorities have a discretion to grant a sole tenancy to the remaining tenant. In exercising this discretion, they should ensure that there are no adverse implications for the good use of their housing stock and their ability to continue to provide for housing need. Where housing authorities decide that they may wish to exercise their discretion in this respect, they must reflect this in their allocation scheme.[21]

There is no information on how this discretion is used in practice. In any event, it must be doubted whether it is really satisfactory to leave such an important issue to the discretion of the local authority. A better approach would be both to impose a duty to inform and advise – both the departing and remaining occupiers – at the earlier stage when the departing joint tenant approaches the local authority for re-housing, as well as requiring the local authority to exercise a discretion along the lines of paragraph 3.9 in the Code of Guidance at the stage of deciding whether to recover possession. This would present a much more 'joined-up' approach to the role of the local authority.[22]

The Law Commission has put forward recommendations to address some of the concerns arising under the present law where one joint tenant serves a notice to quit. Under its proposals, a joint tenant would be able to terminate his or her own interest in the joint tenancy, without bringing the tenancy to an end.[23] Of course, this would mean that the remaining joint tenant is liable to pay the whole rent for the home. If the local authority then wanted to recover possession, it would have to do so in the usual way, which will mean that it has to show a ground for possession.

---

[20] As the applicant did not have a continuing housing need in this case it may be a later court could distinguish it.
[21] ODPM, 'Revision of the Code of Guidance on the Allocation of Accommodation' (November 2002).
[22] S Bright, 'Ending Tenancies by Notice to Quit: The Human Rights Challenge' (2004) 120 *LQR* 398.
[23] Law Commission, 'Renting Homes: The Final Report. Volume 1: Report' (Law Com No 297, 2006) para 2.45. Because the Law Commission scheme is not limited to tenancies, it refers to joint contract-holders rather than joint tenants.

22.3 Fixed Term Leases

Leases for a fixed term generally end by effluxion of time, without any need to serve a notice to quit. There are various ways in which they may be brought to an end earlier, by agreement or following default, but these are discussed in chapter 24. There may also be restrictions that apply on the ending of the lease if the tenancy falls within one of the statutory schemes offering security of tenure; these are discussed in Part Six.

22.4 Statutory Requirements for Residential Tenants

22.4.1 The Requirement of Four Weeks' Notice

By the Protection from Eviction Act 1977, section 5, residential tenants must generally be given at least four weeks' notice. Section 5(1) provides that a notice to quit a dwelling given by a landlord or a tenant shall not be valid unless –

(a) it is in writing and contains such information as may be prescribed, and
(b) it is given not less than 4 weeks before the date on which it is to take effect.

As mentioned earlier, in *Hounslow LBC v Pilling* one of two joint tenants served a notice on the landlord to take effect immediately.[24] The Court of Appeal held that the notice was ineffective, but also said that in any event one joint tenant could not deprive the other of the protection of section 5.

The aim of section 5 is to give the other party time to make alternative arrangements (find a new tenant or a new home). Where it is the landlord/licensor who gives notice, the notice must contain information advising the tenant/licensee that the owner must get a court order before the tenant/licensee can be lawfully evicted and that he may have a right to remain.[25] The section does not apply where no notice to quit is necessary, for example, on the expiry of a fixed term lease.

22.4.1.1 Periodic Licences

Section 5 is not confined to tenancies. Sub-section (1A) applies the same notice requirements to a 'periodic licence to occupy premises as a dwelling'. In *Norris (t/a J Davis & Son) v Checksfield*, Woolf LJ described the periodic licence as 'a new animal'.[26] The Court of Appeal had some difficulty in working out what a periodic licence was, but found that a licence for the period of employment was not periodic, as it did not continue 'for a series of periods until terminated by notice'.[27] This meant that the licence could be ended without notice on the termination of the employment.

---

[24] [1993] 1 WLR 1242 (CA), but on the basis of an earlier authority, *Elsden v Pick* [1980] 1 WLR 898 (CA), the Court of Appeal seemed to accept the principle that if *all* parties agreed, a shorter notice period could be accepted but not agreed to in advance.

[25] Notices to Quit etc (Prescribed Information) Regulations 1988 SI 1988/2201.

[26] [1991] 1 WLR 1241 (CA) 1246.

[27] Unhindered by the problems of terms for uncertain periods that apply to leases, see *Prudential Co Ltd v London Residuary Body* [1992] 2 AC 386 (HL).

22.4.1.2 Exclusions from Section 5

Section 5 does not apply to 'excluded' tenancies or licences entered into on or after 15 January 1989. Excluded tenancies and licences are defined in section 3A of the Act:

(a)   Resident landlord lettings. It excludes tenancies and licences which involve sharing accommodation with the landlord/licensor and which is the landlord's/licensor's only or principal home.[28] Sub-section (3) extends the resident landlord exception to sharing with a member of the landlord's/licensor's family so long as the landlord/licensor has his only or principal home in the same building (provided the building is not a purpose-built block of flats). This resident landlord exception, introduced in 1988, was part of the government's programme of removing controls on resident landlords to encourage letting, and may also reflect concern that in the case of resident landlords a breakdown in the tenancy relationship may require early termination.

(b)   'granted as a temporary expedient to a person who entered the premises … as a trespasser' (subsection (6)).

(c)   granted 'for a holiday only' (sub-section (7)(a)).

(d)   granted 'otherwise than for money or money's worth' (sub-section (7)(b)).

(e)   hostel accommodation let by certain categories of landlord (sub-section (8)).

(f)   granted under the immigration and asylum legislation (sub-sections (7A), (7B) and (7C)).

Most of these exceptions (apart from resident landlords and gratuitous occupation) relate to temporary accommodation where different policy factors come into play.

When notice is given in relation to accommodation provided under the interim housing duties it is arguable that it is unreasonable to terminate the accommodation with immediate effect;[29] and in practice local authorities do give 28 days' notice.[30] The implication from this is that section 5 is not seen as applicable in this situation. Section 5 also (probably) does not apply to premises let for mixed business and residential purposes, according to the Court of Appeal in *Patel v Pirakabaran*.[31]

22.4.2 The Requirement of a Court Order

If the tenant/licensee refuses to leave then, even when a valid notice to quit has been served or a fixed term lease has expired, section 3 of the Protection from Eviction Act 1977 prevents the landlord from recovering possession of a dwelling without first obtaining a court order. Section 3 reads:

---

[28] S 3A(2) – the resident landlord exception.

[29] *R v Newham LBC, ex p Ojuri (No 3)* (1999) 31 HLR 631 (QB).

[30] *Desnousse v LB of Newham* [2006] EWCA Civ 547, [2006] QB 381 [25] and [150], and see the discussion in relation to section 3 at 22.4.2 below.

[31] [2006] EWCA Civ 658, [2006] 1 WLR 3112 [36] (Wilson LJ) and [54] (Sir Peter Gibson). The point was obiter as the case involved s 2. They referred to an earlier Court of Appeal decision in relation to an agricultural holding, *National Trust the Places of Historic Interest or Natural Beauty v Knipe* [1998] 1 WLR 230 (CA), which had held that for the purposes of section 5 the phrase 'let… as a dwelling' did not include premises let as farmland that included farmhouses for residential use. The different meaning of the phrase 'let as a dwelling' in s 5 from ss 1–3 was explained by reference to the statutory genesis of the different sections.

(1) Where any premises have been let as a dwelling under a tenancy which is neither a statutorily protected tenancy nor an excluded tenancy and—

(a)   the tenancy (in this section referred to as the former tenancy) has come to an end, but

(b)   the occupier continues to reside in the premises or part of them,

it shall not be lawful for the owner to enforce against the occupier, otherwise than by proceedings in the court, his right to recover possession of the premises.

(2) In this section 'the occupier', in relation to any premises, means any person lawfully residing in the premises or part of them at the termination of the former tenancy.

…

(2B) Subsections (1) and (2) above apply in relation to any premises occupied as a dwelling under a licence, other than an excluded licence, as they apply in relation to premises let as a dwelling under a tenancy, and in those subsections the expressions 'let' and 'tenancy' shall be construed accordingly.

The Court of Appeal in *Patel v Pirabakaran* considered that this would also apply to mixed use premises.[32]

The policy of the section reflects the fact that English law frowns upon the taking of possession by self-help, and the requirement of a court order also means that if there is an eviction involving force, it will at least be in the context of court appointed bailiffs after notice rather than by private agents, possibly without notice.[33] It also means that if there is any question as to whether the owner's right to possession has arisen, this will also be decided by a court.[34]

If the landlord ignores section 3 and evicts the tenant without a court order, the eviction is unlawful and opens the landlord up to criminal prosecution and potentially large liability for civil damages (see chapter 23).

The effect of section 3 is that even if a tenant has no right to remain in the premises he usually cannot be evicted before the landlord has obtained a court order. Where a tenant is seeking to be rehoused by the local authority this creates a difficulty. If the tenant leaves before the landlord has obtained a possession order, he may be treated as intentionally homeless and therefore not entitled to housing under the main homelessness duty. (See chapter 6 for local authority duties towards the homeless). This is so notwithstanding the remarks of Lord Lowry in *Din (Taj) v Wandsworth Borough Council* that:

It … seems unacceptable that anyone should have to cling to accommodation and defend hopeless cases of ejectment for tactical reasons and thus be compelled by the law to misuse court procedure lest his claim to a house be irretrievably prejudiced.[35]

The Homelessness Code of Guidance for Local Authorities is more ambiguous. An applicant will not be treated as intentionally homeless if he has acted in good faith, but in fleshing this out it says that there will be good faith if he was 'genuinely unaware' that he had a right to remain until a court order or warrant for possession was obtained.[36] The clear implication is that the former tenant is expected to stay put until after the court order; if he

---

[32] [2006] EWCA Civ 658, [2006] 1 WLR 3112.

[33] *Desnousse v LB of Newham* [2006] EWCA Civ 547, [2006] QB 381 [109], [136] and [137].

[34] *Desnousse v LB of Newham* [2006] EWCA Civ 547, [2006] QB 381 [138].

[35] [1983] 1 AC 657 (HL) 679 and 680. See also *R v Newham LBC, ex p Ugbo* (1993) 26 HLR 263 (QB) 266.

[36] DCLG, 'Homelessness Code of Guidance for Local Authorities' (July 2006) para 11.25, see also para 11.27.

leaves before then this is likely to be intentional homelessness unless done in ignorance of the right to stay. So, in *R v London Borough of Croydon, ex p Jarvis* an assured shorthold tenant had been served with a possession notice by her landlord but was told that the local authority would not consider her claim for housing until the landlord had obtained a court order.[37] The judge held that even though this approach had been deprecated by the (then) Code of Guidance and by the House of Lords in *Din*,[38] it was not unlawful. The local authority had reasons – there was a pressing demand for housing for homeless persons and the extra weeks of not having to house Mrs Jarvis would make a significant difference to the public purse. Once a court order has been obtained, however, the tenant is seen as 'threatened with homelessness' and so housing duties arise at this point.[39] Nevertheless it seems wrong that a tenant faced with certain eviction should have to endure the additional stress, costs and delay of a court action.

Section 3 does not apply to excluded tenancies or licences (as defined in section 3A, see 22.4.1.2 above). Nor does it apply to 'statutorily protected' tenancies. This latter exception essentially excludes tenancies that are covered by other statutory schemes that have their own means of offering protection to the tenant. They are defined in section 8(1) to include Rent Act 1977 protected tenancies, Housing Act 1988 assured tenancies, business tenancies within the Landlord and Tenant Act 1954 Part II, farm business tenancies under the Agricultural Tenancies Act 1995, and long residential tenancies under Schedule 10 to the Local Government and Housing Act 1989.

In *Desnousse v LB of Newham* the question arose as to whether section 3 applied to accommodation provided under the interim duties in sections 188 and 190(2)(a) of the Housing Act 1966.[40] In discharge of its housing duty, the local authority arranged for the appellant to have self-contained accommodation with a private company. She was found to be in priority need but intentionally homeless and so was given notice, but she claimed that she could not be evicted without a court order. Although the exclusions in section 3A cover many sorts of transient accommodation they do not cover this situation. There was, however, a previous Court of Appeal decision, *Mohamed v Manek,* that had held that section 3 did not apply to a licence of accommodation secured in discharge of the section 188 duty.[41] A number of strands can be seen in the reasoning of the earlier case: that the provision of accommodation under the interim duties was a public law matter, properly reviewable by judicial review, and private law rights arise only at a later stage when there was a right to accommodation under the main homeless duty; that temporary accommodation was not occupied 'as a dwelling'; and that Parliament had never intended section 3 to apply in relation to the interim duties. In *Desnousse v LB of Newham* the Court of Appeal confirmed that section 3 does not apply to licences provided under the interim duties, leaving open the question whether it would apply to tenancies in similar circumstances.[42]

There was, however, a strong dissent by Lloyd LJ in relation to how human rights arguments applied in this situation. As the possession action was taken by a private landlord

---

[37] (1993) 26 HLR 194 (QB).
[38] *Din (Taj) v Wandsworth LBC* [1983] 1 AC 675 (HL).
[39] *R v Newham LBC, ex p Khan* [2000] All ER (D) 580 (QB) [30].
[40] [2006] EWCA Civ 547, [2006] QB 831.
[41] (1995) 27 HLR 439 (CA).
[42] [2006] EWCA Civ 547, [2006] QB 831. Granting tenancies in this situation would be unusual.

and not a public authority human rights were not directly engaged but the court still had a duty under section 3 of the Human Rights Act 1988 to construe the legislation compatibly with the ECHR. The eviction did involve an interference with the right to a home but was in accordance with law, the key question was one of proportionality.[43] In his view, the disadvantages of requiring a court order (expense, and delay in recovering property that could be used for others awaiting housing) did not outweigh the important safeguards provided by a court order (ensuring that the occupier had notice of eviction, that the eviction process was conducted by court bailiffs, and ensuring that occupation had been lawfully ended). On his view, therefore, section 3 now needed to be read as requiring a court order in this situation. The majority disagreed. In their view, the safeguards built into the Housing Act 1996, together with the practice of giving 28 days' notice, meant that sufficient procedural safeguards were in place; to hold that a court order is necessary would, according to Tuckey LJ, 'seriously hamper the ability of local authorities to discharge their duties under the 1996 Act'.[44]

22.5 Disability and Possession

By section 22(3) of the Disability Discrimination Act 1995 it is unlawful for a manager of premises to discriminate against a disabled person occupying those premises by, inter alia, evicting the disabled person, unless the discriminatory act is justified (in accordance with section 24). In the case of *Manchester City Council v Romano* the Court of Appeal held that this meant that in cases where the court had discretion over whether or not to order possession, it would be ordered only if the landlord believed eviction was necessary in order not to endanger the health or safety of others.[45] More recently, in *Mayor and Burgesses of LB of Lewisham v Malcolm*, the Court of Appeal confirmed that this approach applies even if the ground for possession relied on gives the court no discretion.[46] In this case a secure tenant who suffered from schizophrenia had put in an application under the right to buy but before this process was completed entered into an (unlawful) sub-letting. Under section 93(2) of the Housing Act 1985 this sub-letting brought the secure tenancy to an end. The local authority served a notice to quit and then issued proceedings for possession. The majority of the Court of Appeal held both the notice to quit and possession proceedings to be unlawful discriminatory acts, and therefore ineffective.

These cases illustrate that landlords need to be extremely careful when managing tenants with disabilities. There can be discrimination even if the landlord does not know of the disability and even though other (non disabled) tenants in the same situation would have been treated similarly. Arden LJ refers to the policy behind the disability legislation as being:

> … that landlords should make adjustments for actions by disabled people by reason of their disability and should not evict tenants with a disability without justification.[47]

---

[43] *Desnousse v LB of Newham* [2006] EWCA Civ 574, [2006] QB 831 [106].
[44] *Desnousse v LB of Newham* [2006] EWCA Civ 574, [2006] QB 831 [155].
[45] [2004] EWCA Civ 834, [2005] 1 WLR 2775.
[46] [2007] EWCA Civ 763.
[47] *Mayor and Burgesses of LB Lewisham v Malcolm* [2007] EWCA Civ 763 [50].

22.6 Other Landlord Remedies if the Tenant Refuses to Leave

22.6.1 The Tenant Holding Over

Two ancient statutes provide the landlord with a (little used) remedy if the tenant refuses to leave when required to do so. The idea underlying them is to give the landlord compensation if, for example, relying on the expectation that the tenant is going to leave on a particular date he lines up a new tenant only to find that the tenant does not leave (although it is not restricted to this situation).[48] Both statutes give the landlord the right to recover double rent during the period which the tenant wrongfully holds over. Section 1 of the Landlord and Tenant Act 1730 covers the situation where the landlord has ended the lease and the tenant stays on. Section 1 reads:

> In case any tenant ... shall wilfully hold over any lands, tenements, or hereditaments after the determination of such term or terms, and after demand made and notice in writing given for delivering the possession thereof by his or their landlords or lessors ... then and in such case, such person or persons so holding over shall, for and during the time he, she, and they shall so hold over or keep the person or persons entitled out of possession of the said lands, tenements and hereditaments as aforesaid, pay to the person or persons so kept out of possession ... at the rate of double the yearly value of the lands, tenements, and hereditaments so detained, for so long time as the same are detained ...

The Distress for Rent Act 1737 (the main focus of which was the remedy of distress) deals with the situation when the tenant has served notice to quit but fails to leave. Section 18 states:

> ... in case any tenant or tenants shall give notice of his, her, or their intention to quit the premises by him, her, or them holden, at a time mentioned in such notice, and shall not accordingly deliver up the possession thereof at the time in such notice contained, that then the said tenant or tenants, ... shall from thenceforward pay to the landlord or landlords, lessor or lessors, double the rent or sum which he, she, or they should otherwise have paid, ... and such double rent or sum shall continue to be paid during all the time such tenant or tenants shall continue in possession as aforesaid.

The statutes are acknowledged to be penal in nature and together form a single code. In *Oliver Ashworth (Holdings) Ltd v Ballard (Kent) Ltd* the tenant had purported to end the lease by serving a break notice but the notice was thought to be invalid as it contained an error.[49] In the event, following the House of Lords' decision in *Mannai Investments Co Ltd v Eagle Star Life Assurance Co Ltd* the notice turned out to be effective.[50] In the meantime, the tenant stayed on after expiry of the notice and the landlord wrote on the basis that the notice had been defective and sued for rent arrears on the basis that the tenancy continued. It also put in an alternative claim for double rent under the 1737 Act. In a judgment that explores statutory construction techniques in some detail, Laws LJ held that the 1737 statute applied only if the landlord was treating the 'former tenant' as a trespasser:

---

[48] *Oliver Ashworth (Holdings) Ltd v Ballard (Kent) Ltd* [2000] Ch 12 (CA) 39.
[49] [2000] Ch 12 (CA).
[50] [1997] AC 749 (HL).

The Act of 1730 addresses specifically the situation where a landlord has given notice to quit, and the tenant 'wilfully' holds over. Nothing is more obvious than the statute's concern to redress the wrong to a landlord arising where his tenant continues in occupation as a trespasser, and where that is the very fact of which the landlord complains.

It seems to me to be plain that s 18 of the 1737 Act is concerned with the same mischief.

… the right to double rent conferred by s 18 of 1737 Act only arises where: (a) the tenant holding over after his own notice to quit is in fact a trespasser (thus, the notice must be valid); and (b) the landlord treats him as such.[51]

The landlord needs to be careful in this situation if he accepts 'rent' from the former tenant: the act of acceptance may be construed as a waiver of the right to double rent, or as acceptance of the occupier as tenant, thus creating a new tenancy.[52]

22.6.2 Eviction without Court Order

If the tenancy is not within any of the statutory schemes and, in the case of a residential tenancy is excluded from the Protection from Eviction Act 1977, then the tenancy must be ended in accordance with the common law rules and any contractual provisions. There is no need for a court order. Nonetheless, it is usually safest for the landlord to obtain a court order as there is a risk that forced eviction may amount to a criminal offence. By section 6 of the Criminal Law Act 1977:

(1) … any person who, without lawful authority, uses or threatens violence for the purpose of securing entry into any premises for himself or for any other person is guilty of an offence, provided that –

(a) there is someone present on those premises at the time who is opposed to the entry which the violence is intended to secure; and

(b) the person using or threatening the violence knows that that is the case.

---

[51] [2000] Ch 12 (CA) 38.
[52] *Doe d Cheny v Batten* (1775) 1 Cowp 243. See also ch 3.

23

UNLAWFUL EVICTION AND HARASSMENT

23.1	Introduction
23.2	The type of behaviour that goes on
23.3	The size of the problem
23.4	The victims of unlawful eviction and harassment
23.5	The background to regulation
23.6	The offences of unlawful eviction and harassment
23.7	The response of the agencies
23.8	Civil remedies for illegal eviction and harassment
23.9	Other remedies
23.10	Reform?

23.1 Introduction

Chapter 22 sets out the procedure which a landlord needs to follow in order to bring a residential lease to an end (generally four weeks' notice, and obtaining a court order). However, doing things 'by the book' can take a long time and be expensive. In *Nwokorie v Mason*, for example, the Court of Appeal acknowledged that it could take up to six months to recover possession even though the tenant had no security (28 days' notice to quit, a period awaiting a court hearing, and a period up to three months before possession is given according to the court order).[1] Further, it may be that the court is unlikely to grant possession on the facts. The landlord may, therefore, be tempted to take things into his own hands and short-circuit the 'due process' requirements by, for example, removing the tenant's possessions and changing the locks. The landlord's conduct may well constitute a civil offence under the general law, such as trespass, breach of the covenant of quiet enjoyment and nuisance (and, in the commercial sector, the general law will still be the appropriate channel for an aggrieved tenant to follow). In the residential sector, however, special controls have been put in place to control such abuses. This chapter looks at the laws that have been put in place to discourage landlords from such behaviour.

---

[1] (1993) 26 HLR 60 (CA).

23.2 The Type of Behaviour that Goes On

In addition to the obvious attempts to evict tenants, such as changing locks, landlords can also resort to other means to make life so unpleasant for tenants that they are effectively left with little choice but to leave. Harassment can take a variety of forms. A research project by the Campaign for Bedsit Rights lists some:

> An examination of reported cases – those which have reached the courts, and they are only a fraction of actual incidents – reveals that harassment and illegal eviction takes many forms. It can be subtle or direct, involving physical or mental violence, cruelty and intimidation. It includes such acts as;
>
> — refusing to allow tenants access to parts of their letting such as the bathroom or kitchen or only allowing access at restricted times,
> — stopping tenants from having guests or visitors,
> — constant visits by the landlord or landlord's agent without warning and at unsociable hours,
> — offering the tenant money to leave,
> — threatening the tenant,
> — entering the tenant's home without permission,
> — allowing the property to get into such a bad state of repair that it is uncomfortable or dangerous to stay there,
> — starting building works and leaving them unfinished or sending in builders without notice or at unreasonable times,
> — removing or restricting services such as hot water or heating or failing to pay bills so that services are cut off,
> — harassment because of the tenant's race, sex or sexuality,
> — forcing the tenant to sign agreements which reduce their rights,
> — theft of the tenant's belongings.[2]

A report on harassment of older people tells stories of elderly tenants suffering from a variety of forms of abuse, such as landlords refusing to collect rent so that rent arrears would give a ground for recovering possession, financial abuse in the form of overcharging for services, lack of respect for privacy and neglecting to repair the property.[3] Individually some of these acts of harassment, such as the landlord turning up unannounced, may seem relatively minor, but when they occur frequently, or with vulnerable tenants, they can, and do, cause severe stress and anxiety.

These accounts suggest that unlawful eviction and harassment are both deliberate and blameworthy. Often, however, there can be unlawful eviction from mistakes and incompetence. So, for example, in *Wandworth LBC v Osei-Bonsu*, the local authority repossessed the property without a court order, acting (following legal advice) on the (wrong) assumption that a notice to quit by one of the two joint tenants was effective.[4] This was unlawful

---

[2] P Jew, *Law and Order in Private Rented Housing: Tackling Harassment and Illegal Eviction* (London, Campaign for Bedsit Rights, 1994) 14. See also Milner-Holland, 'Report of the Committee on Housing in Greater London' (Cmnd 2605, 1965) App III 267–8, and A Marsh and others, 'Harassment and Unlawful Eviction of Private Rented Sector Tenants and Park Home Residents' (DETR, 2000) ch 3.

[3] N Carlton and others, *The harassment and abuse of older people in the private rented sector* (Bristol, The Policy Press, 2003).

[4] [1999] 1 WLR 1011 (CA). The assumption was wrong because less than the required 28 days' notice had been given but as this was before the Court of Appeal decision had held that a short notice was ineffective in *Hounslow LBC v Pilling* [1993] 1 WLR 1242 (CA) the legal advice had mistakenly assumed the notice to be effective (see chs 22 and 24).

eviction even though the remaining joint tenant was not currently in occupation (because he was subject to an ouster injunction due to domestic violence). A further example, reflecting the kind of situation that occurs not infrequently, is given by the facts of *Regalgrand Ltd v Dickerson*.[5] The tenants were behind with the rent and the landlord gave notice. The landlord entered the flat the day after the notice had expired and found some items of furniture but very few personal belongings. He assumed that the tenants had left, removed their possessions and changed the locks. Again, this amounted to unlawful eviction. Very commonly unlawful eviction and harassment stems not from wilful action but from ignorance of the law, leading to landlords overstepping the boundaries.[6]

23.3 The Size of the Problem

It is difficult to have a clear picture of the level of the problem. Research conducted for the DETR states:

> It is difficult to assess the changing incidence of harassment and illegal eviction because of the lack of consistent and comprehensive data. The study found no consensus over whether it was declining or increasing. Experience varied between local authorities. It is clear that although the private rented sector was further liberated in 1997, it did not make a concern with unlawful action by landlords a thing of the past.[7]

There are no central statistics kept relating to the number of complaints made to local authorities.[8] Nor are there any centrally collated statistics on the number of civil actions bought.[9] The number of prosecutions brought is tiny, and decreasing, but this reflects the emphasis being placed on conciliation and also the financial constraints on local authorities that limit the number of prosecutions that they can afford to bring. In 1996, there were only 70 trials for unlawful eviction (with 31 convictions) and 54 trials for harassment (with 23 convictions).

The very small numbers of prosecutions for harassment and illegal eviction does not reflect the true scale of the problem. A survey by Rauta and Pickering found that 9 per cent of private renters had suffered from harassment,[10] although, as later DETR research shows, tenant perceptions of what constitutes harassment tends to be wider than the legally defined offences.

Whilst tenant surveys show this high level of harassment, the proportion of cases that actually get reported is much less – the study by Jew suggested that as much as 80 per cent

---

[5] (1997) 29 HLR 620 (CA).

[6] N Carlton and others, *The harassment and abuse of older people in the private rented sector* (Bristol, The Policy Press, 2003); A Marsh and others, 'Harassment and Unlawful Eviction of Private Rented Sector Tenants and Park Home Residents' (DETR, 2000).

[7] A Marsh and others, 'Harassment and Unlawful Eviction of Private Rented Sector Tenants and Park Home Residents' (DETR, 2000) para 3.95.

[8] A Marsh and others, 'Harassment and Unlawful Eviction of Private Rented Sector Tenants and Park Home Residents' (DETR, 2000) para 3.59.

[9] A Marsh and others, 'Harassment and Unlawful Eviction of Private Rented Sector Tenants and Park Home Residents' (DETR, 2000) para 3.62.

[10] I Rauta and A Pickering, *Private Renting in England 1990* (Government Social Survey Department and DoE, 1992) 50.

of harassment and unlawful eviction is unreported.[11] Such a high degree of under-reporting is due to several factors: fear of landlord reprisal; ignorance of the availability of legal channels for complaint (many landlords and tenants sharing the view that the landlord has the right to behave in this way), and the fact that is it usually is easier to simply get away from the acrimonious situation by moving on rather than by pursuing past wrongs (particularly as there is little long-term security left in the private sector).[12] As Jew noted:

> … people with … severely limited security of tenure are very unlikely to exercise their right to seek the help of the local authority regarding harassment, as they can be evicted from their homes very quickly and legally.[13]

Under-reporting seems to be highest amongst certain (vulnerable) groups – tenants with no security and single parents.

23.4 The Victims of Unlawful Eviction and Harassment

Certain tenant groups are more vulnerable than others. A survey in 1990 found that tenants with no security were most likely to suffer from attempts to make them leave.[14] This is similar to the observations made by the Milner-Holland Committee.[15] Single parents were the most likely group to suffer harassment[16] but tenants on low incomes or from black or racial minorities were also more likely to be victims.[17] The more recent DETR research confirms the picture that it is those in the most vulnerable categories, living on benefits in bedsits or in houses in multiple occupation (HMOs), that are most likely to experience harassment: lone parents, the very young, those with drink, drugs and behavioural problems, ethnic minorities and women rather than men.[18]

23.5 The Background to Regulation

In the early 1960s, the problems of harassment came to the political fore. The 1957 Rent Act had introduced a measure of decontrol in the private rented sector. Some housing was removed from the strict security of tenure regime immediately but other housing only became decontrolled when the sitting tenant left, known as 'creeping decontrol'. One result of

---

[11] P Jew, *Law and Order in Private Rented Housing: Tackling Harassment and Illegal Eviction* (London, Campaign for Bedsit Rights, 1994).

[12] D Cowan, 'Harassment and unlawful eviction in the private rented sector – a study of in(-)action' [2001] *Conv* 249.

[13] P Jew, *Law and Order in Private Rented Housing: Tackling Harassment and Illegal Eviction* (London, Campaign for Bedsit Rights, 1994) 33.

[14] 18% of tenants in this group: I Rauta and A Pickering, *Private Renting in England 1990* (Government Social Survey Department and DoE, 1992) 51 Table 7.12.

[15] Milner-Holland, 'Report of the Committee on Housing in Greater London' (Cmnd 2605, 1965).

[16] I Rauta and A Pickering, *Private Renting in England 1990* (Government Social Survey Department and DoE, 1992) 52 Table 7.13.

[17] P Jew, *Law and Order in Private Rented Housing: Tackling Harassment and Illegal Eviction* (London, Campaign for Bedsit Rights, 1994) 91.

[18] A Marsh and others, 'Harassment and Unlawful Eviction of Private Rented Sector Tenants and Park Home Residents' (DETR, 2000) paras 3.77 and 3.97.

this was that landlords now had an incentive to get rid of sitting tenants so that they could be replaced by tenants paying a higher rent. Peter Kemp writes:

> In the late 1950s and early 1960s, stories began to appear in the local press about intimidation of tenants, evictions and homelessness.
>
> What transformed the situation, however, was the storm of publicity surrounding the west London landlord Peter Rachman. His nefarious activities came to light in the wake of the Profumo scandal in 1963. It turned out that one of the call girls involved in the Profumo 'sex and security' scandal had earlier been Rachman's mistress. The addition of slum landlordism to the already potent media cocktail of sex and national security allowed the press to inject new life into the Profumo affair.[19]

Although the story of Rachman is closely associated with the laws regulating unlawful eviction and harassment, his tactics were, in fact, quite different from the activities of landlords who were most affected by the legal controls. In practice, it was the small landlords who were most likely to get rid of tenants without any regard for due process. Rachman, though not a good landlord, often used money to get rid of tenants, and the main public outcry over Rachman related to his charging exorbitant rents for slum property. At the height of his involvement in housing, he owned around 1,000 tenancies. He tended to buy up the short ends of long leases of houses which were occupied by controlled tenants paying low rents. Most houses were in bad repair. He would then buy out the controlled tenants and replace them with higher paying tenants, often immigrants who were finding it difficult to get homes in a time of housing shortage. The method of getting tenants to leave was not always so generous, he also turned to other less-acceptable ways of persuading tenants to leave. But while Rachman has come 'to symbolize the unacceptable face of private landlordism in Britain and gave to the English language a new word – Rachmanism',[20] harassment was not a key part of his methods, his 'success' was in the policy of letting slum housing for high rents.[21]

When the Labour government came to power in October 1964 following the Rachman affair they had a mandate to offer urgent assistance to tenants. This they did by passing the Protection from Eviction Act 1964 which made it an offence to evict a tenant without first obtaining a court order. A year later this was replaced by Part III of the Rent Act 1965, making illegal eviction and harassment into criminal offences. The current provisions are now contained in the Protection from Eviction Act 1977 (as amended by the Housing Act 1988). By section 1(2) it is an offence to unlawfully deprive a residential occupier of his occupation of premises. This covers things such as excluding the occupant from the premises by changing the locks without either having served a proper notice or obtaining a court order. By section 1(3) it is an offence to harass the residential occupier by disturbing him or withdrawing services if this is likely to cause the occupant to leave or not pursue a right or remedy in respect of the premises. This would cover, for example, persistently turning off the gas and electricity supplies to the premises in the hope that this will deter

---

[19] P Kemp, 'Burying Rachman' in J Goodwin and C Grant (eds), *Built to Last?* 2nd edn (London, ROOF, 1997) 114.

[20] P Kemp, 'Burying Rachman' in J Goodwin and C Grant (eds), *Built to Last?* 2nd edn (London, ROOF, 1997) 115.

[21] For further information on Rachman, see D Nelken, *The Limits of the Legal Process, A Study of Landlords, Law and Crime* (London, Academic Press, 1983) 1–5.

the tenant from reporting the landlord to the local environmental health office or causing the tenant to leave. Further details of both offences are given below.

Small landlords are more likely to resort to unlawful methods to get the tenant to leave. They often have a much closer relationship with their tenants, particularly if resident, and are less likely to be tolerant of tenant misbehaviour than larger, more commercially oriented, landlords. Any dispute can quickly become acrimonious. The Milner-Holland Committee was set up to investigate housing conditions in Greater London: reporting in 1965 it found that abuse was concentrated in 'stress areas' where there was overcrowding, multi-occupation and small-time landlords.[22] Small landlords are also less likely to pre-vet tenants thoroughly and therefore more likely to take on undesirable tenants and to encounter difficulties with rent payments. A study by Jew found that the most common cause of harassment and illegal eviction was rent arrears, often caused by delays in housing benefit payment or restrictions in the level of benefit.[23] Other common reasons for unlawful action are delays in possession proceedings, and the inclusion of a greater number of vulnerable households with social problems in the private rented sector.[24] Ignorance of the law amongst small landlords is also a very significant factor in harassment cases.[25] The research conducted for the Department of the Environment, Transport and Regions (DETR) also found that it is these smaller, sideline landlords renting out cheaper, lower quality property, who are most likely to come to the attention of local authorities and other voluntary agencies dealing with harassment complaints.[26]

Although the 1960s legislation was a response – in part – to the Rachman scandal, the activities constrained by the legislation do not really affect Rachman style landlords. These more commercial landlords seldom resort to illegal tactics. The only landlord malpractices to be treated as criminal following the Rachman scandal were unlawful eviction and harassment and not, for example, profiteering or winkling (tempting the tenant to leave by financial inducement).[27]

23.6 The Offences of Unlawful Eviction and Harassment

The offences of unlawful eviction and harassment are set out in section 1 of the Protection from Eviction Act 1977:

Section 1

(2) If any person unlawfully deprives the residential occupier of any premises of his occupation of the premises or any part thereof, or attempts to do so, he shall be guilty of an offence

---

[22] Milner-Holland, 'Report of the Committee on Housing in Greater London' (Cmnd 2605, 1965).

[23] Similar findings were reached by Shelter in 1990: L Burrows and N Hunter, *Forced Out: A Report on the Harassment and Illegal Eviction of Private Tenants after the Housing Act 1988* (London, Shelter, 1990).

[24] A Marsh and others, 'Harassment and Unlawful Eviction of Private Rented Sector Tenants and Park Home Residents' (DETR, 2000) para 3.96.

[25] P Jew, *Law and Order in Private Rented Housing: Tackling Harassment and Illegal Eviction* (London, Campaign for Bedsit Rights, 1994).

[26] A Marsh and others, 'Harassment and Unlawful Eviction of Private Rented Sector Tenants and Park Home Residents' (DETR, 2000) para 3.79.

[27] See D Nelken, *The Limits of the Legal Process, A Study of Landlords, Law and Crime* (London, Academic Press, 1983) *passim*.

unless he proves that he believed, and had reasonable cause to believe, that the residential occupier had ceased to reside in the premises.

(3) If any person with intent to cause the residential occupier of any premises –

(a)   to give up the occupation of the premises or any part thereof; or

(b)   to refrain from exercising any right or pursuing any remedy in respect of the premises or part thereof;

does acts likely to interfere with the peace or comfort of the residential occupier or members of his household, or persistently withdraws or withholds services reasonably required for the occupation of the premises as a residence, he shall be guilty of an offence.

(3A) Subject to subsection (3B) below, the landlord of a residential occupier or an agent of the landlord shall be guilty of an offence if –

(a)   he does acts likely to interfere with the peace or comfort of the residential occupier or members of his household, or

(b)   he persistently withdraws or withholds services reasonably required for the occupation of the premises in question as a residence,

and (in either case) he knows, or has reasonable cause to believe, that the conduct is likely to cause the residential occupier to give up the occupation of the whole or part of the premises or to refrain from exercising any right or pursuing any remedy in respect of the whole or part of the premises.

(3B) A person shall not be guilty of an offence under subsection (3A) above if he proves that he had reasonable grounds for doing the acts or withdrawing or withholding the services in question.

(3C) In subsection (3A) above 'landlord', in relation to a residential occupier of any premises, means the person who, but for –

(a)   the residential occupier's right to remain in occupation of the premises, or

(b)   a restriction on the person's right to recover possession of the premises,

would be entitled to occupation of the premises and any superior landlord under whom that person derives title.

Both subsections apply to protect 'residential occupiers', defined as follows:

Section 1
(1) In this section 'residential occupier, in relation to any premises, means a person occupying the premises as a residence, whether under a contract or by virtue of any enactment or rule of law giving him the right to remain in occupation or restricting the right of any other person to recover possession of the premises.

The sections therefore cover not only tenants but also licensees.

Although section 1(2) is commonly referred to as unlawful eviction and section 1(3) as harassment, those words do not appear in the subsections. Section 1(2) requires deprivation of 'occupation' and section 1(3) requires the intention that the acts done are likely to cause the occupier to give up 'occupation' or refrain from exercising rights. In *R v Yuthiwattana* the Court of Appeal said that for the purposes of section 1(2) it was necessary for the unlawful deprivation to have the character of 'eviction'.[28] This need not be permanent and might include deprivation for a period. An isolated 'locking out' (such as the overnight

---

[28] (1984) 80 Cr App R 55 (CA).

exclusion in *Yuthiwattana*) will not come within section 1(2), but may come within the definition of harassment.

It is not only the landlord himself who may be prosecuted for harassment – under sub-section (3A) his agent may also be guilty and under sub-section (3) 'any person' with intent can commit the offence. By section 1(2) it will be an offence not only to evict an occupier whose licence or tenancy is continuing but also a tenant whose tenancy has come to an end but who has not been served with any necessary court order under section 3 of the Act (see chapter 22).

Under sub-section 1(3) it is necessary for the prosecutor to prove that there was a specific intent to cause the occupier to leave or to refrain from exercising a right or pursuing a remedy. This intent is often difficult to prove and the Housing Act 1988, responding to fears that the deregulation of the private sector would lead to higher levels of harassment, introduced a new offence in sub-sections 1(3)(A–C) that removes the need to prove intent. Notwithstanding the removal of the need to prove intent there has been no significant change in the number of prosecutions being brought.[29]

In order to commit the offence of harassment it is not necessary that the act complained of must also be actionable under the civil law as a breach of contract or tort.[30] Thus, the offence of harassment may be committed if the landlord refuses to let the occupier have a replacement key (having lost the original)[31] or if the landlord prevents the tenant from using toilets near his room (when other toilets remained available).[32]

Although these sub-sections clearly criminalise unlawful eviction and harassment, they have not been wholly effective in either punishing offenders or sending out a message to the community that interfering with residential occupation is wrong. While in some cases few would dispute that the landlord has behaved wrongfully, as where the landlord sends in 'the heavies' and violence is involved or threatened,[33] in other cases the conduct is less obviously wrongful as, perhaps, with the situations referred to earlier in *Wandworth LBC v Osei-Bonsu*[34] and *Regalgrand Ltd v Dickerson*.[35] It is hard to push the message that unlawful eviction and harassment are wrong if few would judge the landlord as behaving badly. This, perhaps, explains the result in *Schon v London Borough of Camden*.[36] The landlord was installing a bathroom above the tenant's flat and needed to strengthen the floor of the bathroom. This could be done either with access from the tenant's flat (the landlord's preferred option) or from above. The tenant was offered alternative accommodation for the expected two week period of the works but turned it down. The landlord went ahead and did the work from above but the ceiling of the tenant's flat collapsed. Given that in *R v Yuthiwattana*[37] it had been said that leaving premises for a 'period' might be deprivation of occupation for the purposes of section 1(2), it might be thought that making the tenant

---

[29] P Jew, *Law and Order in Private Rented Housing: Tackling Harassment and Illegal Eviction* (London, Campaign for Bedsit Rights, 1994) 80–4. There does not appear to have been any further significant change since this report.
[30] *R v Burke* [1991] 1 AC 135 (HL).
[31] *R v Yuthiwattana* (1984) 80 Cr App R 55 (CA).
[32] *R v Burke* [1991] 1 AC 135 (HL).
[33] For example, *Afzal Mohammed Madarbakus* (1992) 13 Cr App R (S) 542 (CA).
[34] [1999] 1 WLR 1011 (CA), see text accompanying n 4.
[35] (1997) 29 HLR 620 (CA), see text accompanying n 5.
[36] (1986) 18 HLR 341 (QB).
[37] (1984) 80 Cr App R 55 (CA).

leave for two weeks could involve harassment. The Court of Appeal in *Schon* held, however, that the offence of harassment was not committed. It could, perhaps, have been said that as the collapse was accidental there had been no 'intent', but the reason in fact given for saying that no offence had been committed was that as the landlord only intended the tenant to be forced out for two weeks this did not amount to forcing her to give up occupation. Glidewell LJ adopted a quite different approach to 'occupation' than had been used in the earlier case of *Yuthiwattana*, saying that a tenant remains in occupation if physically absent for a period intending to return.[38] This result may simply reflect the court's perception of the morality of the landlord's conduct. The landlord behaved quite reasonably in *Schon* by offering substitute accommodation. Had the landlord gone about things differently, and caused the tenant to give up occupation for the same intended two week period but by sending the 'heavies' in, it is tempting to ask whether the court would not then have found the offence of harassment committed.

The ambiguity over the criminality of these offences is compounded by the fact that it the tenant is often not without fault himself. In many cases there are serious rent arrears, or the tenant may be pursuing a disreputable lifestyle, or abusing the landlord's property. It is not always clear therefore that the landlord has greater 'moral blame' for what transpires than the tenant. In addition, tenancy disputes are often perceived as being civil matters – for resolution between the two parties and not involving a wrong against society, in many ways akin to past attitudes to domestic violence.[39] There is also a belief held by some that the landlord as property owner is entitled to exercise dominion over his property and to exclude undesirable occupiers.[40]

23.7 The Response of the Agencies

Whilst the police are able to prosecute section 1 offences, it is the local authorities that have taken the most active role in law enforcement and section 6 also gives them the power to bring prosecutions. Many local authorities have Tenancy Relations Officers whose job includes dealing with harassment and illegal eviction complaints, although there is considerable variation amongst authorities as to the level of resources dedicated to anti-harassment work,[41] and the priority given to it. There is also considerable variance between authorities whose work is largely reactive to complaints and those proactively involved in education and training.[42]

---

[38] (1986) 18 HLR 341 (QB). Adopting the meaning of 'occupation' used in the Rent Act 1977 for determining who is in occupation for the purposes of being a protected tenant. Hill is critical of inconsistent approaches being used for the meaning of 'occupation': J Hill, 'Section 1 of the Protection from Eviction Act 1977: The Meaning of "Occupation"' [1987] *Conv* 265.

[39] P Jew, *Law and Order in Private Rented Housing: Tackling Harassment and Illegal Eviction* (London, Campaign for Bedsit Rights, 1994) 17; D Cowan and A Marsh, 'There's Regulatory Crime, and then there's Landlord Crime: from "Rachmanites" to "Partners"' (2001) 64 *MLR* 831, 839.

[40] A view supported by some of the quotations in D Cowan, 'Harassment and unlawful eviction in the private rented sector – a study of in(-)action' [2001] *Conv* 249.

[41] P Jew, *Law and Order in Private Rented Housing: Tackling Harassment and Illegal Eviction* (London, Campaign for Bedsit Rights, 1994) ch 2; A Marsh and others, 'Harassment and Unlawful Eviction of Private Rented Sector Tenants and Park Home Residents' (DETR, 2000) ch 4.

[42] A Marsh and others, 'Harassment and Unlawful Eviction of Private Rented Sector Tenants and Park Home Residents' (DETR, 2000).

The prosecution rate for reported offences is low. In line with many 'regulatory crimes'[43] the regulators tend to pursue a compliance strategy and see prosecution as a last resort. Cowan and Marsh argue that this approach is especially strong with landlord crime as there is a need for local authorities to work with landlords as 'partners' in local housing strategies rather than to castigate them as 'Rachmanites'.[44] As a result, the usual response will be to try to resolve the problem informally, perhaps by issuing a warning letter or a caution, rather than by prosecuting. This is often found to be effective in preventing further harassment.[45] Further, the handling of harassment claims can also be seen as a 'gateway' to controlling homelessness applications, and tenancy relations officers can be viewed as part of the homelessness service.[46] In terms of helping landlords to become 'good landlords', and reducing homelessness, local authorities often then seek to resolve problems and educate rather than prosecute.

Even if prosecution is thought appropriate, it is often difficult to bring a successful action for many reasons: the high standard of proof required by criminal courts, the reluctance of tenants to act as witnesses through rear of reprisals, mistrust of the judicial system, the length of time it takes for cases to reach the courts (between six months and two years), the fact that tenants move away during this time and because tenants see no benefit for them in prosecuting.[47] Cowan remarks that Tenancy Relations Officers consider that prosecution is seldom worth it:

> Prosecution takes too long, is too costly, does not solve any underlying problems, and, whilst a prosecution is viewed as a deterrent, the penalties are viewed as derisory.[48]

Penalties given tend to be low. Of those found guilty in 1990, three were given an immediate custodial sentence and 77 were fined – only seven of these being fined more than £500.[49] The low level of sentences suggests that magistrates do not regard harassment and illegal eviction as a serious offence. In an era of 'best value', the time and effort required to bring a successful prosecution, coupled with the low benefit, means that there is little incentive for local authorities to prosecute.[50]

Given the difficulties in pursuing prosecutions, some authorities advise complainants to bring civil actions (discussed below), which not only offer the advantage of financial

---

[43] 'Business related crime' rather than 'ordinary crime' (although unlike many regulatory crimes, unlawful eviction and harassment does have a victim).

[44] D Cowan and A Marsh, 'There's Regulatory Crime, and then there's Landlord Crime: from "Rachmanites" to "Partners"' (2001) 64 *MLR* 831. See also D Cowan, 'Harassment and unlawful eviction in the private rented sector – a study of in(-)action' [2001] *Conv* 249, 259

[45] P Jew, *Law and Order in Private Rented Housing: Tackling Harassment and Illegal Eviction* (London, Campaign for Bedsit Rights, 1994) 61.

[46] D Cowan, 'Harassment and unlawful eviction in the private rented sector – a study of in(-)action' [2001] *Conv* 249, 263.

[47] P Jew, *Law and Order in Private Rented Housing: Tackling Harassment and Illegal Eviction* (London, Campaign for Bedsit Rights, 1994) 68; A Marsh and others, 'Harassment and Unlawful Eviction of Private Rented Sector Tenants and Park Home Residents' (DETR, 2000) ch 5.

[48] D Cowan, 'Harassment and unlawful eviction in the private rented sector – a study of in(-)action' [2001] Conv 249, 262. Fines are also described as derisory by P Jew, *Law and Order in Private Rented Housing: Tackling Harassment and Illegal Eviction* (London, Campaign for Bedsit Rights, 1994) 88.

[49] The maximum fine then in the magistrates court being £5,000: in the Crown Court it is unlimited.

[50] D Cowan and A Marsh, 'There's Regulatory Crime, and then there's Landlord Crime: from "Rachmanites" to "Partners"' (2001) 64 *MLR* 831, 854.

compensation for the tenant but also have a lower standard of proof. Costs are, however, a significant issue: the cost of obtaining an injunction alone could start at £1000 or more and legal aid may not be perceived as worthwhile particularly if the tenancy was shortly to run out in any event. Further, if a tenancy is an assured shorthold or there is or more than one occupier in the property, the level of damages is often negligible.[51]

23.8 Civil Remedies for Illegal Eviction and Harassment

23.8.1 Introduction

From the tenant's perspective the criminal law may avenge a perceived injustice but it does little to help his plight. An occupier threatened with eviction or enduring repeated harassment is more likely to want to pursue a civil action and either obtain an injunction, restraining the landlord's conduct or allowing the tenant to re-enter his home,[52] or obtain financial compensation. At common law, the landlord's behaviour may involve trespass, the tort of conversion if any possessions are deliberately interfered with,[53] nuisance, breach of the covenant of quiet enjoyment or assault. In *McCall v Abelesz*, it was argued that breach of section 1 of the Protection from Eviction Act 1977 would found civil liability as well as being a criminal offence but the Court of Appeal rejected this.[54]

In addition to these common law rights, tenants have also been given a statutory right to damages by sections 27 and 28 of the Housing Act 1988. It was intended that the statutory right would act as a deterrent to landlords by depriving the landlord of any financial gain arising from unlawful eviction. The statutory right to damages followed concerns that the partial deregulation of the private rented sector by the 1988 Housing Act would lead to high levels of harassment and illegal eviction, with landlords seeking to replace Rent Act regulated tenants (paying a fair rent) with Housing Act tenants paying a market rent and with little security of tenure (under the assured shorthold).[55] Where statutory damages are given, it is not possible also to recover damages for the same 'loss' under the general law (see 23.8.3.5 below).

23.8.2 Common Law Remedies

Both the injunction and damages are useful remedies for ejected occupiers. If an injunction is given but the landlord ignores it, he will commit a contempt of court for which there may be imprisonment or a fine may be imposed.[56] In a case involving the local authority of

---

[51] A Marsh and others, 'Harassment and Unlawful Eviction of Private Rented Sector Tenants and Park Home Residents' (DETR, 2000) paras 5.11–5.16.

[52] See, for example, *Warder v Cooper* [1970] 1 Ch 495; *Drane v Evangelou* [1978] 1 WLR 455 (CA).

[53] Torts (Interference with Goods) Act 1977.

[54] [1976] QB 585 (CA).

[55] As mentioned above, the criminal offence was also strengthened at this time, removing the need to prove intent.

[56] In *Saxby v McKinley* (1996) 29 HLR 569 (CA) an immediate custodial sentence for 28 days was imposed on a landlord.

Southwark, Munby J decided that the public shame of the judgment would suffice as a penalty: seeing just how badly Southwark's representatives had treated the occupier was punishment enough without imposing a financial penalty that would ultimately be passed on to local taxpayers.[57]

The general principle for damages in tort actions is that the plaintiff be compensated for his loss. This can include general damages for the loss of the right to occupy and for distress, inconvenience and hardship caused by the eviction,[58] as well as special damages.[59] In *Ramdath v Daley* the Court of Appeal upheld the award of £510 to cover living out expenses after eviction and £2,647 for the cost of items taken from the property as special damages in addition to £2,000 by way of general damages.[60]

It may also be possible to recover exemplary and aggravated damages. These two measures of damages have frequently been confused by judges but, as Nourse LJ pointed out, they are intended to serve different purposes:

> Aggravated damages are awarded to compensate the plaintiff for injury to his proper feelings of dignity and pride and for aggravation generally, whereas exemplary damages are awarded in order to punish the defendant.[61]

Aggravated damages of £1,000 were awarded in *Nwokorie v Mason* for conduct that was calculated to cause humiliation and shame and to be thoroughly offensive to the occupant's feelings.[62] Although Lord Devlin in *Rookes v Barnard*, regarded aggravated damages as being compensatory, they can only be given when the defendant's motive or conduct aggravated the injury to the plaintiff.[63] This has led to some confusion as to whether they are therefore not only compensatory, but contain a punitive element to them as well. The Law Commission suggest that they should be labelled 'damages for mental distress', emphasising that they are concerned to compensate and not to punish the wrongdoer.[64] The significance of the wrong-doer's motive or conduct is that it 'aggravates' the injury done, and therefore warrants a greater compensatory sum.[65]

Exemplary damages serve a quite different function. They are clearly punitive.[66] Although punitive damages cannot generally be awarded for a civil wrong there are certain exceptional categories in which they are allowed, and wrongful eviction cases can come within the second category admitted by Lord Devlin in *Rookes v Barnard*:

---

[57] *R (on the application of Bempoa) v Southwark LB* [2002] EWHC 153 (Admin).

[58] For example, in *Melville v Bruton* (1996) 29 HLR 319 (CA) the Court of Appeal assessed damages for inconvenience, discomfort and distress at £500 and in *King v Jackson* (1997) 30 HLR 541 (CA) £1,500 was held appropriate for breach of the covenant of quiet enjoyment that the wrongful eviction involved.

[59] In *Murray v Aslam* (1994) 27 HLR 284 (CA) an award of £5,703 was made in respect of trespass to goods.

[60] (1993) 25 HLR 273 (CA).

[61] (1993) 25 HLR 273 (CA) 277.

[62] (1993) 26 HLR 60 (CA). See also *McMillan v Singh* (1984) 17 HLR 120 (CA); *Jones v Miah* (1992) 24 HLR 578 (CA).

[63] [1964] AC 1129 (HL).

[64] Law Commission, 'Aggravated, Exemplary and Restitutionary Damages' (Law Com No 247, 1997) Part I paras 1.7–1.9.

[65] Law Commission, 'Aggravated, Exemplary and Restitutionary Damages' (Law Com No 247, 1997) Part II para 1.1.

[66] If the landlord has been prosecuted successfully and punished, it may be that exemplary damages cannot be awarded, although the law is unclear: see Law Commission, 'Aggravated, Exemplary and Restitutionary Damages' (Law Com No 247, 1997) Part II paras 1.120–1.127.

Where a defendant with a cynical disregard for a plaintiff's rights has calculated that the money to be made out of his wrong doing will probably exceed the damages at risk, it is necessary for the law to show that it cannot be broken with impunity … Exemplary damages can properly be awarded whenever it is necessary to teach a wrongdoer that tort does not pay.[67]

It is clear that this can cover wrongful eviction, as Lord Hailsham LC remarks:

How, it may be asked, about the late Mr Rachman, who is alleged to have used hired bullies to intimidate statutory tenants by violence or threats of violence into giving vacant possession of their residences and so placing a valuable asset in the hands of the landlord? My answer must be that if this is not a cynical calculation of profit and cold-blooded disregard of a plaintiff's rights, I do not know what is.[68]

In order to recover exemplary damages, though, the tenants must be able to show that the landlord knew that what he was doing was against the law or that he had a reckless disregard as to whether what he intended to do was legal or illegal, and a decision to carry on doing it because the prospects of material advantage outweigh the prospects of material loss.[69] In *Ramdath v Daley* it was not possible to award exemplary damages against the landlord's agent because it had not been shown that the agent had sufficient (financial) interest to come within this category.[70] In *Drane v Evangelou*, the evicted tenant was awarded £1,000 exemplary damages for the 'monstrous behaviour' of the landlord 'to teach the landlord a lesson'.[71] Even if the tenant has not been a 'model tenant' and has not behaved with propriety, this cannot be taken account of so as to reduce the damages.[72] Where the action is framed in contract for breach of the covenant of quiet enjoyment, it is not possible to claim exemplary damages or damages for injured feelings and mental distress.[73]

In an unreported County Court decision, *Daley, James, Wiseman, Reynolds v Mahmood and Rahman*, the judge awarded general damages, special damages, aggravated damages and exemplary damages, coming to more than £100,000, as a response to the landlord's 'outrageous' behaviour that had a serious effect on the health of the tenants and on their employment prospects.[74]

23.8.3 Statutory Damages under Sections 27 and 28 of the Housing Act 1988

23.8.3.1 Introduction

In the years immediately following the introduction of sections 27 and 28 some very substantial awards were made to evicted tenants: £31,000 in *Tagro v Cafane*,[75] £35,000 in

---

[67] [1964] AC 1129 (HL) 1227.

[68] *Cassell & Co Ltd v Broome* [1972] AC 1027 (HL) 1079.

[69] *Cassell & Co Ltd v Broome* [1972] AC 1027 (HL) 1079. Provided that the motive of profit is there, exemplary damages can be awarded even though no profit was in fact made. They therefore differ from restitutionary damages: see Law Commission, 'Aggravated, Exemplary and Restitutionary Damages' (Law Com No 247, 1997) Part II paras 1.100–1.101.

[70] (1993) 25 HLR 273 (CA).

[71] Lord Denning MR, although Lawton LJ and Goff LJ seem to categorise the award as aggravated damages.

[72] *McMillan v Singh* (1985) 17 HLR 120 (CA).

[73] *Bratchett v Beaney* [1992] 3 All ER 910 (CA).

[74] Central London CC 12 August 2005 (HHJ Medawar QC).

[75] [1991] 1 WLR 378 (CA).

Canlin and Gray v Berkshire Holdings,[76] and £20,278 in *Chappel v Panchall*.[77] Since then the level of awards has been tempered in the light of the Court of Appeal fleshing out the limitations on the legislative provisions and the increased use of assured shorthold tenancies which, as will be seen, has a marked impact on valuations made under section 28.

23.8.3.2 Liability of Landlord

Section 27 of the Housing Act 1988 provides for liability if a landlord, or any person acting on behalf of the landlord, unlawfully deprives a residential occupier of his occupation of the whole or part of any premises (or attempts to do so) or harasses the occupier causing the occupier to leave. This is similar to the criminal offences of unlawful eviction and harassment. In *Tagro v Cafane* Lord Donaldson MR referred to sub-section (1) as actual eviction and sub-section (2) as constructive eviction.[78] In *Abbott v Bayley* it was accepted that bringing in new tenants and threatening forceful eviction was likely to cause the occupier to leave.[79] Section 27 states:

(1) This section applies if, at any time after 9th June 1988, a landlord (in this section referred to as 'the landlord in default') or any person acting on behalf of the landlord in default unlawfully deprives the residential occupier of any premises of his occupation of the whole or part of the premises.

(2) This section also applies if, at any time after 9th June 1988, a landlord (in this section referred to as 'the landlord in default') or any person acting on behalf of the landlord in default –

(a)   attempts unlawfully to deprive the residential occupier of any premises of his occupation of the whole or part of the premises, or

(b)   knowing or having reasonable cause to believe that the conduct is likely to cause the residential occupier of any premises –

(i)   to give up his occupation of the premises or any part thereof, or

(ii)   to refrain from exercising any right or pursuing any remedy in respect of the premises or any part thereof,

does acts likely to interfere with the peace or comfort of the residential occupier or members of his household, or persistently withdraws or withholds services reasonably required for the occupation of the premises as a residence, and, as a result, the residential occupier gives up his occupation of the premises as a residence.

(3) Subject to the following provisions of this section, where this section applies, the landlord in default shall, by virtue of this section, be liable to pay to the former residential occupier, in respect of his loss of the right to occupy the premises in question as his residence, damages assessed on the basis set out in section 28 below.

Under section 27 it is the landlord who is liable for statutory damages, even if the conduct complained of has been committed not by the landlord himself but by someone acting for him.[80] This can create problems of recovery if the reason why there is an agent is because the landlord is abroad and out of the jurisdiction.[81]

---

[76] September 1990 Legal Action 10.
[77] December 1991 Legal Action 19
[78] [1991] 1 WLR 378 (CA) 382.
[79] (1999) 32 HLR 72 (CA).
[80] *Sampson v Wilson* [1996] Ch 39 (CA); *Francis v Brown* (1997) 30 HLR 143 (CA).
[81] As was recognised in *Francis v Brown* (1997) 30 HLR 143 (CA).

By section 27(8) the landlord will have a defence if he believed, and had reasonable cause to believe, that the residential occupier has ceased to reside in the premises or, where liability arises by virtue of the doing of acts or withdrawal of services, the landlord had reasonable grounds for acting in the way in which he or she did. The local authority landlord sought to rely on this defence in *Wandworth LBC v Osei-Bonsu*, the argument being that they had reasonably believed that the wife's notice to quit was valid and that the husband had moved out.[82] In the Court of Appeal, Simon Brown LJ admitted to finding this a difficult point but in the end held that the local authority did not have 'reasonable cause' for their belief that the notice to quit was valid.[83]

23.8.3.3 *Measure of Damages*

Section 28 sets out the appropriate measure of damages where a claim is brought under section 27. It is essentially a comparison of the value of the property with and without the interest of the evicted occupier. Section 28 provides:

(1) The basis for the assessment of damages referred to in section 27 (3) above is the difference in value, determined as at the time immediately before the residential occupier ceased to occupy the premises in question as his residence, between –

(a) the value of the interest of the landlord in default determined on the assumption that the residential occupier continues to have the same right to occupy the premises as before that time; and

(b) the value of that interest determined on the assumption that the residential occupier has ceased to have that right.

(2) In relation to any premises, any reference in this section to the interest of the landlord in default is a reference to his interest in the building in which the premises in question are comprised (whether or not that building contains any other premises) together with its curtilage.

By section 28(3) three important assumptions are made in making this comparative valuation:

(a) that the landlord is selling his interest on the open market to a willing buyer;

(b) that neither the residential occupier nor any member of his family wishes to buy; and

(c) that it is unlawful to carry out any 'substantial development' of any of the land in which the landlord's interest exists or demolish the whole or part of the building on that land. This excludes the possibility that the land could now be turned to commercial office use, for example. It would not, however, exclude developments covered by the general development order.[84] In practice, this provision is a compromise between the aim of depriving landlords of all financial gain and the possibility of damages being awarded out of all proportion to the tenant's loss.

The basis of damages awards under section 28 represents a considerable shift from the normal compensation-based approach to damages. The measure of damages is the benefit

[82] [1999] 1 WLR 1011 (CA).
[83] A somewhat hard decision given that the case that confirmed that such a notice is not valid; *Hounslow LBC v Pilling* [1993] 1 WLR 1242 (CA), had not then been decided: see n 4.
[84] See Housing Act 1988 s 28(6).

which the defendant has obtained from his unlawful act; it is not criminal legislation[85] and is best viewed as restitutionary. The clear aim of this is to ensure that the landlord stands to gain nothing from his wrong conduct and therefore has no incentive to throw the occupier out without following the correct procedures. The result if he does so is likely to be a windfall gain to the former occupant.

Applying section 28 can be difficult in valuation terms. It is necessary to work out the value of the immediate landlord's interest in the whole building (assuming he – and not a superior landlord – is the landlord at fault) with the occupier present and the value without the occupier in. This is a notoriously difficult valuation exercise, especially if the building has many occupants, and the courts have frequently been handicapped by the poor quality of valuation evidence produced as Dillon LJ notes in *Jones v Miah*:

> The difficulty here is formidable, since none of the four professional valuers who were called to give evidence gave the judge any assistance at all. This may have been because of the ineptitude of these four individual valuers, or it may have been because the habits of thought of valuers trained in the processes of valuing interests in land are so different from the habits of thought of lawyers who seek to apply the formula under section 28 that there is no meeting of minds, and the valuers can never bring their mind to understand what the calculation is that the lawyers are wanting them to make.[86]

The valuation based on the occupier being present must take account of the level of security and rights of the occupier, and the impact on value of any other occupiers in the property.[87] In *Wandworth LBC v Osei-Bonsu* the valuation evidence adduced and agreed was that the vacant possession value of the house was around £60,000, but with a secure tenant with lifelong security it would be £30,000.[88] On appeal, because this figure had been accepted it could not be reopened, but the Court of Appeal clearly considered that the wrong basis had been used. The occupier was, in fact, in a precarious position and could have been lawfully evicted following service of a proper notice to quit by his wife. The appropriate measure of damages would take account of this and then would have been no more than £2,000, rather than the £30,000 awarded at first instance. The fact that valuation must take account of the occupier's degree of security means that awards in the private sector are contained as the majority of lettings are assured shortholds that can be ended within a relatively short timescale. In some cases it may mean that there is no difference between the valuation with vacant possession and with the tenant in occupation, in which case no statutory damages will be available.[89]

23.8.3.4 Reducing the Damages to Reflect the Tenant's Conduct

Section 27(7)(a) provides that the court may reduce the damages to such amount as it thinks appropriate if the conduct of the occupier, or any person living with him 'was such that it is reasonable to mitigate the damages for which the landlord in default would otherwise be

---

[85] *Jones v Miah* (1992) 24 HLR 578 (CA).

[86] (1992) 24 HLR 578 (CA) 588; see also *Tagro v Cafane* [1991] 1 WLR 378 (CA) where one side failed to produce valuation evidence; *Nwokorie v Mason* (1993) 26 HLR 60 (CA).

[87] *King v Jackson* (1997) 30 HLR 541 (CA).

[88] [1999] 1 WLR 1011 (CA).

[89] *Melville v Bruton* (1996) 29 HLR 319 (CA); *King v Jackson* (1997) 30 HLR 541 (CA) (no statutory damages as only 6 days left of tenancy).

liable'. In *Wandworth LBC v Osei-Bonsu* the former occupier was said to have triggered the whole train of events leading to his eviction by being violent to his wife (which led to the ouster against him, the notice to quit served by his wife, and the landlord reclaiming possession).[90] The effect was that the Court of Appeal reduced by two-thirds the damages that would otherwise have been payable. In *Regalgrand Ltd v Dickerson* the Court of Appeal confirmed that failure to pay the rent can be conduct making it reasonable to mitigate.[91] That failure, together with the fact that the tenants had already decided to move out and had started to move their possessions, meant that damages were reduced on appeal from £12,000 to £1,500.

23.8.3.5 Statutory and Common Law Damages?

Section 27(5) is designed to prevent double recovery of damages:

> Nothing in this section affects the right of a residential occupier to enforce any liability which arises apart from this section in respect of his loss of the right to occupy premises as his residence; but damages shall not be awarded both in respect of such a liability and in respect of a liability arising by virtue of this section on account of the same loss.

This means that it is not possible to recover general and exemplary damages at common law in addition to section 28 damages as it should not be possible to recover twice over for the same loss. So, in *Francis v Brown* it was not possible to recover exemplary damages as the statutory damages 'went beyond what was needed to compensate' the former tenant.[92] The position in relation to aggravated damages is less settled. In *Nwokorie v Mason*, Dillon LJ said that section 27(5) requires aggravated damages to be set-off against the statutory damages, but later cases suggest that it is possible to recover aggravated damages in addition to the statutory damages. This was argued for by Bridge on the basis that:

> … landlords resigned to be hung for a sheep as well as a lamb would otherwise have no incentive to evict with minimum force.[93]

This is supported by the remarks of Sir Iain Glidewell in *Francis v Brown*, and in the county court case of *Fairweather v Ghafoor* aggravated damages were awarded in addition to statutory damages.[94]

Consequential damage, such as damage to goods, can be recovered in addition to statutory damages as they are for a different loss.

23.8.3.6 Re-instating the Tenant

Section 27(6) provides that the landlord will not be liable for damages if the occupier is reinstated before the proceedings are finally disposed of. In practice, there will often be reluctance on the occupier's part to return to the premises, especially as, according to *Tagro v Cafane*, it seems that the occupier has a choice between accepting reinstatement or refusing

---

[90] [1999] 1 WLR 1011 (CA). The notice was given before the Court of Appeal decision in *Hounslow LBC v Pilling* [1993] 1 WLR 1242 (CA) had held that a short notice was ineffective (see chs 23 and 25).
[91] (1997) 29 HLR 620 (CA).
[92] (1998) 30 HLR 143 (CA) 150.
[93] S Bridge, 'Damages for Eviction: Confusion Compounded' [1994] *Conv* 411, 414.
[94] [2001] CLY 4164 (Cty Ct).

reinstatement and pursuing a claim for damages.[95] However, if the offer to reinstate was made before the proceedings were begun, section 27(7) states that the court may reduce the damages to such amount as it thinks appropriate if it was unreasonable of the occupier to refuse the offer. If the occupier is reinstated he may still be able to claim damages under the general law, as in *McCormack v Namjou* where £4,760 was awarded in the form of general, aggravated and exemplary damages.[96]

23.9 Other Remedies

In cases of severe harassment, the local authority may be able to resort to other measures. In *R v Secretary of State for the Environment, ex p Royal Borough of Kensington and Chelsea*, Taylor J confirmed that a local authority may, in extreme cases, be able to compulsorily purchase the property where the effect of the harassment means that the tenant does not have proper housing accommodation.[97]

There may also be the possibility of using the Protection from Harassment Act 1997. Although this was passed primarily to address the problem of stalking and the like, the wording is wide enough that it may be of use in landlord and tenant cases. Harassment is widely defined by section 1, which prohibits a person from pursuing a course of conduct that is harassment and which he knows, or ought to know, amounts to harassment. By section 7(2) harassment includes alarming a person or causing a person distress. Harassment can be both a criminal offence (section 2) and provide a civil remedy (section 3).

Local authorities are most likely to use the Protection from Harassment Act 1997 to respond to problems between occupiers in local authority housing. The DETR report in 2000 said that it had not been used in the private rented sector and would probably be of little use as the 1997 Act was unlikely to catch behaviour that was not already covered by the Protection from Eviction Act 1977.[98]

23.10 Reform?

Overall, notwithstanding the variety of ways in which the law can respond to unlawful eviction and harassment, it is not clear that the law at present is particularly effective. The DETR report makes a number of suggestions for change, grouped into three categories. The first category relates to the national picture and suggests a clearer and more effective framework for local authorities to work in, by giving guidance to local authorities and the police on their roles, and the creation of an arbitration service. The second category is concerned with increasing the effectiveness of the response to harassment and

---

[95] [1991] 1 WLR 378 (CA).
[96] [1990] CLY 1725 (Cty Ct).
[97] (1987) 19 HLR 161 (QB). Presumably the aim is to maintain the tenancy following compulsory purchase.
[98] A Marsh and others, 'Harassment and Unlawful Eviction of Private Rented Sector Tenants and Park Home Residents' (DETR, 2000) paras 5.17–5.20.

unlawful eviction by promoting best practice more widely. This would include things such as clearer lines of responsibility within local authorities, better publicity of the help available to tenants, greater accessibility to help for tenants, more pro-active work, and training for law enforcers so as to emphasise the seriousness of the offence. The final category relates to the law itself and includes suggesting that the law be simplified and clarified, to include a re-examination of the scope and value of damages available under the Housing Act 1988.[99]

---

[99] A Marsh and others, 'Harassment and Unlawful Eviction of Private Rented Sector Tenants and Park Home Residents' (DETR, 2000) 11–2.

24

ENDING A LEASE EARLY

24.1   Introduction
24.2   Ending a lease for tenant breach: forfeiture
24.3   The Law Commission's termination scheme for tenant default
24.4   Tenant termination for landlord default?
24.5   Ending a lease for breach: repudiation
24.6   Tenant insolvency
24.7   Mortgagee possession and residential leases
24.8   Surrender
24.9   Abandonment
24.10   Break clauses
24.11   Merger
24.12   Frustration
24.13   The effect of termination on sub-tenants

24.1 Introduction

This chapter looks at the situations in which the lease can be brought to an end early. This may be through consensual action, such as surrender, or it may be non-consensual, such as when the landlord forfeits the lease following a breach of covenant by the tenant. Given that a periodic tenancy can be brought to an end by a notice to quit, the need to end a lease early is more likely to arise in relation to fixed term leases. This means that the law discussed in this chapter is of most significance to commercial leases and long residential leases.[1] It must not be forgotten that if the lease comes within one of the statutory schemes of protection discussed in Part Six, there will be additional rules that apply on ending the lease.

---

[1] Most agricultural and residential tenancies are either periodic tenancies or short fixed terms. Even in these cases, the parties may sometimes wish to end the tenancy earlier than is possible by notice or effluxion of time.

24.2 Ending a Lease for Tenant Breach: Forfeiture

24.2.1 Introduction

The landlord may be able to end the lease early for tenant default if there is a forfeiture clause. Most commercial and long residential leases provide for the landlord to be able to end the tenancy in the event of the tenant breaching a covenant or condition.[2] The law is based on the doctrine of 're-entry' whereby forfeiture occurs by the landlord re-entering the property, at which point the tenancy ends.[3] This right of forfeiture has been described as analogous to the contractual doctrine of repudiation.[4] Historically, re-entry would occur by the landlord physically entering into possession ('actual re-entry'). Nowadays, most forfeiture occurs constructively through the issue of court proceedings rather than by physical re-entry.[5] Indeed, as will be seen, in the case of residential leases it is only possible to forfeit by court order, and even then there are further restrictions that apply. In all cases of constructive re-entry the tenancy ends at the date of the commencement of the court proceedings and not, as might be expected, when the court orders forfeiture. Accordingly, it is at the point of re-entry that the tenant's obligations under the lease come to an end, although he will be liable to pay 'mesne profits' for his occupation thereafter.

Forfeiture can have severe consequences for the tenant. It means the loss of possession of premises which may be a home or business site, but can also result in large financial loss where the lease was purchased for a capital sum or the tenant's interest has a premium value (for example, where the current rent is less than the market rent). There are other personal and financial costs associated with the need for relocation. Indeed, the costs to the tenant may be out of all proportion to the landlord's loss caused by breach. Although there is an opportunity to apply for relief against forfeiture (which is discussed below at 24.2.2.7), the effect of the doctrine of re-entry is that at the actual moment of termination there has been no opportunity for the merits of termination to be aired before a court.

As will be seen, when it comes to hearing the case for granting relief the courts have tended to lean against forfeiture where it would be unconscionable. So, there has been a reluctance to allow forfeiture where the landlord has suffered no irreparable damage or where that damage is disproportionately small compared to the loss that will be suffered by the tenant. If relief against forfeiture is granted, the forfeiture is set aside and the effect is as if the lease has never been forfeited. If it is not given, the forfeiture stands. Between forfeiture and the application for relief being heard, Sir Robert Megarry VC speaks of a

---

[2] The only modern day example of a condition is where the lease provides for forfeiture in the event of the tenant becoming bankrupt: Law Commission, 'Termination of Tenancies for Tenant Default' (Law Com CP No 174, 2004) para 2.5.

[3] This right of re-entry is capable of being a legal interest: Law Property Act 1925 s 1(2)(e). Although the express grant of such a right is a registrable disposition under the Land Registration Act 2002 s 27(2)(e), the registrar 'need not make any entry regarding such right in the registered title of the reversionary estate': Land Registration Rules 2003 r 77.

[4] In *Abidogun v Frolan Health Care Ltd* [2001] EWCA Civ 1821, Arden LJ says: '… the right to bring the lease to an end by accepting repudiation is … a forfeiture'.

[5] Actual re-entry is no longer allowed if the premises are let as a dwelling and there is someone lawfully residing in them: Protection from Eviction Act 1977 s 2 (see 24.2.2.5).

'twilight period' during which the lease has a shadowy existence, 'it cannot be said to be dead beyond hope of resurrection'.[6]

The law on forfeiture is highly complex. The law on forfeiture for non-payment of rent has developed separately from the law on forfeiture for breach of other covenants, and is discussed separately below. Further, the common law is overlaid by statutory interventions, some of which apply to constructive re-entry but not actual re-entry, and some of which apply differently to actions commenced in different courts. Forfeiture also brings to an end derivative interests (such as mortgages and sub-tenancies), although the interest holders may also have the right to apply for relief (discussed at 24.2.6 below).

There have been several Law Commission papers relating to forfeiture.[7] The most recent, in October 2006, states:

> 1.3 The law of forfeiture is in urgent need of reform. As we stated in our Consultation Paper: 'it is complex, it lacks coherence, and it can lead to injustice'. The time has come for its abolition and its replacement by a simpler, more coherent statutory scheme based on what is appropriate and proportionate in the circumstances.

The reform proposals put forward by the Law Commission are discussed below at 24.3.

What follows is an outline of the law of forfeiture. For further details, the reader should refer to specialist texts.

24.2.2 Forfeiture for Breach other than Non-Payment of Rent

A lease is not automatically ended when the tenant is in breach and the right to forfeit arises, the right of re-entry simply gives the landlord the option of forfeiture. If the tenant has breached the lease by, for example, assigning the lease to a new tenant without the landlord's consent, the landlord may choose to continue the lease if he is happy with the new tenant. The landlord may then 'waive' the breach. If, however, the landlord wishes to end the lease, he must first serve a notice under section 146 of the Law of Property Act 1925 and after a 'reasonable time' can then end the lease either by bringing possession proceedings or by peaceably repossessing the property.[8]

Chart 24.1 shows the main steps to taking forfeiture action where the breach is something other than non-payment of rent.

24.2.2.1 Waiver (Step 2)

If the landlord does wish to forfeit, it is important that he does not in the meantime do any unequivocal act which recognises the continuing existence of the lease as this will waive his right to forfeit. Waiver occurs only when the landlord or his agent is aware of facts giving rise to the breach, but can occur quite unintentionally as, for example, when the landlord's

---

[6] *Meadows v Clerical Medical & General Life Assurance Society* [1981] Ch 70 (Ch).

[7] Law Commission, 'Provisional Proposals Relating to Termination of Tenancies' (Law Com WP No 16, 1968); Law Commission, 'Codification of the Law of Landlord and Tenant: Forfeiture of Tenancies' (Law Com No 142, 1985); Law Commission, 'Landlord and Tenant: Termination of Tenancies Bill' (Law Com No 221, 1994); Law Commission, 'Landlord and Tenant Law: Termination of Tenancies by Physical Re-entry' (Law Com CD, 1998); Law Commission, 'Termination of Tenancies for Tenant Default' (Law Com CP No 174, 2004); Law Commission, 'Termination of Tenancies for Tenant Default' (Law Com No 303, 2006).

[8] If violence is used, this may lead to criminal liability: Criminal Law Act 1977 s 2.

Chart 24.1: Forfeiture other than for Non-payment of Rent

Step 1	**Right to forfeit must have arisen (breach)**
Step 2	**Landlord has not waived breach**
Step 3	**Serve section 146 notice** Note: *breach of repair* in residential/commercial lease of more than 7 years with at least 3 years left: may need court leave to proceed further (LP(R)A 1938)
Step 4	**Re-entry (actual or constructive)** Note: residential leases require court order
Step 5	**Application for relief from forfeiture**
Step 6	**Broad discretion to relieve** Relief usually given if breach is remedied

managing agent sees a new tenant in occupation and the landlord's office accepts payment of rent without this information having been passed onto it. In *Central Estates (Belgravia) Ltd v Woolgar (No 2)* the landlord intended to forfeit a lease as the tenant was convicted of running a brothel at the premises.[9] The office staff were informed of this but one of the clerks did not get the message and demanded the rent. Even though the tenant knew that the landlord planned to forfeit, the clerk's action had the effect of waiving the breach.[10]

Waiver operates only to prevent forfeiture for the breach, other remedies may still be available.

Some breaches are treated as 'once for all' breaches while others are treated as 'continuing' breaches. It is not always clear whether a breach is a 'once for all breach' or a 'continuing' breach, but the distinction matters because an act of waiver removes the possibility of forfeiture if there has been a 'once for all breach' whereas with a 'continuing' breach it is as though it is broken anew each day and so the landlord can forfeit on this ground even if he has, in the past, waived the breach. Denning LJ explains in *Wolfe v Hogan*:

> A breach of covenant not to use premises in a particular way is a continuing breach. Any acceptance of rent by the landlord after knowledge only waives the breaches up to the time of the acceptance of rent. It does not waive the continuance of the breach thereafter and, notwithstanding his previous acceptance of rent, the landlord can still proceed for forfeiture on that account. Indeed, in the case of a continuing breach the acceptance of rent after knowledge is only a bar to a claim for forfeiture if it goes on for so long or is accepted in such circumstances that it can be inferred that the landlord has not merely waived the breach but has also affirmatively consented to the tenant continuing to use the premises as he has done …[11]

Examples of 'once for all breaches' include a failure to build something by a particular date or underletting in breach of an alienation covenant. Examples of continuing breaches include the breach of a user covenant (as Denning LJ refers to) and breach of a covenant to keep in repair.

---

[9] [1972] 1 WLR 1048 (CA).
[10] Even a 'without prejudice' acceptance of rent is waiver: *Davenport v R* (1877) 3 App Cas 115.
[11] [1949] 2 KB 194 (CA) 205–6.

24.2.2.2 Section 146: Notification and Opportunity to Remedy (Step 3)

The Object of Section 146

In relation to breach of covenants other than for non-payment of rent,[12] section 146 of the Law of Property Act 1925 requires the landlord to notify the tenant of the breach[13] and to give an opportunity to remedy the breach or make compensation before forfeiting the lease:

> (1) A right of re-entry or forfeiture under any proviso or stipulation in a lease for a breach of any covenant or condition in the lease shall not be enforceable, by action or otherwise, unless and until the lessor serves on the lessee a notice –
>
> (a) specifying the particular breach complained of; and
> (b) if the breach is capable of remedy, requiring the lessee to remedy the breach; and
> (c) in any case, requiring the lessee to make compensation in money for the breach;[14]
>
> and the lessee fails, within a reasonable time thereafter, to remedy the breach, if it is capable of remedy, and to make reasonable compensation in money, to the satisfaction of the lessor, for the breach.

The object of this notice procedure was set out by Slade LJ in *Expert Clothing Service & Sales Ltd v Hillgate House*:

> In a case where the breach is 'capable of remedy' within the meaning of the section, the principal object of the notice procedure provided for by section 146(1), as I read it, is to afford the lessee two opportunities before the lessor actually proceeds to enforce his right of re-entry, namely (1) the opportunity to remedy the breach within a reasonable time after service of the notice, and (2) the opportunity to apply to the court for relief from forfeiture [see 24.2.2.7 below]. In a case where the breach is not 'capable of remedy' there is clearly no point in affording the first of these two opportunities; the object of the notice procedure is thus simply to give the lessee the opportunity to apply for relief.[15]

Later he adds,

> An important purpose of the section 146 procedure is to give even tenants who have hitherto lacked the will or the means to comply with their obligations one last chance to summon up that will or find the necessary means before the landlord re-enters.[16]

Section 146 applies to most leases and covenants, apart from covenants for the payment of rent.[17] The section cannot be contracted out of[18] and any provision in a lease which has the same effect as a forfeiture clause will be treated as such even if the landlord

---

[12] The law on forfeiture for non-payment of rent developed separately and is excluded from s 146 by the Law of Property Act 1925 s 146(11).

[13] This must be carefully and accurately specified, even though the *Mannai* 'reasonable recipient' test applies to s 146 notices: *Akici v LR Butlin Ltd* [2005] EWCA Civ 1296, [2006] 1 WLR 201.

[14] A landlord who does not want compensation need not ask for it: *Lock v Pearce* [1893] 2 Ch 271 (CA).

[15] *Expert Clothing Service & Sales Ltd v Hillgate House* [1986] Ch 340 (CA) 351.

[16] [1986] Ch 340 (CA) 358.

[17] Law of Property Act 1925 s 146(11); for limited exceptions see s 146(8) and (9). It is unclear if s 146 applies to forfeiture for denial of title: see Law Commission, 'Termination of Tenancies for Tenant Default' (Law Com CP No 174, 2004) para 2.54.

[18] Law of Property Act 1925 s 146(12).

appears to have secured a way of ending the lease for breach without it technically being a forfeiture.[19]

The notice must be served in accordance with section 196 of the Law of Property Act 1925. In the case of breach of a repairing covenant the landlord will not be able to forfeit the lease unless it can prove, in accordance with section 18(2) of the Landlord and Tenant Act 1927, that sufficient time has elapsed since service was known to the tenant (or under-tenant or the person who last paid the rent) to enable the repairs to be executed.

Capable of remedy

If the breach is 'capable of remedy' the section 146 notice must require the tenant to remedy it; if it is not, the notice need only specify the details of the breach and require compensation. This phrase has caused some difficulty. In one sense, no breach can ever truly be remedied in that the breach itself has occurred.[20] Nevertheless, the intent of section 146 is to prevent the landlord from forfeiting where the breach can be put right without any harm being caused to the landlord:

> ... the concept of capability of remedy for the purpose of section 146 must surely be directed to the question whether the harm that has been done to the landlord by the relevant breach is for practicable purposes capable of being retrieved.[21]

The point of the distinction between covenants capable of remedy and those not so capable is that it determines the wording must be used in the section 146 notice. As Kerr LJ pointed out in *Bass Ltd v Morton Ltd* the distinction does not go to the:

> ... substance of the rights and obligations of the parties, but merely to the form of the notices which must be given pursuant to the section.[22]

In trying to work out what 'capable of remedy' means the courts have drawn distinctions between different types of covenants. Thus, a negative covenant (such as a covenant not to use the property for a particular purpose) is said to be unlikely to be capable of remedy, particularly if it is regarded as a 'once and for all' breach. In contrast, the breach of a positive covenant (such as a covenant to decorate or build) can generally be remedied by the required act being done – even if this is after the time prescribed by the covenant.[23] The distinction is not, however, a convincing tool for answering the question of whether or not the breach is capable of remedy, particularly if the focus is to be on the question of whether, in the words of, Staughton LJ in *Savva v Houssein*, 'the mischief caused by the breach can be removed.'[24]

In *Akici v LR Butlin Ltd* Neuberger LJ considered that the law had become too technical. He preferred to assume that most breaches are capable of remedy, particularly as

---

[19] Law of Property Act 1925 s 146(7). See *Clarke (Richard & Co) v Widnall* [1976] 1 WLR 845 (CA); *Plymouth Corporation v Harvey* [1971] 1 WLR 549 (Ch).

[20] See Harman J in *Hoffman v Fineberg* [1949] Ch 245 (Ch) 253, and Neuberger LJ in *Akici v LR Butlin Ltd* [2005] EWCA Civ 1296, [2006] 1 WLR 201 [64].

[21] *Expert Clothing Service & Sales Ltd v Hillgate House* [1986] Ch 340 (CA) 355.

[22] [1988] 1 Ch 493 (CA) 527.

[23] *Expert Clothing Service & Sales Ltd v Hillgate House* [1986] Ch 340 (CA) 355.

[24] [1996] 2 EGLR 65 (CA) 66.

compensation can be given for the breach.[25] A number of recent cases support this approach. In *Savva v Houssain*, for example, the tenant had put up advertising signs in breach of a (negative) covenant yet the Court of Appeal held that this breach could be remedied by removing the signs.[26]

Nonetheless, short of new House of Lords authority, there are two types of covenant that Neuberger LJ accepted are, as a matter of principle, incapable of remedy. The first is a covenant against illegal or immoral use; said to be incapable of remedy because of the 'stigma' that attaches. In *Rugby School (Governors) v Tannahill*, the premises were used as a brothel in breach of a covenant not to use them for illegal or immoral purposes.[27] In holding the breach incapable of remedy, Greer LJ said that the:

> … result of committing the breach would be known all over the neighbourhood and seriously affect the value of the premises. Even a money payment together with the cessation of the improper use of the house could not be a remedy.[28]

The second is a covenant against sub-letting. In *Scala House & District Property Co Ltd v Forbes*, the Court of Appeal held that the breach of a covenant not to assign, underlet or part with possession was not a breach capable of remedy.[29] In *Bass Ltd v Morton Ltd*, Bingham LJ felt that this statement was too formalistic – an unlawful subletting could be brought to an end, undertakings given and compensation made without any continuing damage to the landlord.[30] Anxious to contain the authority of *Scala House*, Neuberger LJ held in *Akici v LR Butlin Ltd* that a covenant against parting with possession or sharing possession, falling short of creating or transferring a legal interest, was capable of remedy.[31]

A tenant who has breached an irremediable negative covenant may still be able to keep the lease if he is granted relief against forfeiture (see 24.2.2.7 below).

Reasonable Time

Where a breach is capable of remedy the tenant must be given a 'reasonable time' to remedy it (which means that the forfeiture proceedings will take longer). In *Expert Clothing Service & Sales Ltd v Hillgate House* the tenant had an obligation to reconstruct the premises and even though by the date of service of the section 146 notice he was already 15 months behind the specified start date, Slade LJ commented that he should still be given a 'reasonable time' to begin construction.[32]

It may, however, become clear that the tenant has no intention of remedying the breach,

---

[25] [2005] EWCA Civ 1296, [2006] 1 WLR 201 [64]–[65]. Neuberger LJ suggests that the positive/negative distinction has grown from the distinction found in relation to passing the burden of freehold covenants, but that it is unhelpful to translate this to the statutory jurisdiction between remediable and non-remediable breaches found in s 146: [70].

[26] [1996] 73 P & CR 150 (CA).

[27] [1935] 1 KB 87 (CA).

[28] [1935] 1 KB 87 (CA) 91.

[29] [1974] QB 575 (CA).

[30] [1988] 1 Ch 493 (CA) 541. In *Akici v LR Butlin Ltd* [2005] EWCA Civ 1296, [2006] 1 WLR 201 Neuberger LJ is highly critical of the reasoning in *Scala House* [67] and [74]. See also the comments of Harman J in *Van Haarlam v Kasner* [1992] 36 EG 135 (Ch) 142, where he suggested that trivial breaches of negative covenants may be remediable.

[31] [2005] EWCA Civ 1296, [2006] 1 WLR 201 [73].

[32] [1986] Ch 340 (CA).

in which case the landlord can proceed with the forfeiture action.[33] In *Shirayama Shokusan Co Ltd v Danovo Ltd* the tenant operated the Saatchi art gallery through a lease which had a rent based upon turnover and which required tickets to be priced at an agreed figure.[34] In breach of this, the gallery ran a 'two for one' offer with Time Out magazine. A section 146 notice was served but it soon became clear that the tenant would not stop running the offer as it had a further four months of advertising arranged with Time Out and did not intend to break the contract. In this event, it was held that the landlord was able to continue the forfeiture proceedings fourteen days after serving the section 146 notice. Similarly, if there is a breach that is not capable of remedy, then a short time may be held reasonable, as in *Scala House & District Property Co v Forbes* where fourteen days was held sufficient following breach of a covenant against sub-letting.[35]

If the tenant does remedy the breach and pay compensation within the reasonable time prescribed by the section 146 notice, the landlord is not able to forfeit the lease.

24.2.2.3 Breach of Repairing Covenant

In the case of forfeiture for breach of repairing covenants it may be necessary to obtain a court order before forfeiting. This is because of the effect of the Leasehold Property (Repairs) Act 1938. A landlord seeking to forfeit for breach of repairing covenant where the lease was initially for seven years or more and has at least three years left unexpired must include in his section 146 notice advice to the tenant of his right to serve a counter-notice within 28 days. If the tenant does serve such a counter-notice claiming the protection of the statute, the landlord is unable to bring proceedings in respect of the repairing covenant without leave of the court. Leave will not be given unless the landlord proves, on the balance of probabilities,[36] one of five grounds set out in section 1(5):

(a) that the immediate remedying of the breach in question is requisite for preventing substantial diminution in the value of his reversion, or that the value thereof has been substantially diminished by the breach;

(b) that the immediate remedying of the breach is required for giving effect in relation to the premises to the purposes of any enactment, or of any byelaw or other provision having effect under an enactment, or for giving effect to any order of a court or requirement of any authority under any enactment or any such byelaw or other provision as aforesaid;

(c) in a case in which the lessee is not in occupation of the whole of the premises as respects which the covenant or agreement is proposed to be enforced, that the immediate remedying of the breach is required in the interests of the occupier of those premises or of part thereof;

(d) that the breach can be immediately remedied at an expense that is relatively small in comparison with the much greater expense that would probably be occasioned by postponement of the necessary work; or

(e) special circumstances which in the opinion of the court, render it just and equitable that leave should be given.

---

[33] Sir Nicholas Browne-Wilkinson (as he then was) in the Court of Appeal in *Billson v Residential Apartments Limited* [1992] 1 AC 494 (CA) 508.

[34] [2005] EWHC 2589 (Ch).

[35] [1974] QB 575 (CA).

[36] *Associated British Ports v Bailey plc* [1990] 2 AC 703 (HL).

The Act does not apply to agricultural leases but covers both residential and commercial leases. The purpose of the Act is to prevent landlords from harassing tenants with long lists of dilapidations, which may not be very material but which would generate a great deal of uncertainty for tenants who could not be sure that landlords would not proceed to forfeit the lease. In the *Associated British Ports* case, for example, the tenants were being asked to repair a dry dock at a cost of £600,000 even though it would probably never be used for ship repair again.[37] As Lord Templeman pointed out:

> In practice many a tenant lost his lease or submitted to an increased rent or substantial expenditure rather than face the expense and uncertainty of a forfeiture action.[38]

The effect of the Act is to ensure that a landlord can only pursue a remedy for breach of the repairing covenant if the repair is necessary in the sense of one of the five grounds. Even if one of these grounds is proven the tenant may still apply for relief in the subsequent forfeiture proceedings.[39]

24.2.2.4 Internal Repair

A similar and overlapping provision exists in relation to internal decorative repairs. By section 147 of the Law of Property Act 1925, the tenant is able to apply for relief when the landlord has served a notice relating to internal decorative repairs. By section 147(1), if the court:

> … having regard to all the circumstances of the case (including in particular the length of the lessee's term or interest remaining unexpired) … is satisfied that the notice is unreasonable, it may, by order, wholly or partially relieve the lessee from liability for such repairs.

This means that the court can not only grant relief from forfeiture but also from liability for the repairs. The section does not cover, inter alia, repairs necessary or proper for getting the property into a sanitary condition or structural repairs[40] or any statutory liability to keep the house 'reasonably fit for human habitation'.[41] The section covers all leases, of any length.

24.2.2.5 Re-entry (Step 4)

If the breach has not been remedied once a 'reasonable time' has elapsed after service of the section 146 notice, the landlord is able to re-enter the premises by peacefully possessing them or by issuing court proceedings. In the case of a residential lease, forfeiture can only occur by court order. Section 2 of the Protection from Eviction Act 1977 states:

> Where any premises are let as a dwelling on a lease which is subject to a right of re-entry or forfeiture it shall not be lawful to enforce that right otherwise than by proceedings in the court while any person is lawfully residing in the premises or part of them.

---

[37] *Associated British Ports v Bailey plc* [1990] 2 AC 703 (HL).
[38] *Associated British Ports v Bailey plc* [1990] 2 AC 703 (HL) 709; see also *Hamilton v Martell Ltd* [1984] 1 Ch 266 (Ch) 278.
[39] On the 1938 Act see also ch 12; P Smith, 'A Review of the Operation of the Leasehold Property (Repairs) Act 1938' [1986] *Conv* 85.
[40] Law of Property Act 1925 s 147(2)(ii).
[41] Law of Property Act 1925 s 147(2)(iii).

This section was held by the Court of Appeal in *Patel v Pirabakaran* also to apply to mixed use premises. In the words of Wilson LJ:

> I suggest that three main considerations underlie the limited prohibition in s 2 against what, in *Billson v Residential Apartments Ltd* [1992] 1 AC 494 at 536, Lord Templeman described as the 'dubious and dangerous' method of enforcing a right of forfeiture by re-entry without due process of law: (a) A tenant should not be at risk of returning home to discover that, unbeknown to him, he and his family have been locked out and are homeless. If they are to be evicted, the eviction should be conducted in an orderly fashion, upon at least some prior notice, by officers subject to court direction. (b) If there is to be an issue as to whether the landlord is entitled to forfeiture under the terms of the tenancy, it is preferable, particularly in relation to a home, for the court to determine it in advance of eviction rather than in proceedings brought by the tenant for an injunction and damages in the wake of it or in criminal proceedings against the landlord under s 1 of the 1977 Act. (c) If there is to be an issue as to whether the tenant is entitled to relief against forfeiture pursuant to s 146(2) of the 1925 Act, it is, again, preferable, particularly in relation to a home, for the court to determine it in advance of eviction rather than in its wake. I see no reason why these considerations should not apply to a tenant for whom the premises represent not only his home but also his place of business.[42]

Apart from these situations, there is no requirement for the landlord to forfeit by legal proceedings. If the landlord chooses to forfeit by peaceable re-entry this is, in practice, usually affected out of business hours, to avoid the risk of committing an offence under section 6 of the Criminal Law Act 1977. This Act makes it an offence to use or threaten violence without lawful authority for the purposes of securing entry into any premises where, to the knowledge of the entrant, there is someone present who is opposed to the entry. Hence in the *Billson* case it was at 6am that the landlord's agents re-entered the premises, changed the locks and put up notices stating that the lease had been forfeited.[43] There can also be 'constructive' physical re-entry where, for example, the landlord allows a third party into occupation and grants a new tenancy to that person.

The availability of such a self-help remedy is at odds with most modern trends. In the *Billson* case, the House of Lords had to decide whether a tenant was able to apply for relief where the landlord had peaceably re-entered. With what was arguably a straining of the language in section 146(2),[44] the House of Lords overturned a controversial Court of Appeal decision and held that the tenant did have the right to apply for relief. In reaching this decision their Lordships were heavily influenced by the desire to reduce the incentive for landlords to pursue what Lord Templeman termed 'the dubious and dangerous method of determining the lease by re-entering the premises'.[45] The dislike of self-help remedies was expressed by Nicholls LJ in his dissenting judgment in the Court of Appeal:

> Nor can it be right to encourage law-abiding citizens to embark on a course which is a sure recipe for violence … The policy of the law is to discourage self-help when confrontation and

---

[42] [2006] EWCA Civ 685, [2006] 1 WLR 3112 [37].

[43] *Billson v Residential Apartments Ltd* [1992] 1 AC 494 (HL).

[44] S 146(2) refers to a landlord who 'is proceeding' – which suggests something currently ongoing. The House of Lords read this as including 'proceeds', which could include a past action. See below at 24.2.2.7 for further discussion.

[45] *Billson v Residential Apartments Ltd* [1992] 1 AC 494 (HL) 536.

a breach of the peace are likely to follow. If a tenant, who is in breach of covenant, will not quit but persists in carrying on his business despite the landlord's right of re-entry, the proper course for a responsible landlord is to invoke the due process of the law and seek an order for possession from the court.[46]

Against this, it has to be said that peaceable re-entry is fast and effective[47] and will be especially attractive where the tenant has abandoned the premises and is therefore unlikely to seek relief.[48]

The Law Commission have blown hot and cold over the continuing availability of self-help possession. In 1985 it recommended that actual re-entry should be banned for all leases:

> ... the loss of [a] ... tenancy is usually a serious matter for a tenant ... and we do not think it should ever occur except by consent or with the authority of the court.[49]

By contrast, in the 1998 consultative document it was seen as an effective management tool, enabling a landlord to protect the value of its investment and the income stream without the need to apply for a court order. The current proposals replace the self-help system with a summary termination procedure which is designed to provide landlords with a similar management tool while providing greater protection for tenants (see 24.3 below).

24.2.2.6 *The Necessity of Re-entry?*

The ability to end a contract for breach is not confined to leases and it has been argued that the law relating to forfeiture of leases represents the application of more general principles of contract law.[50] In *Clark (WG) (Properties) Ltd v Dupre Properties Ltd* forfeiture was seen as an application of the law on repudiation of contracts:

> Whenever there has been a breach of covenant, for example a repairing covenant, which has not been remedied within the time specified in the notice, the landlord is treating the tenant's breach as repudiatory and, by serving proceedings claiming forfeiture of the lease, is accepting that repudiation.[51]

The significance of this argument is that:

> ... [if] forfeiture is but an example of the determination of an agreement in accordance with the principles of the law of contract, re-entry is not to be regarded as some ancient rite deriving its significance from the medieval mysteries of landlord and tenant law; it is merely one kind of unequivocal act exercising the landlord's option to determine the lease, and is essential (to the exclusion of other modes of exercising the option) only if the lease so provides.[52]

Support for this is given in the Australian case of *Progressive Mailing House Pty Ltd v Tabali Pty Ltd*, where Mason J said that:

---

[46] *Billson v Residential Apartments Ltd* [1992] 1 AC 494 (HL) 525.

[47] See Brooke LJ in *Kataria v Safeland plc* [1998] 1 EGLR 39 (CA) 41, who suggests landlords should be at liberty to peaceably possess as there are no fast track procedures enabling landlords to obtain possession orders speedily.

[48] For a general discussion of self-help remedies in property law, see A Clarke, 'Property Law' (1992) 45 *CLP* 81.

[49] Law Commission, 'Codification of the Law of Landlord and Tenant: Forfeiture of Tenancies' (Law Com No 142, 1985) para 3.8.

[50] AJ Bradbrook and CE Croft, *Commercial Tenancy Law in Australia* (Sydney, Butterworths, 1990) 295–7.

[51] [1992] Ch 297 (Ch) 309.

[52] AJ Bradbrook and CE Croft, *Commercial Tenancy Law in Australia* (Sydney, Butterworths, 1990) 297.

... re-entry is essential only where the parties stipulate that advantage shall not be taken of a forfeiture except by an entry upon the land.[53]

On this view it might be possible for a landlord to reserve power to effect forfeiture by, for example, simply serving notice on the tenant (in cases not regulated by statute). In practice, however, leases are not drafted in this way and even if they were, the landlord would still have to serve a section 146 notice before forfeiting and the tenant would be able to apply for relief.[54] Given the dislike of self-help remedies, it would also be an undesirable development.

24.2.2.7 Relief Against Forfeiture[55](Steps 5 and 6)

Equitable and Statutory Jurisdiction

In view of the harsh results of forfeiture, equity intervened early on to grant the tenant relief from forfeiture in certain situations. These situations were initially limited to instances when the tenant was prevented from strict compliance with the contractual provisions through unavoidable accident, fraud, surprise or ignorance which did not constitute wilful neglect or misconduct.[56] This was part of equity's general jurisdiction to intervene in order to prevent unconscionable insistence on strict legal rights, seen also in the development of the equity of redemption in mortgages.[57] This equitable jurisdiction was soon supplemented by statutory powers to relieve against forfeiture,[58] the development being traced by Lord Templeman in *Billson v Residential Apartments Ltd*:

> Before the intervention of Parliament, if a landlord forfeited by entering into possession or by issuing and serving a writ for possession, equity could relieve the tenant against forfeiture but only in cases under the general principles of equity whereby a party may be relieved from the consequences of fraud, accident or mistake or in cases where the breach of covenant entitling the landlord to forfeit was a breach of the covenant for payment of rent ...
>
> In 1881 Parliament interfered to supplement equity and to enable any tenant to be relieved from forfeiture. The need for such intervention was and is manifest because otherwise a tenant who had paid a large premium for a 999 year lease at a low rent could lose his asset by a breach of covenant which was remediable or which caused the landlord no damage. The forfeiture of any lease, however short, may unjustly enrich the landlord at the expense of the

---

[53] (1985) 57 ALR 609 (HC of Australia) 618.

[54] See reference to 'action or otherwise' in s 146(2). In *Richard Clarke & Co Ltd v Widnall* (1976) 33 P & CR 339 (CA) the landlord had the right to end the lease on three months' notice for tenant breach. This was treated as giving the tenant the right to apply for relief against forfeiture whether or not it was technically a forfeiture clause.

[55] As the Law Commission observes: 'It is not easy to state the present law about relief in a way which is both brief and accurate. The substantive rights of the parties vary in some respects according to whether proceedings are brought in the High Court or in a county court. There are uncertainties and anomalies. And the law is in part statutory and in part non-statutory, the statutory part being contained in a number of different enactments, some of which are old and even (in parts) obsolete.': Law Commission, 'Termination of Tenancies for Tenant Default' (Law Com CP No 174, 2004) para 2.17.

[56] *Eaton v Lyon* (1798) 3 Ves Jun 691.

[57] See generally: RP Meagher, WMC Gummow and JRF Lehane, *Equity Doctrines and Remedies* 3rd edn (Sydney, Butterworths, 1992) ch 18 esp [1805]-[1815].

[58] The extent to which there remains an equitable jurisdiction to relieve outside of the statutory jurisdiction is unclear: see Law Commission, 'Termination of Tenancies for Tenant Default' (Law Com No 303, 2006) para 1.12. In *Billson v Residential Apartments Ltd* [1992] 1 AC 494 the majority of the Court of Appeal held that there was no residual equitable jurisdiction to relieve from forfeiture.

tenant. In creating a power to relieve against forfeiture for breach of covenant Parliament protected the landlord by conferring on the court a wide discretion to grant relief on terms or to refuse relief altogether. In practice this discretion is exercised with the object of ensuring that the landlord is not substantially prejudiced or damaged by the revival of the lease ... [59]

The statutory power to grant relief is now contained in section 146(2) of the Law of Property Act 1925:

Where a lessor is proceeding, by action or otherwise, to enforce such a right of re-entry or forfeiture, the lessee may, in the lessor's action, if any, or in any action brought by himself, apply to the court for relief; and the court may grant or refuse relief, as the court, having regard to the proceedings and conduct of the parties under the foregoing provision of this section, and to all the other circumstances, thinks fit; and in case of relief may grant it on such terms, if any, as to costs, expenses, damages, compensation, penalty, or otherwise, including the granting of an injunction to restrain any like breach in the future, as the court, in the circumstances of each case, thinks fit.

This subsection enables the tenant to apply for relief when the landlord 'is proceeding' to forfeit the lease. This has been interpreted by the House of Lords in *Billson v Residential Apartments Ltd* as enabling the tenant to apply any time after the service of a section 146 notice up until the point when the landlord has forfeited the lease by issuing and serving a writ for possession, recovered judgment and entered into possession pursuant to that judgment.[60] The tenant is also able to apply for relief when the landlord has forfeited by peaceable re-entry and not by court order, the absence of a time limit being balanced by the fact that delay on the part of the tenant in applying for relief will be taken account of in deciding whether or not to grant relief.

Discretion

In *Hyman v Rose*, Earl Loreburn LC stressed that the court is given a free discretion to consider all the circumstances and the conduct of the parties:

[When] the Act is so express to provide a wide discretion, meaning, no doubt, to prevent one man from forfeiting what in fair dealing belongs to someone else, by taking advantage of a breach from which he is not commensurately and irreparably damaged, it is not advisable to lay down any rigid rules for guiding that discretion.[61]

Since then the courts have maintained that this discretion should remain unfettered. In many cases the courts adopt the approach put forward by Lord Wilberforce in *Shiloh Spinners Ltd v Harding*, even though he was then addressing the equitable jurisdiction to relieve and not the statutory jurisdiction:

[It] remains true today that equity expects men to carry out their bargains and will not let them buy their way out by uncovenanted payment. But it is consistent with these principles that we should reaffirm the right of courts of equity in appropriate and limited cases to relieve against forfeiture for breach of covenant or condition where the primary object of the bargain is to secure a stated result which can effectively be obtained when the matter comes before the

---

[59] *Billson v Residential Apartments Ltd* [1992] 1 AC 494 (HL) 534–5.
[60] [1992] 1 AC 494 (HL).
[61] [1912] AC 623 (HL) 631, commenting on s 14(2) of the Conveyancing Act 1881 which was replaced by s 146(2) of the Law of Property Act 1925.

court, and where the forfeiture provision is added by way of security for the production of that result.

The word 'appropriate' involves consideration of the conduct of the applicant for relief, in particular whether his default was wilful, of the gravity of the breaches, and of the disparity between the value of the property of which forfeiture is claimed as compared with the damage caused by the breach.[62]

In the Saatchi art gallery case, *Shirayama Shokusan Co Ltd v Danovo Ltd* (see 24.2.2.2 above), the judge refused the tenant relief against forfeiture because of the deliberate disregard it had shown for the landlord's rights in continuing to run not only the existing ticket offers in breach of the lease, but also entering new ones after it knew that this was an issue.[63]

When the breach has been remedied relief will generally be given, unless there are exceptional circumstances:

> ... for example, if the breaches have been gross and wilful or it appears that the tenant is not likely to comply with his obligations in the future.[64]

Proportionality

Proportionality is also very important – whether the harm that would be suffered by the tenant through forfeiture is disproportionate to the harm occasioned to the landlord through the breach,[65] and whether the landlord's gain if no relief is granted is out of proportion to the harm he has suffered. In *Southern Depot Co Ltd v British Railways Board*, Morritt J was faced with three breaches of covenant, two of which were wilful.[66] Nevertheless, unlike in the exercise of the equitable jurisdiction, the wilfulness was only one factor amongst many. Under the equitable jurisdiction, relief can only be given for a deliberate and wilful breach in exceptional circumstances.[67] Morritt J preferred to focus not on wilfulness but on proportionality – the essential question was:

> ... whether the damage sustained by [the landlord] ... is proportionate to the advantage it will obtain if no relief is granted and, if not, whether in all the circumstances it is just that [the landlord] ... should retain that advantage.[68]

On the facts, relief was given – otherwise the landlord would obtain an advantage worth not less than £1.4 million from breaches which had caused it no lasting damage.

This approach restricts the situations in which relief will be denied, so long as the tenant is willing and able to pay for past errors. Lasting damage is rare – most breaches can be made good through payment. Even in cases where there has been breach of covenants designated as incapable of remedy (such as covenants against underletting and immoral user), the courts have been willing to give relief. So, in immoral use cases it is sometimes noted that the 'stigma' is short-lived. In *Ropemaker Properties Ltd v Noonhaven Ltd*, the premises

---

[62] [1973] AC 691 (HL) 723.
[63] [2005] EWHC 2589 (Ch).
[64] *Cremin v Barjack Properties Ltd* [1985] 1 EGLR 30 (CA) 32.
[65] See, for example, *Central Estates (Belgravia) Ltd v Woolgar (No 2)* [1972] 1 WLR 1048 (CA) 1053.
[66] [1990] 2 EGLR 39 (Ch).
[67] See Lord Wilberforce, *Shiloh Spinners Ltd v Harding* [1973] AC 691 (HL) 725.
[68] [1990] 2 EGLR 39 (Ch) 44.

were used for prostitution, described as being a breach of the 'utmost gravity'.[69] Millet J said that where there has been immoral user it:

> will … be in only the rarest and most exceptional circumstances that the court will grant relief … particularly where the breach of covenant has been both wilful and serious.[70]

Nevertheless, on the facts relief was granted taking account, inter alia, of the fact that the lease had substantial value (loss of the lease would cause substantial financial loss to the tenant 'out of all proportion to their offence or to any conceivable damage caused' to the landlord and give an 'adventitious profit' to the landlord), that the immoral user had ended and that it was unlikely to recur.[71]

Third Party Rights
Another factor that will be relevant to the court is whether third party rights are involved, as where the landlord has re-let the property or sold its own interest following forfeiture.

The general approach has been to focus on the landlord's conduct and to be more willing to grant relief where the landlord acted hastily in re-letting the property – the issue of a third party being a relevant factor in considering whether or not to grant relief.[72] If relief is given after a disposition, the lease is capable of binding the third party but the court is also able to grant a form of relief that allows priority to the third party. In *Fuller v Judy Properties Ltd*, the Court of Appeal granted relief but did not allow this to affect the third party.[73] The end result in *Fuller* was that the new third party tenant was in possession and the old (relieved) tenant became the immediate reversioner in relation to the new lease.[74]

24.2.3 *Forfeiture for Non-payment of Rent*

In the case of forfeiture for non-payment of rent, there is no need to serve a section 146 notice but at common law it is necessary to serve a formal demand for rent on the tenant, subject to contrary intention. This demand must be served between the hours of sunrise and sunset. There is a statutory modification of this rule that means that there is no need for a formal demand if the rent is half a year in arrears and there are insufficient goods on the premises to be distrained.[75] In practice, however, most leases contain a provision that the

---

[69] [1989] 2 EGLR 50 (Ch) 56.

[70] [1989] 2 EGLR 50 (Ch) 56.

[71] It was also said that relief would have been given (had the point arisen on the facts) in *Central Estates (Belgravia) Ltd v Woolgar (No 2)* [1972] 1 WLR 1048 (CA) (use as a brothel) where the value of the landlord's estate had not suffered, the tenant stood to lose a lot, and the use did not continue for long; and in *Van Haarlam v Kasner* [1972] 1 WLR 1048 (Ch) (offences under the Official Secrets Acts) in view of the severe disproportionality that forfeiture would entail and noting that 'Nothing he did in the flat was *qua* tenant offences'.

[72] See, for example, *Bhojwani v Kingsley Investment Trust Ltd* [1992] 39 EG 138 (Ch).

[73] (1991) 64 P & CR 176 (CA).

[74] For criticism, see J Martin, 'Casenote Editor's Note' [1992] *Conv* 343. See also *Bank of Ireland Home Mortgages v South Lodge Developments* [1996] 1 EGLR 91 (Ch) in which the leaseholder's mortgagee was granted relief in the form of a reversionary lease and the landlord, who had acted unreasonably in granting a new lease, had to pay the premium of £48,000 received for the new lease, as well as costs, to the mortgagee.

[75] Common Law Procedure Act 1852 s 210.

Chart 24.2: Forfeiture for Non-payment of Rent

Step 1	**Need for formal demand (strict procedural requirements)**
	UNLESS:
	—lease exempts need (usual)
	—half year's arrears and insufficient goods for distress
Step 2	**Court proceedings stop if arrears and costs paid before trial**
Step 3	**Tenant able to apply for relief from forfeiture**

NB. This chart is highly simplified. For a full account see: Law Commission, 'Termination of Tenancies for Tenant Default' (Law Com CP No 174, 2004) paras 2.18–2.29

right of re-entry arises when rent is in arrears, whether or not lawfully demanded.[76] The process of forfeiture for non-payment of rent is outlined in chart 24.2.

It has been possible from an early date for the Court of Chancery to give relief against forfeiture for non-payment of rent. As with forfeiture more generally, the right to forfeit is seen as a means of securing performance, in this instance the payment of the money. The tenant is effectively entitled to relief if he pays all rent arrears and costs, even if he has a persistent record of late payment and arrears. This result stems from a variety of equitable and statutory jurisdictions.[77] In some respects this is surprising. The tenant may have an appalling record of payment but so long as he pays the arrears[78] he can keep the lease.

24.2.4 Forfeiture for Denial of Title

There is an implied condition in every lease that the tenant shall not do anything to prejudice or deny the title of the landlord. This covenant has feudal origins but is now explained as an implied term resting in contract law.[79] If the tenant denies or disclaims the landlord's title, the landlord is entitled to forfeit the lease. In *W G Clark (Properties) Ltd v Dupre Properties Ltd* this doctrine was seen as analogous to repudiation of contract and as amounting to the tenant saying: 'You are not my landlord; I am not in the relationship of landlord and tenant with you.'[80]

Modern cases tend to treat the doctrine narrowly,[81] and the ability to forfeit for denial of title was described by Lord Denning MR in *Warner v Sampson* as 'inappropriate at the present day'.[82] It is condemned by the Law Commission as 'unnecessary and anachronistic' and under their reform proposals, it will no longer be possible for breach of the implied condition not to deny or disclaim the landlord's title to trigger termination.[83] Under

---

[76] 'The law concerning formal demands for rent is obsolete': Law Commission, 'Termination of Tenancies for Tenant Default' (Law Com No 303, 2006) para 1.12 (5).

[77] *Howard v Fanshawe* [1895] 2 Ch 581; Common Law Procedure Act 1852 ss 210 and 212; County Courts Act 1984 ss 138 and 139(2); Supreme Court Act 1981 s 38(1).

[78] In some cases even after the landlord has regained possession, see Common Law Procedure Act 1852 s 210.

[79] *Abidogun v Frolan Health Care Ltd* [2001] EWCA Civ 1821.

[80] [1992] Ch 297 (Ch) 303.

[81] *Abidogun v Frolan Health Care Ltd* [2001] EWCA Civ 1821.

[82] [1959] 1 QB 297 (CA) 315.

[83] Law Commission, 'Termination of Tenancies for Tenant Default' (Law Com No 303, 2006) para 1.12.

the present law, it has been accepted that relief against forfeiture may be available for denial of title.[84]

24.2.5 Residential Leases

A landlord is only able to forfeit a residential lease by court order.[85] Further, by section 81 of the Housing Act 1996,[86] a landlord is unable to forfeit premises let as a dwelling[87] for failure to pay a service charge or administration charge unless the tenant has admitted liability or it has been finally determined as payable by a leasehold valuation tribunal, court or arbitral tribunal. The landlord is unable to forfeit until after a 14 day period has expired from this determination.

There has been a particular problem with long residential leases as forfeiting the lease for a relatively minor breach could lead to a windfall for the landlord. The Commonhold and Leasehold Reform Act 2002 introduced two changes to deal with this mischief. One ensures that insignificant financial arrears cannot give rise to a right to forfeit. Section 167 provides that there can be no forfeiture of a long lease of a dwelling[88] for unpaid rent, service charges or administration charges unless the amount owed is more than £350 or has been outstanding for more than three years.[89] The second change, overlapping with section 81 of the 1996 Act, is that by section 168 of the 2002 Act a landlord under a long lease of a dwelling is not able to serve a section 146 notice (to commence forfeiture proceedings) for breach of *any* covenant or condition unless the tenant has admitted the breach or the breach has been finally determined by a court or arbitral tribunal as having occurred.

As seen in chapter 13, disputes over service charges are common, and it is not unusual for leaseholders to withhold sums in an attempt to exert some kind of leverage over the landlord, believing themselves to be in the right. This can backfire horribly if the landlord uses non-payment as a ground to forfeit, and the combined effect of sections 81 of the 1996 Act and section 167 of the 2002 Act is that the landlord cannot forfeit a valuable lease for relatively minor sums, or for sums that are contested. With long leases the effect of section 168 of the 2002 Act is that forfeiture is not possible if *any* breach is contested until it has been resolved by a judicial hearing.

The kind of issues that can arise are illustrated in *Mohammadi v Anston Investments Limited*.[90] The tenant had been withholding rent and service charge payments in protest at the state of repair. She brought an action for damages, and in its counterclaim the landlord sought judgement for arrears and claimed possession by forfeiture. Of course, under the doctrine of re-entry this brought the lease to an end and the tenant was left applying for relief from forfeiture. At first instance, relief was given on terms that included payments of substantial arrears in respect of the service charge (and interest). The Court of Appeal held

---

[84] *W G Clark (Properties) Ltd v Dupre Properties Ltd* [1992] Ch 297 (Ch); *Abidogun v Frolan Health Care Ltd* [2001] EWCA Civ 1821. For a discussion of relief: see 24.2.2.7.

[85] Protection from Eviction Act 1977 s 2 (see 24.2.2.5).

[86] Amended by the Commonhold and Leasehold Reform Act 2002.

[87] This section is not restricted to long leases.

[88] Broadly, leases of more than 21 years: see Commonhold and Leasehold Reform Act 2002 ss 76 and 77.

[89] Rights of Re-entry and Forfeiture (Prescribed Sum and Period) (England) Regulations 2004 SI 2004/3086.

[90] [2003] EWCA Civ 981.

that in view of section 81 of the Housing Act 1996 forfeiture was effective only in respect of the (small) ground rent component, and so the terms of relief should be similarly limited.[91]

24.2.6 Derivative Interests[92]

All derivative interests, such as under-leases and mortgages, also fall with the tenant's lease. By section 146(4) under-lessees (and those deriving title under them)[93] can also apply for relief:

> ... the court may, on application by any person claiming as under-lessee any estate or interest in the property comprised in the lease or any part thereof, either in the lessor's action (if any) or in any action brought by such person for that purpose, make an order vesting, for the whole term of the lease or any less term, the property comprised in the lease or any part thereof in any person entitled as under-lessee to any estate or interest in such property upon such conditions as to execution of any deed or other document, payment of rent, costs, expenses, damages, compensation, giving security, or otherwise, as the court in the circumstances of each case may think fit, but in no case shall any such under-lessee be entitled to require a lease to be granted to him for any longer term than he had under his original sub-lease.

Sub-tenants and mortgagees have very different interests to protect. The sub-tenant will be primarily interested in continuing occupation, the mortgagee in preserving the value of its security. The application must be made before the landlord has regained possession,[94] but there is no obligation on the landlord to give notice of forfeiture to holders of derivative interests. This is clearly unsatisfactory and commonly leads to, for example, mortgagees discovering that a lease has been forfeited long after the event.[95]

Relief can take two forms: the grant of a new tenancy to the claimant[96] or an order retrospectively vesting the old tenancy in the claimant.[97] Relief is, however, sparingly given in these circumstances. In the words of Harman J:

> ... this remains a jurisdiction to be exercised sparingly because it thrusts upon the landlord a person whom he has never accepted as tenant and creates in invitum a privity of contract between them. It appears to me that I ought only to vest the head term in the under-lessees upon the footing that they enter into covenants in all respects the same, or at least as stringent, as the covenants in the head-lease.[98]

---

[91] Money judgement was given for the service charge arrears.

[92] See generally, S Tromans, 'Forfeiture of Leases: Relief for Underlessees and Holders of Other Derivative Interests' [1986] *Conv* 187.

[93] S 146(5)(e). There have been inconsistent court decisions as to who comes within this definition: see Law Commission, 'Termination of Tenancies for Tenant Default' (Law Com CP No 174, 2004) paras 7.13–7.16.

[94] *Rogers v Rice* [1892] 2 Ch 170 (CA); Law Commission, 'Termination of Tenancies for Tenant Default' (Law Com No 303, 2006) para 2.31.

[95] Law Commission, 'Termination of Tenancies for Tenant Default' (Law Com No 303, 2006) para 4.8.

[96] Law of Property Act 1925 s 146(4). In *Bank of Ireland Home Mortgages v South Lodge Developments* [1996] 1 EGLR 91 (Ch) a mortgagee was granted relief in the form of a reversionary lease after the landlord had re-let the property.

[97] Law of Property Act 1925 s 146(2); *Escalus Properties Ltd v Robinson* [1996] QB 231 (CA).

[98] On the facts the sub-tenants were not willing to agree to this and so relief was denied: *Creery v. Summersell and Flowerdew & Co Ld* [1949] Ch 751 (Ch) 767.

24.3 The Law Commission's Termination Scheme for Tenant Default

24.3.1 Problems with the Law on Forfeiture

The Law Commission identifies a number of flaws with the law on forfeiture. Quite apart from its complexity and its lack of coherence it is severely hampered by being founded on the doctrine of re-entry. The fact that the lease ends when re-entry occurs is detrimental to both the landlord and tenant. In the words of Stuart Bridge, the Law Commissioner behind the 2006 termination of tenancies report:

> ... the re-entry fiction taints the process ...
>
> This is, obviously, detrimental to the tenant. Unless he or she does something, they will be out. But, it is not that great to the landlord either, as the equally pernicious law of waiver may turn around and bite him ...
>
> If you were asked to design a workable system governing the termination of tenancy by landlords in response to default by the tenants, you wouldn't start here. And once it is accepted that recovering possession by self-help is, as it should be, the rare exception rather than the general rule, then it becomes obvious that the starting point for any reform should be termination by order of the court. Unless, and until, the court makes an order terminating the tenancy, the tenancy should continue. That is the most important principle underlying the reforms to the law which the Law Commission [recommends].[99]

It is not only the doctrine of re-entry (and waiver) that is criticised. Also seen as unsatisfactory are the section 146 notice procedure, the existence of two distinct regimes for non-payment of rent and other breaches, the fact that relief does not focus on whether the tenant is a satisfactory tenant, and that holders of derivative interests are not given notice of the forfeiture.

24.3.2 An Outline of the Law Commission's Scheme[100]

The Law Commission has proposed abolition of the law on forfeiture and its replacement with a statutory scheme for termination of tenancies for tenant default. Although there is considerable support for the Law Commission's scheme, whether or not it is enacted will depend on whether there is the political will to devote Parliamentary time to the reform process. The principles on which the scheme is set out are referred to by Stuart Bridge:

> It envisages a scheme which requires the early exchange of necessary information; which is transparent; and, which sets out clearly what the landlord must do in order to terminate and what criteria the court must adopt in deciding whether or not the tenancy should be terminated. There should be as few unnecessary pitfalls as possible.[101]

---

[99] S Bridge, 'Commercial Leases Past and Present: the Contribution of the Law Commission' in S Bright (ed), *Landlord and Tenant Law. Past, Present and Future* (Oxford, Hart, 2006) 80.

[100] This chapter contains a summary of the scheme. For the details refer to Law Commission, 'Termination of Tenancies for Tenant Default' (Law Com No 303, 2006). There are, for example, differences for 'post commencement' and 'pre-commencement' tenancies. The scheme will not apply to assured tenancies or specified tenancies under the Housing Act 1985.

[101] S Bridge, 'Commercial Leases Past and Present: the Contribution of the Law Commission' in S Bright (ed), *Landlord and Tenant Law. Past, Present and Future* (Oxford, Hart, 2006) 81.

Under the proposals, the landlord is only able to apply for termination if an 'explanatory statement' has been given to the tenant, preferably at the beginning of the tenancy, unless the court has dispensed with this requirement.[102] This explains that the landlord is able to seek termination if there is tenant default.

The right to seek termination follows from 'tenant default', described as the gateway to the statutory scheme. Tenant default involves breach by the tenant of a covenant of the tenancy.[103] There will no longer be a need for the lease to contain a forfeiture clause as the right to take termination action will be a statutory right (which can be excluded) rather than a contractual right.

There will be two forms of termination action: a termination claim or a summary termination procedure.

24.3.2.1 Summary Termination Procedure

The summary termination process is intended only for cases in which the premises have been abandoned or where there is no reasonable prospect of defending a termination claim, for example, because the tenant has ceased trading. The aim is to provide the landlord 'with an accelerated means of terminating a tenancy outside the court process'.[104]

The summary termination process will begin with the landlord serving a summary termination notice within six months of knowledge of the tenant default, specifying the default and the date (one month after service) when the tenancy will end. Of course, if the tenant has abandoned the property there is unlikely to be any response. The tenant does, however, have the opportunity to apply to the court within this month for an order discharging the notice. If no tenant application is made (or if it is dismissed), the tenancy will terminate at the end of the month and the landlord may recover possession. It will still remain possible during the following six months for the tenant to apply to the court for an order, which could, for example, order a new tenancy or the payment of compensation. The process is outlined in Chart 24.3.

Chart 24.3: Summary Termination Procedure under the Law Commission Scheme

Step 1	**Tenant default**
Step 2	**Consider if summary termination is available**
Step 3	**If so, serve summary termination notice on tenant and holders of derivative interests and to 'the occupier' at the premises**
Step 4	**No response, tenancy ends after one month**
Step 5	**Notice opposed by application for discharge**
Step 6	**Landlord able to show no realistic prospect of court refusing a termination order**
Step 7	**Within six months, tenant/derivative interest holder can apply for post-termination order** (which can be a new tenancy or compensation)

---

[102] The draft Landlord and Tenant (Termination of Tenancies) Bill annexed to the Law Commission report provides that the court can dispense with this requirement if it thinks it 'just and equitable' do so: cl 5(1).

[103] Also breach by a previous tenant (where there has been an unlawful assignment), or a breach of covenant by a guarantor.

[104] Law Commission, 'Termination of Tenancies for Tenant Default' (Law Com No 303, 2006) para 2.36.

The summary process cannot be used in a number of different situations: if anyone is lawfully residing on the premises, if the unexpired term of the tenancy is more than 25 years,[105] in circumstances that fall within the Leasehold Property (Repairs) Act 1938, or if the lease excludes termination by summary process. The summary termination procedure provides the landlord with a (relatively) quick way of recovering the property where it is clear that the tenant will not be complying with the lease and has no need for the premises. If the landlord's notice seeking summary termination is unopposed, the lease will end without the need for a court order.

24.3.2.2 Termination Claim

The first step in any termination will be service of a default notice: a prescribed form of written notice setting out the details of the breach, and what needs to be done to put it right (which can include payment of compensation).[106] This notice should be served not only on the tenant but on any person with an interest secured on the tenancy, that includes not only sub-tenants and mortgagees but also chargees, and those with an option to purchase or right of pre-emption.[107] This notice will need to be served within six months of the landlord knowing of the tenant default and proceedings must be commenced within six months of the date of service of the notice (or, if later, the date by which any default was to be remedied).[108] A major purpose of the default notice is, according to the Law Commission, to encourage negotiation between the parties. The time limit is to displace the doctrine of waiver. The landlord has six months from the service of the notice (or the date given for remedial action to be completed) in which to commence a termination claim. The process is outlined in Chart 24.4.

With the termination claim, a number of orders are available to the court and conditions can be imposed by the court.[109] The order made must be appropriate and proportionate in the circumstances, and there is a detailed checklist of factors that the court is to take account of. The aim of this list is to maintain consistency while promoting flexibility. The fact that a tenant has remedied a breach does not preclude the court from making a termination order where it is otherwise appropriate or proportionate; this reflects the fact that a persistent defaulter may be a highly unsatisfactory tenant and yet, if the law were otherwise, could survive in occupation by making good the default. The scheme would also replicate, as far as possible, the protection offered to tenants by the 1938 Act.

The orders available follow.

---

[105] These leases will often have a significant capital value and premature 'termination may bestow an unjustifiable and disproportionate windfall on the landlord at the tenant's expense': Law Commission, 'Termination of Tenancies for Tenant Default' (Law Com CP No 174, 2004) para 8.19.

[106] The Law Commission endorses the approach of Neuberger LJ in *Akici v LR Butlin Ltd* [2005] EWCA Civ 1296, [2006] 1 WLR 201 that most breaches are capable of remedy on the basis that late performance, coupled with financial compensation, will usually be possible: Law Commission, 'Termination of Tenancies for Tenant Default' (Law Com No 303, 2006) para 4.43.

[107] The Law Commission prefers to describe them collectively as holders of qualifying interests, rather than as members of a derivative class. There are two further classes covered: those with a right to assignment (for example a guarantor who has made good the tenant's default) and those with a right to an overriding lease.

[108] The court will be able to dispense with any of the requirements concerning tenant default notices if it thinks it just and equitable to do so.

[109] This is not to limit other possible orders that the court may make.

Chart 24.4: Termination Claims under the Law Commission Scheme

Step 1	**Tenant default**
Step 2	**Serve tenant default notice on tenant and holders of derivative interests**
	—within 6 months of knowledge of default
	—detailing breach and necessary remedial action
Step 3	**Within six months,[a] apply for court order**
Step 4	**Court order:**
	—termination order
	—remedial order
	—order for sale
	—(for derivative interests) transfer order
	—(for derivative interests) new tenancy
	—joint tenancy adjustment order
	—no order

[a]Of service of default notice, or deadline for remedying.

(a)   A termination order on the grounds specified by statute which will end the tenancy and any derivative interests on a specified date.

(b)   A remedial order, which will set out with what the tenant needs to do to remedy the default. The effect of the remedial order is to stay the landlord's termination claim for three months from the day the tenant is to complete the remedial action. If the tenant fails to remedy as required, the landlord can apply for the matter to return to court.

(c)   An order for sale of the tenancy by a court appointed receiver (a new but very important idea).[110] Any sale will need to comply with the provisions on dealing contained in the lease, for example requiring consent. The proceeds will be used to pay the receiver's costs, the landlord's costs and sums owed to the landlord, to satisfy secured creditors, and pay the balance to the tenant. This order could be used, for example, where it is clear that because of the tenant's unsatisfactory behaviour, the lease should be brought to an end but doing so would result in an unfair windfall to a landlord. It would achieve the dual aims of enabling the landlord to get rid of an unsatisfactory tenant whilst permitting the defaulting tenant to recoup any capital value in the lease.

(d)   A transfer order, for the lease to be transferred to the holder of a derivative interest (again, subject to the lease's provisions on dealings).

(e)   A new tenancy order, granting a new tenancy to a derivative interest holder.

(f)   A joint tenancy adjustment order, intended for where only some of joint tenants wish to continue to hold an interest in the property.

(g)   No order where, for example, the tenant default is trivial and has little consequence for the landlord.

---

[110] The Law Commission refer to a precedent ordering sale: *Khar v Delbounty Ltd* (1998) 75 P & CR 232 (CA).

24.4 Tenant Termination for Landlord Default?

A major change proposed in the Law Commission Report of 1985[111] was for a statutory tenant termination scheme to be available, along the same lines as the landlord termination scheme that was being proposed at that stage. It was felt that both the landlord and tenant should have similar weapons in their armoury. It was also suggested that the tenant termination order could be coupled with a right to damages to compensate the tenant for losses suffered as a consequence of having to move. By the time that the Law Commission produced its draft Bill in 1994, the tenant termination scheme was not included, priority being given to enacting the less controversial landlord termination order scheme.[112] It has not reappeared since.[113]

It is hard to defend a system that allows only one party to end the relationship for breach, especially as breach of certain covenants, such as repair, could have a severe impact on the tenant's commercial interests or enjoyment of the home. Any rights the tenant has to end the lease must, therefore, flow from the common law on repudiation (considered next) but given the strength of the case for a tenant termination order scheme put in the earlier Law Commission report, it is regrettable that it has been dropped.

24.5 Ending a Lease for Breach: Repudiation

24.5.1 Landlord Breach

As mentioned earlier, the doctrine of forfeiture has often been seen as analogous to repudiation. A contract can be brought to an end if one party breaches the contract in a serious manner that goes to the heart of the contractual obligation. The other party then has the option of accepting this (repudiatory) breach as bringing a contract to an end, or of electing to continue the contract. A repudiatory act is one which shows an intention no longer to be bound by the contract:

> ... a contract may be repudiated if one party renounces his liabilities under it – if he evinces an intention no longer to be bound by the contract ... or shows that he intends to fulfill the contract only in a manner substantially inconsistent with his obligations and not in any other way ... [114]

Although there is no reason in principle why this should not apply to leases, it was assumed for some time that repudiation was inapplicable to leases because the essence of a lease was the conveyance of an estate. On this view, as the estate is granted at the beginning of the lease there has already been substantial performance as soon as the lease is entered into and repudiation can not therefore occur.[115] It is, however, the case that leases have

---

[111] Law Commission, 'Codification of the Law of Landlord and Tenant: Forfeiture of Tenancies' (Law Com No 142, 1985).

[112] Law Commission, 'Landlord and Tenant: Termination of Tenancies Bill' (Law Com No 221, 1994).

[113] Law Commission, 'Termination of Tenancies for Tenant Default' (Law Com CP No 174, 2004) para 1.17.

[114] *Shevill v Builders Licensing Board* (1982) 149 CLR 620 (HC of Australia) 625–6 (Gibbs CJ).

[115] *Total Oil Great Britain Ltd v Thompson Garages (Biggin Hill) Ltd* [1972] 1 QB 318 (CA) 324.

become more complex contracts, and for some tenants the on-going servicing package is as important as the grant of the estate itself. In such cases, breach of any of these important obligations should be capable of amounting to a repudiatory act.

This approach was applied by Stephen Sedley QC (sitting as an assistant recorder) in *Hussein v Mehlman*, when he acknowledged the 'tide of the general law' recognising that the foundation of a lease is contractual.[116] The landlord's breach involved a consistent failure to comply with the statutory repairing obligation set out in section 11 of the Landlord and Tenant Act 1985 (see chapter 12): there was no heating, the ceiling of one bedroom had collapsed, water pipes had burst, a flat roof extension was leaking and there was damp in the hall. On these facts, it was held that the landlord's conduct constituted a repudiatory breach, which the tenant could accept by vacating the premises and returning the keys without incurring further rent liability.

Not all breaches will be repudiatory, however. In *Nynehead Developments Ltd v RH Fibreboard Containers Ltd*, for example, the judge considered that the appropriate remedy for uncontrolled parking on the forecourt of business premises should be damages rather than repudiation as the breach was not sufficiently serious as substantially to deprive the tenant of the whole benefit of his contract.[117]

As it would be highly unusual for a lease to give a tenant an express contractual right to terminate for breach, the acknowledgement that a lease can be ended by a repudiatory act by the landlord provides the tenant with a useful remedy against the landlord.[118] When the Law Commission discussed extending the termination order scheme to tenants it was felt important that the tenant should also be given a right to damages upon termination, otherwise the right to end the lease would be little used in practice.[119] To allow such recovery following a repudiatory breach would be in line with contract law.[120]

Although only a County Court decision, *Hussein v Mehlman* has been treated as correct by the Court of Appeal in *Chartered Trust Plc v Davies* [121] and by the High Court in *Nynehead Developments Ltd v RH Fibreboard Containers Ltd*.[122] As Lloyd LJ observed in *Reichman v Beveridge*, however, there has been no *decision* of the Court of Appeal to the effect that 'a lease could be brought to an end by the tenant's acceptance of a repudiatory breach by the landlord'.[123] It would be most unfortunate if this comment were to reintroduce doubt in this area. If there is a serious breach by the landlord the tenant needs a

---

[116] [1992] 2 EGLR 87 (Cty Ct). See also S Bright, 'Repudiating a lease – contract rules' [1993] *Conv* 71; C Harpum, 'Leases as Contracts' (1993) 52 *CLJ* 212.

[117] [1991] 1 EGLR 7 (Ch).

[118] For a residential tenant who might look to the local authority for substitute housing, the fact that a breach is sufficiently serious to be repudiatory means that it is likely that he is not 'intentionally homeless' as it would not have been 'reasonable for him to continue to occupy' within the Housing Act 1996 s 191.

[119] Law Commission, 'Codification of the Law of Landlord and Tenant: Forfeiture of Tenancies' (Law Com No 142, 1985) paras 17.13–17.17.

[120] In *Reichman v Beveridge* [2006] EWCA Civ 1659, Lloyd LJ did not accept that a *landlord* would be able to recover damages if he accepted the tenant's abandonment as a repudiatory act. This decision was, however, based on old authority specifically to do with the landlord's ability to recover rent (a debt). It is, therefore, distinguishable and should not prevent a tenant from being able to claim damages following a repudiatory breach.

[121] (1998) 76 P & CR 396 (CA). Henry LJ said that the trial judge had been entitled to come to the view that there had been a substantial interference with the tenant's business driving her to bankruptcy and that this was a repudiation of the lease.

[122] [1991] 1 EGLR 7 (Ch).

[123] [2006] EWCA Civ 1659 [10].

remedy that enables him to walk away and find new business premises or a new home; a
remedy sounding in damages only may be inadequate.

Other jurisdictions have accepted that leases can be ended by a repudiatory act. In the
US, for example, a tenant has been allowed to treat a lease as at an end and avoid further
rent liability when the landlord was in breach of a warranty of habitability (although the
cases frequently talk of the tenant 'rescinding' rather than accepting a repudiatory breach).
So, for example, in *Pugh v Holmes,* Larsen J said that the:

> ... tenant may vacate the premises where the landlord materially breaches the implied war-
> ranty of habitability ... Surrender of possession by the tenant would terminate his obligation
> to pay rent under the lease.[124]

24.5.2 Tenant Breach

In other jurisdictions repudiation has more often been used by the landlord against the
tenant. When the tenant abandons the property this is seen as a repudiatory act which the
landlord can accept and then use as a basis to claim post-repudiation losses from the
tenant.[125] Where it is the tenant who has committed a repudiatory act we run into the
question of how the contractual doctrine of repudiation interacts with traditional landlord
and tenant law.[126] If the same act can give rise to a right to forfeit or a repudiatory breach,
and the landlord is free to elect to treat it is a repudiatory breach, this may give him a way of
ending the lease without giving the tenant any right to relief. It would, however, be
undesirable and contrary to equitable principles developed over many years for repudiation
to be used to circumvent controls designed to protect tenants from unconscionable
behaviour by landlords. There is little authority on this point but the Court of Appeal in
Abidogun v Frolan Health Care Ltd took the view that it is not possible to avoid section 146 by
arguing that the landlord is accepting a repudiatory breach. In the words of Buxton LJ:

> It does not ... follow from the interaction of those two parts of the law that the protection for
> a tenant, as has been provided by Parliament in section 146, can be avoided by recourse to a
> purely contractual doctrine such as that of repudiatory breach.[127]

24.6 Tenant Insolvency

The effect of the tenant becoming insolvent will depend upon whether the tenant is a
company or an individual and the different type of insolvency involved. Insolvency is a
complex area of law and the reader should refer to specialist texts for detailed guidance.[128] In

---

[124] 486 Pa 272, 405 A 2d 897 (1979) (SC of Pennsylvania) 907. See also *Steele v Latimer* 214 Kan 329, 521 P 2d 304
(1974) (SC of Kansas); *Teller v McCoy* 162 WVa 367, 253 SE 2d 114 (1978) (SC of Appeals of West Virginia).
[125] *Highway Properties Ltd v Kelly, Douglas & Co Ltd* [1971] SCR 562, (1971) 17 DLR (3d) 710 (SC Canada); *Progressive Mailing House Pty Ltd v Tabali Pty Ltd* (1985) 157 CLR 17, 57 ALR 609 (HC Australia) and see
ch 16.
[126] An issue that does not arise with landlord breach as there is no statutory regulation of tenant termination for
landlord breach.
[127] [2001] EWCA Civ 1821 [52].
[128] See P McLoughlin, *Commercial Leases and Insolvency* 3rd edn (London, Butterworths, 2002).

the case of a company, insolvency can lead to administration,[129] receivership, a company voluntary arrangement, a company voluntary liquidation or compulsory liquidation. In the case of an individual it can lead to bankruptcy or an individual voluntary arrangement.

The tenant becoming insolvent will often lead to the lease ending early. This can be because it triggers a right of forfeiture and the landlord elects to end the lease so that it can re-let the property. With some forms of insolvency, it is necessary to obtain the leave of the court before being able to forfeit the lease. The landlord may not always want to forfeit the lease; although the tenant is insolvent there may be others who are liable to make rent and service charge payments, such as earlier tenants or guarantors, and in a weak property market with falling values the rent passing under the lease may be greater than would be available on a new letting.[130]

In the case of bankruptcy and company liquidation it is, however, also possible for the trustee in bankruptcy or liquidator to disclaim the lease on the grounds that it is 'onerous property'. Onerous property is defined by the Insolvency Act 1986 sections 315(2) (bankruptcy) and 178(2) (company liquidation) as being:

> any unprofitable contract, and
> any other property comprised in the bankrupt's estate which is unsaleable or not readily saleable, or is such that it may give rise to a liability to pay money or perform any other onerous act.

The effect of disclaimer is set out in sections 315(4) and 178(4) of the Insolvency Act 1986:

> A disclaimer under this section –
>
> (a) operates so as to determine, as from the date of the disclaimer, the rights, interests and liabilities of the company in or in respect of the property disclaimed; but
> (b) does not, except so far as is necessary for the purpose of releasing the company from any liability, affect the rights or liabilities of any other person.

In cases of personal insolvency, the disclaimer discharges the trustee in bankruptcy from all personal liability in respect the property by virtue of section 315(3)(b) of the Insolvency Act 1986.

A person with an interest in the disclaimed property, or who is under a liability in relation to it, is able to apply for an order to have the disclaimed property vested in them by sections 181(2) and 320(2) of the Insolvency Act 1986. According to Lord Nicholls, this is a 'statutory re-creation'.[131]

Lord Nicholls summarises the 'essential scheme' by which the disclaimer provisions seek to facilitate the winding up of the insolvent affairs:

> Unprofitable contracts can be ended, and property burdened with onerous obligations disowned. The company is to be freed from all liabilities in respect of the property. Conversely, and hardly surprisingly, the company is no longer to have any rights in respect of the property.

---

[129] For a discussion of administration and leases, see P Levaggi and D Marsden, 'Expensive quandary' (10 March 2007) *EG* 174.

[130] This was the case in the leading case of *Hindcastle Ltd v Barbara Attenborough Associates Ltd* [1997] AC 70 (HL).

[131] *Hindcastle Ltd v Barbara Attenborough Associates Ltd* [1997] AC 70 (HL) 89.

The company could not fairly keep the property and yet be freed from its liabilities.

Disclaimer will, inevitably, have an adverse impact on others: those with whom the contracts were made, and those who have rights and liabilities in respect of the property.[132]

Applying the approach of the House of Lords in *Hindcastle Ltd v Barbara Attenborough Associates Ltd,* the consequence of disclaimer will depend on the type of landlord and tenant situation involved: whether there has been an assignment of the lease, and whether there are any guarantors.[133] In the following section, L1 is the original landlord, T1 is the original tenant, T2 an assignee of T1, ST is a sub-tenant, and G is the guarantor.

(a)   L and T1 only (the lease has not been assigned), T1 is insolvent: all liabilities end and the lease ceases to exist.

(b)   L, T1 and G (there was a guarantor and the lease has not been assigned), T1 is insolvent: the liabilities of T1 end, but the liability of G continues. The lease ceases to exist, but the rights and liabilities of others remain 'as though' the lease had continued.

(c)   L, T1 and T2 (the lease has been assigned), T2 is insolvent: the liability of T2 ends, but the liability of T1 continues (assuming that it is a pre-1996 lease or that an authorised guarantee agreement has been entered).[134] The lease ceases to exist, but the rights and liabilities of others remain 'as though' the lease had continued.

(d)   L takes possession: all future liabilities end.[135]

(e)   L and T1, sub-letting to ST, T1 is insolvent: the liability of T1 to L and to ST ends, but the sub-tenancy continues.

The potential impact of tenant insolvency on the liability of others is illustrated by the facts of *Hindcastle Ltd v Barbara Attenborough Associates Ltd.*[136] The lease was a 20 year lease, entered into before the Landlord and Tenant (Covenants) Act 1995 (and so with original tenant liability, see chapter 18). The lease had been assigned from T1 to T2, with a guarantor, G2, and finally to T3. While T3 was tenant, the initial rent of £13,626 per annum was increased under the rent review provisions to £37,500 per annum. T3 became insolvent and the liquidator disclaimed the lease: the fall in property values meant that the lease had no value and was unsaleable. As the lease was an 'old lease', T1 and T2 remained liable on the leasehold covenants, and G2 was liable under the wording of the guarantee. L obtained judgment against T1, T2 and G2 for £50,000. T1 and T2 both went into liquidation, and T2's liquidator purported to disclaim its liability. Tenant insolvency can, thus, have severe commercial ramifications, not only on the particular tenant and its landlord but also on others.

As well as earlier tenants and guarantors, disclaimer can also have a big impact on the landlord. This is illustrated in the case of *Christopher Moran Holdings Ltd v Bairstow.*[137] The lease was a 20 year commercial lease with upward only review. By the date of the first review, in a time of property recession, the rent under the lease was more than £160,000 per

---

[132] *Hindcastle Ltd v Barbara Attenborough Associates Ltd* [1997] AC 70 (HL) 87.

[133] *Hindcastle Ltd v Barbara Attenborough Associates Ltd* [1997] AC 70 (HL).

[134] If it is a pre-1995 lease, T1 remains liable post assignment; if it is a post-1995 lease and T1 provided an AGA on assignment, T1 remains liable in respect of T2's obligations: see ch 18.

[135] *Active Estates v Parness* [2002] EWHC 893 (Ch).

[136] [1997] AC 70 (HL).

[137] [2000] 2 AC 172 (HL).

annum but the current market rent had plummeted to nearer £35,000. The tenant went into voluntary liquidation and the lease was disclaimed. By section 178(6) of the Insolvency Act 1986 a person suffering loss as a consequence of disclaimer is deemed a creditor and can claim for damages in the winding up. The landlord put in a claim for £5.3 million. The law report focuses on the appropriate method of calculating damages, the House of Lords stating that a discount must be made for early receipt. Some commentators suggested that the effect of this decision was to give the tenant a 'rolling break' clause, but the reality is that few companies could afford to go into voluntary liquidation in order to avoid the rental liability.

More recently, tenants have tried to use company voluntary arrangements (CVAs) to escape rental liability. Powerhouse, the electrical retailer, planned to close 32 of its underperforming stores and put together a CVA that involved the landlords of those stores receiving some compensation, but otherwise releasing Powerhouse and, importantly, its parent company as guarantor, from liability. It was feared that if this scheme was successful it could devastate commercial property values as the financial strength of parent company guarantees is very important to property valuation. In *Prudential Assurance Co Ltd v PRG Powerhouse Ltd*, Etherton J held that the CVA was ineffective as it unfairly prejudiced the interests of the landlord within the meaning of section 6(1)(a) of the Insolvency Act 1986.[138] The judgment does not mean that CVAs can never be used to deprive landlords of recourse to guarantees, but on the particular facts the use of the CVA was unfairly prejudicial as:

> ... the votes of those unsecured creditors who stood to lose nothing from the CVA, and everything to gain from it, inevitably swamped those of the Guaranteed Landlords who were significantly disadvantaged by it.[139]

24.7 Mortgagee Possession and Residential Leases

The issue of mortgagee re-possession can arise in relation to private residential tenancies if the landlord defaults on mortgage payments or in the case of long residential leases if the leaseholder defaults on the mortgage.

24.7.1 Residential Leases

Given that long leases have usually been purchased for large capital sums it is common for there to be a mortgage secured on the leasehold estate. If the mortgagor/leaseholder defaults on mortgage payments, the mortgagee may re-possess the property and sell the lease with vacant possession.[140]

---

138 [2007] EWHC 1002 (Ch).

139 [2007] EWHC 1002 (Ch) [108]. For discussion, see S McClary, 'Sparks still Flying' (5 May 2007) *EG* 76.

140 There is a possible argument that the tenant then should notify the landlord of the action, and if he fails to do so he may be liable to pay a penalty of three years' rack rent to the landlord under s 145 of the Law of Property Act 1925. This section is, however, virtually unused and the usual understanding of one of the few cases on it, *Buckley v Buckley* (1787) 1 TR 647 is that it would not apply in this situation as the mortgagee's claim is not adverse

24.7.2 Residential Tenancies

If a tenancy was entered into before the mortgage, then it is likely that the mortgagee takes subject to the tenancy (the tenancy being an interest that overrides by virtue of paragraph 1 or 2 of Schedule 3 to the Land Registration Act 2002). But if, as will be the norm, the tenancy is entered into after the mortgage and the mortgagee's interest is duly registered, the mortgagee can evict the tenant in the event of the landlord defaulting on the mortgage. In practice the lender may choose to allow the tenant to stay until the lease runs out, and use the rental receipts towards the mortgage repayments. Mortgages which have not been taken out as 'buy-to-let' mortgages will usually require the mortgagor to obtain the mortgagee's consent to a letting, but whether the letting is authorised or not will affect only the question of whether or not the mortgagor is in default simply by virtue of granting the tenancy. It does not affect the question as to whether the tenancy is binding on the mortgagee.

There has been a significant rise in mortgage repossessions since 2004 and although the figures are not broken down between home owners and buy-to-let borrowers, it is thought that some of this is attributable to the unrealistic budgeting of buy-to-let borrowers who are not able to meet mortgage payments during void periods. Of course, this makes tenants vulnerable as few tenants will know whether a property is mortgaged when they agree to rent it, nor will they know the landlord's credit status.

24.8 Surrender

24.8.1 A Consensual Act

Surrender occurs when the lease is brought to an end early by agreement between the parties.

A surrender is a consensual transaction between the landlord and the tenant. It derives its effect from the terms of the transaction, not from the terms of the lease or tenancy that is surrendered.[141]

As Lord Millett explains in *Barrett v Morgan*:

A surrender is simply an assurance by which a lesser estate is yielded up to the greater, and the term is usually applied to the giving up of a lease or tenancy before its expiration. If a tenant surrenders his tenancy to his immediate landlord, who accepts the surrender, the tenancy is absorbed by the landlord's reversion and is extinguished by operation of law.

A surrender is ineffective unless the landlord consents to accept it, and is therefore consensual in the fullest sense of the term. In *Coke's Commentary upon Littleton* (1832), vol. II, s.636, p. 337b the nature of surrender is described as follows:

---

to or inconsistent with the landlord's title. Even if this is not a correct understanding, Seabourne and Paton have argued that *Buckley* should be read this way to make it consistent with the Human Rights Act 1998. They also argue for abolition of s 145: G Seabourne and E Paton, 'Time to Eject the Three Years' Rack Rent Penalty' [2006] 70 *Conv* 451.

[141] *Kay v LB of Lambeth; Leeds CC v Price* [2006] UKHL 10, [2006] 2 AC 465 [141].

'Surrender, *sursum reddito*, properly is a yielding up an estate for life or yeares to him that hath an immediate estate in reversion or remainder, wherein the estate for life or yeares may drowne *by mutuall agreement betweene them*'. [emphasis added by Lord Millett]

On its surrender the tenancy is brought to an end prematurely at a time and in a manner not provided for by the terms of the tenancy agreement.[142]

As a consensual act, a jointly held interest can be surrendered only if all parties agree.

24.8.2 *Express or by Operation of Law*

Surrender can be either express or implied by operation of law. An express surrender must be by deed.[143] If it is in writing only it can be effective in equity as a specifically enforceable contract to surrender provided that the writing complies with section 2 of the Law of Property (Miscellaneous Provisions) Act 1989 (see chapter 4). Where there is an agreement to surrender a protected business tenancy, the landlord must serve a 'health warning' notice in a prescribed form on the tenant and the tenant must sign a declaration.[144]

Leases surrendered by operation of law are excepted from these formality requirements by section 52(2)(c) of the Law Property Act 1925. In practice, the majority of leases are probably surrendered by operation of law rather than by deed. In order for this to occur, there must be unequivocal acts which indicate that both parties agree that the lease is at an end. As explained by Gibson LJ in *Bellcourt Estates Ltd v Adesina*, surrender by operation of law:

[29] … requires not only the re-delivery by the tenant of possession of the demised premises, but also the acceptance by the landlord of that re-delivery. Otherwise the landlord is entitled to look to the tenant to pay the rent throughout the whole of the term of the tenancy, it not having been agreed that the tenant should have the right to surrender the tenancy prematurely … Accordingly, the landlord's consent is necessary. No deed or other writing is required, but the conduct of the parties must unequivocally amount to an acceptance that the tenancy has been surrendered.

[30] The doctrine of surrender by operation of law is founded on the principle of estoppel, in that the parties must have acted towards each other in a way which is inconsistent with the continuation of the tenancy. That imposes a high threshold which must be crossed if the tenant is to be held to have surrendered and the landlord is to be held to have accepted the surrender.

[31] The effective re-delivery of possession by the tenant and its acceptance by the landlord are vital. Thus there will be a surrender when the tenant returns the keys of the premises and the landlord accepts them in circumstances which indicate that the tenancy thereafter no longer exists. The landlord must take possession in such a manner as to estop him from denying that the tenancy is at an end.[145]

---

[142] [2000] 2 AC 264 (HL) 270–71.
[143] Law of Property Act 1925 s 52. There is no exception for leases created orally or short leases.
[144] Landlord and Tenant Act 1954 s 38(A); Regulatory Reform (Business Tenancies) (England and Wales) Order 2003 SI 2003/3096 Sch 3 and 4.
[145] [2005] EWCA Civ 208.

Although handing in the keys and abandoning the premises can amount to an implied surrender, they will do so only in circumstances where it is clear that the landlord has accepted this and it would then be inequitable for him to rely on the fact that there has been no surrender by deed.

24.8.3 *Varying a Lease: Surrender and Regrant*

A common form of implied surrender is where a new lease is granted to the tenant in substitution for the old lease. Much more difficult is the case where parties have negotiated for variations to the lease. This is because the parties will usually think that they are just making a few changes to the lease, whereas in law the effect of these changes may be to treat the old lease as replaced by a new lease, known as 'surrender and regrant'. This can have important and unintended consequences. So, for example, surrender will release the original tenant and any guarantor.[146] If variations were agreed after 1 January 1996 in relation to a lease originally entered into before that date, it may mean that the lease is no longer governed by the old covenant liability regime but is instead a new tenancy governed by the Landlord and Tenant (Covenants) Act 1995, something that will be to the disadvantage of the landlord (see chapter 18). It can also affect the identity of the tenant, as was argued (unsuccessfully on the facts) in *Jenkins R Lewis Ltd v Kerman*.[147] The landlord sought to end the protected agricultural tenancy on the grounds that the tenant (B), with whom the original tenancy contract was made, had died. There had, however, been later variations to the tenancy and the current tenant argued that these changes had brought a new tenancy into being, which would mean that the landlord was unable to use B's death as a reason to end the lease.

In *Jenkins R Lewis v Kerman* the parties had agreed to rent increases; this was insufficient to amount to surrender and regrant. This leads to the question of which variations will count. The answer is, surprisingly, not related to how big the changes are. What matters is what the changes relate to: it is only variations 'altering the nature of the pre-existing item of property'[148] that have been held to imply the surrender of the old tenancy and the creation of a new one. Further, the only variations held to have this effect are variations which involve an extension of the term and the addition of further land. These will always lead to a deemed surrender, even if they are only minor changes.[149] Reducing the term or removing some of the land from the lease does not lead to surrender and regrant.

It is difficult to find any rational basis for the rules on surrender and regrant. They are clearly not related to the parties' intentions; often the possibility of there being a new lease will simply not have occurred to them and will be the last thing they want. As Neuberger J noted in *PW & Co Milton Gate Investments Ltd*, the rules on surrender and regrant illustrate the fact that the proprietary nature of leases can lead there to be results inconsistent with

---

[146] Although under the common law, *any* variation will release the guarantor (*Holme v Brunskill* (1878) 3 QBD 495) the lease is often drafted so that the guarantee will continue even if there is a variation. A deemed surrender will, even with this drafting, end the guarantee.

[147] [1971] 1 Ch 477 (CA).

[148] Russell LJ in *Jenkin R Lewis Ltd v Kerman* [1971] 1 Ch 477 (CA).

[149] *Friends' Provident Life Office v British Railways Board* [1996] 1 All ER 336 (CA) 345 and 350. See also *In re Savile Settled Estates* [1931] 2 Ch 210; *Jenkin R Lewis Ltd v Kerman* [1971] 1 Ch 477 (CA); *Baker v Merckel* [1960] 1 QB 657 (CA).

the contractual intention of the parties.[150] Nor does the estoppel explanation really work. Whereas it may make sense to describe the landlord who 'accepts' the tenant's keys as estopped from denying surrender, it makes no sense in a context where both the landlord and the tenant have assumed that their pre-existing relationship is continuing. There is, however, a practical advantage to the seemingly arbitrary rules. If it is accepted there will be some cases in which the changes are so significant that the only sensible thing to say is that there is a new lease, the merit of having a simple rule that all additions (but not reductions) to the term or the premises will cause a surrender and regrant is that it promotes certainty, enabling the parties to predict the consequences of their actions.[151]

24.9 Abandonment

A tenant who no longer wishes to occupy premises may simply abandon them. The landlord then has a choice: he can treat the lease as continuing and continue to sue for rent as it falls due, or he can accept the tenant's abandonment as bringing the lease to an end but will then be unable to sue for future losses. This is discussed more fully in chapter 16.

24.10   Break Clauses[152]

24.10.1 Introduction

Break clauses give the parties the opportunity to end the lease before the expiry of its term. In commercial leases this is often at the five year point.[153] Break clauses are therefore important in supporting flexibility. They are most commonly used in business tenancies as fixed term leases tend to be longer than is usual in the residential sector,[154] and many residential tenancies are periodic. (But they are, nonetheless also used in residential tenancies.) Indeed, they are increasingly common in commercial leases, particularly in the secondary market,[155] and increasingly likely to be exercised.[156]

---

[150] 2004] EWHC 1994 (Ch), [2004] Ch 142 [79].

[151] For further discussion of this see S Bright, 'Variation of Leases and Tenant Liability' in P Jackson and DC Wilde (eds), *The Reform of Property Law* (Aldershot, Dartmouth, 1997).

[152] See S Murdoch, 'Commercial Leases: Future Directions' in S Bright (ed), *Landlord and Tenant Law. Past, Present and Future* (Oxford, Hart, 2006) 93–5.

[153] N Crosby, C Hughes and S Murdoch, 'Monitoring the 2002 Code of Practice for Commercial Leases' (ODPM, March 2005) 300.

[154] With long residential leases, the lease is a saleable asset and the leaseholder who wishes to move will simply sell the lease.

[155] N Crosby, C Hughes and S Murdoch, 'Monitoring the 2002 Code of Practice for Commercial Leases' (ODPM, March 2005) 300. In 2003, 25% of leases in the IPD (prime properties) had break clauses; questionnaire evidence suggested 45% of the overall commercial lease market had break clauses.

[156] The 2006 Strutt & Parker IPD Lease Events Review suggests that in 2005, 41% of tenants with an option to break their lease exercised this option, an increase of 30% on the previous year. There has been an increase year on year since 2000. This research is based on an analysis of over 60,000 leases. Breaks were exercised more commonly in large, over-rented, office units than other office units (at market rent or under-rented) and than retail spaces. Other research suggests that rates are much lower, at 15%-20%: N Crosby, C Hughes and S Murdoch, 'Monitoring the 2002 Code of Practice for Commercial Leases' (ODPM, March 2005) 301.

A significant number of commercial leases, however, still do not contain break clauses at all even though many commercial tenants state that they would terminate leases if this option were available.[157] What many tenants want is complete flexibility to manage exit strategies; the problem is that even if a lease does contain a break clause it is likely to be tied to a specific time which may well not coincide with the tenant's needs.

24.10.2 Pre-Conditions for Exercising Break Clause

It used to be common to attach strict pre-conditions to the operation of break clauses (for example, requiring the tenant to be in complete compliance with its leasehold obligations in order to be able to rely on the break clause), and there are many cases involving issues of interpretation and compliance. In practice, strict pre-conditions can make the clause effectively inoperable. Reviewing the case law, Sir Andrew Morritt C in *Fitzroy House Epworth Street (No 1) Ltd v The Financial Times Ltd*[158] stated that 'such provisions have to be strictly complied with because equity has no power to relieve a party in breach',[159] there is a need for consistency[160] and the 'the court should not rewrite the parties' contract'.[161] The effect can be seen in *Bairstow Eves (Securities) Ltd v Ripley* where, although the tenant had recently repainted the premises, he was unable to exercise the break clause because he had not decorated within the last year as required by the covenant.[162]

As tenant's advisers have caught on to this, modern leases are unlikely to include pre-conditions that require absolute compliance. Although a requirement that the tenant is not in default with rent is still the norm,[163] modern clauses tend to require 'substantial' or 'material' performance of non-rent obligations. In *Fitzroy House,* the lease required there to be 'material compliance' in order for the break clause to be exercisable.[164] The tenant had undertaken a substantial programme of repair costing around £1 million, but there was not complete compliance with the tenant's obligations and the breaches were more than trivial. Counsel for the landlord argued that there was not, therefore, 'material' compliance but the Court of Appeal disagreed. 'Materiality' is to be determined objectively[165] as a question of fact, assessed by reference to the landlord's ability to re-let or sell the property without either delay or additional expense. On the facts, as the outstanding defects were insubstantial and would have no effect on the landlord's ability to find a new tenant (or on the terms of a new tenancy), there was material compliance with the repair covenant and the tenant had validly exercised the break clause.

---

[157] 71% would terminate leases on some space if possible: CBI/GVA Grimley, 'Survey of Property Trends Supplement' Winter 2006/07. Manufacturers, especially the engineering sector, were least likely to want to terminate leases; those in the distribution and retailing sectors most likely.

[158] [2006] EWCA Civ 329, [2006] 1 WLR 2207 [17].

[159] Citing *Finch v Underwood* (1876) 2 Ch D 310 (CA).

[160] Citing *Simons v Associated Furnishers Ltd* [1931] 1 Ch 379 (Ch).

[161] Citing *Bairstow Eves (Securities) Ltd v Ripley* [1992] 2 EGLR 47 (CA).

[162] *Bairstow Eves (Securities) Ltd v Ripley* [1992] 2 EGLR 47 (CA).

[163] N Crosby, C Hughes and S Murdoch, 'Monitoring the 2002 Code of Practice for Commercial Leases' (ODPM, March 2005) 301.

[164] *Fitzroy House Epworth Street (No 1) Ltd v The Financial Times Ltd* [2006] EWCA Civ 329, [2006] 1 WLR 2207.

[165] Sir Andrew Morritt C specifically rejected the view that material meant 'what is fair and reasonable between landlord and tenant': [16].

The Business Lease Code 2007 suggests even less onerous pre-conditions:

The only pre-conditions to tenants exercising any break clauses should be that they are up to date with the main rent, give up occupation and leave behind no continuing subleases.[166]

The times at which break clauses can be exercised can be a problem, particularly in relation to the linkage between break clauses and rent review. The tenant may intend the break clause to give him the opportunity to exit if the rent on review is too high; but in practice the break clause often has to be operated before the new rent is known. It is, however, the case that in practice break clauses are often used by tenants not because of rental change but for wider operational reasons.[167]

24.10.3 Notices and Break Clauses

Until the House of Lords' decision in *Mannai Investments Co Ltd v Eagle Star Life Assurance Co Ltd*, service of break notices constituted a trap for the unwary.[168] A break clause will usually specify when notice must be served in order to exercise it. In *Mannai* the leases provided that not less than six months' notice must be served, 'such notice to expire on the third anniversary of the term commencement date'. The tenant served notice to end the leases on 12 January 1995, although the third anniversary was in fact 13 January 1995. The House of Lords, by a 3–2 majority, held that the notice was effective notwithstanding the error, adopting a 'commercially sensible construction'.

24.10.4 Joint Interests

If there is a joint tenancy all tenants must act together to surrender the tenancy or to operate a break clause,[169] the difference between this and serving a notice to quit being that surrender/break ends an existing contract and therefore requires the consent of all contracting parties whereas a notice to quit simply fails to renew the contract.

24.10.5 Landlord Break Clauses

Landlord break clauses are seldom made conditional. If the landlord of a business tenancy within the Landlord and Tenant Act 1954 wishes to exercise the break clause he will also need to prove a ground under section 30(1) as a reason for not granting the tenant a new lease.[170]

---

[166] Joint Working Group on Commercial Leases, 'The Code for Leasing Business Premises in England and Wales 2007' (2007) para 3.

[167] N Crosby, C Hughes and S Murdoch, 'Monitoring the 2002 Code of Practice for Commercial Leases' (ODPM, March 2005) 301.

[168] [1997] AC 749 (HL). For further discussion of *Mannai*, see ch 2.

[169] *Hounslow LBC v Pilling* [1993] 1 WLR 1242 (CA); *Hammersmith and Fulham LBC v Monk* [1992] 1 AC 478 (HL).

[170] For an explanation of s 30 and the grounds of opposition, see ch 21.

24.11 Merger

If the tenant acquires the reversion immediately expectant to his term, or a third party acquires both the leasehold term and the reversion, the position at common law was that the lease would merge with the reversion, bringing the lease and all covenants to an end. This would apply provided that the estates were held in the same capacity, for example, both were held by trustees, or absolutely. This result would not necessarily reflect what the holder intends. A tenant of a flat who, for example, acquires the freehold reversion to the block may want the lease to continue as an independent and saleable asset. Equity therefore mitigated the approach of the common law by having regard to the intention of the parties:

> The Court of Equity ... had regard to the intention of the parties, and, in the absence of any direct evidence of intention, they presumed that merger was not intended, if it was to the interest of the party, or only consistent with the duty of that party, that merger should not take place.[171]

Statute has now followed this equitable approach and section 185 of the Law of Property Act 1925 provides that:

> ... there is no merger by operation of law only of any estate the beneficial interest in which would not be deemed to be merged or extinguished in equity.

The result is that if the circumstances are such that there would be no merger in equity, there is now no merger at law.[172] In some cases, merger may well be the intention underlying the acquisition, as in cases of individual enfranchisement, or where the tenant exercises an option to purchase the landlord's reversion. Where merger is desired it is best to state expressly that this is the intention.

The fact that both estates can rest in the same person sits uncomfortably alongside *Rye v Rye*, in which the House of Lords held that it is not possible for a man to grant a lease to himself.[173] Although *Rye v Rye* concerned the grant of a tenancy, the underlying reasoning – based upon the impossibility of contracting with oneself – would appear to apply equally to cases when the second interest is acquired later. In a leasehold context it was noted in *Rye v Rye* that if the landlord and tenant are the same person the covenants are meaningless, and the distress remedy is inappropriate.[174] Although contractually this may appear an oddity, leases and reversions are, of course, separate items of property. Nueberger J uses this to explain how one person can hold both interests:

> The reason why it is possible for a lease to be assigned to the reversioner, or the reversion to be transferred to the lesssee, without the lease thereby automatically ending, is not so much because it is open to the parties to agree a proviso against merger; it is more because a lease involves not only a contract, but also an estate in land.[175]

This was, however, insufficient to persuade Viscount Simonds in *Rye v Rye* that there was not a problem with the emptiness of the leasehold covenants in relation to the grant of

---

[171] *Capital and Counties Bank Ltd v Rhodes* [1903] 1 Ch 631 (CA) 653 (Cozens-Hardy LJ).
[172] *Capital and Counties Bank Ltd v Rhodes* [1903] 1 Ch 631 (CA) 654 (Cozens-Hardy LJ).
[173] [1962] AC 496 (HL).
[174] See, for example, Viscount Simonds at [1962] AC 496 (HL) 505.
[175] *Re Friends' Provident Life Office* [1999] 1 All ER (Comm) 28 (Ch).

leases when the landlord and tenant were the same person. Of course, in the case of later acquisition, covenant enforceability depends not upon the contractual relationship but upon the relationship of privity. In cases of later acquisition the non-enforceability of the covenants is admitted, but Millett LJ has described them as:

> ... in abeyance because of the circuity of action which would be involved in any attempt by either party to enforce them ... [and] enforcement would be permitted once the circuity was eliminated by, for example, an assignment.[176]

Although it is difficult to explain doctrinally how the cases on merger can co-exist with the *Rye v Rye* line of cases, both streams of authority are now well-established and it is unlikely that either will be upset.

24.12 Frustration

It is possible for a lease to be brought to an end by frustration if something happens, without the fault of either party, that would make performance substantially different from that originally contracted for. An extreme example could be if the land that is the subject of the lease disappeared into the sea, as occurred in the nuisance case of *Holbeck Hall Hotel Ltd v Scarborough Borough Council*.[177]

As the supervening event must make performance substantially different it will be rare for a lease to be ended by frustration given that the primary obligation of the lease is the grant of possession of the land for a time and that most problems that occur can be remedied. Indeed, until the House of Lords decision in *National Carriers Ltd v Panalpina (Northern) Ltd*[178] it was doubted whether frustration applied to leases at all.[179] In that case, however, it was accepted that the doctrine of frustration does apply to leases: in the words of Lord Simon, there is 'nothing about the fact of creation of an estate or interest in land which repels the doctrine of frustration'.[180] Further, it was recognised that a lease is about more than the simple grant of an estate that is fully executed at the moment the lease is entered. Instead, again in the words of Lord Simon, 'a lease is partly executory; rights and obligations remain outstanding on both sides throughout its currency'.[181]

Frustration will apply only if the parties themselves have not made contractual provision for the effect of the unforeseen event. It is common for commercial leases to allocate certain risks through the insurance arrangements. So, for example, a lease will usually require insurance to be taken out against fire. If the building is destroyed by fire, the lease may provide for the rent to be suspended for a set period to enable rebuilding to take place. It is

---

[176] *Ingram v IRC* [1997] 4 All ER 395 (CA) 426–7 (Millet LJ, dissenting). This case concerned the grant of a lease by a nominee to his principal, not merger. In the House of Lords, Millet LJ's reasoning was supported.

[177] [2000] QB 836 (CA).

[178] [1981] 1 AC 675 (HL).

[179] In *Cricklewood Property and Investment Trust Ltd v Leighton's Investment Trust Ltd* [1945] AC 221 (HL) there was a difference of opinion between the Law Lords: Viscount Simon LC and Lord Wright thought that frustration could apply (but would be extremely rare), Lords Russell and Goddard thought that it never could, and Lord Porter reserved his opinion.

[180] [1981] 1 AC 675 (HL) 705.

[181] [1981] 1 AC 675 (HL) 705.

also common to give mutual termination rights to the parties if the property has not been reinstated within a specified period; this making the position much clearer than having to rely on the somewhat uncertain doctrine of frustration. It does not follow, however, that risks that have not been contractually allocated will therefore lead to frustration. In *Panalpina* certain risks had been contractually allocated, but not the risk of the premises becoming unusable because of third party acts. On the facts of *Panalpina*, a ten year lease of a warehouse was not frustrated by a twenty month road closure, even though during this period the tenant had to continue to pay rent for a warehouse that could not be used for the intended purpose, and suffered the upheaval and expense of relocating. The fact that the use could resume after a break, however, made it impossible to succeed in a frustration argument.[182]

In practice, leases will rarely be frustrated, particularly as leases tend to be relatively long term relationships. As Lord Hailsham remarked:

> Long term speculations and investments are in general less easily frustrated than short term adventures and a lease for 999 years must be in the longer class.[183]

It is in the case of the largely executory, shorter term leases that a frustration argument is most likely to succeed.

There has been no judicial consideration of whether a lease can be ended by frustration after it has been assigned. It is argued by Murphy, Roberts and Flessas that it cannot be as the assignee does not have a contractual relationship with the landlord:

> … since at its core the doctrine is based on the destruction of the basis or 'substratum' of the bargain, it is difficult to see how it is applicable after a lease has been passed on by assignment. … [The] assignee is bound by the covenants which touch and concern the land simply because they are incidental to the estate, the term of years, he acquires in the assignment. The only bargain such an assignee enters into is with his assignor before taking the assignment (unless, as may happen in some commercial contexts, the assignee is required to enter into a new set of direct covenants with the landlord.)[184]

24.13 The Effect of Termination on Sub-tenants

24.13.1 The Position at Common Law

In this section, the term 'head-tenancy' will be used to refer to the lease between the landlord and the tenant, and 'sub-tenancy' to the lease between the tenant and the sub-tenant.

Under the common law, the general position is that if the head-tenancy fails, then so will the sub-tenancy. In the case of the head-tenancy being forfeited, the sub-tenancy will also come to an end, although as seen earlier, the sub-tenant has a right to apply for relief from forfeiture under section 146(4) of the Law Property Act 1925. The terms of any relief given

---

[182] [1981] 1 AC 675 (HL) 697–8 (Lord Wilberforce).

[183] [1981] 1 AC 675 (HL) 691. See also Deane J in Australian case of *Progressive Mailing House Pty Ltd v Tabili Pty Ltd* (1985) 157 CLR 17, 57 ALR 609 (HC Australia), 635–636.

[184] T Murphy, S Roberts and T Flessas, *Understanding Property Law* 4th edn (London, Sweet & Maxwell, 2004) 154.

are at the discretion of the court and any term granted cannot be for any longer term than the original sub-tenancy.

Similarly, where the head-lease is ended by either party serving a notice to quit this will also bring the sub-tenancy to an end:

> The interest of the sub-tenant was created out of the term created by the lease and was, therefore, always subject to termination in accordance with the terms of the lease.[185]

Before 1994, however, there was some judicial support[186] for the view that an upwards notice to quit served by the head-tenant on the head-landlord would not end the sub-tenancy, even though a downwards notice to quit served by the head landlord would do so. In *Pennell v Payne*[187] the Court of Appeal overturned the earlier decision and held that when the head-tenancy is ended by an upwards notice to quit, the sub-tenancy – lawful or not – will also come to an end. As Simon Brown LJ pointed out, this may well result in the head-tenant being exposed 'to a liability to his sub-tenant in damages for breach of his expressed or implied covenant of quiet enjoyment.' The House of Lords confirmed the correctness of the result in *Pennell v Payne* in *Barrett v Morgan*.[188]

The earlier misunderstanding about the effect of an upwards notice to quit had, however, been relied upon with serious consequences in the case of *PW v Milton Gate Investments Ltd*.[189] In this case the parties to a commercial lease had assumed that a tenant could end the lease by exercising a break clause whilst leaving the sub-leases in place. The head-lease provided that if the tenant exercised the break clause it would pay financial compensation equivalent to nine months' rent, unless 75 per cent of the lettable area of the premises was sub-let with permitted sub-leases having at least five years left to run. The clear intention was that the tenant was free to break without penalty provided there were permitted sub-lettings. Neuberger J held that it was not possible to contract out of the rule in *Pennell v Payne*. Although he accepted that there can be strong arguments for allowing parties to agree their own contracts:

> … a tenancy is not merely a contract: it is and it creates an estate in land. When a tenant grants a sub-tenancy, he is granting a subsidiary estate out of the estate vested in him by the head-tenancy. As a matter of principle, it would seem to follow ineluctably that, if and when the head-tenancy determines, and the estate thereby created ceases to exist, any subsidiary estate carved out of it, including any sub-tenancy, must also determine. It is, I suppose, an example of the maxim nemo dat quod non habet … If that is the right analysis, it is difficult to see how a sub-tenancy can survive a destruction of the head-tenancy simply because the landlord and head-tenant agree that it should.[190]

Further,

> … the fact that a lease creates an estate does sometimes produce results which do not accord with the plain contractual intention of parties.[191]

---

[185] *Kay v LB of Lambeth; Leeds CC v Price* [2006] UKHL 10, [2006] 2 AC 465 [142].
[186] A Court of Appeal decision: *Brown v Wilson* (1949) 208 LT Jo 144 (CA).
[187] [1995] QB 192 (CA).
[188] [2000] 2 AC 264 (HL).
[189] [2004] EWHC 1994 (Ch), [2004] Ch 142.
[190] [2004] EWHC 1994 (Ch), [2004] Ch 142 [73].
[191] [2004] EWHC 1994 (Ch), [2004] Ch 142 [79].

Continuing in the same vein, he later remarks that this area of law turns on

> ... the tenurial nature of a lease ... [It also provides a very good example] of how that tenurial nature can, on occasion, result in the contractual intention of the landlord and tenant, however unequivocally and forcibly expressed, being thwarted, not by virtue of public policy or statute, but by the limitations placed on the freedom to agree by reason of the inherent nature of the leasehold estate. As I see it, just as a tenant cannot grant a sub-tenancy for a term exceeding that of the head-tenancy, so can a tenant not effectively agree with his landlord that a sub-tenancy will survive the expiry of the head-tenancy according to its terms.[192]

It is interesting that these remarks were made sometime after the House of Lords decision in *Bruton*;[193] they indicate that the proprietary qualities of leases do mark them out from other forms of contracts, and from the 'non-estate' tenancies in *Bruton* itself.

Not all commentators would agree with the approach taken by Neuberger J. The case clearly does reveal the tension that can result between adopting a property law perspective and a contractual perspective in the context of leases. In response to Neuberger J's reference to the *nemo dat* rule, Professor Kenny remarks:

> ... if we allow the concept of an estate to be given any significance at all in the twenty-first century in relation to the relationship between landlord and tenant, then in any event the estate to which we should give effect, is the estate agreed upon by the parties. In the example in question [the facts in *PW & Co v Milton Gate Investments*] what is agreed upon is clearly a sub-tenancy the term of which survives the prior determination of the head-tenancy. There is no difficulty in principle in giving effect to that and the maximum *nemo dat quod non habet* is completely irrelevant because in the example the person who does have the estate in question out of which the sub-tenancy compares [sic] assents in any event.[194]

The position is quite different if the head-lease is brought to an end by surrender or merger. The sub-tenancy then is not affected. This is known as the rule in *Mellor v Watkins*.[195] The explanation for this is given by Lord Millett in *Barrett v Morgan*:

> Although a person such as a sub-tenant having a derivative interest may benefit by the surrender and consequent extinguishment of the estate out of which his interest is derived, he cannot be prejudiced by it. It is a general and salutary principle of law that a person cannot be adversely affected by an agreement or arrangement to which he is not a party. So far as he is concerned, it is res inter alios acta ... In *Coke's Commentary upon Littleton*, vol. II, s.636, p. 338b the effect of a surrender on third parties such as sub-tenants is stated as follows:

> 'having regard to the parties to the surrender, the estate is absolutely drowned ... But having regard to strangers, who were not parties or privies thereunto, lest by a voluntary surrender they may receive prejudice touching any right or interest they had before the surrender, the estates surrendred hath in consideration of law a continuance ...'[196]

---

[192] [2004] EWHC 1994 (Ch), [2004] Ch 142 [81].
[193] *Bruton v London and Quadrant Housing Trust* [2000] 1 AC 406 (HL).
[194] P Kenny, 'Freedom of Contract for Landlord and Tenant' [2004] 68 *Conv* 351, 352.
[195] (1874) LR 9 QB 400.
[196] [2000] 2 AC 264 (HL) 271.

Explaining this phrase, 'a continuance' he says:

> ... when the head-tenancy is surrendered, it is treated as continuing until its natural termina-
> tion so far as this is necessary to support the derivative interest of the sub-tenant.[197]

Where the head-lease has been surrendered 'with a view to the acceptance of a new lease
in place thereof', the rights and liabilities of the sub-tenant and the new head-tenant will
take effect as if the original head-lease had remained on foot and not been surrendered.[198]
In *PW & Co v Milton Gate Investments* Neuberger J explains the position in surrender as an
exception to the general rule and of 'great antiquity'.[199] As shown earlier, he held that no
new exceptions to the general rule could be made simply because this is what the parties
have agreed to.

There is also a practical reason given for distinguishing notice to quit and surrender
cases. If the sub-tenancy survives the termination of the head-lease there will be a problem
for the landlord; the absence of privity between the head-landlord and the sub-tenant would
mean that the landlord is unable to enforce obligations in the sub-tenancy. In the words of
Simon Brown LJ in *Pennell v Payne*:

> Against an upwards notice to quit ... landlords are defenceless: they are in no position to
> ensure that they become entitled to the benefit of the sub-tenant's covenants.[200]

Statute has addressed this problem in relation to surrenders through section 139(1) of the
Law of Property Act 1925 by deeming the reversion of the head-lease to be:

> ... the reversion for the purpose of preserving the same incidents and obligations as would
> have affected the original reversion had there been no surrender or merger thereof.

There is, however, no similar statutory solution that applies in cases not involving surrender
or merger, and this is referred to by Neuberger J in *PW & Co v Milton Gate Investments* as
supporting the view that in other cases the sub-tenancy will not survive determination of the
head-tenancy.[201]

In *Barrett v Morgan* the sub-tenant argued that a notice to quit served by agreement
was governed by the surrender approach (not ending the sub-tenancy) as it was
consensual, and therefore different from the usual notice to quit rule.[202] The head-
landlord and head-tenants both wanted to end the head-lease and sub-lease so that the
land could be sold with vacant possession. It had been thought (as it turned out, wrongly)
that if the head-tenant served a notice to quit this, being an upwards notice to quit, would
not end the sub-tenancy. So it was agreed that the head landlord would serve a
(downwards) notice to quit, and the head-tenants agreed not to serve a counter-notice
under the Agricultural Holdings Act 1986. The Court of Appeal had accepted the
argument that just as a surrender does not end a sub-tenancy because it is a 'consensual'
act so, too, a notice to quit served by agreement was consensual and thus ineffective to

---

[197] [2000] 2 AC 264 (HL) 271.
[198] Law of Property Act 1925 s 150.
[199] [2004] EWHC 1994 (Ch), [2004] Ch 142.
[200] [1995] QB 192 (CA) 202.
[201] [2004] EWHC 1994 (Ch), [2004] Ch 142 [85].
[202] [2000] 2 AC 264 (HL).

determine the sub-tenancy. Although the Court of Appeal had been keen to distance itself from the language of 'collusion', with its attendant innuendo, that had been used by the trial judge, it is hard to resist the conclusion that its approach was influenced by the fact that this was a 'scheme' concocted to find a way around the statutory controls. The House of Lords disagreed. It held that the notice to quit was effective to end the sub-tenancy. The fact that it was served by consent could not be used by the sub-tenant to argue that the surrender rather than the notice to quit rule should be used. Consent was relevant in the case of surrender because absent consent they could be no termination. A notice to quit was effective whether or not there was consent.

This set of rules, both the special rule for surrender and the general rule that applies in notice to quit cases, stems clearly from the proprietary nature of leases. They have no application to *Bruton* tenancies, as was confirmed in *Kay v LB of Lambeth; Leeds CC v Price*[203] when *Bruton* style occupiers had sought to argue that their interests survived a surrender of the licence held by their 'landlord':

> ... the *Mellor v Watkins* principle and the *Pennell v Payne* principle can have no relevance to a case in which a tenancy has been granted by someone without any estate in the land in question.[204]

24.13.2 Protected Residential Tenancies

24.13.2.1 Assured Tenancies

The common law rule that a sub-tenancy comes to an end if the head-tenancy ends by forfeiture or notice to quit is modified in relation to assured tenancies. Section 18 of the Housing Act 1988 provides that should the head-tenancy be ended, the sub-tenancy will continue to be assured, so long as the head landlord (who now becomes the immediate landlord) is not within any of the categories of landlord unable to grant an assured tenancy, such as the Crown or a local authority. Section 18 provides:

(1) If at any time –

(a)   a dwelling-house is for the time being lawfully let on an assured tenancy;[205] and

(b)   the landlord under the assured tenancy is himself a tenant under a superior tenancy; and

(c)   the superior tenancy comes to an end, then, subject to subsection (2) below, the assured tenancy shall continue in existence as a tenancy held of the person whose interest would, apart from the continuance of the assured tenancy, entitle him to actual possession of the dwelling-house at that time.

(2) Subsection (1) above does not apply to an assured tenancy if the interest which, by virtue of that subsection, would become that of the landlord, is such that, by virtue of Schedule 1 to this Act, the tenancy could not be an assured tenancy.

---

[203] [2006] UKHL 10, [2006] 2 AC 465.
[204] [2006] UKHL 10, [2006] 2 AC 465 [143].
[205] If, therefore, the sub-tenancy was granted in breach of an alienation covenant it will not be protected by s 18.

24.13.2.2 Secure Tenancies

The basic common law rule will apply on the termination of a secure head-tenancy, so the sub-tenancy will fall if the head-tenancy comes to an end, other than by surrender.[206] If the head-tenancy is surrendered, the sub-tenancy will bind the local authority and the part sublet may be a secure tenancy subject to complying with the 'separate dwelling' requirement in section 79 of the Housing Act 1985.

---

[206] *Acme Housing Association and Royal Borough of Kensington and Chelsea v Chevska*, Legal Action 17 (June 1987), cited in D Hoath, *Public Housing Law* (London, Sweet & Maxwell, 1989) 214, n 24.

25

ENFRANCHISEMENT AND THE RIGHT TO BUY

25.1	Introduction
25.2	Social tenants and enfranchisement
25.3	The right to buy
25.4	The right to acquire
25.5	The preserved right to buy
25.6	Enfranchisement of long leasehold houses – the Leasehold Reform Act 1967
25.7	Enfranchisement of flats
25.8	Limited rights under the Landlord and Tenant Act 1987
25.9	Enfranchisement of flats under the Leasehold Reform, Housing and Urban Development Act 1993
25.10	The future of renting and long leaseholds

25.1 Introduction

This chapter looks at the various statutory rights that have been given to tenants and lease-holders to 'upgrade' their interest. In many cases this upgrading will be to a freehold interest (through the process known as enfranchisement), but often this is not possible. So, for example, a secure tenant who wishes to buy the flat that he lives in will need to do so by way of a long lease. The details of these various statutory schemes are inevitably complex and the aim of this chapter is not to provide comprehensive coverage of the law (for this the reader will need to refer to the various specialist texts available) but to provide an outline of when (and why) tenants have been given these kinds of rights.

Although most legislation on enfranchisement is of recent origin there have been movements supporting enfranchisement for over a hundred years, the first Bill being presented (unsuccessfully) in 1884. The first major piece of legislation on enfranchisement was the Leasehold Reform Act 1967 which applied to private sector leaseholders. It gave tenants with long leases of houses the right to buy the freehold or extend their leases in return for compensation. Long leaseholders of flats were given the collective right to purchase the freehold at market value under the Leasehold Reform, Housing and Urban Development Act 1993, or to individually extend their leases. There are also limited rights to enfranchise contained in the Landlord and Tenant Act 1987, which gives a right of first refusal if the landlord proposes to dispose of his interest or a right to acquire if there has been a serious management failure. In the public sector, council tenants who are renting property on a periodic basis were given the right to buy (RTB) by the Housing Act 1980; although it is not generally referred to as an enfranchisement right it does give them the right to buy the freehold to their homes at a substantial discount from market value. Tenants of registered social landlords (RSLs) were given (a more limited) right to acquire (RTA) by the Housing Act 1996.

There are similarities between the RTB (and RTA) given to social tenants and the enfranchisement rights given to long leaseholders. In both cases the end result is that the tenant or leaseholder ends up as an owner-occupier, albeit that in the case of flats this owner-occupation of necessity takes the form of a long lease. Of course, for the private leaseholder this is merely reinforcing his existing status as an owner-occupier: in the private sector enfranchisement rights are given only to long leaseholders and not renters. Enfranchisement does two main things for the long leaseholder: it provides a solution to the 'wasting asset' problem, and it gives the leaseholder (collectively in the case of flats) control over the management of the property. The issues facing long leaseholders and the arguments for enfranchisement are discussed in chapters 7 and 11. For the social tenant enfranchisement marks a very significant shift from the status of 'renter' to that of 'owner'. This is primarily ideologically and financially motivated: the tenant no longer pays rent to a landlord but invests in a capital asset. That ownership also gives greater security is of secondary significance: the secure and assured tenancies can also provide life-time security, albeit the landlord may be able to obtain possession if a discretionary ground for possession exists and a court considers it reasonable.[1]

Similar issues can occur in relation both to leasehold enfranchisement and RTB. Leasehold enfranchisement has been consistently opposed by landlords on the grounds that it interferes with freedom of contract and property rights. In the public sector, resistance to RTB has formed part of the central versus local government struggle, with claims that it is an undue interference with locally determined policies and priorities and reduces the social housing stock. The question of how much the tenant should pay to exercise the right has also been contentious in both sectors. In the case of leasehold enfranchisement, the issue has focused on whether the leaseholder should be paying simply for acquisition of the site on the basis that he has effectively already paid for the house/flat, or whether the purchase price should include a sum that reflects the value that is released by the leasehold and freehold interests coming together (discussed more fully below). In the case of RTB, the tenant gets a discount from the full capital value of the house/flat but the level of discount has varied according to whether it is seen as reflecting the discounted worth of a house with a sitting tenant in and the value of rent paid, or as a tap to control the flow of take-up of RTB.[2] Initially both RTB and leasehold enfranchisement were rights given only to resident tenants.[3] This is still the case

---

[1] Indeed, given the high rates of mortgage default and re-possession, the security of owner-occupation turns out for many on low incomes to be illusory.

[2] That is, the higher the level of discount, the more people will opt for RTB; through changes to the level of discount the government is able to influence the popularity of RTB. See further 25.3.6.

[3] Surprisingly in the case of enfranchisement. Before 1950, twenty different Enfranchisement Bills had been put forward but only one of these restricted the right to enfranchise to residential tenants.

with RTB but the residency tests have now been removed for leasehold enfranchisement. As Davey notes:

> It was never clear why in principle the 1967 and 1993 Acts had included a residence require-ment, if those Acts were based on the theory that the leaseholder had already paid for the house or flat built on the land. Maybe it was simply to restrict the claim to those who other-wise stood to lose their residence on expiry of the lease. But, this would seem to confuse the rationale of the Rent Acts with the rationale of enfranchisement measures designed to benefit successors in title of original leaseholders who had built or paid for the house. In more recent times, the residence requirement seems to have been a tactical concession to large landowners to limit the operation of the scheme.[4]

No comparable rights exist in the commercial or agricultural sectors. The primary force behind the rights given to social tenants is the government's desire to extend home ownership. The RTB has proven to be attractive to the electorate and its popularity has also helped to implement the aim of reducing the state's role in housing provision. Capital receipts from council house sales form an important part of public expenditure planning. The rights given to long leaseholders stem from years of unrest with the mismatch that leaseholders had between the perception of themselves as owner-occupiers and the reality of the lease as a wasting asset under the control of rapacious or disinterested freeholders. These concerns simply do not arise in the commercial and agricultural sectors.

25.2 Social Tenants and Enfranchisement

25.2.1 Policy

Various statutory rights have been given to social tenants as part of the policy to promote low-cost home ownership (LCHO), essentially schemes designed to assist those at the margins into owner occupation. In addition to these statutory rights given to tenants, there have also been a number of schemes enabling both local authorities and RSLs to sell to social tenants on a voluntary basis. The scheme that has had the greatest impact, however, is undoubtedly the statutory RTB. The RTB was first given as a statutory right to council tenants in 1980, giving tenants of a certain standing a RTB the freehold with a discount. RTA is a similar right that was given to RSL tenants in 1996, but with lower discounts and fewer properties eligible.

The fact that such extensive rights have been given to social tenants is not, however, an indication that the legal relationship of tenancy is somehow not working. Instead they should be seen as part of the political and ideological push for greater home ownership. The policy background to RTB and RTA is quite different from that to leasehold enfran-chisement. There is much housing policy literature available on the RTB and recent government publications offer a variety of justifications for extending home ownership (briefly discussed in chapter 5). Cowan and Marsh state that:

---

[4] M Davey, 'Long Residential Leases: Past and Present' in S Bright (ed), *Landlord and Tenant Law. Past, Present and Future* (Oxford, Hart, 2006) 166.

The right to buy policy had its origins in the government's antipathy to council housing and desire to create a property owning democracy.[5]

RTB is now an established aspect of housing policy, assisting in the creation of mixed tenure communities and freeing up social housing for those in greatest need. What it does show, however, is that tenancy is perceived of as a less perfect goal than outright ownership. Renting cannot offer many of the advantages of ownership: there is no opportunity to build an asset base that can provide financial security for retirement and the hope of an inheritance for family members, and there is not the same degree of control and autonomy over the home. Nor does it satisfy the 'innate desire' to own one's own home (a desire arguably fuelled by propaganda and fiscal incentives over the years) or offer the same degree of 'ontological security'[6] as home ownership.[7] The advantages are not all one way, however. With ownership comes greater responsibility and greater financial risk; LCHO is now reaching households with relatively low and unstable incomes, where the cost of unexpected repair items or the loss of a job can be ruinous. As the government acknowledged in 1998, 'for some people, the cost and strain of home ownership is too much'.[8] There have been particular problems with flats where, having bought under the RTB, the leaseholders have found themselves landed with big service charge bills. Local authorities are undertaking major works to deal with the backlog of disrepair, not simply because of the desire to bring homes up to the Decent Homes Standard.[9] Although average bills are well below £10,000 a small minority face bills above £10,000 following major refurbishment programmes.[10] Even sums at the more modest end of the range can be difficult to meet and householders are having to finance costs by borrowing against the security of the property.[11]

25.2.2 The Impact on Stock

Councils have had a discretion to sell their housing at a 30 per cent discount with ministerial consent since 1951 but it was not until the RTB was introduced that sales occurred in significant numbers across the country. Since then more than 2 million homes in Great Britain have been transferred into home ownership under the RTB. The pattern of RTB sales is shown in Figure 25.1.

---

[5] D Cowan and A Marsh, 'Analysing New Labour housing policy' in D Cowan and A Marsh (eds), *Two Steps Forward* (Bristol, The Policy Press, 2001) 3.

[6] A sense of belonging and continuity of self.

[7] For a fuller discussion of the 'value of home ownership', see D Cowan, *Housing Law and Policy* (Basingstoke, Macmillan, 1999) 326–33.

[8] DETR, 'A Financial Incentive for Local Authorities to Buy Back Homes from Leaseholders or Others in Difficulty – A Consultation Paper' (1998) para 10.

[9] For an explanation of the Decent Homes Standard, see ch 12.

[10] DCLG, 'Assessment of the impact of the cost of repairs for Right to Buy leaseholders' (Housing Research Summary, Number 227, 2006). According to the DCLG News Release 2007/0066, 'Government Helps Local Authority Leaseholders to Pay Major Works Bills' (29 March 2007) some bills are as high as £58,000. A recent survey by London Councils showed that of 143,000 council leaseholders in 26 London Boroughs, just over 9,000 (6.3%) were facing major works bills of £10,000 or more.

[11] The government is working with local authorities to find ways to make it easier for leaseholders to pay, for example, by developing plans for equity release and equity loans: DCLG News Release 2007/0066, 'Government Helps Local Authority Leaseholders to Pay Major Works Bills' (29 March 2007).

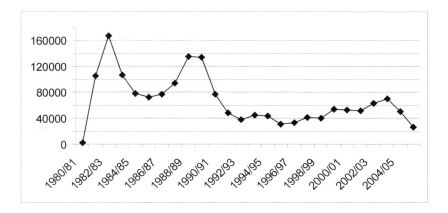

Figure 25.1 Right to Buy Sales of Local Authority Dwellings to Owner Occupation: England
Source: ODPM Live tables, Chart 642

RTB sales are still very significant. Even though the actual numbers of sales are much lower now than the high figures seen from 1980 to 1982 when the first flush of interest in the RTB reached its peak, the lower numbers are a reflection of there being a much smaller council house sector. The rate of sales as a proportion of stock was, in 2003, just as high as in the 1982 peak.[12] The increase in sales from 1987-89 was probably due to the rise in rents and the boom in house prices at that time. Since 2003, there has, however, been a real drop, which is probably explained by caps on discount that were introduced in 2003 (see 25.3.6).

Commenting on the impact of RTB, Forrest and Murie write:

Selling council houses was the most substantial element in the privatisation policies of the Conservative governments between 1979 and 1997 and was a privatisation which benefited ordinary working families rather than the wealthy or those able to shift their investment portfolios around. Over those years some 2.3 million public sector dwellings have been sold to homeowners and a further 250,000 through stock transfers. Most of these have been under the right to buy introduced in the Housing Act 1980.

Those who have bought have mostly bought good houses at cheap (discounted) prices, and in general they had benefited from house price inflation. In some cases, they have bought because it is cheaper to buy than to rent …

Evaluating council house sales over 17 years is complex. The policy has not operated in a vacuum. It has formed part of the general reshaping of housing policy.[13]

The impact of the RTB has been dramatic, both in terms of housing stock but in relation to housing policy itself. In terms of stock, it is the better quality housing that has been the most popular, with relatively few flats being sold (flats represent 30 per cent of the stock but

---

[12] S Wilcox, 'A financial evaluation of the right to buy' in S Wilcox, *UK Housing Review 2006/07* (Coventry, Chartered Institute of Housing and London, Council of Mortgage Lenders, 2006) 14.

[13] R Forrest and A Murie, 'The big sell off' in J Goodwin and C Grant (eds), *Built to Last?* 2nd edn (London, ROOF, 1997) 147.

only 4 per cent of RTB sales).[14] Until recently it has been tenants in the middle age group that have made up the bulk of purchasers. For much of the time councils have been unable to reinvest the proceeds in building new stock and this has caused a decline in both the amount of housing available and in the quality of the remaining stock. As better off tenants have left the social rented sector opting for home ownership, RTB has also led to the local authority sector being occupied by the lowest income groups and more marginalised members of society. The winners are those who have been able to access home ownership, the losers are those:

> … who find that the declining supply and range of choice in council housing increases waiting time, restricts their choice or means that they will not obtain a house at all.[15]

Over time, as the more attractive housing has been removed from the sector and social housing has become increasingly available only to those in great housing need, the RTB has itself changed:

> The evidence from more recent sales suggests that more council house buyers are buying to enable them to move on rather than to secure the home they are attached to. Consistent with this is the fact that these purchasers are younger …
>
> This may well indicate that the Right to Buy is now a mature policy operating in a system already transformed by its early impact. The Right to Buy has changed the system and has been changed by it – with its relevance and appropriateness reduced. At the same time as the policy has matured it has become more complex. It is no longer a simple uniform policy offering a new and straightforward package.[16]

The fact that most remaining local authority tenants are on very low incomes means that there are limited prospects for them to access home ownership, even through the RTB. The nature of the stock left as council housing also limits the numbers wanting to buy. The government has therefore turned to other routes to expand home ownership and make it available to tenants. A variety of shared ownership schemes have been available for a number of years. Under these schemes the purchaser buys a proportion of the property from a social landlord and pays rent on the remaining share. There are opportunities to 'staircase', that is to increase the owned share in stages up to 100 per cent ownership. There are also various 'HomeBuy' schemes available similarly offering the opportunity to purchase a share of the equity in a home. Social HomeBuy enables social tenants of landlords that choose to offer the scheme to buy a share in their existing home. New Build HomeBuy and Open Market HomeBuy are available to existing social tenants and those on the housing register, as well as key workers and other first-time buyers, to enable them to buy a share in the equity of a home newly built with public subsidy or on public sector land or on the open market. The details of these are beyond the scope of this book and the schemes are not confined to social tenants or those in housing need. Nonetheless they do reveal the extent of the government's continuing push to enable social tenants to become home owners.

---

[14] P Malpass and A Murie, *Housing Policy and Practice* 5th edn (Basingstoke, Palgrave, 1999) 255.
[15] P Malpass and A Murie, *Housing Policy and Practice* 5th edn (Basingstoke, Palgrave, 1999) 257.
[16] P Malpass and A Murie, *Housing Policy and Practice* 5th edn (Basingstoke, Palgrave, 1999) 258.

25.3 The Right to Buy

25.3.1 The Qualifying Period for RTB

The RTB is given by the Housing Act 1985 to someone who has been a secure tenant[17] for at least five years.[18] This period was increased from two years by the Housing Act 2004 to 'encourage tenants to make a longer term commitment to the community before they can buy'.[19] This period includes not only the existing tenancy but also any earlier period spent as a 'public sector tenant', which will include as a tenant of a RSL or other local authority.[20] It is also possible for an assured tenant of an RSL to have a 'Preserved RTB' (PRTB) if he previously held a secure tenancy with a local authority;[21] this is designed with stock transfer in mind to ensure that secure tenants do not lose the RTB when the housing stock is transferred from the local authority to the RSL.

The extension of the qualifying period to five years was part of a package of changes introduced by the Housing Act 2004 'with a view to tackling exploitation of the rules by property developers and tenants'. Hopkins and Laurie describe the 2004 Act changes as falling into two categories:

> Those aimed at direct exploitation of the scheme (primarily thought to be instigated by companies) and those intended more generally to make the RTB a less attractive proposition as a purely financial investment.[22]

25.3.2 The Need for a Secure Tenancy

The statutory right is available only so long as the secure tenancy continues. This can be very important as the status of a secure tenant is not necessarily co-terminus with continued occupation. So, for example, if a joint tenant serves a notice to quit on relationship breakdown this will end the tenancy (in accordance with *Hammersmith and Fulham LBC v Monk*)[23] as well as any hopes the remaining occupier has of completing a purchase under the RTB (as occurred in *Bater v Bater*).[24] A secure tenant who is bankrupt loses the RTB.[25] Where a possession order is granted this will also end the statutory RTB.[26] A tolerated trespasser therefore has no RTB, but if the secure tenancy is later revived the tenant will then be able to exercise the RTB. In this situation, the secure tenant will not, however, be able to continue with an application made before becoming a tolerated trespasser and will need to make a

---

[17] For the meaning of secure tenant, see ch 6.

[18] For tenancies beginning on or after 18 January 2005: Housing Act 1985 s 119. When first introduced there was a three-year qualifying period for the RTB. Some RSL tenants may have the RTB if they became tenants before 15 January 1989 and are secure tenants.

[19] Hansard HL vol 664 col 1328 (16 September 2004) (Lord Bassam of Brighton).

[20] Housing Act 1985 Sch 4.

[21] Housing Act 1985 s 171 Sch 9A.

[22] N Hopkins and E Laurie, 'Housing or Property? The Dynamics of Housing Policy and Property Principles in the Right to Buy' (2006) 26 *LS* 65, 77.

[23] [1992] 1 AC 478 (HL).

[24] [1999] 4 All ER 944 (CA).

[25] Housing Act 1985 s 121.

[26] Housing Act 1985 s 121.

fresh RTB application.[27] The interaction of RTB and possession orders has led to some diffi-culties in the case law. A colourful example is *Bristol CC v Lovell*.[28] Mr Lovell, a secure tenant, had an admitted RTB which remained only to be completed by the formal grant of the freehold to him by the local authority. The Council believed that he was using the house as a shop to sell drugs, not unlikely given the following description by Lord Hoffmann:

> It has been suitably adapted to the trade, with steel grilles over doors and windows, kennels for Rottweiler dogs, surveillance cameras to check visitors, a radio scanner tuned to police fre-quency and equipment for locating covert listening devices.[29]

The council bought a possession action alleging nuisance and annoyance to neighbours. Mr Lovell sought an injunction forcing the council to complete the grant of the freehold. The issue before the House of Lords was whether there was a discretion as to the order in which the two cases were heard: if possession was given then this would end the RTB, on the other hand if the injunction was heard first it was accepted that the court would have no real discretion to deny the remedy sought and Mr Lovell would then become the freehold owner. The House of Lords held that there was a discretion to hear the cases in the order which justice and convenience required. There is an obvious concern that tenants committing serious antisocial behaviour should not be able to complete a purchase before a landlord is able to take effective action. The Housing Act 2004, therefore, gives landlords greater control in cases where anti-social behaviour is involved: they can seek an order suspending the RTB on the grounds of anti-social behaviour,[30] and the landlord's obligation to complete the RTB sale is suspended where some type of court action relating to anti-social behaviour is pending.[31]

The conflict between RTB and possession will be much more difficult in cases where the tenant has done nothing wrong. The judge then will have to undertake an extremely difficult balancing act. Where both the possession action and the RTB are arguable claims, the judge does have a duty to investigate the merits as a whole. In *Basildon DC v Wahlen*[32] the tenant had succeeded to his mother's tenancy in a home he had been living in for almost 30 years. The council sought possession on Ground 16 (under occupation, with suitable alternative accommodation being offered), and the tenant sought to exercise his RTB. The price of the property was agreed. The Court of Appeal agreed that the district judge had been right to hear the possession action and the claim for an injunction to enforce the RTB together. When he does so, however, he must engage in a very difficult balancing act. Things that could point in the tenant's favour would include long established occupation of the property, a move that would be unusually disruptive, the fact that there is no breach by the tenant, and that the tenant genuinely intends to complete the RTB. Factors that could point in favour of the local authority would include any persistent or serious breaches by the

---

[27] *Islington LBC v Honeygan-Green* [2007] EWHC 1270 (QB). This stems from the statutory wording of s 121 but is also supported by policy as a tolerated trespasser who does not pay rent should not benefit from the lower purchase price set by an earlier RTB application: [50] and [53].

[28] [1998] 1 WLR 446 (HL).

[29] [1998] 1 WLR 446 (HL) 452.

[30] Similar powers are given to RSLs in relation to tenants with the RTA or the PRTB: Housing Act 1996 s 17 (RTA) and Housing Act 1985 s 171C (PRTB), both as amended by the Housing Act 2004.

[31] Housing Act 1985 ss 121 and 138, both as amended by the Housing Act 2004.

[32] [2006] EWCA Civ 326.

tenant, and a genuine desire to 'better deploy its housing stock'. The significance of the fact that in this particular case a three bedroomed property would be under occupied can be overstated, for example, the tenant may in due course start a family. What was not relevant, however, was the fact that the council would lose a property from its housing stock; this loss is simply a consequence of the RTB policy. Weighing these matters is something for the district judge to do. In this case, he had failed to do that and the Court of Appeal remitted the case for a retrial. As Neuberger LJ remarked, the court will have an:

> ... unenviable task, in that the balancing exercise to be carried out will involve comparing factors which are largely incommensurate with each other.[33]

25.3.3 The Property

The RTB gives a right to buy a freehold from the landlord or, if the landlord is itself a leaseholder or the property is a flat, a right to a lease for 125 years (or for five days fewer than the council's own lease).[34] The important distinction between a flat and a house is complex. Section 183(2) of the Housing Act 1985 provides that a dwelling will be a house if it:

> ... is a structure reasonably so called; so that –
>
> (a) where a building is divided horizontally, the flats or other units into which it is divided are not houses;
> (b) where a building is divided vertically, the units into which it is divided may be houses;
> (c) where a building is not structurally detached, it is not a house if a material part of it lies above or below the remainder of the structure.

If the property does not fall within this definition of a house, section 183(3) states that it will be a flat.

If another flat in the same building has already been bought under the RTB then the length of the lease will be determined by reference to the remaining term of the lease granted to the first purchaser.[35] If, for example, a flat was sold on a 125 year lease under the RTB in 1987, a tenant buying a flat in 2006 would only obtain a lease for 106 years.

25.3.4 Sharing the RTB

Where a secure tenancy is a joint tenancy, the RTB belongs jointly to all of the joint tenants or to one or more of them as agreed between themselves, provided that such person or persons occupies the house as his only or principal home.[36] The right can also, and importantly, be exercised jointly with up to three members of the tenant's family, which includes his spouse and members who have lived with him for the last 12 months.[37]

It is not unusual for the money for the purchase to be put up by other members of the family (and not always resident relatives). It may be that this financial contribution towards

---

[33] [2006] EWCA Civ 326 [30].
[34] Housing Act 1985 s 118 (1).
[35] Housing Act 1985 Sch 6 Part III para 12 (3).
[36] Housing Act 1985 s 118 (2).
[37] And other family members with the landlord's consent: Housing Act 1985 s 123.

the purchase price, combined with the parties' intentions, is sufficient to give the contributors an interest in the property itself (rather than simply a claim in debt). In such a situation, difficult questions of property law can arise in working out exactly how the beneficial interest in the property is shared. Often, the details of how shares in the property are to be owned are not discussed. In determining how the purchase price has been paid, one question is whether the RTB discount (the reduction in the purchase price from full market value 'allowed' to the secure tenant) should be categorised as equivalent to a cash contribution being made towards the purchase by the tenant. If so, in the context of determining the how the property is owned in equity, both those supplying the purchase monies and the tenant will be seen as contributing towards the acquisition. As Hopkins and Laurie show, the tendency is to recognise the discount as a contribution by the RTB tenant, although the working out of this is not always satisfactory and there are inconsistent approaches.[38] Funding by relatives can sometimes be exploitative of the council tenant, particularly where the tenant is elderly and the relatives persuade the tenant to exercise the RTB. Once the right has been exercised, the relatives may evict the former tenant or arrange for the title to be transferred once the discount repayment period has expired (see 25.3.6 below).

25.3.5 Exceptions

There are certain exceptions from the RTB. These fall into two broad categories: those who occupy the dwelling house as a result of employment, and housing particularly suited for certain categories of people.[39] The idea underlying both of these exceptions is to preserve stock which fulfils very particular kinds of need. The employment exception protects property from the RTB only if the home is 'within the curtilage of a building which … is held mainly for purposes other than housing purposes'.[40] It did not, for example, enable Dorset County Council to retain housing for lecturers at an agricultural college even though the housing was proximate to the college and clearly made it easier for lecturers to perform their duties.[41] Homes that are particularly suitable for occupation by elderly persons are exempted,[42] as is housing for the disabled (mentally or physically) if special facilities are also available to them.[43]

A further exception was introduced by the Housing Act 2004 to address exploitation revealed by research commissioned by the Office of the Deputy Prime Minister (ODPM).[44] Exploitation can occur prior to a regeneration scheme being implemented. In the words of Lord Bassam of Brighton as government spokesman:

---

[38] N Hopkins and E Laurie, 'Housing or Property? The Dynamics of Housing Policy and Property Principles in the Right to Buy' (2006) 26 *LS* 65.
[39] Housing Act 1985 Sch 5.
[40] Housing Act 1985 Sch 5 para 5(1)(a).
[41] *Dyer v Dorset CC* [1988] QB 346 (CA).
[42] Housing Act 1985 Sch 5 paras 10 and 11.
[43] Housing Act 1985 Sch 5 paras 7 and 9.
[44] ODPM, 'Exploitation of the Right to Buy Scheme by Companies' (Housing Research Summary, Number 177, 2003).

... when tenants know that demolition is likely, they are able to buy at a discount knowing that when the property has to be repurchased using compulsory powers they will be entitled to full market value plus home loss compensation. This adversely affects the financial viability of regeneration schemes.[45]

Homes due to be demolished are now exempted from the RTB.[46]

25.3.6 The Price and Discount

The valuation of the dwelling-house is based on its vacant possession price.[47] As well as ignoring the fact that there is a sitting tenant in calculating the sale price, section 127(1)(b) of the Housing Act 1985 requires the valuer to disregard any improvements made by the secure tenant and any failure to keep the premises in good internal repair.

The secure tenant buys his dwelling-house at a discount which is determined by the length of time that he has been a secure tenant and by whether he is purchasing a house or a flat. Originally, the same discount rate applied to both houses and flats, but with the disproportionately poor take-up of flats a preferential discount had to be introduced. The rationale for the discount is explained by Hopkins and Laurie:

> When the RTB was introduced, it provided for an initial discount for houses of 33%, following three years' qualifying residence, with a further 1% for each complete year of tenancy, to a maximum of 50% ...
>
> The discount awarded to RTB purchasers was claimed by the Conservative Government of the day to comprise two distinct elements. The initial minimum 33% discount was said to be a reflection of the fact that a council house will have a sitting tenant:
>
> 'Clearly, the sitting tenant valuation is always significantly less. Indeed, in the private sector a discount could be materially greater than 33 per cent if a sitting tenant were in occupation.'
>
> The government claimed that the main cause for the discount was the fact of residence and, in this initial 33%, no account was taken of any rent paid by the tenant. The years of rent paid by the RTB tenant were taken into account in the principle of the additional 1% that was awarded over the initial qualifying period. The government was keen to distinguish between the element of the discount that reflected the existence of a sitting tenant and the increase attributable to the fact that a tenant had been in occupation and paying rent. [footnotes omitted][48]

Forrest and Murie argue, however, that since the early days:

> ... the discount rate has become no more than a balancing act between providing sufficient incentive to maintain sales and generating a certain level of capital receipts.[49]

It is, however, no longer the case that the sole aim is to maintain high sales levels. A number of changes were introduced by the Housing Act 2004 which limit the impact of

---

[45] Hansard (HL) vol 664 col 1377 (16 September 2004).

[46] Housing Act 1985 s 138 and Sch 5 and 5A.

[47] Housing Act 1985 ss 126 and 127.

[48] N Hopkins and E Laurie, 'Housing or Property? The Dynamics of Housing Policy and Property Principles in the Right to Buy' (2006) 26 LS 65, 68.

[49] R Forrest and A Murie, 'The big sell off' in J Goodwin and C Grant (eds), Built to Last? 2nd edn (London, ROOF, 1997) 148.

RTB. The actual amount of discount available to any individual will depend upon whether they have to satisfy the two or the five-year qualifying periods. As with the qualifying residence requirement, the qualifying period for the discount can be spent in different homes, with different landlords and need not be continuous. A tenant who needs a five-year qualifying period will obtain a 35 per cent discount for houses and 50 per cent for flats. Additional discount is available for each extra year of residence: in the case of houses this is one per cent for each year up to a maximum of 60 per cent, in the case of flats it is two per cent for each extra year up to a maximum of 70 per cent.[50] There are also maximum discounts set according to the area which the house is situated in, and these will apply even if the amount calculated by reference to the percentage would be greater. In areas of housing pressure with high levels of homelessness and high property prices, the maximum RTB discount has been reduced to £16,000.[51] There is a further limitation on discount contained in the 'cost floor' rules: under these the RTB discount cannot reduce the price of the property below what the landlord has spent on it during the previous ten years, whether on buying, building, improving, repairing or maintaining.[52] The effect of this is that purchasers of newer properties (or of properties that have recently undergone major renovation) will obtain very little discount.

25.3.7 Repayment of Discount

To prevent tenants cashing in on the discount by immediately reselling the dwelling house for its true value, the landlord is able to demand that the discount be repaid if a non-exempt resale occurs within a specified period, originally three years but extended to five years by the Housing Act 2004. This is secured by a covenant included in the conveyance to the RTB purchaser.[53] Repayment will be triggered by any 'relevant disposal', that is, a sale or grant of a new lease for over 21 years at more than a rack rent.[54] Certain 'non commercial' disposals are exempt, for example, disposals to certain family members, transmission on death, or a transfer following a court order on marriage breakdown.[55]

The repayment rules were originally based upon the actual amount of the discount given. For RTB applications made before 18 January 2005, the entire discount had to be repaid if there was a further sale of the property within one year, two-thirds if the sale was in the second year, and one-third if the sale was in the third year. Thereafter, no discount was repayable. Following the 2004 Act changes, for RTB applications made from 18 January 2005 onwards, the discount repayable was one hundred per cent for a sale during the first year after purchase, four-fifths during the second year, three-fifths during the third year, four-fifths during the fourth year, one-fifth during the fifth year, and nothing thereafter. At the same time, further changes were made to the repayment rules to prevent tenants profiteering from house price rises. Where the RTB has been exercised after 18 January 2005 the discount repayable will be based upon the resale value of the property at that time

---

[50] Housing Act 1985 s 129.
[51] Housing (Right to Buy) (Limits on Discount) (Amendment) Order 2003 SI 2003/498.
[52] Housing Act 1985 s 131; The Housing (Right to Buy) (Limits on Discount) Order 1998 SI 1998/2997.
[53] Housing Act 1985 s 155.
[54] Housing Act 1985 s 159.
[55] Housing Act 1985 s 160.

(disregarding any improvements done).[56] An example of how this works is given on the website of Wrexham County Borough Council:

> For example, if your home was valued at £100,000 at the time you bought it from your land-lord, and you received a discount of £20,000, that means that your discount was 20%.
>
> If your home is valued at £150,000 when you wish to sell it and you want to sell within the second year of purchase, you will have to repay £150,000 x 20% discount x 4/5 i.e. £24,000.

25.3.8 Preventing Abuse

The changes in the Housing Act 2004 also seek to deal with other abuses of RTB. The ODPM research showed there was some exploitation by companies offering council tenants incentives, in the form of a capital sum:

> … to take up the RTB in order for these households to then lease their property to the company and to sign a commitment to sell their home after the … discount repayment period.[57] [This is known as a deferred resale agreement].

The government has tackled deferred resale agreements by providing that if the RTB purchaser agrees to transfer the property to a third-party, either before the RTB purchase or during the discount repayment period, this will trigger repayment of the discount from the date that the agreement is entered into.[58] Strictly, this will also catch such agreements made with relatives who provide funding, but it is likely that some kind of exemption will be made. Nothing has been done to prevent a council tenant buying with RTB discount and then immediately letting the property out at market rents.

25.3.9 Right of First Refusal

Although not related to price or discount, a further change introduced by the Housing Act 2004 shows that the government is also concerned about the impact on housing stock. In line with an approach that had already been adopted for rural housing,[59] there is now a right of first refusal that applies where the RTB has been exercised on or after 18 January 2005. This provides that if there is a relevant disposal within ten years, the property must first be offered to the former landlord or to another social landlord in the area at full market value.[60] Again, this works by inserting a covenant into the RTB conveyance. This right of first refusal has also been applied to RTA, PRTB (the right given to former secure tenants after stock transfer to a housing association) and voluntary disposals by social landlords.

---

[56] Housing Act 1985 ss 155A and 155C.

[57] ODPM, 'Exploitation of the Right to Buy Scheme by Companies' (Housing Research Summary, Number 177, 2003).

[58] Housing Act 1985 s 163A.

[59] Housing Act 1985 s 157 provided that in designated rural areas, National Parks, and Areas of Outstanding Natural Beauty, social landlords could either impose a right of first refusal or require that houses that had been bought through RTB could be sold only to people who have lived or worked locally for at least three years.

[60] Housing Act 1985 s 156A.

25.3.10 Process and the Nature of the Right

The process begins when the tenant gives an RTB claim form to the landlord.[61] The landlord then has a period of four weeks to confirm to the tenant whether there is an RTB[62] and, assuming this is so, the landlord must then send a separate offer notice (known as a section 125 notice) setting out the price that the tenant will have to pay[63] and the terms and conditions of the sale, including – in the case of flats – estimated service charges and improvement costs for the next five years. As soon as all matters relating to the grant are agreed the landlord comes under a duty to transfer the freehold or grant the long lease[64] (although if the tenant is four weeks in arrears with the rent or other tenancy outgoings there is no such obligation while this payment is outstanding).[65]

During the period between the application being made and the transfer being completed, the question may arise as to the nature of the right. In *Bater v Bater* a couple had accepted the local authority's offer to sell to them under the RTB but before the process was completed the couple split up and the secure tenancy was brought to an end by the wife serving a notice to quit.[66] The husband argued that the RTB was 'property' and made an application under the matrimonial legislation for the avoidance of the 'disposition of property' that had occurred by his wife serving the notice to quit. In support of the argument that the RTB was property, his counsel relied on the facts that the right can survive a change of landlord, a change of secure tenant, and can be shared with other members of the tenant's family. This, it was argued, satisfied the requirements of being property laid out by Lord Wilberforce in *National Provincial Bank Ltd v Ainsworth*[67] ('definable, identifiable by third parties, capable in its nature of assumption by third parties, and [having] … some degree of permanence or stability'). Roch LJ rejected this, adopting the remarks of Balcombe LJ in *Bradford MCC v McMahon* that the RTB is:

> … a creature of statute and sui generis; if it is helpful to equate it to some more general right recognised by the courts I would prefer to describe it as analogous to a personal equity.[68]

As Lord Hoffmann stated in *Bristol CC v Lovell*:

> … the 1985 Act does not bring into existence a deemed contract. It misses out the contractual stage of normal conveyancing and creates a statutory right to a conveyance. The only remedy provided for the enforcement of this right is an injunction …
>
> The tenant acquires no proprietary interest whatever until the grant of the freehold.[69]

---

[61] Housing Act 1985 s 122.
[62] Housing Act 1985 s 124.
[63] If unhappy, the tenant can require the value of the house to be determined by the district valuer: Housing Act 1985 s 128.
[64] Housing Act 1985 s 138.
[65] Housing Act 1985 s 138(2).
[66] [1999] 4 All ER 944 (CA).
[67] [1965] AC 1175 (HL) 1248.
[68] [1994] 1 WLR 52 (CA) 60.
[69] [1998] 1 WLR 446 (HL) 453, 455. In *Islington LBC v Honeygan-Green* [2007] EWHC 1270 (QB) Nelson J said that a tenant does not acquire a proprietary interest in the property as a result of the application for the right to buy: [52].

With regard to the transfer itself, there are detailed statutory provisions dealing with the content of the freehold or leasehold conveyance, governing terms such as easements and covenants,[70] as well as terms more specific to the RTB such as the discount repayment[71] and the covenant giving a right of refusal to the landlord.[72] The most detailed provisions relate to the grant of a leasehold flat.[73] They provide that the ground rent cannot exceed £10 a year, and impose an implied repairing covenant on the landlord in relation to the structure and exterior of the dwelling-house and of the building, and a duty to repair any other property over which the tenant has rights. There is also an obligation to maintain services to a reasonable level, together with an implied covenant to rebuild or reinstate in the event of destruction by causes such as fire.

Schedule 6 also provides for the recouping of expenses by the local authority in connection with leasehold repairs and improvements. Once five years have expired since the exercise of the RTB, the landlord of a long leasehold flat can require the tenant to pay a reasonable contribution towards the landlord's costs. Within the first five years the local authority's ability to do so is limited by reference to the estimated service charges and improvement costs that were provided by the landlord in its section 125 notice, plus inflation. In relation to works that were not itemised in the notice, the tenant is only liable for the estimated annual average amount for works of repair. The tenant may be able to obtain a loan from the local authority landlord to assist with these costs.[74] After five years there are no such restrictions and, as seen earlier, long leaseholders can be hit by very substantial service charge bills following major works of repair being undertaken. Former local authority flats, particularly in high rise tower blocks, are often very difficult to resell in the open market.

A secure tenant is able to enforce the RTB even against a landlord reluctant to sell. When the RTB was first introduced in the Housing Act 1980, several Labour local authorities were opposed to it. The legislation contains strong powers to ensure that the tenant is able to exercise the RTB. Under section 138(3) of the Housing Act 1985, the tenant is able to enforce the RTB by injunction. An alternative remedy is open to the tenant without there being any need to go to court where the council delays in processing the application. The effect of this remedy is that after a set period during which the council fails to answer the tenant's notices, the tenant can deduct rent paid from the eventual purchase price.[75]

The Secretary of State also has power under the Housing Act 1985 to intervene and take over sales under the RTB where the local authority appears to be defeating the purpose of the legislation.[76] He may, for example, act after complaints from RTB applicants. Where the Secretary of State does exercise powers under section 164, then ultimately he can transfer the freehold or grant a long lease to any applicant tenant. Indeed, the Secretary of State's

---

[70] Housing Act 1985 Sch 6.
[71] Housing Act 1985 Sch 6A.
[72] Housing Act 1985 s 156A.
[73] Housing Act 1985 Sch 6, Part III.
[74] Housing Act 1985 ss 450A–450C.
[75] Housing Act 1985 s 153A.
[76] Housing Act 1985 s 164.

general powers in this area are extensive.[77] The Secretary of State intervened in Norwich in 1981 after the Council was accused of excessive delays, of overpricing their houses and of including onerous covenants in the conveyances and grants. The local authority sought judicial review. In *Norwich CC v Secretary of State for the Environment* it was found that Norwich County Council had acted in good faith but that nonetheless the Secretary of State had the right to intervene, subject to scrutiny by the courts.[78]

The landlord is also able to serve a notice to complete on a tenant who is delaying things.[79] If nothing happens, the landlord can serve a second notice to complete; if the tenant still fails to act then after 56 days the RTB claim is deemed withdrawn.[80]

25.4 The Right to Acquire

The RTA, similar to the RTB, was given to RSL tenants by the Housing Act 1996.[81] The RTA does not apply to all RSL properties, but only those built or acquired by a RSL on or after 1 April 1997. Most other aspects of the RTA operate in a similar manner to the RTB, for example there are qualification periods and certain properties are exempted. The discounts available, however, are much more limited and range from £9,000 to £16,000, depending upon location. As with RTB, the discount is repayable in whole or in part if the property is sold within a five-year period of exercising the RTA. The impact of the RTA so far has been very small. It appears that annually only a few properties are sold under the RTA,[82] whereas the numbers being sold by housing associations through RTB, PRTB, and rent to mortgage sales are much more substantial.[83]

25.5 The Preserved Right to Buy

A local authority secure tenant who becomes an assured housing association tenant as a result of stock transfer has a PRTB by virtue of sections 171A-171H of the Housing Act 1985 as long as he remains in the same property. This operates on the same basis as the RTB in that area.

---

[77] Housing Act 1985 ss 165–170.
[78] [1982] QB 808 (CA).
[79] Housing Act 1985 s 140.
[80] Housing Act 1985 s 141.
[81] Ss 16, 17.
[82] 312 units were sold as SHG subsidised outright sales in 2001/02, a figure that includes sales by Voluntary Purchase Grant as well as RTA sales. In 2002/03, the figure was 395 units and in 2003/04, it was 573 units. Under the Voluntary Purchase Grant scheme, housing associations are able, on a voluntary basis, to obtain funds from the Housing Corporation to provide discounts of between £9,000 and £16,000 to secure or assured tenants to assist with the purchase of homes. Cambridge Centre for Housing and Planning Research, 'Housing Associations in 2004: Dataspring Briefing Paper' (2005) 7.
[83] In 2003/04, for example, more than 14,500 units were sold in this way: Cambridge Centre for Housing and Planning Research, 'Housing Associations in 2004: Dataspring Briefing Paper' (2005) 8. Rent to Mortgage was a scheme introduced in 1993 under which rent payments could be converted to mortgage payments. Even from the beginning many criticisms were made of this scheme and its long term effectiveness was doubted; the scheme ended in July 2005, the government noting a very low take-up and high administrative costs.

25.6 Enfranchisement of Long Leasehold Houses – the Leasehold Reform Act 1967

25.6.1 Introduction

As seen in chapters 7 and 20, campaigning for enfranchisement of long residential leaseholds began as long ago as the nineteenth century. The first steps taken sought to address problems of insecurity and chapter 20 describes how in the first instance Part I of the Landlord and Tenant Act 1954 gave the tenant a degree of security through a continuation tenancy. The fact that the landlord of such a continuation tenancy was able to recover possession on certain grounds and to receive a rack rent in the meantime meant that this measure did not succeed in relieving the injustice to tenants at the expiry of their leases. By the mid-1960s enfranchisement was becoming an urgent political issue. Large areas of South Wales had been developed in the late eighteenth century under the building lease system. As these leases were now nearing the end of their terms the harshness of the long leasehold system was more evident. Tenants on some estates were able to extend their leases on a voluntary basis on reasonable terms whereas other landlords were taking a much more commercial approach. By 1966 the government was persuaded that tenants of long leases should be given the right to enfranchise and the principle underlying the Leasehold Reform Act 1967 (LRA 1967) was that 'the land belongs in equity to the landowner and the house belongs in equity to the occupying leaseholder'.[84]

The LRA 1967 created the right to acquire the freehold of premises by enfranchisement, or the right to an extended lease, expiring fifty years after the date of expiry of the existing lease. These new rights applied to tenants of lower value houses held on 'long leases' at a 'low rent'. The rent under the extended lease, based on the principle that the house belongs in equity to the leaseholder, is to be a ground rent which represents the letting value of the site (a 'modern ground rent'). Since 1967 this right has been amended on several occasions. The result is a complex and detailed piece of legislation. The overall impact of the amendments has been to extend the reach of the legislation in relation to the enfranchisement provisions (but not the lease extension provisions). It is no longer confined to lower value homes. Significantly, residency requirements initially restricted the scope of the legislation so that only tenants who had occupied the house as the only or main residence for specified time periods could qualify. These residency tests have now been removed.[85]

The basis for calculating the sum that the tenant must pay in order to enfranchise has also changed. The initial valuation approach required the tenant to pay a sum equivalent to what the freeholder could have received on selling its reversionary interest on the assumption that the tenant had extended his lease by 50 years. This was controversial. Whilst it meant that the freeholder was no worse off in investment 'largesse' terms, it sometimes resulted in very substantial 'windfall' profits to a tenant who enfranchised towards the end of the lease. This is because the cost of the reversionary interest (which is

---

[84] Ministry of Land and Natural Resources, 'Leasehold Reform in England and Wales' (Cmnd 2916, 1966) para 4.

[85] Except where it is a business tenancy or the house contains a flat with a tenant qualifying under the Leasehold Reform, Housing and Urban Development Act 1993 (in which case the tenant must have been occupying the house as his only or main residence for at least two years: LRA 1967 ss 1(1B), (1ZB)).

all that the tenant has to pay) is less than the true value of acquiring the freehold to the tenant: if the tenant buys the reversionary interest, he is able to 'unlock' the 'marriage value'. Marriage value flows from the merger of the landlord and tenant interests: the sum of the reversionary interest and the tenant's leasehold interest as independent interests is less than the vacant possession value of a freehold (with both interests merged). It is this value that is released when they are brought together that is known as the marriage value. As an example, let us assume that a house is worth £100,000 with vacant possession. The value of the existing tenancy with fifty years unexpired is, say, £85,000. The value of the freeholder's reversion is £5,000. The marriage value would be:

$$£100,000 - (£5,000 + £85,000) = £10,000$$

It is only by the landlord's and the tenant's interests coming together (marrying) that this sum can be released. The initial valuation approach gave no account to marriage value. In the example given, the £10,000 would be profit for the tenant. Houses brought into the enfranchisement regime by the later amendments have a different valuation basis used that takes account of the marriage value and involves the leaseholder paying a higher sum for enfranchisement.

The 1967 legislation did not extend to flats, allegedly because 'different considerations of equity apply and there would be many practical difficulties in providing for enfranchisement of flats'.[86] What these 'different considerations of equity' are for long leasehold flats is unclear. Although the flat owner has not built the property as in the building lease, he has effectively paid for its construction through the premium and his moral claim must be as strong as that of the house owner. Whilst there are admittedly 'practical difficulties' with enfranchisement of flats (not least, that enfranchisement rights must be collective), this does not explain why the right to extend the lease could not be given to flat owners. A more significant fact was probably that enfranchisement of flats was simply not then a significant issue on the political agenda.

25.6.2 Qualifying Conditions

In order for the 1967 Act to apply various conditions must be satisfied.

25.6.2.1 There Must be a Tenancy of a House

The broad purpose of section 2 is to distinguish between houses (which can be enfranchised under the LRA 1967) and flats (which cannot). The distinction is not always straight-forward.[87] By section 2(1) the Act includes 'any building designed or adapted for living in and reasonably' called a house, providing that it can still be called that at the time of the claim.[88] This means that it will exclude purpose-built hotels or blocks of flats as they cannot reasonably be called houses.[89] It will also exclude other residences that cannot be described as

---

[86] Ministry of Land and Natural Resources, 'Leasehold Reform in England and Wales' (Cmnd 2916, 1966) para 8.
[87] This is never an easy line to draw. As seen earlier, the RTB legislation also has a complex definition.
[88] *Mallett & Sons (Antiques) Ltd v Grosvenor West End Properties* [2006] EWCA Civ 594, [2006] 1 WLR 2848.
[89] *Malekshad v Howard De Walden Estates Ltd* [2002] UKHL 49 [87].

'buildings', for example, caravans[90] and houseboats.[91] It is, however, possible for 'mixed-use' premises, perhaps a building containing a shop as well as a home, to still be a house so long as it can be reasonably so called (and even though it could also be reasonably called something else).[92]

The approach recognises that houses tend to be divided vertically, and flats horizontally. The fact that a house is further horizontally divided into flats does not prevent the whole being a 'house'. But, of course, there can be many variations on this: duplex flats, and houses which 'dog leg' can, for example, have basements running under a neighbouring property. Section 2(2) tackles this problem by providing that a house will be excluded if a 'material part lies above or below a part of the structure not comprised in the house'. There have been various attempts to explain materiality: Stephenson LJ in the Court of Appeal in *Parsons v Trustees of Henry Smith's Charity*[93] looked to whether it was material to the tenant's use of the house, and Nourse LJ in *Duke of Westminster v Birrane*[94] linked it to whether enfranchisement of that part would lead to technical problems with covenant enforceability. The issue came before the House of Lords in *Malekshad v Howard De Walden Estates Ltd* where both of these tests were disapproved of.[95] Materiality is to be judged in relation to the house for which enfranchisement is sought (not the adjoining premises that it goes above or below) and is a question of fact and degree, Lord Scott stating:

> The relative size of the part may be a factor; the price-enhancing quality of the part may be a factor; the extent to which the part derives or provides support or protection from or for other parts of the house may be a factor. No doubt other factors might come into play in a particular case.[96]

To address the practical issues that might follow from permitting enfranchisement when non-material parts go under or above adjoining premises, section 2(5) provides for the possibility of severance of this part.

Certain premises surrounding the house can also be included in the enfranchisement claim. Section 2(3) states that there will be included:

> … any garage, outhouse, garden, yard, and appurtenances which at the relevant time are let to him with the house and are occupied with and used for the purposes of the house.

In *Methuen-Campbell v Walters*, though, a paddock at the end of the garden could not be included in the tenant's claim.[97]

25.6.2.2 The Value of the House

When initially enacted, the 1967 Act did not extend to housing with high rateable values and

---

[90] *R v Rent Officer of Nottinghamshire Registration Area, ex p Allen* [1985] 2 EGLR 153 (QB).
[91] *Chelsea Yacht & Boat Co Ltd v Pope* [2000] 1 WLR 1941 (CA).
[92] *Tandon v Trustees of Spurgeon's Homes* [1982] AC 755 (HL) 767. Tenancies coming within Part II of the Landlord and Tenant Act 1954 (business tenancies) may come within the LRA 1967 depending on the length of the lease and the length of the tenant's residency: see LRA 1967 ss 1(1ZC) and 1(1B).
[93] [1973] 1 WLR 845 (CA).
[94] [1995] QB 262 (CA).
[95] [2002] UKHL 49
[96] [2002] UKHL 49 [96].
[97] [1979] 2 WLR 113 (CA).

applied only to long leases at a 'low rent'. Since then, these limitations have been removed for enfranchisement claims but there remain limits that apply for claims to lease extensions.

25.6.2.3 There Must be a Long Lease

By section 3 a lease for a term of years certain exceeding 21 years will be a long lease.

25.6.2.4 Tenant for Two Years

There is no longer a requirement that the leaseholder must have occupied the house as his only or main home for a specific period, but section 1(1)(b) does specify that the claimant must have been tenant for the last two years.

25.6.2.5 The House Must Not be Exempt

Certain properties cannot be enfranchised because of the identity of the landlord, for example National Trust properties and Crown property.[98] Where the tenancy was entered into after 1 November 1993 there are further exempted properties: houses let by charitable housing trusts[99] and certain 'great houses'.[100]

25.6.3 The Price of Enfranchisement

25.6.3.1 The Valuation Basis

In order to enfranchise, the tenant must pay a sum to compensate the landlord for his loss of the reversion. There are two different approaches to valuation adopted in the legislation. The first is that found in the LRA 1967, applicable to enfranchisement of the lower value houses within the scope of the legislation as initially enacted. In this section, this is referred to as the original valuation basis. This proceeds on the premise that the house belongs in equity to the tenant. The price of enfranchisement is the value of the reversionary interest based on the site value alone and ignoring any element of 'marriage value' (explained above at 25.6.1). The second approach, referred to here as the modern valuation basis, applies to enfranchisement of houses brought within the LRA 1967 by later legislative extensions, and to enfranchisement under the 1993 Act. This results in the cost of enfranchisement being higher as it includes a share of the marriage value. Under the modern valuation approach the tenant pays for the value of the landlord's reversion plus (where the unexpired lease is no more than 80 years) 50 per cent of the marriage value. The two approaches are summarised in Table 25.1.

25.6.3.2 Principles of Valuation

Valuation is an important aspect of all enfranchisement claims, whether enfranchisement of houses under the LRA 1967, or collective enfranchisement of flats under the Leasehold Reform, Housing and Urban Development Act 1993 (discussed later).

Valuation is a specialist area; it is technical and complex. It is also often contested; the valuers for the landlord and leaseholder are likely to place different figures on the interests

---

[98] LRA 1967 ss 32 and 33.
[99] LRA 1967 ss 1(3), (3A).
[100] LRA 1967 s 32A.

Table 25.1: Setting the Price of Enfranchisement

Original Valuation Approach	Modern Valuation Approach
Value of landlord's reversion on site only basis	Value of landlord's interest + 50 per cent of marriage value (if unexpired lease is no more than 80 years)

to be valued. For our purposes, it is useful to understand the broad principles underlying the approach to valuation but the details of how they apply are extremely technical and complicated.

Enfranchisement under any of the Acts will include a sum reflecting the value of the landlord's interest. Under the original valuation basis, this is taken as the value of the right to receive ground rents for the site value; this is expanded on in the following section. Under the modern valuation basis, the value of the landlord's interest is made up of two components: the capitalised income stream from the leasehold rents, and the value of the right to vacant possession at the end of the lease. The first reflects that fact that the landlord has the right to receive the rent payable under the lease for the remainder of the term; the value of this is 'capitalised', that is, it is given a present value reflecting the aggregated projected rental income over the remainder of the term. Capitalisation will also take some account of the perceived security of the income stream. Although there will be considerable variation in practice, it often works out to be a sum representing about 15 times the current ground rent and will be a relatively small proportion of the premium payable by the tenant on enfranchisement. The second component takes the value of the freehold with vacant possession (that is, the amount that a property would sell for empty, without any tenants), and discounts it by an annual percentage rate, known as the deferment rate, to reflect the fact that the landlord is receiving payment now and not having to wait until the end of the lease. In *Arbib v Earl Cadogan* the Lands Tribunal described it thus:

> The deferment rate is the rate of compound interest that would be needed to be earned on an investment made at the valuation date, in order to produce at the end of the term the capital value which has been determined as being the value as at the valuation date of the interest, which value will however accrue only at the end of the term.[101]

A simple illustration of what the deferment rate is provided on the website of lawyers Bircham Dyson Bell:

> ... the value of the right to receive £100 in a year's time will be £94 if the deferment rate is 6%, £93 if 7%. That may be only a small difference, but if the value was £1 million rather than £100, the difference would be £10,000.[102]

For some time, Leasehold Valuation Tribunals had usually applied a deferment rate of 6 per cent in Central London where property was financially safe, but higher deferment rates elsewhere. In an important case, *Earl Cadogan and Cadogan Estates Ltd v Sportelli*, the Lands

---

[101] [2005] 3 EGLR 139 (Lands Trib) [87].
[102] www.bdb-law.co.uk.

Tribunal heard extensive valuation evidence and concluded that the appropriate deferment rate would normally be (whatever the location) 5 per cent for flats and 4.75 per cent for houses (the higher rate for flats reflecting the greater management problems associated with flats).[103] This decrease in the usual deferment rate means that many leaseholders will have to pay more to enfranchise.

25.6.3.3 Valuation under the LRA 1967

The qualification requirements for enfranchisement have changed over the years but the original valuation basis still applies for those properties that qualify under the original criteria. For those that qualify only because of later extensions of the scope of the Leasehold Reform Act 1967 the modern valuation basis is used to work out how much the leaseholder must pay in order to enfranchise. The differences are shown in Table 25.2, and discussed further in the text below.

Table 25.2: Enfranchisement of Long Leasehold Houses

Qualification under	Section 1(1)	Sections 1A, 1AA or 1B
Eligibility	House Long tenancy Tenant for last 2 years Low rent (defined by s 4(1)) Lower value house (defined by s 1(1)(a))	House Long tenancy Tenant for last 2 years
Valuation Basis	Original Valuation Basis (s 9(1)): open market value of reversion on assumption that lease has been extended for 50 years and tenant not buying	Modern Valuation Basis (s 9(1A)): open market value of reversion, can include half of marriage value, assumes 'continuation' tenancy (except for highest value houses), 'injurious affection' payments
Costs	Tenant must pay landlord's reasonable legal and valuation costs	

25.6.3.4 Houses within the Original Limits: The Original Valuation Basis

The price that the tenant has to pay to enfranchise or to extend his lease has proven highly controversial. Section 1 of the Act states that the tenant has a right to acquire on fair terms. The original compensation provisions of the 1967 Act followed through the premise underlying the legislation, that the house belonged in equity to the tenant. Given that this premise was itself questioned by many, it is inevitable that many saw the compensation provisions as totally inadequate.

On enfranchisement the price payable by section 9(1) is the open market value of the reversion on the assumption that the tenant has no right to acquire the freehold but that he

---

[103] [2006] RVR 382 (Lands Trib). NB. The Court of Appeal has given leave to appeal.

has exercised his statutory right to extend the lease for fifty years. Following amendment in 1969, there is a further assumption that the tenant (or other member of his family) is not buying or seeking to buy, that is, it assumes someone other than the tenant is buying so that the premium that a tenant may pay in order to stay and to release the 'marriage value' is not built into the price.

An illustration of how this is calculated is given in Table 25.3, based on an example used

Table 25.3: How the Original Valuation Basis Works

Based on lease with 36 years unexpired, fixed annual ground rent of £15, and an estimated freehold vacant possession value of £75,000

The Value of the Income Stream for the Unexpired Term   Ground rent £15   Years Purchase for 36 years @ 7% is 13.035 (figure drawn from tables)   So £15 × 13.035 = £195   (£195 is taken as today's value of the right to receive £15 a year for the next 36 years)
The Value of the 'Reversion' in the Site   Present freehold vacant possession value of the house = £75,000   Site value taken as 30% of that value £75,000 × 30% = £22,500   (that is, the percentage of the freehold value of the house thought to be attributable to the land)   Modern ground rent taken as 7% of site value £22,500 × 7% = £1,575 per annum   Years purchase in perpetuity, deferred for 36 years @ 7% is 1.25   So, £1,575 × 1.25 = £1,969
The Purchase Price   The price of enfranchisement is, therefore, the aggregate of the value of the income stream for the unexpired term, plus the value of the reversion: £195 + 1,969 = £2,164

on the web-site of the Leasehold Advisory Service.[104] In practice, as there is no real value in the reversion beyond the existing term plus the assumed 50 year lease extension, the value of the reversion is usually taken as being the modern ground rent in perpetuity.[105] The price of enfranchisement is, therefore, based on the capitalised income stream for the unexpired term, plus the capitalised modern ground rent thereafter. This explains the illustration given in Table 25.2. Where the unexpired term of the lease is very short, there may some value in the right to recover possession at the end of this term plus the fifty year extension and so in this situation an additional element may form part of the purchase price.

The effect of the 1967 formula is that a tenant with a lease nearing the end of its term could acquire the freehold for a relatively small sum and then sell the premises at their market value. This was considered by many to result in undeserved windfall profits for the former tenant. An extreme example was a tenant who had paid a low price for a lease before

---

[104] www.lease-advice.org.
[105] *Official Custodian v Charities v Goldridge* (1973) 26 P & CR 191 (CA) 205.

the 1967 Act (and, therefore, without the prospect of enfranchisement), bought the freehold at 28 per cent of its proper value and sold it less than a year later for a profit of £116,000, equivalent to a 636 per cent profit.[106]

25.6.3.5 Other Houses: Modern Valuation Basis

When the Leasehold Reform Act was extended in 1974 to include houses with a higher rateable value, a different basis of valuation was applied by section 9(1A) to properties newly brought within the legislation. The price payable was the amount that the freehold would fetch on the open market on the assumption that at the end of the tenancy the tenant had the right to remain in possession of the house under Schedule 10 of the Local Government and Housing Act 1989.[107] The formula expressly provides that the price is to be reduced by the extent to which the value increased as a result of improvements by the tenant (or a predecessor in title) at the tenant's expense.

In addition, the tenant could now be viewed as a competitor bidder and so the purchase price should reflect the fact that he is a special purchaser who would pay more in order to be able to unlock the marriage value.[108] Where marriage value is payable, the tenant is taken by section 9(1D) to be entitled to one-half of it (unless the unexpired term exceeds 80 years in which event the marriage value is taken to be nil).[109]

As the scope of the Act was further extended (in 1996 and 2002), the assumption of there being a right to remain (the continuation tenancy) was removed for houses at the highest value.

The landlord may also be entitled to 'injurious affection' payments. This is to compensate him for damage to the value of his other interests which is caused by the sale of this property. The freeholder therefore receives compensation for any reduction – caused by the sale – in the value of other land he owns and compensation for any loss of rights in such other land (for example, where the sale prevents a development partly on retained land).

These amendments bring the valuation provisions for expensive housing into line with the market value approach adopted for enfranchisement of flats under the Leasehold Reform, Housing and Urban Development Act 1993 (see below).

An illustration of how the modern valuation basis works, based on an example given on the web-site of the lawyers Bircham Dyson Bell,[110] is given in Table 25.4.

25.6.4 The Right to an Extended Lease

As an alternative to enfranchisement, sections 14 and 15 of the Leasehold Reform Act 1967 entitle the tenant to acquire an extended lease for fifty years from the expiry of the existing lease on terms corresponding to those in the existing lease. After the original term date the rent will, by section 15(2)(a) be a:

---

[106] *James v United Kingdom* (1986) 8 EHRR 123 [18] and [29].
[107] Or Part 1 of the Landlord and Tenant Act 1954: see ch 20.
[108] *Norfolk v Trinity College, Cambridge* (1976) 32 P & CR 147 (Lands Trib).
[109] LRA 1967 s 9(1E).
[110] www.bdb-law.co.uk.

… ground rent in the sense that it shall represent the letting value of the site (without including anything for the value of the buildings on the site) for the uses to which the house and premises have been put since the commencement of the existing tenancy.

This rent is subject to revision after 25 years.[111]

Few tenants chose to extend the lease rather than to buy the freehold. It is a much less attractive right and can only be exercised once.[112] Thereafter, the tenant has no right to either further renewal or to a right to remain under Schedule 10 of the Local Government and Housing Act 1989.

Table 25.4: How the Modern Valuation Basis Works

Example from 27 Poolebay Place, London SW1, The Westbourne Estate

The value of the landlord's interest: income stream + reversion
The value of the income stream for the unexpired term
Ground rent currently payable £160
Years purchase for 13.65 years @ 5.5% is 9.427
So £160 × 9.427 = £1,508
(£1,508 is taken as today's value of the right to receive £160 a year for the next 13.65 years)
The Value of the 'reversion'
Value of freehold interest with vacant possession £1,370,000
Deferred 13.65 years @ 6%[a] is 0.4514
So £1,370,000 × 0.4514 = £618,418
(£618,418 is taken as the present value of the right to the freehold in 13.65 years time)
So, the value of the landlord's interest is £1,508 + £618,418 = £619,926
Landlord's share of marriage value
Value of freehold interest with vacant possession £1,370,000
Less
Value of landlord's interest excluding marriage value £619,926
Value of tenant's interest excluding marriage value £442,500
(for the lease of 13.65 years)
Marriage value (£1,370,000 − (£619,926 + £442,500) = £307,574
50% of marriage value = £153,787
Enfranchisement price
Value of landlord's interest £619,926, plus 50% of marriage value £153,787
= £773,713

[a]Following the decision in *Earl Cadogan and Cadogan Estates Ltd v Sportelli* [2006] RVR 382 (Lands Trib) the deferment rate is now likely to be 5%.

[111] LRA 1967 s 15(2)(b).
[112] LRA 1967 s 16.

25.6.5 Landlord's Overriding Rights

25.6.5.1 Redevelopment rights

By section 17(1) of the LRA 1967 the landlord is able to resist the tenant's claim to extend the lease if he wishes to resume possession of the property on the ground that for the purposes of redevelopment he proposes to demolish or reconstruct the whole or a substantial part of the house and premises. If the lease has already been extended, the landlord can claim possession on this ground at any time 'not earlier than twelve months before the original term date'.

25.6.5.2 Landlord Occupation

By section 18 the landlord is also able to resist a claim for enfranchisement or an extended lease if he wishes to resume possession on the ground that it, or part of it, is or will be reasonably required by him for occupation as the only or main residence of the landlord or of a person who is at the time of the application an adult member of the landlord's family.

This right is only available to landlords who acquired their interest on or before 18 February 1966.

25.6.5.3 Compensation

If the landlord is able to resume possession on either of the grounds in section 17 or 18, compensation is payable to the tenant in accordance with Schedule 2.

25.6.6 No Contracting Out

Section 23 of the Leasehold Reform Act 1967 prohibits the parties from contracting out of its protection.

25.6.7 Estate Management Schemes

In order to meet the fears that enfranchisement would make good estate management difficult, section 19 of the Act enabled the landlord to apply (within certain time limits that have now expired) for an estate management scheme to be approved by the court. Schemes are essentially a means to enable landlords to continue to enforce covenants against the owners of enfranchised property and so to retain powers of management in respect of the property.

25.7 Enfranchisement of Flats

Enfranchisement of flats has always been a much more difficult issue than enfranchisement of houses because of the practical problems stemming from the interdependency of the units and the collectivity of interests. An individual tenant cannot buy the freehold of an individual flat – the freehold subsists in relation to the whole building and individual flats can only be owned on a leasehold basis. Any 'enfranchisement' must, therefore, be of the whole building. Even after 'enfranchisement', the landlord/tenant relationship remains, it is simply that the purchasing tenants will be collectively in control of the landlord. There may well be continuing difficulties in managing the property as any collective of people will have differing views on standards of repair, etc. In addition, it will often be the case that not all tenants participate in the enfranchisement process – any unsatisfactory lease structures will then remain and there may be friction between the tenant controlled landlord and the non-participating tenants.

25.8 Limited Rights under the Landlord and Tenant Act 1987[113]

The limited rights to enfranchise contained in the Landlord and Tenant Act 1987 formed part of the response to the problems of management highlighted by the Nugee Report in 1985.[114] Some of the problems identified by the Nugee Committee – such as poor communications, lack of say in the appointment of managing agents, and inadequate information being provided – can be addressed by the tenants taking control of the management. The 1987 Act as a whole was directed towards strengthening the tenant's hand in management. There were also two provisions enabling the tenants to acquire the freehold to the block. The first, contained in Part I, gives the tenants a right of first refusal whenever the landlord intends to dispose of the premises. This right stands apart from the management driven reforms and gives some recognition to the wider claims that leaseholders have to own their own properties, albeit that the right here arises only if the landlord chooses to make a voluntary disposal. The second, contained in Part III, gives a compulsory right to acquire the landlord's interest when the landlord is in serious breach of his management obligations.

25.8.1 The Right of First Refusal (Part I)

Before making a 'relevant disposal' of premises within Part I of the Act, section 1 requires the landlord to offer them to qualifying tenants.

25.8.1.1 Qualifying Tenant (section 3)

Most residential tenants qualify, not only long leaseholders. Some tenants are excluded: protected shorthold tenants (within section 52 of the Housing Act 1980, the predecessor to assured shortholds), tenants with employment related accommodation, assured tenants and assured agricultural tenants (within the Housing Act 1988), business tenants and tenants who have more than two flats in the premises.

25.8.1.2 Relevant Disposal (section 4)

A relevant disposal is defined in section 4(1) as being a:

---

[113] See ME Percival, 'The Landlord and Tenant Act 1987' (1988) 51 *MLR* 97, CP Rodgers, 'Residential Flats – A New Deal?' [1988] *Conv* 122.

[114] Nugee Committee, 'Report of the Committee of Enquiry on the Management of Privately Owned Blocks of Flats' (London, 1985). See also AJ Hawkins, 'The Nugee Committee Report – the Management of Privately Owned Blocks of Flats' [1986] *Conv* 12; and ch 11.

... disposal by the landlord of any estate or interest (whether legal or equitable) in any such premises, including the disposal of any such estate or interest in any common parts of any such premises.

By section 4A (added in 1996) a contract to create or transfer an interest in land will also be a relevant disposal. There is, however, a long list of exceptions contained in subsection 4(2) such as a gift to a member of the landlord's family or a disposal by way of security for a loan. Whilst these particular exceptions are readily comprehensible, others can too easily be used as a means for avoiding the legislative controls. So, for example, a disposal by a body corporate to a company that has been an associated company for at least two years will not be a relevant disposal. By doing this and selling the shares in the associated company it is possible to avoid the legislative controls.[115]

25.8.1.3 Premises (section 1)

The right of first refusal applies to buildings where more than 50 per cent of the use is residential and more than 50 per cent of the flats are owned by qualifying tenants. Section 1 states:

(2) Subject to subsections (3) and (4), this part applies to premises if –

(a)   they consist of the whole or part of a building; and
(b)   they contain two or more flats held by qualifying tenants; and
(c)   the number of flats held by such tenants exceeds 50 per cent of the total number of flats contained in the premises.

(3) This Part does not apply to premises falling within subsection (2) if –

(a)   any part or parts of the premises is or are occupied or intended to be occupied otherwise than for residential purposes; and
(b)   the internal floor area of that part or those parts (taken together) exceeds 50 per cent of the internal floor area of the premises (taken as a whole); and for the purposes of this subsection the internal floor area of any common parts shall be disregarded.

So, for example, whether a block with shops at high street level and residential accommodation above qualifies will depend on whether the commercial floor area is greater than the residential floor area. In working out the relative proportions (of floor area and qualifying tenants) it is necessary to identify the relevant 'building' but this is not always straightforward, especially as there is no statutory definition of 'building' (see 25.8.1.5 below).

25.8.1.4 Exempt/Residential Landlords

Certain landlords are exempted from the legislation, for example, a local authority or a charitable housing trust.[116] In addition, premises owned by a resident landlord are exempted. The landlord is treated as resident if the premises are not purpose-built, he has occupied a flat in

---

[115] For other avoidance methods see A Thomas and others, 'The Landlord and Tenant Act 1987: Awareness, Experience and Impact' (DoE, 1991) 70–3.
[116] LTA 1987 ss 1(4), 58(1).

the premises as his only or principal residence for at least twelve months and the building contains two or more flats.[117]

25.8.1.5 The Disposal Procedure

A landlord intending to make a relevant disposal must first offer the premises to the qualifying tenants by serving a section 5 notice on the qualifying tenants. This must contain particulars of the main terms of the proposed disposal, including the price.

Getting the offer notice right is important and may be difficult if it is proposed to dispose of more than one structure. If there is more than one building, section 5(3) requires the landlord to sever the transaction so as to deal with each building separately. 'Building' is not, however, defined by the statute and although there is now case-law addressing this it is by no means straightforward to identify what a 'building' is. In *Denetower Ltd v Toop* two blocks of flats were divided by a road leading to shared garages and the Court of Appeal held that 'building' did not cover only bricks and mortar but would include gardens let with the flats as well as the access road.[118] In *Kay Green v Twinsectra Ltd* the Court of Appeal held that when a development of four buildings was sold which were surrounded by gardens and amenity land, each building should be considered separately.[119] On the other hand, in *Long Acre Securities Ltd v Karet,* the judge noted that the legislation simply did not contemplate the disposal of an 'estate', in this case a mix of residential and commercial premises linked by party walls and with a single access way and car parking area.[120] As the legislation was not clear he adopted an interpretation that furthered the purpose of the legislation and held that building:

> … must have been intended by Parliament to include more than one structure where the occupants share the use of the same appurtenant premises.

In practice, the greater the linkage between the structures in both physical terms and in terms of sharing amenities and services, the more likely there is to be 'one building'.

After the offer notice is served the tenants are given not less than two months to state whether they wish to accept the offer. If they wish to do so then an 'acceptance notice' must be served on the landlord by the 'requisite majority of qualifying tenants' (which, broadly, means more than 50 per cent of the qualifying tenants).[121] There are special provisions concerning the timing of notices if the landlord proposes a sale by auction.[122]

If the tenants accept the offer, the landlord is not permitted to dispose of the property to anyone other than the purchaser nominated by the tenants within a prescribed time, which must be not less than two months after the acceptance notice is served in order give the tenants time to proceed with the purchase.[123] The landlord can, however, decide not to go ahead with the disposal at all.[124]

---

[117] LTA 1987 ss 1(4) and 58(2).
[118] [1991] 1 WLR 945 (CA).
[119] [1996] 1 WLR 1587 (CA).
[120] [2004] EWHC 442 (Ch), [2005] Ch 61.
[121] LTA 1987 ss 6, 18A.
[122] LTA 1987 s 5B.
[123] LTA 1987 ss 5A(5), 6.
[124] LTA 1987 s 8(3).

If the qualifying tenants do not accept the offer, the landlord is free to dispose of the property during a 12 month period beginning on the expiry of the notice, provided the disposal is not on more favourable terms than offered to the qualifying tenants.[125]

25.8.1.6 Enforcement Provisions

If the landlord does make a disposal in breach of the provisions in the Act (for example, without first serving a section 5 notice) the tenants can require the new landlord to provide details of the terms of the disposal and compel the new landlord to transfer the property to their nominated purchaser on identical terms.[126] In order to avoid continuing uncertainty as to the purchaser's title, the request for details must be within four months of the requisite majority of qualifying tenants receiving notice that the disposal has taken place.[127] As the Court of Appeal remarked in *Belvedere Court Management Ltd v Frogmore Developments Ltd* it is surprising that the Act, having recognised that a disposal might occur without following the correct procedures, did not then impose a duty on the new landlord not to dispose of his interest, or give effective rights to the tenant against the subsequent purchaser.[128]

Amongst the many criticisms made of the original drafting of the Act was that the sanctions for non-compliance were relatively weak. Section 10A, added in 1996, now makes it a criminal offence to make a relevant disposal without complying with the provisions of the Act.

25.8.2 The Right of Compulsory Acquisition (Part III)

By section 29, the right to apply for a compulsory acquisition order is only available either:

(a)   when the landlord has failed to discharge his management obligations including those relating to repair, maintenance, improvement or insurance and the situation is likely to continue; or

(b)   when a manager, appointed under Part II of the Act,[129] has been acting for the preceding three years.

This provision is directed at blocks held predominantly on long leases. The premises must consist of the whole or part of a building and contain at least two flats held by qualifying tenants. Qualifying tenants here have a different meaning than in Part I. In order to qualify the tenant must have a long lease (generally, one exceeding 21 years)[130] and must not be the tenant of more than two flats.[131] In addition, at least 50 per cent of the internal floor area must be residential.[132]

---

[125] LTA 1987 s 7.
[126] LTA 1987 ss 12A, 12B, 12C and 13.
[127] LTA 1987 s 11(3).
[128] [1997] 1 QB 858 (CA).
[129] See ch 11.
[130] LTA 1987 s 59(3).
[131] LTA 1987 s 26.
[132] LTA 1987 s 25(4).

When initially enacted, 50 per cent of the qualifying tenants were able to exercise the right but this was amended by the Leasehold Reform, Housing and Urban Development Act 1993 to require the support of 'not less than two-thirds' of the qualifying tenants.[133] This is in line with the general view adopted at the time of the 1993 legislation that compulsory acquisition of the landlord's interest requires substantial support from the tenants. Whether it was ever appropriate to apply this to the Part III right given that it is exercisable only if the landlord has seriously neglected his responsibilities as a property owner is questionable, but it is even more surprising that the two-thirds requirement has been retained given that compulsory enfranchisement under the 1993 now only requires support from half of all flats.

The price payable on compulsory acquisition is either that agreed between the parties or, if the matter is referred to a leasehold valuation tribunal, section 31(2) requires the consideration to be:

> ... an amount equal to the amount which, in their opinion, that interest might be expected to realise if sold on the open market by a willing seller on the appropriate terms and on the assumption that none of the tenants of the landlord of any premises comprised in those premises was buying or seeking to buy that interest.

25.8.3 The Effectiveness of the 1987 Act

Overall, the LTA 1987 has been disappointing.[134] The initial wording has been heavily criticized. In *Denetower Ltd v Toop*,[135] Sir Nicholas Browne-Wilkinson VC, described it as 'an ill-drafted, complicated and confused Act', a criticism that was said by Sir Thomas Bingham MR to be 'understated' in *Belvedere Court Management Ltd v Frogmore Developments Ltd*.[136] Although the Housing Act 1996 made a considerable number of amendments to it, problems remain. In addition, an early study of the 1987 Act in operation found that there was a marked lack of awareness of the Act and of its provisions and implications. In relation to the right of first refusal various difficulties were encountered in exercising the right:

— lack of interest of some of the residents living in the block effectively penalises those who do want to buy the freehold to their flat;
— it was difficult to raise sufficient money;
— it was difficult to meet the statutory deadlines;
— the venture was stressful and time consuming.[137]

Many of these problems stem from the fact that it can be very difficult to organise the collective action required by the tenants within the deadlines imposed for responding to the landlord; although some of the deadlines have been lengthened since the study the reality is

---

[133] LTA 1987 s 27(4).
[134] See also PF Smith, 'A Nasty Measure – Part I of the Landlord and Tenant Act 1987' (1992) 12 *LS* 42.
[135] [1991] 1 WLR 945 (CA).
[136] [1997] 1 QB 858 (CA). See also D Wood, 'Mapping the Recent Past' in S Bright (ed), *Landlord and Tenant Law. Past, Present and Future* (Oxford, Hart, 2006) 16.
[137] A Thomas and others, 'The Landlord and Tenant Act 1987: Awareness, Experience and Impact' (DoE, 1991).

that can be extremely hard to co-ordinate a diverse group of tenants. The rights of first refusal in the 1987 Act have also proved easy to evade, as seen, for example, in *Belvedere Court Management Ltd v Frogmore Developments Ltd*.[138]

Commenting on its impact Davey regards it as a weak Act, largely ignored by landlords. As he continues, however:

> … by and large, the primary remedies contained in the Act have been by passed by other more direct forms of relief for beleaguered tenants, not least the right to enfranchise dealt with below.[139]

It is to these more general enfranchisement rights that we now turn.

25.9 Enfranchisement of Flats under the Leasehold Reform, Housing and Urban Development Act 1993

During the 1980s pressure built up for something of more general application to be done about long leases of flats.[140] The Nugee Report of 1985 highlighted the management problems that exist. Tenants and other interested bodies became increasingly concerned over the diminishing asset problem: at about the mid-point of a 99 year lease and often earlier, the leasehold interest ceases to increase its value, or even to maintain its value. The tenant will then find it difficult to sell the lease, in part because lenders are reluctant to accept a mortgage over a leasehold interest which is of diminishing value. During the 1980s the early long leasehold flats were reaching this critical stage in the lease's life and the unfairness of the leasehold system became more visible. In addition, enfranchisement was an important part of the government's plan to extend home ownership.

Part I of The Leasehold Reform, Housing and Urban Development Act 1993 (LRHUDA 1993) gives qualifying tenants of long leasehold flats the collective right to enfranchise at market value, or the individual the right to extend their leases by ninety years at market value. Again, the legislation has undergone later amendment; not all of the amendments inserted by the Commonhold and Leasehold Reform Act 2002 have yet been brought into force.

25.9.1 The Collective Right to Enfranchise

The procedure for enfranchisement set out in Part 1, Chapter 1 of the 1993 Act is complex. This is an inevitable consequence of granting rights collectively, but it is also the result of an effective lobbying campaign during the progress of the Act on behalf of landlords opposed to the principle of compulsory enfranchisement. Some of the concessions made to landlords,

---

[138] [1997] 1 QB 858 (CA).

[139] M Davey, 'Long Residential Leases: Past and Present' in S Bright (ed), *Landlord and Tenant Law. Past, Present and Future* (Oxford, Hart, 2006) 163.

[140] For further criticisms of long leasehold tenure see Building Societies Association, 'Leaseholds – Time for a Change?' (London, 1984); JBC Neo, 'Problems of Private Flat Ownership in England and Wales – Is Strata Title the Solution?' (RICS, 1990).

such as a residency requirement to prevent enfranchisement by absentee leaseholders, have since been removed.[141]

There are two basic eligibility requirements: there must be qualifying leaseholders, and the premises must qualify.

25.9.1.1 Does the Tenant Qualify?

(i) There must be a long lease
Generally, this means that the lease must have originally been granted for more than 21 years, but some additional leases will qualify, such as leases granted in pursuance of the right to buy under the Housing Act 1985.[142]

(ii) No need for a low rent
When initially enacted the tenant would qualify only if the lease was for a low rent.[143] This requirement was repealed by the Commonhold and Leasehold Reform Act 2002.

(iii) It must not be a business lease
That is, it must not be a lease to which Part II of the Landlord and Tenant Act 1954 applies.[144]

(iv) The tenant cannot qualify for more than two flats
A person who would otherwise be a qualifying tenant of three or more flats cannot be a qualifying tenant of any.[145] Associated companies are considered to be the same person.

The purpose of this restriction was to prevent someone from buying interests in several flats and taking advantage of enfranchisement. However, given that enfranchisement is no longer perceived as a right directed only to residents it is hard to justify the continuation of this restriction.

25.9.1.2 Do the Premises Qualify?

Working out whether the Act applies to particular premises also requires running through a series of tests.

(i) The premises must be 'a self-contained building or part of a building'[146]
The building must either be detached or it must be capable of being divided vertically into a part that could be redeveloped independently of the remainder of the building with services provided without causing significant interruption for occupiers of the remainder of the building.

---

[141] See M Davey, 'Long Residential Leases: Past and Present' in S Bright (ed), *Landlord and Tenant Law. Past, Present and Future* (Oxford, Hart, 2006) 164. The residency requirement was probably crucial for the Conservative government to get Parliament, especially the House of Lords, to accept the legislation. It also reflected the then provisions of the LRA 1967.

[142] LRHUDA 1993 s 7.

[143] LRHUDA 1993 s 8.

[144] LRHUDA 1993 ss 5(2)(a) and 101.

[145] LRHUDA 1993 s 5(5).

[146] LRHUDA 1993 s 3(1)(a).

(ii) There must be two or more flats held by qualifying tenants[147]

(iii) At least two-thirds of the flats must be held by qualifying tenants[148]

(iv) No more than 25 per cent of the floorspace can be used for non-residential purposes[149]

The legislation applies only to premises that are predominantly residential. This means that for every one unit of commercial space there will need to be at least three equivalent sized units of residential space for the building to qualify. Initially, a higher percentage of residential use was required (90 per cent). Even under the lower threshold, it is still unlikely that, for example, premises consisting of shops with a row of flats above will qualify for enfranchisement as of right. The concern is to ensure that residential leaseholders do not, in effect, become managers of commercial property. If there were a higher percentage of commercial use permitted, it would also make the cost of enfranchising extremely expensive for tenants – as it is, even one commercial unit can greatly increase the cost of enfranchising and may make it prohibitive. In contrast, under the Landlord and Tenant Act 1987 premises are only excluded if more than 50 per cent of the floorspace is used for non-residential purposes – the justification given for the differing figure being that under the 1987 Act the landlord will only be disposing of the property if either he is a bad landlord or he is acting voluntarily. Under the 1993 Act disposals are compulsory.

(v) Converted houses with no more than four flats and a resident landlord are excluded.

The premises do not qualify if the property is not purpose-built, has no more than four units and the landlord has owned the property since before the conversion and he (or an adult member of his family) has lived there as his only or principal home for not less than 12 months.[150]

(vi) The landlord must not be exempt.

Some landlords are exempt from the enfranchisement provisions.

(a)   where the landlord is a charitable housing association and the flat is part of its housing accommodation provided by it in pursuit of its charitable purposes.[151]

(b)   National Trust properties.[152]

(c)   the 'great houses' exemption.[153] This exempts only a small number of properties. The exclusion is drafted by reference to properties for which conditional exemption has been given for inheritance tax purposes. The idea is that it should exempt houses which are comparable with National Trust properties in terms of quality, national importance and the degree of public access. The reason given for the exemption is that proper care of enfranchised property could not be ensured unless they remained in common ownership and it was feared that the schemes of management that can be established under the Act would be unsatisfactory.

---

[147] LRHUDA 1993 s 3(1)(b).
[148] LRHUDA 1993 s 3(1)(c).
[149] LRHUDA 1993 s 4(1).
[150] LRHUDA 1993 ss 4(4), 10.
[151] LRHUDA 1993 s 5(2)(b).
[152] LRHUDA 1993 s 95.
[153] LRHUDA 1993 s 31.

(d)   Crown property.[154] Although Crown property is formally exempted, the policy is to treat many Crown properties as if they were governed by the Act.

(e)   Cathedral closes.[155]

25.9.1.3 Sufficient Support for Enfranchisement

In addition to the eligibility criteria, there must also be sufficient support amongst tenants for there to be a collective enfranchisement claim: at least one-half of all the flats must support enfranchisement.[156] This is to ensure that a minority is not able to enfranchise against the will of the majority.

25.9.1.4 The Property to be Enfranchised

The question of which property can be acquired is not straightforward. Let us assume that the tenants live in a block of twelve flats with one commercial shop unit, a communal garden and a physically separate row of garages, two of which are allocated to the shop and the remainder let to residential tenants under their flat leases. In this situation, the nominee purchaser can claim the freehold to:

(a)   'the relevant premises' (the block of flats).

(b)   'appurtenant property', that is 'any garage, outhouse, garden, yard, or appurtenances belonging to, or usually enjoyed with, the flat'[157] (the garages which are let to the residential tenants).

(c)   property which the tenant 'is entitled under the terms of the lease of the flat to use in common with the occupiers of other premises'[158] (the communal garden).

Although the nominee purchaser is entitled to claim the freehold to all of these as part of the enfranchisement, the claim can be limited to only some of the property if that is what is preferred.[159]

If there is an intermediate lease between the freehold and the qualifying tenant, the nominee purchaser must buy the leasehold interest between the leases of qualifying tenants and the freeholder.[160] This does not apply, however, when the intermediate lessor is a public sector landlord letting on secure tenancies.

While the nominee purchaser has no right to claim appurtenant property or shared property which is not held by qualifying tenants, in our example, the garages used by the shop, the freeholder may require the nominee purchaser to acquire property additional to that specified in the purchaser's initial notice. This is so if the property

(a)   would for all practical purposes cease to be of use and benefit to [the landlord], or

(b)   would cease to be capable of being reasonably managed or maintained by him.[161]

---

[154] LRHUDA 1993 s 94.
[155] LRHUDA 1993 s 96.
[156] LRHUDA 1993 s 13(2)(b)(ii). When initially enacted, two-thirds of all qualifying tenants also had to support enfranchisement.
[157] LRHUDA 1993 s 1(7).
[158] LRHUDA 1993 s 1(3)(b).
[159] LRHUDA 1993 s 1(5).
[160] LRHUDA 1993 s 2.
[161] LRHUDA 1993 s 21(4).

This will prevent the landlord from being left with a commercially redundant property.

In addition, the freeholder has a right to leaseback certain units.[162] Schedule 9, Part II states that any flats in the premises let on secure or introductory tenancies by a local authority or let by a housing association freeholder to a tenant who is neither a secure tenant nor a qualifying tenant must be leased back to the local authority or housing association. Neither the nominee purchaser nor the freeholder have an option. The idea behind this is to ensure that secure tenants renting from local authorities and tenants of housing associations will continue to have the same landlord.

Schedule 9, Part III provides that where the property includes non-residential parts and/or flats not let on long leases, the freeholder will have the right to leaseback all or some of these parts. The leaseback will be for 999 years at a peppercorn rent. This will enable the landlord to continue to manage any commercial or rental units he wishes to.

25.9.1.5 *The Price of Enfranchisement*

Whereas the original valuation basis under the 1967 Act was widely acknowledged to be confiscatory in effect, the intention was that the 1993 Act would have a fairer system of compensation for the landlord, based on normal valuation practice. The provisions for calculating the cost of enfranchisement are set out in Schedule 6.

The price of enfranchisement is the aggregate of three elements: the value of the landlord's reversion, 50 per cent of the marriage value, and injurious affection payments. In addition the nominee purchaser has to pay the landlord's reasonable professional costs.[163]

The open market value of the freeholder's interest[164]

This is effectively the price at which the freeholder could sell his interest to a third party; the 'special bid' that tenants would make to purchase is ignored at this stage. It is assumed that the freehold is being sold subject to existing leases and that there is no right to enfranchise or extend leases. Any increase in value attributable to tenant's (or a predecessor's) improvements is to be disregarded.

The overall intention is therefore for the reversion to be valued on normal valuation principles, looking to the value of rents passing, the reversionary value when leases expire and any security rights of tenants.

Fifty per cent of the 'marriage value'

Marriage value has been explained earlier (see 25.6.1 above). In the case of collective enfranchisement, it is a misnomer as there is no 'marriage' after such enfranchisement; the tenants' interests do not merge with the freehold. Here the so-called marriage value comes from the fact that the participating tenants are, after enfranchisement, collectively in control and so able to grant themselves longer leases without having to pay for them.

It is defined in Schedule 6, paragraph 4(2):

> … the marriage value is any increase in the aggregate value of the freehold and every inter-mediate leasehold interest in the specified premises, when regarded as being (in consequence

---

[162] LRHUDA 1993 s 36 and Sch 9 Parts II and III.
[163] LRHUDA 1993 s 33.
[164] LRHUDA 1993 Sch 6 para 3.
[165] LRHUDA 1993 Sch 6 para 4(2A).

of their being acquired by the nominee purchaser) interests under the control of the participating tenants, as compared with the aggregate value of those interests when held by the person from whom they are to be so acquired, being an increase in value -

(a) which is attributable to the potential ability of the participating tenants, once those interests have been so acquired, to have new leases granted to them without payment of any premium and without restriction as to length of term, and

(b) which, if those interests were being sold to the nominee purchaser on the open market by willing sellers, the nominee purchaser would have to agree to share with the sellers in order to reach agreement as to price.

If the leases have more than 80 years to run, marriage value is taken to be nil.[165]

A simple illustration of how these first two components of the purchase price work follows in Table 25.5.[166]

Table 25.5: The Cost of Collective Enfranchisement

Property: a block with 10 flats on leases with 50 years unexpired, ground rents of £60 per annum

Open market value of lease of each flat	£160,000
Aggregate value of leasehold interests	£1,600,000
Open market value of freeholder's reversion	£30,000
Vacant possession value of block	£2,000,000
Marriage Value £2,000,000 − (£1,600,000 + £30,000) = £370,000	
Collective cost to tenants	
(reversion + half marriage value) (£30,000 + £185,000) = £215,000	
Average cost per tenant assuming full participation £21,500	

In addition to the £21,500 in the example given, the tenants may have to compensate the landlord for injurious affection and to pay his costs.

In practice there will often not be full participation, nor is there any provision in the Act as to how the price of enfranchisement is to be shared by the participating tenants. As marriage value is based on the number of participating tenants, the more tenants that are involved the greater the sum that the landlord will receive. Of course, after enfranchisement, the non-participating tenants may seek lease extension which would result in a premium to the new landlord; landlords have therefore sought to argue that an additional 'hope value' should be included in the premium payable on enfranchisement. However, the Lands Tribunal in *Earl Cadogan and Cadogan Estates Ltd v Sportelli* found no case for inclusion of

---

[166] This is based on an example given by the housing minister, Sir George Young, at the time the 1993 Act was passing through Parliament. The illustration has been changed only to reflect the fact that the split in marriage value is now 50–50 whereas initially the freeholder was to receive 'at least half' of the marriage value.

[167] [2006] RVR 382 (Lands Trib). Nb the Court of Appeal has given leave to appeal.

hope value in cases under 1993 Act jurisdiction as there is no reference to hope value in the Schedules relating to valuation.[167]

Injurious Affection Payments[168]

The price will also include sums for 'injurious affection', a phrase explained earlier in relation to the 1993 amendments to the 1967 Leasehold Reform Act (25.6.3.5 above).

25.9.1.6 *The Process of Collective Enfranchisement*

In practice, pursuing enfranchisement claims can be extremely difficult and requires perseverance, especially in larger blocks. In order to begin it is necessary to obtain details of everyone with an interest in the property, and section 11 of the 1993 Act gives a qualifying tenant a right to obtain information about superior interests and details of the other tenants.

The enfranchisement claim itself begins when the requisite majority of qualifying tenants serve an initial notice on the landlord;[169] from this time onwards they are liable to pay the landlord's costs. The initial notice must specify the proposed premium (which must be a realistic figure),[170] give details of the property over which the enfranchisement right is being claimed, and give the name of the nominated purchaser[171] (which will usually be a company). In the future, acquisition will have to be through a RTE company (right to enfranchise company) but the relevant provisions,[172] inserted by the Commonhold and Leasehold Reform Act 2002, have yet to be brought into force.

It may be that not all leaseholders wish to participate, and some who start out planning to be involved may want to withdraw later.[173] There will, in the future, be a right to participate which will require all qualifying tenants to be given a formal invitation to participate.[174] For those that do participate, the LEASE website recommends that there should be a formal participation agreement prepared to:

> … govern the joint actions prior to and during the collective enfranchisement procedures – rights of voting, the negotiation and agreement of terms and, most important, the individual leaseholder's financial contributions.

There will need to be lawyers and valuers instructed, usually it will be necessary to create a company to acquire the freehold, and leaseholders will need to raise money to cover the costs and also to pay for the enfranchisement itself.

After the initial notice, the landlord must serve a counter-notice by a date specified in the initial notice (which must be at least two months after the initial notice being served).[175] In the counter-notice the landlord can do one of three things:[176]

---

[167] LRHUDA 1993 Sch 6 para 5.

[169] LRHUDA 1993 s 13.

[170] *Willingale v Globalgrange Ltd* (2001) 33 HLR 17 (CA).

[171] LRHUDA 1993 s 15.

[172] LRHUDA 1993 ss 4A, 4B, 4C, 13(2)(b)(ii).

[173] Those who do not participate will still end up with a new landlord, the legal entity created by the enfranchising tenants in order to acquire the freehold.

[174] LRHUDA 1993 s 12A; inserted by the CLRA 2002 but not yet brought into force.

[175] LRHUDA 1993 ss 1(8), 13(3)(g), 21(1). A court has no discretion to vary this timetable: *Brick Farm Management Ltd v Richmond Housing Partnership Ltd (No 2)* [2006] EWHC 1004 (Ch).

[176] LRHUDA 1993 s 21.

— accept the claim, and either agree the terms or propose alternative terms;
— contest the tenants' entitlement; or
— state that he intends to apply to exercise the redevelopment right.

Where a counter-notice stating the intention to redevelop has been served the landlord can apply to the court for an order under section 23 declaring:

> ... that the right to collective enfranchisement shall not be exercisable in relation to those premises by reason of that landlord's intention to redevelop the whole or a substantial part of the premises.

This applies only in a narrow set of circumstances: where not less than two-thirds of all the long leases are due to terminate within the period of five years and the landlord intends to demolish, reconstruct or carry out substantial works of construction on the whole or a substantial part of the premises, and cannot reasonably do so without obtaining possession.

If the landlord fails to serve a counter-notice, the court will, if the initial notice was correctly served, order a transfer of the freehold on the terms set out in the initial notice.[177]

In practice, there are very many referrals to the Leasehold Valuation Tribunal in relation to enfranchisement claims.

25.9.2 Estate Management Schemes

Within two years of the relevant sections of the 1993 Act coming into force, landlords were able to apply for a scheme of management in respect of property likely to be enfranchised.[178]

25.9.3 The Right to an Extended Lease

As an alternative to collective enfranchisement, Part 1, Chapter II of the 1993 Act, gives individual qualifying tenants a right to an extended lease. This right is available if the tenant has been a qualifying tenant of the flat for the last two years.[179] In outline this means that he must have a long lease, but there is no restriction on the total number of flats he can own.[180] A leasehold extension cannot be pursued at the same time as a collective enfranchisement claim is under way.[181]

There is no need for the premises as a whole to qualify. Extension will be by surrender of

---

[177] The court has no discretion to vary these terms (which is why the premium proposed in the initial notice must be realistic): *Willingale v Globalgrange Ltd* [2000] 2 EGLR 55 (CA).

[178] LRHUDA 1993 s 69, there are two main exceptions to the two year time limit: with consent from the Secretary of State on the basis of there being a change in circumstances (s 72(1)) and applications from certain public bodies (s 73).

[179] LRHUDA 1993 s 39.

[180] LRHUDA 1993 s 39(4). A head lessee cannot, however, exercise the right to individual lease extension: *Howard de Walden Estates Ltd v Les Aggio; Earl Cadogan and Cadogan Estates Ltd v 26 Cadogan Square Ltd* [2007] EWCA Civ 499. In the two cases heard in the joint appeal the head lease included common parts and parking areas as well as the flats (and in one case also included office space); the Court of Appeal held that the headlessee was unable to exercise the right to lease extension in relation to the flats. Central to this conclusion was the fact that the LRHUDA 1993 made no provision as to a number of important matters that would arise if lease extension were allowed, such as how to deal with covenants of common parts.

[181] LRHUDA 1993 s 54.

the unexpired portion of the lease followed by the grant of a new one, to expire ninety years after the expiry date of the present lease and will be at a peppercorn rent.[182] Apart from that, the new lease will be on identical terms. A renewed lease can be extended again by the same procedure.[183] The price payable is, by section 56, required to be assessed under Schedule 13. As with collective enfranchisement claims, there are three components: the diminution in the value of the landlord's interest prior to the grant of a new lease and once the new lease is granted, 50 per cent of the marriage value, and injurious affection payments. Marriage value in this context is defined in para 4(2) as:

> … the difference between the following amounts, namely –
>
> (a)   the aggregate of –
>   (i)   the value of the interest of the tenant under his existing lease,
>   (ii)   the value of the landlord's interest in the tenant's flat prior to the grant of the new lease, and
>   (iii) the values prior to the grant of that lease of all intermediate leasehold interests (if any); and
> (b)   the aggregate of –
>   (i)   the value of the interest to be held by the tenant under the new lease,
>   (ii)   the value of the landlord's interest in the tenant's flat once the new lease is granted, and
>   (iii) the values of all intermediate leasehold interests (if any) once that lease is granted.

If the tenant's lease has more than 80 years unexpired, paragraph 4(2A) provides that marriage value is taken to be nil.

Again, the tenant has a right to serve a notice on the landlord requesting information about superior interests in the property[184] and the process is begun by the tenant serving a notice under section 42 on the 'competent landlord' (that is, the landlord with a sufficient interest in the property to be able to grant the 90 year extension).[185] The notice must specify the premium that the tenant is proposing to pay which must, according to the Court of Appeal in *Cadogan v Morris,* be a realistic figure.[186] From this point, the landlord may require the tenant to pay a deposit of the greater of £250 or ten per cent of the proposed premium.[187] The landlord must respond to the initial notice by the date specified (which must be at least two months from the date of service of the notice). As with collective enfranchisement, the landlord by the counter-notice can do one of three things:

> (a)   admit the tenant's claim (and either accept the proposed terms or suggest alternatives);[188]

---

[182] LRHUDA 1993 s 56.

[183] LRHUDA 1993 s 59.

[184] LRHUDA 1993 s 41.

[185] LRHUDA 1993 s 40. This will not always be the immediate landlord: as, for example, where the immediate landlord is not the freeholder and has a lease which expires in a few years.

[186] (1998) 77 P & CR 336 (CA).

[187] Leasehold Reform (Collective Enfranchisement and Lease Renewal) Regulations 1993 SI 1993/2407 Sch 2.

[188] In suggesting alternatives, the landlord's sought for premium does not have to be realistic but can be any price: *9 Cornwall Crescent London Ltd v Kensington and Chelsea LBC* [2005] EWCA Civ 324, [2006] 1 WLR 1186 (criticised at (2005) 155 NLJ 942). The significance of the landlord's figure is different from the tenant's: if the tenant puts in an unrealistic amount (low) the landlord may be stuck with transferring the freehold for this amount by default if he fails to serve a counter-notice whereas a (high) landlord figure would be referred to a leasehold valuation tribunal.

(b)   contest the tenant's entitlement;

(c)   state that he intends to apply to exercise the right to terminate for redevelopment.[189]

The landlord is given the right to apply to the court for possession of such an extended lease on the grounds that he wishes to redevelop 'any premises in which the tenant's flat is contained'.[190] In *Majorstake Ltd v Monty Curtis* the question arose as to what 'premises' meant in this context.[191] It may be expected that only if the landlord is planning a major redevelopment project of an entire floor or building that the ground can be used, but in *Majorstake Ltd v Monty Curtis* the Court of Appeal held (interpreting the statutory wording but with a degree of unease at the outcome) that it could be used even if the landlord was essentially redeveloping just the flat plus a small adjoining area. As Neuberger LJ pointed out, this could be a way of a landlord depriving the tenant of his right to renew.[192] The ground can only be exercised by application to a court either within 12 months of the expiry date of the original lease or within five years of the expiry date of the renewed lease.[193] If possession is given, the landlord may have to pay compensation under Schedule 14.

When the legislation was first introduced as a bill, this right to a lease extension was only to be available to tenants who would not otherwise qualify for enfranchisement, the aim being to give primacy to enfranchisement. Wider availability of the right was resisted on the grounds that tenants might prefer lease extension to enfranchisement. The Government had to give way on this point and the right was made available to all tenants qualifying under section 39.

25.9.4 The Effect of the 1993 Act

Whilst enfranchisement of houses under the 1967 Act and the RTB have both been popular, collective enfranchisement of flats has been less successful. Many of the difficulties that have been encountered in exercising the rights under the 1987 Act also exist in relation to collective enfranchisement claims under the 1993 Act. A study of the 1993 Act reporting in 1998 found only a small number of leaseholders successfully enfranchising under the Act; indeed, only a minority of those who started down the road to enfranchisement stuck with it, the majority did not go ahead.[194] Leaseholders were put off by a mix of the complexity of the process, poor professional advice, and the uncertainty over costs. It is not only the cost of the premium itself but there were often very high fees payable to lawyers and other professional advisers. Perhaps the biggest factor was, however, the attitude of the freeholder: most respondents who had given up said that they only thing that would revive their interest in enfranchisement was a less obstructive attitude from the freeholder, reflecting the extent to which the process depends upon a good relationship with the freeholder. Interestingly, more

---

[189] LRHUDA 1993 s 45.

[190] LRHUDA 1993 ss 45(2)(c), 47.

[191] [2006] EWCA Civ 1171, [2006] 3 WLR 1114.

[192] [38]. May LJ, dissenting, held that it could be used only if the landlord was developing an existing recognisable unit, such as an entire floor, including the tenant's flat. [2006] EWCA Civ 1171, [2006] 3 WLR 1114 [65]-[66].

[193] LRHUDA 1993 s 61.

[194] I Cole and others, 'The Impact of Leasehold Reform: Flat Dwellers' Experiences of Enfranchisement and Lease Renewal' (DETR, 1998).

leaseholders successfully enfranchised without invoking the statutory procedure than did by resorting to the process of the 1993 Act.

The study also found that lease renewal was less popular than enfranchisement, tending to be used by those with a short time remaining in their lease or who had no problems with leasehold management (and thus no management incentive to enfranchise) or who were unable to enfranchise. However, it is not uncommon on a sale of a flat for the lender of the incoming purchaser to insist upon the right to a new lease being exercised so as to strengthen the value of the security offered on the mortgage.

25.10 The Future of Renting and Long Leaseholds

The story of enfranchisement does raise questions about the nature of the leasehold relationship.

The promotion of home ownership as the tenure of choice suggests that renting is very much the non-ideal, the refuge for those unable to access home ownership. The enormous popularity of the RTB has generated its own problems. Combined with insufficient investment in social new build, there is simply not enough social housing to go round. Investment in reaching the decent homes standard has led to significant improvements in the physical attributes of social housing, but there is not enough of it: between 1997 and 2007 the number of people on council house waiting lists rose by 600,000 to 1.6 million. The relentless promotion of home ownership continues, with new schemes being launched to attract those whose financial resources are too restricted to enable them to buy 100 per cent shares in the home. But renting clearly does have a future. A healthy rental sector (both social and private) is seen by governments of all persuasions as necessary to alleviate the housing crisis.

It is to be hoped that the new legal framework proposed by the Law Commission for rented homes will be adopted to support the rental sector. One of the aims of this is to provide a legal context in which government policy can be delivered particularly in relation to social rented housing.[195]

The story of long leasehold is rather different. Most of those pursuing enfranchisement of flats do so for negative reasons, as a response to problems with high service charges, maintenance and management problems, and poor communications with landlords and managing agents.[196] A much smaller group seek enfranchisement for the positive benefits that it can offer. The problems with long leasehold tenure run deep. Leaseholders perceive themselves to be 'owner-occupiers', particularly because of the large financial investment that they make in their homes, and are often surprised to discover that they only partially enjoy the three characteristics that are strongly associated with home ownership: exclusive use and benefit, control, and rights of disposal.[197]

---

[195] A Arden and M Partington, 'Housing Law: The Future' in S Bright (ed), *Landlord and Tenant Law. Past, Present and Future* (Oxford, Hart, 2006) 215.

[196] I Cole and others, 'The Impact of Leasehold Reform: Flat Dwellers' Experiences of Enfranchisement and Lease Renewal' (DETR, 1998).

[197] See S Blandy and D Robinson, 'Reforming Leasehold: Discursive Events and Outcomes, 1984–2000' (2001) 28 *JLS* 384, 394–6. See also I Cole and D Robinson, 'Owners yet Tenants: The Position of Leaseholders in Flats in England and Wales' (2000) 15 *Housing Studies* 595.

Leaseholders have … [entitlement to use but not security of tenure] because of their time-limited lease and the spectre of forfeiture by the freeholder. 'Control' encompasses the power to establish how the dwelling is to be used, and the power to make changes to the dwelling. Again, control by leaseholders is limited because their use of, and any potential changes to, their own dwelling will affect other occupiers. On the third test, the right of disposal, leaseholders are in the same position as freeholders, but only until the lease expires. In summary, leaseholders in flats appear to stand outside the conventions of home ownership in some key respects.[198]

Additionally, individual leases often make inadequate provision for managing the property, problems that are discussed more fully in chapter 11. Although far from being an unqualified success, enfranchisement does at least offer the means for leaseholders to alleviate the problems with the long leasehold system. But it cannot deliver what Robertson states leaseholders 'really demanded, the ownership rights and associated control of personal space that were core to British cultural notions of homeownership'.[199]

The commonhold legislation was passed to provide the answer but it has not been popular with developers and suffers from various technical defects. So far, only a handful of commonhold schemes have been established, even though it is arguable that commonhold offers a better deal for the owner of the flat. Until developers are willing to embrace commonhold (and it offers a better deal for them), purchasers of flats will not have the choice.

When introducing the 1993 Act Sir George Young, as housing minister, stated that it aimed to 'move away from leasehold as a form of tenure'.[200] In response to a consultation on leasehold reform published by the DETR, 36 per cent of respondents (mostly leaseholders) thought that leasehold should be abolished.[201] Clarke has suggested that it should no longer be possible to sell long residential leases for more than 21 but less than 999 years, and that freeholds should automatically be transferred to tenant owned management companies.[202] This has not happened yet but it is now time for such a root and branch reform to be put on the table.

---

[198] S Blandy and D Robinson, 'Reforming Leasehold: Discursive Events and Outcomes, 1984–2000' (2001) 28 *JLS* 384, 395.

[199] D Robertson, 'Cultural Expectations of Homeownership, Explaining Changing Legal Definitions of Flat 'Ownership' within Britain' (2006) 21 *Housing Studies* 35, 47.

[200] Standing Committee B Hansard HC vol III col 73 (12 November 1992).

[201] DETR, 'Residential Leasehold Reform in England and Wales: Summary of Proposals and an Analysis of Responses' (1998) paras 12 and 13.

[202] D Clarke, 'Long Residential Leases: Future Directions' in S Bright (ed), *Landlord and Tenant Law. Past, Present and Future* (Oxford, Hart, 2006) 186–9.

BIBLIOGRAPHY

Accreditation Network UK, 'Code of Standards for Larger Developments for Student Accommodation Managed and Controlled by Educational Establishments' (2007)
—— 'Code of Standards for Larger Developments for Student Accommodation Not Managed and Controlled by Educational Establishments' (2007)
Adams, J, 'Another View of AGAs' (10 August 1996) *EG* 68
Albon, R and Stafford, DC, *Rent Control* (London, Croom Helm, 1987)
Aldbourne Associates and IRIS Consulting, 'Interim Evaluation of Tenant Participation Compacts' (ODPM, October 2003)
Aldridge, T, 'Consent to assignment and underletting – plus ça change' (1989) 133 *SJ* 1277
Allen, T, *Property and the Human Rights Act 1998* (Oxford, Hart, 2005)
Anon, 'The Percentage Lease – Its Functions and Drafting Problems' (1948) 61 *Harvard L Rev* 317
Anon, 'Reassessing Rent Control: Its Economic Impact in a Gentrifying Housing Market' (1988) 101 *Harvard L Rev* 1835
Anthony, G, 'The Modern Lease' (Conference Paper, 41st Joint Oxford Study Weekend, 2007)
Arden, A and Partington, M, 'Housing Law: Past and Present' in S Bright (ed), *Landlord and Tenant Law. Past, Present and Future* (Oxford, Hart, 2006)
—— 'Housing Law: The Future' in S Bright (ed), *Landlord and Tenant Law. Past, Present and Future* (Oxford, Hart, 2006)
Ashworth, A, 'Social Control and "Anti-Social Behaviour": The Subversion of Human Rights' (2004) 120 *LQR* 263
Association of British Insurers, 'Report of the ABI Working Party on the Landlord and Tenant (Covenants) Act 1995' (January 1996)
Association of Retirement Housing Managers, 'Code of Practice' (2006)
Aston, J, Hill, D and Williams, C, 'Landlords' responses to the Disability Discrimination Act' (DWP, Research Report 429, 2007)
Atiyah, PS, *The Rise and Fall of Freedom of Contract* (Oxford, Clarendon Press, 1979)
Audit Commission, 'Local Authority housing rent income: Rent collection and arrears management by local authorities in England and Wales' (June 2003)
Audit Commission and Housing Corporation, 'Housing: Improving services through resident involvement' (June 2004)
Balchin, P and Rhoden, M, *Housing Policy: an Introduction* 4th edn (London, Routledge, 2002)
Ball, M and Glascock, J, 'Property Investment Funds in the UK' (London, CML, 2005)
Ball, M, 'Buy to Let. The Revolution – 10 Years On' (ARLA, September 2006)
Bamforth, N, 'The Application of the Human Rights Act 1998 to Public Authorities and Private Bodies' (1999) 58 *CLJ* 159
—— 'The True "Horizontal Effect" of the Human Rights Act' (2001) 117 *LQR* 34
Barker, K, 'Review of Housing Supply – Delivering Stability: Securing our Future Housing Needs' (HM Treasury and ODPM, March 2004)
Barnard, L, 'No premium put on transparency' (10 June 2006) *EG* 61
Barr, W, 'Charitable Lettings and Their Legal Pitfalls' in E Cooke (ed), *Modern Studies in Property Law, Vol 1: Property* (Oxford, Hart, 2001)
Barrass, D, 'It's the devil's own job' (16 September 2006) *EG* 190
—— 'Cost-efficient measures' (30 September 2006) *EG* 180
Barry, M, 'Engaged tone' ROOF September/October 2004 28
—— 'What works elsewhere' ROOF September/October 2004 28
Baum, A, *Commercial Real Estate Investment* (Oxford, Chandos Publishing, 2000)

Beatson, J, '"Public" and "Private" in English Administrative Law' (1987) 103 *LQR* 34

Berg, A, 'Thrashing through the Undergrowth' (2006) 122 *LQR* 354

Berger, L, 'The New Residential Tenancy Law – Are Landlords Public Utilities?' (1981) 60 *Nebraska L Rev* 707

Berkeley Hanover Consulting, Davis Langdon Consulting and the University of Birmingham, 'Economics of the Park Homes Industry' (ODPM, October 2002)

Bernstein, R and Reynolds, K, *Handbook of Rent Review* (London, Sweet & Maxwell, 1981-)

Biles, M, 'Tenancy Deposit Schemes' (2005) 9 *Landlord & Tenant Rev* 165

Birch, J, '30:30 Vision' ROOF September/October 2005 36

—— 'Lessons Learnt' ROOF January/February 2007 29

Birchall, J, 'Council Tenants – Sovereign Consumers or Pawns in the Game?' in J Birchall, *Housing Policy in the 1990s* (London, Routledge, 1992)

Birks, P, 'Before We Begin: Five Keys to Land Law' in S Bright and J Dewar (eds), *Land Law. Themes and Perspectives* (Oxford, OUP, 1998)

Blake, J, 'The New Providers' in J Goodwin and C Grant (eds), *Built to Last?* 2nd edn (London, ROOF, 1997)

Blandy, S, 'Housing standards in the private rented sector and the three Rs: regulation, responsibility and rights' in D Cowan and A Marsh (eds), *Two Steps Forward* (Bristol, The Policy Press, 2001)

Blandy, S and Hunter, C, 'Judicial Directions in Landlord and Tenant Law' in S Bright (ed), *Landlord and Tenant Law. Past, Present and Future* (Oxford, Hart, 2006)

Blandy, S and Robinson, D, 'Reforming Leasehold: Discursive Events and Outcomes, 1984-2000' (2001) 21 *JLS* 384

Boddy, M, *Building Societies* (London, Macmillan, 1980)

Bodiguel, L and Cardwell, M, 'Evolving Definitions of "Agriculture" for an Evolving Agriculture?' [2005] 69 *Conv* 419

Bootle, R and Kalyan, S, *Property in Business: A Waste of Space* (London, RICS, 2002)

Bradbrook, A, 'The Application of the Principle of Mitigation of Damages to Landlord-Tenant Law' (1976) 8 *Sydney L Rev* 15

Bradbrook, AJ and Croft, CE, *Commercial Tenancy Law in Australia* (Sydney, Butterworths, 1990)

Bramley, G, 'The Sudden Rediscovery of Housing Supply as a Key Policy Challenge' (2007) 2 *Housing Studies* 221

Brett, M, *Property and Money* 2nd edn (London, Estates Gazette, 1997)

Bridge, S, 'The Unusual Case of Sneyd Hill Pottery' (1987) 50 *MLR* 655

—— 'Damages for Eviction: Confusion Compounded' [1994] *Conv* 411

—— 'Former Tenants, Future Liabilities and the Privity of Contract Principle: The Landlord and Tenant (Covenants) Act 1995' (1996) 55 *CLJ* 313

—— 'Putting it Right? The Law Commission and the Condition of Tenanted Property' [1996] *Conv* 342

—— 'Commercial Leases Past and Present: The Contribution of the Law Commission' in S Bright (ed), *Landlord and Tenant Law. Past, Present and Future* (Oxford, Hart, 2006)

Bright, S, 'Repudiating a lease – contract rules' [1993] *Conv* 71

—— 'Uncertainty in Leases – Is it a Vice?' (1993) 13 *LS* 38

—— 'Variation of Leases and Tenant Liability' in P Jackson and DC Wilde (eds), *The Reform of Property Law* (Aldershot, Dartmouth, 1997)

—— 'Beware the informal lease: the (very) narrow scope of s.54(2) Law of Property Act 1925' [1998] *Conv* 229

—— 'Winning the battle against unfair contract terms' (2000) 20 *LS* 331

—— 'Leases, Exclusive Possession and Estates' (2000) 116 *LQR* 7

—— 'Liability for the Bad Behaviour of Others' (2001) 21 *OJLS* 311

—— 'Avoiding Tenancy Legislation: Sham and Contracting Out Revisited' (2002) 61 *CLJ* 146

—— 'The Concept of the Tolerated Trespasser: An Analysis' (2003) 119 *LQR* 495

—— 'Managing or Leasing' [2005] 69 *Conv* 352

—— 'Protecting the Small Business Tenant' [2006] 70 *Conv* 137

—— 'Street v Mountford Revisited' in S Bright (ed), *Landlord and Tenant Law. Past, Present and Future* (Oxford, Hart, 2006)

—— 'Tolerated Trespasser or New Tenancy' (2006) 122 *LQR* 48

—— 'Article 8 again in the House of Lords: Kay v Lambeth LBC; Leeds CC v Price' [2006] 70 *Conv* 294

—— 'Unfairness and the Consumer Contract Regulations' in A Burrows and E Peel (eds), *Contract Terms* (Oxford, OUP, 2007)

Bright, S and Bakalis, C, 'Anti-Social Behaviour: Local Authority Responsibility and the Voice of the Victim' (2003) 62 *CLJ* 305

Bright, S and Bright, C, 'Unfair Terms in Land Contracts: Copy-out or Cop Out?' (1995) 111 *LQR* 655

Bright, S and McFarlane, B, 'Proprietary Estoppel and Property Rights' (2005) 64 *CLJ* 449

British Property Federation, 'Declaration on Sub-letting' (20 April 2005)

British Property Federation, 'Letting in the Future, Housing Manifesto 2006'

British Retail Consortium, Response of the British Retail Consortium to the 2004 consultation on UORR

Building Societies Association, 'Leaseholds – Time for a Change?' (London, 1984)

Burnett, J, *A Social History of Housing 1815-1985* 2nd edn (London, Methuen, 1986)

Burney, E, *Crime and Banishment: Nuisance and Exclusion in Social Housing* (Winchester, Waterside Press, 1999)

Burrows, L and Hunter, N, *Forced Out: A Report on the Harassment and Illegal Eviction of Private Tenants after the Housing Act 1988* (London, Shelter, 1990)

Burton, J, '*Retail Rents, Fair and Free Market*?' (London, Adam Smith Research Trust, 1992)

Buxton, R, 'The Human Rights Act and Private Law' (2000) 116 *LQR* 48

Cabinet Office, 'Reform of Public Sector Ombudsmen Services in England, Consultation Paper' (August 2005)

Calvert, H, *Social Security Law* (London, Sweet & Maxwell, 1978)

Calvert, JR, 'Service Charge Study Update' (Loughborough University Enterprises Ltd, November 2005)

Cambridge Centre for Housing and Planning Research, 'Housing Associations in 2004: Dataspring Briefing Paper' (2005)

Campbell, S, 'A Review of Anti-Social Behaviour Orders' (Home Office Research Study 236, 2002)

Cardwell, M, 'Agricultural Tenancies: Future Directions' in S Bright (ed), *Landlord and Tenant Law. Past, Present and Future* (Oxford, Hart, 2006)

Carey Jones, O, 'ARLA Members Survey, Source and Tenure of Property in the Residential Rental Market, First Quarter 2005' (Leeds, ARLA, March 2005)

Carlton, N and others, *The harassment and abuse of older people in the private rented sector* (Bristol, The Policy Press, 2003)

Carnegie, AR, 'Terminability of Contracts of Unspecified Duration' (1960) 85 *LQR* 392

Carr, H and others, *The Housing Act 2004. A Practical Guide* (Bristol, Jordans, 2005)

Carr, H, Cowan, D and Hunter, C, 'Policing the Housing Crisis' (2007) 27 *Critical Social Policy* 100

Carr, H, Sefton-Green, D and Tissier, D, 'Two steps forward for tenants?' in D Cowan and A Marsh (eds), *Two Steps Forward* (Bristol, The Policy Press, 2001)

Cave Review of Social Housing Regulation, 'Independent review of regulation of social housing: A call for evidence' (DCLG, December 2006)

Cave, M, 'Every Tenant Matters: A review of social housing regulation' (June 2007)

CBI/GVA Grimley, 'Survey of Property Trends Supplement' Winter 2006/07

Centre for Rural Research, 'Farm Diversification Activities: benchmarking study 2002. Final Report to DEFRA' (University of Exeter, 2002)

CESCR, 'General Comment 4 on the Right to Adequate Housing (Art 11(1))' (United Nations, 13 December 1991)

—— 'Concluding Observations of the Committee on Economic, Social and Cultural Rights: Canada' (22 May 2006) UN Doc E/C.12/CAN/CO/4 – E/C.12/CAN/CO/5

Citizens Advice Bureau, 'Falling short, the CAB case for housing benefit reform' (June 1999)

—— 'Home Remedies: the challenges facing publicly funded housing advice, meeting the challenge of access to justice' (May 2004)

Clarke, A, 'Property Law' (1992) 45 *CLP* 81

Clarke, D, 'Rent Reviews in Residential Tenancies' [1989] *Conv* 111

—— 'Long Residential Leases: Future Directions' in S Bright (ed), *Landlord and Tenant Law. Past, Present and Future* (Oxford, Hart, 2006)

Clarke, DN and Adams, JE, *Rent Reviews and Variable Rents* 3rd edn (London, Longman, 1990)

Clarke, DN, 'Tenant's Liability for Non-Repair' (1998) 104 *LQR* 372

Cobb, N, 'Patronising the mentally disordered? Social landlords and the control of "anti-social behaviour" under the Disability Discrimination Act 1995' (2006) 26 *LS* 238

Coke, E, *The first part of the Institutes of the laws of England, or, A Commentary upon Littleton* 19th edn (London, J & WT Clarke and others, 1832)

Cole, I and others, 'The Impact of Leasehold Reform: Flat Dwellers' Experiences of Enfranchisement and Lease Renewal' (DETR, 1998)

Cole, I and Robinson, D, 'Owners yet Tenants: The Position of Leaseholders in Flats in England and Wales' (2000) 15 *Housing Studies* 595

College of Estate Management, 'Valuing for fair rents: the law and valuation of regulated residential tenancies' (2001)

Collins, H, *Regulating Contracts* (Oxford, OUP, 1999)

Commission for Racial Equality, 'Statutory Code of Practice on Racial Equality in Housing' (2006)

Cornish, WR and Clark, G de N, *Law and Society in England 1750-1950* (London, Sweet & Maxwell, 1989)

Cowan, D, *Housing Law and Policy* (Basingstoke, Macmillan, 1999)

—— 'From allocations to lettings: sea change or more of the same? in D Cowan and A Marsh (eds), *Two Steps Forward* (Bristol, The Policy Press, 2001)

—— 'Harassment and unlawful eviction in the private rented sector – a study of in(-)action' [2001] *Conv* 249

Cowan, D and Hitchings, E, '"Pretty boring stuff": District Judges and Housing Possession Proceedings' (2007) 16 *Social & Legal Studies* 363

Cowan, D and Marsh, A, 'Analysing New Labour housing policy' in D Cowan and A Marsh (eds), *Two Steps Forward* (Bristol, The Policy Press, 2001)

—— 'There's Regulatory Crime, and then there's Landlord Crime: from "Rachmanites" to "Partners"' (2001) 64 *MLR* 831

—— 'From need to choice, welfarism to advanced liberalism? Problematics of social housing allocation' (2005) 25 *LS* 22

Cowan, D and McDermont, M, *Regulating Social Housing, Governing Decline* (Abingdon, Routledge-Cavendish, 2006)

Cowan, D and others, 'Section 38 Landlord and Tenant Act 1954 – Failed Applications' Urban Research Summary No 9 (ODPM, 2003)

Cowan, D and others, 'District Judges and Possession Proceedings' (2006) 33 *J of L and Society* 547

Crabb, L, 'Restrictions on Assignment of Commercial Leases: A Comparative Perspective' (2006) 35 *Common L World Rev* 93

Craig, P, *Administrative Law*, 5th edn (London, Sweet & Maxwell, 2003)

Credland, S, 'Local Authority Progress and Practice, Local authorities and the Homelessness Act 2002 six months on' (London, Shelter, February 2003)

—— 'Local Authority Progress and Practice, Local authorities and the Homelessness Act 2002 – the first year' (London, Shelter, July 2003)

Crew, D, 'Put up or Get Out' ROOF March/April 2007 46

—— 'The Tenant's Dilemma' (CAB, June 2007)

Crook, ADH, 'Housing conditions in the private rented sector within a market framework' in S Lowe and D Hughes (eds), *The Private Rented Sector in a New Century: revival or false dawn?* (Bristol, The Policy Press, 2002)

Crook, ADH and Kemp, P, 'Private Landlords in England' (Housing Research Summary, Number 54, DETR, 1996)

Crook, ADH and others, 'Repair and Maintenance by Private Landlords' (Housing Research Summary, Number 138, DETR, 2000)

Crook, ADH, Hughes, J and Kemp, P, 'The Supply of Privately Rented Homes: Today and Tomorrow' (York, Joseph Rowntree Foundation, 1995)

Crosby, N, 'An Evaluation of the Policy Implications for the UK of the Approach to Small Business Tenant Legislation in Australia' (August 2006)

Crosby, N, Gibson, V and Murdoch, S, 'UK Commercial Property Lease Structures: Landlord and Tenant Mismatch' (2003) 40 *Urban Studies* 1487

Crosby, N, Hughes, C and Murdoch, S, *Monitoring the Code of Practice for Commercial Leases, Interim Report* (ODPM, April 2004)

—— 'Monitoring the 2002 Code of Practice for Commercial Leases' (ODPM, March 2005)

Cullen, S and Potterton, R, 'Must a Surety Guarantee an AGA?' (11 May 1996) *EG* 118

Cullingworth, B, 'Council Housing Purposes, Procedures and Priorities' (DoE, 1969)

Currie, H, 'The Scottish System of Licensing Houses in Multiple Occupation' in S Lowe and D Hughes (eds), *The Private Rented Sector in a New Century: revival or false dawn?* (Bristol, The Policy Press, 2002)

Dale, G, 'Landlords, tenants and the changing world of insurance' (23 September 2006) *EG* 190

Daunton, MJ, *House and Home in the Victorian City* (London, Edward Arnold, 1983)

Davey, M, 'A Farewell to Fair Rents?' (1992) 14 *JSWFL* 497

—— 'Privity of Contract and Leases – Reform at Last' (1996) 59 *MLR* 78

—— 'Neighbours in law' [2001] *Conv* 31

—— 'Long Residential Leases: Past and Present' in S Bright (ed), *Landlord and Tenant Law. Past, Present and Future* (Oxford, Hart, 2006)

Davis, M and Hughes, D, 'What's Sex got to do with it?' [2005] 69 *Conv* 318

DCA, 'Judicial Statistics England and Wales for the Year 2005 (revised)' (Cm 6903, August 2006)

—— 'Statistics on Mortgage and Landlord Possession Actions in the County Court' Third-quarter 2006 Table 1b

DCLG, 'Revision of the Code of Guidance on the Allocation of Accommodation' (November 2002)

—— 'Review of Arms Length Housing Management Organisations' (June 2006)

—— 'Tackling Overcrowding in England: A Discussion Paper' (July 2006)

—— 'Homelessness Code of Guidance for Local Authorities' (July 2006)

—— 'Guide on Effective Rent Arrears Management' (August 2006)

—— 'Landlord and Tenant Act 1954: Review of Impact of Procedural Reforms' (August 2006)

—— 'Housing in England 2004/05' (October 2006)

—— 'Monitoring the Longer-Term Impact of Choice-Based Lettings' (Housing Research Summary, Number 231, 2006)

—— 'Priority review of the uptake by social landlords of legislative powers to tackle anti-social behaviour' (Housing Research Summary, Number 232, 2006)

—— 'Anti-social behaviour intensive family support projects' (Housing Research Summary, Number 230, 2006)

—— 'Assessment of the impact of the cost of repairs for Right to Buy leaseholders' (Housing Research Summary, Number 227, 2006)

—— 'Dealing with "Problem" Private Rented Housing' (Housing Research Summary, Number 228, 2006)

—— 'Evaluating Homelessness Prevention' (Homelessness Research Summary, Number 3, 2006)

—— 'English House Condition Survey 2005' Headline Report (January 2007)

—— 'Allocation of Accommodation: Choice Based lettings. Code of Guidance for Local Housing Authorities' (January 2007)

—— 'Landlord and Tenant Act 1954: Section 57' (Consultation Paper, February 2007)

—— 'Small businesses will get better deal from landlords says Cooper' Press Release 061 (23 March 2007)

—— News Release 2007/0066, 'Government Helps Local Authority Leaseholders to Pay Major Works Bills' (29 March 2007)

——, 'Tenant Empowerment: A consultation paper' (June 2007)

—— 'Delivering Housing and Regeneration: Communities England and the future of social housing regulation' (Consultation, June 2007)

—— 'Discrimination Law Review: A Framework for Fairness. Proposals for a Single Equality Bill for Great Britain' (Consultation paper, June 2007)

—— 'Homes for the future: more affordable, more sustainable' (Cm 7191, July 2007)

—— 'Arms Length Management Organisations: Early impacts and process lessons from Rounds 1 to 3' (Housing Research Summary, Number 237, 2007)

—— Live Tables on rents, lettings and tenancies, 'Table 731: Private tenancies and rents, by type of tenancy'

—— Live Tables, Chart 732: 'Private and local authority rents and tenures by tenancy type: 1995/96, 2004/05, 2005/06'

—— Live Tables, Chart S807, 'How good landlord is at keeping residents informed of things that affect them as tenants'

—— Live Tables, Private Renters, S547 'Weekly mean and median rents net of services by type of letting'

—— Survey of English Housing, Live Tables, S101, 'Trends in tenure'

—— Survey of English Housing, Live Tables: Table S405 'Tenants in receipt of housing benefit'

—— Survey of English Housing, Live Tables: Table S505 'Percentage of tenants receiving housing benefit by letting type'

—— Survey of English Housing, Live Tables: Table S510 'Trends in letting'

De Moor, A, 'Landlord and tenant in French law: a recent statute' (1983) 3 *OJLS* 425

DEFRA, 'Tenanted Land Survey – England 2006, Summary of Results' (15 March 2007)

Delargy, M, 'Tackling rent arrears' ROOF September/October 2004 25

—— 'Show me the money' ROOF September/October 2004 26

Densham, A, 'Agricultural Tenancies. Past and Present' in S Bright (ed), *Landlord and Tenant Law. Past, Present and Future* (Oxford, Hart, 2006)

Derham, R, 'Equitable Set-Off: A Critique of Muscat v Smith' (2006) 122 *LQR* 469

DETR, 'Limiting Fair Rent Increases: A Consultation Paper' (May 1998)

—— 'A Financial Incentive for Local Authorities to Buy Back Homes from Leaseholders or Others in Difficulty – A Consultation Paper' (1998)

—— 'Residential Leasehold Reform in England and Wales: Summary of Proposals and an Analysis of Responses' (1998)

—— 'Monitoring the Code of Practice for Commercial Leases' (April 2000)

—— 'Quality and Choice: A Decent Home for All, The Housing Green Paper' (April 2000)

—— 'Quality and Choice: A Decent Home for All, The Way Forward' (December 2000)

—— 'Views on the large scale voluntary transfer process' (Housing Research Summary, Number 110, 2000)

—— 'Business tenancies legislation in England and Wales: the Government's proposals for reform' (2001)

Disability Rights Commission, 'Code of Practice – Rights of Access: services to the public, public authority functions, private clubs and premises' (2006)

Dixon, M, 'The non-proprietary lease: the rise of the feudal phoenix' (2000) 59 *CLJ* 25

—— 'A Failure of Statutory Purpose or a Failure of Professional Advice?' [2006] 70 *Conv* 79

—— 'Leasehold Covenants and Equitable Set-Off' [2006] 70 *Conv* 460

DoE, 'Local Government in England: Government Proposals for Re-organisation' (Cmnd 4584, 1971)

—— 'Housing: The Government's Proposals' (Cm 214, 1987)

—— 'Consultation Paper on Commercial Property Leases' (27 May 1993)

—— 'Access to Local Authority Housing: a Consultation Paper' (1994)

Donahue Jr, C, 'Change in the American Law of Landlord and Tenant' (1974) 37 *MLR* 242

Donnison, DV, *The Government of Housing* (Harmondsworth, Penguin, 1967)

Donnision, D and Ungerson, C, *Housing Policy* (Harmondsworth, Penguin, 1982)

Dowden, M, 'Guaranteed to cause disputes' (20 July 1998) *EG* 162

DTLR, 'Tackling Anti-Social Tenants, A Consultation Paper' (April 2002)

DWP, 'Building Choice and Responsibility: a radical agenda for Housing Benefit' (October 2002)

—— 'Housing Benefit Sanctions and Antisocial Behaviour – a consultation paper' (May 2003)

—— 'Local Housing Allowance Evaluation 10, Local Housing Allowance Final Evaluation: Implementation and Delivery in the Nine Pathfinder Areas' (October 2006)

—— 'Action to tackle nuisance neighbours' Press Release (5 June 2006)

—— 'A new deal for welfare: empowering people to work: consultation report' (Cm 6859, 2006)

Dymond, A, 'Houses in Multiple Occupation – The New Definition' [2006] *J of Housing L* 50

Edwards, C and Krendel, P, *Institutional Leases in the 21st Century* (London, EG Books, 2007)

Effron, J, 'The Contractualisation of the Law of Leasehold' (1988) 14 *Monash U L Rev* 83

EJS, 'The formula for success' [2006] 70 *Conv* 9

Ellery, S, 'Decade of Discrimination' ROOF November/December 2006 20

English, J, 'Building for the masses' in J Goodwin and C Grant (eds), *Built to Last?* 2nd edn (London, ROOF, 1997)

Errington, A and others, 'Economic Evaluation of the Agricultural Tenancies Act 1995' (DEFRA, 2002)

Evamy, M, *Bluewater: Vision to Reality* (London, Lendlease, 1999)

Fancourt, T, 'Licences to Assign: Another Turn of the Screw?' [2006] 70 *Conv* 37

Feldman, D, *Civil Liberties and Human Rights in England and Wales* 2nd edn (Oxford, OUP, 2002)

Fitzpatrick, S and Pawson, H, 'Welfare Safety Net or Tenure of Choice? The Dilemma Facing Social Housing Policy in England' (2007) 22 *Housing Studies* 163

Flint, J, 'Reconfiguring Agency and Responsibility in the Governance of Social Housing in Scotland' (2004) 41 *Urban Studies* 151

Fogel, S, 'Blundell Memorial Lecture: Landlord and tenant reform – I' (10 August 1996) *EG* 64

Fogel, S and Moross, T, 'Landlord and Tenant (Covenants) Act 1995: How has Practice been Affected?' Blundell Memorial Lecture (1996)

Fogel, S and others, *Leasehold Liability* (Bristol, Jordans, 2000)

Fogel, S and Slessenger, E, 'Must a Surety Guarantee an AGA?' (8 August 1996) *EG* 59

Ford, M, 'Breathing New Life into Ailing Shopping Centres' [1994] 4 *Property Rev* 116

Forrest, R and Murie, A, 'The big sell off' in J Goodwin and C Grant (eds), *Built to Last?* 2nd edn (London, ROOF, 1997)

Fox, L, 'The Meaning of Home: a Chimeral Concept or a Legal Challenge?' (2002) 29 *J of L and Society* 580

—— *Conceptualising Home* (Oxford, Hart, 2007)

Francis Committee, 'Report of the Committee on the Rent Acts' (Cmnd 4609, 1971)

Frankena, M, 'Alternative Models of Rent Control' (1975) 12 *Urban Studies* 303

Freedman, P, 'The last chance to get things right?' (1 July 2006) *EG* 149

—— 'Service Charges' (Conference Paper, 41st Joint Oxford Study Weekend, 2007)

Gardner, S, 'The Proprietary Effect of Contractual Obligations under Tulk v Moxhay and De Mattos v Gibson' (1982) 98 *LQR* 279

Gauldie, E, *Cruel Habitations: A History of Working-Class Housing 1780-1918* (London, George Allen & Unwin Ltd, 1974)

Genn, H, *Paths to Justice: What People do and think about going to law* (Oxford, Hart, 1999)

Gibbard, R and Ravenscroft, N, 'The Reform of Agricultural Holdings Law' in P Jackson and DC Wilde (eds), *The Reform of Property Law* (Aldershot, Dartmouth, 1997)

Gibbard, R, Ravenscroft, N and Reeves, J, 'The Popular Culture of Agricultural Law Reform' (1999) 15 *J of Rural Studies* 269

Glendon, M, 'The Transformation of American Landlord-Tenant Law' (1982) 23 *Boston College L Rev* 503

Goodchild, B and Syms, P, 'Developing and managing market renting schemes by housing associations' (Joseph Rowntree Foundation, Findings, No 213, February 2003)

Goodland, R, 'Developments in tenant participation: accounting for growth' in D Cowan and A Marsh (eds), *Two Steps Forward* (Bristol, The Policy Press, 2001)

Gordon, D, 'The Burden and Benefit of the Rules of Assignment' [1987] *Conv* 103

Government Policy on Leasehold Property in England and Wales (Cmd 8713, 1953)

Goymour, A, 'Proprietary Claims and Human Rights – A "Reservoir of Entitlement"?' (2006) 65 *CLJ* 696

Gray, K, 'Property in Thin Air' (1991) 50 *CLJ* 252

Gray, K and Gray, S, 'Civil Rights, Civil Wrongs and Quasi-Public Space' [1999] EHRLR 46

—— *Elements of Land Law* 4th edn (Oxford, OUP, 2005)

Gross, DH 'Calculation of rental under commercial percentage lease' (1974) 58 ALR 3d 384

Haley M, 'Business Tenancies: Parting with Occupation' [1997] *Conv* 139

—— 'The statutory regulation of business tenancies: private property, public interest and political compromise' (1999) 19 *LS* 207

—— 'Compensation for Tenants' Improvements' (1991) 11 *LS* 119

—— 'Business tenancies and interventionism: the relegation of policy?' (1993) 13 *LS* 225

—— 'The Landlord and Tenant Act 1954: The Need for Continuing Occupation' [1998] *Conv* 218

—— 'Section 25 Notices: A Tenant Confused?' [2002] *Conv* 292

——, 'Business Tenancies: Renewal and Authorised Guarantee Agreements' [2000] *Conv* 566

Hall, M, 'Labour's great homes robbery is straight out of the Stalin textbook' The Express 13 July 2006 10

Hammar, M, 'Time to Unite' Private Renter Issue 4 in ROOF March/April 2006

Harloe, M, *Private Rented Housing in the United States and Europe* (London, Croom Helm, 1985)

—— *The People's Home? Social Rented Housing in Europe and America* (Oxford, Blackwell Publishers, 1995)

Harpum, C, 'Leases as Contracts' (1993) 52 *CLJ* 212

—— 'The Law Commission and Land Law' in S Bright and J Dewar (eds), *Land Law: Themes and Perspectives* (Oxford, OUP, 1998)

—— (ed), *Megarry & Wade, The Law of Real Property* 6th edn (London, Sweet & Maxwell, 2000)

Harvey, J and Houston, D, 'Research into the Single Room Rent Restrictions' (DWP, 2005)

Harwood, M, 'Leases: Are they still not Really Real?' (2000) 20 *LS* 503

Hawkey, E, 'Intensive care' ROOF Jan/Feb 2002 32

—— 'Bidding Wars' ROOF May/June 2007 20

Hawkings, H, 'Shopping centres – turnover rents on the increase' (22 September 1990) *EG* 28

Hawkins, AJ, 'The Nugee Committee Report – the Management of Privately Owned Blocks of Flats' [1986] *Conv* 12

Hayek, FA and others, *Verdict on Rent Control* (London, Institute of Economic Affairs, 1972)

Hayek, FA and others, *Rent Control, A Popular Paradox* (Vancouver, Fraser Institute, 1975)

Hecht, NS 'Variable Rental Provision in Long Term Ground Leases' (1972) 72 *Columbia L Rev* 625

Heighton, M 'Turn over the issues' (3 February 2002) *EG* 214

Hepple, BA, 'Intention to Create Legal Relations' (1970) 28 *CLJ* 122

Hewitt, G, 'The Modern Lease' (Conference Paper, 41st Joint Oxford Study Weekend, 2007)

Hicks, JF, 'The Contractual Nature of Real Property Leases' (1972) 24 *Baylor L Rev* 443

Higgins S, 'The Continuation Conundrum: Part II of the Landlord and Tenant Act' [1997] *Conv* 119

Hill & Redman's *Law of Landlord and Tenant* (LexisNexis Butterworths)

Hill, J, 'Section 1 of the Protection from Eviction Act 1977: The Meaning of "Occupation"' [1987] *Conv* 265

Hills, J, 'Ends and means: The future roles of social housing in England' (CASE Report 34, February 2007)

Hinojosa, JP, 'On Property Leases, Licenses, Horses and Carts: Revisiting *Bruton v London and Quadrant Housing Trust*' [2005] 69 *Conv* 114

HM Treasury and ODPM, 'Housing policy: an overview' (July 2005)

—— 'The Government's Response to Kate Barker's Review of Housing Supply' (December 2005)

—— 'Extending home ownership' (2005)

Hoath, D, 'Rent Books: The Law, Its Uses and Abuses' (1978-9) 1 *JSWL* 3

—— *Public Housing Law* (London, Sweet & Maxwell, 1989)

Hohfeld, WN, 'Some Fundamental Legal Conceptions as Applied in Judicial Reasoning' (1913) 23 *Yale LJ* 16

Holbrook, J and Billingham, N, 'Rethinking possession orders' (2007) 157 *NLJ* 506

Holmans, A, 'Housing and Housing Policy in England 1975-2002' (ODPM, January 2005)

Holmans, A, Stephens, M and Fitzpatrick, S, 'Housing Policy in England since 1975: An Introduction to the Special Issue' (2007) 22 *Housing Studies* 147

Holmes, C, *A New Vision for Housing* (London, Routledge, 2006)

Home Office, 'Tackling Anti-Social behaviour in 2005: summary of survey results' (10 January 2006)

—— 'A guide to anti-social behaviour orders' (August 2006)

—— 'Respect Action Plan' (10 January 2006)

—— 'New House Closure Powers for Neighbours from Hell' Press Release (30 May 2007)

Honore, T, *The Quest for Security: Employees, Tenants, Wives* (London, Stevens, 1982)

Hopkins, N and Laurie, E, 'Housing or Property? The Dynamics of Housing Policy and Property Principles in the Right to Buy' (2006) 26 *LS* 65

Horsley, T, 'Tolerated Trespass: latest court rulings and best practice' (Housing Quality Network, September 2006)

Housing Corporation, 'The Regulatory Code and Guidance' (August 2005)

—— 'Service Charges: value for money?' (March 2007)

—— 'Housing Corporation requirements in relation to resident involvement' (Circular, May 2007)

HRH Duke of Edinburgh (Chair), *Inquiry into British Housing* (London, National Federation of Housing Associations, 1985)

Hughes, D and Davis, M, 'Human Rights and the Triumph of Property' [2006] 70 Conv 526

Hunt, M, 'The "Horizontal Effect" of the Human Rights Act' [1998] *PL* 423

Hunter, C and Nixon, J, 'Taking the blame and losing the home: women and antisocial behaviour' (2001) 23 *JSWFL* 395

Hunter, C, Nixon, J and Shayer, S, 'Neighbour Nuisance, Social Landlords and the Law' (Coventry, Chartered Institute of Housing, 2000)

Hunter, D and others, 'The exercise of judicial discretion in rent arrears cases' DCA Research Series 6/05 (October 2005)

Hurndall, A (ed), *Property in Europe* (London, Butterworths, 1998)

IHOS, 'Housing Ombudsman Service Annual Report and Accounts' (2006)

Ilbery, B and others, 'Research into the potential impacts of CAP reform on the diversification activities of tenant farmers in England – baseline study' (Coventry University and University of Hull, March 2006)

Institute of Rent Officers and Rental Valuers, 'A Report on Good Practice in Assessing and Registering Fair Rents' (Southampton, 1998)

Investment Property Forum, 'Response to the DoE consultation paper on Commercial Leases' (London, IPF and Association of British Insurers, 1993)

—— 'The Size and Structure of the UK Property Market' (Research Findings, July 2005)

Jenkins, Lord Justice (Chair), 'Leasehold Committee: Final Report' (Cmd 7982, 1950)

Jew, P, *Law and Order in Private Rented Housing: Tackling Harassment and Illegal Eviction* (London, Campaign for Bedsit Rights, 1994)

Joint Committee of the House of Commons and House of Lords on Human Rights, 'The Meaning of Public Authority under the Human Rights Act' (HL Paper 39, HC 282, 23 February 2004)

Joint Working Group on Commercial Leases, 'The Code for Leasing Business Premises in England and Wales 2007' (2007)

Joseph Rowntree Foundation, 'The impact of housing benefit changes on help to secure private rented accommodation' (Housing Research Findings No 213, June 1997)

Jourdan, S, 'All bark and no bite' (7 April 2007) *EG* 98

Joyce, J, 'Analysing the Changes' (17 December 2006) *EG* 86

Kavanagh, A, 'The Elusive Divide between Interpretation and Legislation under the Human Rights Act 1998' (2004) 24 *OJLS* 259

Kemp, P, 'Burying Rachman' in J Goodwin and C Grant (eds), *Built to Last?* 2nd edn (London, ROOF, 1997)

—— 'The Origins of Council Housing' in J Goodwin and C Grant (eds), *Built to Last?* 2nd edn (London, ROOF, 1997)

—— *Housing Benefit: Time for Reform* (York, Joseph Rowntree Foundation, 1998)

—— *Private Renting in Transition* (Coventry, Chartered Institute of Housing, 2004)

Kemp, P, and Rugg, J *The Single Room Rent: Its Impact on Young People* (Centre for Housing Policy, University of York, 1998)

Kenny, P, 'Fair Rents – Fair to Whom?' [1999] *Conv* 169

—— 'Freedom of Contract for Landlord and Tenant' [2004] 68 *Conv* 351

Kerr, J, *Business Tenancies: New Farms and Land 1995-97* (London, RICS, 1994)

Kiddle, C, 'RSR Briefing Paper 1: The Population of Registered Social Landlords 1989-2005' Dataspring Briefing Paper (Cambridge Centre for Housing and Planning Research, July 2006)

Kleysteuber, R, 'Tenant Screening Thirty Years Later: A Statutory Proposal To Protect Public Records' (2007) 116 *Yale LJ* 1344

Labour Party, 'Business Manifesto 2001'

Land Registry, 'Report on consultation July 2005: Presentation of prescribed information in registrable leases' (July 2005)

Latham, R, 'Tolerated Trespassers, the Interim Solution' (2006) *Legal Action* 32 (May)

—— 'Tolerated Trespassers, the Problem and the Solution' (2006) *Legal Action* 35 (May)

Laurie, E, 'The Homelessness Act 2002 and Housing Allocations: All Change or Business As Usual?' (2004) 67 *MLR* 48

Law Commission, 'Provisional Proposals Relating to Termination of Tenancies' (Law Com WP No 16, 1968)

—— 'Landlord and Tenant: Report on the Landlord and Tenant Act 1954, Part II' (Law Com No 17, 1969)

—— 'Covenants Restricting Dispositions, Alterations and Change of User' (Law Com No 141, 1985)

—— 'Codification of the Law of Landlord and Tenant: Forfeiture of Tenancies' (Law Com No 142, 1985)

—— 'Landlord and Tenant Law: Privity of Contract and Estate: Duration of Liability of Parties to Leases' (Law Com CP No 95, 1986)

—— 'Landlord and Tenant: Reform of the Law' (Law Com No 162, 1987)

—— 'Commonhold – Freehold Flats and Freehold Ownership of other Interdependent Buildings' (Cm 179, July 1987)

—— 'Landlord and Tenant: Privity of Contract and Estate' (Law Com No 174, 1988)

—— 'Compensation for Tenants' Improvements' (Law Com No 178, 1989)

—— 'Landlord and Tenant: Distress for Rent' (Law Com No 194, 1991)

—— 'Domestic Violence and Occupation of the Family Home' (Law Com No 207, 1992)

—— 'Business Tenancies: A Periodic Review of the Landlord and Tenant Act 1954 Part II' (Law Com No 208, 1992)

—— 'Landlord and Tenant: Responsibility for State and Condition of Property' (Law Com CP No 123, 1992)

—— 'Landlord and Tenant: Termination of Tenancies Bill' (Law Com No 221, 1994)

—— 'Landlord and Tenant: Responsibility for State and Condition of Property' (Law Com No 238, 1996)

—— 'Aggravated, Exemplary and Restitutionary Damages' (Law Com No 247, 1997)

—— 'Landlord and Tenant Law: Termination of Tenancies by Physical Re-entry' (Law Com CD, 1998)

—— 'Renting Homes 1: Status and Security' (Law Com CP No 162, 2002)

—— 'Renting Homes 2: Co-occupation, Transfer and Succession' (Law Com CP No 168, 2002)

—— 'Renting Homes' (Law Com No 284, 2003)

—— 'Termination of Tenancies for Tenant Default' (Law Com CP No 174, 2004)

—— 'Unfair Terms in Contracts' (Law Com No 292, 2005)

—— 'Housing: Proportionate Dispute Resolution, An Issues Paper' (March 2006)

—— 'Renting Homes: The Final Report. Volume 1: Report' (Law Com No 297, 2006)

—— 'Renting Homes: The Final Report. Volume 2: Draft Bill' (Law Com No 297, 2006)

—— 'Termination of Tenancies for Tenant Default' (Law Com No 303, 2006)

—— 'Encouraging Responsible Letting: Consultation Paper' (July 2007)

—— 'Housing: Proportionate Dispute Resolution – the Role of Tribunals' (Law Com CP No 180, 2007)

—— 'Encouraging Responsible Letting' (Law Com CP No 181, 2007)

Leasehold Advisory Service, 'Chairman's Report', *Annual Report 2006* (London, 2006)

Leasehold Committee, 'Final Report' (Cmd 7982, 1950)

Lee, P and Murie, A, *Poverty, Housing Tenure and Social Exclusion* (Bristol, The Policy Press, 1997)

Lee, R, 'Rent Control – The Economic Impact of Social Legislation' (1992) 12 *OJLS* 543

—— 'The Private Sector: The Regulatory Landscape' presented at a workshop in London on Ensuring Responsible Renting organised by the Law Commission on 23 March 2006

Lester, A and Pannick, D, 'The Impact of the Human Rights Act on Private Law: The Knight's Move' (2000) 116 *LQR* 380

Levaggi, P and Marsden, D, 'Expensive quandary' (10 March 2007) *EG* 174

Levison, D, Barelli, J and Lawton, G, 'The Accelerated Possession Procedure: the Experience of Landlords and Tenants' (DETR, 1998)

Lewison, K, *The Interpretation of Contracts* 3rd edn (London, Sweet & Maxwell, 2003)

Lister, D, 'The nature of tenancy relationships: landlords and young people' in S Lowe and D Hughes (eds), *The Private Rented Sector in a New Century: revival or false dawn?* (Bristol, The Policy Press, 2002)

Lizieri, C and Kutsch, N, *Who Owns the City 2006* (University of Reading Business School, March 2006)

Lord Chancellor's Department, 'Report of the Review Body on Civil Justice' (Cm 394, 1988)

—— 'Commonhold, A Consultation Paper' (Cm 1346, 1990)

—— 'Enforcement Review Consultation Paper 5: Distress for Rent' (May 2001)

Loveland, I, 'Fixing Landlords with Liability for the Anti-Social Behaviour of their Tenants' [2005] *J of Planning L* 273

—— 'Tolerated Trespass: a Very Peculiar Legal Creature' (2007) 123 *LQR* 455

Lowe, S, 'Homes and castles' in J Goodwin and C Grant (eds), *Built to Last?* 2nd edn (London, ROOF, 1997)

Luba, J, *Repairs: Tenants' Rights* 2nd edn (London, Legal Action Group, 1991)

Luxton, P, 'Are You Being Served? Enforcing Keep-Open Covenants in Leases' [1998] *Conv* 396

Lyons, TJ, 'The Meaning of "Holiday" under the Rent Acts' [1984] *Conv* 286

Malpass, P, 'The road from Clay Cross' in J Goodwin and C Grant (eds), *Built to Last?* 2nd edn (London, ROOF, 1997)

—— *Housing Associations and Housing Policy: A Historical Perspective* (Basingstoke, Macmillan, 2000)

Malpass, P and Murie, A, *Housing Policy and Practice* 5th edn (Basingstoke, Macmillan, 1999)

Markus, K, 'Leonard Cheshire Foundation: What is a Public Authority?' [2003] *EHRLR* 92

Marsh, A, 'Restructuring social housing rents' in D Cowan and A Marsh (eds), *Two Steps Forward* (Bristol, The Policy Press, 2001)

Marsh, A and others, 'Harassment and Unlawful Eviction of Private Rented Sector Tenants and Park Home Residents' (DETR, 2000)

Martin, J, 'Casenote Editor's Note' [1992] *Conv* 343

Massey, D and Catalono, A, *Capital and Land: Landownership by Capital in Great Britain* (London, Edward Arnold, 1978)

Maxwell, D, *Shifting Foundations: Home Ownership and Government Objectives* (London, Institute for Public Policy Research, 2005)

McClary, S, 'Sparks still Flying' (5 May 2007) *EG* 76

McFarlane, B and Simpson, E, 'Tackling Avoidance' in J Getzler (ed), *Rationalising Property, Equity and Trusts* (London, LexisNexis UK, 2003)

McLoughlin, P, *Commercial Leases and Insolvency* 3rd edn (London, Butterworths, 2002)

McMeel, F, 'Prior Negotiations and Subsequent Conduct – The Next Step Forward for Contractual Interpretation?' (2003) 119 *LQR* 272

Meagher, RP, Gummow, WMC and Lehane, JRF, *Equity Doctrines and Remedies* 3rd edn (Sydney, Butterworths, 1992)

Megarry, R and Wade, HWR, *The Law of Real Property* 4th edn (London, Stevens & Sons, 1975)

—— *The Law of Real Property* 5th edn (London, Steven & Sons, 1984)

Merrill, TW, 'Property and the Right to Exclude' (1998) 77 *Nebraska L Rev* 730

Merrill, TW and Smith, HE, 'Optimal Standardization in the Law of Property: The Numerus Clausus Principle' (2000) 110 *Yale LJ* 1

Millington, A, *Property Development* (London, Estates Gazette, 2000)

Milner-Holland, 'Report of the Committee on Housing in Greater London' (Cmnd 2605, 1965)

Ministry of Land and Natural Resources, 'Leasehold Reform in England and Wales' (Cmnd 2916, 1966)

Monopolies and Mergers Commission, 'The Supply of Beer: A Report on the Supply of Beer for Retail Sale in the United Kingdom' (Cm 651, 1989)

Moorhouse, JC, 'Optimal Housing Maintenance under Rent Control' (1972) 39 *Southern Economics J* 93

Morgan, J, 'Repairing the Breach: Proudfoot v Hart Revisited' [1994] *Conv* 145

Mowbray, A, *The Development of Positive Obligations under the European Convention on Human Rights by the European Court of Human Rights* (Oxford, Hart, 2004)

Mullen, T, 'Stock Transfer' in D Cowan and A Marsh (eds), *Two Steps Forward* (Bristol, The Policy Press, 2001)

Mullins, D and Murie, A, *Housing Policy in the UK* (Basingstoke, Palgrave Macmillan, 2006)

Mullins, D and Niner, P, 'A Prize of citizenship? Changing access to social housing' in A Marsh and D Mullins (eds), *Housing and Public Policy: Citizenship, Choice and Control* (Buckingham, Open University Press, 1998)

Murdoch, S, 'Residential use and the 1954 Act' (1 May 1993) *EG* 101

—— 'Reform of Part II of the Landlord and Tenant Act 1954: Silk Purse or Pig's Ear?' Conference Paper, 5th Biennial Property Conference (March 2004)

—— 'Commercial Leases: Future Directions' in S Bright (ed), *Landlord and Tenant Law. Past, Present and Future* (Oxford, Hart, 2006)

Murie, A and Nevin, B, 'New Labour Transfers' in D Cowan and A Marsh (eds), *Two Steps Forward* (Bristol, The Policy Press, 2001)

Murphy, T, Roberts, S and Flessas, T, *Understanding Property Law* 4th edn (London, Sweet & Maxwell, 2004)

National Audit Office, 'Improving social housing through transfer' (HC 496, 19 March 2003)

National Centre for Social Research and ODPM, 'Survey of English Housing, 2003 – 2004' (SN 5506, October 2006)

Neave, M, 'Recent Developments in Australian Residential Tenancies Laws' in S Bright (ed), *Landlord and Tenant Law. Past, Present and Future* (Oxford, Hart, 2006)

Nelken, D, *The Limits of the Legal Process, A Study of Landlords, Law and Crime* (London, Academic Press, 1983)

—— 'Getting the Law out of Context' (1996) 19 *Socio-Legal Newsletter* 12

Neo, JBC, 'Problems of Private Flat Ownership in England and Wales – Is Strata Title the Solution?' (RICS, 1990)

Neuberger, D, 'Our Not so Flexible Friend' (30 September 2000) *EG* 139

Neuberger, J and Long, G, 'Policy Briefing: Housing Benefit' (Shelter, August 2005)

Nicholls, D, 'My Kingdom for a Horse: The Meaning of Words' (2005) 121 *LQR* 577

Nixon, J and others, 'Housing Cases in County Courts' (The Policy Press in association with the Joseph Rowntree Foundation, 1996)

Nixon, J and others, 'Tackling Antisocial Behaviour in Mixed Tenure Areas' (ODPM, March 2003)

Northfield Committee, 'Report of the Committee of Inquiry into the Acquisition and Occupancy of Agricultural Land' (Cmnd 7599, 1979)

Nugee Committee, 'Report of the Committee of Inquiry on the Management of Privately Owned Blocks of Flats' (1985)

ODPM, 'Housing benefit and the private sector' (Housing Research Summary, Number 95, 1999)

—— 'Tenancy Money, Probity and Protection' (Consultation Paper, November 2002)

—— 'Revision of the Code of Guidance on the Allocation of Accommodation' (November 2002)

—— 'Tenants Managing: Evaluation of Tenant Management Organisations in England' (Research Summary 174, 2002)

—— 'Sustainable Communities: Building for the Future' (February 2003)

—— 'A Guide to Social Rent Reforms in the Local Authority Sector' (February 2003)

—— 'English House Condition Survey 2001: Private Landlords Survey' (December 2003)

—— 'Exploitation of the Right to Buy Scheme by Companies' (Housing Research Summary, Number 177, 2003)

—— 'Private Landlords Survey: English House Condition Survey 2001' (Housing Research Summary, Number 205, 2003)

—— Statement by the ODPM in relation to the Regulatory Reform (Business Tenancies) (England and Wales) Order 2003

—— 'A Decent Home – the definition and guidance for implementation' (February 2004)

—— 'Commercial property leases: options for deterring or outlawing the use of upwards only rent review clauses' (May 2004)

—— 'Anti-Social Behaviour: Policy and Procedure, Code of Guidance for local housing authorities and housing action trusts' (August 2004)

—— 'Licensing in the Private Rented Sector. Consultation on the Implementation of HMO Licensing, Regulatory Impact Assessment, Housing Bill, Part 2' (November 2004)

—— 'Piloting choice-based lettings: an evaluation' (Housing Research Summary, Number 208, 2004)

—— 'National Framework for Tenant Participation Compacts' (March 2005)

—— 'Sustainable Communities: Homes for All, A Strategy to Choice Based Lettings' (June 2005)

—— 'HomeBuy-Expanding the Opportunity to Own, Government's Response to Consultation' (September 2005)

—— 'Enabling local authorities to contract their Anti-Social Behaviour Order functions to organisations managing their housing stock, Consultation Paper' (November 2005)

—— 'Sustainable Communities: Homes for All, A Five Year Plan from the Office of the Deputy Prime Minister' (Cm 6424, 2005)

—— 'Respect Action Plan' (10 January 2006)

—— 'English House Condition Survey 2003: Annual Report' (March 2006)

—— 'A Respect Standard for Housing Management: Consultation Paper' (April 2006)

—— 'English House Condition Survey 2003: Private Landlords Survey' (April 2006)

—— 'Tenancy Deposit Protection: Consultation on Secondary Legislation' (June 2006)

—— Housing, Planning, Local Government and the Regions Committee, 'Decent Homes' Fifth Report HC (2003–04)

—— Live Tables on Stock, Table 114

Office of National Statistics, Survey Division, 'Omnibus Survey' (SN 4145, March 1998)

OFT, 'Unfair Contract Terms Guidance' (OFT 311, February 2001)

—— 'Unfair contract terms' Bulletins 27 and 28 (OFT 743, September 2004)

—— 'Land agreements: Understanding Competition Law' (December 2004)

—— 'Guidance on Unfair Terms in Tenancy Agreements' (OFT 356, September 2005)

Oliver, D, 'Functions of a Public Nature under the Human Rights Act' [2004] *PL* 329

Orwin, CS, *A History of English Farming* (London, Nelson and Sons, 1949)

Papps, P, 'Anti-social Behaviour Strategies-Individualistic or Holistic?' (1998) 13 *Housing Studies* 639

Parkinson, N, 'Securing the Future' ROOF Nov/Dec 2006 44

Partington, M and Hill, J, *Housing Law: Cases, Materials and Commentary* (London, Sweet & Maxwell, 1991)

Pawlowski, M, 'Occupational Rights in Leasehold Law: Time for Rationalisation?' [2002] *Conv* 550

—— 'Unilateral Tenancies and Licences' (2005) 9 *Landlord & Tenant Rev* 161

Pawson, H, 'Reviewing Stock Transfer', paper delivered to the Housing Studies Association Spring Conference 2004

Pawson, H and Fancie, C, *Maturing assets: The evolution of stock transfer housing associations* (Bristol, Policy Press in association with the Joseph Rowntree Foundation, 2003)

Pawson, H and others, 'Local Authority Policy and Practice on Allocations, Transfers and Homelessness' (DETR, 2001)

Pawson, H and others, 'The Use of Possession Actions and Evictions by Social Landlords' (ODPM, June 2005)

Penner, J, 'The "Bundle of Rights" Picture of Property' (1996) 43 *UCLA L Rev* 711

Percival, ME, 'The Landlord and Tenant Act 1987' (1988) 51 *MLR* 97

Phang, A, 'Specific Performance-Exploring the Roots of "Settled Practice"' (1998) 61 *MLR* 421

Phillipson, G, 'The Human Rights Act, "Horizontal Effect" and the Common Law: a Bang or a Whimper?' (1999) 62 *MLR* 824

Pitt, B, 'Lost in Translation: Housing Management, Antisocial Behaviour and the Law' (conference at Oxford Brookes University, 22 September 2004)

PKF Consultants, 'Tenancy Deposits Implementation. Scoping Study Report' (ODPM, August 2005)

Policy Action Team, 'National Strategy for Neighbourhood Renewal, Report of Policy Action Team 8: Anti-Social Behaviour' (March 2000)

Prichard, AM, 'Tenancy by Estoppel' (1964) 80 *LQR* 370

Prichard, A, 'Fair Rents and Market Rents' (1992) 142 *NLJ* 965

Purvis, J, 'A mandate for disclosure' (17 March 2007) *EG* 152

Quinn, RM and Phillips, E, 'The Law of Landlord-Tenant: A Critical Evaluation of the Past with Guidelines for the Future' (1969) 38 *Fordham L Rev* 225

Rabin, EH, 'The Revolution in Residential Landlord-Tenant Law: Causes and Consequences' (1984) 69 *Cornell L Rev* 517

Radlett, D and Luo, Y, 'Hoodies out … or in?' (2006) 156 *NLJ* 1501

Rafferty, R, 'Benefit of the Doubt' ROOF November/December 2005 17

Ramsay, P, 'What is Anti-Social Behaviour?' [2004] *Crim LR* 908

Rauta, I and Pickering, A, *Private Renting in England 1990* (Government Social Survey Department and DoE, 1992)

Reich, C, 'The New Property' (1964) 73 *Yale LJ* 733

Reynolds, L, *Safe and Secure? The private rented sector and security of tenure* (Shelter, 2005)

Rhodes, D, 'The Modern Private Rented Sector' (York, Joseph Rowntree Foundation, 2006)

Rhodes, D and Bevan, M, 'Private Landlords and Buy to Let' (York, The Centre for Housing Policy, University of York, September 2003)

Rhodes, D and Kemp, P, 'Rents and returns in the residential lettings market' in S Lowe and D Hughes (eds), *The Private Rented Sector in a New Century: revival or false dawn?* (Bristol, Policy Press, 2002)

Richards, J and Goodwin, J, 'Changing Duties' in J Goodwin and C Grant (eds), *Built to Last?* 2nd edn (London, ROOF, 1997)

RICS, 'Guidance Notes for Valuers Acting in reviews of Rent at Arbitration under the Agricultural Holdings Act' (1986)

—— 'International Leasing Structures' (Paper Number 26, May 1993)

—— *Service Charge Residential Management Code* (Coventry, RICS, 1997)

—— *Rent Only Residential Management Code* 2nd edn (Coventry, RICS, 2002)

—— RICS response to the government consultation on banning UORR (30 Sept 2004)

—— 'Tenant Satisfaction Index: Tune into Tenants' (2005)

RICS Code of Practice, *Service Charges in Commercial Property* (Coventry, RICS Books, 2006)

RICS Commercial Leases Group, *Commercial Property Leases in England and Wales, Code of Practice* (London, Furnival Press, December 1995)

RICS Policy Unit, *A Code of Practice for Commercial Leases in England and Wales* 2nd edn (2002)

Riseborough, M, 'More control and choice for users? Involving tenants in social housing management' in A Marsh and D Mullins, *Housing and Public Policy: Citizenship, Choice and Control* (Buckingham, Open University Press, 1998)

Rivers, J, 'Proportionality and Variable Intensity of Review' (2006) 65 *CLJ* 174

Roberts, N, 'Access to Quasi-Public Spaces – Whose Visitor?' [2007] 71 *Conv* 235

Robertson, D, 'Cultural Expectations of Homeownership, Explaining Changing Legal Definitions of Flat 'Ownership' within Britain' (2006) 21 *Housing Studies* 35

Robinson, M, 'Once Upon a Time' (1999) 115 *LQR* 389

Robinson, P, *Leasehold Management: A Good Practice Guide* (Coventry, Chartered Institute of Housing, National Housing Federation and the Housing Corporation, 2003)

Rodger, R, *Housing in Urban Britain 1780-1914* (Cambridge, CUP, 1995)

Rodgers, CP, 'Residential Flats – A New Deal?' [1988] *Conv* 122

—— 'Fair rents and the market: judicial attitudes to rent control legislation' [1999] *Conv* 201

ROOF, 'Homefront: Deposit Dodge' ROOF May/June 2007 6

Rook, D, 'Property Law and the Human Rights Act 1998: a Review of the First Year' [2002] *Conv* 316

Ross, M, *Commercial Leases* (London, Butterworths, 1998)

Routley, P, 'Tenancies and Estoppel – After Bruton v London & Quadrant Housing Trust' (2000) 63 *MLR* 424

Ryland, DS, 'EC Leasing practices: Germany, France, Netherlands and Belgium' (4 July 1992) *EG* 110

Scamell, EH (ed), *Precedents for the Conveyancer* (London, Sweet & Maxwell, 1970-)

Scott, P, *The Property Masters* (London, E & FN Spon, 1996)

Seabourne, G and Paton, E, 'Time to Eject the Three Years' Rack Rent Penalty' [2006] 70 *Conv* 451

Select Committee on Business Premises, 'Business Premises' HC (1920)

Shelter, 'Home truths, The reality behind our housing aspirations' (August 2005)

Shone, S, 'EC leasehold regimes: a comparison' (21 March 1992) *EG* 92

Slessenger, E and Cullen, S, 'Is the guarantor on the hook?' (25 July 1998) *EG* 102

Smith, PF, 'A Dent in Street v Mountford' [1987] *Conv* 220

—— 'Confined to the Contract' [1989] *Conv* 216

—— 'A Nasty Measure – Part I of the Landlord and Tenant Act 1987' (1992) 12 *LS* 42

—— 'What is Wrong with Certainty in Leases?' [1993] *Conv* 461

—— 'Repairing Obligations: A Case Against Radical Reform' [1994] *Conv* 186

—— 'Presuming Reality or Not Seeking Ambiguities' [1999] *Conv* 346

Smith, R, 'The Running of Covenants in Equitable Leases and Equitable Assignments of Legal Leases' (1978) 37 *CLJ* 98

Smith, RJ, *Property Law* 5th edn (Harlow, Longman, 2006)

Somerville, P, 'Allocating housing – or 'letting' people choose? in D Cowan and A Marsh (eds), *Two Steps Forward* (Bristol, The Policy Press, 2001)

Sparkes, P, 'Forfeiture of Equitable Leases' (1987) 16 *Anglo-American L Rev* 160

—— 'Purchasers in Possession' [1987] *Conv* 278

—— 'Co-Tenants, Joint Tenants and Tenants in Common' (1989) 18 *Anglo-American Law Review* 151

—— 'Certainty of Leasehold Terms' (1993) 109 *LQR* 93

—— *A New Landlord and Tenant* (Oxford, Hart, 2001)

Spenceley, J and Whitehead, C, 'Housing Associations in 2005' (Cambridge, Dataspring, April 2006)

Spencer, JR, 'The Defective Premises Act 1972 – Defective Law and Defective Law Reform, Part III' (1975) 34 *CLJ* 48

Spencer-Silver, J, 'Landlord's continuing liability' (14 August 1993) *EG* 69

Staughton, C, 'How do the Courts Interpret Commercial Contracts?' (1999) 58 *CLJ* 303

Stephens, M, Burns, N and MacKay, L, 'The limits of housing reform: British social rented housing in a European context' (2003) 40 *Urban Studies* 767

Stephens, M, Whitehead, C and Munro, M, 'Lessons from the Past, Challenges for the Future for Housing Policy: an Evaluation of English Housing Policy 1975 – 2000' (ODPM, 2005)

Sternberg, S, 'The Commercial Landlord's Duty to Mitigate upon a Tenant's Abandonment of the Premises' (1984-85) 5 *Adv Q* 385

Sternlieb, G and Hughes, J, *The Future of Rental Housing* (Piscataway NJ, Centre for Urban Policy Research, 1981)

Stevens, D, 'Covenants and the chain of indemnity' (22 May 1999) *EG* 152

Stevens, R, 'The Contracts (Rights of Third Parties) Act 1999' (2004) 120 *LQR* 292

Stimpson, M, 'A step too far' Private Renter Issue 7 September 2006 in ROOF September/October 2006

Swadling, W, 'Property: General Principles' in P Birks (ed), *English Private Law* (Oxford, OUP, 2000)

Swenarton, M, *Homes Fit for Heroes* (London, Heinemann Educational Books, 1981)

Tayleur, T, 'The Effect of Disclaimer: A Tale of Two Cases' [1997] *Conv* 24

Tenant Involvement Commission, 'What Tenants Want: Report of the Tenant Involvement Commission' (National Housing Federation, 2006)

Tettenborn, A, 'Absolving the Undeserving: Shopping Centres, Specific Performance and the Law of Contract' [1998] *Conv* 23

Thomas, A and others, 'The Landlord and Tenant Act 1987: Awareness, Experience and Impact' (DoE, 1991)

Thompson, MP, *Co-ownership* (London, Sweet & Maxwell, 1988)

Thornton, R, 'Enforceability of Leasehold Covenants' (1991) 11 *LS* 47

Tiplady, D, 'Recent Developments in the Law of Landlord and Tenant: The American Experience' (1981) 44 *MLR* 129

Trade and Industry Committee, 'Pub Companies' HC (2004-05) 128-1

Treitel, GH, *The Law of Contract* 11th edn (London, Sweet & Maxwell, 2003)

TRIG, 'Final Report' (DEFRA, 2003)

Tromans, S, 'Forfeiture of Leases: Relief for Underlessees and Holders of Other Derivative Interests' [1986] *Conv* 187

UN Economic Commission for Europe, 'Guidelines on Social Housing' (draft) (2005)

UN Economic Commission for Europe, 'Guidelines on Social Housing: Principles and Examples' (April 2006) UN Doc ECE/HBP/137

Underkuffler-Freund, L, 'Takings and the Nature of Property' (1996) 9 *Canadian J L & Juris* 161

Universities UK/SCOP 'Code of Practice for the Management of Student Housing' (20 February 2006)

Uthwatt, Lord (Chair), 'Leasehold Committee: Interim Report on Tenure and Rents of Business Premises' (Cmd 7706, 1948 – 1949)

Wade, HWR, 'The Future of Certiorari' (1958) 17 *CLJ* 169

Wade, W, 'Horizons of Horizontality' (2000) 116 *LQR* 217

Waite AJ, 'Repairs and Deduction from Rent' [1981] *Conv* 199

Walker, AG, 'Landlord and Tenant (Covenants) Act 1995: Sureties for tenants and assignees' (1998) 2 *Landlord & Tenant Rev* 124

Walsh, B, 'Shopping centres: why are turnover rents not more popular?' (2 April 1988) *EG* 20

Walker, B and others, 'Social housing tenants' attitudes and reactions to rent levels and rent differentials' (DETR, 2000)

Walter, P, 'Landlord and Tenant (Covenants) Act 1995: A Legislative Folly?' [1996] *Conv* 432

Watchman, P, 'Fair Rents and Market Scarcity' [1985] *Conv* 199

White, J, 'Business out of charity' in J Goodwin and C Grant (eds), *Built to Last?* 2nd edn (London, ROOF, 1997)

White, R, 'A storm is brewing in the fraternity' (12 April 2007) *EG* 188

Wilcox, S, *UK Housing Review 2005/2006* (Coventry, Chartered Institute of Housing and London, Council of Mortgage Lenders, 2005)

—— 'A financial evaluation of the right to buy' in S Wilcox, *UK Housing Review 2006/07* (Coventry, Chartered Institute of Housing and London, Council of Mortgage Lenders, 2006)

Wilde, D, 'Certainty of Leasehold Term' (1994) 57 *MLR* 117

Wilkinson, H, 'Fresh Thoughts from Abroad' [1994] *Conv* 428

Wilkinson, HW, 'Landlords' repair covenants – when is the breach?' (1995) 145 *NLJ* 1793

Willan, PN di C, 'Fair rents or unfair rents?' (1995) 145 *NLJ* 348

Willett, H, 'Turnover Rents – Coming out of Recession' (1997) 1 *Landlord & Tenant Rev* 90

Williams, A, 'Terminating Assured Shorthold Tenancies' (2006) 156 *NLJ* 1550

Williams, PJG, 'The tenant's lot is a happier one' (11 February 2006) *EG* 160

Winter, M, *Agricultural Land Tenure in England and Wales* (London, RICS, 1990)

Wood D, 'Mapping the Recent Past' in S Bright (ed), *Landlord and Tenant Law. Past, Present and Future* (Oxford, Hart, 2006)

Woolf, H, 'Public Law – Private Law: why the divide?' [1986] *PL* 220

Woolf, Lord, 'Access to Justice: Final Report to the Lord Chancellor on the civil justice system in England and Wales' (London, July 1996)

INDEX

abandonment and arrears *see under* rent
absolute covenants
  and alienation 523–4
  and user 418–19
affordability 171, 172–4
  and welfare payments 465–70
    background 465
    housing benefits *see* housing benefit system
agents, management 338–9
agricultural tenancies 19–20, 257–70
  alienation 542
  and assured tenancies 208
  avoidance of statutory protection 262–3
  decline 261, 268–9
  disputes 341–2
  farm business tenancies *see* farm business tenancies
  improvements, compensation right 411–12
  policy/legislative
    history 52, 257–8
    impact post-1995 267–9
  reform proposals 269–70
  rent reviews 496–8
    and scarcity 463
  repair obligations 382
  security of tenure 258–61, 268
    possession grounds 259–60
    rent mechanism 260, 261
  succession on death 551
alienation covenants 515, 522–45
  as absolute covenants 523–4
  agricultural tenancies 542
  commercial leases *see* commercial leases, alienation
    clauses
  disposition in breach
    common law 542–3
    residential tenancies 541, 543–4
  formalities 544–5
  as fully qualified covenants *see under* fully qualified
    covenants, and reasonableness
  long residential leases 541–2
  premises as family home 537–40
    background 537
    occupation rights 538
    transfer of tenancy 538–40
  private renting 537
  public sector tenancies
    general rule 535
    right to exchange 535–6
    right to take in lodgers 537, 540–1
    sub-letting 536–7
    transfer 536, 541

residential tenancies 534
  see also public sector tenancies *above*
  disposition in breach 543–4
  reform proposals 540–1
  as restriction on dealings 522–3
allocation of housing 103–4, 190–202
  background 190–1
  and discrimination 104, 191
  private renting 201–2
  social housing *see under* social housing
alterations *see* improvements
anti-social behaviour 177, 314–26
  background 314–15
  complaints to ombudsman 344
  and disability discrimination 318, 620–3
  eviction 322–6, 594, 599, 604, 610, 617–20
  extra-legal responses 318
  injunctions 318–20
  introductory and demoted tenancies 189–90, 214–15,
    594
  landlord responsibility for tenant behaviour 330–2
  legal responses 316–18
  and licensing 337, 387–8, 389
  orders (ASBOs) 320–1
  and private rented housing 325–6
  problem estates 215
  remedies 325
  and right to buy 750
  as social housing problem 315–16
  tenancy terms against 329–30
arms length management organisations (ALMOs) 169,
    336, 339–40
assignee tenant *see under* leasehold covenants, enforce-
    ment
assignment 518
  commercial leases 530–1
  equitable 574, 580
  formalities 544–5
assured shorthold tenancies 187–8, 196–7, 203–4
  and possession 636–8
assured tenancies 204–10
  exclusions 207–10
  fixed term, rent review 493
  grounds for possession 600 *Table*
  and housing associations 218–19
  and long residential leases 633
  only/principal home requirement 206–7
  and possession 607–8
  separate dwelling requirement 205–6
  and shorthold *see* assured shorthold tenancies
  sub-tenants, termination effect 741

tenancy rights 204–5
tenant as individual, requirement 206
termination 210
authorised guarantee agreement (AGA) 135, 242, 531,
        569, 570, 575, 585, 665
avoidance 144–7
by agreement 146–7
by re-routing 145–6

bankruptcy 726–8
Barker review 149–50, 171
Best Value 175–6, 316, 340
in Housing and Homelessness (BVHH), framework
        336
break clauses 18, 135, 243, 533, 732–4
background 732–3
joint interests 734
landlord 734
and notices 734
pre-conditions 733–4
business efficacy test 361, 373–4
business expansion scheme 168
business property see commercial property sector
business tenancies see commercial tenancies

capital gains tax, exemptions 166
Cave review 180–1, 340, 344
certainty of term 37, 72–7, 92–3
background 72–3
and contractual licence 75–6
indeterminate leases 73
justification of requirement 73–4
and periodic tenancies 76
statutory solution 75
summary of rule 76–7
cesser of rent 513
change of landlord 551–7
background 551
deeds and registration 552
large-scale voluntary transfer (LSVT) 552–7
notifying residential tenancies 552
change of tenant
assignment 518
commercial leases 530–1
background 517–18
residential tenancies 221, 534–41
subletting 518–19
taking in a lodger 519
choice
choice based letting (CBL) 199–200
of property 105
Clay Cross councillors 450
clear lease 18, 131
commercial leases 18–19, 130–8, 241–3, 252–5
see also commercial property sector
alienation clauses 135, 252–3, 530–4
assignment 530–1
background 530
in practice 533–4
sub-letting 135, 531–2

assignment 530–1
change factors 131–3
codes of practice 132–4, 242–3, 253–4, 333
on alienation 533–4
on break clauses 734
on deposit 501
on insurance 428, 431–2
on rent 483–5
RICS service charge code 425 Table, 436, 440–1
on service charges 436
on use 418
company liquidation 726–8
compensation for non-renewal 658–60
confidentiality 133, 446, 483, 485
consumer focus 137–8
deposits 501
dilapidations 135, 395–8, 709
and estate management see estate management
flexibility 136, 241–3
and valuation 137
improvements, compensation right 235–6, 411–13
information rights 120
and institutional lease 17–18, 130–1, 242–3
lengths 135
management see estate management, leasehold
modern rent review clause 132, 135, 477–90
assumptions/disregards see hypothetical lease
        below
background 477–8
comparability 484–5
construction principles 485–90
duration of hypothetical term 487
formula for review 478–9
headline rents/incentives 489–90
hypothetical lease 479–82, 487
machinery for review 478
periods of review 478
presumption of reality 486–7
rent review provisions 487–8
time of the essence 488–9
upward only rent review (UORR) 132, 135, 242–3,
        253, 254, 482–4
new tenancy
see also under commercial leases, security
agreement 650–1
duration 660–1
grounds for opposition 652–3
holding 662–3
impact of legislation 665–6
rent 661–2
tenant/landlord interests 663–4
terms 660–6
original tenant liability 18, 131–2, 242, 526, 562–8
patterns 134–5
renewal rights see commercial leases, security
rent controls 465
rent reviews see modern rent review clause above
repair covenants 354–6, 361, 364–72
security 238–9, 252, 645–66
background 645

compensation for non-renewal 658–60
continuation 646–7
court, application 652
demolition 655–7
end of term options 646–7
and estate management *see* estate management
information requirement 645–6
interim rent, application 651–2
Landlord and Tenant Act 1954, part II, criteria for application 244–51
landlord's need to occupy property 657–8
new tenancy *see* new tenancy *above*
suitable alternative accommodation 654
termination *see* termination *below*
uneconomic subletting 654–5
sub-letting 135, 243, 531–2, 533–4
termination
by landlord 648–50
by tenant 647–8
commercial property sector 13–18, 51, 235–55
see also commercial leases
business purposes, definition 250
choice/flexibility, promotion 241–3
contracting out 239–41, 252, 645
dispute resolution 341–2
as investment 16–18
Landlord and Tenant Act 1954, operation 244
legislative framework 238–9
market, size/categories 13–15
policy/legislative history/proposals 52, 235–8
rents
see also commercial leases, modern rent review clause; rents
cesser of rent 513
commercial rent arrears recovery (CRAR) 511, 512–13
range 447 *Table*
restrictive alienation provision, concern 252–3
service charges *see* services charges
tenancies, need for 245–6
commercial rent arrears recovery (CRAR) 511, 512–13
commonhold 13, 231–2, 313–14, 785
communication, and tenant satisfaction 334
company liquidation 726–8
competition law 422–3
complaints 343–4
conditional alienation 525–6
construction
of contracts 113–15
and leases 115–16
contracts
construction 113–15
fairness *see* fairness, and contracts
leases as 28, 29–35, 329–30
application of contract law 30
background 29
business efficacy test 361, 373–4
changes in US 33–4
construction/rectification 115–16
contractual interpretation 60–1

for possession only 30–1
for possession plus 31–3
rectification 115
rental, model contracts 138
unfair *see* Unfair Contract Terms Act 1977; Unfair Terms in Consumer Contracts Regulations 1999
council housing *see* local authority housing
covenants
disclaimer of landlord's title 124, 716–17
enforceability 37–8, 560–90
express 121
implied *see* implied covenants
non-derogation from grant 30–1, 33, 123–4, 416–17
for quiet enjoyment 30, 121, 122–3, 392–3, 693
release from liability 38

damages
to landlord for breach of repairing covenant
long leases, recovery 395–6
measure of 397–8
to tenant 400–1
and unlawful eviction *see* unlawful eviction, statutory damages
death *see* succession on death
Decent Homes Standard (DHS) 169–70, 348–50
deeds, requirements 106–7
at best rent 107
exceeding three years 106
reform proposals 107
taking effect in possession 107
demolition, and estate management 631–3, 655–7
demoted tenancies *see* anti-social behaviour, introductory and demoted tenancies
demunicipalisation 163
denial of title 124, 716–17
deposits *see* rent, security deposits
destitution
see also homelessness
and human rights 279–80
differential rents 473
disability discrimination 104, 303–5
see also special needs housing, allocation/management
and anti-social behaviour 318, 620–3
and improvements 409–10
and possession 678
disclaimer
effect 589–90
of landlord's title 124, 716–17
onerous property 726
discrimination 104, 191
disability 303–5
and human rights law 285, 548–9
and landlord's consent 519–20
disputes 341–6
background 341
commercial/agricultural 341–2
residential *see under* residential tenancies
distress for rent *see under* rent

domestic violence, and possession 623
dwelling, separate, definition 37, 205–6

employment related tenancies 215, 216
    and possession 597, 600, 626–7
enfranchisement
    see also low-cost home ownership; right to acquire
        (RTA); right to buy (RTB)
    case for 227–9
    of flats *see* flats, enfranchisement
    and future of renting/long leaseholds 784–5
    and human rights 272–3, 287–8
    long leasehold houses *see* long leasehold houses,
        enfranchisement
    and social tenants 743–85
environmental health legislation 385–6
equitable assignment 574, 580
equitable leases 111–12, 573–4, 580
equitable set-off 404
    exclusion 405
equity rents 473–5
estate management 299–303
    see also management
    commercial leases, grounds for opposing renewal
        demolition/reconstruction/works 655–7
        landlord's need to occupy property 657–8
        uneconomic subletting 654–5
    core services 299–300
    and enfranchisement of long leasehold houses 768
    and flats, enfranchisement 781
    leasehold 300–1, 305–10
        contractual duties 306–8
        controlling access to property 308–10
        importance 305–6
    possession, residential tenancies, grounds 628–35
        background 628
        death of tenant 634–5
        demolition/reconstruction/works 631–3
        over-crowding 630
        owner-occupation 634
        special needs housing, allocation/management
            633–4
        student accommodation, vacation lets 635
        suitable alternative accommodation (SAA) 628–9
        temporary accommodation during repairs 629–30
        under-crowding 630–1
        winter lets 635
    and social landlords 301–3
estates, leases as 28–9
estoppel
    and leases 110
    tenancy by 94–5
eviction
    anti-social behaviour 322–6
    and human rights 282–4
    and possession *see under* possession
    residential tenancies 219, 604 *Table*
    secure tenancies 217–18
    unlawful *see* unlawful eviction
    without court order 680

exclusions
    access, human rights 309
    assured tenancies 207–10
    business tenancies 250–1
    equitable set-off 405
    local authority housing, allocation 201
    recoupment right 405
    secure tenancies 214–17
    social *see* social exclusion
    unfair *see under* Unfair Terms in Consumer Con-
        tracts Regulations 1999
exclusive possession 68, 70–2, 75
    absence 79–81, 211–12
    contractual lease 95
    and implied periodic tenancy 89–90
    and multiple occupation 97–9
    other than tenancy 82–4
    and tenancy at will 87–8
    and tolerated trespassers 86–7
express covenants 121
extended lease right
    flats, enfranchisement 781–3
    long leasehold houses, enfranchisement 766–7

fairness, and contracts 124–30
    background 124–5
    Unfair Contract Terms Act 1977 125–6
    UTCCR *see* Unfair Terms in Consumer Contracts
        Regulations 1999
family home, and relationship breakdown *see* alienation
    covenants, premises as family home
farm business tenancies (FBT) 261–2, 263–7
    business/agricultural conditions 264
    compensation for improvements 265–6
        consisting of planning permission 266–7
    dispute resolution 267
    lettings 263–4
        formalities 264–5
    rent review 265, 496–7
    rents 497
fitness for purpose, implied covenant 354, 358–64
    common law position 361
    reform proposals 363–4
    situation in most tenancies 358–9
    statutory warranty 361–3
    warranty of habitability (US) 359–61
fixed term leases 93
    assured tenancy 493
    termination 674
fixtures 413
flats, enfranchisement 229, 230–1, 768–9, 774–84
    collective 774–81
        background 774–5
        and business leases 775
        and converted houses 776
        cost 779–80
        injurious affection payments 780
        landlord exemption 776–7
        long lease requirement 775
        low rent requirement 775

and marriage value 778–9
non-residential uses of floorspace 776
and open market value of freeholder's interest 778
premises qualifications 775–7
premises as self-contained/part of building 775
price 778–9
process 780–1
property requirements 777–8
sufficient support requirement 777
tenant qualifications 775
two flats limit 775
two or more flats held by qualifying tenants 776
two-thirds flats requirement 776
estate management schemes 781
extended lease right 781–3
and Leasehold Reform, Housing and Urban Develop-
    ment Act 1993 774, 783–4
forfeiture 35–6
background 702–3
breach other than non-payment of rent 703–15
    background 703
    breach capable of remedy 706–7
    decorative repair 709
    notification 705–6
    re-entry 709–11, 711–12
    reasonable time requirement 707–8
    repairing covenant 708–9
    steps 704 *Chart*
    waiver 703–4
and derivative interests 718
and human rights 288
and non-payment of rent 715–18
    background 715–16
    denial of title 716–17
    steps 716 *Chart*
problems 719
relief against 35–6, 712–15
    discretion 713–14
    equitable/statutory legislation 712–13
    proportionality 714–15
and residential leases 439–40, 717–18
third party rights 715
formalities 105–10
agreements for lease 108–10
estoppel 110
lease registration requirements 108
legal lease, requirements 105–6
non-observance 110–12
    background 110–11
    enforcing agreements 111–12
    tenancy implied from possession 111
freehold land, positive covenants in 225–6
frustration 31–3, 736–7
fully qualified covenants, and reasonableness 419–21
and alienation 524–30
    and agreed circumstances/conditions 526
    background 524–5
    conditional alienation 525–6
    reasonable refusal 528–9
    reasonableness principles 526–30

unreasonable refusal 529–30
improvements 407–9
private sector tenancies 537
user 419–21

grant, non-derogation from 30–1, 33, 123–4, 416–17
gypsy caravan accommodation 281–2

harassment 56–8, 185, 187, 455, 681–91
background 681
background to regulation 684–6
by occupiers 283, 327–8, 332
civil remedies *see under* unlawful eviction
level of problem 683–4
offences 686–9
Rachman 11, 159, 685–6, 693
reform proposals 698–9
response of agencies 689–91
statutory damages *see under* unlawful eviction
types of 682–3
victims 684
Hills review 8–9, 152, 153, 179, 180, 218
holiday lets, and assured tenancies 208
home
importance of 47–8
only/principal 206–7, 213–14
homelessness
see also destitution, social housing, allocation
applicants and secure tenancies 216
definitions 195
extent of duties 193–5, 200
settled/temporary accommodation 195–7
houses, enfranchisement 12, 229–30, 759–66
case for reform 227–9
houses in multiple occupation (HMOs) 97–9, 169, 176,
    290, 351
licensing 26, 58, 300, 325–6, 386–91
    background 176, 386, 389–90
    conditions 388–9
    and housing authority strategy 388
    mandatory 386–7
    in Northern Ireland 390–1
    and private renting, local authority powers 389
    regulatory regime 389
    selective 387–8
standards and repair 351, 358
housing action trusts (HATs) 163, 553
housing affordability *see* affordability
housing allocation *see* allocation of housing
Housing Association Grant (HAG) 451
housing associations 7–8, 155–66, 218–19
see also social housing
assured tenancies 218–19
diversification 181
early development 155–6
expansion of sector 164–5
as funder/regulator 164
management role 166
private finance 165
rents, historical development 451

right to acquire (RTA) 165–6, 171–2, 222, 744, 745–6, 758
    starter/probationary tenancies 218
    and stock transfer 165, 189, 336
    tenants' statutory rights 189–90
housing benefit system 173–4, 202, 466–8
    reform 468–70
Housing Corporation 159, 164, 172, 340
Housing Health and Safety Rating System (HHSRS) 384
housing injunctions 318–20
Housing Inspectorate, key lines of enquiry (KLE) 302
housing, international rights to 293–6
housing law
    and common law 35
    early legislation 184–5
    private renting see under private renting
    social renting see under social renting
housing management 174–7
housing policy 143–4, 149–50
    central control v local government autonomy 157–8
    current issues 168–77
    owner-occupation, expansion 158–9
    state provision, development 155–6
    summary 181–2
housing supply 170–2
housing tenure see tenure
human rights 45, 271–98
    background 271
    Convention rights
        and destitution 279–80
        and discrimination 285
        and enfranchisement 287–8
        and eviction 282–3, 324, 608, 610–13, 677–8
        exclusion from property 309
        and forfeiture 288
        and HMO registration 390–1
        interpretation 277–9
        and interpretation of legislation 291–3
        margin of appreciation/discretion 278–9
        positive obligations 279, 331
        positive/negative obligations 283–4
        procedural provision 280–1
        and protection of property 286–91
        and rent controls 287, 289–90, 455–8
        and repair duty 283, 392
        and respect for home 281–2
        and succession 549
        Article 3 279–80
        Article 6 280–1
        Article 8 281–4
        First Protocol, Article 1 286–91
    in domestic law 271–3
    international rights to housing 293–6
    and interpretation of legislation 291–3
    and liability to third parties 330–2
    and possession 610–13
    public authority, definition 273–7
    and residential tenancies, termination 677–8

illegal eviction see eviction, unlawful; unlawful eviction

implied covenants 121–4
    background 121–2
    covenant for quiet enjoyment 30, 121, 693
    disclaimer of landlord's title 124, 716–17
    non-derogation from grant 30–1, 33, 123–4, 416–17
improvements
    compensation rights
        agricultural tenancies 260, 262, 265–7, 411–12
        commercial leases 235–6, 412–13
        secure tenancies 413
    and disability legislation 409–10
    fully qualified covenants 407–9
    and repair 367
    tenant's right 406–10
incorporeal hereditaments 247–8
Independent Housing Ombudsman Scheme 343–4, 403
indeterminate leases 73
indexation, of rent 475–6
information to tenants 117–20
    commercial leases 120
    general rights 118–19
    reform proposals 119
    weekly residential tenancies 117
inherent defects 367–8
injurious affection payments
    flats, enfranchisement 780
    long leasehold houses, enfranchisement 766
institutional lease 130–1
insurance 121, 426–32
    contractual provisions 426–7
    cost/choice 427–8
    effecter 428–30
    proceeds, application 430–1
    protection of other party 428–30
    and uninsured risk 431–2
international rights to housing 293–6
investment grade property 15

joint tenancies, and notice to quit 670

labels 145
land
    agreements 423
    and landlords' wealth 46–7
    and tenants' wealth 47–8
land registration rules 108, 133
Landflex leases 137, 432–3
landlord
    breach, repudiation for 723–5
    break clauses 734
    change see change of landlord
    commercial see commercial property sector; under commercial leases
    damages see under damages
    default, tenant, termination for 723
    and enfranchisement of long leasehold houses see under long leasehold houses, enfranchisement
    leasehold see under leasehold covenants, enforcement
    long leases see under long residential leases

original liability *see under* leasehold covenants, enforcement
registered *see* registered social landlords (RSLs)
repair *see under* repair covenants
resident *see* resident landlord exceptions
social *see* voluntary transfer
superior 586–7
title, disclaimer 124, 716–17
unlawful eviction, liability 694–5
large-scale voluntary transfer (LSVT) 8, 163–4, 552–7
Law Commission
  alienation 523–4, 534, 539, 540–1, 542, 544, 545, 549, 550
  business tenancy reform 240, 241, 245, 650
  commonhold 231
  covenant liability 38, 561–2
  damages 692
  distress 512
  housing disputes 58, 344, 345, 346
  improvements 412–13
  landlord termination scheme 719–22
    principles 719–20
    summary termination procedure 720–1
    termination claim 721–2
  lanlord and tenant reform 51–2
  renting homes scheme 222–4
    alienation 534, 540–1, 545
    consumer approach 40, 58, 107, 119, 138, 183
    contract as basis for protection 204
    contracting capacity 77
    housing standards 364
    possession, judicial discretion 602
    security 608, 628, 637–9
    six-month moratorium 203, 637–8
    succession 549, 550
    termination 598, 608, 673
    unfair contract terms 130
  repair 354, 355–6, 357, 362, 363–4, 374–5, 376, 377, 380, 382–3, 391, 394, 395, 398, 409
  responsible renting 58, 176, 179, 341
  tenant termination 723, 724
  user 418–19
leases
  agricultural *see* agricultural tenancies
  commercial *see* commercial leases
  as contracts *see* contracts, leases as
  elements 67–77
    background 67–8
  equitable 111–12, 573–4, 580
  as estates 28–9
  formalities *see under* formalities
  history/classification 27–8
  institutional 130–1
  in legal map 26–7
  management *see* estate management, leasehold
  property based rules 29, 35–9
  and property and contract 39–41
  and rectification 115–16
  repairs *see* repairs
  residential *see* long residential leases

as split-ownership 48–50
terminology 4–5, 22–3
variation *see* variation
vitiating factors 112
leasehold covenants, enforcement
  anti-avoidance 563, 578
  assignee tenant, new leases 574–5
  assignee tenant, old leases
    covenants which touch and concern land 571–2
    equitable assignments of legal leases 573–4
    equitable leases 573–4
    legal relationships 571
    liability following further assignment 572
    liability while a tenant 570–2
  background 559–60
  between tenants 587–8
  continuing liability 560–2
  disclaimer, effect 589–90
  guarantors of former tenants, under new leases 585
  guarantors of former tenants, under old leases
    liability to contracting landlord 583–4
    liability to new reversioners 584–5
  impact of 1995 Act 585–6
  and management companies and new leases 586
  new and old leases 562
  new reversioner, new leases 580–1
  new reversioner, old leases
    equitable leases/assignments 580
    legal leases 578–80
  new reversioner, pre-assignment breaches 581–3
  original landlord liability, new leases 576–8
  original landlord liability, old leases 575–6
    limitations 576
  original tenant, liability 563–70
    common law limitations 564–6
    contractual limitations 564
    during statutory continuation 565–6
    notification of arrears as condition for claim 566–7
    release 565
    right to overriding lease 567–8
    statutory limitations 566–8
    under new leases 568–70
    variations to lease 564–5, 567
  and superior landlord 586–7
leasehold notices 59–63
legislation, human rights interpretation 291–3
legislative intervention 51–9
  avoidance 58–9, 144–7
  limitations 55–8
  and policy 51–2
  and property rights 52–4
licences 78–84
  exclusive possession *see* exclusive possession
  HMO licensing *see* houses in multiple occupation, licensing
  licencee or lodger 71, 79, 145
liveability 350
local authority housing 7
  see also public authorities; social housing

allocation 197–201
    choice based letting (CBL) 199–200
    exclusion criteria 201
    needs basis 197–8
    reasonable preference 198–9
    sustainable communities, promotion 200
autonomy 157–8
best value 175–6, 336, 339–40
changing role, post 1980 160–4
management delegation 339–40
and public law *see under* public law
rent reviews 496
rents, historical development 449–51
residualisation 162–3
right to buy (RTB) 160–2, 745–58
secure tenancies *see* secure tenancies
tenants' statutory rights 188–9
voluntary transfer *see* voluntary transfer
Local Government Ombudsman 332, 343–4, 403
Local Housing Allowance 174, 468–70
Local Reference Rent (LRR) 466
long leasehold houses, enfranchisement 12, 227–30,
        641–2, 759–68, 764 *Table*
    background 759
    basis of valuation 759–60, 762, 766, 767 *Table*
        see also original valuation basis; principles of valu-
            ation *below*
    compensation 768
    compulsory acquisition right 772–3
    contracting out 768
    estate management schemes 768
    exemptions 762
    and extended lease right 766–7
    first refusal 769–73
        enforcement 772
        exempt landlords 770–1
        human rights challenge 272–3, 287–8
        premises 770
        qualifying tenant 769
        relevant disposal 769–70, 771–2
        and residential landlords 770–1
    injurious affectation payments 766
    landlord occupation 768
    Landlord and Tenant Act 1987
        effectiveness 773–4
        limited rights 769
    landlord's compensation 768
    landlord's redevelopment rights 768
    long lease requirement 762
    marriage value 760
    original valuation basis 764–6
    principles of valuation 762–4
    redevelopment rights 768
    and residential landlords 770–1
    setting price 763 *Table*
    tenancy requirements 760–1
    two years' tenancy 762
    value of house 761–2
long residential leases 12–13, 138, 139, 225–34
    alienation 541–2

case for reform 226–9
and commonhold 231–2, 313–14
continuing rights of occupation 641–2
drafting 138
enfranchisement
    of flats *see* flats, enfranchisement
    see long leasehold houses, enfranchisement
future developments 784–5
and landlord's recovery of damages 395–6
management 310–14
    and commonhold 231–2, 313–14
    Landlord and Tenant Act 1987 311–12
    problems 227, 310–11, 313
    RTM *see* right to manage
proposals for future 232–3
repair problems 227–8, 230
security
    continuing rights of occupation 641–2
    protection, qualification for 642–3
    termination/continuation 643–4
statutory controls 232, 233 *Table*
termination/continuation 643–4
variation 139
low-cost home ownership 745–6

maintenance *see* repair duty
management
    agents' use 338–9
    ALMOs 169, 336, 340
    and anti-social behaviour *see* anti-social behaviour
    codes 333–4
    communication and tenant satisfaction 334
    contractual obligations 306–8
    and disability 303–5
    estate *see* estate management
    housing 174–7
    housing associations 166
    insurance *see* insurance
    local authority delegation 339–40
    long residential leases *see under* long residential leases
    repairs *see* repair covenants; repair duty
    residential tenant involvement 335–8
    RTM *see* right to manage
    servicing *see* service charges
    social housing
        consultation rights 334–5
        ensuring compliance 340–1
    third parties *see* landlords, and third parties
    user *see* user
management companies 586
marriage value
    flats, enfranchisement 778–9
    long leasehold houses, enfranchisement 760, 766, 767
mediation 343, 403
merger 735–6
mesne profits 78, 470
mortgagee possession 728–9
mortgagor arrears, and possession 635–6, 728–9
multiple occupation 97–9
    see also houses, in multiple occupation

non-derogation from grant 30–1, 33, 123–4, 416–17
Northern Ireland, HMO licensing 390–1
notice seeking possession (NSP) 597–8, 610
notices
    break clauses 243, 533, 732–4
    leasehold *see* leasehold notices
Nugee Report 12–13, 118, 230, 769
nuisance liability 327–32, 329, 392–3
    and possession *see* possession, and nuisance/annoy-
        ance

obsolete covenants 421
occupation
    as beneficiary 84
    categories 77–95
    leases *see* leases
    licence *see* licence
    multiple 97–9
        see also houses in multiple occupation
    non-consensual 77–8
    prior to sale 82–3
    service 83
    tenancy *see* tenancy
    tolerated trespass 84, 85–7, 405–6, 470, 606–7
Office of Fair Trading (OFT) 129–30
ombudsman
    Independent Housing Ombudsman Scheme 343–4,
        403
    Local Government Ombudsman 332, 343–4, 403
ombudsmen schemes 343–4
onerous property 726
original tenant liability *see* leasehold covenants, enforce-
    ment
over-crowding 351–2, 630
owner-occupation
    current issues 178–9
    expansion 158–9, 166–9
    possession for 634
    promotion 160–1

periodic tenancies 89–93
    assured, rent review 491–3
    certainty of term 76
        and repugnance 92–3
    implied 89–92
        from possession 111
    notice to quit 669–73
        background 669–70
        and joint tenancies 670
        and relationship breakdown 670–3
permissive waste 375–7
perpetually renewable leases 93–4
PFIs (private finance initiatives) 169
policy
    definition 143–4
    importance 141, 143
    and legislative intervention 51–2
positive covenants in freehold land 225–6
possession

commercial leases *see under* commercial leases, secu-
    rity
residential tenancies
    and assured shorthold tenancies 636–8
    and assured tenancies 607–8
    and breach of tenancy 617–18
    and deterioration in condition 623–4
    and disability *see* disability discrimination, and
        anti-social behaviour
    and domestic violence 623
    and employment related tenancies 626–7
    estate management grounds *see under* estate man-
        agement
    eviction issues 615–16
    exercise of discretion 601–2
    grounds, in outline 599–602
    and human rights 282–4, 610–13
    and mortgagor arrears 635–6
    notice seeking 597–8, 610
    and nuisance/annoyance 617–18
        grounds 618
        possession order, type 618–19
    orders
        discretionary grounds 603–5
        execution 608–9
        mandatory grounds 602–3
    and premiums 625–6
    and reasonableness 599–601
    reform proposals 638–9
    and rent arrears 613–16
        background 613
        as discretionary ground 613–14
        eviction issues 615–16
        as mandatory ground 614–15
    and secure tenancies 605–7
    and social landlords, use of actions 609–10
    statutory grounds 596–7
    if tenancy induced by false statements 624–5
premises
    business
        for business purposes 250
        definition 246
    as family home *see under* alienation covenants
    and flats, enfranchisement 775–7
    occupation of 246–8
        for business purposes 250
        by related persons 249–50
        incorporeal hereditaments 247–8
        multiple users 248–9
    right of first refusal, definition 770
    right to manage (RTM) definition 312
premiums, and possession 625–6
preserved right to buy (PRTB) 749, 758
pretence 145–6
private finance initiatives (PFIs) 169
private renting
    alienation covenants 537
    allocation 201–2
    and anti-social behaviour 325–6
    current issues 179–80

and decent homes 349–50
HMOs, local authority powers 389
Housing Act 1988 187–8, 203–10
  legislation pre-1988 185–7
  sector 9–12, 150–1, 167–8, 182
  v social renting 151–2, 153–4
  standards and repair 352–3
  succession *see under* succession at death
privity of estate 570–2
properties acquired for development, shortlife tenancies
      215–16
proportionality 278
  and forfeiture, relief against 714–15
public authority
  see also local authority housing
  definition for human rights 273–7
  and disability discrimination 304–5
public health powers 385–6
public houses 361
  tied leases 421–2, 423
public law 41–6
  background 41–2
  compelling local authority action 45–6
  as ground of challenge 42–3
  liability to third parties 330–2
  and private law challenges 43–4
  remedies 344–5

qualified covenants 418–19
  and alienation 524

Rachman era 176, 684–6
Real Estate Investment Trusts (REITs) 18, 179
receiver/manager, appointment 402
reconstruction, and estate management 631–3, 655–7
recoupment right 403–4
  exclusion 405
rectification
  of contracts 115
  and leases 115–16
registered social landlords (RSLs) 8, 163, 180–1, 637
  allocation policies 103–4, 198, 201
  assured tenancies 188, 595–6
  complaints 343–4
  demoted assured shorthold tenancies 219, 637
  and human rights 274–7
  management of communities 166
  rent
    levels 451, 452
    review provisions 472
  starter tenancies 218, 317
  tenant involvement in management 335, 339–40
    antisocial behaviour 328
    and Ground 8
    and local housing allowance 469
    regulation of 180–1, 340
regulatory controls 41, 383–91
  HMO licensing 386–91
  public health powers 385–6
  unfitness 383–4

regulatory crimes 690
REITs (Real Estate Investment Trusts) 18, 179
relationship breakdown
  and family home *see* alienation covenants, premises
      as family home
  and periodic tenancies, notice to quit 670–3
renewal, and repair 365–7
rent 443–513
  abandonment and arrears
    approaches 506–10, 732
    recovery of lost rent 39
  affordability *see* affordability
  arrears *see under* possession
  background 443
  books 117
  cesser of 513
  collection 504–5
  controls *see* rent controls *below*
  deposits *see* security deposits *below*
  differential 473
  distress for rent 511–13
    abolition and CRAR 512–13
    background 511
    problems 511
  ensuring payment *see* payment
  equity 473–5
  guarantees 500–1
  and housing benefits *see* housing benefit system
  indexation 475–6
  late payment charges 504
  mean weekly 452 *Table*
  overpayment 499
  payment 499–505
    background 499–500
    guarantees 500–1
    late, charges 504
    remedies *see* remedies for non-payment *below*
  v purchase, reasons 15–16
  rates of return 445–6
  references 500
  remedies for non-payment 505–13
    background 505–6
    distress for rent *see* distress for rent *above*
    recovery of rent 506–11
    set off 511
  rent-service 443
  review *see* rent reviews *below*
  review, upward only (UORR) 132, 135, 242–3, 253,
      254, 482–4
  security deposits 202, 501–4
    commercial 501
    residential *see* residential tenancies, deposits
  set off 511
  setting 443–7
  sliding scale 475–6
  social *see* social renting
  step-up 473
  turnover 473–5
Rent Assessment Committee (RAC) 464–5
rent controls 453–65

approaches 453–4
avoidance 464–5
commercial 465
constitutional challenges
    European 455–8, 460
    US 458–9, 460
early development 156
effects 454–5
fair rents 460
    and scarcity 461–3
and human rights 288–90
pre-1988 185–6
residential 221, 460–5
rent reviews 471–99
agricultural leases 496–8
background 471–2
commercial see commercial leases, modern rent
        review clause
differential rents 473
equity rents 473–5
judicial variation 498–9
local authority housing 496
residential 490–6
    background 490–1
    and commercial approach 493, 495–6
    fairness guidance 493–4
    fixed term assured tenancy 493
    periodic assured tenancy 491–3
sliding scale rent 475–6
step-up rents 473
turnover rents 473–5
variation issues 472
rental contracts, model contracts 130, 138
renting homes scheme see under Law Commission
repair covenants 121, 361, 368–70, 394–406
commercial leases 135
council tenants' Right to Repair 401
landlord's remedies 394–400
    damages, see under damages
    rights of entry 394–5
    specific performance 398–400
tenant's remedies 400–6
    alternative remedies 402–3
    council tenants' Right to Repair 401
    damages 400–1
    receiver/manager, appointment 402
    recoupment see recoupment right
    repudiation 402
    set-off see equitable set-off
    specific performance 401
    tolerated trespasser 405–6, 470
    witholding rent 403–5
repair duty
Article 8 283
covenants see repair covenants
definition of repair 364–5, 370–1
duty of care 380382
enforcement 394
implied obligations
    agricultural leases 382

at common law 373–5, 392–3
    duty of care 380–2
    statutory 377–82, 391–4
    on tenant 375–7
and improvements see improvements
and inherent defects 367–8
notification of disrepair 372
reform proposals 382–3, 391–4
and renewal 365–7
Right to Repair 401
standard 371
    see also under standards
statutory 219, 377–82, 391–4
repairs and standards see under repairs
repossession see possession
repudiation 31, 402, 507, 723–5
landlord breach 723–5
tenant breach 725
resident landlord exceptions
collective enfranchisement 776
disability laws 104
minimum notice 675
right of first refusal 770
right to manage (RTM) 312
tenancy laws 186, 209
residential leases 138, 139
see also residential tenancies
residential long leases see long residential leases
residential property
legislative intervention 52
long leases 12–13
Residential Property Tribunal Service (RPTS) 345
residential tenancies
see also residential leases
alienation see under alienation covenants
databases 104
deposits 501–4
    and access 501–2
    regulation 502–4
disputes
    see also under Law Commission
    judicial action 342–3
    mediation 343, 403
    ombudsmen schemes 343–4
    public law remedies 344–5
    tribunals 345
eviction 219, 604 Table
and forfeiture 717–18
involvement in management 335–8
landlord's obligation to repair 219
legislation
    current 219–22
    early 184–5
minimum notice provision 219
ombudsmen schemes 343–4
reform proposals see under Law Commission
rent 449–72
    control see rent controls
right to buy/acquire 221–2
security 221, 595–639

background 595–6
    protection *see* protection schemes
service charges *see* service charges
succession *see under* succession at death
tenant's right to transfer tenancy 221, 534–42
termination, statutory requirements 674–8
    court order requirement 675–8
    excluded tenancies/licences 675
    four weeks' notice 674–5
    and periodic licences 674–5
voluntary transfer *see* voluntary transfer
restraint of trade 422
RICS Service Charge Code, for commercial property
    434, 436, 440–1
right to acquire (RTA) 165–6, 221–2, 758
    see also enfranchisement, and social tenants
    statutory rights 743–5
right to buy (RTB) 160–2, 221–2
    see also enfranchisement, and social tenants
    discount 167 *Table*, 753–4
        prevention of abuse 755
        repayment 754–5
        right of first refusal 755
    exceptions 752–3
    impact on stock 7, 160–2, 172
    nature of right 757–8
    need for secure tenancy 749–51
    price 753
    process 756
    property, definition 751
    qualifying period 749
    reserved 758
    sharing of 751–2
    statutory rights 743–5
right to manage (RTM) 312–13
    management functions 313
    premises 312
    sufficient support 313
Right to Repair 401

secure tenancies 139, 210–18
    and asylum seekers 216
    definition 210–11
    demoted tenancy 190, 214–15, 317, 325, 595
    employment related tenancies 215, 216
    eviction 217–18
    exclusions 214–17
    grounds for possession 218, 600 *Table*
        see also possession, residential tenancies
    and homeless applicants 216
    and improvements 409
    improvements, compensation right 411–13
    introductory tenancy 214
    landlord condition 212
    and long leases 215
    only/principal home requirement 213–14
    period of security 218
    and possession 605–7, 609–10
    and properties acquired for development 215–16
    and right to buy (RTB) 749–51

separate dwelling requirement 211
short term lets while works effected 217
and specific businesses 217
student lets 217
sub-tenants, termination effect 742
temporary housing leased from private sector 216–17
tenancy requirement 211–12
tenant condition 212–14
tenant as individual, requirement 212
variation 139
security
    commercial leases *see under* commercial leases
    importance 591–2
    long residential leases *see under* long residential leases
    residential tenancies, protection *see* possession, resi-
        dential tenancies
    trends 593–4
security deposits *see* rent, security deposits
selection 103–4
separate dwelling requirement
    assured dwelling 205–6
    secure tenancies 211
service charges 432–42
    aims 432–3
    consultation
        and commercial tenants 440
        of residential tenants 335, 438–40
    controls 434–7
        statutory 437–8
    disputes 433–44
    and forfeiture of residential leases 717
    long residential leases, problem with 230
    mixed use premises 441–2
    RICS code *see* RICS Service Charge Code, for com-
        mercial property
service occupancy 83
set-off *see* equitable set-off
sham 145
shorthold tenancies *see* assured shorthold tenancies
Single Room Rent (SSR) 466–7
sliding scale rent 475–6
social exclusion 162–3
    and housing 174–6
social housing 8–9
    see also housing associations; local authority housing;
        voluntary transfer
    allocation 152, 153, 191–3
    and anti-social behaviour *see* anti-social behaviour
    and choice 173–4
    consultation rights 334–5
    cost of repair 352, 355
    definition 154–5
    and employment rates 174
    enfranchisement *see* enfranchisement, and social ten-
        ants
    ensuring compliance 340–1
    and estate management 301–3
    homelessness duties *see* homelessness
    and private sector 202

and relationship breakdown *see* relationship breakdown
role 153
tenancy agreements 138
voluntary transfer *see* voluntary transfer
social renting
  current issues 180–1
  definition 151–3
  housing association rents 451
  legislation 188–90
  local authority rents 449–51
  v private renting 151–2, 153–4
  reform proposals 223–4
  rent restructuring 452–3
  residential rent levels 451
social tenant, enfranchisement *see* enfranchisement, and social tenants
special needs housing, allocation/management 633–4
specific performance
  landlord's remedy 398–400
  tenant's remedy 401
split-ownership 48–50
standards
  ensuring good standards 353–64
    background 353–4
    regulatory controls *see* regulatory controls
  and repair 347–8, 348–53
    see also repair covenants
    cost of repair 352, 355
    decent homes 169–70, 348–50
    liveability 350
    overcrowding 351–2
    private renting 352–3
statutory succession *see* succession on death
step-up rents 473
student lets
  and secure tenancies 217
  vacation lets 635
sub-leases *see* sub-letting
sub-letting 518–19
  commercial leases 135, 531–2
    uneconomic 654–5
  public sector tenancies 536–7, 541
sub-tenants
  liability 546
  protected status 545–6
  termination effect 737–42
    assured tenancies 741
    at common law 737–41
    secured tenancies 742
succession on death 221, 546–51
  agricultural leases 551
  residential tenancies 546–51
    background 546–7
    as possession ground 634–5
    private sector 547
    public sector 547–9
    public/private comparison 549–51
suitable alternative accommodation (SAA) 628–9
  and commercial leases 654

superior landlord 586–7
surrender 729–32
  as consensual act 729–30
  express or by operation of law 730–1
  and regrant 39, 731
sustainable communities, promotion 150, 175, 178, 200

tenancy
  see also tenant
  assured *see* assured tenancies
  at sufferance 78
  at will 87–9, 212, 245–6
  by estoppel 94–5
  employment related 215, 216
  induced by false statements 624–5
  periodic *see* periodic tenancies
  shorthold 187–8, 196–7, 203–4
  state of housing *see* standards, and repair
Tenancy Reform Industry Group (TRIG) 269–70
tenant
  see also tenancy
  abandonment, recovery of lost rent *see under* rent, abandonment and arrears
  breach, repudiation for 723–5
  change *see* change of tenant
  choice 553
  and communication 334
  and competition 416–17
  covenants between, enforcement 587–8
  default *see* forfeiture; Law Commission, termination scheme
  enfranchisement *see* enfranchisement, and social tenants
  fixtures, removal 413
  holding over 679–80
  as individual 206, 212
  insolvency 725–8
  termination for landlord default 723
tenant management organisations (TMOs) 335, 337, 339
tenant participation compacts (TPCs) 176, 336
Tenant's Charter 188–9
tenure
  agricultural *see* agricultural tenancies, security of tenure
  divisions 150–1
  and housing decency 170, 349 *Table*
  and housing stock 158 *Table*
  patterns, pre-1979 159
term certainty *see* certainty of term
third parties
  and forfeiture 715
  human rights, and liabilities 330–2
  landlords *see* landlords, and third parties
  public law, and liabilities 330–2
title, landlord's disclaimer 124, 716–17
tolerated trespasser 70, 84, 85–7, 405–6, 470, 606–8, 749
tort liability 326–9
transfer *see* alienation covenants; change of landlord;

change of tenant; landlords, consent; succession
     on death; voluntary transfer
trespassers 77–8
  see also tolerated trespasser
tribunals 345
turnover rents 473–5

underlease *see* sub-letting
Unfair Contract Terms Act 1977 125–6
Unfair Terms in Consumer Contracts Regulations 1999
     126–30, 494
  and core terms 128
  exclusions 128
  and mandatory statutory 128
  'plain intelligible language' 129
  potentially unfair terms 129–30
  renting homes proposals 130, 138
  scope 127
  test of fairness 128–9
unfitness 383–4
United States, nautre of law 33–4
unlawful eviction 56, 681–99
  background 681
  civil remedies 691–3
     background 691
     common law 691–3
  offences 686–9
  reform proposals 698–9
  response of agencies 689–91
  statutory damages 693–8
     background 693–4
     double recovery 697
     and landlord liability 694–5
     measure of damages 695–6

re-instatement 697–8
tenant's conduct and reduction 696–7
upward only rent review (UORR) 132, 135, 242–3, 253,
     482–4
user 415–26
  absolute/qualified covenants 418–19
  clause, obsolete covenants 421
  clause width and variation 417–21
  clauses restricting trade 421–3
  covenants to keep open 423–6
  enforcement of covenants 425, 426
  fully qualified covenant, and reasonableness 419–21
  restrictions 415–16
  tenants and competition 416–17

variation
  see also rent reviews
  long residential leases 139
  and original tenant liability 567
  secure tenancies 139
  surrender and regrant 39, 731
voluntary transfer 552–7
  amount of stock 554
  background 552–3
  impact on tenants 555–7
  process/tenant consultation 554–5
voluntary waste 375–7

warranty
  see also fitness for purpose, implied covenant
     of habitability (US) 359–61
waste, voluntary/permissive 375–7
winter lets 635
works, and estate management 631–3, 655–7